Using Windows NT

QUE DEVELOPMENT GROUP

CONTRIBUTING AUTHORS:

BOB BRANCHEK
ROBERT EIDSON
CHARLES KINDEL
RON PERSON
KAREN ROSE
MICHAEL ROSS
ALLEN G. TAYLOR
JACK WOEHR

Using Windows NT

Copyright © 1993 by Que® Corporation

Library of Congress Catalog Number: 93-84807

ISBN: 1-56529-101-8

95 94 93   6 5 4 3 2 1

Interpretation of the printing code: the rightmost double-digit number is the year of the book's printing; the rightmost single-digit number, the number of the book's printing. For example, a printing code of 93-1 shows that the first printing of the book occurred in 1993.

Using Windows NT is based on Windows NT.

Publisher: David P. Ewing

Associate Publisher: Rick Ranucci

Director of Publishing: Michael Miller

Managing Editor: Corinne Walls

Marketing Manager: Ray Robinson

CREDITS

Title Managers
Walter R. Bruce, III
Brad Koch

Acquisitions Editor
Sherri Morningstar

Product Directors
Joyce Nielsen
Timothy S. Stanley

Production Editors
Lori Cates
Susan Pink

Editors
Jo Anna Arnott
Elsa M. Bell
H. Leigh Davis
Kelly D. Dobbs
Robin Drake
Donald R. Eamon
Phil Kitchel
Diana Moore
Linda Seifert
Colleen Totz

Technical Editors
Lee Hart
Charles Kindel

Figure Specialist
Wilfred Thebodeau

Editorial Assistant
Jill Stanley

Book Designer
Amy Peppler-Adams

Cover Designer
Jay Corpus

Indexers
Michael Hughes
Joy Dean Lee
Johnna VanHoose

Production Team
Angela Bannan
Claudia Bell
Danielle Bird
Ayrika Bryant
Paula Carroll
Charlotte Clapp
Brook Farling
Teresa Forrester
Mitzi Gianakos
Joelynn Gifford
Michelle Greenwalt
Carla Hall
Heather Kaufman
Bob LaRoche
Sean Medlock
Tim Montgomery
Ryan Rader
Caroline Roop
Tonya Simpson
Amy Steed
Tina Trettin
Susan VandeWalle
Mary Beth Wakefield
Donna Winter
Lillian Yates

Composed in *Cheltenham* and *MCPdigital* by Que Corporation

ABOUT THE AUTHORS

Bob Branchek, president of Bob Branchek Associates, Inc., provides training and consulting for Microsoft's Windows NT and Digital's OpenVMS systems. He teaches system administration classes at New York University and is the writer and on-camera talent for several video training courses.

Robert Eidson, based in Lake Oswego, Oregon, has attained Microsoft's highest rating: Microsoft Consulting Partner. His firm, Graphic Systems Applications, Inc., provides software planning and development of applications using a wide range of components, including C, C++, Visual Basic, Excel, and Word for Windows. He is experienced at re-engineering UNIX applications to run using the Windows and Windows NT operating systems. He also provides corporate mainframe application downsize re-engineering to Windows and Windows NT. His Fortune 500 clients are involved in such areas as engineering, medicine, aerospace, finance, and manufacturing.

Charles Kindel is the author of the popular Windows shareware applications WinPrint and INIedit. As a consultant and contract programmer, he has been responsible for the development of several commercial Windows applications. He now works full-time for a small software company in the Pacific Northwest and is a proud new father. He would like to dedicate the work he did on this book to Julie and Christine.

Ron Person is one of the original Microsoft Consulting Partners, Microsoft's highest rating for Microsoft Excel and Word for Windows consultants. He has written more than 14 books for Que Corporation, including *Using Excel 4 for Windows*, Special Edition; *Using Word for Windows 2*, Special Edition; *Using Windows 3.1*, Special Edition; and is coauthor of Que's *Using Access for Windows*. Ron Person & Co. is based in San Francisco and is a leader in teaching Visual Basic for Applications to corporate developers.

Karen Rose has written five books for Que Corporation, including *Using Windows 3.1*, Special Edition and *Using Word for Windows 2*, Special Edition. Karen has taught Word for Windows and desktop publishing for Sonoma State University and Ron Person & Co. She currently publishes handmade books under the name Little Red Book Press in Santa Rosa, California.

Michael Ross is president of Ross Data Systems, a consulting company specializing in Windows and Windows NT application design and development. Michael designed and codeveloped numerous successful retail Windows applications, including Gupta Corporation's Quest and IBM Corporation's Legato.

Allen G. Taylor is president of Computer Power, a computing consulting firm in Portland, Oregon, that specializes in system development, software design, database design, and technology marketing. He is a best-selling author, nationally recognized speaker, and adjunct professor of computing science at Linfield College.

Jack Woehr (a.k.a "Jax") is in charge of Windows NT development for Cygnus Supports of Mountain View, California. He is the creator of Jax4th for Windows NT. His articles often appear in *Embedded Systems Programming* and *Dr. Dobb's Journal* magazines. He can be reached by E-mail at jax@cygnus.com. Jax says "thanx" to Eric Fogelin and Jonathan Manheim of Microsoft.

ACKNOWLEDGMENTS

Trademark Acknowledgments

All terms mentioned in this book that are known to be trademarks or service marks have been appropriately capitalized. Que cannot attest to the accuracy of this information. Use of a term in this book should not be regarded as affecting the validity of any trademark or service mark.

Microsoft, Microsoft Excel, MS-DOS, Microsoft Word, Microsoft Mouse, and PowerPoint are registered trademarks and Windows is a trademark of Microsoft Corporation.

Trademarks of other products mentioned in this book are held by the companies producing them.

Corporate Acknowledgments

Screen Reproductions in this book were created using Collage Plus from Inner Media, Inc., Hollis, New Hampshire.

Thanks to CD-ROM, Inc., of Golden, Colorado, for generous assistance with CD-ROM-related information.

CONTENTS AT A GLANCE

TABLE OF CONTENTS

II Working with Windows NT

5 Managing Files with the File Manager 125

III Using Windows NT Accessories

10 Using Microsoft Mail 321

IV Using Windows NT Applets

V Running Applications under Windows NT

VIII Appendixes

Introduction

The phenomenal success of Windows, which came of age with the release of Windows Version 3.0, surprised many people. The success didn't surprise the engineers and evangelists at Microsoft, who have praised Windows since the beginning, and it didn't surprise users who have appreciated the benefits of a graphical interface, multitasking, and connectivity between applications for years. However, Windows' success did surprise people accustomed to the command-line interface of DOS, who didn't really think computers should be easy to use. Computers, after all, are serious business tools.

With the success, however, came many criticisms. Probably the biggest criticism was how Windows used memory. A pesky item called system resources became a familiar term to many Windows users. Even though you had plenty of memory, when Windows ran low on system resources, you had to start closing applications. Windows 3.1 increased the system resources, eliminating much of the problem; however, system resources still limit how many applications you can run at the same time. It is time for a version of Windows that solves this and other problems, and prepares users for more powerful applications.

Windows NT is such a version of Windows. Windows NT is a product that has been waiting in the Microsoft wings for quite some time. If the country could apply the cost of the Windows NT development time to the deficit, it would make a big dent.

Although Windows NT looks like Windows 3.1, it is quite a different product altogether. Windows NT is a complete operating system. That's right, you do not have to load DOS before you load Windows NT. Load NT and you are ready.

NT has many advanced features built into it. For example, Windows NT is a 32-bit operating system, which means you can perform operations quickly. Windows NT uses a flat 32-bit memory module, which means you don't have to configure memory as you did with DOS. Using the analogy of memory as land, instead of thinking about little plots of land here, there, and yonder, all you do is think about the great open spaces.

Windows NT performs true *preemptive multitasking*. That means you have better, more fluid performance when running multiple applications. For example, when you format a diskette, you can continue working in another application. You do not have to wait for the diskette to finish formatting before you can continue working, as you would with Windows 3.1.

Many positive features of Windows 3.1 and Windows for Workgroups are still available in Windows NT. For example, Windows NT includes the TrueType font technology, object linking and embedding (OLE), drag-and-drop moving and copying, and built-in multimedia extensions.

Microsoft's solution to increasing the productivity of groups through networking is maintained in Windows NT. Windows NT makes connecting a network of computers easy. In fact, if you have a network adapter installed in your computer, Windows NT automatically installs networking capability.

Most networks require one computer to act as a dedicated *server*, which controls the network; however, Windows NT, right out of the box, shares the networking overhead between all the computers on the network. This reduces the cost of the network. Most networks also require a system administrator who has had technical training. In the peer-to-peer network used by Windows NT, each user is responsible for his or her own system, and each user controls who can and can't access his or her files and printer.

Windows NT also includes three powerful applications to help you and your workgroup work together:

- **Mail** is a message-passing system. People in your workgroup can send messages, memos, and files to others in the workgroup. A network *postoffice* stores and forwards mail, so that you can pick up your mail when it is convenient to you.

- **Schedule+** is a personal or group scheduling application. It helps you manage your time and appointments, and it monitors when groups of people are available for a meeting. It ties into Mail so that you can notify people of a meeting and confirm when the meeting time is added to their schedule.

- **ClipBook** enables everyone in your workgroup to share data. It acts like a central scrapbook for everyone in the workgroup. Workgroup users can paste or link data from the ClipBook into their documents. When the chart, table, or data in the ClipBook changes, everyone in the workgroup gets the updated version.

Windows NT does not stop at peer-to-peer networking. Often, you need the power associated with a dedicated server, a computer that is dedicated to serving files to users attached to the network. With a separate product, Windows NT Advanced Server, you can add a server with full security to your Windows NT network.

How This Book Is Organized

This book is divided into seven parts, beginning with the most basic information and progressing to the most advanced. At the end of the book are two appendixes that describe how to install Windows NT and one of the boot files.

Part I—Getting Started with Windows NT

Part I, *Getting Started with Windows NT*, includes two chapters for those who are new to Windows. If you have never used Windows, these two chapters are a must, because they introduce you to Windows NT and provide basic information about operating windows, menus, and dialog boxes. This information is not repeated in individual chapters. Even if you have been using Windows for a while, you might want to scan Chapters 1 and 2 for tips.

Chapter 1, "Introducing Windows NT," gives you a good overview of Windows NT. In this chapter, you learn some of the basic concepts that make Windows NT unique and powerful. You learn why Windows NT is an operating system superior to DOS.

Chapter 2, "Operating Windows NT," teaches you how to perform basic Windows functions. You learn how to start Windows and about the two different modes of running Windows. You also learn how to start an application and use its menus and dialog boxes. You learn how to run multiple applications simultaneously and cut and paste information between documents in different applications. You also learn that many things you do in one Windows application are the same in all Windows applications, making it easier to become familiar with more Windows applications.

Part II—Working with Windows NT

Part II, *Working with Windows NT*, includes chapters that detail the essential elements of Windows, including how to get help, how to use the File Manager, and how to use the Control Panel. In these chapters, you learn how to customize Windows and how to use features shared by all Windows applications.

Chapter 3, "Getting Help," begins with an overview of the application's features and commands. Many Windows and Windows NT applications, including the Windows NT accessories, include easy-to-use on-line documentation in the form of Help files. You can access Help through a menu, and the Help files in each application work similarly. Windows Help also enables you to search for information by choosing from an index of key topics.

Chapter 4, "Controlling Applications with the Program Manager," presents the Program Manager, which is the heart of Windows NT. When you start Windows NT, the Program Manager is what you see on-screen. This highly customizable manager of your Windows session includes several group windows, each containing a group of program item icons that you use to start applications. You can create your own program item icons, and you can organize them inside your own custom windows.

Chapter 5, "Managing Files with the File Manager," shows how you can use the File Manager to copy or move files or groups of files. You also learn to delete or rename files, create or remove directories, format disks, view files in almost any order, and search for files that meet specified criteria. You learn to share your directories with other members on a network. You also see how to get information from the shared directories of other members on the network. The File Manager makes extensive use of NT's drag-and-drop feature to manage files.

Chapter 6, "Embedding and Linking Windows NT Applications," introduces *object linking and embedding*, or OLE, which is another exciting Windows NT innovation. OLE breaks down the barriers between applications, enabling you to create compound documents made up of pieces from several applications. Importantly, linked objects retain their connection to their originating applications, so they can be automatically updated. You can edit and update embedded objects from within the document where they are embedded. For OLE to work, you need a server application (used to create an object) and a client application (where the object is embedded or linked).

If you use Windows NT on a network, you learn to reduce work among group members by using the ClipBook. The ClipBook is like a scrapbook in which you can store your personal clippings. The network ClipBook can share text, tables, and charts with anyone on your network. If network members link to data in the ClipBook, their document updates whenever the data in the ClipBook updates. The ClipBook makes it easy to keep a group document up-to-date.

Chapter 7, "Customizing with the Control Panel," shows how to take control of the Control Panel, which includes a suite of applications you can use to customize your Windows environment. A Colors application enables you to choose screen colors; a Desktop application enables you to choose background patterns and a screen saver; and a Sounds application enables you to assign sounds to events. A Fonts application enables you to easily install new fonts, and a Printers application enables you to install and connect printers. You can customize your keyboard, your mouse, and your numeric formats. You can set the time and date, install multimedia drivers, and establish network connections. The Network application in the Control Panel gives you the capability to change or control how Windows works within your network.

Chapter 8, "Managing Fonts," introduces one of Windows' most exciting features—TrueType, a font technology that provides you with high-quality fonts on any printer. TrueType scalable font outlines adapt to any screen and any printer that Windows NT supports (at any resolution) and are instantly available to Windows NT and Windows applications. To preserve your investment in other types of fonts, TrueType works seamlessly with existing font technologies, such as downloadable and PostScript fonts.

Chapter 9, "Using the Print Manager," shows you how to use the Print Manager to *spool* print jobs. When you print a file from a Windows application, you don't have to wait impatiently until your printer is finished printing before you can start using your computer again. Instead, the Print Manager spools print jobs to the printer, taking over management of printing functions while you continue working. You can use the Print Manager also to install new printers.

When you are printing in Windows NT on a network, you can use the Print Manager to monitor your print job even if it is printing on a printer located at someone else's computer.

Part III—Using Windows NT Accessories

Part III, *Using Windows NT Accessories*, teaches you how to use the free accessory applications that come with Windows NT. Windows NT accessory applications include a word processor, a painting application, a communications application, a macro recorder, multimedia applications, and others. You can use these applications to accessorize your primary applications.

Chapter 10, "Using Microsoft Mail," discusses Mail, a full-featured electronic mail system that comes as part of Windows NT. By using Mail, you can send, receive, and store messages over the network. You can even attach files to messages, so you can send a message that includes the backup document, spreadsheet, or charts.

Chapter 11, "Using Schedule+," discusses how to help you and everyone in your network workgroup schedule your time, meetings, and common resources, such as meeting rooms. Schedule+ can be used as a personal scheduler to help you keep appointments. It even prints schedules in standard time management notebook sizes. Schedule+ is also designed to work with Mail to make it easy to review when a group of people have a common block of time available for a meeting. Mail incorporates a note for scheduling and confirming group meetings.

Chapter 12, "Using Windows NT Write," discusses Write, a simple but powerful word processing application that comes free with Windows NT. In Write, you can enter, edit, and format text just as in any word processor, and you can add tabs, headers, and footers. Write lacks advanced features such as spell checking and automatic tables of contents, but it is upward-compatible with more powerful word processors such as Word for Windows, making Write a perfect springboard for moving up to an advanced word processor. Write is an OLE client, into which you can embed objects.

Chapter 13, "Using Windows NT Paintbrush," discusses Paintbrush, a fun and colorful painting program you can use to create illustrations in a rainbow of colors and shades. Use Paintbrush's many painting tools to create fanciful works of art or serious illustrations for business use. Paintbrush is an OLE server that you can use to create objects embedded in client documents.

Chapter 14, "Using Windows NT Terminal," shows how you can use Terminal (if your computer is equipped with a modem) to manage your communications. For easy access to modems or on-line services that you use frequently, such as CompuServe, you can create files containing all the information you need to make a connection. Use Terminal to connect to another computer and to upload and download files.

Chapter 15, "Using Desktop Accessories," describes each of the smaller accessory programs that come with Windows. Using the Cardfile, you can keep track of names and addresses in a file that looks like a stack of index cards. You can even automatically dial a phone number on a cardfile card, if your computer has a modem. Use Notepad for keeping notes on your computer. Notepad is a mini word processor that enables you to type text and store the information in a text file. If you work with an IBM mainframe, you can use this book to help you learn how to use the 3270 Terminal Emulator application. Similar to Windows NT Terminal, 3270 Terminal Emulator makes Windows NT act as a 3270 terminal. Start up the Calculator to do quick calculations, or complex scientific calculations, and copy the results into your primary application. Use the clock when you need to watch the time, minimizing the clock to an icon at the bottom of your screen. Use the Character Map application to find those normally difficult-to-find characters that you want to place in your documents. Character Map displays all the characters in a type set.

If you are using Windows NT in a workgroup network, you have additional accessories to help you use the network. Chat is a simple two-way typing screen on which you and anyone else in your workgroup can type simultaneously. You can *chat* back and forth in Chat and get more immediate results than sending a message by Mail.

Finally, are you tired of work? Need a break? You will find information on the three games that come with Windows NT—FreeCell, Solitaire, and Minesweeper.

Chapter 16, "Using Multimedia," discusses what multimedia is, and introduces the multimedia accessory programs that come with Windows NT that you can use with your multimedia equipment. Sound Recorder enables you to create your own music, blend and mix tunes, and record your own voice. Media Player enables you to play existing music and video files. To take advantage of multimedia, you need to equip your PC with a sound board, a CD-ROM drive, and speakers. Optionally, you can add a MIDI-based keyboard, a microphone, a VCR, and other equipment. With a multimedia-equipped PC (or MPC), you can create your own multimedia productions or take advantage of animated, speaking stories and reference libraries available for purchase.

Part IV—Using Windows NT Applets

Part IV, *Using Windows NT Applets*, includes chapters that describe how to use two of the *applets*, or mini-applications, that come free with some Windows applications such as Word for Windows and Microsoft Excel. Applets create objects embedded within a document and can be opened only from within another application.

Chapter 17, "Using Microsoft Draw," concentrates on Microsoft Draw, one of several OLE-based applets that come free with some Windows applications such as Word for Windows, Microsoft Publisher, and PowerPoint. Draw is a drawing program that creates editable, layerable, colorful objects. As an object-oriented application that creates lines, squares, and shapes that you can resize, move, or reshape, Draw is a good complement to Paintbrush, which is a bitmap application that creates paintings in one layer. As an applet, Draw can be used only from within a client application, such as Word for Windows or Microsoft Excel.

Chapter 18, "Using Microsoft Graph," demonstrates the benefits of easy-to-use graphing that Microsoft Excel users have enjoyed for years. All the power of Excel is available to owners of applications such as Word for Windows which include, for free, the Microsoft Graph applet. You can use Graph to create line, bar, column, pie, scatter, combination, and 3-D graphs in a variety of styles, and you can type the data you want to use as the basis for your graph. Also, you can copy or import existing data. Like Draw, Graph is an applet that you can use only from within an OLE-capable client application.

Part V—Running Applications under Windows NT

Part V, *Running Applications under Windows NT*, teaches you how to use Windows applications together and how to use the Command Prompt window and DOS applications in Windows.

Chapter 19, "Running Windows Applications," teaches you about NT's powerful capability to share data between applications. You can run more than one application, switch between applications, and exchange data between applications. Tips help you integrate some of the most commonly used Windows applications such as Microsoft Excel and Word for Windows.

Chapter 20, "Using the Command Prompt," shows you how to use the character-based window to issue commands and start programs. This chapter shows you how to manage the Command Prompt window, and how to start DOS programs and OS/2 1.x and POSIX applications from the window.

Chapter 21, "Customizing PIFs," shows you how to optimize the performance of DOS applications by customizing PIFs. A PIF is a program information file that contains technical specifications. Although a PIF already exists for many DOS applications, you can improve performance by optimizing the PIF for your own computer configuration. In this chapter, you also learn how to create a PIF for DOS applications that don't have one.

Chapter 22, "Running DOS Applications," demonstrates how you can use your existing DOS applications during a Windows NT work session. You can run DOS applications in a special window, and you can copy and paste data between DOS and Windows applications using simple Windows techniques.

Chapter 23, "Tuning Windows NT," shows you how to improve Windows NT performance with a few simple adjustments to Windows NT. Turn to this chapter to get the most out of your computer and Windows.

Chapter 24, "Using Windows NT and OS/2 2.1," discusses some of the differences and similarities between Windows NT and OS/2. This chapter provides information that you will need if you operate both operating systems on computers, and need to share information.

Part VI—Networking with Windows NT

Part VI, *Networking with Windows NT*, shows you how nicely interwoven networking is with Windows NT. In this part, you discover all the networking features that Windows NT offers, including setting up workgroups and securing your systems.

Chapter 25, "Networking with Windows NT," begins with a short description and definitions to help you understand how networks work. In this chapter, you learn many different terms that Windows NT uses for networking, and see many of the features that you can use to create a network with Windows NT.

Chapter 26, "Creating Workgroups," describes the feature of grouping together network users who use the same type of information. This chapter describes what a workgroup is and how to set up and manage a workgroup.

Chapter 27, "Understanding Windows NT Advanced Server," introduces you to client/server networking. Advanced Server is the product you use for high-performance, high-security networking. In this chapter, you learn about Advanced Server and the features that this product offers.

Chapter 28, "Connecting Windows NT to Network Operating Systems," contains precisely the information you need if you use other network operating systems currently. This chapter describes what you must do to attach another network operating system to a Windows NT network.

Chapter 29, "Understanding File Security in Windows NT," discusses how Windows NT secures files. You learn about permissions, and how each of the file systems that NT works with manages file security.

Chapter 30, "Understanding System Security in Windows NT," is an important chapter for networking. Because many users share information, you must ensure that a system cannot be accessed by unauthorized users. This chapter discusses Windows NT system security and utilities that are available for you to secure a system.

Part VII—Administering Windows NT

Part VII, *Administering Windows NT*, contains information that helps you manage your computer and network, and deal with problems when they arise.

Chapter 31, "Using the Administrative Applications," introduces the network-administration applications that come with Windows NT. You learn to control users with the User Manager, manage a hard disk using the Disk Administrator, back up and restore hard disk files using Backup, log, and view system errors and security using Event Viewer, and monitor the network performance using Performance Monitor.

Chapter 32, "Troubleshooting Windows NT," provides solutions to the problems that everyone runs into now and then. Many times, you will find that the fix is simpler than you expect.

Chapter 33, "Help, Support, and Resources," tells you who to call to get answers to pressing questions and where to turn for ongoing support. Despite all your best efforts at finding the answer yourself, sometimes you need help.

Part VIII—Appendixes

Appendix A, "Installing Windows NT," provides information that you need when installing Windows NT. You will find the installation easier than you might expect.

Appendix B, "Understanding MultiBoot," describes the file that Windows NT creates if you install the MultiBoot mechanism that enables you to load either Windows NT or DOS from the same hard disk.

How to Use This Book

To use this book, start with Part I, especially if you are a beginner. To get right to work, go to the specific chapters that interest you. To become more familiar with Windows NT, focus on Part II, where you can learn the details of working with Windows NT.

Two important reference tools begin and end the book: a table of contents and an index. When you are not sure exactly what you want to learn, browse through the table of contents at the beginning of the book to get an overview of Windows NT features and applications. Then turn to the chapter that seems most relevant. If you know exactly what you want to find, look it up in the index at the end of the book. After you become familiar with Windows, take some time to browse through the table of contents to look for features you might have passed over when you were a beginner. You are likely to learn some valuable tips.

Tip, note, and caution boxes appear at appropriate locations throughout the book to provide information that increases your productivity, improves your understanding, or warns you of potential traps. These boxes also provide important information you need to ensure that you do not make an error, lose data, or damage software or equipment.

Getting Started with Windows NT

Introducing Windows NT

W indows NT is the new 32-bit operating system that promises to take the personal computer world by storm. In this chapter, we look at where personal computer operating systems have come from and where Windows NT is going, as well as examine features that make Windows NT interesting, novel, and unique.

Where Does Windows NT Fit in the Scheme of Things?

First, there was MS-DOS. There had been other microcomputer disk operating systems before MS-DOS, possibly better operating systems, but MS-DOS was the one that conquered the world.

That innocent age when the single-task command prompt was acceptable ended in the late 1980s, with the success of the Apple Macintosh (and the cult success of the Commodore Amiga).

Nosediving prices of Industry Standard Architecture (ISA) motherboards, the widespread availability of equally inexpensive peripheral support, and the hundreds of thousands of titles of software packages provided insurance for MS-DOS. Nevertheless, the handwriting on the office partition was clear: "Weighed and found wanting."

The graphical aspect of the emerging user interfaces threatened the dominance of MS-DOS. In addition, multitasking operating systems offered the advanced computer user a substantial productivity advantage over single-tasking systems, TSR programs notwithstanding.

Although neither the Mac nor the Amiga (both of whose unique operating systems addressed various shortcomings of the DOS world) possessed the market acceptance to boost MS-DOS out from below, the threat of UNIX descending crushingly from above also loomed large as the world of commerce became increasingly desperate for an economical migration path to just the type of interconnectivity and interoperability of complex multiuser applications that UNIX provides.

As the 1980s drew to a close, two new application platforms emerged from Redmond. The first was Windows, which grew out of a speculative Microsoft/IBM collaboration called TopView, about which the best that can be said is that it was truly funny. Microsoft Windows was at first greeted with a heartfelt round of apathy, even (we are told) within Microsoft itself, where Bill Gates became the main defender of a software development project only its father could love.

The early Windows offered a GUI of a sort, multitasking of a sort, memory management of a sort, and hardware independence of a sort. It was also sort of buggy. I take that back: It was a lot buggy.

The second and, at first glance, more serious contender was OS/2. Although its detractors style OS/2 as "Today's operating system on yesterday's computers, tomorrow," OS/2 offers genuine memory protection, genuine multitasking, and a clean upward migration path from MS-DOS. Just as OS/2 began to assume significance in the minds of prospective upgrade customers, trouble emerged.

What Engineers have joined together, that shall Bean Counters put asunder. Corporate jealousies led to a noisy and acrimonious rupture in the decade-long collaboration of IBM and Microsoft, a collaboration easily as fruitful as any other in the field of computer technology since Charles Babbage and Ada Byron invented and programmed the difference engine.

The result of the divorce was that IBM took OS/2 in-house. In concentrating, characteristically, on the top of the market, IBM failed to communicate its vision of the future to the average computer user—the user who led the computer revolution of the 1980s. This average user's consent must be secured for new software to have more than marginal significance. And who is this average computer user? You are. I am.

Meanwhile, Windows continues to evolve, nurtured by the creativity of one of the best-managed, most relaxed, and happiest large corporations in America today. Whereas OS/2 seems destined to remain a hothouse exotic carefully tended in Fortune 500 companies, Microsoft

Windows has become widespread with the consumer-priced, consumer-styled, consumer-targeted version 3.0/3.1.

Windows is clearly the people's choice. Partly by means of revised team management practices that have over the years increased Microsoft's capability to deliver reliable and well-documented system software, partly by means of a sophisticated marketing organization, and partly by the power of the idea whose time has come, Microsoft Windows has triumphed on the 286/386/486 architecture.

Thousands of commercial Windows applications come to market each year, with probably an equal number of shareware applications appearing on computer bulletin boards around the world.

Programmers, home enthusiasts, receptionists, order-takers, bookkeepers, and CEOs all can be heard calling out to one another, "How do I save my settings in Program Manager? Can I drag and drop between WordPerfect and Notepad? What does this line in WIN.INI mean?"

All this success is despite the fact that Windows 3.1 is an elephant balancing on top of a very small rubber ball labeled "MS-DOS." For every Windows 3.1 user, there comes a time when the ball rolls and the elephant falls over with a thud. The secret sign by which Windows users recognize one another is the three-finger salute, the trained reflex gesture of pressing the Ctrl+Alt+Del keys to restart the machine. (Does nostalgia compel Microsoft to use the same salute for the login prompt of Windows NT?)

This brings us to the subject of this book: Windows NT. The difference between Windows NT and Windows 3.1 is that Windows NT is all elephant and no ball.

At the application level, Windows NT looks like and behaves pretty much like Windows 3.1. At the same time, the excellence of Windows NT is most noticeable in the areas where Windows 3.1 performs poorly.

Under Windows NT, applications multitask like a jazz dance troupe. Under Windows 3.1, applications multitask like a clog dance troupe.

Windows NT responds like lightning to the critical interrupts of a desktop computer (disk, communications port, network card, and so on), whereas Windows 3.1 responds to these same interrupts with all the alacrity of a government official responding to a congressional subpoena.

Windows NT manages memory like H. Ross Perot manages money, whereas Windows 3.1 manages memory like H. Ross Perot manages presidential campaigns.

Stated in computerese, Windows 3.1 is a neat hack on top of klunky MS-DOS. In contrast, Windows NT is a genuine operating system.

Understanding the World of 32-Bit Processing

- MS-DOS and the 8086 microprocessor
- The 80286
- The 80386 and beyond
- 16 bits versus 32 bits
- Portable operating systems
- Advanced computer hardware

MS-DOS was designed to run on the Intel 8086 microprocessor. This microprocessor primarily handles 8-bit and 16-bit values. It has a 20-bit address bus that can directly address 1 megabyte of memory.

8086 memory is addressed in 64K segments. To access the entire memory model supported by this microprocessor, segment registers are used to determine which page of 64K is being addressed. Pages overlap every 16 bytes. Segment arithmetic is a compulsory discipline for MS-DOS programmers that is as popular and enjoyable a study as the memorization of irregular third declension Latin nouns is for high school students.

The registers of an 8086 microprocessor are 16 bits wide. (A 16-bit register can hold a value between 0 and 2^{16} minus 1, that is, between 0 and 65,535.) Applications for the 8086 microprocessor can be written to manipulate values of any size, but the 16-bit processor must work twice as hard, for instance, to handle 32 bits. This is especially true when values are transferred from internal registers to main memory, because data transmission on the external data bus whereby a microprocessor communicates with external memory is one of the slowest aspects of any microprocessor's operation.

The operating system of an 8086-based computer, along with all application programs and their data, must fit in the 1 megabyte of memory addressable by the 20-bit data bus. (A 20-bit address bus allows 2^{20} unique addresses, that is, 1,048,576 bytes. This is known also as a "K of Ks," that is, 1024 × 1024, which is 1 megabyte.)

To add a further limitation, MS-DOS traditionally permits applications to use only the lower 640K of this 1-megabyte address space, on the assumption that the upper 384K would be occupied by system ROM and other hardware. This limitation has been improved in the latest releases of MS-DOS, but the assumption of the limitation is present in the design of software for MS-DOS.

The memory model of the 8086 running MS-DOS seemed spacious to computer users accustomed to the 16-bit address bus of the Intel 8080 and Zilog Z80 microprocessors inside their Osborne and Kaypro computers, respectively. In these computers, the operating system and application were stuffed into 64K.

While the 16-bit 8086 was becoming the focus of the personal computer revolution, carrying the 16-bit MS-DOS operating system with it, 32-bit microprocessors more than twice as powerful as the 8086 were available. Notable among these were the members of the Motorola 68000 family. The Motorola 68020, in particular, offered both a 32-bit data path and a 32-bit address path, capabilities huge in comparison with the 8086. (2^{32} is 4,294,967,296, or in terms of memory address space, 4 gigabytes.)

Also arriving late in the 1980s was the novel Reduced Instruction Set Computer (RISC) of the sort that Microsoft has chosen for its first non-Intel Windows NT support (MIPS R4000, DEC Alpha). The culture of the RISC user community was heavily influenced by earlier exposure to Motorola 68000 family processors. Environments such as the Sun 3 workstation familiarized these users with the convenience offered by 32-bit computing, 32-bit registers, and 32-bit address space.

As the high end of desktop computer users in the early 1980s explored 32-bit processing's flat (not divided into 64K segments) memory address spaces, the speed of complex numerical calculations in 32-bit registers, and the rapid transfer of data on 32-bit external data buses, MS-DOS users continued to struggle along with 16-bittedness, rendered marginally more tolerable by the advent of the Intel 80286.

The 80286 microprocessor is still a 16-bit microprocessor with an instruction set that is a complete superset of the 8086 instruction set, but it operates at a higher speed and addresses a larger memory model with its 24-bit address bus. (2^{24} is 16,777,216, or in terms of memory address space, 16 megabytes.) The 80286 performs the same functions as the 8086, but with greater efficiency. The 80286 also presented the MS-DOS world with a novelty that the community was ill-prepared to put to use: hardware support for protected virtual memory.

It was to the 80286 that the first genuine virtual memory implementation of Microsoft Windows was targeted. It was to the 80286 that the original design of OS/2 was targeted.

Another advantage of the 80286 was that 16-bit peripheral cards became available. These cards could perform I/O operations such as video and hard disk control much more rapidly than the 8-bit cards common in the personal computers designed around the 8086 and 8088.

By the mid-1980s, the Intel 80386—a 32-bit microprocessor with sophisticated protected virtual memory support—was ready. Serious attention began to focus on 32-bit operating systems. Soon Windows 3.0 and OS/2 2.0 entered development. Both continued support of the 16-bit model, which was imposed on early application software by the 8086/80286 platform. Windows 3.1 itself is a 32-bit program emulating a 16-bit environment for the benefit of older applications, a staggering concession in speed and efficiency made in the interest of economy to the user and the shelf-life of software.

With the arrival of affordable 32-bit 80386 machines, the average MS-DOS user began to shoulder the burden of installing, learning, and using complicated memory-management software designed to allow 16-bit MS-DOS to continue as the operating system of the 80386 while allowing large applications such as computer-aided design (CAD) programs to take full advantage of the immense memory model offered by that microprocessor.

Windows NT vastly simplifies things by offering a flat, 32-bit (4-gigabyte) virtual memory model for all applications on all supported microprocessors, Intel and non-Intel alike. An application must be compiled on its appropriate runtime microprocessor platform; aside from instruction set and certain low-level details of peripheral hardware, however, the environment presented to Windows NT applications is identical, regardless of microprocessor platform.

Windows NT was designed to be a portable operating system. An operating environment similar to Windows 3.1 on the 286/386/486 is now available on a multitude of desktop platforms. The benefit to the user, in this instance, of moving up to Windows NT is that familiar applications will become available and run in an essentially identical manner in different work environments.

Additionally, Microsoft Win32s (pronounced *Win-32-ess*) is an important part of the picture as drawn by Microsoft. Win32s constitutes a support mechanism to allow many 32-bit applications coded for Windows NT to run under Windows 3.x, with certain limitations.

For the former MS-DOS user, the add-on memory manager package vanishes, whereas general and widespread access to applications running at 32-bit speed materializes.

Incidental to the impact of the advance of operating system software for 32-bit architectures is the advance in peripheral hardware that offers 80486 users extremely fast 32-bit I/O cards, such as IDE disks with 1-millisecond access time. The Windows NT flexible strategy with regard to software device drivers, along with its inherent 32-bittedness, is poised to fully accommodate the emerging VESA bus technology.

Understanding Preemptive Multitasking, Multithreading, and Protected Virtual Memory

- Protected operating systems
- Windows 3.1 protection versus Windows NT protection
- Windows 3.1 multitasking versus Windows NT multitasking
- Multiprocessor support in Windows NT

Windows NT embodies a protected operating system. It takes over and controls the entire machine, hardware and software. Every instruction the central processing unit executes on an NT machine is subject to constraints imposed by that operating system and proceeds at the indulgence of Windows NT. If the favor of the operating system is withdrawn due to bad behavior by an application program, Windows NT terminates the program and returns the resources allocated for use by the program to the pool of available resources from which properly executing programs may draw.

Windows 3.1 also runs in a protected environment, but the implementation of that protection is hampered by the limitations imposed by the underlying MS-DOS. The benefit to the user, in this instance, of moving up from Windows 3.1 to Windows NT is a suite of stable applications running on a nearly uncrashable computer.

Windows NT implements virtual memory. It divides memory into pages and assigns these pages to programs. Although Windows NT performs according to its design, no program can access the memory of another application without the consent of that application, or the operating system, or both.

Windows 3.1 also implements virtual memory, but not nearly as cleanly as Windows NT. Again, the limitation is the underlying MS-DOS, which has certain fixed ideas (bordering on obsessive) about how memory is mapped. The benefit to the user, in this instance, of moving up from Windows 3.1 to Windows NT is speedier runtime access to a practically unlimited amount of memory.

Windows NT multitasks, that is, runs multiple applications concurrently, by sharing processor cycles between the applications so that all the applications execute with perceived concurrency.

Windows 3.1 also multitasks, but does so based on a voluntary round-robin model imposed by the single-file access capabilities of MS-DOS.

The unfortunate side effect of the round-robin model is the phenom-enon familiar to all Windows users: A program gets hold of the proces-sor and refuses to yield to any other application. In contrast, Windows NT imposes preemption on multiple tasks. That is, a task always yields execution to another task in a timely manner. The benefit to the user, in this instance, of moving up from Windows 3.1 to Windows NT is smooth execution of multiple applications, none of which can seize the processor, or processors, indefinitely.

Inherent in the Windows NT model of multitasking are multiple threads of execution that can be launched by a single application. Under Win-dows 3.1, an application might launch other applications, but within its own task space there is only a single execution path.

Windows NT provides multitasking that is no longer limited to the sys-tem itself: It's now accessible at the application level. With the advent of multiply-threaded applications on the desktop, word processors, for example, will no longer go catatonic while spooling a print job.

Windows NT supports multiple processors. You and I, the average us-ers, have been "done" every few years by the marketeers of advances in computer hardware. Therefore, it will come as no surprise to discover that we are about to be "done" again. Desktop computers with central processing complexes, rather than central processing units, are already here. It is likely that by 1996 or so, a desktop computer containing four ultraspeed microprocessors will cost the same as today's single-80486-based desktop. The benefit to the user, in this instance, of mov-ing up from Windows 3.1 to Windows NT is that the upgrade path to emerging hardware platforms will appear seamless.

Windows NT Security

■ Advantages of operating system and file system security as offered by Windows NT

Some elements of the Windows NT operating environment find no cor-respondence in Windows 3.1. Strikingly, Windows NT is designed as a secure operating system. Windows NT treats files and devices similarly, in that access to both is subject to a security check based on access permissions established by the file or device owner or by the Adminis-trator of the system. At first glance, it might appear that in moving up to Windows NT you have lost a personal computer and gained a bu-reaucracy; however, the advantages of such a setup in the workplace are many.

Users can sit down in front of the same computer at different times without fear that one user has tangled up the system for another user.

Because each session with Windows NT starts with a login requiring an ID and a password, it is easy for the possessor of the Administrator password to establish who can overwrite what or who can change which settings.

The majority of settings that the typical Windows user sets to his or her taste (for instance, screen colors or printer preference) are user-specific. The user logging on gets his or her own last saved preferences. The Administrator secures against the individual user only the system-wide settings, such as which printers are available, which graphic mode Windows NT comes up in, which users can access the system, and which sets of programs and files are universally accessible.

Windows NT Networking and Administration

- PC Networks move up toward UNIX
- Windows NT's built-in LAN Manager
- Remote procedure calls
- Administrative tools

The UNIX world has long known the benefits of remote logins and distributed applications, pieces of which run on multiple machines. Users of MS-DOS-based networks have been afforded only a shadow of these benefits, largely in the form of shared disk access and, to a lesser extent, remote application launching. The benefit to the user, in this instance, of moving up from Windows 3.1 to Windows NT is a new world of network functionality and multiuser capabilities.

Networking capabilities are built into Windows NT. Although Windows NT has its own LAN Manager networking, it is an open networking system and permits the installation of add-on networking protocols. It's easy in this context to see why security is built into every level of Windows NT, including the file system. In many workplaces, peer-to-peer networking has replaced the client-server model. Windows NT support for networking is flexible and equally at home in a peer-to-peer role and as a network client or server.

Most pleasingly, Windows NT networking is compatible with many types of desktop environments. Not everyone in a workgroup is forced to upgrade to Windows NT. The Windows NT goal is to support mixed workgroups, which include also Windows 3.x, MS-DOS, and UNIX nodes.

Furthermore, Windows NT supports the Remote Procedure Call (RPC), which allows applications executing on one machine to assign subordinate operations to other machines on a network. Mainframe-like applications, such as databases consisting of persistent distributed objects or highly parallelized scientific software, now verge on becoming practical and perhaps common in the workplace.

The degree of detailed administrative control that the administrator may exercise over remote access to a server/workstation running Windows NT is very fine indeed.

Readers who have some administrative experience in multiuser environments should note the ease and convenience of carrying out Windows NT administrative chores. If you've ever struggled through the labyrinth of UNIX administration, even with the aid of the come-lately graphics tools provided for that purpose, you'll breathe a sigh of relief as you teach yourself Windows NT.

The Administrative Tools program group in the Windows NT Program Manager is shown in figure 1.1. This group contains some of the graphic-interface tools that make Windows NT system administration possible, because little of an administrative nature can be or needs to be done at the command prompt.

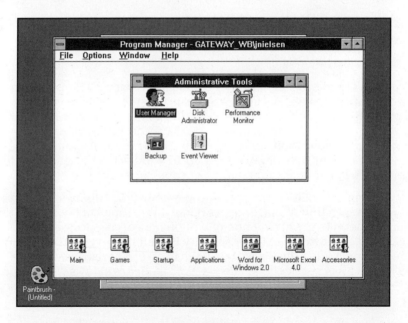

Fig. 1.1

The Program Manager's Administrative Tools Group.

Figure 1.2 shows the Tape Backup manager. This program enables the scheduling of automated tape backups—complete or incremental—by authorized backup managers and individuals possessing the proper privilege level. It also enables users to back up their own files.

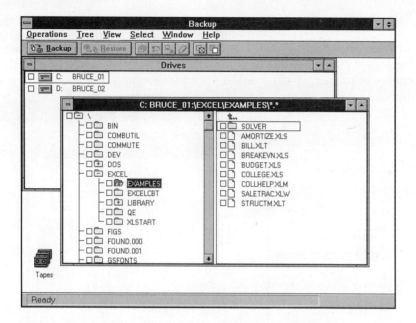

Fig. 1.2

The Windows NT
Backup program
for tape drives.

The Disk Administrator, shown in figure 1.3, enables the authorized
user to format disks in the desired file systems, divide disks into volumes, and establish striped, mirrored, and spanning sets, along with
other disk management chores.

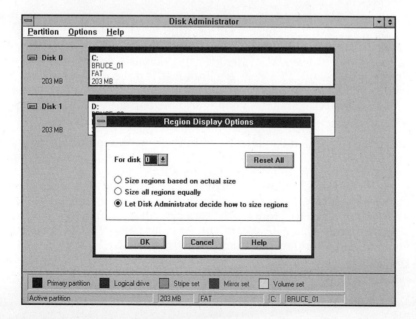

Fig. 1.3

The Windows NT
Disk Administra-
tor for hard disk
administration.

The Event Log records system information on various transactions that may be of interest to the Administrator account holder. The events can be viewed as a list or clicked for more detailed information, as shown in figure 1.4. (This figure shows the detailed record in connection with the failure of the network to start at system powerup.)

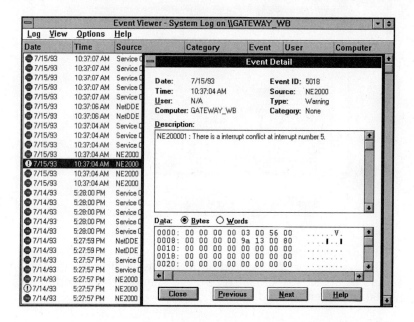

Fig. 1.4

The Windows NT Event Viewer for reviewing system events.

Figure 1.5 shows the Registry Editor. Although individual Windows applications may still have .INI files containing their last saved configurations, the Windows NT system uses a database of configuration and driver information. This Registry Database is not a plain ASCII text file, and it can be altered only by an authorized user. The Registry Database is a Windows NT installation configuration, and the REGEDIT32 program exists to allow delicate and critical configuration changes.

The best advice that can be offered to the novice administrator regarding the REGEDIT32 program has already been offered by Windows NT Setup, which by default declines to install the icon for the REGEDIT32 program in the Administration Tools program group. This is as clear a "don't mess" warning as can reasonably be offered under the GUI metaphor. If you place this tool in the Administrative Tools program group under Program Manager, you might consider using the File Properties menu option to rename its icon to "System Mangler," just to remind yourself of its potential.

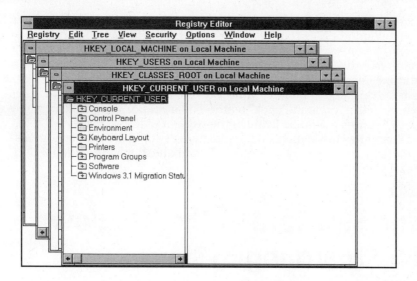

Fig. 1.5

The Windows NT
Registry Editor.

The User Manager, shown in figure 1.6, enables the administrator to
maintain and update user accounts, including various privileges and
group memberships.

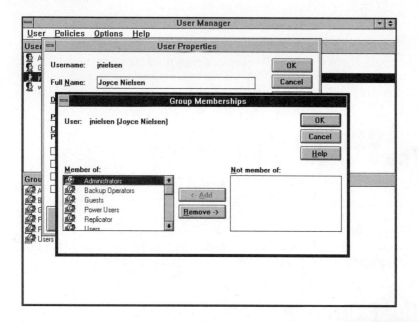

Fig. 1.6

The Windows NT
User Manager
program for add-
ing and editing
the accounts of
authorized users.

Like all the better Windows applications that we use more than once, Windows NT security and administrative tools are graphic, menu-driven, and self-explanatory. Administrative operations present cautionary dialog boxes when you're about to make important or irrevocable changes. All tools have extensive online help. Unlike in UNIX, it is relatively safe to blunder your way into administering your own system with the "hunt and click" method of mouse-driven self-teaching. We UNIX veterans could be living in the twilight of the RTFM era. (RTFM, or Read The Fine Manual, is the plaintive cry of UNIX system administrators in response to bothersome E-mail questions forwarded by puzzled users.)

The Structure of the Windows NT Operating System

- The microkernel
- The executive
- User-mode subsystems
- File systems
- Other design features

The design of Windows NT reflects a profound truth of the computer world: The designer can't imagine what the user might want in the future. This truth is the stumbling block of many other systems, but forms the cornerstone of Windows NT design layering.

The Microkernel

The innermost layer of Windows NT is a microkernel that controls the interaction of software with hardware. This kernel is essentially the only portion of the NT system specific to the hardware platform on which Windows NT is running. The microkernel runs at the highest level of privilege afforded by the microprocessor architecture. Thus, application software cannot interfere with its execution.

The Executive

At the next hierarchical level above the microkernel is the Windows NT executive, also operating at the highest level of privilege. In interaction with the microkernel, the Windows NT executive provides fundamental system services, such as virtual memory management, file system, process creation, and input and output. However, neither of these two layers provides the operating environment for application software, such as word processors, spreadsheets, or the marvelous FreeCell solitaire game distributed with Windows NT. And there's the rub.

User Mode Subsystems

The actual operating environment, any operating environment, for applications running on a Windows NT machine is provided by separate load-on-call protected user-mode subsystems running at a lesser level of protection than the microkernel and executive. Most of what you have come to recognize as the "operating system" of your computer is, with Windows NT, effectively an application program.

This approach of providing application-level services as installable subsystems, formerly found only on high-end workstations and mainframe computers, is now available on your desktop. The implications of this aspect of Windows NT design for business and engineering software are staggering.

Win32 Subsystem

Windows NT currently ships with five protected user-mode subsystems. The most important is Win32, which forms the native application programming interface for software intended to run specifically on a Windows NT machine. Other user-mode subsystems execute calls to Win32 services to provide the system services their own applications expect.

MS-DOS Subsystem

There is also an MS-DOS subsystem that runs good, old MS-DOS applications in a window or full screen, much as does Windows 3.1. Under Windows NT, however, such applications have lost more of their capability to trash the overall system. Included in Windows NT, MS-DOS support is support for modern, 32-bit MS-DOS applications written under the new DOS-32 API.

Win16 Subsystem

The Win16 subsystem loads when a Windows NT user attempts to run a Windows 3.x application. In the current release, it does a creditable job of nearly seamless support under Windows NT for all the familiar applications, while we await the anticipated deluge of Win32 applications.

POSIX Subsystem

The Windows NT POSIX subsystem runs applications coded in compliance with the POSIX standard from the UNIX application world and recompiled for the Windows NT system. Experienced UNIX users will find that many of their favorite terminal-session-oriented tools and filters port easily to Windows NT under this subsystem. Already there is excitement among the developer community about a quick technology infusion in the form of Windows NT POSIX subsystem ports of the popular suite of Stallman et al's GNU Project utilities and compilers.

The OS/2 subsystem currently supports OS/2 1.x character-based applications. The intent is to support the full range of OS/2 application programs in future releases, but here Omar Khayyam's advice in the *Rubaiyat* applies: "Take the cash and let the credit go."

More User-mode Subsystems?

These five subsystems would seem to be enough to keep most programmers and users occupied for years. The story does not end here, however.

Due to the layered design of Windows NT, there is nothing to prevent Microsoft or a third-party developer of sufficient acumen and resources from developing other protected user-mode subsystems to provide an application interface to popular software found on other operating systems. For instance, the PICK system remains popular for accounting and object-oriented databases. One wonders how long it will be before PICK applications appear running under a Windows NT PICK subsystem.

Other Design Aspects

Certain subtle aspects of Windows NT design promise considerable long-term benefits to the end user. Windows NT is more programmer-friendly than Windows 3.x. The programming model is complex but consistent. Formerly tedious aspects of Windows memory management are vastly simpler in Windows NT than in Windows 3.x.

Windows NT input and output services are factored neatly for multitasking. The main message loop that forms the heart of a Windows program is not quite as liable to become, in a given application, the rat's nest it might easily have been in Windows 3.x, because repetitious and mechanical chores are best delegated to dedicated Windows NT threads.

At the most profound level, Windows NT is Microsoft's latest stab at producing a more object-oriented operating system. Windows NT is described by Microsoft as the threshold of reaching a truly object-oriented operating environment somewhere between the mid-90s and the turn of the century—or at least the step before the threshold. In this domain, it appears to professionals that a substantial portion of the design goals which Microsoft set for itself at the start of the Windows NT project has been achieved successfully.

The Object of Objects

In an object-oriented environment, each aspect of the software accumulation that constitutes the moment-by-moment interaction of applications and operating system is an entity. This entity is self-contained, exists in an atmosphere of rough-and-ready equality with other software entities, and possesses distinct and well-understood channels of communication with all other objects with which it must interact.

In practice, this means that applications will become smaller, more numerous, and have simpler and clearer functionality. Because they are self-contained and possess well-understood channels of communication, they will be able to operate with any other application. The commercial goal to be attained in this brave new world of objects is that you will no longer have to buy a word processor, spell checker, thesaurus, printer driver, and font package from one vendor or one clique of vendors: Any spell checker will work with any editor, which will work with any printer driver, which will work with any thesaurus, and so on.

However, the glacial movement of Microsoft across the Windows years toward "true" object-oriented systems may yield to the empirical truth that no programming methodology ever answers all problems.

Truth Is Beauty

The computer programmer derives satisfaction from the aesthetic just as any creative individual does. And Windows NT is, in many ways, beautiful to the eyes of the programmer. Because more milk comes from contented cows, we may anticipate in the future of Windows NT a steady flow of cleaner software possessing expanded functionality, in contrast with the problematic first-generation Windows applications characteristic of Windows 3.x.

While you are waiting for all these next-generation wonder-applications to appear, the protected user-mode subsystems permit the current generation of applications, which you have carefully selected and diligently assimilated into your work style, to continue to operate under Windows NT. At present, the DOS and WIN16 subsystems support the majority of popular Windows 3.x, MS-DOS, and character-based OS/2 1.x applications, as well as a new generation of 32-bit MS-DOS applications that are just appearing.

File Systems, Protection, and Recovery

Consistent with the overall design of Windows NT that you have just examined, Windows NT's handling of file systems is flexible and layered. File systems, like user-mode subsystems, are installable. Installing Yet Another File System requires only the initiative of a programming team and some code designed in conformance to the requirements of Windows NT. Windows NT already supports three file systems: FAT, HPFS, and the Windows NT native NTFS.

In a manner similar to most other modern operating systems (but in contrast to Windows 3.x), Windows NT also treats devices as files. Programs open devices by calls to the Win32 API function OpenFile(), not with Windows 3.x calls such as OpenComm(). This model of the device-as-file has had a long trial run in the UNIX world and is a welcome upgrade to Windows NT over previous Microsoft operating systems.

To the user, the most significant aspect of a file system is the hard disk drive, where the great mass of active data resides. Physical disk drive control is an affair to be handled between the disk drive, its controller, the computer ROM BIOS, and the low-level Windows NT microkernel.

At the user and application level, Windows NT allows different file systems to be installed on different logical drives, where they can be manipulated by user-mode subsystems that recognize the particular file system.

Disk drives are divided into partitions, each of which has a filing system assigned to it. Often, a partition may be divided into more than one logical drive, that is, a drive with a unique identifying letter assigned to it, such as C or D.

The FAT File System

The file system that we have grown to know and tolerate under MS-DOS and Windows 3.x is called the FAT (File Allocation Table) file system. All user-mode subsystems shipped with the first release of Windows NT recognize and can manipulate files and directories on FAT partitions. Win32 applications can easily read data from and write data to a FAT partition without, in most instances, paying much attention to the partition type.

File and directory names on a FAT partition are limited to eight characters with an optional three-character extension, just as they are under MS-DOS. These names are effectively converted to uppercase.

FAT files may optionally possess certain attributes that can be detected and altered by the operating system and the application program. The optional attributes that a file may possess are found under MS-DOS, that is, Read-only, Hidden, System, and Archive.

This limited attribute structure, along with other technical limitations, such as maximum uninterrupted data length in a file, and performance make the FAT file system undesirable for a multiuser, secure operating system such as Windows NT.

Windows NT correctly handles the FAT file system and even boots off a FAT disk. On FAT partitions, however, files cannot be assigned security attributes, which are essential to the security scheme of Windows NT. FAT partitions are therefore generally not suitable for networking.

With the first upgrade of OS/2, users were introduced to the more sophisticated High Performance File System (HPFS), which is the second of the installable file systems supported under this release of Windows NT. In the category of desirability under Windows NT, HPFS ranks somewhere between FAT and NTFS.

The HPFS File System

HPFS allows faster hard disk access than FAT, which was really designed for floppy disks. HPFS doesn't partition a disk, but rather organizes it into volumes. Whereas FAT allows only about eight megabytes in its largest data structure, HPFS allows 16 contiguous megabytes.

HPFS was designed to cache write information in the interests of efficiency, instead of writing data immediately to the physical disk. Under the Windows NT HPFS installable file system, Windows NT assumes the responsibility for caching write data, and performs it in a fashion compatible with the Windows NT native NTFS.

The disk organization of HPFS also reserves some space in order to provide some recovery capabilities after disk errors.

HPFS uses a B-tree type structuring of its records for faster seeking of files and retrieval of their data. A B-tree is a binary branching tree of any type of linked data records that is reorganized each time a data record, or node, is added or deleted. The tree is reorganized so that it remains balanced, that is, with an equal depth and equal number of branches descending from each level of the tree. This leads to more dependable tree-searching, or file-searching, times.

HPFS file names can be up to 255 characters, relieving the user of the need to invent a meaningful eight-character name for every file object, an intellectual exercise which lost its entertainment value about a week after MS-DOS 1.1 was released.

HPFS is supported to aid the execution of OS/2 programs and to ease the burden on the user of migration from OS/2 to Windows NT. Certain special features of HPFS are either not supported or replaced by Windows NT system operations (such as disk caching). Many users install both operating systems on their systems, and it is convenient to be able to exchange files easily between two disk devices.

The New Technology File System

The native file system of Windows NT is called the New Technology File System (NTFS). This file system is quite different from FAT, and more sophisticated than HPFS, although similar in many respects.

Like HPFS, NTFS divides all storage media into volumes rather than partitions. NTFS takes the novel approach that everything on a volume is a file or part of a file, including unallocated disk space. The maximum volume size and maximum file size are identical under NTFS: 2^{64} bytes.

Like HPFS, NTFS uses a B-tree structure to speed file access. In addition, the more distributed structure of NTFS reduces the amount of seeking that has to be performed to gather all the data pertaining to a file or directory.

NTFS file names are accessible to non-NTFS filing systems over a network because NTFS automatically generates both an NTFS file name (up to 255 Unicode characters) and a legal MS-DOS file name for the same file. NTFS preserves the case of characters in file names. There is no practical limit to the length of path names passed to NTFS.

Every NTFS file has an owner. Every NTFS file has an access control list (ACL) that determines who can access the file and under what circumstances. The NTFS file system is an integral part of Windows NT system security.

In contrast with the simplicity of FAT file identification (the old system of eight plus three characters and four possible file attributes), NTFS file names and attributes present an almost bewildering complexity. The file name itself is an attribute; there are long lists of attributes which aid in supporting file system security and integrity and the interoperability of the file systems that Windows NT supports. Even the set of attributes is extensible under this powerful file system, because every aspect of file data is an attribute.

Despite the FAT file system's general inefficiency and unsuitability for the majority of Windows NT installations, some sound reasons remain for keeping one or more FAT partitions available. For instance, it may be some time before Windows NT adequately supports a tape backup drive. In the meantime, it's nice to be able to take advantage of Windows NT MultiBoot to boot MS-DOS off a small (say, 20-megabyte) MS-DOS partition and use MS-DOS software to back up your hard disks, including the partitions that Windows NT occupies. This convenience is available only if you decline Windows NT Setup's seductive invitation to convert to NTFS.

NTFS is a recoverable file system. Although writes are cached, which would normally increase the risk of a power failure damaging a volume, a transaction log is maintained that makes powerup recovery of file system integrated, rapid, and reliable. Maintaining the transaction log adds to overhead in comparison with merely caching write data, but it is economical in comparison with directly writing all data to disk.

On recovery from a power failure, NTFS notes transactions that were not completed and backs out of the transactions, maintaining the integrity of the filing system. The data from an initiated disk write that was never completely logged due to the system crash may be lost, but the filing system is unlikely to be rendered inconsistent and therefore unusable.

But power failures don't necessarily cost any data loss: Windows NT offers uninterruptable power supply (UPS) support. An uninterruptable power supply unit, which is typically an optional hardware installation, is capable of sending an interrupt to the computer it supports. The Windows NT operating system is prepared to respond to such an interrupt with a rapid and orderly shutdown of the system on residual battery power provided by the UPS.

Of course, despite all precautions, Stuff Happens. This is why Windows NTFS fault tolerance is enhanced in a number of ways.

Periodic backups are directly supported with Administrator software tools that enable a variety of backup operations for full and incremental data preservation on removable media (for example, digital tape).

Disk striping enables the file system to be configured such that data words are written to multiple disks, to each of two to 32 disks.

Striping may optionally include an extra parity bit. *Disk mirroring*, the option of redundantly recording the same data on more than one fixed disk, is also an optional feature of Windows NT and is supported for all installed file systems. Of the published schemes of employing redundant arrays of inexpensive disks (RAID), Windows NT supports RAID 0, 1, and 5.

An element of NTFS provided for convenience is *disk spanning*, the capability to conjoin different physical and logical devices into one NTFS volume.

All the features, utilities, and options just explored are accessible, as mentioned, through typical Windows easy-to-learn graphical utilities, such as the Disk Administrator and the Tape Backup utility.

Summary

In this chapter, you examined Windows NT, a portable, multitasking, multiuser, secure, and fault-tolerant operating system. Its modern design is based in part on what its designers perceive to be the best aspects of existing operating systems and in part on novel approaches. User-mode subsystems and installable file systems not only aid in preserving user investment in software designed for the earlier MS-DOS, Windows, OS/2, and UNIX operating environments, but also point to a future of the interoperability of popular applications across operating system boundaries. In addition, the well-understood Windows user interface provides handy and accessible tools for administering the complexity inherent in an advanced system like Windows NT.

The Windows NT native interface offers an upward path to powerful, easy-to-use, graphic-oriented, 32-bit applications portable between Windows NT installations on different hardware platforms. Strong built-in network and multiprocessing support suggest that Windows NT is poised to take advantage of powerful new hardware coming on-line in the middle of this decade and will thus remain an attractive target for application development into the next century. Useful application programs make today's powerful 32-bit computer useful, so Windows NT appears poised to emerge as one of the champions of the desktop operating systems wars.

Operating Windows NT

Windows NT is a graphical operating system that makes it easier to use your computer. Under Windows NT, each application runs in a *window* on your screen that you can open or close. You can run multiple applications at the same time, each in its own window, and you easily can switch between applications. Your knowledge of one application transfers to each new application you use because each Windows NT application operates in a similar way.

What you learn in this chapter will help you operate any Windows NT application. It contains important information about operating Windows NT in the form of full explanations and suggests alternative ways of accomplishing tasks. After completing this chapter, you should learn how to start and manage applications with the Program Manager, as described in Chapter 4, and how to manage your disk and files with the File Manager, as described in Chapter 5. From there, you can jump to any other chapter in this book.

In this chapter, you learn that Windows NT is easy to operate and that operating one Windows NT application is similar to operating another. This "learning carry-over" is important—when you start a new Windows NT application, you already understand most of the concepts necessary to operate it. You know how to choose, find, and use most commands.

This chapter shows you how to control the location, size, and status of windows that contain applications. You also learn the three methods of choosing commands and working with applications. The first method uses a mouse and is excellent for graphics applications and for learning new applications. The second method uses the keyboard—touch typists usually prefer this method of choosing commands and entering data. The third method uses shortcut key combinations and improves everyone's efficiency.

Starting Windows NT

If you have not yet installed Windows NT, turn to the Appendix to learn how. After it is installed, Windows NT is easy to start.

When you start your system with Windows NT installed, you are offered a menu that allows you to choose which operating system you would like to boot. If you select Windows NT or Windows NT Advanced Server, you see several messages describing the components of Windows NT as they successfully load.

Finally, you'll be presented with the Windows NT Desktop and the message `Press Ctrl+Alt+Del to log on`. Windows NT's perception of Ctrl+Alt+Del is a little less deadly than your computer's use for the special keystroke under DOS—you use it to log in rather than to restart your system.

When you press Ctrl+Alt+Del, you'll see the Windows NT login dialog box (see fig. 2.1).

Fig. 2.1

The Windows NT login dialog box.

The system administrator logs in with `Administrator` and the appropriate password. If you're not the system administrator, you should log in using the password the administrator assigned you when your account was created. If you enter an incorrect password, you see a message that says `The system could not log you on`. Make sure your user name and domain are correct, then type your password again. You'll be returned to the login dialog when you click the OK button.

After your password has been confirmed, the Program Manager appears on your screen as a window that contains other windows and icons (see fig. 2.2). The windows inside the Program Manager window, such as the open *Main* window in the figure, contain icons that represent applications. The icons (pictures with names below them) at the bottom of the Program Manager window represent closed windows.

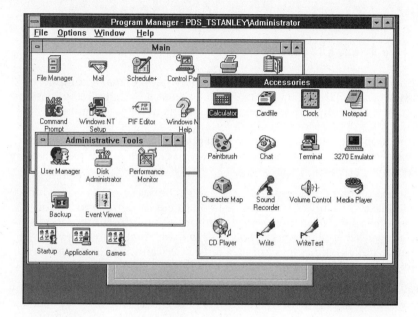

Fig. 2.2

The Program Manager with the Main, Accessories, and Administrative Tools groups open.

When you first install Windows NT, you see that the Program Manager contains the Main window, which includes utilities to help you manage files, work with DOS, customize Windows NT, and install new printer drivers. The Program Manager also includes the Accessories window, which includes applications you can use to accessorize your main applications; the Games window, which contains three games you can use to learn how to use Windows NT; the Administrative Tools window, which the system administrator uses to manage the computer; the Startup window, which you can place applications in to start when Windows NT starts; and, if Windows detects existing Windows applications, an Applications window, which contains your Windows NT and DOS applications.

As you'll learn in this chapter and in Chapter 4, you can customize your Windows NT start-up screen in many ways. You can create new windows and new icons to go in the windows. Each icon can represent an application or an application and a data file (so that when you start the application the data file opens automatically). The applications and files can be located in different directories on your disk, and different icons can represent the same application in different windows. If you customize your Program Manager, windows and icons different from those shown in figure 2.2 may appear when you start Windows NT on your computer.

Working in the Windows NT Environment

Windows NT uses concepts that, for many people, make computers easier to use. The basic organizational concept is that all applications run on a desktop, and each application runs in its own window. Windows NT can run multiple applications just as you can have stacks of papers on your desk from more than one project. You can move the windows and change their size just as you can move and rearrange the stacks of papers on your desk.

Just as you can cut, copy, and paste parts between papers on your real desktop, Windows NT enables you to cut or copy information from one application and paste the information into another. Some Windows NT applications even share *live* information; when you change data in one application, Windows NT automatically updates linked data in other applications.

Making entries, edits, and changes to information is similar in all Windows NT applications. The basic procedure is as follows:

1. Activate the window containing the desired application.

2. Select the text or graphics object you want to change.

3. Choose a command from the menu at the top of the application.

4. Select options from a dialog box if one appears and complete the command by choosing OK or pressing Enter.

Learning the Parts of the Windows NT Screen

Figure 2.3 shows a Windows NT desktop containing multiple applications, each in its own window. The parts of a typical Windows NT screen are labeled in the figure.

With the *mouse pointer*, you can control Windows NT applications quickly and intuitively. It enables you to choose commands, select options, and move on-screen items. When you move the mouse, the mouse pointer moves accordingly. The mouse pointer changes shape at different locations on-screen to indicate that it has different capabilities at that point. You select items on-screen by positioning the pointer on the item to be selected and then pressing or holding down the mouse button. You use three actions to control the pointer in Windows NT: *clicking*, *double-clicking*, and *dragging* (see table 2.1 later in this chapter).

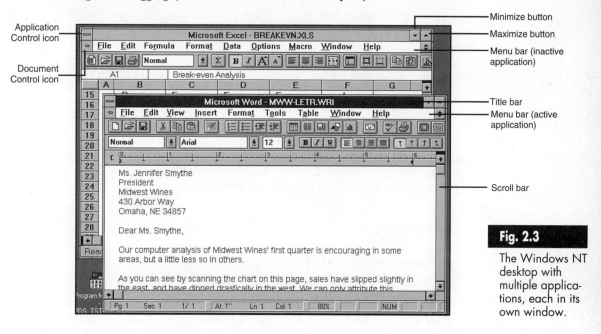

Application Control icon

Document Control icon

Minimize button

Maximize button

Menu bar (inactive application)

Title bar

Menu bar (active application)

Scroll bar

Fig. 2.3

The Windows NT desktop with multiple applications, each in its own window.

The *Control icon* opens a menu that contains commands to control window location, size, and status (open or closed). Each application and each document window has its own Control icon and menu. The *application Control icon* appears at the left edge of the application title bar. The *document Control icon* appears at the left edge of the document title bar (if the document window is smaller than full-screen) or at the left edge of the menu bar (if the document window is full-screen). To open an application Control menu, press Alt, space bar; to open a document Control menu, press Alt, hyphen (-). You can open either menu by clicking the pointer on the Control icon.

The *title bar* at the top of each window contains the name of the application. After you save a file, the title bar also shows the file name. The title bar is one color when the window is active and another color when the window is inactive. (The *active window* is the window on top; it contains the currently running application.)

Menu names are located in the *menu bar* directly under the title bar. Windows NT applications use the same menu headings for common functions (such as **F**ile, **E**dit, **W**indow, and **H**elp) to make it easy for you to learn new applications. Select a menu by clicking on it with the left mouse button or by pressing Alt and then the underlined letter in the menu name. (This book shows the letter you press in **bold** type: for example, **F**ile.)

Icons are small pictorial representations. Some icons in Windows NT represent applications in memory that do not currently occupy a window. Icons appear along the bottom of the desktop or within the Program Manager window. To reduce the clutter of a filled desktop, you can minimize windows to icons. When you want to work with the application, restore icons into windows by using mouse techniques or the Control menu.

Application windows are the windows containing applications. *Document windows* appear inside application windows and contain documents. In many (but not all) applications, you can have several document windows open at a time; you switch between them by pressing Ctrl+F6 or by selecting the document you want from the **W**indow menu.

In applications, you use *scroll bars* to move up and down in a document or from left to right in documents wider than the screen.

You can *maximize* a window by clicking on the Maximize button—an upward pointing arrow at the top right of the window—so that it occupies the full screen, or you can minimize a window by clicking on the Minimize button—a downward pointing icon at the top right of a window. Double-click the minimized icon to return it to a window. (When a window is maximized, you can *restore* it to its previous size.) You also can minimize, maximize, and restore windows by choosing commands from the application or document Control menu.

You can resize a window by dragging its *window border* with the mouse or by choosing the **S**ize command from the Control menu. You can move a window without resizing by dragging its title bar with the mouse or by choosing the Move command from the Control menu.

Using the Mouse and the Keyboard

The *mouse* is a hand-held pointing device that controls the position of a pointer on-screen. As you move the mouse across your actual desktop or mouse pad, the pointer moves across the screen in the same direction. The mouse acts as an extension of your hand, enabling you to point to objects on-screen. The mouse works well for people unfamiliar with a keyboard, for new users, or for people using graphics and desktop publishing applications.

To use a mouse, hold it so that the cable extends forward from your fingers and the mouse's body nestles under the palm of your hand. Place your index finger and second finger on the buttons. Move the mouse on your desk to move the pointer on-screen; click the left mouse button to make a selection. (Windows NT and Windows NT applications use the left button to indicate most selections, but you can use the Control Panel to make the right button the selector button if you find that button more convenient.) The most common use of the mouse is to select menus, commands, text, graphics objects, or windows so that you can change them with a command. In graphics applications and desktop publishing applications, you usually use the mouse to select menus, options, and icons and to select and move objects on-screen.

The mouse senses movement through the rotating ball on its undercar-riage. To use a mouse, your desktop surface must be smooth and clean. If possible, do not run the mouse on paper or cardboard surfaces; the lint from paper or cardboard can clog the ball and cause the pointer to skip. The ideal surface is a specially designed mouse pad. If you have an optical or laser mouse, you may have a special surface on which you must move your mouse.

To use a mouse, you need a clear area on your desk next to the key-board. You don't have to clean your whole desktop—you need only a six- or eight-inch square of space for the mouse. Using the Control Panel, you can increase or decrease the sensitivity of the mouse so that you need a smaller or larger area to move the mouse.

To select an object or menu item using the mouse, follow these steps:

1. Move the mouse so that the tip of the mouse pointer, usually an arrow, is on the name, graphics object, or text you want to select.

2. Quickly press and release the left mouse button.

Throughout this book, this two-step process is called *clicking*. Clicking the mouse button twice in rapid succession while pointing is called *double-clicking*. Double-clicking produces an action different from click-ing. In a word processing application, for example, you click to position the insertion point, but you double-click to select a word.

You can use the mouse also for *dragging*. Dragging selects multiple text characters or moves graphic objects such as windows. In figure 2.4, a sentence in the Write word processor is selected.

To drag with the mouse, follow these steps:

1. Move the mouse so that the tip of the pointer is on the object or at the beginning of the text you want to select. (When over text, the pointer appears as an I-beam.)

2. Press and hold down the mouse button.

3. While holding down the mouse button, move the mouse. If you are dragging a graphical object, the object moves when you move the mouse. If you are selecting text, the highlighted text area expands when you move the mouse.

4. Release the mouse button.

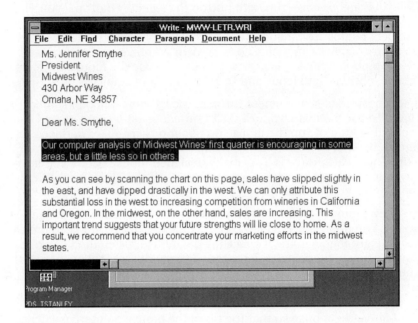

Fig. 2.4

Selected text in an application.

The mouse is a useful tool, but you can use the keyboard to do nearly everything you can do with the mouse. (Table 2.1 describes keyboard actions in detail.) The mouse and the keyboard work as a team for controlling Windows NT applications. You can perform some tasks more easily with the mouse and some more easily with the keyboard. Most Windows NT applications can perform all functions with either. Experiment with the mouse and the keyboard and use each where it works best for you.

Understanding Windows NT Terminology

Table 2.1 introduces terms, mouse actions, and keystrokes that describe certain actions. The first part of the table contains general terms describing Windows NT actions. The next part defines keystrokes and mouse actions that produce consistent results in most Windows NT applications. Refer to this table as you continue reading *Using Windows NT*.

Table 2.1 Basic terminology of Windows NT and of this book	
Term	**Definition**
Special Terms Used in Windows NT	
Choose	Execute a command or complete a dialog box.
Select	Select an item to activate it so that you can change it. Selecting a command or option turns it on but does not complete it. Selected options show a black dot or an *X*. Selected text appears in reversed type. Selected graphics appear enclosed by a dashed line or fenced in by boxes known as handles.
Unselect or Deselect	Remove the selection.
Mouse Terms	

Note: A comma indicates that you release the first key before pressing the second key. A plus (+) indicates that you press and hold down the first key and then press the second key.

Point	Move the mouse so that the arrow pointer is on the desired menu name, command name, or graphic object, or so that the I-beam pointer (used in text) is where you want the insertion point (cursor) to be.
Pointer	The on-screen symbol controlled by the mouse. As you move the mouse on the desk, the pointer moves on-screen. The pointer changes shape to indicate the current status and the type of

continues

Table 2.1 Continued	
Term	**Definition**
	functions and selections available. An arrow means that you can select menus, commands, or objects. An I-beam means that the pointer is over text that you can edit. A two-headed or four-headed arrow means that you can move the edge of the item. An hourglass means that you must wait while the application works. A crosshair means that you can draw.
I-beam	When the mouse pointer is in an area of text that you can edit, the pointer appears as a vertical I-beam. Reposition the flashing insertion point (cursor) by positioning the I-beam and clicking.
Mouse button	The mouse usually has two buttons. (Some mice have three.) Normally, clicking the left button completes an action; clicking the center or right button does nothing in Windows NT. (Clicking the right mouse button performs a specific function in some Windows NT applications.) You can switch the action of the left and right buttons through the Control Panel.
Click	Quickly press and release the mouse button as you point to the item indicated. Clicking is used to reposition the insertion point in text, select a menu, choose a command from a menu, or select an option from a dialog box.
Drag	Select multiple text characters or move objects by pointing to them and holding down the left mouse button as you move the mouse.
Double-click	Rapidly press and release the left mouse button twice as you point to the indicated item. Double-clicking on an icon or file name opens an application or window related to that icon or file name.
Shift+click	Press and hold down the Shift key as you click. Use Shift+click to select multiple consecutive file names or to select text between the current insertion point and where you press Shift+click.
Ctrl+click	Press and hold down the Control (Ctrl) key as you click. Use Ctrl+click to select multiple nonconsecutive file names or item choices.

Term	Definition

Keyboard Actions

Note: A comma indicates that you release the first key before pressing the second key. A plus (+) indicates that you press and hold down the first key and then press the second key.

Alt, *letter*	Press and release the Alt key and then press *letter*. This action opens a menu without choosing a command.
Alt+*letter*	Press and hold down the Alt key as you press *letter*. This action opens a menu or selects an option in a dialog box.
Letter	Press the indicated letter to choose a command in a menu. To choose a command, press the letter in the command that is underlined on-screen (this book shows the letter you are to press in bold type). Press **M**, for example, to choose the **M**ove command. You can press the uppercase or lowercase letter.
Arrow key	Press the appropriate directional arrow key.

Keystrokes to Control Windows NT

Note: A comma indicates that you release the first key before pressing the second key. A plus (+) indicates that you press and hold down the first key and then press the second key.

Alt+Esc	Activate the next application window or icon on the desktop. Pressing Alt+Esc does not restore icons into windows.
Alt+Tab	Activate the *next* application window or icon. Restores icons into windows. Only the "cool switch" window, containing the application's name and icon, shows until you release Alt+Tab, making it faster to cycle through application windows than to use Alt+Esc.
Alt+Shift+Tab	Activate the *previous* icon or application. Restore icons into a window. Only the "cool switch" window, containing the application's name and icon, shows until you release Alt+Shift+Tab.

continues

Table 2.1 Continued

Term	Definition
Ctrl+F6	Activate the next document window (if an application has multiple document windows open).
Ctrl+Tab	Activate the next group window within the Program Manager.
Ctrl+Esc	Display the Task List window, from which you can activate an application by selecting from a list of currently running applications.
Alt+space bar	Select the Control menu for the active application icon or window so that you can control the location, size, and status of the window.
Alt+hyphen (-)	Select the Control menu for the active *document* window within the *application* window so that you can control the location, size, and status of the document window.

Keystrokes to Control the Menus

Note: A comma indicates that you release the first key before pressing the second key. A plus (+) indicates that you press and hold down the first key and then press the second key.

Alt	Activate the menu bar.
Alt, *letter*	Select the menu indicated by *letter* (*letter* is <u>underlined</u> on-screen; *letter* is displayed in **bold** in this book).
letter	Choose (execute) the command in the menu indicated by *letter*.
Arrow keys	Select but do not choose the next menu (use the right or left arrows) or the next command (use the up or down arrows).
Enter	Choose (execute) the selected command in the menu.
Esc	Close the current menu without making a choice. Press Esc a second time to deactivate the menu bar and return to the document.

Term	Definition

Keystrokes to Control Dialog Boxes

Note: See table 2.2 in the upcoming section, "Selecting Options from Dialog Boxes," for more information.

Arrow keys	Select or scroll file names in a list box. Select round option buttons in a group.
Tab	Select the next text box, list box, group of options, or button.
Shift+Tab	Select the *previous* text box, list box, group of options, or button.
Alt+*letter*	Select the option, text box, or list box specified by *letter* (*letter* is <u>underlined</u> on-screen; *letter* is displayed in bold in this book).
Space bar	Select or deselect the active check box or button.
Enter	Choose the bold or outlined button (usually the OK button). This action completes the command or opens another dialog box.
Esc	Close an open dialog box without making any changes.

Controlling the Windows in Windows NT

Just as you move papers on your desktop, you can move and reorder windows on-screen. In fact, you can resize windows, expand them to full size, shrink them to a small icon to save space, and restore them to their original size.

All these activities take place by choosing options on a Control menu or with a mouse action. Every application and document window has a Control menu icon located at the left edge of the window's title bar. Figure 2.5 shows an open application Control menu.

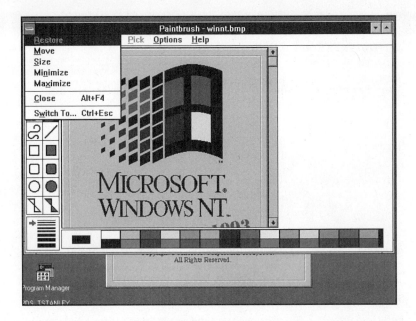

Fig. 2.5

The Paintbrush
Control Menu.

In an application window, the Control menu icon looks like a space bar
in a box. To activate it with the keyboard, press Alt, space bar. In a
document window in an application, the Control menu icon looks like a
hyphen in a box. To activate it with the keyboard, press Alt, hyphen (-).
To activate either Control menu with the mouse, click on the Control
menu icon.

Many of the commands in a document Control menu are the same as
those in an application Control menu. The application Control menu,
however, controls the application window; the document Control menu
controls the document window within the application. The commands
in a Control menu are given in the following chart.

Command	Action
Restore	Restores an icon or maximized window to its previous window size. The shortcut-key combination is Ctrl+F5 (for a document window).
Move	Moves the currently selected icon or window to a new location when you press the arrow keys. The shortcut-key combination is Ctrl+F7 (for a document window).
Size	Resize a window by moving its edge. The shortcut-key combination is Ctrl+F8 (for a document window).

Command	Action
Minimize	Minimize a window into an icon. In most cases, this command applies only to application windows.
Maximize	Increase an application window or icon to its full size. The shortcut-key combination is Ctrl+F10 (for a document window).
Close	Exits an application or closes a document window. If changes were made to the current file since the last save, the application asks whether you want to save the file. The shortcut-key combinations are Alt+F4 (for an application window) and Ctrl+F4 (for a document window).
Switch To	Displays the Task List so that you can switch to a different application. The shortcut-key combination is Ctrl+Esc.
Next Window	Activates the next document window in applications that enable multiple documents to run simultaneously; works only when multiple document windows are open. The shortcut-key combination is Ctrl+F6.

When you size or move a window using the mouse pointer, the mouse pointer changes appearance to indicate what change you can make. The different mouse-pointer appearances are listed and described in the following chart.

Pointer Appearance	Mouse Action
⟺	Drag the edge left or right.
⇕	Drag the edge up or down.
⬂	Drag the corner in any direction.
✛	Drag the window to a new location.

 NOTE You can change cursors in the Control Panel. See Chapter 7 for more information.

Moving a Window or an Icon

With Windows NT, you can move a window to any location on-screen. You can arrange applications on your Windows NT desktop as neatly or as messily as your real desktop.

To move a window with the mouse, activate the window by clicking on it; then place the pointer on the window's title bar, press and hold down the mouse button, drag the outline of the window to the new location, and release the button. Move icons in the same way.

To move a window with the keyboard, activate the window you want to move by pressing Alt+Tab or Alt+Esc until the window is active. Select the Control menu by pressing Alt, space bar or Alt, hyphen; then choose **M**ove. A four-headed arrow appears, and the window borders turn gray. Press the arrow keys to move the shadowed borders to where you want the window and then press Enter.

To move a program or group icon with the keyboard, press Alt+Esc to select the icon. Press Alt, space bar to display the Control menu and then select **M**ove from the Control menu. Press the arrow keys until the icon is where you want it.

You cannot move a maximized window (if you open the Control menu in a maximized window, the Move command is dimmed—unavailable). To move a maximized window, you must restore it to a smaller size (see the following section).

Changing the Size of a Window

To change the size of a window with the mouse, activate the window by clicking on it. Move the pointer to one edge or corner of the window until the pointer changes into a two-headed arrow (see the preceding chart). Press and hold down the mouse button and drag the double-headed arrow to move the edge or corner of the window and resize the window. When the window is the size you want, release the mouse button.

To change the size of a window with the keyboard, press Alt+Tab or Alt+Esc to activate the window you want to resize. Choose the Control menu and select **S**ize to display a four-headed arrow in the window. Press the arrow key that points to the edge you want to resize. A double-headed arrow jumps to the edge you selected. Press the appropriate arrow key to move the selected edge. When the window is the size you want, press Enter. To return the window to its original size, press Esc while the edges are shadowed.

You cannot size a maximized window (if you open the Control menu in a maximized window, the Size command is dimmed—unavailable). To size a maximized window, you must restore it to a smaller size (see the following sections on maximizing, minimizing, and restoring).

Moving Two Edges at the Same Time

To move two edges at once with the mouse, move the pointer to the corner of a window so that the pointer becomes a two-headed arrow tilted at a 45-degree angle. Drag the corner to its new location and release the mouse button.

To move two edges at once with the keyboard, choose the Control Size Command so that a four-headed arrow appears. Press the arrow key that points to the first edge you want to move (for example, press the left arrow to select the left edge); then press the arrow key that points to the second edge of the corner. A double-headed arrow appears pointing to the corner you selected. Press the arrow keys to move that corner to its new location; press Enter to fix the corner.

Maximizing a Window to Full Size

When you are working in an application, you may find it convenient to maximize the application window so that it fills the screen. If the application includes document windows, you can maximize the document windows so that they fill the entire inside of the application window. When you maximize a window, you hide other windows and icons, but they are still active.

To maximize a window with the mouse pointer, click the Maximize button at the top right of the window (the up arrow) or double-click in the title bar. Restore the window to its previous size by clicking the Restore icon that appears at the top right of the window (the double arrow that appears only in a maximized window) or by double-clicking in the maximized window's title bar.

You can maximize or restore windows with the keyboard by choosing the Control Maximize or Control **R**estore command. When a window is already restored, the **R**estore command is unavailable (it appears in gray) in the menu.

You cannot move or size a maximized window.

Minimizing and Restoring Windows and Icons

When you have too many windows on-screen, you can clean up the screen by changing windows into icons. As you know, *icons* are small pictorial representations of an application (or, in the Program Manager, of a closed group window). Usually, application icons are stored at the bottom of the screen (see fig. 2.6). Icons usually show a name, symbol, or shape that indicates the application they represent. They also can show their active file or document. The icons at the bottom of figure 2.6 are for the Excel,Clock, Paintbrush, Chat, File Manager, ClipBook Viewer, Print Manager, and Program Manager applications. In the figure, Word for Windows and its document are sized and positioned at less than the maximum so that you have immediate access to the applications shown as icons at the bottom of the screen.

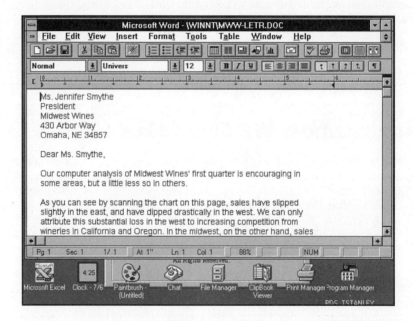

Fig. 2.6

Icons representing applications available in memory that are not in a window.

Application icons represent applications that are in memory but not in a window. Windows NT applications can continue running even when minimized into an icon. The Clock application, for example, continues to tell time.

With a mouse, you can reduce a window to an icon by clicking on the Minimize button (the down-arrow located at the right edge of the application's title bar). Restore an icon into a window by double-clicking on the icon (if you cannot see the icon, move the window covering it). You also can restore an icon to a window by activating the Task List and selecting the application from the list (to activate the Task List, double-click on the desktop background or press Ctrl+Esc).

From the keyboard, you can minimize windows into icons by pressing Alt, space bar to display the Control menu and then choosing Minimize. To restore an icon to its previous size with the keyboard, choose **R**estore from the Control menu. Or, press and hold down Alt+Tab until the icon is selected. When you release Alt+Tab, the selected icon restores itself into a window.

To select an icon but not restore it, press Alt+Esc until the icon is selected. Press Alt, space bar to display the Control menu for that application. Choose any of the Control commands such as **R**estore, Maximize, or **C**lose.

You can close an application by choosing the Control **C**lose command. If you made changes to the file since the last save, you are asked whether you want to save the changes. Some DOS applications require special closing procedures. For full details on DOS applications, refer to Chapter 22.

Using Menus and Dialog Boxes

Every Windows NT application operates in a similar way. As you have already learned, you can move and resize all windows the same way in every application. You also execute commands in the same way in all Windows NT applications. Commands are listed in menus whose names appear at the top of the window. You can choose commands from a menu by using the mouse or the keyboard (many timesaving shortcuts exist for choosing commands, too). If a command needs information from you, a dialog box appears after you choose the command. You can use the mouse or the keyboard to choose options or enter values in dialog boxes.

Choosing Menus and Commands

When a menu is selected as shown in figures 2.7 and 2.8, its commands appear in a list. If you're not sure where to find a command, try browsing through the menus until you find the command you need. Many applications use similar commands for similar actions—a practice that makes learning multiple Windows NT applications easier.

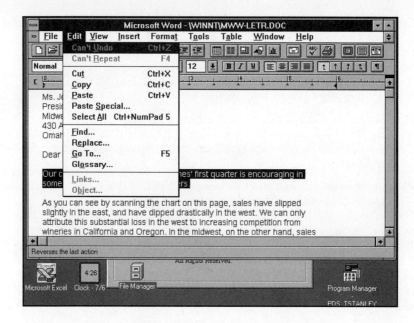

Fig. 2.7

Microsoft Word's
Edit menu.

To choose a command with the mouse, follow these steps:

1. Position the tip of the mouse pointer on the menu name in the menu bar and click the left mouse button.

2. Click on the command name in the menu.

To choose a command with the keyboard, follow these steps:

1. Press and release the Alt key to activate the menu bar.

2. Type the underlined letter in the name of the menu you want.

3. Type the underlined letter in the name of the command you want.

   or

   Press the down arrow to select the command you want and then press Enter.

Another way to choose commands with the keyboard is to press Alt, Enter to open the first menu, press the left and right arrows to open adjacent menus, and then press the up and down arrows to select the command you want from the open menu. Press Enter to choose the selected command.

You can choose commands that appear in a menu in solid black (bold) type. You performed all the steps necessary to activate a command that appears in bold.

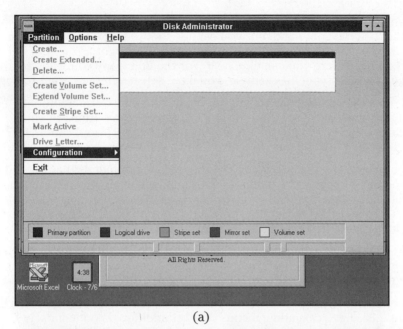

(a)

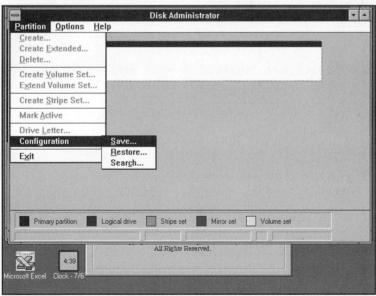

(b)

Fig. 2.8

Disk Administrator's Partition menu with cascading menu option selected (a), then with the cascading menu open (b).

You cannot choose commands that appear in gray in a menu. You can see the gray command, but you cannot choose it. If a command you want to choose appears in gray, you probably forgot a step that is required before you can choose it. For the **E**dit **C**opy command to appear in bold type, for example, you must select what you want to copy.

Command names followed by an ellipsis (...) display an additional dialog box or window from which you can choose options or enter data. If you choose **E**dit **F**ind... from a Windows NT application, for example, a box appears in which you type the word you want to find.

Commands with a check mark to the left are commands that toggle on and off. A check mark indicates the command is on; no check mark indicates the command is off. In Windows NT Write, for example, a check mark next to the **B**old command in the **C**haracter menu indicates that bold is *on* for the currently selected text.

Commands with key combinations listed to the right have shortcuts. In Word for Windows, for example, the **E**dit **C**opy command lists a shortcut of Ctrl+C. To copy text, you can choose **E**dit **C**opy or press Ctrl+C.

Commands with an arrowhead next to them (such as Configuration in fig. 2.8a) have cascading menus that list additional commands. In Disk Administrator, the Configuration command in the **P**artition menu has a triangle to its right, indicating that a list of configuration options appears when you choose the Partition Configuration command. You must choose the configuration option that you want from this list.

If you don't want to make a choice after displaying a menu, click the pointer a second time on the menu name or click outside the menu. If you are using the keyboard, press Esc to back out of a menu without making a choice and press Esc a second time to return to the document.

Backing Out of Menus, Edits, and Dialog Boxes

When you are in doubt about the command you are about to choose or the edit you are about to make, you can escape. Press the Esc key to cancel the current dialog box or edit. Press the Esc key to close the open menu but leave the menu bar active; press Esc a second time to leave the menu bar and return to your document. If you are in a dialog box, you can choose the Cancel button to cancel selections you made. Clicking on the Cancel button or pressing Esc closes the dialog box.

Many Windows NT applications have an Undo command. If you complete a command and then decide you want to undo it, check under the Edit menu for an **U**ndo command.

Many commands have associated key combinations, many of which appear to the right of the command on the pull-down menu. Figure 2.7 shows the shortcut key combinations available under the **E**dit menu in the Word for Windows application. You can press Ctrl+C to copy selected text, for example, or press F5 to go to a specific page. (Notice that some of the commands are gray and therefore unavailable.)

Selecting Options from Dialog Boxes

Some commands need additional information before you can complete them. To use the Format **N**umber command in Excel, for example, you must specify which predefined or custom numeric and date formats you want to use. The command displays a dialog box containing a list from which you can choose existing predefined or custom formats and a text box in which you can type new custom formats.

Commands that require more information display a *dialog box*—a window similar to those shown in figures 2.9 and 2.10. Dialog boxes like the one in figure 2.9 have areas for you to enter text (see the File **N**ame text box) or to select from a scrolling list of choices (see the **D**irectories list). Many applications also include drop-down list boxes with lists that appear only when you select the box and press the down-arrow key or click on the down arrow on the right side of the window. Figure 2.10 shows that dialog boxes can have round option buttons and square check boxes. The round option buttons are clustered in groups, and you can select only one of the options. The square check boxes, like the Parity Chec**k** box in figure 2.10, are by themselves, and you can turn each on or off. After you select options or make text entries, you accept the contents of the dialog box by choosing the OK button (press Enter); you can cancel the dialog box by choosing the Cancel button (press Esc).

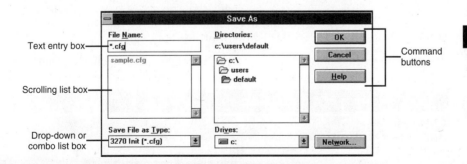

Fig. 2.9

The Save As dialog box with a text-entry box, a scrolling-list box, a drop-down list box, and command buttons.

The five areas of a dialog box are summarized in table 2.2.

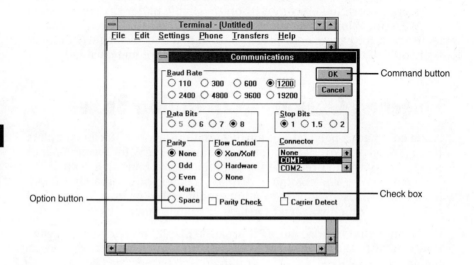

Fig. 2.10

The Communications dialog box in the Terminal application, with round option buttons and square check boxes.

If a dialog box hides something that you want to see on-screen, you can move the dialog box with the mouse by dragging the dialog box by its title bar to a new position. With the keyboard, press Alt, space bar to open the dialog Control menu and then choose **Move**. The arrow turns into a four-headed arrow; press any arrow key to use the four-headed arrow to move the dialog box. Press Enter when the dialog box is where you want it. (You can cancel the move before you press Enter by pressing Esc.)

Using the Mouse in Dialog Boxes

To select an option button or check box, click on it. Clicking on a check box the first time puts an *X* in it, signifying that the check box is selected. Clicking on a check box a second time turns off the *X*. To turn off a round option button, click on one of the other buttons in the group.

To select command buttons such as OK, Cancel, Yes, or No, click on them.

Table 2.2 Areas of a dialog box	
Area	**Use**
Text box	Type text entries manually. Press the Backspace key to erase characters if you make a mistake.
List box	Select a listed item by scrolling through the list and selecting one item. The selected item appears in highlighted text (and also may appear in the text box above the list).

Area	Use
Drop-down or Combo list box	Display the list by selecting the list and then pressing the down-arrow key, or clicking the arrow on the right side of the list. Press the down-arrow to select the item you want from the list or click on the item you want to select.
Option button	Select one option from a group of option buttons. (You can select only one option button in each group.) Option buttons are round and have darkened centers when selected. To remove a selection, select a different option in the same group.
Check box	Select multiple options from a group of check boxes. Check boxes are square and contain an X when selected. To deselect a check box, select it a second time.
Command button	Complete the command, cancel the command, or open an additional dialog box for more alternatives. Pressing Enter chooses the command button that appears in bold.

To select a text box so that you can type in it, click in the box. Reposition the cursor by moving the I-beam to a new location and clicking. The flashing insertion point is where your typed characters or edits appear. Select multiple characters by holding down the mouse button and dragging the I-beam across the text you want selected. (Text entry and editing is described in "Editing Text in Text Boxes" later in this chapter.)

To select from a scrolling-list box, select the list box by clicking in it. Scroll through the list by clicking on the up or down arrow in the scroll bar at the right side of the box. Make large jumps through the list by clicking in the shaded area of the scroll bar. Drag the square in the scroll bar to new locations for long moves. When the desired selection appears in the list box, click once on that selection.

Some Windows NT applications use drop-down list boxes. These list boxes appear like figure 2.11 when closed and like figure 2.12 when opened. To select from a drop-down list box, click on the down arrow to the right side of the text box. When the scrolling list appears, select from it in the same way you select from any scrolling-list box—click on the item you want.

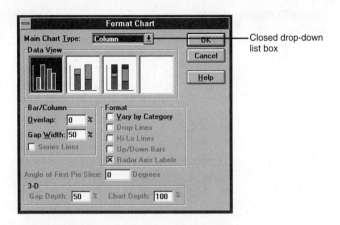

Closed drop-down list box

Fig. 2.11

A closed drop-down list box.

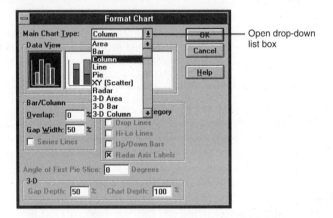

Open drop-down list box

Fig. 2.12

An open drop-down list box.

Mouse Shortcut in Dialog Boxes

In some dialog boxes, double-clicking on an option button or an item in a list selects that option and simultaneously chooses the OK command button. In the Open dialog box, for example, you can double-click on a file name to select and open the File. Experiment with the dialog boxes in your applications to determine whether double-clicking is a viable shortcut.

Using the Keyboard in Dialog Boxes

With the keyboard, you can select from dialog boxes in one of two ways. With the faster method, you use Alt+*letter*. You press and hold down Alt while you press the underlined letter in the name of the item you want. With the second method, you move among items in a dialog box by pressing Tab.

To select from a group of round option buttons, access the group of option buttons by pressing Alt+*letter*, where *letter* is the underlined letter in the name of the group of option buttons. A dashed line encloses the active option button. Move the selection to another button in the same group by pressing the arrow keys. For example, in the Communications dialog box shown in figure 2.10, press Alt+B to select the **B**aud Rate group and then press arrow keys to select the baud rate you want.

To select a check box, press Alt+*letter*, where *letter* is the underlined letter in the name of the check box. Each time you press Alt+*letter*, you toggle the check box between selected and deselected. An *X* appears in the check box when the box is selected. You also can toggle the active check box between selected and deselected by pressing the space bar. A dashed line encloses the active check box. In the Communications dialog box in figure 2.10, press Alt+k to select the Parity Chec**k** option; press Alt+k again or press the space bar to deselect the option.

To make an entry in a text box, select the text box by pressing Alt+*letter*, where *letter* is the underlined letter in the name of the text box. Press Alt+N, for example, to select the File **N**ame text box in the Save As dialog box shown in figure 2.9. Type a text entry or edit the existing entry by using the editing techniques described in the upcoming section, "Editing Text in Text Boxes."

To select from a list of alternatives in a scrolling-list box, select the list box by pressing Alt+*letter*, where *letter* is the underlined letter in the name of the list box. When the list box is active, use the up- or down-arrow key or PgUp or PgDn to move through the list. The text in reversed type is selected. (To display a drop-down scrolling list by using the keyboard, press Alt+*letter* to activate the list and then press Alt+down-arrow to drop the list. Select items by pressing the up- or down-arrow keys.)

To select a command button, press Tab or Shift+Tab until a dashed line encloses the name of the button you want. Press the space bar to select the active button shown by the dashed enclosure. You can select the button in bold, usually the OK button, at any time by pressing Enter. Press Esc to choose the Cancel button and escape from a dialog box without making any changes.

Changing Directories in a List Box

In many Windows NT applications, the Save As and Open dialog boxes contain hierarchical **Directories** and Drives lists with icons (other dialog boxes used for locating files may have similar lists). See figure 2.13 for an example. To change the directory, you must navigate through this hierarchical list.

The topmost entry in the **D**irectories list represents the current drive. To its left is an icon that represents an open folder, indicating that the contents of the drive are displayed. The entries below it represent directories. They have closed folder icons, indicating that the directory contents are not listed, or they have open folder icons, indicating that the directory contents are listed. To see what's in a directory, you must open this folder.

When you open a folder, any subdirectories contained within the directory are listed below the directory in the **D**irectories list, and any files contained in the directory are listed in the File **N**ame list. Figure 2.13 shows the Windows NT Write Save As dialog box; other dialog boxes may have lists that look slightly different or have different list names.

To open a directory or subdirectory in a **D**irectories list, follow these steps:

1. Select the **D**irectories list.

2. Scroll the **D**irectories list to display the directory you want to open.

   Mouse: Click on the down arrow. (Click and hold down the down arrow to scroll continuously.)

   Keyboard: Press Tab to advance to the Directories list; press the down or up arrows to scroll the list.

3. Select and open the directory.

   Mouse: Double-click on the directory you want to open.

   Keyboard: Select the directory by pressing the up or down arrow. Press Enter or choose OK to open the directory.

4. Open the subdirectory in a directory by using the same technique as for opening a directory.

You can close a subdirectory by using the reverse procedure: select an open directory higher in the hierarchy than the subdirectory you want to close and press Enter (or double-click on the higher directory).

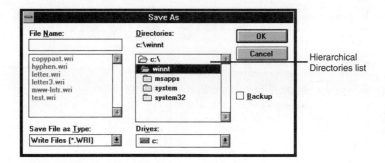

Fig. 2.13

A hierarchical
Directories list.

Editing Text in Text Boxes

You can use the text-editing techniques you learn in this section in all
Windows NT applications. These editing techniques are described for
text boxes inside dialog boxes, but they also work when you're editing
text in other locations in Windows NT applications.

To edit text in a text box with the keyboard, select the text box by
pressing Alt+letter or by pressing Tab until the text box is selected. (All
text inside the box usually is selected.) To replace selected text, begin
typing; the new characters you type replace the selected text.

To edit text in the text box with the mouse, position the I-beam pointer
over the text where you want the insertion point to be and click. To
delete multiple characters, drag across the characters so that they are
selected and then press Del.

To deselect text in the text box, click somewhere else in the text or
press End, Home, or the right or left arrow. When you select text, the
characters you type are inserted at the insertion point. (The insertion
point is the vertical flashing bar.)

To delete a character to the right of the flashing insertion point, press Del.
Press Backspace to delete a character to the left of the insertion point.

Replace existing text with new text by selecting the text you want to
replace and then typing. To select text with the keyboard, move the
insertion point to the left of the first character, press and hold down
Shift, and press the right arrow. Select with the mouse by dragging the
I-beam across the text as you hold down the mouse button.

When you are editing text in an application, you can use **E**dit commands such as **U**ndo, **C**opy, and **P**aste, but these commands do not
work in dialog boxes. However, the keystroke equivalents Ctrl+C,
Ctrl+X, and Ctrl+V do work.

Starting, Using, and Quitting Applications

When you start Windows NT, the Program Manager appears. With the Program Manager, which is always running in Windows NT, you can easily start applications that you work with frequently.

The Program Manager usually contains one or more open windows, called *group windows.* The Program Manager also usually contains one or more *group icons,* which are closed group windows (refer to the earlier section, "Controlling the Windows in Windows NT," to learn how to open and close group windows). Inside each group window are one or more *program item icons.* A program item icon represents an application (and sometimes an associated data file).

Shortcut Keys for Editing

Some Windows NT applications include shortcut keys for editing text. These keys may work in some parts of the application, such as a formula bar, but may not work in others. Experiment to find the shortcuts that can help you.

Key	Action
Shift+left-arrow or Shift+right-arrow	Adds the next adjacent character to the selection
Shift+down-arrow	Selects to next line
Shift+up-arrow	Selects to preceding line
Shift+PgUp or Shift+PgDn	Selects to top or bottom of page or screen
Shift+Home	Selects to beginning of line
Shift+End	Selects to end of line
Ctrl+Shift+left-arrow or Ctrl+Shift+right-arrow	Selects a word each time you press the left or right arrow
Ctrl+Shift+Home	Selects to start of document
Ctrl+Shift+End	Selects to end of document

With the mouse, you can click where you want to begin to select text, press and hold down the Shift key, and click where you want the selected text to end. The text between the clicks is selected. In some applications, such as Word for Windows and Excel, you can select a word by double-clicking anywhere within the word.

The easiest way to start an application is from its program item icon. You can start your application by using the mouse or the keyboard. You also can start an application with the File Manager, whether or not the application has a program item icon (described in Chapter 5).

When you run multiple applications, you will want to switch easily among them. You can cycle through running applications by pressing shortcut keys, or you can use the Task List to switch to the application you need.

When you are finished using an application, exit it before you exit Windows NT (especially with DOS-based applications). The procedure for exiting is similar in most Windows NT applications. Exit DOS applications by using the appropriate technique for that application—even though the DOS application is running under Windows NT.

If the Program Manager does not appear when you start Windows NT, someone may have customized Windows so that the Program Manager displays as an icon at the bottom of the screen. Double-click on the Program Manager icon or press Alt+Tab enough times to display the Program Manager window or a box showing its name. When you release the Alt and Tab keys, the Program Manager window opens.

If you cannot see the Program Manager because Windows NT is customized so that an application starts when you start Windows NT, minimize the application (by choosing the Control Minimize command or clicking on the Minimize button—the downward-pointing arrow at the top right of your screen). After you minimize the application so that it appears as an icon at the bottom of your screen, you can see the Program Manager.

Starting Applications

When you installed Windows NT, you had the choice of assigning Windows NT and DOS applications to groups. *Group windows* store all applications related to a specific task together. With group windows, you can find and start applications and get data for a job you do frequently. Chapter 4 goes into depth about setting up group windows in the Program Manager.

If you requested it during the installation, Windows NT made program item icons for each application and put them in an Applications group. This group appears within the Program Manager as a group window or a group icon at the bottom of the window. If you open the group icon into a window, the program item icons are displayed. You can start the applications from the icons. Figure 2.14 shows the Program Manager with group windows, group icons, and program item icons. Application icons appear at the bottom of the screen to represent running applications.

If you did not install the applications into a group (or if you added a new application to your system or want to regroup your applications), read Chapter 4 and create your own customized program item icons to hold applications.

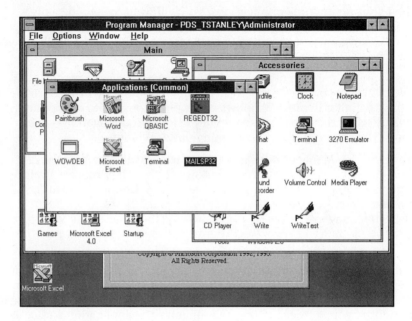

Fig. 2.14

Grouping applications and data together in the Program Manager.

To learn how to start applications from the File Manager, read Chapter 5.

Starting Applications from Icons

To start an application from a program item icon, follow these steps:

1. Open the Program Manager. It usually is open when you start Windows NT. If you just installed Windows NT, the Main group window appears open in the Program Manager window. If the Program Manager is not open, follow the appropriate instructions:

    Mouse: Double-click on the desktop. When the Task List appears, double-click on the name Program Manager. If you can see the Program Manager icon, double-click the icon to open it into a window.

    Keyboard: Press Ctrl+Esc. When the Task List appears, press the arrow keys to select the name Program Manager, and then press Enter. As an alternative, press Alt+Tab until you see the Program Manager, then release both keys.

2. Open the group icon or activate the group window that contains the application you want to start.

    Mouse: In the Program Manager window, click on the group window you want. If the correct group window is not open, double-click on the group icon you want in the Program Manager window.

    Keyboard: Press Ctrl+Tab until the group window you want activates. If the application is inside a group icon, press Ctrl+Tab to select the icon and then press Enter.

3. Start the program item that contains the application or the application and document you want.

    Mouse: Double-click on the program item icon containing the application or application and document you want to start.

    Keyboard: Press the arrow keys to select the program item icon you want to start and press Enter.

Starting Applications with Commands

You may not want applications you use infrequently to clutter the Program Manager. Instead of starting applications from icons, you can start applications and their related data documents by using the **File Run** command in the Program Manager. To start an application by using **File Run**, follow these steps:

1. Choose the **File Run** command from the menu bar. The Run dialog box appears (see fig. 2.15).

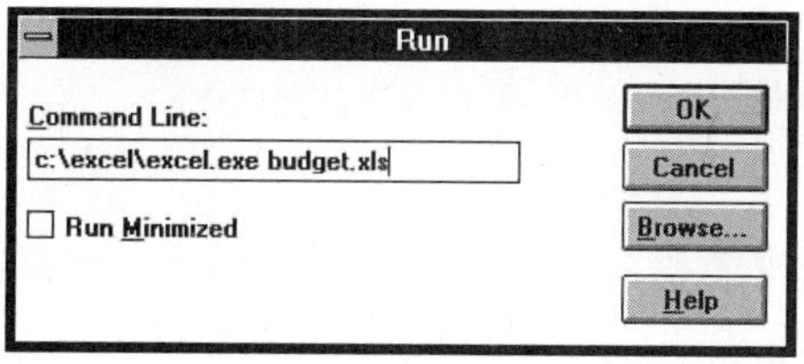

Fig. 2.15

The Run dialog box.

2. Type the full path name and application name in the **C**ommand Line text box.

3. To open a document with the application, type a space after the application name and type the name of the document. If the document is in a different directory from the application, also specify the path name of the document. For example, type the first of the following lines to start Excel, which is located in the EXCEL directory, and open the file BUDGET.XLS, also in the EXCEL directory. Type the second of the following lines if the file BUDGET.XLS is in the FINANCE directory:

C:\EXCEL\EXCEL.EXE BUDGET.XLS

C:\EXCEL\EXCEL.EXE C:\FINANCE\BUDGET.XLS

4. If you want the application to shrink to an icon when it starts, select the Run **M**inimized check box.

5. Choose OK or press Enter.

If you are not sure of the path or name of the application you want to start from the Run dialog box, choose the **B**rowse button and select the program from the Browse dialog box. When you choose OK or press Enter, the application's path and name appear in the **C**ommand Line text box. You can return to the command prompt while you run Windows NT. To start the command prompt from the Program Manager, open the Main group window. Select the Command Prompt icon with arrow keys and press Enter, or double-click on it. When you are finished working from the command prompt, type **EXIT** at the prompt and press Enter to return to Windows NT and the Program Manager.

Working with Applications

Many operations are similar from application to application in Windows NT. Nearly all Windows applications, for example, start with the File and Edit menus. The File menu includes commands for opening, closing, saving, and printing files. The Edit menu includes commands for cutting, copying, and pasting and other editing commands specific to the application. Operating menus and dialog boxes is the same in all applications and is the same in applications as in Windows NT itself; you learned these techniques in the earlier section on Learning Windows NT Techniques. Selecting text and objects also is similar in most Windows applications.

Opening, Saving, Printing, and Closing Files

When first started, many applications present you with a new, empty document—a blank page, if the application is a word processing or graphics or desktop publishing application; an empty worksheet, if the application is a spreadsheet application. If you finish working on one file, you can start a new file by choosing the File **N**ew command. Your application may ask you for information about the type of new file to start.

To open an existing file, choose the File **O**pen command. An Open dialog box similar to the one shown in figure 2.16 appears. In the Drives box, select the drive that contains your file. In the **D**irectories box, select the directory containing your file and choose OK to display the list of files in that directory. From the list of files presented in the File Name text box, select the file you want to open and choose OK or press Enter. (The File Name text box lists only files with the application's extension; to list other types of files, type a different extension in the File Name text box.)

The File menu contains two commands for saving files: Save As and Save. Use the File Save or File Save As command the first time you save a file so that you can tell Windows NT where to save it and so that you can name your file. You also can choose Save As to create a new version of an existing file by giving the file a new name. The Save As dialog box is often similar to the Open dialog box shown in the preceding figure; in it, you must specify the drive and directory to which you want to save your file and name the file. File names are limited to eight characters with a three-character extension, usually supplied by the application. After you type the file name, choose OK or press Enter to save the file. After you name your file, you can choose the File Save command to save the file without changing its name or location. This command replaces the original file.

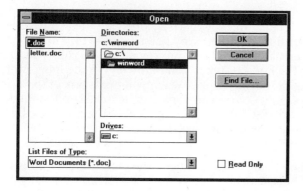

Fig. 2.16

The Open dialog box in a Windows NT application.

Printing your file may take two steps. Often you first must make some choice about the printer by using a command in the File menu named something like Print Setup or Target Printer. Use this command to identify the printer you want to use or to change the paper orientation. (After you make these selections, you need not access this menu again until you want to change the setting.) After you identify the printer you will use, you can choose the File Print command to print your document. You are presented with a dialog box that asks for details about the print job: how many copies to print; what range of pages to print; and other options depending on the application. Make your selections and then choose OK or press Enter. In some applications, such as Windows NT Write and Aldus PageMaker, you can change the printer setup by choosing a special "Setup" command in the Print dialog box.

To close a file, you often can choose the **File Close** command. Applications that don't allow more than one document to be open at once, however, usually don't include a **File Close** command; instead, to close the current file, you open a new file or exit the application. If you choose **File Exit**, you exit the application. When you close or exit, most Windows applications prompt you to save any changes you made since you last saved your document.

Scrolling in a Document

Most applications include scroll bars at the right and bottom edges of the screen. You can use the vertical scroll bar at the right to scroll up and down in your document. You can use the horizontal scroll bar to scroll left and right. To scroll a small distance, click on the arrow at either end of either scroll bar; you will scroll in the direction the arrow points. To scroll a larger distance, click in the grey area next to the arrow or drag the scroll bar box to a new location. In many applications, the scroll bars are optional: if you want more working space, you can turn them off.

You can scroll using the keyboard by pressing the arrow keys to move a character or line at a time or by pressing the PgUp or PgDn keys to move a screen at a time. The Home key usually scrolls you to the left margin, and the End key takes you to the end of the line or the right side. Holding down the Ctrl key when you press any other scrolling key extends the scroll: Ctrl+Home, for example, takes you to the beginning of your file; Ctrl+End takes you to the end of the file; Ctrl+the left- or right-arrow key moves you a word at a time rather than a character at a time. Most applications have many shortcuts for scrolling.

If you scroll by using the scroll bars, the insertion point does not move; it remains where it was before you scrolled. If you scroll by using the keyboard, the insertion point moves as you scroll. Scroll bars are shown in figure 2.17.

Using Simple Editing Techniques

Editing text and objects is similar in all Windows NT applications. When you're working with text, in your document or in a dialog box, the mouse pointer turns into an I-beam when you move it onto editable text. You can use the I-beam to move the insertion point and to select text. The flashing vertical insertion point is where text appears when you type.

You can use the mouse or the keyboard to move the insertion point. To use the mouse, position the I-beam where you want the insertion point to move and click the left mouse button. (If you cannot see the insertion point, it may be under the I-beam; move the mouse a little to move the I-beam.) To use the keyboard to move the insertion point, press the arrow keys. For a complete description of how the arrow keys work, refer to the box in the "Starting, Using, and Quitting Applications" section earlier in this chapter. Many keyboard shortcuts also are listed in that box.

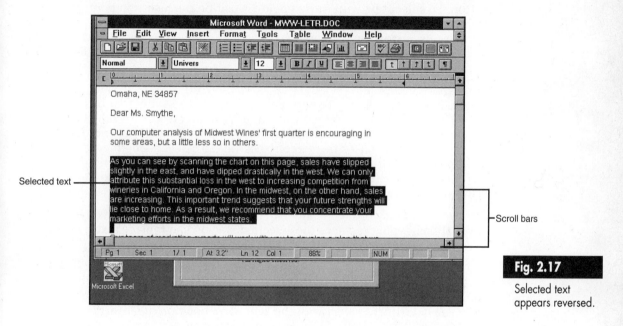

Selected text

Scroll bars

Fig. 2.17

Selected text
appears reversed.

To insert text at the insertion point, simply type. Most applications push existing text to the right to make room for the new text (although some applications allow you to select an *overtype* mode). To delete text to the left of the insertion point, press the Backspace key. To delete text to the right of the insertion point, press the Delete key.

Most applications contain an "oops" function: the **Edit Undo** command. This command undoes your most recent edit—use it when you make an edit you instantly regret.

T I P

Selecting Text and Objects

You can sum up one of the most important editing rules in all Windows applications in three simple words: *Select, then Do.* You must select text or an object before you can do anything to it (if you don't select first, the application doesn't know where to apply your command).

To select text and objects, you can use the mouse or the keyboard. To select text with the mouse, position the I-beam at the beginning of the text you want to select, click and hold down the left mouse button, drag to the end of the text you want to select, and release the mouse button. To select text with the keyboard, position the insertion point at the beginning of the text you want to select, press and hold down the Shift key, use arrow keys to move to the end of the text to select, and then release the Shift key. Selected text appears reversed, as shown in figure 2.17.

Many shortcuts exist for selecting. To select a word with the mouse, double-click on the word. To select a word using the keyboard, hold down Ctrl+Shift while you press the left- or right-arrow key. To select a length of text with the mouse, you can drag until you touch the end of the screen, which causes the screen to scroll. To select a length of text with the keyboard, position the I-beam where you want the selection to start, hold down the Shift key, and scroll to the end of the selection by using any keyboard scrolling technique.

After you select a word, you can turn it bold or change its font. In most applications, typing replaces the selection, so you can replace text by selecting it and typing the new text. If a graphic is selected, you can resize it.

To select an object, such as a picture, with the mouse, click on the object. (To select multiple objects, hold down Shift while you click on each one in turn.) To select with the keyboard, position the insertion point beside it, hold down Shift, and press an arrow key to move over the object. Selected objects, such as graphics, usually appear with *selection handles* on each side and corner.

Copying and Moving

After you select text or an object, you can use the Edit menu to copy or move it. The commands all Windows applications use to copy and move are Edit Cut, Edit Copy, and Edit Paste. The Edit Cut command removes the selection from your document; Edit Copy duplicates it. Both commands transfer the selection to the Clipboard, a temporary holding area. The Edit Paste command copies the selection out of the Clipboard into your document at the insertion point's location. Your selection remains in the Clipboard until you replace it with another selection.

To copy a selection, choose Edit Copy, move the insertion point where you want the selection duplicated, and choose Edit Paste. To move a selection, choose Edit Cut, move the insertion point where you want it moved, and choose Edit Paste. Many shortcuts exist for copying and moving. Shift+Delete usually cuts a selection, and Shift+Insert usually pastes the Clipboard's contents. Many Windows NT applications also take advantage of Windows NT's *drag and drop* feature: you can use the mouse to drag a selection to its new location and drop it into place.

Because the Clipboard is shared among all applications running under Windows NT, you can move or copy a selection between documents and between applications as easily as you can move and copy within the file you are working in. The next two sections explain how to switch between documents and applications.

Switching between Document Windows

In many—but not all—Windows NT applications, you can open more than one file and switch between the files easily. Use these techniques when you want to copy or move information from one document to another. To open multiple files, choose the **File Open** command multiple times. If your application doesn't support multiple documents, it closes the current file, asking you whether you want to save any changes you made since you last saved.

If your application supports multiple documents, each document opens in its own document window as shown in figure 2.18. You can use the document control menu, at the left of the menu bar, to control the size and position of the document window. You also can control the document window using the restore, minimize, and maximize buttons that appear at the right end of the menu bar.

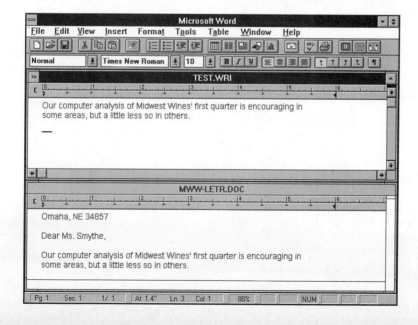

Multiple document windows.

You will find the document Control menu icon in one of two places. If the document is maximized in the application window, the document Control menu icon is found to the left of the menu bar. However, if the document window is not maximized—appears as a window in the application window—the document Control menu icon can be found at the left end of the document title bar. Click on the box or press Alt+hyphen to open the document Control menu.

The file you opened most recently is the active file; usually it appears in the top window, and it may hide the other document windows. In some applications, such as Word for Windows, you can use the **Win**dow **Arrange** All command to arrange your document windows so that they all are visible (if you have many files open, the windows may be very small).

To switch between document windows with the mouse, click on the window you want to activate. If the window you want to activate is not visible, you may need to move or size the active window on top (move a window by dragging its title bar; size it by dragging its border). To switch between document windows with the keyboard, choose the **W**indow menu and select the document you want from the list of open windows. In most applications, you can hold down Ctrl while you press the F6 key to switch between open document windows within an application.

Switching between Applications

When you run several applications, you need an easy way to switch between the windows.

If you are using a mouse, *activate* another window (or bring it to the top of the stack of windows) by clicking on it. If you cannot see the window of the application you want, use a keyboard technique or move the top windows as described in the earlier section, "Controlling the Windows in Windows NT." If the application you want is in an icon, double-click on the icon to open it into an active window.

If you are using the keyboard, press and hold down Alt+Tab to cycle through the application windows. A dialog box appears on-screen showing the name and icon of the next application. As you hold down the Alt key, each time you press Tab, the next icon and application name appear in the box. Release the Alt+Tab keys when the title of the application you want appears. You also can press Alt+Esc to cycle through application windows, but this method is slower because each window must be completely redrawn before the next window appears.

Whether you use the mouse or the keyboard, you can use the Task List to switch among many applications (see fig. 2.19). The Task List shows which applications are currently running. You can switch between applications by choosing the one you want from the list.

Fig. 2.19

The Task List
window.

To switch among applications using the Task List, follow these steps:

1. Activate the Task List.

   Mouse: Double-click on the desktop background.

   Keyboard: Press Ctrl+Esc; or press Alt, space bar and choose the Switch To command.

2. Choose the application you want active.

   Mouse: Double-click on the application you want active.

   Keyboard: Press the down arrow to select the application you want and then press Enter.

The following chart lists the command buttons in the Task List window.

Command Button	Action
Switch To	Activates the selected application in the Task List.
End Task	Exits the selected application in the Task List.
Cancel	Exits the Task List without making a choice.
Cascade	Arranges all open application windows in an overlapping cascade from top left to bottom right.
Tile	Arranges all open application windows to fill the screen with equal-sized windows.
Arrange Icons	Arranges all application icons along the bottom of the desktop.

Quitting Windows NT Applications

Most Windows NT applications abide by the same design rules. Fundamental commands such as saving and quitting are common across different applications. To quit a Windows NT application, follow these steps:

1. Activate the application by following the appropriate instructions:

   Mouse: Click on the application window.

   Keyboard: Press Alt+Tab until the application appears; or press Ctrl+Esc to display the Task List, press the down-arrow key to select the name of the desired application, and then press Enter.

2. Choose the **File Exit** command from the application's menu.

You also can exit an application by selecting the application Control menu (press Alt, space bar) and choosing **Close** or by double-clicking on the Control menu icon. For most applications, the shortcut key for Control **Close** is Alt+F4.

If you alter documents without saving them, you are prompted to save your changes before the application quits.

To run a non-Windows (DOS, OS/2 character mode, or POSIX) application from Windows NT, follow the normal procedure to quit or exit that application. Make sure that you save before quitting because you may or may not be prompted to save your work before the application quits. Depending on your Windows NT settings and on how the DOS application was started, you may return immediately to Windows NT, or you may return to an empty (inactive) window. If you return to an inactive window, press Alt, space bar to display the Control menu. Choose the **Close** command to close the window and return to normal Windows operation.

Ending the Session

When you are ready to end your Windows NT session, you need to either log off the system or shut down Windows NT. If you will be turning off your machine, you'll want to shut down Windows NT so that it has the opportunity to write out any unsaved disk data. If you'll be using your machine later or expect that someone else will use your machine, you can log out without turning off your machine.

To log off while applications are running, follow these steps:

1. Activate the Program Manager if its window is not open and on top of the other windows by following the appropriate instructions:

   Mouse: Click on any exposed part of the Program Manager window or double-click on the Program Manager icon to open the Program Manager window.

   Keyboard: Press Ctrl+Esc to display the Task List. Press the up or down arrow to highlight the name *Program Manager*, then press Enter.

2. Choose the **File** Logoff command to close the Program Manager and log off of Windows NT. Choose this command by using the appropriate instructions:

   Mouse: Click on the **File** menu, then click on the **L**ogoff command.

   Keyboard: Press Alt **F**, and then **L**. As a keyboard shortcut, you can press Alt+F4 to exit the Program Manager and log off of Windows NT.

3. Choose OK when the message advising you that `This will end your Windows session.` appears.

   Mouse: Click on the OK button.

   Keyboard: Press Enter.

   If you don't want to log off of Windows NT, choose Cancel rather than OK.

4. If a Windows NT application is still running with a document containing unsaved changes, you are prompted to save your changes. Choose **Y**es to save changes, **N**o to discard changes, or **C**ancel to return to Windows NT. If you choose **Y**es to save changes to an unnamed file, the application's Save As dialog box appears and you must name and save the file. If a DOS, POSIX, or OS/2 application is still running, Windows NT tells you to return to the application and quit it in the usual way before you can exit Windows NT.

You can also log off of your Windows NT session by using the Program Manager's Control menu. The Control menu is the square icon at the left edge of the Program Manager title bar. Normally, you use the Control menu to close an application's window; however, when you close the Program Manager window, you also log off of Windows NT. To close Windows NT from the program Manager Control menu, follow these steps:

1. Open the Program Manager's Control Menu.

   Mouse: Click on the Control Menu icon.

   Keyboard: Press Alt+Spacebar.

2. Choose the **C**lose command.

   Mouse: Click on the Close command.

   Keyboard: Type **C**.

3. Choose OK when the message advising you that `This will end your Windows session.` appears.

   Mouse: Click on the OK button.

   Keyboard: Press Enter.

   If you don't want to log off of Windows NT, choose Cancel rather than OK.

4. If an application is still running that contains a file with unsaved changes, you are prompted to save changes.

If you want to shut down your system, you can follow these steps:

1. Activate the Program Manager if its window is not open and on top of the other windows by following the appropriate instructions.

   Mouse: Click on any exposed part of the Program Manager window or double-click on the Program Manager icon to open the Program Manager window.

   Keyboard: Press Ctrl+Esc to display the Task List. Press the up or down arrow to highlight the name *Program Manager*, then press Enter.

2. Choose the **F**ile **S**hutdown command to close the Program Manager and log off of Windows NT. Choose this command by using the appropriate instructions:

   Mouse: Click on the **F**ile menu and then click on the **S**hutdown command.

   Keyboard: Press Alt **F**, and then **S**.

3. Press OK when the message advising you that `Shutting down will end your Windows session.` appears.

   Mouse: Click on the OK button.

   Keyboard: Press Enter.

   If you don't want to log off of Windows NT, choose Cancel rather than OK. This dialog box also has a checkbox marked `Restart` `when shutdown is complete.` If this box is checked, Windows NT immediately restarts itself after the shutdown is complete. This is useful when you want to completely restart the system—as when you have made a configuration change, for example.

4. If a Windows NT application is still running with a document containing unsaved changes, you are prompted to save your changes. Choose **Yes** to save changes, **No** to discard changes, or Cancel to return to Windows NT. If you choose Yes to save changes to an unnamed file, the application's Save As dialog box appears and you must name and save the file. If a DOS, POSIX, or OS/2 application is still running, Windows NT tells you to return to the application and quit it in the usual way before you can exit Windows NT.

Summary

In this chapter, you learned how to start Windows NT and how to understand the terms used in Windows NT. You learned the parts of the Windows NT screen, and you learned that you can choose from menus by activating the menu bar with the Alt key and then pressing the underlined letter of the command or by clicking with the pointer on the menu name and then on the command name. You also learned how to choose options from dialog boxes, which appear for commands that need additional information. You can choose options in dialog boxes by holding down the Alt key and pressing the underlined letter for that option or by clicking with the pointer on that option.

Windows NT gets its name from the way the screen looks and works: each application appears in a window that you can size, move, minimize, or maximize by using a mouse or the keyboard.

All Windows NT's applications work similarly. Techniques you learn for operating Windows NT carry through to the applications, and techniques you learn for operating one application are similar in all applications. You can use multiple applications at the same time.

Windows Applications are built to work together—especially true of the OLE-based *applets* that can be shared among Windows applications. To learn about OLE, or object linking and embedding, read Chapter 6; to learn about applets, refer to Part IV.

When you are comfortable running the desktop applications, you will want to run fully featured Windows and DOS applications and exchange data between them. When you reach that level of involvement with Windows, read the chapters in Parts V and VI. They explain how to integrate Windows applications so that they pass and share data; the chapters also explain how to run non-Windows— or DOS—applications within a window.

Working with Windows NT

PART

II

OUTLINE

Getting Help

W indows applications and accessories have extensive Help screens to help you find information about procedures, commands, techniques, and terms. The tools in Windows Help enable you to search for topics, print Help information, annotate the Help screens with your own notes, and copy information from the Help screens to the Clipboard for use in other applications.

Although different Windows applications come from different software manufacturers, most manufacturers use the Help application supplied by Microsoft, the manufacturer of Windows. The Help applications in many different programs, therefore, all work similarly. You can learn the basics of using Help in one application and translate what you know to all your other Windows applications.

Although Help is part of your Windows application, Help also is a separate application. As such, Help runs in a separate window that overlays your application window. If you expect to use it frequently, you can leave Help open and easily switch between your application and the Help window. You also can minimize Help to an easily accessible icon at the bottom of your screen.

This chapter uses the Help screens in Cardfile as examples. Many Windows accessories and applications use the same kinds of commands and procedures as the Cardfile Help. Each application's Help screens are different, however, and you can learn how to use an application's Help by selecting the **H**ow to Use Help command from the **H**elp menu.

Understanding Windows Help

You start Help by choosing a command from the **Help** menu or by
pressing the F1 key. Figure 3.1 shows the Help pull-down menu for the
Cardfile accessory. Different Windows applications may have more or
fewer Help menus or buttons.

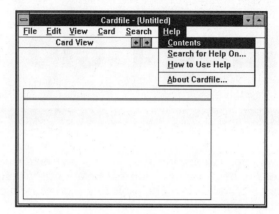

Fig. 3.1

The Help pull-
down menu for
the Cardfile
application.

The following list defines the commands you find in the **Help** menu:

Command	Purpose
Contents	A table of contents of all Help topics
Search for Help on	Enables you to search the Help information for specific topics
How to use Help	Basic instructions for using Help
About Cardfile	Information about the current ap-plication, including copyright, the licensed user informa tion, and the current Windows mode and memory and system resources information

To start Help, follow these steps:

1. Choose the **Help** menu.

2. Select the **Contents** command to display the Help contents
   (see fig. 3.2).

   or

   Select the **Search for Help on** command to display the Search
   dialog box (see fig. 3.6).

In most applications, you can start Help also by pressing the F1 key.

When you start Help by choosing the **H**elp **C**ontents command, the Help window usually has three sections: the menu bar, the button bar, and the Help text area. Figure 3.2 shows the Cardfile's Help window.

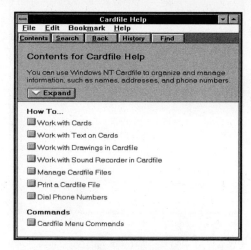

Fig. 3.2

The Cardfile Help screen, showing the Contents for Cardfile Help topic.

Using the Contents Window

The Contents for Cardfile Help window lists main help topics. For example, there are seven different How To... main topics and one Commands main topic.

To the left of each main topic is a button. By choosing the main topic button, you list subtopics for that main topic. For example, choosing Work with Cards lists three subtopics, as shown in figure 3.3.

Each subtopic contains a small button to its left. Choosing the small button displays help for that subtopic. For example, choosing Duplicating Cards (see fig. 3.3) displays the Duplicating Cards help window, which is shown in figure 3.4.

In addition to viewing the subtopics for one main topic, you can view all the subtopics. To view all the subtopics, click the Expand button. Note that when you choose the Expand button, all subtopics display in the Help window, and the Expand button is replaced by the Collapse button. Use the Collapse button to display only the main headings again.

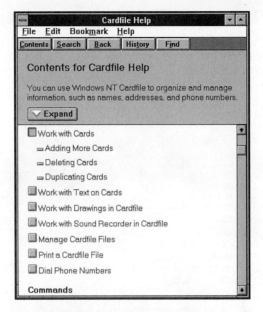

Expand the main
topics to view
Help subtopics.

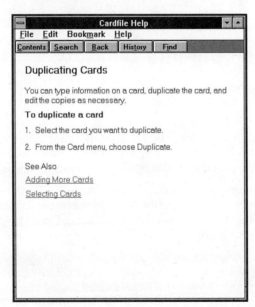

Selecting a
subtopic displays
help information
for that topic.

Jumping between Topics in Help

The underlined topics listed in some Help windows (see fig. 3.4) are
known as *jumps* and are used to display additional information about

the topic. Some Help screens may contain graphic jumps, which appear in a second color. When you move the mouse cursor over a jump on a Help screen, the mouse pointer changes to a pointing hand. Selecting a jump shows additional information about the item. Most frequently, jumps are used to display help on related topics to the current help window.

To select a jump using a mouse, just move the mouse over a jump, and the mouse pointer changes to a hand icon. Click once to select the item. To select a jump using the keyboard, press the Tab key to move to the next jump or press Shift+Tab to move to the previous jump and then press the Enter key.

Displaying a Definition

Some Help topics contain words underlined with a dashed line. The dashed line indicates that a *popup* is linked to this word. Generally speaking, a popup displays the definition for the underlined word.

To display the word's popup, click on the word. Click a second time to remove the popup box. If you are using a keyboard, press the Tab key until the dashed underline is selected, then press Enter to display the popup box. Press Enter a second time to remove the box.

Getting Help for a Dialog or Alert Box

Many Windows applications are designed to give you help as you work. When a dialog box or alert box with which you are unfamiliar appears, try pressing the F1 function key. This action may display *context-sensitive help*, or information related to what you are doing at the moment.

In many applications, if you press F1 when a dialog box appears, you see the explanation of what each item in the dialog box does.

If you Press F1 when an alert or error box appears, you see an explanation of the cause of—and possibly a solution for—the error.

Getting Help Quickly with the Button Bar

Help screens may have buttons on a button bar. (Some applications may use different Help buttons.) These buttons enable you to jump to a specific Help screen or perform other functions. Some buttons you may see are Contents, Search, Back, History, and Find.

You choose a button by clicking with the mouse pointer or by pressing the underlined key.

Seeing Help's Table of Contents

Selecting the Contents command in the Help pull-down menu or pressing F1 in a Windows application opens the Help Contents window. Figure 3.5 shows the Cardfile Help Contents screen.

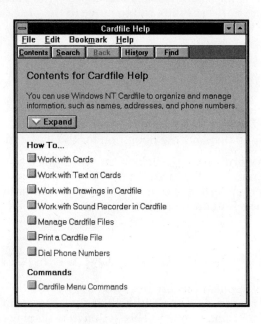

The Help window uses the standard Windows controls: scroll bars (vertical and horizontal as needed), minimize/maximize buttons, and the application control button in the top-left corner. You can resize the Help window as needed.

The Contents screen typically shows a short description of the screen's contents and the major topics (How To... and Commands) for the screen. Each major topic is divided into subtopics, which you can view by choosing each main topic's button, or by choosing the Expand button.

Searching for Topics by Key Word

You can use Help's Search button to quickly find information about a particular topic. By using *key words*—words associated with Help topics—you can display on-screen a list of topics that contains information about the key word.

To search for a Help topic, follow these steps:

1. On the Help Button Bar, choose the **S**earch button.

2. From the Search dialog box shown in figure 3.6, select a phrase or word from the Type a **w**ord list, or type the word for which you are searching in the text box. The list box scrolls to the first entry that most closely matches the characters that you type.

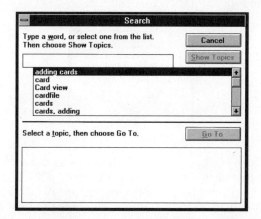

Fig. 3.6

The Search
dialog box.

3. Choose **S**how Topics or double-click on the desired topic in the list box.

4. The lower topic list box shows a list of all topics that you can select.

5. Select a topic and then choose **G**o To to display the Help screen for this topic.

   To cancel the search, select Cancel or press the Esc key.

Retracing Your Path through Help

If you move through different Help topics or search for different keywords, you may occasionally want to retrace this path to review previous topics. You can perform this step by choosing the **B**ack button to see the Help topic you previously viewed. Help tracks the topics that you previously viewed; using the **B**ack button shows these topics in reverse order until the Help Contents screen appears.

Reviewing Previous Help Screens

To see a list of all the topics you covered, and even jump back to a previous topic, use the History button. The History button presents a list of up to 40 previously viewed Help screens. You can jump quickly to a Help topic from this list. To use the History button, follow these steps:

1. Choose the History button. The History window (shown in figure 3.7) displays up to the last 40 topics viewed.

2. Choose a topic by double-clicking on (or pressing arrow keys to select) the topic and then pressing Enter.

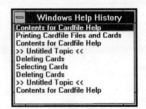

Because the history list appears in a window and not a dialog box, this list remains visible until closed. Windows handles the history list in this way so that you can keep the list visible until you no longer need to select previously used Help screens. To close the history list, press Alt+F4 or double-click on the Control menu icon at the top-left corner of the window.

Searching for Help Information with Find

You can use Help's Find button to search for text in the help file. Find is different than Search. Instead of searching for main topics in the current help file, Find enables you to search through a selected help file for specific information.

To use Find, follow these steps:

1. Choose the Find button. The Search dialog box, shown in figure 3.8, displays on the screen.

2. Type the information for which you are searching in the Search For: text box. In this text box, you can type key words or phrases. Or, choose the drop-down arrow and select a word or phrase that you previously used.

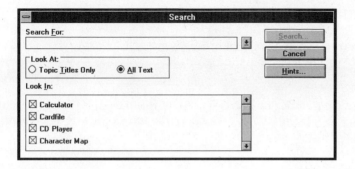

Fig. 3.8

Use the Find button to search through multiple Help files for information.

3. In the Look At: group of control buttons, choose Topic Titles Only to search main topics, or choose All Text to search through all of the text of each help file.

4. Select help files to include in the Look In scroll box. To include a help file listed in the Look In scroll box, mark the associated check box.

5. Choose Search to begin searching. The Topics Found window appears on the screen, listing the topics that contain the search text (see fig. 3.9).

Fig. 3.9

The Topics Found window displays topics you are searching for using the Find button in the Help window.

6. Choose the topic that you want information about. Press Alt+F4 to close the Topics Found window.

The Search dialog box offers you great flexibility in searching for information. You can use the AND, OR, and NOT keywords to limit or expand your search capabilities. For example, type CARDS AND PRINTING to search for topics that include both the word *CARDS* and the word *PRINTING*. To search for information that includes the words *MEDIA* or *VIDEO*, type MEDIA OR VIDEO in the Search For text box. To see more examples, choose the Hints button in the Search dialog box.

T   I   P   You can use the NEAR keyword in the Search For text box to find
information when one word is *near* another word—that is, when one
word is within a certain number of words of the other word. For example, PRINT NEAR SAVE displays all topics in which the words
PRINT and *SAVE* are within eight words of each other. You can
change the number of words using the **H**ints button to display the
Search Hints dialog box. *At the bottom of the dialog box, change the
number in the NEAR means within 8 words text box.*

Customizing Help for Your Work

Help is more than just a list of procedures or word definitions. You can
print Help screens, copy screens into word processors, and even annotate your notes so that Help becomes customized to the kind of work
you do.

Adding Custom Notes to Help Topics

You can customize Help information in a Windows application to make
Help information more useful to you or to coworkers. You might want
to include your company's default settings, for example, in a Help window on document formatting, or you may want to attach a note that
names the templates for mailing labels to a built-in Help window that
describes creating mailing labels. You can use Annotations to add
these notes.

A Help window is marked as having annotated text when it has a paper
clip icon next to the topic. To create an annotation, follow these steps:

1. Display the topic that you want to annotate.

2. Choose the **E**dit **A**nnotate command from the menu bar. The
   Annotate dialog box appears (see fig. 3.10).

3. Type notes or choose the **P**aste button to paste text you previously cut or copied to the Clipboard. By default, text wraps as
   you type. Press the Enter key to start a new line.

4. To copy text in the Annotation text box, select the text and then
   choose the **C**opy button.

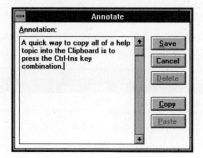

Fig. 3.10

Annotate help
topics using
the Annotate
dialog box.

5. Choose the **S**ave button.

   A paper clip icon appears to the left of the topic title in the Help window.

To view an annotation, follow these steps:

1. Select the topic with an annotation.

2. With the mouse, click on the paper clip icon or use the Tab key to highlight the paper clip icon and press Enter.

3. Make all changes to the annotation and choose the **S**ave button. To return to the topic without making changes, choose Cancel.

To remove an annotation, follow these steps:

1. Select the topic with the annotation.

2. Click on the paper clip icon with the mouse or use the Tab key to highlight the paper clip icon and press Enter.

3. Choose the **D**elete button in the Annotate window.

The paper clip icon disappears from the Help topic, and the Annotate window is deleted.

Marking Special Places in Help

Bookmarks enable you to mark Help topics that you frequently reference. A bookmark is a named location. By assigning a bookmark to a location in Help, you can at any time choose this bookmark's name from a list to quickly go to the location.

To create a bookmark, follow these steps:

1. Display the Help topic that you want to add to the bookmark list.

2. Choose the Bookmark Define command from the menu bar.

   The Bookmark Define dialog box, shown in figure 3.11, shows a list of existing bookmarks.

Fig. 3.11

Insert quick reference marks using the Bookmark Define dialog box.

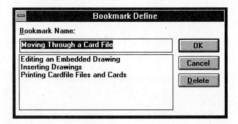

3. In the **Bookmark Name** text box, type a bookmark description or accept the default topic.

4. Choose OK or press Enter.

To quickly go to a location you previously marked with a bookmark, follow these steps:

1. Choose the Bookmark menu.

2. From the lower part of the menu, select the bookmark name you entered. With the mouse, click on the desired bookmark. With the keyboard, press the number associated with the bookmark. If more than nine bookmarks are available, select **More** to see the next group of nine bookmarks.

To delete a bookmark, follow these steps:

1. Choose the Bookmark **Define** command.

2. Select the name of the bookmark to delete.

3. Choose the **Delete** button.

Running Help for Other Applications

In some Help windows (especially those for newer applications), you can read Help information for more than just the application in which you are currently working. From within a Help window, you can open other applications' help files, or you can use the File Manager to open Help for an application.

After you start Help, you can open another application's help window
by following these steps, with the Help window active:

1. Choose the **File O**pen command. The Open dialog box appears
   (see fig. 3.12).

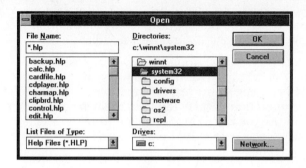

Fig. 3.12

Open other help
files using the
Open dialog
box.

2. Select or type into the File **N**ame list box the filename with an .HLP
   extension to view.

3. Choose OK or press Enter.

Printing Help Information

Often, having a printed copy of the Help topic in which you are interested can help you more clearly understand the topic. When the topic
for which you want information is in the Help window, choose the **F**ile
Print Topic command to print the topic on the current printer. The
entire text for the current Help topic prints. Choose the **F**ile **P**rint Setup
command to select a printer or to change printer options.

> Some of the handiest information you can print or copy from Help is
> an application's shortcut keys. If you didn't get a shortcut keystroke
> template for the keyboard attached to your computer, look under
> the Help contents for a topic called Keyboard Shortcuts, or a similar
> name. Copy these topics to a word processor and reorganize them,
> or print the topics directly from Help. You then can use a photo-
> copier to reduce the printouts for pasting onto 3×5 cards for easy
> reference.

T I P

Copying Help Information to Another Application

You can create a collection of Help topics by copying Help information and pasting this data into a word processor document file. You can copy and paste into another application any information you see in a Help window. The information transfers as editable text.

Depending on the Windows application you are using, you can copy information from a Help window in two ways. In some applications, you are limited to copying all the text information in a Help window. To perform this operation, display the Help topic in which you are interested and choose the **E**dit **C**opy command from the menu bar. The full text of the window is copied to the Clipboard so that you can paste text into another application.

In other Help applications, you can selectively copy Help information. To perform this action, take the following steps:

1. Display the Help topic you want to copy, and choose the **E**dit **C**opy command. The Copy dialog box appears (see fig. 3.13).

   To copy the entire Help topic, press Ctrl+Ins instead of choosing the **E**dit **C**opy command. Then skip to step 4. The entire topic is copied to the Clipboard.

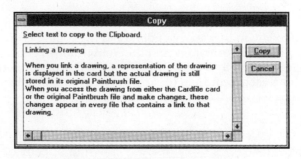

Fig. 3.13

Copy help topics to the Clipboard using the Copy dialog box.

2. Select the portion of the text that you want to copy. With the mouse, drag across desired text; with the keyboard, move the insertion point to the beginning of the selection, then use Shift and the arrow keys to select.

3. Choose the **C**opy button to copy the selected text to the Clipboard.

4. Switch to the application into which you want to paste the information, position the insertion point, then choose the **E**dit **P**aste
   command.

Shortcut Keys in Help

Several shortcut keys are available in Windows Help, which also are
common to many Windows applications:

Key	Function
F1	In an application, starts the Help application and displays the Help contents for that application. If the Help window is active, the Contents for How to Use Help topic appears.
Shift+F1	In many applications, including Word for Windows and Excel, turns the mouse pointer into a question mark. To get information, you then can click on a command or a screen region, or press a key combination.
Tab	Moves to the next jump (underlined topic) in the Help window.
Shift+Tab	Moves to the previous jump in the Help window.
Ctrl+Tab	Highlights all jumps in a topic.
Ctrl+Ins	Copies the current Help topic to the Clipboard.
Shift+Ins	Pastes the Clipboard contents in the Annotate dialog box.
Alt+F4	Closes the Help window.

Exiting Help

While using the Help screens, you can minimize the Help window to an
icon, or you can exit Help. To minimize Help to an icon, click on the
minimize button or choose the Control Minimize command.

To exit Help, choose the **F**ile **E**xit command or press Alt+F4.

Summary

Help in Windows applications is a useful feature. Not only can you learn about individual commands, many applications also include numbered lists to help you with complex procedures.

An important aid to learning more about many Windows applications is to press F1 when a dialog box or alert box appears. The Help window that appears describes the options available in the dialog box. In some dialog boxes, you can get Help by choosing a Help button.

Some Windows applications even include help to aid you in changing from one application to another. Microsoft Excel, for example, contains a keystroke Help feature that accepts Lotus 1-2-3 keystrokes and then uses those keystrokes to demonstrate how to do the equivalent feature in a Microsoft Excel worksheet. You can learn as you work. Word for Windows has a similar feature that enables you to learn Word for Windows, even as you use WordPerfect keystrokes and commands.

Controlling Applications with the Program Manager

The Program Manager is the application and document coordinator for Windows NT. The Program Manager helps you keep together software applications and their associated data by organizing related applications and data into groups.

With the Program Manager, you can group together applications and files according to the way you work, and you can start an application and (optionally) an associated data file.

The Program Manager contains windows and icons that help you quickly find and run applications and documents you use frequently. The Program Manager contains the following parts:

Part	Definition
Program item icon	An icon that represents an application or an application with an associated document. Opening such an icon starts the application and opens the document (if one is associated with the icon). You can have a program item icon for each task you perform with an application— in other words, you can have multiple program item icons for the same application. Program item icons can be copied and moved to different group windows. Create your own program item icons by following the steps in "Adding Applications and Documents to a Group," later in this chapter.
Group icon	An icon that represents a collection of program item icons. Opening such an icon displays the group window where you can see the program item icons belonging to that group. The icon visually displays whether the group is a personal group or a common group.
Group window (personal)	A window in the Program Manager containing a collection of program item icons visible only to the current user. Usually a group window contains program item icons that relate to a specific type of work. A group window can contain multiple program item icons that start the same application. Group windows save you time by grouping together similar program item icons, making it easy to start applications and documents related to that group. Create your own group window by following the steps in "Creating Personal Groups of Applications and Documents," later in this chapter.
Group Window (common)	A window in the Program Manager containing a collection of program item icons visible to every user. Discernable from a personal group window in that the title bar of the group window says *Common*. If a user is allowed to make changes to this group, it will affect all users who also see the group.

The Program Manager opens as soon as you start Windows NT and remains as a running application while Windows NT runs. Closing or quitting the Program Manager shuts down Windows NT. The Program Manager remains ready for you to choose the group of applications and documents you want to work with. The Main group window, shown in figure 4.1, appears inside the Program Manager when Windows NT starts for the first time. After you begin using Windows NT, you probably will customize your Program Manager to fit your own work habits. If you do, the Program Manager will look different from the figure when you start Windows NT.

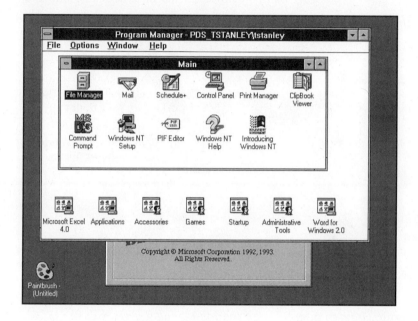

Fig. 4.1

The Program Manager displays Group windows, Group icons, and Program Item icons.

At the bottom of figure 4.1, you can see other groups. You can create groups like these that contain the applications and documents you use. When you installed Windows NT, you had the option of letting Windows NT create the Applications group for you from applications that Windows NT found on your hard disk. Regardless of whether you had this group created, you still have the Main group, the Startup group, the Accessories group, the Administrative Tools group, the Games group, and optionally the Applications group. Following is a list of the contents of these groups.

Group	Contents
Main group	Includes system applications that help you control files, control printing, set up peripherals, customize the desktop, and manage files.
Startup group	Includes applications that Windows NT activates immediately on startup.
Accessories group	Includes desktop accessories that come with Windows NT, such as a simple word processor, calendar, calculator, and so on.
Administrative Tools group	Includes applications that the system administrator uses to manage the system such as the User Manager and Event Viewer.
Games group	Includes three games, Solitaire, FreeCell, and Minesweeper, to help relieve the stress of working for long hours at your computer.
Applications group	Includes any applications that Windows NT found on your computer during installation.

Operating the Program Manager

Learning how to operate the Program Manager gives you the power to group applications and documents together in the same way you work with them. You also can start applications and documents quickly.

Figure 4.1 shows the four major parts of the Program Manager. Because the Program Manager is a Windows NT application, it resides in its own application window. The Program Manager window can contain many group windows or group icons. A *group window* and a *group icon* are two different views of a group of applications and data. A group window reveals all the program item icons. Group windows can be minimized to group icons; group icons can be changed back (restored) to group windows.

In figure 4.1, the Main group window is inside the Program Manager window. The Main group window contains program item icons that represent applications.

Figure 4.2 shows another group window, called Daily Business, opened on top of the Main group window. The Daily Business group contains program item icons referencing applications such as Excel, Word for Windows, and Paintbrush; a single document that is used on a daily basis is associated with each application. Each of these applications and its associated document is represented by a program item icon. Each program item icon can contain one application and one associated document. That is why you see several Excel and Word for Windows icons—each contains a different associated document.

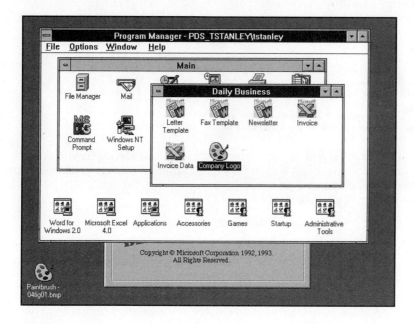

Fig. 4.2

You can create customized groups containing applications and documents.

Each program item icon represents an application and an associated document. Program item icons in the Daily Business group have been given names such as Letter Template, Fax Template, Newsletter, Invoice, Invoice Data, and Company Logo. When you create your own groups and program item icons, you can name them to fit the task they perform.

Icons of applications that are running can be dragged on top of the Program Manager window or on top of one of the group windows.

These icons may appear to be in the Program Manager, but they really are not; they merely overlap the Program Manager in the same way that windows overlap. If you reselect the Program Manager window by clicking it or pressing Ctrl+Esc, you see the Program Manager window without the overlapping icon.

You can start applications from the program item icons in a group window or from the File Manager (discussed in Chapter 5). Once an application is running, it occupies its own window. Applications also can be shown as icons on the desktop, but you should not confuse these icons with program item icons. The easiest way to tell them apart is that program item icons appear *inside* the Program Manager window, whereas icons that represent running applications appear *outside* the Program Manager window (unless you drag the icon on top of the Program Manager window). You can switch between applications that are running in a couple of ways, as described in Chapter 2.

Starting Applications from a Group Window

When you open a group window in the Program Manager, you see program item icons. Each icon refers to an application and, optionally, an associated *document,* or file of data. Sometimes the associated document is simply a new, empty document.

To open a group window, follow these steps:

1. Open the Program Manager (if it isn't open) by double-clicking the Program Manager icon or by pressing Ctrl+Esc and choosing the Program Manager from the Task List.

2. Activate the group window or open the group icon containing the program item you want to start. Click a group window to activate it; double-click a group icon to open it; or press Ctrl+Tab until the icon or window is selected (then press Enter if you need to open a group icon).

You can start an application in the active group window with a mouse by double-clicking the program item icon. If you are working with the keyboard, however, follow these steps:

1. Select the icon in the active group window by pressing the arrow keys until the program item name is highlighted.

2. Press Enter.

Moving an application to the Startup group causes Windows NT to start the application automatically when you start Windows NT. You can add any application you like to the Startup group (for details, see the section "Adding Applications and Documents to a Group").

Check the Program Item Properties

If you try to start a program item but the application does not start, or the application starts but the document cannot be found, check the program item's properties. The name or directory path to the application or document files may be incorrect. Files may have been moved, renamed, or erased.

To check the path and file name, activate the Program Manager and the appropriate group window. Select the program item icon and then choose the **File Properties** command. Change the path, application file name, or document file name in the **Command Line** text box. You can use **Browse** to find the correct path and file name for the application. The File Properties command is described in more detail in "Creating Groups of Applications and Documents," later in this chapter.

Customizing Groups

You don't have to limit yourself to the Windows NT Applications group that may have been created automatically for you. You can create your own customized groups to match the way you work, putting together applications and associated documents that you use to do specific jobs.

Creating and Deleting Groups

You can create your own groups to fit the way you work. Your groups can contain collections of applications and documents you use together for a task. The applications and documents can be located in different places on your disk, yet they appear together in the group window. Items in a group can contain just an application or an application and one associated document.

There are two types of program groups that you can create in Program Manager: *personal program groups* and *common program groups*.

A personal program group is a group that an individual user creates and uses. Windows NT stores the personal program group information with your logon name. When you log on to Windows NT, your personal program groups display in Program Manager. Only you can access the program items stored in a particular personal program group.

A common program group, on the other hand, is a program group that appears to all users who log on to Windows NT. A common program group contains program items that are available to all Windows NT users. Not just anyone using Windows NT can create a common program group. Only a system administrator has the rights to create or change a common program group.

You can visually tell the difference between a personal program group and a common program group. When you view these groups as icons, the personal program group appears with a picture of a person in the icon. The common program group appears with a picture of a computer system in the icon. Likewise, when viewing program group windows, a common group window contains the word *common* in the title bar of the program group window, whereas the personal group contains only the name of the program group in the title bar.

T I P Create common program groups that any user can access. For example, store applications that any user can use in common program groups. Individual users, however, should store customized documents or programs that only the user accesses in personal program groups.

Program Items Contain One Application and Document

Each program item contains either one application and no associated document, or one application and one associated document. Groups can contain many program items that start the same application but have different documents. For some applications like Word for Windows and Excel, however, each program item starts a different instance of the same application. This arrangement results in multiple copies of the application— a waste of memory when the application is large. (Not all applications will run multiple copies. You can have multiple program item icons for applications that will run only a single copy and each icon can have a unique associated document, but only one copy of the program will run.)

If you want an application to start with multiple documents, create an auto-opening macro that runs from the document specified by the program item. When the application and that document start, the auto-opening macro loads the other documents that are also needed. In Microsoft Excel 4, for example, you can create a Workbook that Windows NT associates with Excel. The Workbook opens all worksheets, charts, and macros that were open when you last selected File Save Workbook from Excel. Auto-opening macros and worksheets for Microsoft Excel are described in *Using Excel 4 for Windows NT,* Special Edition; auto-opening macros for Word for Windows are described in *Using Word for Windows 2,* Special Edition. Both books are published by Que Corporation.

Creating Groups of Applications and Documents

Before creating groups, determine the type of applications or documents that you plan to store in each group. If you plan to store applications or documents that everyone using Windows NT needs access to, create a common group. However, if you plan to store applications or documents that only you need access to, create a personal group.

 NOTE Only administrators and power users can create common program groups. Other users can only create personal groups.

If you are creating common groups, you may want to create a separate group for each application. In that group, you can create a program item to start the application. Additionally, you can create program items to start individual templates using that application.

If you are creating personal groups, you may want to create groups based on tasks that you perform during the day. Imagine the tasks you perform each day. Divide those tasks into related groups, such as writing proposals, managing a project timeline and budget, or contacting clients and sending follow-up letters. Each of these groups of tasks can become a group window. Within each group window, you add program item icons representing the applications and documents needed to get that work done.

To create your own group, start with the Program Manager window active and follow these steps:

1. Choose the **F**ile **N**ew command.

2. Select the **P**ersonal Program Group option or the **C**ommon Program Group option.

3. Choose OK or press Enter. The Program Group Properties dialog box appears (see fig. 4.3).

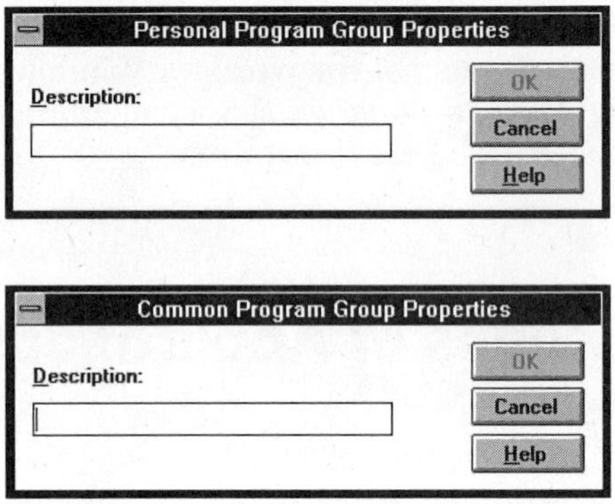

Fig. 4.3

The Program Group Properties dialog box for both personal groups and common groups.

4. Type in the **D**escription text box the title you want under the group icon or as the title of the group window. Do not make an entry in the **G**roup File text box; Program Manager automatically creates a GRP file for the group you are creating.

5. Choose OK or press Enter.

The new group window you have created remains open on-screen. If you want to add applications and data to the window, leave it open. If you want to minimize the group window so that it appears as an icon, double-click the Control menu icon of the new group window. As a shortcut, press Ctrl+F4 to change the group window to an icon.

Protecting a Program Group

If you want to prevent changes to a group, designate it as a "read-only" group. Start the File Manager, select the group file (usually this is a file located in your Windows NT directory with a GRP extension), and choose the **F**ile **P**roperties command. In the Properties dialog box, select the **R**ead Only option from the Attributes group.

When you make a program group read-only, you can make no further changes to the Group window, unless you remove the read-only attribute. For example, you cannot add new program items to or delete program items from the protected group. You also cannot move or rearrange the program item icons in the protected group.

Adding Applications and Documents to a Group

After you create and title a new group window, include in the window the applications and documents you use in this group. The applications and documents you put in a group are called *program items*; they appear as item icons in the group window.

> Microsoft recommends that you do not include more than 40 program items in a single group.
>
> **T I P**

NOTE Remember, only administrators and power users can add program items to a common program group. If you are not an administrator or a power user, you can add program items only to a personal group.

To add items, applications, and documents associated with an application to a new or existing group, follow these steps:

1. Select the group window that will contain the program item.

2. Choose the File New command.

3. Select Program Item from the New Program Object dialog box.

4. Choose OK or press Enter. The Program Item Properties dialog box appears (see fig. 4.4).

5. Select the **Description** text box and type the title you want to appear under the program item icon.

6. Select the **Command** Line text box and type the path name, file name, and extension of the program for this item. If you are unsure of the path and program file name, choose **Browse** to display a list of files and directories (see fig. 4.5). Select the directory

containing the application from the **D**irectories list, select the application from the File **N**ame list, and choose OK. (To open a higher, or *parent*, directory, select the parent directory in the **D**irectories list—the one indicated by an "open folder" icon—and choose OK. To attach to a network directory, use the Net**w**ork button.) When you choose OK, the Program Item Properties dialog box reappears with the path and application name copied into the **C**ommand Line text box.

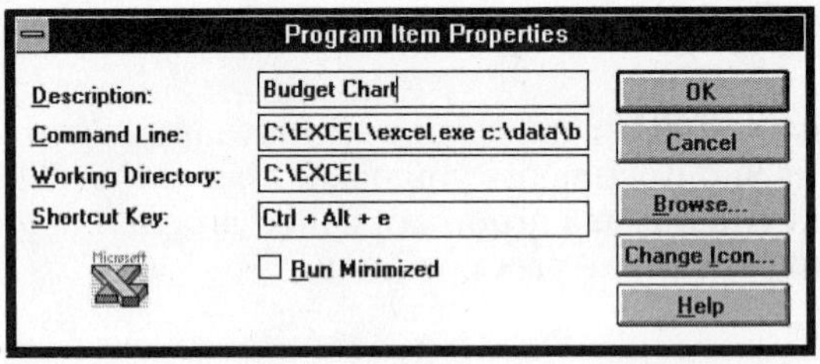

Fig. 4.4

Use the Program Item Properties dialog box to add a program item to a program group.

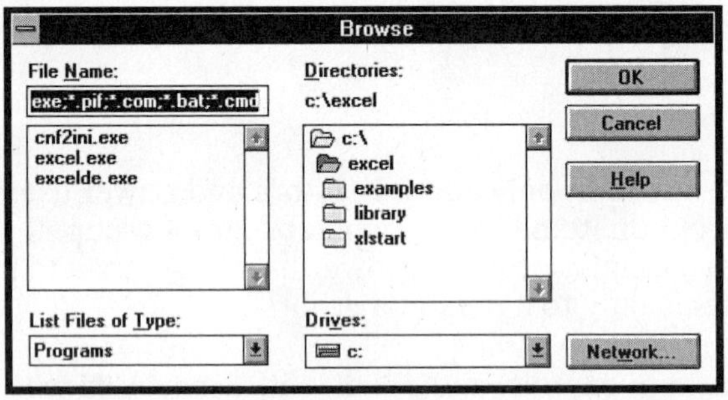

Program Item Properties

Description:	Budget Chart
Command Line:	C:\EXCEL\excel.exe c:\data\b
Working Directory:	C:\EXCEL
Shortcut Key:	Ctrl + Alt + e
	☐ **R**un Minimized

OK
Cancel
B**r**owse...
Change **I**con...
Help

Fig. 4.5

The Browse dialog box.

Browse

File **N**ame: exe;*.pif;*.com;*.bat;*.cmd

cnf2ini.exe
excel.exe
excelde.exe

Directories: c:\excel

c:\
excel
examples
library
xlstart

List Files of **T**ype: Programs

Dri**v**es: c:

OK
Cancel
Help
Network...

7. If you want a document such as a spreadsheet, letter, or data file to open with the application, type a space after the file name in the **C**ommand Line text box and then type the path and file name of the document. A completed command line where the application and document are in separate directories might look like this:

    C:\EXCEL\EXCEL.EXE C:\BUDGETS\JUNE.XLS

8. In the **W**orking Directory text box, enter the directory you want to be active when you start this application (your program defaults to this directory when opening or saving files).

9. Select the **S**hortcut Key text box and press Shift, Shift+Ctrl, or Ctrl while you type a character or function key. You see a shortcut key combination such as Ctrl+Alt, plus your character; press this key combination to switch to the application if it is running.

10. Normally, Windows NT chooses an icon to represent the program item you are creating. If more than one icon is available

to represent the item, the Change Icon button turns bold. Choose the Change Icon button and select the icon you want to represent the application and document. Move through the icons using the scroll bar below the icon window. Choose OK or Cancel to return to the Program Item Properties dialog box.

11. Select the Run Minimized icon if you want the application to be minimized to an icon on start-up.

12. Choose OK or press Enter.

To use icons other than those shown, choose Change Icon to display the Change Icon dialog box. In the File Name text box, enter PROGMAN.EXE or MORICONS.DLL, including the full path where those files are located (usually in your Windows NT directory). To access icons in the MORICONS.DLL file, for example, enter *C:\WINNT\SYSTEM32\MORICONS.DLL*. You also can choose the Browse button to locate these files.

Figure 4.6 shows a Program Item Properties dialog box that has been filled out to start Word for Windows and one document template. A program item can have only one document associated with an application.

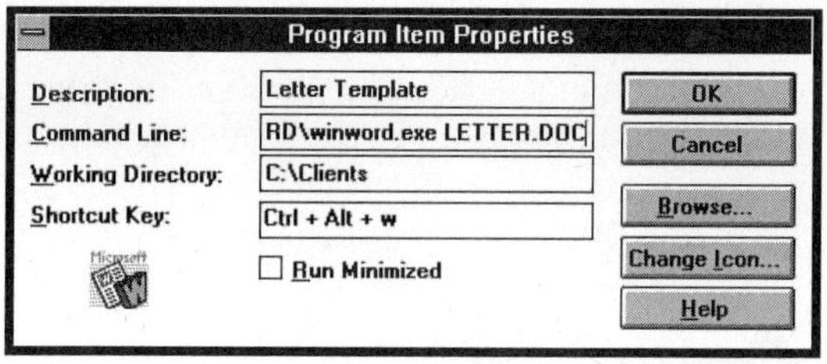

Fig. 4.6

A Program Item Properties dialog box that specifies an application and one document.

By default, the Browse window initially shows only application files (files with the extensions EXE, COM, BAT, or PIF). To see all the files in the directory, select the All Files option from the List Files of Type box in the Browse dialog box.

Creating a Program Item Icon

Another way you can create a program item icon is to run the File Manager and the Program Manager side by side, locate in the File Manager the application for which you want to create an icon, and drag the file name from the File Manager into the Program Manager. A program item icon appears in the group window where you drop the file name. You can use the File Properties command (described in the next section, "Redefining Groups and Program Items") to associate a document to the application.

Redefining Groups and Program Items

When you gain experience with groups and program items, you may want to change the names you have assigned them or change the document associated with a specific program item. You can make these changes easily.

To change the title of a group, follow these steps:

1. Select the group icon whose name you want changed (you cannot change the name of an open group window).

2. Choose the **File Properties** command.

3. Select the **Description** text box and type a new description. This text becomes the new title.

4. Choose OK or press Enter.

When you want to change the title of a program item icon, or when you want to change the application associated with an application, follow these steps:

1. Select the program item icon you want to change.

2. Choose the **File Properties** command.

3. Change the icon title in the **Description** text box or change the application or document name in the **Command Line** text box.

4. Choose OK or press Enter.

Deleting Groups

If you no longer use any of the program items in a group, or if you find a group unnecessary, you can delete the entire group so that it no longer appears in the Program Manager window. Deleting the group removes the group window and its program items from the Program Manager window; it does not delete the application files or data files from disk. To delete a group, follow these steps:

1. If the group window is open, minimize it to an icon by clicking its minimize button or by pressing Ctrl+F4.

2. Select the group icon you want to delete by clicking it or by pressing Ctrl+Tab until the group icon is selected.

3. Choose the **File Delete** command or press the Del key.

4. Choose **Yes** to delete the group.

Deleting Program Items

As your job changes, or as you become more familiar with Windows NT and groups, you frequently will want to keep a group but move or delete a program item in that group. Deleting the program item only removes the icon from the group window; it does not delete the application or data file from disk. To delete program items, follow these steps:

1. Open the group window containing the program item.

2. Select the program item by clicking it or by pressing an arrow key to select it.

3. Choose the **File D**elete command or press the Del key.

4. Choose **Yes** when asked to verify deletion.

Moving and Copying Program Items

As you become more familiar with your work habits in Windows NT, you may want to change the contents of your groups. That may mean copying or moving program items between groups. You also may find that one program item can be useful in more than one group window (you can use it repeatedly for different jobs). If that happens, don't re-create the program item in the multiple groups; instead, move or copy the existing program item to other groups where it is needed.

To move a program item to another group using a mouse, open the group window containing the program item and drag the program item onto the destination group window. You also can drag a program item from one group onto a group icon, but you have no control over where the program item is positioned in the destination window.

To move a program item using the keyboard, open the group window containing the program item. Select the program item to be moved by pressing the arrow keys. Choose **File M**ove (or press F7); when the Move Program Item dialog box appears, select the name of the destination group window and choose OK or press Enter.

To copy a program item to another group using a mouse, follow these steps:

1. Open the group window containing the program item. Open the destination group window if you want to position the icon in a specific place or position the destination group icon where you can see it.

2. Press and hold down the Ctrl key and drag the program item icon where you want it in the destination group window or over the destination group icon.

3. Release the mouse button.

To copy a program item to another group using the keyboard, follow these steps:

1. Open the group window containing the program item.

2. Use the arrow keys to select the program item to be copied.

3. Choose the **File** **C**opy command.

4. Select the destination group's name from the **To** Group list in the Copy Program Item dialog box.

5. Choose OK or press Enter.

Duplicating a Program Item

To duplicate a program item in a group window, hold down the Ctrl key and use the mouse to drag the program item to a new position in the same group window. Release the mouse button to copy the program item in the original group window.

Controlling the Program Manager

The Program Manager is always available in Windows NT. It may appear on-screen in its own window or as the Program Manager icon. Activate the window or the icon to use the Program Manager.

If you can see the Program Manager or its icon, you can activate it by clicking anywhere on the Program Manager window, by double-clicking the Program Manager icon, or by pressing Alt+Tab until the Program Manager icon or window is selected, and then releasing both keys.

If you cannot see the Program Manager window or icon, you can activate it by pressing Ctrl+Esc or double-clicking the desktop to activate the Task List. The Task List is shown in figure 4.7. From the Task List, select the Program Manager by clicking its name or by pressing the up- or down-arrow key. Choose the **S**witch To button or press Enter to activate the Program Manager.

Fig. 4.7

Use the Task List
window to switch
to an application.

Using Menu Commands with the Program Manager

You can operate the Program Manager by using menus, mouse actions, or shortcut keys. The menu commands for the Program Manager are as follows:

Command	Action
File New	Adds a new group item to a group or creates a new group
File Open	Starts the selected program item and its associated document
File Move	Moves a program item to another group
File Copy	Copies a program item to another group
File Delete	Deletes a group or program item
File Properties	Changes the description, program name, document name, or icon for a program item
File Run	Starts the application whose name you enter, with or without a document (the application does not have to be a program item)
File Logoff	Logs the current user off of Windows NT, closing all open files, enabling another user to log onto the system
File Shutdown	Logs the current user off of Windows NT and prepares the system to be shut off or restarted

continues

Command	Action
Options **A**uto Arrange	Rearranges icons automatically in the selected group window when you change the window
Options **M**inimize on Use	Shrinks the Program Manager window to an icon when another application starts
Options **S**ave Settings on Exit	When a check mark appears next to this item, Windows NT will save all changes to window sizes and positions to pre-serve the current environment for your next Windows NT session
Options Save Settings Now	Saves all the current changes that you have made to Program Manager
Window Tile	Arranges windows side by side so that each window is visible
Window **A**rrange Icons	Arranges all group icons in a row at the bottom of the screen or all program item icons into neat rows in a selected group window
Window # (group names)	Selects a group and opens or activates its window
Help	Defines Program Manager terms and explains its operation

Using the Mouse with the Program Manager

By using the mouse, you can open different groups, activate windows, and start items quickly. If you are familiar with how the mouse works in Windows NT, you can guess how most of the Program Manager operates. Following are some of the basic mouse actions:

Mouse Action	Result
Click an item in the active window	Selects the item
Click a window	Activates the window
Double-click a Program Item icon	Starts the program item (the application and its associated document)

Mouse Action	Result
Double-click a Group icon	Opens the Group icon to a Group window
Drag an item or window title	Moves the item within its group window or moves the group window within the Program Manager window

Using Shortcut Keys with the Program Manager

Although the mouse is the most intuitive method of operating the Program Manager, you can touch-type your way through almost any Windows NT application—including the Program Manager. Following are the shortcut keys you can use to operate the Program Manager:

Key	Result
Arrow keys	Moves the selection between items in the active group window
Ctrl+F6 or Ctrl+Tab	Moves selection to the next group window or icon
Enter	Starts the selected program item (the application and its associated document) or opens the selected group icon
Shift+F4	Arranges group windows in tiles
Shift+F5	Arranges group windows in a cascade
Ctrl+F4	Closes the active group window
Alt+F4	Logs the user off from Windows NT (you are given a chance to cancel the action)

Minimizing the Program Manager to an Icon for Easy Access

Figure 4.8 shows the Windows NT desktop with the Program Manager minimized to an icon in the bottom left corner. Whenever you need room on the desktop or want to remove visual clutter, minimize the

Program Manager window to an icon. When the Program Manager shrinks to an icon, all the group windows remain "inside" the Program Manager icon. To minimize the Program Manager, click the minimize button (the down triangle) at the right edge of the Program Manager title bar. If you use the keyboard, follow these steps to minimize the Program Manager window:

1. Select the Program Manager Control menu (press Alt+space bar).

2. Choose the Minimize command.

To restore the Program Manager from an icon to a window, double-click the icon. If you use the keyboard, follow these steps:

1. Press Ctrl+Esc to display the Task List.

2. Press the up- or down-arrow key to select the Program Manager from the list.

3. Press Enter.

You can specify that the Program Manager minimize to an icon automatically whenever you start an application. To make this specification, choose the Options Minimize on Use command from the Program Manager's menu bar. A check mark appears next to the Minimize on Use option when it is selected. To turn off this command, choose it again.

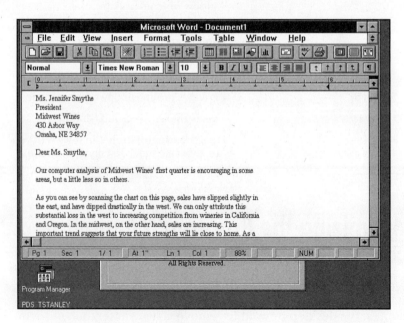

Fig. 4.8

The Program Manager has been iconized to give more space on the desktop.

Opening Group Windows

Before you can open program items (applications and their associated documents), you must open the group window that contains the items. Group windows usually are stored as icons at the bottom of the Program Manager window (see fig. 4.9). The name of the icon appears below each icon.

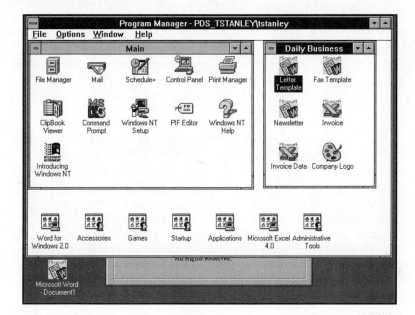

Fig. 4.9

The icons that represent groups, stored at the bottom of the Program Manager window.

If you are using a mouse, double-click the group item icon to open it into a window.

If you are using the keyboard, select and then open an icon by pressing Ctrl+F6 or Ctrl+Tab until the group icon you want is selected. Once it is selected, press Enter. If you find it difficult to read the names under each group icon, choose the **W**indow command in the menu bar and then select the group name from the list at the bottom of the menu.

Sizing Group Windows

When you have multiple windows, you may want to change their sizes to see multiple groups or to maximize one group window so that it fills the inside of the Program Manager. You can resize a group window using the same window-sizing principles you learned in Chapter 2. If you are unfamiliar with window sizing, minimizing, and maximizing, you may want to review Chapter 2.

To resize a group window with a mouse, move the pointer to a window edge until the pointer changes to à two-headed arrow. Drag the window edge to a new location and release the mouse button. To resize a group window with the keyboard, press Alt and the hyphen (–) to access the document Control menu; choose the **S**ize command. Press the arrow key that points to the edge you want to move and then press the arrow keys to move the edge. When the window is sized as you want it, press Enter.

> **Maximizing a Group Window**
>
> Double-click the title bar of a group window to maximize the window. You can restore a maximized window to its previous window size by clicking the restore icon (a double-headed arrow in the upper-right corner of the window).

You can maximize, minimize, and restore group windows in the Program Manager just as you can do with windows (described in Chapter 2). To maximize, minimize, and restore with the mouse, click the arrowhead icons located at the right edge of each group window's title bar. The up arrowhead maximizes a window; the down arrowhead minimizes the window to an icon; the double arrowhead restores a maximized window to its previous size.

If you have many group windows, you may find it easier to move between groups if you minimize group windows you are not using. Another method of minimizing a group window with the mouse is to double-click the document Control menu icon. This icon is located at the left edge of the title bar of each group window. If you double-click this icon in an application window, you close the application window; but because group windows cannot be closed, they become icons when you double-click the document Control menu icon.

Arranging Group Windows and Icons

You can arrange group windows and icons manually, or you can use commands in the Program Manager to arrange them. If you want to manually move a group window, drag its title bar with the mouse pointer. To move a group window with the keyboard, press Alt and the hyphen (-), choose **M**ove, move the group window with the arrow keys, and press Enter.

If you want a cascading arrangement of overlapping group windows, like that shown in figure 4.10, choose **W**indow **C**ascade or press Shift+F5.

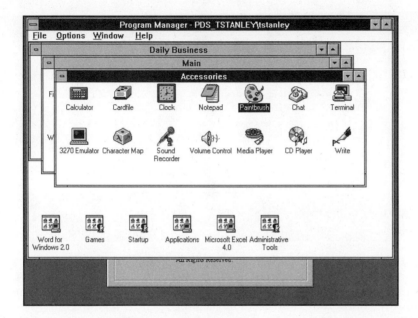

Fig. 4.10

Using **W**indow **C**ascade to overlap group windows.

Cascading group windows are useful when you are working with primarily one group, when you have a large number of program items in each window, or when you have so many group windows that tiling produces small windows. When you have too many group windows to fit in a single cascade, Windows NT overlaps cascades. (The window that was active before you issued the command is the window on the top of the cascade.)

You can arrange group windows in tiles so that you can see a portion of all open group windows (see fig. 4.11). To achieve this arrangement, choose **W**indow **T**ile or press Shift+F4. Tiling group windows is useful if you need access to the program items from multiple groups. To tile multiple group windows, choose the **W**indow **T**ile command.

You can arrange group icons in the Program Manager window. If you want to move a group icon to a new location, drag the icon with the mouse to its new location. If you are using the keyboard, press Ctrl+Tab until the group icon is selected, press Alt and the hyphen (-) to open the document Control menu, choose the **M**ove command, press the arrow keys to move the group icon, and press Enter when you want to fix the icon's location. To arrange all the group icons at the bottom of the Program Manager window, first select any group icon and then choose the **W**indow **A**rrange Icons command.

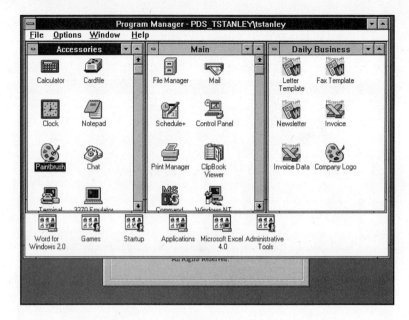

Fig. 4.11

Using **W**indow
Tile to fill the
Program
Manager with a
portion of all
group windows.

To arrange the program item icons in a group window, select the group
window and then choose the **Window Arrange Icons** command. If you
want Windows NT to automatically arrange program item icons whenever you open or resize a window, choose the **O**ptions **A**uto Arrange
command. A check mark appears next to the **A**uto Arrange command
when it is on. Choose the command again to turn it off.

Changing Groups with the File Manager

You can perform many of the operations you just learned from the File
Manager. You also can use the File Manager to prevent accidental or
unauthorized changes, such as deletions of program items. You learn
how to do this in Chapter 5.

Restoring the Program Manager

If you have been running an application, the Program Manager may
have been minimized to an icon. If you want to restore the Program
Manager icon to a window, double-click the Program Manager icon if
you can see it.

If you cannot see the icon or are using a keyboard, press Ctrl+Esc to display the Task List (see fig. 4.7). The Task List enables you to activate applications that are running in Windows NT but that are not visible (and Program Manager is always running when Windows NT is running). From the Task List, press the up- or down-arrow keys until Program Manager is highlighted; press Enter to start the Program Manager.

Quitting the Program Manager

When you log into Windows NT, the Program Manager automatically starts, displaying your program groups and program items. The Program Manager is always running and available because it is the central coordinator for any applications running in Windows NT. When you close or quit the Program Manager, you also log off of Windows NT.

When you are ready to quit Windows NT, follow these steps:

1. Save the data in your application and then quit the application.

2. Activate the Program Manager, opening the icon into a window, if necessary.

3. Choose the **File Logoff** command. The Logoff Windows NT dialog box, shown in figure 4.12, displays.

4. Choose OK or press Enter.

Logoff Windows NT

This will end your Windows session.

OK   Cancel

Fig. 4.12

One way of quitting Program Manager is by logging off from Windows NT using the Logoff Windows NT dialog box.

A quick way to log off Windows NT is to press Alt+F4 when Program Manager is the active application.

T I P

Windows NT ensures that all your data is saved, closing all windows that you had open, including the Program Manager. Windows NT redisplays the Welcome window telling you to press Ctrl+Alt+Del to log on.

A second way to quit Program Manager is to shut down Windows NT. Shutting down Windows NT prepares your computer to be shut off. If you plan to shut off your computer, follow these steps:

1. Save the data in your application and then quit the application.

2. Activate the Program Manager, opening the icon into a window, if necessary.

3. Choose the **File S**hutdown command. The Shutdown Computer dialog box, shown in fig. 4.13, displays.

    The dialog box contains a checkbox—**R**estart when shutdown is complete. Mark this box to reboot the computer after Windows NT completes the shutdown procedures.

4. Choose OK or press Enter. When shutdown completes, you can safely turn off the computer.

Fig. 4.13

Choose to shut down Windows NT when you want to turn off or reboot the computer.

Summary

In this chapter, you learned how the Program Manager can help you organize your applications and their associated documents into groups that match the way you work. You can use the Program Manger to create groups for each different type of work you do.

From here, you will want to learn how to manage the files on your disk: how to copy, move, and erase the files as well as how to create new directories. The File Manager displays trees showing the files in each directory and showing how directories are organized. The File Manager also displays the corresponding file lists next to the tree. Copying or moving with a mouse is as easy as dragging a file name to the disk or directory where you want it to go and dropping it in. With the File Manager, you may find that managing your hard disk and floppy disks can actually be fun.

Managing Files with the File Manager

T he File Manager in Windows NT is a well-designed tool that acts like an office manager to help you see how files are organized; to manage disks; to copy, move, and erase files; and to start applications. When you first start the File Manager, you see a window divided into left and right sides. The directory tree area on the left shows the tree-like structure in which directories and subdirectories are organized on a hard disk. The right side of the window shows the files and subdirectories found within the directory selected on the left side. You can have multiple directory windows open—each showing the contents of a different directory in the contents list segment.

With the File Manager, you can view and maintain files and directories easily. If you have a mouse, for example, you can copy all the files in a directory to a diskette by dragging the directory's icon on top of the diskette drive icon and releasing the mouse button. Figure 5.1 shows the different parts of the File Manager.

You can connect to *shared* directories on other computers on your network. Likewise, you can designate directories on your hard disk as shared so that other users can access the files in those directories. You use File Manager to connect to shared directories and also to share directories on your computer.

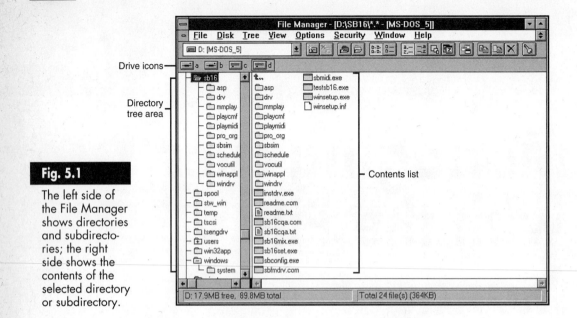

Drive icons

Directory
tree area

Contents list

Fig. 5.1

The left side of
the File Manager
shows directories
and subdirecto-
ries; the right
side shows the
contents of the
selected directory
or subdirectory.

Understanding Storage, Memory, Files, and Directories

The computer does all calculations and work in *electronic memory*.
(Electronic memory is known as *RAM*, Random-Access Memory.) RAM
is where Windows NT and your applications work. The data you work
on also resides in RAM. If the computer loses electrical power, the data,
application, and Windows NT are lost from memory. Because electronic
memory is limited in size and disappears when electrical power is removed, the computer needs a way to store large amounts of data and
applications for long periods of time.

You use *magnetic storage* to store applications and data for long periods of time or when the computer is turned off. Magnetic-storage media
are floppy disks (which are removable and don't contain much space)
or hard disks (which are internal to the computer and have vast
amounts of space). When you start an application or open a data file,
the computer places a *copy* of the information stored in magnetic storage (on floppy disks or a hard disk) into electronic memory (RAM).
If power is lost, the magnetic copy still is available.

You save the work in magnetic *files*, which store the data on a floppy
disk or hard disk. Over time, you may have hundreds or even thousands of files. Searching for a specific file among the thousands of file
names that the File Manager displays could be very time-consuming.

To make the job of finding files easier, hard disks usually are organized into *directories*. If you think of the hard disk as a filing cabinet, directories are like the drawers in the filing cabinet. In a filing cabinet, each drawer can hold a different category of document. In a hard disk, each directory can hold a different category of file. The files in a directory can be *applications* (also known as *programs*) or *documents*.

Within a filing-cabinet drawer, you can further segment the drawer with file folders. Within a hard disk, you can segment a directory by putting subdirectories under it. *Subdirectories* also hold files.

The process of organizing a hard disk is similar to organizing a filing cabinet. With File Manager commands, you can create, name, and delete directories and subdirectories. (Some networks, however, may prevent you from altering or creating directory structures.) For example, you may want a WINWORD directory for word processing jobs. Within the WINWORD directory, you may want subdirectories with names such as BUDGETS, SCHEDULE, LETTERS, and REPORTS.

Large computers and networks have multiple hard disks, each disk with its own drive letter. In figure 5.1, there are four disks, as shown by the icons for drives A, B, C, and D. Each disk acts like a separate filing cabinet and can have its own unique directories and subdirectories.

Understanding the File Manager's Display

Before you use File Manager, you will find it helpful to understand the different characteristics of the File Manager display. Recognizing the display features enables you to more quickly perform file management tasks like listing the contents of a directory or finding the total space used by a group of files.

You will find the Windows NT File Manager very similar to the Windows for Workgroups File Manager.

Windows NT File Manager Display

When you first start the File Manager, the *directory window* is divided into two parts. In figure 5.1, the *directory tree*, with the expanded structure of directories and subdirectories on drive C, occupies the left portion of the window. The *contents list* on the right shows the files in the D:\SB16 directory.

The plus and minus signs shown in the directory tree designate expandable and collapsible branches. The directory icons in the directory tree do not display plus and minus signs by default. To display them, select the Indicate Expandable Branches command from the Tree menu. At the top of the directory window (just below the menu bar) are icons that represent the available *disk drives*. The title bar shows the *directory path* for the currently selected directory.

Notice the *status bar* at the bottom of the File Manager. On the right, the bar always displays the number and sum total size of the files on the selected subdirectory. When the directory tree portion of the window is active, the left portion of the bar shows the available storage on the active disk. When the contents list is active, this area shows the total size in bytes of the selected files. Scroll bars appear on the right side and bottom of the directory tree and at the bottom of the contents list. If either segment contains more information than it can show at once, the scroll bar is shaded.

The directory tree contains miniature folder icons, which represent directories and subdirectories. The contents list shows files as miniature icons that represent documents. If you have selected Indicate Expandable Branches from the Tree menu, a plus sign (+) in a directory or subdirectory icon indicates that additional subdirectories are inside the icon. A minus sign (–) in a subdirectory icon indicates that the directory can be collapsed inside its parent directory. A folder icon without a plus or minus sign indicates that it is the lowest level of subdirectory.

When a directory or subdirectory icon is expanded, as shown in figure 5.1, you can see the underlying subdirectories. Notice the vertical lines and indentations that show how directories and subdirectories are dependent. When a directory or subdirectory is open, its icon changes to look like an open folder, and its contents are displayed in the contents list.

At any given time, the File Manager's *focus* is on only one area of the window: the drive bar, the directory tree, or the contents list. The area that has a selection with a highlighted background has the focus. In the area with the focus, you can use the arrow keys on the keyboard to change the selection. Press Tab to move the focus between areas.

The File Manager can display multiple directory windows at one time to show the file contents of any directory or subdirectory you select. To make comparing disk contents or copying or deleting files easy, open multiple directory windows onto different disks and directories.

Just below the menu bar is the *toolbar*. The *buttons* on the toolbar enable you to quickly access several frequently used File Manager commands. Each button represents one of the menu commands. You can customize the toolbar so that it includes buttons for whatever commands you want (see "Customizing the Toolbar" later in this chapter). See "Using the Toolbar with the File Manager" in this chapter to learn how to use the toolbar.

Also located on the toolbar (at the left end) is a drop-down list of all the drives available for you to use, including *network drives*, which are directories being *shared* by other users. The *share name* and a *computer name* may appear next to the names of network drives in this list.

When a directory is shared, it is represented in the directory tree as a folder with a hand underneath it (see fig. 5.2). The SB16 directory in the figure is shared.

Operating the File Manager

As with most Windows NT applications, you can operate the File Manager with the mouse, by touch typing, or with shortcut keys. Use the method that is most convenient for you. A combination of mouse actions and typing is fast and flexible.

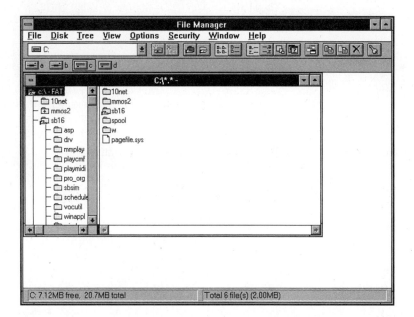

Fig. 5.2

The directory window in the File Manager includes a toolbar.

Using Commands with the File Manager

Table 5.1 lists the commands available in the File Manager. You can
select these commands with either the keyboard or mouse.

Table 5.1 File Manager commands

NT, NTAS, or both	Command	Description
Both	**Disk Connect Network Drive...**	Connects to a particular network drive (displayed only if you are on a network)
Both	**Disk Copy Disk...**	Copies the contents of one diskette to another diskette of the same capacity
Both	**Disk Disconnect Network Drive**	Disconnects the computer from a drive (displayed only if you are on a network)
Both	**Disk Format Floppy...**	Formats a diskette
Both	**Disk Label Disk...**	Creates or changes the volume label on disks or diskettes
Both	**Disk Select Drive...**	Selects a different disk drive
Both	**Disk Share As...**	Makes a disk directory available to other users (this command is available only if you are on a network)
Both	**Disk Stop Sharing...**	Makes a shared disk directory unavailable to other users (this command is available only if you are on a network)
Both	**File Associate...**	Associates a selected document file with an application so that you can open a document in an application by opening only the document file
Both	**File Copy**	Copies selected files or directories to a new location

NT, NTAS, or both	Command	Description
Both	**File Copy to Clip**board	Copies a file to the Clipboard
Both	**File C**reate Directory	Creates a directory or subdirectory within the currently selected directory or subdirectory
Both	**File D**elete	Deletes selected files or directories
Both	**File E**xit	Exits and closes the File Manager
Both	**File M**ove	Moves selected files or directories from one location to another
Both	**File O**pen	Starts the selected application, opens a directory window of the selected directory, or opens the selected document and starts the application associated with the document
Both	**File P**rint	Prints the selected text file to the current printer
Both	**File Properties**	Displays some information about a selected file and allows changes to a file's Read Only, Hidden, Archive, and System attributes
Both	**File Re**name	Renames a selected file or directory
Both	**File R**un	Starts a selected application with a data file (if one is associated) or with a start-up argument (if one is associated)
Both	**File Search**	Searches for file or directory names that meet naming patterns you set; you can search the entire disk with this command
Both	**File S**elect Files	Selects files and directories in the active directory window
NTAS	**Mail S**end Mail	Sends a mail message with selected files attached to the message

continues

Table 5.1 Continued

NT, NTAS, or both	Command	Description
Both	Options Confirmation...	Controls confirmation messages
Both	Options Customize Toolbar	Adds, removes, and rearranges the buttons on the toolbar
Both	Options Drivebar	Displays a bar with drive buttons for each drive connected to your computer. Selecting a drive button displays the contents of that drive in the File Manager window.
Both	Options Font	Changes the font, font style, and font size used to display directory and file information
Both	Options Minimize on Use	Minimizes the File Manager to an icon when you start an application
Both	Options Open New Window on connect	Opens a new window when you connect
Both	Options Save Settings on Exit	Enables the automatic saving of current settings of all options in the Options menu
Both	Options Status Bar	Displays the status bar at the bottom of the File Manager for information about the selected files or directories
Both	Options Toolbar	Displays the toolbar at the top of the File Manager with buttons for quickly carrying out several File Manager commands
Both	Security Permissions...	Permissions; applies only to NTFS volumes
Both	Security Auditing...	Auditing; applies only to NTFS volumes
Both	Security Owner...	Owner; applies only to NTFS volumes

NT, NTAS, or both	Command	Description
Both	**Tree Collapse Branch**	Collapses the lower level subdirectories into the selected directory
Both	**Tree Expand All**	Expands all directories and subdirectories; files are not shown
Both	**Tree Expand Branch**	Expands the selected directory to show all lower subdirectories
Both	**Tree Expand One Level**	Expands the selected directory to show the next level
Both	**Tree Indicate Expandable Branches**	Uses plus (+) and minus (–) symbols to indicate whether a directory contains subdirectories
Both	**View All File Details**	Shows all information about the files and file attributes (name, size, date, and time most recently edited, and attributes)
Both	**View By File Type...**	Limits the files displayed to the specified types and/or to files whose names match specified parameters
Both	**View Directory Only**	Displays only the contents list
Both	**View Name**	Shows the file and directory name in the current directory window
Both	**View Partial Details...**	Shows selected information about the files (you select what you want to show)
Both	**View Sort by Date**	Sorts file names by last modification date (oldest dates first)
Both	**View Sort by Name**	Sorts file names by name (alphabetical order)

continues

Table 5.1 Continued

NT, NTAS, or both	Command	Description
Both	View Sort by Size	Sorts file names by size (from largest to smallest)
Both	View Sort by Type	Sorts file names by type (alphabetically by extension name)
Both	View Split	Moves the dividing line between the directory tree and the contents list
Both	View Tree and Directory	Displays the directory tree on the left and the contents list on the right
Both	View Tree Only	Displays only the directory tree
Both	Window #	Activates the indicated window; all open windows' names are assigned a number in the list
Both	Window Arrange Icons	Arranges minimized directory window icons in a row at the bottom of the screen
Both	Window Cascade	Arranges windows so that they cascade in overlapping fashion from top left to lower right
Both	Window New Window	Opens a new directory window
Both	Window Refresh	Rereads the disk and updates the active window to match the disk contents
NT	Window Tile Horizontally	Arranges open windows horizontally so that the contents of all windows are visible
NT	Window Tile Vertically	Arranges open windows vertically so that the contents of all windows are visible

Using the Keyboard with the File Manager

To operate the File Manager by using keystrokes, use this section as a quick reference. This section lists the keyboard shortcuts; complete instructions for procedures using these keystrokes are in following sections.

When you are in the *drive icon area*, use the keystrokes in the following list:

Keystroke	Action
Tab or F6	Moves the active area between the disk-drive icons, the directory tree, and the contents list
Ctrl+*letter*	Selects and opens the drive specified by *letter*. For example, Ctrl+C selects drive C and displays the directories on this drive in the directory tree area.
← or →	Moves the selection among the drive icons if you have tabbed into the drive area of the window
Enter	Opens the selected drive and displays the contents of the drive in the directory tree area of the window

When you are in the *directory tree area*, use the following keystrokes:

Keystroke	Action
↑ or ↓	Moves the selection to a directory or subdirectory above or below the currently selected directory in the directory-tree section of the window
→	Selects the first subdirectory (the daughter) within the currently selected and open directory when you are in the directory-tree section of the window
←	Selects the directory that contains the current subdirectory (the parent) when you are in the directory-tree section of the window

continues

Keystroke	Action
Ctrl+↑ or Ctrl+↓	Restricts selections to a subdirectory level within the current directory
PgUp	Selects the directory one window up
PgDn	Selects the directory one window down
Home	Selects the root directory for the disk
End	Selects the last directory in the window
letter	Selects the next directory or subdirectory, beginning with *letter*
- (hyphen)	Collapses the selected directory. (The minus sign key also works.)
+ (plus)	Expands the selected directory one level
* (asterisk)	Expands all branches in the selected directory
Ctrl+*	Expands all branches on the disk

When you are in the *contents list area*, use the keystrokes in the following list:

Keystroke	Action
PgUp	Selects the file or directory one window up
PgDn	Selects the file or directory one window down
Home	Selects the first file or directory in the window
End	Selects the last file or directory in the window
letter	Selects the first file or directory beginning with *letter*
Shift+arrow	Selects all files or directories over which you move the selection highlight
Shift+F8	Selects nonadjacent files; keeps current selections as you move the selection highlight without selecting additional files. Press the space bar to select or deselect files; press Shift+F8 to return the arrow keys to normal.

Keystroke	Action
Ctrl+/ (slash)	Selects all items
Ctrl+\ (backslash)	Deselects all items except the one that was selected when you started
↑,↓	Moves the selection between files or directories
←, →	Scrolls the contents window left or right
space bar	Selects or deselects the current file or directory when moving the selection with Shift+F8
Enter	Opens a directory if the directory is selected or starts an application if an application or the associated data file is selected

Using the Mouse with the File Manager

If you have a mouse, the File Manager can be much easier to use. The mouse makes selecting and copying nonadjacent files very easy. The following chart lists some activities and the mouse actions you do to achieve them.

Activity	Mouse Action
Select a directory	Click on a directory in the directory tree area
Select a file	Click on a file in the contents list
Select multiple and adjacent files	Click on the first file; press Shift+click on the last file
Select multiple nonadjacent files	Ctrl+click on each file
Start an application file or open a document file	Double-click on the application an associated document file
Expand a directory one level	Double-click on the icon with the plus sign (+) to the left of the directory you want to expand
Collapse a directory one level	Double-click on the icon with the minus sign (–) on the open folder icon above the directory you want to collapse

continues

Activity	Mouse Action
Copy a file	Drag the file name onto another disk drive
Move a file	Drag a file name into a different directory on the same disk drive

Using the Toolbar with the File Manager

If you are working with File Manager, you can quickly execute many File Manager commands with the toolbar, which is located immediately below the menu bar. To execute a command, click the button on the toolbar for that command. File Manager comes with a default set of buttons in the toolbar, which are described in the following table. The table lists the icons in left to right order as they appear in File Manager. You can also customize the toolbar so that it includes buttons for the commands you use most frequently (see "Customizing the Toolbar," later in this chapter).

Icon	Button Name	Description
	Connect Network Drive	For connecting to a network drive
	Disconnect Network Drive	For disconnecting from a network drive
	Share As	For sharing a directory with other users on a network
	Stop Sharing	Stops the sharing of a directory with other users
	View Name	Changes the display to show only file names
	View All File Details	Changes display to show all file details
	Sort By Name	Sorts files alphabetically by file name
	Sort By Type	Sorts files alphabetically by file name extension

Icon	Button Name	Description
	Sort By Size	Sorts files by size, from largest to smallest
	Sort By Date	Sorts files by date, starting with most recent files
	New Window	Opens a new directory window
	Copy	Copies selected files or directories to a new location
	Move	Moves selected files or directories from one location to another
	Delete	Deletes selected files or directories
	Permissions	Applies only to NTFS volumes

Selecting and Opening Files and Directories

File Manager follows the primary rule of all Windows NT applications: *Select, then Do.* When you want to work on a file or directory in the File Manager, you first must find and select the file or directory. After you select a file, you can display information about the file and start, copy, move, or delete the file. After you select a directory, you can find information about the directory contents, copy or move the directory, or open the directory to see the subdirectories or files it contains.

Selecting a New Disk Drive

Before you can work with files and directories, you must be in the correct disk drive. The disk drives available in the computer appear as icons under the directory window title bar. The currently selected drive appears outlined. If the focus is on the drive icon bar, the currently selected drive also displays with a dark background. To change to a new drive with the mouse, click on the drive icon you want to activate.

When using the keyboard to change to a new drive, first notice whether the focus is in the drive icon area of the window. Press the Tab key to move the focus among the three screen areas.

If the focus is in the drive icon bar, change to a new drive by pressing the left- or right-arrow key to move the focus to a different drive; then press Enter. The highlight moves behind the drive you selected.

If the focus is in the directory tree or contents list area of the window, press Ctrl+*letter* to change to a different drive, where *letter* is the drive's letter. (If you change to a diskette drive containing an unformatted disk, File Manager prompts you to format the diskette. Refer to the later section, "Formatting Diskettes," to learn how.)

In File Manager, you can also select the drive you want to work with by using the drop-down list at the left end of the toolbar (see fig. 5.3). The advantage to using the drop-down list is that you can easily see the shared directory associated with the drive letter.

To open this list, click the down arrow to the right of the list or press F2. Click the drive you want to activate or use the up- or down-arrow keys to select the drive you want to activate and press Enter.

Drive list —

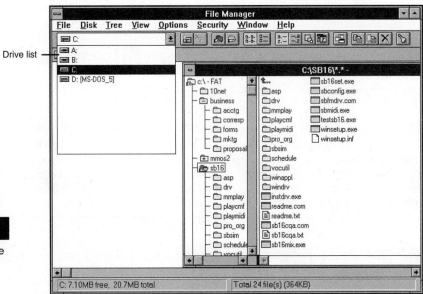

Fig. 5.3

Selecting a drive using the drive list on the toolbar.

Selecting, Expanding, and Collapsing Directories

The directory window, shown in figure 5.1, always displays in the File Manager window. It may be either in its own window or in an icon at the bottom of the File Manager window. The directory tree area in the left half of the File Manager shows the hierarchical structure of the area of the disk you are currently examining.

Select One Directory at a Time

You can select only one directory at a time in a given directory window. You can, however, open multiple directory windows, each displaying a different directory. Open more than one directory when you want to see the contents of multiple directories at one time. Copying files between directories is easier when you open a source-directory window and a destination-directory window. To learn how to open a second File Manager window, refer to the upcoming section, "Opening and Selecting Directory Windows."

To select a directory using the mouse, click on the directory or subdirectory you want. If you cannot see the directory, use the vertical scroll bar on the directory tree area to scroll it into sight before clicking. If you need files in a subdirectory, open the directory above the desired subdirectory first, as described later in this section.

To select a directory using the keyboard, follow these steps:

1. Press Tab if necessary to move the focus to the directory tree area of the window.

2. Press Ctrl+*letter* to change to the drive that contains the files you want.

3. Select a directory from the tree with the keys described in "Using the Keyboard with the File Manager," earlier in this chapter.

After you select a specific directory, you may want to see the subdirectories beneath it. Or you may want to collapse the fully expanded directory structure so that you can see the directories at a higher level. Figure 5.3 shows a directory structure with directories expanded. The BUSINESS directory is a parent directory that has been expanded to show the ACCTG, CORRESP, FORMS, MKTG, and PROPOSAL subdirectories beneath it. Collapsed directories do not show the subdirectories they contain.

Directory icons appear as file folders. If a directory icon contains a +
(plus) sign, the directory contains subdirectories. If a directory icon
contains a – (minus) sign, the directory can be collapsed so as not to
display its subdirectories. If the directory icon does not contain a +
(plus) sign, no subdirectories are contained within this directory
or the plus and minus signs are hidden. To display them, choose
the **Tree** I**ndicate Expandable Branches** command.

To expand or collapse a directory or subdirectory with the mouse,
use one of the following mouse actions:

- Double-click on the + (plus) sign in a directory icon if you want to
  expand the directory one level.

- Double-click on the – (minus) sign in a directory icon if you want
  to collapse the directory.

To expand or collapse a directory or subdirectory with the keyboard,
follow these steps:

1. Select the directory or subdirectory.

2. Press one of the following keys:

Key	Action
- (hyphen)	Collapses the selected directory
+ (plus)	Expands the selected directory one level
* (asterisk)	Expands all subdirectories in the selected directory
Ctrl+* (asterisk)	Expands all subdirectories on the disk

To expand or collapse directories with the menu commands, follow
these steps:

1. Select the directory or subdirectory.

2. Choose one of the following commands:

Command	Action
Tree Expand One Level	Expands the selected directory to show all subdirectories at the next lower level
Tree Expand **B**ranch	Expands the selected directory to show all lower subdirectories

Command	Action
Tree Expand **A**ll	Expands all subdirectories on the disk
Tree **C**ollapse Branch	Collapses the lower level subdirectories into the selected directory

Opening and Selecting Directory Windows

You can have many directory windows that show the contents of individual directories. Figure 5.4 shows the File Manager with numerous directory windows. Notice that each directory window displays a different directory, and even different disks. For any directory window, you have the option of displaying just the directory tree, just the list of files in the directory, or both. Use the **V**iew command to select one of these three options. As you see later in this chapter, having multiple windows open onto different directories and disks is a convenient way to copy or move files with a mouse.

To open a new directory window, choose the **W**indow **N**ew Window command. The new window will display the path name of the previously active window in the title bar, followed by a colon and 2, which indicates that the window is the second one associated with this particular directory. When you choose another directory, however, the path name in the new window changes.

> To cycle through all the open directory windows, press Ctrl+F6. To arrange all the directory windows on-screen, choose the **W**indow **C**ascade command or the **W**indow **T**ile command.

T I P

Each file within a directory window displays an icon that helps identify its type of file. These icons are shown in the following list.

Icon	Type of File
Directory Tree icons	
	Open directory or subdirectory
	Closed directory or subdirectory

continues

Icon	Type of File
Contents List icons	
▭	Application or batch file having the extension EXE, COM, PIF, or BAT (choosing one of these files may start an application)
🗎	Document file associated with an application (choosing one of these files starts the application that created the file)
🗋	Other files
Shared directory icon	
🗁	Directory that is shared with other users

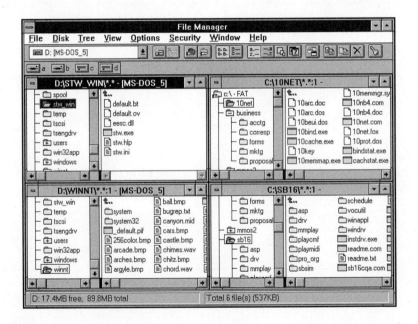

Fig. 5.4

Directory windows, each displaying the contents of different directories.

Suppose that you have multiple directory windows open and want a specific window to be active. If you are using a mouse and can see the window you want, click on a portion of this window to make it active.

If you are using a keyboard, press Ctrl+F6 until the window you want is active or select the **W**indow menu and choose the name of the window you want from the menu. (If you have more than nine windows open, the **M**ore Windows command appears at the bottom of the **W**indow menu. Choose it to select from a scrolling list of open windows.)

A quick way to open a new window in File Manager is to double-click on a disk drive icon. Double-click on the icon for disk drive A, for example, to open a new window displaying the contents of a diskette in drive A. Double-click on the current drive icon to duplicate the window currently displayed. Often, follow this step by tiling your windows so that you can see the contents of all open windows. A shortcut to tiling your windows vertically is to press Shift+F4.

T I P

Changing or Closing Directory Windows

Each directory window usually contains both a directory tree and a contents list. However, you can change this to another **V**iew option for any given window. You might be doing some intensive disk management, for example, and need to display multiple directory windows for easier moving and copying. To save screen space, you can display one directory tree together with multiple contents lists. To do this, follow these steps:

1. With a single directory window open, choose the **V**iew **Tr**ee Only command.

2. For each directory whose contents you want to see on-screen, open a new window.

3. Select each window in turn and choose the **V**iew Directory **O**nly command. Leave one window in tree-only format and use it for quick perusals of the directory structure.

4. Choose **W**indow **T**ile if you want to see all the open directory windows at all times. If you have more than a few windows open, you might need to maximize the File Manager window to work effectively.

Directory windows are document windows, so you can use the mouse or document Control menu to resize, move, or close each window. Activate the window you want to change by clicking on it or by pressing Ctrl+F6 until it is on top of the other windows.

To close the active directory window using a shortcut key, press Ctrl+F4.

To control the active window with the keyboard, press Alt+hyphen (-) to display the Control menu. The Control menu lists all the commands necessary to move, resize, or close the window.

Selecting More Than One File or Directory

Before you can act on a file, you must select it. In some cases (when copying or deleting files, for example) you may want to select multiple files before choosing any command.

To select a single file with the mouse, click on the file name. To select multiple adjacent files, click on the first file, press and hold down the Shift key, and click on the last file. All files between the two files you clicked on are selected. To select nonadjacent files, click on the first file and hold down the Ctrl key as you click on other files. If you want to retain current selections but deselect a file, Ctrl+click on the file you no longer want selected.

To select a single file with the keyboard, press the arrow keys to move the selection to the file name you want. To select multiple adjacent files, move the selection to the first file, press and hold down the Shift key, and press an arrow key. To select nonadjacent files, select the first file, press Shift+F8, press an arrow key to move to the next file to be selected, and press the space bar. Move to the additional files you want to select and press the space bar. To deselect a file and retain other selections, move to the selected file and press the space bar. Press Shift+F8 to return to normal mode (selecting a single file at a time).

If you want to select all files in a directory window with a given extension, select a contents list window and choose the File Select Files command. The dialog box shown in figure 5.5 appears.

In the Files text box, type the name for the file you want to select. You can use the familiar DOS wild card characters in the file name.

Use wild cards, such as * and ?, to search for a group of files or directory names or to search when you don't know the exact name of the file or directory. In the example shown in figure 5.6, the pattern E*.XLS searches for all file names beginning with E and having the extension XLS (an Excel worksheet). Although the file name must begin with E, the rest of the file name can be any group of letters (as specified by *).

Fig. 5.5

The Select Files dialog box with *.* specified.

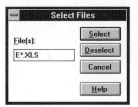

Fig. 5.6

The Select Files dialog box with E*.XLS specified.

To select all files in the window, choose the **S**elect button while the Files text box displays *.*. If you want to deselect certain files, change the **F**iles parameter and choose **D**eselect. Choose **C**lose when you finish making the selection(s).

A quick way to select all the files in a selected contents list is to press Ctrl+/. To deselect all files but one, press Ctrl+\.

T I P

Canceling Selections

If you select the wrong file or directory, you can cancel it. To cancel a single selection with the mouse, click on another file or directory. If you select multiple files and want to cancel one but retain the others, press and hold down the Ctrl key as you click on the file you want to deselect.

To cancel a single selection with the keyboard, press an arrow key to select another file or directory. If you select multiple files or directories and want to cancel one but retain the others, press Shift+F8, press the arrow keys to enclose the incorrect selection with the dashed focus line, and press the space bar. Deselect any other incorrect selections and press Shift+F8 to return to normal selection mode.

To cancel a selection while the Select Files dialog box is on-screen, change the Files parameter to *.* and choose the **D**eselect button.

Searching for Files or Directories

Losing a file is frustrating and wastes time. With Windows NT, you can search disks or directories for file names similar to the file you have misplaced. To search for a file by its name or part of its name, follow these steps:

1. Select the disk drive you want to search.

2. Select the directory (if you want to search a single directory).

   If you do not know the specific directory that contains a file, select the parent directory of all subdirectories that might contain the file.

3. Choose the **File Search** command. The Search dialog box appears (see fig. 5.7).

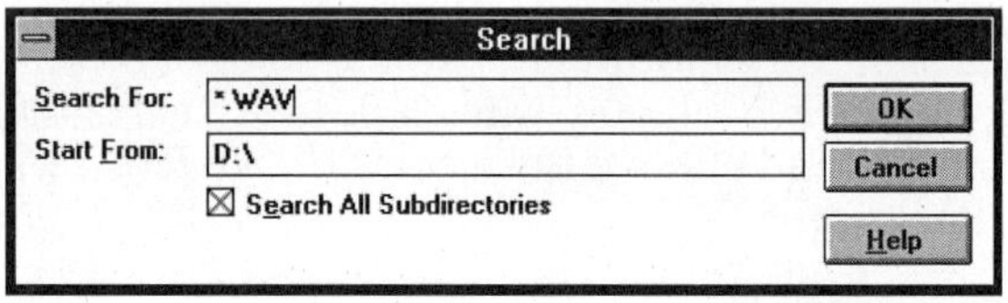

Fig. 5.7

The Search
dialog box.

4. Type in the **Search** For text box the name of the file for which you are searching. You can use a pattern of DOS wild cards in the file name.

5. To search all directories on the current disk, specify the root directory in the Start **From** text box. By default, Windows NT searches all subdirectories beneath the directory you select. To search the specified directory only, turn off the **Search** All Subdirectories option.

6. Choose OK or press Enter.

A Search Results window, like the one shown in figure 5.8, displays the paths and file names of all files that match the pattern you were seeking. When you see the file or application you want in the Search Results window, start the document or application by double-clicking on it with the mouse or by selecting it and pressing Enter. You can start documents and applications together if the document has been associated with an application, as explained in "Associating Documents with an Application," later in this chapter.

When you use wild cards in a name pattern, remember that the * wild-card character finds any group of characters in the file name in the same or following positions. The ? wild-card character matches any single character within the file name that is in the same position as ?.

Suppose that you know the directory in which a file is located and the date or time at which the file was last saved, but you don't know the file name. You can display the time and date of all the files in the directory window to help you locate that specific file. Choose the View All File Details command to show the time and date on which files were last saved. This command also indicates file attribute(s) at the right.

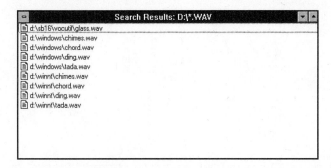

Fig. 5.8

The Search Results window.

If you want to save screen space, you can choose the View Partial Details command and specify which particular file details to display in the Partial Details dialog box (see fig. 5.9).

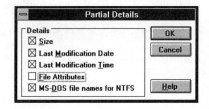

Fig. 5.9

The Partial Details dialog box.

Note that one of the choices, MS-DOS file names for NTFS, gives the eight-character file name with a three-character extension alias for a long NTFS name.

To sort the files in the directory window by name, type, size, or date, choose the corresponding Sort By command under the View menu. Figure 5.10 shows a directory window after choosing the View Sort By Date command.

Some Windows NT applications, such as Word for Windows, can search through their document files and return a list of all files that contain specific words or phrases. An application's search facility can be more effective and precise than the File Manager's search command.

T I P

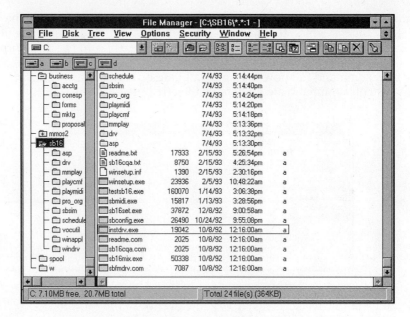

Fig. 5.10

A directory
window sorted
by date (the
newest files are
displayed first).

Controlling File Manager Windows and Displays

You can arrange the windows and files in a way that makes it easy to get work done, whether copying files between directories, making backup copies to disk, or deleting files. The following sections explain how to manipulate the appearance of the Windows NT display screen.

Arranging Directory Windows and Icons

You can arrange directory windows and icons in four ways. You can arrange them by manually sizing and positioning them, by cascading them to show all the window titles, or by placing them in tiles to show each window's contents. You also can minimize windows so that they appear as icons.

To arrange directory windows in a cascade like that shown in figure 5.11, choose the Window Cascade command or press Shift+F5. The active window becomes the top window in the cascade.

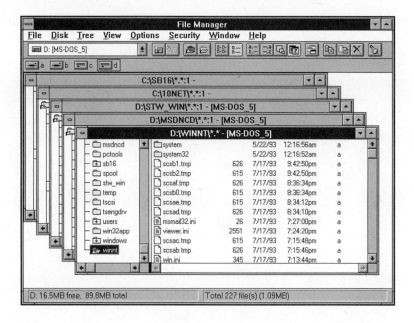

Fig. 5.11

Windows NT in
a cascade
arrangement.

In Windows NT, File Manager provides two ways to arrange directory
windows in tiles (see fig. 5.12). Choose the **W**indow Tile **H**orizontally
command to distribute directory windows in tiles that are arranged one
on top of the other. Choose **W**indow **T**ile Vertically to distribute directory windows in tiles that are arranged side by side.

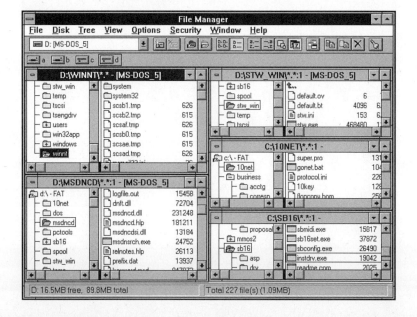

Fig. 5.12

Windows NT
in a tile
arrangement.

When windows are arranged by cascading or by tiling, you still can use each directory window's Control menu to move a window. Chapter 2, "Operating Windows NT," describes how to use the Control menu to move a window.

T   I   P
You can save time if you minimize to icons directory windows that you use frequently (see fig. 5.13). When you want to work with the directory contained within the icon, maximize the icon. To minimize a directory window into an icon, click on the minimize button (the down arrow at the top right of the window). Alternatively, press Alt+hyphen (-), N (for Minimize). To maximize a directory icon into a window, double-click on the icon; alternatively, select the icon by pressing Ctrl+F6 and then press Alt+hyphen (-), X (for Maximize). Remember that you move among icons with the keyboard by pressing Ctrl+F6 or Ctrl+Tab. Chapter 2, "Operating Windows NT," describes how to minimize windows, maximize icons, and move both windows and icons.

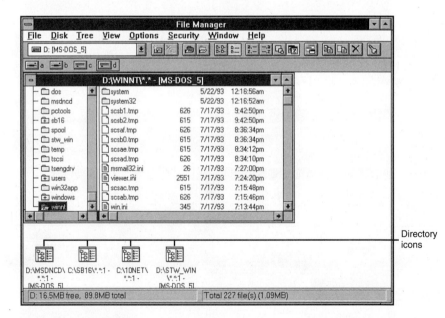

Fig. 5.13

Directory icons keep frequently used directory windows available.

Directory icons

Specifying File-Display Details

You can specify what file information appears in the directory window. View Name shows only the file names and extensions. View All File Details shows all file information. The View Partial Details command enables you to select the information you want displayed. To display file information, follow these steps:

1. Activate the directory window you want to change. If you want to change the display of all subsequent windows you open, activate the directory tree area.

2. Choose the appropriate command. The following chart lists the commands that affect the window display.

Command	Description
View Name	Displays only names and directories
View All File Details	Displays the name, size, date and time last saved, and file attributes
View Partial Details	Selects a custom display showing one or more of the following file characteristics:
	Size—displays the file size in bytes
	Last Modification Date— displays the last date the file was modified and saved
	Last Modification Time— displays the last time the file was modified and saved
	File Attributes—displays one of the following letters for different attributes:
	A Archive
	S System
	H Hidden
	R Read Only

3. If you chose **View** **P**artial Details, choose OK or press Enter after you select one or more of the options.

You can sort the directory window by any of the characteristics displayed. Use the **View** Sort By commands as explained later in this section. If you want to change a file's attributes, use the **File** Properties command, described later in this chapter.

Figure 5.14 shows the Partial Details dialog box from which you can select the different file characteristics you want to display. Figure 5.15 shows two directory windows, each displaying different sets of file characteristics.

The Partial Details dialog box.

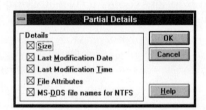

Two directory windows, each showing different file characteristics.

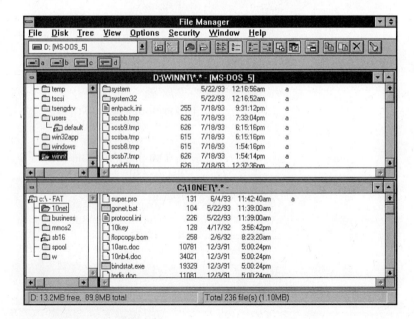

Hiding the Status Bar

You can change some characteristics of the File Manager window. For example, you can hide the status bar at the bottom of the File Manager window.

Leave the Status bar turned on to see available storage and the number of files. The status bar displays important information about the active window. If the directory tree is selected, the status bar shows the available storage on the disk and the number of files in the current directory. If the contents list is selected, the disk storage information is replaced by the number of selected files and the total size of the selected files.

If you want to find out how much room you have on a disk, change to that disk and look at the status bar.

You may want to remove the status bar from the bottom of the File Manager so that you can display more files. In general, however, you should display the status bar so that you can monitor the available disk storage. To turn on the status bar, choose the **O**ptions **S**tatus Bar command. A check mark appears next to the command when the option is on. Choose the command again to turn off the status bar. (This action also removes the check mark.) All directory windows you open subsequently also omit the status bar.

Hiding the Toolbar and Drivebar

You can choose to display or not display the toolbar and drivebar. If you need more room to display files, or do not use the toolbar, you may want to turn off one or both of these options. To turn off the toolbar, choose the **O**ptions **T**oolbar command. Choose the command again to turn the toolbar on. To turn off the drivebar, choose the **O**ptions **D**rivebar command. Choose the command again to turn the drivebar on. A check mark appears next to these commands when the options are on. When you turn off the option, the check mark is removed.

Changing the Font

By default, File Manager displays directory and file names in 8-point MS Sans Serif font. This small font is generally optimal for displaying as many entries as possible while still remaining readable. You can change the font, however, with the **O**ptions **F**ont command.

Choose **O**ptions **F**ont; then select the desired font (typeface), font style, and size from the appropriate list boxes. As you make selections, the Sample box changes to reflect the current state of the File Manager display font. When you are satisfied, choose OK or press Enter.

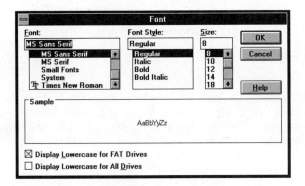

By default, characters in the File Manager appear in upper- and lower-case letters, exactly as you enter them. If you want text in the File Manager window to display in uppercase letters, choose the **O**ptions **F**ont command. The dialog box shown in figure 5.16 appears. Turn off the **L**owercase option to display file and directory names in uppercase letters.

Fig. 5.16

The Font dialog box.

Updating a File Manager Window

You may need to update a directory window. For example, you may have switched diskettes. As a result, you may activate the File Manager and not see a file you have just saved—a scenario that is more than a little disconcerting. Don't panic; the file is there. All you have to do is to choose the **W**indow **R**efresh command (as a shortcut, press F5). If you still cannot find the file in the directory in which you thought you saved the file, you may have saved it to a different directory or disk. Use the **F**ile Search command to find the file.

Sorting the Display of Files and Directories

Finding files or directories is much easier if you rearrange the contents of a directory window. You can order the window contents alphabetically by file name, alphabetically by file extension, by file size, or by the last date the file was saved. To reorder a window's contents, choose one of the commands in the following chart to sort the window.

Command	Description
View Sort by Name	Sorts alphabetically by file name
View Sort by Type	Sorts alphabetically by file extension
View Sort by Size	Sorts by file size from largest to smallest
View Sort by Date	Sorts by last date modified, most recent first

You don't have to display the file date or size in the directory window to sort by those attributes. If you want to see the file's date and size in the directory window, use the View All File Details or View Partial Details command.

Filtering Out Unwanted Files from the Display

Another way to easily find a specific type of file in a directory window is to limit the number of files displayed. You can set criteria to filter files so that only files of the type you want are displayed. Specify the type of file to be displayed when you want to see only application files or only document files that end with a specific extension.

To include in the directory window only the files you want, follow these steps:

1. Activate the directory window in which you want to specify the type of file you want to display.

2. Choose the View By File Type command. The dialog box shown in figure 5.17 appears.

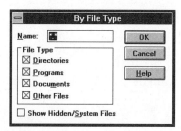

3. Select the **N**ame text box and type a file pattern to display only the files matching the pattern you specify (you can use the wild cards * and ?). Alternatively, select one of the following options:

Option	Description
Directories	Displays only directories or subdirectories
Programs	Displays only files with file extensions of EXE, COM, PIF, or BAT
Docu**m**ents	Displays document files and files that have been associated with an application with the **F**ile **A**ssociate command
Other Files	Displays all other files that are not directories, applications, or documents
Show Hidden/ **S**ystem files	Displays hidden files or system files

4. Choose OK or press Enter.

Changing a File's Attributes

Each file on a disk has a set of *attributes*, or descriptive characteristics. Attributes describe whether the file has been backed up, is part of the operating system, is hidden from normal viewing, or can be read but not written over. With the File Manager, you can display file attributes and change them.

You can display the file attributes in the current directory window by choosing the View **A**ll File Details command. If you want to see only the attributes, choose the View **P**artial File Details command and select the attributes option. This process is described in "Specifying File-Display Details," earlier in this chapter.

To change a file's attributes, select the file or files you want to change and then choose the **F**ile P**r**operties command. The Properties dialog box appears. Select the attribute you want changed and choose OK or press Enter. The following is a list of the attributes you can change.

Attribute	Description
Read Only	Sets the R or read-only attribute, which prevents a file from being changed or erased. Set this attribute for a file when you want to prevent someone from accidentally changing a master template or erasing a file critical to system operation.

Attribute	Description
Archive	Sets the A or archive attribute. Marks with an A any file that has changed since being backed up using the DOS BACKUP, RESTORE, or XCOPY commands. If no A appears, the file has not changed since you (or someone else) backed it up.
Hidden	Sets the H or hidden attribute, which prevents files from displaying.
System	Sets the S or system attribute, which prevents files from displaying. Some files that belong to the operating system are hidden so that they aren't accidentally erased.

Reducing the Chance of Erasing Critical Files

If you want to ensure that a file isn't accidentally changed or erased, set the attributes to Read Only and Hidden or System. These attributes prevent the file from being changed and hide the file from standard display.

Display Hidden or System Files with the View Include Command

Assigning the Hidden or System attribute to hide files is a good way to prevent tampering or accidental erasure. As an experienced Windows NT user, however, you may need to see these files to change, erase, or copy them. To display files with the Hidden or System attribute, choose the View By File Type command and select the Show Hidden/System Files check box.

Viewing the Properties of a File or Directory

You can view the properties of a file or directory in the Properties dialog box. The file name, path, file size, and the date and time the file or directory was last changed are displayed.

The Properties dialog box in File Manager includes more information. For example, you also will find information on the version number, copyright, and company name of a program if the selected item is a program file.

Displaying Warning Messages

During some File Manager operations, a warning message appears and asks you to confirm the action about to take place. If you select a directory and choose File Delete, for example, you may be asked to confirm the deletion of each file and the removal of the directory. If you find the confirmation messages annoying, you can turn them off—but remember that these warning messages appear to prevent you from making mistakes. If you turn off the messages, you have no warning for potentially hazardous actions!

Turn off warning messages by choosing the Options Confirmation command and deselecting the desired options from the Confirmation dialog box (see fig. 5.18). Choose OK or press Enter after choosing an option. Turn a confirmation message back on by reselecting the option so that the check box contains an X.

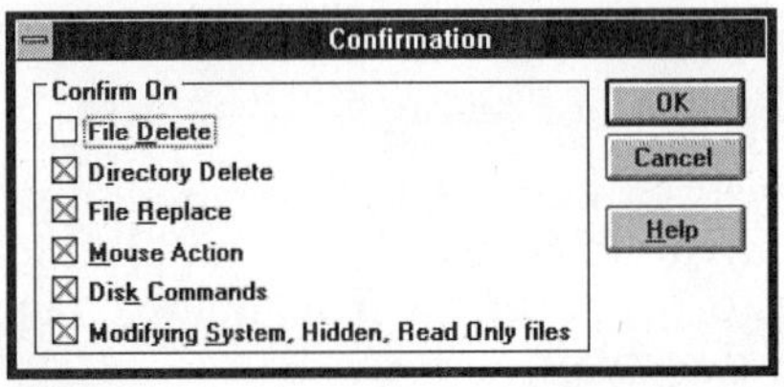

Fig. 5.18

The Options
Confirmation
dialog box.

The following is a list of the options in the Confirmation dialog box and the messages whose display they control.

Option	Action Confirmed by Message
File Delete	Each file being erased
Directory Delete	Each directory being erased
File Replace	One file being copied or moved over another
Mouse Action	Any mouse action involving moving or copying
Disk Commands	Each disk being copied over or formatted
Modifying System, Hidden, Read Only files	Each action on a system, hidden, or read only file

As you gain more experience and confidence with the computer, you may want to turn off these messages. If you are a beginner or have difficulty accurately positioning the mouse, you may want to leave these messages on.

Customizing the Toolbar

The toolbar comes with a default set of buttons for quickly accessing some of the more commonly used File Manager commands. However, you can add and remove buttons from the toolbar so that the commands you use most frequently are accessible from the toolbar. There is a button available for every File Manager command. You can remove buttons that you do not use, add buttons for the commands you use frequently, and move buttons around to arrange them in whatever order you want. You can also return to the default set of buttons at any time.

Removing a Toolbar Button

To quickly remove a toolbar button when you are using a mouse, put the tip of the mouse pointer on the button on the toolbar, hold down the Shift key, and drag the button off the toolbar. When the toolbar button is off the toolbar, release the mouse button.

To remove a toolbar button using the Customize Toolbar dialog box, follow these steps:

1. Choose the **O**ptions Customize Tool**b**ar command or double-click in the background of the toolbar.

   This displays the Customize Toolbar dialog box shown in figure 5.19.

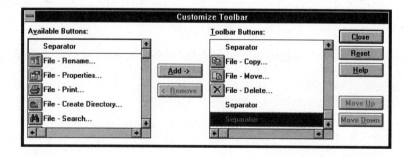

Fig. 5.19

Customize your toolbar in the Customize Toolbar dialog box.

2. Select the button you want to remove from the **T**oolbar Buttons list.

3. Choose the **R**emove button.

4. Repeat steps 2 and 3 for each button you want to remove.

5. Choose the **C**lose button.

Adding a Toolbar Button

To add a button to the toolbar, follow these steps:

1. Double-click anywhere on the background of the toolbar.

   or

   Choose the Options Customize Toolbar command.

   The dialog box shown in figure 5.19 appears. All available toolbar buttons are listed in the Available Buttons list on the left side of the dialog box. All buttons currently displayed on the toolbar are listed in the Toolbar Buttons list on the right.

2. Select the button you want to add from the Available Buttons list. Use the scroll bar to find the button you want, if necessary.

3. Choose the Add button. The button is added to the Toolbar Buttons list on the right side of the dialog box.

   The button is inserted immediately above the button that was selected in the Toolbar Buttons list when the Add button was chosen. Use the Move Up and Move Down buttons to locate the button wherever you want on the toolbar.

4. Repeat steps 2 and 3 to add buttons you desire.

5. Choose the Close button.

   If you run out of room to add more buttons, you must remove buttons for commands that you use less often.

Rearranging Toolbar Buttons

To quickly move a toolbar button to a new location when you are using a mouse, put the tip of the mouse pointer on the button on the toolbar, hold down the Shift key, and drag the button to its new location on the toolbar, then release the mouse button.

You can arrange the buttons on the toolbar in any order you want. To move a toolbar button using the Customize Toolbar dialog box, follow these steps:

1. Choose the Options Customize Toolbar command or double-click in the background of the toolbar to display the Customize Toolbar dialog box shown in figure 5.19.

2. Select the button from the Toolbar Buttons list that you want to move.

3. Choose the Move **U**p button to move the button up the list. This action will move the button to the left on the toolbar.

   or

   Choose the Move **D**own button to move the button down the list. This action will move the button to the right on the toolbar.

4. Repeat steps 2 and 3 for each button you want to move.

5. Choose the Close button.

Restoring the Default Toolbar

You can restore the default toolbar by following these steps:

1. Double-click anywhere on the background of the toolbar.

   or

   Choose the **O**ptions Tool**b**ar command.

   This displays the Customize Toolbar dialog box.

2. Choose the **R**eset button.

3. Choose the Close button.

Managing Files and Disks

Working with a hard disk, which can store thousands of files, can be confusing. Problems arise if you do not erase unnecessary files or do not make backup copies of files in case the hard disk fails.

In this section, you see how easy it is to erase unwanted files, copy files to other disks, or move files between directories. You also learn how to create directories so that you can organize a disk to fit your work and data.

Copying Files or Directories

Copying files is an important part of keeping work organized and secure. When organizing files, you may want to copy a file to make it accessible in two different locations. A more important reason for copying files is security.

The hard disk on which you store files is a mechanical device and has one of the highest failure rates among computer components. Should the hard disk fail, the cost of replacing the disk is insignificant compared to the cost of the hours you worked accumulating data on the disk. One way to prevent the loss of this data is to make a set of duplicate files on backup diskettes.

If you have copied files with DOS commands, you will find copying files and directories much more fun with Windows NT and a mouse. All you do is drag the files you want to copy from one location in the File Manager to another.

T I P Before you copy multiple files or a directory full of files, make sure that you have enough storage space on the destination disk. To do this, select the destination disk-drive icon, activate the directory tree area, and check the amount of available storage displayed in the status bar at the bottom of the screen. Then activate the directory window that contains the files you want to copy and select the files. (If you are copying an entire directory, you must select all the files in the directory.) Check the status bar again to see how much storage these files occupy. Compare the amount of space occupied by the files you want to copy with the amount of space left on the destination disk to make sure that the destination disk can receive all the files.

Follow these steps to copy files with a mouse:

1. Make sure that both the source and destination are visible.

   The *source* is the item you want to copy. It can be a file in the contents list or a directory from the contents list or the directory tree.

   The *destination* can be a directory icon in the directory tree or the contents list. It also can be a directory icon at the bottom of the File Manager window or a disk drive icon at the top of the File Manager window.

2. Activate the part of the File Manager screen that contains the source file or directory. If you are copying an entire directory, you can activate the directory tree or the contents list.

3. Select the file(s) or directory to be copied.

   If you want to copy more than one file, select multiple files. You can select only one directory at a time from the directory tree area, but you can select multiple directories in the contents list. When you copy a directory, you copy all the files and subdirectories in the directory.

4. To copy the files, drag the directory or the individual files to the destination (see fig. 5.20). Press and hold down the Ctrl key if the destination is on the same disk as the source files. Do not hold down the Ctrl key if the destination is on a different disk than the source files.

You cannot drag a window to copy it, but you can use keyboard techniques to copy an entire window.

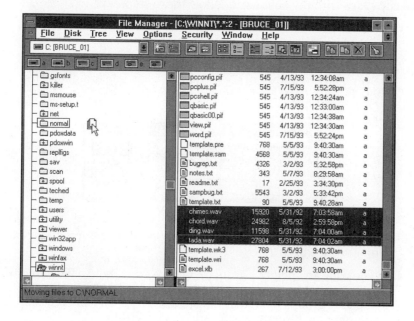

Fig. 5.20

Dragging files to a disk or directory to make copies.

5. When the file icon is over the destination, release the mouse button; release the Ctrl key if you were using the Ctrl key.

If the destination has a file with the same name as the file you are copying, you are asked to confirm that the destination file can be replaced by the copy.

Copying Many Files into Multiple Directories

A directory icon can serve as the destination for a file or files that you copy. If you want to copy files into several different directories quickly, this technique is useful. For each directory into which you want to copy the file or files, open a window by selecting the directory in the directory tree and then choosing the Window New Window command. Minimize each new window to an icon at the bottom of the File Manager screen by clicking the

continues

continued

> minimize button at the top right of the window. (Make sure that your original directory window is smaller than the File Manager window so that you can see the icons.) Then drag the files you want to copy onto the directory icons.

To copy files with the keyboard, follow these steps:

1. Activate the window that contains the files or directories you want to copy.

2. Select the files or directories you want to copy. If you want to select a large number of files, you can use wild card characters in step 4.

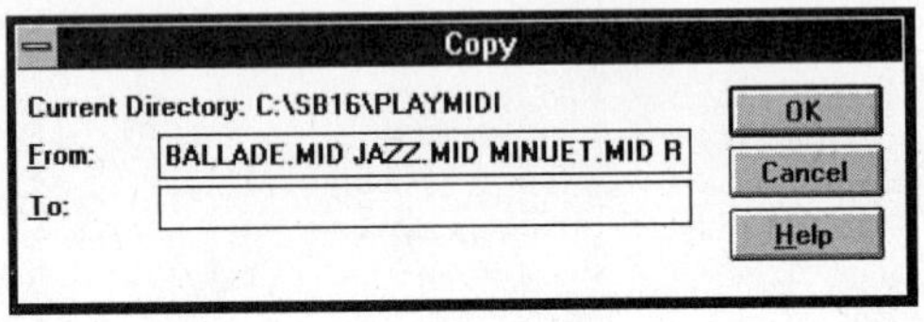

Fig. 5.21

The Copy dialog box showing the files being copied.

Copy
Current Directory: C:\SB16\PLAYMIDI
From: BALLADE.MID JAZZ.MID MINUET.MID R
To:
OK   Cancel   Help

3. Choose the **File Copy** command or press F8. The Copy dialog box appears (see fig. 5.21).

4. If you want to specify a group of files to copy, type a file-name pattern in the **From** text box. Use the wild card characters * and ? to specify groups of similar file names. To specify an entire directory, type the directory path, such as *C:\BUDGET*.

5. Type the path name of the destination location in the **To** text box.

6. Choose OK or press Enter.

If the destination has a file with the same name as the file you are copying, you are asked to confirm that the destination file can be replaced by the copy.

Use the wild card characters * and ? in the **From** text box of the Copy dialog box to copy multiple files with similar names. Remember that the * wild card matches any group of letters; the ? wild card matches any single letter in the same location. Following are some examples:

File Name Pattern	Files Matched
PROJ*.XLS	PROJ05.XLS
PROJECT?.XLS	PROJECTA.XLS
SM?TH.DOC	SMITH.DOC

File Name Pattern	Files Matched
	SMYTH.DOC but not SMITHS.DOC
*.XL?	anyname.XLS anyname.XLC anyname.XLW
.	all file names

Moving Files or Directories

You can move files just as easily as you can copy them. Moving files puts them in a new location and removes the originals from the old location. You move files when you need to reorganize a disk. You can move files or directories to a new directory or disk. Moving a directory moves both the directory's files and subdirectories.

Selecting All Files in a Directory

If you want to move all the files in a directory, you can select all the files in the current window by choosing the File Move command and typing *.* in the From text box. Or, you can do the following:

1. Choose the File Select Files command.

2. Type *.* in the File(s) text box.

3. Choose Select or press Enter.

To move files or directories with the mouse, follow these steps:

1. Activate the source and destination directory windows.

2. Select the files or directories you want to move.

3. To move, drag the file or directory to the destination if the destination is on the same disk. If the destination is on a different disk, press and hold down the Alt key as you drag to move a file, files, directory, or directories.

4. Release the mouse button when the icon or file is over the destination.

5. If you are asked to confirm the move, consider whether you are copying or moving and how the files will change. Then choose **Yes** to complete the action, **No** to stop a single move, or Cancel to cancel all moves.

Using the Mouse to Move or Copy Files

The following chart summarizes the mouse actions you use to move or copy files with the mouse:

Desired Action	Mouse Action
Copy to a different disk	Drag or Ctrl+drag
Copy to the same disk	Ctrl+drag
Move to a different disk	Alt+drag
Move to the same disk	Drag or Alt+drag

To move files or directories with the keyboard, follow these steps:

1. Activate the source and destination directory windows.

2. Select the files or directories you want to move.

3. Choose the **File** **Move** command or press F7.

4. If you did not select files in step 2, type in the **From** text box the names of the files to be moved. Use wild cards if you want to move multiple files with similar names.

5. In the **To** text box, type the destination path name, drive, and directory.

6. Choose OK or press Enter.

Creating Directories

Creating directories on a disk is like adding new drawers to a filing cabinet. Creating directories is an excellent way to reorganize or restructure the disk for new categories. After you build directories and subdirectories, you can put existing files in them using the **File** **Move** and **File** **Copy** commands.

To make new directories, follow these steps:

1. Activate the directory tree area. (This step is unnecessary if you want to put the new subdirectory under the currently selected directory.)

2. Select the directory under which you want a new subdirectory.

3. Choose the File Create Directory command. The Create Directory dialog box appears (see fig. 5.22).

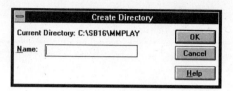

Fig. 5.22

The Create
Directory
dialog box.

4. Type the name of the new directory. Directory names are the same as file names and can have eight letters in the file name and three letters in the extension.

5. Choose OK or press Enter.

Adding new subdirectories is like growing new branches on a tree. New subdirectories must sprout from existing directories or subdirectories. If you want to create multiple layers of subdirectories, first create the directories or subdirectories that precede the ones you want to add.

Create a Directory without Selecting a Directory

You can create a directory at any location without selecting the parent directory by typing the full path name in the Name text box of the Create Directory dialog box.

Renaming Files or Directories

Unless you do everything perfectly the first time, there will come a time when you want to rename a file or directory. To rename a file or directory, select the file or directory from a directory window and choose the File Rename command. When the Rename dialog box appears, type the new file name and choose OK or press Enter.

You can rename a group of files with a similar name or the same extension. To rename a group of files, select the files you want to rename and choose the File Rename command. Use the wild cards * and ? in the From and To text boxes to indicate the parts of the names you want to change. Choose OK or press Enter to rename the files. Renaming with wild cards can save you a great deal of typing, as shown by the following example:

Original File Names	From	To	Resultant File Names
ACNTAR.XLS	ACNT*.*	ACCT*.*	ACCTAR.XLS
ACNTAP.XLS	ACNT*.*	ACCT*.*	ACCTAP.XLS
ACNTTRND.XLC	ACNT*.*	ACCT*.*	ACCTTRND.XLC

Deleting Files or Directories

Delete files or directories when you want to remove old work from the disk. Deleting files gives you more available storage on a disk. Deleting directories that don't contain any files makes very little difference in storage space.

Unless you have prepared the hard disk with special software, you cannot recover files or directories after you delete them. Be very careful to select only the files or directories you want to delete. If you aren't sure about deleting files or directories, turn on the warning messages by choosing the Options Confirmation command and selecting the warning messages you want.

T I P

Be careful that you do not accidentally select a directory when you select files to be deleted. If you select a directory and choose File Delete, all the files in the directory as well as the directory itself are deleted. Deleting entire directories can be convenient, but it also can be a real surprise if it is not what you wanted to do.

If you want to confirm each file or subdirectory being deleted, choose the Options Confirmation command and make sure that the File Delete and Directory Delete boxes are selected.

To delete files or subdirectories, follow these steps:

1. Activate the directory window that contains the files you want to delete. Activate the directory tree area if you want to delete only directories.

2. Select the files or directories you want to delete; alternatively, use wild cards in step 4.

3. Choose the File Delete command or press the Del key. The Delete dialog box appears.

4. If you did not select the files you want to delete, type their names in the Delete text box. Use DOS wild cards to select multiple files. For example, type *.* in the Delete text box to specify every file in the current directory.

5. Choose the OK button. If the Confirm File Delete dialog box appears, asking you to confirm deletions, choose **Yes** when appropriate or choose Yes to **All** to confirm deletion of several files.

   Use the **O**ptions **C**onfirmation command to specify the types of deletions that require a confirmation. Only by selecting options in the Confirmation dialog box will you see a Confirm File Delete dialog box in step 5.

Copying Disks

Make duplicate copies of diskettes whenever you need another diskette for secure storage off-site or when you need a duplicate of original program disks. To copy an entire disk to another disk, the disks must be the same size and capacity. If the original is a 3 1/2-inch high-density diskette, the destination diskette must be the same. To duplicate a disk, follow these steps:

1. Protect the original disk by attaching a write-protect tab on 5 1/4-inch diskettes or sliding the protect notch open on 3 1/2-inch diskettes.

2. Insert the original diskette in the source disk drive.

3. Insert the diskette to receive the copy (the destination disk) in the second disk drive. If you don't have a second disk drive, don't be concerned; you can switch diskettes in a single drive.

4. Choose the **D**isk **C**opy Disk command. The Copy Disk dialog box appears. If you have only one disk drive, skip to step 7.

5. In the **S**ource In list, select the drive letter for the source drive.

6. In the **D**estination In list, select the drive letter for the destination drive (even if it is the same as the source drive).

7. Choose OK.

8. If you have only a single disk drive, you are instructed to switch the source disk and destination disk in and out of the single drive. Windows NT prompts you to exchange disks.

The **Disk Copy Disk** command formats the destination disk if it is not already formatted. If the destination disk contains data, the data is lost.

Formatting Diskettes

You usually cannot use new diskettes until you format them (some diskettes come already formatted). Formatting prepares diskettes for use on a computer. Formatting is similar to preparing a blank book for use by writing in page numbers and creating a blank table of contents. If a diskette contains data, formatting completely erases all existing data. Part of the process of formatting is checking for bad areas on the diskette's magnetic surface. All bad areas found are identified so that data is not recorded in these areas.

To format a diskette, follow these steps:

1. Put the diskette to be formatted in the disk drive.

2. Choose the **Disk Format** Disk command. The Format Disk dialog box appears.

3. Select the disk drive that contains the diskette to be formatted in the **Disk** In drop-down list box.

4. Select the appropriate diskette size in the **C**apacity drop-down list box.

5. If you want to assign a label to the diskette, type the label in the **L**abel text box.

6. Select **Q**uick Format to save time if the disk has been formatted and you're reasonably sure that the diskette does not have bad areas.

7. Choose OK. A message box warns you that formatting will erase all data on the disk. If you're sure, choose **Y**es.

8. After this diskette is formatted, you are given the chance to format additional disks.

Format an entire box of diskettes at one time and put a paper label on each disk when it is formatted. This system lets you know that open boxes contain formatted diskettes; paper labels confirm that the diskettes are formatted.

Labeling Disks

Although you may be accustomed to putting a paper label on diskettes, both hard disks and diskettes can have magnetically recorded labels, known as *volume labels*. Volume labels appear at the top of the directory tree area when the drive with the volume label is active. Not all disks have or need this kind of label.

You just learned how to create a volume label when you format a diskette. If you want to create or change a volume label on a previously formatted disk, select the drive icon and choose the **D**isk **L**abel Disk command. When the Label Disk dialog box appears, type a label name of up to 11 characters and choose OK or press Enter.

Printing Files

You can send text files directly to the printer from the File Manager. For example, many software applications come with last-minute corrections and additional information stored in a text file. The information usually is not in the printed manual. These text files, which usually have the extension TXT, contain information such as helpful tips, corrections to the manual, and hardware configuration settings not covered in the manual. It often is helpful to print these files.

When you print with the File Manager, you send the file to the default printer. To change the default printer, use the Control Panel as described in Chapter 7, "Customizing with the Control Panel."

To print a file with the File Manager, the file must be associated with an application. To print a file using the File Manager, follow these steps:

1. Activate the directory window that contains the file or files you want to print.

2. Select the file or files you want to print.

3. Choose the **F**ile **P**rint command.

4. Choose OK or press Enter.

You also can use File Manager's drag and drop feature to print; see the section, "Using the File Manager's Drag and Drop Feature," later in this chapter.

Starting Applications and Documents

Using the Program Manager and group windows is the best way to start frequently used applications. As described in Chapter 4, "Controlling Applications with the Program Manager," you can use the Program Manager to group together a frequently used application and an associated document to make them readily accessible.

On some occasions, however, the application you want to start may not be in a group window. When this happens, start the application directly from the File Manager. You can start any application from the File Manager.

Starting an Application

Starting an application from the File Manager is easy with the mouse: just open the directory window that contains the application and double-click on the name of the application.

Starting an application with the keyboard is almost as easy: open the directory window that contains the application, select the application name, and press Enter. Alternatively, choose the **File Open** or **File Run** command.

Application file names end with EXE or COM. You may have to start some DOS applications by double-clicking on a file with the extension BAT or PIF, as described in Chapter 22, "Running DOS Applications."

You can specify some document or data files so that they start an application. Choosing this associated document or data file starts the application and loads the document or data as well.

If an application is associated with a specific file extension, you can start an application by using the same starting procedures on a document file. Pretend the document file is the application you want to start. Windows NT starts the associated application and then loads the selected document file.

If you want to start an application with a document or with special arguments that modify how the application runs, choose the **File Run** command. In the **C**ommand Line text box, type the directory path and full application name. Press the space bar and type the name of the document you want the application to load. Choose OK or press Enter.

If you want the application to minimize to an icon as soon as it starts, select the Run **M**inimized check box from the Run dialog box before choosing OK.

See the section "Using the File Manager's Drag and Drop Feature" to learn how you can start an application by dragging a document icon onto an application icon.

Associating Documents with an Application

One of the convenient features of Windows NT is its capacity to start an application when you choose an associated document. An associated document is one that runs with a particular application. When you choose an associated document, Windows NT finds the application that runs the document, starts the application, and then loads the document. Many Windows NT applications create associations for their own files by modifying the Windows NT Registry when the application is installed. You also can add associations to fit your applications and work habits.

Spreadsheet files with the extension XLS, for example, are associated with Microsoft Excel. This association is made automatically because installing Excel modifies Registry. You may be in an office with people who use Lotus 1-2-3. Because Excel can open and save Lotus 1-2-3 files, you can associate Lotus 1-2-3 files with the Excel application. Once you associate a Lotus 1-2-3 file with Excel, you can choose this 1-2-3 file to make Excel start and load the 1-2-3 worksheet and charts.

To associate a document file with a specific application, follow these steps:

1. Activate the directory window that contains the data file (document file) you want to associate with an application.

2. Select the name of the file you want associated. Windows NT associates document files to applications by checking the file extension of the document file.

3. Choose the **F**ile **A**ssociate command. This brings up the Associate dialog box (see fig. 5.23). The extension for the document you selected is listed in the **F**iles with Extension text box.

4. Scroll through the list box attached to the **A**ssociate With text box. Find the name of the application you want to associate with all files using the extension shown in the **F**iles with Extension text box. Select the application name if you find it.

If necessary, type the full path and file name of the application. If you're unsure of the correct directory path, you can search for it by choosing the **B**rowse button.

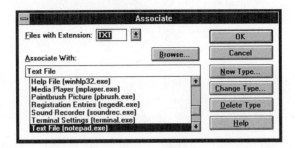

Fig. 5.23

The Associate
dialog box.

5. Choose OK or press Enter.

Some DOS applications, such as WordPerfect, can use any file extension for data documents. In this case, you must associate each of the different file extensions you use with WordPerfect to the WordPerfect application.

Some DOS applications may not start directly from an associated file. Other applications may start but not run with optimal configuration. If either is true for the document files you are using, refer to Chapter 21, "Customizing PIFs," for information on creating a PIF.

Using the File Manager's Drag and Drop Feature

The File Manager's drag and drop feature enables you to print files, link or embed files, create program item icons, and start applications by dragging File Manager icons or file names with a mouse. You also drag and drop icons to copy and move files, as described in other sections in this chapter.

To use the drag and drop feature, you need to be able to see two things on your screen: the File Manager, or source, displaying the file you want to drag; and the destination, displaying the icon or document where you want to drag the file. Before you drag and drop File Manager icons, arrange windows on your screen so that you can see both. In some cases, such as when you are starting an application, the File Manager is both source and destination, so you must open two File Manager windows.

To learn how to use the drag and drop feature for copying and moving, see the sections in this chapter on "Copying Files or Directories" and "Moving Files or Directories."

Using Drag and Drop to Print

To print a file using the drag and drop feature, you must be able to see the file you want to print in the File Manager, and you must be able to see the Print Manager program icon or window on your desktop. If the Print Manager is not running, start it from the Program Manager.

You also must be sure that the document you want to print is associated with its application. To learn how to do that, refer to the section in this chapter on "Associating Documents with an Application."

To use the drag and drop feature to print, follow these steps:

1. Start the File Manager, if necessary, and locate the file you want to print.

2. Start the Print Manager, if necessary.

3. In the File Manager, position the mouse pointer over the file you want to print. Click and hold down the left mouse button and drag the file onto the Print Manager window or icon.

   As you drag, you see a changing icon. When the icon appears as a page with a plus sign (+) inside it, and you are sure that you are on top of the Printer Manager window or icon, release the mouse button.

If a message box appears telling you that no association exists for the file or that the association data is incomplete, then you must complete the association or use the application to print your file.

Using Drag and Drop to Link or Embed

One of the easiest ways to link or embed a file into a document is to drag the file name from the File Manager onto the open document. Embedding a file in this way creates a package, which appears in the document as an icon. You can edit the package, or you can double-click on the icon to start the application containing the embedded file. To learn more about linking and embedding, refer to Chapter 6.

To use the drag and drop feature to link or embed a file, follow these steps:

1. Start the File Manager, if necessary, and locate the file you want to link or embed.

2. Start the application containing the document into which you want to link or embed a file, if you haven't already, and open the document. Display the location in the document where you want to insert the linked or embedded file.

3. In the File Manager, position the mouse pointer over the file you want to link or embed. Click and hold down the left mouse button and drag the file onto the document where you want the file to be linked or embedded.

   As you drag, you see a changing icon. When the icon appears as a page with a plus (+) sign inside it, and you are sure that you are on top of the document icon into which you want to link or embed the file, release the mouse button.

Using Drag and Drop to Create a Program Item Icon

You can quickly create a program item icon in the Program Manager by dragging a program file from the File Manager onto the Program Manager. Follow these steps:

1. Start the File Manager and locate the application for which you want to create a program item icon.

2. Activate the Program Manager and display the group window in which you want to add your new program item icon.

3. Arrange the File Manager and Program Manager windows so that you can see both the application for which you want to create the program item icon and the group window in which you want to create it.

4. Drag the application file name from the File Manager onto the Program Manager. Release the mouse button when the application name is over the group window where you want to create the program item icon.

Using Drag and Drop to Start an Application

You can quickly start an application by dragging a document file icon onto an application icon. The application starts, and the document opens. Follow these steps:

1. Start the File Manager and open two windows: one displaying the directory containing the document file you want to open and one displaying the directory containing the application you want to start. Choose the **W**indow **N**ew Window command to open a new window or double-click on a disk-drive icon.

2. Tile the two windows by choosing the **W**indow **T**ile command.

3. Scroll each window so that you can see both the document and the application file names.

4. Drag the document file name onto the application file name. Release the mouse button when the document file name is over the application file name.

Working with Networks in Windows NT

When you are using Windows NT on a network, you can share directories with other users in your workgroup. You can open the files in any directory that has been designated as *shared* by another user, and you can *share* any of your directories so that the files in that directory can be shared by other users. The File Manager is where you connect to directories that others have shared and where you share directories on your computer that you want others to have access to.

Connecting to Shared Directories

You can connect to any directory that has been designated as shared by any user on your network (to learn how to share a directory, see the next section, "Sharing a Directory"). You connect to a directory using the File Manager. When you connect to a directory, File Manager creates a *network drive* for that directory and assigns a letter to that drive. You can view the files in that directory by selecting the drive icon assigned to that directory, or by selecting the drive from the drive list in the toolbar. You open files in the directory in exactly the same way you open a file on your own hard disk. Whether or not you can modify the file depends on the level of access the owner of the directory has granted to other users.

Connecting to a Network Directory

To connect to a shared directory, follow these steps:

1. Click the Connect Network Drive button on the toolbar.

   or

   Choose the **Disk Connect Network** Drive command.

   The Connect Network Drive dialog box shown in figure 5.24 appears.

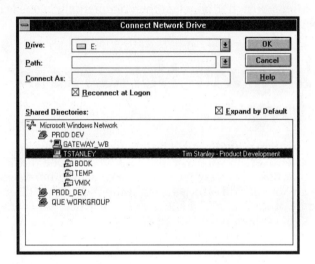

Fig. 5.24

Select the directory you want to connect to in the Connect Network Drive dialog box.

2. By default, File Manager assigns the next available drive letter on your computer to the directory you select to connect to. To assign a different letter, open the **D**rive list and select a letter from the list.

3. Enter the path for the shared directory in the **P**ath box.

   The path includes the computer name where the directory is located, and the share name assigned to that directory. The computer name is preceded by double backslashes and is separated from the share name by a single backslash. For example, \\SALESMAN\SALES.

   There are three methods for entering the path:

   If you know the path for the directory, you can type it directly in the **P**ath text box.

   or

You open the **P**ath drop-down list and select a path from a list of recently used paths.

or

Double-click on a workgroup icon in the list **S**how Shared Directories (or select the icon with the arrow keys and press Enter) to expand the workgroup. Select a name from the list of computer names listed under the workgroup to display a list of shared directories in the Shared Directories box. When you find the directory to which you want to connect, select it.

4. If you want to automatically reconnect to this shared directory at startup, select the Reconnect at Logon checkbox.

5. Choose OK or press Enter.

When you connect to a shared directory, a new window for that directory will appear if the **O**pen New Window on Connect option in the **O**ptions menu is selected. To select this option, choose the **O**ptions **O**pen New Window on Connect command. A check mark appears next to the command when it is turned on. If you do not want a new window to open each time you connect to a shared directory, turn this option off.

Disconnecting from a Network Drive

To disconnect from a network drive, follow these steps:

1. Click the Disconnect Network Drive button on the toolbar.

or

Choose the **D**isk **D**isconnect Network Drive command.

The Disconnect Network Drive dialog box shown in figure 5.25 appears.

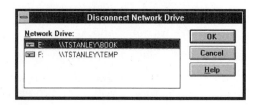

Fig. 5.25

Use the Disconnect Network Drive dialog box to disconnect from a shared directory.

2. Select from the **D**rive list the drive you want to disconnect.

You can select additional directories from the list if you want to disconnect from more than one directory at once. To select more than one directory, click on the first directory, hold down the Ctrl key, and click on subsequent directories. To deselect a directory, hold down the Ctrl key and click on the directory. To use the keyboard, select the first directory, press Shift+F8, use the up- and down-arrow keys to move to the next directory, and press the space bar. Move to additional directories and press the space bar. To deselect a directory and retain the other selections, move to the selected directory and press the space bar. To return to selecting a single directory at a time, press Shift+F8 again.

3. Choose OK or press Enter.

Sharing and Unsharing a Directory

You can designate any directory on your computer as shared. When you share a directory, you can assign a *share name* and *password* to that directory. You can also specify what type of access users have to the shared directory. Once you have shared a directory, other users have access to the files in that directory. The computers that have the directories you want to share must be on, and logged on to the network.

Just as you can share a directory, you can *unshare* or stop sharing the directory. When you stop sharing a directory, you return the directory to its original state; only you can access information in the directory.

Sharing a Directory

To share a directory, follow these steps:

1. Using either the mouse or the keyboard, select the directory you want to share.

2. Click the Share As button on the toolbar.

   or

   Choose the **D**isk Share **A**s command.

   The New Share dialog box shown in figure 5.26 appears.

3. The name of the directory you selected in step 1 is the default name of the shared directory. If you want, type a new name in the **S**hare Name box.

4. The path of the directory you selected in step 1 appears in the **P**ath box. If you selected the wrong directory in step 1, type in the path for the correct directory.

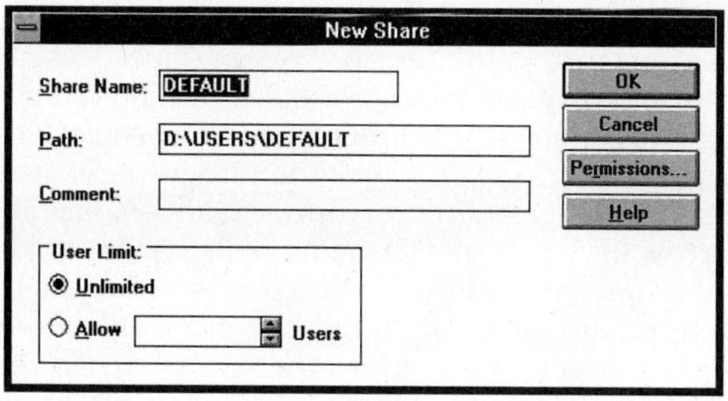

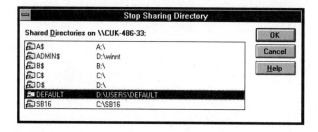

Fig. 5.26

The New Share dialog box is used to share a directory on your computer.

5. Type a comment in the **C**omment box if you want. This comment appears next to the share name in the Connect Network Drive dialog box and can be helpful for other users when those users are looking for a particular shared directory to connect to.

6. If you wish to limit the number of users who may share the directory, click the Allow radio button and set the number of users.

7. Choose OK or press Enter.

Unsharing a Directory

To stop sharing a directory, follow these steps:

1. Click the Stop Sharing button on the toolbar.

   or

   Choose the **D**isk **S**top Sharing command.

   The Stop Sharing dialog box appears (see fig. 5.27).

Fig. 5.27

Select the directories you want to stop sharing in the Stop Sharing dialog box.

2. Select the name of the directory you want to stop sharing in the Shared **D**irectories list.

You can select additional directories from the list if you want to stop sharing more than one directory at once. To select more than one directory, click the first directory, hold down the Ctrl key, and click subsequent directories. To deselect a directory, hold down the Ctrl key and click the directory. To use the keyboard, select the first directory, press Shift+F8, use the up- and down-arrow keys to move to the next directory, and press the space bar. Move to additional directories and press the space bar. To deselect a directory and retain the other selections, move to the selected directory and press the space bar. To return to selecting a single directory at a time, press Shift+F8 again.

3. Choose OK or press Enter.

Changing the Share Name or Comment for a Shared Directory

You can use the **Disk Share As** command to change the share name or comment for a shared directory. To change any of these properties, follow these steps:

1. Using the mouse or keyboard, select the directory you want to modify.

2. Click the Share As button on the toolbar.

   or

   Choose the **Disk Share As** command.

   The Shared Directory dialog box shown in figure 5.28 appears.

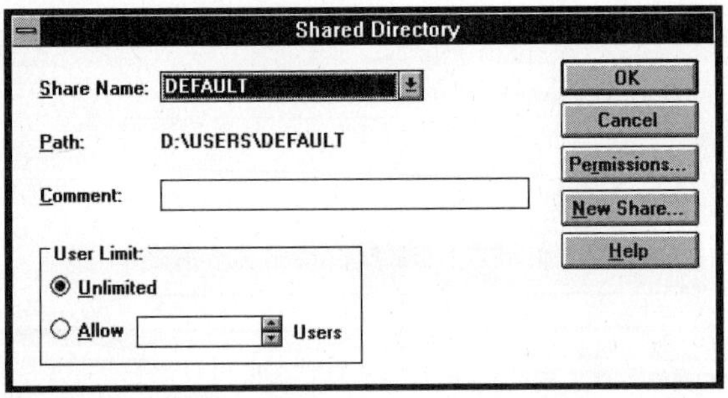

Fig. 5.28

The Shared Directory dialog box looks just like the New Share dialog box discussed earlier.

Shared Directory
Share Name: DEFAULT
Path: D:\USERS\DEFAULT
Comment:
User Limit:
● Unlimited
○ Allow _____ Users

OK
Cancel
Permissions...
New Share...
Help

3. Change the entries in the **S**hare Name or **C**omment boxes, as desired.

4. Choose OK or press Enter.

Viewing Workgroup Directories

You can find out which directories are being shared in the workgroups on your network. To view the directories in the workgroups on your network, follow these steps:

1. Click the Connect Network Drive button on the toolbar.

   or

   Choose the **D**isk Connect Network Drive command.

   The Connect Network Drive dialog box shown earlier in figure 5.24 appears.

2. Double-click the workgroup whose directories you want to view in the **S**how Shared Directories On list, or use the arrow keys to select the workgroup and press Enter.

3. Select the computer whose directories you want to view from the list of computer names under the workgroup name.

   A list of shared directories appears in the **S**hared Directories box.

4. In the **S**hared Directories box, select the shared directory to which you want to connect.

5. Choose OK or press Enter.

   As an alternative to selecting a directory and choosing OK, simply double-click on the directory to which you want to connect in the **S**hared Directories list.

Your computer will probably have a specified limit to the number of local or network drives to which it can be connected. If you attempt to connect to a network drive and your computer has already used all the drives it has available, then you will get a warning message. This message says that the drive letter you specified in the **D**rive pull-down list is invalid.

The number of drives your computer can be connected to is specified in the CONFIG.NT file, which is probably located in your C:\WINNT\SYSTEM32 directory. Using the Windows NT Notepad, you can open the CONFIG.NT file and change the LASTDRIVE command to allow additional network drives. The LASTDRIVE command will appear in the form,

```
LASTDRIVE=F
```

In this case drive F is the last allowable drive. Change the last letter and save the CONFIG.SYS file back to its original directory. You must exit Windows NT and restart your computer before you will be able to take advantage of the extra drives you can now connect.

Viewing the Users of a Shared Directory

If you are sharing directories with other users, you may want to know which of those directories are being used by others at any time, or you may want to know which users are using specific files. For example, if someone else is using a file of yours in a directory you are sharing, you may want to find out who is using the file. You may want to know who is using one of your shared files so you can warn them if you need to turn off your computer. Some files also restrict the access or capabilities of other users while they are being shared. In that case you may want to ask the user to stop using the file so another user can have full access.

To view the names of users of a directory or file, follow these steps:

1. Using the mouse or keyboard, select the directory or file you want to check.

2. Choose the **F**ile Properties command or press Alt+Enter.

3. Choose the **O**pen By button to display the Network Properties dialog box (see fig. 5.29). The **O**pen By button only appears in the Properties for dialog box when you have selected a shared directory or file in step 1.

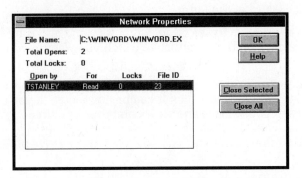

The Network Properties dialog box displays a list of shared files that are in use by others.

4. Choose OK twice or press Enter twice to return to the directory window.

Closing a File in a Shared Directory

If someone is using one of your files in a directory you have shared, you cannot open that file. If you want to be able to access your file, you can close the file. Be aware that the person using the file at the time you close it may lose data. Use the procedure described in the previous section to learn who is using the file and then ask the person to close the file.

If you must forcefully close a shared file regardless of the other user, follow these steps:

1. Select the directory in which the file is located or select the file itself.

2. Choose the File Properties command (or press Alt+Enter).

3. Choose the Open By button.

4. Select the file you want to close from the Open By list.

5. Choose the Close Selected button.

6. Choose OK twice or press Enter twice to return to the directory window.

 **NOTE** Besides enabling you to share files and directories from one computer to the next, you can attach to network servers using Windows NT and the File Manager. The way that you attach to a server depends on the type of server you are attaching to. For more information about networking with Windows NT, see Part VI of this book, "Networking with Windows NT."

File Security

If you are running Windows NT and currently have an NTFS partition selected, you will find that the commands in the Security menu are available to you. These commands are not available when any other file system is selected because those systems don't support file security. The choices in the Security menu enable you to administer permissions, auditing, and ownership of the files and directories on a volume.

Changing File Permissions

To change the permissions on a file or directory, first select that file or directory in the File Manager's window. When you select the Permissions command from the Security menu, you see the Directory Permissions dialog box, which contains a list of permissions that apply to the currently selected file

Each entry in the list shows a name and the access permissions that the name has over the directories. The Type of Access combo box at the bottom of the screen enables you to quickly change the permissions for the selected user or group. The following permissions are available:

Term	Method
No Access	Completely restricts access—the user or group cannot even detect the existence of the file.
List	The named user or group can see the file.
Read	The named account or group can read from the file.
Write	The named account or group can write to the file.
Delete	The named account or group can delete the file or directory.
Execute	The named account can read the file, but only for use as an executable image.
Change Permissions	The named account or group is allowed to change permissions on the named files or directories.
Take Ownership	The named account can assume ownership of the file or directory.
Change	This shortcut combines the Execute, Read, Write, and Delete choices.
Add	This shortcut combines Write and Execute privileges for files only.
Add and Read	This shortcut combines Read, Write, and Execute privileges for files, and Read and Execute privileges for directories.
Full Control	This shortcut gives complete control of the directories and files to the named account.

If you make a change to permissions while the Replace Permissions on Subdirectories option is checked, you change the permissions on the files and subdirectories below the subdirectory you have selected. This is useful when you want to exclude a user or group from an entire directory structure in one step.

If you need to change the access for someone else, pressing the Add button reveals a second dialog box: the Add Users and Groups dialog box.

This dialog box enables you to change the access for several groups or users at a time. You can select a user, click the **A**dd button, then select another user or group and click **A**dd again. Each time you click the **A**dd button, the selected name is added to the list in the lower half of the dialog box. Selecting a type of access changes that access for the users when you click the OK button. The users you've added will be displayed in the first Directory Permissions dialog box when you dismiss the Add Users and Groups dialog box.

If you have selected a user in the Add Users and Groups dialog box and that user already had access permissions set in the Directory Permissions dialog box, the new setting overrides the old.

Note that settings for an individual override the settings given to that individual for a group. For example, even though the user *Andy Warhol* might be a member of the group *Everyone*, specifically revoking Andy Warhol's rights to a directory overrides the access granted by the group *Everyone*.

Setting File Auditing

Windows NT provides for file auditing, which allows an administrator to track the usage of each file on the Windows NT system. You should use auditing judiciously because it causes a performance impact on file access. When you select the Auditing choice in the **S**ecurity menu, you see the Directory Auditing dialog box.

This dialog box shows the users who already have auditing enabled. The list box shows the name of the group or user who is audited, whereas the check boxes at the bottom of the dialog box show which events are audited. Note that each group or user might have different events selected to be audited. Auditing can be enabled for the success or failure of the following access attempts:

Term	Method
Read	Taking ownership of the file or directory
Write	Writing the file or directory
Execute	Executing the file or directory
Delete	Deleting the file or directory
Change Permissions	Changing permissions on the file or directory
Take Ownership	Taking ownership of the file or directory

If a user attempts to perform one of these operations and the appropriate auditing control is enabled, the system event log records an event describing the access.

You can change the audited events by clicking on the user name in the list and checking the appropriate boxes at the bottom of the dialog box. When you press OK to leave the dialog box, your changes are saved for each of the users you altered. If you need to set up auditing for a group or user who is not in the list, click on the Add button. This reveals the Add Users and Groups dialog box.

You can use this dialog box to add more users and groups to the list in the Directory Auditing or File Auditing dialog box. You can select any name and click the Add button to move it to the list at the bottom of the dialog box. You can add more than one user or group by selecting the name and clicking the Add button again. When you click the OK button, the list of names you've built is moved back into the Directory Auditing or File Auditing dialog box.

Changing File Ownership

When you select the Ownership option from the Security menu, you see the Owner dialog box, which shows the ownership of a given file or directory.

The Close button dismisses the box without changing the ownership of the file. The Take Ownership button instructs Windows NT to let the current user try to assume ownership of the selected directory or file. This does not work if the Take Ownership privilege is not set on the file for the current user.

Summary

You can go in three directions from here. One option is to finish the next few chapters in this section and learn how to customize Windows NT with the Control Panel, how to manage fonts, and how to use the Print Manager. In Chapter 7, you learn how to use the Control Panel to change screen colors, select a new desktop background, install new printers, and control the mouse speed. Chapter 8, "Managing Fonts," teaches you about TrueType and shows you how to install new fonts. Chapter 6, "Embedding and Linking," teaches you about creating compound documents. Chapter 9, "Using the Print Manager," teaches you how to control printing, in a stand-alone mode and on a network.

The second direction you may go is toward learning how to use Windows NT accessory applications in Part III and learning to use Windows NT applets in Part IV. Accessory applications include many day-to-day desktop tools, including a word processor, a painting application, and a communications application. Windows NT applets are mini-applications that you use from within the primary applications.

The third option is to go to Chapters 19 and 21 and learn how to use Windows NT to run applications you already have. In these chapters, you learn how to copy and paste text and numeric data among Windows NT and DOS applications and how to link text or graphics data among Windows NT applications.

Sharing files is one of the first things that most workgroups do.

Embedding and Linking Windows NT Applications

I f you are accustomed to working with one application, the value of linking or embedding data is not always immediately apparent. After you begin to link and embed data, however, you will see how much it can improve your communication. The following list describes examples of how linking and embedding can work with various applications:

- Linking a mailing list in a Windows NT database or worksheet to a mail-merge data document in a Windows NT word processor

- Creating sales projections, financial analysis, inventory reports, and investment analysis with Microsoft Excel or Lotus 1-2-3 for Windows NT and then linking or embedding them into Windows NT word processing documents

- Maintaining client reminder letters and callbacks by linking PackRat, a personal information manager, to Word for Windows through the WordBASIC macros that come with PackRat

- Embedding in Word for Windows or Ami Pro, drawings or schematics that can be updated from within the word processor using Microsoft Draw

- Linking Microsoft Excel to a Windows NT database or SQL Server to monitor and analyze inventory

- Creating a compound document composed of pieces of text, graphics, and other data from many users on a network; updating the shared data in the ClipBook updates the compound document

- Posting a changing graph or worksheet table in the ClipBook so that everyone on the Windows NT network can have the most current data

Figure 6.1 shows an example of a letter that has links to a Microsoft Excel worksheet and chart.

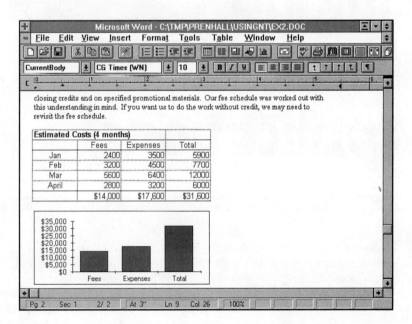

Fig. 6.1

A letter with links to a spreadsheet.

Throughout this chapter, the *server* is the file or data in an application that is supplying data. The *client* is the application receiving information. Some applications function as both server and client. Other applications may be one or the other, but not both. Microsoft Write and Cardfile, for example, are clients—they only receive information. Windows NT Paintbrush however, is a server—it only can supply information.

Copying, linking, or embedding data between Windows NT applications may use the same or similar commands, and the results may appear the same on-screen or in the document. Each fits a different situation, however, and has unique advantages and disadvantages. The following table describes the different ways to transfer data, and the advantages and disadvantages of each method.

Table 6.1 Transferring data

Copying   Use when you do not want to update data. Data must be replaced to be updated.

Advantages

- Data does not change when other parts of the document update.

- Less memory and storage are required to use or save the document.

Disadvantages

- Pictures may print at lower resolution if copied as a bitmap.

- Updating data requires redoing each copy and paste of data.

Linking   Use when you need to update one original in the server and have the changes cascade into multiple client documents.

Advantages

- Less memory is required than for an embedded object.

- Many client documents can be updated by changing one server document.

- Older Windows 3.X applications that cannot embed objects can still link data.

Disadvantages

- Links between the server and the client may be broken if the server file names or path names are changed or deleted.

- Automatically updated links may slow down Windows NT operation.

- Server data must be saved, and the name and path name must be maintained.

continues

Table 6.1 Continued

Embedding	Use when you have only a few client documents that may need updating and you want to include the server data (an *embedded object*) as part of the document.

Advantages

- Client document and server data are stored as a single file; you do not have to maintain links, path names, and server files.

- Server data is saved as part of the client document.

- You can stay within the client document and use the server application to update the embedded object.

Disadvantages

- Documents containing embedded objects are larger than other documents because they contain both client and server data.

- Updating an embedded graphic may result in a file with less printer resolution than the original.

- Each client document must be updated individually.

Two additional methods of transferring data within Windows NT applications are not described in this chapter. Applications such as Word for Windows and Microsoft Excel can open files created by the application, or they can use a command, such as Insert File in Word for Windows, to link to an on-disk file created by another application.

Microsoft Excel, Word for Windows, Lotus 1-2-3 for Windows, and Ami Pro can open files created by other applications. Files that are opened like this become part of the document and cannot be updated except by replacing them. To open another application's file, you must install file converters that come with the Windows application.

Applications that can link to a file on disk, such as Word for Windows, enable you to link their documents to Microsoft Excel, Lotus 1-2-3, WordPerfect, or dBASE files. When the file on disk changes, you can update the Word for Windows document to reflect the new data.

Different Windows NT applications sometimes use different commands to implement object linking and embedding. For example, to insert an embedded object in a Word for Windows document, you choose the Insert Object command; to do the same in Windows NT Write, you choose Edit Insert Object. Even when the applications use the same commands, the underlined letters in the commands (shown in bold in this book) may be different. To edit an embedded object in Word for Windows, the command is Edit Object; in Write, the command is Edit Object.

The following procedures describe the commands and active letters for some of the more frequently used applications. Not all applications that have object linking and embedding capability have all the features described in this chapter.

Viewing Data in the Clipboard

Windows NT transfers copied or linked data between applications using the Clipboard. The Clipboard is a temporary storage area for data being transferred or linked. The Clipboard takes its name from an artist's clipboard, where cut items are stored until they can be pasted down in new locations. (If you are using Windows NT, see the following section titled, "Viewing and Using Data in the ClipBook Viewer.")

If you need to see the information currently in the Clipboard, open the ClipBook Viewer application located in the Main program window. Inside the ClipBook Viewer window, you can see the contents or a description of the Clipboard's contents.

Use the File Save command and File Open command to save Clipboard contents as files that can be retrieved for later use. In the View menu, you can see the different ways in which the current contents can be pasted. When you copy a selection into the Clipboard, Windows NT queries the application to see which formats it supports. Windows NT lists all these formats in the View menu and selects the one that gives the best copy. Normally, the View Default Format command is selected. If you want to paste the Clipboard contents in a different format, you can choose a different format in the View menu or use the Edit Paste Special command of the client document.

Viewing and Using Data in the ClipBook Viewer

When you use Windows NT, you have a Clipboard available for transferring cut or copied information between applications on your computer. But you have an additional tool at your disposal, a ClipBook.

The ClipBook serves two purposes. First, the ClipBook acts as a personal scrapbook that stores multiple *clippings*. Each different clipping can be on a *page* in the ClipBook. In the ClipBook, you can see a table of contents, thumbnail views, or a full window view of each clipping. From the collection of clippings, you can choose the one you want to use. The second way to use the ClipBook is as a shared scrapbook. If you designate a page as shared, others in your NT workgroup can use the data on the page.

Your workgroup can use data, such as text, tables, and graphics, in shared ClipBook pages, which could reduce everyone's workload. For example, you can draw a company logo and copy that logo to a shared page in your ClipBook. Others in your workgroup can use that logo at any time by pasting or embedding the logo into their documents. You don't have to run around giving everyone a copy.

The ClipBook also enables workgroup members to link to a shared page in a ClipBook. For example, you may have created a timetable and chart using Microsoft Excel. Three different people need your timetable and chart for reports that they must update each week. The workload for your workgroup can be significantly reduced if you copy the timetable and chart into shared pages of your ClipBook. The three people in your workgroup can then paste linked copies of the timetable and chart from your ClipBook into their reports. Each week when you update your Excel timetable and chart, their reports automatically update.

Displaying the ClipBook

Windows NT displays the Clipboard and ClipBook in the same ClipBook application. The ClipBook application is located in the Main program group window of the Program Manager.

The Clipboard is where data is *temporarily* stored when it is being transferred within or between applications. This is where data is stored when you do an **E**dit Cu**t** or **E**dit **C**opy. You can view the information currently stored in your Clipboard in the Clipboard window of the ClipBook Viewer application, shown in figure 6.2.

The contents of the Clipboard remain there until you cut or copy new data into the Clipboard or until you clear the contents with the **E**dit **D**elete command. The ClipBook viewer also has a ClipBook window. If you need to store information and retain it when you cut or copy other information, you can copy the contents of the Clipboard into a page in the ClipBook. The contents of a ClipBook page can be copied back to the Clipboard at any time. You can also *share* pages in your ClipBook so that other users on your network can connect to your ClipBook and transfer the information from shared pages into documents on their computers. ClipBook pages, therefore, can be a shared resource, just like a printer or directory.

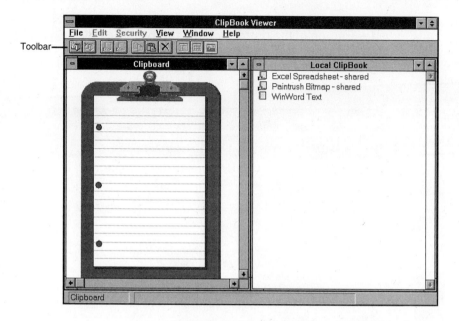

Toolbar

Fig. 6.2

You can store information to the Clipbook viewer for later retrieval.

To view the contents of your Clipboard and ClipBook, choose the Main group in Program Manager, and then double-click on the ClipBook Viewer icon. You also can use the arrow keys to select the icon, and then press Enter.

> You can start the ClipBook or Clipboard from within some applications by selecting the application control menu and choosing the Run command. The application control menu appears as a long dash at the top-left edge of each application's title bar. Click the long dash or press Alt+space bar to open the menu. After you choose the Run command, a Run dialog box appears. Use this dialog box to choose the Clipboard option and OK to run the ClipBook or Clipboard.
>
> **T I P**

The ClipBook Viewer screen appears (see fig. 6.2), with a Local ClipBook window and a Clipboard window. One or both of these windows may be minimized to icons, which appear at the bottom of the screen. Restore icons to windows by double-clicking the icon, or pressing Ctrl+Tab to select the icon and pressing Enter.

The ClipBook Viewer has a menu bar with commands for carrying out various functions. If you are using a mouse, use the toolbar, which is just under the menu bar in figure 6.2. The toolbar gives you ready access to many of the most frequently used commands. See the following table for a description of the buttons on the toolbar. The buttons in the table are listed from left to right, the order in which they appear on the toolbar. These different functions are discussed in the sections that follow.

Table 6.2 Toolbar Functions

Button	Name	Function
	Connect	Connects you to the ClipBook on another user's computer
	Disconnect	Disconnects you from the ClipBook on another user's computer
	Share	Shares the selected ClipBook page with other users
	Stop Sharing	Stops sharing the selected ClipBook page with other users
	Copy	Copies the selected ClipBook page onto the Clipboard
	Paste	Pastes the contents of the Clipboard into a new page in the ClipBook
	Delete	Deletes the contents of the Clipboard or the selected ClipBook page
	Table of Contents	Displays a list of ClipBook page titles in the ClipBook window
	Thumbnails	Displays small graphical representations of each page in the ClipBook window
	Full Page	Displays the contents of the selected page in the ClipBook window

Saving the Information in the Clipboard

There are two ways to save information stored in the Clipboard. You can save Clipboard contents as a file on-disk or as a page in the ClipBook.

To save the contents of the Clipboard in a file, choose the **F**ile Save **A**s command from the ClipBook menu. Clipboard files are automatically given the extension CLP and can be saved in either NT or Windows 3.1 format. You can then use the **F**ile **O**pen command in the ClipBook application to retrieve the contents of a file and put the contents back in the Clipboard. Once in the Clipboard, you can use the information to paste, link, or embed as you would any Clipboard content.

The second way to save the contents of the Clipboard is to store the data as a *page* in the Local ClipBook. Viewing and using ClipBook pages is much easier and quicker than working with Clipboard files. You can also share ClipBook pages so that other users can use the information in those pages, which you cannot do with Clipboard files.

NOTE If others in your workgroup will be linking to shared pages within your ClipBook, save the source document before you copy its data into the ClipBook. Linked data will refer back to the original source document by referencing its file name. When you change the data in the source document, all documents containing linked data will update.

To store data as a page in the ClipBook, follow these steps:

1. Save the original document if others in the workgroup will be linking to the data. Use a file name and directory that will not change.

2. Select the data (text, table, graphics, and so on), and copy it to the clipboard. Most applications use the **E**dit **C**opy command.

3. Activate the ClipBook application found in the Main group of the Program Manager.

4. Click in the Local ClipBook window or press Ctrl+Tab to activate the Local ClipBook window.

5. Click the Paste button on the toolbar or choose the **E**dit **P**aste command.

    The Paste dialog box appears (see fig. 6.3).

6. Type a name for the page in the Page Name box.

7. If you want to share the page with others in your workgroup, select the Share Item Now option.

8. Choose OK or press Enter.

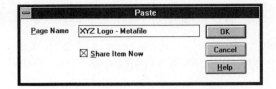

This pastes the data that is currently in the Clipboard into a page in the ClipBook.

If you selected the Share Item Now option, the Share ClipBook Page dialog box appears. With this dialog box, you specify how others will share the page. See "Sharing ClipBook Pages" for more information on this dialog box. When you have made the selections you want, choose OK or press Enter.

Sharing Pages in Your ClipBook

You can share pages in your ClipBook if you want other users to have access to the information in those pages. For example, you may have financial data or standard contract text that others in your workgroup could use in their own documents to save time. The ClipBook offers a simple and convenient way of sharing this common information across a network.

When you share a page in your ClipBook, the contents of that page become a shared resource, no different than a shared printer or shared directory. These contents are available to workgroup members connected to your ClipBook. You can limit the type of access to shared pages by creating a set of access rights for specific users and groups of users. This set of access rights determines whether included users and user groups have read-only permission, permission to modify the contents, or no access at all.

There are two steps involved in sharing pages in your ClipBook with other users. First, you must designate the pages as shared. You can specify that a page is shared when you create the page or at any later time. Once a page is shared, anyone who wants to use it must *connect* to your ClipBook.

Sharing a ClipBook Page

The following steps describe how to share a page. If you selected the Share Item Now check box while creating a page in the ClipBook, begin the following process at step 3. If you want to identify an existing ClipBook page as shared, begin with step 1. To indicate that a page in your ClipBook is shared, follow these steps:

1. Using the mouse or keyboard, select the page you want to share.

2. Click on the Share button on the toolbar, or choose the **File S**hare command.

   The Share ClipBook Page dialog box, shown in figure 6.4, displays.

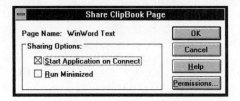

3. Select the **S**tart Application on Connect option if you want the application that created the data in the shared page to start up automatically when the page is transferred to another computer.

4. If you do not want to change the default access rights for your page, click the OK button or press Enter to finish up, and then skip the following steps. The default access rights for your page are set to *Read and Link* for all members of the group *Everyone*. This access type prevents modification to the contents of the page and provides a link from the data back to the original source document. The link is updated if the source document changes.

5. If you want to change access rights for specific users or user groups, select the **P**ermissions button.

   The ClipBook Page Permissions dialog box, shown in figure 6.5, displays.

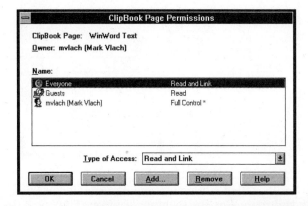

6. If you want to remove a user or user group from the access list, select the name from the **N**ame group and then click the **R**emove button.

7. If you want to change access rights for an existing user or user group, select the name and then select a new access type from the Type of Access group.

There are multiple levels of access you can grant to users and user groups for a shared page. If you want to prohibit specific users/groups from getting any type of access, select the No Access option. Select the Read option to prevent a user/group from modifying the contents of the page. Select the Read and Link option to allow Read access with the data linked back to the source document. Select the Change option to allow a user/group to modify the contents of a page. Finally, select the Full Control option to give a user/group unlimited access to the shared page.

8. Click the Add button to add new users or user groups to the access list.

The Add Users and Groups dialog box, shown in figure 6.6, displays and the user group names managed by your computer are displayed in the Names list. To list user names as well as groups, click the Show Users button. To add one or more users/groups with a specific access type, select the name(s) from the Names list, select the Add button, and then change the access rights by selecting an option from the Type of Access group.

Fig. 6.6

The Add Users and Groups dialog box.

If you want to select from members of a specific user group, select a name and then click the Members button. The Local Group Membership dialog box, shown in fig 6.7, is displayed. Select a name and then click the Add button to include it in the access list.

If the name selected is another user group that you also want to view, select the **M**embers button again from this dialog box.

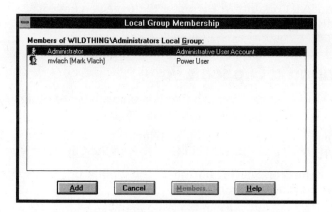

Fig. 6.7

The Local Group
Membership
dialog box.

To list user and user group names managed by another computer in your workgroup, select a different computer name from the **L**ist Names From group. If you don't know what computer the user/ group is listed on, click the **S**earch button. This displays the Find Account dialog box, shown in figure 6.8. Specify the user/group search string, select where you want to search, then select the **S**earch button to start. If found, the name is added to the Search **R**esults list. Select the name and then click the **A**dd button to include the name in the access list.

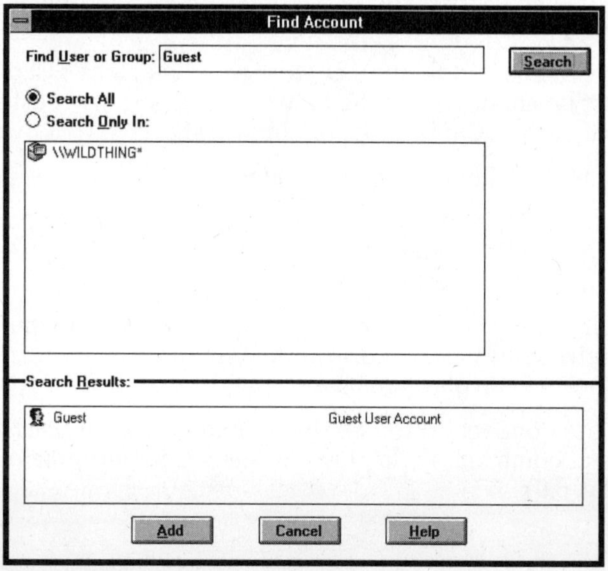

Fig. 6.8

The Find Account
dialog box.

9. Choose OK or press Enter to accept any changes made at each dialog level. Click Cancel or press Esc to abandon any changes.

In the Table of Contents, the icon for the page you have just shared has a hand displayed beneath it.

Unsharing a ClipBook Page

You can stop sharing a page so that it is unavailable to others on the Windows NT network by following these steps:

1. Using the mouse or keyboard, select the page that you want to stop sharing in the Table of Contents in the ClipBook window.

2. Click the Stop Sharing button on the toolbar or choose the File Stop Sharing command.

Pages that are not shared will not display the sharing hand icon when viewed in the Table of Contents view.

Connecting to the ClipBook on Another Computer

If you want to use the information from someone else's ClipBook, you must first connect to that ClipBook. You will then have access to any shared pages in that ClipBook. After you are connected to another's ClipBook, you can paste their shared data, link to their data, or copy their data into your ClipBook.

Before you can connect to another workgroup member's ClipBook, that person must be connected to the network. That person must specify which pages of their ClipBook he or she will share.

To connect to the ClipBook of someone in your workgroup:

1. Choose the Main group in Program Manager, and then double-click the ClipBook Viewer icon or use the arrow keys to select the icon and press Enter.

   The ClipBook Viewer window appears. You may see the contents of your previous cut or copy in the Clipboard. Your Local ClipBook will display your pages.

2. Click the Connect button on the toolbar or choose the File Connect command to display the Select Computer dialog box (see fig. 6.9).

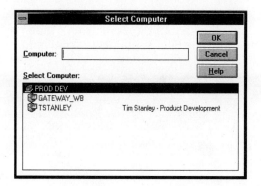

Fig. 6.9

The Select
Computer
dialog box.

Type or select the name of the computer you want to connect in
the **C**omputer name box. There are three methods for entering the
name of the computer:

- Type the name of the computer directly in the **C**omputer text
  box if you know the name.

- Select the name from the **S**elect Computer list box by clicking the down arrow next to the edit box or by pressing the
  down arrow key. Then select a computer from the list of
  computers you connected to recently.

- Double-click on a workgroup icon in the **S**elect Computer list
  box to expand the workgroup. Select a name from the list of
  computer names listed under the workgroup. The name will
  appear in the Computer name box.

3. Choose OK or press Enter.

   A ClipBook window displaying a list of pages in the ClipBook on
   the other computer will appear (see fig. 6.10).

Now that you can see the shared pages in the other ClipBook, you can
use them just the same as you would pages from your own Local
ClipBook.

To view all the Windows at once, choose the **W**indow Tile Horizon-   **T I P**
tally or **W**indow **T**ile Vertically command.

When you want to disconnect from the shared ClipBook, activate the window containing the shared ClipBook from which you want to disconnect, then choose the File Disconnect command.

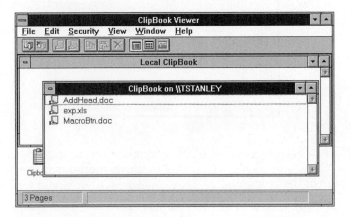

Fig. 6.10

Viewing
ClipBook pages
from another
computer.

Using ClipBook Pages

To use the contents of a page in your Local ClipBook or the ClipBook to which you are connected, you must first copy the contents of the page to your Clipboard. To do this, select from the Local or connected ClipBook window the page whose contents you want to use. Then click the Copy button on the toolbar or choose the Edit Copy command (or press Ctrl+C). The contents of the page will appear in the Clipboard window. You can now paste this information into any of your Windows NT applications using the application's Edit Paste or Edit Paste Special command.

To learn how to link or embed items from the ClipBook, see the following sections titled "Passing Linked Documents to Other Computer Users" and "Linking Data between Computers."

Viewing ClipBook Pages

You can view ClipBook pages in one of three ways. To view a list of all the pages in the ClipBook, choose the View Table of Contents command. Shared pages appear with the sharing hand underneath. The Thumbnails view, shown in figure 6.11, displays a small picture for each page with the name of the page beneath the picture. Shared pages have a small hand beneath the picture. Choose the View Thumbnails command to see this view. To view the contents of the selected page, choose the Full Page command or press Enter.

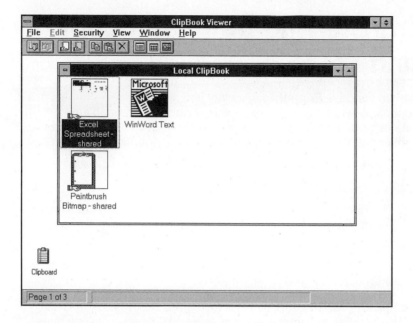

Fig. 6.11

Displaying a
Thumbnail view
of the ClipBook
contents.

T I P

You can use the mouse to quickly move between the Table of
Contents view and the Full Page view or Thumbnail view. To toggle
from the Table of Contents view to the Full Page or Thumbnail view,
double-click in the Table of Contents. To toggle back, double-click in
the ClipBook window. Double-clicking displays the Full Page or
Thumbnail view, whichever was previously displayed.

Deleting in the Clipboard or ClipBook

You can clear the contents from the Clipboard by selecting the Clipboard window and pressing the Del key or by choosing the **E**dit **D**elete
command. Choose Yes when the message box asking you to confirm
your choice appears.

To delete a page from the ClipBook, select the page you want to delete,
and then press the Del key or choose the **E**dit **D**elete command. Choose
OK when asked to confirm your choice.

Transferring Data with Copy and Paste

Copying and pasting—the same way you move text or graphics in a document—is the simplest method of transferring small amounts of data or graphics between applications. To copy from one Windows application to another Windows application, follow these general steps:

1. Select the text, cells, or graphic in the originating document.

2. Choose the **Edit Copy** command.

3. Switch to the receiving document—the application in which you want to paste the data.

4. Position the insertion point where you want the data to appear in the document.

5. Choose the **Edit Paste** command.

Text pastes into the document as formatted text. Microsoft Excel worksheet cells or ranges paste in as a table. Graphics paste in as pictures. None of them are linked to the server document. If you double-click on the picture, however, it loads into Microsoft Draw and becomes an embedded object.

Linking Data between Applications

Linking documents together is another way to transfer data between Windows applications. Links in a client document create references to data in a server application or a server document from the same application. The actual data still is stored in the server document; a copy is sent through the link to the client document.

Changing a single server document can update all the client documents that depend on its data. Another major advantage to linking documents is that client documents are smaller than documents containing embedded objects because the data still resides in the server document.

The disadvantage to using links is that you must maintain the links to a server document. If the location or name of the server document changes, you must update the reference by editing the link. If you give the client document to another user, you also must provide the server documents to make updating possible.

Creating a Link

Creating a link between Windows applications capable of linking is as easy as copying and pasting. When you give the paste command, you have the option of either making the link update automatically or requiring a manual update.

The command to paste in a link may vary between applications. The client document may use a command such as **E**dit **P**aste Link or **E**dit Paste Sp**e**cial with a dialog box that contains a Paste Link button. If your client application contains a Paste Link command, you may not need to continue past step 6 in the following procedure.

> If your server application does not have linking capability, you will not see an **E**dit **P**aste Link command or **E**dit Paste Special command with a following Paste Link button.
>
> **T   I   P**

To create a link, follow these steps:

1. Start both Windows applications—the server and the client—and open their documents. Activate the server document.

2. Save the server document using the name that it will keep during all future transactions. (You must save the server document to create a link.)

3. Select the text, range of cells, graphic, or database records that you want to link.

4. Choose the **E**dit **C**opy command.

5. Activate the client document that will receive the data, and position the insertion point where you want the link to appear.

6. Choose the **E**dit Paste Link command to paste in the link immediately. (If your application has a Paste Link command, you do not need to continue.)

   or

   Choose the **E**dit Paste Special command.

   A Paste Special dialog box similar to the one in figure 6.12 appears. Notice that the dialog box displays the source of the link and presents a list of different ways in which the linked data can appear.

Fig. 6.12

The Paste
Special
dialog box.

7. From the **D**ata Type list, select the form in which you want your linked data. These link types are described in table 6.3.

   Selecting some data types may disable the Paste **L**ink button because this type of data may not be able to maintain a link. If this occurs, you can paste the data or insert the data as an embedded object.

8. Choose the Paste **L**ink button.

When you choose the Paste Link button, Windows NT creates an automatically updating link. To have the link update only when you manually request it, see the section "Controlling Manual versus Automatic Updates" later in this chapter.

When you create a link, the data from the server may appear in different forms in the client document. Your data may appear as tabbed text, a formatted table, a picture, or a bitmap. Each server application has different forms in which it enables its data to appear. Generally, choose the type that gives graphics resolution or transfers the most text formatting. Table 6.3 describes some of the types.

Some applications enable you to reformat linked data and retain the format when the linked data is updated. In Word for Windows, for example, this is done by using switches within the {LINK} field codes. An example of a LINK field code produced by the **E**dit Paste Sp**e**cial command is as follows:

```
{LINK ExcelWorksheet C:\\FINANCIAL\\FORECAST.XLS
Result \* mergeformat \r \a}
```

In this example, a range of cells named Result within the Microsoft Excel worksheet was copied and pasted into the Word for Windows document as Formatted Text (RTF). The different arguments that specify the form for the linked data are as follows:

\r	Formatted Text (RTF)
\t	Unformatted Text
\p	Picture
\b	Bitmap

Any manual changes to the format of the linked data are preserved by the following switch:

```
\* mergeformat
```

You do not need to type this field code into the Word document; the code is automatically pasted in according to the selections you have made in the Paste Special dialog box.

Table 6.3 Data types stored in the Clipboard	
Data Type	**Type of Link Created**
Object	Data is an embedded object. All data is stored in an object. No link is maintained with the source worksheet or chart.
Formatted Text	Text transfers with formats. Worksheets (RTF)appear formatted in tables. Data can be edited or reformatted. If Paste **L**ink was chosen, a LINK field that links to the source document is inserted. If **P**aste was chosen, the data appears as unlinked text.
Unformatted Text	Text is unformatted. Worksheets appear as unformatted text with cells separated by tabs.
Picture	Some graphics, text, database tables, and worksheet ranges appear as pictures. (A picture preserves formatting and resolution from the original application—usually resulting in a high-quality image on-screen and when printed.) They can be formatted as pictures, but text cannot be edited. Unlinking changes them to Microsoft Draw objects.
Bitmap	Some graphics, text, and worksheet ranges appear as bitmap pictures. (A bitmap appears at screen resolution and may be distorted if resized.) They can be formatted as pictures, but text cannot be edited in Word. Resolution is poorer than that of a picture.

Passing Linked Documents to Other Computer Users

To make changes in the linked data in a client document containing a link, you must have both the server application and the server document available. When you give a document containing links to someone else, make sure that they have access to the server document and application. If you must share a document with someone who does not own the server application, you can use embedded objects instead of linked data. You also can convert the link to simple pasted data by breaking the link.

Breaking the link changes linked word processing and worksheet information into text—as though the text were typed in the client document. Graphics become pictures or bitmaps.

To break a link, follow these steps:

1. In the client document, select the linked data.

2. Choose the **E**dit Lin**k**s or **F**ile Lin**k**s command (or a similar command). The Links dialog box appears, as shown in figure 6.13.

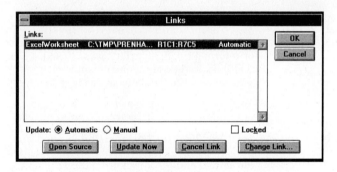

Fig. 6.13

Editing links using the Links dialog box.

3. If you did not select the links you want to break in step 1, select the links now from the Links list.

4. Choose the **C**ancel Link button.

If you want to remove linked data rather than break the link, just select the linked data and press the Del key.

Editing Linked Data

To edit linked data with a mouse, double-click on the data in the client document. The server application activates and loads the file necessary to update the data. After you have made changes to the data, from within the server application, choose the **F**ile **U**pdate command or the **F**ile E**x**it and Return to document command to update the linked data and exit the server application. (Commands may vary somewhat, depending on the server application. If the server application does not start and load the client document, do so manually.)

Some applications can specify that linked data will not update automatically. To edit linked text or worksheet data that does not update
automatically, follow these steps:

1. Select the linked data.

2. Choose the **Edit Links** or **File Links** command.

3. If you did not select the linked data in step 1, select the links now
   from the **Links** list.

4. Choose the **U**pdate Now button or its equivalent in your
   application.

Linking Data between Computers

If you are connected to a Windows NT network, you can link data between computers, just as you can link data between applications on a
single computer as described in the section "Linking Data between
Applications." When changes are made to the source data stored in a
ClipBook, the data updates in all client documents linked to the data.

Before you can link data from another computer, the data must be created in an application on the other computer, copied to the Clipboard
on that computer, and then saved in a page in that computer's
ClipBook. This page in the ClipBook must be designated as a shared
page so that others on the network can link to it.

Linking to the Server's Clipboard

To link to data stored in another computer's ClipBook, you must first
connect to the other computer's ClipBook. Connecting to another
ClipBook in your workgroup is described earlier in the section "Connecting to the ClipBook on Another Computer."

A ClipBook window will appear listing all the shared pages in the other
computer's ClipBook. This window is shown in figure 6.10.

To link data from another computer on the Windows NT network to
your computer, begin by preparing your Windows NT application to
receive linked data. Follow these steps:

1. Activate your Windows NT application and document that you
   want to contain linked information. Press Alt+Tab until the application appears, or press Ctrl+Esc and select the application. If you

need to start the application, activate the Program Manager and start your application.

2. Position the insertion point in the document where you want the linked information to appear.

3. Activate or start the ClipBook application. Press Alt+Tab until the ClipBook appears, or press Ctrl+Esc and select the ClipBook. If you need to start the ClipBook, activate the Program Manager and start your ClipBook.

Now, with your ClipBook application active, connect to another computer's ClipBook:

1. Click the Connect button or choose the **File Connect** command.

2. Select the workgroup and computer name to which you want to connect.

3. Choose OK or press Enter.

Connecting to another computer's ClipBook is described in greater detail in this chapter's section titled "Connecting to the ClipBook on Another Computer."

Finally, select the page in the other computer's ClipBook and link it into your document:

1. Select the ClipBook page to which you want to link. Click on the page or press arrow keys to select the page.

2. Click the Copy button on the toolbar or choose the **Edit Copy** command to copy the page contents into your Clipboard.

3. Activate the application and document that will receive the information. (The insertion point must be where you want the information to appear.)

4. Choose the **Edit Paste Special** or **Edit Paste Link** command. The command you use depends on how your application creates linked data.

   A Paste Special dialog box appears. The dialog box displays the source of the link and lists several formats in which the linked data can be displayed.

5. From the **Data Type** list, select the format you want to use for your linked data. See table 6.3 for a description of the different formats.

   Selecting some data types may disable the Paste Link button because this data type may not be able to link. Some applications may not be able to link with any data type in which case the Paste Link button will be disabled for all data types. If this occurs, you may be able to paste or embed the data. Pasting or embedding across the network is described in a later section, "Embedding Data from Another Computer."

6. Choose the Paste Link button.

The data you paste in will appear in your document. For example, figure 6.14 shows a Microsoft Word for Windows document containing a chart linked to a Microsoft Excel chart.

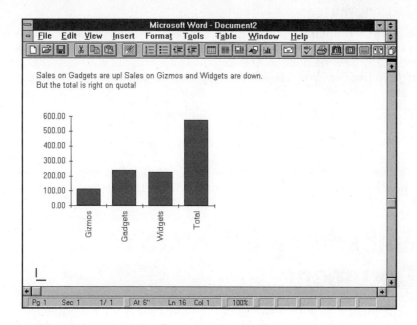

Fig. 6.14

A Word document with a linked chart from Excel.

Updating Linked Information

Changing the file from which the data originated, the source, will update all the links across the network. Linking data from one computer to another via the ClipBook actually creates a link to the file containing the original data. When the original file changes, any documents that contain the linked data will update. Because this link references the original file name that was the source of the data, you should not move the source file or change its name.

In some Windows NT applications, such as Windows NT Write, you are unable to see where the original data is linked to. In some applications, such as Word for Windows, you can see the formula that creates the link. For example, if you select the View Field Codes command, you view the link between Word for Windows and Excel. To link an Excel chart into a Word for Windows document, Word uses a code such as the following:

```
{LINK \\\\SALESMAN\\NDDE$ "$month sales xlc.OLE" Chart \*
  mergeformat \p \a}
```

If you have a document containing linked data, you can update the linked data if you can share the directory and file that created the source data. To update the linked data, start the application that created the source data, and then access the directory containing the shared file. Update the data document and resave it into the same directory with the same file name.

When you reopen a document that contains data linked across the network, you may get a dialog box asking whether you want to automatically link the document to applications outside your current application. Choose Yes to relink with the source document for the linked data.

You may encounter a situation in which you no longer want your client document to change when the source data changes. Some applications enable you to break a link, which then changes the linked data into pasted or embedded data. Each application has its own command or keystroke for breaking links. Once a link has been broken, you must update the data manually; it will not update when the source changes.

Embedding Data into a Document

Embedding is another method of inserting data from one application into another. Embedding enables a server document to store its data directly within a client application's document. A picture from Windows NT Paintbrush, for example, can be stored within a Windows NT Write letter.

Embedding objects gives you an alternative to pasting or linking data. It also gives applications more power because you can access one application's features from within another application. From within Word for Windows, for example, you can start Microsoft Excel and store the data from a worksheet or chart directly within the Word document.

Linking data has some advantages, but also comes with inherent problems. Linked data requires you to keep track of where the server files are located, to make sure that the server file names do not change, and to make sure that anyone receiving your client document receives all the server files.

Embedding the linked data directly within the client document eliminates those file management problems, but creates another issue. The
document becomes quite large because the client document contains
both server and client data.

Windows NT applications make use of powerful embedding tools called
OLE-based applets. Applets are small applications that add functionality
to larger applications. From within Windows NT Write, for example, you
can start applets that are bundled with other Windows NT applications,
such as Microsoft Draw and Microsoft Graph. This gives Write the
power of a drawing package far more powerful than Paintbrush and
a charting package with 3-D charts. Some of the applets available for
Windows NT applications are described in Part IV.

In a client document, you can embed objects created by OLE-based
applets or by stand-alone applications that function as OLE servers.

Creating an Embedded Object

You can create embedded objects in two ways, both of which produce
the same results. In the first method, you insert an object into a client
document, starting the server application so that you can create a
drawing, worksheet, or chart. When you close the server application,
the object is embedded in the client document. In the second method,
you start the server application, copy the data, and embed it in the
client document.

> Applets cannot run by themselves. Some applets must be started
> from within an OLE-capable application. If you are using an applet
> that cannot run by itself, use the Insert Object method of starting the
> applet and embedding an object.

T I P

To insert an embedded object, follow these steps:

1. Move the insertion point to where you want the object.

2. Choose the **E**dit **I**nsert Object or **I**nsert Object command (or a
   similar command in your application). A dialog box similar to the
   one in figure 6.15 appears, showing applications from which you
   can embed objects.

3. From the **O**bject Type list, select the type of object you want to
   insert and then choose OK or press Enter.

Fig. 6.15

The Object
dialog box lists
applications from
which you can
insert objects.

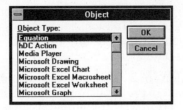

4. Create the data you want in the server application.

   You can create the server data from scratch or copy existing data into the server document from the Clipboard.

5. Embed the server data with one of the following techniques as appropriate to the application creating the object.

   ■ Choose the File Exit and Return to document (or just File Exit) command to close the application and update the embedded object. Answer Yes if a dialog box asks you whether you want to update the object in your client document.

   ■ Choose the File Update command to update the embedded object but keep the application and object open. (Some applications, such as Microsoft Excel, do close.)

   ■ If the server application supports multiple document windows, close the document window containing the object in order to update the object but keep the application open.

For an application to appear in the Object Type list, the application must be registered with Windows NT and must be capable of producing embedded objects. Applications capable of object linking and embedding are registered when you install them in Windows NT.

If you already have a document that you want to embed, you need to use the second method, described in the following steps:

1. Start the server application and create the text, chart, worksheet, or database you want to embed. (Unlike linked data, you do not have to save the data you are creating because it is stored within the client document.)

2. Select the data and choose the Edit Copy command.

3. Switch to the client application, open the document, and position the insertion point where you want to embed the object.

4. Choose the Edit Paste Special command. A dialog box similar to figure 6.16 appears.

Fig. 6.16

The Paste
Special
dialog box.

5. Select the *application* Object item, such as Paintbrush Picture Object, from the **D**ata Type list.

6. Choose the **P**aste button.

Editing Embedded Objects

Embedded objects are very easy to edit. Just double-click on the embedded object. With the keyboard, select the object and then choose the **E**dit *application* Object command at the bottom of the Edit menu (the command may vary slightly). The server application that you used to create the object starts (or activates if it is already running) with the object in its window. You then can edit the object using the same application you used to create it—without leaving your client application.

To update the object when you are done editing or formatting it, use the same procedures used to exit when you created it.

- Choose the **F**ile **E**xit and Return to document (or just **F**ile **E**xit) command to close the application and update the embedded object.

- Close the document window containing the object to close the object but keep the application open.

- Choose the **F**ile **U**pdate command to update the embedded object but keep the application and object open. (Some applications, such as Microsoft Excel, do close.)

Embedding Data from Another Computer

When you are working with Windows NT, not only can you embed data from one application into another on your computer, but you can embed data from another computer on your network into an application on your computer. Embedding data, known as *objects*, from another computer is an advantage if you do not want your document to change whenever the source data changes. For example, you may want to embed a portion of an Excel cost estimate table into a Word document. By embedding the table in the Word document, changes to the original Excel worksheet will not appear in your document, but you will be able to easily change the cost estimate table with your copy of Excel as necessary.

Before you can embed an object from another computer, the object must be created in an application on the other computer, copied to the Clipboard on that computer, and then copied to a page in the ClipBook. The page in the ClipBook must be shared by the other user before you can proceed to embed the object in a document on your computer (see "Sharing the Pages in Your ClipBook"). Not all Windows NT applications are capable of creating objects that can be embedded. A Windows application must have OLE capability for embedding to work.

To embed an object from another computer, you must first connect to the other computer's ClipBook. Connecting to another ClipBook in your workgroup is described earlier in the section "Connecting to the ClipBook on Another Computer." When you connect, a ClipBook window will appear and list all the shared pages in the other computer's ClipBook.

To embed data from another computer on the Windows NT network to your computer, begin by preparing your Windows NT application to receive the embedded data. Follow these steps:

1. Activate your Windows NT application and document that you want to contain the data.

2. Position the insertion point in the document where you want the embedded data.

3. Activate or start the ClipBook application.

Now, with your ClipBook application active, connect to another computer's ClipBook. Follow these steps:

1. Click the Connect button or choose the **File C**onnect command.

2. Select the workgroup and computer name to which you want to connect.

3. Choose OK or press Enter.

Connecting to another computer's ClipBook is described in greater detail in this chapter's section titled "Connecting to the ClipBook on Another Computer."

Finally, select the page in the other computer's ClipBook and embed its contents into your document. Follow these steps:

1. Select the ClipBook page whose contents you want to embed. Click on the page or press arrow keys to select the page.

2. Click the Copy button on the toolbar or choose the **E**dit **C**opy command to copy the page contents into your Clipboard.

3. Activate the application and document that will receive the object. (The insertion point must be where you want the embedded object to appear.)

4. Choose the **E**dit Paste Sp**e**cial or **I**nsert Object command. The command you use depends on how your application creates embedded objects.

   A Paste Special dialog box appears. The dialog box displays the source of the object and lists several formats in which the selected object embedded.

5. From the **D**ata Type list, select the format you want to use for the embedded object. See table 6.3 for a description of the different formats. Some data types may not allow embedding.

6. Choose the Paste button.

The object you embed will appear in your document. For example, a Microsoft Excel chart can be embedded as an object into a Word for Windows document. The chart still appears as it did in Excel, but it is not linked to the original file that created the chart.

An embedded object contains all the data used to create the object. If you have a copy of the application that created the object on your computer, you can edit the object. To edit the object, double- click it. This action will start the application and load the object so that it can be edited. When you finish editing, use the **F**ile E**x**it or similar command to close the application. You will be asked whether you want to update the embedded object. Choose Yes to accept the changes. For example, if you embedded an Excel chart in a Word document, you could double-click on the chart, and Excel will start and load the chart. You could then reformat the chart and close Excel to see the newly formatted chart in your Word document.

Embedding Data as Packages

In addition to linking or embedding data, you can bundle data as a package and embed in your client document an icon that represents that data. The icon, a small picture, can represent part of a document or an entire document. Only applications that support object linking and embedding can support packages of embedded data. Figure 6.17 shows a document containing packaged data.

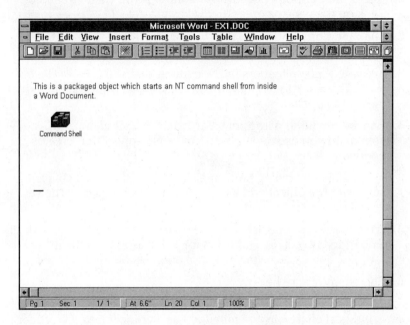

Fig. 6.17

A packaged object embedded into a document.

Embedded packages act the same as embedded objects. When activated, they open the server application and display the data contained in the package. Besides data, embedded packages can contain sound, voice, or animation, as described in Chapter 16. You also can add a label or create your own icon to represent the data.

The situations in which you may want to embed a package of data are as follows:

- A memo refers to a previous report that you want to package with the memo so that the reader can review it. Instead of inserting a lengthy report in the memo, you embed a package containing the report. Double-clicking on the package icon explodes it into the entire report.

- A new product proposal you have written gets to the point right away, but you want to make sure that all the supporting detail is included in case there are additional questions. You package the worksheets, charts, and notes and embed them in the proposal so that readers can delve into detail only if they want.

- A sales report has variances that you need to explain. Rather than break up the flow of the report, you package the variance report as notes. Each note is embedded at the proper location in the report.

To package objects, your application must support object linking and embedding. There are different methods of creating packages that depend on when your application was written and whether you want to embed or link a package. In some applications, creating an embedded package is as easy as dragging a file from the File Manager and dropping it onto a document. For other applications, you may need to use the File Manager or the Object Packager, which is found in the Accessories group, to package embedded or linked files.

The Object Packager appears in figure 6.18. The left side of the Object Packager displays the icon that represents the data. The right side shows the name of the object, such as a file name or a picture of the object.

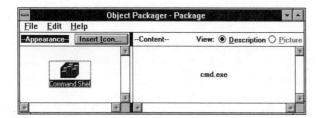

Fig. 6.18

An object appears in the Object Packager.

Activating Package Contents

A package may contain any form of Windows NT document, including multimedia files containing sound or animation. To activate the package so that it delivers its contents, double-click on the package icon. Or, select the package and then choose the **E**dit Package **O**bject command (or a similar command, such as **E**dit Package **O**bject). A cascading menu may appear to the side; if it does, choose **A**ctivate Contents to start the application and load the embedded data. (In some applications, using the keyboard to edit a packaged object only enables you to edit the object using the Object Packager.)

Packaging Entire Files

Files can be packaged and embedded using the Object Packager or the File Manager. The File Manager method is easy and enables you to link a package to the server document, but the Object Packager offers you the chance to change the icon and add a custom label.

Packaging a File with the Object Packager

To include the entire contents of a file or document in the package, follow these steps:

1. Open the Object Packager found in the Accessories application window.

2. Select the Content window by clicking or pressing Tab.

3. Choose the File Import command.

4. Select the file you want to package and choose OK.

Figure 6.18 shows how a package and its description appear in the Object Packager. Notice that the default icon associated with the imported file appears on the Appearance side of the Object Packager. The Content side shows a description.

At this point, you can change the appearance of the icon or the label attached to the icon. Both features are described later in this chapter.

To embed the package into a document that has object linking and embedding capability, follow these steps:

1. With the Object Packager still active, make sure that the Appearance side is active by clicking on it or pressing Tab until the title Appearance is selected.

2. Choose the Edit Copy Package command.

3. Activate the client application and open the document. Move the insertion point where you want the package icon to appear.

4. Choose the Edit Paste command.

    or

    Choose Edit Paste Special and then select Package Object as the Data Type and choose Paste.

The package appears in the document as the icon you saw in the Object Packager.

Packaging Files with the File Manager

Windows NT applications can use the Clipboard to copy files from the File Manager and paste them as objects directly into an application that supports object linking and embedding.

Some Windows NT applications that have object linking and embedding enable you to drag a file from the File Manager and drop it into a client document. The file then becomes an embedded package.

4. Choose the **E**dit **P**aste command.

   The existing icon is pasted into Paintbrush, where you can modify it. If you want to create an icon, start with step 5.

5. Use the Paintbrush to modify or create an icon. Use the **F**ile **S**ave command if you want to save a copy of the icon.

6. Select the icon you have drawn and then choose the **E**dit **C**opy command.

7. Activate the Object Packager.

8. Select the Appearance side and choose the **E**dit **P**aste command.

Use the procedures described previously to paste the package with its new icon into a document.

Editing an Icon's Label

Each package is labeled by the file name if you packaged a document or by the object type if you packaged part of a file. You can create your own label or file name.

To change a label while the package is in the Object Packager, select the Appearance side of the Object Packager and choose the **E**dit La**b**el command. Enter a new name in the Label dialog box that appears and then choose OK.

Editing Existing Package Icons

To change the icon or label of an existing package in a client document, select the icon and then choose the **E**dit Package **O**bject command (or a similar command). From the cascading menu that appears, choose the **E**dit Package command. Object Packager loads the package, enabling you to use the preceding procedures to change the icon's appearance or label.

Sizing and Moving Package Icons

You can size and move a package within Windows NT Write and other applications in the same way that you size or move other graphic objects. For information on how to do this in Windows NT Write, refer to Chapter 12.

Managing Links

Keeping track of the many links that create a complex document can be difficult. The Edit Links command makes the job considerably easier. When you choose Edit Links, the Links dialog box displays to show you a list of all the links, their types, and how they update (see fig. 6.21). From the buttons and check box, you can update linked data, lock links to prevent changes, cancel the link, and change the file names or directories where the linked data is stored.

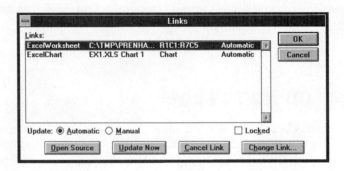

To select multiple adjacent links, click on the first link in the Link dialog box and then Shift+click on the last. To select or clear multiple nonadjacent links, hold down the Ctrl key as you click on the links.

Updating Links

To update individual links in a client document to reflect changes in the original document, select the linked data and then choose the Edit Links command. When the Links dialog box appears, select the links you want to update and then choose the Update Now button.

When you want to update all the links in an entire document, select either the entire document or all the links in the Link dialog box and choose the Update Now button. In some applications, shortcuts exist for updating links. For example, in Word for Windows, you can update a link by selecting it and pressing the F9 key.

Controlling Manual versus Automatic Updates

Some client/server applications enable you to specify whether a link should automatically update itself or should be updated only manually.

You may want to use manual links if you have many links that change frequently, because numerous automatic links can slow down Windows NT.

You also may want to use manual links if you want the client document to update selectively. This may occur if you have Microsoft Excel linked to a mainframe database, so inventory charts can be analyzed every ten minutes. A manually controlled link from Microsoft Excel into a Word for Windows document, however, updates an inventory report only when you request an update.

When you use the Edit Paste Special command to create a link, it is created as an automatic link. To change a link to a manual link, follow these steps:

1. Select the linked data or graphic.

2. Choose the Edit Links command. The Links dialog box appears.

3. Select the Update option that specifies when you want updates.

   Manual   Link updated when you specify

   Automatic   Link updated when source data
                       changes

4. Choose OK or press Enter.

To update a manual link, use the procedure described in "Updating Links," an earlier section of this chapter. Some applications enable you to update a link by selecting the linked data and pressing a shortcut key, such as F9. To prevent a link from updating, lock the link by using the next procedure.

Locking a Link to Prevent Accidental Changes

You may want to prevent accidental updating of a link but still want updates at your discretion. You can do this by locking or unlocking the related link. To lock or unlock a link, select the linked data and choose the Edit Links command. Select the link you want to lock or unlock and then select or clear the Locked check box.

Unlinking Inserted Files or Pictures

To unlink the server document and change the result into normal text or graphics that do not change when the server changes, select the linked data and choose the Edit Links command. Then choose the Cancel Link button. A dialog box appears, asking you to confirm that you want the link cancelled. Choose Yes to cancel the link.

Editing Links When Server File Names or Locations Change

If a server document's location, file name, or the linked range within the document changes, you need to change the link. If you do not change the link, the client document cannot find the correct server document or the correct data within the document.

To update a link, choose the Edit Links command, select the link you need to edit, and then choose the Change Link button. The Change Link dialog box shown in figure 6.22 appears. Within this dialog box, you can edit the Application, File Name, or Item text boxes to match the application, path and file name, and range name for the new server. (The Item is the range name or bookmark that describes the linked data within the document.)

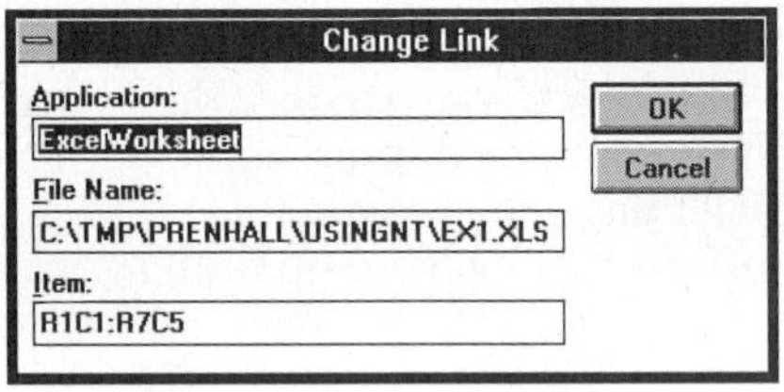

Fig. 6.22

Changing a link using the Change Link dialog box.

Summary

This chapter gave you the techniques you need to create compound documents—documents created from many different applications and collected together. Word for Windows and the Windows applications with which it can exchange data create the most powerful document-building system available.

For information on using applets to add features to any application capable of object linking and embedding, read Chapters 17 and 18.

Customizing with the Control Panel

The Control Panel gives you the power to customize Windows NT. You can add printers and fonts; change window colors, background patterns, or date and time formats; set Windows NT for different languages, keyboards, and date/time/currency formats; add a screen saver; or control how your computer interacts with a network.

Operating the Control Panel

The Control Panel icon, a program item icon within the Main group window of the Program Manager, looks like a personal computer with a clock and a mouse (see fig. 7.1).

To open the Control Panel, follow these steps:

1. Open the Program Manager.

2. Activate the Main group window.

3. Open the Control Panel by double-clicking on its icon or by pressing the arrow keys to select it and then pressing Enter.

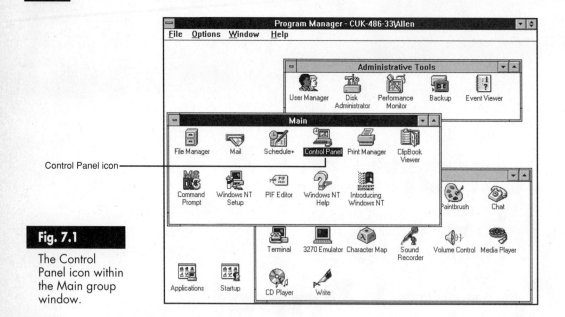

Control Panel icon

Fig. 7.1

The Control Panel icon within the Main group window.

When you start the Control Panel, its window shows the icons you see in figure 7.2. Each icon represents an application you can use to customize some feature of Windows NT. Although many of the Control Panel applications are standard with Windows NT, others appear only when you install certain equipment. A Network icon appears if you are connected to a network.

To use one of these Control Panel applications to customize Windows NT, choose the application that fits your needs. Double-click on its icon or press the arrow keys to select the icon and then press Enter. The following chart lists the icons in the Control Panel and describes what each application does.

Icon	Description
Color	Changes the colors in the desktop and other parts of the Windows NT environment.
Fonts	Adds or removes TrueType and other fonts; turns TrueType on or off.
Ports	Configures the printer and communication ports (COM1 through COM$) and defines how they work. Establishes IRQ interrupt settings.

Icon	Description
Mouse	Adjusts how fast the pointer moves when you move the mouse and the speed at which you double-click; enables or disables the mouse "trails"; and enables you to reverse the left and right mouse buttons.
Desktop	Changes the patterns or pictures used as the desktop background; specifies how icons align themselves on the desktop and icon title word wrapping; and controls the operation of the screen saver.
Keyboard	Changes the keyboard's rate of repeating.
Printers	Adds or removes printer drivers and defines which features they use; connects printers to the appropriate port or network queue.
International	Changes display and operation between different languages, keyboards, and formats for numbers, date, time, and currency.
System	Specifies the startup operating system, and allows specification of environment variables and virtual memory allocation.
Date/Time	Resets the computer's date and time.
Network	Controls how you interact with your network, if installed.
Cursors	Changes the mouse cursor images.
Drivers	Installs and configures your system's multimedia drivers, including sound boards, CD Audio, or MIDI.
MIDI Mapper	Sets up MIDI devices (for details, refer to Chapter 16, "Using Multimedia").
Sound	Sets the sounds used for different Windows NT events.
Server	Provides local server management.

continues

Icon	Description
Services	Manage system services.
Devices	Manage peripheral devices.
UPS	Configures the uninterruptible power supply.

The Control Panel, showing icons representing different applications used to customize Windows NT.

Customizing Windows NT with Color

One of the first changes many Windows NT users want to make is to customize their screens. You can pick colors for window titles, backgrounds, bars—in fact all parts of the window. Predesigned color schemes range from the brilliant Florescent and Hotdog Stand schemes to the cool Ocean and dark Black Leather Jacket schemes. You also can design and save your own color schemes and blend your own colors.

Using Existing Color Schemes

Windows NT comes with a list of predefined color schemes. Each color scheme maps a different color to a different part of the screen, and you can select from existing color schemes, or you can devise your own schemes (described in the next section). Figure 7.3 shows the Color dialog box. To select one of the predefined color schemes on the list, follow these steps:

1. Choose the Color icon to display the Color dialog box shown in figure 7.3.

2. Select the Color **S**chemes drop-down list box by clicking on the down arrow.

3. Select a named color scheme from the list. The colors in the demonstration window show how Windows NT will appear with these colors.

4. Choose OK if you want to use the displayed color scheme.

   or

   Return to step 2 to select another color scheme.

Fig. 7.3

The Color dialog box.

Using the Keyboard with a Drop-Down List Box

To use the keyboard to select from a drop-down list box, first select the list by pressing Alt+letter. In some dialog boxes, this automatically drops down the list. In others, you must press Alt+ the down-arrow key to drop down the list so that you can see its contents. In the Color dialog box, as in some others, display the list by pressing Alt+S and then pressing the down- and up-arrow keys to cycle through the items on the list.

Creating Color Schemes

You can select all or some of the colors for different parts of your Windows NT desktop. For example, you can select different colors for the inactive and active title bars, for the border, for regular and highlighted text, and so on. You can use existing colors or blend your own, as described later in this chapter. To create new color schemes, follow these steps:

1. Open the Control Panel.

2. Choose the Color icon.

3. Select the Color **S**chemes list box and select the scheme that most closely matches the color combination you want.

4. Choose the Color **P**alette button to display the right side of the Color dialog box as shown in figure 7.4.

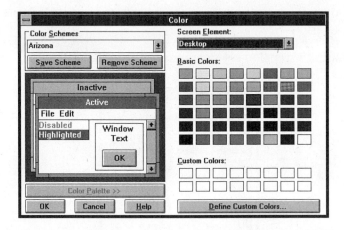

Fig. 7.4

Expanding the Color dialog box to choose your own colors.

5. Click in the demonstration window on the window element you want to change. (Some elements require that you click more than once. For example, clicking on the OK button once enables you to change the Button Shadow; clicking additional times enables you to change the Button Text, Button Face, and Button Highlight— although not necessarily in that order. To see which element you have selected, read the Screen Element text box.) Alternatively, choose the window element you want to change from the Screen Element drop-down list.

6. Select a new color for this element from the Basic Colors palette and click on the color you want. Alternatively, press Tab to move to the **B**asic Colors palette (a dotted line surrounds the current

color), press the arrow keys to move between colors, and press the space bar to select a color. As soon as you select the color, the demonstration window shows the change.

7. Choose one of these alternatives for the colors you have selected:

■ If you want to color another window element, return to step 5.

■ If you want to use these colors now but not in another scheme, choose OK or press Enter.

■ If you want to save these colors so that you can use them now or return to them at any time, choose the Save Scheme button and type a name in the Color Schemes list box.

■ If you want to cancel these colors and return to the original scheme, choose Cancel.

To remove a Color Scheme, select the scheme you want to remove from the Color Schemes drop-down list box and choose the Remove Scheme button. Choose Yes to confirm.

Blending Your Own Colors

Windows NT lets you blend your own colors and custom-design your own color schemes. In addition to the 48 colors in the Basic Colors palette, Windows NT can display up to 16 additional blended colors in the Custom Colors palette. You can use the colors you create for the Custom palette as you do the Basic palette. Figure 7.5 shows the Custom Color Selector box, which you can use to blend your own colors.

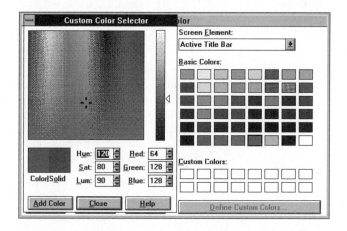

Fig. 7.5

Blending your own colors with the Custom Color Selector.

In the Custom Color Selector, you can create colors in one of two ways, described in the steps that follow. You can either use the mouse to point to the color you want and then adjust its luminosity; or you can use the keyboard or mouse to define exactly how much hue, saturation, and luminosity, or red, green, and blue goes into the color.

To blend your own colors, follow these steps:

1. Choose the Color icon from the Control Panel.

2. Choose the Color Palette button to open the Color dialog box shown in figure 7.4.

3. If you want the color you have created to appear in a specific box on the **C**ustom Colors palette, select the box by clicking on it. With the keyboard, press Alt+C, move to the box with the arrow keys, and press the space bar.

4. Choose the **D**efine Custom Colors button. The Custom Color Selector dialog box shown in figure 7.5 appears.

5. Select the color you want from the Custom Color Selector dialog box.

6. If you want a solid color (rather than blended), select S**o**lid by pressing Alt+O or by double-clicking on the solid side of the Color/Solid box.

   Mouse: Click the pointer in the Color Refiner box to select the color you want; a crosshair appears where you clicked, and the color you selected appears in the Color/S**o**lid box. You also can drag the mouse pointer around in the Color Refiner box while holding down the mouse button; a crosshair appears when you release the mouse button. This first step selects the color's hue and saturation. Next, drag the arrowhead up or down along the side of the vertical luminosity bar to adjust the luminosity (brightness) of the color. (You can adjust the color in small increments by clicking on the up or down arrows to the right of each text box.)

   Keyboard: Select the **R**ed, **G**reen, or **B**lue box and adjust the value in the box by typing new numbers or by clicking the up or down arrow on the right side of the box to increase or decrease the number. Select the **H**ue, **S**aturation, or **L**uminosity box and adjust the value in that box by typing new numbers or by clicking the up or down arrows. The Color/S**o**lid box shows what the color appears like in a large area.

> **Hue, Saturation, Luminosity, and Dithering**
>
> | | |
> |---|---|
> | *Hue* | Amount of red/green/blue components in the color |
> | *Saturation* | Purity of the color; lower saturation colors have more gray |
> | *Luminosity* | How bright or dull the color is |
> | *Dithering* | Dot pattern of colors that can be displayed to approximate colors that cannot be displayed—in the Custom Color selector, these are the blended colors |

7. Choose the **A**dd Color button to add this color to the Custom Color palette. Each time you choose the **A**dd Color button, a new color is added to the next box in the Custom Colors palette.

8. Return to step 5 if you want to add more colors to the Custom palette.

   or

   Choose Close to close the Custom Color Selector window.

You can assign custom colors to any part of your window by following the steps described in the preceding section, "Creating Color Schemes."

Customizing the Desktop

Changing colors is just one way you can customize the desktop. You also can change the pattern used in the desktop background, add a graphical wallpaper as a background, change the border width of windows, adjust the positioning of icons, and more.

To think of how color, pattern, and wallpaper interact on your screen, imagine the Windows NT desktop (screen background) as a wall. The wall can have a color selected from the Color dialog box (refer to fig. 7.4) and a pattern selected from the Desktop dialog box (see fig. 7.6). You also can hang wallpaper over the entire wall or just a part of the wall.

Wallpaper options you select here can include both patterns that come with Windows NT—including some wild and colorful ones—and designs you create or modify with Windows NT Paintbrush.

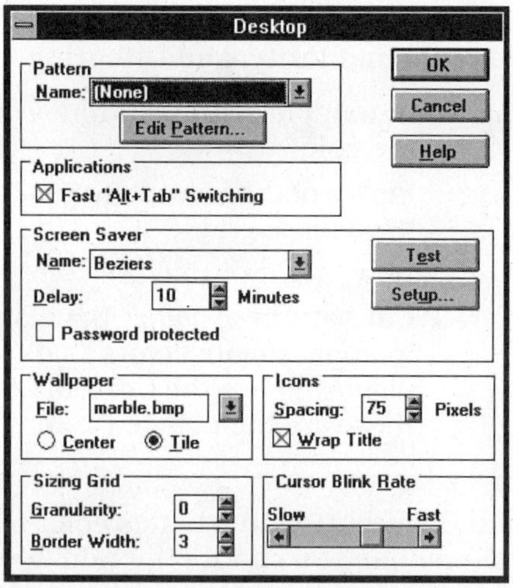

Fig. 7.6

The Desktop
dialog box.

You can put wallpaper over just the center portion of the desktop, or
you can tile the desktop with wallpaper, with the wallpaper repeating
as necessary to fill the area. Tiling wallpaper may put wallpaper pieces
edge-to-edge to fill the screen. Even when wallpaper fills the screen,
icon titles show through with the desktop's color and pattern.

Customizing the Background Pattern

Earlier in this chapter, you learned how to change the desktop's background color using the Color dialog box. In this section, you learn how
to put a pattern over the desktop's color. The pattern is a small grid of
dots that repeats to fill the screen. The Sample area of figure 7.7 shows
how a background pattern appears. Windows NT comes with predefined patterns you can select; you also can create your own. The
color of the pattern is the same as the color selected for Window Text
in the Color dialog box.

To choose an existing desktop pattern, follow these steps:

1. Choose the Desktop icon to display the Desktop dialog box shown
   in figure 7.6.

2. Click on the Edit **P**attern button to open the Desktop-Edit Pattern
   dialog box. Click on the down arrow to the right of the pattern
   Name list box. Select a pattern from the list. Some of the built-in
   repetitive patterns you can select are 50% Gray, Boxes, Diamonds,
   Scottie, and Weave.

3. Choose OK to add the pattern to the desktop. Alternatively, use
   the following procedure to edit the pattern just selected.

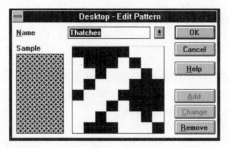

Fig. 7.7

The Desktop-Edit Pattern dialog box.

You can edit or create new patterns only if you have a mouse. To edit an existing pattern or create a new pattern, follow these steps:

1. Choose the Desktop icon.

2. Choose the Edit **P**attern button to display the Desktop-Edit Pattern dialog box shown in figure 7.7.

3. Select an existing pattern from the **N**ame drop-down list box or type a new name if you want to create a new pattern.

4. Click in the editing grid in the location where you want to reverse a dot in the pattern. Watch the Sample area to see the overall effect.

5. Continue to click in the grid until the pattern is what you want.

6. When you are finished creating or editing, continue with one of the following options:

   ■ If you want to change an existing pattern, choose the **C**hange button.

   ■ If you want to add a new pattern, type a new name in the **N**ame list box and choose the **A**dd button.

To remove an unwanted pattern from the list, select the pattern and choose the **R**emove button. Confirm the deletion by choosing **Y**es. The **R**emove button is available only immediately after you select a new pattern name.

A pattern appears behind program icon names. It may make the names hard to read, especially if you are using wallpaper as well. If you plan to use wallpaper (see the next section), don't use a pattern.

T I P

Wallpapering Your Desktop with a Graphic

Using a graphic or picture as the Windows NT desktop is a nice personal touch. For special business situations or for custom applications, you may want to use a color company logo or pictorial theme as the wallpaper for your desktop.

Windows NT comes with a collection of graphics for the desktop. You can modify these images or draw new images for the desktop with the Windows NT Paintbrush application. For high-quality pictorials, use a scanner to create a digitized black-and-white or color image.

Figures 7.8 and 7.9 show two of the several wallpaper patterns that come with Windows NT. Most of the patterns must be tiled to fill the entire screen, which you learn how to do in the upcoming steps.

Wallpaper is created from files stored in a bitmap format. These files end with the BMP extension and, to be used as wallpaper, must be stored in the Windows directory. You can edit BMP formats with the Windows NT Paintbrush application. You also can read and edit files with PCX format in Paintbrush and then save them in BMP format to use as a desktop wallpaper.

T   I   P   Bitmap images displayed as the desktop wallpaper use more memory than a colored or patterned desktop. If you run low on memory, remove the wallpaper.

To select wallpaper, follow these steps:

1. Choose the Desktop icon.

2. Select the Wallpaper **F**ile drop-down list box.

3. Select a wallpaper from the list.

4. Select **C**enter to center the wallpaper in the desktop; select Tile to fill the desktop with the wallpaper. Tile uses multiple copies of the wallpaper, if necessary.

5. Choose OK or press Enter.

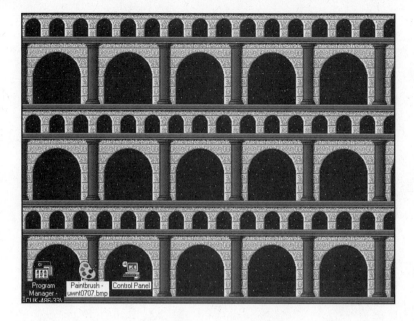

Fig. 7.8

The Arches wallpaper as a desktop background.

Creating Desktop Wallpapers

You can create your own desktop wallpapers in one of four ways:

- Buy clip art from a software vendor. If the clip art is not in PCX or BMP format, use a graphics-conversion application to convert the image to one of these formats. Use Windows NT Paintbrush to read PCX format and resave the figure in BMP format.

- Download a graphics file from a bulletin board system (BBS) or from an online service such as CompuServe or America Online. If the file is not a BMP file, you must use a graphics-conversion application to convert the file to the BMP format.

- Scan a black-and-white or color picture using a digital scanner. Scanners create TIFF files with the extension TIF. Use a graphics-conversion application to convert the TIF file to a BMP file for use as a wallpaper or to a PCX file to use with Paintbrush.

- Modify an existing desktop wallpaper or create a new one with Windows NT Paintbrush. Use Paintbrush to read BMP or PCX files. After you edit them with Paintbrush, save the files with the BMP format.

Store your new BMP (bitmap) graphics files in the WINNT directory so that they appear in the Wallpaper File drop-down list of the Desktop dialog box.

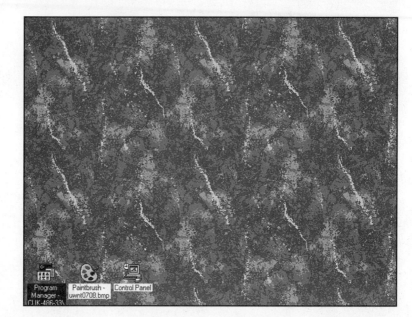

Fig. 7.9

The Marble wallpaper as a desktop background.

To remove a wallpaper file from the Wallpaper File drop-down list, delete or remove its BMP file from the WINNT directory. To remove the wallpaper from the desktop, repeat the preceding steps but select None in step 3.

Using the Screen Saver

A screen saver application prevents an image from burning into your screen by replacing a document screen with pictures or patterns. You can specify the delay before the screen saver activates, and you can set up various attributes—including a password—for most of the screen savers.

To select and set up a screen saver, follow these steps:

1. Open the Control Panel and choose Desktop.

2. Select the Screen Saver Name drop-down list and press the down or up arrow to select the screen saver you want.

   Choose Test to see what the screen saver looks like.

3. Select Delay and enter the number of minutes after you quit using your computer that the screen saver should appear.

4. Choose Set**u**p to set various parameters for your screen saver. The parameters for each are different; figure 7.10 shows the Setup dialog box for the screen saver Beziers. Choose OK or press Enter.

5. Choose OK or press Enter to close the Desktop dialog box.

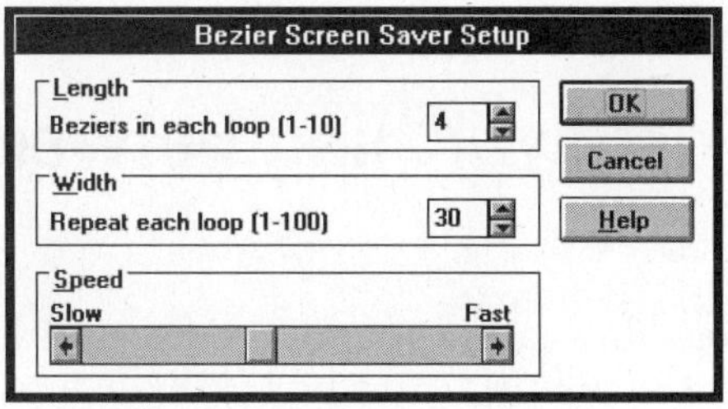

```
          Bezier Screen Saver Setup
 ┌Length──────────────────────┐   ┌──────┐
 │ Beziers in each loop (1-10)  4 ▲▼│  │  OK  │
 ┌Width───────────────────────┐   ┌──────┐
 │ Repeat each loop (1-100)    30 ▲▼│ │Cancel│
 ┌Speed───────────────────────┐   ┌──────┐
 │ Slow              Fast        │  │ Help │
 │ ◄         ▯            ►       │
```

Fig. 7.10

The Setup dialog box for the Bezier screen saver.

Spacing and Aligning Icons on the Desktop

If the names of your application or program item icons overlap, you may want to change the automatic spacing of the icons. At the same time, you also can turn on a grid that helps you align icons in a neat and orderly row.

To change the spacing between icons, choose the Icons **S**pacing text box from the Desktop dialog box and type the desired number of pixels (screen dots) of separation between icons. The width you specify applies to both the icon and its label. The maximum number of pixels you can specify for spacing is 512.

When your icon titles are long, you can put them on multiple text lines by selecting the **W**rap Title check box; if you want the names all on one line, unselect the **W**rap Title option.

To line up icons more easily, turn on an invisible grid that icons "snap to." With the grid on, move and then release an icon close to the desired location; the icon "snaps to" the nearest grid line. Use the grid to help put all the icons on the same line. When the grid is on, it also affects window sizing so that the window edges align with the grid.

To turn on the invisible "snap to" grid system, select the **G**ranularity text box in the Desktop dialog box and type the desired number of screen dots between grid lines. If you have a mouse, you can click on the up or down arrows next to the box to change the numbers. You can enter numbers between 0 and 49; each increment of 1 moves the icons 8 pixels or screen dots apart. Enter 0 to turn off the grid.

To change the border width on most windows, select the **B**order Width option in the Desktop dialog box and type a new number or click on the up or down arrows. Widths can range from 1, the narrowest, to 50, the widest. A border width value of 3 to 5 makes it easy to use the mouse to grab the window border for resizing. Windows you cannot resize have a fixed border width you cannot change.

Selecting Fast Switching between Applications

The Desktop application enables you to use the Alt+Tab keys to display quickly in the center of your screen a box with the next application's name.

Select this setting—the default when Windows NT is installed—with the Fast "Alt+Tab" Switching check box in the Desktop dialog box. When this option is enabled, you can select another running application by holding down the Alt key as you press the Tab key. When you see the name of the application you want to switch to, release the Alt key. The application is then restored. Press the Alt+Esc key combination to return to your original application.

Adjusting the Cursor Blink Rate

Some people are driven frantic by a rapidly blinking cursor; others fall asleep when the cursor blinks too slowly. Whichever group you happen to fall in, remember that you can control the blink rate. To change the cursor blink rate, select the Cursor Blink **R**ate option in the Desktop dialog box and press the right- or left-arrow keys. If you have a mouse, drag the box in the gray scroll bar or click on the left or right arrows. Watch the sample cursor to see the resulting blink rate.

Customizing Date/Time

Use the Control Panel's Date/Time icon to change the date or time in your computer system. Open the Date/Time icon from the Control Panel to display the Date & Time dialog box shown in figure 7.11. You can also change the time zone, and decide whether to have Windows NT automatically adjust for daylight saving time.

To change the date or time, select either the **D**ate or the **T**ime option and press Tab to move between the month, day, and year or hour, minute, second, and AM or PM. With the mouse, click on the up or down arrows to scroll rapidly to the date or time you want or type the new date or time. To change the time zone, click on the down arrow to the right of the Time **Z**one: field to pull down the time zone selection list. Click on the appropriate time zone for your location.

Fig. 7.11

The Date/Time dialog box.

Choose OK or press Enter when the date, time, and time zone are set correctly.

Change the formats in which Windows NT displays the date or time by opening the Control Panel's International icon and selecting the **T**ime Format Change button. Changing date and time formats is explained in "Customizing International Settings" later in this chapter. Often you need to select only the country to change the date and time formats accordingly.

Creating Formats in Windows NT Applications

With some Windows NT applications, including Word for Windows and Excel, you can create your own custom date and time formats if you need a format different from the predefined formats.

Changing Keyboard Speed

Although changing the keyboard speed doesn't result in a miracle that makes you type faster, it does speed up the rate at which characters are repeated. You also can change the delay before the character repeats.

Change the keyboard repeat rate by choosing the Keyboard icon from the Control Panel window. The dialog box shown in figure 7.12 appears. Select the **R**epeat Rate and press the right or left arrow, or click on the arrows with the mouse, to change the repeat rate. Set the **D**elay Before First Repeat in the same manner. Test the repeat rate by selecting the **T**est box; press and hold down one letter key.

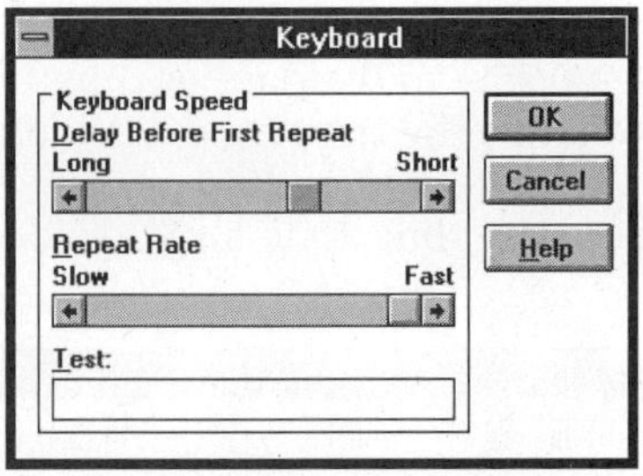

Fig. 7.12

The Keyboard
dialog box.

T I P   Four of the most commonly repeated keys are the arrow keys. Use
the **R**epeat Rate option to set the repeat rate that is most comfortable for you when you press an arrow key. To test the speed of the
arrows in the **T**est text box, you first must type text in the box.

Changing the Behavior
of the Mouse

If you are left-handed or if you like a "hot-rod" mouse, you will want to
know how to modify your mouse's behavior. Open the Mouse icon on
the Control Panel to display the Mouse dialog box shown in figure 7.13.
To change the speed at which the pointer moves as you move the
mouse, select the **M**ouse Tracking Speed option. Press the left or right
arrow to adjust the speed at which the pointer moves. Alternatively,
click on the scroll bar with the mouse.

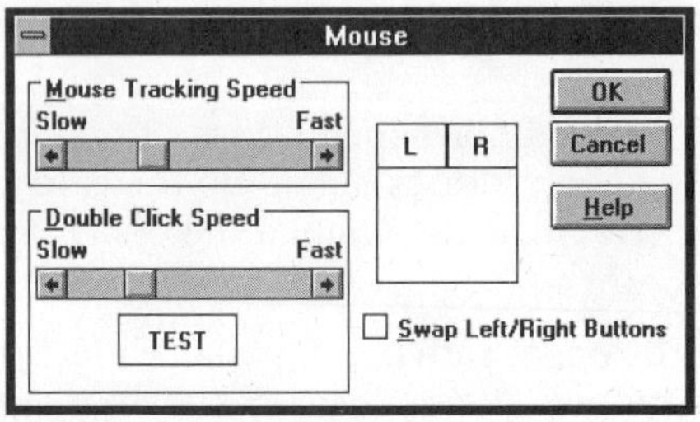

Fig. 7.13

The Mouse
dialog box.

If you use the mouse with your left hand, you may find the mouse more
comfortable to use if you reverse the left and right mouse buttons. Select the **S**wap Left/Right Buttons check box. Press the left and right

mouse buttons and watch the test *L* and *R* to see the result. This option takes effect immediately, so you need to use the Right mouse button to unselect the button swapping.

Another customizable feature is the rate at which Windows NT recognizes double-clicks with the mouse. Some people—especially beginners—double-click the mouse slowly. As you gain experience with Windows NT, the speed at which you double-click increases. To change the double-click response rate, select the **D**ouble Click Speed scroll bar. Drag the square in the gray scroll bar to the left or right to change the response rate. Double-click in the TEST box to test the new rate; the TEST box will change colors when you have successfully double-clicked.

Changing Mouse Cursors

If you want to use a different cursor shape, you can use the Cursors icon in the Control Panel to display the Cursors dialog box (see fig. 7.14). When you select a cursor from the list, you can see a picture of the cursor in the sample box at the right side of the window. To change the shape of the cursor displayed for the named context, click on the item in the list box you want to change, then click the **B**rowse... button.

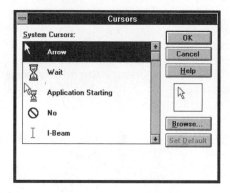

The Cursors dialog box.

The Browse dialog box lists files that contain static cursors or cursor animations. Static cursors are in files with extensions of CUR. They show a cursor that doesn't change as time goes by. Animated cursors, however, show a cute animation. The animated cursor HORSE.ANI, for example, shows a running horse as your mouse cursor. As time goes by, the cursor redraws itself so that the horse seems to trot in place. You can select any of the animated cursor files and see a demonstration of the animation in the box at the right side of the Browse dialog box (see fig. 7.15). If you select a static cursor, its image is shown in the sample box as well.

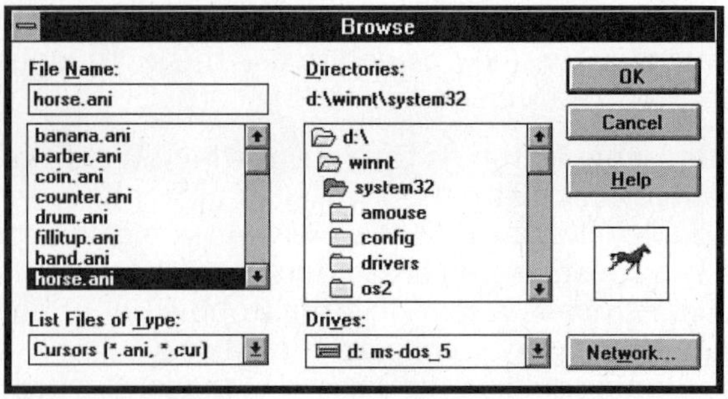

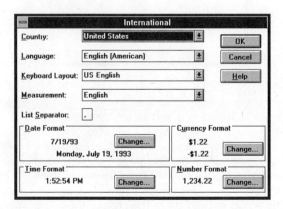

Fig. 7.15

The Browse
dialog box.

Clicking OK in the Browse dialog box brings you back to the Cursors
dialog box and makes your change to the selected cursor. If you click
Cancel in the Browse box, your change is not made.

You can restore the normal Windows NT cursor by clicking the Set
Default button in the Cursors dialog box.

Customizing International Settings

Another advantage with Windows NT applications is the ability to
switch between different international character sets, time and date
displays, and numeric formats. The international settings you choose in
the Control Panel affect applications, such as Excel, that take advantage
of these Windows NT features. Choose the International icon from the
Control Panel window to see the International dialog box shown in
figure 7.16.

Fig. 7.16

The International
dialog box.

> **Check with Vendors for International Software Versions**
>
> Although you can use the International dialog box to change
> language and country formats, doing so does not change the lan-
> guage used in menus or Help information. To obtain versions of
> Windows and Microsoft applications for countries other than the
> United States, check with your local Microsoft representative.
> Check with the corporate offices of other software vendors for
> international versions of their applications.

To set up Windows NT with a country format, language, and measurement system different from those of the United States, follow these
steps:

1. Choose the International icon from the Control Panel window.

2. Select the **C**ountry drop-down list box and select a country. Watch
   the sample formats in the **D**ate, **T**ime, **C**urrency, and **N**umber
   boxes change. Changing the country also may change default paper sizes in your applications.

3. Select the **L**anguage drop-down list box and select the language
   you use. Changing this option enables your applications to accurately sort words that may contain non-English characters, such
   as accent marks.

4. Select the **K**eyboard Layout drop-down list box and select the
   international keyboard style you use. Changing this option enables you to use key-characters specific to your language.

5. Select the **M**easurement drop-down list box and select either
   English (for inches) or Metric (for centimeters).

6. Select the List **S**eparator text box and type the character you want
   to use to separate lists. Applications, such as Excel, use the separator character to separate a list of arguments used in math
   functions.

7. Make custom changes to the **D**ate, **T**ime, **C**urrency, or **N**umber
   Format boxes as necessary. (Details on how to make these
   changes follow.)

8. Choose OK or press Enter.

If the number, currency, date, and time formats do not change to what
you want when you select a **C**ountry setting, you can change their formats manually. The following instructions explain how to make these
manual adjustments.

To change the number format when the International dialog box is already open, follow these steps:

1. Select the **N**umber Format box by clicking on its Change button or by pressing Alt+N. The International-Number Format dialog box appears (see fig. 7.17).

International - Number Format

1000 Separator:	，
Decimal Separator:	.
Decimal Digits:	2
Leading Zero:	○ .7 ◉ 0.7

OK
Cancel
Help

2. Select the formatting option you want:

Option	Result
1000 **S**eparator	Changes the character separating thousands
Decimal Separator	Changes the character separating decimal and whole numbers
D**e**cimal Digits	Changes the number of decimal digits displayed
Leading zero	Specifies whether a leading zero displays in front of decimal numbers

3. Choose OK or press Enter.

4. Examine the sample format.

5. Return to step 2 to make additional changes or choose OK to accept the new format.

Change the currency format in the same way you changed the number format. Select the **C**urrency Format box by choosing the Currency Format Change button or by pressing Alt+U. The International-Currency Format dialog box displays (see fig. 7.18). Then select options from the drop-down list boxes or type your entry. The following mini-table lists the options available:

Option	Result
Symbol **P**lacement	Selects from a drop-down list the placement and spacing of the currency symbol.
Negative	Selects how you want negative currencies to appear.

Option	Result
Symbol	Specifies the currency symbol (you may have to select a different keyboard to type the character you want).
Decimal Digits	Specifies the number of decimal digits.

Changing date and time formats in the International dialog box changes the default date and time formats in most Windows NT applications. It also changes how they display in the Windows NT accessories. Choosing the country usually changes the date and time to that country's standard. To make specific changes, however, choose the **D**ate Format or **T**ime Format box from the International dialog box and select from the lists presented.

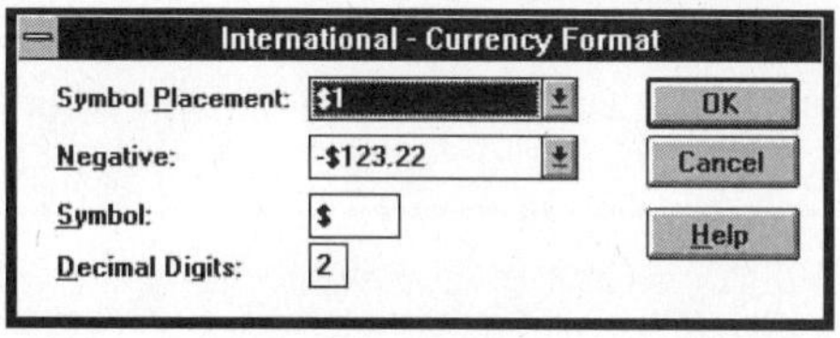

Fig. 7.18

The International-Currency Format dialog box.

When you choose the **D**ate Format option or click on its Change button, the dialog box shown in figure 7.19 appears. Notice that the formatting group at the top of the dialog box is for short dates, such as 7/12/93, and the bottom formatting group is for long dates, such as July 12, 1993. With many Windows NT applications, you can format dates so that they spell out the full month or day. The following table lists date format options:

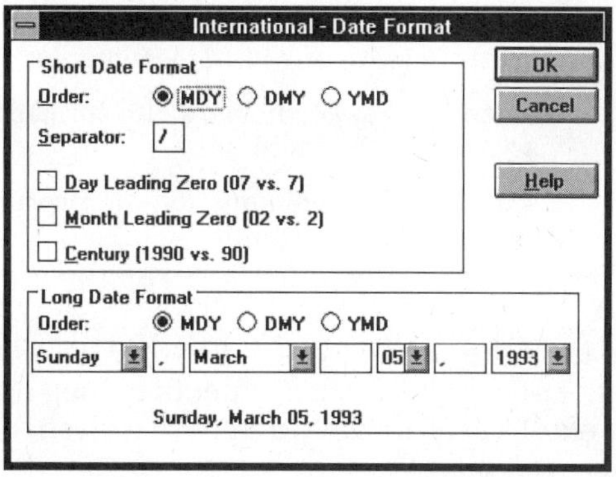

Fig. 7.19

The International-Date Format dialog box.

Short Date Format Options

Option	Result
Order	Changes the order in which month (M), day (D), and year (Y) display.

Short Date Format Options

Option	Result
Separator	Changes the character separating the month, day, and year (for example, the / in 7/12/93).
Day Leading Zero	Changes how day digits display (for example, 7/1/93 or 7/01/93).
Month Leading Zero	Changes how month digits display (for example, 7/1/93 or 07/1/93).
Century	Changes how years display (for example, 1993 or 93).

Long Date Format Options

Note: When you change the long date format, watch the sample date at the bottom of the dialog box. (No sample date appears for short date formats.)

Option	Result
Order	Changes the order in which month (M), day (D), and year (Y) display.
Day of the week	Changes between full day name or abbreviated name.
Month	Changes from full month name, abbreviation, or numeric (with or without leading zeros).
Day	Changes between numeric day formats (with or without leading zeros).
Year	Changes between numeric year formats (the last two or all four year digits).

Be careful not to miss the Separator text boxes. These boxes contain the character that appears between segments of long dates. Type the character you prefer to use—usually a period, a slash, or a comma.

The long date format boxes are dynamic; they change order as you select different MDY orders. If you use a keyboard, move between the boxes by pressing Tab.

Display a drop-down list in the selected box by pressing Alt+ down arrow.

When you choose the **T**ime Format option or click on its Change button, the dialog box shown in figure 7.20 appears.

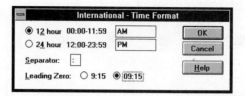

Fig. 7.20

The International-
Time Format
dialog box.

Select new time formats in the same way you did date formats. The time-format options are given in the following chart:

Option	Result
12 hour 00:00-11:59	Displays times from a 12-hour clock.
24 hour 12:00-23:59	Displays times from a 24-hour clock.
AM/PM boxes	Specifies the 12-hour time formats you want (for example, am and pm or AM and PM). If you select the 24-hour format, use the single text box to type a time zone abbreviation (such as EST for Eastern Standard Time).
Separator	Specifies the character separating time segments.
Leading Zero	Selects leading zeros for times.

Adding and Configuring Printers

When you buy a new printer and connect it to your computer, you must install and configure the printer to operate under Windows NT. Installing a printer activates a *printer driver*, enabling Windows NT to recognize your printer and access the printer's features. Configuring a printer tells Windows NT where and how the printer is connected to your computer.

The Control Panel gives you a way to add printer drivers not installed initially with Windows NT. Drivers for most popular printers were included in your original Windows NT installation; others are available on a disk from your printer dealer, printer manufacturer, or Microsoft. To install a new printer, follow this procedure:

1. Double-click the Printers icon in the Control Panel window. In the window that is displayed, pull down the **P**rinter menu, as shown in figure 7.21.

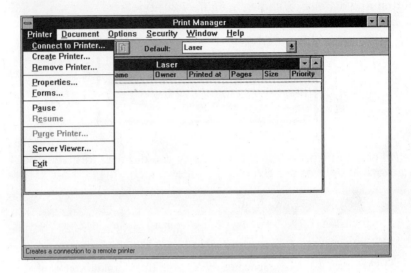

The Print Manager window.

2. From the menu, select Create Printer.... The Create Printer dialog box appears, as shown in figure 7.22.

The Create Printer dialog box.

3. Enter a name in the Printer **N**ame field.

4. Select the most appropriate printer driver from the **D**river drop-down list.

5. Enter a description in the **D**escription text box.

6. From the Print to drop-down list box, select the port where the printer is located. For information about sharing printers, see Chapter 9.

7. When you select the OK button to confirm the new printer, the Printer Properties dialog box appears. Figure 7.23 shows the box's appearance for a laser printer.

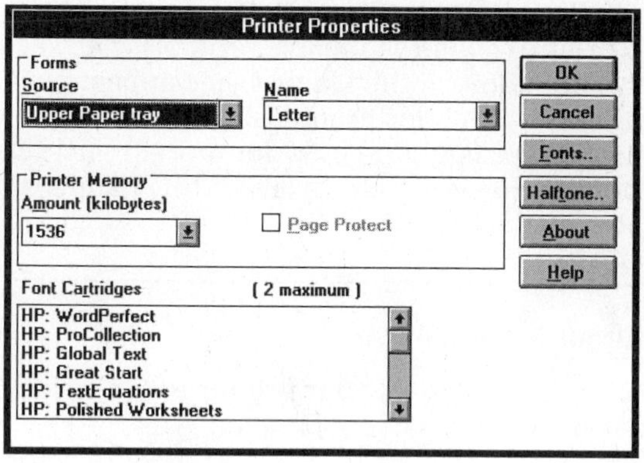

Fig. 7.23

The Printer Properties dialog box.

You can specify the default source and size of paper, and the amount of memory installed in the printer. You can also identify any font cartridges installed. Other printers—dot-matrix printers in particular—will have different Printer Properties dialog boxes that are appropriate for the features of the selected printer.

Pressing the Details button shown in figure 7.22 brings up the Printer Details dialog box, which controls such things as times of availability, priority, and whether jobs are to be printed to additional ports. The Job Defaults... button in the Printer Details dialog box leads to yet another dialog box, where you can specify paper size and orientation. You can also press buttons for additional options, including graphics resolution, the Color/Monochrome toggle, and halftone color adjustment.

Windows NT gives you a bewildering array of choices for configuring your printers. Fortunately, the default settings work fine in most cases.

The Connect to Printer... choice on the Printer menu shown in figure 7.21 allows you to connect to network printers located on remote nodes on the network. The Remove Printer... option on the same menu removes (or deinstalls) the currently selected printer.

After a printer has been installed on the system, you can modify its characteristics by selecting Properties from the Printer menu. The Printer Properties dialog box that appears is identical to the Create Printer dialog box shown in figure 7.22.

Do not confuse this box with the Printer Properties dialog box shown in figure 7.23, which you can reach from this dialog box by selecting the Set**u**p button. Microsoft should resolve this name conflict. Until they do, be aware of it.

The Settin**g**s... button in the higher level Printer Properties box leads to a dialog box in which you can specify the **T**ransmission Retry Timeout interval. The default interval is 45 seconds. The Print Manager keeps trying to print to an unresponsive printer for 45 seconds. If the printer has not responded by then, a message appears on-screen. If you are transmitting a very complex graphics image to the printer, it is conceivable that the printer might be busy for more than 45 seconds before it can respond to the computer again. If this happens, set a longer **T**ransmission Retry interval.

Printing without a Printer Driver

You have three alternatives if your printer is not included in the Create Printer dialog box's list of **D**rivers:

- Call Microsoft or your printer manufacturer to obtain a driver. Install your printer by selecting Other... from the **D**river list.

- Switch your printer into a printer-emulation mode so that it duplicates an industry-standard printer, such as the Epson FX-80 (dot matrix), HP LaserJet (laser printer), or Apple LaserWriterPlus (PostScript). You might have to change switches on your printer to put it into emulation mode. Select the driver for the printer being emulated.

- Select the Generic/Text Only driver as the last resort. This driver prints text and numbers but does not print graphics or enhanced text.

Refer to the PRINTERS.WRI files in the Windows NT directory to get specific help on special settings for your printer. Use the Write application to read these files. Some printer drivers come with their own README files that you can read also with the Notepad or Write application.

T I P If you are having trouble printing large files, try increasing the Transmission Retry value.

> You can add memory to many laser printers. If your laser printer has more memory than is standard, be sure the proper value is listed in the Printer Memory box in the Printer Properties dialog box (see fig. 7.23).
>
> **T I P**

Connecting to and Disconnecting from Network Printers

If you are connected to a network printer, you can print from Windows NT to that printer. To connect to a network printer, follow these steps:

1. From the Print Manager **P**rinter menu, select **C**onnect to Printer. The Connect to Printer dialog box appears on-screen.

2. If you know the name of the printer to connect to, type that name in the **P**rinter text box. If you do not know the name of the printer to connect to, select the printer to connect to from the **S**hared Printers list box.

   You can display the printers you can connect to in the **S**hared Printers list box by double-clicking on the workgroup or domain names in the box. Each printer associated with a workgroup or a domain is shown below the workgroup or domain name in the list box. When you select a printer from the list, its name appears on the **P**rinter text box.

3. Choose OK to connect to the printer that you selected.

To disconnect from the network printer, repeat the preceding steps, selecting the printer from the Network Printer Connection dialog box and choosing the **D**isconnect button.

Removing Printers from Windows NT

Removing a printer saves only a small amount of disk space, but it unclutters the printer selection and setup dialog boxes. To remove a printer driver, choose the Printers icon from the Control Panel, displaying the Print Manager dialog box. Select the printer by clicking on its icon at the bottom of the Print Manager window, then selecting **R**emove Printer… from the **P**rinter menu. Windows NT asks you to confirm whether you want to remove the printer.

Working with Fonts

Fonts are families of differently shaped and sized characters. Printers that operate under Windows NT can use different fonts, change the font size, and enhance fonts with attributes like bold, underline, and italic.

You add or remove fonts from Windows NT when you add a new printer or when you purchase new fonts to give more capability to a laser printer. Normally, Windows NT adds fonts automatically when you install a new printer.

If you add software fonts or enhance your printer, you may need to install additional fonts after the printer is installed. For some printers, Windows NT needs font information to display fonts on the screen (*screen fonts*) as well as font information to print data to the printer (*printer fonts*). Some types of printers, such as dot-matrix and inkjet printers, use the screen fonts for printing.

For printers that contain their own fonts internally, Windows NT needs to know only how the fonts should appear on-screen. The font information for printers with internal fonts can be found on one of the original Windows NT installation disks, on the disk that came with the printer, or on the disk that came with the software fonts (*soft fonts*).

Adding and Removing Fonts

Windows NT includes a number of fonts. These fonts are used on-screen to represent a similar font that your printer uses. If you use a dot-matrix or inkjet printer, the screen fonts also are used as the printer fonts.

If you format characters for your printer with a font that is one of Windows NT's screen fonts, Windows NT uses the screen font of the appropriate size. If no screen font exists to match the font you select for your printer, Windows NT substitutes a font of the closest size and type. When you install a printer or add soft fonts to Windows NT, you also add to Windows NT's built-in screen fonts that match the capabilities of the printer. Windows NT adds support for TrueType fonts. These fonts are scalable fonts that are printed exactly as they are seen on-screen, no matter which printer you have installed. (To learn more about TrueType, see Chapter 8.)

Fonts available in Windows NT may be proportional or non-proportional. Characters in *proportional* fonts vary in width so that characters can be more closely packed and appear more like typeset characters. Characters in *non-proportional* fonts are all the same width so that characters are evenly spaced and appear more like typewritten text.

Non-proportional fonts, such as Courier, are measured by their width, characters per inch (*cpi*). Such fonts can be measured this way because each character has the same width. Proportional fonts are measured by their height in *points* (72 points per inch) because each character has a different width. In Windows NT applications, you see character sizes specified in a **P**oints text box or scrolling list. Remember that the larger the point size, the taller the character. A 12-point character is approximately the same size as a 10-cpi character.

Fonts may also be serif or sans serif. *Serif* fonts have small marks at the ends of character strokes. *Sans serif* fonts are straighter and do not have the small strokes at the end of characters. Serif fonts, such as Times New Roman, are easier to read in body copy. Sans serif fonts, such as Arial, more often are used for headings, charts, and displays.

The following fonts are available in Windows NT:

Font	Description
Arial	A proportional sans serif font. Arial is a TrueType font that resembles the popular Helvetica font.
Courier	A non-proportional serif font similar to that used by typewriters. Courier is a bitmap or vector font.
Courier New	A non-proportional serif font commonly used by typewriters. Courier New is a TrueType font.
Modern	A proportional sans serif font used with plotters.
MS Sans Serif	A proportional sans serif font. It is a bitmap font.
MS Serif	A proportional serif font. It is a bitmap font.
Roman	A proportional serif font used with plotters.
Script	A proportional font that looks like handwriting and is used with plotters.
Small Fonts	Eight very small proportional fonts.
Symbol	A proportional font containing mathematical symbols. Symbol is a TrueType font.
Symbol (bitmap)	A proportional font containing mathematical symbols.
Terminal 8×8	A non-proportional font that looks like the font on a non-graphics video terminal.
Times New Roman	A proportional serif font commonly used in newspapers and magazines. Times New Roman is a TrueType font that resembles the Times font.
Wingdings	A proportional font containing desktop publishing symbols, such as arrows, boxes, circled numbers, and so on, used to draw attention to parts of a document. Wingdings is a TrueType font.

Adding Fonts to Windows

You can see the available font sets and their shapes in the Fonts dialog box. You also use the Fonts dialog box if you purchase additional fonts for your printer and want to add them to Windows.

To add new fonts, follow these steps:

1. Choose the Fonts icon from the Control Panel to display the dialog box shown in figure 7.24.

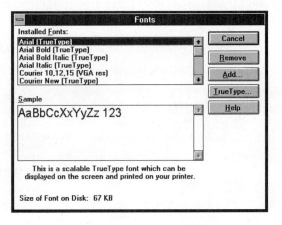

The Fonts dialog box.

2. Choose the **A**dd button. The Add Fonts dialog box appears.

3. Specify the location of the font files by using the Drives and **D**irectories list boxes. Then select the font files that you want to install from the List of **F**onts. To select more than one font at a time, press Shift-click.

   If you want to use the fonts from their current drive or directory, rather than copying them to the Windows directory, unselect the **C**opy Fonts to Windows Directory option. (Windows' default is to copy the fonts.)

4. Choose OK to install the fonts.

For details about installing fonts, refer to Chapter 8.

Removing Fonts from Windows

Some fonts, especially soft fonts (stored on your hard disk) take up considerable memory. If you do not use them, you may want to remove them. Do not delete font files without first using the following procedure to remove the fonts from Windows.

Use the Control Panel to Remove Fonts

Windows keeps track of the location of font files. Do not manually delete font references in the WIN.INI file or delete font files from the hard disk unless you have first used the Control Panel to re-move fonts from Windows. If your fonts have been "messed up," you may have to reinstall the fonts so that your system can handle the fonts correctly.

To remove a font from Windows, follow these steps:

1. Choose the Fonts icon from the Control Panel.

2. Select the font you want to remove from the Installed **F**onts list.

3. Choose the **R**emove button.

4. Confirm that you want to remove the font.

This process removes the font from memory but does not remove the files from disk. If you want to add the files again later, you can leave them on the disk or copy them to diskette. Use the File Manager to remove the font files you no longer need.

CAUTION: Do not remove the MS Sans Serif font. Windows uses this font for titles, menus, and dialog boxes.

TrueType Fonts

TrueType fonts are *scalable* fonts that can be sized on the screen (and to the printer) in any size, enabling the printed text to closely match the appearance of the screen text. TrueType fonts also ensure that the text will be printed at high quality on all types of supported printers.

You can choose not to use the TrueType fonts; Windows will instead use screen and printer fonts. If the exact printer font is not available, Windows substitutes a printer font similar to the screen font. Your printed output may be slightly different from the screen display of your text in the Windows application. The line lengths and page breaks when printed are the same as on the screen, however.

The Fonts dialog box enables you to set one TrueType font option when you choose the **T**rueType button: setting the **S**how Only TrueType Fonts in Applications option enables you to use only TrueType fonts in Windows NT applications. Non-TrueType fonts are not shown.

Setting Up Communication and Printer Ports

Serial ports are hardware connections in the computer to which you connect some printers and all modems. Unlike LPT (parallel ports), serial ports (also called COM ports) must be set up so that Windows knows the speed (baud rate) of data to be sent to the port and how to package information it sends. Use the Ports icon from the Control Panel to set up COM ports. If you do not have a serial printer or a modem, you do not need to set up serial ports.

To set up a serial port, follow these steps:

1. Choose the Ports icon from the Control Panel. The Ports dialog box appears (see fig. 7.25).

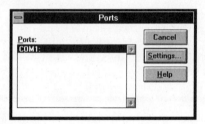

Fig. 7.25

The Ports dialog box.

2. From the **P**orts list box, select the COM port you want to set up. Click on the port or use the arrow keys to select it. Only serial ports that are actually installed on your computer are shown in the dialog box.

3. Choose the **S**ettings button to display the Settings dialog box (see fig. 7.26).

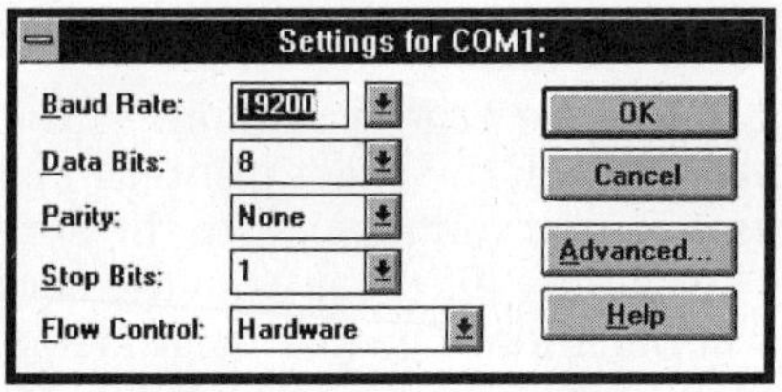

Fig. 7.26

The Settings for COM1: dialog box.

4. Select the options needed by the device you have connected to the specified COM port. Refer to your printer, plotter, or modem

manual for these settings. The options you select must be compatible with the communications parameters of the device to which you are communicating. The options are as follows:

Option	Description
Baud Rate	Changes the speed at which information is sent to the port. Most modems in use are 2400 baud or 9600 baud, although the number of even higher baud rate modems is increasing. Printers generally use 9600 baud. Check your printer settings to make sure that you use the correct value.
Data Bits	Changes the amount of information sent in each package of data. The setting is usually 7 or 8.
Parity	Changes the type of error-checking performed. Most PC software uses None as the parity setting.
Stop Bits	Changes how data packets are marked. The setting usually is 1.
Flow Control	Changes how the computer and the device signal each other when a packet of data is received. Refer to the manual for your communication device to determine what kind of handshaking is used.

Additionally, choose the **A**dvanced button to display the Advanced Settings dialog box. Not all serial ports enable you to make advanced settings. See the section "Advanced Port Settings" for more information.

5. Choose OK to close the Settings dialog box and accept the COM port settings.

6. Choose Close to close the Ports dialog box and accept all changes made to the COM ports.

Advanced Port Settings

The Advanced Port settings enable you to specify the base Input/Output port address and Interrupt request number used by your COM ports. These settings must match those installed in your computer. The normal settings for the COM ports are as follows:

Port	I/O Address	Interrupt
COM1:	03F8	4
COM2:	02F8	3
COM3	03E8	4
COM4	02E8	3

To make changes to these settings, follow these steps:

1. Choose the Ports icon from the Control Panel. The Ports dialog box appears.

2. Select the COM port that you want to modify. Click on the port or use the arrow keys to select it.

3. Choose the Settings button to display the Settings dialog box.

4. Choose the Advanced button, which displays the Advanced Settings dialog box for the port you selected.

5. Enter the Base I/O Port Address in the text box or select the down arrow to see a standard list of values. With the keyboard, press Alt+down arrow to see the list. Select the desired port address.

6. To change the Interrupt, select the Interrupt Request Line (IRQ) and change the value as in step 5.

7. Select OK to return to the Settings dialog box; then select OK to save your changes for that port.

8. Make any needed changes to the other ports with the same procedure; then select Close to exit the Ports setup application.

Setting System Sounds

A beeping computer is one thing when you're up playing Nintendo games after the kids have gone to bed. But it's something else entirely when you are at work and each earsplitting beep tells your coworkers you have made another embarrassing computer mistake.

To turn off the warning beep, choose the Sound icon from the Control Panel, select the Enable System Sounds check box to remove the *X* in it, then choose OK. This action disables all beeping for all applications used in Windows NT.

You also can use the Control Panel's Drivers application to add support for any sound devices installed on your computer. This enables you to choose your own sounds for various Windows NT events, such as the Default Beep, Questions dialog box, or when you start or exit Windows NT.

To specify these settings, first use the Drivers application to install the sound drivers for your device. (See the "Configuring for Sound Devices" section later in this chapter for that procedure.) Then you can set the sounds for various Windows NT events by following these steps:

1. From the Control Panel, choose the Sound icon.

2. The Sound dialog box shows the available Windows Events in one list box and the sound Files list in another list box (see fig. 7.27). Sound files normally have a WAV file extension. If your sound files are stored in another drive or directory, select the drive or directory from the Files box.

3. Select the Event that you want to change. The file being used for that event is selected in the Files box. Select another sound file if you want to change it.

4. Choose the Test button to see how the sound file sounds.

5. Repeat steps 3 and 4 for other Windows NT events.

6. When you have set sounds for all the events, choose OK.

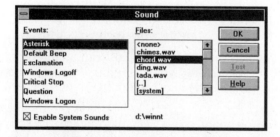

Fig. 7.27

The Sound dialog box.

Using the Network Icon

The Network icon in your Control Panel opens the Network Settings dialog box, which enables you to change the way Windows NT perceives your network. You can use this icon to enable or disable network processing, or to update, remove, or configure network cards or protocols.

If you want to change the name of your computer or the workgroup your computer has created, you can press the Change... buttons near the Computer Name: and Workgroup: fields at the top of the dialog box. A simple dialog box appears, asking you for the new name of your workgroup or computer.

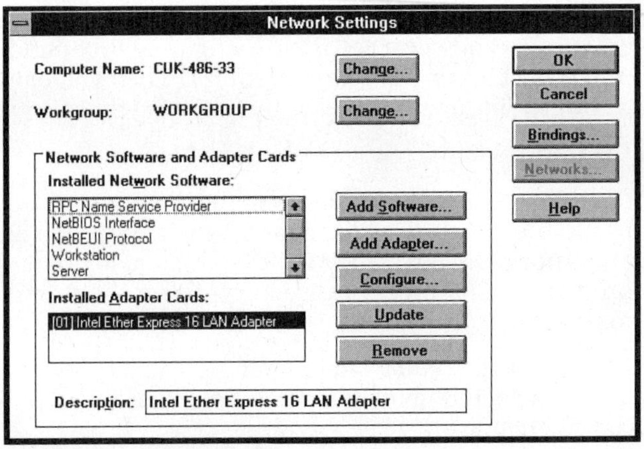

Fig. 7.28

The Network
Settings dialog
box.

If you've installed a new network interface card, you should click the
Add Adapter button. This results in a dialog box that tries to detect and
configure your new card. The dialog box is specific to your card; it displays your card's options and enables you to choose them. You should
carefully compare the settings in the dialog box against the settings on
your card to be completely sure they match perfectly. Otherwise, operating Windows NT with your network card will be erratic at best.

If you have changed the configuration of your adapter without actually
installing a different adapter, you can jump directly to the adapter-
specific configuration box using the Configure button in the Network
Settings dialog box.

The Update button enables you to load updated drivers or protocols
for your network card. Windows NT prompts you for the proper disk
drive or directory for the setup files, but the dialog boxes that follow
are specific to the network vendor.

You can view the protocol bindings in place by pressing the Bindings
button. This results in the Network Bindings dialog box, shown in
figure 7.29.

This dialog box shows which network protocols are used in communicating with other machines. In this example, the lowest binding is the
Intel Ether Express 16 LAN Adapter Driver, which manages a protocol
that in turn communicates with the NetBEUI Protocol. NetBEUI sends
commands and requests through the NetBIOS Interface. There are
other bindings listed, and those are automatically used when appropriate. You can use the Enable and Disable buttons to change which bindings are in effect for your machine. You can use the arrow buttons at
the end of the window to scroll the list box.

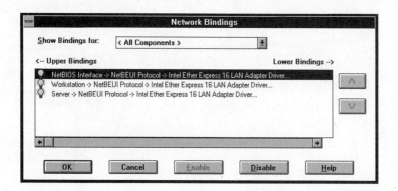

Fig. 7.29

The Network Bindings dialog box.

Configuring for Sound Devices

Windows NT adds the ability to install *drivers* for multimedia devices, such as sound boards or CD-ROM drives. Windows NT comes with some sound drivers; other drivers are part of the added device. If you add a sound board, for instance, it may come with its own custom drivers but also can use the included Windows NT sound drivers.

Using sounds has its limitations. If you are running a communications application in the background, a sound "task" in the foreground may cause data loss.

To install a driver, follow these steps:

1. From the Control Panel, select Drivers.

2. The Drivers dialog box shows a list of drivers that are standard with Windows NT (see fig. 7.30).

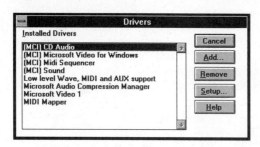

Fig. 7.30

The Drivers dialog box.

3. If you have one of the listed devices, select from the Installed Drivers list, choose Setup, and skip to step 5.

4. To see additional drivers, choose **A**dd. The Add dialog box includes the List of Drivers. Select yours from the list. To use a driver installed in a drive or directory other than your Windows directory, select Unlisted or Updated Driver and then select OK. The Install Driver dialog box asks you for the disk with the driver file. Or use the Browse button to select the drive or directory that contains the driver file. Select OK to return to the Drivers dialog box.

5. Each driver installed has different settings you can select with the **S**etup button. You can select the Port and Interrupt, for example, for the Creative Labs Sound Blaster board.

6. Some driver settings dialog boxes have a Test button for testing your settings. Some also may have Help available for additional information.

7. To complete the driver installation, select OK until you exit back to the Control Panel. As you exit, a dialog box advises that you need to restart Windows NT to enable most drivers. Select the Restart Now button to exit and restart Windows NT so that the installed drivers are available to Windows NT.

If you remove a device from your computer, you may want to remove its driver also, to save a little disk space. Do not delete any required device driver files—Windows NT will not work properly.

The System Option

If you click on the System icon on the Control Panel, the System dialog box shown in figure 7.31 appears.

The System dialog box gives you a peephole into some of the most fundamental processes taking place under the surface of the operating system. There are three functional areas, and two buttons that lead to additional dialog boxes. The functional areas are Operating System, System Environment Variables, and User Environment Variables. The two buttons are Virtual **M**emory... and **T**asking....

Setting Startup Defaults

The **S**tartup field is contained in the Operating System box. Listed in the field is the current default operating system, if you are using MultiBoot to choose which of two or more operating systems to start when you turn on your system or reboot. A drop-down menu lists the other installed operating systems. If you want to change the default, do so by selecting another operating system from the menu.

The Show list for field determines how long MulitBoot will display the list of alternate operating systems before starting the default. You can enter any number between 0 and 999 seconds.

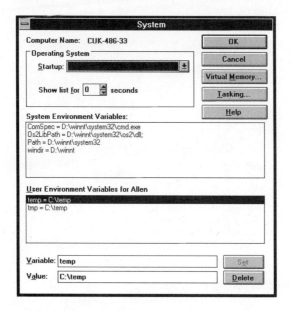

Fig. 7.31

The System
dialog box.

Setting System Environment Variables

The variables listed in the System Environment Variables box contain information that the operating system uses to find programs, allocate memory, and control application behavior. You cannot change these variables from this dialog box. The display is strictly for your information.

The User Environment Variables are used by applications rather than by the system. You can add, delete, or change them from this dialog box. Add a new environment variable by selecting the Variable field and typing the new variable name, then selecting the Value field and entering its value. Choose the Set button to add the new variable to the user environment variables list. To delete a user environment variable, select it in the User Environment Variables box, then choose the Delete button. To change an existing user environment variable, select it in the User Environment Variables box, then modify the entries in the Variable or Value fields below, as desired. When you are finished with the change, choose the Set button to complete the operation.

Configuring Virtual Memory

The Virtual Memory... button leads to the Virtual Memory dialog box, which is shown in figure 7.32.

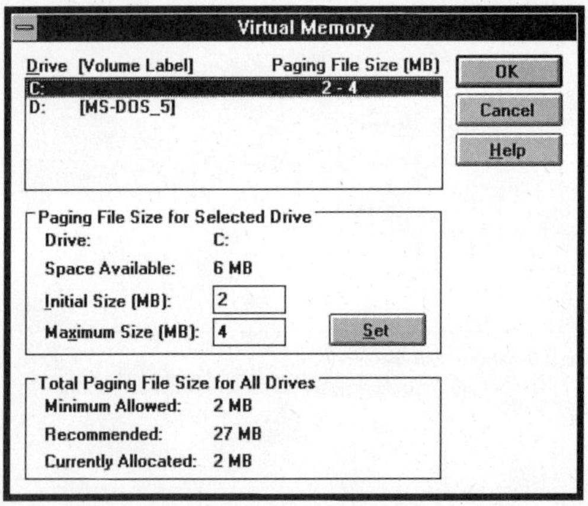

Fig. 7.32

The Virtual Memory dialog box.

The virtual memory system is one of Windows NT's most powerful features. It enables you to run a program that is larger than the memory you have installed in your computer, or to simultaneously run a combination of programs that are larger. Not all parts of all of those programs are active at the same time. With a virtual memory system, a certain portion of your hard disk storage is set aside as "virtual" memory. Inactive code or data in memory is swapped out to the virtual memory area on disk to allow other, active material to be read into RAM and used. All the programs involved "think" they are completely loaded into RAM and behave normally.

The main disadvantage of using memory is speed. Disk storage is about 100,000 times slower than RAM. When your flow of execution needs something that has previously been swapped out to disk, you have to wait a while to get it. This delay is often perceptible, even to us slow humans. However, a little delay is often a small price to pay for the ability to run something that you wouldn't be able to run at all without virtual memory.

Figure 7.33 shows that for the example system, the paging file is on drive C and ranges from 2 to 4M in size. The amount of space currently available on that drive is 6M. The minimum page file NT allows is 2M. In the example system, it may expand up to 4M if necessary, then shrink back down to 2M as demand for memory slackens. NT recommends a page file of 27M for a system with as much disk space as the example system has. This is clearly not feasible here because there is only 6M of free space.

Because the amount of disk space allocated to paging is so much less than the recommended value, the operator of this system will probably experience frequent messages from NT to shut down unneeded processes, as the amount of swap space approaches the 4M limit. If demand for swap space exceeds the upper limit, NT could fail in a manner that damages files. From the Paging File Size for Selected Drive box, you can change both the Initial Size and the Maximum size of the paging file. If you have plenty of free disk space, you will want to set both of these figures higher. For optimum performance, set the maximum at the value recommended by NT.

Configuring the Tasking Option

The Tasking... button on the system dialog box leads to another dialog box, which is considerably easier to deal with than the Virtual Memory dialog box. Shown in figure 7.33, the Tasking dialog box gives you control of resource allocation in a multitasking situation.

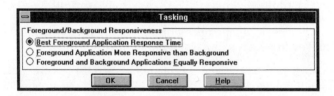

Fig. 7.33

The Tasking dialog box.

One window on the desktop has a different color border from all the rest. This window has "the focus," and the task running in it is considered the *foreground* task. Other tasks that are running at the same time are background tasks. The foreground task is the one the user is paying attention to at the moment. Usually this is the one you want to devote the most system resources to, so that it can give the user the best response time. There are degrees, however, of how much extra priority you may want to give to the foreground task. The tasking dialog box gives you three options. The default option is Best Foreground Application Response Time. The next option, Foreground Application More Responsive than Background, gives the background tasks more resources. The third option, Foreground and Background Applications Equally Responsive, gives all the background applications the same amount of system resources that the foreground application receives. This dialog box does not give you the ability to allocate fewer resources to the foreground application than the background applications are receiving.

The MIDI Mapper Option

The MIDI Mapper option gives the user control, from the desktop, of the way a MIDI musical device connected to the system (such as a sound card, synthesizer, or electronic saxophone) plays sounds. The MIDI Mapper dialog box shown in figure 7.34 enables you to edit **s**etups, **P**atch Maps, and **K**ey Maps for a specific musical instrument.

Fig. 7.34

MIDI Mapper dialog box.

Setups have to do with the routing of sound signals from source devices to destination (playing) devices. Patch maps enable you to make specific customizations of signal routing and volume control to the destination device. Key maps provide the ability to automatically change the key in which a musical composition is played.

MIDI is a complex technology that has been used for several years by professional musicians to create, score, and play their most demanding musical compositions. Until recently, it has been quite expensive. With NT, much of the power of MIDI can be realized with no more than a personal computer and a music synthesizer. MIDI mapper enables you to change the settings of an electronic instrument, such as a synthesizer, and to "map" the way sound signals are transferred between the instrument and your computer. By altering the mapping, you can change the way music sounds, or the way various channels blend with each other.

T I P   Don't use MIDI Mapper at all unless you have a very good understanding of MIDI concepts and terminology, and understand what results your changes are likely to produce.

The Server Option

If the system running NT is being used as a server by remote users, the Server option on the Control Panel gives a real-time snapshot of how active those remote users are. Figure 7.35 shows the Properties dialog box.

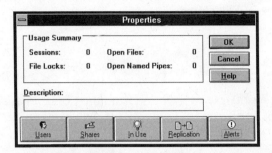

Fig. 7.35

The Properties dialog box displayed by the Server option on the Control Panel.

The number of sessions and file locks currently active, as well as the number of open files and open named pipes, is displayed. By pressing the buttons at the bottom of the dialog box, you can tell the identities of remote users and the shared resources they are using. You can also disconnect one or all remote users, allow or disallow remote directories to be copied to this computer, and decide which computers will receive administrative alerts.

The Services Option

Windows NT provides a number of optional services to users. Some of these are started automatically when Windows NT boots up. Others must be started manually. From the Services dialog box (fig. 7.36), you can start or stop any service, as well as change its startup status from automatic to manual or vice versa.

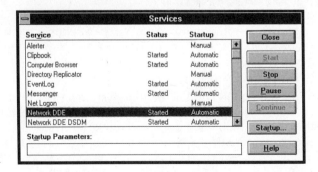

Fig. 7.36

The Services dialog box.

Figure 7.36 shows that Network DDE was started automatically and is currently active. You can press the **S**top button or the **P**ause button to change its run status; however, **S**tart and **C**ontinue are grayed out because Network DDE is already running.

The Devices Option

When you select the Devices Option from the Control Panel, the Devices dialog box shown in figure 7.37 is displayed.

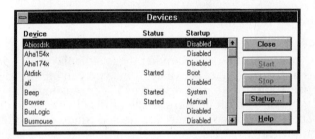

Fig. 7.37

The Devices dialog box.

There are many possible devices. Many are not connected to your computer and are disabled. Others are available and may or may not have been started, either automatically or manually. From this dialog box, you can start or stop any device, as well as change its default start-up type. Possible types are **B**oot, **S**ystem, **A**utomatic, **M**anual, and **D**isabled.

The UPS Option

If you have an uninterruptible power supply (UPS) connected to your system to protect you from a power outage, use the UPS option on the Control Panel to set up Windows NT to work with it. Figure 7.38 shows the UPS dialog box.

The UPS should be installed on one of your system's COM ports so that it can communicate its status to the computer. From the UPS dialog box, you can specify which COM port, and tell Windows NT about some of the specific characteristics of your UPS, such as whether it has a power failure signal, a low battery signal, or the ability to be shut down remotely by the computer. Additional characteristics that vary from one UPS to another include battery life and recharge time. From this dialog box, you can also set the time interval between a power failure and the first warning message to appear on users' screens. You can also set the delay between the first message and subsequent messages.

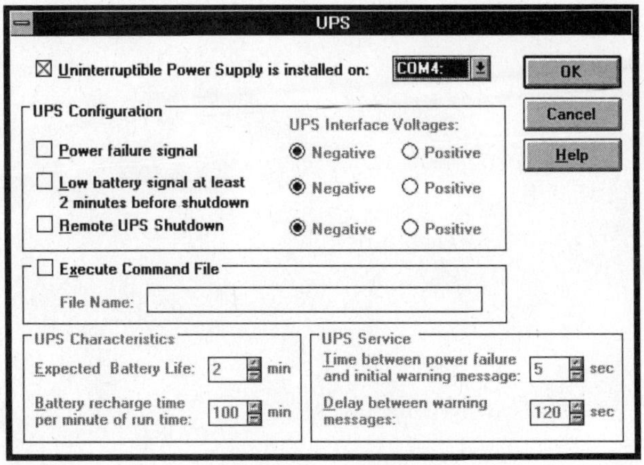

Fig. 7.38

The UPS dialog box.

Summary

Working with the Control Panel is something you need to do only to get your system working better, to customize your system, or to add fonts, printers, or drivers to your system.

Managing Fonts

The days of limited font selections—when the one or two fonts that came with the printer were the only fonts you had—are long gone. Fortunately, with Windows NT and TrueType, the days of complex solutions to the problem of limited font selections also are gone. TrueType brings you easily accessible, built-in, scalable fonts that don't care what kind of printer or display monitor you have.

Windows NT comes equipped with only a few TrueType fonts, but you can easily add more fonts to your system. Many font manufacturers offer TrueType fonts, so you aren't limited to using only TrueType fonts with Windows. You still can use any downloadable fonts that you may have purchased previously. You also can use, if you want, the fonts built into the printer along with the TrueType fonts.

Understanding Fonts

Loosely defined, a *font* is a style of type, or the way the letters and numbers look—whether straight-sided *sans serif* fonts or *serif* fonts with strokes (serifs) that extend from the ends of each line (see fig. 8.1). Fonts can appear wide and rounded, or thin and condensed. Fonts can have an old-fashioned appearance or look contemporary. Type design is an art form hundreds of years old, and thousands of type styles are available.

Despite the many type styles in existence, only a few basic categories of type styles exist: serif, sans serif, script, symbol, and decorative fonts are the most common styles. Serif type styles are characterized by thick and thin lines with tiny strokes (or serifs) at the ends of each line. Because these fonts are considered more readable than other fonts, you see serif type styles used in most books, magazines, and newspapers. Sans serif type styles have lines of uniform thickness and have no strokes (or serifs) at the end of each line. Because these fonts are easier to read from a distance, sans serif type styles are frequently used in signs and bold headlines. Script type styles resemble hand-writing; symbol type styles replace characters with mathematical or *dingbat* symbols. Finally, decorative type styles each have a specialized appearance.

The terminology used to describe fonts and type styles can be confus-ing. Windows defines a font as a type and the style: Times regular is a font; Times New Roman italic is a font; Arial bold is a font. Each font may appear in a wide range of sizes. Fonts are grouped in type families: the Times New Roman family includes Times New Roman regular, Times New Roman bold, Times New Roman italic, and Times New Ro-man bold italic. Most serif and sans serif type families come in four font styles: regular, bold, italic, and bold italic. Symbol and decorative type styles usually include only a single font style.

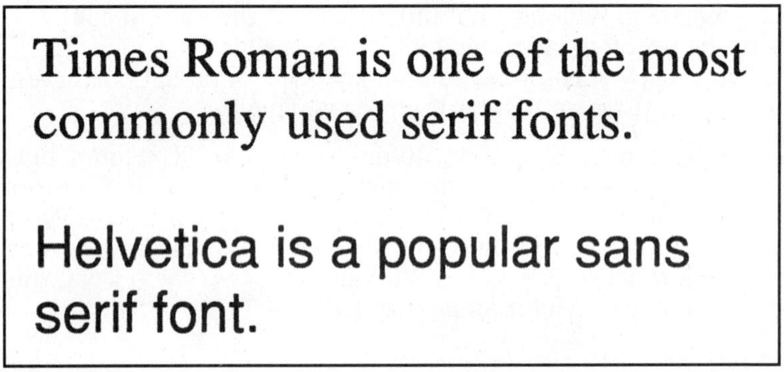

Times Roman is one of the most commonly used serif fonts.

Helvetica is a popular sans serif font.

Fig. 8.1

Times Roman is one of the most popular serif fonts; Helvetica is a common sans serif font.

Type is measured in *points*, and an inch contains 72 points. A typical type size for a newspaper may be 9 or 10 points. Books frequently are printed in 10- or 11-point fonts. Subheadings are larger: 12, 14, or even 18 points. Titles range from 18 points up to about 36 points. Screaming headlines in a newspaper may measure more than 100 points.

Early computers used *monospace* type, which resembled an old type-writer with each character occupying the same horizontal width on a page. A narrow *i* occupied the same space as a wide *w*. The fonts on many computers today, however, are *proportional* rather than monospace: each character's width is appropriate to the character. An *i* occupies much less horizontal space than a *w*. Although you are going to use proportional fonts for most work, Windows also provides a monospace font (Courier New).

Type does more than deliver words to a reader. Type makes the text easier or harder to read, determines how much text fits on a page, creates a mood, and sets a tone. Don't use type carelessly; pick the font best suited to the job.

Understanding How Computers Use Fonts

With so many fonts available, you may find it comforting to know that most computers have access to only a select group of fonts. This knowledge greatly simplifies the job of selecting the right font for the task. (And you can always add more fonts to the system as you grow more discriminating about the fonts you use.)

Computers gain access to fonts in several ways. Fonts may be built into the operating system, such as Windows NT TrueType fonts. Fonts may be built into the printer, as in many PostScript printers, some HP LaserJet models, and most dot-matrix printers. Fonts also may be added to the printer with a cartridge or added to the computer hard disk as soft fonts, which are downloaded to the printer either before or as the fonts are needed.

The fonts that reside in the computer or on the printer are stored in one of two ways, either as bitmap representations or as scalable outlines.

Bitmap fonts store a unique bitmap (or graphic) image for each font in each size (see fig. 8.2).

When you want to print a 10-point Helvetica bold capital E, the computer searches for that specific bitmap. Bitmap fonts can quickly consume a large amount of storage space on the computer, in the printer, or in both. Many downloadable and cartridge fonts use bitmap technology.

Scalable outline fonts store an outline of each character in a font and, when needed, scale the outline to size (see fig. 8.3).

Because only one outline is scaled to create all sizes, scalable fonts usually consume far less disk storage space than do bitmap fonts. PostScript fonts, TrueType fonts, and fonts built into the HP LaserJet III are scalable fonts.

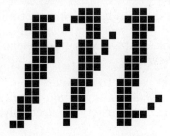

No matter how you store fonts in your system, each font must fulfill two roles: it must appear on-screen and print on the printer. Before TrueType, computers needed separate screen and printer fonts because monitors have a different resolution than printers. Even scalable fonts depended on bitmap fonts for on-screen display because these fonts could be scaled only to printer resolution.

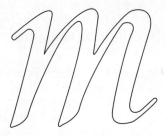

With the introduction of TrueType, however, a single font outline fulfills both roles. The TrueType outline scales to any resolution—screen resolution, dot-matrix printer resolution, laser printer resolution, or high-quality typesetting resolution.

TrueType fonts, therefore, have two space-saving advantages over other fonts: these fonts are scalable, so only one picture of each character is needed (rather than an image for each character in each size) and these fonts are *device-independent*, so only one version of the font must reside in the system.

Windows offers another advantage over DOS in using fonts. Some DOS applications each require separate font files, which means that you must reinstall the same font for each separate application (these duplicated font files can quickly consume a large amount of disk space). Windows, however, shares resources among applications. After you install a font in Windows, the font is available to all Windows applications that support multiple font usage.

Using TrueType Fonts

Windows NT comes with TrueType font technology built in, along with 14 TrueType fonts in five families. These scalable fonts are installed in Windows and are ready to use immediately.

Three of the TrueType families are Times New Roman, Arial, and Courier New (see fig. 8.4). Each family includes regular, bold, italic, and bold italic fonts. The Symbol font is made up of only a single font. The Wingdings font also is a single-font family. Times New Roman, a serif font, is similar to the popular Times Roman font. Arial, a sans serif font, is similar to Helvetica.

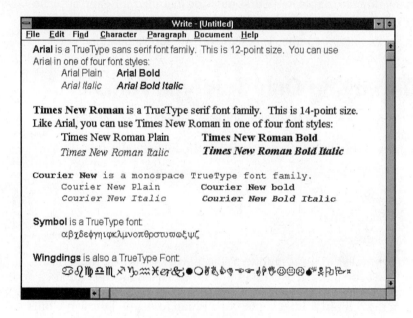

Fig. 8.4

The Windows TrueType fonts.

TrueType offers the following advantages over other alternatives for producing fonts on-screen and on the printer:

- TrueType is a scalable font, so only a single version of each font is stored in the computer. A single outline can produce a font of any size. In contrast, bitmap fonts store a different picture for each font in each size and either consume massive amounts of storage or severely limit the number of sizes available.

- TrueType fonts adapt to both the screen and the printer. A single outline suffices for both and produces equally high quality on both screen and printer. Most other fonts, however, require separate screen and printer fonts. To save disk space, many fonts come in limited screen sizes only, rendering blocky representations of a size you request that is not stored as a screen font.

■ Whether you use a laser printer or a dot-matrix printer, TrueType fonts print on all printers that Windows supports. Many other fonts are printer specific, so you're tied to using a single printer or, if you switch printers, you may switch to a different set of fonts, which results in different line breaks and page breaks. With TrueType, you can print the same fonts on all printers.

A final advantage of TrueType over many downloadable fonts is that TrueType fonts are immediately available to all Windows applications; many downloadable fonts first must be installed for each application you use.

Because of the benefits, TrueType is a Windows default.

Displaying Only TrueType Fonts

When you installed Windows NT, you selected a printer driver for the printer that you use. That printer, of course, has built-in fonts. For example, an HP III LaserJet printer has the following fonts built in:

CG Times

Courier

Line Printer

Universe

When you list fonts, Windows NT displays the printer fonts, in addition to TrueType fonts, and bitmap fonts (discussed more in the next section). When you choose a font to use in an application, you may select from the built-in printer fonts, the bitmap fonts, or TrueType fonts.

Because of the advantages of TrueType fonts listed in the preceding section, many users decide to only use TrueType fonts. Instead of listing all fonts available to Windows NT, you can list only TrueType fonts, and avoid displaying a long list of fonts, many of which you don't use.

Using the Control Panel, you can limit the fonts that Windows displays to only TrueType fonts. To display only TrueType fonts, follow these steps:

1. Display the Windows NT Program Manager and open the Main window.

2. Choose the Control Panel by double-clicking the Control Panel icon or by pressing arrow keys to select the Control Panel icon. Press Enter. The Control Panel window appears.

3. Choose the Fonts icon by double-clicking it or by pressing arrow keys to select it and then pressing Enter. As shown in figure 8.5, the Fonts window appears.

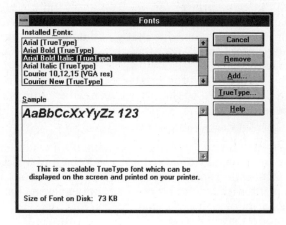

Fonts currently installed are listed in the Installed Fonts list box.

4. Choose the **TrueType** button. The TrueType dialog box appears (see fig. 8.6).

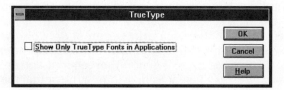

5. To display only TrueType fonts in applications, select the **S**how Only TrueType Fonts in Applications option.

6. Choose OK. The Fonts dialog box is again the active dialog box.

7. Choose Close.

Now, only TrueType fonts display in applications.

Using Non-TrueType Fonts

Although TrueType offers significant advantages, for some people TrueType also has a big disadvantage: Windows ships with only a few TrueType fonts. You may need more fonts, and as a result, you may have already invested in non-TrueType fonts.

Fortunately, you can continue to use the existing fonts and also the new TrueType fonts.

Non-TrueType fonts come in various styles and may be *built-in fonts*, which are built into the printer (as are PostScript fonts, LaserJet III fonts, and many dot-matrix fonts). Fonts may come as *cartridge fonts*, which are contained in a cartridge that you plug into a printer and which act like printer fonts. Another way to add non-TrueType fonts to the system is with *soft fonts*, also known as downloadable fonts. Built-in and cartridge fonts reside in the printer. Soft fonts reside in the computer and are downloaded to the printer as needed (this process may happen by default, or you may need to use a command to download the fonts).

Although the fonts you add may have scalable outlines to use on the printer, these fonts usually display bitmap screen fonts. This may be true of both printer and soft fonts. Screen fonts come from one of two sources. For printer fonts with no corresponding screen fonts, Windows includes a set of generic bitmap screen fonts in serif, sans serif, and symbol models, available in 8-, 10-, 12-, 14-, 18-, and 24-point sizes; a Courier screen font is available in 10-, 12-, and 15-point sizes. Some printer fonts have corresponding screen fonts that match the printer fonts, and when you install them, you decide the sizes to include. Because a bitmap font file can be quite large—especially the larger font sizes—the number of bitmap screen font sizes is limited.

Bitmap screen fonts have long presented a problem to people concerned with making a screen display closely match the printed output. Bitmap screen fonts fail to match printer output in two ways. First, if you don't have screen fonts to specifically match the printer fonts, Windows substitutes the closest generic screen font and spaces the on-screen characters as closely as possible to the actual font's print requirements. The line and page breaks may be correct, but don't count on accurate letter and word spacing. Second, if you specify a size that doesn't match an available screen font size, Windows scales the nearest bitmap size to the size you want, which often results in a jagged-looking letter. (At large point sizes, Windows may substitute a vector font, designed for use on plotters. *Vector fonts* appear on-screen as outlines.)

TrueType solves at least part of the problem of mismatched screen appearance and printer output. With TrueType, Windows creates display fonts in one of two ways. If no screen font specific to the font exists, Windows substitutes the nearest TrueType font, accurately scaling the font to size. If, for example, you choose the Bookman font (which is installed in your PostScript printer but for which you have no corresponding screen font), Windows substitutes the serif TrueType font Times New Roman for the screen display. Therefore, with TrueType, fonts look better than if Windows scales a bitmap screen font to size.

However, even with TrueType, if Windows detects a screen font specifically designed to match the printer font, the screen font is used for display, rather than the TrueType font (see the section "Using Non-TrueType Fonts with TrueType," for more information).

Another solution to the problem of mismatched screen and printer fonts is a type management application (such as Adobe Type Manager, which scales screen fonts, or Agfa Type Director, which creates bitmap screen fonts from scalable printer fonts).

Working with Mismatched Screen and Printer Fonts

If the printer font doesn't have a matching set of screen fonts, Windows uses its own screen fonts to try to match the printer fonts. These screen fonts may not be as accurate as custom screen fonts, however, and you may see discrepancies between the text on-screen and the text as printed.

This difference between screen and printer fonts can cause the following problems:

- Words wrap at a different place on-screen than they do in print.

- Titles or sidebars extend further than expected.

- On-screen text extends past the margin set in the ruler.

- On-screen text in tables overfills cells in tables.

- Bold or italic formatting causes lines to appear longer on-screen than the lines look when printed.

Another cause of mismatched screen fonts and printer fonts arises when fonts unavailable in the printer are used on-screen. This problem can occur because selecting a font—even a font unavailable on the current printer—is possible in many applications. (Understanding this quirk can be useful if you want to create a document for printing on another printer.) If you use a font not available in the printer in the document, Windows substitutes a font close in style and size to the unavailable font. Windows tries to find a similar typeface and size. If the requested size isn't found, Windows substitutes the next smaller size.

You can remedy these issues in one of two ways. First, if you are using soft fonts or a font manager, make sure that you generate and install the screen fonts that go with the printer's soft fonts. Second, use fonts available in the printer. You can tell if a font is in the current printer because a small printer icon appears to the left of the font name in your application's Font list.

Using Non-TrueType Fonts with TrueType

TrueType fonts work side by side with non-TrueType fonts. As discussed previously in this chapter, Windows NT displays an associated screen font for a non-TrueType font, if one is available. However, if no screen font is available, Windows represents the font on the screen using a similar TrueType font.

Many printer fonts don't include corresponding bitmap screen fonts. In previous versions of Windows before Windows NT, applications depended on the generic Windows screen fonts to supply screen fonts for these printer fonts. Windows' *font metrics* files provided information to help the application in spacing characters and words more accurately and increasing the similarity between screen display and printed output. TrueType, however, takes over the job of supplying screen fonts for printer fonts that don't have screen fonts. One advantage of using TrueType scalable screen fonts is that you can scale these fonts to any size. Bitmap screen fonts, however, are not scalable and when you request a size not included on the disk (such as 11 or 13 points), Windows fashions a rather jagged-looking font from the nearest available font size.

One disadvantage, however, exists when using TrueType screen fonts. TrueType substitutes the nearest TrueType font for the font you request so that the on-screen representation of a PostScript font, such as Helvetica (for which you may not have a specific screen font), looks exactly the same as the TrueType font Arial, shown in figure 8.7. You see the difference between the two fonts when you print. Although line and page breaks remain accurate, character and word spacing are inaccurate when Windows substitutes a TrueType screen font for the printer font you request.

To get an accurate screen display, you must either use TrueType fonts only, which look the same on-screen and on the printed page, or you must provide a screen font that matches the printer font. If you have a screen font that matches the printer font, TrueType uses this screen font rather than scaling the closest TrueType font. Therefore, you see a screen display that closely matches the printed page. The tradeoff is that bitmap screen fonts take up extra disk space, but the screen display is more accurate.

Adding New Fonts

You can easily add fonts to a computer, whether they are TrueType fonts or another kind of font.

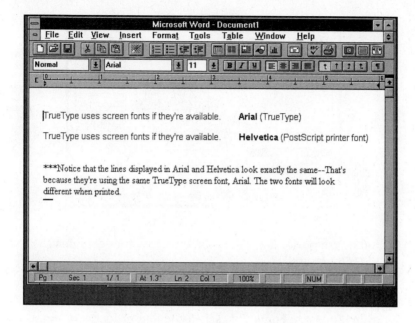

Fig. 8.7

TrueType
displays non-
TrueType printer
fonts with a
TrueType
scalable font if
no correspond-
ing screen font
exists.

To install TrueType fonts, you can use the Fonts program you see in the Windows Control Panel. To install some downloadable or cartridge fonts, you may need to use special installation software that comes with the fonts. Printer-resident fonts are usually installed by default when you install a printer.

Before you add a new font, be sure that the original font diskettes are available. You need these disks during the installation process.

To add a new font to the system by using the Fonts application, follow these steps:

1. Display the Windows Program Manager and open the Main Window.

2. Choose the Control Panel.

3. Choose the Fonts icon. The Fonts window appears. Fonts currently installed are listed in the Installed Fonts list box.

4. Choose the Add button. The Add Fonts dialog box, shown in figure 8.8, appears.

5. In the Drives list, select the drive that contains the font you want to add.

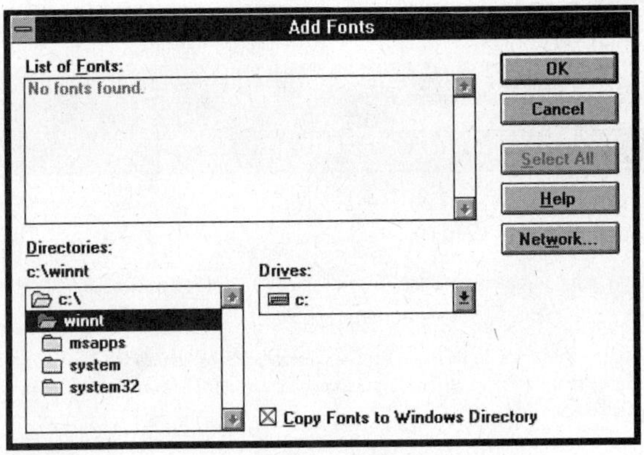

Fig. 8.8

The Add Fonts dialog box.

6. In the **Directories** list, select the directory that contains the font you want to add.

   The fonts in the directory and drive you selected appear in the List of **F**onts box.

7. From the List of **F**onts box, select the font or fonts you want to add.

   If you want to add all the fonts, choose the **S**elect All button.

8. If you decide not to add the fonts to the system, but rather, to use the fonts from the current drive and directory, deselect the **C**opy Fonts to Windows Directory so that no X appears in the check box.

   Use this option only if you want to use the fonts occasionally and don't want to use up disk space by storing these fonts permanently.

9. Choose OK to add the font or fonts to the system.

10. Choose Close to close the Fonts window.

When you install fonts by using the Font Installer, you install both the screen fonts and printer fonts at the same time.

If you are adding fonts by installing a new font cartridge, you must set up the printer to recognize the new cartridge. If the fonts are built into the print driver, you need do nothing more. If, however, you don't have access to the fonts after you installed the printer and set up the cartridge, you need to install the fonts. Use the Font Installer or check the font documentation to see if you must use a special font installation application.

To set up a new font cartridge, take the following steps:

1. Turn off the printer and insert the cartridge. Turn the printer back on.

2. From the Main group in the Program Manager, choose Control Panel.

3. From the Control Panel, choose Printers.

4. From the Installed **P**rinters list, select the printer into which, in step 1, you inserted the new font cartridge.

5. Choose **S**etup.

6. From the Ca**r**tridges list, select the name of the cartridge you inserted.

7. Choose OK to close the Setup dialog box. Then choose Close to close the Printer dialog box. Close the Control Panel.

Using Fonts in Windows Applications

After installation, fonts become available for use in all Windows applications. Because you may have several kinds of fonts installed in Windows, special icons identify each font. By looking at these icons, which appear to the left of the font names in font list boxes, you can tell whether a font is a TrueType font, a printer font, or a Windows system font.

In the font list (from Word for Windows, a word processing application) shown in figure 8.9, you can see that TrueType fonts display a TT icon to the left of the TrueType font, and printer fonts display a printer icon.

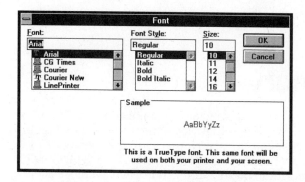

Fig. 8.9

In most Font lists, you can identify fonts by the icons that appear to the left of the font name.

Removing Old Fonts

You can remove from Windows a font that you no longer need. Removing fonts saves memory on a computer with limited memory or a computer running memory-hungry applications. If you remove the disk file, you also save disk space (but you must reinstall this font to be able to use the font again in future work sessions).

To remove a font, follow these steps:

1. Display the Windows Program Manager and open the Main Window.

2. Choose the Control Panel.

3. Choose the Fonts icon. The Fonts window appears. Currently installed fonts are listed in the Installed Fonts list box.

4. In the Installed Fonts list box, select the font you want to remove.

5. Choose the Remove button.

   A dialog box confirms that you want to remove the font. To proceed with removing the font, choose Yes.

6. If you also want to remove the font files from the disk, select the Delete Font File From Disk check box.

   Do not delete font files from the disk if you unselected the Copy Fonts to Window Directory option when you installed the fonts (in other words, if you were using fonts from the original disks rather than copying the fonts to Windows). Doing so deletes the font files from the original font disk, and you cannot reinstall these fonts.

7. Choose Yes or choose Yes to All to remove several fonts at once.

   You return to the Fonts dialog box.

8. Choose Close.

Don't remove the MS Sans Serif font, which is used in Windows dialog boxes.

Summary

Without doing anything special, you have access to Windows TrueType fonts, scalable fonts that look the same on-screen and on the printer. TrueType fonts offer many advantages over other kinds of fonts and work with any printer Windows supports. TrueType fonts consume less disk space than bitmap fonts and provide a more accurate screen display than other fonts. Three TrueType font families come free with Windows: Times New Roman, Arial, and Courier—each font is available in plain, bold, italic, and bold italic styles. Windows also includes the TrueType font Symbol, available only in plain style.

You also can use soft, or downloadable, fonts with Windows, as well as printer-resident fonts and cartridge fonts. If the fonts that come with Windows and the printer don't give you enough variety, you can purchase and easily install additional fonts.

Nearly every stand-alone Windows application takes advantage of the fonts in Windows. To learn more about using applications, refer to Chapter 1, which covers basic Windows operations. To learn more about specific applications, turn to other Que books, such as *Look Your Best with Word for Windows*, by Susan Plumley; *Using Word for Windows 2*, Special Edition, by Ron Person and Karen Rose; *Using PowerPoint* by James G. Meade; *Using Microsoft Publisher*, by Kathy Murray; and *Using Excel 4 for Windows*, Special Edition, by Ron Person.

Using the Print Manager

Applications designed to run on the Windows family of operating system products share not only a common graphical interface but also printing resources. In DOS applications, such as Lotus 1-2-3 and WordPerfect, printer drivers are built into each application. These drivers—a driver for each different printer—translate the text or data you want to print into commands understood by the printer. But Windows family applications have no printer drivers. Instead, these applications, such as Excel and Word for Windows, use the printer drivers built into Windows NT. (Some applications, such as WordPerfect for Windows, can use both their own printer drivers and the Windows drivers.) Windows NT has a special application, the Print Manager, that manages printing for all Windows applications. The Print Manager is initially located in the Main group window.

The Print Manager springs into action when you issue the command to print a file, causing two things to happen. First, the Print Manager intercepts text or graphics output and sends it not to the printer, but to a *buffer*, or *queue*, where files waiting to be printed are lined up (or queued) for printing. Second, these output files are routed, in the order received, to the printer.

Windows NT gives the Print Manager control over the printing rather than let the application control printing (as happens with DOS applications), so you can continue using the application or switch to another application while the Print Manager handles the print job. You don't have to wait for the document to print before you can start working on something else.

> **You Cannot Use an Application until the File Reaches the Print Manager**
>
> While the Print Manager is printing a file, you can continue working with the application. If you print a large file, however, you may have to wait a while for the file to reach the Print Manager. You can't use the application while the application sends the file to the Print Manager. (You can use other applications, however.) Be patient; the file reaches the Print Manager more quickly than it takes to print!

Printing a File

The procedure for printing may vary slightly from application to application, but the basic steps remain the same when you print from a Windows application. Usually, two steps are required.

First, you set up the printer you plan to use by selecting its icon from the Print Manager window. Next, choose **P**rinter **P**roperties Set**u**p and **P**rinter **P**roperties Deta**i**ls **J**ob Defaults... to set up things the way you want them.

The second step in printing from a Windows NT application is to print the file by choosing the **F**ile **P**rint command. Depending on the application, in this step, you identify the number of copies to print, the range of pages to print, and other choices. (For details about printing with Windows NT applications, refer to the application documentation or to a Que book, such as *Using Excel 4 for Windows*, Special Edition or *Using Word for Windows.*)

After you have issued the print command from the Windows application, the Print Manager takes over, transferring information and instructions to the printer as you work.

> **T I P**
>
> To print a Windows file, you must install the correct printer drivers when you install Windows NT or use the Windows NT Control Panel to install the printer drivers after you install Windows NT. Windows NT already supports most popular printers. You can set up the printer from the Print Manager by choosing the **Printer Properties Setup** command.

Although the Print Manager manages the task of printing, you manage the Print Manager. You can open the Print Manager window to see which files are in the queue to print on which printer, and you can make changes. For example, you can pause the printing, pause individual print jobs, or cancel a print job. These procedures and more are explained in following sections of this chapter.

Different Printers Produce Different Results

Printers have different characteristics and capabilities. Some laser printers print at a resolution of 300 dots per inch; some dot-matrix printers print at a much coarser resolution. Some printers have built-in fonts that you may want to use; with others, you rely on the Windows TrueType technology to supply fonts. Some printers have enough memory to print a full page of graphics; others have limited memory. Before you print a document, become familiar with your printer's capabilities and limitations.

Using the Print Manager Window

Activate the Print Manager in the same way you activate other applications: Double-click the program icon, or use the arrow keys to select the Print Manager icon and press the Enter key. The Print Manager icon is located in the Program Manager's Main program group.

When you activate the Print Manager, the Print Manager window opens on-screen. It can show the status of current print jobs and enable you to change several things about the print jobs, such as orientation, print resolution, and halftone color.

Understanding the Print Manager Window

The Print Manager window contains printer status icons that, when opened, show the status of the print queue for the selected printer. The window shows you which printers are active, which printers are printing, which files are being printed, and which other files are in the queue for printing. The window also can show you the time and date you sent the file to the printer and the size of the file. Figure 9.1 shows a sample Print Manager window.

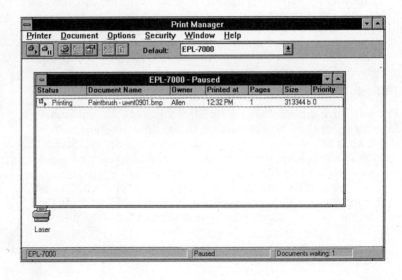

Fig. 9.1

The Print Manager window showing the status of a print job.

The Print Manager window contains several menus and a toolbar to control printing. The following chart lists the **P**rinter menu choices and their uses. These choices apply to the currently selected printer, as indicated by the selected icon at the bottom of the Print Manager window.

Option	Description
Connect to Printer...	Creates a connection to a remote printer
Create Printer...	Creates a new printer and installs the required drivers
Remove Printer...	Deletes the selected printer

Option	Description
Properties...	Displays and permits the configuration of the printer, the driver and shares (shares are printers located on other nodes on the network)
Forms...	Displays the forms database on the selected printer
Pause	Stops printing on the selected printer temporarily
Resume	Restarts the selected printer after pausing
Purge Printer...	Deletes all documents on the selected printer
Server viewer...	Displays the printers on the server

The **D**ocument menu controls the printing of individual documents. Options in this menu are explained in the following:

Option	Description
Remove Document	Deletes the selected document from the printer
Details...	Displays information about the document
Pause	Pauses printing of the selected document
Resume	Resumes the printing of the selected document
Restart	Restarts the printing of the selected document

The **O**ptions menu enables you to decide whether to show or hide the toolbar at the top of the window and the status bar at the bottom. You may also decide whether to save the new settings when you exit the Print Manager.

The **S**ecurity menu displays permissions and the events currently being audited on the selected printer. It also allows a user with a high enough privilege level to take ownership of the selected printer. The Audit function records which user or group of users has used the printer. The owner of a printer can change the privilege levels of other users.

The **W**indow menu gives you the familiar choices for cascading or tiling windows and arranging icons, along with refreshing the selected window. It also enables you to select a printer and view its current status.

Start the Print Manager from the Program Manager

The Print Manager starts by default when you print a document. You can run the Print Manager, however, even if you aren't printing. You might do this when you want to change settings, add a new printer, or delete an old one. In the Program Manager, activate the main window. Then double-click the Print Manager icon or press the arrow keys to select the Print Manager icon and press Enter. To close the Print Manager, choose the **P**rinter Exit command.

Figure 9.2 shows the status window for the EPL-7000 printer, obtained by double-clicking the EPL-7000 icon in the Print Manager window. Important facts about each document in the queue are given, including the document name, owner, time the file was sent to the print queue, number of pages, number of bytes, and priority. The printer is paused and five documents are in the print queue. The fifth one, UWNT0707.BMP is selected. None of the documents is currently being printed, as shown by the blank Status column.

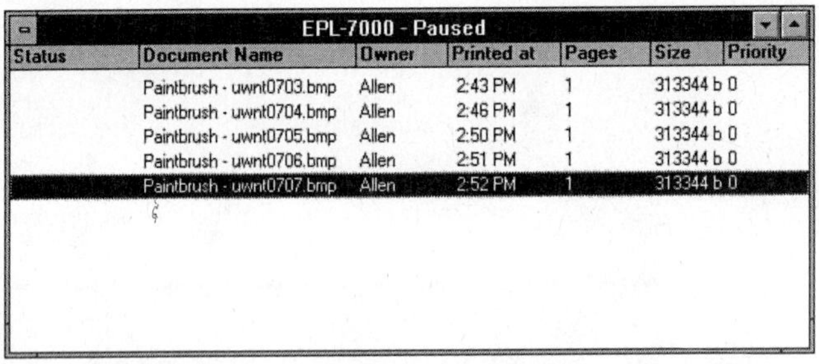

Status	Document Name	Owner	Printed at	Pages	Size	Priority
	Paintbrush - uwnt0703.bmp	Allen	2:43 PM	1	313344 b	0
	Paintbrush - uwnt0704.bmp	Allen	2:46 PM	1	313344 b	0
	Paintbrush - uwnt0705.bmp	Allen	2:50 PM	1	313344 b	0
	Paintbrush - uwnt0706.bmp	Allen	2:51 PM	1	313344 b	0
	Paintbrush - uwnt0707.bmp	Allen	2:52 PM	1	313344 b	0

EPL-7000 - Paused

Fig. 9.2

The printer status window with queued documents.

You could remove the selected document from the print queue by selecting **R**emove Document from the **D**ocument menu. Any document in the queue can be removed in this manner. Selecting **D**etails... from the **D**ocument menu displays the Document Details dialog box shown in figure 9.3.

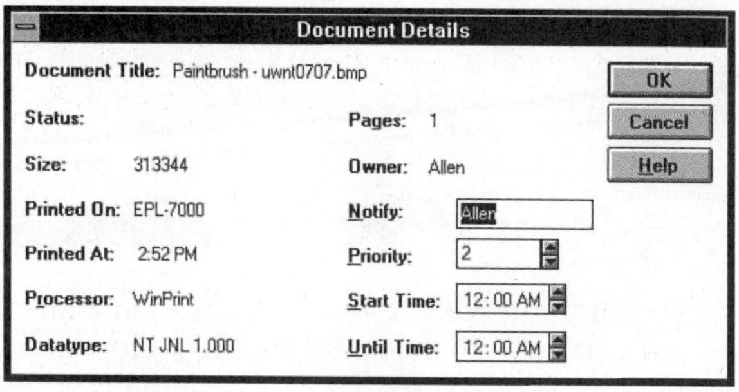

┌───┐
│ ═ Document Details   │
│ Document Title: Paintbrush - uwnt0707.bmp   ┌──────┐ │
│   │ OK │ │
│ Status: Pages: 1   └──────┘ │
│   ┌──────┐ │
│ Size: 313344   Owner: Allen   │Cancel│ │
│   └──────┘ │
│ Printed On: EPL-7000   Notify: [Allen] ┌──────┐ │
│   │ Help │ │
│ Printed At: 2:52 PM   Priority: [2   ]▲▼ └──────┘ │
│   │
│ Processor: WinPrint   Start Time: [12:00 AM]▲▼ │
│   │
│ Datatype: NT JNL 1.000 Until Time: [12:00 AM]▲▼ │
└───┘

Fig. 9.3

The Document Details dialog box.

In this dialog box, you can set a specific print time, indicate who should be notified when the job runs, and change the print priority. You may want to schedule the print job at a time when system usage is low. By setting a higher priority to a print job, you force it to run before jobs of lower priority that are earlier in the queue. Figure 9.3 shows that the priority for UWNT0707.BMP has been raised from 0 to 2; the highest priority is 99. You can also selectively pause files higher in the queue to allow those listed lower to be printed first. Note that once a file has been sent to the printer, pausing it has no effect. Printers with large memories, particularly laser printers, may continue to print long after the Print Manager has put the printer into Pause mode.

Stopping the Printer after Print Manager Has Sent It a Job

The printer may print *buffered* information long after you delete the file currently printing. To stop the printer, you may have to reset it to clear the print buffer. You can reset the printer by turning it off and back on again (or by selecting the printer's reset option, if one is available).

Changing the Printer Priority

Because Windows NT can print in the background as you work in the foreground, the PC must divide resources between these two tasks. The foreground task always has a priority at least equal to the priority of the background tasks, including printing. Because this priority affects the entire system, it is not set from the Print Manager, but from the System selection on the Control Panel. If you select Tasking... from the System dialog box, you can set foreground and background responsiveness to one of three states. The default is Best Foreground Application Response Time. To give background processes more CPU time, choose Foreground Application More Responsive than Background. To give the background processes as much time as possible, select Foreground and Background Applications Equally Responsive.

Displaying Print Manager Alerts

Occasionally, the printer needs attention. For example, if you're printing envelopes and you need to insert the next envelope, your printer may alert you to load the envelope. Paper may jam in the printer, to which your printer alerts you of a problem. The Print Manager handles these alert messages by flashing either the Print Manager icon or the inactive title bar to let you know a message is waiting. When you activate the Print Manager, the message is displayed on the screen.

Using the Print Manager Window in Windows NT

The Print Manager window in Windows NT displays icons for all the printers available for your use. These printers are

- Printers connected to your computer

- Printers connected to your computer and designated as shared so that others on your network can use them

- Printers connected to other computers on your network and designated as shared and available for your use

The *default printer*, which is the printer used automatically when you issue the Print command in Windows applications, is specified in the toolbar. If you open a printer's icon, its window lists the files currently in the print queue for that printer. To the left of each file name is an icon indicating whether the file is currently printing or paused. Figure 9.4 shows a print queue in which the first file is printing, the second one is paused, and the third file is selected but is neither printing nor paused.

Next to each file name is the log-on name of the person who sent the file to the printer. The Status column indicates the status of the file—for example, whether it is printing, paused, or stopped because of an error. The other columns indicate the time the file was added to the print queue, the number of pages, the file size in bytes, and the print job priority.

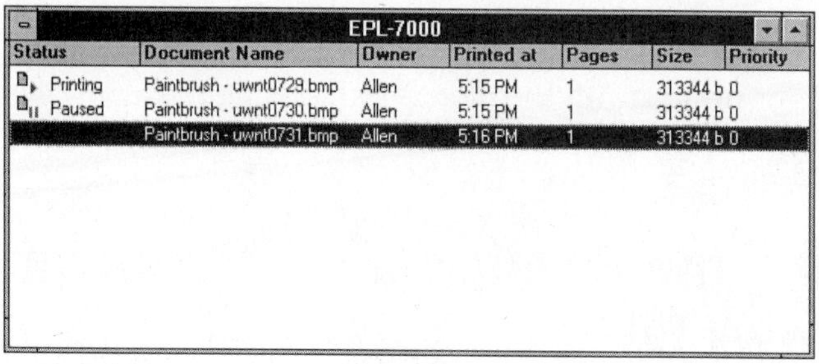

EPL-7000						
Status	Document Name	Owner	Printed at	Pages	Size	Priority
Printing	Paintbrush - uwnt0729.bmp	Allen	5:15 PM	1	313344 b	0
Paused	Paintbrush - uwnt0730.bmp	Allen	5:15 PM	1	313344 b	0
	Paintbrush - uwnt0731.bmp	Allen	5:16 PM	1	313344 b	0

Fig. 9.4

The Printer status window with an active print queue.

At the top of the Print Manager window, just below the menu bar, is the toolbar. It contains several buttons that you can use to control your print jobs, as described in Table 9.1. There is a corresponding menu command for each of these buttons.

Table 9.1 Toolbar functions in the Print Manager

Icon	Button Name	Function
	Connect to Remote Printer	Connects to any shared printer on your network
	Disconnect Network	Disconnects from a network printer
	Display Printer Properties	Displays the Printer Properties dialog box, enabling you to reconfigure the printer
	Pause Printing Document	Temporarily stops the selected document from printing
	Resume Printing Document	Resumes printing of the selected document
	Delete Document	Removes the selected document from the print queue
	Display Document Details	Gives detailed information about the document

To use the toolbar buttons, you first must select the printer or file on which you want to carry out an action. Select the printer or file by clicking the file or printer with the mouse or by using the arrow keys to move the selection bar. Then click the appropriate button.

Pausing the Printing of a Document in Windows NT

The Print Manager enables you to control the order in which documents print by pausing them. In addition to pausing a printer, you can also pause any document in the queue of a printer connected to your computer. For printers on your network but not connected to your computer, you can pause only your own documents.

While a printer or document is paused, the word Paused appears in parentheses in the Status column. When you pause the printer or document, the printer continues to print all text in the printer's buffer; therefore, printing may not stop immediately.

To pause printing, follow these steps:

1. Select the printer or document you want to pause in the Print Manager window.

2. Click the Pause Printing Document button on the toolbar, or choose **P**rinter **P**ause or **D**ocument **P**ause from the Print Manager menu.

To resume printing, follow these steps:

1. Select the printer or document for which you want to resume printing in the Print Manager window.

2. Choose **P**rinter **R**esume or **D**ocument **R**esume from the Print Manager menu.

Deleting a Document from the Queue in Windows NT

When working with Windows NT, you can delete any of the documents on your printer, even those from another user to be printed on your shared printer. If you are printing on a shared printer that is not connected to your computer, you can delete only documents that you created.

To delete a document from the print queue, follow these steps:

1. Select the document you want to remove from the queue.

2. Click the Delete Document button on the toolbar, or choose **Docu**ment **R**emove Document, or press Del.

3. Choose OK or press Enter if a confirmation message box appears.

 NOTE   If you exit the Print Manager by using the **P**rinter E**x**it command, a message box appears and warns you that all pending print jobs will be canceled. Choose OK if your intention is to cancel all print jobs, including those sent to your printer by others on the network.

Using Separator Files

In Windows NT, you can insert a printed separator file between printed documents. This can help you identify the owner of documents on shared printers or simply separate your documents on your own printer. You can use a simple standard separator page, or you can create a custom separator page (or pages) that can include custom fonts and graphics.

To print a separator file, follow these steps:

1. From the Print Manager, choose **P**rinter.

2. Choose **P**roperties....

3. Click the Details... button to display the Printer Details dialog box, which is shown in figure 9.5.

4. Type the name of your separator file in the **S**eparator File field. Alternatively, you can click the Separator File browse button to the right of the field. It will list all the files in the current directory with the SEP extension.

5. Click OK until you get back to the Print Manager. This activates the separator file, which will be printed between every job.

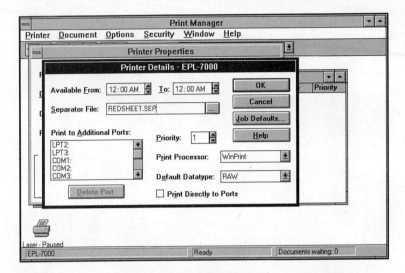

Fig. 9.5

Specifying a
separator file.

Closing the Print Manager Window

If the Print Manager started when you selected to print from an application, the Print Manager shuts down when printing is complete. If you started the Print Manager from the Main program group, however, you must exit the Print Manager manually after printing ends. You also can minimize Print Manager so that you can drag and drop files from the File Manager.

Be careful; if you exit the Print Manager while print jobs are outstanding in the queue, the print jobs are canceled. To close the Print Manager window without canceling print jobs, minimize the window by clicking the minimize button (the down arrow at the top right of the window) or choosing the Minimize command from the Control menu. If the window is minimized to an icon, the Print Manager shuts down after printing is completed.

To exit the Print Manager immediately, choose the **P**rinter E**x**it command.

CAUTION: When you exit the Print Manager while print jobs are still pending, not only your print jobs but also any jobs sent by users sharing your printer are canceled. Be careful! You may want to use the Chat facility available on Mail or send a Mail message to the person who is printing before you exit the Print Manager.

Installing Printers from the Print Manager

You can use the Print Manager to add, configure, or remove a printer on your system—just as you can use the Printers application in the Control Panel. Before you add a printer, be sure to have your original Windows NT diskettes on hand—they contain the necessary printer driver.

To add, configure, or remove a printer using the Print Manager, follow these steps:

1. Choose the Print Manager icon from the Main window in the Program Manager.

2. Choose **P**rinter, then Cre**a**te Printer. The Create Printer dialog box appears.

3. Enter the name of the printer in the Printer **N**ame text box.

4. Select a printer driver for your printer in the **D**river drop-down list box.

5. Enter a description for the printer in the D**e**scription text box (optional).

6. Select the port the printer is attached to from the Print **t**o drop-down list box. You can select a parallel or serial port that is attached to your computer. If you are on a network, you can select a printer attached to another computer on the network.

7. Choose the Details… button.

8. When the Printer Details dialog box appears on the screen, change any of the following and choose OK:

Available **F**rom	The beginning time that the printer is available during the day
To	The ending time that the printer is available during the day
Separator File	The file name that you want printed on a sheet of paper to indicate a new print job
Print to **A**dditional Ports	Assign other printers that you can print to so that your document prints to the first available printer

Priority	Set the priority of the printer
Print Processor	Choose a print processor other than Windows NT
Default Datatype	Indicate the format of the information printed
Print Directly to Ports	When selected, Windows NT bypasses the spooler and sends your document directly to the printer

9. Choose the Settings... button. Change the settings for the port you have attached the printer to, then choose OK.

10. If you want to share this printer on the network, check the box in the bottom half of the screen and enter a Share Name and a Location.

11. When all the data has been entered, click OK in the Create Printer dialog box.

12. If the system lacks the needed driver, it prompts you to insert an installation disk. Install any needed printer driver.

13. Click OK to return to the Print Manager. The new printer has been installed. The printer's icon now shows a hand under it, denoting a shared printer, as shown in figure 9.6.

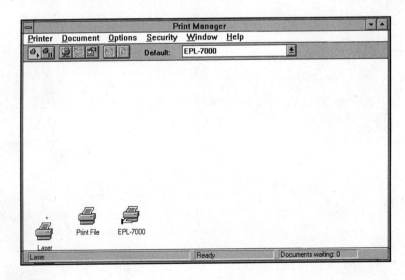

Fig. 9.6

EPL-7000 is now a shared printer.

NOTE You can set the default printer without using the **Printer** Setup command in the Print Manager in Windows NT.

continues

continued
Pull down the Default list in the toolbar and select the printer that you want to be the default printer.

Printing to a File

On occasion, you may want to print to a file rather than to the printer. If you want to print a desktop-published document on a high-resolution typesetter owned by a service bureau, for example, you can more easily print from an EPS (Encapsulated PostScript) file. You create an EPS file by selecting a PostScript printer and then printing to an EPS file (by selecting a PostScript printer, you instruct Windows NT to create a file that is PostScript-compatible). To print to a file, you must create a printer object that prints to a file.

To print to a file, follow these steps:

1. If the Print Manager isn't running, choose the Print Manager icon in the Main group in the Program Manager.

2. Choose Create Printer from the Printer menu.

3. Give the new virtual printer a name, a driver appropriate for the printer that will eventually print the file, and a Print to selection of FILE, as shown in figure 9.7. (FILE is one of the last entries in the Print to drop-down list.)

4. If the driver for the printer you have named has not already been installed, Windows NT Setup pops up a dialog box that prompts you for the full path of the Windows NT distribution files on your installation disks, suggesting A:\ as the default. Follow instructions to install the driver.

5. Choose OK. The new printer window appears in the Print Manager window. You can minimize it to join the other printer icons at the bottom of the window.

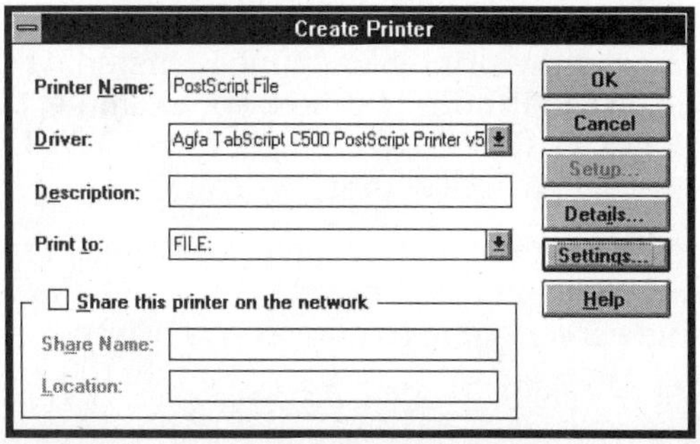

Fig. 9.7

The Create Printer dialog box for printing to a file.

Now when you print from an application, you will be prompted for a path and file name. The print destination will be the file rather than a printer.

NOTE   You do not have to install a new printer to be able to print to a file. You can change a current printer to print to a file using the **P**rinter **P**roperties menu selection from the Print Manager. Then, choose FILE from the Print **t**o drop-down list box. Finally, choose OK to close the Printer Properties dialog box.

Printing on a Network in Windows NT

If you are using Windows NT and are connected to a network, you can print on network printers. A *network printer* is a printer connected to a computer on the network that other users on the network can print to. Before you can print on a network printer, that printer must be designated as *shared* by the person using the computer that the printer is connected to. In the same way, you must *share* a printer connected to your computer before other users can print on it.

Connecting to a Network Printer

Before you can connect to a network printer, you need to install the *printer driver* for that printer on your computer. See the section "Installing Printers from the Print Manager" for instructions on how to install a printer driver from the Print Manager. Then follow these steps.

1. Click the Connect to Printer button on the toolbar, or open the **P**rinter menu and choose **C**onnect to Printer. The Connect to Printer dialog box is displayed (see fig. 9.8).

2. Type the name of the printer to connect, including the server name, in the **P**rinter text box. For example, type **\\TSTANLEY\TSS_HPIIISI** to connect to the TSS_HPIIISI printer on the TSTANLEY server.

   If you do not know the name of the printer, select the printer from the **S**hared Printers list box. Double-click the workgroup name and the server name to display the printers available, as shown in fig. 9.9.

3. Choose OK to connect to the printer.

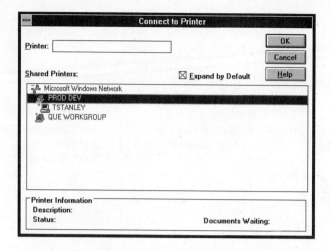

Fig. 9.8

The Connect to Printer dialog box.

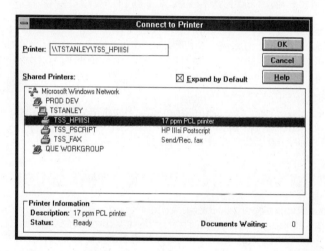

Fig. 9.9

Select a printer to connect to, using the Shared Printers list box.

A printer window appears in the Print Manager for the printer you connected to. However, if Windows NT does not have a printer driver installed for the printer you selected to connect to, the Connect to Printer message box is displayed. If you choose OK from this message box, you can install a printer driver.

Updating Network Queue Status

The Print Manager regularly updates the status of network printer queues displayed in the Print Manager window. However, you can manually update the status if you want an up-to-the-minute status report. To manually update the status of network printer queues, choose the **W**indow Refresh command or press F5.

Printing on a Network

If you share printers with others on a local area network, printing with the Print Manager is a little different from the single-user case. Additional Print Manager options, such as **N**etwork Settings and Network **C**onnections, become available in the **O**ptions menu. You also have the option to bypass the Print Manager, which is sometimes a faster way to print on a network.

Viewing a Network Print Queue

When you print to a network printer, the Print Manager lists the files you previously sent to a printer. By opening the printer's window, you can see all the files everyone on the network has sent to the same printer. Seeing this list can give you an idea of how much time will pass before the printer prints your job.

To view a network print queue, open the Print Manager window, then double-click the target printer's icon.

Viewing Other Network Print Queues

If you have access to a number of printers on a network, you can view queues for all the printers before deciding which printer to use—even printers that aren't installed or activated. Before you can print to a printer, you must install it by using the **P**rinter Cre**a**te Printer command in the Print Manager or by choosing the Printers application in the Control Panel. See Chapter 7, "Customizing with the Control Panel," for details about installing printers.

Setting Printer Security

With the **S**ecurity **P**ermissions... choice from the Print Manager menu, the owner of a printer can specify the level of access to the printer that various groups of users will have. Full Control is the highest level of access, and No Access is the lowest. Between them are Manage Documents and Print. A person with Print access can print but do nothing else. A person with Manage Documents access may alter settings for a document, and pause, resume, restart, or delete it from the print queue.

The **S**ecurity **A**uditing... choice allows you to track printer usage. You can specify which groups, individual users, or specific actions to audit.

The **S**ecurity **O**wner... command gives a person with Full Control permission the opportunity to take ownership of the printer. A printer's owner can change the permission levels of all other users.

Correcting Printing Problems

Occasionally, problems arise when you try to print. If you run into trouble, read through the following checklist. Sometimes, the solution to printing problems is simpler than you expect. Many printer difficulties arise from installation and setup errors that you can correct by using the **P**rinter **P**roperties... command. (You also can use the Printers application in the Control Panel to do the same thing. See Chapter 7.)

- *Is the printer plugged in and turned on?*

- *Is the printer out of paper?*

- *Do you have the right printer cable, and is it correctly connected to the printer and the computer?*

- *Is the printer driver installed in Windows NT?*

  To install printers for Windows NT, use the **P**rinter **C**reate **P**rinter... command in the Print Manager, or the Printers application in the Control Panel.

- *Did you select the correct printer name when you installed the printer?*

  Choose the **P**rinter **P**roperties... command in the Print Manager. Then check which printer driver is listed. Make sure that you have the right one.

- *Is the correct printer selected as the default printer?*

  Check the toolbar.

- *Is the printer connected to the correct port?*

  Choose the **P**rinter **P**roperties... command in the Print Manager or the Printers application in the Control Panel to make sure the correct port is shown in the Print to list box.

■ *Are the port settings correct?*

Use the Ports application in the Control Panel to select the port settings. If the serial printer loses text, try reducing the baud rate.

■ *Are the paper source, size, and orientation correct?*

Check the **File Print** Setup command in the application. You also can choose the **Printer Properties...** command in the Print Manager or the Printers application in the Control Panel and select **Setup**.

■ *Is TrueType enabled?*

Choose the Fonts application in the Control Panel; then choose the **TrueType** button and select the **Enable TrueType** fonts option.

■ *Is the font cartridge all the way in the slot?*

Push the cartridge in firmly.

■ *Are the soft fonts properly installed?*

Check the installation manual that came with the font package or choose the Fonts application in the Control Panel and then choose the **Add** button to add fonts.

■ *Was the printer turned off after you downloaded fonts?*

Download the fonts again.

■ *Is the printer short on memory?*

A printer that lacks enough memory may not print all the fonts or graphics you expect; printers like the HP LaserJet with 512K of memory may not have enough memory to print multiple fonts or large graphics. You must either print smaller graphics or buy more memory for the printer.

Summary

The Print Manager really can speed up work because you can print in the background as you work in the foreground. Now that you know how to use the Print Manager, you may want to learn more about preparing printers to work with Windows applications. Part III, "Using Windows NT Accessories," discusses each of the various applications.

PART

III

Using Windows NT Accessories

Using Microsoft Mail

A workgroup can accomplish far more when everyone can communicate easily. Mail is a program that enables you and others in your workgroup to send and store *messages*, which are text notes that you send to or receive from other users on your network. You also have the option of attaching files to a message, for example, a word processing document, or spreadsheet file. Mail is a stripped-down version of Microsoft's full-featured mail application. Although it lacks some of the more high-powered electronic mail features, Mail's design meets the needs of small groups of users who work together.

In some ways, Mail offers features more powerful than mail applications not designed specifically for use on a Windows network. You can accomplish the following tasks (among others) with Mail:

- Send messages to coworkers
- Receive messages
- Attach files to messages
- Work with messages and files away from the office
- Create linked files across the network
- Embed objects in messages and files

Starting Mail

Mail is a message system built around a Postoffice. The Mail Postoffice can be set up on any workgroup member's computer. The workgroup member whose computer stores the Postoffice directory administers the mail system. See "Administering the Postoffice" for details on creating and maintaining the Postoffice.

Before any workgroup member can begin to send and receive mail, the member must set up a user account with the Postoffice (see "Creating Your User Account"). The administrator can set up the account or the user can do it. After the member has a user account, the Postoffice acts as a collective mail drop with an Inbox folder and an Outbox folder for the member, as well as a Sent Mail folder that holds copies of the messages the user sends.

You don't need to be logged on to the network (*on-line*) to work with your messages and their attached files. If you work *off-line*, you don't have to deal with mail interruptions; you can even work with messages off-site. The "Using Mail Off-Line" section, later in this chapter, describes how to work with your messages off-line.

T I P   A Postoffice must be created before the first person in a workgroup can use Mail. If no one has set up a Postoffice, refer to the section "Administering the Postoffice" near the end of this chapter for information on how to set up a Postoffice.

T I P   If you have already created a user account and need only to sign in and check your mail, refer to the following section, "Signing In to Mail."

The first time you start Mail, you must connect to an existing Postoffice, and you must create a user account if the Postoffice administrator hasn't already created one for you. See "Creating Your User Account" for details on how to set up a user account. To start mail and connect to a Postoffice, follow these steps:

1. Select and open the Main group window within the Program Manager.

2. Find the Mail icon in the Main window of the Program Manager. It looks like a gold-plated mail slot (see fig. 10.1). Select this icon and press Enter, or double-click the icon.

The first time you execute this step, Mail displays the Welcome to Mail dialog box (see fig. 10.2).

The Mail icon ——————

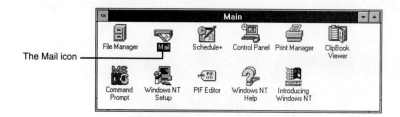

Fig. 10.1

The Mail icon in the Main program group.

Fig. 10.2

Windows NT greets new users and invites them to connect to an existing Postoffice.

3. Select the **C**onnect to an Existing Postoffice option. Then choose OK or press Enter. The Connect to Postoffice dialog box opens (see fig. 10.3).

Fig. 10.3

The Connect to Postoffice dialog box.

4. Type the path in the text box. Use the format *computername**sharename*. (The term *computername* refers to the name of the computer and the drive on that computer where the Windows NT software is installed. The term *sharename* refers to the directory on *computername* containing your workgroup's Postoffice.)

5. Choose OK or press Enter.

6. If the Postoffice directory is password-protected, Mail displays the Enter Shared Directory Password dialog box (see fig. 10.4). Type the password in the text box (the characters appear as asterisks); then press Enter.

   If the Postoffice directory isn't password-protected, this dialog box doesn't appear.

Fig. 10.4

The Enter Shared Directory Password dialog box.

7. Mail displays a dialog box that asks whether you have an account (see fig. 10.5).

Fig. 10.5

The dialog box that asks whether you have an account.

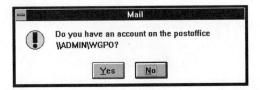

Choose **Yes** if the administrator has created an account for you. Choose **No** if you need to set up your account. See the following section for details on how to set up an account.

Creating Your User Account

If you do not already have a user account set up for you when you connect to a Postoffice, as described in the previous section, and you select No when you are asked whether you have an account on the postoffice, you are presented with the Enter Your Account Details dialog box, as displayed in figure 10.6.

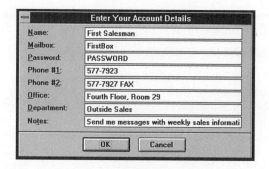

Fig. 10.6

The Enter Your
Account Details
dialog box.

To set up a user account, follow these steps:

1. In the Enter Your Account Details dialog box, enter your name in
   the Name text box, a name for your mailbox in the **M**ailbox text
   box, and a password in the **P**assword text box. All other details
   are optional. (The details are described following these steps.)

2. After you complete the information in the dialog box, choose OK
   or press Enter.

In the Enter Your Account Details dialog box, you must enter the
following information:

- *Name.* Enter a name of up to 30 characters.

- *Mailbox.* Enter a mailbox name not longer than 10 characters.

- *Password.* If you don't want to use the default password (*PASS-
  WORD*), type a unique password of up to 8 characters.

Because Postoffice is indifferent to case, you can use any combination of upper- and lowercase letters for your name, mailbox name,
and password. Be sure to use words that are simple and easy to
remember.

T I P

The following details in the dialog box are optional:

- *Phone #1 and Phone #2.* Enter one or two phone numbers (for
  example, enter your office phone number and your fax number).
  You can use up to 32 characters for each number.

- *Office.* Enter up to 32 characters describing your office location
  (for example, *fourth floor, room 12*).

326

■ *Department.* Enter up to 32 characters identifying your department name (for example, *Packaging* or *New Sales*).

■ *Notes.* Enter a note of up to 128 characters.

NOTE After you establish your user account, Mail creates the MSMAIL.INI file and the MSMAIL.MMF message file in your Windows directory. The MMF file records all your messages and addresses (MSMAIL.MMF is the default file name). Every user should have a uniquely named MMF file.

Signing In to Mail

You need to connect to the Postoffice and create your user account only once. Subsequently, you can sign in to Mail each time you start Windows, using one of the following methods:

■ Go through the normal sign-in and password procedures

■ Set up the Mail icon's properties to bypass the normal sign-in procedure

To use the normal Mail start-up and sign-in procedures, follow these steps:

1. Choose the Mail icon in Program Manager's Main group window to start Mail. The Mail Sign In dialog box appears (see fig. 10.7).

Fig. 10.7

The Mail Sign In dialog box.

2. Check your Mailbox **N**ame to be sure that it is correct.

3. In the **P**assword text box, type your password (Mail displays asterisks in place of the characters you type) and then press Enter. The Mail Inbox window opens (see fig. 10.8).

NOTE If security is a concern in your business or organization, be sure to create a password. Don't use the default password (*Password*).

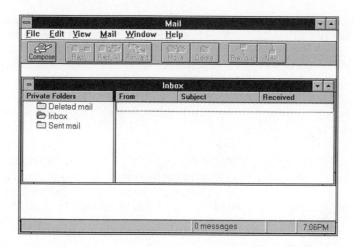

Fig. 10.8

The Mail application window and Inbox window at start-up.

To skip the sign-in procedures when you start Mail, follow these steps:

1. Select the Mail icon in the Main group window in Program Manager.

2. Choose **F**ile **P**roperties or press Alt+Enter to display the Program Item Properties dialog box.

3. In the **C**ommand Line text box, at the end of the path statement, type a space, your mailbox name, another space, and then your password. Choose OK and start Mail.

NOTE   If you are concerned about the security of your data, don't type your password in the command line.

You can automatically start Mail when Windows NT starts by dragging a copy of the Mail icon to the Program Manager Startup group window (for details on using Program Manager, see Chapter 4, "Controlling Applications with the Program Manager").

T I P

Using Help

Like most Windows applications, Mail comes with its own Help file and on-line Help system. To access Help, you can press F1, choose **H**elp Contents, or choose **H**elp Index. If you access Help from a dialog box or while a command in the menu is selected, Mail displays Help for that dialog box or command. If you choose **H**elp **C**ontents, the Mail Help Contents window opens. In this window, expansion buttons reveal topic lists (see fig. 10.9). See Chapter 3, "Getting Help," for a detailed explanation of how to use the help facility.

Quitting Mail

Quitting Mail is slightly different from quitting other applications. You can exit and sign out of Mail or you can exit without signing out. If you exit and sign out, applications that require the Postoffice (such as Schedule+) close when Mail closes, and you must sign in again if you restart Mail. To quit and sign out of Mail, choose **F**ile **E**xit and Sign Out.

If you exit without signing out, other applications dependent on the Postoffice can run, and you don't have to sign in again when you restart Mail. To quit without signing out of Mail, choose **F**ile **E**xit, press Alt+F4, or open the Control menu of the Mail window and choose the **C**lose command.

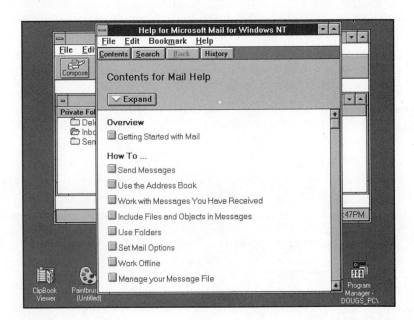

Fig. 10.9

The Mail Help Contents window with a selected topic.

  If no applications dependent on the Postoffice are running when you exit Mail, choosing **F**ile **E**xit signs you out of Mail.

Sending Messages with Mail

Sending messages to group members is a two-step operation. First you compose and address your message; then you send the message. Mail gives you some options to consider, but sending a message can be as simple as making a phone call.

Composing the Message

To prepare a message, you first must display the Send Note window (see fig. 10.10). You display the window in one of three ways: by choosing the Compose button on the toolbar (refer to fig. 10.8), by choosing the **M**ail Compose **N**ote command, or by pressing Ctrl+N.

When composing your message, you first address the message by specifying the recipient in the **T**o text box. If you want to copy the message to other recipients, use the **C**c text box. You can type the address of the recipient or choose the address from a list of addresses. The next two sections describe manual and automatic addressing of messages.

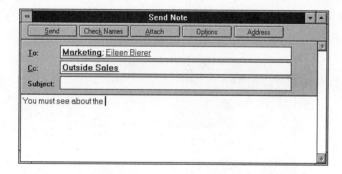

Fig. 10.10

The Send Note window.

Manual Addressing

If you decide to address your message by typing addresses in the **T**o and **C**c text boxes, you need to type only the first few characters of an address; then press Alt+K. Mail completes the entry from its address list.

To address the message manually, follow these steps:

1. In the **T**o text box, enter the name of the person(s) or group(s) to receive the message. To include multiple names, type a semicolon and a space between the names.

2. To send a copy of the message to another person or group, type the name(s) in the **Cc** text box. To include multiple names, type a semicolon and a space between the names.

3. If you want to check your entries in the **To** and **Cc** text boxes, choose the Chec**k** Names button in the Send Note dialog box.

If the entries don't match names in the Mail address list of users, an information box appears, instructing you to check the names you have typed.

If the entries match the Mail address list, the names appear underlined in the **To** and **Cc** text boxes.

Automatic Addressing

Mail manages an address list. New addresses are automatically added to the address list when you send a message to an address you have not sent to previously. The address list enables you to keep a list of people or groups to which you frequently send messages. It reduces typing and incorrect addresses. To address your message by using the address list, follow these steps:

1. Choose the **Ad**dress button in the Send Note dialog box or choose the **M**ail A**d**dress command. The Address dialog box appears (see fig. 10.11).

Fig. 10.11

Use the Address dialog box to select addresses for your messages.

2. In the Postoffice List, select the names of people or groups to whom you want to send the message. Then choose the **T**o button in the Address dialog box. The names appear in the To text box.

3. In the Postoffice List, select the names of people or groups to whom you want to send copies of the message. Then choose the **Cc** button in the Address dialog box. The names appear in the Cc text box.

4. Choose **OK** or press Enter.

A later section of this chapter, "Sending the Message," describes other features of the Address dialog box.

The selected names appear in the **To** and **Cc** text boxes of the Send Note dialog box. Mail underlines the names that match names in its records.

Completing the Message

After you have addressed the message, press Tab to move to the Subject text box, or click the box. Then type the subject, using up to 480 characters (a brief subject is more considerate than a lengthy one). You don't need to list a subject, but a subject listing helps workgroup members to sort and prioritize incoming mail. After you finish typing the subject, press Tab to move to the text editing area. Your subject text appears in place of "Send Note" in the title bar of the Send Note window.

In the text editing area, you can type and edit text as you do in many Windows text editing or word processing programs, such as Write or Notepad. You can do any of the following tasks:

■ Type letters, numbers, and symbols from the keyboard.

■ Select and delete text by pressing Del or by choosing **Edit Delete**.

■ Change fonts. You have only two choices: the Windows default (Times New Roman) or a nonproportional typewriter typeface. Choose **View Change Font** to toggle between these fonts.

■ Select and copy text to the Windows Clipboard by choosing **Edit Cut** or **Edit Copy**.

■ Insert text copied from other Windows applications or other messages, that is, any text stored in the Clipboard, by placing the insertion point where you want to insert the text and choosing the **Edit Paste** command. To copy between messages, you must close the message you copied from and open the message you are copying to. You cannot have two Send Note windows open at one time.

■ Insert special characters from the Windows Character Map.

TIP You can cancel a message in the Send Note window at any time by pressing the Esc key.

Saving or Storing the Message

After you finish entering the message, you can send the message immediately (as described in the next section). Occasionally, you may want to save the message as a text file, for example, if you want to use the text in the message in another application, or you may want to store it in a folder for sending later.

To save a message as a text file, choose the **F**ile **S**ave As command to display the Save Message dialog box. A truncated version of the text you entered in the Subject box is used for the default file name that appears in the File **N**ame text box. The extension TXT is added to the file name.

You can store your message to send later by moving or copying it to a folder. Mail comes with three default folders: Deleted Mail, Inbox, and Sent Mail. You can also create your own folders. (See "Creating and Using Folders" later in this chapter.) You can store your message temporarily in a folder and open and send the message later. To store a message in a folder, follow these steps:

1. To copy the message, choose **F**ile **C**opy. The Copy Message dialog box appears.

   To move the message, choose **F**ile **M**ove or click the Move button on the toolbar. The Move Message dialog box appears.

   The Copy Message and Move Message dialog boxes are identical except for the name on the title bar (see fig. 10.12).

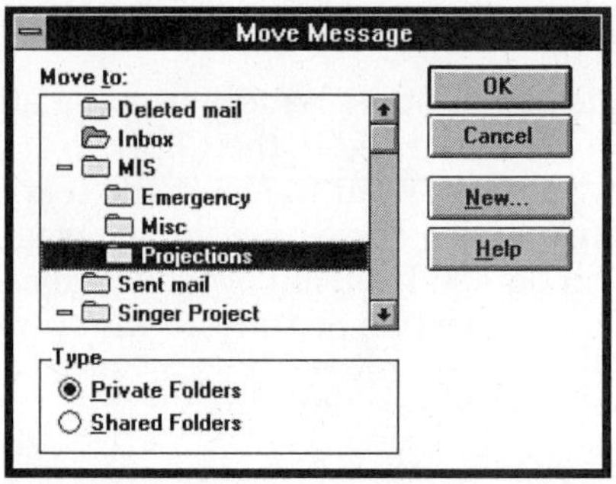

Fig. 10.12

The Move Message and Copy Message dialog boxes are identical except for name and function.

2. Select a folder in the Move **T**o or Copy **T**o list box.

   As in any list, you can scroll the list to find a name that does not show in the box. You cannot scroll horizontally to see beyond the right side of the box.

3. Choose OK or press Enter.

Mail moves or copies the message to the new folder and displays your Inbox window. When you select the folder that the message was moved or copied to, the listing of the message appears with a gray envelope and note icon next to it.

> If you frequently send a message to the same addresses, copy a version to a new folder called Templates. (For a description of how to create a new folder, see "Creating and Using Folders" later in this chapter.) When you need to send that message, drag its template to the Outbox, adjust the text and address information as necessary, and send the message. Mail sends the message, but the template copy remains intact in the Template folder.
>
> **T I P**

Sending the Message

You can send a Mail message immediately after you compose it, or you can retrieve and send messages from any folder available to you. The Inbox window displays folder icons (Deleted Mail, Inbox, Sent Mail, and any folders you have created) to the left of the message listing. (To learn how to create a folder, see "Creating and Using Folders," later in this chapter.)

To send a message immediately, choose the **S**end button in the message's Send Note window after you finish addressing and composing the message. Mail delivers the message to the Inbox of the addressee(s).

To send a stored message from the Inbox window, select and open the folder in which you stored the message. You can use either of these two methods to select and open the folder: double-click the folder; or press Tab to move to the folder list, use the direction keys to select the desired folder, and then press Enter. The title bar displays the name of the new folder, and Mail lists the stored messages by priority, addressee, subject, and date and time sent.

From the folder, you can send a message in the following ways:

■ Select a message and open it by double-clicking the message name or pressing Enter. You can change the addresses if necessary.

■ Click the message name and drag it to the Outbox (see fig. 10.13). Mail opens the Send Note window with the message title in the title bar. You can change the addresses if necessary.

Finding Addresses

Remembering all the names of all the users on the network and the many different groupings may be difficult; however, Mail gives you a way to remember all the names and find them easily.

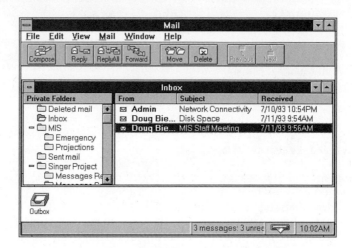

Fig. 10.13

To send the selected message, drag it to the Outbox.

If you are familiar with the name, you will want to use the first method. In the **To** text box of the Send Note window, begin typing a name; then press Alt+K. Mail completes the name if it finds a matching name in the address list (for a description of this process, see "Composing the Message," earlier in this chapter).

Four other methods of entering addresses use the Address dialog box. With the Send Note window or any message open, choose the **Ad**dress button or choose the **M**ail A**d**dress command. Mail displays the Address dialog box (refer to fig. 10.11). Then use one of the following methods:

■ Type the first letter of the name you want to find. The displayed list of users scrolls to the names beginning with that letter. Typing *S*, for example, may scroll the list to Sales Group, which may be followed by Sam Taylor, Scot, and any other names that fit in the list box. Select the desired name in the list box.

■ Click the Search button in the Address dialog box (it shows a magnifying glass icon) or press Ctrl+F. The Name Finder dialog box appears, as shown in figure 10.14. In the text box, type as much of the name as you remember; then choose Find. Name Finder searches for all instances of the specified characters. When the search is complete, Mail lists the matching names in the address list box; select the name you want. If the address you want doesn't appear, modify what you typed in the Name Finder box and try again.

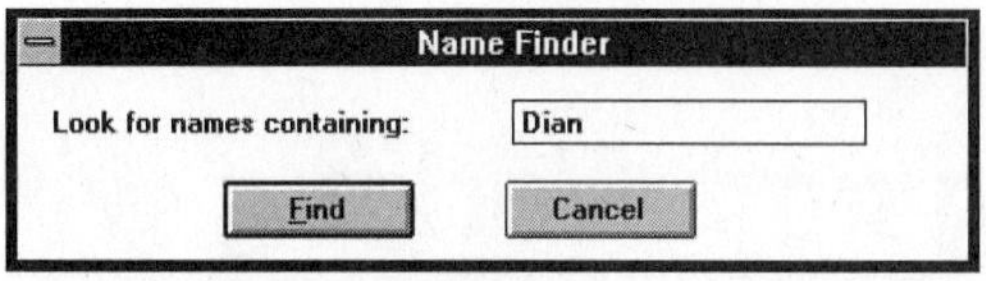

Name Finder	
Look for names containing:	Dian
Find	Cancel

Fig. 10.14

Use the Name Finder to find and select users.

■ Click the Directory button in the Address dialog box (it shows an address book icon) or press Ctrl+L. The Open Directory dialog box appears, listing two directories—your Personal Address Book and the Postoffice list. Select the directory you want to use and choose OK. The list of users in the selected directory appears in the Address dialog box.

■ Click the Personal Address Book button in the Address dialog box (it shows an index card file icon) or press Ctrl+P. This address book records all users to whom you have sent a message and all personal groups you have created. Search for names alphabetically, select the users, and choose the **To** or **Cc** button in the Address dialog box to add these names to the To or Cc text box.

You can select more than one user from the list in the Personal Address Book. To select more than one user, click on the first user, hold down the Ctrl key, and click on subsequent users. To deselect a user, hold down the Ctrl key and click on the user. To use the keyboard, select the first user, press Shift+F8, use the up- and down-arrow keys to move to the next user, and press the space bar. Move to additional users and press the space bar. To deselect a user and retain the other selections, move to the selected user and press the space bar. To return to selecting a single user at a time, press Shift+F8 again.

T I P

Getting Details on a User

Even if Mail finds a name that matches your search criteria, you may not be sure that you have found the right address. If you are unsure, you can look at the information provided by the user when he or she first set up the account. To display the detail information, follow these steps:

1. Open the Address dialog box by clicking the Address button on the toolbar or choosing the Mail Address command.

2. Find a potential addressee by using any of the methods described in the preceding "Finding Addresses" section.

3. Choose the Details button in the Address dialog box. An information dialog box appears, with the addressee's name in the title bar.

Reading and Working with Messages

All of your incoming messages are stored in your Inbox folder. At your convenience, you can read your messages, then you have several options for processing your messages. You can store them in a folder of your choice, forward them to other users, reply to them, print them, or delete them. Each of these tasks can be accomplished very easily in Mail, which enables you to use your electronic mail system to streamline communications with your coworkers.

Reading Messages

Mail notifies you in a couple of different ways when you receive an incoming message. If you are working in another Windows application, you may hear your computer beep to indicate that new messages have come in. You can control how Mail notifies you and how frequently it checks for new mail by using the Mail Options command as described later in this chapter.

If you are viewing your Inbox in Mail when a message from another user arrives, your computer will beep, your mouse pointer will briefly change to an envelope icon, and the new message will be listed in the Inbox folder's list of messages. An icon of a closed envelope appears next to the listing, indicating that the message has not been read.

If Mail is reduced to an icon on your desktop when a message arrives, your computer will beep and the icon will change to show an envelope popping out of the mail slot. If you want to know when a message has arrived when you are working in another application, you can minimize Mail, that is, reduce it to an icon on your desktop, and arrange your application windows so that you can see the Mail icon on your desktop. That way, when a message arrives, you will see the Mail icon change (as well as hear a beep) and you can quickly restore Mail to a window and read the message.

To read a message, follow these steps:

1. Switch to Mail and open the Inbox folder by double-clicking on the Inbox folder icon or pressing the Tab key to move to the Private Folders window, using the arrow keys to select the Inbox folder, and pressing Enter.

2. Double-click on the listing of the message you want to read in the right side of the Inbox window or press the Tab key to move to the right side of the Inbox window, select the message you want to read with the arrow keys, and press Enter.

   The selected message is displayed in a window, as shown in figure 10.15.

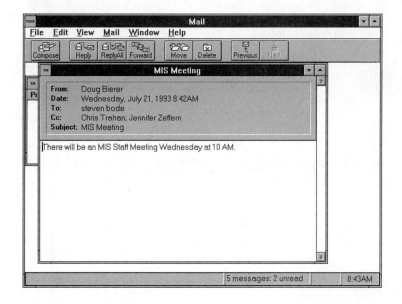

Fig. 10.15
When you open a message, it appears in its own window.

After you read a message, you can reply to the message, forward the message to another address, print the message, store the message in a folder, save the message as a text file, or delete the message.

Replying to Messages

Replying to a letter is cordial, but not always expedient. In the electronic mail environment, replying to a message may lead to problems in disk storage space and may slow down the network. Replying to every message received also may prove too great a task or one of low priority. If you need confirmation that an addressee has received your message, Mail offers a Return Receipt option (see "Setting Message Options" later in this chapter).

Nevertheless, you may need to send a reply message to workgroup members. You can reply to just the sender of a message or to every recipient of the message. To reply to a message, follow these steps:

1. If you are already viewing the message you want to reply to, click the Reply or ReplyAll button on the toolbar or choose the Mail Reply or Mail Reply to All command.

   or

   Double-click on the folder in the left side of the Mail window that contains the message you want to reply to or press the Tab key to move to the left side of the window, use the arrow keys to select the folder containing the message, and press Enter. Select the message you want to reply to from the list and click the Reply or ReplyAll button on the toolbar or choose the Mail Reply or Mail Reply to All command.

   A Reply Note window appears (see fig. 10.16). The addressee(s) is listed in the To and Cc text boxes and RE appears at the beginning of the Subject text box, indicating that this message is a reply to another message. RE also appears in the title bar, followed by the text from the Subject box, The text editing area contains a copy of the original message text.

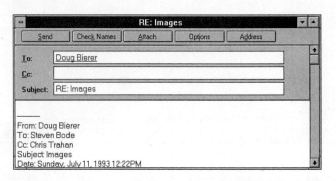

Fig. 10.16

The addressee and subject fields in a reply are automatically inserted.

2. Using the usual editing techniques, compose your reply in the text area of the reply window.

3. Add or delete names in the **T**o and **C**c text boxes as necessary. Separate the names with semicolons.

4. Choose the **S**end button in the reply window. Mail sends the reply message to all the addressees.

Forwarding Messages

In this information-driven age, the ability to pass information to others quickly is a great advantage. Because your workgroup may depend on this shared information, you can easily forward to any name or group in your address list any message that you can access.

To forward a Mail message, follow these steps:

1. With the message displayed in its Send Note window or selected in the folder's list of messages, choose the Forward button on the toolbar, or choose the Mail Forward command.

   Mail displays the message in a Send Note window and FW appears at the beginning of the Subject text box.

2. Change addresses, change the subject, or modify the text as necessary.

3. Choose the **S**end button in the Send Note window; Mail sends the message.

Deleting Messages

If you have no reason to save a message, you should delete it to conserve disk space and reduce the clutter in your Mail folders. You can move files to the Deleted Mail folder at any time. When you quit Mail, the program deletes these messages. To delete a message or messages, use one of the following techniques:

1. While viewing the message (or with the message selected in a folder), choose the Delete button on the toolbar, press the Del key, or choose the File Delete command. Mail moves the message to the Deleted Mail folder.

   or

   Double-click on the folder in the left side of the Mail window that contains the message you want to delete or press the Tab key to move to the left side of the window, use the arrow keys to select the folder containing the message, and press Enter. Select the message you want to delete from the list and click the Delete button on the toolbar, drag the message to the Deleted Mail folder, or choose the File Delete command.

You can select several messages at once and delete them with one command. To select more than one message, click on the first message, hold down the Ctrl key, and click on subsequent messages. To deselect a message, hold down the Ctrl key and click on the message. To use the keyboard, select the first message, press Shift+F8, use the up- and down-arrow keys to move to the next message, and press the space bar. Move to additional messages and press the space bar. To deselect a message and retain the other selections, move to the selected message and press the space bar. To return to selecting a single message at a time, press Shift+F8 again. When you have selected all the messages you want to delete, click the Delete button on the tool bar, drag the message to the Deleted Mail folder, or choose the File Delete command.

If you mistakenly delete a message, you can open the Deleted Mail folder and move the message back to its former folder or to any other folder. When you exit Mail, the program deletes the messages in the Deleted Mail folder; at that point, you cannot retrieve them.

Printing Messages

You can easily print a message, either as you view it or by selecting from the list of messages in a folder. To print a message, follow these steps:

1. If you are already viewing the message, choose the File Print command (or press Ctrl+P).

   or

   Double-click on the folder in the left side of the Mail window that contains the message you want to print or press the Tab key to move to the left side of the window, use the arrow keys to select the folder containing the message, and press Enter. Select the message you want to print from the list and choose the File Print command (or press Ctrl+P).

TIP   You can select two or more messages at once from the list of messages in a folder and print them with one command. To select multiple messages, click on the first message, hold down the Ctrl key, and click on subsequent messages. To deselect a message, hold down the Ctrl key and click on the message. To use the keyboard, select the first message, press Shift+F8, use the up- and down-arrow keys to move to the next message, and press the space bar. Move to additional messages and press the space bar. To deselect a message and retain the other selections, move to the selected message and press the space bar. To return to selecting a single message at a time, press Shift+F8 again.

The Print dialog box appears (see fig. 10.17).

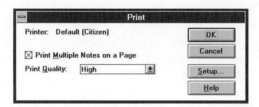

Fig. 10.17

Mail's Print dialog box.

2. If you have selected more than one message to print, select the Print Multiple Notes on a Page option. The messages will print continuously, one after another. Deselect this option if you want a new page for each message.

3. Choose the desired print quality from the Print Quality drop-down list.

4. Choose OK or press Enter.

 NOTE Embedded objects in a message will print, but you can print attached files only from their original application (see "Attaching and Embedding in Mail" later in this chapter). You must use Excel, for example, to print an Excel spreadsheet—even if you received it as part of a message.

Finding Messages

Mail provides a convenient way to find messages you need to reference, forward, copy, or otherwise use in your work. Using the Message Finder, you can specify the criteria that are used for finding messages, based on the text in the To, From, Subject, and Text fields of the message. For example, you can search for all messages sent to a specific person or for messages containing a particular word or phrase. You can search all folders for a message or limit the search to a particular folder. When the search is completed, the headings for all of the messages that meet the criteria you specified are listed in the Message Finder window. From this list, you can select messages to read, reply to, forward, print, or delete. You can run the Message Finder as many times as you want, specifying different search criteria each time, and you can reduce a Message Finder window to an icon on your Mail desktop so that you can rerun a search at a later time using the original criteria that you specified in that Message Finder window.

To search for a message, follow these steps:

1. Choose the File Message Finder command. The Message Finder window opens (see fig. 10.18).

   When you first open a Message Finder window, the title bar will display the words Message Finder and a number indicating what instance of the Message Finder this window is.

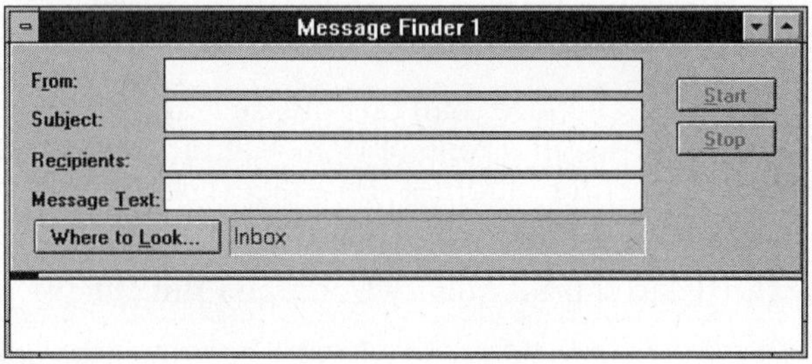

Fig. 10.18

The Message Finder locates messages by using search criteria that you specify.

2. In each text box, enter as much information about the message as you know: in the From text box, type the name of the sender; in the Subject text box, type the subject; and in the Recipients text box, type the names of the To and Cc workgroup members.

   If you type criteria into more than one of the text boxes, Message Finder will find only messages that meet each and every one of the conditions specified. For example, if you type *Peter* in the From text box and *Budget Reports* in the Subject text box, Message Finder will locate only messages that are from Peter and about budget reports.

3. If you know which folder may hold the message, choose the Where to Look button in the Message Finder window. The Where To Look dialog box opens; select the Look in All Folders option, or select a specific folder in which you want to search. Then choose OK or press Enter to close the Where To Look dialog box.

4. Choose the Start button in the Message Finder window. The Message Finder searches all the folders or the folder you specified for any match to the specified criteria.

   Mail lists the titles of the matching messages in the Message Finder window. If you see the message you are looking for before the search is completed, you can choose the Stop button to end the search.

You can select any message from the list of message titles in the Message Finder window and read, reply to, forward, print, move (to any folder), or delete it using the methods described in the previous sections.

NOTE When you delete a message from the Message Finder, Mail also deletes the message from its folder.

T I P

If you often search for messages using the same criteria, you need to set up a Message Finder window for those particular criteria only once. When you have finished searching for messages using these criteria, minimize the Message Finder window to an icon on your Mail desktop. When you need to repeat a search using these criteria, double-click on the icon or press Ctrl+Tab until the icon is selected, press Enter to restore the Message Finder window, and select the Start button. Message Finder icons on the Mail desktop are saved when you exit Mail, so that they will be available whenever you use Mail. You can set up as many Message Finder windows, each with different search criteria, as you want.

Attaching Files to a Message

Mail allows you to easily attach a file to a message, so that the recipient of the message receives an actual copy of the file along with the message. For example, if you want to distribute a copy of a document you have been working on to several coworkers, you can address a message to those coworkers explaining what the document is about and attach the document file to the message. Each of the addressees will receive the message and a copy of the file. Think how much quicker and easier this is than hand-delivering a diskette with the file on it to each of your coworkers.

There are three methods for attaching a file to a message. The first method works well if you are already working in Mail and working on a message. With this method, you can quickly select the file or files you want to attach to the message as you compose the text for the message. The second two methods use File Manager. If File Manager is already opened, it may be to your advantage to use one of these methods. For example, if you need the facilities in File Manager for finding a file that you want to attach to a message (see Chapter 5, "Managing Files with the File Manager"), you can find the file and then attach a message to it all from within File Manager.

Attaching Files to Messages in Mail

If you are working in Mail and know what file you want to attach to a message and where it is located, it is easiest to attach the file from Mail. To attach a file to a message as you compose the message in Mail, follow these steps:

1. While composing the text in the Send Note window, position the insertion point at the point in the text where you want to insert a file or files.

2. Choose the **A**ttach button in the Send Note window. The Attach dialog box appears (see fig. 10.19).

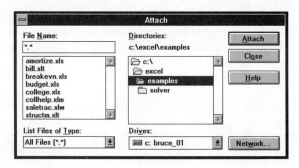

Fig. 10.19

You can select a file to attach to a message in the Attach dialog box.

3. Use the Attach dialog box (as you do any Open dialog box) to locate and select the file you want to attach to your message.

4. Choose the **A**ttach button or double-click the file name. The Attach dialog box remains on-screen and a file icon corresponding to the type of file you selected, for example, the Paintbrush icon for BMP files or the WinWord icon for Word DOC files, appears at the insertion point in the text.

5. Repeat steps 3 and 4 for as many files as you need to attach and then choose the Close button in the Attach File dialog box.

6. When you have finished composing the message, send it as you would any message.

Attaching Files to Messages with File Manager

There are two methods for using the File Manager to attach files to a message. If you are already working on a message in Mail and want to use the File Manager to locate and attach a file to the message, use the first method. On the other hand, if you are working in File Manager and decide you want to send a file to another user with a message attached to it, use the second method. In the end, the results of any of the methods described here or in the previous section for attaching a file to a message (or a message to a file) are the same; the recipient will receive a message in his or her Inbox with the attached file or files. Attached files can be opened by the recipient using the application that originally created the file.

To attach a file to a Mail message that you are already working on using File Manager, follow these steps:

1. Switch to Program Manager and open the File Manager in the Main program group (see Chapter 5, "Managing Files with the File Manager," for details on how to open File Manager).

2. Arrange your File Manager and Mail windows so that you can see both at the same time (see Chapter 2, "Operating Windows").

3. In File Manager, locate and select the file or files you want to attach to the message.

4. Drag the files from the File Manager to the locations in the text in the Mail message where you want them to appear. A file icon appears in the text to mark the location of the embedded file or files.

5. Finish composing the message and send it as you would send any message.

Drag a file or group of files from File Manager directly to your Outbox. A Send Note window appears with the files attached in the text box. Then just add explanatory text, addresses, and a subject.

Viewing and Saving Attached Files

When you receive a message with attachments, you probably want to view the attached files. Mail cannot display these files; you must have an application that can display the attachment's contents. To display a picture created in Paintbrush, for example, you must have the Paintbrush application installed on your computer. You can open a text file in most text editing, word processing, or desktop publishing applications, however.

To view an attached file, you use one of two methods. The first technique is to double-click the attachment icon or select it and choose **F**ile **O**pen. If the file's extension is associated with its application, Windows starts the application and the application loads the attached file. If the file is not associated with an application, you can create an association (see Chapter 5, "Managing Files with the File Manager") or you can use the following method for viewing the file:

1. Select the attachment's icon and choose **F**ile Save **A**ttachments. Mail displays the Save Attachment dialog box. The message attachments are listed in the **A**ttached Files list box (see fig. 10.20).

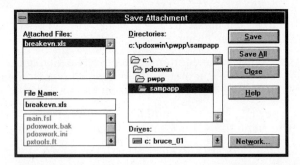

Fig. 10.20

Saving attachments from Mail.

2. Select the attached file or files you want to save. If desired, change the drive, directory, and/or file name with the **D**rives and **D**irectories list boxes and File **N**ame text box. Then choose the **S**ave button in the Save Attachment dialog box. Alternatively, you can choose the Save **A**ll button to save all attachments.

   Mail changes the Cl**o**se button to a **D**one button and saves the file or files in the current directory.

3. Choose the **D**one button. The Save Attachment dialog box closes.

4. Open the file by using File Manager or by loading the file into an application that can display it.

Embedding an Object in a Message

To embed an object in a message, follow these steps:

1. In the application containing the data you want to embed, select the data and copy it to the Clipboard. (The usual command for this step is **E**dit **C**opy.)

2. Switch to the Send Note window and place the insertion point where you want to embed the object.

3. Choose **E**dit Paste **S**pecial. The Paste Special dialog box appears (see fig. 10.21).

Fig. 10.21

Use the Paste Special dialog box to embed an object in a message.

4. In the **D**ata Type list box, select the form in which you want your linked data. (See Chapter 6, "Embedding and Linking Windows NT Applications," for more information on data types.)

5. Choose the **P**aste button in the Paste Special dialog box. Mail returns to the Send Note window and displays an object (a replica of the original object) in the text at the insertion point.

Embedding a File in a Message

When you need to embed an entire file from an application that has Object Linking and Embedding capability, follow these steps:

1. Save the file you want to embed.

2. In the Send Note window, place the insertion point where you want to insert the object and choose **Edit Insert from File**. The Insert from File dialog box appears (see fig. 10.22).

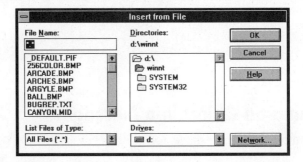

3. Select the file.

4. Choose OK.

The object (that is, its icon) appears at the insertion point.

Creating an Object for Embedding

Occasionally, you may need to create objects to illustrate a point. When you need a quick chart, picture, or other object, you can use Mail to create it. Follow these steps:

1. In the Send Note window's text area, place the insertion point where you want to insert the object; then choose **Edit Insert Object**. The Insert Object dialog box appears, listing the available Windows OLE applications (see fig. 10.23).

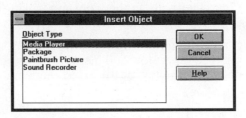

2. Select the application you want to use to create the new object.

3. Choose OK. The application opens.

4. Create the object. Then choose the originating application's **F**ile **U**pdate command or simply close the application. The object appears at the insertion point in the Send Note window.

Managing Messages with Mail

Just as you manage the files on your hard disk with the File Manager, you can manage the messages you send and receive with the facilities provided in Mail. Mail provides several options that can help you keep track of your messages.

Setting Message Options

Mail can reduce the number of interruptions and the time you spend on the phone or in conference with individuals. To reduce the interruptions to work and help focus time effectively, you can put a priority on mail messages; this lets the receiver know how important the message is and whether it should be handled immediately. (When setting the priority on a message, don't forget the tale about the boy who cried wolf too many times.)

If you just need a quick acknowledgment that someone has received your message, don't force them to write a note back to you. Instead, send your message with a return receipt requested. As soon as they open your message a postcard is sent back to you telling you that your message was opened.

To set these message options while in the Send Note window, choose the Options button. Mail displays the Options dialog box (see fig. 10.24).

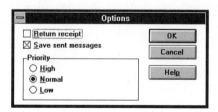

Fig. 10.24

Message options can save time and effort.

In this dialog box, you can set the following options:

■ *Priority.* Choose the name of an addressee in the Send Note dialog box; then specify a priority of **H**igh, **M**edium, or **L**ow in the Options dialog box. The priority rating will appear in the addressee's Inbox message list. Repeat this action for each addressee.

■ *Return Receipt.* If you choose this option, the message displays a yellow sealed envelope icon and a red exclamation point to the right of the folder's From column. When the addressee opens the message, Mail sends you a postcard message, confirming delivery (see fig. 10.25).

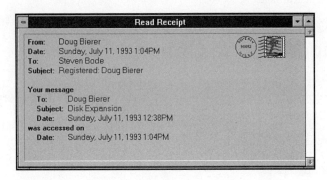

Fig. 10.25

You get a postcard when an addressee has read a return receipt message.

■ *Save Sent Messages.* Choose this option to retain (in your Sent Mail folder) a copy of the messages you send.

Creating and Using Folders

A workgroup may exchange hundreds of messages per week and thousands in a month. Keeping track of this electronic paper can be a nightmare without an orderly filing system. Mail provides folders as the means for storing and organizing messages sent and received, as described in the next sections.

Adding Folders

When you first open your account, Mail includes three folders: Deleted Mail, Inbox, and Sent Mail. The Inbox and Sent Mail folders may overflow, because Mail brings into the Inbox folder every message you receive, and stores in the Sent Mail folder a copy of every message you send. You can add folders to handle this overflow. The folders can be private folders for your exclusive use or shared folders used by any workgroup member with shared folder access privileges. For example, use shared folders for messages concerning a shared project.

Mail displays folders as yellow folder icons with names below each icon in the left side of the Mail window. To add a folder, follow these steps:

1. Choose File New Folder. The New Folder dialog box appears (see fig. 10.26).

Fig. 10.26

The New Folder
dialog box.

2. In the **Name** text box, type a name for the folder. The name can use any combination of characters, including spaces. For efficiency, keep the names of your folders brief.

3. In the Type section, choose the **P**rivate or **S**hared option:

   Private   Messages stored in a private folder can be viewed only by you.

   Shared   Messages stored in a shared folder are accessible to other users in your Postoffice. To set the access level other users have to messages in a shared folder, choose the **O**ptions button in the New Folder dialog box, and select or deselect the Read, Write, and Delete options in the Other Users Can group.

4. Choose OK or press Enter.

   An icon of a folder will appear next to the name of the folder in the folders section in the left side of the Mail window. Folders are listed alphabetically by name. By default, the folder will be a top-level folder, that is, it will not be subordinate to any other folders. The following section shows you how to add subfolders.

Adding Subfolders

A single-level filing system may not handle all your messages. Mail enables you to create multiple levels of subfolders. You can gather messages from general to specific categories. For example, you may have a folder named Projects that contains messages sent by all project man-agers. You can then have subfolders subordinate to the Project folder for each of the specific projects.

To create a subfolder, you normally select the folder to contain the subfolder; then follow the steps to create a new folder. The new folder is created as a subfolder of the selected folder (the *parent folder*). To create a subfolder with no parent folder selected, however, follow these steps:

1. In the New Folder dialog box, choose the **O**ptions button to expand the dialog box.

2. Type the name of the subfolder in the **N**ame text box.

3. In the Level section, select the Su**b**folder Of option. (The **T**op Level Folder option creates a folder independent of all other folders.)

4. In the Su**b**folder Of file list, select the name of the parent folder.

5. Choose OK or press Enter.

   An indented listing for the new folder appears beneath the listing for the parent folder. You have the option of displaying or not displaying the subfolders of a parent folder. When the subfolders are not displayed, a plus sign appears next to the parent folder. To expand the listing to show the subfolders, click the plus sign or press the Tab key to move to the folders list, use the arrow keys to select the parent folder you want to expand, and press the plus sign on the keyboard. To collapse a listing, click the minus sign next to the parent folder or select the parent folder with the key-board and press the minus sign.

Moving, Renaming, and Deleting Folders

Essentially, anything you can do with a message, you can do with a folder. This section describes how to manage your folders.

To move a folder or subfolder to another folder, drag the folder from its existing location to the location where you want it. Alternatively, with the folder selected, choose **F**ile **F**older Properties or press Alt+Enter. The Folder Properties dialog box appears, displaying the settings for that folder (see fig. 10.27). Select the Su**b**folder Of option and specify the folder that you want to use as the parent of the selected folder.

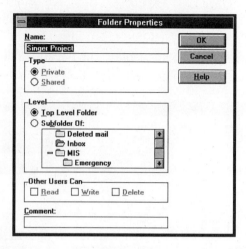

Fig. 10.27

Use the Folder Properties dialog box to change the properties of a folder.

To rename a folder, type the folder's new name in the **Name** text box of the Folder Properties dialog box. Choose OK or press Enter, and the folder's new name appears under the selected folder.

 You cannot change the name of the Inbox, Sent Mail, or Deleted Mail folders.

To delete a folder, select the folder and then press Del, choose **File Delete**, or press Ctrl+D. A message box appears to warn you that deleting a folder also deletes the folder's contents, including messages, attachments, embedded objects, and subfolders. If you still want to delete the folder, choose the **Yes** button in the warning box; if you don't want to delete the folder, choose the **No** button or press Enter.

Backing Up Message Files

Electronic messaging eliminates the excessive use of paper, but it increases the number and kind of messages sent. Mail keeps all your messages in folders, and keeps all the folders in the MSMAIL.MMF file. (As mentioned earlier, you can rename your MMF file; MSMAIL.MMF is the default name.) Your Personal Address Book, generated as you add addressees to your messages, is also part of the MMF file. You should back up your MMF file regularly to protect the data stored in it.

To back up your MSMAIL.MMF file (the message file), follow these steps:

1. Choose **M**ail **B**ackup. Mail displays the Backup dialog box (see fig. 10.28).

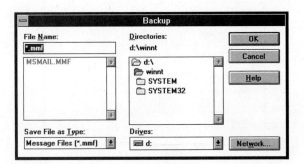

Fig. 10.28

The Backup
dialog box.

2. In the File **N**ame text box, type the name you want to use for the backup copy of the current MMF file you are using.

3. Specify the drive and directory in which you want to save the backup file.

4. Choose OK.

If the mail file you normally use becomes corrupted, Mail displays a dialog box asking you to locate your backup file. When you select your backup file, Mail re-creates your mail contents as they existed when you created that backup file.

Controlling the Mail System

Most people keep their mail and telephone systems at home organized with an address book; in the office, many people used index card files and Rolodex thumb files until computers came along. These methods have one thing in common: You must establish a *protocol* for using the system, especially with a group of people dependent on the information's accessibility and integrity. The protocol is a set of procedures for using your Personal Address Book and common rules for your workgroup. This section explains what you can do to modify and organize your Mail options to enhance your personal productivity.

Setting Up Your Personal Groups

Mail enables you to define groups of addresses for easy message addressing. This makes it convenient to send a message to a task team or to all the people working for you. To set up groups, follow these steps:

1. Choose Mail Personal Groups. The Personal Groups dialog box appears (see fig. 10.29).

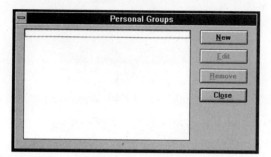

Fig. 10.29

The Personal Groups dialog box.

2. Choose the **New** button in the dialog box. The New Group dialog box appears (see fig 10.30).

Fig. 10.30

The New Group dialog box.

3. Type the name of the new group in the New group name text box. Then choose the **C**reate button in the dialog box or press Enter.

   The Personal Groups dialog box appears (see fig. 10.31). The name of the dialog box changes to reflect the name of the group you typed at the beginning of this step. This dialog box resembles the Address dialog box that you can access when you are composing a message. You can search for group member names, get details, and select names one at a time or in sets.

4. Choose the **A**dd button for each member or group selected. The group member names appear in the Group Members list box. (If you prefer, you can type the names you want to add in the Group Members text box.)

5. Choose OK or press Enter.

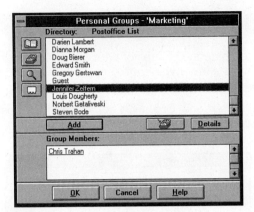

Fig. 10.31

Selecting groups
of users.

To edit an existing personal group, follow these steps:

1. Choose the Mail Personal Groups command.

2. In the Personal Groups dialog box, select the group you want to edit.

3. Choose the Edit button.

4. Add and remove members from the group using the Add and Remove buttons.

5. Choose OK and then choose Close.

To delete a personal group, follow these steps:

1. Choose the Mail Personal Groups command.

2. Select the group you want to remove from the list of groups.

3. Choose the Remove command.

4. Choose the Close button.

Building Your Personal Address Book

Each time you send a message, Mail adds the addressees of the message to your Personal Address Book. Mail saves this address book in your MMF file. You can also add addresses to your Personal Address Book even if you are not sending a message to these addresses.

Adding an Address

To add a name to your Personal Address Book, follow these steps:

1. Choose **M**ail A**d**dress Book. The Address Book dialog box appears (see fig. 10.32).

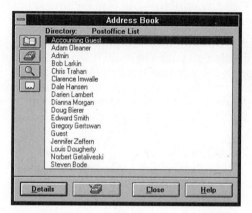

Address Book

Directory: Postoffice List

> Accounting Guest
> Adam Oleaner
> Admin
> Bob Larkin
> Chris Trahan
> Clarence Imwalle
> Dale Hansen
> Darien Lambert
> Dianna Morgan
> Doug Bierer
> Edward Smith
> Gregory Gertswan
> Guest
> Jennifer Zeffern
> Louis Dougherty
> Norbert Getaliveski
> Steven Bode

Details   **C**lose   **H**elp

Fig. 10.32

The Address Book dialog box is used for maintaining your Personal Address book.

2. Choose the Open Directory icon, which looks like an open address book, to display the Open Directory dialog box.

3. Select Postoffice List and choose OK.

    The Address Book directory will now list all of the users in your Postoffice. You can select one or more names from the list and add them to your Personal Address book.

4. Select the names from the list that you want to add to your Personal Address book.

    To select more than one name from the list at one time, click on the first name, hold down the Ctrl key, and click on subsequent names. To deselect a name, hold down the Ctrl key and click on the name. To use the keyboard, select the first name, press Shift+F8, use the up- and down-arrow keys to move to the next name, and press the space bar. Move to additional names and press the space bar. To deselect a name and retain the other selections, move to the selected name and press the space bar. To return to selecting a single name at a time, press Shift+F8 again.

    To search for a name in the Postoffice list, click on the Search button, which looks like a magnifying glass, or press Tab until the Search button is selected and press Enter. Type the name or part of the name in the Name Finder dialog box that appears and choose Find. Every name that contains the text string that you typed in the dialog box will be listed in the Address Book dialog box. You can then select the name or names you want to add to your Address Book.

5. Click on the Add Names button at the bottom of the dialog box, which looks like a Rolodex file with an arrow pointing into it, or press the Tab key until the Add Names button is selected and press Enter.

    If you need to find out more about a name that you have selected before you add it to your Personal Address Book, choose the De-tails button to display the detailed information associated with that name. If you decide you want to add the name, you can choose the Add Names button at the bottom of the dialog box. Then choose the Close button to return to the Address Book dialog box.

6. When you have finished adding names, choose the Personal Address Book button, which looks like a Rolodex file (without an arrow pointing into it). You will see the names you added to your Personal Address book in the list of names.

7. Choose Close.

Several shortcut keys make maintaining your Personal Address Book easier and faster. These shortcuts are described in the following table:

Action	Keys
Open a new directory	Ctrl+L
Open your Personal Address Book	Ctrl+P
Find a name	Ctrl+F
Enter a new address	Ctrl+N
Add a name to your Personal Address Book	Ctrl+A
Close the Address Book	Esc

Creating a Custom Address

If your Windows NT network has a gateway connecting your workgroup to electronic mail systems on other computers or networks, you can add to your address book the addresses of the people on those other mail systems. Follow these steps:

1. Choose the New Address button in the Address Book dialog box (it looks like a single index card). The New dialog box appears (see fig. 10.33).

Fig. 10.33

The New dialog box is used for creating custom addresses.

2. Select Custom Address in the Create what kind of entry list and choose OK or press Enter. The New User dialog box appears.

3. Type the new user's name in the Name text box (the dialog box title bar adopts the name of the new user). Type the E-mail address and E-mail type in the appropriate text boxes; then choose the Add User button, which shows an index file with an arrow pointing to it. Mail adds the new user to your Personal Address Book.

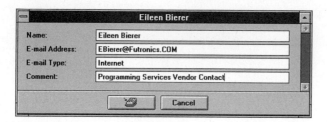

Fig. 10.34

Adding a user from another network.

4. Choose Cancel or press Esc to return to the Address Book dialog box and then choose Close.

Setting Mail Options

You can set Mail options for sending, receiving, and deleting messages.

To access these global settings, choose **M**ail **O**ptions to access the Options dialog box (see fig. 10.35). All options in the dialog box are selected by default.

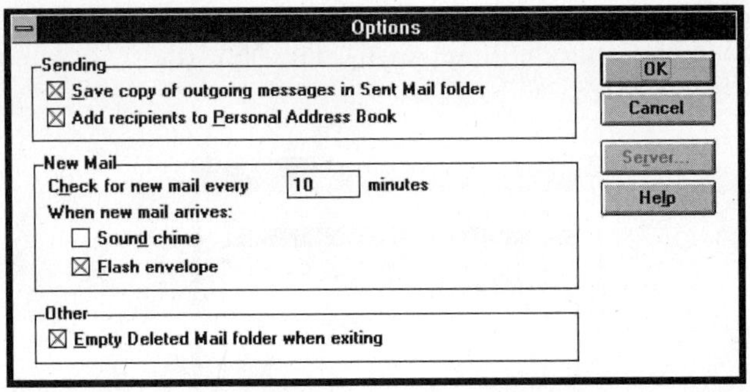

Fig. 10.35

The Options
dialog box.

The following list describes the options in the dialog box:

Option	Function
Save copy of outgoing messages in Sent Mail folder	Saves a copy of each message you send
Add recipients to Personal Address Book	Adds all the addressees to whom you send a message to your Personal Address Book.
Check for new mail every *XXXX* minutes	Specifies how frequently Mail should check for new messages. Type the number of minutes in the text box.
When new mail arrives	Controls how Mail notifies you of new message arrivals. Choose Sound Chime if you want Mail to sound a chime or beep from the computer's sound system. Choose Flash Envelope if you want Mail to change its desktop icon from a plain mail slot to a mail slot with letters sticking through it.
Empty Deleted Mail folder when exiting	Mail automatically empties the Deleted Mail folder when you exit the program.

Controlling How You View Folders

Mail gives you several options for controlling how you view folders and sort their contents. Many of these options are available on the View menu (see fig. 10.36) or by using the buttons along the top of the folder window (see fig. 10.37). Some viewing options are available only by using the mouse.

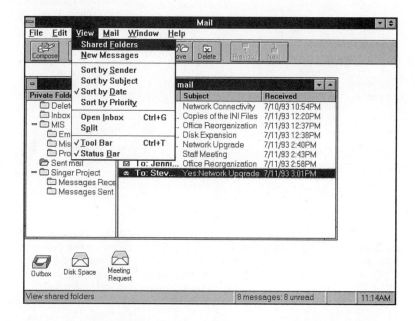

Fig. 10.36

The View menu.

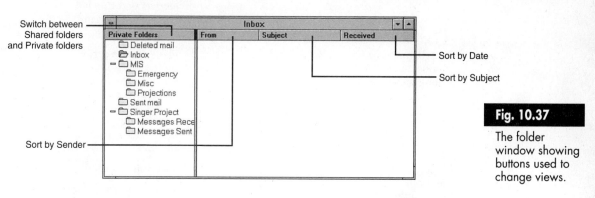

Fig. 10.37

The folder window showing buttons used to change views.

The following table summarizes Mail's folder-viewing options.

Action	View Menu	On-Screen Option
Choose private or shared folders	View Shared Folders or View Private Folders	Click the Shared Folders or Private Folders button bar to toggle between these two views

continues

Action	View Menu	On-Screen Option
Open a folder	No equivalent	Select a folder and press Enter or double-click a folder
Search for new messages	View **New** Messages or View Open **In**box	Open the Inbox folder (Ctrl+G)
Sort messages by sender	View Sort by **S**ender	Click the From button bar
Sort messages by subject	View Sort by Sub**j**ect	Click the Subject button bar
Sort messages by date and time	View Sort by **D**ate	Click the Received button bar
Sort messages by priority	View Sort by Priority	No equivalent
Redistribute window space for folder and message lists	View S**p**lit selects the vertical line between the folder list and the Messages list, which you control with arrow keys or the mouse.	Place mouse arrow on the black line between the Folders button bar and the From button bar; when the arrow changes to a white line with black arrows pointing left and right; click and drag the line.
Redistribute window space among messages	No equivalent	Place mouse arrow on the black line between the From and Subject or the Subject and Received button bars; click and drag the line
Display or remove the toolbar from beneath the menu	View **T**ool Bar	No equivalent
Display or remove the status bar* from the bottom of the window	View Status **B**ar	No equivalent

The status bar displays an explanation of a menu command, the number of messages in a selected folder (and how many are unread), the time of day, and a disconnected net-work icon if you are working off-line or the incoming message icon if you are working on-line when a message arrives.

Changing Your Password

You can change your Mail password. Changing your password on a regular basis is advised because security systems depend on limited access to your data and passwords may be spread around.

To change your password, follow these steps:

1. Choose **M**ail **C**hange Password. The Change Password dialog box appears (see fig. 10.38).

Fig. 10.38

The Change Password dialog box.

2. Type your old password in the **O**ld Password text box. Mail displays asterisks in place of the characters you type.

3. Type your new password in the **N**ew Password text box and then type the new password again in the **V**erify New Password text box. If the characters typed in the **V**erify New Password text box match the password typed in the **N**ew Password text box, the OK button becomes available for selection. Retype your new password in the Verify New Password text box if the OK button remains gray.

4. Choose OK or press Enter. Write your password down and keep it somewhere safe in case you forget it.

If you forget your password, see your Postoffice Administrator. The Administrator can change your password (see "Controlling User Accounts," later in this chapter).

Using Mail Off-Line

Mail assumes that you do all your work at a single computer and on the network, but sometimes you may need to work when the Postoffice server computer isn't available (for example, on weekends, holidays, and after work hours). You also may use a portable computer, with which you want to work away from the network. In these cases, Mail enables you to work off-line.

By default, Mail stores your MSMAIL.MMF (or other MMF) file in your computer's WINNT directory. The MSMAIL.INI file also must be in the WINNT directory. In some situations (for example, to conserve local disk space), you may choose to rename and store your MMF file on the Postoffice server computer. Before you can work off-line, however, you must move your MMF file to a directory on your local computer.

T I P	Be prepared to work off-line by having your MMF file stored locally.

To move your MMF file to your local drive, use Windows File Manager. You cannot use the Mail **B**ackup command in Mail because it leaves a copy of your MMF file intact and other users may send messages to this MMF file while you are off-line. For information on moving files, see Chapter 5, "Managing Files with the File Manager."

To work off-line, follow these steps:

1. With your computer disconnected from the network, start Mail. A message box appears, telling you that Mail didn't find your network files. Choose OK.

2. Another message box asks whether you want to work off-line. Choose OK again. The Mail Sign In dialog box appears.

3. Type your password and choose OK or press Enter. If Mail cannot find your MSMAIL.MMF file, it displays a dialog box asking you to type the path and name of your message file.

4. Type or otherwise designate the path (usually, C:\WINNT) and file name for your MMF file and then choose OK or press Enter. Mail displays your Inbox folder as usual and you can begin working with messages.

You may face the situation of working on both a desktop computer and a laptop and wanting to maintain the same message files on both. If both computers have Windows NT installed, you can maintain your Mail files on your laptop while you travel and update your desktop when you return. To use this method of working off-line with Mail:

1. Delete or move the MSMAIL.MMF file (or your MMF file with a personalized name) from your laptop's Windows directory. This will later force the laptop to ask you for the directory of your MMF file.

2. Copy the MSMAIL.INI file from your desktop computer to the Windows directory of your laptop.

3. Copy your MSMAIL.MMF file (or your MMF file with a personalized name) from your desktop computer to a diskette. This diskette file will be used as your Postoffice while you are on the road.

4. Do not run Mail on your desktop computer while you are using Mail on your laptop. Doing so will cause you to lose messages when you return and copy the laptop's MMF file back to the desktop computer.

5. When you are ready to work with mail on your laptop, start Mail on your stand-alone system with the diskette containing the MSMAIL.MMF file in the diskette drive.

6. When Mail asks for the path to your MSMAIL.MMF file, specify the diskette drive.

7. Work with Mail on the laptop as usual.

8. When you return to your networked desktop computer, copy the current version of your MSMAIL.MMF file from the diskette you used with the laptop back into your Windows directory on your desktop computer. Do this before you start Mail on your desktop or you will lose messages that people have sent to you while you were gone.

While working off-line, as you send, reply to, or forward messages, Mail places these messages in your Outbox, where they become part of your MSMAIL.MMF file. When you next start Mail on-line, Mail sends these messages immediately.

Importing and Exporting Folders

Workgroups by definition must share information—sometimes, whole folders of information. When creating a folder, if you choose to share it, the whole workgroup has access privileges to that folder. You control the access by giving users read, write, or delete capabilities for the folder (see "Creating and Using Folders," earlier in this chapter), but sometimes you may need to give all the messages you have in a folder to another workgroup member. In this case, you can export the folder to another member's MMF file or that member can import the folder from your MMF file.

To import or export a folder, follow these steps:

1. To import a folder, choose File Import Folder; the Import Folders dialog box appears (see fig. 10.39).

   or

   To export a folder, choose File Export Folder; the Export Folder dialog box appears (similar to fig. 10.39).

2. Specify the drive, directory, and MMF file name for the target folder (when importing a folder) or the destination folder (when exporting a folder).

3. Choose OK or press Enter. Mail displays a modified version of the Import Folders dialog box (see fig. 10.40) or the Export Folders dialog box (similar to fig. 10.40). This version of the dialog box lists the folders for the MMF file that you selected in step 2.

4. In the Folders To Import or Folders To Export list, choose All Folders or Selected Folders. If you choose Selected Folders, specify the folder or folders you want to import or export (to select multiple folders, click on the first name, press the Shift key, and click on the last name to select a sequential range or Ctrl-click individual names).

5. Choose the Options button. The Options dialog box appears (see fig. 10.41); select All Messages or Messages Received or Modified. If you choose the latter option, specify beginning and ending dates in the From and To text boxes.

Fig. 10.39

Select the MMF file name from which you want to import folders in the Import Folders dialog box.

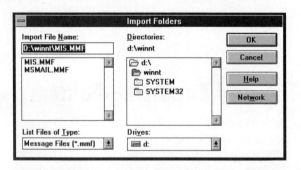

Fig. 10.40

After choosing an MMF file, you can select which folders you want to import.

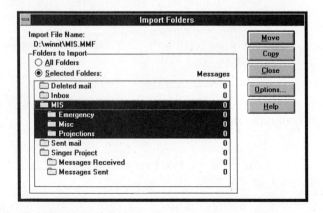

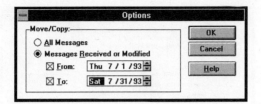

Fig. 10.41

You can import all messages or only those for a range of dates.

6. Choose OK or press Enter to close the Options dialog box.

7. Choose the **M**ove or Co**p**y button. Mail moves or copies the folder and files to the appropriate MMF file. If you are importing the folder, it appears in your list of folders.

Administering the Postoffice

Any member of the workgroup can be the Postoffice administrator, but these responsibilities usually go to a member whose computer system offers the most storage space and the fastest performance features. The administrator must have this computer turned on for the workgroup to use Mail on-line. More minor administrative tasks are covered in the Microsoft Windows NT manual, but this section presents the basic administrator skills.

Creating the Postoffice

The first task of the Postoffice administrator is to create the Workgroup Postoffice (WGPO). You may recognize this task as a variation of the directions for creating a user account. To create a Postoffice, follow these steps:

1. Check the hard disk storage space available for applications and tools. You need 360K disk space for an empty Postoffice and 16K disk space for each user account. In addition, each user must have enough disk space to hold the size and number of messages he or she expects to send and receive. Remember that a large Postoffice could require tens of megabytes of storage.

2. Start Mail. This must be the first time you start Mail anywhere on the network. Mail displays the Welcome to Mail dialog box; in this version of the dialog box, you specify whether you want to connect to an existing Postoffice or create a new one (see fig. 10.42).

Fig. 10.42

The Welcome to
Mail dialog box.

3. Choose the Create a **n**ew Workgroup Postoffice option.

4. Choose OK or press Enter. A message box appears, reminding you of your responsibilities as a Postoffice administrator and advising that only one Postoffice per workgroup should exist.

5. The message then asks if you want to create a new Postoffice. Choose **Y**es or press Enter.

6. The Create Workgroup Postoffice dialog box appears, asking you where you want to place the WGPO (see fig. 10.43). Select the location where you want to create the Postoffice from the **C**reate WGPO in list box and the **D**rives combo box. When you have selected the location, choose OK or press Enter. The Enter Your Administrator Account Details dialog box appears (see fig. 10.44). Notice that the details for the administrator are the same as those for the user accounts.

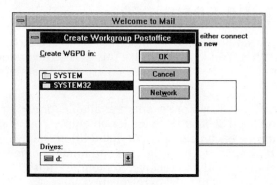

Fig. 10.43

The Create
Workgroup
Postoffice
dialog box.

7. In the dialog box, enter your name in the **N**ame text box, a name for your mailbox in the **M**ailbox text box, and a password in the **P**assword text box. All other details are optional. Choose OK or press Enter.

Mail displays a reminder to share the WGPO directory. Other users must have full access to the WGPO directory that Mail creates on the Postoffice Administrator's computer. The procedure for sharing the WGPO directory is explained in the next section.

Fig. 10.44

The administrator is the first user defined on the system.

8. Choose OK or press Enter. Mail creates the new Postoffice as the subdirectory WGPO in the directory you selected in step 5.

9. A final message box appears reminding you to share the WGPO directory. Choose OK when you read the message.

Sharing the WGPO

Immediately after creating the WGPO directory, you must share this directory so that other users have full access to it. Until you do so, other users will be unable to create an account on the Postoffice. To share the WGPO directory, follow these steps:

1. In File Manager, select the Postoffice directory (the default directory is C:\WINNT\WGPO).

2. Choose **D**isk Share **A**s. The New Share dialog box appears (see fig. 10.45).

3. Type a different name for the Postoffice or keep the default WGPO in the **S**hare Name text box.

   The Share name is the name Windows assigns to a directory that you share with other users. It does not have to be the same name as the directory itself.

4. Select the Pe**r**missions button. The Access Through Share Permissions dialog box appears (see fig. 10.46).

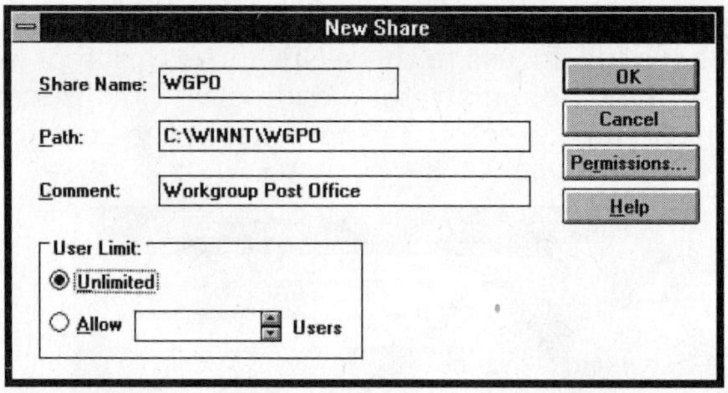

Fig. 10.45

The New Share dialog box in File Manager.

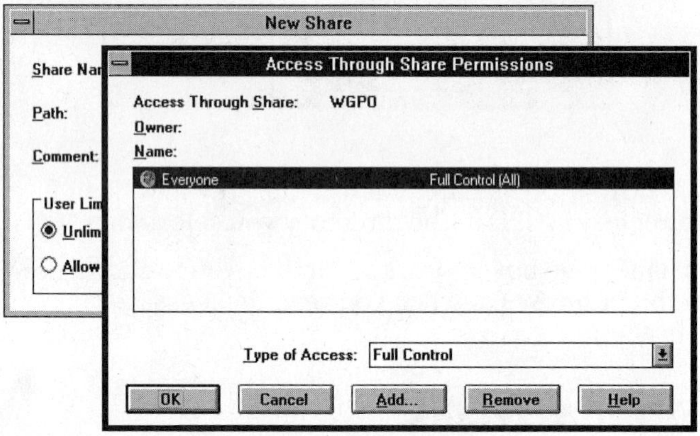

Fig. 10.46

The Access Through Share Permissions dialog box.

5. Ensure that Type of Access is Full Control. Then choose OK or Press Enter. You return to the New Share dialog box.

6. Choose OK or press Enter.

Controlling User Accounts

The Postoffice Administrator should control the creation and removal of user accounts. To remove a user account, follow these steps:

1. Choose the **M**ail **P**ostoffice Manager command. Mail displays the Postoffice Manager dialog box (see fig. 10.47). The dialog box lists the users by drive and path (specified above the list box).

2. Select the name of the user you want to delete and choose the **D**etails button. A user details dialog box appears, with the user's name on its title bar. The dialog box shows the information that the user or administrator provided when creating the account (refer to fig. 10.6). Look over the information to be sure this is the account you want to delete and then choose OK.

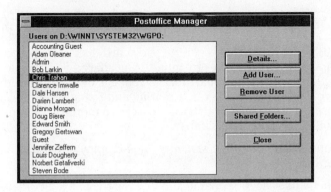

Fig. 10.47

You can add or delete users with the Postoffice Manager dialog box.

3. In the Postoffice Manager dialog box, choose the **R**emove User button. A confirmation box appears. Choose **Y**es if you are sure you want to remove this user; choose **N**o or press Enter if you don't want to remove this user from the mail system.

To add a user, follow these steps:

1. In the Postoffice Manager dialog box, choose the **A**dd User button. An Add User dialog box appears (the dialog box shows the details for the user—refer to fig. 10.6).

2. Specify the user's name, mailbox name, and password in the **N**ame, **M**ailbox, and **P**assword text boxes. The rest of the information in the dialog box is optional.

3. Choose OK or press Enter. The new user's name appears in the user list in the Postoffice Manager dialog box.

 This procedure doesn't create an MMF file for the new user. Mail creates the MMF file when the user first signs in to Mail.

To modify user account information, follow these steps:

1. In the Postoffice Manager dialog box, select the name of the user whose information needs to change; then choose the **D**etails button. The user's details dialog box appears.

2. In the details dialog box (the user's name appears on the title bar of the dialog box), change any or all of the information fields (for example, change the password if the user needs a new one).

3. Choose OK or press Enter. Be sure to inform the user of the changes you made.

Compressing the Size of the Postoffice

The Postoffice Administrator can recover hard disk storage space on the administrator's computer by monitoring shared folders and compressing them when additional storage space is needed. Shared folders can be created by any user (see "Creating and Using Folders"); any user can access the messages in a shared folder. To monitor and compress shared folders, follow these steps:

1. Choose **M**ail **P**ostoffice Manager. Mail displays the Postoffice Manager dialog box.

2. Select a user account name and choose the Shared **F**olders button. Mail displays the Shared Folders dialog box, which shows the current status of shared folders. This information includes the number of shared folders, the total number of messages in the shared folders, the collective byte count of the shared folders, and the number of bytes you can recover by compressing the shared folders.

3. If desired, choose the Compress button. Mail compresses the files.

 Be absolutely certain that no users are using the shared folder before you compress it. Warn all users before you attempt to compress the folder.

4. Choose Close to return to the Shared Folders dialog box.

Renaming, Moving, or Removing the Postoffice

Occasionally, you may need to re-create, relocate, or remove the Postoffice. Other workgroups may need to network with yours, which means that the two Postoffices must share information and folders; if both Postoffices have the same name, one name must change. Sometimes when disk space becomes sparse, relocating the Postoffice can be a temporary solution. If you forget your administrator password, you must remove the old Postoffice, create a new one, and reestablish user accounts in the renamed Postoffice system. For all of these tasks, you use File Manager.

To rename a Postoffice, select the Postoffice directory (WGPO by default) and then choose **D**isk Share **A**s. Type a new name in the Share Name text box. Share the directory with the new name as described in the section "Sharing the WGPO," earlier in this chapter.

If you need to move the Postoffice, for example, to a new computer, or to a different drive on your current computer, there are several steps you need to complete. To move a Postoffice, follow these steps:

1. Inform all users that they must Exit and sign out of Mail.

2. Open File Manager and select the WGPO directory.

3. Choose the **F**ile **M**ove command.

4. Type the new path name for the WGPO directory in the **T**o text box.

5. Choose OK or press Enter.

6. Share the new directory as described earlier in Sharing the WGPO.

7. Using Notepad or another text editor, modify the following line in the Postoffice administrator's MSMAIL.INI file:

   ```
   ServerPath=DRIVE:\DIRECTORY
   ```

   where DRIVE is the letter designator for the drive the directory is on, for example, D:\, and DIRECTORY is the path name for the relocated WGPO, for example, \WINNT\WGPO.

8. Instruct all users to modify the following line in the [Microsoft Mail] section of their MSMAIL.INI file, using Notepad or another text editor:

   ```
   ServerPath=\\COMPUTERNAME\SHARENAME
   ```

   where COMPUTERNAME is the name of the computer on which the WGPO directory is located, and SHARENAME is the share name that you assigned to the WGPO directory in step 6.

 NOTE Do not attempt to move your Postoffice unless you feel comfortable with each of the steps outlined above. Seek help from a more experienced user if necessary. Also, you may want to assist other users with step 8 if they are not familiar with working with text files.

To remove a Postoffice, select the Postoffice directory and then choose **F**ile **D**elete or press Del.

Summary

Mail can be a valuable tool to reduce wasted time while increasing communication within your workgroup. The key to making it work is to keep information succinct. This saves you time in composing the message and saves the recipient time in reading it. And studies have shown that the shorter the message, the more likely it is to be understood. Don't obfuscate the obvious!

Although Mail can help your workgroup, electronic mail can also hurt companies that have a poor or bureaucratic culture. Companies like this soon get swamped by electronic mail. They get mired down in the morass of "for your information" and "this is what I did, was it OK?" so that soon no one reads their messages. In fact, one manager confided to us that on returning from vacation and seeing all the electronic mail waiting, the manager just erased all of it. His response was, "If it's really important they'll call me on the phone."

One advantage to Mail is that it enables you to use Schedule+. This scheduling program makes it easy for you to schedule conference rooms or quickly confirm that three decision-makers are available at the same time for an important meeting. No longer do you need to spend so much time on the phone that you get calluses on your ear. To learn more about Schedule+, see Chapter 11.

Using Schedule+

Schedule+ is a tool for keeping track of your appointments, meetings, and tasks. Schedule+ serves as a personal scheduling tool and as a tool for scheduling others in your workgroup, if you are working with Windows NT.

The *Appointment Book* is your place in Schedule+ for assigning time-specific events, such as your appointments and meetings (see fig. 11.1). You can schedule in the Appointment Book one-time-only events or events that occur at regular intervals—for example, a weekly staff meeting. For recurring events, you need to enter the event into your appointment book only once and specify the time interval for its recurrence. Schedule+ then fills in the appropriate slots in your appointment book for all subsequent occurrences of the event.

Schedule+ also acts as a group scheduling tool that enables you to see when others in your workgroup have slots open in their calendars so that you can schedule meetings during these times. After you schedule these meetings, Schedule+ sends a message to those people you have requested to attend. Potential attendees can, in return, accept or decline your proposed time. Schedule+ then communicates back to you the responses to your request.

The *Task List* is the place in Schedule+ to list anything you must accomplish that is not necessarily assigned to a specific time period, as is an appointment (see fig. 11.2). The Task List is, essentially, a to-do list of all the tasks you need to complete, either by a specific date or whenever you can.

Items in the task list remain listed until you complete the task and delete the item from the list. You also can specify the starting and due dates for each task on the list. After you specify its starting and due dates, the task appears on your to-do list on a specific date; overdue tasks—those tasks you fail to complete by the due date—appear in red in the Task List. You can also assign a priority to each task and sort your tasks by those priorities.

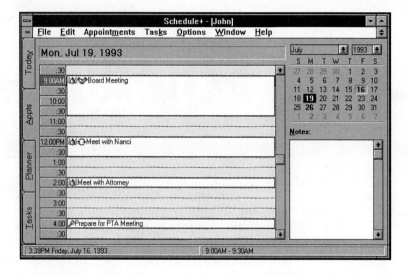

Fig. 11.1

The Schedule+ window, showing the Appointment Book.

The Schedule+ *Planner* displays the busy and free times in your schedule in a day-by-time grid, which enables you to view several days at a time (see fig. 11.3). If you are working *on-line*—that is, you are connected to the mail server on your network—you can view the busy and free times of others in your workgroup as well. The mail server is the computer on which the Postoffice is located; through the mail server, communication among computers collected together in a workgroup occurs. (See Chapter 10, "Using Microsoft Mail.") The primary function of the Planner is to help you schedule meetings with others in your workgroup at times that do not conflict, a topic that is covered in this chapter (see "Scheduling a Meeting" for detailed discussion of how to use the Planner). You can also use the Planner to get an overview of your time committments over a period of several days.

Starting Schedule+ from the Program Manager

Schedule+ is started from the Main group in the Windows Program Manager. Unless you are already signed in to Mail, you must sign in to Schedule+. To sign in, you must have a user account with Mail and know your mail box name and password. (See Chapter 10, "Using Microsoft Mail," for information on Mail.)

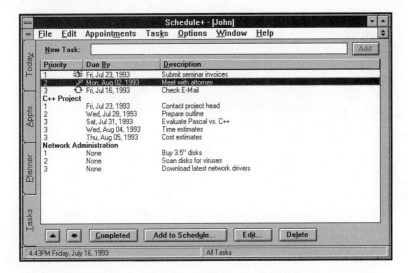

Fig. 11.2

The Schedule+ window, showing the Task List, with an item in the list selected.

To start and sign in to Schedule+, follow these steps:

1. Open the Program Manager, and choose the Main group (see fig. 11.4).

2. Choose the Schedule+ icon by double-clicking on the icon or selecting the icon with the arrow keys and pressing Enter. The Mail Sign In dialog box appears (see fig. 11.5).

3. Type your mailbox name in the **Name** text box of the Mail Sign In dialog box, as shown in figure 11.5.

4. Press the Tab key or click the **Password** text box, and type your mailbox password in the **Password** box. (Asterisks rather than alphabetical characters appear in the text box as you type to prevent someone else from reading your password.)

5. Choose OK or press Enter.

After Schedule+ opens, the Appointment Book is displayed in the Schedule+ window, with the current date displayed, as shown in figure 11.3. You perform most of your work with Schedule+ within the Schedule+ window. The title bar of the window displays your name, and tabs along the left side of the window list the Appointment Book (**Appts**), the **Planner**, and the Task List (**Tasks**). Clicking on a tab or pressing Alt+*letter* takes you to the appropriate feature. A Today tab enables you to return immediately to your Appointment Book schedule for the current day. When you are viewing or responding to meeting requests, you are working in a different window and you will not see your name in the title bar or tabs along the side of the window. Also, if you are viewing someone else's schedule, which you will learn how to do in this chapter, you will see that person's name in the title bar.

After you sign in to Schedule+, you are working with Schedule+ *on-line*. Working on-line with Schedule+ means you are connected to your network's mail server and can use the features of Schedule+ that take advantage of your network. You can view the schedules of others in your workgroup, for example, and schedule meetings based on your coworkers' available time (see the sections, "Working with Another User's Appointment Book and Task List" and "Scheduling a Meeting," later in this chapter).

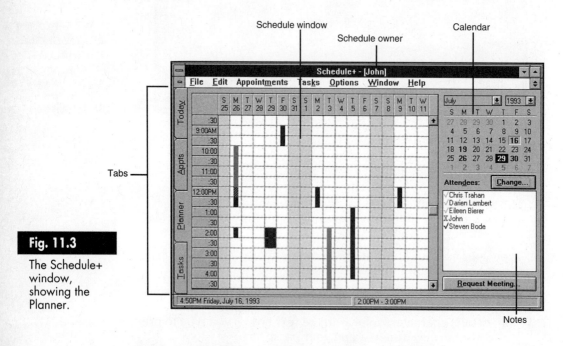

Fig. 11.3

The Schedule+ window, showing the Planner.

Working with Schedule+ Off-Line

You also can work *off-line*, which simply means working with Schedule+ without being connected to your Postoffice. Normally, when you are working on-line, your scheduling information is saved in a *local file*, located on your computer and in a *network file*, located on the computer where the Postoffice is located. If the computer serving as the network's mail server is temporarily off-line, for example, or you want to work on your portable or home computer, working off-line is your only option.

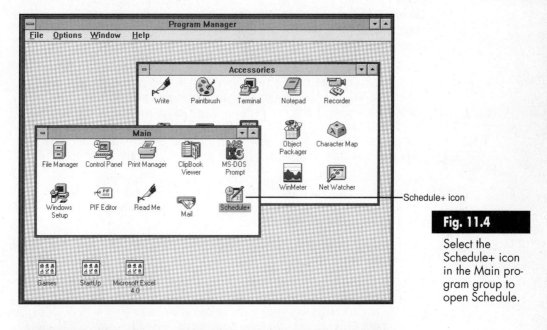

Schedule+ icon

Fig. 11.4

Select the Schedule+ icon in the Main program group to open Schedule.

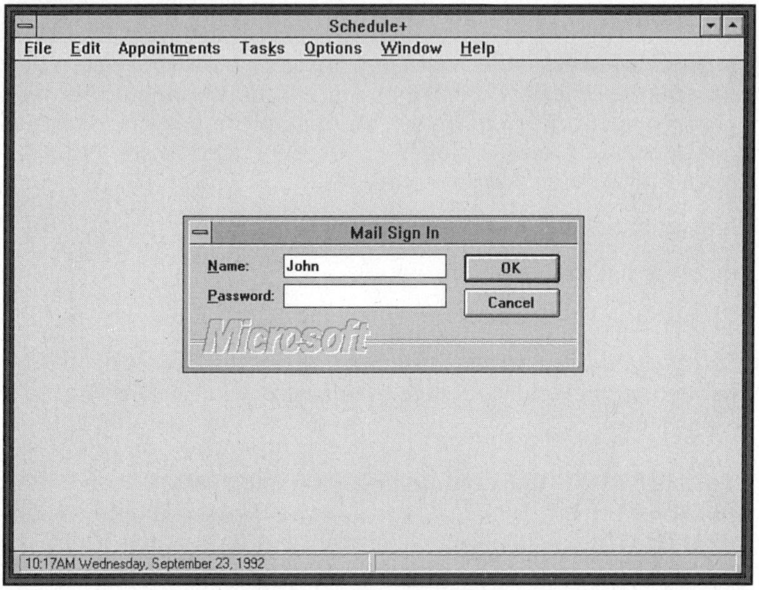

Fig. 11.5

The Mail Sign In dialog box.

If you want to work on another computer that is not connected to your network—for example, your portable computer—you need to copy the file with your scheduling information to that computer. And then, when you return to your office, you need to copy the file back onto your computer (the one connected to the network) so that the information on the *network file,* the file located on the computer with the Postoffice, can be updated.

If you neglect to copy the file back to your networked computer, then when others view your schedule—for example, to schedule a meeting—they will not see any appointments you made while using Schedule+ away from your office. Keep in mind, that when you work with Schedule+ off-line, whether it is on your networked computer or on another computer, you will not have access to anyone else's schedule and will not be able to use the workgroup scheduling features.

If you are already working on-line with Schedule+ on your networked computer, choose the **File Work** Offline command. You may want to do this if you receive a lot of messages, and want to be able to work uninterrupted for a period of time.

If you want to work with Schedule+ on a stand-alone computer, that is, on a computer that is not connected to your network, follow these steps:

1. Copy the file named SCHDPLUS.INI from the C:\WINNT subdirectory on your networked computer to the C:\WINNT directory on your stand-alone computer. (See Chapter 5, "Managing Files with the File Manager" for instructions on how to copy a file.)

   The SCHDPLUS.INI file contains information on your setup of Schedule+. Unless you make changes in how Schedule+ is set up on your networked computer, for example, if you make changes in the General Options dialog box, you only need to copy this file once to your stand-alone computer.

2. Log on to Schedule+ on your networked computer.

3. Insert a diskette into your floppy drive.

4. Choose the **File Move Local** File command.

5. Select the correct drive designation from the Drives drop-down list and, if necessary, change the directory in the **Directories** list.

6. Choose OK or press Enter.

   Your Schedule+ file, containing all the information from your Appointment Book, Task List, and Planner, is moved onto the floppy diskette. The name of the file is your mailbox name with the extension CAL.

7. Log on to Schedule+ on your stand-alone computer with the floppy diskette inserted in the floppy drive.

8. When you are prompted for the location of your local file, specify the floppy drive.

9. Work with your schedule as usual, with the exception that you cannot do group scheduling.

10. When you next log on to Schedule+ on your networked computer, use the **F**ile Move **L**ocal File command to move your scheduling file back to the WIN directory in your networked computer.

or

Use File Manager to copy the file from the diskette to the WIN subdirectory on your networked computer.

When you open Schedule+ on your networked computer, your Schedule+ file will automatically be updated on the mail server (assuming you are working on-line).

To work off-line when your computer is connected to a network, choose the **F**ile **W**ork Offline command. To return to working on-line, choose **F**ile **W**ork Online. You may want to work off-line while using your networked computer to prevent interruptions from Mail or Chat or to prevent others from using files on your drives.

If you are connected to your mail server, as described in Chapter 10, you can display a Messages window (see fig. 11.6). This window is where you receive and view replies to your requests for meetings or requests from others in your workgroup for meetings. See "Reading Responses to a Meeting Request" and "Responding to a Meeting Request" later in this chapter for details on how to use the message window.

Using the Appointment Book

The Schedule+ Appointment Book is where you assign your appointments and meetings to specific time slots. A time slot can contain up to six appointments or tentative appointments. Each appointment is listed in its own section of the time slot. When you fill in a time slot in the Appointment Book, that time period is blocked out on the Planner as busy time so that you or others viewing your Planner know not to schedule anything else during that time. Tentative appointments do not show up on your Planner as busy time, however, so when others look at your schedule, they see that time as open.

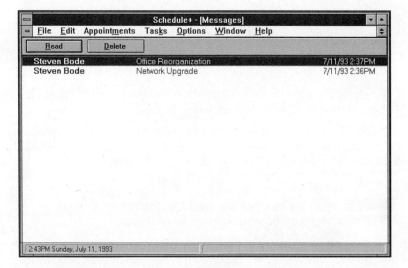

Fig. 11.6

The Messages window in Schedule+.

If you need to schedule an appointment that recurs at regular time intervals, you can enter the appointment once in your Appointment Book and specify at what intervals and for how long a period you want that event to appear on your schedule. You also can attach a reminder to any or all appointments so that a pop-up message box appears on-screen to remind you of an appointment.

Adding an Appointment

Adding appointments to your Appointment Book involves several steps. You must designate the date on which the appointment takes place. You also must indicate on the appropriate page of your Appointment Book the starting and ending times of the appointment. Finally, you must include a description of the appointment. You also may want to designate the appointment as tentative or private and set up a reminder of the appointment to appear at a specified time beforehand.

There are two methods for adding an appointment to your Appointment Book. The first method is the quickest and works well if you do not need to designate options, such as making the appointment private or tentative or setting a reminder for the appointment. With this method, you select the time slot and enter a text description of the appointment directly on the page of your Appointment Book. The second method uses the New Appointment command in the Appointments menu. This method is slower but more powerful, because you have several options that are not available with the first method. You can select a time slot for your appointment from a display showing several days of your schedule at a glance, and you can designate the appointment as private or tentative and set a reminder from the Appointment dialog box.

To add an appointment to your schedule, your Appointment Book must be on-screen in the Schedule+ window that displays your name in the title bar. If you are not in that Schedule+ window, choose the **W**indow menu from the menu bar, select your name from the **W**indows menu by clicking with the mouse or using the arrow keys and pressing Enter; or type the number that appears next to your name on the menu. Your personalized Schedule+ window appears. If your Appointment Book is not currently displayed in your personalized Schedule+ window, click on the **A**ppts tab along the left side of the window or press Alt+A.

Adding an Appointment Directly in Your Appointment Book

To add an appointment in your Appointment Book, you must first display the page for the date of the appointment. You can use the small *calendar* located in the upper-right corner of the Appointment Book (refer to fig. 11.1) to select the appointment date by following these steps:

1. Click the arrow to the right of the month box in the calendar. A drop-down list of months appears; click the desired month. The name of the month you chose from the drop-down list appears in the month box, and the calendar changes to show the dates of that month in the year that appears in the year box. The Appointment Book also changes to display whatever date is selected in the calendar.

2. If you need to change the year, click the arrow to the right of the year box to display a drop-down list of years. Click the year in which the appointment is to take place. The year you selected appears in the year box and the dates in the calendar change to those of the chosen month in that year.

3. To set the exact day of the appointment, click that date in the month calendar. The date you have chosen appears at the top of your appointment book, including the exact day of the week on which the appointment is to take place.

You also can use the calendar to set the date of your appointment by pressing Alt and then using the arrow keys to select the desired day in the calendar. The date you select in the calendar appears in color and the schedule changes to that date. To select a different month, press Shift+Alt and use the arrow keys to select the desired month. As you press Shift+Alt+*arrow key,* the month shown in the drop-down list and the month in the schedule change.

Another method of setting the date for your appointment uses the Go To Date dialog box. To set an appointment date with the Go To Date dialog box, follow these steps:

1. Choose **E**dit **G**o To Date or press Ctrl+G; the Go To Date dialog box appears (see fig. 11.7).

Fig. 11.7

The Go To Date
dialog box.

2. Type the desired date in the Go To Date dialog box.

   or

   Use the right- and left-arrow keys to move to different parts of the date and type the numbers of the new date. (You also can click on the up or down scroll arrows to the right of the date box until the correct date appears.)

3. After you have finished entering the correct date, choose OK or press Enter. The correct day and date appears at the top of the page in your Appointment Book.

If you are working in the Planner, you can quickly move to a date and time in the Appointment book by double-clicking on the square of the date and time to which you want to move. The Appointment book will display with the date and time you selected.

After you set the date for your appointment, you must set the beginning and ending times of the appointment and enter a description of the appointment. (After these times are set, the total time of the appointment is blocked off in your Planner.) Enter the time and description for the appointment by following these steps:

1. Click the time the appointment begins in the column of half hour time periods that lies along the left side of the Appointment Book and drag the mouse pointer down to the ending time for the appointment and release the mouse button. The entire time for the appointment is highlighted.

   or

   Press Shift+Tab to move to the time column of the appointment list. Use the up- or down-arrow keys to move to the beginning time of the appointment, press the Shift key and use the down arrow to move to the end time, and release the Shift key. The time period for the appointment is highlighted.

2. Type a description for the appointment.

   As soon as you start typing, the highlighted time slot is displayed with a white background, with green lines before and after the time. The text description for the appointment appears inside the box. If you type beyond the limits of the box, the box will scroll to allow you to continue adding text. When you select another time slot or appointment, the green borders will disappear from this time slot. You do not have to press Enter when you have finished typing the description.

Adding an Appointment by Using the New Appointment Command

To designate any appointment as tentative or private (or both) and to set up a reminder for an upcoming appointment, you must use the Appointment dialog box. Just as when you add an appointment directly to your Appointment Book, you can select the time for your appointment and enter a description for it. You can also view the time slots for several days at a glance by using the Choose Time option in the Appointment dialog box, and then selecting the time for your appointment from this display of time slots. To set an appointment using the Appointment dialog box, follow these steps:

1. Choose Appointment New Appointment, or press Ctrl+N. The Appointment dialog box appears, as shown in figure 11.8.

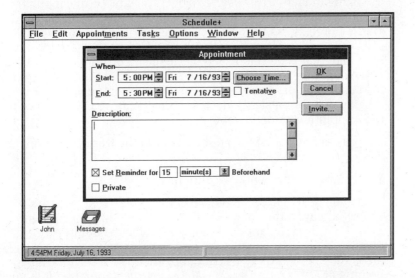

Fig. 11.8

The Appointment dialog box.

2. Set the start and end times and dates for the appointment in the **S**tart and **E**nd boxes.

   To set the times and dates using the mouse, click in the part of the time or date that you want to change to select it and then type in a new number, or click on the up or down arrows on the right side of the time and date boxes to change the entry in the selected slot.

   To set the times and dates using the keyboard, press the Tab key to move to the starting or ending time or date you want to change, and then use the right- and left-arrow keys to select the part of the time or date you want to change. Then type in a new entry or use the up and down arrows on the keyboard to select a new entry.

   If you chose the date and the time slot for a new appointment as described at the beginning of the previous section, using the small calendar in the upper-right corner of the Appointment Book, the date and the beginning and ending times for the appointment appear in the **S**tart and **E**nd boxes of the Appointment dialog box. If the dates and times that appear in the **S**tart and **E**nd boxes are correct, you can skip this step.

   To view the time slots for several days of your schedule at a glance, choose the Choose **T**ime button. The Choose Time dialog box, shown in figure 11.9, appears. You can select a time slot for the new appointment with the mouse by clicking on the starting time on the day you want to schedule the appointment and dragging to the ending time. To use the keyboard to select a time, use the right- and left-arrow keys to select the day for the appointment, and then use the up- and down-arrow keys to select the starting time, press the Shift key, and use the down-arrow key to select the ending time. If you want to schedule the appointment for a date that is not displayed in the dialog box, follow steps 1-3 at the beginning of the previous section to select the date from the small calendar in the upper-right corner of the dialog box. When you have finished selecting a time, choose OK to return to the Appointments dialog box.

3. Enter a description of the appointment in the **D**escription text box.

4. You can select the Tentati**v**e option.

   When you designate an appointment as tentative, it appears against a gray, rather than white, background in your Appointment Book, and the appointment is not blocked out in your Planner. When you or others in your workgroup view your schedule in the Planner, this time slot appears open. Designate an appointment as tentative if you want to get the appointment in your

Appointment Book so you won't forget it, but are not ready to make a final committment to the time for the appointment and don't want to eliminate that time slot for others who are trying to schedule meetings.

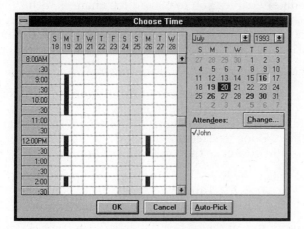

Fig. 11.9

The Choose Time dialog box displays several days of your schedule at a glance.

5. To set a reminder for the appointment, select the Set **R**eminder check box and enter the amount of time you want to be reminded before the appointment. (See "Setting Appointment Reminders," later in this chapter, for details on how to set reminders for appointments.)

   After you set a reminder for an appointment, a bell icon appears next to that appointment in your Appointment Book (refer to fig. 11.1).

6. To designate an appointment as private, select the **P**rivate check box.

   When you designate an appointment as private, others in your workgroup cannot view the appointment in your schedule (see "Viewing or Modifying Another User's Appointment Book or Task List"). After you make an appointment private, a key icon appears next to the appointment in your Appointment Book (refer to fig. 11.1).

7. Choose OK or press Enter.

The appointment now appears in your Appointment Book on the scheduled date, as well as in the Planner if it is not a tentative appointment, just as you described it in the Appointment dialog box.

After you have entered an appointment in your Appointment Book, you can edit that appointment or you can designate the appointment as a recurring appointment.

Editing an Appointment

As often happens, you may need to change the details of an appointment after you have recorded the appointment in your Appointment Book. Schedule+ enables you to make such changes with a few easy edits, whether the changes involve the appointment's description, a complete change in day or time, or selecting one of the options described earlier, such as a reminder or making the appointment private.

To change the description of an appointment, follow these steps:

1. Display the page in your Appointment Book for the date of the appointment you want to edit. Follow steps 1-3 at the beginning of the section entitled "Adding an Appointment Directly in Your Appointment Book" to select the date from the small calendar in the upper-right corner of the Appointment Book.

2. Double-click the time slot containing the appointment you want to edit or press the Tab key to select the appointment then choose the **Edit** Edit Appt command (or press Ctrl+E).

   The Appointment dialog box appears (refer to fig. 11.8).

3. Edit the text that appears in the **D**escription text box of the Appointment dialog box as you would edit the text in any dialog box, using the Backspace, Delete, and arrow keys.

4. If necessary, change the time for the appointment. See the previous section for details on how to change the time.

5. Choose OK or press Enter.

   You can also select or deselect the Tentati**v**e, **P**rivate, or Set **R**eminder For options in the Appointment dialog box by marking or unmarking the appropriate check boxes. (See "Adding an Appointment Using the New Appointment Command," earlier in this chapter, and "Setting Appointment Reminders," later in this chapter, for information on these options.)

T I P   You can change the description and time slot for an appointment without using the Appointment dialog box. To change the description, select the appointment, and edit the text in the time slot, as you edit any text. To change the beginning time for the appointment, click on the top edge of the time slot and drag the appointment to the new starting time. The duration of the appointment will stay the same; only the start time changes. To extend the time slot for the appointment, click on the bottom edge of the appointment and drag the edge to the new ending time.

Moving an Appointment

Moving an appointment to a new date and time is easy. To move an appointment, follow these steps:

1. Display the page in your Appointment Book for the date of the appointment you want to move. Follow steps 1-3 at the beginning of the section "Adding an Appointment Directly in Your Appointment Book" to select the date from the small calendar in the upper-right corner of the Appointment Book.

2. Click on the time slot for the appointment you want to move or press the Tab key to select the appointment.

3. Choose the **E**dit Mo**v**e Appt command (or press Ctrl+O). The Move Appointment dialog box appears (see fig. 11.10).

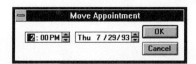

Fig. 11.10

The Move Appointment dialog box.

4. Set the new time and date for the appointment.

   To set the times and dates using the mouse, click in the part of the time or date that you want to change to select it and then type in a new number or click on the up or down arrows on the right side of the time and date boxes to change the entry in the selected slot.

   To set the times and dates using the keyboard, press the Tab key to move to the starting or ending time or date you want to change, and then use the right- or left-arrow keys to select the part of the time or date you want to change. Type in a new entry or use the up and down arrows on the keyboard to select a new entry.

5. Choose OK or press Enter.

Schedule+ moves the appointment to the new day and time in your Appointment Book.

Copying an Appointment

You may be able to save time by copying an existing appointment to another time slot in your Appointment Book rather than having to reenter the appointment. To copy an appointment, follow these steps:

1. Display the page in your Appointment Book for the date of the appointment you want to copy. Follow steps 1-3 at the beginning of the section "Adding an Appointment Directly in Your Appointment Book" to select the date from the small calendar in the upper-right corner of the Appointment Book.

2. Click on the time slot for the appointment you want to move or press the Tab key to select the appointment.

3. Choose the **E**dit **C**opy Appt command (or press Ctrl+Y).

4. Select the new date and time for the appointment, as described at the beginning of the section "Adding an Appointment Directly in Your Appointment Book."

5. Choose the **E**dit **P**aste command (or press Ctrl+V).

A copy of the original appointment appears at the new day and time in your Appointment Book.

T I P If you have a recurring appointment, use the Recurring Appointment feature in Schedule+ to set an appointment that repeats at a consistent interval. To learn how to work with repetitive appointments, see the following section titled "Creating a Recurring Appointment."

Deleting an Appointment

If you want to delete an appointment from your Appointment Book, follow these steps:

1. Display the page in your Appointment Book for the date of the appointment you want to delete. Follow steps 1-3 at the beginning of the section "Adding an Appointment Directly in Your Appointment Book" to select the date from the small calendar in the upper-right corner of the Appointment Book.

2. Click on the time slot for the appointment you want to delete or press the Tab key to select the appointment.

3. Choose the **E**dit **D**elete command or press Ctrl+D.

Schedule+ removes the appointment from your Appointment Book and from your Planner.

Setting Appointment Reminders

You can tell Schedule+ to notify you in advance of any or all appointments listed in your Appointment Book by setting up a *reminder*. After you set a reminder, a pop-up message box appears on-screen at a designated time interval before the specified appointment. You can set a reminder when you are creating a new appointment, or you can add a reminder to an existing appointment. You also can choose an option that sets reminders for all new appointments as you add those appointments to your Appointment Book.

To set a reminder for an existing appointment, follow these steps:

1. Display the page in your Appointment Book for the date of the appointment on which you want a reminder. Follow steps 1-3 at the beginning of the section "Adding an Appointment Directly in Your Appointment Book" to select the date from the small calendar in the upper-right corner of the Appointment Book.

2. Double-click the appointment or press the Tab key to select the appointment and choose the **E**dit **E**dit Appt command (or press Ctrl+E).The Appointment dialog box appears (refer to fig. 11.8).

3. Select the Set **R**eminder For option by placing a mark in the check box.

   The text box and the Beforehand field to the right of the Set **R**eminder For check box list the amount of time and the time interval before the reminder appears.

4. To set a different time interval for the length of time before the appointment reminder appears on-screen, type a new number in the text box immediately to the right of the Set **R**eminder For check box. Then select the appropriate time interval—minutes, hours, days, weeks, or months—by clicking the down-arrow box to the right of the second text box and selecting the interval from the Beforehand drop-down list that appears.

5. Choose OK or press Enter.

To set a reminder for a new appointment, use the method described in "Adding an Appointment by Using the New Appointment Command" to add the new appointment. Follow steps 3 and 4 while you are in the Appointment dialog box to set the reminder.

After you set a reminder for an appointment, a bell icon appears next to the appointment in your Appointment Book.

T   I   P
To set reminders for all new appointments, choose the **Options** **G**eneral Options command and select Se**t** Reminders Automatically in the General Options dialog box. Specify the length of time before the appointment you want reminders to appear and choose OK or press Enter. With this option set, every new appointment will automatically have a reminder set for it. To turn off all reminders, choose the **F**ile Turn Off Re**m**inders command. When you do this, the command toggles and changes to **F**ile Turn On Re**m**inders command. Choose this command to turn all reminders back on. You can toggle back and forth between these two options by successively selecting these commands.

Creating a Recurring Appointment

If a certain appointment recurs on a regular basis, you can save time by entering the appointment once in your Appointment Book and designating that appointment as a *recurring appointment*. Schedule+ enters the recurring appointment in your Appointment Book at the designated times for as long a time period as you specify.

To create a recurring appointment, follow these steps:

1. If the appointment you want to make recurring already exists, select that appointment using the techniques described in previous sections. If you have not already entered the appointment in your Appointment Book, select the time slot for the appointment using the techniques outlined in the section "Adding an Appointment."

2. Choose the Appoint**m**ents New **R**ecurring Appt command or press Ctrl+R. The Recurring Appointment dialog box appears, as shown in figure 11.11.

3. Choose the **C**hange button to display the Change Recurrence dialog box (see fig. 11.12).

4. Select one of the options in the This Occurs group.

   When you select a frequency option, such as **W**eekly from the This Occurs group, the check boxes immediately to the right change. In figure 11.12, these check boxes appear as days of the week because the **W**eekly option button has been selected. The different collections of check boxes that appear for each This Occurs option are listed in the following table:

Occurs option	Frequency that check boxes appear
Daily	Every day or Every weekday
Weekly	Every Week On (specify which days of the week)
Bi-Weekly	Every Other Week On (specify which days of the week)
Monthly	Specify which day of every month; for example, first Monday or day seven of every month
Yearly	Specify a date, for example, March 1 of every year, or a particular day, for example, the first Monday of March

5. Select from the check boxes to the right of the This Occurs group to specify the frequency of the recurring appointment.

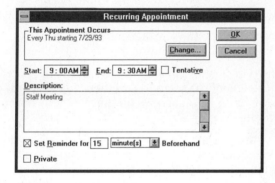

The Recurring Appointment dialog box.

6. To specify starting and ending dates for the recurring event (that is, the first date the event occurs and the last date it occurs), select the **S**tarts and **En**ds options in the Duration box and edit the date entries in the two fields.

    To set the times and dates using the mouse, click in the part of the time or date that you want to change to select it and then type in a new entry or click on the up or down arrows on the right side of the date boxes to change the entry in the selected slot.

    To set the times and dates using the keyboard, press the Tab key to move to either the Starts or Ends date, and then use the right- or left-arrow keys to select the part of the date you want to change. Type in a new entry or use the up and down arrows on the keyboard to select a new entry.

If you select the **E**nds option but do not change the end date, the appointment is automatically set to recur for one year from the date of the page currently displayed in the Appointment Book. Alternatively, you can select the N**o** End Date option, in which case the appointment is set to recur indefinitely (until you change the end date or delete the recurring appointment).

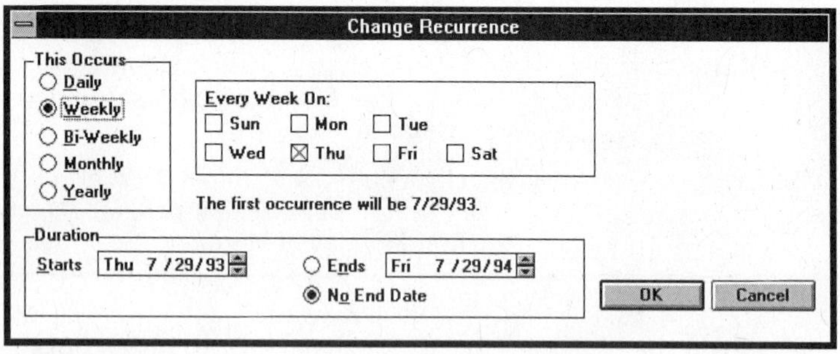

Fig. 11.12

The Change Recurrence dialog box.

7. Choose OK or press Enter to return to the Recurring Appointment dialog box.

8. If necessary, change the starting and ending times for the appointment using the **S**tart and **E**nd boxes.

    To set the times using the mouse, click in the part of the time that you want to change to select it and then type in a new entry or, click on the up or down arrows on the right side of the time boxes to change the entry in the selected slot.

    To set the times using the keyboard, press the Tab key to move to the starting or ending time you want to change, and then use the right- or left-arrow keys to select the part of the time you want to change. Type in a new entry or use the up and down arrows on the keyboard to select a new entry.

9. If you are working with an appointment not already entered, type a description of the appointment in the **D**escription text box. If the appointment is already described, skip to the next step.

10. Select any or all Tentative, **P**rivate, or Set **R**eminder For options, as described in detail in the "Adding an Appointment" and "Setting Appointment Reminders" sections earlier in this chapter.

11. Choose OK or press Enter.

The appoinment is now entered in your Appointment Book for every date that falls within the criteria designated in the Change Recurrence dialog box. A circular arrow icon is displayed next to recurring appointments in your Appointment. The circular arrow can be seen in figure 11.1.

Editing or Deleting
a Recurring Appointment

You can edit or delete any particular occurrence of a recurring appointment in your Appointment Book by using the same method as for editing or deleting a regular appointment. (See the section "Editing an Appointment," earlier in this chapter, for details.) You also can edit or delete *all* occurrences of a recurring appointment.

To delete all occurrences of a recurring appointment, follow these steps:

1. Choose the Appointments Edit Recurring Appts command to display the Edit Recurring Appointments dialog box (see fig. 11.13). The dialog box lists all the recurring appointments currently entered in your Appointment Book.

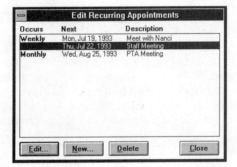

2. Select the recurring appointment you want to delete by clicking it or press the up- or down-arrow keys on the keyboard until the item is selected.

3. Choose the **D**elete button; the selected recurring appointment is removed from the appointment list in the dialog box.

4. Choose the **C**lose button. Schedule+ removes the recurring appointment from your Appointment Book and your Planner.

To edit all occurrences of a recurring appointment, follow these steps:

1. Choose the Appointments Edit Recurring Appts command to display the Edit Recurring Appointments dialog box (refer to fig. 11.13).

2. Select the recurring appointment you want to change by double-clicking the appointment in the dialog box list or by using the arrow keys to select the item and choosing the **E**dit button.

3. Choose the **E**dit button. The Recurring Appointment dialog box is displayed (refer to fig. 11.11).

4. Make the desired changes in the Recurring Appointment dialog box, as described in the preceding section "Creating a Recurring Appointment." To change the time interval for the recurring appointment, choose the **C**hange button, make the desired interval changes in the Change Recurrence dialog box (refer to fig. 11.12), and choose OK or press Enter to return to the Recurring Appointment dialog box.

5. Choose OK or press Enter to return to the Edit Recurring Appointments dialog box.

6. Select another appointment to edit or choose **C**lose. Schedule+ makes the appropriate changes in all the occurrences of the recurring appointment in your Appointment Book and Planner.

Adding Notes to Your Appointment Book

Sometimes you may want to make a note for a particular day that is not associated with an appointment in the Appointment Book. To accommodate such a need, Schedule+ enables you to add notes to the pages of your Appointment Book. These notes are displayed in the **N**otes box in the lower-right corner of the Appointment Book. Notes apply to a specific day but need not be associated with a particular time slot.

To add a note to your Appointment Book, follow these steps:

1. Change to the date in your Appointment Book to which you want to add your note, if not the current date. See the steps outlined at the beginning of the section "Adding an Appointment Directly in Your Appointment Book" for details on how to select the date in your Appointment Book.

2. Click inside the **N**otes text box, or press Alt+N.

   The Notes text box is in the lower-right corner of the Appointment book as shown in figure 11.1. An insertion point appears inside the Notes box where you can start entering text.

3. Type the text for the note into the **N**otes box.

   If you need more room for notes than appears in the box, just keep typing. The text scrolls up as you continue to type, just as with any text you type. You can use the scroll bar to the right of the **N**otes box to move up and down within the box, just as with other Windows programs.

Just as you can add notes to your Appointment Book, you can edit your notes or delete them altogether, as with any text. To edit or delete a note, click inside the Notes box or press Alt+N and edit or delete the text of your notes as you would edit text in any Windows application, using the Del, Backspace, and arrow keys.

You can set an option to display a pop-up reminder message on days that have notes. The reminder message appears on-screen when you first open up Schedule+ on a day that has notes associated with it. Although you would be able to see the notes in your Appointment Book when you open Schedule+ anyway, adding a reminder to your notes serves to bring your attention immediately to those notes as soon as you open Schedule+. When you select this option, it applies to all days that have notes associated with them. Choose the Options General Options command, select the Set Reminders for Notes option, and choose OK or press Enter.

If you need to locate any particular appointment or note within your Appointment Book, you can use the Find command in the Edit menu to search for strings of text. This command is especially helpful if you know you have scheduled an appointment regarding a specific topic or with a person you remember, but you cannot remember on what day.

To find text in your Appointment Book, follow these steps:

1. Choose the Edit Find command or press Ctrl+F to display the Find dialog box (see fig. 11.14).

2. Type the text string you want to locate in the Search For text box.

3. Choose one of the three search options: Forward from Today, Backward from Today, or Whole Schedule.

   The first two search options search through your Appointment Book in the stated direction from the current date only. The last searches the entire Appointment Book.

4. Choose the Start Search button.

Fig. 11.14

The Find dialog box.

If the text you specified is found, the Appointment Book page for the day in which the text occurs is displayed and the text is highlighted. The Find dialog box stays open and the Start Search button changes to the Find Next button so you can continue your search using the same text string by choosing the Find Next button. After you have located the appointment or note you want, choose the Cancel button or press Esc. If the Find dialog box covers text that you need to see, you can move it by clicking on the title bar and dragging the dialog box to a new location, or by pressing Alt+space bar, choosing Move from the control menu, using the arrow keys to move the dialog box, and pressing Enter.

Using the Task List

The Task List in Schedule+ is where you can list tasks you need to accomplish but that are not necessarily associated with a specific block of time, as is an appointment. You can keep in this list a running collection of what you want to accomplish, removing items as each task is completed. You can designate a *starting time* and *due date* for a task. The starting time determines when the task becomes *active* in your Task List. If you have the Show Active Tasks options selected (see "Sorting Projects and Tasks" later in this chapter), only those tasks that are active are displayed. The due date is when the task is noted as *overdue*. When a task becomes overdue, it will continue to be listed in your task list but will be displayed in red typeface.

You can create recurring tasks that are added to your Task List at specific time intervals. You can even attach a reminder to a task so that a pop-up message box appears on-screen to remind you to start the task. You can assign a priority to a task, according to the importance of the task's completion. You then can sort tasks by priority, due date, or description.

You also can create a *project* and add tasks to that project. You can then view all the tasks associated with a particular project. A project is simply a grouping of all tasks associated with a particular job, for example, all the tasks associated with creating a budget or opening a new office.

Adding a Task to Your Task List

As you work with your Task List, you are certain to discover that, as you finish certain tasks, you need to add others to the list. To add a new task to your Task List, follow these steps:

1. If you are not already in the Schedule+ window that bears your name, choose the Window menu, and select your name (or type the number listed next to your name) from the menu.

2. If your Task List is not displayed in the Schedule+ window, click
   the **T**asks tab along the left side of the window or press Alt+T. The
   Task List appears on-screen (refer to fig. 11.2).

3. Choose the **T**asks New **T**ask command, or press Ctrl+T, to display
   the Task dialog box (see fig. 11.15).

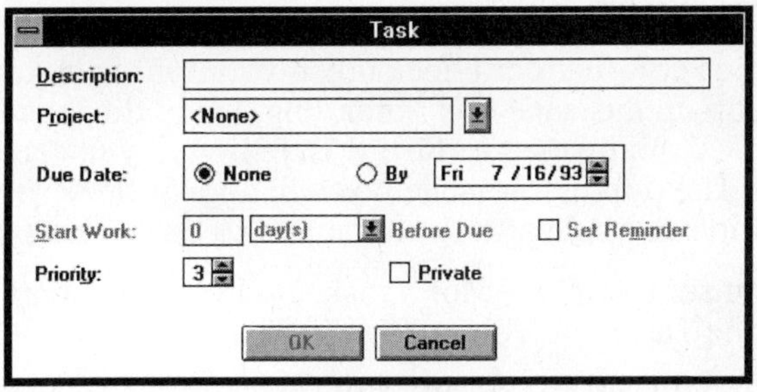

Fig. 11.15

The Task dialog
box.

4. Type a description of the task in the **D**escription text box.

5. To add the task to a specific project you have created, select the
   project from the **P**roject drop-down list by clicking the arrow to
   the right of the Project field. (See "Adding a Project" later in this
   chapter.) Select *None* from the list if you do not want to add the
   task to a project.

6. To specify a due date for the task, select the **B**y option in the Due
   Date box. Select **N**one if you do not want to specify a due date. (If
   you select **N**one, skip to step 10.)

   If you select the **B**y option, you must change the date in the date
   field to the desired due date. (If the correct due date already
   appears in the date field, skip to step 8.)

7. To change the date, click in the date field and edit the date by
   using the arrow, Del, and Backspace keys. Alternatively, you can
   click the up and down arrows to the right of the date field until
   the desired date is selected.

   After you specify a due date for a task, the **S**tart Work and Set
   Re**m**inder options are enabled. You may use these options to designate a starting date for your work on the task and to set a reminder for yourself to start the task on the designated starting
   date.

8. To specify a starting time for the task in the **S**tart Work box, type
   a number in the text box and then click on the arrow to the right
   of the Before Due field. Select a unit of time—days, weeks, or

months—from the Before Due drop-down list. (If you do not want to specify a starting time, type 0 in the text box; the unit of time becomes unimportant if 0 is entered into the Start Work box.)

The time interval you specify in the **S**tart Work box and Before Due field determines how long before the due date the task becomes active in your Task List—that is, before the task is actually displayed in your Task List.

9. Select the Set Re**m**inder check box if you want Schedule+ to display a pop-up message box reminding you of the task on the starting date. (You must set a starting date before you can select this option.) The pop-up message box will appear on-screen in whatever Windows application you happen to be working.

   After you set a reminder for a task, a bell icon appears next to the task in the Task List (refer to fig. 11.2).

10. If you do not want the default priority assigned to a new task, select a new priority level from the Priority box by clicking the up and down arrows to the right of the box.

    Priority levels range from 1 to 9 or from A to Z (if you prefer to use letters).The highest priority level is 1, or A if you are using letters. If you use both numbers and letters to prioritize your tasks, numbers have a higher priority than letters; that is, 9 has a higher priority than A. The default level is 3, or C.

    For the best time management in your day, you should have one to three A or 1 level tasks. These are tasks that must get done. They are necessary to achieving your most important goals. You might have three to five B or 2 level tasks. These are supporting tasks or daily work type of tasks. Frequently, they are the mundane but necessary tasks to keep your job functioning, but they may not advance your career.

    Finally, there are the C or 3 level tasks or tasks at an even lower level. These tasks are the ever-present administrivia that can clutter your day and keep you from advancing your career, spending time with your family, or meeting personal goals. They are such tasks as returning non-mandatory phone calls, attending meetings where you are not a contributor, cleaning out filing cabinets, and so on. Everyone needs an occassional level C or 3 task to give their brain or body a moment to unwind, but try to stay away from them until you are forced to move them into the level B or 2 priority.

11. To prevent other users from viewing this task, select the **P**rivate check box.

After you designate a task as private, a key icon appears next to the task in the Task List (refer to fig. 11.2).

12. Choose OK or press Enter. The new task now appears in your Task List.

Adding a Project

Just as you can create and add new tasks to your Task List, you can create projects and add to them those tasks associated with each project. After tasks are added to projects, you can choose to view the tasks grouped by project in the Task List.

To add a project to your Task List, follow these steps:

1. With the Task List displayed, choose the Tasks New Project command. The Project dialog box appears, as shown in figure 11.16.

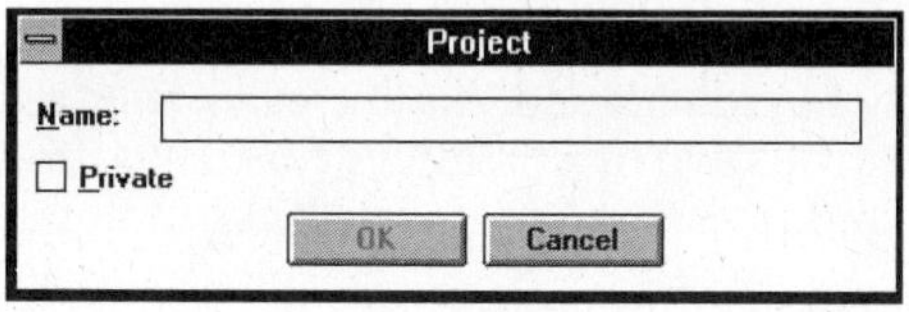

Fig. 11.16

The Project dialog box.

2. Type a name for the project in the Name text box.

3. To make the project private, select the Private check box.

   After you make a project private, that project cannot be viewed by other users. A key icon is displayed in the Task List next to projects that have been designated as private.

4. Choose OK or press Enter.

The new project appears in your Task List. The title for a project appears in bold in the Task List (refer to fig. 11.2). If tasks are grouped by project, all of the tasks for a given project will be listed under the title for the project.

Tasks are assigned to a project by selecting the project's name from the Project list in the Task dialog box for that task, as described in the section, "Adding a Task," earlier in this chapter. Existing tasks also may be added to a new project by clicking the task name on the Task List and dragging and dropping the task under the new project's name on the list, as discussed in the following section, "Editing Tasks and Projects," which concerns moving tasks from a project.

Tasks assigned to a project are listed under the project name on the Task List only after the View by Project option in the Tasks menu is turned on. To turn on the View by Project option, choose the Tasks View by Project command. A check mark appears next to this command if it is selected. To turn off the View by Project command, choose the command again. If View by Project is not turned on, all tasks are listed together on the Task List and project names do not appear in the Task List.

Editing Tasks and Projects

Sometimes you must change the description of a task or project or alter other aspects of a task in your Task List. You may even need to delete a task or project altogether—especially if you have completed it. Schedule+ enables you to edit or delete any existing tasks or projects in your list.

To edit or change a task, follow these steps:

1. With the Task List displayed, double-click the task you want to edit, or select the task by clicking it (or using the arrow keys to highlight it) and pressing Enter. The Task dialog box appears.

2. Edit the task Description in the Task dialog box by using the arrow, Del, and Backspace keys and adding any new text necessary.

   You also can change the task's due date and starting date, set a reminder for the task, change the priority level, or designate the task as private in this dialog box, as discussed in the section "Adding a Task," earlier in this chapter.

3. Choose OK or press Enter.

Changes you make in the Task dialog box are reflected in the task's listing in the Task List after you choose OK or press Enter.

> **T I P** To change the priority level of a task without using the Task dialog box, select the task in the Task List and click the up or down arrow at the bottom of the Task List.

You can edit a project name the same way you edit a task name. To edit a project name, follow these steps:

1. Double-click the project name in the Task List, or select the project by clicking it (or using the arrow keys to highlight it) and pressing Enter. The Project dialog box appears.

2. Edit the text in the **N**ame text box of the Project dialog box.

3. Choose OK or press Enter to transfer the changes to the project name from the dialog box to the Task List.

To delete a task, follow these steps:

1. With the Task List displayed, select the task you want to delete.

2. Click the Delete button at the bottom of the Task List, or press Alt+L. The task is removed from the Task List.

After you complete a task, you may want to keep a reminder that the task is finished. Schedule+ enables you to insert a note about the completed task in your Appointment Book at the same time you remove the task from your Task List.

To remove a completed task from the Task List and insert a note in your Appointment Book about the completed task, select the task and choose the **C**ompleted button at the bottom of the Task List. Schedule+ inserts the description of the task in the notes section of your Appointment Book for the day on which the Task was completed

You can delete a project and all its associated tasks simultaneously. To delete a project and its tasks, follow these steps:

1. Select the project in the Task List, and choose the Delete button. A message box appears informing you that the project and all its tasks will be deleted.

2. Choose OK.

The project and all its tasks are removed from your Task List.

To delete a project without deleting its tasks, you must first move all the tasks from that project on the Task List. You can perform this operation by clicking on each task and dragging and dropping the task in an area of the Task List where tasks not associated with the project are listed. You also can double-click on the task, or select the task and press Enter, to display the Task dialog box. Select *None* from the **P**roject drop-down list, and choose OK or press Enter. After all the tasks have been moved from the project, select the project name and choose the Delete button to remove it from the Task List.

To copy a task from one project to another, first select the task you want to copy in the Task List. Holding down the Ctrl key, drag and drop the task on or under the name of the project to which you want the task copied.

Adding a Task to Your Appointment Book

Some tasks should be completed at specific times or on specific dates. To ensure you don't forget this type of task, you can add a task to a time slot in your Appointment Book. To add a task to your Appointment Book:

1. Click on the Tasks tab or press Alt+T to select the Task List.

2. Select the task you want to schedule by clicking on it or pressing the up- or down-arrow keys.

3. Choose the Add To Schedule button. This displays the Choose Time dialog box.

4. Select the date from the calendar and the time slot to which you want to assign the task.

5. Choose OK or press Enter.

The tasks will still appear in your Task List but they will also be shown in the Appointment Book.

Adding a Recurring Task

If you must complete a certain task on a regular basis, you can save yourself time by entering the task once in your Task List and then designating the task as a recurring task. Schedule+ then enters the task at the designated times for as long a time period as you specify.

To create a recurring task, follow these steps:

1. Choose the Task New Recurring Task command to display the Recurring Task box (see fig. 11.17).

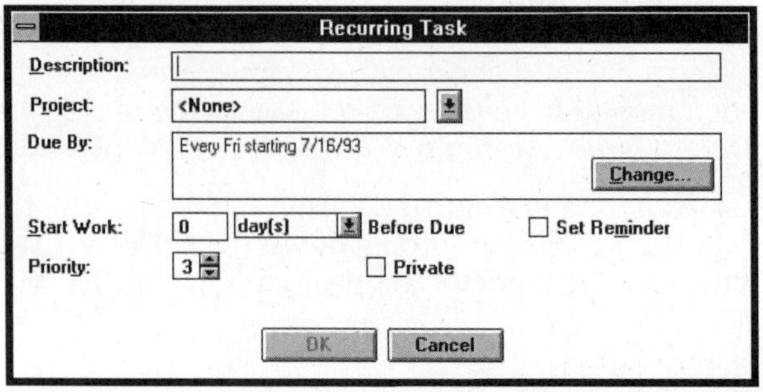

Fig. 11.17

The Recurring Task dialog box.

2. Type a description of the task in the **D**escription text box of the Recurring Task dialog box.

3. To add the recurring task to a specific project you have created, select the project to which you want to assign the task from the **P**roject drop-down list. Select *None* from the list if you do not want to add the task to any project.

4. Choose the **C**hange button to display the Change Recurrence dialog box (refer to fig 11.8).

5. Refer to the "Creating a Recurring Appointment" section for details on how to set up the recurring task.

6. Choose OK or press Enter to return to the Recurring Task dialog box.

7. Follow the steps outlined in "Adding a Task to Your Task List" to finish creating the recurring task.

8. Choose OK or press Enter.

The recurring task now appears in your Task List for every day that falls within the criteria designated in the Change Recurrence dialog box. A circular arrow icon is displayed next to each listing of a recurring task in the Task List (refer to fig. 11.2).

Editing a Recurring Task

You can edit or delete any occurrence of a recurring task in your Task List by using the same method as for editing or deleting a regular task. (See the section "Editing a Task," earlier in this chapter, for details.) You also can edit or delete *all* occurrences of a recurring task.

To delete or edit all occurrences of a recurring task, follow these steps:

1. Choose the **T**asks Edit Re**c**urring Tasks command to display the Edit Recurring Tasks dialog box (refer to fig. 11.18). The dialog box lists all the recurring tasks currently entered in your Task List.

2. Follow the steps outlined in "Editing a Recurring Appointment" to select, delete, or edit the task.

3. Choose **C**lose. Schedule+ makes the appropriate changes in all occurrences of the recurring task in your Task List.

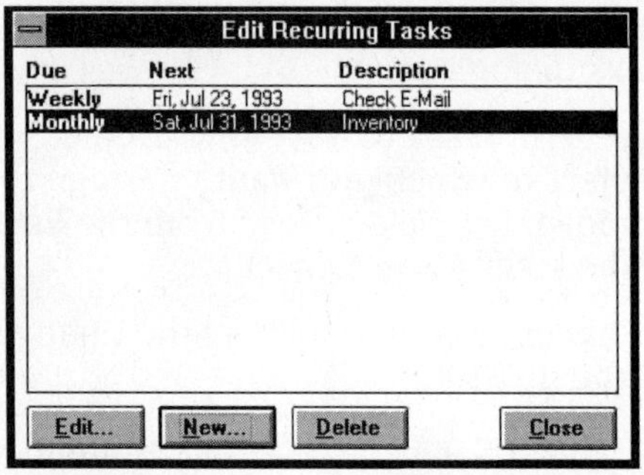

```
┌─────────────────────────────────────────┐
│ ═                Edit Recurring Tasks       │
│ Due        Next            Description       │
│ Weekly     Fri, Jul 23, 1993   Check E-Mail  │
│ Monthly    Sat, Jul 31, 1993   Inventory     │
│                                              │
│                                              │
│                                              │
│                                              │
│                                              │
│                                              │
│                                              │
│  [ Edit... ]  [ New... ]  [ Delete ]  [ Close ] │
└─────────────────────────────────────────┘
```

Fig. 11.18

The Edit Recurring Tasks dialog box.

Sorting Projects and Tasks

Tasks can be arranged in several ways on your Task List. You can display your tasks arranged by project, for example, and you can sort tasks by priority, due date, or description. You also can restrict your Task List to displaying only *active* tasks—that is, tasks with no starting or due dates, or tasks with a starting date that has arrived, or you can display all tasks, including tasks that have not yet become active.

To view your tasks organized by project on the Task List, choose the Tasks View By Project command (or press Ctrl+Shift+V). Return to viewing your tasks ungrouped by project by choosing the Tasks View By Project command (or pressing Ctrl+Shift+V) again.

You can sort your tasks by priority, due date, or description. If your tasks are grouped by project, your tasks will be sorted within each project. Tasks that are not part of a project are grouped and sorted together, separate from tasks assigned to projects.

To sort your tasks by priority, click the Priority button at the top of the Task List, or choose the Tasks Sort By Priority command.

To sort your tasks by due date, click the Due By button at the top of the Task List, or choose the Tasks Sort by Due Date command.

To sort your tasks by description, click the Description button at the top of the Task List, or choose the Tasks Sort By Description command.

To view only your active tasks on the Task List, choose the Tasks Show Active Tasks command. To return to viewing all your tasks, choose the Tasks Show Active Tasks command again.

Scheduling a Meeting

One of the most powerful and useful features of Schedule+, when you are connected to the mail server in Windows NT (or working *on-line*), is that Schedule+ enables you to schedule meetings with others in your workgroup without ever leaving your desk or making a phone call. When you work on-line with Schedule+, everyone in a workgroup can access the schedules of the others in that workgroup. This accessibility enables anyone in the workgroup to schedule a meeting at a time that does not conflict with the appointment times for the others who are to attend the meeting.

When you schedule a meeting, you can select who you want to attend the meeting and suggest a date and time for the meeting, based on times that appear to be open in the schedules of the people you want to attend. After you have scheduled a meeting, a request is sent to each of the people you have asked to attend. You have the option of attaching a message to this request, for example, to explain more about the agenda for the meeting. This request appears in the form of a message in the message window in Schedule+, as well as in the Inbox in Mail. Each potential attendee can then reply to your request by declining, accepting, or tentatively accepting the proposed meeting time. Those people responding have the option of attaching a text message to their reply. Responses to meeting requests appear in your message window in Schedule+ and in your Inbox in Mail.

Schedule+ gives you several options for designating how much other users can access your schedule. You can designate any of the following levels of access:

- Users have no access to your schedule.
- Users can view your free and busy time slots without actually viewing your appointments.
- Users can actually read your appointments and tasks.
- Users can create or modify your appointments and tasks.

You can also assign an assistant, who has complete access to your schedule, act for you in scheduling meetings and responding to meeting requests.

You can schedule a meeting from your Appointment Book or from your Planner. The Planner (refer to fig. 11.2) displays blocks of time for several days at a glance in a day-by-time grid. When you—or others in your workgroup whose schedules you are viewing—have an appointment, that appointment is represented in the Planner by a vertical line running through the time slot allotted for the appointment. Your appointments are represented by a blue line and the appointments of others in your workgroup are represented by a gray line. A calendar in the upper-right corner of the Planner window, similar to the one in the Appointment Book, enables you to change the days displayed in the Planner.

Not only can you view the schedules for everyone in your workgroup, including your own, but you also can mark out a block of time when you want to schedule a meeting, select the people you want to attend the meeting, and send meeting requests (along with an optional message) to each person you want to attend the meeting. If the people you have asked to attend a meeting reply positively, the meeting time is marked in the Planners of all attendees.

Just as you can schedule a meeting, so can you schedule a resource; for example, a meeting room or slide projector. In order to schedule a resource, the Postoffice Administrator has to set up a Mail account on the Postoffice for that recourse (see Chapter 10, "Using Microsoft Mail"). If you then grant full access privileges to other users for that account, anyone can view the schedule for that resource and book the resource during any open time slot. Or, someone can be designated as the assistant for the resource, so that all requests for the resource must be confirmed by the assistant.

Scheduling a Meeting by Using the Planner

To schedule a meeting using your Planner, follow these steps:

1. If you are not already in your schedule window, choose the **W**indow menu and select your name (or type the number next to your name).

2. If your Planner is not already displayed, click on the *Planner* tab along the left side of the window or press Alt+P.

3. Notice who is already listed in the Attendees list in the lower-right corner of the Planner window. Choose the **C**hange button to select the additional attendees. The Select Attendees dialog box appears (see fig. 11.19).

4. Select the people you want to attend the meeting from the Directory box at the top of the dialog box.

   If the list does not include the names of the people you want to send a request to, click on the Directory button (the icon of the open book) or press Ctrl+L and select a new directory in the Open Directory dialog box. To make the directory you have selected the default directory, choose the Set **D**efault button. Choose OK or press Enter.

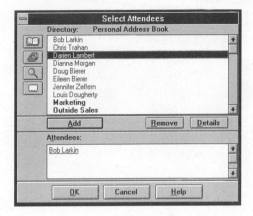

Fig. 11.19

The Select
Attendees
dialog box.

5. Choose the **A**dd button; the names of the people you selected appear in the Attendees box.

6. After you finish selecting the attendees, choose OK.

   If the Attendees list in Planner includes people you don't want to attend, you can click on their names in the Attendees box. The schedules for these people are not shown in the Planner, and these people are not sent a meeting request.

7. Click on the beginning time for the proposed meeting in the Planner and drag to the ending time for the meeting.

   or

   Use the arrow keys to select the beginning time, hold down the Shift key, and use the arrow keys to move to the end time.

   Be sure to select a time when everyone you want to attend is available.

To quickly find a time when everyone in your attendees list is available, select a time slot in the grid equal to the length of time the meeting is scheduled for and choose the Appointments Auto-Pick (or press Ctrl+A).

T I P

---

8. Choose the **R**equest Meeting button to display the Send Request dialog box (see fig. 11.20).

9. Type the subject of the meeting in the Subject box.

   What you type in the subject box is also used as the description of the appointment in everyone's Appointment Book.

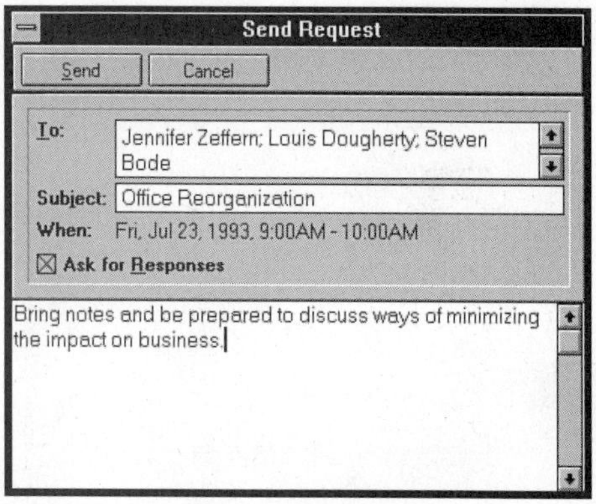

Fig. 11.20

The Send Request
dialog box.

10. By default, the recipients of your request are asked for a response. If you don't want a response, deselect the Ask For **R**esponses check box.

11. Press the Tab key or click in the message area, and type a message to accompany the request. You do not have to include a message.

12. Choose the **S**end button.

A messsage box informing you that the meeting was successfully booked appears. Click on OK or press Enter to return to the Planner. A hand-shaking icon is displayed next to meetings in your Appointment Book.

T I P   The following are some tips for selecting from the Personal Address Book:

■ To view the names in your Personal Address Book, click on the Personal Address button (the index file icon) or press Ctrl+P.

■ To search for a name in the names list, click on the Find button (the magnifying glass icon) or press Ctrl+F, type the name in the Name Finder dialog box, and choose the **F**ind button.

■ To select two or more names listed consecutively in the names list, click the first name (or use the arrow keys to select the first name), hold down the Shift key, and click on the last name (or use the arrow keys to select the last name).

■ To select two or more names *not* listed consecutively, click on the first name (or use the arrow keys to select the first name), hold down the Ctrl key, and click on the other names you want to select (or use the arrow keys to select a name and press the space bar). To deselect a name in the list, hold down the Ctrl key and click on the name (or hold down the Ctrl key, use the arrow keys to select the name, and press the space bar).

For additional information about the Personal Address book—for example, if you want to add names to your address book—see Chapter 10, "Using Microsoft Mail."

Scheduling a Meeting by Using the Appointment Book

To set up a meeting using your Appointment Book, follow these steps:

1. If you are not already in your schedule window, choose the **W**indow menu and select your name (or type the number next to your name).

2. If your Appointment Book is not already displayed, click on the *Appts* tab along the left side of the window or press Alt+A.

3. Select a proposed time for the meeting. This time can be changed after you view the schedules of the other people you want to attend the meeting.

4. Choose the Appoint**m**ents **N**ew Appointment command (or press Ctrl+N) to display the Appointment dialog box (refer to fig. 11.8).

5. To view the free and busy times of the people you want to invite to the meeting, choose the Choose **T**ime button to display the Choose Time dialog box (see fig. 11.21).

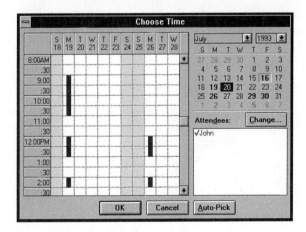

6. Choose the **C**hange button to display the Select Attendees dialog box (refer to fig. 11.19).

7. Complete steps 4-6 described in the "Scheduling a Meeting by Using the Planner" section, earlier in this chapter.

8. If conflicts arise with the time you originally selected in your Appointment Book, select a new time in the Choose Time dialog box.

T I P   To quickly find a time when everyone in your attendees list is available, select a time slot in the grid equal to the length of time the meeting is scheduled for and choose the Auto-Pick button. If you do not like the scheduled time choosen by Auto-Pick, continue to choose the Auto-Pick button to see other times that meet everyone's schedule.

T I P   If you do not need to view the busy and free times of the proposed attendees, you can choose the **Invite** button in the Appointment dialog box to go directly to the Select Attendees dialog box.

9. Type a description of the meeting in the **D**escription box.

10. Choose OK or press Enter.

The Send Request dialog box is displayed (refer to fig. 11.20).

11. Complete steps 9-12 described in the "Scheduling a Meeting by Using the Planner" section, earlier in this chapter.

Scheduling a Resource

You can use Schedule+ to schedule a resource, just as you would schedule a meeting. For example, you may need to schedule a meeting room, a portable computer, or an overhead transparency projector. Before you can schedule a resource, the Postoffice Administrator must create a mail account for that resource and someone has to open up Schedule+ and set up the resource so that it is either accessible to all users or has an assistant assigned to it who will handle the scheduling for that resource.

To add a resource, follow these steps:

1. Ask your Postoffice Administrator to create a Mail account for the resource (see Chapter 10, "Using Microsoft Mail").

2. Sign into Schedule+ by using the name and password for the resource.

3. Choose the **O**ptions **G**eneral Options command.

4. Select the This **A**ccount is for a Resource option.

5. Choose OK or press Enter.

6. Choose the **O**ptions Set **A**ccess Privileges command.

7. Select the **C**reate Appointments & Tasks to give all users the ability to schedule the resource themselves.

   If this option is selected, any user can schedule a resource using the methods outlined in the section "Working with Another User's Appointment Book and Task List" later in this chapter.

   or

   Select the Assistant option and assign an assistant to manage the resource.

   If you assign an assistant to the resource, only that person can actually schedule the resource; all requests for the resource go to the assistant. See "Assigning an Assistant for Your Schedule" later in this chapter for details on how to designate an assistant.

Reading Responses to a Meeting Request

After others respond to your meeting requests, their responses appear in the message window of Schedule+, as well as in your Inbox in Mail.

To read these responses, follow these steps:

1. Choose **W**indow Messages to display the message window (see fig. 11.22).

2. Double-click on the response you want to read.

   or

   Select the response you want to read using the mouse or arrow keys and choose the **R**ead button (press Alt+R).

3. To delete a response, select the response using the mouse or keyboard and choose **D**elete.

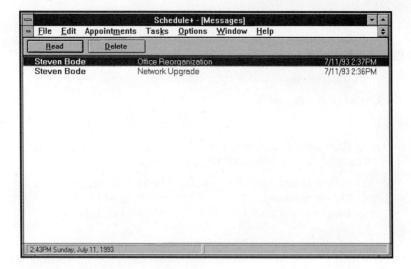

Fig. 11.22

The message
window.

Rescheduling a Meeting

To reschedule a meeting, follow these steps:

1. If you are not already in your schedule window, choose the **W**indow menu and select your name (or type the number next to your name).

2. If your Appointment Book is not already displayed, click on the *Appts* tab along the left side of the window or press Alt+A.

3. Find the meeting in your Appointment Book and move the meeting to the new proposed time. (See the section "Editing an Appointment," earlier in this chapter.)

   At this point, Schedule+ asks whether you want to notify the attendees of the meeting of the change.

4. Choose **Y**es to display the Meeting Request window.

5. If you choose, you can add a message to the request, and choose the **S**end button.

Attendees receive a new meeting request with the new time, to which they can respond as with any meeting request.

Canceling a Meeting

To cancel a meeting, follow these steps:

1. If you are not already in your schedule window, choose the **W**indow menu and select your name (or type the number next to your name).

2. If your Appointment Book is not already displayed, click on the *Appts* tab along the left side of the window or press Alt+A.

3. Select the meeting in your Appointment Book.

4. Choose **E**dit **D**elete Appt (or press Ctrl+D).

   A message box appears asking if you want to notify the meeting attendees of the cancellation.

5. Choose **Y**es to display the Cancel Meeting window.

6. Type a message in the message area, and choose **S**end.

All attendees of the meeting receive a message notifying them of the cancellation and the meeting is removed from everyone's Appointment Books and Planners.

Responding to a Meeting Request

If someone else in your workgroup sends a request to you to attend a meeting, you receive the request in your message window in Schedule+ as well as in your Inbox in Mail. You can read and respond to such requests in the message window.

To read and respond to meeting requests, follow these steps:

1. Choose **W**indow Messages.

2. Double-click the request you want to respond to.

   or

   Select the request using the mouse or keyboard and choose **R**ead (or press Alt+R).

   The Meeting Request window appears, as shown in figure 11.23.

3. Choose the View **S**chedule button to view your schedule.

   To return to the Meeting Request window, choose **W**indow Meeting Request.

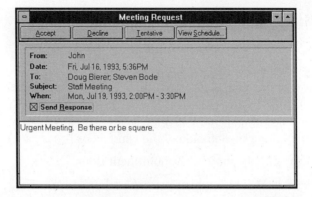

Fig. 11.23

The Meeting
Request window.

4. Choose the **A**ccept button, the **D**ecline button, or the **T**entative
   button.

   If you choose to accept or tentatively accept the request,
   Schedule+ enters the meeting into your Appointment Book.

   The Send Response window appears, as shown in figure 11.24.

5. You can add a message to your response by typing the message in
   the upper portion of the message area.

6. Choose the **S**end button.

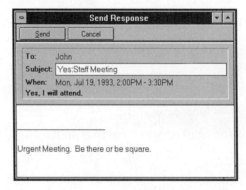

Fig. 11.24

The Send
Response
window.

Assigning an Assistant for Your Schedule

Schedule+ gives you the option of designating another user on your
network as an assistant. That person can then view and change your
Appointment Book as if the book were his own. The assistant also receives meeting requests and responses to meeting requests for the
owner of the Appointment Book. Responses to meeting requests are
logged in the owner's appointment book.

You have the option to have meeting messages sent only to your assistant. Choose **O**ptions **G**eneral Options, select the Send **M**eeting Messages Only to My Assistant check box, and choose OK or press Enter.

Designating an Assistant

To designate another user as your assistant, follow these steps:

1. Choose the **O**ptions Set **A**ccess Privileges command to display the Set Access Privileges dialog box (see fig. 11.25).

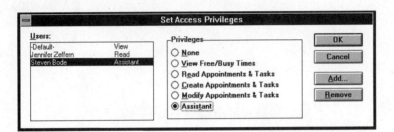

Fig. 11.25

The Set Access Privileges dialog box.

2. Select the user's name from the Users' box if the name is listed.

   or

   Choose the **A**dd button and select the user's name from the names list.

   If the list does not include the name of the person you want to designate as your assistant, click on the Directory button (the icon of the open book) or press Ctrl+L and select a new directory in the Open Directory dialog box.

   Choose the **A**dd button and choose OK or press Enter.

   You are limited to designating one assistant for your schedule at a time.

3. Choose the Assistant option from the Privileges group of options.

4. Choose OK or press Enter.

Removing or Changing Your Assistant

To change your assistant, you must first remove your current assistant and then designate a new assistant, since you can only have one assistant.

418

To remove an assistant, follow these steps:

1. Choose the **O**ptions Set **A**ccess Privileges command.

2. Choose the assistant's name from the **U**sers' box.

3. Select a new access privilege for your assistant.

T I P   You can remove the assistant status and assign the default access privilege to your assistant in one step by selecting the assistant's name from the Users' box and choosing the **R**emove button. The default access privilege is applied to all users except those who have specifically been assigned another access privilege. (See the section "Designating Specific Privileges to a User," later in this chapter.)

Working as an Assistant for Another User

If you are acting as the assistant for someone else's schedule, you must open up that person's Appointment Book before you can work with his schedule.

To open up the owner's Appointment Book, follow these steps:

1. Choose the **F**ile **O**pen Other's Appt. Book command. The Open Other's Appt. Book is displayed (see fig. 11.26).

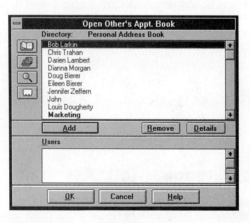

Fig. 11.26

The Open Other's Appt. Book dialog box.

2. Choose the name of the owner from the names listed at the top of the dialog box.

   If the list does not include the name of the person whose Appointment Book you want to open, click on the Directory button (the icon of the open book) or press Ctrl+L and select a new directory in the Open Directory dialog box.

3. Choose the **A**dd button.

4. Choose OK or press Enter.

After you open the owner's Appointment Book, you can schedule meetings and respond to meeting requests just as you do with your own Appointment Book. You receive responses to meeting requests sent by you, and Schedule+ logs the responses in the owner's Appointment Book.

You can act as an assistant for a resource in the same way you assist another user. If you are in charge of scheduling for a conference room, for example, you must be assigned assistant privileges for that resource. You then receive all requests for the resource. After you receive a request, you check for the availability of the resource at the time requested and respond to the request, just as with a meeting request.

Working with Another User's Appointment Book and Task List

In Schedule+, you can view another user's Appointment Book or Task List if the user has granted you that privilege. Several levels of access privileges can be assigned to a user. These levels range from no access to the ability to view and modify another user's Appointment Book or Task List. Each user can designate the level of access any other user has to his Appointment Book and Task List.

Designating Default Access Privileges

If you fail to assign specific access privileges to a user, that user is granted the default access privilege. You can change the default access privilege, which is the privilege granted to all users except those specifically granted another access privilege.

To set the default access privilege, follow these steps:

1. Choose the **O**ptions Set **A**ccess Privileges command to display the Set Access Privileges dialog box (refer to fig. 11.25).

2. In the **U**sers box, select *default* if that option is not already selected.

3. Select one of the access privilege options from the Privileges group.

   The access privilege options are described in table 11.1.

Table 11.1 User access privileges

Option	Description
None	No access.
View Free/Busy Times	User can view the times when you are free or busy but cannot view the descriptions of your appointments.
Read Appointments & Tasks	User can read your appointments and tasks but cannot modify them.
Create Appointments & Tasks	User can add new appointments and tasks to your Appointment Book and Task List.
Modify Appointments & Tasks	User can modify your appointments and tasks.
Assistant	User can act as your assistant, so as to view and modify your schedule, schedule meetings, and reply to meeting requests.

4. Choose OK or press Enter.

Designating Specific Privileges to a User

To designate a specific privilege other than the default privilege to a user, follow these steps:

1. Choose the **O**ptions Set **A**ccess Privileges command.

2. Select the user's name from the **U**sers' box if the name appears there.

   or

Choose the **A**dd button and select the user's name from the names list.

If the list does not include the name of the person whose access privilege you want to set, click on the Directory button (the icon of the open book) or press Ctrl+L and select a new directory in the Open Directory dialog box.

3. Choose the **A**dd button, and click OK or press Enter. Then select the user's name from the Users' box.

4. Select from among the options in the Privileges group. Table 11.1 describes each option.

5. Choose OK or press Enter.

You can determine what access privileges a user has to your schedule by choosing **O**ptions Set **A**ccess Privileges, selecting the user whose access privileges you want to view, and looking in the Privileges group to see which privilege is selected. Choose Cancel to close the dialog box.

Viewing or Modifying Another User's Appointment Book or Task List

If other users grant you access privileges to their schedules, you can work with their schedules. You may be restricted to viewing other users' schedules, but even this privilege can help you schedule a meeting at a time available to everyone you want to invite. If your access level is more extensive, you may have the privilege not only of viewing another user's appointments or tasks but even of adding to or modifying that user's appointments or tasks. Your level of access to another user's schedule depends on what access privilege the user has granted you. (See "Designating Specific Privileges to a User," earlier in this chapter, for details on how access privileges are assigned to a user.)

To work with another user's schedule you must open that user's Appointment Book. To open another user's Appointment Book, follow these steps:

1. Choose the **F**ile **O**pen Other's Appt Book command. The Open Other's Appt. Book dialog box appears, as shown in figure 11.26.

2. Select the user's name from the Directory box if the name is listed, and choose **A**dd.

If the list does not include the name of the person whose Appointment Book you want to open, click on the Directory button (the icon of the open book) or press Ctrl+L and select a new directory in the Open Directory dialog box.

3. Choose OK or press Enter.

The user's Appointment Book appears in your Schedule window. If you do not have access to that user's Appointment Book, you are informed of that restriction. After you have opened a user's Appointment Book, you can work with it in the same way as you work with your own Appointment Book, except that you can perform only those operations for which you have been granted access. To access the user's Task List, click the Task tab on the left side of the Appointment Book or press Alt+T.

Taking Your Appointments, Tasks, and Notes with You

You would be very limited if you were restricted to viewing your Appointment Book, Task List, and notes only on-screen. Schedule+ enables you to print your appointments, tasks, and notes in various formats to carry in your briefcase, insert in your personal scheduling notebook, or post on your wall.

Printing Your Appointments and Notes

To print your appointments and daily notes, follow these steps:

1. If you are not already in your schedule window, choose the **W**indow menu and select your name (or type the number next to your name).

2. If your Appointment Book is not already displayed, click on the *Appts* tab along the left side of the window or press Alt+A.

3. Choose the **F**ile **P**rint command (or press Ctrl+P) to display the Print dialog box (see fig. 11.27).

4. Select a starting date for the printout in the **S**tarting box, and how many days you want the printout to include in the **F**or box.

5. Select how you want your printout organized in the **P**rint drop-down list.

6. Select the print quality you want from the Print **Q**uality drop-down list.

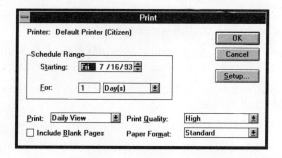

7. Select the size of your printout from the Paper Format drop-down
   list. These paper formats are designed to fit many personal and
   desktop scheduling or time-management systems.

   To change the margins of your printout, choose the Setup button
   to display the Print Setup dialog box (see fig. 11.28). Change the
   settings in the Margins edit boxes and choose OK or press Enter.
   You can also make other changes related to your printer in this
   dialog box.

8. Choose OK or press Enter.

Printing Your Tasks

To print your tasks, follow these steps:

1. If you are not already in your schedule window, choose the
   Window menu and select your name (or type the number next
   to your name).

2. If your Task List is not already displayed, click on the *Tasks* tab along the left side of the window or press Alt+T.

3. Choose to display all your tasks or just your active tasks. (See the section "Sorting Projects and Tasks," earlier in this chapter.)

4. Choose whether to display your tasks by project (see "Sorting Projects and Tasks").

5. Sort your tasks by priority, due date, or description (see "Sorting Projects and Tasks").

6. Choose the **File Print** command.

7. Choose Tasks from the **Print** drop-down list.

8. Choose OK or press Enter.

Customizing Schedule+

Several options are available for customizing the way Schedule+ looks and behaves. You can change the colors used in displaying Schedule+ with the **Options Display** command. You can change the password you use to log into Schedule+ with the **Options Change Password** command. Several other options can be controlled by using the **Options General Options** command.

Changing Schedule+ Colors

To change the colors used in Schedule+:

1. Choose the **Options Display** command to display the Display dialog box (see fig. 11.29).

2. Select the colors you want to use for the different elements of Schedule+ and change the font size for the display, if necessary.

3. Choose OK or press Enter.

Changing Your Password

You must be working on-line when you change your password, since passwords are maintained on the mail server. See the section entitled "Starting Schedule+ from the Program Manager" for details on how to work on-line. To change your password, follow these steps:

1. Choose the **O**ptions **C**hange Password command.

2. Type your current password in the Change Password dialog box.

3. Choose OK or press Enter.

4. Type the new password.

5. Choose OK or press Enter.

6. Type the new password again, to verify your new password.

7. Choose OK or press Enter.

 This password is the same password you use to sign into Mail, so after you change your password in Schedule+, you must use this new password when you sign into Mail.

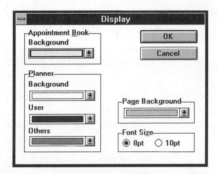

Fig. 11.29

The Display
dialog box.

Changing Other Schedule+ Options

To select other options that affect how Schedule+ works:

1. Choose the **O**ptions **G**eneral Options command to display the General Options dialog box (see fig. 11.30).

2. Change whatever options you want. See table 11.2 for a description of each of the options.

Table 11.2 Description of general options	
Option	**Description**
Startup Offline	After selected, Schedule+ starts up in the off-line mode and creates a *local file* for your schedule. This option is useful when working with Schedule+ installed on a portable or home computer.

continues

Table 11.2 Continued

Option	Description
Set Reminders for Notes	After selected, a reminder pops up on days with a note attached.
Set Reminders Automatically	After this option is selected, a reminder is set for all new appointments, using the default reminder settings.
Sound Audible Alarm	After selected, an audible alarm sounds when a reminder message pops up.
Day Starts at	Determines the starting hour for your workday.
Day Ends at	Determines the ending hour for your workday.
Week Starts On	Determines what day your working week starts on.
Show Week Numbers in the Calendar	After selected, the number for each week is displayed along the left side of the calendar in your Appointment Book.
Send Meeting Messages Only to My Assistant	After selected, only the user you have designated as your assistant receives meeting requests and responses to meeting requests.
This Account is for a Resource	Designates an account as a resource. See "Scheduling a Resource."

Fig. 11.30

The General Options dialog box.

Exiting Schedule+

You can exit Schedule+ in one of two ways: You can quit Schedule+ but stay logged onto Mail, or you can exit Schedule+ and Mail with one command.

To exit Schedule+ only:

Choose the **File Exit** command.

To exit Schedule+ and Mail:

Choose the **File Exit** command and Sign Out.

Summary

Schedule+ can improve how you and the people around you work. You can use Schedule+ to manage your own time, making sure you get back to people on time and don't miss appointments or deadlines. You can even use its Task List to set priorities for all the things you have to do. If you are the type of person who is on the go and can't be tied to a scheduler in your desktop computer, then you can copy Schedule+ to your portable or laptop computer or even print pages that fit in most standard personal time management books or schedulers.

Everyone in your workgroup can take advantage of Schedule+ and stop wasting time doing the meeting room shuffle. Schedule+, combined with Mail's capability to send and acknowledge messages, enables you to check when key people are available for meetings and see which meeting rooms and other facilities are available. Schedule+ uses Mail to notify attendees when the meeting will be. You can even request a return receipt that acknowledges the meeting.

Windows NT can really help you build a team to solve business problems. Use Mail to send and receive messages and pass files and documents to others. It's quick and you don't have to get tied up in conversations about the weekend, traffic, and the spouse and kids. Mail is described in Chapter 10. Don't forget to read Chapter 5 about the File Manager. It's one of the first features most workgroups use. With the File Manager, you can share selected directories between members of the workgroup. No more of the "Nike network" using the running shoes to carry the latest file around to workgroup members. Now, everyone can stay up-to-date with the most current files, templates, and documents.

Using Windows NT Write

W rite is a simple but powerful word processor for Windows. Although it is one of the easiest word processors to use, Write can handle the majority of general business typing needs and produces high-quality results. It offers many of the editing and formatting capabilities commonly found in more advanced applications, including the following:

- Moving and copying text
- Finding and replacing text
- Undoing the last edit
- Setting tabs, indentations, and margins
- Enhancing text with boldface, italic, and underline
- Changing text font and size
- Centering and justifying text
- Adding headers, footers, and page numbers

Write offers an advantage that many DOS applications don't provide: the capability of sharing information with other applications and files. You easily can cut, copy, and paste text and graphics between Write documents. Because Write also is a Windows application, you can move text and graphics between Write and other applications, including Windows NT accessories (such as Notepad and Paintbrush), Windows applications (such as Excel and Word for Windows), and standard DOS applications (such as Lotus 1-2-3). Unlike a more powerful word processor like Word for Windows, Write handles only one document at a time. However, you can have many copies of the Write application open at once, each in a separate on-screen window.

Another advantage to Write is that it uses the same structure of menus, commands, icons, and dialog boxes that all Windows NT applications use. Therefore, what you learn about managing text in Write applies to most of the Windows NT applications involving text. The consistency of the Windows NT environment makes learning new applications quick and easy.

Write files are fully compatible with files created by Word and Word for Windows, Microsoft's full-featured Windows word processors. Word and Word for Windows offer features, such as mail merge, spell checking, and automatic indexes and footnotes, and are ideal for long documents or complex editing tasks. Write is a simpler application, and is ideal for many day-to-day word processing needs.

Creating Write Documents

Creating a Write document is as simple as starting the application and typing the text. Because margins, a font, and tabs are already set, you can begin using Write as soon as you start the application.

Write is similar in operation to other Windows applications, and its screen contains many of the same elements that you see in other Windows applications. Write is a simple application that opens only a single document at a time. In this chapter, however, you learn how to start Write a second time if you want to work on more than one Write document at a time.

Starting Write

With Windows NT running, follow these steps to start Write:

1. Open the Accessories group window from within the Program Manager.

2. With the mouse, double-click the Write icon. With the keyboard, select the Write icon by pressing the direction keys and then pressing Enter.

Starting Write opens a new Write file (see fig. 12.1).

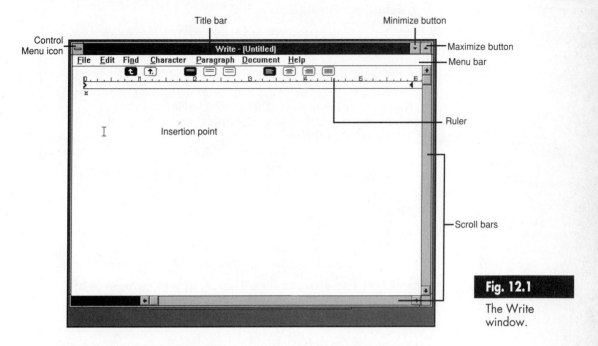

Fig. 12.1

The Write
window.

The Write window includes a title bar at the top, which shows the name
of the document (a new document is known as *Untitled*). Below the title
bar is the menu bar. Maximize and minimize buttons at the top right of
Write's window enable you to shrink the window to an icon or expand
the window to fill the screen. Scroll bars, along the bottom and right
sides, show the relative position in the document and let you move
around in the document.

> You can start Write from a Command Prompt window. At the
> command line, type **WRITE** and press Enter.
>
> **T I P**

As with all Windows applications, Write windows are manipulated by a
Control menu located at the top left of the window. The Control menu
icon looks like a space bar; you open the menu by pressing Alt and the
space bar. The remaining menus control Write and are unique to Write
(although the **F**ile and **E**dit menus work the same way in Write as they
do in most Windows applications). Write's menu operations are covered in following sections of this chapter.

Using Menus and Dialog Boxes

To better work with Write, you may want to review Windows NT's operation. You can choose from a menu by one of these methods:

Mouse: Click the menu heading; then click the command.

Keyboard: Press Alt, press the underlined letter in the menu heading, and then press the underlined letter in the command. Alternatively, press Alt, press the left- or right-arrow key to move to the menu heading, press the up- or down-arrow key to move to the command, and then press Enter.

You can move between areas in a dialog box using one of these methods:

Mouse: Click the text box or option.

Keyboard: Press Tab to move forward or Shift+Tab to move backward to another option area. Alternatively, press Alt plus the underlined letter of the option you want to set.

After you select an area of a dialog box, turn selections on or off by using one of these methods:

Mouse: Click the selection.

Keyboard: To turn on square check boxes or round option buttons, press Alt plus the underlined letter. To turn off a square check box, press Alt plus the underlined letter a second time. To turn off a round option button, press Alt plus the underlined letter of a different option, or press the left- or right-arrow key to move to a different option button. Another way to turn on and off a selected check box is to press the space bar.

After you make the dialog box selections, carry out the command using one of these methods:

Mouse: Click the command button (such as OK or Cancel).

Keyboard: Select the command button (such as OK or Cancel) and press the Enter key.

In the top left of the text area is a flashing insertion point followed by an end mark. The insertion point (sometimes known as a *cursor* in other word processors) is where text appears when you start typing; the end mark shows where the file ends. Move the insertion point by typing text, pressing the arrow keys, or by moving the mouse pointer (an I-beam) to a different location and clicking the mouse button. Remember that you can never move the insertion point beyond the end mark (if you want to move the end mark further down, position the insertion point before the end mark and press Enter as many times as you want).

The ruler, used for quick formatting, is an optional element in the Write window and doesn't appear when you first start Write, but remains on throughout a Write session after you display it in any one document. To learn about the ruler, refer to the sections on formatting text, paragraphs, and the document later in the chapter.

Starting Write and an Existing Document Together

You can open an existing Write document directly from the File Manager if the file ends with the extension WRI. Simply open the document as though you were starting the Write application: Double-click the Write document (a WRI file) with the mouse, or select the document from the keyboard and press Enter. Another way to open Write and an existing document together is to select the WRI file and choose the File Open command.

You also can open Write and a Write document together by associating Write and the document together in a program item icon in the Program Manager. To learn how, refer to Chapter 4, "Controlling Applications with the Program Manager."

Creating a Write Document

The easiest way to create a new Write document is to start Write, which opens a new file. A blank Write window (the document) appears.

In Write, you can work on only one document at a time. You can start a new document (or open a different document) while you are working on an existing Write document, but the existing document closes. If you haven't saved changes to the existing document, you see the dialog box shown in figure 12.2, asking whether you want to save the changes. Choose Yes to save the changes, No to discard the changes, or Cancel to return to the existing document. When you save the existing file, the window clears, and a new, blank document appears. (For details about saving, read the section "Saving and Naming a Write File.")

Fig. 12.2

A dialog box asks whether to save an existing document before creating a document.

Typing in Write

A new Write window is empty except for the blinking insertion point and the end mark. You can begin typing as soon as you open a file. If you make a mistake, press Backspace to back up and erase one character at a time. Alternatively, you can ignore the mistakes and edit them later. (Editing techniques are explained later in this chapter.)

When you reach the end of a line, continue typing. Write by default *wraps* the text to the next line. Press Enter to begin a new paragraph. Press Enter twice to leave a space between paragraphs. As you fill the page, the screen scrolls down (or left and right), keeping the insertion point in view.

Keep Margins Narrower Than the Screen

If the text is wider than the screen, the Write window scrolls left and right as you type. Some people find this annoying. To prevent left-to-right scrolling, set the margins so that the text is narrower than the width of the screen. (Do this by making the margins *wider*.) If you want, you can return the margins to their original settings before you print the document.

Opening an Existing Write Document

To view, edit, or print a file already created and saved, you must open the file.

To open an existing file from within Write, follow these steps:

1. Choose the **File Open** command. The Open dialog box appears (see fig. 12.3), which contains the items listed in table 12.1.

2. From the Drives list, select the drive containing the file you want to open (do this only to open a file on a drive different from the drive currently displayed in the **D**irectories list).

3. From the **D**irectories list, select the directory containing the file you want to open.

4. From the File **N**ame list, select the file you want to open.

5. Choose OK or press Enter.

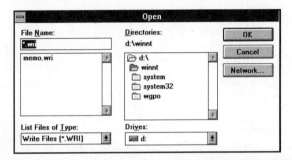

Fig. 12.3

The Open dialog box.

Table 12.1 Parts of the Open dialog box

Item	Description
Drives	From the list, select the drive containing the file you want to open.
Directories	Select the directory containing the file you want to open.
List Files of Type	Select the file type you want to list in the File Name list.
File Name	From the list, select the file you want to open. Or, in the text box, type the name of the file you want to open. (If you want to open a file in a different directory than the one listed in the **D**irectories list, type the full path name.)
OK	Opens the file or directory selected in the list box.
Cancel	Returns to the current document.
Network	Connect to a network drive and browse for documents.

Working with Multiple Write Documents

There is a way to work with multiple Write documents: open the Write application multiple times. Follow the instructions in "Starting Write," earlier in this chapter to start Write the first time from the Windows NT Program Manager. Follow the same procedure to start Write again. You can have a separate document in each Write window, and you can copy or move text (and pictures) between documents using the **E**dit Cu**t**, **E**dit **C**opy, and **E**dit **P**aste commands.

The number of times you can open Write is limited only by the amount of memory in the computer. Because the different copies of Write share parts of their program code, you can open more copies than seems possible for a given amount of memory.

Working with Multiple Copies of Write Is Easy

Working with multiple copies of Write makes comparing different documents, or copying or moving information between documents, easy. There are two ways to work with multiple copies of Write. One is to maximize the Write application you're currently working with, minimize it when you're finished, and then maximize the next Write application. Another is to keep all the Write windows open and overlapping on-screen and to switch between the windows by clicking the one you want with the mouse button or by pressing Alt+Tab.

Moving through the Document

Before you can edit the text, you must be able to move the insertion point through the document. You can use either the keyboard or the mouse to move the insertion point.

To use the mouse to move the insertion point to a different location on-screen, move the I-beam where you want the insertion point and click the mouse button. To scroll to a different area of the document, use the scroll bars at the right and bottom edges of the window. To scroll vertically with a mouse, click the arrows at the top or bottom of the scroll bar at the right edge of the window. Scroll left or right over the document by clicking the arrow at the left or right end of the horizontal scroll bar at the bottom of the screen. Click in the gray area in either scroll bar to jump up or down, or left or right, one screen at a time.

Drag the scroll box in either scroll bar to make a large jump to another position in the document. (The scroll box in the scroll bar indicates your relative position in the document. If, for example, the box is in the middle of the scroll bar, you are near the middle of the document.)

To move with the keyboard, use the techniques listed in table 12.2.

Table 12.2 Keystrokes for moving the insertion point

Movement	Press
Single character	Left-arrow or right-arrow key
Single line	Up-arrow or down-arrow key
Next or previous word	Ctrl+left-arrow key or Ctrl+right-arrow key
Beginning of the line	Home
End of the line	End
Next or previous sentence	Goto (5 on the keypad)+left-arrow or right-arrow key
Next or previous paragraph	Goto (5 on the keypad)+up-arrow or down-arrow key
Top or bottom of window	Ctrl+PgUp or Ctrl+PgDn
Next or previous page	Goto (5 on the keypad)+PgUp or PgDn
Continuous movement	Hold any of the above keys or key combinations
One screen	PgUp or PgDn
Beginning of document	Ctrl+Home
End of document	Ctrl+End

To jump to a specific page, follow these instructions:

1. Choose the Find Go To Page command (or press F4).

2. Type the page number in the Go To dialog box.

3. Choose OK or press Enter.

You Cannot Go Where There Is No Text

Remember, the insertion point cannot travel past the end mark in a document. If you want to move the insertion point farther down, press Enter to add more blank lines to the end of a document.

Selecting and Editing Text

Editing the text you type is one of a word processor's most important capabilities. Write gives you the power to add to, delete from, change, move, copy, or replace text. You even can change your mind and undo the last edit.

You can make simple edits by moving the insertion point and deleting or inserting text. But more complex editing requires that you first *select* the text you want to edit. In fact, the rule "select, then do" applies in Write just as it does in many other Windows applications: You must *select* text before you can *do* something to it.

Inserting and Deleting One Character at a Time

To make simple insertions, place the insertion point where you want to add text and begin typing. The new text is "threaded" into existing text. Simple deletions also are easy. To erase one character at a time, position the insertion point next to the character and press Backspace (to delete characters to the left) or Del (to delete characters to the right). By default, Write reformats the paragraph.

Undoing an Edit

Write lets you change your mind about an edit you just made or a sentence you just typed. To undo, select **Edit Undo** or press Alt+Backspace or Ctrl+Z. You can restore text you just deleted, delete text you just added, or remove formatting. You can even undo an undo.

When you undo typing, the text is removed back to the location of the last nontyping insertion-point movement or the last file save. The Undo Typing command has no character limit. If you find that **Edit Undo** removes too much typing, choose **Edit Undo** a second time to undo the undo.

Notice that the **Edit Undo** command changes depending on the kind of edit you have made. For example, the command may appear as Undo Typing, Undo Formatting, or Undo Editing.

Selecting Text

Many edits you need to make are more complex than simply entering or deleting one character at a time. You may want to change a word, delete a sentence, or move a whole paragraph. Or you may want to change the appearance of text or format a paragraph. To do these things, you must identify the text you want to edit or format by *selecting* it. Selected text appears in reverse video on-screen, as shown in figure 12.4. You can select the text using either the mouse or the keyboard, or a combination of the two.

To select text with the mouse, position the I-beam at the beginning of the text, hold down the mouse button, drag to the end of the text, and release the mouse button. Write also offers time-saving selection shortcuts, such as double-clicking to select a word. The selection bar also is convenient. The *selection bar* is the white space between the left edge of the screen and the left margin of the text. (For example, in fig. 12.4, the selection bar is the blank area between the left edge of the Write window and the left edge of the text in the letter.) When you move the I-beam to the selection bar, the I-beam turns into a right-pointing arrow. You can select a line of text by pointing at the line and clicking the mouse button. Dragging the mouse pointer down the selection bar selects entire lines and paragraphs at a time.

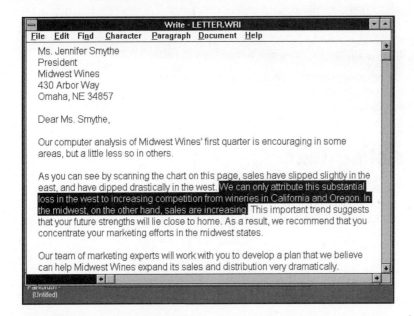

Fig. 12.4

Two sentences selected for editing.

Techniques for selecting with the mouse are shown in table 12.3.

Table 12.3 Techniques for Selecting with the Mouse

Selection	Action
One word	Double-click the word.
Several words	Double-click the first word and drag to the end of the last word.
Any amount of text	Press the mouse button and drag from the beginning to the end of the text.
Between two points	Move the insertion point to the beginning, click, move to the second point, press and hold down Shift, and click at the second point.
One line	Click the selection bar (white space) to the left of the line.
Several lines	Press the mouse button and drag up or down in the selection bar.
Paragraph	Double-click in the selection bar to the left of the paragraph.
Entire document	Press Ctrl and click in the selection bar.

To select text with the keyboard, press and hold down Shift while moving the insertion point with the arrow keys. To select a word at a time, press Shift+Ctrl+left-arrow key or right-arrow key. In fact, by holding down Shift, you can select text while you move the insertion point using any of the techniques described in table 12.2.

To deselect text with the mouse, click once anywhere in the text portion of the window. To deselect text with the keyboard, press any arrow key. Deselected text returns to its normal appearance.

Deleting Text

To delete a block of text, select it and press Delete or Backspace or choose the **E**dit C**u**t command. You also can replace text by selecting it and then typing; Write deletes the selected block and inserts the new words.

When you delete text by pressing Delete or Backspace, the text is erased for good, and you can get it back only by selecting the **E**dit **U**ndo command. But if you delete text by choosing **E**dit C**u**t, you can retrieve it by choosing **E**dit **P**aste (see the next section on "Moving Text").

Moving Text

Any amount of text—a letter, a word, part of a sentence, or several pages—can be moved from one place in a document to another. The process is like "cutting" and "pasting" the text with glue and scissors. Start by selecting the text. Text you cut is stored in the *Clipboard*, a temporary memory space that holds one (and only one) selection at a time.

When you move text, remember that the text is stored in the Clipboard and that the Clipboard holds only one selection at a time. The next text you cut replaces what was in the Clipboard. When you move text, paste the text immediately after cutting so that you do not lose the information.

To move text, follow these steps:

1. Select the text to be moved.

2. Choose the **Edit Cut** command or press Shift+Del or Ctrl+X to cut the text to the Clipboard.

3. Move the insertion point to the new location for the text you cut.

4. Choose the **Edit Paste** command or press Shift+Ins or Ctrl+V to paste the text in its new location.

An Easy Way to Remember the Cut and Paste Keys

Remembering two of the shortcut keys for cutting and pasting is easy. Just think that you want to *shift* text to a new location, so you Shift+Del (Delete) it from one location and Shift+Ins (Insert) it to a new location.

You can use the mouse and these steps as another method for moving text:

1. Select the text to be moved.

2. Using the scroll bars, scroll the screen until you can see the point where you want to relocate the text. (Do not move the insertion point, which deselects the text selected in step 1.)

3. Press and hold down Shift+Alt; click the mouse button where you want the text to appear. The selected text is cut and pasted where you clicked.

Copying Text

You can copy text from one place to another or to several other places in a document. The process is similar to moving, but the original text is left in place.

Copied text is stored in the Clipboard (as is cut text) and can be pasted as often as you like. Remember that cutting or copying another block of text replaces the existing contents of the Clipboard.

To copy text, follow these steps:

1. Select the text to be copied.

2. Choose the **E**dit **C**opy command or press F2, Ctrl+Ins, or Ctrl+C.

3. Move the insertion point to the place in the document where you want to copy the text.

4. Choose the **E**dit **P**aste command or press Shift+Ins or Ctrl+V.

You can paste additional copies of the text in the Clipboard by moving the insertion point and choosing **E**dit **P**aste again.

You can use the mouse and these steps as a shortcut for copying text:

1. Select the text to be copied.

2. Scroll the screen to display where you want the copied text. (Make sure that the text remains selected.)

3. Press and hold down Alt; click the mouse button where you want the text to be copied.

Finding and Replacing Text

You can use Write to help search a document to find or change text— for example, to change a misspelled name or correct an old date. The **Fi**nd menu includes three commands that help you find text and make changes quickly: **F**ind, Repeat **L**ast Find, and **R**eplace.

The **Fi**nd **F**ind and **Fi**nd **R**eplace commands operate through dialog boxes. After you enter the text you want to find or change, Write starts at the insertion point and searches forward through the document. It finds and selects the first occurrence of the text. At this point, you have three choices: you can move the insertion point into the document and edit the text while the dialog box remains on-screen; you can close the dialog box; or you can continue searching for the next occurrence of the text. Close the dialog box when the search is complete. (To move the insertion point between the document and the dialog box, click the document with the mouse or press Alt+F6 on the keyboard.)

If Write cannot match the text you indicated, Write shows a dialog box with the message Text not found.

If this happens, choose the OK button and try a different search word.

Undoing 12 Years of Bad Habits Taught in School

Twelve years of schooling has conditioned most people to write perfect sentences, with perfect structure, and without spelling or grammar errors. The problem is that we are conditioned to try to do all this on the first try. However, people don't work in this way. As a result, many people say "I can't write" and others say "I've got writer's block."

One of the greatest benefits of writing with a word processor is that you need not get it right the first time. Just be concerned with getting the ideas down. You can reorganize and correct them later. You should type your ideas as fast as you can, one idea to a paragraph. Don't worry about spelling or grammar. Never stop writing. When you come across a number, name, date, or fact you don't know, enter a "missing-information" marker and keep typing. If you stop writing to look up a fact or get a book, you can lose ideas and may have to warm up to writing all over again.

Following are some markers you can leave in the text to flag incomplete thoughts:

Marker	Meaning
???	Unknown text
###	Unknown numbers and dates
***	Note to yourself or someone sharing the document

After you have the ideas listed, go back and use the **Edit** commands to reorganize the good material, delete the bad material, and filter out the unnecessary material. Expand the ideas into sentences and paragraphs. Brutally slash out unneeded words, sentences, and paragraphs. Cut and cut until the writing is clear and concise. Use **Fi**n**d F**ind to locate the markers in the document. Then go back and check grammar and spelling.

To find text, follow these steps:

1. Choose the **Fi**n**d F**ind command. Figure 12.5 shows the Find dialog box. Move the dialog box if it obstructs your view of the document.

2. Type the text you want to find in the Find What text box.

3. Select the Match Whole Word Only check box to match only whole words. Select the Match Case check box to match capitalization.

4. Choose the Find Next button or press the Enter key.

5. When Write is finished finding, you see a dialog box that reads Find Complete. Choose OK or press Enter.

Fig. 12.5

The Find dialog box.

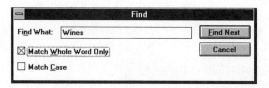

To close the Find dialog box, press Esc or choose Cancel. To repeat the last find, choose Find Repeat Last Find or press F3.

Finding Close Matches

You can use Find Find and Find Replace to find words even when you are not certain which words you want. Do this by using a wild card in the words. For example, the question mark wild card represents unknown characters. If you want to look for *Smith* or *Smythe*, but are unsure whether the name is spelled with a *y* or an *i*, you can search for *Sm?th?*. Write finds occurrences of both *Smith* and *Smythe*.

The following chart lists the wild cards you can use with Find Find and Find Replace. The caret mark (^) is Shift+6 on the keyboard.

Wild Card	Item Selected
?	Any character
^w	Any empty (white) space
^t	Tab
^p	Paragraph end mark
^d	Manual page break

T I P

You can find text in only part of your document by selecting that part before choosing the Find Find command. The Find command then searches only the highlighted text.

Write also enables you to make repetitive changes rapidly throughout the document with the Find Replace command. Some word processors call this a search-and-replace feature.

To change text, follow these steps:

1. Choose the Find Replace command. The dialog box shown in figure 12.6 appears.

2. Type the text you want to find in the Find What text box.

3. Type the text you want to replace the selected text with in the Replace With text box.

4. Check the Match Whole Word Only check box to match only whole words. Check the Match Case box to match capitalization.

5. Choose the Find Next button to select the next occurrence of the text.

6. Select the type of change you want. Following are the selections you can make and a description of the change made:

Find Next	The first time used, it finds the first occurrence of the text. Used subsequently, it finds the next occurrence of the text without replacing the current occurrence.
Replace	Makes the change on the found text and then finds the next occurrence.
Replace All	Changes the specified text throughout the document.

7. When Write is finished replacing, you see a dialog box that reads Find Complete. Choose OK and then choose the Close button.

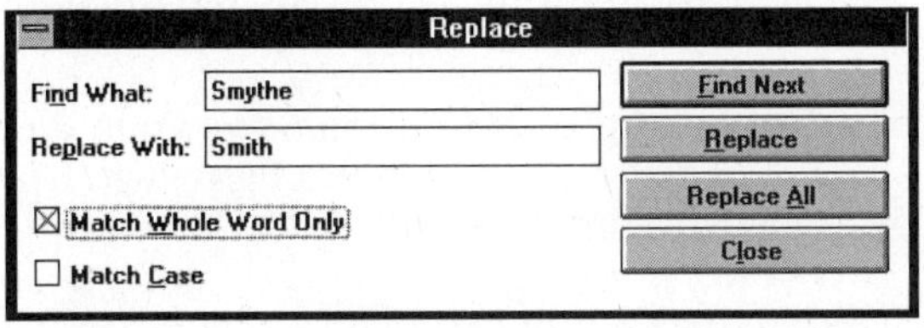

Fig. 12.6

The Replace dialog box.

T I P   You can replace text in only part of your document by selecting that part before choosing the Find Replace command. The Replace All button changes to read Replace Selection.

Formatting Characters

Formatting or enhancing letters and words—by changing the size and style of the letters, or adding boldfacing, underlining, and so on—can improve the appearance of almost any document. Using Write, you have the capacity of enhancing and emphasizing text much like a typesetter.

The Character menu controls the appearance of characters. If you already have typed the characters, you can change their appearance by selecting the text and choosing commands from the Character menu. (If you're not sure how to select text, refer to the earlier section in this chapter, "Selecting Text.") If you have not yet typed the text, position the insertion point where you want the enhanced text to begin, choose the enhancement, and type the text. Choose the enhancement a second time to turn off the enhancement (alternatively, choose Character Regular or press F5 to turn off all enhancements).

Enhancing Text with Boldface, Italic, and Underline

Boldface, italic, and underline are character enhancements you can use to signify something special in the text: a level of meaning, a pause in the thought process, or a change of topic. **Boldface** is useful for calling attention to important text or for creating subheadings in a long document. *Italic* identifies titles and can be used for calling attention to text. <u>Underlining</u> works well for list headings and section breaks. Using these devices consistently helps make reading the document easy and pleasurable.

Many of the character enhancement options, shown in the Character menu in figure 12.7, "toggle" on and off like a light switch—you turn them on the same way you turn them off: by choosing the command. To make plain text bold, for example, you select the text and choose the Bold command; to make bold text plain, you do the same thing. The Character menu shows a check mark next to selected enhancements.

Some enhancements, such as bold and italic, can be used together, so you see two check marks. (Shortcuts for choosing enhancements include Ctrl+*key* combinations, as shown in the **C**haracter menu, and function keys listed in the following steps.)

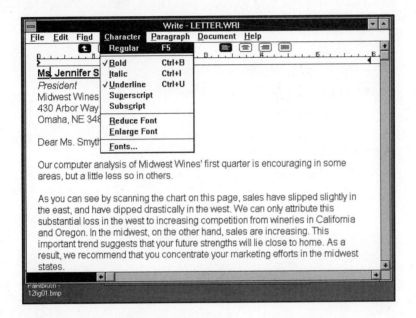

Fig. 12.7

The **C**haracter menu and examples of enhanced text.

You can enhance existing text, or you can enhance new text as you type.

To enhance text, follow these steps:

1. Select the existing text or position the insertion point where you want the enhancement to begin.

2. Choose the **C**haracter menu.

3. Choose one or more of the following commands: **B**old, **I**talic, **U**nderline.

4. Move the insertion point to deselect the text or type the enhanced text and choose the enhancement command a second time to toggle it off.

Several shortcuts exist for quickly enhancing text:

Enhancement	Function Key	Ctrl+Key Combination
Boldface	F6	Ctrl+B
Italic	F7	Ctrl+I
Underline	F8	Ctrl+U

Most fonts (including TrueType fonts) come in four styles: regular, italic, bold, and bold italic. You can add these enhancements through the Character menu or by using shortcuts, but you can also add them through the Font dialog box. To learn how, refer to the section "Changing the Font." Using the Font dialog box is handy when you want to make several changes to the same text because it enables you to change the font, font style, and font size all at once.

Removing enhancements is easy. If text has more than one enhancement, you can remove just the enhancement you don't want.

To remove an enhancement, follow these steps:

1. Select the enhanced text.

2. Choose the enhancement from the Character menu or press the appropriate function or Ctrl+key combination.

To remove all enhancements, follow these steps:

1. Select the enhanced text.

2. Choose the Character Regular command or press F5.

> **T I P**   Because character enhancements toggle on and off, be careful how you select text when you want to remove an enhancement. If, for example, you select a boldfaced word and choose the Bold command, the boldface is removed. But if you select a bold word along with a plain word or character and then choose the Bold command, boldface is applied to both words.

Creating Superscripts and Subscripts

Superscripts (raised text) and *subscripts* (lowered text) are useful in science, math, and footnoting: for example, H_2O or "So proclaimed the King."[4] These features raise or lower the selected text and shrink it slightly so that the changed text fits easily between lines.

To create a superscript or a subscript, select the text to be raised or lowered. Then choose the Character Superscript command to raise the selected text or the Character Subscript command to lower the text.

> **Unavailable Enhancements**
>
> If you try to enhance text but the enhancement doesn't change on-screen or when printed, either the printer isn't capable of printing this enhancement, or you are using a printer driver that doesn't take advantage of the printer's capabilities. Chapter 7, "Customizing with the Control Panel," describes how to get a printer driver to match the printer.

Reducing and Enlarging Text

Another use for Character menu commands is to enhance a passage by changing the size of the type. You can enlarge type to the next larger size or reduce it to the next smaller size. (Write displays only the sizes the printer can print.)

Type sizes are measured in *points* (72 points per inch). A common size for text is 10 points, which produces about six lines of text per vertical inch. Many books and newspapers use 10-point type.

To change the size of characters you are about to type, choose Character Enlarge Font or Character Reduce Font and then type the characters.

To enlarge or reduce text you have already typed, follow these steps:

1. Select the text.
2. Choose the Character Enlarge Font or the Character Reduce Font command.

You can repeat this step, enlarging or reducing the text as large or small as you want.

Another way to change the font size is to use the Character Fonts command, as follows:

1. Select the text to change.
2. Choose the Character Fonts command.
3. Select the size you want from the Size list, or type the size you want in the Size text box.
4. Choose OK or press Enter.

A sample of the font and font size appear in the Sample box.

Changing the Font

With Write, you are not limited to using a single *font* (the style or type-face of characters). Instead, you can choose from several fonts and sizes; with Windows NT and TrueType, the only restriction is the number of fonts that you own (to learn more about TrueType, refer to Chapter 8).

The Font dialog box also enables you to change the font style and size (see fig. 12.8). Table 12.4 lists the parts of the Font dialog box.

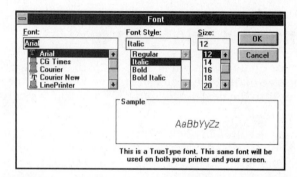

Fig. 12.8

The Font dialog box.

Table 12.4 Parts of the Font dialog box

Item	Description
Font	The Font text box displays the font selected in the Font list. You can select a font by choosing it from the list or by typing its name in the text box.
Font Style	Lists font styles for the selected font.
Size	Lists font sizes available for the selected font.
Sample	Shows a sample of the selected font, along with a message describing the nature of the font.

To choose a font, follow these steps:

1. Select the text to change.

2. Choose the **Character Fonts** command.

3. Select the font you want from the **Font** list, or type the font you want in the **Font** box.

4. Select the style you want from the Font Style list.

5. Select the size you want from the **S**ize list or type the size in the **S**ize box.

6. Choose OK or press Enter.

In the **F**ont list, an icon to the left of each font describes the nature of the font. TrueType fonts have a "TT" icon; printer fonts have a printer icon (screen fonts have no icon).

The font you choose is displayed in the Sample box, along with a message describing the nature of the font. For example, the message accompanying the TrueType fonts shown in the figure explains that the same font will be used both on the screen and by the printer. If you choose a non-TrueType font, a message says, `This is a printer font. The closest matching Windows NT font will be used on your screen.` Using TrueType fonts give you a more accurate screen representation of the final output. To learn more about TrueType, refer to Chapter 8, "Managing Fonts."

Avoid Using Too Many Fonts on a Page

Graphic designers warn against cluttering a page with too many fonts. Although the temptation is great when you have such a wide selection, resist using more than two fonts in a document. Instead, choose one font and vary it with other enhancements. Make titles large, boldface, and centered. Italicize book titles. Make subheads boldface and perhaps one size larger than the text.

How do you choose a font? It depends on the purpose of the document. If a document has a lot of text, most publishers recommend a serif type. *Serifs* are the end strokes on characters that you see in most books and newspapers. Common serif types are Times New Roman and Palatino.

If, however, you are creating a document meant to be easily read from a distance, such as a foil (transparency), poster, or sign, choose a *sans serif* type (type with plain, straight letters). Common sans serif types include Arial and Helvetica.

Determining Fonts and Sizes

To find out what font or size a section of text is, select the text and choose **C**haracter **F**onts. The current font and size are shown selected in the Font dialog box. If you selected text containing more than one font or size, the text boxes are empty; you should select a smaller amount of text.

Linking Text and Data

Through the Windows NT technology called object linking and embedding, or OLE, you can embed or link objects into a Write document. In "Including Pictures in a Document," later in this chapter, you learn how to embed and link pictures.

You also can link text and other data, such as a portion of an Excel spreadsheet, into your Write document. Linked objects retain their connection to the original file, and when you change the original, the linked copy in Write updates to reflect your changes. You can link the same object into many different Write documents—sharing information between documents.

OLE requires two types of applications: a server application, used to create the objects that are linked in a document; and a client application in which objects are linked. Write is an OLE client application. OLE servers include Word for Windows and Excel.

To link text or an object into a Write document, follow these steps:

1. Start the server application (such as Excel) and create the data you want to link into your Write document or open the file containing the data.

2. Save the original data file.

3. Select the data you want to link into Write and choose the Edit Copy command.

4. Switch to your Write document and position the insertion point where you want the linked data to appear.

5. Choose the Edit Paste Link command.

One of two things appears in your Write document, depending on the server application. Either you see an icon representing the data in your Write document, or you see the data itself. When you link text from Word for Windows, for example, you see an icon; when you link data from an Excel spreadsheet, you see a spreadsheet.

If you edit the original data file, the linked data in your Write document updates, by default, to reflect the changes. You can edit the data from within Write or in the server application. Editing links and linked data from within Write is the same as editing a link or a linked picture; to learn how, refer to the sections "Editing a Link" and "Editing Pictures" later in this chapter.

To learn more about object linking and embedding, refer to Chapter 6.

Formatting Paragraphs

Write (like all word processors) defines a *paragraph* as a block of text that ends with a return character (entered when you press the Enter or Return key on the keyboard). A paragraph may be two letters long, two lines long, or two pages long. You can create a new paragraph by pressing Enter at the end of any string of text. Press Enter twice to leave a blank line between paragraphs. Paragraph formatting is preserved when you move or copy text.

Paragraph formatting describes the appearance of a paragraph (or of a single line that stands by itself as a paragraph). Formatting includes characteristics such as centering, line justification, indentation, and line spacing. In Write, some formatting choices were made for you already: text is left-aligned, and no paragraphs are indented. You can change the paragraph format by using the **P**aragraph menu (see fig. 12.9) or the ruler.

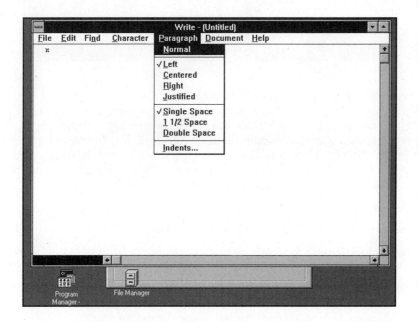

Fig. 12.9

The **P**aragraph menu lists commands for formatting paragraphs.

The optional ruler, shown in figure 12.10, provides a quick way to apply paragraph formatting if you have a mouse. You can use the ruler as a handy alternative to choosing commands from the **P**aragraph menu. (The ruler also is used as an alternative to the **D**ocument **T**abs command for setting tabs.)

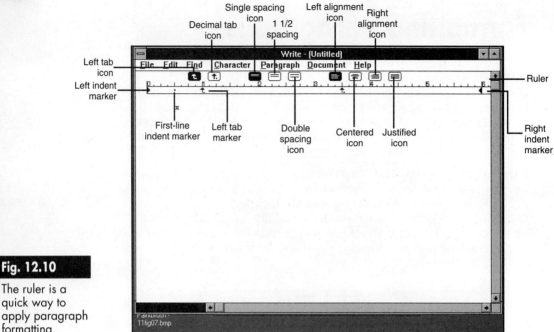

Fig. 12.10

The ruler is a quick way to apply paragraph formatting.

Choosing the **D**ocument **R**uler On command displays the ruler at the top of the screen. The ruler reflects formatting exactly as it occurs in Write's menus; the ruler includes as icons any format settings you have made through menu commands. Therefore, if the insertion point is in a centered paragraph, the centering icon in the ruler is selected (reversed). If you move the insertion point to a left-aligned paragraph, the left-align icon is selected.

The ruler contains the following paragraph formatting features:

- A ruler with inch (or centimeter) markings

- Black triangles that set paragraph indents (within the page margins set with **D**ocument **P**age Layout)

- A white square inside the left-indent triangle or a black square outside the left-indent triangle that indicates a first-line indentation (or a hanging indent if it is to the left of the left indent marker)

- Tab icons for left and decimal tabs

- Three line-spacing icons for single spacing, one-and-a-half spacing, and double spacing

- Four paragraph-alignment icons for left-aligned, centered, right-aligned, and justified paragraphs

To turn on the ruler, choose **D**ocument **R**uler On. To hide the ruler (without losing its settings), choose **D**ocument **R**uler Off. The ruler's zero point begins at the left margin set by the **D**ocument **P**age Layout command, not at the left edge of the page.

The End of Paragraph Mark Holds the Formatting Code

A paragraph's formatting is stored in the paragraph mark that defines the paragraph. This paragraph mark doesn't appear on-screen, but you can delete or select it. If you accidentally delete the paragraph mark, the paragraph merges with the paragraph below it, assuming the lower paragraph's formatting.

You may want to use the paragraph mark to copy a paragraph's formatting. To copy paragraph formatting, select the paragraph mark that belongs to the paragraph with the formatting you want to copy and choose the **E**dit **C**opy command (a quick way to select the paragraph mark is to double-click after the last character in the paragraph). Then select the paragraph mark for the paragraph you want to change and choose the **E**dit **P**aste command. The paragraph formatting is copied from the first paragraph to the second.

Aligning Paragraphs

In Write, paragraphs can be aligned with the left margin, the right margin, both the left and the right margins, or in the center between the margins. The alignment for the paragraph containing the insertion point is identified with a check mark in the **P**aragraph menu. The four different kinds of paragraph alignment are shown in figure 12.11.

How you align text is largely a matter of individual preference, but following a couple of guidelines can improve readability. Left-aligned text tends to be the easiest to read. When you reach the end of a line, your eyes move back to the left margin. If you know exactly where this left margin is, you find it more quickly. Justified text (aligned on both margins) also can be easy to read. The only drawback is that to make both margins even, Write increases the spaces between words. If words are separated by too much space, reading is slower. To help, you can hyphenate long words that appear at the beginning of lines by pressing the hyphen (-) key or the optional hyphen key (Shift+Ctrl+hyphen). Centered and right-aligned text is difficult to read and should be reserved for special effects, such as for headings or short blocks of text.

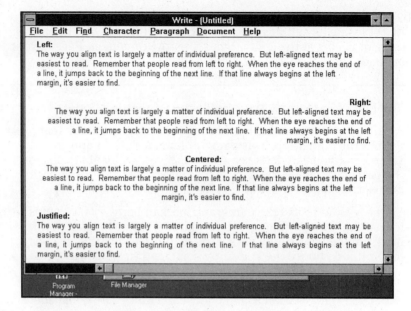

Fig. 12.11

Four ways to align paragraphs.

To change paragraph alignment, follow these steps:

1. Select the paragraphs to be aligned. (To align only one paragraph, position the insertion point anywhere inside the paragraph.)

2. Choose the **P**aragraph menu and select **L**eft, **C**entered, **R**ight, or **J**ustified.

You can restore a paragraph to Write's default format choices—left-aligned, single-spaced, and unjustified with no indentations—by choosing the **P**aragraph **N**ormal command.

To change paragraph alignment with the ruler, follow these steps:

1. Position the insertion point inside the paragraph you want to change.

2. Click the left, center, right, or justify alignment icon.

Using Hyphens to Smooth Justified Text

To justify text (make the margins even on both sides), the computer adds spaces between the words on a line. Doing so sometimes creates large gaps between words, which can make reading difficult. To help avoid wide spaces, hyphenate long words that fall at the beginning of lines. The portion of the word in front of the hyphen moves up to the preceding line, if there's room for it.

Write uses two kinds of hyphens: the normal hyphen, used to join two words (such as *built-in* or *first-rate*), and the optional hyphen, which you insert where a word should break if the word falls at the end of a line.

To insert an optional hyphen between the syllables of a word, press Shift+Ctrl+hyphen. Write doesn't use the optional hyphen unless needed. You can use a dictionary to check the hyphenation of a word.

Suppose that the word *hyphenation* occurs at the beginning of a line of text, but the line above this word has large spaces between the words. Insert optional hyphens by pressing Shift+Ctrl+hyphen in the word like this: *hy-phen-a-tion* (see fig. 12.12). If the line above has room for any portion of the word, these syllables move up, and only the needed hyphen appears.

Spacing Lines in Paragraphs

Lines in paragraphs can be single, one-and-a-half, or double-spaced. You may want to type a document in single space so that you can see the maximum number of lines on-screen; you may want to print a rough draft in one-and-a-half or double space, to leave room for notes when you edit it. The spacing for the paragraph with the insertion point is shown with a check mark in the **P**aragraph menu.

To change paragraph spacing, follow these steps:

1. Select the paragraphs to be spaced. (To change the spacing of only one paragraph, position the insertion point anywhere inside the paragraph.)

2. Choose the **P**aragraph menu and select **S**ingle Space, **1** 1/2 Space, or **D**ouble Space.

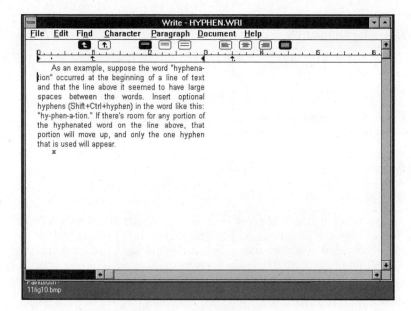

As an example, suppose the word "hyphenation" occurred at the beginning of a line of text
and that the line above it seemed to have large
spaces between the words. Insert optional
hyphens (Shift+Ctrl+hyphen) in the word like this:
"hy-phen-a-tion." If there's room for any portion of
the hyphenated word on the line above, that
portion will move up, and only the one hyphen
that is used will appear.

Fig. 12.12

Using optional
hyphens to
prevent excess
space between
words in justified
text.

To change line spacing with the ruler, follow these steps:

1. Position the insertion point inside the paragraph you want to change.

2. Click the single, one-and-a-half, or double-spacing icon.

Selecting What You Want to Reformat with the Ruler

When no text is selected, the ruler changes margins, spacing, or alignment for only the paragraph with the insertion point. To change several paragraphs, select all the paragraphs you want to change. To select the entire document, press Ctrl and click the selection bar between the left margin of the text and the left edge of the screen.

Indenting Paragraphs

Paragraphs can be indented to set them off from the main body of text—for example, for long quotations. Also, the first lines of paragraphs can be indented so that you do not have to press Tab at the beginning of each paragraph.

Indentations, like all measurements in Write, are measured in inches rather than characters, because Write supports different font sizes and proportional spacing.

Understanding Character Spacing

In *proportional* spacing, the widths of letters are proportional; for example, the letter *i* is narrower than the letter *m*. If margins and indentations were measured in characters, Write would not know how large to make an indentation: An inch might contain 16 *i*'s but only 12 *m*'s. Similarly, varying font sizes means that Write cannot measure the length of a page by lines.

Measurements are calculated in inches and are typed in decimals (rather than in fractions). Half an inch is typed as *.5* rather than *1/2*. Use a negative number for a hanging indent (a *hanging indent* makes the first line start to the left of the left margin or indent).

The **P**aragraph **I**ndents command works through a dialog box, shown in figure 12.13. The settings shown in the figure indent a selected paragraph one-half inch from the left and right margins, and the first line

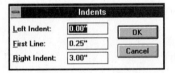

Fig. 12.13

The Indents dialog box.

one-quarter inch from the indented margin.

To indent a paragraph using a command, follow these steps:

1. Select the paragraphs to be indented. (To change the indentation of only one paragraph, position the insertion point anywhere inside the paragraph.)

2. Choose the **P**aragraph **I**ndents command.

3. Type the left indentation value in the **L**eft Indent box. Always enter indentation values in inches, using decimals for fractions of inches (one-half inch is *.5*).

4. In the **F**irst Line box, type the amount of space to indent the first line. Type a negative value to create a hanging indent.

5. In the **R**ight Indent box, type the value of the right indentation.

6. Choose OK or press Enter.

To indent a paragraph with the ruler, use the following steps:

1. Position the insertion point inside the paragraph you want to change.

2. Drag either of the indent markers to the left or right. This method is good for creating paragraphs with double indentations.

To set a first-line indentation, follow these steps:

1. Position the insertion point inside the paragraph you want to indent.

2. Drag the first-line indentation marker (the white box inside the left indentation marker) to the right. The box turns black when it moves away from the left indentation marker.

Hanging Indents Are Useful for Creating Lists

When you want to create a bulleted or numbered list, create a hanging indent, in which the first-line indent is to the left of the left indent. Using the Indents dialog box, you can do this by setting a positive left indent and a negative first-line indent. For example, for bullets to appear at one-quarter inch from the margin and the text of the list at one-half inch from the margin, enter these indentation values:

Left Indent: .5"

First Line: −.25"

To create the same hanging indent with the ruler, drag the left indentation marker (the black triangle at the ruler's left edge) to the .5-inch position on the ruler and drag the first-line indentation marker (the white square inside the left indentation marker) to the .25-inch position on the ruler.

Removing Paragraph Formatting

You can add many different kinds of paragraph formatting to a paragraph, and you can change or remove each one individually. If, for example, the paragraph is centered, but you want it to be left aligned, you simply select the paragraph and select the left alignment command from the **P**aragraph menu or the ruler.

If you want to remove all paragraph formatting at once, select the paragraph (or paragraphs) and choose the **P**aragraph **N**ormal command. The selected paragraphs return to Write's default settings: left-aligned, no tabs or indents, and single spaced.

Formatting a Document

Document formatting affects an entire document and its appearance: headers, footers, and tab and margin settings. The **D**ocument menu controls document formatting; the ruler offers an additional way to set tabs.

In a new Write document, many document formatting choices are made for you already. Margins, for example, are set to 1.25 inches on the left and right, and 1 inch on the top and bottom. Default tab settings are every .5 inch. You can change all these settings and many more.

Adding Headers, Footers, and Page Numbers

You can add one header and one footer to each Write document; headers appear at the top of every page of the printed document; footers at the bottom (you can exclude headers and footers from the first page, if you prefer). You can include automatic page numbers as part of a header or footer.

You can create headers and footers using a special screen and dialog box (see fig. 12.14). The screen, where you type the header or footer text, works like any other Write screen: You can format the header or footer just as you format any Write text. Use the dialog box to specify where on the page to place the header or footer, and whether to include a page number. Headers and footers appear wherever you position them on the page, regardless of the top and bottom margins.

The parts of the Page Header and Page Footer dialog boxes are described in table 12.5.

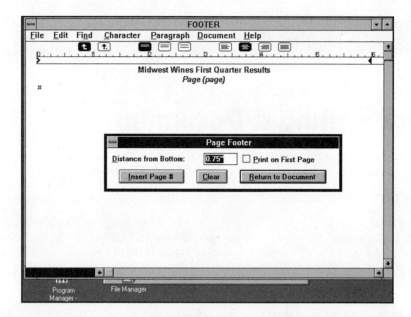

Fig. 12.14

The Page Footer
screen and
dialog box.

Table 12.5 Parts of the Page Header and Page Footer dialog boxes

Item	Description
Distance from Top text box	Where you type, in decimal inches, the distance from the top of the page to the header. (This box appears only when you are creating a header.)
Distance from Bottom text box	Where you type, in decimal inches, the distance from the bottom of the page to the footer. (This box appears only when you are creating a footer.)
Print on First Page check box	Select if you want the header (or footer) to appear on the first page (leave unselected to leave the header or footer off the first page).
Insert Page # button	Inserts the (page) page-number symbol in the header or footer at the insertion point. The page number is printed in this spot.
Clear button	Removes the header or footer.
Return to Document button	Closes the header (or footer) window and returns to the document, saving the settings.

To create a header or footer, follow these steps:

1. Choose the **D**ocument **H**eader or the **D**ocument **F**ooter command.

2. Type the header or footer text. Format the header or footer as you would any document.

3. Activate the Header or Footer dialog box by clicking it with the mouse button, or by pressing Alt+F6.

4. Select the **D**istance from Top or **D**istance from Bottom box and type the distance in decimal inches (1/2 of an inch is .5) for the header or footer to appear from the top or bottom of the page.

5. Select the **I**nsert Page # button to include automatic page numbering. The (page) page-number symbol appears at the insertion point, marking where page numbers will print.

6. Select the **P**rint on First Page box if you want the header or footer to print on the first page of the document. Leave the box deselected if you don't want the header or footer to appear on the first page.

7. Choose the **R**eturn to Document button.

To remove a header or footer, choose the **C**lear button in the Page Header or Page Footer dialog box and choose the **R**eturn to Document button. Pressing Esc in the header or footer dialog box acts the same as choosing the **R**eturn to Document button. If you want to undo a mistake, use the **E**dit **U**ndo command.

Note that a selection in the Page Layout dialog box controls the starting page number in headers and footers. To change the starting page number, choose the **D**ocument **P**age Layout command and type the starting page number in the **S**tart Page Numbers At text box.

Headers and footers do not appear in the document on-screen—you do not see them until you print the document.

Positioning a Header or Footer

Make sure that the position of the header or footer agrees with the top and bottom margins set for the text. Write has default top and bottom margins of 1 inch. Make sure that the headers and footers stay within the margins. Also keep in mind that your printer may have limitations on how close to the edge of a page it can print. Most laser printers, for example, cannot print within one-quarter of an inch from the edge of a page.

Setting Tabs

Write's tab settings apply to the entire document. Write includes preset tabs at every half inch, but you can override these tab settings using the **D**ocument **T**abs command or using the ruler. The tab settings tell the insertion point where to go when you press the Tab key in the document.

You can choose from two kinds of tabs: left-aligned and decimal. A left-aligned tab lines up text from the left; decimal tabs align numbers by a decimal (which is useful for columns of dollar amounts). You also can use the decimal tab as a right-aligned tab, aligning entries that do not contain a decimal point so that the right edge is on the tab setting.

You can have up to 12 tabs in the document.

Setting Tabs with a Menu Command

The Tabs dialog box is shown in figure 12.15 and is described in table 12.6. Set tabs in inches from the left margin (as shown in the figure), not from another tab setting. Press Tab to move between boxes in the dialog box. Remember that tab settings apply to the entire document.

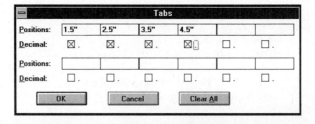

Fig. 12.15

Entering tab measurements in the Tabs dialog box.

Table 12.6 Parts of the Tabs dialog box

Item	Description
Positions	Where you type how far from the left margin to set each tab (type tab settings in decimal inches; for example, a tab one-quarter inch from the left margin is typed as *.25*).
Decimal check boxes	Specifies that the tab above the box is a decimal tab. Click the box or tab to the box and press the space bar to select or deselect this box.
Clear **A**ll button	Clears the tabs you have typed and restores the default 1/2-inch tabs.

To set tabs using the keyboard, follow these steps:

1. Choose the **D**ocument **T**abs command.

2. Type tab positions in decimal inches from the left margin in the **P**ositions text boxes. (Press Tab to move between the boxes.)

3. Select the **D**ecimal boxes to specify decimal tabs.

4. Choose OK or press Enter.

To change or remove a tab setting with the keyboard, follow these steps:

1. Choose the **D**ocument **T**abs command.

2. Select the tab setting you want to change. (Press Tab to move between the boxes.)

3. Type a new tab setting (or press Del to remove the current tab setting).

4. Choose the OK button.

To restore the default tabs at every half inch, follow these steps:

1. Choose **D**ocument **T**abs.

2. Choose the Clear **A**ll button.

3. Choose the OK button.

Change tab locations in a document by changing the tab settings. Suppose that you use tabs to create a table with three columns and then discover you need more space between the columns. You can move the columns by choosing **D**ocument **T**abs and entering the new tab settings. Because the tabs are in the text, the columns move to align on the new settings. If you have a mouse, use the ruler to experiment with spacing (see "Setting Tabs with the Ruler," later in this chapter).

Using the Decimal Tab

Use a decimal tab to line up columns of numbers that include decimals, such as dollar amounts. The decimal positions itself on the tab setting, and the numbers extend before and after the decimal.

You also can use the decimal tab to right-align columns of text or numbers that contain no decimal points. A right-aligned column is useful in an index, a table of contents, or a menu. Figure 12.16 shows a table created entirely with decimal tabs. Notice that the first column in this chart is right-aligned; this effect is created using the decimal tabs.

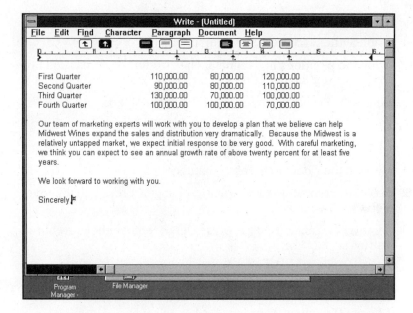

Setting Tabs with the Ruler

If you use a mouse, the ruler may be the easiest way to set tabs in the document. The ruler (shown in fig. 12.16) contains two kinds of tab icons: left and decimal. Set tabs by selecting the icon for the kind of tab you want and then clicking the ruler where you want the tab setting. You can easily move tab settings by dragging the tab arrows left or right. Remove tabs by dragging them down off the ruler. When you move tab settings, any tabbed text in the document moves with them.

To set tabs with a mouse and the ruler, follow these steps:

1. Choose the **D**ocument **R**uler On command to display the ruler.

2. Click either the left-align tab icon or the decimal tab icon to identify the kind of tab you want.

3. Click the blank bar below the numbers on the ruler to set a tab at this point.

By default, the ruler uses inches as a measurement system; if you select centimeters (cm) in the Page Layout dialog box, the ruler displays centimeters instead. To access the Page Layout dialog box, choose the **D**ocument **P**age Layout command.

Setting Margins

Write's margins are preset to 1 inch on the top and bottom, and 1.25 inches on the left and right. With the **D**ocument **P**age Layout command, you can change the margins. You also can specify a starting page number other than 1 for automatic page numbering in headers and footers and can change the measurement system from inches to centimeters.

To set margins, follow these steps:

1. Choose the **D**ocument **P**age Layout command.

2. Select the **L**eft, **R**ight, **T**op, and **B**ottom boxes in turn, and type a decimal measurement for each margin.

3. Choose OK or press Enter.

Choosing **D**ocument **P**age Layout displays the Page Layout dialog box, which you use to change margins (see fig. 12.17). Table 12.7 lists the parts of the dialog box.

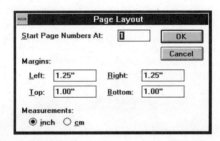

Fig. 12.17

The Page Layout dialog box.

Table 12.7 Parts of the Page Layout dialog box

Item	Description
Start Page Numbers At	Where you type the page number at which automatic page numbering is to start (useful for documents that extend across several files)
Left	Where you type the left margin in decimal inches
Top	Where you type the top margin in decimal inches
Right	Where you type the right margin in decimal inches
Bottom	Where you type the bottom margin in decimal inches
inch and **c**m Measurements	Select either **i**nch or **c**m for the type of measurement you want to use—inches or centimeters

> **Your Printer May Have Margin Limits**
>
> The printer may have mechanical limits that prevent you from using no margins or very wide margins. Most laser printers, for example, must have at least a .25-inch margin on all sides. If you set margins that the printer doesn't allow, you see a dialog box telling you that the printer cannot print with these margins. Enter new margins and try printing again.

Controlling Page Breaks

When you print, Write determines by default where to end one page and begin the next. Write inserts page breaks to start each new page. The number of lines per page depends on line spacing, margin settings, and font size.

If you want precise control over where page breaks occur (or if you simply want to see where page breaks will occur), you can repaginate the document before you print, inserting page breaks where you want them.

Choosing the **F**ile **R**epaginate command displays the Repaginate Document dialog box, shown in figure 12.18.

Fig. 12.18

The Repaginate Document dialog box.

To repaginate with page breaks, follow these steps:

1. Choose the **F**ile **R**epaginate command.

2. Select Confirm Page **B**reaks if you want to confirm each page break.

3. Choose OK or press Enter.

If you didn't select Confirm Page **B**reaks in step 2, Write inserts page breaks and then returns to the document. Page breaks appear as double arrows (>>) in the left margin.

If you selected Confirm Page **B**reaks in step 2, Write displays a page break mark (>>) at the first proposed page break and displays a dialog box you can use to move or confirm page breaks (see fig. 12.19). You can move the page break up or move it back, but you cannot move a page break further down than Write originally positioned it. After you confirm a page break, Write advances to the next proposed page break.

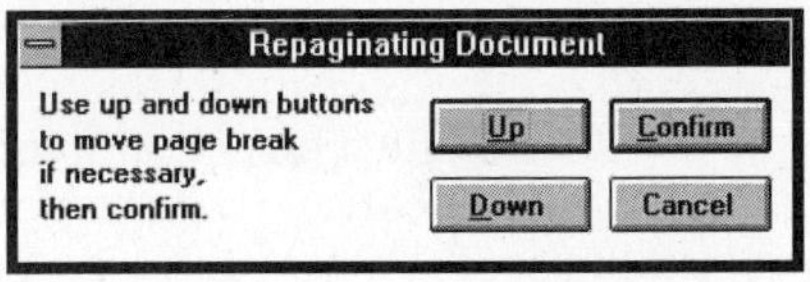

```
┌─────────────────────────────────────────┐
│ ▬    Repaginating Document               │
│ Use up and down buttons   ┌────┐ ┌───────┐│
│ to move page break        │ Up │ │Confirm││
│ if necessary,             └────┘ └───────┘│
│ then confirm.             ┌────┐ ┌───────┐│
│                           │Down│ │ Cancel││
│                           └────┘ └───────┘│
└─────────────────────────────────────────┘
```

Fig. 12.19

Confirming page breaks.

To move or confirm proposed page breaks, follow these steps:

1. Choose the **U**p button to move up the proposed page break. Choose the **D**own button to move down a page break you previously moved up. Select neither button to accept the proposed page break.

2. Choose **C**onfirm.

Another way to force a page break is to move the insertion point to the spot where you want to start a new page and press Ctrl+Enter. The forced page break appears on-screen as a dotted line. To delete a forced page break, move the insertion point just below the line and press Backspace enough times to erase the dotted line.

You also can confirm or delete a forced page break as part of the repagination process. If you're confirming page breaks, when Write encounters a forced page break in the document, it highlights the page break and displays a dialog box asking whether you want to keep it or remove it. Choose **K**eep to keep the break, or choose **R**emove to remove it.

After you repaginate or print a document, you see two changes in the document. Page breaks you entered by repaginating appear as double arrows (>>) in the left margin; page breaks you entered by pressing Ctrl+Enter appear as dotted lines that extend the full width of the page. Additionally, the current page number appears at the bottom left of the window in a status box.

If you made any editing changes, the page numbers shown before repaginating may be incorrect. Repaginate before trusting page numbers or page breaks.

T I P

Including Pictures in a Document

Pictures of all kinds—graphs from Excel or 1-2-3, sketches from Windows NT Paintbrush, clip art from files of graphics, and even scanned images of photographs—can be pasted into Write files, lending a professional effect and increasing communication in finished documents.

There are three ways you can include a picture in a Write document. The first, and simplest, is to copy a picture from a graphics application and paste it into the Write document. The second way is to embed a picture created by a graphics application that supports object linking and embedding (such as Microsoft Paintbrush). You can edit an embedded graphic in Write. The third way to include a picture is to link it from an application that supports object linking and embedding. By default, Write updates linked graphics when you change the original.

Object linking and embedding, or OLE, requires two types of applications: a server application, used to create the objects (such as pictures) embedded or linked in a document; and a client application, in which objects are embedded or linked. Write is an OLE client application.

To learn more about object linking and embedding, read Chapter 6. For details about transferring data between DOS and Windows NT applications, refer to Chapter 22.

Write does its best to accurately represent the picture on-screen. However, the picture is displayed in printer—rather than screen—resolution. If the printer resolution doesn't match the screen resolution (and it probably doesn't), the screen image may appear slightly distorted. But because the picture prints at printer resolution, the graphic will look fine when you print it.

Whether it's copied, embedded, or linked, you can move or size the graphic after you have added it to the Write document.

 You must save a Write document before you can embed or link an object to the document.

Copying a Picture

The Edit commands enable you to copy a picture from another application into a Write document. Figure 12.20 shows a chart copied from Excel and pasted into a Write document.

To copy a picture from one application into another, follow these steps:

1. Open the application containing the picture or chart.

2. Select and copy the picture to the Clipboard. For Windows NT applications, select the portion of the picture you want copied and choose a command such as **E**dit **C**opy. For standard DOS applications, such as 1-2-3, display the picture on-screen and press Alt+PrtSc.

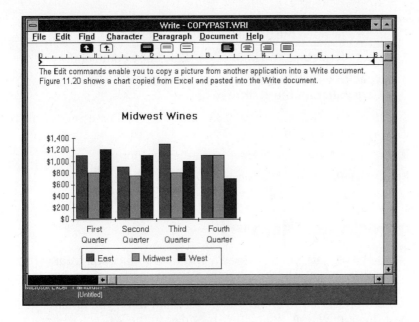

The Edit commands enable you to copy a picture from another application into a Write document. Figure 11.20 shows a chart copied from Excel and pasted into the Write document.

Midwest Wines

Fig. 12.20

A spreadsheet chart copied into a Write document.

3. Close or **Mi**nimize the application.

4. Open or activate the Write file.

5. Position the insertion point where you want the picture.

6. Choose the **Edit Paste** command.

To learn more about using applications together, refer to Chapters 19 and 22.

The result you get when you paste in a copied picture depends on the graphics application you used to create the picture. If the graphics application does not support object linking and embedding, the pasted picture is a static object that retains no connection to the graphics application. To edit the picture, you must create a picture and replace the existing one in your Write document. However, if the application supports object linking and embedding (as does Windows NT Paint-brush, an OLE server), the copied picture is automatically embedded in your Write document when you choose the **Edit Paste** command. You can edit the embedded picture—using the original graphics application—from within your Write document (see the later sections in this chapter, "Embedding Pictures" and "Editing Pictures").

If you want to copy in a picture from an application that supports object linking and embedding, but you do not want the picture to be embedded, follow these steps:

1. Start the sever application, such as Paintbrush, and create the picture or open the file containing the picture.

2. Select the picture and choose the **Edit C**opy command.

3. Switch to your Write document and position the insertion point where you want the picture to appear.

4. Choose the **E**dit Paste Sp**e**cial command. The Paste Special dialog box appears.

5. From the Data Type list, select Bitmap or Picture.

6. Choose Paste or press Enter.

Embedding Pictures

To embed a picture, you can open a graphics application from within the Write document. On the computer, Write opens any application compatible with object linking and embedding technology. You use the graphics application to create the picture and when you update the file or exit the application, the picture is added to the Write document. Figure 12.21 shows a Windows Paintbrush picture being embedded into a Write file. You also edit the picture in Write.

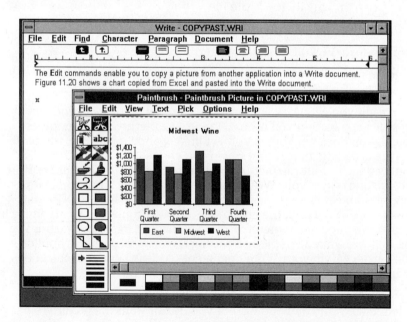

Fig. 12.21

You can embed a Windows Paintbrush picture in a Write document.

To embed a picture in a Write file, follow these steps:

1. Position the insertion point where you want the picture to appear in the Write document.

2. Choose the **Edit Insert** Object command. The Insert Object dialog box appears, listing all applications that support object linking and embedding (see fig. 12.22).

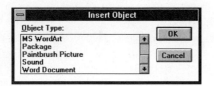

Fig. 12.22

The Insert Object dialog box.

3. Select the application you want to use to create an embedded picture. For example, select Paintbrush Picture.

4. Choose OK or press Enter. Paintbrush opens.

5. Use Paintbrush to create the picture or choose the **Edit Paste** command to paste in a picture from the Clipboard.

6. When you're finished with the picture, choose the **File Update** command to include a copy of the picture in the Write document.

7. Choose the **File Exit** and Return to document command from the Paintbrush menu.

If you get an error telling you of a memory shortage when you choose the **File Update** command, resize the picture to make it smaller and then try again.

When you choose the **Edit Insert** Object command, the Insert Object dialog box lists all the applications on your computer that support object linking and embedding. Because Paintbrush comes free with Windows NT, you always see Paintbrush on the list (unless you have deleted it), but you also see applets like Microsoft Draw if you have installed an application such as Word for Windows, which includes such applications for free. See Part IV, "Using Windows NT Applets," to learn more about these applets.

T I P   When you use the Edit Insert Object command to embed a Paintbrush picture in the Write document, the picture comes in at the full
size of the Paintbrush screen. Write doesn't provide a way to crop
away unneeded portions of the picture. If you want to embed a small
Paintbrush picture, start Paintbrush from the Program Manager
(rather than activating it by choosing **Edit Insert Object**). Select the
picture in Paintbrush, then copy the picture, switch back to Write,
and paste in the picture. The picture comes in at the size you selected, and you can edit the picture in the same way you edit an embedded Paintbrush picture.

Linking Pictures

Linking a picture is similar to embedding a picture—the picture remains connected to the application used to create it. But a linked picture goes a step further: you can update the original, and any Write
documents that contain linked copies are updated by default to reflect
the changes. Like an embedded picture, you can edit a linked file in
Write.

To link a picture to a Write file, follow these steps:

1. Position the insertion point where you want the linked picture to
   appear.

2. Open the application containing the picture you want to link.
   For example, open Microsoft Excel to link a chart.

3. Open the file containing the chart or picture you want to link or
   create a new chart or picture.

4. Save the chart or picture.

5. Select the chart or picture.

6. Choose the **Edit Copy** command.

7. Switch back to the Write document (Alt+Tab switches between
   running applications).

8. Choose the **Edit Paste Link** command.

9. Save the Write file.

Editing a Link

If you have linked a picture or chart in Write, the picture or chart remains connected to the original file. If the original changes, the image in the Write file changes. But there are several ways you can edit the link between the original file and the Write file, using the Links dialog box shown in figure 12.23. Table 12.8 describes the selections in the Links dialog box.

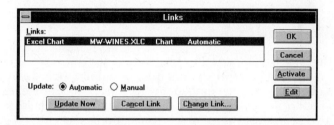

Fig. 12.23

The Links dialog box.

Table 12.8 Parts of the Links dialog box

Item	Description
Links	Lists all the linked files in a Write document. The link you select is the one that the commands in this dialog box will act on.
Update Automatic	Select this option if you want the link in a Write document to update by default any time the original file changes. (This option is Write's default.)
Update Manual	Select this option if you want to update the link manually.
Update Now	Choose this command to update the link (use this command for manually updated links).
Cancel Link	Choose this command to cancel the link between the object in Write and the original file. The formerly linked object in Write will no longer update when the original file changes.
Change Link	Choose this command to change the original file to which the linked object is linked or to update the location of the original file if it has moved to a different drive or directory. You see a dialog box similar to the Open dialog box. Choose the new original file.
Activate	Choose this command to activate the server application.
Edit	Choose this command to edit the linked object, using the server application.

To edit a link, follow these steps:

1. Choose the Edit Links command. The Links dialog box appears.

2. From the Links list, select the link you want to edit.

3. Choose the options you want (see table 12.8).

4. Choose OK or press Enter.

Editing Pictures

From within Write, you can edit pictures that are embedded from, or linked to, Windows Paintbrush or another graphics application that supports object linking and embedding. Editing the picture causes the graphics application to open, with the picture displayed in its window. Although you can start the graphics application using either a mouse or the keyboard, you need a mouse to operate Paintbrush and most other graphics applications.

To edit an embedded drawing using the mouse, follow these steps:

1. Double-click the drawing to open Paintbrush and display the picture.

2. Edit the picture.

3. Choose the File Update command.

4. Choose the File Exit and Return to document command. Or, you can just exit the application, and a message asks whether you want to update the picture in the Write document. Choose Yes to update.

To edit an embedded drawing using the keyboard, follow these steps:

1. Select the picture. Click on the picture or with the keyboard, position the insertion point above the picture you want to edit and press the down-arrow key to select the picture.

2. Choose the Edit Edit Paintbrush Picture Object command. Paintbrush opens, with the picture in its drawing window.

   If you are editing an object created by an application other than Paintbrush, you see its name in the command instead of `Paintbrush`.

3. Edit the picture.

4. Choose the File Update command to update the picture in Write.

5. Choose the File Exit and Return to document command.

    You also can select the embedded object and start the graphics application by double-clicking on the object.

You can edit a linked picture in Write the same way that you edit an embedded drawing. Because you're using the original graphics application to edit the picture, any changes you make are reflected in any other file containing a link to the original picture.

To edit a linked drawing using the mouse, follow these steps:

1. Double-click the drawing to open the graphics application and display the picture.

2. Edit the picture.

3. Choose the File Save command. The picture in the Write document is updated by default.

4. Choose the File Exit command in Paintbrush.

To edit a linked object using the keyboard, follow these steps:

1. In Write, choose the Edit Links command.

2. When the Links dialog box appears, select the file containing the object you want to edit.

3. Choose Edit to display the application, with the object in its drawing window.

4. Edit the object.

5. Choose the File Save command. The object in the Write document updates to reflect the changes you made.

6. Choose the File Exit command.

You also can edit a linked picture by selecting the picture, choosing the Edit Edit...Object command, editing and saving the picture, and exiting the graphics application.

If you have set links to update manually, the Write document will not reflect the changes to the linked picture until you update the link using this process:

1. In Write, choose the Edit Links command.

2. When the Links dialog box appears, select the linked picture you want to update and choose the Update Now button.

3. Choose OK or press Enter.

Moving a Picture

A picture is included in a Write document at the insertion point, but you can move it to another location. A menu command enables you to position the picture wherever you want it relative to the left and right margins; in addition, if the picture exists as a separate paragraph, you can use paragraph formatting commands to align the picture to the left, right, or center of a page. You also can move a picture by selecting and cutting it from one location (or document) and pasting it into another location (or document).

To move a picture to the right or left in a Write document, follow these steps:

1. Select the picture by clicking it or by using the same techniques you use to select a word (position the insertion point before or after the picture, press and hold down the Shift key, and press the left- or right-arrow key).

2. Choose the **E**dit **M**ove Picture command. A square cursor appears at the center of the picture.

3. Move the picture left or right, using the following techniques for the mouse and the keyboard:

   Mouse: Without clicking the mouse button, drag the square insertion point left or right.

   Keyboard: Press the left- and right-arrow keys.

   As you move the picture, a dotted frame moves to show the picture's new position.

4. Click the mouse button or press Enter when the picture is where you want it.

To move a picture up or down on the page, insert or delete lines above the picture using Enter or Backspace. To move a picture to a different place on the page, select it, cut it with **E**dit **Cut**, and paste it with **E**dit **P**aste.

If you change your mind about moving the picture after selecting it, press the Esc key to remove the selection. Choose **E**dit **U**ndo to undo a move.

Use Paragraph-Formatting Commands to Move a Picture

You can center a picture on the page or align it to the right margin by using paragraph-formatting commands. Select the picture and then choose the **P**aragraph **C**entered or **P**aragraph **R**ight command or use the ruler to select the centered or right-aligned icon. You can, of course, align the picture to the left margin by choosing the **P**aragraph **L**eft command or selecting the left-aligned icon on the ruler.

Sizing a Picture

You can change the size of a picture using a process similar to the one you use when you move a picture.

To change the size of a picture, follow these steps:

1. Select the picture by clicking it or by using the same techniques you use to select a word (position the insertion point before or after the picture, press and hold down the Shift key, and press the left- or right-arrow key).

2. Choose the **E**dit **S**ize Picture command. A square cursor appears at the center of the picture, and a dotted line appears on all sides.

3. Size the picture, using the appropriate techniques for the mouse or keyboard:

   Mouse: Without clicking the mouse button, drag the square insertion point to the left, right, or bottom side or corner from which you want to resize the picture and then drag that side or corner to resize the picture.

   Keyboard: Press the left-, right-, or down-arrow key to select the side from which you want to resize the picture (or press the two arrows to select a corner). Press the arrow keys to move the selected side or corner to resize the picture.

   As you size the picture, a dotted frame around it moves, indicating the size to which the picture will grow or shrink.

4. Click the mouse button or press Enter. The picture is redrawn at the new size.

As you resize a picture, its measurements appear in the status box at the bottom-left corner of the window. The measurements appear as X and Y coordinates; the X coordinate refers to the picture's horizontal width; the Y coordinate refers to the vertical height. You usually should make the measurements the same (3X wide by 3Y high, for example) to keep the picture in proportion; try to use whole numbers to prevent distortion.

Printing

Printing with Write involves three steps: installing a printer in Windows NT, selecting the printer you use in Write, and printing the current document.

To install the printer, you must tell Windows NT during installation which printer (or printers) you want to use; alternatively, you can add printers after installation by using the Control Panel. (The Control Panel also is used to set printer connections and default settings for printers. To learn more about using the Control Panel, refer to Chapter 7, "Customizing with the Control Panel.")

Selecting a Printer

To select a printer, you must access the Print Setup dialog box. You can do this by choosing the File Print Setup command or by choosing the Setup button in the Print dialog box. Once a printer is selected, it remains selected for all documents—you won't have to select a printer again unless you want to change to a different printer.

The Print Setup dialog box lists all the printers installed for Windows NT on the computer, as well as options for selecting paper orientation, size, and source. When you select a printer, page orientation, paper size, and paper source, the choices remain in effect until you change them—even after you start a new document. The dialog box also includes an Options button; choose it to select additional information, such as gray scale image type on an HP LaserJet printer, or scaling on a PostScript printer. The Print Setup and Options dialog boxes are shown in figure 12.24.

To identify and set up the default printer, follow these steps:

1. Choose the File Print Setup command or choose the File Print command and choose the Setup button.

2. Select either the Default Printer or another printer from the Specific Printer list.

3. Select the paper orientation: Portrait (vertical pages) or Landscape (horizontal pages).

4. Select a Paper Size and Source from the lists provided.

5. Choose Options to make additional choices, depending on the printer. (The dialog box that appears may contain another Options button, enabling you to set Advanced Options.)

6. Choose OK to close the Options dialog box; then choose OK or press Enter to close the Print Setup dialog box.

Figure 12.24 shows the Print Setup, Document Properties, and Advanced Document Properties dialog boxes for an HP LaserJet IIIsi printer (the Document Properties dialog box you see depends on the printer you select). Table 12.9 describes the contents of the Print Setup dialog box.

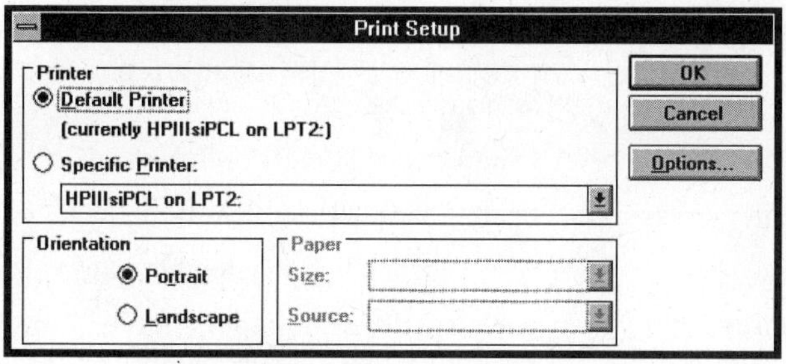

(a)

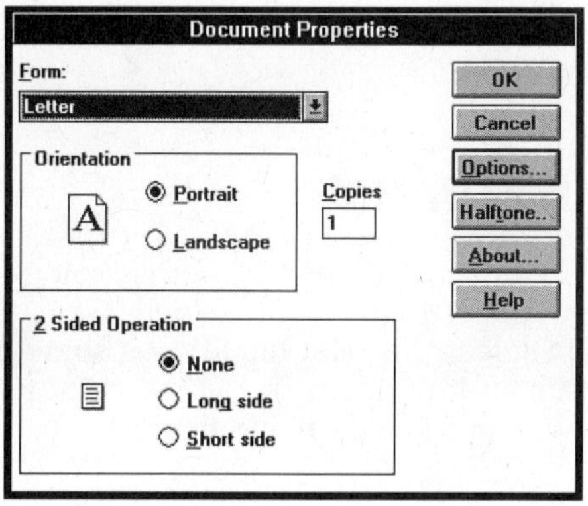

(b)

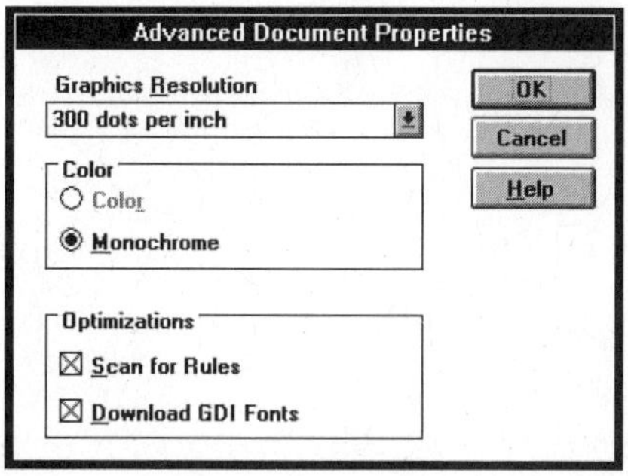

(c)

Fig. 12.24

The Print Setup (a), Document Properties (b), and Advanced Document Properties (c) dialog boxes.

Table 12.9 Parts of the Print Setup dialog box

Item	Description
Default Printer	Select this option to print on the default printer (you choose the default printer in the Control Panel).
Specific **P**rinter	Select a printer from this list if you want to print on any of the other printers installed in Windows NT.
Orientation Po**r**trait	Prints text vertically on the page.
Orientation **L**andscape	Prints text horizontally on the page.
Paper Si**z**e	Select from a list of available paper sizes.
Paper **S**ource	Selects a different paper source, if the printer has more than a single paper tray or bin.
Network	Select a new pointer from those available on your network.

Printing a Document

When you print a document, you have several choices to make. You can select a range of pages to print (by default, Write prints the entire document); you can select the print quality (on some printers you can save time by printing in draft quality); you can print to a file rather than to the printer; and you can select the number of copies and whether they are collated.

To print a document, follow these steps:

1. Choose the **F**ile **P**rint command. The Print dialog box appears (see fig. 12.25).

2. Select the Print Range **A**ll button to print all the pages; select Print Range Se**l**ection to print only the selected text; or select the **P**ages **F**rom and **P**ages **T**o text boxes and type a range of pages to print.

3. From the Print **Q**uality list, select the print resolution you want.

4. Select the Print to Fi**l**e option to print to a file rather than to the printer.

5. In the **C**opies box, type the number of copies you want to print.

6. To collate multiple copies of the document, select Collate Copies (available if your printer supports collating).

7. Choose OK or press Enter.

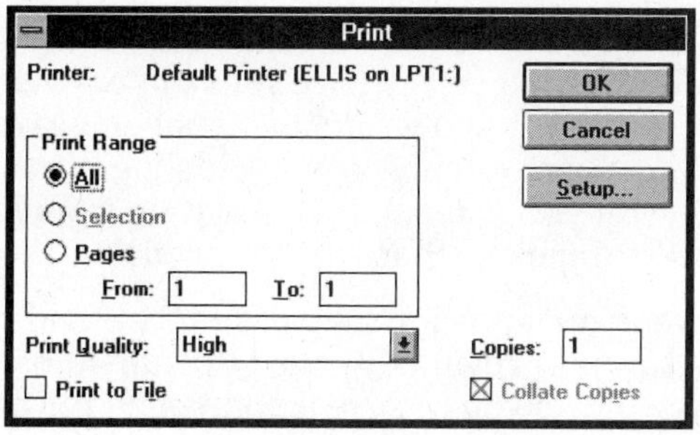

Print

Printer: Default Printer (ELLIS on LPT1:) — OK — Cancel — Setup...

Print Range
◉ All
○ Selection
○ Pages
From: 1   To: 1

Print Quality: High   Copies: 1
☐ Print to File   ☒ Collate Copies

Fig. 12.25

The Print dialog box.

Table 12.10 lists the parts of the Print dialog box shown in figure 12.25.

Table 12.10 Parts of the Print dialog box

Item	Description
Print Range All	Prints all the pages in a file.
Print Range Selection	Prints the selected text.
Print Range Pages From	Begins printing with this page.
Print Range Pages To	Ends printing with this page.
Print Quality	Selects from a list of optional print qualities—draft printing is at a lower resolution and can save printing time.
Print to File	Prints to a text file rather than to the printer (Write prompts you for a file name if you select this option).
Copies	Where you type the number of copies you want to print.
Collate Copies	Collates copies of multiple documents.
Cancel	Returns you to the document without printing.

When you send a document to be printed, Write presents a dialog box that tells you the file is being printed and offers a Cancel button. (Notice that the currently selected printer is named at the top of the dialog box.)

Saving and Naming a Write Document

When you open a new file, you are working in the computer's random-access memory (RAM). If the electricity goes off, or even blinks for a split second, you lose what you wrote if you haven't saved the file. Therefore, save your work often. A good guideline is to save work every 15 minutes. When you save a file, the information from memory transfers to permanent storage on a hard or floppy disk.

Write includes two commands for saving: File Save and File Save As. File Save quickly saves a previously saved document using its current name. File Save As allows you to save an unnamed file or to rename a file you already saved.

The first time you save a document, both File Save and File Save As call up the File Save As dialog box, enabling you to enter the new file name (see fig. 12.26). Using the same dialog box, you can change the directory in which you save the file, and you can select a different file format in which to save the file. Table 12.11 lists the contents of the Save As dialog box.

Table 12.11 Parts of the Save As dialog box

Item	Description
File Name	Where you type the file name (if you already saved the file, the file name appears in this text box).
Directories	Lists available directories; select the directory into which you want to save the file.
Save File as Type:	Enables you to save a file in a format other than Write.
Write Files (*.WRI)	Standard Write format.
Word for DOS (*.DOC)	Microsoft Word format (not Word for Windows NT). Saving in Word format doesn't preserve pictures.
Word for DOS/TXT	Unformatted Microsoft Word text fill only.
Text files (*.TXT)	Windows NT ANSI text format—useful when you send a file via a modem.
Drives	Selects the drive on which you want to save the file.
Backup	Makes a backup copy of the file along with the primary file (the backup copy has the same name as the current file but with the extension BKP for Write files and BAK for Word files).

Item	Description
OK button	Saves the file with the name in the text box. You can press Enter at any time to choose OK.
Cancel button	Returns to the document without saving.
Network	Select a target server from those on the network.

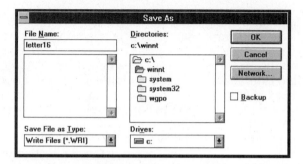

Fig. 12.26

The Save As dialog box.

The next time you save the same file, you can choose either **File Save** (keeping the current file name and replacing the old file) or **File** Save **As** (giving the file a different name and, therefore, creating a new version of the file). Unlike Save **As**, **S**ave isn't followed by a dialog box if the document was saved previously.

Before saving a file, the name `Write-(Untitled)` appears in the document's title bar. After saving, the file name you assigned appears there.

To save and name a file, follow these steps:

1. Choose the **File Save As** command.

2. Select the drive where you want to save the file in the **Drives** list.

3. In the **Directories** list, select the directory in which to save the file. By default, Write saves files in the current directory.

4. In the File **Name** text box, type the file name.

5. If you want to save the file in some format other than Write, select a format from the Save File as **Type** list.

6. To make a backup copy of the file (besides the saved WRI file), select **Backup**. Note that backup Write files use the extension BKP rather than WRI. Backup Word files use the extension BAK.

7. Choose OK or press Enter.

To resave a file with its current name, choose the **File Save** command.

File Systems and File Names

A file name identifies a file so that you can retrieve it later. Windows NT supports installable file systems, which means that Windows NT can use a variety of methods for storing and naming files. Common file systems on NT include OS/2 HPFS, NTFS, and FAT. Each file system has its own advantages and rules for naming files.

A few simple rules apply to most file systems. First, characters in file names can be letters, numbers, or punctuation characters. File names are made up of two parts: the root name (up to eight characters) and the extension (up to three characters). The root name is separated from the file name by a period. Unless you type a different extension, programs usually assign a default extension to files they create. Microsoft Write, for example, uses the extension WRI for all of its files. Usually, you can just type a file's root name and let the program you're using fill in the default extension. Extensions are useful because they identify the application or type of application to which a file belongs.

Naming constraints are the most strict in the FAT file system, which is included in Windows NT for compatibility with DOS disks. FAT file names have a root name of eight or fewer characters and an extension of three or fewer characters. Names in the FAT file system can include letters, numbers, and many punctuation characters, including the following: !, @, #, $, %, -, ^, &, (,), and _ . File names on FAT volumes cannot contain asterisks, question marks, commas, or plus signs.

Exiting Write

After you finish writing or are ready to stop for the day, exit Write and return to the Windows NT desktop by choosing **File Exit** from the Write menu.

If you have not saved the most recent changes, Write reminds you that the document has changed and asks whether you want to save the changes. Select Yes if you want to save the changes, No to discard the changes, or Cancel to cancel the Exit command and return to the document.

Working with Other Applications

Like other Windows applications, Write can share information—not only between Write files, but also between applications. Information you can add to Write files includes graphics created in Windows NT applications (such as Paintbrush) and worksheet data from applications such as Excel. Write also is highly compatible with another Microsoft word-processing application—Word for Windows.

You move or copy information between Windows applications by using the Clipboard and Edit commands, which work in all Windows applications. Cut, copy, and paste text or graphics between documents by using the Edit commands and pressing Alt+Tab to switch between application windows. You can move text between Write files in the same way.

You do not have to have both Windows applications open at the same time to transfer text or pictures. If, for example, the computer's memory is limited, you may not have room for many large applications. If so, cut or copy from one application, close the application, start the other application, and paste the selection. Be sure that you do not delete, cut, or copy another selection before you paste the first selection. If you do, the second cut or copy replaces what is in the Clipboard.

To move or copy a selection between Windows applications or Write files, follow these steps:

1. Open the application that contains the text or picture you want to move or copy.

2. Select the text or picture you want to move or copy.

3. Choose the Edit Cut command (to move the selection) or the Edit Copy command (to duplicate it).

4. Open or activate the Write document to receive the selection.

5. Position the insertion point where you want the selection to appear.

6. Choose the Edit Paste command.

488

Starting a Library of Standard Text

Write offers a way to save time if you work on documents that have repetitive or standard parts: create a *library* of standardized pieces (also known as *boilerplate* text), such as paragraphs for a sales proposal or a legal contract. Save this library as a Write document.

When you need a paragraph contained in the library, just start a new Write application and open this library document. You can copy the paragraph from the library and paste it into the work document (Alt+Tab switches between open applications).

Do not close the Write application holding the library. Instead, keep it as an icon at the bottom of the screen so that you can get to the next standard paragraph quickly. See Chapters 2 and 4 for information on using icons.

You can open several file formats in Write. You can, for example, open a Word for Windows file or an ANSI text file. (To list files with any extension in the File Open dialog box, type *.* in the File **N**ame box to list files in all formats or select the file format you want to open from the List Files of **T**ype list.) When you open these files, you see a dialog box asking whether you want to convert the files to Write format. Sometimes you do, but sometimes you don't. Most Windows applications, for example, save text files in ANSI format, and you must *not* convert these files when you open them in Write. Select the **N**o Conversion option in the dialog box. (If you accidentally convert a Windows NT ANSI format file, close it without saving to return the file to its original format.) If a text file comes from a DOS application such as Word for DOS, select the **C**onvert option in the dialog box to convert the file to Write format.

Copying and Pasting from Standard DOS Applications

Commands to operate standard DOS applications vary. However, copying text or graphics from a standard DOS application and pasting the copy into a Write document is easy. Chapter 22, "Running DOS Applications," describes how to transfer selections between DOS and Windows NT applications.

Word for Windows and Microsoft Word for DOS are advanced word-processing applications used by writers who need features such as mail merge, footnotes, style sheets, a spelling checker, and automatic hyphenation. Word for Windows works in Windows NT like Write but has far more powerful features. Write, Microsoft Word for DOS, and Word for Windows files are compatible, although some features not available in Write are lost in translation between the two applications.

To use a Write file in Word for DOS, follow these steps:

1. Choose the **F**ile Save **A**s command.

2. Type a file name in the File **N**ame box.

3. In the Save File as **T**ype list, select the Word for DOS option.

4. Choose OK. If the file contains pictures, you see a dialog box advising you that the pictures will be deleted. Choose OK to delete the pictures or choose Cancel to return to the document without saving.

5. Open the file in Word for DOS.

If you open the file in Word for Windows, you must be sure that the Windows NT Write filter is installed, which by default translates files. Installing this filter in Word for Windows is described in depth in *Using Word for Windows*, Special Edition, published by Que Corporation.

Summary

The Write word processor is an excellent personal word processor that meets most personal and business needs. The **C**opy, **C**ut, and **P**aste commands make it easy to brainstorm ideas and reorganize thoughts into finished prose. With Write's three levels of formatting (character, paragraph, and document), you easily can format and print impressive-looking letters and reports. When you feel comfortable with the menus, read through this chapter again and look for the time-saving shortcut keys and tips.

If you use simple graphics in business documents, such as organizational charts or floor plans, you may find the Paintbrush application helpful. Chapter 13 explains Paintbrush. Although Paintbrush is only a fundamental drawing application, it incorporates many of the principles used in more comprehensive, professional drawing applications.

Using Windows NT Paintbrush

A computer is a business tool—everyone knows that. Sometimes when you sneak up on someone who has Windows on their PC, however, you find that they are not working—they are playing Solitaire, or creating a masterpiece with Windows NT's fun and colorful painting application, Paintbrush.

Even though Paintbrush is a simple, easy-to-use graphics application, it may be as powerful a graphics application as you will ever need. Paintbrush is fun, but it also is a serious business tool. With Paintbrush, you can create everything from free-flowing drawings to precise mathematical charts, and you can use your creations in other Windows NT applications, such as Windows Write, Windows Notepad, Windows Cardfile, or Word for Windows. You can use your computer "paintings" to illustrate a story, to emphasize an important point in a report, or to clarify instructions.

The following are some of the graphic effects you can create using Paintbrush:

- Lines in many widths, shades, and colors
- Brush strokes in a variety of styles, widths, shades, and colors
- Unfilled or filled shapes with shades or color

■ Text in many sizes, styles, and colors

■ Special effects like rotating, tilting, and inverting

Windows NT Paintbrush is fun, but it also is a tool you can use in your work. People are attracted to pictures. They understand pictures better than they understand text alone. Whatever type of work you do, think about how you can communicate more effectively by using illustrations you create with Windows NT Paintbrush.

Starting Windows Paintbrush

The Paintbrush program item icon is located inside the Accessories group, which may be open as a window or closed as a group icon. Follow these steps to start Paintbrush:

1. If the Accessories group appears as an icon, select the icon and press Enter or double-click on the Accessories group icon. Either method opens the Accessories window.

2. Select the Paintbrush icon and press Enter or double-click on the Paintbrush icon.

Starting Paintbrush opens a new, empty Paintbrush file. You can customize a program item icon, however, so that when you start the application, an existing file opens automatically (see Chapter 4, "Controlling Applications with the Program Manager").

Getting to Know the Paintbrush Window and Tools

The Paintbrush window, like other windows, has a *title bar* across the top, a *menu bar* below the title bar, *scroll bars* on the right and bottom, and a *drawing area* in the middle. Unique to Paintbrush are its three tool areas: the *toolbox* on the left side; the *line-width box* in the bottom-left corner; and the color and shades *palette* along the bottom. Figure 13.1 shows a labeled Paintbrush screen.

To paint, draw, fill, color, shade, write, and edit in Paintbrush, you first must select the appropriate tool, line width, and shade or color. Figure 13.2 labels the individual tools in the toolbox located on the left side of the screen.

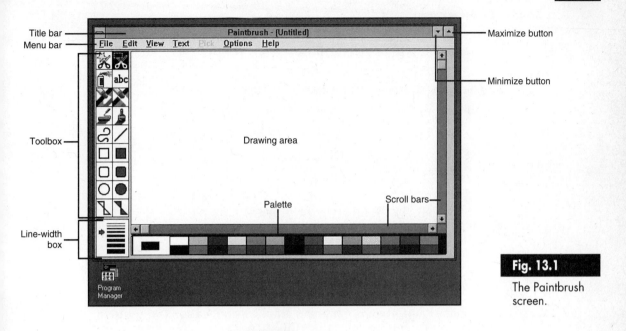

Fig. 13.1
The Paintbrush screen.

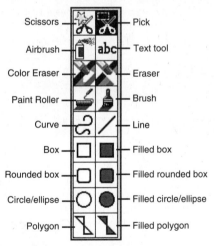

Fig. 13.2
The Paintbrush Toolbox.

On a color system, the palette appears in color. If your system is monochrome, shades of gray are in your palette.

To select a tool, line width, or shade or color, follow the appropriate instructions:

Mouse: Position the pointer on the tool, line, or shade or color you want and click the left mouse button.

Keyboard: Press Tab to move between areas in the window; press the arrow keys to move between selections in the toolbox, line-width box, or palette; press the Ins key to select a tool, line, or shade or color.

The general procedure for using Paintbrush is as follows:

1. Select the tool with which you want to draw from the toolbox.

2. Select the line width you want from the line-width box.

3. Select the color you want from the palette.

4. Move the pointer into the drawing area and draw a shape. (The pointer changes into a different shape in the drawing area, depending on which tool you select.)

To draw an unfilled red box with a wide line, for example, select the unfilled box tool; select a wide line; select red; move the pointer into the drawing area, where the pointer turns into a crosshair; and drag the crosshair while holding down the mouse button. Release the mouse button when the box is the size and shape you want.

Because Paintbrush is a bit-map graphics application (rather than an object-oriented application) the shapes you create are painted on-screen in one layer. You cannot reshape a box or move an object behind another object, but you can select a box and move it some-where else, select a picture of a house and tilt it, select a pattern and flip it, or change the colors of your painting. You also can erase your painting (or part of it) and paint something new.

Using the Keyboard with Paintbrush

Paintbrush is easiest to use if you have a mouse. The instructions in this chapter assume that you have a mouse; if you're using a keyboard, use the following keystrokes in place of the equivalent mouse action:

Mouse Action	Keyboard Equivalent
Click left mouse button	Press Ins
Click right mouse button	Press Del
Double-click left mouse button	Press F9+Ins
Double-click right mouse button	Press F9+Del
Drag	Press Ins+arrow keys

You also can use the keyboard to move around the Paintbrush screen. You may find that some of these techniques work as shortcuts, even if you have a mouse:

Press	To Move
Tab	Among drawing area, toolbox, line-width box, and palette
Arrow	In the direction of arrow
Home	To top of drawing area
End	To bottom of drawing area
PgUp	Up one screen
PgDn	Down one screen
Shift+up arrow	Up one line on-screen
Shift+down arrow	Down one line on-screen
Shift+Home	To left edge of drawing area
Shift+End	To right edge of drawing area
Shift+PgUp	Left one screen
Shift+PgDn	Right one screen
Shift+left arrow	Left one space on-screen
Shift+right arrow	Right one space on-screen

Selecting Tools, Line Widths, and Shades or Colors

When you draw a picture with Paintbrush, you draw it with the tool you select, in the line width you select, and in the shade or color you select. Before you start drawing, select a tool, line width, and shade or color.

To move the pointer from the toolbox to the line-width box and then to the palette with the keyboard, press the Tab key. To move the pointer among the selections in each area, press the arrow keys.

To select a tool or line width with the keyboard, press Insert (Ins). To select a tool or line width with the mouse, position the pointer on the tool or line width you want and press the left mouse button.

The palette offers two choices: foreground and background shade or color. At the left end of the palette, shown in figure 13.3, is a box within a box. The *inner* box is the *foreground* shade or color; the *outer* box is the *background* shade or color. You use the foreground shade or color to create lines, brush strokes, shapes, and text. The background shade or color has three functions: it borders a filled shape; it shadows the edges of text typed with the **S**hadow style; and it becomes the background of the next *new* Paintbrush file you start (but not the current file).

Foreground shade or color (left mouse button)

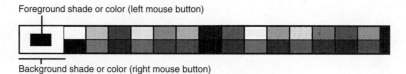

Background shade or color (right mouse button)

Fig. 13.3

The Paintbrush palette.

To select a shade or color from the palette, follow these steps:

1. Move the pointer over the shade or color you want to select.

2. Press the *left* mouse button to select the *foreground* color; press the *right* mouse button to select the *background* color.

If you are selecting colors with the keyboard, press Insert (Ins) to select the foreground color and press Delete (Del) to select the background color.

Using the Paintbrush Tools

The toolbox includes tools for cutting out, airbrushing, typing text, erasing, filling, brushing, drawing curves or straight lines, and drawing filled or unfilled shapes. Most of the tools operate using a similar process: press and hold down the left mouse button, drag the mouse, and release the mouse button. (Three exceptions are the text tool, which works by clicking and typing; the paint-roller tool, which works by pointing and clicking; and the curve tool, which works by clicking, dragging, and clicking.)

Whichever tool you use, the **E**dit **U**ndo command is a useful ally. Use it to undo your most recent action. Keep one rule in mind when you use Undo: *it undoes everything back to when you selected the tool you're using, used a scroll bar, opened another application, or resized the window.* When you select **U**ndo, you may undo one line or ten. To keep Undo useful, reselect the tool each time you draw a successful line or shape.

Several Tools Use the Right Mouse Button to Undo

Several tools, including the selection tools, the line tools, and the shape tools, use the right mouse button to undo. To cancel the line or shape you're currently drawing, click the right mouse *before* you release the left mouse button.

Using the Cutout Tools

 With the Cutout tools, you can draw an enclosure around any part of your Paintbrush drawing. Whatever is inside the enclosure is selected and can be moved, cut or copied (and then pasted), resized, tilted, flipped, or inverted. "Editing the Painting" and "Creating Special Effects," later in this chapter, explain the things you can do with a selected object or area of the painting.

The toolbox has two cutout tools: the *Scissors* is the icon on the left side of the toolbox, and the *Pick* is the icon on the right side of the toolbox. The Scissors cutout tool draws a free-form enclosure. The Pick cutout tool draws a rectangular enclosure. Both tools select everything inside the enclosure—the object and the space around it.

To use the Scissors tool, follow these steps:

1. Select the Scissors tool from the top *left* of the toolbox.

2. Position the mouse pointer where you want to begin the enclosure; press and hold down the left mouse button.

3. Drag the mouse to draw a line that encloses the area you want to select.

4. Release the mouse button at the same place you started drawing the line.

Press the Mouse Button To Cancel a Cutout

If you make a mistake while using either of the cutout tools, click the left mouse button outside the cutout area to cancel the cutout and try again.

To use the Pick tool, follow these steps:

1. Select the Pick tool from the top *right* of the toolbox.

2. Position the mouse pointer where you want to begin the enclosure; press and hold down the left mouse button.

3. Drag the mouse to draw a rectangle around the area you want to select.

4. Release the mouse button.

Figure 13.4 shows an image selected with the pick tool. Notice that the selection box—the box that surrounds the image—is formed of dashed lines.

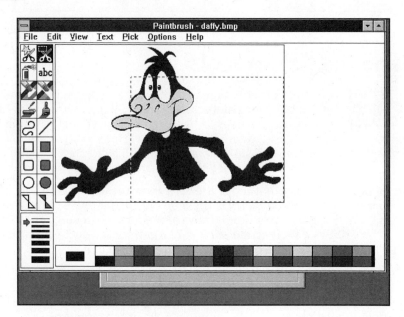

Fig. 13.4

Using the Pick cutout tool to select an object or area.

Expanding the Paintbrush Screen

To enlarge the Paintbrush screen to the full size of the monitor, double-click the Pick cutout tool in the toolbox. You cannot edit the painting in this view, but you can see more of it. To return the screen to the normal editing size, click the mouse button or press the Esc key.

Using the Airbrush Tool

 The Airbrush tool works like a can of spray paint, spraying a mist of color. When selected, the Airbrush tool turns into a crosshair that produces a circular pattern of dots when you click it on-screen (to produce an airbrushed dot) or drag it across the screen (to produce an airbrushed line). The line width you select determines the diameter of the circle of dots; the palette foreground color determines the shade or color that the Airbrush tool sprays. The speed you drag determines the density of dots—if you drag the crosshair slowly, you get a dense pattern of dots; if you drag it quickly, the spray is lighter.

Unlike other tools, the Airbrush draws transparently. Any image under the airbrush spray may remain visible, depending on how densely you spray over the image (see fig. 13.5).

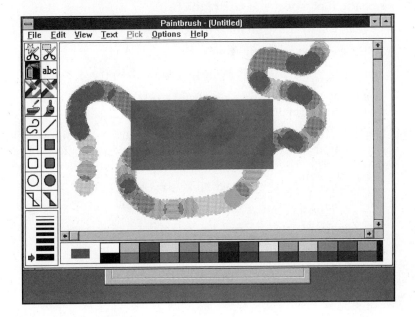

Fig. 13.5

Using the Airbrush tool to draw a circular, transparent mist of dots in the foreground shade or color.

To use the Airbrush, follow these steps:

1. Select the Airbrush tool from the toolbox.

2. Select a line width and foreground color.

3. Position the pointer where you want to begin the airbrush stroke; press and hold down the left mouse button.

4. Drag the crosshair to paint the airbrush stroke.

5. Release the mouse button.

Using the Text Tool

 With the Text tool, you can add words to your computer painting. Paintbrush has limited typing capabilities: text does not wrap from line to line; you must press Enter to begin the next line of text. You can press the Backspace key to erase a letter when you type, but after you click the mouse button, you cannot return to the text to edit it.

The following steps briefly explain how to use the text tool; refer to "Typing Text in Paintbrush," later in this chapter for details about changing the font, style, and size of the text.

To type text, follow these steps:

1. Select the Text tool from the toolbox.

2. Select the color you want your text to be from the palette.

3. Position the I-beam where you want to start typing and click to display the insertion point.

4. Type the text. Press Backspace to erase characters; choose any command from the **Text** menu to change the appearance of the text.

5. Press Enter to begin the next line of text.

Using the Eraser Tools

Paintbrush has two eraser tools: the *Color Eraser* on the left side of the toolbox and the *Eraser* on the right side of the toolbox.

The Color Eraser tool is really a color switcher. It works two ways, and both ways depend on the foreground and background color choices you make in the palette. (The foreground color is the color in the center box at the left end of the palette; you select the foreground color by clicking on the color you want with the *left* mouse button. The background color is the border color in the palette box; you select the background color by clicking on the color you want with the *right* mouse button.)

Dragging the Color Eraser tool across an area in your painting changes every occurrence of the selected foreground color to the selected background color. Double-clicking on the Color Eraser tool in the toolbox changes every occurrence of the selected foreground color in the visible area of your painting to the selected background color. (The Color

Eraser changes only the *selected* foreground color; the Eraser tool, described next, changes *all* foreground color.) Be aware that the Color Eraser tool also erases or alters custom colors blended from the foreground color.

Suppose that you have on-screen a red square with a wide black border. Red is the selected foreground color, and yellow is the selected background color. If you drag across the square with the Color Eraser, the red foreground color turns to yellow, but the black stays black (see fig. 13.6). (If you use the Eraser tool instead of the Color Eraser, the black also turns yellow, as does any area outside the square you drag the Eraser across.)

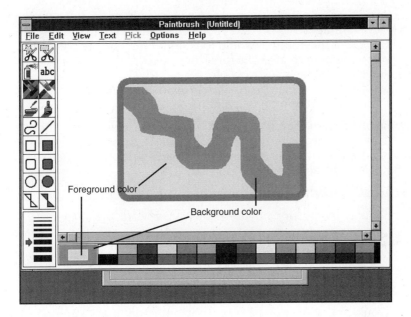

Fig. 13.6

Using the Color Eraser tool to change the selected foreground color to the selected background color.

To use the Color Eraser tool on part of your painting, follow these steps:

1. Select the Color Eraser tool.

2. Select a line width—the width of the area this tool erases depends on the line width you select.

3. Select a foreground color from the palette. When you drag the Color Eraser over your painting, you change this color.

4. Select a background color from the palette. When you drag the Color Eraser over your painting, the foreground color changes to this color.

5. Press and hold down the left mouse button.

6. Drag the Color Eraser tool across the part of your drawing you want to change.

7. Release the mouse button.

The Color Eraser Tool Doesn't Work with Shades

You can paint with shades or colors, but the Color Eraser tool works only with colors. If you work on a monochrome monitor, the Color Eraser tool works the same as the Eraser tool.

The Color Eraser tool makes it easy for you to change a color throughout your painting. Suppose that you used green in your painting and now think that the painting would look better if the green were blue. In the palette, select green as the foreground color and blue as the background color. Double-click the Color Eraser tool to change all the green to blue. (Be sure to select as the foreground color the same shade of green you used in the original painting.)

Double-clicking on the Color Eraser changes the *displayed* portion of the painting. If the painting is larger than the screen and you want to change all the painting, scroll to display each portion and then double-click to change each displayed portion.

To change a color throughout your painting, follow these steps:

1. Display the portion of your painting you want to change.

2. Select a foreground color from the palette. This is the color in your painting that you want to change.

3. Select a background color from the palette. You want the selected foreground color in your painting to change to this color.

4. Double-click the Color Eraser tool in the toolbox. If you don't have a mouse, move the pointer over the Color Eraser tool and press F9+Ins.

The Eraser tool (the tool on the *right* side of the toolbox) "erases" by changing every part of the painting it touches to the background color (see fig. 13.7). It erases everything in the foreground.

To use the Eraser tool, follow these steps:

1. Select the Eraser tool from the toolbox. The width of the area it erases depends on the line width you select.

2. If necessary, select a background color from the palette. Everything in your painting changes to this background color when you pass the Eraser over it.

3. Press and hold down the left mouse button.

4. Drag the Eraser tool across the part of your drawing you want to erase.

5. Release the mouse button.

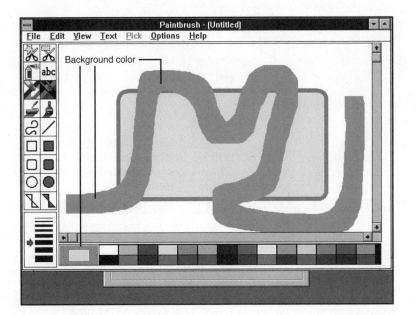

Fig. 13.7

Using the Eraser tool to change all foreground color to the selected background color.

Use the Eraser as a Brush

Because the eraser tool works by converting foreground shades or colors into the background shade or color, you can turn the eraser tool into a giant paintbrush. Select the shade or color you want to paint with as the *background* shade or color; select a wide line width (the wider the line width, the bigger the eraser); and then click and drag the Eraser to draw a wide line of the background color.

Use the Eraser Tool To Erase the Entire Painting

To erase an entire painting, double-click the Eraser tool in the toolbox. Paintbrush asks whether you want to save changes (choose **Yes** if you do, **No** if you do not), closes the current file, and opens a new file. The new file has the same background color as the file you close. (If you want a white background, be sure that white is the selected background color before you use this method.)

Using the Paint Roller

The Paint Roller fills a closed shape with the selected foreground shade or color (see fig. 13.8). You can use it to fill a solid shape (if the shape is filled with a solid color or black or white) or an empty shape enclosed by a border.

The Paint Roller tool looks like a paint roller with paint flowing out of its end. The tip of this flowing paint is the *active* part of the tool—where the selected foreground shade or color flows out from. Because the tip is sharply pointed, you can fill very small shapes with the Paint Roller tool.

If you fill a shape that has a gap in its border, the paint leaks out onto the entire painting. Choose the Edit Undo command, fix the leak, and try again. You can use the View Zoom In command to help patch a leak.

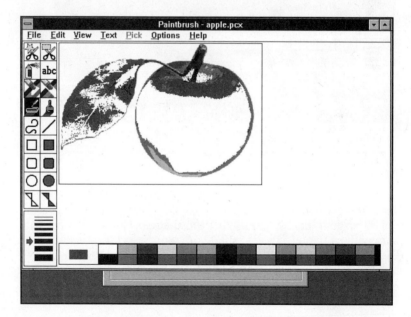

Fig. 13.8

Using the Paint Roller tool to fill a shape with a shade or color.

Be Careful When You Use the Undo Command

The Edit Undo command undoes all edits up to the last time you selected a tool, saved the file, used a scroll bar, or resized the window. If you're filling many areas in a painting with the Paint Roller tool, *set* each successful fill by saving the file or reselecting the Paint Roller tool. If you issue Undo incorrectly, however, you can undo the undo.

To fill a shape using the Paint Roller tool, follow these steps:

1. Select the Paint Roller tool from the toolbox.

2. Select a foreground color from the palette. This color will fill the shape.

3. Position the pointed tip of the Paint Roller tool inside the shape you want to fill. The pointed tip of the Paint Roller tool is where the paint comes out; because the tool is very precise, you can use it to fill even a small shape.

4. Click the left mouse button. The shape fills with the selected foreground color.

The Paint Roller tool is one of the two tools that you can use when you zoom in to edit a portion of a painting in detail (see "Getting Different Views of the Painting," later in this chapter). The other tool that you can use when you zoom in is the Brush tool.

T I P

Using the Brush Tool

 The Brush tool brushes an opaque stroke of the selected foreground shade or color onto your painting (see fig. 13.9). The brush stroke appears in the line width selected in the line-width box.

To use the Brush tool, follow these steps:

1. Select the Brush tool from the toolbox.

2. Select a foreground shade or color from the palette.

3. Position the pointer where you want the brush stroke to begin; press and hold down the left mouse button.

4. Drag the brush to paint a brush stroke.

5. Release the mouse button.

You can use the Brush tool in any of six shapes you choose from the Brush Shapes dialog box (see fig. 13.10). The default square shape paints with a square brush; the round shape paints with a round brush. The straight-line and diagonal-line brushes paint with a thin line and can paint a variable-width brush stroke, as shown in figure 13.9 (fig. 13.9 was painted with the diagonal-line brush shape shown selected in fig. 13.10). No matter what the brush shape, its width is determined by the selected line width.

To select a brush shape, follow these steps:

1. Choose the **O**ptions **B**rush Shapes command. Alternatively, double-click on the Brush tool in the toolbox.

2. Select the brush shape you want to use from the Brush Shapes dialog box (see fig. 13.10).

3. Choose OK or press Enter. Alternatively, double-click on the brush shape you want in the dialog box.

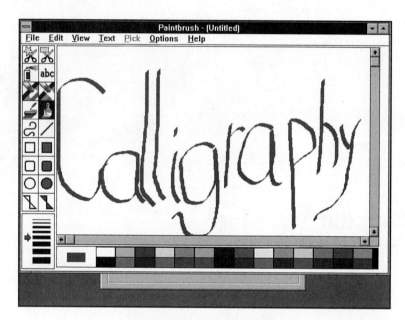

Fig. 13.9

An opaque brush stroke painted with the Brush tool.

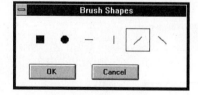

Fig. 13.10

The Brush Shapes dialog box.

Using the Curve Tool

The Curve tool is probably the most unusual tool in the Paintbrush toolbox. Unlike the Brush, you cannot use the Curve tool to draw freehand shapes. Instead, you use the tool to draw very accurate curves.

To use the Curve tool, you use a series of three click-and-drag movements. Follow these steps:

1. Select the Curve tool from the toolbox.

2. If necessary, select a line width and foreground color.

3. Press, drag, and release the mouse button to draw a straight line. Notice that the line appears thin and black.

4. Move the crosshair to one side of the line you drew.

5. Press the left mouse button and drag the pointer away from the line to pull the line into a curve. If this is the shape you want, click the mouse button to complete the line. If you want an S-shaped curve, go to step 6.

6. Move the crosshair to the other side of the line, press and hold down the left mouse button, and drag the pointer away from the line to pull the line in the opposite direction. You now have an S-shaped curve, as shown in the flower stem in figure 13.11.

Fig. 13.11

Using the Curve tool to help draw accurate curves.

You can use a special type of undo with the curve tool: any time before you complete the line, you can click the right mouse button to undo the line and start over.

Draw a Petal Shape with the Curve Tool

To draw a petal shape with the Curve tool, click the mouse button one time to anchor the base of the petal, click a second time at the wide end of the petal, and then click and drag away from the wide end of the petal to form the petal shape. The petal appears as a thin black line until you release the mouse button.

Using the Line Tool

With the Line tool, you can draw a straight line in the foreground shade or color and in the selected line width. When you draw the line, it appears as a thin, black line. When you release the mouse button to complete the line, however, the line appears with the width and color you selected.

As with the Curve tool, you can use the right mouse button to undo an action. To undo the line you're drawing, click the right mouse button before you release the left mouse button.

To draw a line that is perfectly vertical, perfectly horizontal, or at a 45-degree angle, press and hold down the Shift key as you draw (see fig. 13.12).

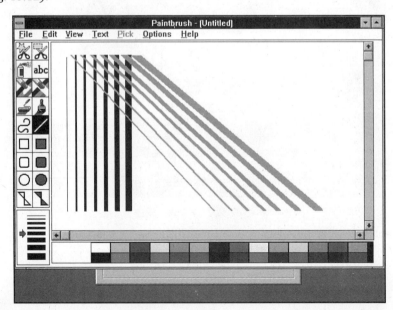

Fig. 13.12

Using the Shift key and the Line tool to draw perfectly horizontal lines.

To use the Line tool, follow these steps:

1. Select the Line tool from the toolbox.

2. Select a line width and foreground color.

3. Position the pointer where you want to start the line; press and hold down the left mouse button. To draw a vertical, horizontal, or 45-degree line, press and hold down the Shift key as you press and hold down the left mouse button.

4. Continue holding down the mouse button and drag the crosshair in any direction to draw a line. If you're holding down the Shift key, keep pressing it, too.

5. Release the mouse button to complete the line. Release the Shift key.

Using the Box and Rounded Box Tools

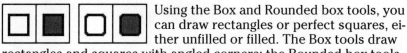 Using the Box and Rounded box tools, you can draw rectangles or perfect squares, either unfilled or filled. The Box tools draw rectangles and squares with angled corners; the Rounded box tools draw rectangles and squares with rounded corners.

An unfilled box line is the selected foreground shade or color. A filled box line is the selected background color, and its fill is the selected foreground color. The border of any box is the selected line width. (If you don't want a border, select the same foreground and background shade or color, or make sure that the selected background color is the same as your painting's background.)

To draw a perfectly square box or rounded box, hold down the Shift key as you draw.

Figure 13.13 shows a selection of rectangles and squares drawn with the various Box tools.

To use the Box tools, follow these steps:

1. Select the Box, Filled box, Rounded box, or Filled rounded box tool from the toolbox. The Box tool appears on-screen as a crosshair.

2. Select a line width, foreground color, and background color.

3. Press and hold down the left mouse button to anchor one corner of the rectangle. To draw a square, press and hold down the Shift key as you draw.

4. Continue holding down the mouse button and drag the crosshair in any direction to draw the rectangle. The rectangle appears as a thin, black line.

5. Release the mouse button when the rectangle is the shape you want. The rectangle takes on the selected line width and shade or color.

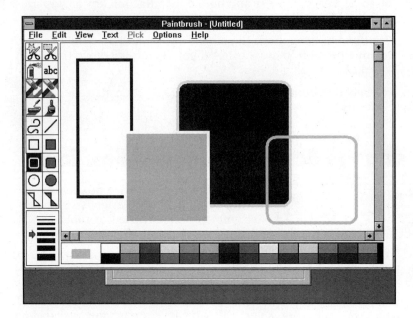

Fig. 13.13

Using the Box and Rounded box tools to draw unfilled or filled rectangles or squares.

Using the Circle/Ellipse Tools

You can use the Circle/Ellipse tools to draw ovals and circles. If you use the unfilled Circle/Ellipse tool, Paintbrush draws the resulting shape in the selected foreground color and leaves the center empty. If you use the Filled Circle/Ellipse tool, Paintbrush draws the border in the selected background color and fills the shape with the selected foreground color. (If you don't want a border, select the same foreground and background shade or color.) With either tool, the border is the selected line width.

The Circle tools draw an oval (ellipse) shape by default; if you want a perfect circle, press and hold down the Shift key as you draw.

Figure 13.14 shows a selection of circles and ellipses drawn with the Circle tools.

To draw an ellipse or circle, follow these steps:

1. Select the Circle/Ellipse or Filled circle/ellipse tool from the toolbox. The Circle/Ellipse tool appears on-screen as a crosshair.

2. Position the pointer where you want to start the ellipse or circle; press and hold down the left mouse button. To draw a perfect circle, press and hold down the Shift key as you draw.

3. Drag the crosshair away from the starting point in any direction. The ellipse or circle appears as a thin black line.

4. Release the mouse button to complete the circle or ellipse. Release the Shift key if you're drawing a circle. The border and fill take on the characteristics you selected.

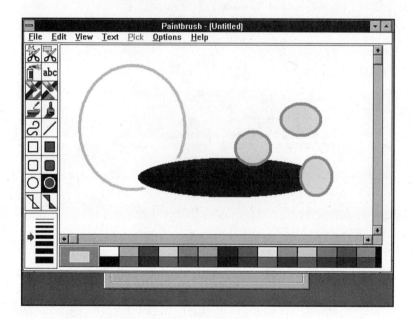

Fig. 13.14

Using the circle tools to draw ovals or circles.

Using the Polygon Tools

You can use the Polygon tools to draw closed multisided shapes (unfilled or filled). If you use the Unfilled polygon tool, Paintbrush draws the polygon in the selected foreground color and leaves the center empty. If you use the Filled polygon tool, Paintbrush draws the border in the selected background color and fills the polygon with the selected foreground color. (If you don't want a border, select the same foreground and background shade or color.) With either tool, the border is the selected line width.

Drawing a shape with a Polygon tool requires three steps: click-drag-release to draw the first side of the polygon; click to define each of the polygon's remaining corners; and double-click to close the polygon.

Figure 13.15 shows a filled polygon.

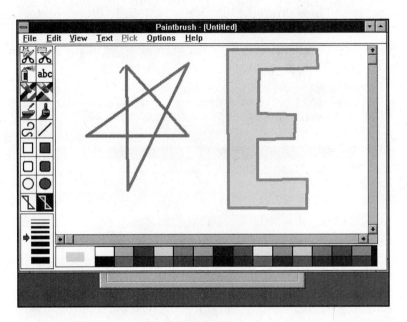

To draw an unfilled or filled polygon, follow these steps:

1. Select the Polygon or Filled polygon tool from the toolbox. The Polygon drawing tool appears on-screen as a crosshair.

2. Position the crosshair where you want to start the polygon and press and hold down the left mouse button.

3. Drag the crosshair to draw the first side of the polygon; release the mouse button when the line is finished. Press and hold down the Shift key to draw a perfectly horizontal, vertical, or diagonal line.

4. Click the left mouse button to define each of the polygon's remaining corner points. The border appears as a thin black line.

5. Double-click the left mouse button to complete the polygon. The end point joins the starting point to close the polygon, and the border and fill take on the characteristics you selected.

Typing Text in Paintbrush

A picture may be worth a thousand words, but sometimes words can help clarify your message. You can use the Text tool to add text to your painting in any of several fonts, sizes, styles, and shades or colors.

As explained in the section titled "Using the Text Tool," typing in Paintbrush has some limitations. You can edit the text you type only until you complete the typing by clicking the mouse button. The text becomes part of the picture, and the only way you can edit the text is to erase it or paint over it. Paintbrush doesn't have a word-wrap feature; when you reach the edge of the screen, you must press Enter to move the insertion point to the next line.

When you type text, it appears in the selected font, the selected style, the selected size, and the selected foreground color. You can change any of these selections *while* you are typing to change the *current* block of text. Alternatively, you can change any of these selections *before* you start typing to set the style for the *next* block of text you type. Each block of text, however, can have only one font, style, size, or color. The fonts available in Paintbrush are the same as those fonts installed in Windows. Figure 13.16 shows some examples of text you can use in your drawings.

To change the font or type style before you begin typing, refer to the upcoming sections on "Enhancing Text" and "Selecting a Font, Style, and Size."

To type text, follow these steps:

1. Select the Text tool from the toolbox.

2. Move the pointer into the drawing area, where it becomes an I-beam.

3. Position the I-beam where you want to start typing and then click the left mouse button. (The I-beam turns into a flashing cursor or insertion point.)

4. Type the text (press Enter when you want to start a new line). If you make a mistake, press Backspace to erase it.

5. Click the mouse button to *set* the text into your painting—after you click the mouse button, you cannot edit the text.

Enhancing Text

A text enhancement is a variation of the selected font. Paintbrush offers several text enhancements: **R**egular, **B**old, *I*talic, Underline, **O**utline, and **S**hadow. You can use as many enhancements as you like at the same time. For example, you can type a bold and underlined title. Select **R**egular to delete all text enhancements. All of these choices and the font, style, and size choices described in the next section are available from the **T**ext menu shown in figure 13.17.

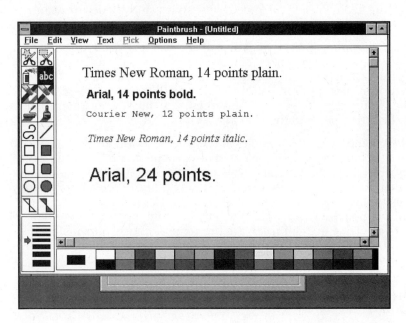

Fig. 13.16

Examples of Paintbrush fonts and styles.

Typed text appears in the selected foreground color, with one exception: shadow text adds a shadow in the selected background color.

If you choose enhancements while the insertion point is flashing inside a block of text, the enhancements apply to the current block of text and to future blocks of text that you type. If you choose enhancements before you click the I-beam on the painting to begin a block of text or after you click the mouse button to end a block of text, enhancements apply to the next block of text that you type.

To select a text enhancement, follow these steps:

1. Choose the **T**ext menu.

2. Select one of the following enhancements:

    Regular

    Bold

    Italic

Underline

Outline

Shadow

3. Repeat the process to select additional enhancements for the same text.

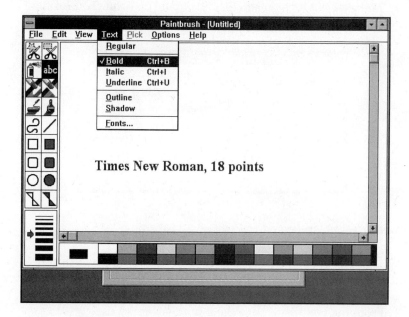

Fig. 13.17

You can select text enhance-ments from the **T**ext menu.

You can select a text enhancement before you begin typing or while you are typing, but after you click the mouse button to set your text into the painting, you cannot change the text enhancement. (For infor-mation on how to erase the text and type new text, see the upcoming section, "Editing a Painting.")

Selecting a Font, Style, and Size

A font is an alphabet of characters that have the same appearance. Fonts that come with Windows (if you are using TrueType) include Times New Roman, Arial, and Courier New. You may have additional fonts supplied by your printer or by font software. Using a dialog box, you can change the font, font style, and font size all at once (font styles are the same as the font enhancements listed in the **T**ext menu). You also can add strikeout and underlining.

If you are not using TrueType, the fonts you have available to use are those fonts installed in your printer or those fonts that you download from your computer. In the Font dialog box (shown in fig. 13.18) you can tell whether a font is a TrueType font, a printer font, or a system font by the icon that appears to the left of the font name in the Font list. TrueType fonts have a "TT" icon; printer fonts have a printer icon; and system fonts have no icon. A sample box shows you how your font, style, and size will look on-screen and when you print. To learn more about TrueType, refer to Chapter 8, "Managing Fonts."

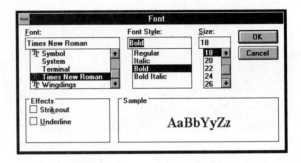

Fig. 13.18

The Font dialog box.

To select a font, style, and size, follow these steps:

1. Choose the Text menu and select the Fonts command.

   The Font dialog box appears, which enables you to change font, style, and size all at once.

2. From the Font list, select the font you want to use.

3. From the Font Style list, select the style you want.

4. From the Size list, select the size you want your text to be.

5. In the Effects group, select Strikeout if you want a line through your text or select Underline if you want text underlined.

6. Choose OK or press Enter.

When you select a font, that font applies to any new text you type and to any text you are currently typing, if you haven't clicked the mouse button.

Editing the Painting

With Paintbrush, you can edit a painting by using the Eraser tools (described earlier in this chapter); the Undo command; the Edit Cut, Copy, and Paste commands; the Pick commands; the Backspace key; and the right mouse button.

As you are editing, be aware that objects in a Paintbrush painting are always completed or uncompleted. Anything uncompleted is subject to edits. You can cancel an uncompleted line or curve, for example, by clicking the right mouse button; you can change the appearance of uncompleted text by making a selection from the Text menu. The method you use to complete an object depends on the object. To complete a straight line, for example, you release the mouse button; to complete text, you click the mouse button.

Using the Undo Command

Use the Undo command to cancel all the work you did up until when you saved the file, selected the tool you're currently using, resized the window, or scrolled the page. For example, if you select a Box tool, draw five rectangles, and choose Undo, you erase all five rectangles. (To undo the Undo, select Undo again.) If you draw four rectangles, select the Rectangle tool, draw one more rectangle, and *then* choose Undo, however, you remove only the most recent rectangle.

Be careful when you use Undo. Save the file or reselect the tool you are using to prevent what you are doing from being undone.

To undo your most recent work, choose the Edit Undo command. Alternatively, press Ctrl+Z.

Using Backspace as an Eraser

While you are working with any drawing tool, you can press the Backspace key to display a temporary eraser that looks like a square with an *X* through it. You can use this eraser to erase the work done with the current tool, but you can erase work done only from the point at which you selected the tool. When you're finished erasing, the eraser turns back into the tool you were using before you pressed the Backspace key.

To use the Backspace eraser, follow these steps:

1. Press the Backspace key. The tool turns into an eraser that looks like a box with an *X* in it; the size of the box depends on the selected line width.

2. Press and hold down the mouse button and drag over the part of your drawing you want to erase.

   Remember that the Backspace eraser removes only what you just drew; you cannot erase a completed painting.

3. Release the mouse button. The Backspace eraser changes back to a drawing tool.

Cutting, Copying, and Pasting

In Paintbrush, you cut, copy, and paste objects just as you do in any other Windows application. You start by *selecting* the object with one of the two cutout tools. Techniques for using the cutout tools are described in "Using the Cutout Tools" earlier in this chapter.

To cut or copy a portion of your painting, follow these steps:

1. Use the Scissors or the Pick cutout tool to select the area you want to cut or copy. A dashed line appears around the selected area.

2. To cut, choose the **E**dit Cu**t** command (Ctrl+X); to copy, choose the **E**dit **C**opy command (Ctrl+C). The selection is cut or copied into the Clipboard.

To paste the portion of the painting you cut or copied, follow these steps:

1. Display the area of the painting where you want to paste the contents of the Clipboard.

2. Choose the **E**dit **P**aste command (Ctrl+V).

The pasted object appears at the top left of the screen and is enclosed by a dotted line to show that the object still is selected. You can move the selection by clicking on it and dragging. For additional information, see "Moving a Selection" later in this chapter.

Copying a Selection to a File

You can save a portion of your painting to a file by using the **E**dit **C**opy To command. When you use this command, name the file and choose a file format. If you don't choose a file format, Paintbrush saves the file in its native format, which ends with the extension BMP. Files that have the extension BMP can be opened in Paintbrush.

To copy part of a painting to a file, follow these steps:

1. Use the Scissors or the Pick cutout tool to select the portion of the painting you want to save to a file.

2. Choose the **E**dit **C**opy To command. The Copy To dialog box appears.

3. Type a file name in the File **N**ame text box and select from the list in the **D**irectories box the directory in which you want to save the file.

4. In the List Files of **T**ype list, select one of the following file formats:

Format	File Extension Assigned
PCX	PCX
Monochrome bitmap	BMP
16 Color bitmap	BMP
256 Color bitmap	BMP
24-bit bitmap	BMP

If you don't select one of these formats, Paintbrush saves the file in Paintbrush bit-map format with the extension BMP.

5. Choose the **I**nfo button to see a dialog box describing the width, height, number of colors, and number of planes in your painting. Choose OK.

6. Choose OK or press Enter.

Pasting from a File

The **E**dit **P**aste **F**rom command enables you to merge the contents of two or more Paintbrush files. When you choose the command, a dialog box appears, listing all the Paintbrush files (those files with the extension BMP). You also can list and open files with the extensions PCX and MSP. When you select one of the listed files, Paintbrush pastes it into the top-left corner of the file currently open. Because the pasted picture arrives selected (as if it were selected with a cutout tool), you easily can move it where you want it on the page.

To paste from a file, follow these steps:

1. Choose the **E**dit **P**aste **F**rom command.

2. If necessary, select the file format of the files you want to list and open. The available selections are as follows:

> **B**MP
>
> **M**SP
>
> **P**CX
>
> All Files

3. From the File **N**ame list, select the file you want to open. (If necessary, first select a different directory from the **D**irectories box.) Alternatively, type the name of the file you want to open in the File **N**ame box.

4. Choose OK or press Enter. The file is pasted in the top-left corner of the screen.

Moving a Selection

You can move an object or area on-screen after you select it with the Scissors or Pick cutout tool. (The object already is selected if you just pasted it.) Paintbrush has several tricks for moving selections. You can move a selection and make it transparent or opaque. You can move a selection and leave a copy of the selection behind. You can *sweep* a selection across the screen and leave a trail of copies of the selected image behind.

To move a selection, follow these steps:

1. Use the Scissors or Pick cutout tool to select an object or area of the drawing. A dashed line encloses the selection.

2. Move the crosshair over the selection (so that the crosshair is inside the dashed line that defines the edges of the selection). The crosshair turns into an arrow.

3. Press and hold down the left mouse button to drag the selection to its new location and make it a *transparent* object. Press and hold down the right mouse button to drag the selection to its new location and make it an *opaque* object.

4. Release the mouse button.

5. Click the mouse button outside the selection to fix the selection in its new location.

If you move a selection transparently, the space between the object and the dashed selection line—usually a white border around the outside edge of the object you want to move—is transparent. If you move opaquely, the white space between the object and the selection line is also opaque and erases whatever is underneath it when you release the mouse button.

To copy a selection, follow the preceding steps for moving a selection, but press and hold down the Ctrl key as you drag the object to its new location. You can copy the selection and make it a transparent object (by holding down Ctrl and dragging with the left mouse button) or an opaque object (by holding down Ctrl and dragging with the right mouse button).

To sweep an image, follow the preceding steps for moving a selection, but press and hold down the Shift key as you sweep the image to its new location and leave a trail of images behind. You can sweep the selection and make it a transparent or opaque image. The faster you sweep the selection, the fewer copies of the image it leaves behind. Figure 13.19 shows an example of sweeping a transparent object.

Getting Different Views of the Painting

You can zoom in to get a closer look at your painting or zoom out to see the whole page. Zoom In mode shows you the pixels, or tiny squares of color, that make up your painting. You can paint *pixels* in the selected foreground color by clicking the dots with the left mouse button and in the background color by clicking the right mouse button. You can use the paint roller tool in Zoom In mode, or you can click and drag the mouse to change all the pixels in a selected area. (Click with the left mouse button to change all selected pixels to the foreground color; click with the right mouse button to change all selected pixels to the background color.) The upper-left corner of the Zoom In view will show a normal view of the Zoom area.

To zoom in for a close-up view of your painting, follow these steps:

1. Choose the **View Zoom In** command (or press Ctrl+N). A zoom box appears to help you define where you want to zoom in.

2. Position the zoom box over the spot on which you want to zoom in.

3. Click the mouse button to zoom in. Paintbrush displays a close-up view of your painting on-screen (see fig. 13.20).

To zoom back out to regular editing view, choose the **View Zoom Out** command (or press Ctrl+O). You also can choose **View Zoom Out** when you are in the regular view to display a reduced picture of the entire page. Choose **View Zoom In** to return to normal size.

You Can Do Some Editing in the Zoom Out View

When you zoom out to see your whole painting, you can cut, copy, and paste selections. You can rearrange a painting that is larger than your screen. You only can paste, move, or sweep the selection as an opaque object, however. To paste, move, or sweep transparently, zoom in to the regular editing view.

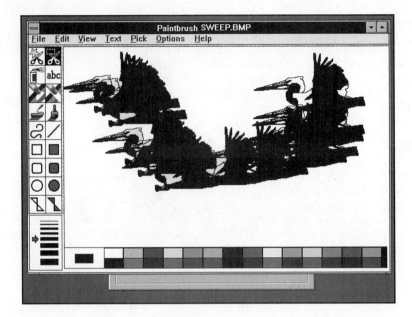

Fig. 13.19

Sweeping an object by holding down the Ctrl key as you drag.

If your painting is larger than your computer screen, you can see more of it by using the **View** Picture command. When you choose **View** Picture, all toolboxes, menus, and scroll bars disappear, and your picture expands to fill the window. You only can view in this mode; you cannot edit your painting in Picture mode.

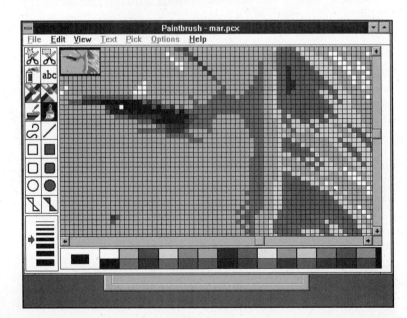

Fig. 13.20

Zooming in to get a closer look at your work.

To view more of your painting, follow these steps:

1. Choose the **View** **View** Picture command or press Ctrl+P.

2. Return to the normal editing view by clicking the mouse button or by pressing the Esc key.

When you're drawing lines or shapes that must line up accurately on-screen, you will find the **View** **Cursor** Position command helpful. **View** **Cursor** Position displays a small window at the top-right corner of the screen. In the window are two numbers that tell you the position of the insertion point or drawing tool on-screen. The position is given in XY coordinates, measured in pixels, from the top-left corner of the painting. The left number is the X-coordinate (the position relative to the left edge of the painting); the right number is the Y-coordinate (the position relative to the top of the painting). If the numbers in the Cursor Position window read *42, 100*, for example, the cursor is 42 pixels from the left edge of the painting and 100 pixels down from the top of the painting.

To display the Cursor Position window, follow these steps:

1. Choose the **View** **Cursor** Position command. The window appears as shown in figure 13.21.

2. Hide the Cursor Position window by choosing the **View** **Cursor** Position command again. Alternatively, double-click the control bar at the top left of the Cursor Position window.

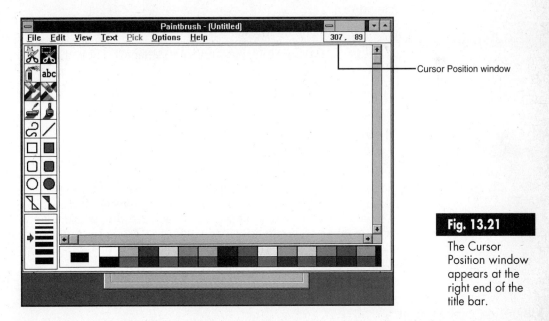

Cursor Position window

Fig. 13.21

The Cursor Position window appears at the right end of the title bar.

If the Cursor Position window is not conveniently located, you can move it to another place on-screen. With the mouse, drag the window by its title bar to a new location. With the keyboard, press Alt+F6 to activate the window; press Alt+space bar to open that window's Control menu; and then choose the **M**ove command to display the four-cornered move arrow. Press the arrow keys to move the window; press Enter to anchor the window in its new position.

Creating Special Effects

Using the **P**ick menu, you can flip, invert, shrink, enlarge, or tilt objects you selected with the Scissors or Pick cutout tool. These special effects can help you refine your Paintbrush painting by altering selected objects in subtle or not-so-subtle ways.

Flipping a Selection

You can flip a selection in two ways: horizontally (left to right) or vertically (top to bottom). Flipping horizontally reverses an image from left to right; you can use this technique to create mirror images by copying the selection and then flipping the pasted copy as shown in figure 13.22. Flipping vertically flips an image from top to bottom, making it upside-down.

To flip a selection, follow these steps:

1. Use the Scissors or Pick cutout tool to select the object or area you want to flip.

2. Choose the **P**ick Flip **H**orizontal command to flip horizontally; choose **P**ick Flip **V**ertical to flip vertically.

Inverting Colors

You can invert the colors in your painting, changing them to their opposite on the red/green/blue color wheel. In an inverted black-and-white painting, for example, black becomes white, and white becomes black; in an inverted green-and-yellow painting, green becomes purple, and yellow becomes blue (any white border area turns black). Use this technique to *reverse* a selected object.

Fig. 13.22

You can create mirror images by flipping a copy of your selection horizontally.

To invert colors, follow these steps:

1. Use the Scissors or Pick cutout tool to select the object or area you want to invert.

2. Choose the **Pick I**nverse command.

Shrinking and Growing a Selection

You can use the **Pick S**hrink + Grow command to reduce or enlarge a selection. After you select the object and choose the command, you drag the mouse to draw a box the size in which you want the resized image to fit. When you release the mouse button, the object fills the box you drew, and the box disappears.

If you choose the **Pick Clear** command before you choose the **Pick Shrink + Grow** command, Paintbrush erases the original selection after resizing the image. (If you choose Clear, make sure that the selected background color in your palette matches the background color in your painting—the area you select will be filled with the background color when you shrink or grow the selection.) If you don't choose **Pick Clear**, you create a resized duplicate of the original.

To shrink or grow a selection, follow these steps:

1. Use the Scissors or Pick cutout tool to select the object or area you want to shrink or grow.

2. Choose the **Pick Shrink + Grow** command.

3. Position the crosshair where you want the new resized image.

4. Press and hold down the mouse button; drag the mouse to draw a box the same size as you want the new, duplicated image. To keep the new image proportional to the original, hold down the Shift key while you press and hold down the mouse button, drag the mouse, and release the mouse button.

5. Release the mouse button. Release the Shift key if you used it.

When you finish shrinking or growing your selection, select a tool to cancel the **S**hrink & Grow command—otherwise, you can shrink or grow your image again and again.

Tilting a Selection

Drawing an angled polygon is a precise science. Fortunately, Paint-brush makes it easy with the **Pick Tilt** command. The Tilt command works a little like the **S**hrink + Grow command: after you select the object and choose the command, drag the mouse to draw a box at the angle at which you want the tilted image to appear. When you release the mouse button, the object appears—tilted—in the box you drew, and the box disappears.

If you choose the **Pick Clear** command before you choose **Pick Tilt**, Paintbrush erases the original selection after tilting the image. If you don't choose **Pick Clear**, you create a duplicate of the original. If you choose **Pick Clear**, make sure that the background color in your painting matches the background color selected in your palette.

To tilt a selection, follow these steps:

1. Use the Scissors or Pick cutout tool to select the object or area you want to tilt.

2. Choose the **Pick Tilt** command.

3. Position the crosshair where you want the tilted object to appear.

4. Press and hold down the mouse button; drag left or right to create a tilted box that is the same shape you want your tilted object to be. Notice that the box you're drawing has a dashed-line border.

5. Release the mouse button. The selected object fills the tilted box you drew, and the box disappears.

Figure 13.23 shows an image before and after it was tilted.

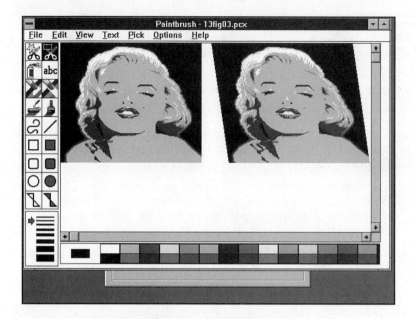

Fig. 13.23

Tilting an image.

Working with Color

Color is a tremendously important component in daily life, giving meaning to what you see. Psychologists have studied color's effects on
people; advertisers use color carefully to attract attention; artists use
color as one of their most important tools. If you have a color monitor,
you can use color in your Paintbrush paintings, and you can use your
colorful paintings in applications such as Windows Write, Word for
Windows, and Aldus PageMaker. If you are lucky enough to have a
color printer, you can print your painting in color.

Computer color is different from pigment color because computer
color is made of light. In Paintbrush, colors are blended from three
primary colors—red, green, and blue—each of which has 255 degrees
of shading. Black is no light: zero red, zero green, and zero blue. White
is pure light: 255 red, 255 green, and 255 blue.

Paintbrush has 28 colors in its palette, including black and white. All
these colors are blended from the three primary colors. You can customize the Paintbrush palette by blending your own colors. If you create a palette of colors you like, you can save it and retrieve it to use in
another Paintbrush painting. (You can retrieve palettes from Microsoft
Draw if they have no more than 28 colors and end with the extension
PAL.)

To customize colors in Paintbrush, start with an existing foreground color and modify it by adding or subtracting amounts of the three primary colors. A sample box at the right side of the Edit Colors dialog box shows you the color you are creating.

To create a custom color, follow these steps:

1. Select from the palette the foreground color you want to alter.

2. Choose the **O**ptions **E**dit Colors command. Alternatively, double-click on the color in the palette you want to customize. The Edit Colors dialog box appears (see fig. 13.24).

3. Increase or decrease the amount of each color (**R**ed, **G**reen, and **B**lue) by clicking the left or right arrows in the scroll bars. Watch the color in the sample box on the right side of the dialog box change when you alter the amount of each color.

4. Choose OK or press Enter to add your custom color to the palette, replacing the color that was there before. Alternatively, choose **R**eset to reset the color to what it was originally.

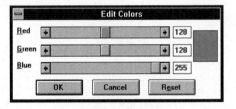

Fig. 13.24

The Edit Colors dialog box.

The colors you customize don't change the current painting, but they make different colors available on the palette. Your custom palette remains in effect when you start a new Paintbrush painting; unless you save the custom palette, the colors are gone when you close the Paintbrush application. If you save a custom palette, you can retrieve it into any Paintbrush file.

To save a custom palette, follow these steps:

1. Choose the **O**ptions **S**ave Colors command. The Save Colors As dialog box appears.

2. Type a name in the File **N**ame box. If necessary, select a different directory in the **D**irectories box or a different drive in the Drives list.

3. Choose OK or press Enter.

When you save a palette, Paintbrush assigns the extension PAL, but you can specify a different extension if you want.

To retrieve a custom palette, follow these steps:

1. Choose the **O**ptions **G**et Colors command.

2. Select a palette file from the File **N**ame list box. (If necessary, first select a directory from the **D**irectories box.) If you know the file name of the palette you want to retrieve, you can type its name in the File **N**ame box.

3. Choose OK or press Enter.

Remember that you can reset a custom color to its original palette shade by selecting the color and choosing the **R**eset button in the Edit Colors dialog box. You can reset a color to its original color even if you have changed it more than once or have saved the palette.

If you customize your palette, the customized version appears in any new document you create until you restart Paintbrush—at which time, you revert to the default 28-color palette.

Setting Up the Page

Page-setup choices affect your printed paintings. Margins, for example, determine where your painting is positioned on the page. You add headers and footers to the top and bottom of your printed pages. (See table 13.1 for a list of the commands you can use in headers and footers.)

To set up your page for printing, follow these steps:

1. Choose the **F**ile Page Se**t**up command. The Page Setup dialog box appears.

2. Select the **H**eader box and type a header to appear at the top of your printed page. Headers appear inside the top margin.

3. Select the **F**ooter box and type a footer to appear at the bottom of your printed page. Footers appear inside the bottom margin.

4. In the Margins box, select the **T**op, **L**eft, **B**ottom, and **R**ight boxes and type the margins you want. Paintbrush warns you if your margins are too large for your painting.

5. Choose OK or press Enter.

When you type the text of the headers and footers, you can include any or all of the commands listed in table 13.1.

Table 13.1 Commands for headers and footers

Command	Function
&d	Includes the current date
&p	Numbers the pages
&f	Includes the file name
&t	Includes the current time
&l	Aligns the header/footer to the left margin
&r	Aligns the header/footer to the right margin
&c	Centers the header/footer between the margins (This command is the default choice.)

Controlling Screen Size and Appearance

Paintbrush determines the capabilities of your computer monitor and the amount of memory your computer has available for printing graphics. With this information, Paintbrush creates an appropriately sized drawing area. You can override the *default* image area by resizing the image area to make it smaller or larger.

To resize the Paintbrush image area, follow these steps:

1. Choose the **O**ptions **I**mage Attributes command.

2. In the **W**idth box, type the width you want for the image area.

3. In the **H**eight box, type the height you want for the image area.

4. In the **U**nits group, select in (inches), cm (centimeters), or pels (pixels).

5. Choose OK or press Enter.

If you plan to expand the size of your painting, keep in mind that a larger painting (or one with colors) uses more of your computer's memory and takes more memory to print. If you expect to print at printer resolution rather than screen resolution (see "Printing Paintbrush Files" later in this chapter), enter the height and width dimensions in pels (pixels, or picture elements) in proportion to the current screen dimensions.

To return to the default image area size, select the **D**efault button. In the same dialog box, you can select whether the palette appears in black and white or color (and hence whether your drawing is in black and white or color). The changes you make in this dialog box don't affect the current Paintbrush document; they take effect when you open a *new* Paintbrush document and remain in effect for all new documents until you change them again.

Saving Paintbrush Files

When you save a Paintbrush file, Paintbrush assigns the extension BMP to the file name and saves the file in Windows bit-map format. If you prefer, you can save the painting in a different format so that you can use it in another application. For example, you can save a file in PCX format to use with several PC painting applications.

To save a Paintbrush file, follow these steps:

1. Choose the **F**ile Save **As** command. The File Save As dialog box appears.

2. Type a file name in the File**n**ame text box; select from the **D**irectories box the directory where you want to save the file.

3. Select the **O**ptions box to select one of the following file formats:

Format	File Extension Assigned
PCX	PCX
Monochrome bit map	BMP
16 Color bit map	BMP
256 Color bit map	BMP
24-bit bit map	BMP

If you don't select one of these formats, Paintbrush saves the file in Paintbrush bit-map format with the extension BMP.

4. Select the **I**nfo box to see a dialog box describing the width, height, number of colors, and number of planes in your painting.

5. Choose OK or press Enter.

To resave your file later without changing the name, select the **E**dit **S**ave command.

Working with Other Applications

The paintings you create in Paintbrush make wonderful illustrations that you can use with many other applications. If the other application does not support object linking and embedding, you can include a Paintbrush painting by copying the painting. (Such a painting remains static in your other application—you cannot change it.) You also can link or embed it in an application that supports object linking and embedding. Linked and embedded paintings can be edited from within the other application.

To copy a Paintbrush painting into another application, follow these steps:

1. Select the painting, or portion of the painting, that you want to copy to another application.

2. Choose the **Edit C**opy command.

3. Start the other application, open the document where you want to copy the painting, and position the insertion point where you want the painting to appear.

4. Choose the **Edit P**aste command.

With some applications, you can insert a Paintbrush file without opening Paintbrush. In PageMaker, you can choose the **File Pl**ace command. In Word for Windows, you can choose **I**nsert **P**icture.

Applications such as Windows Write, Word for Windows, and Page-Maker include commands you can use to move and resize illustrations that you paste into your documents.

When you copy a Paintbrush painting onto the Clipboard (or copy part of a painting), the painting is stored in various formats so that you can paste the painting into documents in other applications. Some applications, however, cannot paste those formats. For those applications, you must remove the formatting before you copy the painting or selection onto the Clipboard.

To remove formatting, follow these steps:

1. Choose the **O**ptions **O**mit Picture Format command.

    A check mark appears next to the command.

2. Select the portion of the painting you want to copy.

3. Choose the **E**dit **C**opy command.

Remember to choose the **O**ptions **O**mit Picture Format command a second time to turn it off for future copies, if necessary.

Embedding and Linking Paintbrush Paintings

Besides being a stand-alone painting application, Paintbrush also is an OLE *server* application. OLE stands for object linking and embedding. A server is an application that can create objects that can be embedded inside or linked to documents created in other applications. Paintbrush can create objects that can be embedded or linked to documents created by applications such as Windows Write and Word for Windows.

For example, you can embed or link a Paintbrush painting (or part of one) inside a letter created in Windows Write or a report created in Word for Windows. When you embed or link objects inside a document, the application used to create that document is functioning as an OLE client. Applications besides Write and Word for Windows also can function as OLE clients.

When a Paintbrush object is embedded or linked in a document, you can start Paintbrush—with the object displayed in its drawing window—from within that document. For example, if a bar chart that you created in Paintbrush is embedded or linked in a letter you created in Write, you can start Paintbrush and edit the bar chart from within your Write document.

Embedding and linking differ in three ways: in the way you get the embedded or linked object from the server document into the client document; in the way the client application stores the object; and in the way you update the object.

Embedding a Paintbrush Object

You can use two different methods to embed a Paintbrush painting inside a document created by a application that supports OLE. You can either copy the painting into the client application's document, or you can use a command in the client program to insert the object. Each way has advantages. If you copy the painting, you can use an existing painting; if you create a painting, you can save it to a separate file that you can embed in other documents. If you embed a painting from within the client document, you cannot use an existing painting, and you cannot save the painting as a stand-alone file, but you can create the painting without leaving the client document.

When you embed an object inside a document, the client application stores the entire object with the client document. For example, you can give someone a disk containing a Write file with an embedded Paintbrush picture, and as long as they have Paintbrush on their computer, they can view, edit, and update the picture. Similarly, if someone gives you a Word for Windows file containing an embedded object created by a graphics application that you do not own, you still may be able to view, edit, and update the picture—because Windows has all the information about the picture, it will use another graphics applications (such as Paintbrush) to display, edit, and update it.

To embed a Paintbrush painting by copying, follow these steps:

1. Start the client application (into which you want to embed your Paintbrush painting) and Paintbrush.

2. In the client application, open the document into which you want to embed the Paintbrush painting. Scroll to display the exact place where you want to embed the painting.

3. In Paintbrush, open the document containing the painting you want to embed in the client document. Or, you can create the painting (save the painting if you want to use it again later).

4. Select the Paintbrush painting (or part of it) that you want to embed.

5. Choose the **E**dit menu and select the **C**opy command.

6. Switch to the client application and position the insertion point in the document where you want to embed the painting.

7. Choose the **E**dit **P**aste command.

The commands for embedding a Paintbrush painting from within a client application vary. In the following example, you see the command for embedding a painting into a Windows Write document. Using this technique, you must create the painting from within your Write document, and you cannot save the painting to use in any other document. (You also can use the same technique to embed many other types of objects besides Paintbrush paintings.)

To embed a Paintbrush painting from within Windows Write, follow these steps:

1. Start Windows Write and open the document into which you want to embed a painting. Position the insertion point where you want the painting.

2. Choose the **E**dit menu and select the **I**nsert Object command. The Insert Object dialog box appears.

3. From the **O**bject Type list, select Paintbrush Painting. Choose OK or press Enter.

   Paintbrush appears on your screen with a new, blank painting window.

4. Create your painting.

5. To add your painting to your Write document without closing Paintbrush, choose the **F**ile menu and select the **U**pdate command. Choose the **F**ile menu and select the E**x**it & Return command when you are ready to close Paintbrush and return to your document.

   Or, to add your painting to your Write document and at the same time, close Paintbrush, choose the **F**ile menu and select the E**x**it & Return command. When a dialog box appears asking whether you want to update your Write document, choose **Y**es.

To embed a Paintbrush painting into a Word for Windows document, choose the **I**nsert menu and select the **O**bject command. From there, the steps are the same as for Write. If you have a different application, check the menus to see which command will work; although the command may not be exactly the same as the commands in Write or Word for Windows, it is likely to be similar.

Be sure to save your Write or Word for Windows file in order to save your Paintbrush painting.

After a Paintbrush object is embedded inside a client application's document, you can edit the object from within that document. In almost any application, you can do that by double-clicking on the object to start Paintbrush. You also can use keyboard commands to edit embedded objects in most applications, but the commands vary. In Write, select the object, choose the **E**dit menu, and select the Edit Paintbrush Picture **O**bject command. In Word for Windows, select the object, choose the **E**dit menu, and select the Paintbrush Picture **O**bject command. Look for a similar command if your application is different.

To update an embedded Paintbrush object, follow these steps:

1. Start Paintbrush from within the client document by double-clicking on the Paintbrush picture or by choosing the appropriate command from the client application's menu.

2. Change the Paintbrush object.

3. Choose the File menu and select the Update command.

4. Choose the File menu and select the Exit & Return command to exit Paintbrush and return to your document.

To learn more about object linking and embedding, see Chapter 6, "Embedding and Linking Windows NT Applications."

Linking a Paintbrush Object

Linking an object from Paintbrush into a client document is similar to embedding. There is only one way to do it, however: you must copy a saved picture into the client document using a special command.

A linked picture is not stored as a complete file inside the client document, as is an embedded picture. Instead, the client document stores a link to the original file. If you give someone a disk with a Write file containing a linked Paintbrush picture, therefore, you also should include the Paintbrush picture on disk.

The advantage to linking is that when you change the original picture, the picture in the client document updates to reflect your changes. Because the client document stores a link to the original, rather than storing the original, you can create a single original picture and link it to many client documents (even if they are created by different applications). All the client documents update to reflect changes to the original.

To link a Paintbrush picture to a client document, follow these steps:

1. In Paintbrush, create or open the picture you want to link to the client document. If you make any changes, you must save the file.

2. Select the portion of the picture you want to link and choose the Edit Copy command.

3. Start the client application and open the document where you want to link the picture. Position the insertion point where you want the picture.

4. Choose the Edit Paste Link command.

Most client documents link objects so that they update automatically when the original object changes. However, you can edit the link in many ways: you can set it for manual update; you can update the link to reflect a new location for an original file that you have moved; or you can link the picture to a different original file.

Like an embedded object, you can edit a linked object from within the client document. The technique for starting the server application is the same as for embedding: you can double-click on the linked picture, or you can select the picture and choose an editing command. The application starts, and you edit and save the picture.

To learn more about linking, see Chapter 6, "Embedding and Linking Windows Applications."

Printing Paintbrush Files

Paintbrush gives you great flexibility in printing paintings. You can print all or part of a painting, in draft or final quality, scaled smaller or larger. Before you print, be sure that you have the correct printer selected and set up.

To select and set up a printer, follow these steps:

1. Choose the **F**ile **P**rint Setup command.

    The Printer Setup dialog box appears.

2. Select a printer from the Printer group. You can select the **D**efault printer or any other printer from the Specific **P**rinter list.

3. Select an option from the Orientation group: Po**r**trait prints your painting vertically on the page; **L**andscape prints it horizontally.

4. If necessary, choose options from the Paper group: to change the paper size, select an option from the Si**z**e list; to change paper source on your printer, select an option from the **S**ource list.

5. Choose OK or press Enter.

Setting up a printer in Paintbrush is the same as in any application. Remember that printer setup choices you make in one Windows application apply to *all* Windows applications. For details about printer setup, refer to Chapter 7, "Customizing with the Control Panel."

To print the Paintbrush painting on the selected printer, follow these steps:

1. Choose the **F**ile **P**rint command. The Print dialog box appears (see fig. 13.25).

2. In the Quality box, select **D**raft or **P**roof. **D**raft prints an unenhanced version of the painting quickly; **P**roof prints an accurate version of the painting. (On some printers, such as laser printers, there is no difference between Draft and Proof printing.)

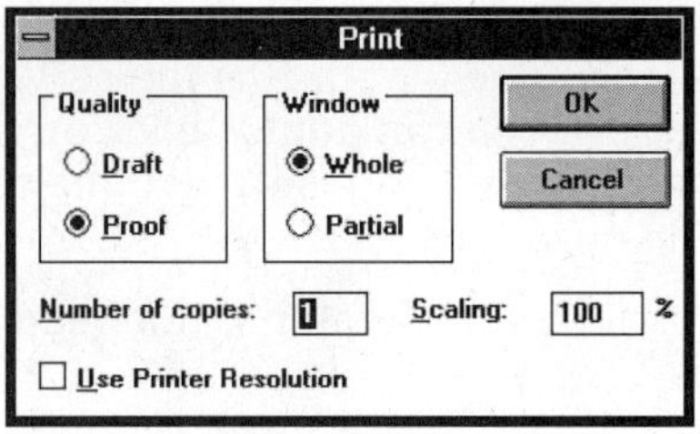

Fig. 13.25

3. In the Window box, select **W**hole or Pa**r**tial. **W**hole prints the entire painting; Pa**r**tial displays the painting on-screen and enables you to drag a crosshair to enclose the part of the painting you want to print.

4. In the **N**umber of copies box, type the number of copies of the painting you want to print.

5. In the **S**caling box, type a percent at which you want to print the painting. *100%* is actual size; *50%* is half size; *200%* is double size, and so on.

6. Select the **U**se Printer Resolution option to print the painting at printer resolution rather than Paintbrush screen resolution. Printer and screen resolution may be different; Paintbrush stretches a painting to make it print the same as it appears on-screen if you do not select **U**se Printer Resolution.

7. Choose OK or press Enter.

Summary

This chapter presented the information you need to use Paintbrush to paint useful illustrations. Now that you know how to create with Paintbrush, use your paintings to enliven the documents you create in other applications. If you find Paintbrush useful but want to do more, you may be ready for a more powerful graphics application.

Using Windows NT Terminal

W ebster's defines communication as the giving or exchanging of information. This definition provides a good start toward explaining what a communications application does. It enables a user to give information to or get information from a variety of sources—a mainframe, a public bulletin board, or another PC. The information may be as varied as corporate manufacturing data, medical or literary information, on-line airline information, budget worksheets, or messages sent to other users of a bulletin board.

Personal computers provide a wonderfully quick way to create letters, track business data, and generate financial information. But users need to share the information created. Information from a mainframe may help create a management report. To transfer the information from place to place—from an office computer to a home computer, for example—you need communications software, such as the Terminal application.

Communications applications use software and hardware components to link computers. The software component translates computer information into a signal that can be transmitted quickly and accurately over telephone lines. The hardware component may be a modem that converts computer signals into telephone signals and connects the computer to the telephone line. The hardware and software components of both your PC and the other computer must use the same methods of communication and the same *protocol* (communication language).

For computers to communicate, they must use the same communication settings, including type of communications port, memory parity (a checking method), stop bits (end of a word), and baud rate (the transmission rate). If you are dialing through a modem, you also may need a telephone number. Once the settings are in place, you can start the communications process.

Normally, to communicate with another computer, you follow this procedure:

1. Start the Terminal application.

2. Use the **S**ettings menu to change settings, if necessary, or use **F**ile **O**pen to open and load settings you saved previously.

3. Use the **P**hone menu to dial the phone line of the other computer.

4. Enter log-on information and then either interact with an on-line computer service or receive or send files in text or binary format and save them to disk.

5. Disconnect from the other computer.

6. Hang up the phone line, using the **P**hone menu.

7. Save the settings using the **F**ile menu if settings have changed or if you want to use them again.

8. Exit the Terminal application.

Starting Terminal from the Program Manager

To start Terminal, choose the Accessories group in the Program Manager and then open the Terminal application. Open this application by double-clicking on it with a mouse or by pressing an arrow key until the icon is selected and then pressing Enter.

Creating and Using Settings Files

If you frequently use Terminal to connect to the same source of information, you may want to save the settings for this communication. This makes reconnecting quick and easy. Settings files contain the information selected in the Settings menu. All commands in the Settings menu are saved except the last three menu items: Printer Echo, Timer Mode, and Show Function Keys.

Creating a Settings File

Choose the File New command to reset Terminal settings back to their default, or normal, state. Choosing File New deletes any phone number entered, clears the Terminal scroll buffer, and resets the communications port to 1200 baud, 8 bits, 0 stop bits, and no parity. If you made changes before choosing New, Terminal asks whether you want to save the existing settings before it resets all options to their default states.

Saving a Settings File

To save any changes made to the currently loaded settings file, choose the File Save command. Save automatically overwrites the existing settings file and saves all currently selected settings options. If the current file is untitled, Save automatically defaults to the Save As command so that you can name the settings file.

To save the current settings under a new file name, choose the File Save As command. The previous settings file remains unchanged. Save As displays the dialog box shown in figure 14.1.

If you enter the name of an existing file, Terminal displays a dialog box asking whether you want to replace the selected file with a Terminal settings file.

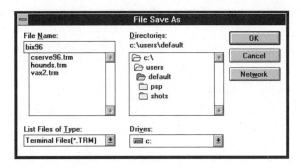

Fig. 14.1

The File Save As dialog box.

T I P   If you save a settings file with the name TERMINAL.TRM, Terminal loads this file as the default when you start the application.

Opening a Settings File

Use the **File O**pen command to load a previously saved settings file. If you have made changes to the currently loaded settings file, Terminal asks whether you want to save any current settings before loading the new settings file. When you choose **File O**pen, the dialog box shown in figure 14.2 appears.

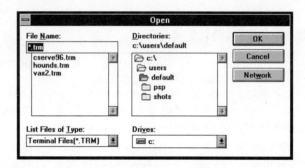

Fig. 14.2

The File Open dialog box.

As shown in figure 14.2, Terminal defaults to the file extension TRM. You can change this extension to anything you want. You can use the Windows Program Manager to create a Terminal program item icon that appears in a group window of the Program Manager. You can associate a particular settings file with this icon so that when you start Terminal, it automatically loads with all the options saved in the settings file.

Leaving Terminal

Choose the **File E**xit command to leave the Terminal application. If you have made any changes to the settings, you are asked whether you want to save the changes before exiting Terminal.

Remember to Hang Up!

If you are currently connected with a modem, Terminal asks whether you want to hang up. Failing to hang up the phone when you exit can leave you connected to a remote computer system, causing you to be billed for unused connect time. Do not worry about being billed for days of use, however; most systems automatically hang up if you have not made an entry in the last few minutes.

Using the Edit Menu

The Edit menu enables you to copy information from an application and paste the information into the Terminal window. You then can send what you paste to the computer to which you are connected.

Suppose that you have written a note in Windows Notepad and want to send it as though you were typing directly into the Terminal program.

Make the Notepad window active, select a block of text, and copy it to the Clipboard. Next, activate Terminal, and when the computer you are connected to requests that you type your message, select **Edit Paste**. Although you are pasting information into Terminal, the computer you are connected to assumes that you are typing the message from the keyboard. The following sections explain how to use the Terminal **Edit** menu to manipulate text from other applications.

Copying Text to the Clipboard

Use normal copying procedures for Windows or non-Windows applications to copy text or numbers into the Clipboard. Terminal purges all blanks at the end of each selected line and ends each line with a carriage return and line feed.

If you want to send graphics through Terminal, you need to send them as a binary file. Sending a binary file is described later in this chapter.

Using the Send Command to Save Steps

To send text directly to another computer, without copying and pasting, wait until the computer you are connected to requests your message. Then select the text, choose the **Edit Send** command, or press

Ctrl+Shift+Ins. Terminal copies the text you pasted to the Clipboard and sends it to the remote computer. This option is particularly useful when you are replying to electronic mail and want to forward part of a message you have received.

Selecting All the Text in Terminal's Buffer

Terminal stores information it has received in an area of memory called a *buffer*. To select the entire contents of Terminal's buffer, choose the Edit Select All command. This option is equivalent to selecting all of Terminal's received messages with the mouse or keyboard.

Clearing Terminal's Buffer

To clear the contents of Terminal's scroll buffer and window, choose the Edit Clear Buffer command. This command clears the data that has scrolled through Terminal's window.

Tailoring Terminal to Your Needs

You can tailor most of Terminal's options to your needs through the Settings menu, where you configure Terminal to match the communication requirements of other computers. The Settings menu enables you to select the default phone number, terminal emulation, terminal preferences, function keys, text transfers, binary transfers, communications parameters, and modem commands. Each operation is described in the following sections.

Using CompuServe

CompuServe is one of the most widely used public databases. Anyone can join CompuServe for a low membership fee. You then can connect to many different types of information services at rates of $8 per hour and up. The information services you can connect to cover a wide range of topics:

Help for Windows and Windows applications

Libraries of free programs and sample files

On-line airline guides that help you find and schedule the lowest air fares

Dow-Jones stock quotes

Wall Street Journal articles and analyses

News reports that have been filed but not yet published

Medical and legal databases

Engineering and technical databases

Games

The settings to connect to CompuServe are as follows:

Settings **P**hone Number	Local CompuServe phone number (call CompuServe for this number)
Settings **B**inary Transfers	**X**Modem/CRC (remember this setting; every time you download files, CompuServe will ask you for this information)

Settings Communications

Baud Rate	1200
Data Bits	7
Stop Bits	1
Parity	Even
Flow Control	Xon/Xoff
Connector	(Choose the COM port your modem is connected to)

Chapter 33 lists some of the CompuServe forums related to Windows NT and Windows applications. These forums are an excellent source of software updates, shareware and freeware programs, access to technical support from Microsoft engineers, and more.

Entering a Phone Number

From the **S**ettings menu, choose Phone **N**umber to specify the phone number you want Terminal to dial. The dialog box shown in figure 14.3 appears when you select this option.

In the **D**ial text box, type the phone number you want to use. The phone number can contain parentheses and dashes. A comma placed anywhere in the text field causes the modem to pause for two seconds before dialing any remaining digits. Use this option when you need to dial 9 to get an outside line and must pause briefly.

In the Timeout If Not Connected In text box, type the time (in seconds) you want Terminal to wait before assuming that the remote computer is not answering the phone. The minimum time allowed is 30 seconds.

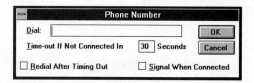

Select Redial After Timing Out to make Terminal automatically redial the phone number after the time limit has been reached.

Select Signal When Connected to have the computer beep to indicate that the connection has been made. This feature can be very useful when you are working on several tasks and want Terminal to signal you when it connects with the remote computer.

Selecting a Terminal Emulation

Choose the Settings Terminal Emulation command to specify which type of terminal you want to emulate. Terminal emulation makes the Terminal program act like one of three industry-standard hardware terminals used with most computers. The dialog box shown in figure 14.4 appears.

Terminal supports three terminal emulations: TTY, VT 52, and VT 100. The TTY emulation recognizes only ASCII text and responds to carriage returns and line feeds. The VT 100 and VT 52 emulations are based on the popular DEC VT 100 and DEC VT 52 terminals. When you select either of these terminal emulations, Terminal responds to all the display requests these terminals have, such as bold, underline, and the DEC line-drawing character set.

Terminal Emulation

○ TTY (Generic)
⊙ DEC VT-100 (ANSI)
○ DEC VT-52

OK
Cancel

Using Arrow and Function Keys During Terminal Emulation

When Terminal emulates VT 52 or VT 100 terminals, your PC keyboard can emulate the VT 52 or VT 100 keyboard. Press the Scroll Lock key to switch from the Windows keyboard to the terminal keyboard. When emulating a terminal, the arrow keys work the same, the F1 through F4 function keys become the PF1 through PF4 keys, and the numeric and punctuation keys are the same. Press the + key on your keyboard for the VT 52 or VT 100 Enter key.

Choosing Terminal Preferences

To modify local terminal parameters, choose the **S**ettings Terminal **P**references command. This specifies how your personal computer accepts the characters it receives—for example, how it wraps lines of text and whether it double-spaces lines. When you choose this command, the Terminal Preferences dialog box appears (see fig. 14.5).

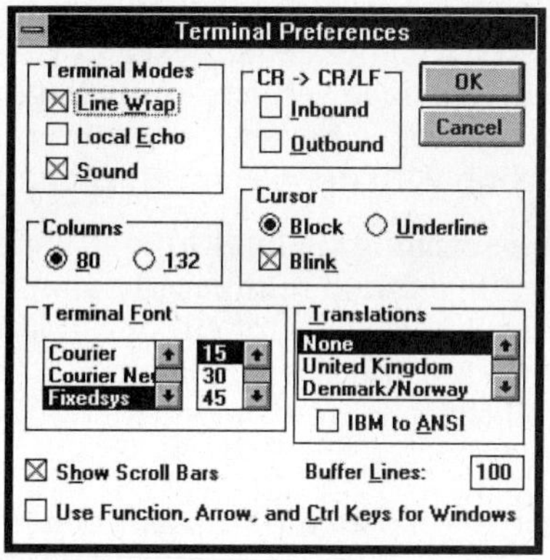

Fig. 14.5

The Terminal Preferences dialog box.

Select the Line **W**rap check box if you want Terminal to wrap characters that pass the last character column displayed in Terminal. Do not check this option if you want Terminal to lose and not display characters that exceed the width of the Terminal display. Select this option if Terminal is set to display 80 columns, but the computer you are connected to sends 132 columns. Selecting Line **W**rap ensures that data is not lost.

Select the Local Echo check box if you want Terminal to echo (repeat on your screen) keystrokes you're sending. Otherwise, Terminal displays outgoing keystrokes on the remote system only. You cannot see them.

In some hardware, the remote system echoes the transmitted keystrokes back to you (a condition called *remote echo*). In this instance, deselect Local Echo to avoid displaying each keystroke twice on your screen. If the remote system is not configured for remote echo or if you are not currently connected, select Local Echo to display the outgoing keystrokes as you type them. By default, the Local Echo setting is deselected.

Select the Sound check box to direct Terminal to sound warning bells (^G characters) coming from the remote system. Disable the bell by deselecting the Sound check box. By default, this setting is selected.

Select the Inbound check box to display incoming carriage returns as carriage returns followed by line feeds. Deselect the Inbound check box to display incoming carriage returns as carriage returns only. By default, the Inbound setting is deselected. If your computer receives the transmission with double-spacing, change this setting.

Select the Outbound check box to display outgoing carriage returns as carriage returns followed by line feeds. Deselect the Outbound check box to display outgoing carriage returns as carriage returns only. By default, the Outbound setting is deselected. If the other computer receives the transmission with double-spacing, change this setting.

Select the width of the scrolling region for your window by specifying in the Columns group the desired number of columns (one character per column). You can select a width of either 80 or 132 characters. If the width you specify is too wide to display in the Terminal window, you may have to scroll right to view the entire document. The default number of columns is 80.

Depending on the type of display monitor you have, you may find that one type of insertion point or cursor is more visible than another. Portable computers especially may require some experimentation to find the best cursor type. Select Block to display the cursor as a block; select Underline to display the cursor as an underscore character. If you want the cursor to blink, select the Blink check box. Deselect the Blink check box if you want the cursor to display without blinking. By default, the Blink setting is selected.

As is true of any good Windows NT application, you can select the font and point size used for the characters on-screen. Select fonts and sizes for the Terminal window from the scrolling-list boxes in the Terminal Font group. All Windows NT display fonts are available for use in the Terminal window.

If you use Terminal in an international environment, you may need to use international character sets. Select the desired character translation from the **T**ranslations scrolling list. By default, Terminal selects the country specified in the International option of Control Panel. You can see and change these settings using the International option in the Control Panel window.

If your message is long or its characters exceed the screen width, you need to scroll the window. You use the scroll bars to scroll with the mouse. If you work strictly with the keyboard, you may want to remove the scroll bars so that you can see more of the screen. Select the **Sh**ow Scroll Bars check box to direct Terminal to display the scroll boxes in the Terminal window. Deselect the **Sh**ow Scroll Bars check box to remove the scroll-bar display. This choice is valid whether or not the Terminal window is maximized.

Terminal keeps the information you send and receive in an area of memory called the *buffer*. You can control the size of the buffer. Enter in the Buffer **L**ines text box the desired size of the buffer in numbers of lines. If you type a number smaller than 25, Terminal allocates a scroll buffer containing 25 lines. The default number of buffer lines is 100. With the mouse, use the scroll bars at the sides of the Terminal window to determine the size of the buffer you need. Scroll backward and forward through the buffer to display the text you typed and received.

If you know that you want to save all the lines you send and receive, use the techniques described in "Receiving Text Files," later in this chapter.

If you want to use the function, arrow, and Ctrl keys to carry out Windows tasks—for example, using Ctrl+Esc to open the Task List—select the Use Function, Arrow, and Ctrl Keys for Windows options. If you want to use these keys to control the software on the remote computer, deselect this option.

After you specify the Terminal Preferences settings, you can use them, discard them, or save them to a settings file.

Creating On-Screen Function Keys

Using function keys is an easy way to automate the communications process. Instead of using the menu items, for example, you can program a function key to dial a number, send your user ID, or hang up. You can display function keys as buttons at the bottom of Terminal's screen, as shown in figure 14.6. Display or hide function keys with the **S**ettings Show **F**unction Keys or Hide **F**unction Keys command.

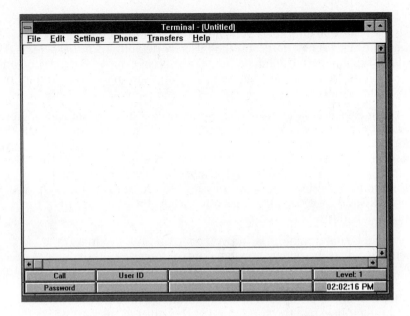

Fig. 14.6

Function keys
display at bottom
of Terminal's
screen.

You can create up to 32 function keys. Because the function keys have
other purposes in Windows, you must press Ctrl+Alt+*function key* to
activate the custom keys.

The 32 possible function keys appear in four *levels* of 8 keys, as you can
see at the bottom of figure 14.6. For convenience, put the keys you use
most often in level 1. You can access level 1 function keys without additional mouse clicks or key presses.

Switch between levels with the mouse by clicking on the level-indicator
button at the far right of the banks of buttons. (This indicator reads
Level:1 in figure 14.6.) Switch between levels with the keyboard by creating a function key in each level that takes you to the next level. The
code you use to define such a key is described later in this chapter.

As you can see in figure 14.7, a function key definition has two parts:
the function key name and the function key command.

To customize function keys, follow these steps:

1. Choose the **S**ettings Function **K**eys command. The dialog box
   shown in figure 14.7 appears.

2. Select a Key Level of 1 through 4 to specify the group of function
   keys you want to create. Usually, you start with level 1.

3. Select the Key Name of the function key you want to customize
   and type the text you want to appear in the button (the label of
   the button). Press Tab to move to the Command text box for that
   key.

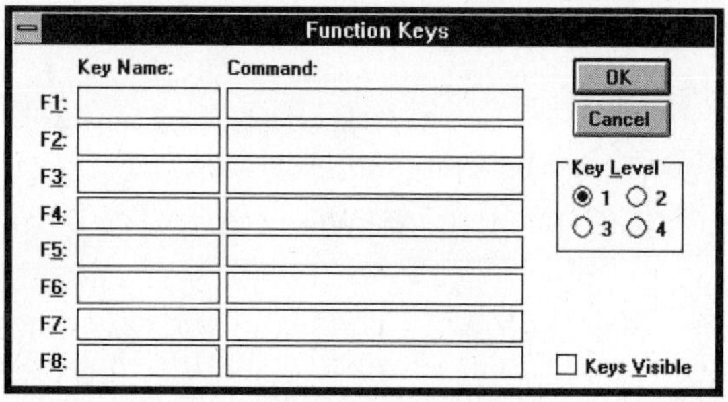

Fig. 14.7

The Function
Keys dialog box.

4. In the Command text box, type the text or commands you want
   the key to perform. A chart later in this section describes those
   commands.

5. Repeat steps 3 and 4 to customize any other function keys in this
   level.

6. Select the Keys **V**isible check box to display the function keys.

7. Choose OK or press Enter.

The Command text boxes can contain any combination of text and
codes from the following chart. The chart lists the actions you may
want a function key to perform and provides the appropriate commands to achieve those actions.

Action	What To Type in the Command Text box
Send Control-A through Control-Z (note that these commands do not include a $)	^A through ^Z
Send a Break code (each number is a unit equal to 117 milliseconds)	^$B*number*
Choose the **Phone Dial** command	^$C
Delay Terminal for *number* of seconds (use this command while waiting for password or log-on response)	^$D*number*
Choose the **Phone Hangup** command	^$H
Change to the level of key group indicated by number (1 through 4); enables you to use the four groups of eight function keys	^$L*number*
Send a caret (^) to the remote computer	^^
Send a NULL character to the remote computer	^@
Send *number* escape code sequences to remote computer	^[*number*

Those codes preceded by ^ are typed with the Shift+6 key and not the Ctrl key.

You can assign the key name *MyLogin* to F1, for example, and type the following commands in the Command text box:

```
^$C^$D10LOGIN^M^$D10PASSWORD^M
```

When you press F1 or click the on-screen button containing this command, Terminal executes the ^$C command and calls the number specified in the active settings file. Terminal waits 10 seconds as specified by ^$D10, sends the string LOGIN and a carriage return (^M), waits 10 more seconds, sends the string PASSWORD, and sends another carriage return (^M).

If you want a key that changes between function-key levels, use a code like the following in that key's Command box:

```
^$L3
```

When you press Ctrl+Alt+*function key* (where *function key* is the key to which this command is assigned), the display changes to show the function keys on level 3.

Displaying Function Keys On-Screen

To display the function keys on-screen when you open a settings file, check the Key Visible check box in the Function Keys dialog box and save the settings file. If you want to toggle between displaying and hiding the on-screen function keys, choose the Settings Show Function Keys command. This command toggles between Show Function Keys and Hide Function Keys.

Changing How Terminal Sends Text

You use text transfers to transmit text files. Text files are usually word processing or mainframe files that do not contain formatting. (To transfer other types of files, see the following section on binary transfers.) Choose the Settings Text Transfers command to set the text-transfer protocol and the text margins. The dialog box shown in figure 14.8 appears.

To transfer text in XON/XOFF mode, select Standard Flow Control. In this mode, the receiving system sends an XOFF message to the transmitting system when the receiving system's input buffer is nearly full. The transmitting system then halts transmission until it receives an XON message from the receiving system, indicating that the input buffer has been cleared.

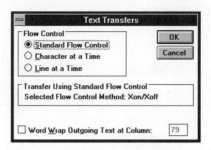

Fig. 14.8

The Text Trans-
fers dialog box.

Select **C**haracter at a Time to transfer text one character at a time. Notice that when you select this option, the dialog box changes, as shown
in figure 14.9.

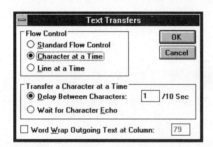

Fig. 14.9

The Character at
a Time option in
the Text Transfers
dialog box.

Select **D**elay Between Characters to specify the delay between characters. Enter the desired delay in tenths of a second in the text box.
Changes are sent at even intervals without regard to whether they have
been received correctly.

Select Wait for Character **E**cho to instruct Terminal to wait until the
receiving computer echoes back its response. In this mode, the transmitting system waits for the transmitted character to be returned by
the receiving system before it sends the next character. The transmitting system compares the two characters to verify that the correct
character was received.

To transfer one line at a time, select **L**ine at a Time from the Flow Control group. The dialog box options change, as shown in figure 14.10.
Select Delay **B**etween Lines to specify the delay between lines. Enter
the desired delay in tenths of a second in the text box. Lines are sent
at even intervals without regard to whether they have been received
correctly.

Select Wait for **P**rompt String to prompt Terminal to wait to receive a
line from the remote system before sending the next line. ^M is the

suggested end-of-line character. Use this method when you have difficulty with character transmission.

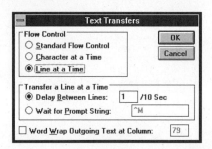

Fig. 14.10

The Line at a
Time option in
the Text Transfers
dialog box.

If the text you are sending may be formatted wider than the width of
the receiving screen, select Word **W**rap Outgoing Text at Column.
(This option frequently is needed when you send text files from a word
processor.) You then can specify the column number at which you
want the text to wrap. For example, if the receiving terminal has a
132-column screen, set the Word **W**rap option to 131 columns. This
setting leaves one character position for the ^M end-of-line code. If you
do not select this option, text is sent as it is formatted.

Selecting Binary Transfers Options

Use a binary transfer when you want to transfer a file in its native
format—for example, an Excel XLS or XLC file, a Lotus WK1 file, a
formatted Word for Windows file, a graphics file like PCX or BMP, or
a compressed PKZIP or archived file.

Choose the **S**ettings **B**inary Transfers command to specify the binary
transfer protocol. The dialog box in figure 14.11 appears. You can
choose either **X**Modem/CRC or **K**ermit protocol; the default binary
transfer protocol is XModem/CRC. Make sure that the sending and
receiving communications applications are using the same protocol.
Some computers or services to which you connect, such as Compu-
Serve, ask you which method of transmission you want to use.

Fig. 14.11

The Binary
Transfers dialog
box.

Transmitting Application Files

If you want to use Terminal to send a Microsoft Excel, Word for Windows, or 1-2-3 file from one PC to another, make sure that both computers are transmitting at the same baud rate and with the same file-transfer protocol—either XModem or Kermit. After you connect with the other PC, test the connection by typing some text in your Terminal window. The text you type should appear on the other PC's screen. When text is typed on the other PC, that same text should appear on your screen.

When you know that you have established the connection, choose the **T**ransfers Send **B**inary File command, select the file you want to send from the scrolling list, and then choose OK.

If the user of the other PC selects the **T**ransfers Receive Binary **F**ile command, you can see the progress of the transfer in the status bar. You also can make Terminal an icon and watch the background color of the icon change as the transfer progresses. You may work in other applications while the transfer is proceeding. When the transfer is complete, the icon flashes.

Selecting Communications Parameters

An important aspect of using your computer to exchange information is setting the communications *parameters*. These communications characteristics ensure that two computers "talk" at the same rate, use the same bundles of information, and use the same dialect. If you are connecting to a commercial database service, such as CompuServe, or with a local bulletin board system, call the service to find out what settings you should use. (Settings for CompuServe are listed in a tip in this chapter.) To change or set parameters, choose the **S**ettings **C**ommunications command (see fig. 14.12).

Select the speed at which you want data to be sent and received by specifying the **B**aud Rate. The maximum baud rate at which you can communicate is a function of many factors, such as the type of modem and the quality and length of the communications line. The default baud-rate setting is 1200. Most telephone communication is done at 1200 or 2400 baud.

Select the number of **D**ata Bits to be transmitted in each character packet. The default **D**ata Bits setting is 8.

Select the number of **S**top Bits to be transmitted. The default **S**top Bits setting is 1.

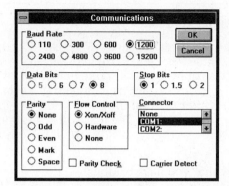

Fig. 14.12

The Communications dialog box.

Select the **P**arity type. Parity is used for detecting errors during transmission. If you selected 8 for the Data Bits setting, select None for the Parity setting. If you select Mark parity, the eighth bit is set to on. If you select Space parity, the eighth bit is set to off. Odd and Even parities calculate the total of the first seven bits; the eighth bit is then set by Terminal to make the total of the eight bits either always odd or always even.

Select the **F**low Control. If XON/XOFF is selected, the receiving system sends an XOFF message to the transmitting system when its input buffer is nearly full. The transmitting system halts transmission until it receives an XON message from the receiving system, indicating that the input buffer has been cleared. If you select Hardware, flow control is handled through the pins on the RS-232 serial cable. If you select None, no flow-control method is used.

Your modem connects your computer to another computer's telephone line or directly to a minicomputer or mainframe computer. For Terminal to send information to the modem, Terminal must know which communication port the modem is connected to. If the serial ports in the back of your computer are not labeled, check with your dealer or support representative to find out which one the modem is connected to. Select the desired communications port from the **C**onnector scrolling list. In Windows NT, you can use COM1 through COM4. Select None when the modem is disconnected because you're using its serial port for a printer or other device.

Select the Parity Chec**k** check box to direct Terminal to replace with a question mark (?) characters that do not match the specified parity. Characters may not match because of transmission errors or noise in the telephone line. Deselect the Parity Chec**k** check box to ignore parity errors. The default Parity Chec**k** setting is deselected.

Hayes-compatible modems have a hardware-connect signal that is set to TRUE when a communications connection is made. Select the Carrier Detect check box to enable Terminal to use this signal to determine whether the Receive Line Signal Detect (RLSD) is set. If you select this check box, Terminal automatically hangs up if the carrier is lost, preventing you from having to select Hangup from the Phone menu before dialing. Deselect the Carrier Detect check box if you do not want Terminal to hang up automatically or if your modem's RLSD is unreliable. The default Carrier Detect setting is deselected.

Changing Modem Options

Change the Settings Modem Commands command to modify the commands Terminal sends to your modem (see fig. 14.13). The correct modem commands for the modem type selected (Hayes is the default) are displayed in the text boxes. You can use these commands as they are or modify them to accommodate the codes used by nonstandard modems. Be sure to check your modem manual for the appropriate commands. In most cases, you need only to select the type of modem you are using from the Modem Defaults group; you need not enter your own commands.

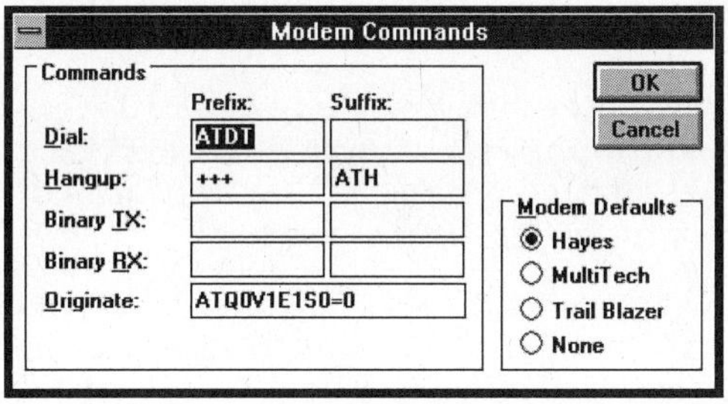

Fig. 14.13

The Modem Commands dialog box showing Hayes commands.

The following chart lists the various text boxes in the Modem Commands dialog box and the kind of information expected by each.

Text Box	Description
Dial	The prefix and suffix appended to the phone number that direct the modem to dial
Hangup	The prefix and suffix that direct the modem to hang up
Binary TX	The prefix and suffix necessary for initiating a binary file transfer

continues

Text Box	Description
Binary **R**X	The prefix and suffix necessary for receiving a binary file transfer
Originate	How Terminal directs the modem to exit answer mode

Consult your modem manual before you modify these commands. If you make a mistake, choose one of the **M**odem Defaults options to reset the settings.

Viewing Text Files from Disk

Before you send a text file you may want to view its contents. Choose the **T**ransfers View Text File to see in the Terminal window the file you request. The dialog box shown in figure 14.14 appears. The *.TXT in the File **N**ame text box appears by default, listing all text files with the extension TXT. Select the file you want to view. Display a file in this fashion when you want to review a file before sending it or when you want to add to the file or replace it with an incoming text file.

To view the file, enter the desired file name in the File **N**ame text box and choose OK or press Enter.

Select **A**ppend LF to add a line feed after each carriage return in the file, producing a new line after each paragraph. Deselect the **A**ppend LF check box to leave carriage returns as they appear in the file. The default **A**ppend LF status is deselected.

Select the **S**trip LF check box to strip line-feed characters after carriage returns. Deselect the **S**trip LF check box to leave carriage returns and line feeds as they appear in the file. The default **S**trip LF status is deselected.

After specifying the options in the View Text File dialog box, choose OK or press Enter. The file you specified is displayed on-screen (see fig. 14.15).

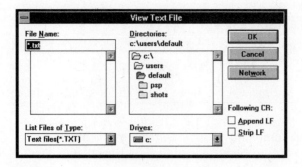

Fig. 14.14

The View Text
File dialog box.

A status bar displays in the lower portion of the Terminal window as
you view the text file. To stop the View Text File from scrolling past,
choose either the Stop button or the Transfers Stop command. To
pause the scrolling text temporarily, choose either the Pause button
or the Transfers Pause command. After you click on the Pause button,
it changes to a Resume button. To restart the suspended file display,
choose either the Resume button or the Transfers Resume command.
Terminal displays the name of the file being viewed, and the scale at
the bottom changes to indicate the portion of the text that has been
displayed.

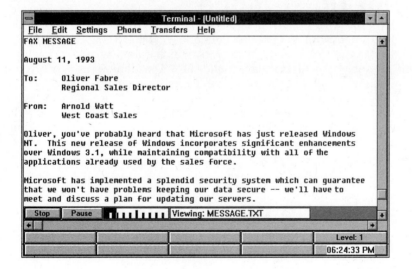

Fig. 14.15

Viewing a text
file before it is
replaced or sent.

Printing Incoming Text from Terminal

Choose the Settings Printer Echo command to print all data received in the Terminal window. When active, this option is preceded by a check mark in the Setting menu. To exit Printer Echo mode, choose the Printer Echo command again. When you exit Printer Echo mode, Terminal sends the printer a form feed to eject the current sheet of paper.

You also can paste information from the Terminal window into a word processing application or the Notepad, where you can edit, save, or print copy. If you receive a large amount of text data, a much more efficient method of printing is to save incoming text to a file. Read "Receiving Text Files" later in this chapter to learn how to save received text directly to a file. Open this file into a word processing application when you want to edit or print it.

Keeping Track of Time with Timer Mode

If you connect with a commercial database, you are charged by the amount of time you are connected, by which database you access, and by your transmission rate (baud rate). Dawdling while you are connected to one of these databases can cost you money, so watch the time. You can have Terminal's clock function as a timer. Just choose the Settings Timer Mode command, and the digital timer is displayed at the lower right when the function keys are visible. To reset the timer to zero, deselect and reselect the Timer Mode command from the Settings menu.

Displaying and Hiding On-Screen Function Keys

To see the function keys as buttons at the bottom of your screen, choose the Settings Show Function Keys command. Once the function keys are displayed, the menu option changes to Hide Function Keys. Select this option to remove the function-key display.

Figure 14.6 showed you how the function keys appear when they are displayed. To program your own function keys, refer to "Creating On-Screen Function Keys," earlier in this chapter.

Making a Call with Terminal

Once you have set all the settings necessary to connect to another computer, choose the **P**hone **D**ial command to dial the other computer's modem and make a connection. The **P**hone menu commands dial a telephone number or hang up from the current connection. The **D**ial option directs Terminal to dial a phone number. By default, Terminal dials the phone number specified in the settings file. If no phone number is in the active settings file, enter the number in the **D**ial option dialog box.

Choose the **P**hone **H**angup command to send the hang-up prefix and hang-up suffix specified in the **M**odem Commands dialog box.

Sending Text Files

To send a text file, choose the **T**ransfers **S**end Text File command. This command sends the text file you select, whether created by Notepad or a word processor. When you choose the **T**ransfers **S**end Text File command, the dialog box shown in figure 14.16 appears.

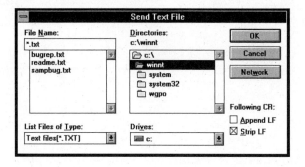

Fig. 14.16

The Send Text File dialog box.

You may choose one of the Following CR check boxes if you want to remove line feeds from the end of each line sent. If the information you receive has overlapping lines (no line feed was sent), select **A**ppend LF. If the information you receive has double-spaced lines, select **S**trip LF. If you are in doubt about how the receiving terminal handles lines, transmit with these boxes cleared. Check the message received by the receiving terminal and then select one of these check boxes so that the text is received the way you want it.

A status bar appears in the lower portion of the terminal window as you send a text file. Click on the Stop button or choose Transfers Stop to cancel the Send Text File option. Click on the Pause button or choose Transfers Pause to suspend the file transfer temporarily. When you click on the Pause button, it changes to a Resume button. This procedure is equivalent to using the Transfers Resume command to restart the suspended file transfer.

Terminal also displays the name of the file being sent. The scale changes to display the portion of the text file that has been sent.

Receiving Text Files

To receive a text file, choose the Transfers Receive Text File command (see fig. 14.17). This command can be used either to receive a text file from the remote system or to capture text coming into the Terminal window and save it to a file.

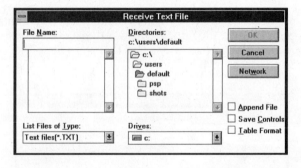

Fig. 14.17

The Receive Text File dialog box.

Use the Directories list box to specify the directory where you want the incoming file saved. In the File Name text box, enter the file name under which you want the text stored.

Select the Append File check box to save incoming text to the end of the file you specify without clearing the current contents of the file. To replace the current file contents with the incoming text, deselect the Append File check box. The default Append File status is deselected.

To save incoming control characters, select the Save Controls check box. Some applications use control characters to format text, set options, and so on. If you are unfamiliar with control characters, try both settings and then open the files with a word processing application and check the results. To strip incoming control characters, deselect the Save Controls check box. The default Save Controls status is deselected.

To save incoming text in tabular format, select the Table Format check box. Terminal puts tab characters between incoming text fields separated by two or more consecutive spaces. Use this setting when you want to receive a Lotus 1-2-3 print file (which contains only characters and spaces) or a Microsoft Excel TXT file (which uses tabs to separate cell values). Clear the Table Format check box to save the file in its current format. The default Table Format status is cleared.

Control buttons appear in the lower portion of the Terminal window as you receive a text file. Click on the Stop button or choose Transfers Stop to cancel the Receive Text File option. Click on the Pause button to stop temporarily storing the incoming text to the specified file. After you click on the Pause button, it changes to a Resume button, and the Transfer Resume command becomes available. Choose the Resume button or the Transfer Resume command to resume storing the incoming text to the specified file.

> **CAUTION:** Choosing the Pause button or the Transfer Pause command to stop temporarily storing incoming text does not prevent the remote system from sending text. The incoming text is not saved while the Receive Text File option is paused. This option is useful for saving (or not saving) parts of a file, but it can cause you to miss data if you select it at the wrong time.

Terminal displays at the bottom of the screen the name of the file in which the incoming text is stored (see fig. 14.17). The Bytes indicator changes to reflect the number of bytes received.

Sending Binary Files

If you are sending formatted word processing files, database files, worksheets, programs, graphics, or compressed files of any type, you probably want to send them as binary files. Choosing the Transfers Send Binary File command enables you to send a file in binary format (see fig. 14.18). The *.* in the File Name text box appears by default to list all the files in the current directory. The file is sent according to the binary transfer protocol established by the Settings Binary Transfer command.

```
┌─────────────────────────────────────────────────────┐
│ ⊟                    Send Binary File                 │
├─────────────────────────────────────────────────────┤
│  File Name:              Directories:      ┌────────┐ │
│  ▓                       c:\users\default  │   OK   │ │
│  ┌──────────────┐  ┌──────────────────┐   └────────┘ │
│  │cserve96.trm ▓│  │ 🗁 c:\          ▓ │   ┌────────┐ │
│  │hounds.trm    │  │  🗁 users        │   │ Cancel │ │
│  │vax2.trm      │  │   🗁 default     │   └────────┘ │
│  │              │  │    🗀 psp        │   ┌────────┐ │
│  │              │  │    🗀 shots      │   │Network │ │
│  │             ▓│  │                 ▓│   └────────┘ │
│  └──────────────┘  └──────────────────┘             │
│  List Files of Type:     Drives:                     │
│  ┌──────────────┐▓┐  ┌──────────────┐▓┐             │
│  │All files(*.*)│ │  │ ▤ c:         │ │             │
│  └──────────────┘─┘  └──────────────┘─┘             │
└─────────────────────────────────────────────────────┘
```

Fig. 14.18

The Send Binary
File dialog box.

To send a binary file, use the **Directories** list box to select the directory containing the file. Select the file from the **F**iles list or type the file name in the File **N**ame text box.

A status bar displays in the lower portion of the Terminal window while you send a binary file. Click on the Stop button to cancel the Send **Bi**nary File command.

Occasionally, a communications error occurs, preventing the transfer of a packet of data in the binary file. When an error occurs, Terminal tries to send the data packet again. After making the maximum number of unsuccessful retries, Terminal cancels the file transfer. The Retries indicator displays the number of times Terminal tried to resend the data packet.

If an error occurs, check with the receiving party to ensure that you are using the same settings. Line noise or static also may cause the problem. If the problem is telephone noise, try sending the file later.

Terminal displays the name of the binary file being sent. The scale at the bottom of the screen shows the portion of the file that has been sent.

Receiving Binary Files

Choose the **T**ransfer Receive Binary **F**ile option to receive a file in binary file format. The file is received according to the binary-transfer protocol established by the **S**ettings **B**inary Transfer command.

To receive a binary file, check to make sure that you are using the same settings as the computer sending the information. Prepare the file you want to receive and choose the **T**ransfer Receive Binary **F**ile command. The dialog box in figure 14.19 appears. Enter the name of the file you want to receive. To receive the file, click on the OK button or press Enter.

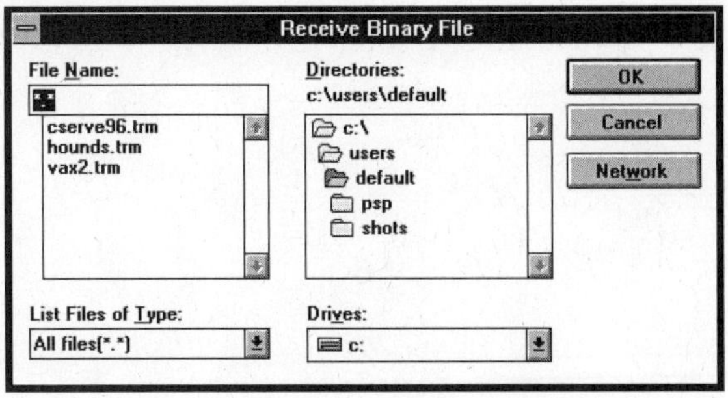

Fig. 14.19

The Receive
Binary File
dialog box.

A status bar displays in the lower portion of the Terminal window as you receive a binary file. Clicking on the Stop button or choosing the Terminal Stop command instructs Terminal to cancel the Receive Binary File option.

Occasionally, a communications error occurs, preventing the transfer of a packet of binary data. When an error occurs, the remote system tries to send the data again. After the remote system makes the maximum number of unsuccessful retries, Terminal cancels the file transfer. The Retries indicator at the bottom of the screen displays the number of times the remote system tried to resend data packets. With XModem/CRC protocol, the maximum number of retries is 20; with Kermit protocol, the maximum number of retries is 5.

Terminal also displays the name of the binary file being received. The scale changes to display the portion of the file that has been received.

Summary

You and a co-worker in the same office—or across the country—may want to use Terminal to send and receive files. Although you cannot communicate directly from Terminal to Terminal, you can leave messages for each other in a public database such as CompuServe or upload and download information from your company's computer.

Many people enjoy using on-line databases and mail services. Companies such as CompuServe offer business information, access to buying services, discussions on many topics, and even games.

Using Desktop Accessories

The desktop accessories that come with Windows NT can help you
perform special tasks related to a current project without leaving
the application. You may be working in Excel, for example, and need to
make a quick note; the Windows NT Notepad is the perfect companion.
When working in Word for Windows NT, you may need to make a quick
calculation; the Windows NT Calculator can do the job. You may want
to make a telephone call but can't remember the phone number; use
the Cardfile to find, and even dial, the number. If you need to insert a
special character or symbol in a Windows NT application; you can select the desired symbol from the Character Map.

These desktop accessories take advantage of one of Windows NT's
most powerful features: the capability of running several applications
simultaneously. As you work in the main application, you can keep the
Windows NT desktop applications running at the same time. You get
quick access to these useful tools—without closing the application in
which you're currently working. Because so little of the computer's
memory is used, the desktop accessories don't slow you down.

The Write, Paintbrush, and Terminal applications are discussed in previous chapters. The PIF Editor, which helps you specify how DOS applications run, is discussed in Chapter 21, "Customizing PIFs." Multimedia
is discussed in Chapter 16, "Using Multimedia." The Object

Packager is discussed in Chapter 6, "Embedding and Linking Windows NT Applications." This chapter covers the smaller desktop applications listed in the following chart.

Application	Description
Notepad	A text editor for medium-size text files.
Character Map	A table of symbols and characters for each of the character sets you have available. Copy one or more characters or symbols from the map and paste them in any Windows NT document that supports multiple fonts.
Cardfile	A computerized stack of cards that stores and retrieves text or graphics. You can quickly find cards that contain a specified word or phrase and use Cardfile's dialer feature to dial telephone numbers.
Clock	A clock that enables you to be a clock watcher as you stare at the screen. Even as an icon, Clock shows the time.
Calculator	An application that works just like a normal or scientific calculator, except that you don't need batteries and someone won't borrow it off your desk.
Chat	A communications tool that lets you have an electronic conversation with another person on your network.
3270 Emulator	A communications product that enables you to access a remote IBM mainframe host application from your computer.
Minesweeper	An analysis game to help you get tense about something other than work.
Solitaire	The classic card game that makes you wonder how 1:00 a.m. arrived so quickly.
FreeCell	A logic puzzle similar to a solitaire card game; however, the cards are all dealt face up.

In this chapter, you learn the features of the Notepad, including how to copy and move text, create a time-log file, and save and print Notepad files. You learn how the Cardfile works as a handy database of names and phone numbers, that even can dial phone numbers for you.

You see how you can quickly start up a computer Calculator to do math and how you can copy results from the Calculator in the current application. You see how the Clock helps you keep track of time. You learn how to contact another user and have an electronic conversation from your computer using Chat. You see how to use your computer as a remote terminal connected to an IBM host computer using 3270 Emulator. Finally, for recreation, you learn how to play Minesweeper, Solitaire, or FreeCell at the end of the day.

All Windows NT accessories can be found in the Program Manager (see fig. 15.1). Notepad, Character Map, Cardfile, Clock, Calculator, Chat, and 3270 Emulator are located in the Accessories group. Minesweeper, Solitaire and FreeCell are located in the Games group. Open the Program Manager window by double-clicking the Program Manager icon or by pressing Alt+Tab until the Program Manager title appears and then releasing the keys. Within the Program Manager, you see different icons and windows. Open the Accessories window by double-clicking on the Accessories icon or by pressing Ctrl+Tab to select the icon and pressing Enter. If the Accessories window is open but underneath another window, click on the window to bring it to the top or press Ctrl+Tab until it appears on the top of the on-screen stack of windows.

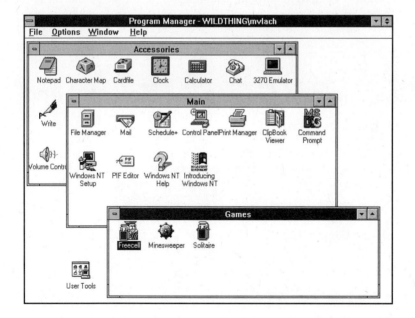

Fig. 15.1

The Program Manager Window.

Writing in the Notepad

Notepad is a miniature text editor. Although with limited functions when compared to an application like Windows NT Write or a professional word processor like Word for Windows or Ami Pro, Notepad is an ideal tool for many purposes. Just as you use a notepad on the desk, you can use Notepad to take notes on-screen while working in other Windows NT applications. Notepad uses little memory and is useful for editing text that you want to copy in a Windows NT or NT command line application that lacks an editing capability.

The Notepad retrieves and saves files in text format. This feature makes Notepad a convenient editor for creating and altering the Windows NT batch files, and other text-based files. Because Notepad stores files in text format, almost all word processors can retrieve Notepad's files.

Another handy use for the Notepad is to hold text you want to move to another application. The Clipboard can hold only one selection at a time, but the Notepad can serve as a text *scrapbook* when you are moving several items as a group.

As a bonus, Notepad also includes a feature for logging time, so you can use Notepad as a time clock, which enables you to know when you opened a file or to monitor the time you spend on a project. Notepad files cannot hold graphics.

Opening and Closing the Notepad and Notepad Files

Open the Notepad application by double-clicking the Notepad icon in the Accessories window or by pressing arrow keys to select the icon and then pressing Enter. A blank Notepad appears (see fig. 15.2).

You can open a new or existing file from within the Notepad application by choosing the File New or File Open command. To open the file, choose the File Open command to display the Open dialog box, select the directory and file you want to open, and choose OK.

As an alternative, you can open an existing text file in Notepad from the Windows NT File Manager, as long as a file association for that extension has been set up for Notepad. To open a text file that has been associated with Notepad, double-click the file name in the File Manager or select the file name and press Enter. Notepad opens and loads the text file.

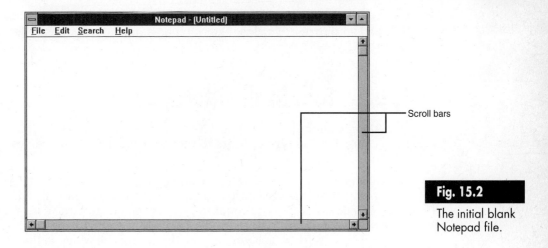

Scroll bars

Fig. 15.2

The initial blank
Notepad file.

Notepad's **File O**pen command looks for files with a TXT extension by
default. To open text files with any other extension, choose the **File
O**pen command, change the *.TXT in the Filename text box to the extension you want to access, and press Enter. A list of files with this
extension appears. To see a list of all files with all extensions, in the
List Files of **T**ype list, select All Files(*.*).

CAUTION: Be careful when you edit with Notepad. Because
Notepad creates text files, you can open and edit important
system, application, and data files. To avoid loss of data or applications, make sure that you open only files with which you are
familiar and that you know are text files.

Incorrectly editing a batch file (BAT), a system file (SYS), or a
Windows NT initialization file (INI) can cause problems with computer or application operation. Before making changes, use the
File Copy command in the Windows NT File Manager to create a
backup copy of the file with a different name (for example,
WIN.BAK). If the system doesn't restart after you make the
changes, use a start-up, or *system*, diskette to start the computer
and then, using the original file name, copy the backup file back
on.

When you open a new file from Notepad, the currently open file closes.
If your file has changed, a dialog box asks whether you want to save the
current changes. Choose **Y**es to save or **N**o to discard the changes.
Choose Cancel to return to the original file.

You can close a Notepad file in two ways: open a new file or close the Notepad application. To close the Notepad application, choose **F**ile E**x**it.

Typing Text in the Notepad

Immediately after you open a new Notepad file, you can begin typing. Each character you type appears to the left of a blinking vertical line known as the *insertion point.*

Unlike most word processing applications, Notepad doesn't by default wrap text to the following line. You must either choose the **E**dit **W**ord Wrap command or press Enter at the end of each line. With Word Wrap turned on, text wraps to fit the width of the Notepad window, no matter how wide the window is. If you change the size of the window, the text rewraps to fit (see fig. 15.3). You can activate Word Wrap at any time. When Word Wrap is active, a check mark appears beside the command on the menu.

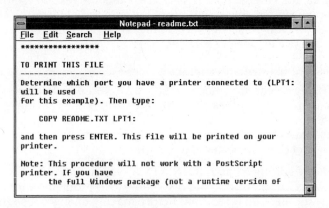

Fig. 15.3

Two examples of text wrapping to fit the Notepad window.

If you choose the **E**dit **W**ord Wrap command again, the word-wrap feature turns off, and text stretches out until it reaches a hard return. Without automatic word wrap, lines can reach up to 160 characters long (if you type beyond the right edge of the window, the page scrolls to the left). When Word Wrap is turned off, no check mark appears beside the command on the menu.

> **T I P**
>
> If you want to edit in Notepad a file from another application, first open the file in the other application and then save the file in text format. Most word processors, spreadsheets, and databases have this option. Some spreadsheets or databases come with a translator utility that converts the applications files to or from text. Open the text file in Notepad by using the Notepad **F**ile **O**pen command.

Moving and Scrolling on the Page

To edit existing text or to add new text in Notepad, you must learn to scroll the page and move the insertion point. Although Notepad pages scroll through the Window, the best way to think of this action is as a Notepad window that moves down a long strip of document. The horizontal and vertical scroll bars along the right bottom edge of the Notepad window (see fig. 15.2) move the window around on this strip of paper. The length and width of the scroll bars represent the entire Notepad document and the scroll box represents the Notepad window's current position on the document. To scroll by line, click on the arrows in the scroll bars. To move one full screen at a time, click in the gray area of the scroll bar. For larger moves, drag the scroll box to a new vertical or horizontal location. With the keyboard, press the PgUp key to scroll up one screen at a time; press the PgDn key to scroll down one screen at a time.

 The horizontal scroll bar appears only when the **W**ord Wrap command is selected (has a check mark to its left) in the Edit menu.

You can move the insertion point by using either the mouse or the keyboard. To move the insertion point with the mouse, position the *I-beam*, (the text-screen mouse pointer) where you want the insertion point and click the mouse button. With the keyboard, use the arrow keys to move the insertion point. As in any word processing application, the insertion point in Notepad travels only where typed characters appear, even if these characters are spaces or Enter characters. You cannot move the insertion point beyond where you already typed.

Keyboard shortcuts for moving the insertion point and scrolling are listed in table 15.1.

Table 15.1 Keyboard commands to move the insertion point and to scroll the screen

Keyboard Command	Action
End	Move to end of line
Home	Move to beginning of line
Ctrl+Home	Move to beginning of document
Ctrl+End	Move to end of document
PgUp	Scroll one screen up
PgDn	Scroll one screen down

T I P   Experienced typists know how to save time by using a combination of techniques for moving around the screen and for selecting and editing text. The quickest way to select text, for example, may be to drag the mouse across the text, but the fastest way to scroll down the page may be to press the PgDn key. If you have both a mouse and the keyboard, you aren't limited to using only one method or the other.

Selecting, Editing, and Formatting Text

You select and edit text in the Notepad the same way you select and edit text in Write.

To add text, move the insertion point to the new text location and start typing (if you use a mouse, position the I-beam where you want the insertion point and click). Delete a single character by moving the insertion point to the left of the character and pressing Del or by moving the insertion point to the right of the character and pressing Backspace.

To delete or replace more extensive amounts of text, you first must select the text. To select with the mouse, press and hold down the mouse button and drag the I-beam across the text you want to select. To select text by using the keyboard, hold down the Shift key and press any arrow key. Select all text in the Notepad document at one time by choosing the **E**dit Select **A**ll command.

To replace selected text, just type new text. To delete text, select the text to delete and choose the Edit Delete command or press the Del key.

You can correct editing mistakes by choosing the Edit Undo command or by holding down Ctrl and pressing Z. Remember that you can undo only the most recent edit.

The Notepad enables you to perform limited formatting by using the File Page Setup command. When you select this command, the Page Setup dialog box appears (see fig. 15.4), where you can change the margins and add a header or footer to the note. In Notepad, you cannot format characters or paragraphs in any way. You can use Tab, the space bar, and Backspace to align text. Tab stops are preset at every eight characters.

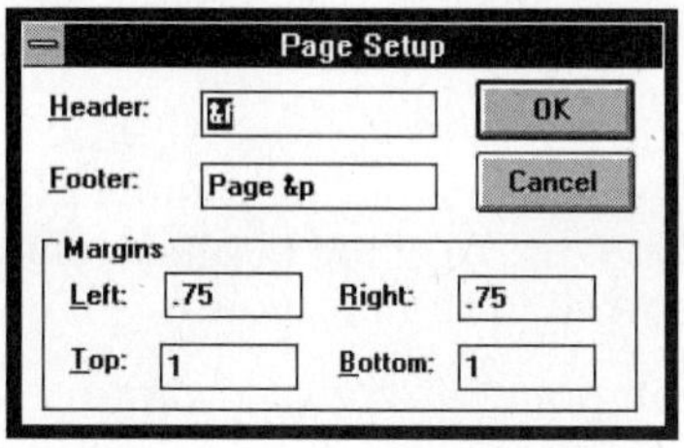

Fig. 15.4

Set margins and insert header/ footer in the Page Setup dialog box.

A handy shortcut for selecting a single word is to double-click on the word. To select a large block of text, click at the beginning of the selection, use the scroll bars to scroll to the end of the selection, and then hold down the Shift key as you click at the end of the selection. All text between the original insertion point and the Shift click is selected.

To select with the keyboard, move the insertion point to the beginning of the selection, press and hold down Shift, and scroll to the end of the selection. Holding down Shift as you scroll or move the insertion point selects all text between the starting and ending points.

Copying and Moving Text

With Notepad's Edit commands, you can cut, copy, and move selected text from one place in a file to another. As in any Windows NT application, text you cut or copy is stored in the Clipboard, a temporary file that holds only one selection at a time. When you paste text, this text is copied from the Clipboard to the document at the insertion point.

To cut, copy, and paste text, follow these steps:

1. Select the text you want to cut, copy, or move (see fig. 15.5).

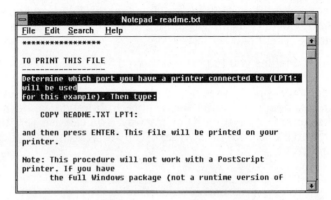

```
┌─────────────────────────────────────────────────────┐
│─               Notepad - readme.txt            ▼│▲│
│ File  Edit  Search   Help                            │
│ ****************                                    ▲│
│                                                      │
│ TO PRINT THIS FILE                                   │
│ ──────────────────                                   │
│ Determine which port you have a printer connected to (LPT1: │
│ will be used                                         │
│ for this example). Then type:                        │
│                                                      │
│      COPY README.TXT LPT1:                           │
│                                                      │
│ and then press ENTER. This file will be printed on your │
│ printer.                                             │
│                                                      │
│ Note: This procedure will not work with a PostScript │
│ printer. If you have                                 │
│        the Full Windows package (not a runtime version of │
│                                                     ▼│
└─────────────────────────────────────────────────────┘
```

Fig. 15.5

Selected text in
reverse type.

2. To move text, choose the **E**dit **Cut** command; to make a duplicate of the text and leave the original in place, choose **E**dit **C**opy. The selected text is stored in the Clipboard.

3. Move the insertion point where you want to paste the text.

4. Choose the **E**dit **P**aste command. The text is copied from the Clipboard in the document at the location of the insertion point.

Remember that you can use keyboard shortcuts: cut using Ctrl+X; copy using Ctrl+C; paste using Ctrl+V. (If you select text and press Del, text is deleted without being copied to the Clipboard. The only way to retrieve this kind of deletion is to immediately choose the **E**dit **U**ndo command.)

Cut or copied text is saved in the Clipboard and stays there until you cut or copy something else. You can paste text from the Clipboard as many times as you like. The Clipboard holds only one item at a time, however; so be sure that you paste things as soon as you cut or copy them.

Searching through Notepad

Notepad's Search command finds and selects any word or phrase. You can search forward or backward through a document, beginning at the insertion point. You can specify whether to search for an exact upper-case or lowercase match or whether to search for any match.

To search for text, follow these steps:

1. Choose the **S**earch **F**ind command. The Find dialog box appears (see fig. 15.6).

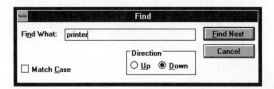

Fig. 15.6

The Find dialog
box.

2. In the Find What text box, type the text you want to find.

3. To find text that exactly matches the text you typed in uppercase and lowercase letters, select the Match Case check box.

4. Select **D**own to search forward from the insertion point; select **U**p to select backward from the insertion point.

5. Choose **F**ind Next or press F3.

The application selects the first occurrence of the word or phrase. The dialog box remains open so that you can continue the search by choosing **F**ind Next again. To return to the document, choose Cancel. If Notepad cannot find the word or phrase, a message box appears and tells you that it cannot find the text. Choose OK to acknowledge the message and then choose Cancel to return to the document. To continue the search after you close the dialog box, choose **S**earch Find Next (or press F3).

NOTE You can find whole, partial, or embedded words or characters. If you want to find a string of characters—even characters located inside another word—type the string of characters in the Find What text box. To find the "search" in researches, for example, type *search* in the text box.

To find only the occurrences of a whole word, enter a space at the beginning and at the end of the word in the Find What text box. To find only the word "search," for example, type <space>*search*<space>. Be aware that this kind of entry, however, doesn't find the word when "search" is followed by a comma or a period.

Creating a Time-Log File with Notepad

By using a simple command, .LOG, you can have Notepad enter the time and date at the end of a document each time you open the file. This feature is convenient for taking phone messages or for calculating the time spent on a project. An example of the Notepad with a time log is shown in figure 15.7. As an alternative to the .LOG command, you can choose the **E**dit Time/**D**ate command to insert the current time and date at the insertion point.

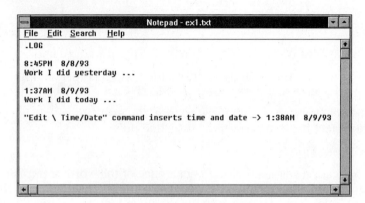

Fig. 15.7

You can track times in a Notepad document in two ways.

To create a time log by default in a document, follow these steps:

1. Move the insertion point to the left margin of the first line in the Notepad document.

2. In capital letters, type the command .LOG.

3. Save the file.

4. Reopen the file.

   When you reopen the Notepad file, the time and date are inserted by default. You now can type a note that describes the project. By entering notes that describe your work between the times, you keep an accurate log of how much time is spent on a project.

5. Save the file again.

6. After you finish the project, reopen the file.

   Again, the time and date are entered by default. Type a log entry that states the project is finished.

To insert the time and date from the keyboard, follow these steps:

1. Move the insertion point where you want to enter the time and date.

2. Choose the **E**dit Time/**D**ate command or press F5.

Notepad takes the time and date information from the computer's internal clock. To make sure that the inserted time and date are accurate, you must set the computer's clock correctly. Use the Control Panel to change the time and date, as described in Chapter 7, "Customizing with the Control Panel."

The format of the time and date are determined by the International application in the Control Panel.

Setting Up the Page for Printing

You can use the File Page Setup command to set the margins for a document and to add a header or footer to a document. Headers and footers print at the top and bottom of each page of a document. Several codes are available to enhance headers and footers.

To set the margins for a document, follow these steps:

1. Choose the File Page Setup command.

2. Set the margins as desired in the Left, Right, Top, and Bottom boxes.

3. Choose OK or press Enter.

To add a header or footer to a document, follow these steps:

1. Choose File Page Setup.

2. In the Header or Footer text box, type the text you want to appear in the header or footer.

You can use any of the following codes in headers or footers:

Code	Result
&d	Inserts current date
&p	Inserts page number
&f	Inserts file name
&l	Left justifies text following code
&r	Right justifies text following code
&c	Centers text following code
&t	Inserts the current time

Saving and Printing Notepad Files

To save and name a Notepad document, follow these steps:

1. Choose the **F**ile Save **A**s command.

2. From the **D**irectories list box, select the directory in which you want to save the file.

   By default, Notepad saves the file in the current directory.

3. In the File **N**ame text box, enter a name.

4. Choose OK or press Enter.

If you previously saved a file but want to save it again with the same file name, choose File **S**ave. The current file replaces the original version.

If you don't enter a file extension, Notepad adds the extension TXT. To save a different kind of file, such as a batch file, enter the file name and add the desired extension.

You can print a Notepad file on the currently selected printer. If you want to select a different printer, follow these steps:

1. Choose the **F**ile P**r**int Setup command.

2. From the **P**rinter list, select the printer you want to use.

3. If the printer you wish to use is not connected to your computer and is located elsewhere on your network, choose the **N**etwork button to display the available printers. Type in the Printer name or select from the **S**hared Printer list. Choose OK or press Enter to continue.

4. Make the selections that pertain to the printer you use: the paper size, orientation, source, and so on. Depending on the printer you select, these selections vary.

5. Choose the **M**ore button to display a dialog box containing additional Advanced Document Properties, depending on what type of printer you selected. Select the options you want.

6. Choose OK or press Enter.

7. Choose OK or press Enter a second time to close the Print Setup dialog box.

To print a Notepad file on the selected printer, follow these steps:

1. Open the file to be printed.

2. Choose the **F**ile **P**rint command.

Although you don't see a dialog box when you issue the **File Print** command, a message box appears that tells you the document is printing. To cancel the print job, select the Cancel button in the message box.

Inserting Symbols with Character Map

The Character Map accessory gives you access to symbol fonts and ANSI characters. One symbol font, Symbol, is included with most Windows NT applications. Other symbol fonts may be built into the printer. Most PostScript printers, for example, include Zapf Dingbats. When you setup and indicate the model of the printer, font cartridges, and so on, the printer tells Windows NT what symbol fonts are available. (Printer fonts appear in character map only when they include a matching screen font.)

ANSI characters are the regular character set that you see on the keyboard and more than a hundred other characters, including a copyright symbol, a registered trademark symbol, and many foreign language characters.

To use the Character Map accessory, you first must start the application from Program Manager. You then can select any characters or symbols from the Character Map dialog box and, by using the Clipboard, insert these items in to any Windows NT application.

Open Character Map by double-clicking the Character Map icon in the Accessories window or by pressing arrow keys to select the icon and then pressing Enter. You are presented with the Character Map dialog box (see fig. 15.8). The dialog box includes a drop-down list box, from which you can select any of the available fonts on the system. After you select a font, the characters and symbols for this font appear in the Character Map table.

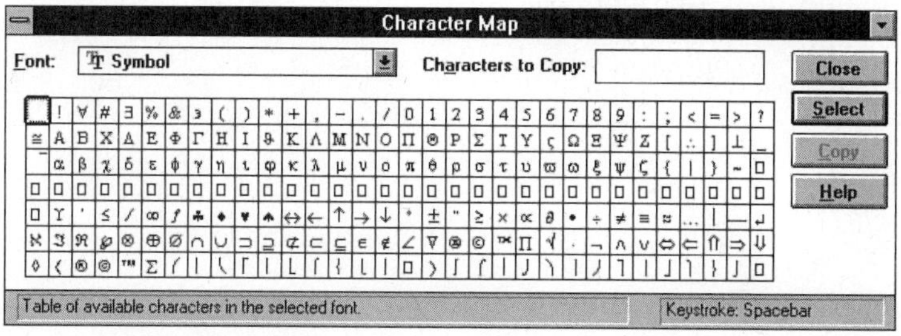

Fig. 15.8

Select characters from the Character Map dialog box for use in Windows NT documents.

To insert characters and symbols in to a Windows NT application, you copy the characters you selected from the Character Map dialog box to the Clipboard and then paste the characters in to the application by using standard Windows NT copy-and-paste procedures.

To insert a character in a Windows NT application from the Character Map, follow these steps:

1. From Program Manager, open the Character Map accessory.

2. Select the font you want to use from the **F**ont list.

    The Character Map displays on-screen the characters for the selected font. Each set of fonts may have different symbols. Some fonts, such as Symbol and Zapf Dingbats, contain nothing but symbols and special characters.

3. You view characters by clicking on them and holding down the mouse button or by using arrow keys to move to the character.

4. Double-click on the character you want to insert or choose the **S**elect button to place the current character in the Ch**a**racters to Copy text box.

5. Repeat steps 2 through 4 to select as many characters as desired.

6. Choose the **C**opy button to copy the characters that appear in the Characters to Copy text box in the Clipboard.

7. Open or switch to the application in which you want to copy the character(s).

8. Place the insertion point where you want to insert the character(s) and choose the Edit **P**aste command.

If the characters don't appear as they did in Character Map, you may need to reselect the characters and change the font to the same font in which the character originally appeared in the Character Map.

T   I   P   If you plan to use the Character Map frequently, you may want to add this application to the StartUp program group in the Program Manager so that Character Map opens when you start Windows NT.

Storing and Retrieving Information in the Cardfile

The Cardfile is like a computerized stack of three-by-five index cards that gives you quick reference to names, addresses, phone numbers, and even graphics. The Cardfile is an excellent way to store free-form information that you may need to retrieve quickly. You even can store *embedded* information, such as a map that you drew in Windows NT Paint, in the Cardfile. Double-clicking on the map brings up Windows NT Paint so that you can edit the map.

Each *card* in a Cardfile has two parts: a single index line at the top and an area for text or graphics below. Cards always are arranged alphabetically by the index line (see fig. 15.9). The active card is the top card on the stack.

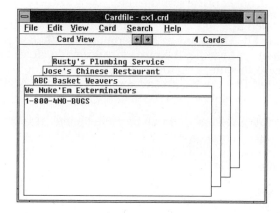

Fig. 15.9

Cards in a Cardfile store information so that you can retrieve it quickly.

You can have as many cards in a Cardfile file as the computer's memory can hold, and you can use as many Cardfile files as the disk can hold.

Accessing the information in a Cardfile file is easy. Display the card you need and read, copy, or print the information the card contains. If the computer is connected to a modem or a phone, you can use Cardfile to dial a phone number.

T I P   Cardfile is convenient for handling small amounts of simple information. Although it can function to keep track of clients or mailing lists, you will be more efficient and less frustrated if you use a true mailing list manager, personal information manager (PIM), or database to handle large or related lists of information. Many of these programs are available for Windows and share information with the major Windows word processors.

Opening and Closing the Cardfile

You open the Cardfile application from the Accessories window by double-clicking on the Cardfile icon or by selecting the icon by using the arrow keys and pressing Enter. After you open the application, a new, untitled Cardfile appears on-screen.

You also can open new or existing Cardfile files from within Cardfile by choosing the **File Open** or **File New** command. When you open a new file from within Cardfile, the currently open file closes. If you made changes to this file, a dialog box asks whether you want to save the changes. Choose **Yes** to save current changes, **No** to discard the changes, or Cancel to return to the file.

You also can simultaneously open a Cardfile file and the Cardfile application by double-clicking on a data file from the Windows NT File Manager or by selecting a cardfile and pressing Enter. Cardfile data files have the extension CRD.

You can close a Cardfile file only by opening a new file or by closing the Cardfile application. To close the Cardfile application, choose Control **Close** or **File Exit**.

Entering Information in the Cardfile

After opening a new Cardfile file, you see a single blank card (see fig. 15.10). The insertion point flashes in the top left corner of the card, just below the double line. This location is where you type information, such as names, addresses, and phone numbers, in the body of the card. To enter information in the card, just begin typing. Use Tab, Backspace, and the space bar to arrange the text. If you reach the right edge of the card, the text wraps to the next line.

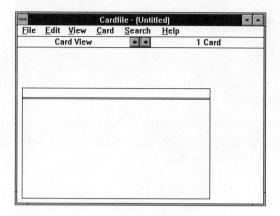

Fig. 15.10

A new Cardfile, displaying a single blank card.

The index line at the top of the card is important: Cardfile arranges cards alphabetically by index lines. After you type the body of the first card, you are ready to enter an index line.

To type text in the index line, follow these steps:

1. Choose the **E**dit **I**ndex command or press F6. The Index dialog box appears (see fig. 15.11).

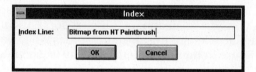

Fig. 15.11

The Index dialog box.

2. In the **I**ndex Line text box, type the text that identifies the contents of the card. Remember that cards are arranged alphabetically by index lines.

3. Choose OK or press Enter. The insertion point returns to the body of the card.

Like the cards in a rotary card file, Cardfile cards always stay alphabetized—even when a card in the middle of the stack is on top. If you want to arrange the Cardfile alphabetically by last name, type the last name first in the index line. You can begin an index line with a number; numbers are listed before letters in alphabetical order.

To edit existing index lines, select the card and choose the **E**dit **I**ndex command or press the F6 key.

Inserting Pictures in a Card

You can paste pictures of all kinds in Cardfile cards: graphs from Microsoft Excel or Lotus 1-2-3, sketches from Windows NT Paintbrush or Microsoft Draw, clip art from files of graphics, and even scanned images of photographs.

Three ways are available to insert a picture in a card:

- The simplest way is to copy and paste to the card a picture from a graphics application that does not support object linking and embedding. After pasting, you cannot edit this picture; you must replace it with another picture.

- You can insert by choosing to embed a picture. The picture must be created by a graphics application that supports object embedding, such as Microsoft Paintbrush or Microsoft Draw. Object linking and embedding is known as OLE. You can edit an embedded graphic from within Cardfile. The advantage of embedded pictures is that these images contain all the information needed to re-create and edit the picture. Embed a picture when you don't need to update many copies of the picture and when you want the data in the picture to go with the cardfile so that the receiver of the cardfile can make changes.

- You can insert a picture by choosing to link the image. The picture must come from an application that supports object linking. By default, Cardfile updates linked graphics when you change the original picture in the original file. Linking is useful when you have one original picture or chart that feeds into multiple documents. By updating the single original, all the documents that use this picture also are updated. A disadvantage of linking is that if you want to send the cardfile to another user, you should send copies of all the linked pictures used in the cardfile.

To learn more about object linking and embedding, see Chapter 6, "Embedding and Linking Windows NT Applications."

Cardfile tries to accurately represent the picture on-screen. The picture, however, is displayed in screen—rather than printer—resolution. If the printer resolution doesn't match the screen resolution (usually the case), the screen image may appear slightly distorted. Because the picture prints at printer resolution, the picture looks fine when printed.

You can include only one picture in a card.

Copying a Picture in a Card

With the Edit commands, you can copy a picture from another application to a Cardfile card. Figure 15.12 shows a bitmap image that was

copied from Microsoft Paintbrush and pasted in a Cardfile card. Some
applications can create pictures that you can use as a pasted picture,
as a linked picture, or as an embedded object.

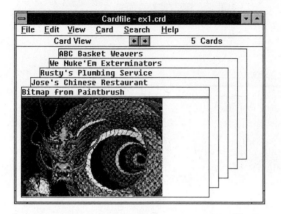

To copy a picture from one application to another, follow these steps:

1. Open the application that contains the picture or chart.

2. Select and copy the picture.

   For Windows NT applications, select the portion of the picture
   you want copied and choose a command such as **E**dit **C**opy. For
   NT command-line applications, such as 1-2-3 for DOS, display the
   picture on-screen and press Alt+PrtSc.

3. Open or activate the Cardfile application and the card in which
   you want to paste the picture.

4. Position the insertion point where you want the picture to appear.

5. Choose the **E**dit Pictu**r**e command.

6. Choose the **E**dit Paste **S**pecial command. The Paste Special dialog
   box appears (see fig. 15.13).

7. From the **D**ata Type list, select an unlinked or nonembedded format for the picture. Selecting a Bitmap or Picture type will paste
   the image in unlinked and nonembedded format.

8. Choose the **P**aste button.

If you attempt to edit a picture that isn't linked or embedded, an alert
box appears with the message Cannot activate static object.

Fig. 15.13

The Paste Special
dialog box
enables you to
paste pictures in
different ways.

> **T I P** Some applications, such as Microsoft Excel, may have more than one
> way to copy a graphic. Edit Copy, for example, copies a graphic that
> you can link or embed, while holding down the Shift key and repeat-
> ing the same procedure copies a bit map picture that you can paste
> and that is neither linked nor embedded. (Pasted bit maps have the
> poorest quality print resolution.)

Embedding Pictures in a Card

Pictures embedded in a card contain the actual data that created the
picture. Windows NT tracks the location of the original application that
created the picture so that you can activate and edit an embedded picture, using the application that created the picture. Embedding a picture is useful when sending a Cardfile file to another user and making
sure that all the picture information is included so that they can edit
pictures used in the cards.

Embedded pictures must be created with drawing or charting applications capable of object linking and embedding, such as Windows NT
Paintbrush, Microsoft Draw, or Microsoft Excel. You can embed a picture in two ways. You can open a drawing or charting application from
within Cardfile and embed the resulting picture or you can create a
drawing or chart in the other application and then copy and embed by
pasting the graphic in a card.

If you already drew a picture or created a chart in a Windows NT application capable of object linking and embedding, then you can embed
the graphic in a card by following the previously listed steps for pasting. However, when you reach step 7, select from the Data Type list the
type for an object, such as *Paintbrush Picture Object*.

If you are in the Cardfile application and want to embed a new object,
follow these steps:

1. Position the insertion point where you want the picture to appear
   in the Cardfile card.

2. Choose the **E**dit Picture command to enable picture editing features. (The **E**dit Picture command is selected when a check mark appears to its left.)

3. Choose the **E**dit **In**sert Object command. The Insert New Object dialog box appears, shown in figure 15.14, listing all Windows NT applications that support object linking and embedding.

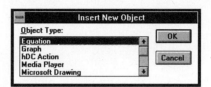

Fig. 15.14

The Insert New Object dialog box enables you to start an OLE application and embed an OLE document.

4. Select the application you want to use from the **O**bject Type list. For example, select Paintbrush Picture.

5. Choose OK or press Enter. The application opens.

6. In the application, create a drawing.

7. After you finish the picture, choose the File Update File Exit and Return command (this command may vary between applications) to embed a copy of the picture in the Cardfile card and close the application.

To preserve the embedded picture, save the Cardfile. You can edit this picture by using techniques described in following sections of this chapter.

Linking Pictures in a Card

Although linking a picture is similar to embedding a picture, the picture is in a file separate from the Cardfile file. A link is created between the Cardfile card and the application document that contains the picture. The advantage of using linked pictures is that you can update the picture in the original application, and any Cardfile card linked to the application is updated. Use linked pictures when you link multiple cards to a single picture and you want only to update the picture one time. The disadvantage to linked pictures is that if you send another user a copy of the Cardfile file, you also should send copies of the picture files to which the picture is linked.

NOTE Do not rename or move the picture or chart file to which a card is linked, or the card will lose the picture the next time you update the card. If the link is lost in this way, use the techniques in Chapter 6 to reestablish the link. If a picture or chart is to be used in only one card, embedding is probably preferable. If you want one original picture or chart to update many cards at the same time, use linking. With linking, a single original picture can be linked to many cards.

To link a picture in a Cardfile file, follow these steps:

1. Position the insertion point where you want the linked picture to appear.

2. Open the application that contains the picture you want to link. Open Microsoft Excel, for example, to link in a chart.

3. Open the file that contains the picture you want to link or create a new chart.

4. Save the chart or picture by using the file name that the file will keep.

5. Select the chart or picture. (Applications may use different commands to select all or part of a picture or document.)

6. Choose the **E**dit **C**opy command.

7. Switch back to the Cardfile card.

8. Choose the **E**dit Pictur**e** command to enable picture editing in cards.

9. Choose the Paste **L**ink command.

Managing the Links between Original Pictures and Cards

If you linked a picture or chart in Cardfile, the picture or chart remains connected to the original file. If the source picture or chart changes, the image in the Cardfile file changes. Renaming, deleting, or moving the file that contains the original picture or chart, however, can destroy the link. As a result, the card loses the picture or chart.

To learn how to re-create or change links between a card and the linked picture or chart, read the sections on managing links in Chapter 6, "Embedding and Linking Windows NT Applications."

Editing Embedded and Linked Pictures

From within Cardfile, you can edit pictures embedded from—or linked to—Windows NT Paintbrush or another application that supports object linking and embedding. Editing the picture causes the application to open, with the picture or chart appearing in the window. To learn how to activate and edit embedded or linked pictures that were previously pasted in a card, read the sections on editing pictures and linked data in Chapter 6. Usually, the procedures for most embedded or linked pictures are similar to the following procedures for Paintbrush.

To edit an embedded Paintbrush drawing by using the mouse, follow these steps:

1. To open Paintbrush and display the picture, double-click on the drawing.

2. Edit the picture.

3. In Paintbrush, choose the **F**ile **U**pdate command.

4. In Paintbrush, choose the **F**ile E**x**it and Return to Document command.

You also can just exit Paintbrush, and a message asks whether you want to update the picture in the Cardfile card. To update the card, choose **Y**es.

To edit an embedded drawing by using the keyboard, follow these steps:

1. Choose the **E**dit Edit Paintbrush Picture **O**bject command. Paintbrush opens, with the picture in the drawing window.

2. Edit the picture.

3. In Paintbrush, choose **F**ile **U**pdate to update the picture in Cardfile.

4. In Paintbrush, choose **F**ile E**x**it and Return to Document.

You can edit a linked picture in Cardfile the same way that you edit an embedded drawing. One major difference is that you must save changes to the original picture or chart. Use standard file saving techniques. Because you're using the original graphics application to edit the picture, all changes you make are reflected in all other files that contain a link to the original picture.

To edit a linked drawing using the mouse:

1. To open Paintbrush and display the picture, double-click on the drawing.

2. Edit the picture.

3. In Paintbrush, choose the **F**ile **S**ave command. By default, the picture in the Cardfile card is updated.

4. In Paintbrush, choose the **F**ile E**x**it command.

To edit a linked drawing using the keyboard:

1. In Cardfile, choose the **E**dit Lin**k** command.

2. After the Links dialog box appears, choose the **E**dit button to display Paintbrush, with the picture in the drawing window.

   Cardfile can accept only one picture. In applications that may have multiple links, you need to first select the link you want to edit before you choose the **E**dit button.

3. In Paintbrush, edit the picture.

4. Choose the Paintbrush **F**ile **S**ave command. The picture in the Cardfile card updates to reflect the changes you made.

5. Choose the **F**ile E**x**it command in Paintbrush.

If you previously set links to update upon command, the Cardfile card won't reflect the changes to the linked picture until you update the link by using the following process:

1. In Cardfile, choose the **E**dit Lin**k** command.

2. After the Links dialog box appears, choose Update Now (see fig. 15.15).

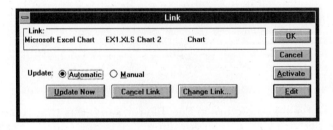

3. Choose OK or press Enter.

If you want a picture to update on command, rather than automatically, choose the **E**dit Lin**k** command and select the Update **M**anual option.

You also can change a link command when the location of the original picture changes (or when you want to link to a different original picture). Choose the Edit Link command, choose the Change Link button, and in the Change Link dialog box that appears, select the new file you want to link to or select the new location for the existing original file. Choose OK or press enter. Finally, you can cancel a link by choosing the Edit Link command and choosing the Cancel Link button. The picture then is no longer linked. To close the Link dialog box, choose OK or press Enter.

Adding Cards

Adding new cards to an existing card file is easy. After you add a new card, the Add dialog box appears, which prompts you to type the index line. When you finish entering the index line, the new card, complete with index line, appears in front of the other cards in the file.

To add a new card, follow these steps:

1. Choose the Card Add command or press F7. The Add dialog box appears.

2. In the Add text box, type an index line for the new card.

3. Choose OK or press Enter.

The new card with the index line you just typed is displayed on top of the stack. The insertion point is at the top left of the card, ready for you to type the contents of the card.

Scrolling through the Cards

Cardfile provides several ways to search through the stack of cards and bring the card you want to the front of the stack. You can scroll through the cards, as described in this section, or you can search through the cards to find a card with specific information, as described in the following section.

In the status bar of the Cardfile window, you see a pair of arrows. You can scroll through the cards, one card at a time, by clicking on these arrows. To scroll backward one card, click left; to scroll forward one card, click right. The PgUp and PgDn keys on the keyboard perform the same tasks. These and other ways of scrolling in the Cardfile are summarized in table 15.2.

Table 15.2 Scrolling the Cardfile	
Direction To Scroll	**Action**
Backward one card	PgUp or click on left arrow
Forward one card	PgDn or click on right arrow
To a specific card	Click on card's index line
To first card	Ctrl+Home
To last card	Ctrl+End
To card with index line beginning with *letter*	Shift+Ctrl+*letter*

Searching through Information in the Cards

You can search through the cards in a Cardfile by the index line or by the information in the body of the card. Both searches use a menu command and a dialog box to locate the card that contains the word or phrase you want to find. A third menu command enables you to quickly repeat the most recent search.

To search through index lines in the Cardfile, follow these steps:

1. Choose the **S**earch **G**o To command or press F4. The Go To dialog box appears.

2. In the **G**o To text box, type any portion of the index line you want to find (even a partial word works), as shown in figure 15.16. Because the search isn't case-sensitive, you can type either upper- or lowercase letters.

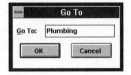

3. Choose OK or press Enter.

After you select OK, the first card with the search string, *Plumbing,* in the index line is brought to the top of the stack.

Moving Quickly to a Card by Using the Index Line

To quickly bring up the first card with a specific beginning letter in the index line, press Shift+Ctrl+*letter*. Press Shift+Ctrl+M, for example, to bring to the top of the stack the first card that has *M* as the first letter of the card's index line.

To search through information in the body of the cards, follow these steps:

1. Choose **S**earch **F**ind. The Find dialog box, shown in figure 15.17, appears.

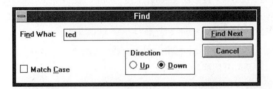

Fig. 15.17

Using **S**earch **F**ind to search through text in the cards themselves.

2. In the **Fi**nd What text box, type any portion of the information for which you want to search (a partial word also works with this search).

3. From the direction options, select **U**p or **D**own and the Match **C**ase option if you want to make the search sensitive to upper- and lowercase.

4. Choose the **F**ind Next button.

Cardfile finds and selects the first occurrence of the word. To continue the search, choose **F**ind Next again. To close the dialog box, choose Cancel. To repeat the most recent search after closing the dialog box, choose the **S**earch **F**ind **N**ext command (or press F3).

> In the Find dialog box shown in figure 15.17, choosing OK or pressing Enter brings to the top of the stack the next card that contains the letters *ted* anywhere in the body of the card. The search may bring up a card that contains the word *interested*. If you are looking for the name *Ted* and want the search to ignore the letters *ted* within words, use the space bar to enter a space before and after the search word: <space>*ted*<space>.

T I P

Duplicating and Deleting Cards

Often, the information on two cards is so similar that duplicating the current card and making minor changes to the duplicate is faster than typing a new card. You may want, for example, two separate cards for two people in the same company—the names and phone numbers are different but the company name and address are the same.

To duplicate a card, follow these steps:

1. Bring the card you want to duplicate to the top of the stack.

2. Choose the **C**ard Du**p**licate command.

Using normal Windows NT text-editing procedures, edit the duplicated card text. (Choose the **E**dit **I**ndex command or double-click the index line to edit the index line.)

You can delete from the Cardfile all cards you no longer need. To delete a card, follow these steps:

1. Bring the card you want to delete to the top of the stack.

2. Choose the Card Delete command. A message box appears, asking for confirmation.

3. Choose OK or press Enter.

Once It's Gone, It's Gone

After you delete a card and save the file to disk, you cannot use the **E**dit **U**ndo command to undo the deletion. Be absolutely certain that you no longer need the information on a card before you delete it.

You can retrieve an important card that you deleted, provided you have not saved the Cardfile to disk after deleting the card. Open a new Cardfile application from the Accessories window and reopen the same file on which you are currently working. A copy of the unedited Cardfile on the disk loads into memory. From the unedited file, copy the card you accidentally deleted and paste it in the file where the card is missing.

Another way to recover from an accidental deletion is to choose the **F**ile **O**pen command and reopen the current file. This method closes the current file. Do not save the changes. Use care when performing this procedure and use this method only when you don't mind losing all changes made since the last time you saved the file.

Editing and Moving Text

You can change, add, or delete text from a card or the index line, move text or graphics from one card to another, transfer data from the Cardfile to another application (such as the Notepad or Windows NT Write), or transfer text or graphics in Cardfile from another application (such as Windows NT Write or Paintbrush).

To edit the text on a Cardfile card, display on-screen the card you want to change. The insertion point flashes at the top left of the card. Use normal editing techniques to edit the text: move the insertion point where you want to make a change by positioning the I-beam and clicking the mouse button or by pressing the arrow keys. Then press Backspace or Del to delete text or just type to insert text. Select longer blocks of text to edit by dragging the mouse across the text or by holding down the Shift key and pressing the arrow keys. Just type to replace selected text or press Del or Backspace to remove the text.

If you want to edit an index line, you must display the card and choose the Edit Index command. If you have a mouse, double-click on the index line of the top card. The Index Line dialog box appears, in which you make the changes.

To move text between cards or to other applications, follow these steps:

1. Bring the card that contains the text you want to move to the top of the stack.

2. Select the text you want to move.

3. Choose the Edit Copy (Ctrl+C) or Edit Cut (Ctrl+X) command.

4. Position the insertion point in another card or application.

5. Choose the Edit Paste (Ctrl+V) command.

Use the Edit Text Command to Work with Text

If you worked with pictures and graphics, you chose the Edit Picture command. While the Edit Picture command is selected, you can't edit text. To edit text again, choose the Edit Text command.

Two more useful editing commands are Undo and Restore. Cardfile *remembers*, and can undo, the most-recent edit—if you use Undo before you make another change. Cardfile also remembers the information on the card before editing began and can restore the card to original condition if you do not turn to another card after editing the first card.

To undo the most recent edit, choose the **Edit Undo** command or press Ctrl+Z. To restore a card to original condition, choose the **Edit Restore** command.

Moving Pictures in a Card

You can move the single picture in a card anywhere in the lower area. To move a picture with a mouse, choose the **Edit Picture** command and then drag the picture to the new location. To move a picture with the keyboard, choose the **Edit Picture** command and then press arrow keys to move the picture.

Viewing a List of Index Lines

After you first open Cardfile, you view the entire first card. You can see all the information on the top card but cannot see more than a few cards at a time. For a quick review of a file's contents, you can look at only the index lines (see fig. 15.18).

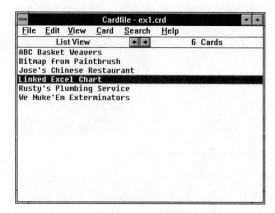

To view a list of the index lines, choose the **View List** command. To restore the full view of the cards, choose the **View Card** command.

As a shortcut, you can double-click on any index line listed in the List View window. The Index dialog box appears with the selected index line highlighted and ready for changes.

Dialing a Phone with Cardfile

If your computer is connected to a Hayes or Hayes-compatible modem, you can use Cardfile to dial a phone number that appears on a card. You must be in the Card view.

When you choose the **C**ard Au**t**odial command or press F5, Cardfile dials the first number that appears on the top card. Figure 15.19 shows Cardfile just after the **C**ard Au**t**odial command has been chosen. Notice that the phone number in the dialog box is the same as the phone number on the top card. To dial another number on the card, select this number before you choose the **C**ard Au**t**odial command. To change the number after choosing Autodial, type the new number in the **N**umber text box in the Autodial dialog box.

```
┌─────────────────────────────────────────┐
│ ─          Autodial                      │
│ N̲umber:  356-5621           ┌──────────┐ │
│                             │    OK    │ │
│ Pre̲fix:   9-                └──────────┘ │
│                             ┌──────────┐ │
│                             │  Cancel  │ │
│ ☐ U̲se Prefix                └──────────┘ │
│                             ┌──────────┐ │
│                             │ S̲etup >> │ │
│                             └──────────┘ │
└─────────────────────────────────────────┘
```

Fig. 15.19

Dialing numbers with Cardfile's Autodial command.

If you select the **U**se Prefix box, Autodial dials the number in the Prefix box before dialing the phone number on the card, which is helpful for long-distance dialing. After you type a prefix in the Prefix box, the prefix remains until you enter a new prefix.

When you type a phone number on a card, be sure that you include the area code (if different from your area code). Leave no spaces between numbers; spaces cause some or all of the phone number to be ignored. Remove parentheses from around the area code; numbers between parentheses are ignored. Hyphens don't interfere with autodialing, so a good format for phone numbers is 707-555-4247.

The first time you use Autodial to dial a number, check the dial settings (choose **S**etup in the Autodial dialog box). All settings, the dial type, port, and baud rate, stay set and don't have to be changed. After you select Setup, a dialog box appears, from which you make the following choices:

1. Depending on the kind of phone line you have, from the Dial Type box, select Tone or Pulse.

2. From the Port box, select COM1, COM2, COM3, or COM4, depending on the port to which the modem is connected.

3. From the Baud Rate box, select 110, 300, 1200, 2400, 4800, 9600, or 19200, depending on the modem's baud rate.

> **Tone or Pulse Phone?**
>
> If you don't know what kind of phone line you have, try the following experiment. Pick up the phone and dial a few numbers. If you hear different tones when you dial, you have a touch-tone phone. If you hear clicks, you have a pulse phone.

To dial a phone number with Autodial, follow these steps:

1. Display the card with the phone number you want to dial. If the number you want to dial is not the first number listed on the card, select the number you want to dial.

2. Choose the **C**ard Autodial command or press F5.

3. Select Pre**f**ix and type a dialing prefix, if necessary.

4. Select **U**se Prefix if you want Autodial to begin dialing with the prefix (usually not needed for local calls).

5. If necessary, choose **S**etup and make the appropriate dialog-box selections.

6. Choose OK or press Enter. The computer dials and displays a message box with instructions.

7. Pick up the phone receiver when instructed to do so by the dialog box.

8. Choose OK or press Enter to complete the connection.

To make Autodial pause or wait during dialing, insert a comma. For example, type a comma after a prefix to add a 5-second delay after the prefix.

Merging Cardfile Data Files and Counting the Cards

You can have as many different Cardfile files as you want. You can have one file for business contacts, one file for personal friends, a file for pictures you use frequently, and so on. On certain occasions, however, you may want to merge multiple Cardfile files into a single file.

A special command appends the contents of an unopened Cardfile to the open Cardfile. The application then alphabetizes all the cards. The unopened file is preserved in original form, and the open file includes both files.

To merge two Cardfile files, follow these steps:

1. Open the Cardfile you want to contain both files.

2. Choose the **F**ile **M**erge command.

3. From the File **N**ame list, select the file you want to merge in the open file.

4. Choose OK or press Enter.

5. If you want to preserve both original files, save the resulting Cardfile file under a new name.

Saving and Printing Cardfile Documents

To print the top card in the stack, choose the **F**ile **P**rint command. To print all the cards in a Cardfile, choose the **F**ile Print All command. No dialog boxes appear after you select the command; the cards just print on the selected printer. You can cancel printing by selecting the Cancel button that appears in the on-screen status box during printing. The cards are printed as actual card representations, which you can cut out and tape to cards on a rotary file.

To select a printer, choose the **F**ile **P**rint Setup command. In the Print Setup dialog box, select a local printer from the **P**rinters list or select a printer on your network by choosing the **N**etwork button (see the Print Setup section described for Notepad for more details).

When Cardfile documents are saved, they receive the default extension, CRD. You can use a different extension, but if you do, Cardfile doesn't list the file in the Open dialog box, and you can't open the file directly from the Windows NT File Manager.

To save and name a Cardfile, follow these steps:

1. Choose the **F**ile Save **A**s command.

2. Type a name in the File Name box.

3. From the Directories list box, select the directory in which you want to save the file. By default, Cardfile saves files in the current directory.

4. Choose OK or press Enter.

To save an existing Cardfile with the same name, choose the **F**ile **S**ave command. The new version of the file replaces the existing version on disk.

If, when you save a file, you assign a file name already in use, Cardfile asks whether you want to replace the original file with the new file. If you do, choose Yes; if not, choose No and type a different name.

Performing Desktop Calculations with the Calculator

Like a calculator you keep in a desk drawer, the Windows NT Calculator is small but saves you time (and mistakes) by performing all the calculations common to a standard calculator. The Windows NT Calculator, however, has added advantages: you can keep this calculator on-screen alongside other applications, and you can copy numbers between the Calculator and other applications.

The standard Windows NT Calculator, shown in figure 15.20, works so much like a pocket calculator that you need little help getting started. The Calculator's *keypad*, the on-screen representation, contains familiar number *keys*, along with memory and simple math keys. A display window just above the keypad shows the numbers you enter and the results of calculations. If your computational needs are more advanced, you can choose a different view of the calculator, the Scientific view (see fig. 15.21).

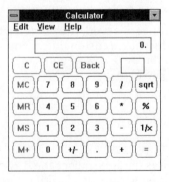

Fig. 15.20

The Standard Calculator.

The Calculator has only three menus: Edit, View, and Help. The Edit menu contains two simple commands for copying and pasting, the View menu switches between the Standard and Scientific views, and the Help menu is the same as in all Windows NT accessories.

Although you cannot change the size of the Calculator (as you can other Windows NT applications), you can shrink the Calculator to an icon for easy availability when working in another application.

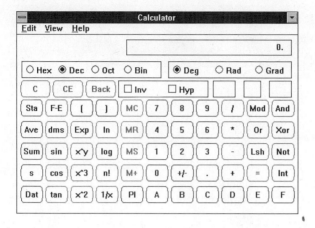

Fig. 15.21

The Scientific
Calculator.

Opening, Closing, and Operating the Calculator

You open the Calculator application by double-clicking on the Calculator icon in the Accessories window or by pressing the arrow keys to select the icon and then pressing Enter. The Calculator opens in the same view (Standard or Scientific) as was displayed the last time the Calculator was used.

You close the Calculator by choosing **C**lose from the Control menu (or pressing Alt+F4). If you use the Calculator frequently, however, don't close it; minimize the Calculator to an icon. As an icon, you can access the Calculator quickly when needed.

To use the Calculator with the mouse, just click on the appropriate number and function keys, like you press buttons on a desk calculator. Numbers appear in the display window as you select them, and the results appear after the calculations are performed.

Operating the Calculator with the keyboard also is easy. To enter numbers, use either the numbers across the top of the keyboard, or you can use the numeric keypad (although you first must press the NumLock key). To calculate, press the keys on the keyboard that match the Calculator keys. If the Calculator button reads +, for example, press the + key on the keyboard (press either the + key near the Backspace key or the + key on the numeric keypad). Table 15.3 shows the Calculator keys for the keyboard.

Table 15.3 Calculator keys

Calculator Key	Function	Keyboard Key
MC	Clear memory	Ctrl+L
MR	Display memory	Ctrl+R
M+	Add to memory	Ctrl+P
MS	Store value in memory	Ctrl+M
CE	Delete displayed value	Del
Back	Delete last digit in displayed value	Backspace
+/–	Change sign	F9
/	Divide	/
*	Multiply	*
–	Subtract	–
+	Add	+
sqrt	Square root	@
%	Percent	%
1/x	Calculate reciprocal	R
C	Clear	Esc
=	Equals	= or Enter

Calculating Percents

To calculate a percentage, treat the % key like an equal sign. For example, to calculate 15% of 80, type 80*15%. After you press the % key, the Calculator displays the result 12.

Working with the Calculator's Memory

You can use the Calculator's memory to total the results of several calculations. The memory holds a single number, which starts as zero; you can add to, display, or clear this number, or you can store another number in memory. After the number in memory appears in the display window, you can perform calculations on the number, just as you can on any other number. When a number is stored in memory, the letter M appears in the box above the sqrt key on the Calculator.

Buttons and keystrokes for using the Calculator's memory are described in table 15.3.

Use the Calculator's Memory To Sum Subtotals

You can use the Calculator's memory to sum a series of subtotals. Sum the first series of numbers, for example, and add this sum to memory by clicking the M+ button or pressing Ctrl+P on the keyboard; then clear the display and calculate the second subtotal. Add the second subtotal to memory. Continue until you add all the subtotals to memory; then display the value in memory by clicking the MR button or by pressing Ctrl+R.

Copying a Number from the Calculator in Another Application

When working with many numbers or complex numbers, you make fewer mistakes if you copy the Calculator results in other applications rather than retyping the result. To copy a number from the Calculator in another application, follow these steps:

1. In the Calculator display window, perform the math calculations required to display the number.

2. Choose the **Edit** **C**opy (Ctrl+C) command.

3. Activate the application you want to receive the calculated number.

4. Position the insertion point in the newly opened application where you want the number copied.

5. From the newly opened application, choose **Edit** **P**aste (or its equivalent).

Keeping the Calculator Handy

If you are working on a Windows NT application that needs several calculations, reduce the Calculator to an icon so that you can activate it quickly. To minimize Calculator to an icon, click the

continues

continued

minimize button in the top right corner or press Alt+space bar and choose the Minimize command. To restore Calculator to a window, double-click the Calculator icon or press Alt+Tab until you see its name and then release the keys.

Copying a Number from Another Application in the Calculator

You can copy and paste a number from another application into the Calculator. After the number is in the Calculator, you can perform calculations with the number and then copy the result back in the application.

A number pasted in the Calculator erases the number currently shown in the display window.

To copy a number from another application in the Calculator, follow these steps:

1. In the other application, select the number.

2. Choose **E**dit **C**opy (or its equivalent) from the application.

3. Activate the Calculator and choose the **E**dit **P**aste command or press Ctrl+V.

If you paste a formula in the Calculator, the result appears in the display window. If you copy *5+5* from Windows NT Write and paste the calculation in the Calculator, the resulting number 10 appears. If you paste a function, such as @ for square root, Calculator performs the function on the number displayed. If, for example, you copy @ from a letter in Windows NT Write and paste in a Calculator displaying the number 25, the result 5 appears.

Numbers and most operators (such as + and –) work fine when pasted in the Calculator display, but the Calculator interprets some characters as commands. The following chart lists the characters that the Calculator interprets as commands:

Character	Interpreted As
C	Ctrl+L (clears memory)
E	Scientific notation in decimal mode; the number E in hexadecimal mode

Character	Interpreted As
M	Ctrl+M (stores current value in memory)
P	Ctrl+P (adds value to memory)
Q	C button or Esc key (clears current calculation)
R	Ctrl+R (displays value in memory)
:	Ctrl if before a letter (:m is Ctrl+M); function-key letter if before a number (:2 is F2)
\	Data key

Using the Scientific Calculator

If you have ever written an equation wider than a sheet of paper, you're a good candidate for using the Scientific Calculator. The Scientific Calculator is a special view of the Calculator.

To display the Scientific Calculator, follow these steps:

1. Activate the Calculator.

2. Choose the **View S**cientific command.

The Scientific Calculator works the same as the Standard Calculator, but adds many advanced functions. You can work in one of four number systems: hexadecimal, decimal, octal, or binary. You can perform statistical calculations, such as averages and statistical deviations. You can calculate sines, cosines, tangents, powers, logarithms, squares, and cubes. These specialized functions aren't described here but are well documented in the Calculator's Help command. To learn more about using Help, refer to Chapter 3, "Getting Help."

Watching the Clock

Windows NT comes equipped with a standard clock, which you can display on-screen in different sizes and views (see figs. 15.22 and 15.23). Even after you shrink the clock to an icon at the bottom of the screen, the hands still are readable in Analog view.

Fig. 15.22

The Clock in
Analog view.

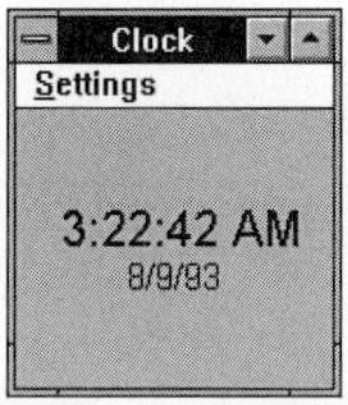

Fig. 15.23

The Clock in
Digital view.

Start the Clock application by double-clicking the Clock icon in the Accessories window or by pressing the arrow keys to select the icon and then pressing Enter. Close the Clock by choosing **C**lose from the Control menu or pressing Alt+F4. By minimizing, rather than closing the Clock to an icon, you can keep the clock visible on-screen; even as a small icon at the bottom of the screen, you can read the time.

The Clock application has one menu—the **S**ettings menu. From this menu you choose whether to display the clock in **A**nalog or **D**igital view. The Analog view shows a round clock face with ticking hands; the Digital view shows a numeric readout of the time. You also can change the font used in the Digital view, remove the title bar, and choose whether or not to display seconds and the date (in the title bar). Windows NT remembers the settings you choose and uses these settings every time you start the Clock application.

The time displayed by the Clock is based on either the computer's internal clock (if the computer has an internal clock) or on the time you type when you start the computer. If the time on the clock is inaccurate, use the Control Panel application to reset the clock as described in Chapter 7, "Customizing with the Control Panel."

T I P   To display just the clock—with no title or menu bar—double-click the clock face or choose the **S**ettings **N**o Title command. (Repeat the procedure to redisplay the title and menu bars.) This technique works in either Analog or Digital view.

Chatting with Other Users on Your Network

When you use Windows NT, you can send Mail to a single person or a group. An organization that uses Mail correctly can cut down on unnecessary meetings and phone tag. But there are occasions when you may not want to use Mail. You want to chat with someone immediately and directly. For example, you can ask questions of anyone else on the network—questions like the following:

> "Susan, can you save this shared file to your local drive so we can shut down the computer the shared file is on?"

Or one of those dreaded messages like:

> "Alrich, where are you? Everyone else is already in the boardroom waiting for your presentation."

When you need to *chat* with someone in your workgroup, use Chat. Chat is an application in the Accessory group. Its icon looks like a telephone and works almost exactly like a telephone.

With Chat, you talk by typing with anyone in your workgroup who is logged on. When you *call* someone, that person is notified of an incoming call. When the person activates his or her Chat application, you can *talk* back and forth with that person by typing in separate portions of the Chat screen. Figure 15.24 shows the Chat screen. The top portion shows what the sender is typing—the bottom portion shows what the receiver is typing. And both people can type and receive messages at the same time. It's as interactive as a telephone.

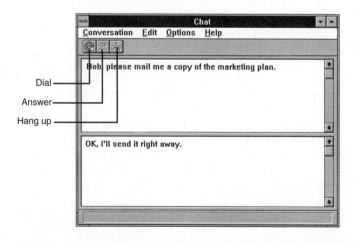

Fig. 15.24

You can chat with someone else in your workgroup using the Chat accessory.

Making a Call

Remember how to use a telephone and you'll remember how to use Chat. You can chat with anyone in your workgroup who is logged on. To call someone, follow these steps:

1. Click the Dial button (notice that the Dial button, first button on the left of the toolbar, looks like a rotary dial from an old phone) on the toolbar or choose the **C**onversation **D**ial command.

   The Select Computer dialog box shown in figure 15.25 appears.

2. Select the computer name of the person you want to chat with.

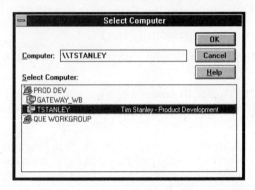

Fig. 15.25

Select the computer name of the person with whom you want to chat.

The status bar at the bottom of the Chat window will show you when the other person is connected. As soon as the status bar shows you are connected, you can begin typing in the top window. As you type, your message appears in the receiver's bottom window.

Answering a Call

The person receiving a call is alerted to an incoming call in one of two ways. If Chat is not running, the incoming call starts as a telephone icon at the bottom of the desktop of the person receiving the call. You see the handset on the telephone bounce as the telephone rings. If you have sound turned on, you hear the ring sound you have designated. If Chat is active in a window, you see a message that someone is calling in the status bar at the bottom of the screen. You see the computer name of the person calling you.

To answer a call, click the Answer button in the toolbar or choose the **C**onversation **A**nswer command. If Chat is an icon, you need to activate the application before you can answer the call. Activate Chat by double-clicking the Chat icon, or by selecting it and pressing Enter. You can begin typing as soon as you answer the call.

Editing, Copying, and Saving Conversations

Chat uses all the Windows NT editing conventions to which you are accustomed. Use the editing keys with which you are familiar from Windows NT Write or most word processors. The receiver sees corrections as you make them. You also have the **E**dit **C**ut, **E**dit **C**opy, and **E**dit **P**aste commands available so that you can transfer text and numbers into Chat.

The **E**dit **U**ndo command is not available because your conversational partner watches everything you type and correct, so there is no reason for after-the-fact editing.

To save a Chat message for later reference, choose the **E**dit Select **A**ll command, and then choose the **E**dit **C**opy command. This puts the entire message in the Clipboard. You can then paste the message into Windows NT Write or a word processor, where it can be saved. Your portion of the window and the receiver's portion must be selected and copied separately. To switch between the two portions of the screen, click in the portion you want or press the F6 key.

> Chat works with text and numbers. If you need to transmit a formatted word processing file, a spreadsheet, a chart, or graphic, attach the file to a Mail message. Because Windows NT enables you to run more than one application at a time, you can send the files attached to a Mail message as you talk over Chat.

T I P

Ending Your Conversation

As with the telephone, a conversation in Chat ends by hanging up. To hang up, click the Hangup button or choose the **C**onversation **H**angup command. The Hangup button looks like a phone receiver coming down onto the phone cradle.

Changing Chat's Appearance and Sound

Like most Windows NT applications, Chat offers numerous features that you can customize so that Chat is more to your personal taste. For example, you can change the background color, change or turn the sound on or off, or change the font.

To change the background color on your typing portion (the upper half) of the screen, follow these steps:

1. Choose the **O**ptions Background **C**olor command.

2. Select the color you want from the **B**asic Colors.

3. Choose OK or press Enter.

T I P You may select a patterned color from the Basic Color group, but the closest solid color will be used. In some cases, you may see no change or a totally black screen.

The **C**ustom Colors option is not available in Chat even though it appears in the Color dialog box, because the Color dialog box is shared between different applications, some of which do have custom color capability.

To change the font your Chat screen uses, follow these steps:

1. Choose the **O**ptions **F**ont command.

2. Select or type the font name in the **F**ont list box.

3. Select a style in the Font Style list.

4. Select a size from the Size scrolling list.

5. Select the **S**trikeout or **U**nderline check box for these effects.

6. Select a character color from the Color combo list.

7. Choose OK or press Enter.

You can use the same font that the person on the other end of the conversation is using by choosing the **O**ptions **P**references command, and then selecting the Use **P**artner's Font or Use **O**wn Font selection.

You may want to display your screen in the side-by-side display shown in figure 15.26. To toggle your chatting Windows NT between vertical and horizontal, choose the **O**ptions **P**references command, and then select either the **T**op and Bottom option or the **S**ide by Side option.

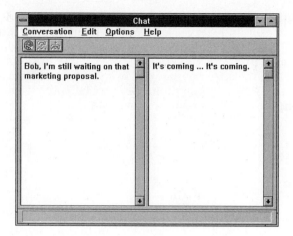

Fig. 15.26

Using Options
Preferences,
you can change
window
orientation.

Chat rings at both the caller's and receiver's personal computers. The sound of the ring depends upon whether you have a sound board, and which sound you have selected to act as the ring. If you do not have a sound board, you hear a beep. If you are a very popular person, you may want to turn the sound off so your office mate isn't disturbed during his or her afternoon nap. To toggle the sound between on and off, choose the **O**ptions Sou**n**d command. Each time you select the command, it changes the sound status.

Like most Windows NT applications with toolbars and status bars, you can turn those options on or off if you need more screen area or do not use them. To toggle the toolbar on and off, choose the **O**ptions **T**oolbar command. To toggle the status bar at the bottom of the screen on or off, choose the **O**ptions Status **B**ar command. If you want to reverse the current condition of the toolbar or status bar, just choose the **O**ption **T**oolbar or **O**ption Status **B**ar command again.

Connecting to a Remote IBM Host Application Using the 3270 Emulator

The 3270 Emulator is similar to the Terminal application discussed previously in that it is used to establish a communications channel with another computer through a virtual terminal window. The main difference between the Terminal application and the 3270 Emulator is that the 3270 Emulator communicates only with specific IBM mainframe host applications. Therefore, it can't be used for tasks like dialing in to a service such as CompuServe. Also, unlike Terminal which uses a standard modem, the 3270 Emulator uses a special hardware adapter and communications protocol for establishing a remote host connection. Once connected, the 3270 Emulator allows you to execute a host application, such as IBM's Customer Information Control System, while working from the comfort of your NT workstation.

Opening the 3270 Emulator and Making a Connection

Open the 3270 Emulator application from the Accessories window by double-clicking on the 3270 Emulator icon or by selecting the icon by using the arrow keys and pressing Enter. After you open the application, a blank 3270 Emulator window appears on-screen (see fig. 15.27).

You connect to a remote IBM host application by selecting the **S**ession **C**onnect command. Assuming that your session settings are correct (this is covered in the next section), and that the network connection to the remote host has been setup correctly, you should receive a sign on message allowing you to login to the remote system. Once you have completed your work on the host application, disconnect from the remote system by selecting the **S**ession **D**isconnect command.

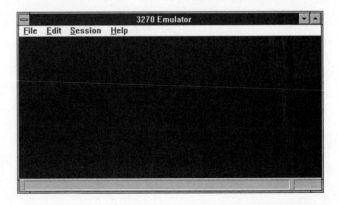

The 3270 Emulator window.

Working in the 3270 Emulator Terminal Window

Once a working connection has been established, the 3270 Emulator window acts just like a dedicated terminal connected to the host.

However, in the NT environment you gain some additional benefits. Because the 3270 Emulator is a Windows NT application, you can copy data from the terminal window to the Clipboard and then paste it back in at another terminal screen location. Since the data is stored on the Clipboard, you can also paste the data into another application such as Word for Windows or Microsoft Excel.

To select text with the mouse, press and hold down the mouse button and drag the I-beam across the text you want to select. To select text by using the keyboard, hold down the Shift key and press any arrow key. To select all text in the terminal window, select the **Edit Select All** command. To copy the text to the Clipboard, select the **Edit Copy** command. To insert the Clipboard contents at the current cursor location, select the **Edit Paste** command. If you want to replace text in the terminal window, select it first as outlined above, and then select the **Edit Paste** command.

You can also print the contents of the 3270 Emulator terminal window by selecting the **File Print** command. If you want to print specific text, highlight it first as outlined above, and then select the **File Print** command. If you need to set up or change the settings for the printer, select the **File Print Setup** command. This displays the standard Print Setup dialog box which allows you to select a printer, change paper size and orientaion, and modify various other parameters which may vary depending on the printer you select.

Changing the Session Settings

Session settings are used by the 3270 Emulator to establish the communications parameters necessary for connecting to a specific remote host. The first time you use the 3270 Emulator, you need to adjust these settings in order to connect to a remote host. Check with your systems administrator for the proper values to use.

If you are going to enter your own session settings from scratch, select the **File New** command to create a set of "defaults," which is essentially a clean slate. However, if you are already working with a set of session settings that you just want to modify, select the **Session Settings** command. In both cases, the 3270 Settings dialog box will be displayed (see fig. 15.28).

To modify the session settings, follow these steps:

1. Set the Host Network **A**ddress field to the 12 digit hexadecimal address of the host you want to communicate with.

2. In the Local Node ID (**X**ID) fields, type the local node ID which identifies your computer. The three digit block number goes in the first box and the five digit node number goes in the second box.

3. This should be sufficient to establish a connection to a remote host. However, once you are connected you may want to review the requirements for the host and fine-tune your settings accordingly. To do so, select the **A**dvanced command which expands the 3270 Settings dialog box as shown in fig. 15.29. If you do not want to modify the Advanced settings, choose OK or press Enter at this point and skip the following steps.

4. Set the Host Code **P**age field to the country code which is required by the remote host. If you are logging on to a system which is located in a different country, you may need to modify this field.

5. Set the **L**ocal Adapter Name field to correspond to the local physical adapter your computer will use to connect to the remote host.

6. Set the Logical Unit **N**umber of the Logical Unit (LU) defined for the remote host. ANY is a legal value you can use if you do not want to specify a particular LU.

7. Type the Local **S**AP Address, the system address point, for your computer.

8. Set the **M**ax Data Length field to match that expected by the Physical Unit used by the remote host.

9. Set the ACK **R**eceive Window field to the maximum number of frames that the 3270 Emulator receives before transmitting an acknowledgement (ACK) to the remote host. Adjust this parameter to maximize performance.

10. Set the ACK Send **W**indow field to the maximum number of frames that 3270 Emulator transmits before waiting for an acknowledgement (ACK) from the remote host. Adjust this parameter to maximize performance.

11. Choose OK or press Enter.

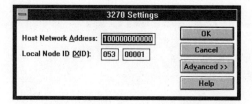

Fig. 15.28

3270 Emulator basic session settings.

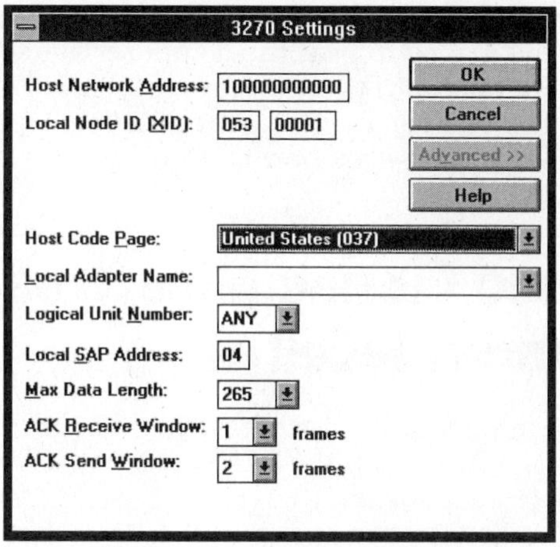

Fig. 15.29

3270 Emulator advanced session settings.

Saving and Opening Session Configurations

Once the session settings for a particular remote host have been setup, you can save the settings in a configuraton file by selecting the **File Save** or **File Save As** command. This will display a dialog box which will allow you to choose a file name and directory location in which to save the session settings. To reopen a previous set of session settings, select the **File Open** command. This will reset the session settings to those that were in effect when the file was saved.

Ask Your Systems Administrator for Configuration Files!

If you are working with multiple hosts, your systems administrator may be able to provide you with default configuration files for the various hosts used in your organization. Check it out! This could save you considerable setup time, leaving you with more on-line time.

Developing Strategic Skills with Minesweeper, Solitaire, and FreeCell

A good reason exists to include Minesweeper, Solitaire, and FreeCell at the end of this chapter: many Windows NT users stay up until the late hours of the evening, trying to beat the computer at a challenging game of Minesweeper, Solitaire, or FreeCell! Now you have a good excuse for playing these games: you can claim that you're developing strategic skills and honing your hand-eye coordination.

Opening and Closing Minesweeper, Solitaire and FreeCell

To open the game applications, double-click the icons in the Games window (they are not located in the Accessories window), or press the arrow keys to select an icon, and then press Enter. Close the games by choosing Exit from the Game menu.

Playing Solitaire

After you start Solitaire, you see a screen like the one shown in figure 15.30. The screen has three active areas: the deck in the upper-left corner of the playing area; the four suit stacks in the upper-right corner of the playing area (which start out empty); and the seven row stacks in the bottom half of the screen. The number of cards in each row stack increases from one to seven, from left to right. The top card in each row stack is face up; all other cards in each stack are face down.

The object of the game is to move all the cards from the row stacks into the suit stacks at the top right of the screen. You must build the stack upward, in sequential order, from Ace to King, one suit per stack. To start the stack, you need an Ace.

To get an Ace, you must either display this card in the lower stacks or turn over an Ace from the deck. The lower stacks build from high cards downward, in suits of alternating colors. You can build a lower stack, for example, starting with the King of Diamonds, the Queen of Spades, the Jack of Hearts, the Ten of Clubs, and so on. When you get an Ace, you can move the card to an upper suit stack and start building the suit stack there.

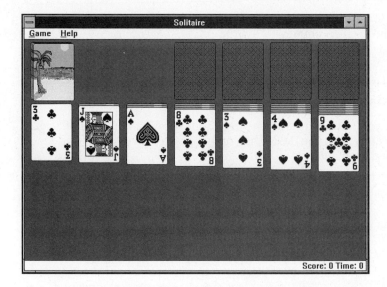

Fig. 15.30

Playing Solitaire.

In the lower stacks, you can move cards between the stacks, or from the deck to the stacks. You can move a single card at a time, or a group of cards. After all the upturned cards are moved from a lower stack, you can turn over the top card on the stack. To turn a card, click it with the mouse button or move the arrow to the card (by using the arrow keys) and press the space bar.

To deal from the deck, select the deck (by clicking the deck or by pressing the arrow keys to move to the deck and pressing the space bar). The dealt card appears to the right of the deck. If you can, move this card to a stack. You can move, for example, a King onto a blank space in the lower stack area.

To move a card (or cards), click and drag with the mouse. (You can move a card quickly from the lower stacks to the upper suit stacks by double-clicking on the card you want to move.) You can use the left- and right-arrow keys to move the selection arrow to the card you want to move: press Enter, use the arrow keys to move the card where you want, and press Enter to complete the move. If you want to move more than one card in a stack, press the up-arrow key to select a card higher up in the stack before you press Enter. If you make an illegal move, Solitaire moves the card to its original location.

Solitaire offers several options. Choose the **G**ame De**c**k command to choose a different deck illustration. Choose the **G**ame **O**ptions command to select the number of cards in each draw (one or three cards) and scoring options. Solitaire even has a **G**ame **U**ndo command to undo the last action.

When you finish playing and want to start a new game, choose the **G**ame **D**eal command.

To learn the rules of Solitaire, browse through the **H**elp command.

Watch the Dealer's Hand!

If you're playing with the deck that shows a hand full of aces, watch what the dealer has up his sleeve! Give it time and you may see amazing things.

Playing Minesweeper

Minesweeper is a game of analysis and tension. It requires a totally different flair than Solitaire.

When you open Minesweeper, you are faced with a grid of squares that represent a mine field (see fig. 15.31). The goal of this game is to mark all the mines; if you step on a mine, the game is over. When you step on a square, three outcomes are possible: the square contains a mine that "blows up," and the game ends; the square contains no mine, and the minesweeper indicates that no mines exist in the surrounding eight squares; or the square contains no mine, and the minesweeper indicates that a certain number of mines exist in the surrounding eight squares (the number that appears in the square).

Fig. 15.31

Minesweeper is a game of analysis and tension.

As you successfully uncover squares without stepping on a mine, the information provided by your minesweeper helps you deduce which squares contain mines. When you know a square contains a mine, you can mark this square, which effectively deactivates this mine. The object of the game is to mark all mines *before* stepping on one.

To uncover a square, click it. If the square contains no mine, either a number appears in the square, indicating the number of mines in the surrounding eight squares, or a blank space appears. If the square contains a number, you can try to deduce and mark which of the surrounding squares contains a mine or mines. To mark a mine, click the square with the right mouse button.

Watch for patterns in the numbers. Once you play a few games, you will begin to see repeating patterns of numbers on the mine field. From those numbers, and the mines you can see, you can deduce where it is safe to take your next step.

Three predefined skill levels, which you select from the **G**ame menu, are available in Minesweeper: **B**eginner, **I**ntermediate, and **E**xpert. The levels differ in the size of the minefield and in the total number of mines per minefield. You also can define custom minefields with the **G**ame **C**ustom command. For more information on the rules of Minesweeper and some strategic hints on playing the game, choose the **H**elp command.

Playing FreeCell

FreeCell is logic puzzle which has a form similar to Solitaire. One of the main differences from Solitaire, however, is that after the initial shuffle there is no luck involved. When you open FreeCell and select the **G**ame **N**ew Game command, you will notice that the cards are are all dealt face up with no hidden cards (see fig. 15.32). The object of the game is to move all the cards from the card columns at the bottom of the window to the "home cells," the four card locations in the top-right corner of the FreeCell window. Each suit of cards should be piled on a different home cell, starting with the Ace. The four card locations in the top-left corner, called the "free cells," are used as temporary locations to hold cards while rearranging the deck. Each free cell can only hold one card.

When you move a card in FreeCell, there are three legal moves you can make. You can move a card from the bottom of a column to an empty free cell. You can move a card from a free cell, or from the bottom of a column, to a home cell if the card is of the same suit and the rank is one greater than the card in the home cell. Aces can always be moved to an empty home cell. Lastly, you can move a card from a free cell, or from the bottom of a column, to the bottom of another column if the card is of opposite color and the rank is one less than the card in the other column. You win the game when all cards have been moved to the home cells. You lose the game when there are no more legal moves which can be made.

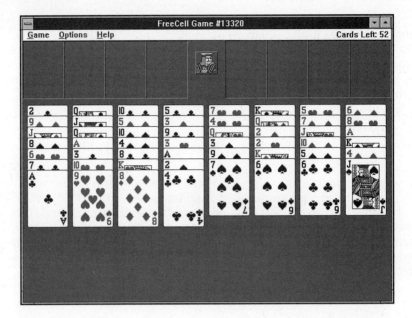

Fig. 15.32

FreeCell is similar to Solitaire, but all cards are dealt face up.

To move a card, click and release the mouse on the card you want to move (the card will be displayed in reverse video). Move the mouse pointer to the location where you want to move the card. If the move is legal, you will see the mouse pointer change to an up or a down arrow, and clicking on that location will move the card. An illegal move attempt will cause a message box to be displayed, indicating that the move is not allowed.

There are 32,000 different games from which to select, each with a different deal of the deck. You can choose one of these games at random by selecting the **G**ame **N**ew Game command, or you can pick a specific game number by selecting the **G**ame **S**elect Game command. This option will display a dialog box in which you can enter the game number. You can restart a current game in progress by selecting the **G**ame **Re**start command.

There are two options in FreeCell. Selecting the **O**ptions **S**tatisitics command shows you your wins, losses, and streaks. When you lose a game, you can replay the same game number without losing the statisitics. Selecting the **O**ptions **M**essages command disables the message box displayed when an illegal move is made.

For more information on the rules of FreeCell and some strategic hints on playing the game, choose the **H**elp command.

You Can't Use Drag and Drop to Move Cards

Unlike Solitaire, FreeCell does not use drag and drop for moving cards. Moves are made by first selecting the card to be moved, and then selecting the location to move to.

Summary

Because Windows NT desktop accessories are so convenient to use, they quickly become part of your daily business tools. The Cardfile is an application you may want to load by default when you start Windows NT. Copy the appropriate program item icon to the StartUp group window in the Program Manager.

After checking appointments and a *To Do* list, you can minimize these accessories to icons, or close the desk accessories if you need maximum memory. The Notepad is a great way to track telephone conversations, ideas about a project in progress, lengthy notes while you work in a spreadsheet, and so on. When needed, you can transfer these notes easily to Windows NT Write or retrieve the TXT file with another word processor.

Using Multimedia

A s computers edge into more and more aspects of everyday life, they take on new roles. Consider these roles: computer as musician, as storyteller, as business presentation tool, as educational tool, and as research assistant.

Multimedia plays a part in each of these roles because it combines two familiar communications media—sound and sight—in a single package and gives you control over producing and delivering sound and visual effects.

You can use multimedia in several ways. With the right equipment, you can play all of the many multimedia packages available commercially. Included are games, stories, full encyclopedias, complete reference texts, and more. You can record simple messages, tunes, or motion pictures and embed them in documents you create in Windows NT applications. If you are adventurous, you can move beyond the simple applications that come with Windows NT to a multimedia authoring application and create original multimedia presentations and applications.

Using multimedia requires that you have the right equipment. You need a CD-ROM player, speakers, and a sound board. All hardware must be compliant to the MPC standard developed by Microsoft and the Multimedia PC Marketing Council. You can supply the equipment you need in one of two ways: by upgrading a present PC or by buying a special multimedia PC equipped with all you need.

Upgrading Your Equipment to Multimedia Standards

To take advantage of multimedia, you need the right equipment. Basically, you need a powerful PC, VGA graphics, a sound board, speakers, and a CD-ROM drive. You can add many optional pieces of equipment, including VCRs, microphones, joysticks, MIDI synthesizers, and music keyboards.

To ensure compatibility among all multimedia software and equipment, the Multimedia PC Marketing Council has established standards for multimedia PC hardware (listed in table 16.1). You can get the right equipment in one of two ways. You can purchase an MPC-compliant computer, ready to play. Several manufacturers sell these MPCs, which include all the hardware (and, often, the software) you need. The second way to get the proper equipment is to upgrade your current system by adding a sound board, a CD-ROM drive, and (if necessary) VGA graphics. Make sure that the equipment you choose conforms to this standard. The best way to accomplish this task is to look for the MPC logo, which ensures compliance; another way is to understand the hardware requirements and purchase equipment that conforms to these standards.

You already may have some of the equipment you need. Your stereo system can serve as the amplifier and speakers, and an MPC-compliant CD-ROM player that you use for music also may play multimedia disks.

Table 16.1 NT multimedia equipment requirements

System Element	Minimum Requirements	Recommended
Computer		
CPU	80386, 25MHz	
RAM	12M	16 M
Diskette	3 1/2-inch, 1.44 M	Same capacity
Fixed disk	75 M	212 M
User input	101-key keyboard, mouse	Same
I/O	1 serial, 1 parallel, 1 joystick*	Same

System Element	Minimum Requirements	Recommended
Graphics		
Display	VGA, 640 5 480, 16 colors	Same, 256 colors
Audio		
Sampling type	Linear PCM	Same
Resolution	8-bit	16-bit
Sampling rate, DAC**	11.025 and 22.05 kHz	44.1 kHz
Sampling rate, ADC**	11.025 kHz, microphone input	22.05 and 44.1 kHz
Melody notes/timbres	6/3 simultaneous	16/9 simultaneous
Percussive notes/timbres	2/2 simultaneous with melody	16/8 simultaneous
External audio input	Microphone	Added stereo input
Internal mixing	CD, synthesizer, and DAC	Added aux. input
Audio Output	Line level, _10 db, stereo***	Same
MIDI I/O	In, Out, Thru, interrupt-driven	Same
CD-ROM Drives		
Transfer Rate	150K/second, 16K blocks	300K/second, 64K (with buffers)
Seek time	1 second	Same
MTBF	10,000 hours	Same
Mode	1	2, form 1 and 2
Subchannels	Q	P and R-W

Joystick input usually is provided by the audio adapter card.

** *DAC is an abbreviation for digital-to-analog converter, a device that converts digital data to audio signals. ADC stands for analog-to-digital converter, which converts audio input signals to digital data.*

*** *Referenced to standard consumer audio line level _0 db = 1 milliwatt into 600 ohms.*

Installing Multimedia Equipment and Drivers

Before you can use a multimedia device, such as a sound board or a CD-ROM player, you first must physically plug the device into the computer; then you must install the device driver in Windows NT; and finally you must set up the hardware. The process is similar to installing a new printer on the system: plugging in the hardware establishes the physical connection; installing the driver tells Windows NT the device exists; setting up the device tells Windows NT how to communicate with the device.

Installing Equipment

Plugging in a device—whether a sound board or a CD-ROM player—isn't difficult. If the device is internal, such as a sound board, turn off the power, remove a few screws from the sides of the *system unit* (the computer box that holds the CPU), and slide off the cover. (You also may have to remove a port cover from the back of the PC to provide external access to the new board's ports.) Boards plug into an area of the PC reserved for boards.

Look at the boards already installed in the PC to see how these circuit boards are attached. Then look at the new board; you can see that the board has ports at one end that must point toward the back of the PC for external access and a wide *tab* on one side of the board that pushes into any of the available slots in the PC. Although you need firm pressure to push the tab into the slot, the process is neither complex nor dangerous. When you are finished, slide the cover back on the PC and replace the screws. (Just think how impressed your colleagues will be when you casually mention that you installed a new board in your PC today.)

CD-ROM players may be internal or external, but either way, these players usually connect to a PC via a cable. If you have the space, you can install an internal CD-ROM player inside the PC (you need an available drive bay). To install an internal CD-ROM, you have to take off the cover of the PC, as you do to install a board. Follow the manufacturer's instructions for connecting the cables inside the PC. If you don't have space inside the PC, add an external CD-ROM player; this installation is a simple matter of connecting cables. Read the documentation that comes with the device for details about attaching multimedia equipment to your PC.

You also may need to attach the multimedia device to other equipment. A sound board, for example, requires speakers (if you have a stereo system, you can connect the sound board to the amplifier and use the stereo's speakers). The documentation tells you how to make this connection. Sound boards often include connectors that make adding a microphone or joystick or connecting to your CD-ROM player simple. Sound boards also usually include a connector for a MIDI musical synthesizer or keyboard, but you may need an additional converter box to operate the MIDI equipment. Check with the sound board documentation or manufacturer.

After attaching the device to the PC, you may need to run a test to check that the device is successfully attached. After you plug in a Sound Blaster board, for example, you run a test to determine whether the board is successfully connected to both the PC and the speakers. If the test is successful, you hear music you never thought could come from a computer. From the test, you learn that the speakers are correctly attached and that the PC and the board are communicating. If the test is unsuccessful, you may have to change the setup. For more information about changing the setup, see "Setting Up a Device Driver" later in this chapter.

Write down all information the test application gives you about the installation. The Sound Blaster test, for example, may tell you that the board is currently using I/O address #220 and Interrupt #7. You may need this information when you install the driver in Windows NT.

Adding Multimedia Drivers

For Windows NT to recognize and communicate with the multimedia equipment you install, you must install the correct device driver in Windows NT. Windows NT comes with many multimedia equipment drivers, which you find listed in Windows NT but which are not yet installed. You know whether Windows NT includes a driver for the equipment when you display a list of existing drivers (step 4 in the following instructions). If the driver you need isn't included, you may be able to use the generic driver that comes with Windows NT. If you learn that the generic driver doesn't work for the equipment, check the documentation for the new equipment to find out whether a Windows NT driver is available (or call the manufacturer).

To install the driver, you must have the original Windows NT installation media (or the media that came with your device, if you are using the manufacturer's driver). The Windows NT media, shipped on either diskettes or CD-ROM, should contain the driver you need for the device.

After the multimedia device is successfully attached, follow these steps to install the driver and set up the device in Windows NT:

1. In the Windows NT Program Manager, open the Main window and then choose the Control Panel. The Control Panel window appears (see fig. 16.1).

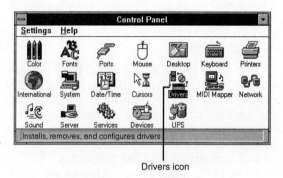

Fig. 16.1

The Control Panel contains the Drivers icon.

Drivers icon

2. Choose the Drivers application by double-clicking the Drivers icon with the mouse or by pressing the arrow keys to select the icon and then pressing Enter. The Drivers dialog box appears (see fig. 16.2).

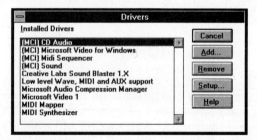

Fig. 16.2

The Drivers dialog box shows a list of the drivers already installed in Windows.

3. Choose the Add button. The Add dialog box appears (see fig. 16.3).

4. Select the equipment's name in the List of Drivers list and choose OK. If the equipment isn't listed, select Unlisted or Updated Driver. A dialog box appears, prompting you to specify a path to the location of the media that contains the device driver (see fig. 16.4).

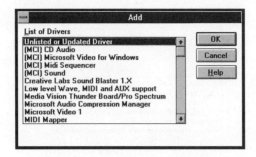

Fig. 16.3

The Add dialog box shows all the drivers that Windows supplies.

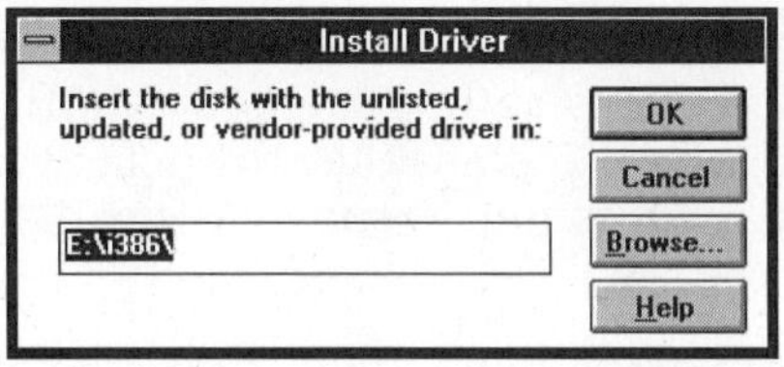

Fig. 16.4

The message tells you exactly which disk to insert.

5. Insert the media that contains the driver into the proper drive. Typcially, this is a diskette inserted into drive A, or a CD inserted into your CD-ROM drive. If the driver is located on a different drive or directory in the PC, or if you are installing from CD-ROM, type the drive and directory names (but not the driver's file name).

   If you don't know where the driver is located, choose Browse (see fig. 16.5). Then select the drive and directory that contains the device driver and choose OK.

6. When you return to the Add dialog box, choose OK. A Setup dialog box may appear, requesting configuration information (see fig. 16.6).

Fig. 16.5

To locate the driver, you can browse through drives and directories.

Fig. 16.6

The Setup dialog box already may show the correct setup information.

7. After referring to the notes you took when you tested the device, select the necessary setup information and choose OK.

8. If Windows NT requires more drivers to go with the driver you installed, Windows NT installs them by default and may ask you for more setup information. Respond to any dialog box that appears and choose OK.

   If, however, the installation is complete, a dialog box advises you that you must restart Windows NT for the installation to take effect.

9. Choose Restart Now to restart Windows NT so that you can use the driver. (If you don't restart, you can use the driver the next time you use Windows NT.)

Setting Up a Device Driver

Windows NT communicates with devices, such as sound boards and CD-ROM players, through only a limited number of channels. When you install and set up the new device, you must make sure that the settings you choose don't conflict with settings already in use by other devices.

Testing after you connect the equipment to your PC is the best way to ensure that no conflict exists. Windows NT warns you about conflicts between hardware drivers when you first start your system and log on. If you receive a warning indicating that a particular driver did not start up, you can view details about the event by choosing the Event Viewer application in the Program Manager Administrative Tools group. A driver that did not start is indicated with a "stop sign" icon at the beginning of the line (see fig. 16.7). Choose the **View** **D**etail command to see a more comprehensive description (see fig. 16.8). The Event Viewer won't tell you which devices are in conflict but it will help you narrow down the problem, so a little investigative work may be called for here. As an example, if your system has a printer installed on LPT1 which is set to IRQ 7, and you install a Sound Blaster card also set to IRQ 7, you will receive a boot up device startup error. The Event Viewer will tell you that the Sound Blaster driver did not start, but it won't tell you why. By process of elimination, you can readily determine that the problem is an IRQ sharing conflict. At this point you should reconfigure the Sound Blaster's IRQ to one that you know is free, reboot your system, and then change the driver's setup to match. If you are unsure of what system resources the device uses, refer to the device's documentation. You also can call the manufacturer or the Microsoft support line (see Chapter 33, "Help, Support, and Resources").

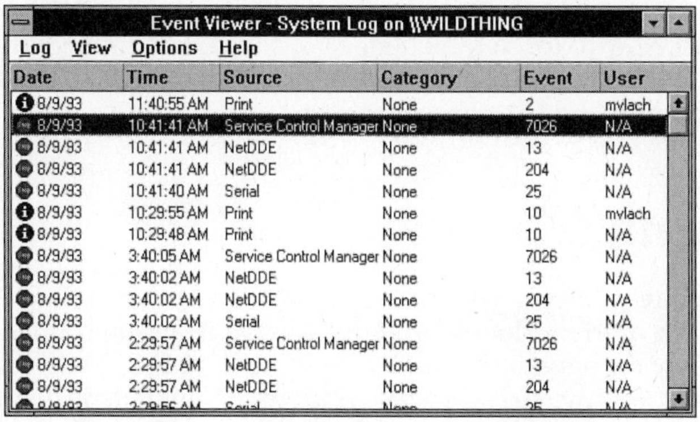

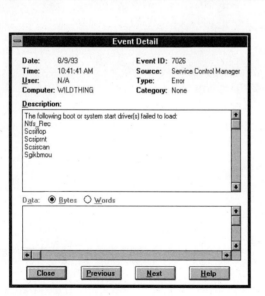

Fig. 16.7

A message in the Event Viewer shows that a driver did not start when starting NT.

Fig. 16.8

Viewing the details of the Event Viewer message.

To make changes to the driver setup, follow these steps:

1. Choose the Drivers icon in the Control Panel. The Drivers dialog box appears.

2. From the Installed Drivers list, select the driver you want to set up.

3. Choose the Setup button. (If the driver requires no settings, the Setup button is dimmed.) The Setup dialog box appears.

4. Select the setup options you need, referring to the device's documentation.

5. Choose OK.

6. When the System Setting Change dialog box appears, choose Restart Now to force the changes to take effect immediately or choose Don't Restart Now and choose Close to close the Drivers dialog box.

Removing a Driver

You can remove a driver you no longer use from the Installed Drivers list. Removing a driver doesn't remove the file from the hard disk, so you can easily reconnect if you subsequently find that you need the driver. Do not remove drivers that Windows NT installed (just to be safe, don't remove any drivers you don't recognize).

To remove a driver, follow these steps:

1. In the Control Panel, choose the Drivers icon. The Drivers dialog box appears.

2. Select the driver you want to remove from the Installed Drivers list.

3. Choose the Remove button. A dialog box appears, asking you to confirm removal of the driver.

4. Choose Yes.

5. Choose Restart Now to force the removal to take effect immediately.

Operating the Sound Recorder

To use sound on a PC, you must add a sound board that conforms to the Multimedia Personal Computer specifications for the PC. You must install the board after adding it, as described in the previous section "Adding Multimedia Drivers." If you use high-level MIDI sound or a synthesizer, you also must install the drivers for these devices.

To record sound, you also need a microphone; the sound board probably has a microphone jack (or port), but you should check the documentation to find out the connector you need. You also need to be sure that the microphone is powerful enough to replicate your voice adequately; check documentation for specifications.

Using the Sound Recorder application, you can play, record, and edit sounds that have the WAVE format (designated by the file extension WAV). You can play these sounds on the speakers, assign sound to events, or embed sounds in applications that support object linking and embedding. You can embed a spoken message, for example, inside an Excel spreadsheet file or a Word for Windows document. (To learn more about object linking and embedding, refer to Chapter 6, "Embedding and Linking Windows NT Applications.")

The Sound Recorder application appears as a small window on-screen that shows a menu across the top, buttons on the bottom, and an oscilloscope-like display in the center. You use the menus to open, edit, and save sound files. You watch the wave-like display to monitor the sound file's progress. You use the buttons to start and stop the Recorder, just like a tape recorder.

Starting the Sound Recorder

To start the Sound Recorder, follow these steps:

1. In the Program Manager, open the Accessories window (see fig. 16.9).

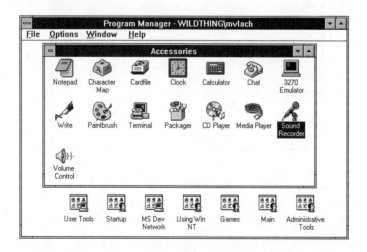

Fig. 16.9

The Sound Recorder icon is among the accessories.

2. Choose the Sound Recorder. (Double-click on the Sound Recorder icon with the mouse or press the arrow keys to select the icon and then press Enter.) The Sound Recorder window appears (see fig. 16.10).

Fig. 16.10

The Sound Recorder window gives you a visual display of sound wave forms.

Opening and Playing Sounds

On a PC, sound is stored as a file, just like other documents. To play a sound, you first must start the Sound Recorder (see the preceding section) and open a sound file recorded in the WAVE format (a file with the extension WAV). Windows NT includes several sound files that use the WAVE format, and you can use Sound Recorder to record, edit, or mix sounds that you create.

To open and play a sound file, follow these steps:

1. Choose the **F**ile menu and select the **O**pen command. The Open dialog box appears (see fig. 16.11).

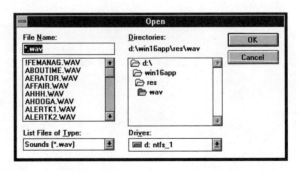

Fig. 16.11

Use the Open dialog box to locate the WAV file you want to open and play.

2. In the Dri**v**es list (if necessary), choose the drive that contains the file and, in the **D**irectories list, select the directory. In the File **N**ame list, select the file you want to open.

3. Choose OK to open the sound file.

   The Length message on the right side of the Sound Recorder dialog box tells you the playing length, in seconds, of the file you opened.

4. Choose the Play button.

   The Position message on the left side of the Sound Recorder dialog box tells you the current position, in seconds, of the sound you are playing.

The status bar reads Playing, and you see a visual representation of the sound waves in the Wave box (see fig. 16.12). You also see the scroll box move to the right as the file progresses.

Fig. 16.12

The Sound Recorder with waves visible.

Each time you choose the Play button, the sound plays from beginning to end. When the file ends (or when you choose the Stop button), Stopped appears in the Status bar.

You can stop the file manually by choosing the Stop button, and you can resume by choosing Play again. You also can move around in a sound file. To move forward by one tenth of a second, click on the right arrow of the scroll bar (to move backward, click the left arrow of the scroll bar). To move one second at a time, click on the shaded part of the scroll bar in the direction you want to move. With a keyboard, press the Tab key to select the scroll bar and press the left- or right-arrow keys to move forward or backward by tenths of a second.

You can move quickly to the end of a sound file by choosing the Forward button or pressing the End key; you can move to the beginning by choosing the Rewind button or pressing Home.

Creating a Sound File

You can create a sound file by recording the sound, by adding to an existing sound file, by inserting one sound file into another, or by mixing together two sound files. To record a voice, you need to attach a microphone. Check the device documentation to learn how.

You can record up to one minute of speech. To record a voice, follow these steps:

1. Choose the File menu and select the New command.

2. Choose the Record button.

3. To record the message, speak into the microphone.

4. Choose the Stop button when you finish.

To record from a stereo, plug the stereo's output attachment into the microphone input port on the sound board (this procedure may require a special connector; check with an electronics store). If you find that recording exactly what you need is difficult, record a little more than you need and delete the extra (described in the following paragraphs of this section).

To record into an existing file, open the file and use the Play and Stop buttons (or the scroll bar) to move to the position where you want to add the new sound. Choose the Record button and speak into the microphone. Choose Stop when you finish and save the file.

You also can merge two sound files. Open the sound file into which you want to add another sound file and use the Play and Stop buttons to move to the place where you want to add another sound file. Choose the Edit menu and select the Insert File command. Select the file you want to insert and choose OK. Save the new file.

Another option is to mix two files so that the sounds of both files play simultaneously. One file may be music and the other file a voice. Open one of the files and use Play and Stop (or the scroll bar) to move to the place where you want to mix in another file. Choose the Edit menu and select the Mix With File command. Select the file you want to mix in and choose OK. Save the new file.

To delete part of a sound file, move to either immediately before or after the point at which you want to delete the sound and choose the Edit menu and select either the Delete Before Current Position or the Delete After Current Position command.

Before you save the sound file, you can *undo* changes at any time by choosing the File menu and selecting the Revert command.

Editing a Sound File

You can edit a sound file after you create it by adding special effects, changing the volume, speeding up or slowing down, adding an echo, or reversing the sound. (If you reverse the file, be sure that you don't include offensive subliminal messages.)

To edit a sound file, follow these steps:

1. Choose the **F**ile menu and select the **O**pen command.

2. Select the file you want to edit and choose OK.

3. Choose the Effect**s** menu and select one of the following commands:

Command	Effect
Increase Volume (by 25%)	Make the sound file 25% louder
Decrease Volume	Make the sound file 25% softer
Increase speed (by 100%)	Double the speed of the sound file
Decrease Speed	Halve the speed of the sound file
Add Echo	Add an echo to the sound
Reverse	Play the sound file backward

By choosing the **F**ile menu and selecting the **R**evert command, you can *undo* changes at any time before you save the sound file.

Saving a Sound File

Be sure to save after you create or edit a sound file.

To save a sound file, follow these steps:

1. Choose the **F**ile menu and select the Save **A**s command.

2. Select the drive where you want to save the file in the D**r**ives list.

3. Select the directory where you want to save the file in the **D**irectories list.

4. Type a file name in the File **N**ame box. Include the file extension WAV to make the file easier to open at a later time.

5. Choose OK.

If you decide not to rename a file, instead of **F**ile Save **A**s, choose **F**ile **S**ave.

Exiting Sound Recorder

When you finish using Sound Recorder, choose the File menu and select the Exit command.

Assigning Sounds to Events

The simplest form of sound on a computer is the sound you can assign to computer-related events, such as pressing the asterisk key or question mark or starting or stopping Windows NT. Windows NT comes equipped with several sound files you can assign to these events (and you can use the Sound Recorder to create custom sounds). You also can turn off system sounds so that the PC operates more discreetly.

To assign sounds to computer events, follow these steps:

1. From the Control Panel, choose the Sound icon. The Sound dialog box appears, showing the available Windows NT Events in one list box and the sound Files in another list box (see fig. 16.13). Sound files usually have the WAV file extension.

Fig. 16.13

Use the Sound dialog box to assign sounds to events.

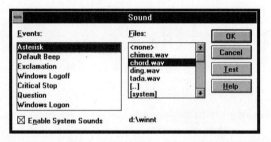

2. If the sound files are stored in another drive or directory, select the drive or directory from the Files text box.

3. Select the Event that you want to change. The sound file currently assigned to this event is selected in the Files text box. Select another sound file to assign a different sound to the event.

4. Choose the Test button to see how the sound file sounds.

5. Repeat steps 3 and 4 to assign sounds to other Windows NT events.

6. After you set the desired sounds for the events, choose OK.

To turn off the PC's warning beep, select the Enable System Sounds check box and choose OK. This action disables all beeping for all applications used in Windows NT.

Operating the Media Player

Using the Media Player application, you can play Windows NT-compatible multimedia sound, animation, and music files. Where Sound Recorder only plays WAVE-format sound, Media Player can play sound, animated video, and MIDI music files as well as controlling a CD-ROM drive for playing audio CDs.

Before you use the Media Player, you must connect the multimedia device (usually a CD-ROM player, VCR, or MIDI synthesizer) to the PC, and you must install the device in Windows NT and set up the driver to run with Windows NT. For more information, refer to the earlier section on "Installing Multimedia Equipment and Drivers."

The Media Player is a small window that contains menus, a scroll bar, and buttons. The menus enable you to open files, select the device to play on, and switch between time, frames, and tracks. The scroll bar follows the progress of the file you play. The buttons play, pause, stop, and eject the media, just like a VCR or CD-ROM player.

Unlike the Sound Recorder, you cannot use the Media Player to create custom files. To create multimedia files, you must purchase a multimedia authoring kit, such as *Multimedia ToolBook* from Asymetrix or *Guide Media Extensions* from Owl International.

Starting the Media Player

The Media Player is a Windows NT accessory, and, therefore, is located in the Accessories window.

To start the Media Player, follow these steps:

1. Activate the Accessories window in the Program Manager. You see the Media Player icon (see fig. 16.14).

2. Choose the Media Player. (Double-click on the Media Player icon with the mouse or press the arrow keys to select the icon and press Enter.) The Media Player window appears (see fig. 16.15).

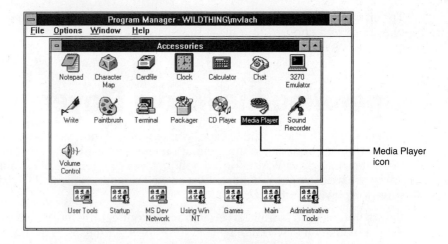

Fig. 16.14

Use the Media
Player icon
to start the
Media Player
application.

Fig. 16.15

The Media Player
window enables
you to open and
play multimedia
files.

Choosing and Configuring a Media Device

Before you can play a multimedia game, movie, or story, you must
specify the device on which you plan to play the game, movie, or story.
Two kinds of devices exist: simple and compound. *Simple* devices play
whatever is physically loaded into the device. To play a *compound* device, you must choose the device and then open the file you want to
play. The listed devices reflect the equipment and drivers you previously installed.

To choose a media device, follow these steps:

1. Choose the **D**evice menu (see fig. 16.16).

2. Select the device that you want to play. Simple devices are not
   followed by a dialog box.

   Compound devices (like **V**ideo for Windows, **M**IDI Sequencer, and
   Sound in fig. 16.16) are followed by a dialog box.

3. If you selected a compound device, select the file that you want to play and choose OK.

Fig. 16.16

The devices listed in the Device menu depend on what is installed on the system.

To configure a device, you can use the Control Panel as described in a previous section, or you can choose the **D**evice **C**onfigure command from the Media Player. The second option is a shortcut, and will display the same dialog accessed by using the Control Panel Driver's **S**etup command (see fig. 16.17). The contents of this dialog will vary depending on the device selected. Make any device driver changes necessary, and select OK or press Enter to continue.

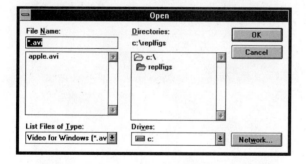

Fig. 16.17

The Open dialog box appears when you select **V**ideo for Windows from the **D**evice menu.

If you installed and configured a midi-music card or sound card with on board midi and attached speakers, you can open and play one of two 2-minute music files included in the Windows NT installation directory: CANYON.MID and PASSPORT.MID.

Opening a File

After you specify a compound device and open a file, you can open a different file to play on the same device, without choosing the device again (unless you want to switch to a different device).

To open a file, follow these steps:

1. Choose the File menu and select the Open command. The Open dialog box appears.

2. Select in the Drives list the drive where the file is located.

3. Select the kind of file you want to list in the List Files of Type list. (Select MIDI Sequencer, for example, to list files with the extensions MID and RMI.)

4. In the Directories list, select the directory that contains the file.

5. In the File Name list, select the file that you want to open.

6. If the file is located elsewhere on your network, select the Network button to choose from a list of other computers to connect to.

7. If the file selected is a Video for Windows file, a second window opens and displays the video image ready for playback (see fig. 16.18).

Fig. 16.18

Displaying the APPLE.AVI animation using Media Player.

8. Choose OK.

Playing a Media File

After you select a device and either insert the media (if you select a simple device) or open a file (if you select a compound device), Media

Player is ready to play. The buttons in the Media Player window enable you to play, pause, stop, and eject the media (if the device supports ejecting).

Choose the following buttons to operate the Media Player:

Button	Action
Play	Begin playing the media in the simple device or begin playing the file in the compound device
Pause	Pause the media (choose either Pause or Play to restart)
Stop	Stop the media (choose Play to restart)
Eject	Eject the media (if the device supports this action)
Rewind/Previous Mark	Rewind the media to the beginning, or move the slider to a left mark if one is set
Page Left	Step back in the media by 10 percent increments
Page Right	Step forward in the media by 10 percent increments
Fast Fwd/Next Mark	Fast forward the media to the end, or move the slider to a right mark if one is set
Mark In	Mark the beginning of a selected section of the media
Mark Out	Mark the end of a selected section of the media
Track Bar	Show the media sequence and indicate the current playing position with the slider, which moves to the right as the media plays

The Media Player can also be displayed in an abbreviated form, showing only the Play button, Stop button, and Track Bar slider (see fig. 16.19). Use the shortcut key Ctrl+W to switch between normal and abbreviated views. If you are working with a video sequence, switching to abbreviated view attaches the buttons and slider to the video window (see fig. 16.20).

Fig. 16.19

The Media
Player's abbre-
viated form
displays only the
Play button, Stop
button, and Track
Bar slider.

Fig. 16.20

Playing the
APPLE.AVI
animation with
the abbreviated
Media Player.

Changing the Scale, Moving to a Different Position, and Making Selections

By default, no scale appears below the slider in Media Player, but three
scales—Time, Frames, and Tracks—are available. The Time scale
shows your progress through the media or file by time. The Frame
scale displays the frame count for a video sequence. The Track scale
counts the tracks as the media or file plays. Because these scales appear below the scroll bar, you can move to a specific position in the file
by watching the scale as you move the slider.

To change the scale, follow these steps:

1. Choose the **S**cale menu.

2. Select the **T**ime command. The Time scale appears (see fig. 16.21).

   You can also select the **F**rames or **T**racks command. The Frames
   scale is shown in figure 16.22, and the Tracks scale is shown in
   figure 16.23.

Fig. 16.21

Track time using
Media Player's
Time scale.

Fig. 16.22

Media Player
displaying the
Frame scale.

Fig. 16.23

Media Player
displaying the
Track scale.

You can move to a different spot in the file by clicking on the left or right arrow on the right side of the track bar; dragging the slider; clicking in the slider bar; or pressing the left-arrow, right-arrow, PgUp, or PgDn keys on the keyboard.

You can select a portion of a media sequence for playback or for copying to the Clipboard using two different methods. With the first method, you use the Mark In and Mark Out buttons to set or remove markers in the track bar. With the second method, you use the **E**dit **S**election command.

To set a selection using the marker buttons, follow these steps:

1. Move the slider in the toolbar to where you want to mark the end point of the selection, then select the Mark Out button. A marker appears at the slider location.

2. Move the slider in the toolbar to where you want to mark the beginning point of the selection, then select the Mark In button. A second marker appears at the slider location. The selection area between the beginning and ending markers displays as a crosshatched band (see fig. 16.24).

3. To move the beginning marker to a new position, move the slider to a new location and select the Mark In button. To move the end marker, move the slider and select the Mark Out button.

Fig. 16.24

The Slider Bar
displays the
progress of the
animation being
played.

To set a selection using the menus, follow these steps:

1. Select the **Edit Selection** command. The Set Selection dialog box displays (see fig. 16.25). Notice that the dialog box displays the selection information in a mode consistent with the Scale type currently selected.

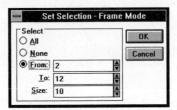

Fig. 16.25

The Set Selection
dialog box.

2. Choose a selection option, either **All**, **None**, or **From**. If you select From, you need to fill in the values for the From, To, or Size fields to select a portion of the media sequence. Notice that the values displayed are consistent with the Scale mode; Time is displayed in seconds, Frames in frame numbers, and Tracks in track numbers.

3. Choose OK or press Enter. The selected region is marked in the toolbar by a cross-hatched band (refer to fig. 16.24).

Setting Media Player Options

Media Player options fall into two main areas. The first set of options control what happens in Media Player when the end of a sequence is reached. The second set of options control how an embedded Media Player object is displayed and played in a target OLE client. The procedures for embedding a Media Player object in an OLE client are covered in the next section.

If you want to change Media Player options, select the **Edit Options** command. The Options dialog box displays (see fig. 16.26). Make your selections and choose OK or press Enter to continue.

Fig. 16.26

The Options
dialog box.

You can select the following end-of-sequence options in the Options
dialog box:

Auto Rewind	Automatically rewinds a media sequence to the beginning when the end is reached.
Auto **R**epeat	Automatically repeats a media sequence when the end is reached.

You can select the following OLE options in the Options dialog box:

Cap**t**ion	Defines the name that is displayed on an embedded media clip object.
Border around object	Turns on or off the border for the icon displayed for an embedded media clip object.
Play in client document	Plays the embedded multimedia sequence from within the target document.
Control bar on playback	Turns on or off display of the abbreviated Media Player control bar during playback of an embedded media sequence.
Dither Picture to VGA Colors	Dithers the colors used in an embedded video object so that it will use the standard VGA palette.

Setting Video Viewing Options

Video for Windows provides its own separate set of options that you can change from the Video Playback Options dialog box (see fig. 16.27). As previously mentioned, you can display this dialog box by selecting the **D**evice **C**onfigure command or by selecting the Control Panel Drivers **S**etup command. Because these options can be used to interactively control how Media Player displays a video sequence during playback, they are discussed in detail here.

The Video
Playback Options
dialog box.

You can select the following video options in the Video Playback Options dialog box:

Zoom by 2	Doubles the size of the video playback window.
Play only if waveform device available	Plays the video sequence only if a sound track associated with the video can access a WAVE playback device.
Always seek to **n**earest key frame	Chooses the nearest full frame when a jump to a nonconsecutive frame occurs.
Skip video frames if behind	Forces Media Player to skip video frames in order to keep up with an associated sound track.
Don't buffer offscreen	Increases the playback rate by eliminating the offscreen buffer used to buffer image data during playback.

Exiting Media Player

After you finish playing the multimedia file or device, choose the File menu and select the Exit command. If the multimedia file or device is not finished playing when you exit, a simple device continues playing, and you must turn off the actual device.

Controlling Volume in Sound and Music Applications

When playing back multimedia sound and music, you can use the Volume Control application to change volume, balance, and mute settings. You can find Volume Control in the Program Manager Applications group (see fig. 16.28). Start Volume Control by double-clicking the icon in the Accessories group, or by selecting the icon with the keyboard arrow keys and pressing Enter. The Volume Control application starts and displays as shown in figure 16.29.

Volume Control icon

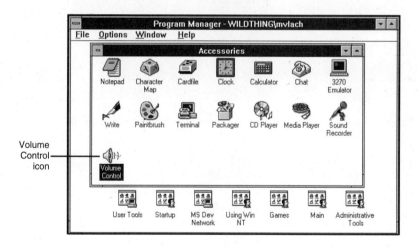

To change the audio settings for your sound card, follow these steps:

1. To change sound volume, move the Master vertical volume slider up or down.

2. To change sound left/right stereo balance, move the Master horizontal balance slider left or right.

3. To mute sound output, push the **M**ute button. This mutes the sound, and the button label changes to Un-**M**ute. Press the button again to unmute the sound.

If you have midi-music installed on your system, either as part of your sound card or as a separate device, you can change the audio settings for it as well.

To change the audio settings for your midi-music synthesizer, follow these steps:

1. Select the **E**xpanded View command from the Control menu, or use the shortcut key Alt+E to display an expanded view of the Volume Control application (see fig. 16.30).

2. To change midi-music volume, move the Synth vertical volume slider up or down.

3. To change midi-music left/right stereo balance, move the Synth horizontal balance slider left or right.

4. To mute midi-music output, click the **M**ute button. The button label changes to Un-**M**ute. Press the button again to unmute midi-music.

Embedding Sound and Video in Applications

One of the promises of multimedia is that you can integrate pieces from different applications into a unified presentation. In its simplest form, a multimedia presentation may consist of a file that contains embedded sound or video.

You can embed sound and video into a file by using one of three methods. The first—and preferable—way is to start from the Media Player or Sound Recorder and copy the media sequence or sound to the Clipboard, then switch to the target application and paste the object into your target document. This is the simplest and most elegant method resulting in a Media Player or Sound Recorder icon being placed in your document. Double-clicking the icon starts Media Player or Sound Recorder and automatically plays the media sequence or sound. The second method is to start from the target application, select that application's Insert Object command, and select a Media Clip or Sound object to insert. This starts Media Player or Sound Recorder. Set up a media sequence or sound, then select the Update command or exit the Media Player or Sound Recorder application in order to update your document. The third method involves using the Object Packager accessory to package a media object together with the related application and embed the object as an icon in the target document. Refer to Chapter 6, "Embedding and Linking Windows NT Applications," for details about how to use the Object Packager.

To embed sound or video in a file, all the applications involved must support object linking and embedding, or OLE. Sound Recorder and Media Player are OLE servers; the application in which you want to embed a sound or video object must be an OLE client.

After a sound or video file is embedded in a document, an icon appears in the document. The icon for a Sound Recorder object is a microphone; the icon for a Media Player object is a reel of film. If the embedded object is a WAVE-format sound file, you can double-click the microphone icon to play the sound. If the embedded object needs the Media Player (as do MIDI or Video for Windows files), when you double-click the film-reel icon, the Media Player appears on-screen. You can choose to have the sequence load and pause or play automatically depending on how you created the object (see the previous section on Media Player).

To embed a multimedia object by starting from the Media Player or Sound Recorder, follow these steps:

1. In the Accessories Window, choose the Media Player or Sound Recorder. (Double-click the respective icon or select the icon by using the arrow keys and pressing Enter.)

2. Set up a media sequence in Media Player or a sound file in Sound Recorder using the steps described in the previous sections. These applications are acting as the OLE servers. Use the Media Player options to mark specific areas of a media sequence for copying to the Clipboard and to control how the object is displayed and played back from your target document.

3. Select the **E**dit **C**opy command from Sound Recorder, or select the **E**dit **C**opy Object command from Media Player to place the object on the Clipboard.

4. From the target application, which is acting as the OLE client, set the insertion point where you want to place the object in your document and select the **E**dit **P**aste command. A Media Player or Sound Recorder icon is displayed in your document (see fig. 16.31).

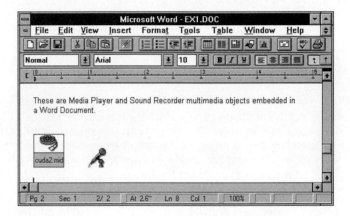

Fig. 16.31

You can package objects in applications using OLE.

5. Save the document.

To embed a multimedia object by starting from the target application, follow these steps:

1. From the target document, which is acting as the OLE client, set the insertion point where you want to place the object in your document and select the **I**nsert **O**bject command. Note that the name for this command varies depending on your application. The Object dialog box displays (see fig. 16.32).

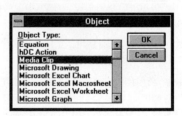

Fig. 16.32

The Object dialog box.

2. Select the Media Clip object type to embed a Media Player object or select the Sound object type to embed a Sound Player object. Choose OK or press Enter to continue. The Media Player or Sound Recorder application is started. Note that no media sequence or sound file is loaded at this point.

3. Set up a media sequence in Media Player or a sound file in Sound Recorder using the steps described in the previous sections. These applications are acting as the OLE servers. Use the Media Player options to mark specific areas of a media sequence for copying to the Clipboard and to control how the object is displayed and played back from your target document.

4. To exit from Media Player, select the **File** **Exit & Return** command. To exit from Sound Recorder, select the **File** **Exit** command. You are prompted to update your target document. Select **Yes** to update and quit the Media Player or Sound Recorder application. A Media Player or Sound Recorder icon is displayed in your document (refer to fig. 16.31).

5. To update your document without exiting the multimedia application, choose the **File** **Update** command. Media Player or Sound Recorder remains open for further editing of the object. A Media Player or Sound Recorder icon is displayed in your document (refer to fig. 16.31).

6. Save the document.

When you double-click the icon in your document using either of the preceding methods, the Sound Recorder or Media Player window starts up and the sound or media sequence plays. If the object is from the Media Player, the options you set for the object when you created it affect whether the Media Player window displays and whether the media sequence plays automatically. If the object is from the Sound Recorder, the Sound Recorder window always displays and the sound file plays automatically. If you don't want a sound to play automatically, embed the sound using the Media Player rather than the Sound Recorder. If you absolutely need to use Sound Recorder and you don't want the sound to play automatically, you can use the third method, which requires that you package the sound file using the Object Packager. Refer to Chapter 6, "Embedding and Linking Windows NT Applications," for details about how to do this.

Using the MIDI Mapper

When you install a device that supports MIDI, such as the Sound Blaster sound card, an application for controlling MIDI devices is added by default. The application, MIDI Mapper, appears as a new icon in the Control Panel. You can use MIDI Mapper to choose a preconfigured MIDI setup for the MIDI device or to create custom setup specifications.

Choosing a MIDI Setup

When installing Windows NT, some predefined MIDI settings designed to work with common MIDI devices are included. A new device probably will conform to one of these settings and, therefore, work flawlessly with Windows NT. However, you can change the settings by using the MIDI Mapper application in the Control Panel. You may need to change these settings if you use a nonstandard MIDI setup or if the device doesn't include a MIDI setup.

To alter a MIDI setting, follow these steps:

1. In the Program Manager, select the Main window and choose the Control Panel. You can see the MIDI Mapper icon if you installed a MIDI device (see fig. 16.33).

Fig. 16.33

The MIDI Mapper icon in the Control Panel window.

MIDI Mapper icon

2. Choose the MIDI Mapper icon. The MIDI Mapper dialog box appears (see fig. 16.34).

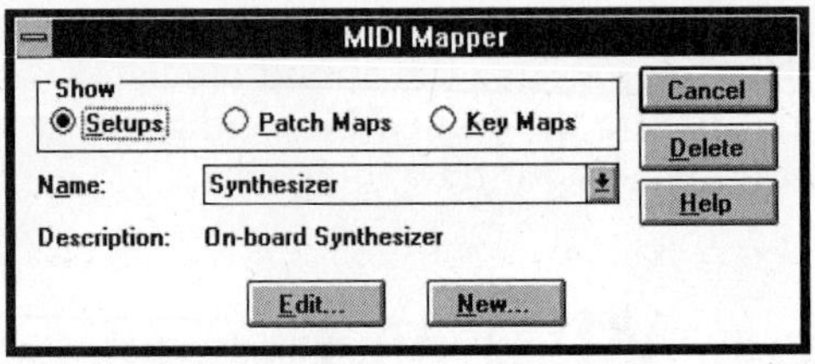

Fig. 16.34

The MIDI Mapper dialog box.

3. Make sure that the Show Setups option is selected. Then from the Name list, select the setup you want to use.

4. Choose Close.

If no setting for the device is listed, first call the manufacturer to see whether an updated MIDIMAP.CFG setup file, which includes a setup for this device, is available. If an updated file is available, make a backup of the existing MIDIMAP.CFG file and copy the new file to the

SYSTEM32 subdirectory in the Windows NT directory. If no setup file is available, you may need to create a custom file.

Creating a Custom MIDI Setup

All MIDI devices conform to certain musical specifications. However, the output is not mapped in a standard way, which is why different MIDI setups are available for different pieces of equipment. Choosing the correct mapping is like using computer keyboards from different manufacturers, each of which uses a proprietary key layout—to get a K on-screen, you have to know where the K key is, and the PC also has to know.

Similarly, Windows NT must know which key and which channel the MIDI device uses for each sound. The process is known as *mapping*, which means that you map the PC keys and channels to the corresponding keys and channels in the device. This way, when you press a key that is supposed to play a middle-octave C from an acoustic grand piano, you get a middle-octave C that sounds like an acoustic grand piano, rather than a high D that sounds as though the note was played by an oboe.

This procedure is complex and requires that you know a great deal about the device. Check the documentation to see whether information is provided about key, patch, and channel mapping; if not, call the manufacturer to get the information (first read through this section so that you understand what information you need). Also be aware that the application you use to play the device must be Windows NT-compatible to take advantage of the settings you create in the MIDI Mapper.

To set up a MIDI device, you need to know whether the device is a base-level or an extended-level synthesizer. *Base-level* synthesizers meet the minimum MIDI requirements; *extended-level* synthesizers can play more notes simultaneously than base-level synthesizers, which produce richer sounds.

Four basic steps are involved in setting up a MIDI device:

1. You must set up the device to receive MIDI messages on multiple MIDI channels. Refer to the device's documentation to learn how to perform this procedure.

2. You must create a key map for both percussion instruments and melodic instruments that play in the wrong key.

3. You must create patch maps for both the percussion and melodic instruments. A patch defines a sound and all of the sound's voices.

4. You must create the channel map for the synthesizer.

Creating key, patch, and channel maps all are similar processes. First, you name the map (if you are creating a map). Then, a table-like chart appears, listing possible specifications. In the left columns, information describes the MIDI source; you cannot change this information. In the remaining columns, however, identified with an underlined letter in the column headings, the information pertains to the destination—the sound device. You can change the settings in these columns. To change the settings, select the box in the same row as the corresponding sound or channel at the left. When you change information in a destination column, you map the instructions going out from the computer to the appropriate sounds on the device.

Creating a Key Map

Create a key map for the synthesizer if the synthesizer doesn't conform to MIDI standards which specify that certain keys play certain sounds or a particular octave. MIDI Mapper provides up to 2,048 key maps for each of 128 patch entries for the 16 allowable patch maps.

If the synthesizer plays certain melodic sounds at registrations different from MIDI standards, you may need to create two types of key maps: a map for percussion sounds and a map for melodic sounds.

To create a key map, follow these steps:

1. Choose the MIDI Mapper application in the Control Panel. (Double-click on the MIDI Mapper icon or press the arrow keys to select the application and then press Enter.) The MIDI Mapper dialog box appears.

2. Select the **Key** Maps option.

3. Choose the **New** button. The New MIDI Key Map... dialog box appears, as shown in figure 16.35.

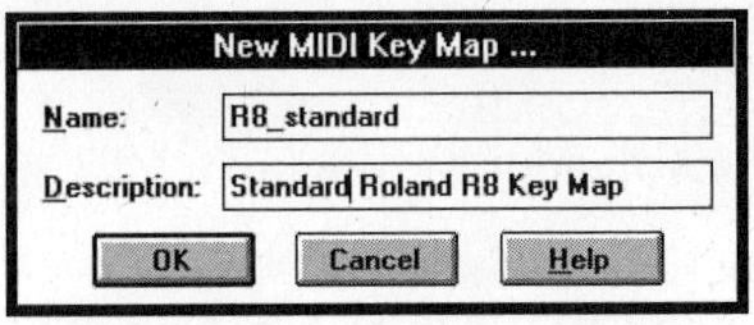

Fig. 16.35

The New MIDI Key Map... dialog box.

| New MIDI Key Map ... |
| **Name:** R8_standard |
| **Description:** Standard Roland R8 Key Map |
| OK   Cancel   Help |

4. In the **Name** text box, type a name (up to 15 characters) for the new MIDI key map. In the **Description** text box, type a description (up to 28 characters).

5. Choose OK or press Enter. The MIDI Key Map dialog box appears, as shown in figure 16.36, with the following columns:

Src Key
Source Key Number. The MIDI-specified keys; you cannot change these keys.

Src Key Name
Source Key Name. The names of the instruments associated with the keys, as specified by MIDI standards; you cannot change these names.

Dest Key
Destination Key Number. The key on the synthesizer that plays when you press the source key; you can change this number to any number from 0 to 127.

6. Select the **D**est Key that you want to change, which causes up and down arrows to appear at the right side of the text box. Click the up arrow to raise the destination key number or click the down arrow to lower the number. You also can press the Tab key to select the existing destination key number and type a new number.

To show the key you want to change, you may need to scroll the window. Click the up or down arrow in the scroll bar or press PgUp or PgDn.

7. Choose OK or press Enter. A dialog box appears, confirming the changes.

8. Choose **Yes** to confirm or **No** to discard the changes (or choose Cancel to return to the MIDI Key Map dialog box).

9. To close the MIDI Mapper dialog box, choose Close.

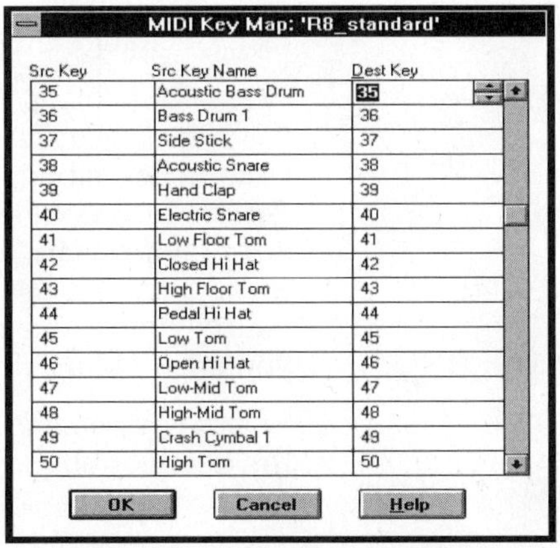

Src Key	Src Key Name	Dest Key
35	Acoustic Bass Drum	35
36	Bass Drum 1	36
37	Side Stick	37
38	Acoustic Snare	38
39	Hand Clap	39
40	Electric Snare	40
41	Low Floor Tom	41
42	Closed Hi Hat	42
43	High Floor Tom	43
44	Pedal Hi Hat	44
45	Low Tom	45
46	Open Hi Hat	46
47	Low-Mid Tom	47
48	High-Mid Tom	48
49	Crash Cymbal 1	49
50	High Tom	50

MIDI Key Map: 'R8_standard'

OK   Cancel   Help

Fig. 16.36

The MIDI Key Map dialog box lists the sounds for keys 35 through 81 (the MIDI-specified percussion keys).

Creating a Patch Map

A patch describes a sound, such as an acoustic grand piano or a dulcimer. If the synthesizer uses patches that differ from the MIDI specifications, you must create a set of patches for percussion instruments and for melodic instruments.

To create a patch, follow these steps:

1. Choose the MIDI Mapper in the Control Panel.

2. Select the **P**atch Maps option and choose the **N**ew button. The New MIDI Patch Map dialog box appears which looks just like the New Key Map dialog box.

3. In the **N**ame text box, type a name (up to 15 characters) for the new MIDI key map. In the **D**escription text box, type a description (up to 28 characters).

4. Choose OK or press Enter. The MIDI Patch Map dialog box appears that contains the following columns (see fig. 16.37):

    Src Patch   *Source Patch Number.* MIDI-specified patch numbers; you cannot change these numbers. Some synthesizers number patches 0 through 127; others number from 1 through 128. Select the sequence the synthesizer uses by choosing a button at the top of the dialog box.

    Src Patch Name   *Source Patch Name.* Names of sounds or instruments associated with the source patch numbers, specified by MIDI standards; you cannot change these names.

    Dest Patch   *Destination Patch.* Patch numbers the synthesizer plays to create sounds described in the Source Patch Name column. If the synthesizer confirms to MIDI standards, these numbers are the same as Source Patch numbers. Otherwise, you must change these numbers.

    Volume %   *Volume by percent.* Volume at which the destination plays the sound.

The default, 100, means that the sound plays at 100 percent. To play louder, set a **V**olume % greater than 100; to play softer, set a number less than 100.

Key **M**ap Name — Links the patch to the correct key map—a custom or an existing key map. Selecting this option shows a list of all existing key map names. Several preexisting key maps exist, such as _1 Octave_, which you can use to map a melodic patch to an octave lower.

5. If the synthesizer's patch numbers start at 0 rather than 1, choose the 0 Based Patches button; if the numbers start at 1 rather than 0, choose the 1 Based Patches button.

6. To change the destination patch number (the patch number in the synthesizer that maps to the existing source patch number), select the appropriate box in the Dest Patch column, which causes an up and down arrow to appear at the right side of the box. Click the up arrow to increase the number; click the down arrow to decrease the number; or press the Tab key enough times to select the patch number you want to change and type a new number. If the patch you want to change isn't visible, use the scroll bar to show more numbers or press Tab enough times to scroll to the number you want to change.

7. To change the destination patch volume, in the Volume % column, select the volume box in the same row as the patch you want to change. Click the up or down arrow to change the number or select the existing number and type a new number.

8. To map the patch to a different key map, in the Key **M**ap Name column, select the key map name box in the same row as the patch you want to map differently. A list of all existing key maps appears. Select the name of the key map that you want the patch to use.

9. Choose OK or press Enter. A dialog box appears that confirms the changes.

10. Choose **Y**es to confirm or **N**o to discard the changes (or choose Cancel to return to the MIDI Patch Map dialog box).

11. Choose Close to close the MIDI Mapper dialog box.

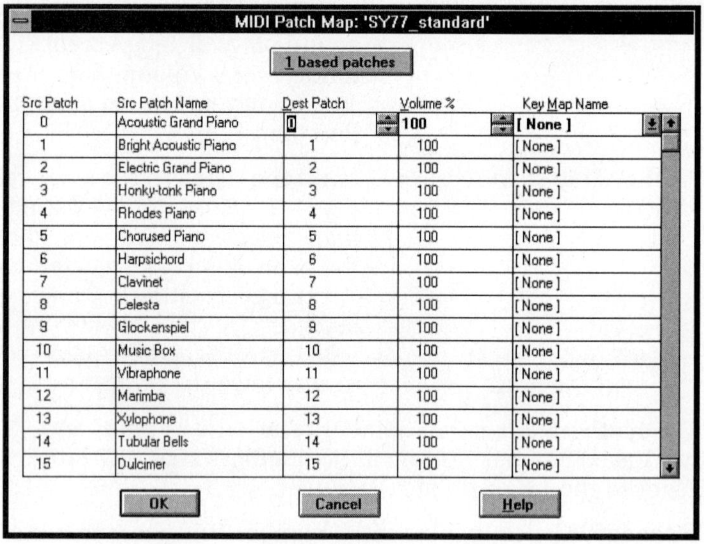

Src Patch	Src Patch Name	Dest Patch	Volume %	Key Map Name
0	Acoustic Grand Piano	0	100	[None]
1	Bright Acoustic Piano	1	100	[None]
2	Electric Grand Piano	2	100	[None]
3	Honky-tonk Piano	3	100	[None]
4	Rhodes Piano	4	100	[None]
5	Chorused Piano	5	100	[None]
6	Harpsichord	6	100	[None]
7	Clavinet	7	100	[None]
8	Celesta	8	100	[None]
9	Glockenspiel	9	100	[None]
10	Music Box	10	100	[None]
11	Vibraphone	11	100	[None]
12	Marimba	12	100	[None]
13	Xylophone	13	100	[None]
14	Tubular Bells	14	100	[None]
15	Dulcimer	15	100	[None]

Fig. 16.37

The MIDI Patch Map dialog box enables you to create or edit a patch map.

Creating a Channel Map

If the channels on the synthesizer don't map to the standard MIDI channels, you need to create a channel map. Sixteen MIDI channels are available; a base-level synthesizer uses channels 13 through 15 for melodic sounds and 16 for percussion sounds; an extended-level synthesizer uses channels 1 through 9 for melodic sounds and 10 for percussion.

To create a channel map, follow these steps:

1. Choose the MIDI Mapper in the Control Panel.
2. Select the **S**etups option and choose the **N**ew button. The New MIDI Setup dialog box appears.
3. In the **N**ame text box, type a name (up to 15 characters) for the new MIDI key map. In the **D**escription text box, type a description (up to 28 characters).
4. Choose OK or press Enter. The MIDI Setup dialog box that appears contains the following columns (see fig. 16.38):

Src Chan	*Source Channel.* MIDI channels specified by the application; you cannot change these numbers.
Dest Chan	*Destination Channel.* Channel the synthesizer uses to play the sounds in the source channel. If the synthesizer supports the MIDI standard, this channel is the same as the source channel. If not, change the channel number.

Port Name	Port you want the channel to use. When you select a box in the **P**ort Name column, a drop-down list appears that shows all the MIDI device drivers connected to ports in the computer. Select the driver for the channel to use (not all channels must use the same port).
Patch **M**ap Name	Name of the patch map to use with the specified channel. When you select a Patch **M**ap Name box, a list of existing patch map names appears; select the patch you want to use. For melodic source channels, select a melodic patch map; for percussion source channels, select a percussion patch map.
Active	Activates or deactivates the selected port (available only if you selected a **P**ort Name). If you select the **A**ctive option (an X appears in the check box), sound from the channel *is* sent to the selected port; if deselected, sound *isn't* sent.

5. If necessary, change the destination channel by using the **D**est Chan option and selecting the appropriate box in the **D**est Channel column, which causes up and down arrows to appear at the right end of the box. Click the up or down arrow to change the number or select the existing channel number and type a new number. You can press the Tab key to move between the boxes in the **D**est Channel column.

6. If necessary, change the name of the port you want the selected channel to use by selecting from the list that appears when you select a box in the **P**ort Name column.

7. If necessary, select the patch map you want each channel to use. To perform this step, select the box in the Patch **M**ap Name column adjacent to the channel whose patch map you want to change.

8. If necessary, activate or deactivate the port by selecting or deselecting the Active option.

9. Choose OK or press Enter. A dialog box appears that confirms the changes.

10. Choose **Y**es to confirm or **N**o to discard the changes (or choose Cancel to return to the MIDI Setup dialog box).

11. Choose Close to close the MIDI Mapper dialog box.

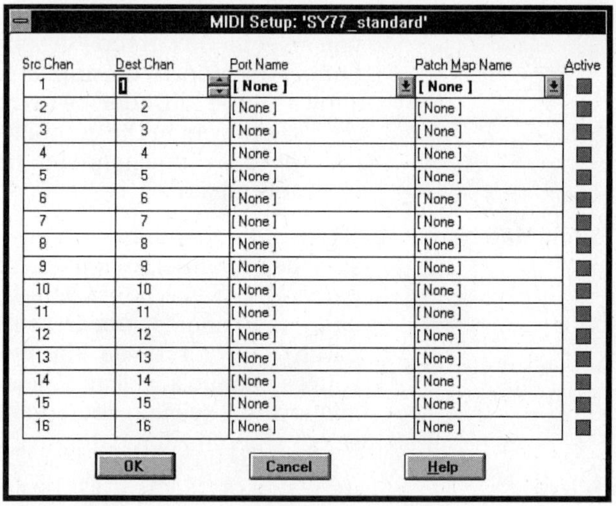

Fig. 16.38

Use the MIDI
Setup dialog box
to map MIDI
channels to
the correct
channels on the
synthesizer.

Editing and Deleting Maps

Besides creating maps, you also can edit existing maps. The process is
the same as the methods you used to create a map (see the previous
sections), but—rather than choosing the New button—you choose the
Edit button in the MIDI Mapper dialog box, and you don't have to supply a name or description.

Similarly, you can delete an existing map by selecting the appropriate
category from the Show group (Setups, Patch Maps, or Key Maps),
selecting the map name from the Name list, and then choosing the
Delete button.

Using the CD Player

If you listen to audio CDs using your CD-ROM drive, you can control
playback of CD tracks by using the Media Player described previously,
or you can use the CD Player application. You can find CD Player in the
Program Manager Applications group (see fig. 16.39). You start it by
double-clicking the icon in the Accessories group, or by selecting the
icon with the keyboard arrow keys and pressing Enter. If an audio CD is
present in the CD-ROM drive, CD Player starts and displays, as shown
in fig. 16.40. If no audio CD is present in the CD-ROM drive, CD Player
displays a warning message and quits.

16 — USING MULTIMEDIA

665

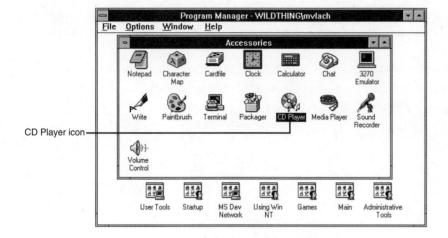

CD Player icon

Fig. 16.39

The CD Player icon in the Program Manager Applications group.

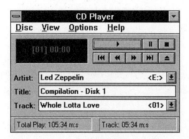

Fig. 16.40

The CD Player application in use.

The primary advantage of using CD Player over Media Player is that you have much better control over playback of tracks. You can create names for the CD title, artist, and tracks. You also can play back tracks in an order that you define by using a *Playlist* (described later). The only disadvantage of using CD Player is that you can't embed a CD audio sequence into another application. For this you need Media Player.

CD Player controls are laid out in similar fashion to those found on a typical hardware CD player. There are four main groups in the CD Player Window: the Toolbar, the Playback controls, the Disk/Track Info fields, and the Status Bar. You can toggle on or off the display of the Toolbar, Disk/Track Info, and Status Bar by selecting the View menu and checking or unchecking the name for each group. Display of the Playback controls can't be disabled.

The functions for each of the items in the four CD Player groups are defined as follows:

The Toolbar buttons:

Selected Order	Plays the tracks in Playlist order
Random Order	Plays the tracks in random order
Single Disk Play	Plays a single CD in Playlist order
Multi Disk Play	Plays tracks from multiple CDs (if the player supports it)
Continuous	Plays tracks continuously in the order selected
Intro Play	Plays the first 10 seconds of each track
Current Track Time	Displays how long the current track has played
Remaining Track Time	Displays the remaining play time for the current track
Remaining Playlist Time	Displays the remaining play time for the current Playlist
Edit Playlist	Starts the Playlist editor dialog box

The Playback controls:

Track/Time Display	Shows track number and time information for the current track
Play	Starts playback for the current track
Pause	Pauses playback for the current track; The Track/Time display blinks
Stop	Stops playback and resets the CD to the beginning of Track 1
Skip Back	Skips to the beginning of the previous track
Fast Reverse	Rewinds the current track
Fast Forward	Advances the current track
Skip Forward	Skips to the beginning of the next track
Eject Button	Ejects the CD from the drive

The Disk/Track Info:

Artist	The name of the artist for the current CD and CD-ROM drive
Title	The title of the CD
Track	The name of the current track

The Status Bar:	
Total Play	Total play time for the entire CD
Track	Total play time for the current track

Playing CDs

CD Player can play single or multiple CDs using a variety of options. This section describes how to use CD Player for basic playback and for single and multiple CD playback with various playback options.

For basic CD playback of individual tracks, perform the following steps:

1. Insert an audio CD into the CD-ROM drive.

2. From the Program Manager Accessories Group, start CD Player by double-clicking its icon, or by pressing Enter from the keyboard after selecting the icon with the arrow keys.

3. When CD Player starts, select the Play button to start playing from Track 1 of the CD.

4. Pause and restart playing by repeatedly selecting the Pause button.

5. Stop playing and move to the beginning of Track 1 by selecting the Stop button.

6. To skip to another track, press the Skip Forward or Skip Back buttons. If playback is stopped, restart playback on the newly selected track by pressing the Play button.

7. To fast forward or rewind within or over track boundaries, select the Fast Reverse or Fast Forward buttons.

8. When you're done with that CD, press the Eject button. Notice that after the CD ejects, the Disk/Track Info fields indicate that there is no audio CD present in the drive.

9. Insert another CD. The Disk/Track Info fields now indicate that a CD is present in the drive.

For continuous single/multiple CD playback with various track ordering and options, use the following steps:

1. If your CD-ROM drive supports single CDs only, the **O**ptions **S**ingle Disk Play command is selected by default and the **O**ptions **M**ultidisc Play command is disabled. If your CD-ROM drive supports multiple CDs, both commands are available. If you choose the multiple CD option, the following steps apply to the currently selected CD.

2. To start playback in Playlist order, select the **O**ptions Selected **O**rder command and press the Play button.

3. To start playback in random order, select the **O**ptions **R**andom Order command and press the Play button.

4. To play the selected CD continuously in the currently selected order, select the **O**ptions **C**ontinuous command and press Play to start playback. This command is a toggle; selecting it again disables continuous play.

5. To get a 10-second preview of the selected CD's tracks in the currently selected order, select the **O**ptions Intro Play command and press Play to start playback. This command is a toggle; selecting it again disables Intro Play.

6. To save your options settings when you quit CD Player, make sure the **O**ptions **S**ave Settings on Exit command is checked.

T   I   P   Use the Toolbar. All of the preceding options are more easily accessed from the Toolbar. Also, there are several useful time information commands supported in the Toolbar that are not accessible elsewhere in CD Player.

Creating and Using a CD Playlist

A Playlist determines the order in which CD Player plays tracks from a single CD or multiple CDs (assuming, of course, that the Selected Order option is enabled). The default Playlist, which is used when CD Player is first started, puts all tracks in CD order. The tracks play exactly as listed on the CD's package. You can modify the track playback order and provide other useful name information by creating a custom Playlist.

Use the following steps to create a custom Playlist:

1. Select the **D**isc Edit Play **L**ist command. The CD Player: Disc Settings dialog box displays (see fig. 16.41). If your CD-ROM drive supports multiple CDs, or you have multiple CD-ROMs connected to your system, you can select from the available drives in the Drive list. The drive you select is used as the current CD in the following steps.

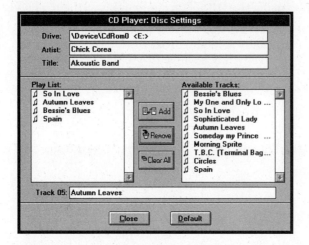

Fig. 16.41

The CD Player:
Disc Settings
dialog box.

2. To create some useful names for the current CD, first select the Artist field and type the name of the artist. Then select the Title field and type the title of the CD.

3. To create some useful track names for the current CD, select the first track in the Available Tracks list, then type a new name in the Track *<number>* field, where *<number>* stands for the currently selected track number. Repeat this process for each of the tracks on the currently selected CD.

4. To add tracks to the Playlist, select one or more tracks from the Available Tracks list and then press the Add button to add them to the Playlist. Repeat this process as many times as you want, and add the tracks in any order that you see fit. You can also add tracks multiple times to the Playlist.

5. To remove tracks from the Playlist, select one or more tracks from the Play List list box, then press the Remove button. If you want to remove all tracks from the Playlist, press the Clear All button.

6. If you want to reset the Playlist to its default CD order, select the Default button.

7. If you are working with multiple CDs, you can select a different drive from the Drive list and repeat the process starting from step 2.

8. When you're finished editing, click the **C**lose button. You are prompted to save your changes. Answer **Y**es, and the new Playlist is used as the CD Player default.

You can use the Playlist also to control playback of individual tracks and drives by using the Data/Track Info fields in the CD Player window:

1. If you have a Playlist set up for multiple CD-ROM drives, switch to a different CD by selecting from the list of names in the Artist field. If you have only a single drive, this field shows only the currently installed drive. Note that the Title field changes automatically to the name defined in the Playlist.

2. After you have selected an Artist, select a track to play from the Track list.

3. Press the Play button to start playback on the selected drive and track.

Summary

Multimedia is an exciting new technology that turns a PC into a sound-and-video-equipped teacher, research assistant, storyteller, or musician. Your computer can look up information, read you a story, play a tune, or any combination of these activities. Not only can you hear what the PC has to say, you also can see what it has to show. Windows NT supplies two multimedia applications and Sound Recorder. Additionally, Windows NT enables you to manage MIDI devices with the MIDI Mapper and to play audio CDs with CD Player.

One way to create custom multimedia presentations is to embed a sound or video object in a document that was created by an application that supports *object linking and embedding*, or OLE. To learn more about object linking and embedding and about using the Object Packager, read Chapter 6, "Embedding and Linking Windows NT Applications."

Using Windows NT Applets

Using Microsoft Draw

T he company that manufactures Windows has a vision for the future. This vision, "Information at Your Fingertips," calls for quick and easy access to the information stored on your computer. With multitasking and a consistent graphical user interface shared by all Windows applications, Windows goes a long way toward actualizing "Information at Your Fingertips." Windows goes even further with a concept—*object linking and embedding*, or *OLE*.

With object linking and embedding, you can use one application within another application, creating a compound document made up of files created by two or more applications. You use a *client* application such as Word for Windows to create the initial document, then use a *server applet*, such as Microsoft Draw, to create and edit embedded objects within the compound document. You never have to leave your primary application.

Microsoft Draw is an applet that comes free with Microsoft Word for Windows, Microsoft Publisher, and other applications. As an applet, it is not a stand-alone application like Windows Paintbrush—you cannot start up Microsoft Draw on its own and create a picture. Instead, you must start Word for Windows, or any other Windows application that supports the OLE concept, and start Microsoft Draw from within a document. Similarly, you cannot save a Microsoft Draw picture as a separate file—your masterpiece exists only as part of your client document.

The Microsoft Draw applet is a good complement to Windows Paintbrush, which comes free with Windows. Two general varieties of graphics applications are available: object-oriented drawing applications and bitmapped painting applications. Each type of application has its benefits.

Microsoft Draw, an object-oriented drawing application, creates objects on the screen. Squares, circles, lines, and freeform shapes created with Microsoft Draw can be edited, moved around, and layered on the screen. (See fig. 17.1 for an example of an illustration created with Microsoft Draw.)

In contrast, a bitmapped painting application, such as Microsoft Paintbrush, works in a single, flat layer on your screen. You can erase and redraw shapes created with Paintbrush, but you cannot edit them.

Fig. 17.1

An illustration created with Microsoft Draw.

Although Microsoft Draw is a simple applet that comes free with some Windows applications, it is nonetheless powerful enough that it may be the only drawing application you need. Draw is a valuable business tool that you can use to make letters, reports, and newsletters more interesting and informative. You can use Draw to create anything from a simple line drawing to a complex color composition—and have fun doing it, too.

Object linking and embedding, an important concept in Windows, furthers the dream of making information easily, quickly, and intuitively available at your fingertips. Many applications support OLE. You can embed a Windows Paintbrush painting in a Windows Write letter—or an Excel spreadsheet in a Word for Windows report. The subject of object linking and embedding is explored fully in Chapter 6.

 NOTE The step-by-step instructions in this chapter are specific to Word for Windows. Other applications use similar—but not identical—commands. A chart follows each set of instructions, describing the commands you need to use Microsoft Draw in other applications.

Starting Microsoft Draw

As an OLE-based accessory application, Microsoft Draw works only from within a document created in your client application—the application that receives the embedded object. Microsoft Draw is called the server because it originates the object. Before starting Microsoft Draw, you need to start Word for Windows or some other application that supports object linking and embedding; then open a new or existing document.

To start Microsoft Draw, follow these steps:

1. Open a Word for Windows document or create a new document.

2. Position the insertion point where you want to insert your drawing.

3. Choose the Insert Object command. The Insert Object dialog box pops up (see fig. 17.2).

4. Select Microsoft Drawing.

5. Choose OK or press Enter. Microsoft Draw pops up in a new window on your screen.

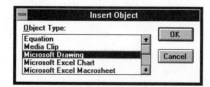

Fig. 17.2

The Insert Object dialog box.

Starting Microsoft Draw from Other Applications

Powerpoint	Choose the **F**ile Insert command. Select Microsoft Drawing from the list of applications.
Publisher	Choose the **E**dit Insert O**b**ject command.
Excel	Choose the **E**dit Insert **O**bject command.
Ami Pro	Choose the **E**dit **I**nsert command and then select New **O**bject.
Windows Write	Choose the **E**dit Insert Object command and then choose Microsoft Drawing from the **O**bject Type list.

Because Windows applets are not stand-alone applications, you cannot save the objects they create as stand-alone files. The way you save Draw objects is to update the client document and save that file. When Word for Windows is your client application, you add the Draw picture to your Word for Windows document and then save the Word for Windows file. The way you add a Draw object to a document is to *update* the client document.

Updating the Client Document

You transfer your Draw object back into the client document in either of two ways. You can update the document without closing Microsoft Draw, or you can close Microsoft Draw when you update your client document. To save your drawing, you must save your client document after you update the drawing.

To update your Word for Windows document without closing Draw, choose the **F**ile **U**pdate command in Draw.

To update your Word for Windows document and also close Microsoft Draw, choose the **F**ile E**x**it and Return to document command. A dialog box pops up asking whether you want to update your client document. Choose **Y**es.

To exit Draw without updating the Word for Windows document, choose the **F**ile E**x**it and Return to document command. When a dialog box pops up asking whether you want to update your client document, choose **N**o.

Updating the client document is the same no matter which client application you are using.

Remember: updating your client document does not save your drawing. Your drawing exists only as part of your client document. To save your drawing, you must save the client document that contains your drawing.

Editing a Microsoft Draw Picture

You can change your Draw picture as easily as you created it. Because it is part of your client document, you must first open the client application and then open the client document containing your Draw picture. Instructions for using Draw's tools to edit your drawing appear throughout the remainder of this chapter. When you finish editing, update your client document as described in the previous section, "Updating the Client Document."

To edit a Draw picture in a Word for Windows document, follow these steps:

1. Locate the Draw picture in your document.

2. With a mouse, double-click on the picture to start Draw, with your picture in its drawing window.

   or

   Select the picture by positioning the insertion point next to it, holding down the Shift key, and pressing the appropriate arrow key to pass the insertion point over the drawing. Then choose the Edit Microsoft Drawing Object command. Draw starts with your picture in the drawing window.

3. Edit your drawing.

4. Update your Word for Windows document.

When you exit Draw and return to your Word for Windows document, you normally see your drawing. If, however, the View Field Codes command is selected, you see a field code in place of your drawing. Choose the View Field Codes command again to turn it off so that you can see your drawing.

T I P

Editing a Draw Object in Other Applications

Powerpoint   Double-click the object or select the object and choose the **Edit Ed**it Microsoft Drawing command.

Publisher   Double-click the object or select the object and choose the **Edit Edit Object** command.

Excel   Double-click the object or click the object with the right mouse button to display the Shortcuts menu and choose the Edit Object command.

Ami Pro   Double-click the object.

Windows Write   Double-click on the object or select the object and choose the **Edit Edit Microsoft Drawing Object** command.

In some applications, you can use Draw to edit pictures that were not created by Draw. Thus, you can do a quick edit on a picture created by an application that does not support object linking and embedding. (You also can use this technique when you don't want to take the time to start the original graphics application or when you don't have the original application.) If you want to try it, just follow the same steps as for editing a Draw object. Be careful, however: after you edit a picture in Draw, it becomes a Draw object.

Understanding the Microsoft Draw Screen

If you have ever used a graphics application before, the Microsoft Draw screen probably looks familiar (see fig. 17.3). Even if you haven't used a graphics application, the screen is intuitive.

As in every Windows NT application, the title and menu bars are along the top of the Microsoft Draw window. On the left side is the toolbox: this has the tools you use to create your drawing. On the bottom is a color palette: you use the top half to choose line color and the bottom half to choose fill color. On the right and bottom sides of the screen are the familiar scroll bars that enable you to move around on your drawing (which is a maximum of 22 × 22 inches wide).

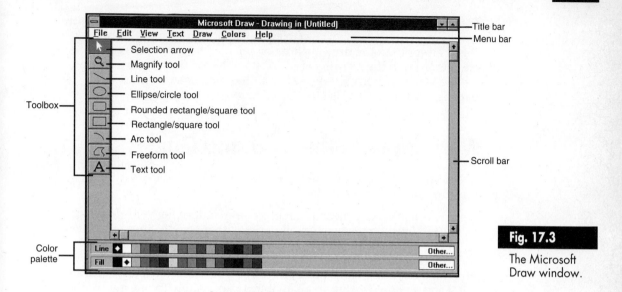

Fig. 17.3

The Microsoft
Draw window.

The general process for creating a drawing is to select menu options to
set frame and fill defaults, select the tool you want to use, select colors
from the palette, and draw your picture in the drawing area. You can
edit any object after you create it in Microsoft Draw. For details about
using the tools, palette, and menu options, refer to the following sections in this chapter.

Although you can operate most Windows applications with either a
mouse or the keyboard, you must use a mouse to use Microsoft Draw.
Some keyboard techniques and shortcuts are available in the application, but most operations require a mouse.

If you want the Microsoft Draw window to appear full-size on your
screen, click the Maximize button at the top right of the Microsoft Draw
window. Use Windows techniques to move between the Draw window
and the Word for Windows window. To learn more about basic Windows techniques, refer to Chapter 2.

Scrolling the Drawing Page

Although you can see only a portion of it, the full Microsoft Draw page
measures 22 × 22 inches. Use the horizontal scroll bar at the bottom of
the screen to scroll left and right and use the vertical scroll bar at the
right to scroll up and down.

Although scrolling enables you to view a part of the page that currently is hidden, in the Full Size view (Draw's default), you cannot draw an object larger than the drawing area or select a group of objects that extends beyond the drawing area. To do either of those, you need to use the Magnify tool. (See the section "Zooming In and Out with the Magnify Tool" later in this chapter.)

Working with the Grid and Guides

Before you begin your drawing, you should know about two helpful drawing aids: the grid and the guides.

The *grid* is a magnetic measurement system underlying your drawing. It's like an invisible piece of graph paper with magnetic lines—12 lines per inch both vertical and horizontal. These lines snap your drawing tool to 1/12-inch increments, forcing your drawn objects to conform to the grid. Using the grid is important when you want to ensure accurate sizing and when you want to align objects accurately to one another.

Guides also are helpful for precise drawing. When you turn on this option, two guides appear as intersecting dotted lines in the middle of the drawing area. You can move each guide independently by dragging it with the Selection arrow. As you drag a guide, its distance from the top of the page (horizontal guide) or left of the page (vertical guide) appears at the arrow's location. When you hold down the Ctrl key, the measurement starts from zero at the guide's starting location, making it easy to measure the size of an object. If the grid is turned on, the guides move in the 1/12-inch increments.

Choose the **D**raw Snap to Grid command to turn on the grid. To turn on the guides, choose the **D**raw Sho**w** Guides command.

Both the grid and the guides are commands you toggle on and off, using the **D**raw menu. A check mark appears to the left of each command when it's turned on. To turn off the grid or guides, select the command a second time (the check mark disappears).

To move a guide, drag it with the Selection arrow. To measure an object using the guides, follow these steps:

1. Drag the guide to one end or side of the object you want to measure.

2. Hold down Ctrl while you drag the guide with the Selection arrow; watch the measurement that appears on your screen.

Choosing a Frame, Fill, Pattern, or Line Style

Each object you draw with Microsoft Draw is a line or a shape. Lines have only one component: line style. Shapes have two components: a frame (the line around the shape's edges) and a fill (the color inside the shape). You can draw a line in any of several line styles. You can draw a shape that is framed or unframed and filled or not filled. You can choose any line style for a framed shape, and you can choose from several patterns for a filled shape.

You can make these choices from a menu at one of two times. Choices made *before* you draw an object become defaults and apply to any subsequent shapes you draw. Choices made *after* you draw and select an object or objects apply only to the selection.

Remember this rule: If no object is selected, choices you make about frame, fill, pattern, and line style become defaults and apply to future objects you draw. If any object is selected, however, your frame, fill, pattern, and line style choices apply only to the selection. (Selected objects have small black handles at each end or corner.)

Frame, fill, pattern, and line style choices are made through the **Draw** menu. The Frame**d** and **F**illed commands toggle on and off. A black diamond or check mark appearing to the left indicates that the commands are on. A black diamond indicates that Frame**d** or **F**illed is selected as a default; a check mark indicates that it is selected only for the currently selected object or objects. If two objects with conflicting frames or fills are selected, no mark appears to the left of the Frame**d** or **F**illed command.

The **P**attern and **L**ine Style commands have submenus (see fig. 17.4) from which you can choose a pattern or line style. These commands also toggle on and off, with a black diamond indicating a default choice and a check mark indicating the currently selected object or objects.

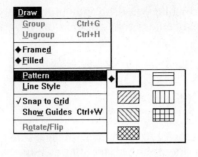

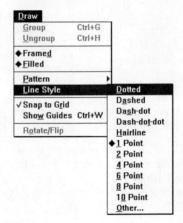

Fig. 17.4

The **P**attern and
Line Style
commands have
submenus.

To specify Frame**d**, **F**illed, **P**attern, or **L**ine Style, follow these steps:

1. Make sure that no object is selected if you want all future objects
   to be framed or filled or if you want to include a pattern or line
   style in all future objects—in other words, if you want to set a
   default.

   or

   Select the object or objects for which you want a frame, fill, pattern, or line style.

2. Choose the **Draw** Frame**d** command to frame an object or objects.

   or

   Choose the **Draw** **F**illed command to fill an object or objects.

   or

   Choose the **Draw** **P**attern command and select a pattern from the
   Pattern submenu to fill an object or objects with the pattern.

   or

Choose the **D**raw **L**ine Style command and select a line style from the Line Style submenu to frame an object or objects with the line style.

Color is another important component in the drawings you create with Microsoft Draw. Use the Line palette at the bottom of the screen (the palette on the top) to select colors for lines and borders around framed shapes. Fills and patterns appear in the color you select from the Fill palette at the bottom of the screen (the palette on the bottom). To select a Line or Fill color, just click the color you want.

Like other choices you make in Draw, you can choose colors *before* you begin your drawing or *after* you draw and select a line or shape. Colors selected before you begin your drawing become the defaults for any subsequent lines or shapes you draw. Colors selected after you draw and select a line or shape apply only to the selection.

In the color palette, default colors appear with a diamond; colors for the currently selected object appear with a check mark. To learn more about using colors, see "Working with Colors" later in this chapter.

Using Microsoft Draw Drawing Tools

Each tool in the Microsoft Draw toolbox has a specific use. Some tools have more than one function. With the Ellipse tool, for example, you can draw an oval or a perfect circle. You can draw a rectangle or a perfect square with the Rectangle/Square tool. Use the Freeform tool to draw a line or a closed polygon.

You first must select a tool before you can use it. To select a tool from the toolbox, click the tool icon in the toolbox. After you select a tool, move the pointer into the drawing area. The pointer changes from an arrow into some other tool. For drawing most objects, the pointer turns into a crosshair.

The next several sections explain how you can use your drawing tool or text tool to create your drawing. Refer to figure 17.3, which shows the nine drawing tools.

Figure 17.5 shows examples of framed and filled shapes created by using a variety of tools, line styles, patterns, and colors.

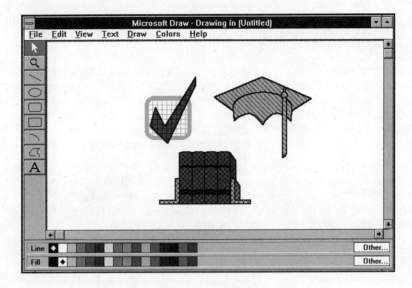

Fig. 17.5

A sampling of framed and filled shapes using a variety of line styles and patterns.

Selecting with the Selection Arrow

The Selection arrow selects text and objects in your drawing, usually so that you can edit them in some way. You can use the Selection arrow in one of two ways. You can point to the object you want to select and click the left mouse button—holding down Shift enables you to select several objects. To select multiple objects in a group, use the Selection arrow to draw a box, or *marquee*, around the group you want to select.

The Selection arrow is particularly important because of one guiding principle that applies in nearly every Windows application: *select and then do*. You first must *select* an object before you can *do* something to it.

To select an object or objects, follow these steps:

1. Click the Selection arrow in the toolbox.

2. Point to the object to select and click the mouse button (hold down Shift to select several objects).

   or

   Drag the Selection arrow in a box around a group of objects you want to select. The box appears as a dotted line while you hold down the mouse button and disappears when you release the mouse button. Be sure to enclose completely each object you want to select.

Many tools in the toolbox revert to the Selection arrow after you use them. After you draw a box and then click elsewhere in the drawing area, for example, the box crosshair turns into the Selection arrow.

Zooming In and Out with the Magnify Tool or View Command

When you first start Microsoft Draw, you see your page in full size—and your drawing is in the actual size it will be when printed. If your drawing is larger than the drawing area, however, you may want to zoom out and see more of the page. You also may want to zoom in and get a close-up look at part of your drawing, particularly if you need to do some detailed editing.

Microsoft Draw offers seven different magnification levels for your picture: 25%, 50%, 75%, Full Size, 200%, 400%, and 800%. You can draw and edit at any magnification. The available magnifications are listed in the View menu. The same choices are available also through the Magnify tool, which offers two advantages. First, the Magnify tool is easy to use—you just point and click. Second, it offers more control—when you point at an object and click the Magnify tool, you zoom in to that specific location on your screen. When you use the View menu, you zoom in to the object you most recently created or edited, regardless of where you want to be.

To magnify your drawing using the Magnify tool, follow these steps:

1. Select the Magnify tool from the toolbox.

2. Position the Magnify tool over the place in your drawing where you want to zoom in or zoom out.

3. Click the left mouse button to zoom in to the next higher magnification.

    or

    Hold down Shift and click the left mouse button to zoom out to the next lower magnification.

4. Click repeatedly to continue zooming in or out.

To magnify or reduce your drawing through a menu, choose the View menu and select 25% Size, 50%, 75%, Full Size, 200%, 400%, or 800%.

Drawing Lines

The Line tool enables you to draw straight lines. Your line appears in the default Line palette color and in the selected Line Style. Remember that black diamonds are used to indicate the default color and line style.

To draw a line, follow these steps:

1. From the **D**raw menu, select the **L**ine Style you want. Select the line color from the color palette.

2. Select the Line tool from the toolbox.

3. Move the pointer into the drawing area.

4. Position the crosshair where you want to start your line.

5. Click and hold down the mouse button.

6. Drag the crosshair to where you want to end your line.

7. Release the mouse button.

A newly drawn line has selection handles at each end, which you can use to edit the line (see "Manipulating Text and Objects" later in this chapter). When you finish drawing a line, you can click the mouse button anywhere in the drawing area to deselect the line you just drew. Then choose the Selection arrow from the toolbox. Figure 18.6 shows the process of drawing a line.

Two constraint keys, Shift and Ctrl, can help you keep a line straight or enable you to draw a line from the center outward. To constrain your line to a 45- or 90-degree angle (especially when you want a perfectly horizontal or vertical line), hold down the Shift key as you draw the line. To draw your line from the crosshair outward in both directions, hold down the Ctrl key as you draw.

Drawing Ellipses, Circles, Rectangles, and Squares

Three tools enable you to draw round and square shapes. The Ellipse/circle tool draws ellipses (ovals) or, when you hold down the Shift key, circles. The Rounded rectangle/square tool draws rectangles with rounded corners or, if you hold down the Shift key, rounded-corner squares. The Rectangle/square tool draws rectangles, or, when you hold down the Shift key, squares. For each tool, holding down the Ctrl key as you draw enables you to draw from the center outward rather than from one corner to another.

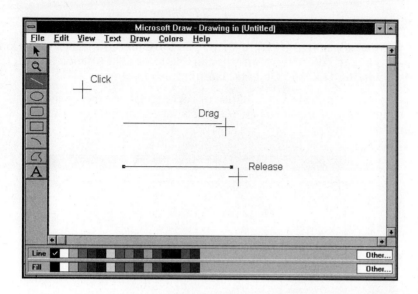

Fig. 17.6

Drawing a line.

You use the same process for drawing ellipses, circles, rectangles, and squares. To draw an ellipse, circle, rounded-rectangle, rounded square, rectangle, or square, follow these steps:

1. From the **Draw** menu, choose the Frame**d** command if you want your shape to have a border; choose the **F**illed command if you want your shape to be filled. Select the **P**attern or **L**ine Style you want. Select the Line color and Fill color you want from the color palette.

2. Select the Ellipse/circle tool to draw an ellipse or circle.

   or

   Select the Rounded rectangle/square tool to draw a rounded rectangle or square.

   or

   Select the Rectangle/square tool to draw a rectangle or square.

3. Move the tool into the drawing area, where it becomes a crosshair.

4. Position the crosshair where you want your shape to start.

   Hold down Shift if you want to draw a perfect circle or a perfect square shape. Hold down Ctrl to draw from the center outward.

5. Click and hold down the mouse button and drag to draw your shape.

6. Release the mouse button when your shape is correct.

As you can see in figure 17.7, a shape you have just drawn has selection handles at each corner, which you can use to edit the shape. (See "Manipulating Text and Objects" later in this chapter.)

When you finish drawing an ellipse or rectangle, click the crosshair anywhere off the object to deselect the shape tool and select the Selection arrow.

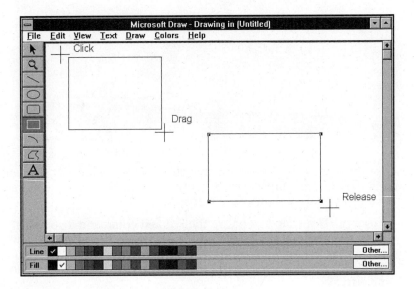

Fig. 17.7

Drawing squares.

Drawing Arcs and Wedges

An arc, as drawn in Microsoft Draw, is one quarter of an ellipse or circle. As with all the tools, two constraint keys can help you draw. Hold down the Shift key to make your arc or wedge a quarter of a perfect circle instead of an ellipse. Hold down the Ctrl key to draw your arc from the center rather than from one corner to another.

The process of drawing an arc is similar to that of drawing any shape in Microsoft Draw. To draw an arc, follow these steps:

1. From the **D**raw menu, choose the Frame**d** command if you want your arc to have a border and the **F**illed command if you want to fill your arc. Select the **P**attern or Line Style you want. Select the Line color and Fill color you want from the color palette.

2. Select the Arc tool from the toolbox.

3. Move the tool into the drawing area, where it becomes a crosshair.

4. Position the crosshair where you want to start your arc.

   Hold down the Shift key if you want to draw a perfect quarter-circle arc. Hold down the Ctrl key to draw from the center outward.

5. Click where you want to start the arc, hold down the mouse button, and drag to where you want to end the arc.

6. Release the mouse button.

As with all tools, you can drag the crosshair in any direction as you draw. To draw an arc that shows the bottom half of a circle or ellipse, drag the crosshair upward.

Drawing Freeform Lines and Polygons

The Freeform tool is one of the most versatile tools in the toolbox. With the Freeform tool, you can draw a curving line, a jagged line, or a closed polygon (see fig. 17.8).

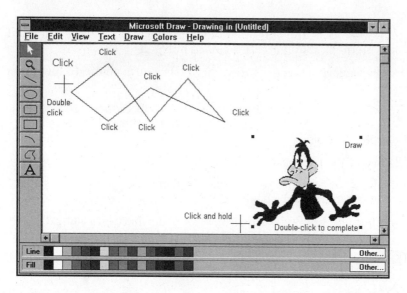

Fig. 17.8

Drawing a polygon is a series of clicks; hold down the mouse button to change the polygon's crosshair to a pencil for drawing freeform lines.

Only one constraint key—Shift—works with the Freeform tool. Holding down Shift while you draw forces line segments to be on the horizontal, vertical, or 45-degree axis. When you're drawing a curved line, holding down Shift still forces each tiny segment of the line to be on one of these axes.

You later can change the frame, fill, pattern, and line style for any freeform object (see the section on "Manipulating Text and Objects"). You can change each segment of a polygon, using the special technique described in "Editing a Freeform Shape" later in this chapter.

To draw a jagged line or closed polygon with the Freeform tool, follow these steps:

1. Select **D**raw Frame**d** for a framed polygon or **D**raw **F**illed for a filled polygon. Select your **P**attern, **L**ine Style, and color defaults.

2. Select the Freeform tool from the toolbox.

3. Move the tool into the drawing area and position the crosshair where you want your jagged line or polygon to begin.

4. Click the mouse button to anchor the first end of the line or polygon.

5. Move the crosshair to the second point on your line or polygon and click again.

6. Continue moving the crosshair and clicking the mouse button to define each point on your line or polygon.

7. Double-click the last point of your line to complete the line.

   or

   Double-click the first point of your polygon to join the last point with the first and create a closed polygon.

To draw a curving line or closed curving freeform shape, follow these steps:

1. Select **D**raw Frame**d** for a framed freeform shape or **D**raw **F**illed for a filled freeform shape. Select your pattern, line style, and color defaults.

2. Select the Freeform tool from the toolbox.

3. Move the tool into the drawing area and position the crosshair where you want to begin your curving line or freeform shape.

4. Click and hold down the mouse button where you want to start your line or shape. Wait until the crosshair turns into a pencil.

5. Still holding down the mouse button, drag the pencil around in the drawing area to draw your line or shape.

6. When you reach the end of your line, double-click the mouse button.

   or

   To close the shape, double-click the line's beginning point.

Adding and Editing Text

A picture may be worth a thousand words, but sometimes words can help clarify your point. You easily can add text to your Microsoft Draw drawing, selecting its font, style, and size. Later, you can select and edit your text as needed.

You can type just one line of text in Microsoft Draw. If you reach the end of the screen, text does not wrap, and you cannot press Enter to start a new line. To stack lines of text, you must type each line separately and drag each line into place using the Selection arrow. Using Microsoft Draw's Snap to Grid feature (in the **D**raw menu), however, enables you to stack lines of text evenly and easily.

As for any object, Windows' *select and then do* principle applies to text: to change the appearance of your text, first select it. If you don't select the text first, choices you make in the Text menu and the palette become the new defaults and apply to anything you do subsequently.

Moving text is no different from moving other objects. Techniques for moving text are discussed later in this chapter in the section "Copying, Moving, and Deleting Text and Objects."

Typing Text

To enter text in your drawing, follow these steps:

1. Choose your text defaults. If a shape is selected in your drawing, you cannot choose text defaults—unselect the shape. From the **T**ext menu, select any of these commands:

Command	Result
Plain (Ctrl+T)	Plain, with no formatting
Bold (Ctrl+B)	Boldface
Italic (Ctrl+I)	Italicized
Underline (Ctrl+U)	Underlined
Left	Left-aligned
Center	Centered
Right	Right-Aligned
Font	A different font
Size	A different size

When you choose the **F**ont or **S**ize command, a list of fonts or sizes pops out to the right of the menu. Select the font or size you want from that list.

Three of the choices in the **T**ext menu—**B**old, **I**talic, and Underline—are style choices, which can be combined. You can type text that is both bold and italic, underlined and bold, or even bold, italic, and underlined. Each style choice selected for the current text has a check mark to its left. To remove all style choices at once, select the **P**lain style.

2. From the Line color palette at the bottom of the screen, select a color for your text.

   If the color palette is not visible, choose the **C**olors Show **P**alette command to display it.

3. Select the Text tool from the toolbox.

4. Move the tool into the drawing area, where it turns into an I-beam. Position the I-beam where you want the left margin of your block of text.

5. Click the mouse button to insert the cursor where you want your text to start.

6. Type the text.

   You can press Shift+Ins to insert text from the Clipboard (even if the text was typed in a different application). Just remember that in Microsoft Draw you can have only one line of text at a time.

7. Press Enter or click the mouse button somewhere off the text to end the text block. The text block and the Selection arrow are selected.

T I P   Colored text sometimes looks best superimposed over a background. To superimpose text, choose one color for your text, draw around the text a shape that is filled with a different color, and then use the **E**dit menu to send the shape to the back of the text. For best readability, be sure that you have plenty of contrast between the two colors.

Editing Text

Text must be selected before you can edit it. Text is selected automatically after you type it and press Enter or click outside the text. If the text you want to edit is not currently selected, point to it with the Selection arrow and click the mouse button.

Like any selected object, selected text has selection handles at each of its four corners. The selection handles indicate that you can move or edit the text.

Once text is selected, you can change its style, alignment, font, or size by choosing commands from the Text menu. To change the color of the text, select a different color from the Line palette at the bottom of your screen.

To select text so that you can change its style, alignment, font, or size, follow these steps:

1. Select the selection arrow from the toolbox.

2. Point at the text you want to change and click the mouse button.

Alternatively, you can change the words by deleting, inserting, or retyping characters. To change the words in a text block, you first must move the insertion point inside the selected text. You cannot just click the text to move the insertion point inside it. To move the insertion point inside the text, follow these steps:

1. Select the text block by clicking it with the Selection arrow.

2. Choose the **E**dit E**d**it Text command.

   or

   Double-click the text block.

   An insertion point appears inside the text block. The insertion point appears exactly where you double-click.

3. Edit the text using standard editing techniques.

   Press the Backspace key to erase characters to the left, or press Del to erase characters to the right. You can select text and retype it, or you can cut, copy, and paste text using commands from the Edit menu.

4. Press Enter or click outside the text block to complete the editing process.

Working with Colors

If you have a color monitor, you can really enjoy Microsoft Draw's colors. The Line and Fill palettes contain up to 16 solid colors (Windows limit) and almost limitless *dithered* colors, blended from the available solid colors. You can apply these colors to any object you create—text or shapes. (If you see fewer than 16 colors, it's because your PC supports fewer colors.)

The color palette at the bottom of the Microsoft Draw window contains colors for Line (top of the palette) and Fill (bottom of the palette). The colors with a black diamond inside them are the defaults. When you select objects created earlier, you may see a check mark inside a color—this means that color is applied to the currently selected object.

You can change your color palette in two ways: by clicking the Other button at the right end of the Line or Fill palette or by using the Colors menu. Use either method to add new colors to your palette or to change existing colors. You also can save palettes for use in future drawings, following the techniques described in the next few sections.

To enlarge your screen space, you can hide the color palette. If the palette is displayed and you want to hide it, choose the Colors Show Palette command. To display the palette, choose the command a second time. The Show Palette command toggles on and off; you see a check mark to its left when it's on.

Coloring Text and Objects

The default color in the Line palette is applied automatically to text, lines, the frame around framed objects, and the foreground in any patterned fill. The default color in the Fill palette is applied automatically to the fill in any filled shape and to the background in any pattern fill.

Default color choices apply to any object you create, but you easily can change the Line or Fill color of an object or text created earlier. Simply select the object (or objects) and choose the Line or Fill color you want. Colors change only for the selected object or objects.

To select a Line or Fill color as a default or to change the Line or Fill color for a selected object, follow these steps:

1. If you want to change the default Line or Fill color, make sure that no object is selected. An easy way to do that is to select the Selection arrow; this cancels all previous selections.

   If you want to change the Line or Fill color for one or more specific objects, select the objects.

2. In the top half of the color palette, click the Line color you want.

   In the bottom half of the color palette, click the Fill color you want.

Using Blended Colors

Although your initial color palette contains only up to 16 solid colors, you can add a rainbow of blended colors to your palette. Working with blended colors requires that you use the most colorful dialog box in Microsoft Draw—the Other Color dialog box (see fig. 18.9). The Other Color dialog box offers a rainbow of colors you can add to your palette or apply to the selected objects. (If you access this dialog box through the Colors menu, its title is Add Color.)

When you are blending colors, remember that computers understand color in terms of light—not pigment. Computers use an additive system for blending colors, whereas pigments use a subtractive system. So forget what you have learned about color wheels. In a computer's mind, pure red and pure green combine to make yellow; pure red, pure green, and pure blue combine to make white.

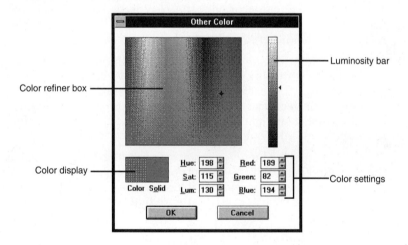

Fig. 17.9

The Other Color dialog box.

You can blend a color using the Other Color dialog box in three ways:

- You can select a color from the Color refiner box (the rainbow-colored box) and a luminosity from the Luminosity bar.

- You can blend your own color by setting its hue, saturation, and luminosity.

- You can blend your own color by setting its levels of red, green, and blue.

In the next section, you learn how you can add blended colors to your palette.

Follow these steps to use the Other Color dialog box to add a color to your objects:

1. Select the objects whose line or fill colors you want to change. Choose Other from the Line or the Fill palette. The Other Color dialog box appears.

2. Use the Color refiner box (the large, rainbow-colored box) to select the color.

   Click the color you like, or, holding down the mouse button, drag the black diamond selection icon onto the color you like. (The color display shows the selected color.)

3. To set your selected color's *luminosity*, or value (lightness or darkness), use the Luminosity bar (the vertical bar to the right of the rainbow-colored refiner box).

   Drag the black triangle icon up to select a lighter color, drag down to select a darker color, or click the area of the bar you want to select. Click the So**l**id box (right side) to select the solid color rather than the dithered color.

4. To select a color by *hue* (color), *saturation* (amount of color), and *luminosity* (brightness), select values from 0 to 239 in the **H**ue, **S**at, and **L**um boxes. Type the value or select the up and down arrows to increase or decrease the value. Values range from 0 (red hue, no saturation [black], and no luminosity [black]) to 239 (red hue, full saturation [pure color], and full luminosity [pure white]).

5. To select a color by blending hues, select values from 0 to 255 in the **R**ed, **G**reen, and **B**lue boxes. Type the value or select the up and down arrows to increase or decrease the value. Values range from 0 (no hues, or black) to 255 (pure hue, or white).

6. To see the color you have selected, look at the Color/Solid box (below the Color refiner box). If it's not one of Windows 16 solid colors, you see a dithered color blended of Windows 16 colors.

Editing the Palette

You can add blended colors to your initial palette, and you can change the existing colors and delete colors in your palette. To edit the palette, use the Colors menu, which accesses the Other Color dialog box described in the previous section. When you're editing the palette, however, the dialog box is named Change Color or Add Color. See the previous section for a description of the Add Color dialog box.

When you edit your palette using the **Colors** menu, you change the Line and Fill palettes simultaneously.

To change, add to, or delete colors from the palette, follow these steps:

1. Choose the **Colors E**dit Palette command.

   The Edit Palette dialog box appears (see fig. 17.10), displaying the colors in the current palette as well as many blank spaces where you can add new colors. Notice that 100 spots are available for colors.

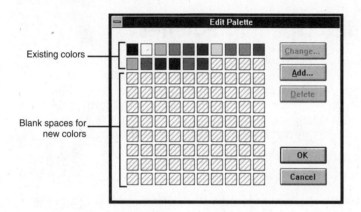

Existing colors

Blank spaces for new colors

Fig. 17.10

The Edit Palette dialog box.

2. Select the existing color you want to change or delete, or select the existing color you want to use as the basis for a new color.

3. Choose **C**hange to change the color you have selected, choose **A**dd to add a color to the next available blank space, or choose **D**elete to delete the selected color.

   If you add or change a color, you advance to the Change Color or Add Color dialog box, described in the previous section as the Other Color dialog box.

4. Make your choices in the Add Color or Change Color dialog box and choose OK or press Enter. You return to the Edit Palette dialog box.

5. Choose OK or press Enter.

The Edit Palette dialog box offers a couple of shortcuts. You can double-click the color you want to edit. You also can drag an existing color to a new square in the color grid to rearrange your palette.

As you have seen in the Edit Palette dialog box, you can have up to 100 colors on your palette. If you have more colors than can fit on your screen, scrolling arrows appear at the left and right ends of your on-screen palette. Click those arrows to see more of your palette.

If you have used the on-screen palette to change the color of an object in your drawing, you later can add that color to your palette.

To add an existing object's color to your palette, select the object whose color you want to add to the palette. Choose the **Colors Add** Colors From Selection command.

If your object contains both a new Line and a new Fill color, both are added to your palette. (If your object contains only one new color, it is added to both palettes.)

Saving and Opening Palettes

When you first start Microsoft Draw, the Line and Fill color palette is displayed at the bottom of the drawing area. It contains 16 solid colors—fewer, if your PC supports fewer. You also can get a different palette—Microsoft Draw includes several—or save a palette you have created yourself, making it available the next time you use Microsoft Draw. This is the way you can share colors among drawings.

To save your custom palette, follow these steps:

1. Choose the **Colors S**ave Palette command.

2. Enter an eight-character file name. Microsoft Draw supplies the extension PAL.

   Microsoft Draw saves the currently displayed color palette in the MSDRAW directory by default. You can save it in a different directory if you want, but if you do, your palette will not show up automatically when you choose the **G**et Palette command later.

3. Choose OK or press Enter.

T I P You can create a palette in Microsoft Draw to use in Windows Paintbrush if the palette contains no more than 28 colors. Paintbrush uses palettes in the same file format as Microsoft Draw (with the same extension), but Paintbrush looks for palette files in the Windows directory. If you are creating a palette for Paintbrush, save it in the Windows NT directory.

To get an existing palette, do the following:

1. Choose the **Colors G**et Palette command. The Get Palette dialog box appears.

2. In the **F**iles list box, select the palette you want to open.

   Change the directory if your PAL file is stored somewhere besides the MSDRAW directory (a subdirectory under MSAPP).

3. Choose OK or press Enter. The new palette is displayed on your screen.

Manipulating Text and Objects

After you draw objects and type text in Microsoft Draw, you can manipulate your drawing in many ways. Everything you create—even text—is an object you can move, layer, or group with other objects. You can resize, reshape, rotate, and flip shapes or grouped shapes (but not text). With Microsoft Draw's object-editing capabilities, you can produce complex and interesting works of art, like the one shown in fig. 17.11.

Fig. 17.11

By creating and editing objects, you can create complex and interesting works of art.

If you don't like the new look, you can choose the **E**dit **U**ndo command to undo your most recent screen action.

Selecting Text and Objects

Remember: Before you can edit any object, you first must select it. When selected, an object has selection handles on its four corners. (Even non-rectangular shapes have four selection handles arranged in a rectangle around the object.) Drag these handles to resize or reshape a selected object.

To review briefly, you can select objects by selecting the Selection arrow and clicking on the object or by drawing a selection marquee around a group of objects you want to select. (For more details, refer to the earlier section "Selecting with the Selection Arrow.") You can select all the objects in your drawing by choosing the Edit Select All command.

Resizing and Reshaping Objects

You can change the shape and size of any selected object, except text, by dragging the selection handles. Two constraint keys apply: Shift to retain proportions and Ctrl to resize and reshape from the center outward. As you're resizing or reshaping the object, a dotted-line bounding box shows you the object's new size or shape.

To change an object's size or shape, do the following:

1. Select the object.

2. To reshape an object, drag any corner handle to a new shape; release the mouse button when the bounding box shows the shape you want.

   or

   To resize the object and keep it proportional, hold down the Shift key while you drag a corner handle.

T I P   You cannot resize or reshape multiple objects simultaneously unless you first group them (see the upcoming section on "Grouping and Ungrouping Text and Objects").

Copying, Moving, and Deleting Text and Objects

You can easily move an object or a text block—just drag it to its new location. Because you can drag only as far as the edge of the drawing area, you may need to zoom out so that you can move on a larger area of the page. You can move a selected group of objects together by dragging one of the objects.

As you're dragging an object to move it, you see a dotted-line bounding box that represents the position of your speeding object (the object reappears when you release the mouse button).

If you prefer, you can use the standard Windows Edit Cut, Edit Copy, and Edit Paste commands to use the Clipboard to copy and move selected objects. This technique is useful when you want to copy or move objects between drawings or between distant spots on the same large drawing. Because you can switch between applications in Windows by sharing the Clipboard, you also can use this technique to copy or move a drawing from Microsoft Draw into an application other than Word for Windows.

To copy or move objects, follow these steps:

1. Select the object or objects you want to copy, move, or delete.

2. To move an object, choose the Edit Cut command.

   To copy an object, choose the Edit Copy command.

3. Move to where you want the object moved or copied.

4. Choose the Edit Paste command.

To remove an object, select it and choose the Edit Clear command or just press the Del or Backspace key.

Working with Layers

Like most drawing applications, Microsoft Draw enables you to work in layers. That is, you can create two or more objects and stack them on top of one another. Menu commands—and keyboard shortcuts—enable you to bring a selected object to the front or send it to the back of other objects.

Classic examples of layering are a shadow box—usually a white box overlapping a darker box of the same size—and text on a different color background.

To move an object to a different layer in your drawing, do the following:

1. Select the object or objects you want to send to the back or bring to the front of another object.

2. To bring the object to the top layer, choose the **Edit Bring to Front** command (or press Ctrl+=).

   To send the object to the bottom layer, choose the **Edit Send to Back** command (or press Ctrl+-).

T I P

If you know an object is hidden somewhere behind some other object and you want to find it, choose the **Edit Select All** command to select all objects. Then look for the hidden object's selection handles. To reveal the hidden object, you must either move the top object (or objects) to the back of the stack or drag the top object off the object you're trying to find.

Editing a Freeform Shape

You can edit a freeform shape in one of two ways. You can resize or reshape it as described in the earlier section on "Resizing and Reshaping Objects." This technique leaves the freeform object in the same general shape. (When dragging its corner handles, however, you may condense or expand the shape if you don't hold down the Shift key to keep it proportional.)

You also can edit the segments that make up the freeform shape. Use the Selection arrow and then a menu command to display control handles you can use to reshape the freeform shape. While you're editing a freeform object, it appears on-screen as an empty shape with a thin, black frame.

To edit a freeform shape, follow these steps:

1. Select the shape by clicking it with the Selection arrow. Four selection handles appear on each corner.

2. Choose the **E**dit E**d**it Freeform command. Control handles appear at the end of each segment of the freeform shape.

3. Drag any control handle to change the shape of the freeform drawing.

   To add a control handle, hold down Ctrl (the arrow turns into a plus sign inside a circle) and click anywhere on the edge of the freeform shape.

   To remove a control handle, hold down Ctrl and Shift (the arrow turns into a minus sign inside a square) and click any existing control handle.

4. Press Enter or click anywhere outside the freeform shape to hide the control handles.

As an alternative to selecting the freeform shape and then choosing the **E**dit Freeform command, you can double-click the freeform shape to display the control handles.

Editing an Arc or Wedge

You can edit an arc or wedge in two ways. Select the arc or wedge with the Selection arrow and resize or reshape it by dragging the corner handles. Hold down the Shift key as you drag to keep the arc proportional. You also can change the arc's degree by first selecting it with the Selection arrow and then choosing a menu command to display special control handles.

To change a wedge's or arc's degree, follow these steps:

1. Select the arc or wedge by clicking it with the Selection arrow. Four corner handles appear.

2. Choose the **E**dit E**d**it Arc command. Two control handles appear—one at each end of the arc or wedge.

3. Drag either control handle in a clockwise or counterclockwise manner to change the degree.

4. Click outside the arc to deselect it.

As an alternative to selecting the arc and then choosing the **E**dit Arc command, you can double-click the arc to display the control handles.

Grouping and Ungrouping Text and Objects

If you want to turn several objects into one (to copy, reshape, or move them together easily, for example), you can select and group them. You then can edit the objects as a single object. However, you cannot re-size, reshape, rotate, or flip text included in the group. Later, you can ungroup grouped objects. If you have resized a group, the ungrouped objects will be the new size.

To group objects, follow these steps:

1. Select all the objects you want to group. (Either hold down Shift while you click each object you want to select or draw a selection marquee around a group of objects.)

2. Choose the **Draw Group** command.

To ungroup a grouped object, do the following:

1. Select the grouped object.

2. Choose the **Draw Ungroup** command.

To select a grouped object, you must click on one of the grouped objects using the Selection arrow. You cannot select a group by clicking between the objects.

Rotating and Flipping Objects

You can rotate a selected object (or selected group) in 90-degree increments to the left (counterclockwise) or right (clockwise). You can flip an object vertically or horizontally. You cannot rotate or flip text.

To rotate or flip an object, follow these steps:

1. Select the object.

2. Choose the **Draw Rotate/Flip** command and select Rotate **L**eft, Rotate **R**ight, Flip **H**orizontal, or Flip **V**ertical.

Importing and Editing Clip Art and Other Pictures

You can import many types of graphics into Microsoft Draw. Among the most interesting are a series of clip-art images that come with Microsoft Draw, which you can import and disassemble to use in whole or in part. Browse through the various clip-art files to see what's available.

To import a picture, follow these steps:

1. Choose the File Import Picture command. The Import Picture dialog box appears.

2. Select the file you want to import from the Files box (change the directory if necessary).

Clip-art files are stored in the subdirectory CLIPART, located inside your Word for Windows directory. These files have the extension WMF, indicating that their format is Windows metafile.

You also can import BMP, PCX, and TIF files. If you import object-oriented images, edit them the same way you edit any Microsoft Draw object. When you import bitmap files (such as those created in Microsoft Paintbrush), Microsoft Draw converts the bitmaps into objects, which you can resize, reshape, or recolor. To restore a bit-mapped image to its original size or shape, select it and double-click any corner handle.

Saving Your Drawing

You can copy your drawing into the client document in either of two ways. You can update the client document without closing Microsoft Draw, enabling you to continue working on your drawing. Or, you can close Microsoft Draw when you update your client document.

When updating your client document, choose the File Update command to update without closing Microsoft Draw. To update the client file and exit Microsoft Draw, choose the File Exit and Return to Document command. For more details, see "Updating the Client Document" earlier in this chapter.

Remember, however: Updating your client document *does not* save your drawing—it merely copies it. To save your drawing, you must be sure to save your client document after you update the drawing.

Summary

Microsoft Draw is a simple but very powerful application. You can use Microsoft Draw to create original works of art to illustrate your Windows application document or to edit existing art. You even can use the clip art that comes with Microsoft Draw as the basis for your own drawings.

To learn more about how to use Microsoft Draw with your application, refer to a Que book specifically describing that application. In *Using Word for Windows*, you learn how you can move, frame, size, and border pictures in Word for Windows, the Windows word processor. *Using Excel 4 for Windows,* Special Edition, explains how to use Draw with the spreadsheet application Excel.

Using Microsoft Graph

With Microsoft Graph, you can create informative and impressive charts that you can incorporate into all Windows applications that have Object Linking and Embedding (OLE) capability. (For a discussion of OLE, see Chapter 6, "Embedding and Linking Windows NT Applications.") Microsoft Graph is an *applet*, or a small application designed to work with Windows applications that have OLE capability. Applets add features to OLE-capable applications. Microsoft Graph is a separate application that embeds charts in Windows applications, such as Microsoft Word for Windows, Ami Pro, or Microsoft Excel. Microsoft Graph comes free with some Windows applications, such as Word for Windows. After you install Word for Windows, Microsoft Graph can be used with other OLE-compatible applications, such as Windows Write.

Using Microsoft Graph, you can turn an overwhelming table of numbers into a chart that shows important trends and changes. You can relegate the detailed numeric table to a location where this much detail doesn't slow down communication. Figure 18.1 shows a Word for Windows document enhanced by a chart. Microsoft Graph is more than a small charting application; Microsoft Graph has all the charting capability of Microsoft Excel 3.0, the most powerful Windows spreadsheet and charting application. Microsoft Graph can even produce 3-D charts with shaded backgrounds, changeable fonts, and movable text.

T I P Many Windows applications include applets, such as Microsoft Graph, WordArt, Microsoft Draw, and Equation Editor. If you receive an OLE applet with one Windows application, you can usually use the applet to enhance documents produced in other Windows applications that have object linking and embedding capability. Besides the applets that come free with many applications, you can buy applets separately to enhance many Windows NT applications.

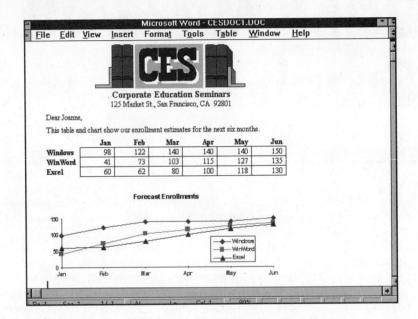

Fig. 18.1

A Word for Windows document enhanced by a chart.

Charts embedded in a Word for Windows document contain both the chart and the data that creates the chart. When you activate Microsoft Graph, the selected chart and the data are loaded so that you can make changes. You cannot save the chart or data separately; both are embedded into the Windows NT application.

T I P   Many tips found in the charting chapters of Que's book, *Using Excel 4 for Windows*, Special Edition, also work in Microsoft Graph.

Creating a Chart

With Microsoft Graph, you can create a new chart in a Windows NT application in several ways. You can select the text and numbers in the data sheet from a table in a word processing document; you can type data into Microsoft Graph directly; you can copy data from any Windows application; you can import data from Microsoft Excel, Lotus 1-2-3, or a text file; or you can import data from an existing Microsoft Excel chart.

To create a chart within a Windows application, select the place in the document in which you want the chart to appear and then follow the instructions for the particular application you are using for inserting a chart. In Write, the word processor included with Windows, for example, you choose the **Edit Insert** Object command. You then select Microsoft Graph from the **O**bject Type list. In Word for Windows (Version 2.0), you choose the **Insert O**bject command and select Microsoft Graph from the **O**bject Type list.

Microsoft Graph opens in an application window on top of the current application. Microsoft Graph opens with default data in the data sheet and chart (see fig. 18.2). The chart reflects the data in a sample data sheet. (If you select data in a Windows application before you start Microsoft Graph, this data is used.) If you change the data in the data sheet, you change the chart. When you close the Microsoft Graph application, you can embed the chart and the related data into an application.

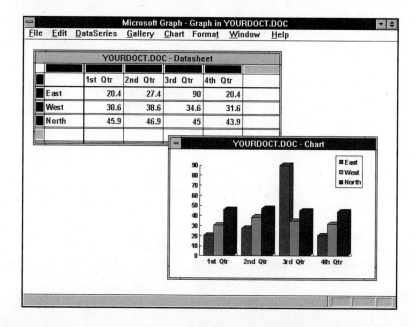

Fig. 18.2

A sample data sheet and chart.

In Microsoft Graph, you can change the data in the sheet in many ways. You also can choose different kinds of charts from the Gallery menu. From the Chart menu, you can add or remove from a chart items such as legends, arrows, and titles. You can change the appearance or position of selected chart items or data in the sheet by using the commands in the Format menu.

Understanding the Data Sheet Layout

The data points from the data sheet are plotted as markers in the chart. Markers appear as lines, bars, columns, data points in X-Y charts, or slices in a pie chart. Microsoft Graph usually uses its default settings when it first creates a chart. A row of data points, therefore, appears in a chart as a series of markers. A series of values appears in the chart connected by a line or as bars or columns that have the same color. In figure 18.3, for example, the row labeled East corresponds to one line in the 3-D line chart.

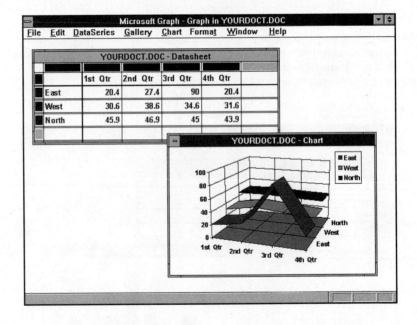

Fig. 18.3

Each row of data translates to a series of data points in the chart.

In the default orientation shown in figure 18.3, known as Series in Rows, the text in the first row of the data sheet becomes the category names that appear below the *category (X) axis* (the horizontal axis). The text in the left column becomes the *series names*, which Microsoft Graph uses as labels for the legend. (The legend is the box that labels the different colors or patterns used by each series of markers.) If you change orientation and want to return to the default orientation, choose the **D**ataSeries Series in **R**ows command.

If the data on the data sheet uses the reverse orientation so that each data series goes down a column, you must choose the **D**ataSeries Series in **C**olumns command. The category names (x-axis labels) are taken from the left column of the data sheet (see fig. 18.4). The series names (legend labels) are taken from the top row.

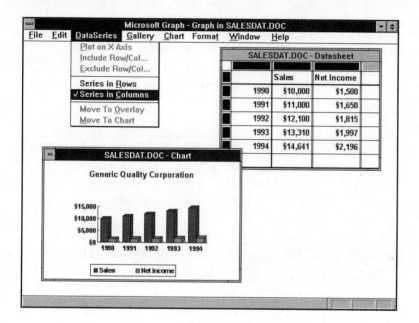

When you create a Microsoft Graph chart, be sure that you have text for each series name (legend labels), text for each category label (x-axis), and a number (or N/A to enter a blank data point) for each data point.

Typing Data for a New Chart

To manually create a chart, type over the numbers and text that appear in the default data sheet. When you change the default data sheet, you update the chart.

If you change numbers or text in the data sheet after you open it, you make corresponding changes in the chart. Rows or columns of data you add to the data sheet are included in the chart. Later sections in this chapter describe methods for editing data and for including or excluding rows or columns from the chart.

Creating Charts from a Table in Your Document

In some Windows applications, you can select data in a document from which you want to create a chart. That data is then loaded into the data sheet in Microsoft Graph as soon as it opens. When this happens, the resulting chart reflects the data in the document.

In the following example, a Word for Windows document contains a table that is quickly converted into a chart. Figure 18.5 shows a table and its subsequent conversion to a chart in a document.

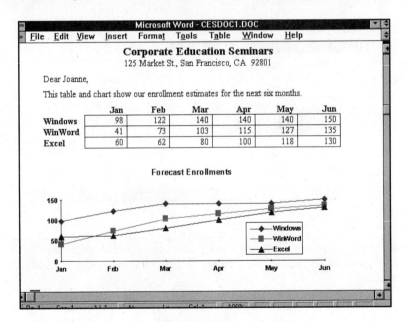

Fig. 18.5

A table and its subsequent chart in a document.

To create a chart from a table in a Word for Windows document, follow these steps:

1. In the table, enter the data and text in the layout you want to appear in a Microsoft Graph data sheet.

   In Word for Windows, use the Table menu or the Table button on the toolbar to insert a table.

2. Select the table.

3. Choose the object linking command.

   In Word for Windows, click on the Graph button in the toolbar or choose the **I**nsert **O**bject command.

4. Select Microsoft Graph from the **O**bject Type list and then choose OK.

   Microsoft Graph starts. After a moment, Microsoft Graph will load the table's data in the data sheet. The chart updates.

5. Format, modify, and size the chart and data sheet. If the data series are in columns, you need to choose the **D**ataSeries Series in **C**olumns command.

6. Choose the **F**ile E**x**it and Return to Document command.

7. To embed the chart in the document, choose **Y**es at the prompt.

Microsoft Graph closes. The chart is inserted after the table, with a blank line in between.

Copying Data from Windows Applications into the Data Sheet

You can copy data from applications and paste them into a Microsoft Graph data sheet to create a chart. You can create a chart from a series of text and numbers aligned on tabs in Word for Windows or Write, or you can copy a range of cells from a Microsoft Excel worksheet. (A following section, "Importing a Microsoft Excel Chart," describes how to import a range from Microsoft Excel or use a Microsoft Excel chart as a basis for a Microsoft Graph chart.)

You must separate data and text in a word processing document by tabs for the information to copy into separate data sheet cells. Figure 18.6 shows the same Word for Windows document used in figure 18.5, but the data and labels are separated by right-align tabs. You must arrange data and text as you want this information to appear in the Microsoft Graph data sheet.

To copy data from a document or Microsoft Excel worksheet and create a chart, follow these steps:

1. Select the tabbed data or range of Microsoft Excel cells. Choose the **E**dit **C**opy command.

2. Move the insertion point to where you want the chart and choose the command to start Microsoft Graph and embed an object.

In Word for Windows, click on the Graph button or choose the **Insert O**bject command. Select Microsoft Graph from the list and choose OK.

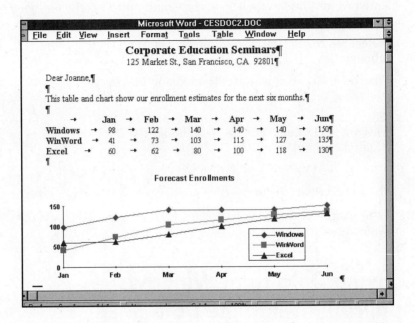

Fig. 18.6

Data and labels separated by tabs.

3. Activate the data sheet in Microsoft Graph by clicking on its title bar and then erase all existing data by choosing the **E**dit Select **A**ll command or pressing Ctrl+A. Then choose the **E**dit Clear command or press the Del key. When the Clear dialog box displays, choose OK or press Enter.

4. Ensure that the top-left cell in the data sheet is selected and choose the **E**dit **P**aste command or press Ctrl+V.

   The data is pasted into the data sheet, and the chart updates.

5. Format, modify, or size the chart and data sheet as necessary.

6. Choose the **F**ile Exit and Return to Document command.

7. Choose **Y**es when asked whether you want to update the chart in the document.

The chart is inserted at the insertion point.

Importing Worksheet or Text Data

You may want to use data from an ASCII text file or a Microsoft Excel or Lotus 1-2-3 worksheet to create a chart. You can save time by importing this data directly into the Microsoft Graph data sheet.

To import data into the data sheet, follow these steps:

1. Move the insertion point to where you want the chart in your document and choose the command to start Microsoft Graph and embed an object. In Word for Windows, click on the Graph button or choose the **Insert Object** command. Select Microsoft Graph from the list and choose OK.

2. Erase all unwanted data from the data sheet and select the cell where you want to locate the top left corner of the imported data. If you are importing an entire chart's worth of data, select the top left cell of the data sheet.

3. Choose the **File Import Data** command. The Import Data dialog box appears (see fig. 18.7). Find and select the file from which you want to import data.

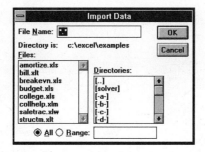

Fig. 18.7

The Import Data dialog box.

4. Specify the amount of data you want imported. To import all data, choose the **All** button. To import a range of data, enter the range or range name in the **R**ange text box.

5. Choose OK or press Enter.

Importing a Microsoft Excel Chart

Microsoft Excel is a powerful worksheet and charting application. With Excel, you can create mathematical models that generate charts. These charts then can be linked to Word for Windows documents. Changing the worksheet changes the chart, which in turn changes the chart in the Word for Windows document.

Importing a Microsoft Excel chart into Microsoft Graph and embedding the resulting chart into your document has advantages over linking a chart. Charts linked back to the original Excel chart change when the Excel data changes; embedded charts don't change. Embedded charts place the chart and chart data in the document so that the document, data, and chart stay together even when copied or moved. Embedded charts can be updated by someone who has Microsoft Graph but doesn't have Microsoft Excel.

To embed a Microsoft Excel chart and the chart's related data into a document, follow these steps:

1. Move the insertion point to where you want the chart and start Microsoft Graph.

   In Word for Windows, click on the Graph button in the toolbar or choose the Insert Object command. Select Microsoft Graph from the Object Type list and choose OK.

2. Choose the File Open Microsoft Excel Chart command. To overwrite existing data in the data sheet, choose OK when prompted.

   The Open Microsoft Excel Chart dialog box appears (see fig. 18.8).

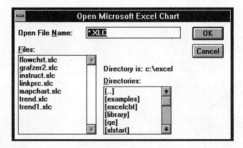

3. Select the drive, directory, and file name of the Microsoft Excel chart, and then choose OK. Microsoft Excel charts use the file extension XLC.

   The chart opens in Microsoft Graph, and the associated data appears in the data sheet. Data series found in rows in Microsoft Excel are in columns in the Microsoft Graph data sheet but the DataSeries Series in command compensates and the chart appears correctly.

4. Format, modify, and size the chart and data sheet.

5. Choose the File Exit and Return to document command.

6. To embed the chart in the document, choose Yes at the prompt.

Editing Existing Charts

Updating existing Microsoft Graph charts embedded in a Windows application is easy. With a mouse, double-click on the chart. With the keyboard, select the chart by moving the insertion point next to the chart, and then pressing Shift+arrow across the chart. After the chart is selected, follow the instructions for editing an embedded object for the application in which you are working. In Word for Windows (Version 2.0), for example, choose the Edit Microsoft Graph Object command.

Entering Data for Overlay Charts

Overlay charts overlay one kind of two-dimensional chart onto another. They make seeing the relationships between different kinds of charts or seeing data with widely different scales easier.

Overlay charts consist of a main chart (the underlying chart foundation that uses the Y-axis on the left) and an overlay chart (the overlay that covers the main chart and uses a second Y-axis on the right). You can create an overlay chart by choosing the Gallery Combination command. You also can create an overlay chart from existing charts by selecting a data series (line, bar, or column) and choosing the DataSeries Move to Overlay command. The selected series is moved out of the main chart and into the overlay chart.

The Gallery Combination command divides the number of data series in half. The first half creates the main chart, and the second half creates the overlay chart. When the total number of series is odd, the main chart receives the larger number of series. If five rows of data existed, for example, the first three rows would be in the main chart and the last two rows would be in the overlay chart.

Editing the Data Sheet

Working in the data sheet is similar to working in a word processing table or a Windows worksheet. Because the data sheet cannot be printed, the data sheet doesn't have a wide range of font formatting options. Another difference is that you can edit cellular data directly in a cell or within an editing box.

Selecting Data

Moving and selecting cells in the data sheet uses many techniques also used in Microsoft Excel. If you use a mouse, you can use the scroll bars to scroll to any location on the data sheet. Click on a cell to make the selection. To select multiple cells, drag the mouse across the cells. To select a row or column, click on the row or column header. To select multiple rows or columns, drag across the headers. To select all cells in the data sheet, click on the blank rectangle at the top-left corner where row and column headings intersect.

> **CAUTION:** Use care when selecting multiple cells, rows, columns, or the entire data sheet. Selecting the entire worksheet and then pressing Del erases the entire worksheet.

If you are using the keyboard, use the keys shown in the following tables to move the insertion point or select cells and the cells' contents.

To move	Press
To a cell	Arrow
To first cell in row	Home
To last cell in row	End
To top left data cell	Ctrl+Home
To lower right data cell	Ctrl+End
A screen up/down	PgUp/PgDn
A screen right/left	Ctrl+PgUp/PgDn

To select	Press
A cell	Arrow
A range (rectangle) of cells	Shift+arrow or F8 (enters Extend mode); Arrow and then F8 (exit Extend mode)
A row	Shift+space bar
A column	Ctrl+space bar
The datasheet	Shift+Ctrl+space bar or Ctrl+A or Edit Select **All**
Undo selection	Shift+Backspace or move an arrow key

Replacing or Editing Existing Data

The easiest way to replace the contents of a cell is to select the cell by moving to it or clicking on the cell and then typing directly over the cell's contents. When you press Enter or select a different cell, the edits take effect.

To edit the contents of a cell, select the cell by moving to it using the arrow keys or by clicking on the cell. Press F2, the Edit key, or double-click on the cell. A simple edit box appears and shows the contents of the cell. You can edit the cell's contents as you edit the contents of any edit box. After you finish editing, choose OK or press Enter.

To break a line chart at one point and continue at another point without dropping to a zero value, enter *N/A* in the appropriate cells in the data sheet. If you enter *0* (zero) in a cell, the line drops to the zero value, but if you enter *N/A*, the line stops and then restarts at the next cell that contains a numeric value.

T I P

Inserting or Deleting Rows and Columns

Microsoft Graph expands the chart to include data or text you add in rows or columns outside the originally charted data. If you add rows or columns of data and leave blank rows or columns, Microsoft Graph doesn't include the blank rows or columns as part of the chart.

To insert or delete rows or columns in the data sheet, select the rows or columns in which you want to insert or delete and then choose the **E**dit **I**nsert Row/Col or the **E**dit **D**elete Row/Col command. The shortcut keys for inserting or deleting selected rows or columns are Ctrl++ (plus) and Ctrl+– (minus), respectively. A dialog box appears if you don't select an entire row or column and asks you to select whether you want to affect the rows or columns that pass through the selected cells.

The Microsoft Graph data sheet cannot have more than 256 columns or 4,000 rows. If you need a larger data sheet, create the chart in Microsoft Excel or an advanced charting application and link or paste the chart in the application.

Copying or Moving Data

Copy or move data in the data sheet by using normal Windows techniques. Select the cells you want to copy or move and then choose the **E**dit **C**opy or **E**dit **C**ut command. (The shortcut keys are Ctrl+C and Ctrl+X, respectively.) Select the cell at the top-left corner of the area where you want to paste the data and choose the **E**dit **P**aste command or press Ctrl+V. The pasted data replaces the original data. To undo the paste operation, choose the **E**dit **U**ndo command.

Including and Excluding Data from a Chart

When you add data or text to the data sheet, Microsoft Graph immediately redraws the chart, even if the data doesn't touch the preceding data. This redraw feature is inconvenient if you want to exclude some rows or columns from the chart.

You can see which rows and columns of data are included because the row or column headings are darkened. Excluded rows or columns are grayed.

To include or exclude a row or column with the mouse, double-click on the row or column heading. The double-click toggles the row or column between included and excluded.

To include or exclude a row or column with the keyboard, select the entire row or column and then choose the **D**ataSeries **I**nclude Row/Col or the **D**ataSeries **E**xclude Row/Col command.

Changing Data by Moving a Graph Marker

Microsoft Graph enables you to move column, bar, lines, or X-Y markers on 2-D charts using the mouse. As you move the data point, the corresponding data changes in the data sheet. This feature is convenient for smoothing a curve so that the chart matches real-life experience or for *fudging* numbers to fit the results you want.

To change values on the datasheet by moving markers on the chart, follow these steps:

1. Open the data sheet and chart. Activate the chart. The chart must be a two-dimensional column, bar, X-Y, or line chart.

2. Hold down the Ctrl key and click on the column, bar, or line marker you want to change. A black *handle* (a small square) appears at the top of the marker.

3. Click on the black handle and drag the handle to the new position. When you drag the black handle, a tick mark on the vertical axis moves, showing you the value of the new location.

4. Release the mouse when the marker reaches the location you want.

The corresponding data in the data sheet changes.

Sizing Your Chart

You get the best results if you resize the chart in Microsoft Graph rather than in the application in which the chart is embedded. Resizing the chart in the application changes the size but doesn't correct text placement, readjust the scale, and so on. By sizing the chart in Microsoft Graph before updating the chart in the application, you use Microsoft Graph to reposition and resize elements in the chart.

Change the size of the chart as you change the size of any window. Drag the borders or corners with the mouse. With the keyboard, press Alt+- to open the document Control menu, choose the **S**ize command, and then use the arrow keys to resize the window. Make sure that the chart's window is the size you want the chart when pasted into the application.

Although you can change the magnification of the graph, doing so doesn't change the size of the chart when pasted in the document. Magnifying is useful when you format or position text or arrows. To magnify or shrink the view of the chart, select the Window menu and choose a percentage to magnify or shrink.

Changing the Chart Type

When Microsoft Graph first opens, the chart appears as a three-dimensional column chart. Many different kinds of charts are available, but you have to select the appropriate one.

Try to choose the appropriate chart before you begin customizing. To change the chart type after you customize, follow the procedure described in the later section, "Customizing an Existing Chart Type."

Selecting the Original Chart Type

When you build charts, you can use any of the 81 predefined chart formats. The easiest way to create charts is to select the predefined chart closest to the chart you want. You then can customize the predefined chart until it fits your needs. To use a predefined chart, follow these steps:

1. Choose the **G**allery command.

2. From the menu, choose one of the following twelve kinds of charts:

> Area
> Bar
> Column
> Line
> Pie
> X-Y (Scatter)
> Combination
> 3-D Area
> 3-D Bar
> 3-D Column
> 3-D Line
> 3-D Pie

After you make a choice, the Chart Gallery dialog box appears. This dialog box shows the different predefined charts. Figure 18.9 shows the gallery available for 3-D column charts.

3. To select a chart type, click on the associated square or type the chart's number and choose OK or press Enter.

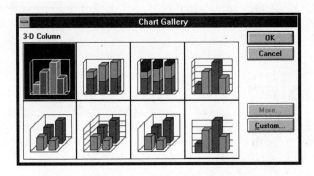

Fig. 18.9

The gallery of predefined formats for 3-D Column charts.

4. If you don't see the kind of chart you want and the **More** button is not grayed, choose the **More** button to see more formats of this kind of chart.

5. If you want a variation from one of the listed charts, choose the **Custom** button.

   The Format Chart dialog box appears (see fig. 18.10). Select the desired options to modify the chart. This dialog box is different for each kind of chart.

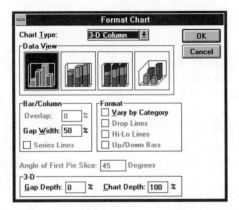

Fig. 18.10

The Format Chart dialog box for 3-D column charts.

6. Choose OK or press Enter.

You can access the customizing options available through the **Custom** button in step 5 at any time by choosing the Forma**t C**hart or Forma**t O**verlay command.

> To select the kind of chart you want, double-click the box in the Gallery that contains the chart. This technique selects the type and chooses OK.
>
> **T I P**

The following table describes the two-dimensional chart types available through the Gallery menu:

Chart	Description
2-D Line	Compares trends over even time or measurement intervals plotted on the category (X) axis. (If the category data points are at uneven intervals, use an X-Y scatter chart.)
2-D Area	Compares the continuous change in volume of a data series
2-D Bar	Compares distinct (noncontinuous) items over time. Horizontal bars show positive or negative variation from a center point. Frequently used for time management.
2-D Column	Compares separate (noncontinuous) items as they vary over time
2-D Pie	Compares the size of each of the pieces making up a whole unit. Use this chart when the parts total 100 percent for the first series of data. Only the first data series in a worksheet selection is plotted.
X-Y (Scattergram)	Compares trends over uneven time or measurement intervals plotted on the category (X) axis
Combination	Lays one chart over another. These charts are useful for comparing data of different kinds or data requiring different axis scales.

The following table describes the three-dimensional charts available through the Gallery menu:

Chart	Description
3-D Area	Uses 3-D area charts for the same kind of data as used in 2-D area charts
3-D Bar	Uses 3-D bar charts for the same kind of data as used in 2-D bar charts
3-D Column	Uses 3-D column charts for the same kind of data as used in 2-D column charts. You can create 3-D column charts with the columns adjacent to each other or layered into the third dimension.
3-D Line	Uses 3-D line charts for the same kind of data as used in 2-D line charts. 3-D line charts also are known as ribbon charts.
3-D Pie	Shows labels or calculates percentages for wedges. Only the first data series from a selection is charted as a pie. Wedges can be dragged out from the pie.

Customizing an Existing Chart Type

You can save work by choosing the kind of chart you want before you customize it. Use the **G**allery command to try different kinds of charts and then customize the kind you decide to use. If you use the **G**allery command to change the kind of chart after customizing, you may lose some of the custom selections.

To change or customize a chart type without losing custom formatting, choose the Forma**t C**hart or Forma**t O**verlay command and then select from the available options.

The Forma**t O**verlay command is only available when the chart is a combination chart.

Forma**t C**hart changes the basic chart type or customizes the main or background chart. Forma**t** Overlay changes or customizes the overlay chart. Figures 18.11 and 18.12 show the Format Chart and Format Overlay dialog boxes that enable you to customize the main or overlay charts. Both use the same options for a given chart type.

Options in the Format Chart and Format Overlay dialog boxes are available only when appropriate for the active chart. For a detailed description of the options available in the Format Chart and Format Overlay dialog boxes, choose the **H**elp command, select Commands and Menus, and then select Format Menu Chart or Format Menu Overlay from the list of topics.

If you didn't choose a combination chart as the first chart type, you still can change the chart to include an overlay. To add data series to an overlay or to create an overlay, select the data series in the data sheet or select the markers in the chart. Choose the **D**ataSeries Move to **O**verlay command. The series you selected will become an overlay.

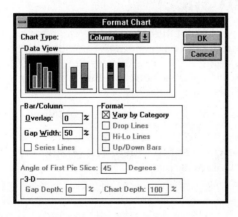

Fig. 18.11

The Format Chart dialog box.

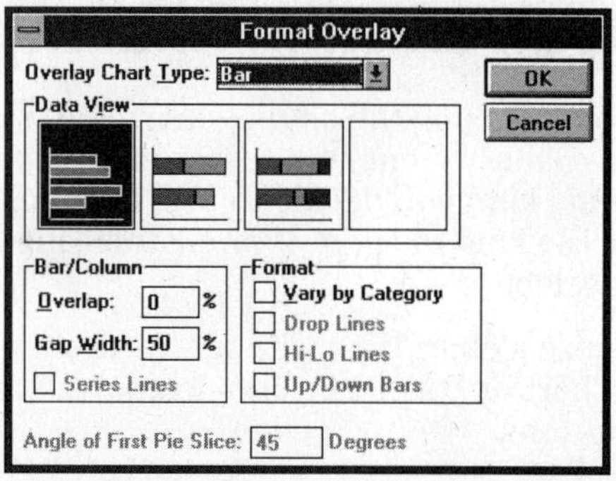

Fig. 18.12

The Format Overlay dialog box.

To remove a data series from the overlay, select the data series or the markers and then choose the **Data**Series **M**ove to Chart command. To completely remove an overlay, move the data series in the overlay back to the main chart.

Formatting the Data Sheet

Formatting the data sheet is important for more reasons than making data entry easier and more accurate. The format of the numbers and dates in the chart are controlled by the formatting of the numbers and dates in the data sheet.

Adjusting Column Widths in the Data Sheet

Numbers, when entered in unformatted cells, appear in General format. If the column isn't wide enough to display the full number, the number's format changes to scientific format. 6,000,000, for example, changes to 6E+6 on-screen. When a scientific number is too large to fit in a cell, the cell fills with # signs.

To change the column width with the mouse, follow these steps:

1. Move the pointer to the vertical line to the right of the column heading that you want to widen. The pointer changes to a two-headed horizontal arrow.

2. Drag the column left or right until the shadow appears where you want. Release the mouse button.

To change the column width with the keyboard, follow these steps:

1. Select a cell in the column you want to change. Change multiple columns by selecting a cell in each column that you want to change.

2. Choose the Forma**t** Column **W**idth command.

3. Enter the column width as the number of characters.

4. Choose OK or press Enter.

Formatting Numbers and Dates

Microsoft Graph has many predefined numeric and date formats. You can choose from these formats to format the data sheet and chart or to create custom formats.

The format of the first data cell in a series defines the numeric or date format for that series in the chart. You even can enter a date, such as *12-24-92*, as a label for a category axis. You then can format the cell with a different date format (such as *d-mmm*, and the date appears as 12-Dec).

Microsoft Graph uses the same numeric and date formatting methods as Microsoft Excel and the same as many of the numeric and date formatting switches used with Word for Windows field codes. Graph has all of Microsoft Excel's custom numeric and date formatting capability.

To format data cells, follow these steps:

1. Select the data cell or range you want to format. You can select entire rows or columns at one time.

2. Choose the Forma**t** **N**umber command.

   The Number dialog box displays a list of different numeric and date formats.

3. From the list, select the numeric or date format you want to apply to the selected data cells.

4. Choose OK or press Enter.

The items in the list may appear strange looking until you understand the symbols used to represent different numeric and date formats. The characters in the list are as follows:

Character	Example	Entry	Result
#	#,###	9999.00	9,999
0	#,###.00	9999.5	9,999.50
$	$#,###	9000.65	$9,001
( )	0.00 ;(0.00)	5.6	$5.60
		–9.834	($9.83)
m	mmm	12	Dec
d	dd	6	06
yy	yy	1991	91
h or m	hh:mm AM/PM	6:12	06:12 AM

is a position holder for commas. Blank values, such as the trailing zeros to the left of the decimal, aren't represented.

0 is a position holder for leading or trailing zeros.

$ displays a dollar sign. Values are rounded when there are no trailing zeros.

( ) parenthesis are used to enclose negative numbers.

m represents months (m = 6, mm = 06, mmm = Jun, mmmm = June).

d represents days (d = 6, dd = 06, ddd = Tue, dddd = Tuesday).

yy represents years (yy = 93, yyyy = 1993).

h represents hours; m following h represents minutes; AM/PM indicates 12-hour clock; no AM/PM indicates 24-hour clock.

Microsoft Graph also enables you to format numbers and dates with a different format for positive, negative, or zero values. A semicolon separates positive, negative, and zero formats. The combination $#,##0.00 ;($#,##0.00), for example, produces different formats for positive and negative numbers, as shown in the following example:

The number	Appears as
89875.4	$89,875.40
–567.23	($567.23)

When a negative format is enclosed in parentheses, the positive format usually has a space between the last digit and the semicolon. This space leaves a space at the end of the positive number to balance the trailing parenthesis on a negative number and helps positive and negative numbers align when a column is right aligned.

Custom Formatting of Numbers and Dates

If you don't find the format you need in the Number Format list, you can create custom formats by typing them in the Format text box. Use the same characters as used in the predefined formats. After creation, a custom format appears at the bottom of the Number Format list for later reuse. Que's book *Using Excel 4 for Windows*, Special Edition, covers creating custom formats extensively.

Adding Items to a Chart

You can add many items to make Microsoft Graph charts more informative and easier to read. Some of the items you add are movable, and some are fixed. Items fixed in position, when selected, appear with white handles at the corners. You cannot move or resize fixed items. You can move or resize items that, when selected, display black handles.

You use the Chart menu to add most items to a chart. For example, you can add titles, arrows, or a legend with this menu. To format an existing item, select the item and use the Format menu.

Adding Titles and Data Values

You can use the Chart menu to add or delete most items from a chart. To add a title to a fixed location on a chart, for example, follow these steps:

1. Choose the **Chart Titles** command. The Attach Title dialog box appears (see fig. 18.13).

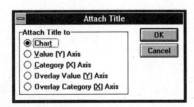

Fig. 18.13

The Attach Title dialog box.

2. Select one of the option buttons.

3. Choose OK or press Enter.

   If you choose Chart or one of the axis options, a default title of Title, X, Y, or Z appears at the appropriate location in the chart.

4. With this default title selected, type the text you want. Press Enter to move to a second line. Edit using normal editing keys.

5. To finish the text, Press Esc or click outside the text.

To remove fixed text, select the text and then press the Del key or choose the Edit Clear command.

To attach numbers or labels that move with the data point in a bar, column, or line chart, follow these steps:

1. Choose the Chart Data Labels command.

2. Select the Show Value or Show Label option. If you are working with a pie chart, you may choose the Show Percent option.

   The Show Value option labels each data point with its numeric value. The Show Label option labels each data point with its category name. The Show Percent option labels each slice in a pie chart with its percentage of the total value.

3. Choose OK or press Enter.

The Chart Data Labels command adds labels to all the data points. To remove the labels, select one of the labels and press Del or choose the Chart Data Labels command and select the None option. Either method removes all labels.

Adding Floating Text

You can use *floating text*, which you use to add comment boxes or to create boxes for embellishing or covering parts of a chart.

To add floating text, make sure that no other text is selected and then type the text you want to float. The text appears in a floating box surrounded by black handles. To complete the box, click outside the box or press Esc.

The black handles on selected text indicate that you can resize and move the text. To move the text, point to any area between two black boxes and drag the text to the new location. To resize the box enclosing the text, point to one of the handles (the pointer changes to a crosshair) and drag the handle. You can format floating text boxes to include colors and patterns, using the Format menu commands.

To use the keyboard to format the text, press the arrow keys until the text you want formatted is enclosed by black or white handles. You cannot use the keyboard to move floating text.

To edit the text in a floating text box, click on the text to select it and then click where you want the insertion point. Use the normal editing keys (Del and Backspace) to edit the text. To delete a floating text box, select the text and then press the Del key or use Edit Clear.

Adding Legends, Arrows, and Gridlines

To add a legend, choose the Chart Add Legend command. The legend appears. Notice that the legend is enclosed with black handles. To move the legend to a fixed location, select the legend and then choose the Format Legend command. Select one of the position options and choose OK. You also can drag the legend to a new location with the mouse. You cannot resize the legend.

To change labels used in the legend, change the series labels in the data sheet.

To add arrows to charts, make sure that an arrow isn't selected and then choose the Chart Add Arrow command. If an arrow is selected, the Chart Delete Arrow command replaces the Chart Add Arrow command. For resizing and pivoting, there are black handles at either end. To change the length of an arrow, point to one of the black boxes and drag the box to the desired length. To pivot the arrow around the head or tail, grab the appropriate box and move the head or tail to a new location. To move an arrow, drag with the pointer on the arrow's shaft. You can format arrows with different heads, thicknesses, or as a line, using the Format menu commands.

To add gridlines to a chart, choose the Chart Gridlines command. The Gridlines dialog box that appears has many check boxes for vertical and horizontal gridlines. To delete gridlines, choose the Chart Gridlines command again and clear the check boxes for the gridlines you no longer want.

Formatting the Chart and Chart Items

After you select a predefined chart format and add chart items, you can customize a chart. You can change the colors, patterns, and borders of chart items; the type and color of the fonts; and the position and size of some chart items. By selecting an axis and then selecting a format command, you can change the scale and the appearance of tick marks and labels. You also can rotate 3-D charts and create picture charts, in which pictures take the place of columns, bars, or lines.

Customize charts by selecting an item in the chart and then choosing a format command, as in the following steps:

1. Select the chart item you want to customize by clicking on the item or by pressing an arrow key until the chart item is selected.

2. Choose the Format menu and select the appropriate command to format the item.

3. Select the changes you want to make from the dialog box that appears.

4. Choose OK or press Enter.

T I P   As a shortcut, you can double-click on any chart item, such as an arrow, bar, or chart background, and this item's Pattern dialog box appears. You then can change the item's pattern, border, color, or line weight or choose one of the buttons in the dialog box to move to another dialog box such as Font, Scale, or Text.

Changing Patterns and Colors

To add patterns or colors to an item, choose the Format Pattern command and select the colors, patterns, shading, and line widths you want for the item. To display the item's Pattern dialog box with a mouse, double-click on the item.

You can return to the default colors, patterns, and borders by selecting the chart items you want to change, choose the Format Patterns command, and then select the Automatic option.

T I P   You are limited to 16 colors, but can blend these colors to create custom colors. To create a custom color palette, choose the Format Color Palette command. After the Palette dialog box appears, select the color you want to replace and then choose the Edit button. When the custom palette appears, type new color numbers or click in the palette and choose OK. The custom color replaces the color you previously selected. To return to the original color settings, choose the Default button.

Formatting Fonts and Text

One font, size, and style are used by the entire data sheet. Each text item in the chart, however, can have a different font, size, or style.

To change an item's font, size, or style, select the item and then choose the Format Font command. Select the font, size, or style you want. With a mouse, double-click on the item and then choose the Font button to tunnel through to the Font dialog box. The Font dialog box resembles Font dialog boxes found in most Windows applications but enables you to select different kinds of character backgrounds.

To rotate or align text, such as the text on an axis, select the text or axis and then choose the Format Text command. Select the text orientation from the options and choose OK.

Formatting Axes

By default, Microsoft Graph scales and labels the axes, but you can select any axis and change the scale, how frequently labels or tick marks appear, and the orientation and font of text.

Microsoft Graph scales charts to even amounts. To rescale charts, select the axis (vertical or horizontal) and then choose the Format Scale command. (A shortcut is to double-click on an axis. When the Pattern dialog box appears, choose the Scale button.) If you select the Category (X) Axis, you can change tick marks styles and spacing or labels spacing along the horizontal axis. If you select the Value (Y) Axis, you can change the vertical axis' beginning and ending values, the number of increments and the kind of tick marks. Figure 18.14 shows the Format Axis Scale dialog box for the Value (Y) Axis, where you can adjust the end points and increments.

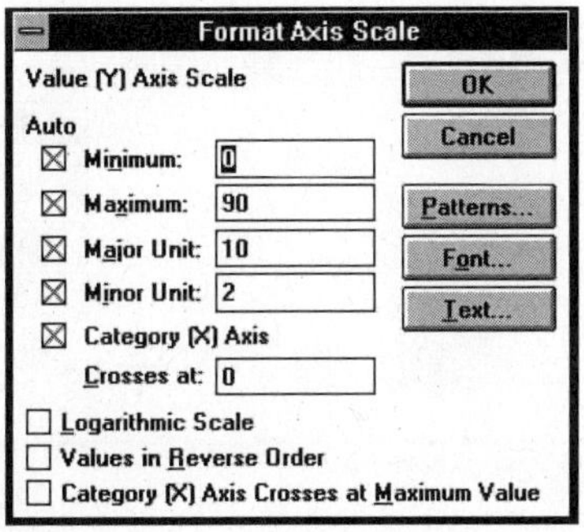

Fig. 18.14

Format Axis Scale dialog box for the Value (Y) Axis.

To thin out the number of tick marks or overlapping labels along the Category (X) Axis, select the axis and then choose the Format **S**cale command. Select the text boxes for either or both Number Of Categories (or Series) Between Tick **L**abels and Number of Categories (or Series) Between Tick Ma**r**ks. If you type *5* in a box, for example, every fifth tick mark and label is displayed. Choose OK or press Enter. Figure 18.15 shows the Format Axis Scale dialog box for the Category (X) Axis where you can adjust the frequency of data labels and tick marks.

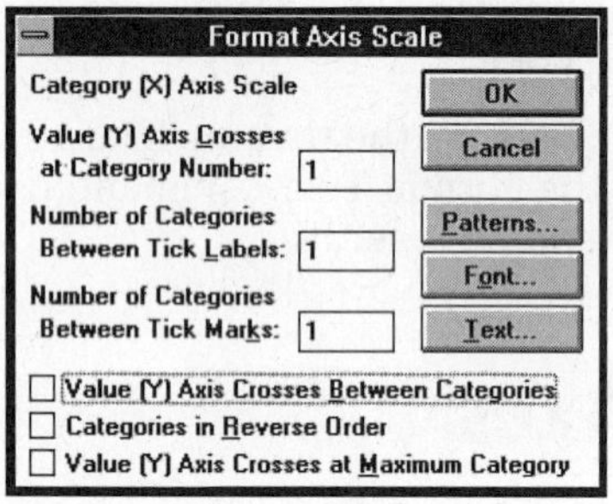

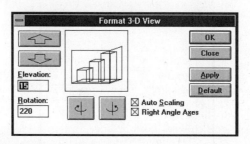

Fig. 18.15

The Format Axis Scale dialog box for the Category (X) Axis.

To change how tick marks appear on an axis scale, double-click on the axis or select the axis and choose the Format **P**attern command.

Rotating 3-D Charts

If a 3-D chart appears so that you don't have a good point-of-view to see the entire chart, you can rotate the chart to show the angle you want (see fig. 18.16). To rotate a 3-D chart, follow these steps:

1. Choose the Forma**t 3**-D View command. The Format 3-D View dialog box appears (see fig. 18.16).

Fig. 18.16

The Format 3-D View dialog box.

2. Change the **E**levation, **P**erspective, or **R**otation by clicking on the appropriate buttons or by typing values. Changing these values affects the wire frame sample chart.

3. When the wire frame sample is oriented so that you can see the chart as you want, choose OK or press Enter.

The **A**pply button enables you to apply the new orientation to the chart and still keep the dialog box open, which helps when you are experimenting. To return to the original orientation, choose the **D**efault button.

Exiting or Updating Graphs

You can keep Microsoft Graph open and update the chart in an application or close Microsoft Graph and update the chart. Updating the chart embeds the chart and that data in the other application. The chart and data cannot be saved separately but must be saved as embedded objects within another application.

To see how a chart or your changes appear in an application, you don't need to close Microsoft Graph. To keep Microsoft Graph open and update the new or existing chart in the document, choose the **F**ile **U**pdate command. You then can use the standard Windows methods for making the application window active. Press Alt+Tab until the application window is selected and then release both keys or press Ctrl+Esc to bring up the Task list, select the application from the list, and choose Switch To.

When you exit Microsoft Graph, you are asked whether you want to update the new or existing chart in the application. To exit Microsoft Graph, choose the **F**ile **E**xit and Return to Document command. If you made changes since the last update, you are prompted to update the chart in the document. Choose Yes to update the chart.

Summary

If you are familiar with charting in Microsoft Excel, use what you learned in Microsoft Excel to learn about Microsoft Graph. For more information about Microsoft Graph, refer to the book *Using Excel 4 for Windows*, Special Edition, published by Que Corporation. Many descriptions, tips, and tricks used in this best-selling book also apply to Microsoft Graph.

Running Applications under Windows NT

Running Windows Applications

T his chapter discusses the environment presented to users of
applications coded specifically for the Windows NT Win32 and
Win16 user mode subsystems. An application coded for Win32 is a
Windows NT application. An application coded for Win16 is a Windows
3.x application. We use the *Win32* and *Win16* shorthand because to
Windows NT, both of these (and several other) application program
interfaces (APIs) are a sort of suboperating system of the Windows NT
operating system. Any number of these subsystems can, in theory, be
launched to allow applications coded for different operating systems to
be executed on a Windows NT workstation.

Under Windows 3.x, OS/2, and certain versions of UNIX and Mach,
users became accustomed to operating systems that ran applications
written for different operating systems. With Windows NT, this aspect
of system software is expanded sufficiently to become nearly bewildering in its complexity.

These capabilities are a tremendous convenience to the user. But when a feature of software interfacing is touted as "transparent to the end-user," this assertion is nearly always made because aspects of the interface are not totally transparent to the end-user. As President Harry Truman said, "If a man prays too loud at church, run home and lock your smokehouse." This principle is applicable to all software marketing claims and to advertising in general!

Application Launching

As you know, Windows NT contains subsystems for MS-DOS, POSIX, OS/2 1.x, and Windows 3.1, enabling you to run those types of applications besides running Windows NT applications. When you start an application, the respective subsystem is responsible for managing that application.

Windows NT can launch any of the supported applications by one of three methods. These three methods are:

- Double-clicking the icon representing the application or one of its projects: either the picture icon representing the application or application project found in the appropriate group in the Windows NT Program Manager, or the application executable icon or one of its associated project icons in the File Manager.

- Using the Program Manager or the File Manager's File Run option to bring up a dialog box into which you can insert either the name of a program or the name of a project whose extension has been associated with an executable by the File Manager's File menu Associate option. You can insert this name in the Run dialog box by typing the name or selecting an executable file with the Browse option of the Run dialog box. Then type any optional command-line arguments, such as the file name of a project.

- Typing in the Command Prompt window the name of a program executable residing in the current directory or in one of the directories in the search path, followed by any command-line arguments, such as the file name of a project. Optionally, you can precede the name of the program with the Command Prompt START command. Doing so launches the desired application asynchronously with the Command Prompt, allowing the latter to continue to be used while the application thus launched is running.

Understanding the Win32 Subsystem

At the heart of Windows NT is the NT kernel. This core body of routines is the major component of that which must be ported across architectures by Microsoft engineers to bring up Windows NT on a new processor. Pretty much all of the essential Windows NT system above the kernel level is written in high-level programming languages and can be recompiled without recoding when Microsoft decides to introduce Windows NT to another hardware platform.

Above the kernel is the NT *executive*. This is the main system services interface, controlling I/O, networking, security, hardware access, and so on. Both the NT kernel and the executive operate at the *highest level of privilege*. This means that they are free to perform operations forbidden to code operating at lower privilege levels. For instance, direct access to computer hardware is performed by kernel and executive code. Nothing in the Windows NT environment other than the kernel and the executive operate at this level of privilege.

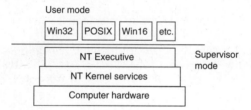

Fig. 19.1

A representation of the NT system's hierarchy.

Figure 19.1 shows the hierarchy of the Windows NT system. Above the hardware itself is the NT Kernel and Executive, operating in supervisor mode (Ring 0 on the Intel 80386 and above). Operating in user mode (Ring 3 on the Intel 80396 and above) are the user-mode subsystems which provide the application program interface.

The API

The kernel and the executive together technically constitute an operating system, but this is still not an application program interface.

The *application program interface*, or API, is the set of routines that defines the mechanisms whereby a specific application can be inserted between the user and the rest of the computer system (hardware and software). In most operating systems, including Windows NT, the application program is sandwiched between two layers of the operating system.

The operating system handles mouse and keyboard input. The operating system passes this input to the appropriate application, then passes the output of the application to (for example) the user, a disk, or a modem. This interaction between the active application and the operating system is the application program interface. To further understand this concept, recognize that Windows 3.x is an alternative API superimposed on the traditional MS-DOS API.

Multiple Application Programming Interfaces

The Windows NT operating system permits multiple, alternative application program interfaces to coexist in one desktop session.

No particular application program interface is hard-coded into the Windows NT kernel and executive. Instead, the application program interface is a type of application program called a *user-mode subsystem*, which is coded with information on how to call the desired low-level hardware and software services from the Windows NT kernel and executive.

Win32 is the most important user-mode subsystem in the Windows NT hierarchy. It is the *native API* of Windows NT. Win32 is the "windows" in Windows NT. Win32, among its other responsibilities, provides the *graphical user interface* (GUI) of Windows NT. This GUI is similar to the one for Windows 3.x. It provides this interface not only for Win32-targeted application programs, but also for other user-mode subsystems so that they can be part of the desktop display and user interaction.

Win32 is an integral part of the user interface for all other user-mode subsystems. These other application program interfaces call Win32 for their display and other services. For instance, the MS-DOS command prompt (see fig. 19.2)—which offers a powerful DPMI environment for compatibility with the most modern MS-DOS applications in addition to its capability to launch applications for any other Windows NT subsystem—appears in its little window by calls to the Win32 subsystem.

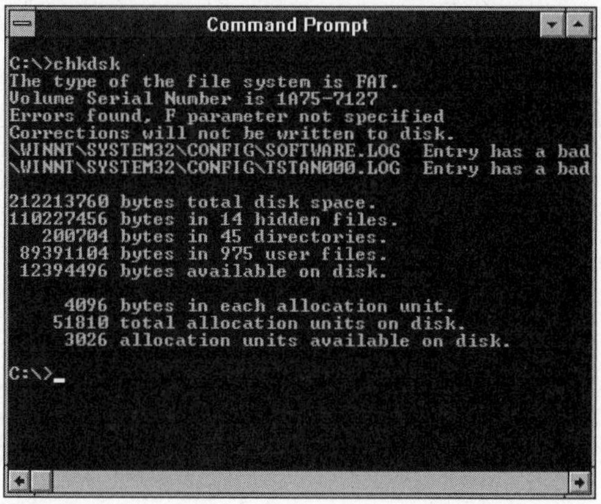

Fig. 19.2

The Command Prompt window displays on-screen by calls made to the Win32 sub-system.

Applications coded specifically to run as native, 32-bit, graphic, mouse-driven applications under Windows NT are Win32 applications. Win32 applications generally are coded by programmers using the Win32 SDK (Software Development Kit), a product sold separately by Microsoft.

The Win32 subsystem is launched automatically at the start of every Windows NT login session, because part of its responsibility is to present the user with the GUI and the Windows NT Program Manager. Without Win32, you would be staring at a blank screen, which would not be very informative or useful!

Win32 Threads and Windows NT Preemptive Multitasking

Native Windows NT applications that use the Win32 GUI to interact with the user look much like good old Windows 3.x applications: The menus look the same, the scroll bars look the same, and so on. Behind this facade of familiarity, however, lurk some surprising capabilities inherent in Win32 that were denied applications running under Windows 3.x.

The most notable is the capability of the Win32 API to draw on the resources of the Windows NT kernel to provide an application with *multiple threads of execution*. We know from Windows 3.x that multiple applications can be launched and run at the same time. All Windows 3.x applications consist of a single thread that is spliced at runtime into the Windows 3.x GUI's single thread of execution for the entire GUI.

Multitasking

Multitasking is a computer operating system's ability to run more than one program at the same time. On computers with one microprocessor, this is achieved by dividing the microprocessor's time among individual tasks to give the appearance that all tasks are running concurrently. On computers having multiple microprocessors, tasks are assigned to different microprocessors.

In both types of multitasking, a portion of the operating system called a *dispatcher* schedules each task's turn at execution, be it in a time slot or on a distinct processor. The Windows 3.1 dispatcher schedules programs as tasks, but doesn't offer any fancier multitasking than merely allowing multiple programs to execute at the same time. The Windows NT multitasker is more sophisticated: its dispatcher not only allows multiple programs to execute at once, but also allows programs to schedule concurrent execution of separate sections of their code. Therefore, a spreadsheet program may be calculating while continuing to allow the user to input data simultaneously, a capability not present in the Windows 3.1 operating environment.

Under Windows NT, a Win32 application multitasks not only by merely appearing on the Windows desktop running alongside other applications (as is the case in Windows 3.1); It may further, under Windows NT, multitask *within itself*, performing multiple operations asynchronously as the Windows NT preemptive multitasking kernel provides each individual thread of execution with processor time.

A Win32 application consists of at least one thread and optionally as many threads as necessary and permitted by the resources allocated to the application.

A notable feature of the Win32 GUI is that it doesn't freeze up the way Windows 3.x does when an application gets busy. For instance, when you launch an application from the Program Manager in Windows 3.x, it's usually impossible to minimize the Program Manager while the new application is loading. This is because Windows 3.x multitasking, such as it is, is based on a cooperative, message-driven model. When a Windows 3.x application receives control of the (single) processor, it keeps that control until it chooses to yield the processor, and a loading application is generally in no position to yield the processor.

By contrast, the Windows NT kernel preempts each thread of execution periodically, based on internal timer interrupts. A program still may voluntarily relinquish the processor(s) on which it is executing. One or more threads of an executing application may even block for a specific event or class of events, that is, relinquish the processor until a certain event has occurred. In any case, every thread is paused at the end of its time slice, which is arbitrated by the Windows NT kernel as a balance between the requirements of the thread and the requirements of the system.

Again, under Windows 3.x, pressing the Alt+Tab combination and holding Alt to browse through running applications freezes the active window. This is not true for Win32 applications running under Windows NT; the active window (along with all other threads of execution, visible or invisible) continues processing.

Remember that under Windows 3.x, any disk access generally prevents other useful work from taking place until the disk access is completed. By contrast, under the Win32 GUI, note the new selection on the gauge that shows the progress during a floppy disk formatting operation (see figure 19.3). If you click the **H**ide button, the gauge disappears and you can minimize the File Manager. Alternatively, you can click another application or use the Task Manager or Program Manager to call up an application to allow work to proceed, despite the fact that intensive disk access is taking place. Other disk operations (at least those that do not involve the floppy disk being formatted) can take place concurrently.

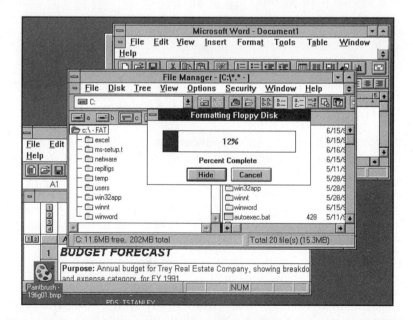

Fig. 19.3

With multi-threading, you can switch to other tasks while performing disk operations in the background.

The preemptive model of multitasking used by Windows NT in native Win32 applications is a boon to the convenience and productivity of the end-user.

Win32 Applications and Remote Files

Some applications implicitly or explicitly use files on one or more remote Windows NT or Windows for Workgroups workstations. The user
who invokes such an application or wants to use any Windows NT application to access remote files must be granted the necessary security
permissions on the remote system to access such files. If a security-
related error occurs in accessing remote files, contact the Administrator account holder of the remote Windows NT workstation in question.
For more information about Windows NT security see Chapter 29,
"Understanding File Security in Windows NT," and Chapter 30,
"Understanding System Security in Windows NT."

Win32 Applications and Distributed Processing

Certain Win32 applications invoke execution threads that run on one
or more remote Windows NT servers rather than on the user's workstation. In this case, just as with files you want to access on a remote
system, certain permissions must be granted to the user by the Administrator of the remote system. If an application you are using returns an
error dialog box associated with the execution of a *remote procedure
call* (RPC), contact the Administrator account holder of the remote
Windows NT workstation in question.

Multitasking and Virtual Memory

It's loads of fun running multiple applications, but doesn't Windows NT
ever run out of memory? The answer is "always and almost never."

Windows NT is a virtual memory system that divides all memory into
4-kilobyte *pages*. At any time, a given page may be in RAM or on disk in
the PAGEFILE.SYS file. A Windows NT session pretty much cannot run
out of memory until not only physical RAM but all of PAGEFILE.SYS (up
to its maximum size) has been exhausted.

The Windows NT virtual memory implementation is more powerful and
more efficient than the virtual memory system of Windows 3.x, 386-
enhanced mode. Despite Windows NT's intensive memory requirements leading to more individual instances of paging to disk, the paging
of memory is smoother and much less noticeable than that of Windows
3.x. And if you ever start to run short, just increase the size of the
Pagefile, as shown in fig. 19.4.

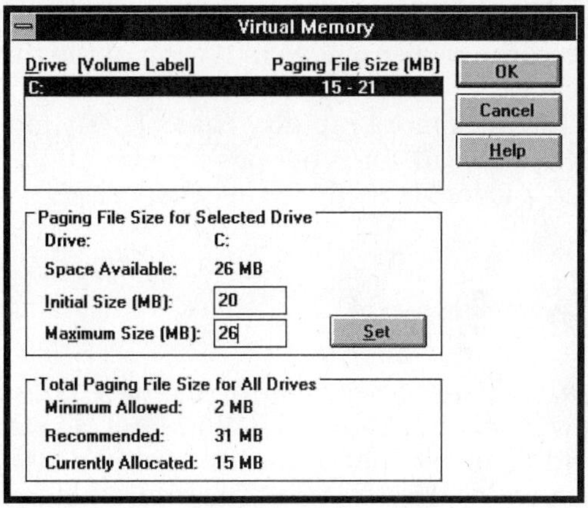

Fig. 19.4

Changing
Windows NT
virtual memory
settings.

Understanding Symmetric Multiprocessing

By providing preemptive multitasking, Windows NT has greatly improved its performance over its DOS-based predecessor. Beyond that, there remains much more to the architecture of the environment in which Windows NT applications execute.

The Windows NT kernel supports symmetric multiprocessing. Although the vast majority of Windows NT users do not have machines that provide multiple microprocessors on which the operating system may execute, Windows NT is designed primarily for just such hardware. This design decision on the part of the Microsoft development teams was based on the reasonable assumption that such multiprocessor hardware, which is already becoming the norm in the high-end workstation market, will repeat computer history and become within a few years as common as single-processor, 386-based desktop machines are today.

How Windows NT Handles Multiple Processors

Windows NT kernel multitasking support is based on a queue of threads, sorted by priority, waiting for execution. The Windows NT kernel is capable of scheduling and dispatching these threads of execution on one processor or many processors.

Picture a casino blackjack dealer. The deck has 52 cards. If three players are at the table, the dealer will deal to each of the three, "hitting" on request. If five players are at the table, the dealer will do the same, but he'll go through the deck more rapidly. That's pretty much how Windows NT dispatches threads or programs for execution. Threads get dealt to whatever "player" is ready for another "card."

Safe at Any Speed

If you are using a single-processor 386- or 486-based desktop, you will have noticed how much more smoothly Windows NT runs than Windows 3.x. In addition, many operations run a good deal faster under Windows NT than under Windows 3.x. The future holds even more: The programmer's jargon describing how Windows NT executes on a multi-processor machine is that it "fairly screams."

If you are the sort who needs to know how fast Windows NT executes, we commend to your attention PERFMON.EXE, the Windows NT performance monitor. PERFMON.EXE is found in the Program Manager's Administrative Tools group as the Performance Monitor, shown in figure 19.5. The Performance Monitor helps track system load so that the adminstrator can see the impact of configuration changes and varying load conditions.

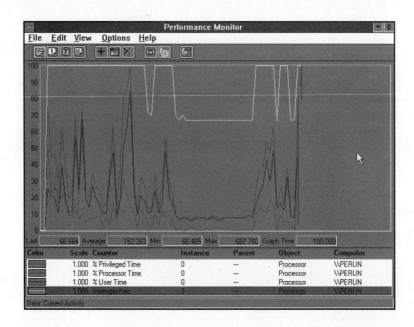

Fig. 19.5

The Windows NT Performance Monitor.

Understanding Win16

As mentioned, Windows NT is prepared to run not only a native Win32 application, but also your favorite Windows 3.x applications. Windows NT does this through the Win16 user-mode subsystem.

Like the Win32 user-mode subsystem, Win16 is a program charged with the responsibility of providing the API for a class of application programs—in this case, Windows 3.x programs.

Win16 works by emulating, or imitating, the environment under which Windows 3.x applications were intended to run.

The Win16 subsystem is not loaded expressly by the user, nor is it loaded automatically at powerup. Instead, it is loaded automatically whenever the user attempts to launch the first Windows 3.x application of a login session. To this extent, it is nearly transparent to the end-user. However, you will notice that the first Windows 3.x application launched during a login session takes a little longer to load than subsequent ones: this is because the first application causes the Win16 subsystem to load and initialize itself, which takes a few seconds.

What Is Win16 Doing?

The Win16 subsystem spends most of its time translating 16-bit Windows 3.x transactions into equivalent 32-bit Win32 transactions. When there is no equivalent transaction, the Win16 subsystem performs some fancy footwork. Well, some of the footwork is fancy; some of it is a little lead-footed! In general, you will find that most Windows 3.x programs execute at about the same speed under Windows NT that they did under Windows 3.x, with some operations noticeably slower and some operations noticeably faster.

Windows on Windows

Microsoft also calls the Win16 subsystem WOW, which means "Windows on Windows." With what you've read so far, it may sound like Win16 opens a largish window inside which Windows 3.x executes in its own little world, but in fact no such thing happens.

Win16 allows Windows 3.x applications to appear on the desktop alongside Win32 applications coded specifically for Windows NT, as shown in figure 19.6. You can't tell merely from static appearance which applications are the Win16 applications and which are Win32 applications.

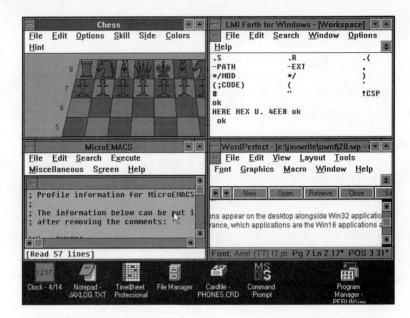

Fig. 19.6

A busy Windows
NT desktop:
Which applica-
tions are Win16
and which are
Win32?

Constraints on Win16 Applications

Under Windows NT, not every Windows 3.x application will run, or run
exactly as it did under Windows 3.x. A problematic application usually
is one that attempts to address hardware directly. This category includes disk optimizers, FAX card software, and tape drive software.

The chain of security is only as strong as its weakest link. It would be
useless for Windows NT to strictly safeguard the operations of Win32
applications, only to ignore the mischief an MS-DOS or Windows 3.x
application can cause.

With this problem in mind, Windows NT interposes layers between an
application and the hardware platform, and just shuts down an offending application. Many of these protection layers were absent in Windows 3.x, so Windows 3.x programs sometimes expect to be able to
perform operations that are not allowed under Windows NT.

Another type of application that may no longer work under Win16 is
one that assumes the presence of the MS-DOS file system on a disk you
have formatted to NTFS. Some disk backup software is in this category.

New applications and device drivers for hardware-specific applications
must be specifically coded for Windows NT to provide the functionality
of the older applications, but do so in a way that doesn't try to short-
circuit any security built into the Windows NT kernel.

Multitasking Win16 Applications

After Windows 3.x applications are launched, they appear and behave as they do in their native Windows 3.x environment. Actually, they behave a little too much like they do in their native environment, which will encourage many users to adopt as quickly as possible a suite of Win32 programs. Win32-specific programs are much more versatile and powerful than corresponding Win16 programs.

Recall the previous discussion about how the Windows NT kernel multitasks the one or more threads that constitute an application running on a Windows NT system. Remember also that user-mode subsystems are themselves applications being run by the same Windows NT kernel.

Although the Win32 subsystem that provides the API to native Windows NT applications is multithreaded, the API that Windows 3.x applications expect and are prepared to deal with is a single thread of messaging between all running applications and the Windows 3.x system. This same environment, including its limitations, is emulated closely by the Win16 subsystem included with Windows NT. Windows 3.x applications running under Win16 exhibit the same sluggishness of control that they exhibit under Windows 3.x.

It is possible to dash around the Windows NT Program Manager, clicking several application icons to launch them all more or less simultaneously. Win32 applications will all start loading at once, but only one Win16 application will launch at a time because that's how Windows 3.x works. Because Win16 is emulating the same messaging system between Win16 client applications, it behaves in the same manner as Windows 3.x.

Here is another example that shows what is happening in the Win16 subsystem. Users of WordPerfect for Windows 3.x may have noticed that when WordPerfect is exited under Windows 3.x, it takes a moment to complete its internal recordkeeping and cleanups. During that time, it does not relinquish the single Windows 3.x thread of execution and thus does not allow other applications whose windows or icons have been revealed by the disappearance of the WordPerfect window to redraw themselves. After a few moments, WordPerfect completes its exit and relinquishes Windows 3.x's single thread of execution, at which point all the icons and windows on the Windows 3.x desktop are instructed to redraw themselves.

The Windows NT desktop presents a more interesting and varied spectacle under these circumstances. When WordPerfect for Windows 3.x running under the Win16 subsystem is closed, all the icons for Win32 applications (and for applications running under user-mode subsystems other than the Win16 subsystem) that are revealed by the disappearance of the WordPerfect window instantly redraw themselves. However, the Win16 applications on the desktop do not redraw themselves until WordPerfect has completed its internal calculations and relinquished the Win16 thread of execution (which is emulating the Windows 3.1 messaging system), at which point the Win16 subsystem is able to send the redraw message to each of the Win16 client applications and process the returning messages.

Win16 shares the strengths and weaknesses of Windows 3.x. An ill-behaved application may still, by refusing to relinquish execution, lock up Win16, just as it could lock up Windows 3.x in the same fashion. However, under Windows NT, a lockup of the Win16 subsystem affects only Windows 3.x applications running under that subsystem: the rest of the desktop, Win32 applications, POSIX applications, and so on, continue to operate normally.

Win16 Application Error Handling

What Win16 does when it is given its turn at the processor is entirely up to Win16. The Windows NT kernel and executive are running in protected memory at a higher level of privilege than all user subsystems. Win32, which provides much of the interface that Win16 draws on, runs in its own protected memory space like all Windows NT applications.

Win16's emulation of Windows 3.x cannot crash the Windows NT operating system or lock up the Windows NT desktop created by Win32. However, Win16 can crash itself and lock itself up just as neatly as the Windows 3.x environment that Win16 is emulating can when afflicted by a runaway Windows 3.x application.

In the event of a Windows 3.x application crash, Win16 usually handles matters itself and presents a Win32-style subsystem-modal dialog box reminiscent of Windows 3.x dialogs regarding runaway applications. A *subsystem-modal dialog box* is a dialog box to which the user must respond before the subsystem presenting the dialog will continue processing. The Win16 subsystem-modal dialog box shown in figure 19.7 suspends all Windows 3.x applications running at the time it pops up until the user has clicked the OK or Cancel button in the dialog box.

After the user responds to the dialog appropriately, Win16 may close the offending application or even shut down the entire Win16 subsystem. In such a case, you can usually relaunch the Win16 subsystem invisibly by simply opening a Win16 application. Under the current release of Windows NT, in those rare instances when the Win16 application or the Win16 subsystem will not restart, logging off and logging in again appears to reset things sufficiently to continue.

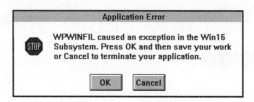

Fig. 19.7

The Win16 subsystem-modal error dialog box.

NOTE In figure 19.7, we purposely generated an application error that caused the Win16 subsystem to suspend all processing in its own domain until the user replies to the subsystem-modal dialog box. This error was produced by exploiting a bug in a preliminary release of Windows NT. Microsoft has already corrected this bug, and it will not appear in your copy of Windows NT. This figure also is not intended to reflect negatively on WordPerfect for Windows, which runs just peachy under Win16.

The suspension of Win16 application processing during the presentation of a subsystem-modal error dialog does not interfere with applications running native under Win32 or under other Windows NT user-mode subsystems, except that none of the Win16 applications will respond, redraw, or minimize. This can leave the display a bit messy if the user chooses temporarily to ignore the subsystem-modal dialog. But the Task Manager is still accessible with Ctrl+Esc, so you can ignore a subsystem error if you don't need any subsystem applications immediately and you don't mind screen clutter. But don't count on being able to get a good look at your wallpaper!

If matters get beyond what Win16 can handle, Windows NT either shuts down the Win16 subsystem (and all running Windows 3.x applications) or enables the user to shut down the problem applications with the Windows NT Task Manager.

All Things Considered

The result for the user of all this complex interaction between related subsystems and the applications exploiting the APIs is that Windows NT native Win32 applications and Windows 3.x Win16 applications can coexist on the same desktop GUI, exchange data through the clipboard and dynamic data exchange, and generally offer all the conveniences to which we have become accustomed…and then some!

Installation and Setup of Win16 Applications

A pleasant surprise about Windows 3.x applications running under the Windows NT Win16 subsystem is that such applications are often easier to install under Windows NT than under Windows 3.x. The MS-DOS attitude that everything stops for disk access is pleasantly lacking in Windows NT. Although the limitations of Windows 3.x are also the limitations of Win16, the Windows NT desktop and other subsystems do not become unusable during a Setup operation. You can perform other tasks while a long, multidisk Setup is running, as long as the tasks revolve around Win32 applications or applications spawned by other subsystems. At appropriate intervals, the requester for the next disk will pop up. Satisfy it, and it goes away. Back to FreeCell!

WIN.INI and SYSTEM.INI

The %SYSTEMROOT%\WINNT directory is the directory returned to a program when it calls for a pointer to the Windows directory. This directory contains WIN.INI and SYSTEM.INI files. These files are only for Win16 applications; Win32 applications do not use them.

Windows 3.x users spend some of their time editing WIN.INI and SYSTEM.INI to make their systems and favorite applications run correctly. Under Windows NT, however, this sort of information is no longer kept in text files. Most of the information about the system and about applications which formerly was contained in INI files is now embedded in the Windows NT Registration Database, covered in Chapter 22, "Running DOS Applications."

Windows 3.x applications running under Windows NT will, however, still occasionally want to look at WIN.INI and SYSTEM.INI, so these files are provided with Windows NT and may be edited to suit the application suite you are running.

Sanity Check Setup

In general, Setup programs for Windows 3.x applications work fine under the Windows NT Win16 subsystem. They correctly copy and expand files, and add or modify program groups. When installing Windows 3.x applications, it's still useful to run on a Windows NT workstation to sanity-check Setup! Not everything that a Windows 3.x Setup will do is appropriate, desirable, or effective for Windows NT.

In particular, watch out for Setup dialogs that request permission
to add or change path or environment variable statements in
AUTOEXEC.BAT, or that try to change settings or install new software
in CONFIG.SYS. The AUTOEXEC.BAT and CONFIG.SYS files have diminished effect on the Windows NT Command Prompt and no effect on the
execution environment of the typical Win32 or Win16 program. You
must take situation-specific action in those cases where Setup attempts
to insert information critical to the correct execution of an application
into these now-unreferenced startup files. For instance, the correct response an attempt by Setup to insert SET statements in
AUTOEXEC.BAT is to edit appropriately the environment variables
associated with your login environment by using the System dialog box
of the Control Panel, as shown in fig 19.8.

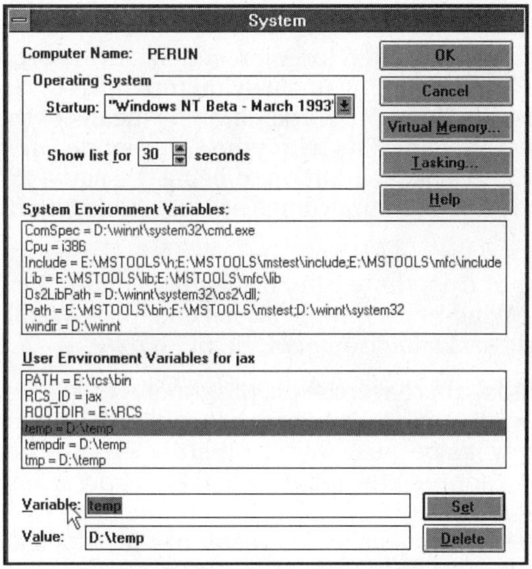

Fig. 19.8

The Control Panel
System dialog
box for changing
environment
variables.

On the other hand, if Setup tries to change CONFIG.SYS, especially to
add drivers to be loaded at bootup, you will have to contact the provider of the program undergoing SETUP to find out how to install the
program correctly under Windows NT.

NOTE When a Windows 3.x Setup wants to change AUTOEXEC.BAT
or CONFIG.SYS, often it offers the alternative of writing
the proposed changes to a separate file for the user to examine later and manually make the necessary adjustments.
Accept this alternative, examine the output file of changes

continues

continued

proposed by Setup, then use your knowledge of the Windows NT environment acquired from this book and from experience to make equivalent adjustments to your login environment or to the common environment of the system.

Win32s

Just in case you are beginning to think you understand the relationship between native Windows NT applications (Win32) and Windows 3.x applications (Win16), there's one more element to add to the confusion: Win32s.

Win16 applications are coded for Microsoft Windows 3.x, which is essentially a 16-bit API resting uneasily on top of MS-DOS. Win16 applications run on a Windows NT workstation by means of the Win16 user-mode subsystem that coexists with other user-mode subsystems, in particular Win32. Win32, in addition to being the native API of Windows NT, provides the hook to important services needed by the Win16 subsystem.

The inverse is not true: there is no mechanism under Windows 3.x whereby 32-bit Windows NT applications coded for Win32 can be run in the 16-bit Windows 3.x environment. Right? *Wrong.*

Maybe it's because there were extra programmers at Microsoft, twiddling their thumbs. Maybe it's because they didn't want us to get too smug. Most likely it's because Microsoft strives for the convenience of the end-user but appreciates the time and effort programmers have invested in software they have coded or are planning to code for Windows NT. Whatever the reason, Microsoft has provided a development and execution environment called Win32s (pronounced *Win-thirty-two-ess*) that allows many Windows NT native Win32 applications to run under good old Windows 3.x.

What Is Win32s?

Win32s consists mainly of two components. The first component of Win32s is a set of *dynamic link libraries* (DLLs) distributed by the software provider along with the Win32s application. You do not have to buy these DLLs; Microsoft provided them to the creator of the software you will be using, and the creator provides them to you on a disk with the software you purchase.

The Win32s DLLs are not necessary to run a Win32(s) application un-der Windows NT. The DLLs are installed by the application's Setup program only if it detects that the application is being installed on a Windows 3.x workstation rather than a Windows NT workstation, and that the same version or a later version of the particular Win32s DLLs is not already installed.

These Win32s DLLs are necessary only for Windows 3.0 and Windows 3.1. Later versions of Windows for DOS will have these DLLs already present and will support Win32s applications out of the box. Setup programs for Windows NT applications designed to run under Windows 3.x will recognize later versions and will not uselessly install the (now-) superfluous DLLs.

The second component in the Win32s system is a set of coding guide-lines that must be followed by the programmer authoring an applica-tion intended to run on both Win32 and Windows 3/4 Win32s. Not all Windows NT native Win32 applications will run on a Windows 3/4 work-station, even if the Win32s DLLs are already installed.

Using a Win32s Application

Consult the manual for the application you would like to run on both Windows NT and Windows 3.x to see whether it is a Windows 3.x appli-cation or a Win32s application. In either case, the application will run under both Windows NT and Windows 3.x, if other system require-ments (memory, disk space, and so on) are met and installation is com-pleted successfully.

 **NOTE** To run Win32s applications under Windows 3.x, your Win-dows 3.x workstation must have at least 2 megabytes of physical RAM (4 megabytes are recommended) and be run-ning in 386-enhanced mode with paging enabled. No, Win32s applications won't run on your 286 box any more than Win-dows NT will!

Win32s applications running under Windows NT sometimes have capa-bilities that are absent under Windows 3.x. These capabilities are the ones that depend on advanced features of Windows NT. Consult the manual for the particular program to determine which features of the program are available when running under Windows 3.x.

Summary

The useful application programs you have become accustomed to under Windows 3.x can still, by and large, be used effectively under Windows NT thanks to the implementation of the Win16 subsystem, which runs 16-bit Windows applications side by side with Windows NT native Win32 subsystem applications. Generally, only minor details of performance differentiate these two types of applications. In some instances, however, Windows 3.x applications will not run correctly under Windows NT, especially when the Windows 3.x application attempts certain types of hardware access that are subject to security under Windows NT.

Users must exercise their best judgment when installing Windows 3.x applications on a Windows NT workstation, because the Setup for some Windows 3.x applications may attempt inappropriate or ineffective environment modifications.

In addition to the conveniences typically associated with the multitasking Windows environment, Windows NT offers enhancements in the form of preemptive multitasking, multiprocessor support, improved virtual memory management, and remote procedure calls allowing threads of applications to execute on remote Windows NT workstations.

Not only can most Windows 3.x applications run under Windows NT, selected Windows NT applications can run under Windows 3/4, if the software provider coded them specifically to do so.

Using the Command Prompt

The capability to conveniently switch between Windows and DOS has always been available in the Windows environment. With the introduction of Windows NT, Microsoft has made this capability substantially more powerful. The Main program group contains the familiar icon labeled *MSDOS Command Prompt*. By activating this icon, you can issue DOS commands, start various subsystem applications, do network administration, and integrate applications using cut-and-paste operations.

What Is the Command Prompt?

The command prompt is a single, character-based interface providing a common access to five operating systems: Windows NT, OS/2 version 1.x, POSIX-compliant programs, Windows 3.1, and DOS. Don't be confused by the MS-DOS application icon. The power of each of these subsystems is at your fingertips after the command prompt is activated.

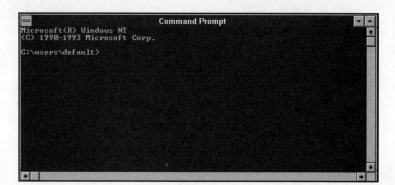

Fig. 20.1

The command
prompt window.

Each of these subsystems operates independently. The command prompt processor evaluates each command you enter, selects the appropriate subsystem, and passes the command line to that subsystem.

Starting the Command Prompt Window

The Command Prompt window can be started either by highlighting its icon and pressing the Enter key or by double-clicking on the icon. Either method causes the Command Prompt to activate and display the Command Prompt window.

You find the Command Prompt window icon in the Program Manager's Main group window. Don't be fooled by the appearance of the icon—MS-DOS. This icon starts the command prompt. Of course, you will most likely issue MS-DOS commands from the command prompt window. However, the command prompt window enables you to issue network commands and start POSIX and OS/2 character-based applications, besides starting MS-DOS applications.

Starting Programs in the Command Prompt

In order to start a subsystem application, you type its name at the command-line prompt and press the Enter key. Any Windows NT, Windows 16-bit, DOS, OS/2 16-bit, or POSIX-based application and batch file can be run from the command prompt. Type any file names, switches, and parameters required to run the application. After you press the Enter key, Windows NT starts the application.

For example, if you type **EXCEL** at the command prompt, Windows NT will start Excel, if it is not already started, and will make Excel the foreground application. Figure 20.2 shows the screen after starting Excel from the command prompt. You can start Excel and load a worksheet by including the name of the worksheet in the command to start Excel—for example, EXCEL C:\SHEET\PROJSTAT.XLS.

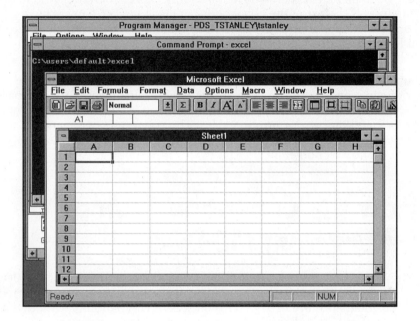

Fig. 20.2

Starting Excel from the command prompt.

Suppose that this worksheet automatically initiates a set of macros known to take a long time to process. You can minimize the application and continue with other work. While the command prompt is minimized and the Excel application is executing, the icon title displays the program or command currently being run.

If the command terminates while the command prompt icon is still minimized, the command you issued to initiate this process disappears from the icon title.

You can start as many command prompts as needed. If you know the applications will take a long time to execute, minimize them and do other work. Because Windows NT changes the icon title as each application finishes, you can monitor the progress of each application easily.

The Command Subsystems

Two kinds of commands are understood by Windows NT: native commands and subsystem commands. You may issue either type of command from the Command Prompt window.

Native commands take full advantage of the 32-bit operating system of Windows NT. Most of the commands familiar to DOS 6.0 users have been reengineered as native system commands. These commands enable you to perform integral tasks such as checking the disk, copying files, configuring devices, and managing a network.

Subsystem commands are 16-bit, non-native commands. These have not been reengineered, and are included with Windows NT for compatibility reasons. Some of these commands, such as SHARE, perform functions that Windows NT now manages. The subsystem commands that perform the same function that is now built into Windows NT actually perform no function at all.

How the Command Prompt Differs from MS-DOS

Windows NT provides a set of 16-bit, non-native commands for the DOS subsystem so that older DOS commands, such as EDLIN, are supported. These commands are provided for backward compatibility. Other commands (such as SHARE, which does memory management), are accepted to provide compatibility with existing files, but these commands have no effect because their functionality is already implemented in Windows NT.

At first, using these commands gives the illusion that the command prompt is useful only for processing DOS commands. This idea is reinforced by the application icon, which is the familiar MS-DOS moniker. Nothing could be further from the truth. Although the DOS commands retain their original name, their underlying functionality has been reengineered to take advantage of Windows NT where applicable.

New Commands

The new environment created by Windows NT resulted in the creation of the following commands:

Command	Explanation
CMD.EXE	Replaces the DOS COMMAND.COM file.
CONVERT	Converts disk file systems from the File Allocation Table (FAT) format or the OS/2 High Performance File System (HPFS) format to the new Windows NT NTFS file system.
FINDSTR	Searches for text in files using regular expressions.
START	Starts a new command prompt window to run a specified program or command.
TITLE	Sets the title of the command prompt window.
WINVER	Displays the Windows NT version number.

Replaced and Obsolete Commands

Some Microsoft DOS commands are now obsolete or have been superseded by built-in Windows NT functionality. The next table summarizes these replaced and obsolete commands:

Command	Explanation
ASSIGN	Redirects requests for disk operations on one drive to a different drive. Not supported in Windows NT.
CTTY	Changes the terminal device used to control the computer system. Not currently supported in Windows NT.
DOSPROMPT	Starts a graphical interface to DOS. Replaced by Windows NT.
EXPAND	Used only for files on the MS-DOS distribution disks; not needed by Windows NT.
FASTOPEN	Starts the Fastopen program, which decreases the amount of time needed to open frequently used files. Windows NT inherent caching is superior to this utility.
FDISK	Configures hard disks for use with MS-DOS. The Disk Manager has replaced FDISK and now prepares hard disks for use with Windows NT.

continues

Command	Explanation
JOIN	Joins a disk drive to a directory on another disk drive. The increased partition size and improved file systems in Windows NT have eliminated the need to join drives.
MIRROR	Records information about disks in the system. The processes supplied by MIRROR are not supported by Windows NT.
SYS	Copies the MS-DOS system files and the MS-DOS command interpreter, COMMAND.COM, to the floppy disk in the drive you specify. Windows NT will not fit on a standard 1.2M or 1.44M floppy disk.
UNDELETE	Restores files deleted by DEL. Is not supported by Windows NT.
UNFORMAT	Restores a disk erased by the FORMAT command. Not supported by Windows NT.

Command Syntax Used in the Command Prompt

Commands supplied in the command prompt require at least the complete command name to execute. You may also supply parameters, switches, and values. Windows NT evaluates the information supplied on the command line and determines from the command name which subsystem will receive the command, parameters, switches, and values. Any command supplied to the command prompt can be entered in the following format:

commandname [*parameters*] [*switches*] [*values*]

In the syntax line, *commandname* refers to the name of the command. For example, CHKDSK and DIR are command names.

Some commands need parameters to identify the task to accomplish. A parameter defines or creates the object on which you want Windows NT to act. Sometimes a command needs more than one parameter. For example, ATTRIB requires the name of a file and a switch. For example:

ATTRIB -r MyFile.txt

uses the ATTRIB command with the -r switch to remove read-only attributes from MyFile.txt.

Switches control or modify how the command performs a task. Switches are coded with a forward slash (/) and usually are followed by words, letters, or numbers. Some commands do not require switches, whereas others may require several. If a command has more than one switch, type each in order and separate them with a space.

Data values help a command determine how to interpret a switch. A value is coded with a starting colon (:) or equal sign (=) followed by a word, letter, or number. The words, letters, and numbers must immediately follow the colon or equal sign, with no intervening spaces.

Changing the Command Prompt Appearance

You can change the appearance of the command prompt, thereby changing the size of the window and the fonts that display in the window, for example. Windows 3.1 enables you to change the fonts displayed in the window by using the window's Control Menu box. However, Windows NT enables you to have more control over the appearance of the window.

The command prompt defaults to a window capable of displaying 25 lines that are 80 characters long. If these limits are inappropriate for the commands you intend to use, you can change them.

Changing the Font Size

The default font size in the Command Prompt window is 8x12, which means that each character is 8 pixels wide and 12 pixels high. You can change the character size to make the font smaller or larger. If, for example, you changed the font size from the 8x12 default to 10x18, each character would be twice as big.

On the other hand, changing the font size to 4x6 changes the font to half the size. Figure 20.3 displays three command prompt windows displaying different-sized fonts.

To change font size, select Fonts from the Control menu. When you do, the Font Selection dialog box, shown in figure 20.4, displays on-screen. Choose the particular font size from the Font list box in the Font Selection dialog box.

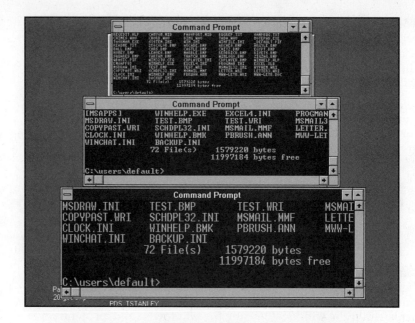

Fig. 20.3

Command prompt windows displaying fonts that are 4X6, 8X12, and 10X18.

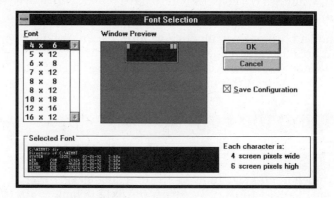

Fig. 20.4

Change the font size from the Font Selection dialog box.

Follow these steps to change the font size:

1. Select the Control-Menu box of the Command Prompt window.

2. Select **F**onts from the drop-down menu. The Font Selection dialog box displays on the screen (shown in fig. 20.4).

3. Select the particular font size combination desired from the **F**ont list box, then choose OK to have your selection take effect.

Windows NT displays an example of your choice in the Selected Font window. Press OK to accept the new selection and return to the Command Prompt window.

Changing the Default Window Settings

Change the default window settings by choosing Settings from the Control-Menu. When you do, the Command Prompt dialog box appears on-screen. From this dialog box, you can set the Command Prompt to appear full screen or in a window. Choose Full Screen to display only the command prompt on the screen. Choose Window to display the Command Prompt in a Window on the Windows NT Desktop.

Select the Save Configuration check box to save changes that you make to the Command Prompt. The next time you start the Command Prompt, Windows NT will display the Command Prompt with the settings that you made.

Select the QuickEdit Mode option to alter how you copy information from the Command Prompt window. With this option marked, you can select information in the window to copy using the mouse. If you do not mark this option, however, you must choose Edit, Mark from the Control menu to select information in the window to copy.

The Terminate button enables you to close the Command Prompt window. You generally close any programs running in the Command Prompt window, then type EXIT to close the command prompt window. However, if a command prompt window locks up, or the program in the Command Prompt window stops responding, you can use the Terminate button to close the window. Use this button only as a last resort.

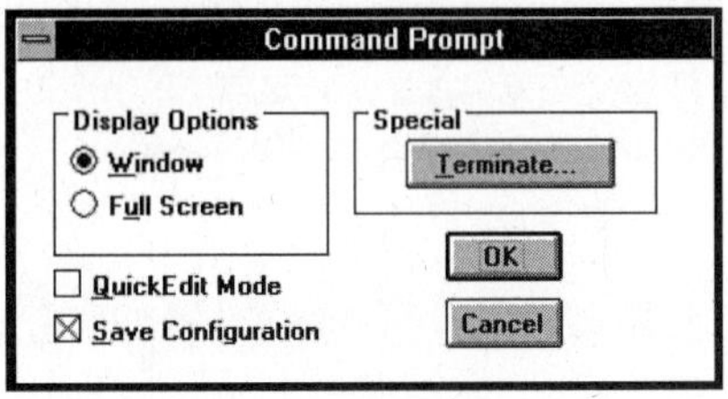

Fig. 20.5

Change Command Prompt window settings from the Command Prompt dialog box.

T I P

Sometimes it is convenient to switch from the windowed prompt to a full screen prompt. Some reasons for this are that too much data was being displayed in the windowed prompt or you just did not want the distraction of other applications on the screen while concentrating on this application. Whatever the reason, switching is done by using the Alt+Enter key combination while the Command Prompt window is the current process.

Setting the Screen Size and Position

To change the screen size and position

1. Select the Control menu.

2. Select Screen Size and Position from the dropdown menu list. This causes the Screen Size and Position dialog box to appear.

3. Change the number of rows and columns that will be displayed in the Command Prompt window by pressing the up or down arrows in the corresponding Width and Height boxes of the Screen Buffer Size box.

4. Select Save **W**indow Size and Position if you want the command prompt to always be the same size and appear in the same location on the screen.

    This is a convenient way to set up the Command Prompt window so that it is available for your use but does not take up much monitor space.

5. Choose OK to accept the changes and close the dialog box.

Fig. 20.6

Change the size and position of the Command Prompt window using the Screen Size And Position dialog box.

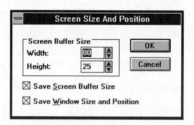

Changing Command Prompt Colors

You change the command prompt colors by opening the Control menu and then selecting Screen C**o**lor from the drop-down menu. When the Screen Colors dialog box appears, you can change text and background colors to any of 16 colors.

You can change the screen text and background colors and the popup text and background colors. These changes are all done by following these steps:

1. Select one of the option buttons: Screen Text, Screen Background, PopUp Text, or PopUp Background.

2. Select one of the 16 color choices provided in the dialog box. Notice that the color immediately changes in the display box that corresponds to the selected button option. This enables you to easily match text and background colors.

3. Select **S**ave Configuration if you want Windows NT to use these selections each time the Command Prompt window is activated.

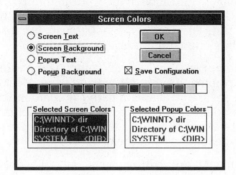

Fig. 20.7

Change Command Prompt window colors from the Screen Colors dialog box.

Using the Command Prompt

You enter commands in the Command Prompt window just as you enter commands from DOS—by typing them at the command-line prompt. Figure 20.8 shows the use of the VER subsystem command. Many of the DOS commands have been reengineered to operate using the 32-bit, native mode capabilities of Windows NT.

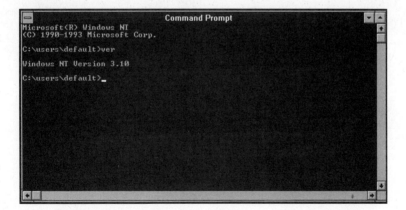

Fig. 20.8

Entering the VER native mode subsystem command.

Windows NT provides this command prompt window to conveniently perform system and network command activity. System commands are used to perform a variety of maintenance tasks or to configure the MS-DOS or OS/2 subsystems. Network commands enable you to perform network tasks such as starting and stopping services or adding groups.

Using System Commands

Some system commands have been incorporated into the new command processor, CMD.EXE, and reside in memory at all times. This makes them very fast. They are also quick to use, because they are accessible from the Command Prompt window.

The Command Prompt window is the common place where both system and network commands are entered and used. Most commands familiar to DOS users are available in native mode Windows NT system commands. Other commands, such as XCOPY, are not included in CMD.EXE. They are external, which means that they are stored in their own file and must be loaded from the disk.

Native mode commands are written specifically to take advantage of Windows NT's ability to use 32-bit commands. Most commands DOS users are familiar with are native mode commands. Following is a list of native mode commands that are incorporated into CMD.EXE and are always available.

Table 20.1 Native mode system commands			
ATTRIB	ECHO	PATH	TREE
CALL	ERASE	PAUSE	TYPE
CHCP	EXIT	PRINT	VER
CHDIR (CD)	FC	PROMPT	VERIFY
CHKDSK	FIND	RECOVER	VOL
CLS	FINDSTR	REM	XCOPY
CMD	FOR	RENAME (REN)	WINVER
COMP	FORMAT	REPLACE	>
CONVERT	GOTO	RESTORE	>>
COPY	HELP	RMDIR (RD)	<
DATE	IF	SET		
DEL	KEYB	SHIFT			
DIR	LABEL	SORT	&
DISKCOMP	MKDIR (MD)	START	&&
DISKCOPY	MODE	SUBST	( )
DOSKEY	MORE	TIME	^

Native mode commands are typed at the command prompt. Figure 20.5 shows the VER command and its results. Native mode commands retain the same degree of functionality as in MS-DOS because Windows NT provides the capability to continue using applications that depend on MS-DOS. It is entirely possible that some applications expect these commands to be available for use. The commands will be available and supported as long as MS-DOS continues to be a supported subsystem.

Reviewing DOS Commands

Windows NT includes some non-native 16-bit commands of the MS-DOS subsystem that enable you to use older MS-DOS commands for activities such as file editing and graphing. These commands are included mainly to provide MS-DOS compatibility.

Some MS-DOS subsystem commands, such as SHARE, duplicate services performed by Windows NT. These commands are retained in the overall operating system solely to provide compatibility with existing files. The following table lists the non-native commands in Windows NT.

Command	Purpose
APPEND	Allows programs to open data files in specified directories as if they were in the current directory.
BREAK	Sets or clears Ctrl+C checking.
DEBUG	Runs Debug.
EDIT	Starts the MS-DOS editor.
EDLIN	Starts EDLIN.
EMM	Allows MS-DOS to emulate expanded memory.
EXE2BIN	Converts .EXE files to binary format.
GRAFTABL	Enables Windows NT to display an extended character set in graphics mode.
GRAPHICS	Loads a program that can print graphics.
LOADFIX	Loads and runs programs above the first 64K of memory.
LOADHIGH	Loads a program into the upper memory area.
MEM	Displays the amount of used and free memory for the MS-DOS subsystem.

continues

Command	Purpose
NLSFUNC	Loads country-specific information.
QBASIC	Starts the QBasic programming environment.
SETVER	Sets the MS-DOS version number that Windows NT reports to a program.
SHARE	Starts the share program.

Reviewing CONFIG.SYS Commands

To configure the subsystem environment, MS-DOS must have certain commands in the CONFIG.SYS file. Commands such as DEVICE and LASTDRIVE are used frequently. For compatibility, CONFIG.SYS continues to be used, is required, and must be placed in the root directory of the current boot drive. Following is a list of the annotated commands required for CONFIG.SYS.

Command	Purpose
BUFFERS	Allocates memory.
COUNTRY	Enables MS-DOS to use international time, dates, currency, and other parameters.
DEVICE	Loads device drivers into memory.
DEVICEHIGH	Loads device drivers into high memory.
DOS	Specifies that MS-DOS maintain a link to the upper memory area.
DRIVEPARM	Defines parameters for block devices.
FCBS	Specifies the number of file control blocks that can be open simultaneously.
FILES	Sets the number of files that the command prompt can access at one time.
INSTALL	Loads a memory-resident program into memory.
LASTDRIVE	Specifies the maximum number of drives that can be accessed.
SHELL	Specifies the name and location of the command interpreter you want Windows NT to use.
STACKS	Supports the dynamic use of data stacks to handle hardware interrupts.
SWITCHES	Forces an enhanced keyboard to behave like a conventional one.

These commands affect only the MS-DOS subsystem. Some, such as BUFFERS and BREAK, are no longer used because corresponding services are provided by Windows NT. They are retained for compatibility.

Reviewing Network Commands

Network commands can now be executed in the Command Prompt window. (All network commands begin with *net*.) These commands are similar to LAN Manager 2.1 commands but have changed to take advantage of Windows NT. They provide a variety of services such as account management, configuration, file management, help, message management, and session management.

The following is an annotated list of the network commands available in the Windows NT environment using the command prompt.

Network Command	Command Purpose
Net Accounts	Displays or sets the role of servers in a domain.
Net Config	Displays configurable services that are running.
Net Config Server	Displays or changes settings for the server service.
Net Continue	Reactivates suspended services when typed at a server.
Net File	Displays the names of all open shared files on a server.
Net Group	Adds, displays, or modifies global groups.
Net Help	Provides a list of commands and topics for which help is available.
Net Helpmsg	Provides help with a network error message.
Net Localgroup	Adds, displays, or modifies local groups.
Net Name	Adds, deletes, or displays aliases on a workstation.
Net Pause	Pauses services on shared printers.
Net Print	Displays or controls print jobs and printer queues
Net Send	Sends messages or files to other computers on the network.

continues

Network Command	Command Purpose
Net Session	Lists or disconnects sessions between a server and workstations.
Net Share	Creates, deletes, or displays shared resources.
Net Start	Starts a service or displays a list of started services.
Net Start Alerter	Starts the Alerter service.
Net Start Eventlog	Starts the Eventlog service.
Net Start Messenger	Starts the Messenger service.
Net Start Nbt	Starts the NetBIOS over TCP/IP service.
Net Start Netlogon	Starts the Netlogon service.
Net Start Server	Starts the Server service.
Net Start SNMP	Starts the Simple Network Management Protocol service.
Net Start TCPIP	Starts and configures the TCP/IP service.
Net Start Telnet	Starts the TELNET service.
Net Start Workstation	Starts the Workstation service.
Net Statistics	Displays the statistics log.
Net Stop	Stops a network service.
Net Time	Synchronizes the workstations' clocks.
Net Use	Connects a workstation to shared resources.
Net User	Adds or modifies user accounts or displays user account data.
Net View	Displays a list of servers.

These network commands, issued in the command prompt, provide an easy and convenient way to quickly tackle network problems or get operational information. Figure 20.6 shows a typical response to network commands in the command prompt.

When the Net Accounts network command is issued in the Command Prompt window, information for the local account is displayed. This is a convenient way for the network administrator to access network information and services anywhere in the system.

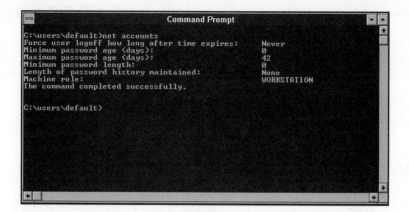

```
                              Command Prompt
C:\users\default>net accounts
Force user logoff how long after time expires:      Never
Minimum password age (days):                        0
Maximum password age (days):                        42
Minimum password length:                            0
Length of password history maintained:              None
Machine role:                                       WORKSTATION
The command completed successfully.


C:\users\default>
```

Fig. 20.9

Displaying network information in the Command Prompt window.

Running Windows NT Applications from the Command Prompt

You can start applications from the Command Prompt window as shown at the beginning of this chapter. You saw how to run a Windows NT application, such as Excel, simply by typing the application name at the command prompt. The application begins running immediately, making the application the current application.

Suppose that you need to run Excel while you are using the Command Prompt window. Type **EXCEL** and press the Enter key. Excel begins to execute, and is ready for you to use. When you exit Excel, the Command Prompt window returns to the foreground.

While you are running the application initiated from the command prompt, you cannot return to that Command Prompt window to issue other commands until you exit the application. However, you may start another Command Prompt window to issue other commands from the command prompt. Like DOS, however, the application that you start must either be on the search path or you must provide the path when you invoke the command. The search path consists of all subdirectories identified in the PATH environment variable located in the AUTOEXEC.BAT file.

Running OS/2 1.X and POSIX-Compliant Applications

Although IBM's 32-bit OS/2 2.X is not supported by Windows NT, you can run 16-bit OS/2 1.X, DOS, or POSIX applications from the Windows

NT command prompt, just as if you were launching them in their native environments. Windows NT decodes any command you enter, and decides which subsystem to call to execute it. It then invokes the appropriate subsystem, which executes the command. The command may start a large application running, or a small one. It may do something as simple as specifying a path to be searched for data files. In any case, when the operation is completed, the subsystem returns control to the main Windows NT command processor.

What Is POSIX?

POSIX is an internationally accepted standard for operating systems that is strongly endorsed by the United States government. The standard is maintained by the Institute of Electrical and Electronic Engineers (IEEE). It is a young standard, and thus incomplete. The current version, IEEE 1003.1, covers basic operating system functions, but is silent on many important issues. These issues are being addressed by standards committees. As time goes on, new sections will be added to subsequent revisions of the standard.

The purpose of the POSIX standard is to make the many popular varieties of UNIX and UNIX-like operating systems compatible with each other at the source code level. *Source code compatibility* means that you should be able to take the source code for a program that runs under one operating system, transport it to a different operating system, compile it, and have it run without errors. The U.S. government administers a certification process that tests an operating system/hardware platform combination for adherence to IEEE 1003.1.

Theoretically, any application developed on a certified POSIX system should be able to migrate to any other certified POSIX system, be compiled on the new system, and run without errors. At present, very little migration of this kind is taking place. Because POSIX is still a "work in progress" and promises to remain in that state for the immediate future, true modification-free migrations of major applications are more dream than reality. However, things are improving. As time passes and more of the operating system functions are covered by the specification, migration will become progressively easier.

What Does it Mean to Be POSIX-Compliant?

Some operating system vendors (such as Microsoft) claim that their operating systems are POSIX-compliant. Others claim POSIX-conformance, whereas a third group claims to be POSIX-certified.

The only one of the three terms that is officially recognized is POSIX-certified. A POSIX-certified operating system has been tested by one of the seven NIST (National Institute of Standards and Technology) testing laboratories and certified to adhere to the FIPS 151-2 standard. This is the Federal standard that is equivalent to IEEE 1003.1. POSIX certification applies only to the combination of hardware and software tested. Thus, if an operating system is certified on an IBM PS/2 Model 95, the certification does not extend to other Intel 486-based machines, or even other PS/2 models.

Obtaining POSIX certification for even the few most popular hardware platforms is time-consuming and expensive. As a result, vendors of operating systems that run on open architecture hardware, such as Intel-based personal computers, tend to claim POSIX compliance or POSIX conformance. These terms can be used interchangeably, and neither has any official standing. They mean that the vendor's own engineers have tested their product against the standard and found it to conform. Such testing, although not exactly impartial, does give an indication that the vendor thinks adhering to standards is important, and that they are moving their product in the direction of cross-platform portability.

Simultaneously Running Multiple DOS, OS/2, and POSIX Applications

Because Windows NT is a true multitasking operating system, it is possible to run multiple applications at the same time. You can run them in any combination. For instance, you could run a native NT application, an OS/2 application, a DOS application, and a POSIX-compliant application all at the same time. Alternatively, you could run two or three OS/2 applications at the same time, or two DOS applications and one POSIX-compliant, or any combination that you choose. The speed of your processor and the size of your memory determines how many of these you can activate and still get reasonable performance from all of them.

To launch an OS/2 or POSIX-compliant application, simply open a Command Prompt window by double-clicking on the MS-DOS Command Prompt icon in the Main window of the Program Manager. At the prompt in the window, enter the command to start your application. To start a second application, just select another instance of the Command Prompt window from the Program Manager. You can do this as many times as you want, within the performance limitations of your machine. As jobs complete, they will return the resources that they had been using to the operating system, allowing the remaining jobs to run faster.

With Windows NT's default settings, the application that has the focus tends to get the lion's share of the available CPU cycles. Processes running in the background tend to run more slowly. You can change this resource allocation if you want (see Chapter 21). Generally, if all the jobs you are running at the same time are I/O-bound, or if they are all CPU-bound, you will notice performance degradation as more jobs are added. On the other hand, if you have a good mix of I/O-bound and CPU-bound jobs, they will all complete much sooner than if you had run them one after the other.

Command Symbols and Filter Commands

Command symbols and filters are nothing more than special symbols utilized by the command prompt to manage the flow of data during the time a command is being executed. These symbols and filters are the same ones used in the DOS operating environment.

The > symbol, for example, redirects information feedback from a command to some other destination than the computer screen. For example

```
DIR *.DOC > MYDOCS
```

is a subsystem command requesting a directory listing of all files ending in .DOC. The > symbol tells Command Prompt to create a file named MYDOCS and put the normal output of DIR into that file rather than display the information on your screen.

The >> symbol causes output of a subsystem command to be appended to some prior file. This is especially handy if, for example, you create a batch file that creates directory listings of particular data files and you want all subdirectories to appear in the same report. By redirecting the output of DIR and appending it to the same file name, output of DIR will appear all together when this common file is printed.

Sometimes, application programs expect to receive operating instructions from you. To accomplish this, you must enter the data using the keyboard. If the data is substantially the same each time you use the command, it might be more convenient to create a batch file containing the command data and modify this batch file as required for each subsequent use. When you use the application in this manner, include the < symbol to obtain the "keyboard" information from your batch file.

If MYANSR.TXT contains appropriate information expected by the MYAPP.EXE application, entering the following command at the command prompt would be an easy way to then execute the application:

```
MYAPP.EXE < MYANSR.TXT
```

MYAPP.EXE expects to obtain information from you through the keyboard. You put the correct answers in MYANSR.TXT and use the < symbol to obtain keyboard input by MYAPP.EXE from MYANSR.TXT.

Available Filter Commands

There are three filter commands (Sort, More, and Find) available that really can provide substantial help when you understand just how to use them.

SORT

SORT is a filter command used to organize data in a file and produce a file arranged in a predetermined order. It is considered a filter program because it is used to sort and organize (filter) data. SORT has the following syntax:

```
SORT switches InputFileName > SortedFileName
```

The following are possible switches that you can use with SORT:

/R	Enables you to reverse the sort order
/+n	Enables you to indicate the column to use when sorting, where n is the column number

You can sort the file on any column or set of columns, and in ascending or descending order. This gives you the opportunity to organize the data meaningfully for further processing.

MORE

MORE is another filter application used to help you manage data you need to read. MORE gives you the ability to read a file one screen at a time without having to control the specific amount of data that gets displayed on the screen at any one time.

MORE has the following command syntax:

```
MORE /E /C /P /S /Tn +n < d:\path\filename.ext
```

The following are the possible switches:

/E	Enable extended features
/C	Clear screen before displaying page

/P	Expand form feed characters
/S	Squeeze multiple blank lines into a single line
/T*n*	Expand tabs to *n* spaces (default 8)
+*n*	Start displaying the first file at line *n*
filename	File to be displayed

If extended features are enabled, the following commands are accepted at the -- More -- prompt:

P *n*	Display the next *n* lines
S *n*	Skip the next *n* lines
F	Display the next file
Q	Quit
=	Show line number
?	Show help line
<space>	Display next page
<ret>	Display next line

FIND

FIND is a command that also provides filtering properties. You use it to locate files that contain some particular "string" of data. You can use FIND to locate all files that either contain the string of data you are looking for or do not contain the string. The following command syntax shows how FIND can be used to filter data:

FIND [/V] [/C] [/N] [/I] "*string*" [[*drive:*][*path*]*filename*
[...]]

The following switches are used:

/V	Displays all lines *not* containing the specified string
/C	Displays only the count of lines containing the string
/N	Displays line numbers with the displayed lines
/I	Ignores the case of characters when searching for the string

| `"string"` | Specifies the text string to find. |
| `[drive:][path]filename` | Specifies a file or files to search. If a path name is not specified, FIND searches the text typed at the prompt or piped from another command. |

Automating Repetitive Tasks with Batch Files

Batch files have always been a staple in the programmer's library of tools. They enable you to simplify routines and repetitive tasks. A batch program is a text file that contains one or more commands understood and processed by the command subsystems. Using commands such as IF and GOTO enables you to make conditional tests and do program branching which, when other commands are also involved, enables you to write extensive programs capable of performing many tasks.

Command Prompt Help Is Available from Several Sources

Help is available from Windows NT help files and from within the Command Prompt window for all commands. If you do not know which specific command to use or how to use it, try typing **HELP** and pressing Enter at the command prompt. If you do, Windows NT responds by listing all of the commands for which help is available and a brief description of each command, as shown in the following list.

```
ACLCONV    Converts OS/2 LANMAN SERVER access control
           lists.
AT         Schedules commands and programs to run on a
           computer.
ATTRIB     Displays or changes file attributes.
BREAK      Sets or clears extended Ctrl+C checking.
CALL       Calls one batch program from another.
CD         Displays the name of the current directory or
           changes the current directory.
CHCP       Displays or sets the active code page number.
CHDIR      Displays the name of the current directory or
           changes the current directory.
```

CHKDSK	Checks a disk and displays a status report.
CLS	Clears the screen.
CMD	Starts a new instance of the Windows NT command interpreter.
COMP	Compares the contents of two files or sets of files.
CONVERT	Converts FAT or HPFS volumes to NTFS; you cannot convert the current drive.
COPY	Copies one or more files to another location.
DATE	Displays or sets the date.
DEL	Deletes one or more files.
DIR	Displays a list of files and subdirectories in a directory.
DISKCOMP	Compares the contents of two floppy disks.
DISKCOPY	Copies the contents of one floppy disk to another.
DOSKEY	Edits command lines, recalls Windows NT commands, and creates macros.
ECHO	Displays messages, or turns command echoing on or off.
ENDLOCAL	Ends localization of environment changes in a batch file.
ERASE	Deletes one or more files.
EXIT	Quits the CMD.EXE program (command interpreter).
FC	Compares two files or sets of files, and displays the differences between them.
FIND	Searches for a text string in a file or files.
FINDSTR	Searches for strings in files.
FOR	Runs a specified command for each file in a set of files.
FORMAT	Formats a disk for use with Windows NT.
GOTO	Directs Windows NT to a labeled line in a batch program.
GRAFTABL	Enables Windows NT to display an extended character set in graphics mode.
HELP	Provides Help information for Windows NT commands.
IF	Performs conditional processing in batch programs.
KEYB	Configures a keyboard for a specific language.
LABEL	Creates, changes, or deletes the volume label of a disk.
MD	Creates a directory.
MKDIR	Creates a directory.
MODE	Configures a system device.

MORE	Displays output one screen at a time.
MOVE	Moves one or more files from one directory to another directory on the same drive.
PATH	Displays or sets a search path for executable files.
PAUSE	Suspends processing of a batch file and displays a message.
POPD	Restores the previous value of the current directory saved by PUSHD.
PRINT	Prints a text file.
PROMPT	Changes the Windows NT command prompt.
PUSHD	Saves the current directory, then changes it.
RD	Removes a directory.
RECOVER	Recovers readable information from a bad or defective disk.
REM	Records comments (remarks) in batch files or CONFIG.SYS.
REN	Renames a file or files.
RENAME	Renames a file or files.
REPLACE	Replaces files.
RESTORE	Restores files that were backed up with the BACKUP command.
RMDIR	Removes a directory.
SET	Displays, sets, or removes Windows NT environment variables.
SETLOCAL	Begins localization of environment changes in a batch file.
SHIFT	Shifts the position of replaceable parameters in batch files.
SORT	Sorts input.
SUBST	Associates a path with a drive letter.
START	Starts a separate window to run a specified program or command.
TIME	Displays or sets the system time.
TITLE	Sets the window title for a CMD.EXE session.
TREE	Graphically displays the directory structure of a drive or path.
TYPE	Displays the contents of a text file.
VER	Displays the Windows NT version.
VERIFY	Tells Windows NT whether to verify that your files are written correctly to a disk.
VOL	Displays a disk volume label and serial number.
XCOPY	Copies files and directory trees.

The Help Switch

You can get help for individual commands from the Command Prompt window. Add the /? parameter to the command to display specific help for the command.

For example, suppose you want to display help for the Net Accounts command. At the command prompt, type **NET ACCOUNTS /?** and press Enter. Figure 20.10 displays the help information in the Command Prompt window.

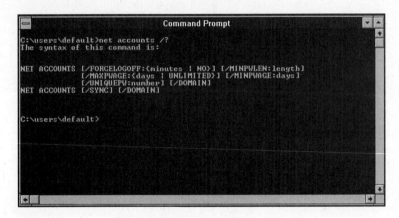

Help from Windows NT

Help is available also from the Windows NT hyperlinked help system. To use this system, double-click on the Windows NT Help icon located in the Main program group. This Help system is shown in figure 20.11.

In the Help window, select Access the Command Reference Help to display an alphabetically indexed hypertext file.

As shown in figure 20.12, two windows display on the screen. The first window, Commands, displays alphabetized commands. The second window, Command Reference, initially displays the following topics:

Command List

What's New and Different from MS-DOS?

What's New and Different from LAN Manager 2.1?

In the Command Reference window, click on one of the three topics. Information associated with that topic displays in the Command Reference window.

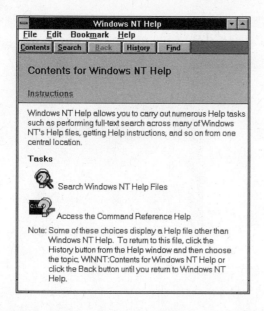

Fig. 20.11

The Windows NT
Help system.

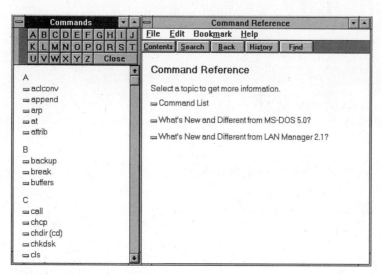

Fig. 20.12

Command
Reference help
for the Command
Prompt window.

Suppose that you want to display information about the command
CHKDSK. Scroll through the Commands window until you find CHKDSK.
Then, click on the command. Information for that command displays in
the Command Reference window, as shown in figure 20.13.

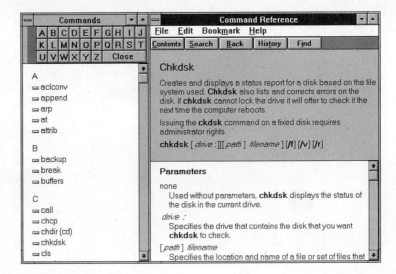

Fig. 20.13

Displaying help
for CHKDSK
using the
Windows NT
Help system.

Summary

In this chapter, you learned that Windows NT provides a command prompt windowed interface to two programming subsystems: system commands and network commands.

Access to system commands and network commands is provided by the command prompt. Many subsystem commands are named the same as their DOS counterparts but have been reengineered to take advantage of capabilities available in Windows NT.

A substantial help system is available from the command prompt and from the Windows NT help system. This help system provides explanations of the Windows NT components and how to use them.

Each of the systems available through the Command Prompt provides a rich array of commands for use with the system. Batch programs can be developed using the native system commands and network commands available from the subsystems.

Windows NT provides the ability to run applications written for it, Windows 3.1, DOS, OS/2, or POSIX applications. Windows NT is multitasking, provides support for these diverse operating environments, and makes it possible to operate all of them at the same time. This retains the value of the application by allowing it to run in its native host environment, unchanged.

Customizing PIFs

A PIF (Program Information File) is a file that provides Windows NT with the information the program needs to run a DOS application. PIFs contain such information as how much memory the application needs and what video mode is required. Windows NT creates PIFs for most popular DOS applications. If Windows NT does not have the information on how to create a PIF for the DOS application, you can create your own PIF using the instructions in this chapter. This chapter also describes how to improve DOS application performance and how to modify PIFs to decrease the use of memory by DOS applications.

Creating and Using PIFs

When you start a non-Windows (DOS) application, Windows NT looks for a PIF designed for that application. If Windows NT finds the PIF, the application uses that information instead of the standard settings in the default PIF. Windows NT uses the default PIF, _DEFAULT.PIF, unless a specific application PIF is located.

You can set up a PIF in three ways:

- Have the Windows Setup application create a PIF for you.
- Use or modify the default PIF.
- Use the PIF that came with the DOS application.

T I P PIFs created by the Windows Setup application are stored in the directory containing Windows NT (usually \WINNT). After they are created, you can move the PIF anywhere on disk. For example, you may want to locate the PIF for a particular application in that application's directory to reduce the number of files stored in the Windows NT directory.

The Windows Setup application creates a PIF for your DOS application when you first install Windows NT or when you run Windows Setup to install an application. Windows Setup searches your hard disk for the Windows NT applications and DOS applications listed in the APP.INF file. Windows NT can create PIFs for any DOS applications listed in the APP.INF file.

If an application PIF is not created or if an application does not come with a PIF, Windows NT uses the default PIF. If settings need to be changed in the default PIF so that the application works correctly with Windows NT, you can modify the default PIF by using the PIF Editor.

Many DOS applications provide a PIF. For example, when you install Lotus 1-2-3 Release 2.4, a 123R24.PIF file is installed. Generally, you should use the PIF that comes with an application, because its settings are optimized.

Creating a PIF with Windows Setup

The Windows Setup application is used when you initially install Windows NT to find and create PIFs and program item icons for applications on disk. You also can run the Windows Setup program at any later time to install applications you did not originally install. The Windows Setup program item icon is located in the Main group window.

When you use Windows Setup to install a DOS application, it creates and sets up a PIF for that application in the Windows NT directory (usually C:\WINNT). The Setup application searches the drives you specify and lists any applications it finds. Setup lists only the DOS applications that the APP.INF file provides PIF information on. When you install Windows NT, APP.INF is placed on your hard disk in the C:\WINNT\SYSTEM32 directory. APP.INF contains the recommended settings for many of the most popular DOS applications. If an application is not listed in the APP.INF file, Windows NT does not provide a PIF for that application when SETUP is run.

NOTE The Windows Setup application reads the APP.INF file when it executes. APP.INF is located in the SYSTEM32 directory underneath the directory in which you installed Windows NT.

APP.INF contains a series of sections that provide the Windows Setup application with information. These sections are used by Setup to create and maintain PIF information for DOS applications. They contain all of the settings necessary to support DOS application execution within the Windows NT environment. The [AppExes] section, for example, contains a large number of DOS application entries for which Windows NT already knows the PIF information. If a DOS application is not in this list, but the application is on your hard disk, Windows NT does *not* create a PIF for the application when Setup is run.

Windows NT makes creating PIFs easy if you use the Windows Setup application. Although most DOS applications run well using the default PIF, you may need more memory or a special feature available only if the application runs with a custom PIF. In that case, you can modify the PIF Windows Setup creates by using the PIF Editor.

To run Windows Setup and create a PIF after you have installed Windows NT, follow these instructions:

1. Activate the Main group window in the Program Manager.

2. Start the Windows NT Setup application. The Windows NT Setup dialog box appears.

3. Choose the **O**ptions Set Up **A**pplications command.

4. Select the drive to search or choose to search the current path from the list box. Choose the **S**earch Now button.

5. If Windows NT cannot determine the application that matches an EXE or COM file name, you can select the application from a list of possible matches. For example, WP.EXE may be the EXE file name for more than one word processor.

6. When the Set Up Applications dialog box appears, select, from the list box on the left, the DOS applications for which you want PIFs.

7. Choose the **A**dd button to add the applications to the list box on the right. Setup creates PIFs for these applications. Figure 21.1 shows the Set Up Applications dialog box with two applications selected for setup.

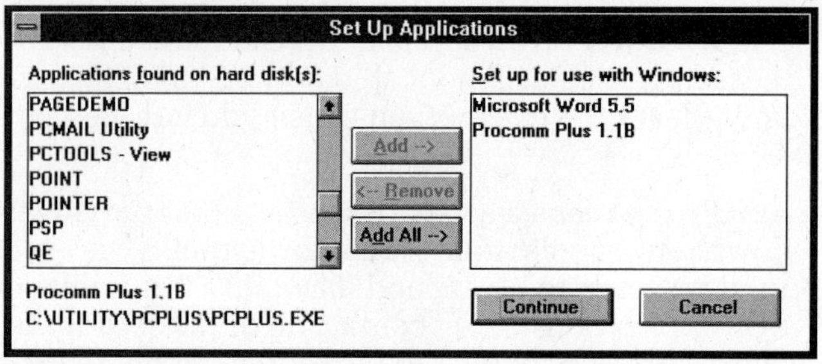

Fig. 21.1

Using the Set Up Applications dialog box to set up applications in Windows NT.

8. Choose Continue if you want Windows NT to create PIFs for the DOS applications in the list on the right side of the dialog box.

9. Close the Windows NT Setup window.

If you did not have an Applications group previously, Setup creates one for you. In addition to the PIF created and stored in the \WINNT directory, Setup creates a program item icon to match your application.

If you select applications to be set up that already have been set up, you may get more than one program item icon for an application. To delete unwanted program item icons, select them in the Program Manager and press the Del key.

Open the Applications group in the Program Manager and run the added DOS application by choosing its program item icon. If the application does not run or does not run with a feature you desire, modify the PIF with the procedures described later in this chapter.

Creating a PIF by Dragging and Dropping

One of the easiest ways to create a PIF is through *dragging and dropping*. This easy technique works with DOS application files that Windows NT recognizes and for which Windows NT has PIF information.

To create a PIF and program item icon by dragging and dropping, follow these steps:

1. Arrange the Program Manager and File Manager side by side on-screen.

2. In the Program Manager, open the group window in which you want to create a program item icon.

3. In the File Manager, display the DOS application file for which you want to create a PIF.

4. Drag the application's file folder from the File Manager to the group window.

    If more than one DOS application uses that same file name, a scrolling list appears.

5. If the scrolling list appears, select the name of the DOS application and then choose OK.

In the group window where you released the file folder icon, a generic DOS application icon appears. If Windows NT cannot find an existing PIF for the application, it creates a PIF in the \WINNT directory.

You can use the process described next to change the generic DOS icon to an icon designed for that application.

From the Program Item Properties dialog box, you can add a specific icon by completing the following steps:

1. Choose the Change Icon button.

    The Change Icon dialog box appears.

2. In the File Name box, type the name of the file containing icons and then choose OK. You also can use the Browse button to search for files containing icons.

    Default icons are found in C:\WINNT\SYSTEM32\PROGMAN.EXE. Icons specifically designed for many DOS applications and generic tasks are found in C:\WINNT\SYSTEM32\MORICONS.DLL. Files that contain icons use the extensions EXE (for Windows applications), DLL, and ICO. Not all EXE or DLL files contain icons. You can buy libraries of icons as files and save them to your \WINNT\SYSTEM32 directory for use with any application.

    When you choose an icon file, the Current Icon list displays the icons available, as shown in figure 21.2.

Fig. 21.2

Select application-specific icons from the MORICONS.DLL file.

3. Choose an icon from the Current Icon list.

4. Choose OK twice.

If you already have created a program item icon for any Windows or DOS application, you can change the program item icon in the Program Manager by selecting the icon and then choosing the **File** **P**roperties command. When the Program Item Properties dialog box appears, choose the Change **I**con button and follow the previous steps.

Manually Creating a PIF

If you need to edit or create a PIF and want to have control over the settings, use the PIF Editor. The PIF Editor is located in the Main group if you installed Windows NT as a new application. The icon for the PIF Editor looks like a luggage tag.

> **T   I   P**   Many popular DOS applications use the default PIF and run without a problem. However, in most cases, you want to create a PIF because the default PIF operates with settings that fit the widest range of applications. Creating a PIF specific to your DOS applications in- creases the applications' speed and improves their memory use when operating under Windows NT.

When you start the PIF Editor, a window displays a new, untitled PIF with the standard settings. Every PIF has two sets of options that match the different modes in which Windows NT runs. When you edit a PIF, you see the options available for the current Windows mode:

- Standard mode options for running the application in standard mode

- 386-enhanced mode options for running the application in 386- enhanced mode

Usually, the PIF Editor displays the PIF settings for the current mode in which Windows NT is running. You may want to select PIF options for a mode that is not the current Windows NT mode. For example, you may want to create a PIF for an application in standard mode, even though you currently are running Windows NT in 386-enhanced mode. To switch modes in the PIF Editor, choose the mode you want from the **M**ode menu.

The PIF Editor window changes slightly depending on which mode is being displayed. Figure 21.3 shows the default settings of the PIF Editor window that appears when Windows NT is operating in standard mode; figure 21.4 shows the default settings of the PIF Editor window that appears when 386-enhanced is the current mode. The **A**dvanced button on the screen in 386-enhanced mode has a second window available for advanced options, shown in figure 21.5. Most PIF options apply only in the mode in which they are selected. To create a PIF, do the following:

1. Choose the PIF Editor from the Main group window in the Program Manager to start the application.

2. Fill in the appropriate text boxes and options as described in the section "Understanding PIF Editor Options."

3. Choose **F**ile **S**ave, name the file, and save it.

4. Choose **F**ile **N**ew to start a new PIF or choose **F**ile E**x**it to close the PIF Editor.

 NOTE Before testing a PIF, close all other applications in Windows NT. If you encounter a problem, you can restart the computer without losing data in another application. After the application runs by itself, test it while running other applications.

```
┌──────────────────────────────────────────────────────┐
│ ▭           PIF Editor - (Untitled)            ▾ ▴ │
├──────────────────────────────────────────────────────┤
│  File   Mode   Help                                   │
├──────────────────────────────────────────────────────┤
│  Program Filename:    [                            ]  │
│  Window Title:        [                            ]  │
│  Optional Parameters: [                            ]  │
│  Startup Directory:   [                            ]  │
│  Video Mode:          ◉ Text   ○ Graphics/Multiple Text │
│  Memory Requirements: KB Required  [128]              │
│  XMS Memory:          KB Required [0]   KB Limit [0]  │
│  Directly Modifies:   ☐ COM1   ☐ COM3   ☐ Keyboard    │
│                       ☐ COM2   ☐ COM4                 │
│  ☐ No Screen Exchange         ☐ Prevent Program Switch │
│  ☒ Close Window on Exit       ☐ No Save Screen        │
│  Reserve Shortcut Keys: ☐ Alt+Tab  ☐ Alt+Esc  ☐ Ctrl+Esc │
│                         ☐ PrtSc    ☐ Alt+PrtSc        │
├──────────────────────────────────────────────────────┤
│  Press F1 for Help on Program Filename.               │
└──────────────────────────────────────────────────────┘
```

Fig. 21.3

The PIF Editor options and defaults for Windows NT in standard mode.

When you start a DOS application for which Windows NT cannot find a PIF, Windows NT starts the application using the default PIF options for the current mode. You can override these default options by modifying the default PIF. The default PIF is named _DEFAULT.PIF and is in the \WINNT directory. For example, in 386-enhanced mode, Windows NT always starts DOS applications in full-screen mode. You can modify the _DEFAULT.PIF and change the Display Usage option so that applications start in a window instead of in a full screen.

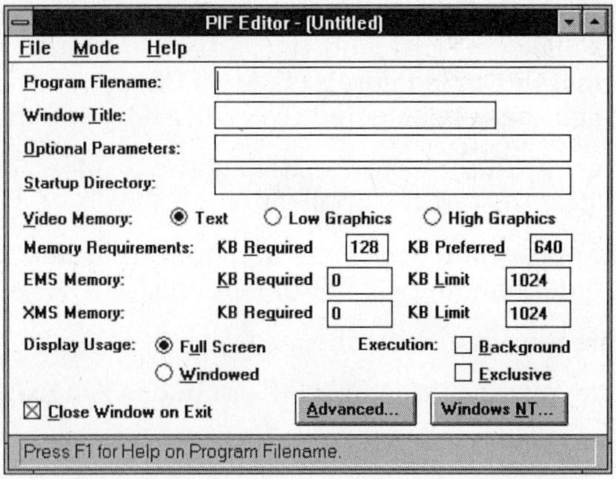

Fig. 21.4

The PIF Editor options and defaults for Windows NT in 386-enhanced mode.

```
PIF Editor - (Untitled)
File   Mode   Help

Program Filename:     [                        ]
Window Title:         [                        ]
Optional Parameters:  [                        ]
Startup Directory:    [                        ]
Video Memory:    (•) Text   ( ) Low Graphics   ( ) High Graphics
Memory Requirements:  KB Required [128]  KB Preferred [640]
EMS Memory:           KB Required [0]    KB Limit [1024]
XMS Memory:           KB Required [0]    KB Limit [1024]
Display Usage: (•) Full Screen      Execution: [ ] Background
               ( ) Windowed                    [ ] Exclusive
[X] Close Window on Exit   [Advanced...]  [Windows NT...]
Press F1 for Help on Program Filename.
```

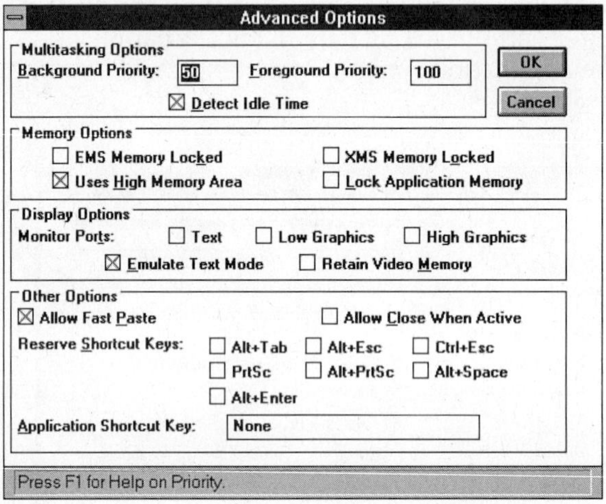

Fig. 21.5

The advanced PIF Editor options and defaults for Windows NT in 386-enhanced mode.

```
Advanced Options
┌Multitasking Options──────────────────────┐   [OK]
│Background Priority: [50]  Foreground Priority: [100]│ [Cancel]
│        [X] Detect Idle Time               │
┌Memory Options────────────────────────────┐
│ [ ] EMS Memory Locked    [ ] XMS Memory Locked│
│ [X] Uses High Memory Area [ ] Lock Application Memory│
┌Display Options───────────────────────────┐
│Monitor Ports: [ ] Text  [ ] Low Graphics  [ ] High Graphics│
│        [X] Emulate Text Mode  [ ] Retain Video Memory│
┌Other Options─────────────────────────────┐
│ [X] Allow Fast Paste       [ ] Allow Close When Active│
│Reserve Shortcut Keys: [ ] Alt+Tab [ ] Alt+Esc [ ] Ctrl+Esc│
│               [ ] PrtSc  [ ] Alt+PrtSc [ ] Alt+Space│
│               [ ] Alt+Enter               │
│Application Shortcut Key: [None]           │
Press F1 for Help on Priority.
```

NOTE Make sure that you make a backup copy of _DEFAULT.PIF before you modify it. If your new default PIF does not work as planned, you can return to the original default PIF settings by copying your backup file over the modified file.

When you change _DEFAULT.PIF, leave the Window Title option blank. You must provide a Program Filename, however, because the PIF Editor checks that this text box is filled before it enables you to save the PIF. Type **DEF.BAT** (you can use whatever program file name you like, but it must have an EXE, COM, or BAT extension) in the Program Filename box. Type over this program file name when you make a new PIF.

Editing a PIF

You may have to edit a PIF in the following circumstances:

- The application runs using the _DEFAULT.PIF, but it needs operating memory, or speed improvements.

- The application is in a different directory than the one listed in the Program Filename text box of the PIF.

- The Startup Directory option, which specifies the data directory, is different from the directory you want or the directory expected by the application.

- You want to start an application with a special parameter.

- You want to ensure that an application swaps to disk when not in use, freeing more memory for additional applications (the Prevent Program Switch option in standard mode).

- An application has been upgraded and requires more memory or uses additional graphic memory.

Naming and Running Applications from a PIF

Before you edit a PIF, make a backup copy of the original PIF, using an extension such as PAK instead of PIF. If the edited PIF gives you trouble, return to the original settings by renaming the PAK file to PIF.

If you start the application by choosing the application file name from the File Manager or from within a program item, the PIF name must have the same name—WP.EXE and WP.PIF, for example. If the PIF has the same name as the application file name, when you choose an application file name, the corresponding PIF is executed. If you have several WordPerfect PIFs (all for the same version of WordPerfect), each with unique settings, start the application by choosing the PIF or create a program item icon in the Program Manager for each of the PIFs.

 **NOTE** If you start the application by choosing the application file name, Windows NT looks for the PIF file name that matches the application's name. For example, if you are in the File Manager and click on WP.EXE to launch WordPerfect, Windows NT looks for WP.PIF. Windows NT looks for the PIF in

continues

continued

two places—the \WINNT directory and the directory associated with the application (such as \WP60 for WordPerfect). Windows NT does *not* search the directories in your PATH statement.

Editing a PIF

To edit a PIF, follow these steps:

1. Choose the PIF Editor application from the Main group.

2. Choose **File O**pen and change to the directory containing the PIF to be edited.

   Windows Setup stores PIFs in the \WINNT directory. The default PIF, _DEFAULT.PIF, is in the \WINNT directory. PIFs have the extension PIF.

3. Select and open the PIF you want to edit. The PIF Editor window appears, showing the current PIF settings (see fig. 21.6). Choose **F**ile Save **A**s and save a backup copy of the PIF with an extension such as PAK.

4. Make changes to the text boxes or selections in the PIF Editor window. If you are in 386-enhanced mode, choose the **A**dvanced button to see additional PIF options.

   See "Understanding PIF Editor Options" later in this chapter, for a detailed discussion of all the PIF options.

5. Choose **F**ile Save **A**s and name the PIF with a PIF extension.

6. Choose **F**ile E**x**it to quit the PIF Editor or minimize it to an icon so that it is readily accessible for further editing after you test the application.

T I P   To get help specific to any item in the PIF Editor window, select the item by clicking on it or by tabbing to the item and then pressing the Help key, F1. A Help window displays information about the item you selected. Press Alt+F4 to close the Help application.

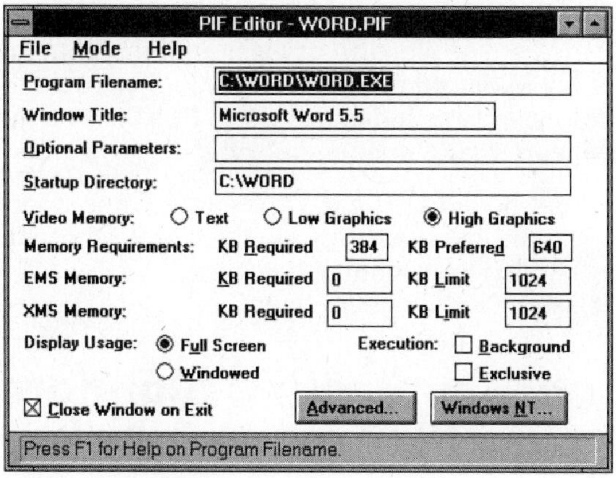

Fig. 21.6

The WORD.PIF in the PIF Editor shows the settings for Microsoft Word 5.5 in 386-enhanced mode.

Starting an Application in a Data Directory

To specify an active directory after the application starts, type that directory name in the **S**tartup Directory text box in that application's PIF. Because you can have multiple PIFs for the same application, you can make each PIF start the application in a different directory. Be aware, however, that some applications require that the start-up directory be the same as the application's directory. Some applications look in the application directory for additional files needed at start-up so that the application can successfully locate those files; the current directory must be the application's directory.

Understanding PIF Editor Options

Windows NT provides the ability to run in one of two modes: standard and enhanced. Standard mode is a protected mode that allows Windows to access all available memory (not just the first megabyte of memory). This mode takes advantage of the protected-mode hardware of the computer.

Enhanced mode is the second protected mode used by Windows NT (it is the default). This mode provides all of the features of standard mode, plus it provides virtual memory.

Virtual memory is nothing more than disk space used by Windows NT as though the disk space were an extension of main memory. For example, if there is 8M of real memory and a 30M virtual memory file is allocated, Windows NT provides access to this 38M memory just as though all 38M were really main memory.

The PIF Editor text boxes are nearly the same for standard and 386-enhanced modes, although each mode does have some different text boxes. The boxes also look similar in design.

PIF Options Common to Standard and 386-Enhanced Mode

The following paragraphs describe the PIF Editor text boxes that are similar for both standard and 386-enhanced mode.

The **P**rogram Filename text box entry specifies the name of the application's executable file or start-up file. You type this file name from the command prompt to start the application. Type the full path name and application name, including the file extension. Most application file names have the extension EXE or COM. Batch files that run commands or start applications have the extension BAT. For example, an entry for WordPerfect 6 would be `C:\WP60\WP.EXE` and an entry for Lotus 1-2-3 Release 2.4 would be `C:\123R24\123.EXE`.

The Window **T**itle text box entry is the description that appears in the application's window title bar when it displays in a window and the title under the application's icon when it is minimized. Type the name you want to appear in the application window title bar and under the icon. If you leave the Window **T**itle text box blank, Windows NT uses the application name (for example, WordPerfect), for the window title bar and for the icon name when you minimize the application. The title entered in the Window **T**itle text box is used only if the application is started using the **F**ile **R**un command (using the PIF file name) or if it is started from the File Manager. (If you associate the PIF to an icon, the icon name entered in the **D**escription text box in the Program Item Properties dialog box overrides the description in the PIF's Window **T**itle text box. The icon description, therefore, appears in the application's window title bar when it displays in a window and as the title under the application's icon when minimized.)

In the **O**ptional Parameters text box, type any parameters you want added to the application when it starts, such as which file to open. These parameters or arguments are the ones you type after the file name when you start an application from the command prompt. If you frequently use different parameters, type a question mark in this box, and Windows NT prompts you for the optional parameter when you run the PIF. Parameters can be up to 62 characters in length.

Some examples of optional parameters follow:

- *filename* loads the specified file when WordPerfect 6 starts.

- */m=macroname* starts the specified macro when WordPerfect 6 starts.

- */l* opens the last document you worked on in your previous Microsoft Word session.

- *-wfilename* retrieves the specified file when Lotus 1-2-3 starts.

If you launch an application by typing the application's file name after choosing **F**ile **R**un from the Program Manager or File Manager, and the PIF has the same name as the application file, any parameters you supply on the **F**ile **R**un command line automatically override those supplied in the **O**ptional Parameters box for this PIF.

The **S**tartup Directory text box entry defines the drive and directory made current before the application starts. For example, you may keep all your word processing files in a directory called \WPDOCS, but your word processor is located in \WP60. If you want the word processor to have \WPDOCS as the file directory when it starts, enter **C:\WPDOCS** in the **S**tartup Directory box.

You also can specify a **S**tartup Directory in a program item icon by entering a directory in the **W**orking Directory box with the **F**ile **P**roperties command from the Program Manager. Settings made in Program Manager override settings made in PIF Editor.

If the application has a default settings file that includes a default startup directory (like WordPerfect and Lotus 1-2-3), the **S**tartup Directory in the PIF or the **W**orking Directory in a program item icon are overruled.

PIF Options for Standard Mode

The following sections describe the standard mode PIF Editor settings (see fig. 21.3). The Memory Requirements options specify how much memory the application uses; the Directly Modifies options, Prevent Program Switch option, and No Screen Exchange option affect how much memory is left for other applications to use.

Video Mode

Video mode is used to determine how the material displayed on a computer monitor appears and what capabilities are provided. Text mode provides text-only information display. Graphics mode provides all of the graphical features expected from Windows-type programs.

Option	Description
Text	Select this option when the application uses only text mode. This Video mode option tells Windows to set aside only enough memory to save an application's text display so that you can switch back and forth between the application and Windows. The Text option reserves the least amount of memory possible for saving the display. You cannot display graphics screens when this option is set.
Graphics/MultipleText	Select this option when the application displays graphics. This choice causes Windows to set aside more memory for saving the screen because the application is using video data. You should choose this option in most cases.

Memory Requirements

Every application program requires computer memory in which to execute. *Standard* (conventional) memory refers to all computer memory up to 640K. Extended (XMS) memory is all of the memory above 640K up to a 1M limit.

Option	Description
KB **R**equired	Type the amount of memory in kilobytes required by the DOS application to run. This setting tells Windows the minimum conventional memory that must be available to load the application. The KB **R**equired setting is less than the amount listed in the application user manual because the amount listed includes memory required for DOS and other parts of the system. Usually, you should start with the default setting of 128. Start the application with no other

Option	Description
	applications running to see whether it starts. If the application does not start, raise the KB **R**equired setting in increments of 64 until the application does run. If you try to start a DOS application and the required amount of memory is not available to the system, you receive an error message from Windows, and you cannot start the application.

XMS Memory

These options tell Windows how much extended memory to use for applications requiring XMS memory specification. Because Windows enables the use of extended memory as long as it is available, you can leave these options at the standard settings of 0.

Option	Description
KB Required	Type the number of kilobytes of extended memory recommended by the application manual if your application uses extended memory that prescribes to the Lotus/Intel/Microsoft/AST Extended Memory Specification Version 2.0 or later. This setting is the minimum amount needed to start the application. Unless you are positive that the application you are creating the PIF for uses extended memory, leave this setting at 0. The 0 setting prevents applications from using XMS memory. Few DOS applications use extended memory.
KB Limit	Type the maximum amount of extended memory needed by the application. This setting prevents the application from taking all extended memory for itself by setting an upper limit. Leave the setting at 0 to prevent the application from gaining access to any extended memory, or set the option to –1 to give the application all the extended memory it requests. Use the –1 setting only if the application requires large amounts of extended memory, because this setting slows down the system significantly.

Directly Modifies

Some applications cannot share resources with other applications. The Directly Modifies settings group defines which resources cannot be shared. You cannot switch back to Windows without quitting the application if you choose these options.

Option	Description
COM1, COM2, COM3, COM4	Select one of these check boxes if the application uses COM1, COM2, COM3, or COM4. Selecting an option prevents other applications from using the COM port selected for this application. The application using a PIF with this selection does not swap from memory onto a hard disk, so you cannot fit as many additional applications in Windows.
Keyboard	Select this option if the application directly controls the keyboard.

No Screen Exchange

Select this option to prevent copying and pasting between DOS applications using the Clipboard. If you select this option, you cannot copy screens with the Print Screen or Alt+PrtScrn key. Selecting this option conserves memory.

No Save Screen

Select this option so that Windows does not save the screen information when you switch to another application. When you choose the No Save Screen option, Windows no longer retains in memory the screen information for the application, and the memory becomes available. Use this option only when the application has the capability to retain its own screen information and has a "redraw screen" command.

Prevent Program Switch

Select this option to prevent switching from the application back to Windows. Selecting this check box prevents you from using Alt+Tab,

Alt+Esc, or Ctrl+Esc to switch back to Windows NT. You must exit the application to return to Windows NT. This option conserves memory.

Close Window on Exit

Select this option to close the window in which the DOS application is displayed when you exit the DOS application.

Reserve Shortcut Keys

Select the Reserve Shortcut Key options to select the key combinations you want to use for carrying out functions in the application instead of for use by Windows.

Option	Description
Alt+Tab	Select this option to reserve the Alt+Tab shortcut key for this application. Windows uses Alt+Tab to toggle between applications.
Alt+Esc	Select this option to reserve the Alt+Esc shortcut key for this application. Windows uses Alt+Esc to switch to the next application.
Ctrl+Esc	Select this option to reserve the Ctrl+Esc shortcut key for this application. Windows uses Ctrl+Esc to switch to the Task List.
PrtSc	Select this option to reserve the PrtSc shortcut key for this application. Windows uses Print Screen to copy a full screen to the Clipboard.
Alt+PrtSc	Select this option to reserve the Alt+PrtSc shortcut key for the application. Windows uses Alt+PrtSc to copy a full screen (or active Window) to the Clipboard.

PIF Options for 386-Enhanced Mode

The 386-enhanced options appear in two dialog boxes (see figs. 21.4 and 21.5). The basic PIF options are similar to the PIF options in standard mode. The descriptions of Program Filename, Window Title, Optional Parameters, and Startup Directory are described in "PIF Options Common to Standard and 386-Enhanced Mode." The advanced options, described later in this chapter, fine-tune the application for running in 386-enhanced mode.

Many of the standard mode PIF options are duplicated for 386-enhanced mode. For example, if you set the **P**rogram Filename option in standard mode and then use the **M**ode command to switch to the settings for 386-enhanced mode, Windows NT duplicates the same settings in 386-enhanced mode. This duplication is especially helpful when you run Windows NT frequently in standard or 386-enhanced mode and you need to set PIF options for both modes. The most notable exception, however, is the **O**ptional Parameters setting, which you use to supply command-line parameters to an application when you start it. You must set this option independently for each mode.

Video Memory Options

The **V**ideo Memory options determine the video mode for the program. Different methods of displaying graphics require different amounts of memory, and these options ensure that Windows NT sets aside enough memory for the video mode used by the software. These modes are Text, Low Graphics, and High Graphics. Use the lowest memory mode possible so that more memory is available for Windows NT. If the application does not have sufficient video memory, it does not start, and a warning message appears. If you switch from a graphics mode to one that requires less memory, Windows NT releases the video memory no longer needed. However, you are prevented from switching back to graphics if another application is using the memory. To ensure that video memory is reserved for your application so that this does not happen, select the High Graphics option and, from the advanced portion of the dialog box, select the Retain Video **M**emory check box. This means that your applications will always be able to switch memory modes, but less memory will be available for other applications.

Option	Description
Text	Requires the least amount of memory. Graphics will not display. Use this mode if the DOS application will not be displaying graphics. This mode makes more memory available for Windows NT.
Low Graphics	Low-resolution graphics will display such as CGA monitors.
High Graphics	Requires the most amount of memory. Select this option and the Retain Video **M**emory check box in the Advanced Options dialog box to ensure that high-resolution memory is always available for the application. Choose this option if you are using a VGA (or better) monitor.

Memory Requirements Options

Windows NT and DOS applications view conventional memory very differently. Windows NT treats all memory—conventional, extended, and virtual (disk-based) memory—as one large pool of memory. DOS is a single-tasking operating system, and a DOS application assumes that it is the only application running and that it can use unlimited conventional memory (0K to 640K). When a DOS application makes a request for a block of conventional memory, Windows NT satisfies that request by giving it a block of memory from the pool. The Memory Requirements PIF settings enable you to specify the upper and lower limits of memory that a DOS application receives.

Option	Description
KB **R**equired	Type the minimum amount of conventional memory that must be free for the application to start. Windows NT does not start the application if available memory is less than the amount specified in the KB **R**equired text box. If you are unsure of what to enter, leave the setting at 128. Do not enter the amount of memory recommended by the user manual—this figure is inflated to account for drivers and DOS. Generally, you should use a KB **R**equired setting just high enough to load the application without Windows NT issuing an insufficient memory error message, but low enough that you can load the application when memory is tight. If the application does not run due to insufficient memory, close all other applications and increase the KB **R**equired setting in 64K increments until the application runs. Enter –1 to give the application all available conventional memory up to 640K. You should avoid using this setting; in most cases, using a setting of –1 sets aside a full 640K, which is too much for most applications.
KB Preferre**d**	Type the maximum amount of memory you want the application to use if the memory is available. The default 640K is the maximum; most applications use much less. Use –1 to give the application as much memory as possible up to 640K. Most applications run more efficiently with more memory, but remember that Windows NT shares a pool of memory and you do not want one application taking more memory than it uses. Be frugal with this setting if you know your application will not need the upper limit of 640. If you decrease the KB Preferre**d** amount to 512K, you conserve 128K for other applications because this application cannot use more than 512K of memory.

EMS Memory Options

When running in 386-enhanced mode, Windows NT uses only extended memory; however, Windows NT simulates expanded memory for applications that need the memory or that perform better when expanded memory is available.

Option	Description
KB Required	This setting is the minimum amount of memory required for the application to run. Leave this setting at 0 (no expanded memory) for most applications. Entering a required amount does not limit the amount of expanded memory used, but if less memory is free than what is specified by **K**B Required, the application does not start and displays a warning message.
KB Limit	Enter the maximum amount of expanded memory you want the application to use. Windows NT gives the application as much expanded memory as it needs, up to the limit you specify in this text box or until no more memory is available. The default setting is 1024. Set to 0 to prevent the application from having any expanded memory. A setting of –1 gives the application unlimited memory, but this setting can slow the performance of other applications.

XMS Memory Options

The XMS Memory settings configure Windows NT for an application that uses the Lotus-Intel-Microsoft-AST Extended Memory Specification (XMS). Few applications use XMS; generally, you can leave these options at their default settings.

Option	Description
KB Required	Type the minimum amount of extended memory recommended by the user manual for the application. If the application uses XMS memory, the computer must have the amount of memory specified by this option, or the application does not start. Leave this setting at 0 for most applications.

21 — CUSTOMIZING PIFS

Option	Description
KB Limit	Type the maximum amount of extended memory you want the application to use. The default setting of 1024 gives the application as much extended memory as it requires, up to 1024K or until no more memory is available. Leave this setting at 0 to prevent the application from using extended memory. Few DOS applications use extended memory.

Display Usage Options

The Display Usage options govern whether a program uses the entire computer screen (Full Screen) or only a portion of the screen. Full screen provides the same look and feel as if the application were running DOS. A windowed display will be smaller than the entire monitor area and appear more like the windows native to Windows NT.

Option	Description
Full Screen	Select this option to start the application in a full-screen display rather than in a window. Running an application in a full screen saves memory and is required for some applications running in high video modes. You can switch between full-screen applications and Window applications quickly by pressing Alt+Tab.
Windowed	Select this option to start the application in a window. Running in a window provides the advantages of easily activating other applications and copying and pasting data portions of a screen.

You quickly can switch from a window to full-screen display using Alt+Enter, and the application reverts to the application set color scheme. You can toggle between windows and the full screen by pressing Alt+Enter.

Execution Options

In 386-enhanced mode, Windows NT is a multitasking environment for DOS applications. Although Windows NT appears to be running multiple applications, Windows NT really can run only one application at a time. Windows NT must share the computer time between each running application by using *time slicing*. Each application gets a portion of the total processor time. To run multiple DOS applications simultaneously with all of them continuing to run while you are working in one of them, the DOS PIFs must be set up so that one application runs in the foreground, where it is active, and the other application runs in the background. The PIFs that Windows Setup and the installation application create make sure that all DOS applications run in the foreground and background. You can change the proportion of time each application receives by modifying the Execution options in an application's PIF.

Option	Description
Background	Select this check box to enable the application to run in the background while you use another application. For example, a mail-merge application or database search can run in the background while you complete a letter with a word processor in the foreground. The amount of processor time allocated to the application while in the background is set using one of the Advanced PIF options.
Exclusive	Select this check box to suspend all other applications while this application is in the foreground. All other applications are halted—even if the applications have their **B**ackground option selected. This option gives an application all the processor time. Usually, this option can be left unchecked.

The Close Window on Exit Option

Select the **C**lose Window on Exit option to close the window when you exit the DOS application. Do not select this option if the DOS application leaves information on the screen after it terminates. Windows NT will close the window and this DOS information will be lost.

The Advanced Button

Choosing the **A**dvanced button displays the Advanced Options dialog box for additional 386-enhanced mode PIF options (refer to fig. 21.5). These options are described later in this chapter, in the section titled "Advanced PIF Options for 386-Enhanced Mode."

The Windows NT Button

Choosing the Windows NT button displays the Windows NT Options dialog box, which allows DOS applications running under Windows NT to have custom startup files. This feature is described in the section "Creating Custom Startup Files," later in this chapter.

Advanced PIF Options for 386-Enhanced Mode

The advanced options, like the other PIF options, have been included in the PIF editor to allow Windows NT a way of providing operational compatibility with Windows 3.1.

By using the advanced options in 386-enhanced mode, you can modify a PIF for better memory use and performance for the DOS application. To display the Advanced Options dialog box, choose the **A**dvanced button at the bottom of the basic PIF Editor dialog box. This button displays only when the PIF Editor is in 386-enhanced mode. Use the **M**ode menu to switch to the 386-enhanced PIF Editor if the **A**dvanced button does not appear. (Although you can edit a 386-enhanced PIF while running standard-mode windows, the PIF options take effect only when operating in 386-enhanced mode.)

Figure 21.5 shows that the Advanced Options dialog box is divided into four areas: Multitasking Options, Memory Options, Display Options, and Other Options. Using these options, you can adjust your PIF for best performance and memory usage.

Multitasking Options

The Multitasking options control how a DOS application shares processing time with other DOS applications. When you are running two (or more) DOS applications at the same time and one (or more) of them is running in the background, you need a way to control how much processor time each application gets in relation to the other applications. Windows NT enables you to control this ratio through the Multitasking Options group.

Option	Description
Background Priority	Type a value between 0 and 10000 to specify the background priority for this DOS application. The default background priority is 50. This value is meaningful only when compared to **B**ackground and **F**oreground Priority settings for the other running DOS applications.
	To figure the percentage of processor time allocated to a DOS application, total the **F**oreground Priority for the active DOS application with the **B**ackground Priority for all DOS applications running in background at that time. Divide the priority (**F**oreground or **B**ackground Priority) of an application by the total. For example, the total priority of three applications is 200 (one foreground application with a priority of 100 and two background applications, each with a priority of 50). The background activity gets 50 out of a total of 200, or 25 percent of the processor time allocated to DOS applications.
	If an application's Execution: **B**ackground check box is turned off, the application cannot run in the background. Therefore, any number you enter in the **B**ackground Priority box does not have any effect.
Foreground Priority	Type a value between 0 and 10000 to specify the foreground priority for the application. The default foreground priority is 100. The value has no meaning unless another DOS application is running in the background.
Detect Idle Time	Select this option so that Windows NT gives processor resources to other applications when this application is idle (waiting for input from you, for example). This option enhances the performance of your computer and should be selected in most cases. If an application is running slowly, deselecting this option may help in some circumstances.

Memory Options

Sometimes it is necessary not to have the advanced memory management features of Windows NT operate for every application. Applications may need to have all of their memory remain constant (locked) because of the type of processing in which they may be engaged.

If a program is in the process of transmitting data from its local memory through a modem to some other application, suddenly having the memory swapped to disk could be very disruptive. Being able to lock the memory prevents these problems.

Option	Description
EMS Memory Locked	Select this option to prevent the application's expanded memory from swapping to hard disk. This setting improves the application performance because the application remains in memory; however, selecting this option can force other applications to swap more frequently and slow down their performance.
XMS Memory Locked	Select this option to prevent the application from swapping memory to hard disk. Selecting this check box improves the application performance because the application remains in memory; however, selecting this option can force other applications to swap more frequently and slow down their performance.
Uses High Memory Area	Select this option to enable the application to use the high memory area (HMA). If HMA is available, each application can allocate its own HMA.

HMA is used by some memory-resident utilities such as networks. If a memory-resident utility is using HMA when you start Windows NT in 386-enhanced mode, no other applications can use HMA.

Select Uses High Memory Area for most applications. This option makes more memory available for the application if needed. If the application does not use the additional memory, HMA is not wasted. The default setting of 1024 gives the application as much extended memory as it requires, up to 1024K or until no more memory is available. |

continues

Option	Description
Lock Application Memory	Select this option to prevent conventional memory from swapping to the hard disk. Selecting this option improves the performance of this application but decreases overall system performance. Use the settings previously described to lock EMS and XMS memory.

Display Options

Some applications directly access the computer's hardware input and output ports to control the display adapter. Windows NT must monitor the application's interface with the hardware ports to ensure that when you switch applications, the video display is restored correctly. Use the default settings for most applications.

These selections control the amount of memory Windows NT reserves for the application display when the application starts. Generally, these settings should not be changed. If you change the application's display mode during operation, Windows NT releases unused memory to other applications if you go to a less memory-intensive mode; Windows NT attempts to use additional memory if you go to a more memory-intensive mode. If additional memory is not available, the screen image may be lost. Use the High Graphics and Retain Video Memory options to ensure that memory is available if you lose the display when you switch graphics modes.

The first three options in the following list are Monitor Ports selections:

Option	Description
Text	Select this option to have Windows NT monitor video operations when the application is running in text mode. Few applications require this option.
Low Graphics	Select this option to have Windows NT monitor all video operations when the application is running in low-resolution graphics mode. Few applications require this option.
High Graphics	Select this option when the application displays graphics in high-resolution graphics mode. EGA and VGA graphics adapters display applications in high-resolution graphics mode. The High

Option	Description
	Graphics option requires about 128K of memory. Select this option and the Retain Video Memory option to make sure that you have enough memory to run any application. Be aware, however, that these selections reduce the amount of memory available to all applications.
Emulate Text Mode	Select this option to increase the rate at which the application displays text. Leave this option selected for most applications. If your application has garbled text, if the cursor appears in the wrong place, or if the application doesn't run, try clearing this check box.
Retain Video Memory	Select this option so that Windows NT retains extra video memory and does not release it to other applications. Some applications, such as Microsoft Word, use more than one video mode. When Word switches from text to graphics mode, Windows NT usually releases the memory for the video mode not in use. If memory becomes scarce, Word may not be able to switch back to a previous video mode. Selecting this check box and the correct video memory option ensures that you always have enough memory available to switch back to an application and to view the screen.

The application may lose its display if you select this option under low-memory conditions and then change to a more memory-intensive video display. The display is lost because Windows NT cannot dynamically free the memory needed for the new display mode. |

IBM's VGA display adapter is not affected by the settings you make in the Monitor Ports options. Any settings made are ignored by these types of display adapters.

T I P

Other Options

The Other options enable you to customize Windows NT even further when in the 386-enhanced mode.

Option	Description
Allow Fast **P**aste	Usually, this option is selected. Most applications can accept information pasted from the Clipboard using the fastest method. If you paste into a DOS application and nothing happens, clear this check box on the application's PIF.
Allow **C**lose When Active	Select this option to enable Windows NT to close the application without requiring you to use the application's Exit command. Select this option to exit Windows NT without closing all active DOS applications first. Because you do not have to exit the application before closing the window, no reminder to save work in progress appears. Windows NT does display a message box asking whether you are sure that you want to close the active application.
Reserve **S**hortcut Keys	Select the key combinations you want available for an application when it runs in the foreground. Usually, these key combinations are reserved for use by Windows NT. This option enables you to use special keys in your application that Windows NT may otherwise reserve for its use. Two more shortcut keys are available in 386-enhanced mode than in standard mode: Alt+Enter, which toggles a DOS application between full screen and windows and Alt+Space, which activates an application window's Control menu.
Application Shortcut Key	Specify the shortcut-key combination you want to use to activate the application so that the application moves from background to foreground. The shortcut combination must include Alt or Ctrl. You can include combinations of letters, numbers, and function keys. To specify a shortcut-key combination, select this option and press the key combination you want. For example, select this option and press Alt+W. (To remove the current shortcut key, select this option and press Shift+Backspace.)

Option	Description
	Select your shortcut-key combinations carefully. After the application is loaded, the shortcut keys specified activate that application and do not work as shortcut keys for other applications.

Be Careful Selecting the Allow Close When Active Option

Selecting the Allow Close When Active check box can result in loss of data and file damage. This option enables Windows NT to close an application before the application has the chance to close its open files. The files may be damaged, and you lose any changes made to these files.

This problem occurs most frequently with accounting and database software. These applications keep files open while operating. If you quit the application with Allow Close When Active selected, the open files may be left open—ruining the data files with which you were working.

Creating Custom Startup Files

The Windows NT button in the PIF editor gives you the ability to set some parameters that are specific to Windows NT. Choosing this button results in a dialog box with two text boxes (see fig. 21.7).

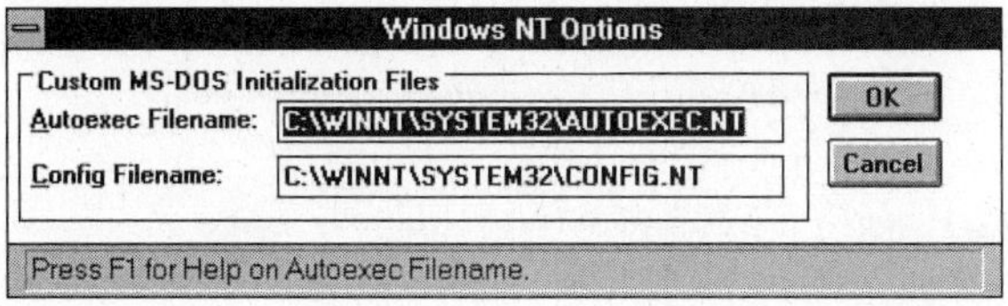

Fig. 21.7

The Windows NT Options dialog box.

The Windows NT Options dialog box allows DOS applications running under Windows NT to have custom startup files. In the Autoexec Filename box, you can specify a special AUTOEXEC.NT file that is run in place of the normal AUTOEXEC.NT file when your DOS application runs with this PIF. Similarly, the Config Filename field allows you to name a file to load in place of the normal CONFIG.NT file. These alternate files are effective only for these PIF files. You can use these files when your application requires special drivers, environment variables, or configuration settings in order to run.

Changing Settings of a Running Application

Besides using the PIF Editor to define PIF option settings, you can change some PIF options while the application is running in 386-enhanced mode. You can change an application's display option between full screen and windows. You also can change the percentage of processor time the application receives when it is active or in the background.

To change settings for an application running in 386-enhanced mode, follow these steps:

1. Press Alt+space bar to quickly access the Control menu.

2. Choose the Settings command from the application's Control menu.

   A settings dialog box for the application appears (see fig. 21.8).

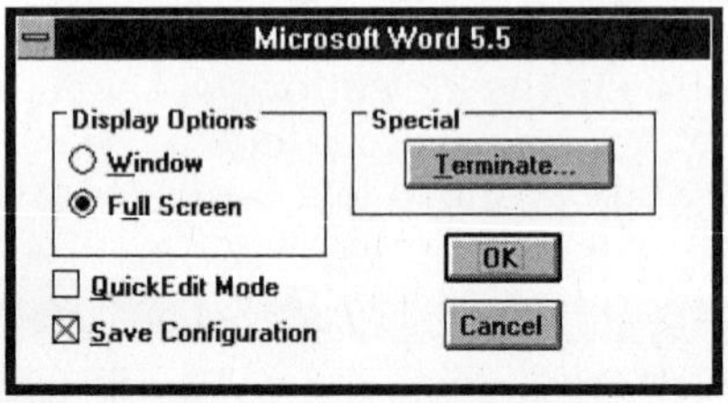

Fig. 21.8

Changing applications as they run with the settings dialog box.

3. Select the option you want to change.

Switching Back to Full Screen

If you press Alt+space bar while running a full-screen DOS application in 386-enhanced mode, the application is put into a window, and the Control menu appears. To return to full-screen mode from a window, press Alt+Enter or choose Settings from the application's Control menu, select Full Screen, and choose OK.

Some applications use Alt+space bar for their own purposes. Remember to reserve this shortcut key in the PIF for the application if you want to retain the shortcut key for the application's purposes, and you do not want to return to Windows NT. If Alt+space bar is used by the application, open the Control menu by pressing Alt+Enter (which puts the application in title bar) to open the Control menu.

The following sections list the options you can change as the application runs.

Display Options

The Display Options change how the application appears. A faster method of switching display options is to press Alt+Enter to alternate between full-screen and windowed modes.

Option	Description
Window	Displays the application in a window
Full Screen	Displays the application in a full screen

The QuickEdit Mode Option

The QuickEdit Mode option controls how you select information to copy in the Command Prompt window. With this option marked, you can use the mouse to select information in the Command Prompt window to copy to the Clipboard. If you leave this option unmarked, however, you must use the Edit Mark Selections option from the Control Box menu to select information to copy to the Clipboard.

The Save Configuration Option

The Save Configuration option enables you to record changes that you make to the Command Prompt window. For example, if you select this option, then make changes to the fonts that you display in the Command Prompt window, Windows NT saves the changes you made to the fonts. Each Command Prompt window you open will display using the font change. However, if you do not mark the Save Configuration option, you loose any Command Prompt setting changes when you close the Command Prompt window.

The Terminate Option

Use the **T**erminate option as a last resort. Choose this option when you cannot exit or quit the application in any other way. Terminate closes the application and gives you the chance to return to Windows NT to save open files in other applications. Save the files in all other applications and then close the applications and exit Windows NT. If you are unable to exit Windows NT, press Ctrl+Alt+Del.

If you choose a PIF to start a DOS application but the application does not start or operate correctly, use the PIF Editor to edit the PIF.

Some of the most common problems and their solutions follow:

Problem	Solution Using the PIF Editor
Application file not found	Check the application path name and the file-name extension in the **P**rogram Filename text box.
Associated files not found	Type the application's path name in the **S**tartup Directory text box.
Insufficient memory to start	Increase the Memory Requirements: KB **R**equired setting. You may need to increase the EMS Memory: **K**B Required or XMS Memory: KB Re-**q**uired setting if your application requires EMS or XMS memory.
Add-in applications don't run	Increase the Memory Requirements: KB **R**equired setting.
Special keystrokes don't work	Reserve keystrokes for the application's use in the Reserve **S**hortcut Keys group (choose the **A**dvanced button in a 386-enhanced mode PIF to see these options).

Customizing DOS Applications with Multiple PIFs

Sometimes, you may need to start the same DOS application in different ways. You can create a different PIF for each of the ways in which you want the DOS application to run. Assign a different program item icon to each PIF or start each PIF directly from the File Manager. For example, you may want to specify different start-up directories for different types of work, or you may want to specify a different application macro to run for each of the PIFs.

You also may want a different memory configuration for the different times you run the application. You may need to invoke WordPerfect with a large amount of memory reserved, for example.

Another good use for several PIFs is to invoke specific applications parameters. For example, you can name a PIF WP-M.PIF to invoke WordPerfect and run a macro provided in the **O**ptional Parameters by using the /m=*macroname* parameter. You also may have a PIF named WP-F.PIF that has a ? in the **O**ptional Parameters text box so that you can provide a file name to automatically load.

Running DOS Batch Files

You can run DOS batch files from within Windows NT by creating a PIF for them. Creating a PIF for a batch file is the same as creating a PIF for any application. Although you can run some DOS batch files without creating a corresponding PIF, the following sections illustrate some of the advantages to running batch files from a PIF.

Running a Batch File from a PIF

You can run a batch file from a PIF in the same way you run any DOS application. By creating a PIF to prepare Windows NT for the batch file, you can set up the Windows NT environment correctly. For example, you may want to load a terminate-and-stay-resident (TSR) application along with one of your DOS applications.

To run a TSR and then a DOS application in the same DOS session, use the Notepad accessory to create a batch file like the following:

```
C:\tsrpathname\tsr.EXE
C:\application_pathname\application.EXE
```

Save this batch file with the extension BAT.

Create a PIF to run this batch file by using the path name and file name of the batch file entered in the **P**rogram Filename box. When the PIF runs, the file first opens a DOS session with the parameters set by the PIF. Then the PIF runs the batch file. The batch file loads the TSR and then loads and runs the application. When you quit the application, the session ends; Windows NT recaptures the memory; and the window closes, if a window was used.

When you create a batch file to run more than one application, for example a TSR and a DOS application, enter into the PIF the settings for the most demanding application in the batch file. The DOS session started by the PIF has the settings for the most difficult to operate DOS application.

The following batch files illustrate how you can run batch files to do chores or procedures unavailable through the File Manager. This one-line batch file prints a listing of the files and directory names in the current directory to most non-PostScript printers connected to the LPT1 parallel port. After the batch file runs, you need to turn the printer off-line and press the form feed button to eject the page.

Type **DIR>LPT1:** into the Notepad and save the file with the name DIRPRINT.BAT. Open the PIF Editor and choose the **F**ile **N**ew command. Type **DIRPRINT.BAT** in the **P**rogram Filename box. Choose the **F**ile Save **A**s command and enter a name for the file name.

You now can print the current directory by choosing the DIRPRINT.PIF from the File Manager. If you use this command frequently, you may want to use the **F**ile **N**ew command with the Program **I**tem option in the Program Manager to create a program item icon that starts this PIF and prints the directory. When the batch file runs, the DOS session closes, and control returns to Windows NT.

Keeping a DOS Session Open after a Batch File Finishes

When you run a batch file under Windows NT, whether from a PIF or not, the DOS screen closes, and control returns to Windows NT. Windows NT reclaims the memory the batch file used.

You may want the DOS window or screen to remain open so that you can read results from a DOS application. For example, when you are writing batch files to run from PIFs, you may want to see the batch file operations on-screen to ensure that they have run correctly. If the window or screen immediately closes when the batch file finishes, you probably cannot see what happens.

To make Windows NT execute the batch commands and then keep the DOS screen open, you must add the line C:*pathname*\COMMAND.COM as the last line of your batch file (where *pathname* is the directory containing COMMAND.COM). On a network, you can use the variable name *%COMSPEC%* instead. %COMSPEC% is a DOS environment variable that stores the location of DOS. Because %COMSPEC% always contains the current location of the COMMAND.COM file, no matter how the system is configured, you will want to use it as the last line of any batch file for which the DOS screen should remain open.

For example, if you want a batch file to display file names in wide format for the current directory and then keep the list on-screen, the batch file appears as follows:

```
DIR /W
%COMSPEC%
```

When you run a PIF that keeps the DOS screen open, don't forget to type **EXIT** and press Enter to return to Windows NT.

T I P

Creating a Program Item Icon for a Batch File

After you have created a PIF that runs your batch file, you can assign a program item icon to the PIF so that you can run the PIF by choosing an icon in the Program Manager. To create a program item icon for your batch file, complete the following steps:

1. Activate the group window in the Program Manager in which you want the icon.

2. Choose the **F**ile **N**ew command.

3. Select the Program **I**tem option and choose OK.

4. Type the label for the icon in the **D**escription box.

5. Type the path and file name for the PIF in the **C**ommand Line box. Use the **B**rowse button to find and select the file if you cannot remember the name.

6. Choose the Change **I**con button.

7. Type the name of the file containing icons in the **F**ile Name box. If you do not have a library of icons, enter the name of a file that contains icons that came with Windows NT. These files usually are found in C:\WINNT\SYSTEM32\PROGMAN.EXE or C:\WINNT\SYSTEM32\MORICONS.DLL. Choose OK.

8. From the **C**urrent Icon list, select the icon you want in the Program Manager.

9. Choose OK twice.

Ensuring that Batch File Variables Have Enough Memory

DOS reserves a small amount of memory in which to store names and numbers. This memory is the DOS environment. Usually, the DOS environment stores information such as COMSPEC (the location of COMMAND.COM), PATH (directories in the path), and PROMPT (the appearance of the command prompt). The DOS environment also can store variables used by batch files. Variables are changeable items in a batch. For example, if a batch file asks that you type a number, the number is stored in an environment variable.

The amount of memory available in the DOS environment is important to you if you want to run batch files from within Windows NT that use a large number of variables. Batch files that create DOS menuing systems, batch files that ask for many user prompts, or batch files that set up networks all need a larger DOS environment than Windows NT usually sets aside.

One way of expanding the DOS environment is to use Notebook to add a line to your CONFIG.SYS file:

```
SHELL=C:\pathname\COMMAND.COM /E:512 /P
```

This line loads COMMAND.COM with an environment of 512 bytes. The /P parameter indicates that COMMAND.COM is loaded; you must include this parameter.

Because the amount of DOS environment may change, you may want to use the PIF to expand the environment memory and to run the batch file or application. The following modifications to a PIF expand the DOS environment so that it can store variables that may be used by the batch file:

Program file name:	COMMAND.COM
Title:	*filename*.PIF
Optional Parameters:	/E:384 /C C:*pathname**filename*.BAT

These changes create a DOS environment of 384 bytes and then run any application or batch file (COM, EXE, or BAT) that follows the /C. In this case, the batch file *filename*.BAT runs.

Passing Variable Data from a PIF to a Batch File

You can pass variable data from a PIF to a DOS batch file. This enables you to create a batch file that changes how it operates depending upon which variables are passed to it. For example, the same batch file can add different directories to the DOS PATH depending upon which PIF ran the batch file. With this arrangement, you can set up a program item icon tied to each PIF so that double-clicking on an icon adds a new directory to the PIF. You also can create a PIF that prompts you to enter information. The batch file then uses that information to operate. This example is just one way in which you can control DOS from within Windows NT.

Use Notepad to create a batch file that adds a variable directory name to the current DOS PATH. (By adding a directory to the PATH, any file in the PATH can be run from anywhere on the disk without entering the file's full path name.) Save this one-line batch file to the name PATHCHNG.BAT:

```
SET PATH=%PATH%;%1
```

This line tells DOS to attach a directory name stored in the variable %1 to the current path, stored in the variable %PATH%. The PATH then should be set equal to this new path that includes an additional directory. The variable %1 stores what is entered in the **O**ptional Parameters line of the PIF that ran PATHCHNG.BAT.

For example, if you occasionally need to add the Paradox 3.5 directory to your DOS path, you can create a PIF with C:\PDOX35 in its **O**ptional Parameters box. The **P**rogram Filename should be PATHCHNG.BAT. When the PIF runs, the optional parameter C:\PDOX35 is stored in %1 in the DOS environment. The PATHCHNG.BAT batch file runs. The SET PATH line then adds the directory in %1 to the existing PATH.

You can make this type of PIF more flexible by typing a question mark in the **O**ptional Parameters box. When the PIF runs, Windows NT prompts you for the **O**ptional Parameter. What you type in the prompt box is stored in the variable for use by the batch file.

You can enter multiple variables in the **O**ptional Parameters box. Separate each variable with a space. Each variable then is passed to the batch file as *%1*, *%2*, *%3*, and so on depending upon the order in the PIF Editor.

Passing Variable Data from a Batch File to a PIF

Just as a PIF can pass variable data to a batch file, a batch file can pass variable data to a PIF. In a batch file, the DOS command SET can store a value in an environment variable. The contents of the environment variable then can be retrieved by using the variable name enclosed in percent signs, *%variable%*. That variable then can be read by a PIF. The **P**rogram Filename, Window **T**itle, **O**ptional Parameters, and **S**tartup Directory boxes in the PIF Editor can all receive DOS environment variables.

Summary

In this chapter, you learned what a PIF is and how Windows NT works with a PIF. You learned how to create, edit, and optimize PIFs. You also learned how to use the PIF Editor.

Now that you know how to work with PIFs, you may want to experiment and optimize the performance of your DOS applications. PIFs are one of the keys to making DOS applications run efficiently within Windows NT.

Running DOS Applications

When you use Windows NT, you don't need to give up your useful MS-DOS applications. In fact, you will find that Windows NT adds new dimensions to MS-DOS applications.

With Windows NT, you can load more than one application, whether the applications are DOS, Windows, POSIX, or OS/2 character mode applications. In Windows NT, you can run multiple DOS, Windows 3.x, Windows NT, POSIX, and OS/2 character mode applications simultaneously. You can copy text or graphics from one application and paste the text into another application or paste text or graphics into a Windows or Windows NT application. You can run DOS applications in a window just like a Windows application. Multiple DOS and Windows applications can continue working, even when in the background (not in the topmost window).

NOTE Windows NT can multitask DOS applications. When multitasking, each application that runs shares a portion of computer resources by taking advantage of the 80386 and 80486 processor's capability of making *virtual* computers (or simulating two or more computers within your machine). Each DOS application receives a portion of memory and a portion of processing power. Windows NT provides more memory to each application than when running with DOS. Windows NT treats all memory—actual and virtual (disk based) memory—as one large pool of memory. When

continues

continued

a DOS application makes a request for a block of memory, Windows NT satisfies this request by giving the application a block of memory from the *pool*. A DOS application shares both memory and CPU time with all other active applications and now is one application among many sharing the computer's resources, which Windows NT governs. You can run DOS applications in a window or as a full-screen display.

When you start a DOS application, Windows NT looks for the Program Information File (PIF) for the application. A PIF is a file that provides Windows NT with the information needed to run the DOS application. PIFs contain information, such as how much memory the application needs and what video mode is required. If Windows NT finds the PIF, the information within this file is used rather than the standard settings in the default PIF. Many popular DOS applications can use the default PIF without a problem. By default, PIFs are created for most DOS applications during installation.

If you dislike the configuration used in the default PIF settings, you can use the PIF Editor to create or modify existing PIFs. Chapter 21, "Customizing PIFs," describes how to create and modify PIFs.

The Command Prompt Window

If you have used Windows 3.1, you probably are familiar with the MS-DOS window. The Command Prompt window is similar to the MS-DOS window in that you can run MS-DOS applications. However, the Command Prompt window is more than just a way to run DOS programs. From the Command Prompt window, you can start Windows NT applications, OS/2 character-based applications, and POSIX-compliant applications. You can control network operations, issue MS-DOS commands and TCP/IP commands. The Command Prompt window enables you to perform many tasks that you otherwise perform through Windows—only you can issue command line syntax to perform the functions.

Understanding How Windows NT Handles DOS Applications

Windows NT manipulates memory, applications, and disk storage to load or run multiple applications simultaneously. If you understand how this process works, you can get better performance from the computer.

Running DOS Applications in a Window or a Full Screen

You can have multiple DOS applications running in separate windows or on full-screen and switch quickly between the applications. Figure 22.1 shows Lotus 1-2-3 Release 2.3 and WordPerfect 6.0, each running in separate windows.

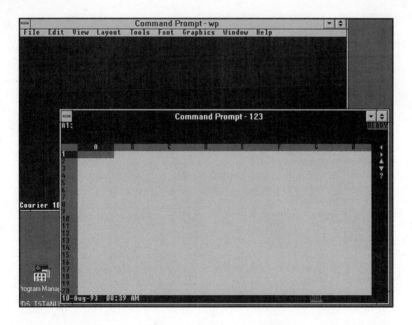

Fig. 22.1

Lotus 1-2-3 and WordPerfect in separate windows.

Applications designed for Windows NT or DOS use memory differently. Windows NT distributes memory efficiently among Windows applications because Windows applications use memory cooperatively.

DOS applications, however, don't have the memory-management capabilities of Windows applications. Most DOS applications, unlike Windows applications, aren't designed for multitasking. A DOS application, due to design, *thinks* that it is the only application running and therefore hogs memory and CPU time and doesn't share data easily. Windows NT expands the horizons of a DOS application by controlling certain properties of the application, such as memory, CPU time, and video mode, and thereby gives DOS applications multitasking capabilities. Windows NT can have both multiple Windows applications and multiple DOS applications active.

When a DOS application runs in a full-screen under Windows NT, the computer display appears as though only the DOS application is running. Appearances, however, can deceive. Pressing Ctrl+Esc returns you to the Windows NT Task Manager, and you then can choose a different DOS or Windows application from the Task List. The Windows NT Task Manager lists all open applications. Windows NT keeps the DOS application open but shrinks the application to an icon at the bottom of the screen, similar to the icons shown at the bottom of figure 22.2.

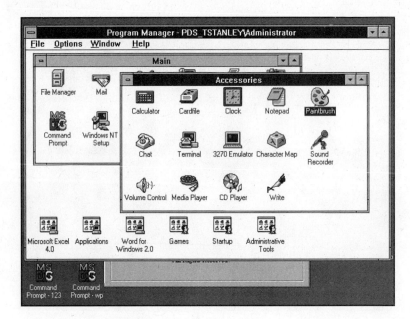

Fig. 22.2

DOS applications minimized to icons when not in use.

If your DOS applications are running in a window and you press Ctrl+Esc, the Task List appears above the DOS application window. You can always switch to a DOS application by pressing Ctrl+Esc to display the Task List and then select the application. You also can press Alt+Tab to switch among applications.

During the Windows NT installation process, Setup builds Program Information Files (PIFs) for the DOS applications on which Setup has information. This setup information is stored in the APPS.INF file. When a PIF is created by Windows NT Setup, the file is created with full-screen mode selected as the default. To have a DOS application start in a window, use the PIF Editor to edit the application's PIF. Choose the **W**indowed option from the Display Usage group.

> **T I P**
>
> If you want to switch a DOS application between full-screen and window modes, press Alt+Enter. Pressing Alt+Enter at any time toggles the display between full-screen and windowed.

NOTE Even when running under Windows NT, DOS applications use the DOS screen and printer drivers. You must install the DOS application and the print and screen drivers as described in the application's installation instructions. The DOS application doesn't use the printer drivers available in Windows NT.

Running the Command Prompt in a Window

To run DOS commands (internal or external) from within Windows NT, choose the Command Prompt icon from the Main group window in the Program Manager. Usually, the command prompt appears in a full-screen when started. Figure 22.3 shows the command prompt running in a window. From the command prompt, you can issue DOS commands, such as DIR and FORMAT. To quit the command prompt, type **EXIT** and press Enter.

Fig. 22.3

Running the command prompt from Windows NT.

Running DOS Memory-Resident Applications

Some DOS applications are designed to load into memory simulta-neously with other DOS applications. You can then call up these *resident* applications *over the top of* the active DOS application. These applications are referred to as *pop-up* or *terminate-and-stay-resident* (TSR) applications. One of the more familiar DOS TSR applications is SideKick.

If you must run a DOS TSR, start the TSR directly from Windows NT. You then can switch to and from the application as you switch between any DOS application. If necessary, create a PIF for the TSR application. (Refer to "Creating PIFs" in Chapter 21 for more information.)

You can start the DOS TSR application by creating a program item icon for the TSR in Program Manager and then double-clicking the icon. You also can set up a PIF for the TSR so that the TSR *pops-up* with the same keystroke that activates the TSR in DOS. Some TSRs require a key com-bination that Windows NT reserves (such as Alt+Esc). Here, you must create a PIF by using the PIF Editor and selecting the Reserve **S**hortcut Keys option for this key combination. After you create the PIF and re-serve the shortcut key, pressing this key combination activates the TSR application rather than performing the usual Windows function.

Depending on whether you load the TSR from the Program Manager, using a program item icon, or from the command prompt, Windows NT behaves differently. When you load the TSR from the Program Manager, the TSR is loaded, and Windows NT displays a message that tells you to press Ctrl+Z when you are finished using the TSR (see fig. 22.4).

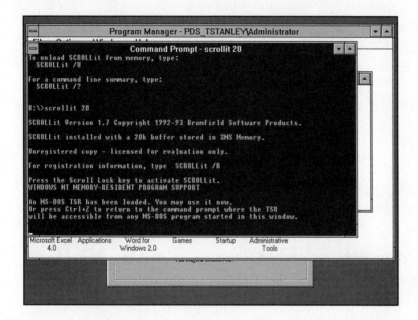

Fig. 22.4

The message Windows NT displays when a TSR is loaded.

When you press Ctrl+Z, Windows NT removes the TSR from memory and ends that DOS session, returning you to Windows NT. To close the TSR and end the DOS session, you must type **EXIT** at the C:\ prompt, which results in the message telling you to press Ctrl+Z to return to Windows NT. When you load the TSR from the command prompt while operating in enhanced mode, again, the TSR is loaded but no message is displayed. To close the TSR and return to Program Manager, you must type **EXIT** at the C:\ prompt, which immediately returns you to the Program Manager without you having to press Ctrl+Z.

You also can switch to a TSR application using standard Windows methods rather than by pressing the key combination that usually activates the application. Use the Task Manager to activate a TSR or press Alt+Tab until the TSR is activated and then release the Alt key.

Often, you may want to use a DOS TSR with a specific application, and therefore want the TSR to load only when the application loads. You can do this by creating a DOS batch file that loads the TSR and the DOS application. You then create a PIF that runs the batch file. Use the PIF Editor to create the PIF and put the batch file name in the **P**rogram file name text box of the PIF Editor.

Loading and Running DOS Applications

You can start DOS applications in four ways:

- Choose an application icon from a group window like the DOS Application group in the Program Manager.

- Choose the application file name from the directory window in the File Manager.

- Choose the application PIF name from the directory window in the File Manager.

- Choose Run from the File menu in the Program Manager or File Manager and then enter the path, file name, and all arguments for the application.

Because Windows NT must understand the special requirements of some DOS applications, however, Windows NT needs to use PIFs.

Understanding Why Windows NT Uses PIFs

When starting a DOS application, Windows NT looks for an application's PIF. A PIF is a *program information file*. A PIF tells Windows NT how much memory the application requires and how the application interacts with the keyboard and screen. If a PIF cannot be found for an application, Windows NT starts the application with standard default settings. Most DOS applications run correctly when using these standard settings. Many DOS applications don't need special PIFs. If a DOS application doesn't run correctly or as you prefer when using the default PIF or the PIF created by Windows NT, then create or modify the application's PIF with the PIF Editor, supplied with Windows NT.

Usually, you can start a DOS batch file (a file with the extension BAT) as you start any DOS application. Windows NT also runs DOS applications started and controlled by a batch file. Occasionally, DOS applications may not run when started from a batch file under Windows NT because the combined memory requirements of the batch file and the application exceed the memory limits set by the application's PIF. Here, create a PIF for the batch file and increase the memory required in the application PIF to make room for the batch file. If you create a PIF for a batch file, give the PIF the same name as the batch file; for example, call the two files DOWNLOAD.BAT and DOWNLOAD.PIF. See Chapter 21, "Customizing PIFs," for more information on PIFs.

Starting a DOS Application from the Program Manager

You can install DOS applications in Windows NT during the initial installation process or at a later time. If you install DOS or Windows applications at a later time, you may want to run the Windows NT Setup application from the Main group of the Program Manager.

When you use Setup to install a DOS application, and Windows NT contains information on that application, Setup creates and adds an application icon to the Application group. If an Application group doesn't exist, Setup creates one. Setup also installs a PIF for the application in the WINNT directory.

You can start a DOS application from a program group window in the Program Manager by choosing the application icon in the same way you start Windows applications—double-click on the icon or press an arrow key to select the icon, then press Enter. Starting applications from icons is described in detail in Chapter 4, "Controlling Applications with the Program Manager." Figure 22.5 shows the WordPerfect application icon selected in the Applications group in the Windows NT Program Manager. In this figure, the four DOS applications have different icons. Chapter 4 also explains how to select alternative icons to represent program items you create or modify.

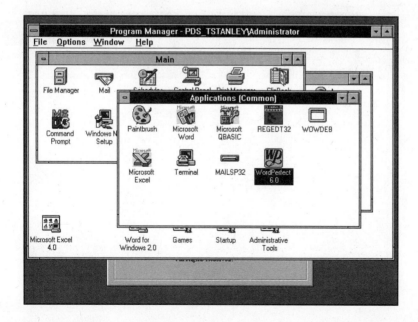

Fig. 22.5

Starting the WordPerfect application from the icon.

Starting a DOS Application from the File Manager

You can start a DOS application by choosing either the application or PIF from the Windows NT File Manager. Select the application file (or PIF) and press Enter or double-click on the file name. Application file names are recognizable because the file extensions are COM, EXE, or BAT. Figure 22.6 shows the WordPerfect file name, WP.EXE, in the WP60 directory. The lower directory window shows the PIF that starts WordPerfect, WP.PIF, in the Windows NT directory. You can start WordPerfect by double-clicking on either the PIF or the WP.EXE file.

Do Not Run Applications That Modify the File Allocation Table

From Windows NT, don't run any DOS utility or application that modifies files or the File Allocation Table (FAT). Utilities you should not use include applications used to unerase or undelete files and those that defragment or compact the disk. Use only those utilities that are written specifically for Windows NT.

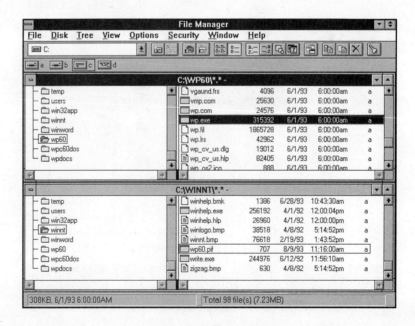

Fig. 22.6

You can start DOS applications from either the filename or PIF in the File Manager.

Customize PIFs to Run Applications with Different Settings

If you start applications by choosing the PIF rather than the application file, you can create a different PIF for different start-up requirements. Each PIF starts the same application but with different Windows or application parameters. Suppose you want to start WordPerfect 6.0 with the /m-*macroname* parameter so that WordPerfect runs the macro specified by *macroname*. You can type the following command at the command prompt:

    WP /M-*MACRONAME*

You can enter this start-up command and the argument in the **O**ptional Parameters text box of the PIF Editor when you create the WordPerfect PIF. If you start WordPerfect this way, the *macroname* macro runs when WordPerfect starts. This macro may load documents or change default settings. You also may want to run WordPerfect with large memory limits when working on a book and want WordPerfect to run faster, or you may need to run WordPerfect with minimum memory limits to run WordPerfect alongside other applications in Windows NT standard mode.

You can create different PIFs to handle these scenarios; to start WordPerfect with one of the sets of options, just select the PIF that contains the desired options. You can create program item icons in the Program Manager for each of these PIFs—making it easy to access the application using the different settings. To learn how to create a program item for a PIF, see Chapter 21.

Controlling DOS Applications

Windows NT adds a great deal of power to your work, even if you don't run Windows NT applications. You can run, and switch between, multiple DOS, and Windows applications. If you work with DOS applications, this feature enables you to copy a table of numbers from Lotus 1-2-3 and paste them into WordPerfect, or you can copy a number from accounting or checkbook applications, such as Quicken, and paste into Lotus 1-2-3. You can copy and paste information, minimize and maximize the application, and move the window or icon. The time you save definitely makes using Windows NT with DOS applications worthwhile.

Switching among Applications

Windows NT uses the same key combinations to switch among all applications, whether they are Windows NT applications or another application supported by Windows NT.

The following table highlights ways in which you can switch among DOS applications:

To switch, press	when DOS applications are...
Alt+Tab	full-screen or windowed. Each application's title bar appears. Releasing keys displays the application.
Alt+Enter	full-screen or windowed. Each windowed or full-screen application appears.
Ctrl+Esc	full-screen or windowed. This displays a Task List of all applications running. Choose the desired application.
Double-click on window	windowed. Click on background window to make window active in foreground.

To switch from an active DOS application to another application, take the following steps:

1. Press and hold down the Alt key and press Tab. Keep holding down Alt and pressing Tab until the window or title bar of the application you want to activate appears.

2. Release Alt.

A gray box displaying the title of a window appears. Each time you press Alt+Tab, a different title from an open window displays in the box. When the title appears for the application you want, release Alt. By showing only the titles as you press Alt+Tab, Windows NT can switch quickly among applications. Release Alt when you see the title bar of the desired application. The selected application becomes active.

You also can switch among applications by pressing Alt+Esc. This procedure takes longer if you have multiple applications in Windows NT. Pressing Alt+Esc immediately activates the next application, which may not be the one you want. Activating this application takes time. After the application is active and the screen is drawn, you must again press Alt+Esc to activate the next application. A faster method is to press Alt+Tab until you see the title of the application you want.

You also can switch to the Task Manager by pressing Ctrl+Esc. After the Task List appears, you can choose the application you want to activate from the list.

Some DOS applications occasionally suspend the keyboard. During these times, using Alt+Tab, Alt+Esc, or Ctrl+Esc may not work. To switch back to Windows NT, return to the application's standard operating mode (this action may require pressing Esc) and then press Alt+Tab or Ctrl+Esc. If you are displaying a graph in Lotus 1-2-3, for example, press Esc to return to the spreadsheet or menu and then press Alt+Tab.

If you have DOS applications in windows, you can click the mouse from window to window. Position the windows on-screen so that each window is seen and switch between them.

Printing and DOS Applications

The Windows NT Print Manager controls printing from all applications that you use in Windows NT. When you print using the DOS application, Print Manager intercepts the information going to the printer, and places that information in line with any other application that prints to the printer. You do not have to worry about a DOS application corrupting information being sent to the printer by a Windows NT application.

Using the DOS Application Control Menu

All DOS applications have an application Control menu similar to Windows applications. Use the application Control menu to copy and paste information, to minimize and maximize the application, and to control the application's use of system resources.

Whether the DOS application is in a window or full-screen, you can activate the Control menu by pressing Alt+space bar. If the DOS application is in a window, you also can activate the Control menu by clicking on the Control menu bar to the left of the window title. The Control menu is shown in figure 22.7.

If you activate the Control menu when the application is full-screen, Windows NT minimizes the application into an icon and then brings up the Control menu.

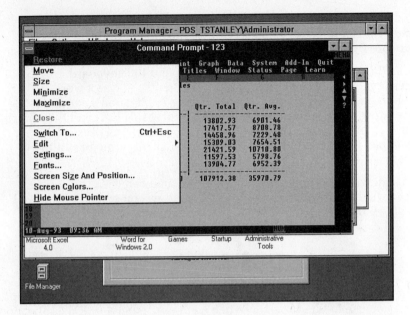

On the Control menu, you see the commands to Restore, Move, or Size a DOS application window. Of course, because the application is in a window, you also can accomplish these tasks by using the mouse. The Minimize and Maximize commands shrink the application to an icon or expand an icon to a window or full-screen. Because the application's icon also has a Control menu, you can restore or move the icon just as you manipulate a windowed or full-screen application. The Close and Edit commands are described in a following section of this chapter.

Changing Font Size in DOS Application Windows

You can make a DOS application easier to read by changing the size of the font used in a DOS application window. To change the font size, take the following steps:

1. Choose the DOS application Control menu by clicking on it or by pressing Alt and then the space bar.

2. Select the Fonts command. The Font Selection dialog box appears as shown in figure 22.8.

3. From the Font list, select a font size.

The Window Preview and Selected Font boxes show you how the font looks on-screen.

4. To save this size for the next time you run this application, select the **S**ave Configuration check box.

5. Choose OK.

Changing the font size doesn't affect how a DOS application operates but only helps to make the DOS application more readable when working in a window.

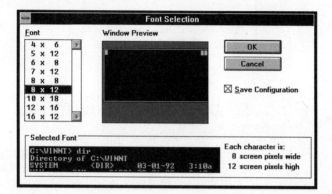

Fig. 22.8

Use the Font Selection dialog box to change character size in a DOS window.

Changing Window Size

Many DOS programs enable you to change the screen so that you can display more information on-screen. For example, you can change the number of rows and columns that display in Lotus 1-2-3 from the default 80 columns and 25 rows to 80 columns and 50 rows. Windows NT can accommodate the larger display, enabling you to change the number of columns and rows that appear in the Command Prompt window. Although Windows NT automatically detects the correct number of columns and rows to display in a Command Prompt window, you also can change the display manually.

To change the number of columns and rows that Windows NT displays, follow these steps:

1. Choose the DOS application Control menu by clicking on it or by pressing Alt and then the space bar.

2. Select the Screen Size And Position command. The Screen Size And Position dialog box appears as shown in figure 22.9.

3. Change the Width and Height settings by typing a new number or by clicking on the scroll arrows.

4. To save this size for the next time you run this application, select the Save **W**indow Size and Position check box.

5. Choose OK.

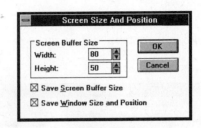

Using a Mouse in DOS Applications

If the DOS application supports a mouse and the Windows NT mouse driver is loaded, you can use the mouse normally when the application is running full-screen. You can do all the things the application usually enables you to do with a mouse—bring up menus, select objects, and so on.

You can use the mouse whether you are operating the DOS program full-screen or in a window. If you are operating the DOS program in a window, then you use the same pointer to control the DOS program that you use to control Windows NT applications. Running the DOS program full-screen, the pointer displays as a block in text mode, or as an arrow in graphics mode.

A DOS application that doesn't support a mouse still can use a mouse for some Windows features when the application is running in a window. You can use the mouse to select areas to copy or to choose commands from the Control menu.

Scrolling in DOS Application Windows

While a DOS application is in a window, you can use the mouse as you do with any window, to click on the minimize and maximize buttons at the top right or to resize the window by dragging an edge. When an application's screen is larger than what the window can display, vertical, and horizontal scroll bars appear. You can use keystrokes or the mouse to scroll the window and display the DOS application screen. You cannot scroll to see more than usually appears on a single screen. With the mouse, you also can select areas of a DOS text or graphics screen to be copied.

When you run a DOS application in a window, the Control menu includes a Scroll command. This command enables you to scroll with the keyboard. The Scroll command is a menu choice from the Edit command. You use this command to see parts of the file that cannot fit on-screen. This command scrolls the application's full screen of information in the window. You cannot scroll the window over more information than appears in the application's normal DOS screen.

To scroll with the keyboard, select the Control menu by pressing Alt+space bar, select Edit, and then choose the Scroll command. The window title changes to show that you are in Scroll mode; if you are in WordPerfect and the window title is WordPerfect, the window title changes to Scroll WordPerfect. Now press the arrow keys, PgUp, PgDn, Home, or End to scroll the window. When you finish scrolling, press Esc or Enter to exit scrolling mode.

Copying and Pasting Information between Applications

When you run DOS applications under Windows NT, you can copy and paste information among applications. Although you can copy and paste with DOS applications, such as Lotus 1-2-3 for DOS and WordPerfect 6.0 for DOS, you don't have the more powerful features of Windows NT available, such as a common menu system, linked data, or embedded objects.

DOS applications running under Windows NT can use the Windows NT Clipboard. This feature enables you to copy data from a DOS application to a Windows application, from a Windows application to a DOS application, or between two DOS applications. Windows NT keeps the copied information in the same Clipboard used by all Windows applications; once copied, you then can paste the information into a Windows or DOS application.

> **Copying and Pasting DOS Graphics May Give Varying Results**
>
> Some DOS applications handle screen graphics in nonstandard ways. This limitation may make capturing the contents of a screen in graphics mode difficult or impossible. You may find that the color palette changes or text characters, for example, disappear when copied from a DOS application and pasted into another application. However, you can capture full or partial screens of many applications, which then can be pasted into Windows applications, such as Windows NT Write, Ami Pro, Word for Windows, Microsoft Excel, Aldus PageMaker, or Aldus Freehand. Most DOS and Windows applications can copy and paste text and numeric data indiscriminately, if the receiving application is in a mode that can receive the text or numbers you type.

Copying or Capturing DOS or Windows NT Screens

You can copy either a full or partial screen of text or a full-screen graphic from a DOS application. DOS applications can receive pasted text but are incapable of receiving pasted graphics. Windows applications can receive pasted text, and Windows applications designed to work with graphics can receive pasted graphics.

Copying or Capturing a Full Screen

To capture a text or graphics screen, press the PrtScrn (Print Screen) key. The entire display is copied to the Clipboard, and you then can paste the image into other applications or save the image with the ClipBook Viewer (found in the Main window of the Program Manager). With some keyboards, you need to use Shift+PrtScrn rather than PrtScrn to capture the entire display.

If the screen is a DOS text application, you capture the information as text characters that you can paste as text into other applications. If the screen is a DOS graphic or a Windows application, the screen is captured as a bitmap graphic, which can be pasted into Windows applications that accept bitmap graphics.

> Capture full Windows or DOS application screens with the PrtScrn
> key and paste them into applications, such as Word for Windows,
> Ami Pro, or Aldus PageMaker as a way of quickly producing polished
> documentation or training materials.

T I P

To see exactly what you copy to the Clipboard, start the ClipBook
Viewer from the Main program group. Maximize the window to see
the entire copied contents. As you view the Clipboard contents, notice
that all the text from the screen was copied, including text from the
application's work area, any displayed menu names and file names,
and any text in the background. Figure 22.10 shows the contents of
the ClipBook Viewer after a full-screen capture of WordPerfect 6.0,
which was running in a window. Because the full screen was captured,
you can see the Program Manager with the program icons in the
background.

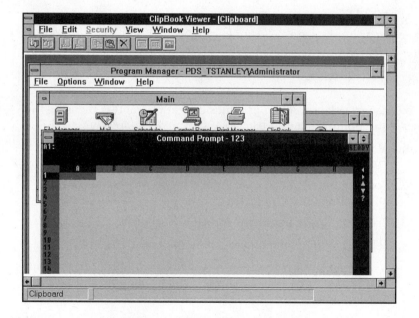

Fig. 22.10

The ClipBook
Viewer displays
or saves screens
that you capture.

Copying or Capturing a Partial Screen

You can capture only the active window by pressing Alt+PrtScrn. If
PrtScrn or Alt+PrtScrn doesn't work, these key combinations probably
are reserved as shortcuts in an application's PIF. See Chapter 21 for
more information on PIF reserved keys.

To copy a partial screen of text or graphics by using the mouse, follow these steps:

1. Activate the DOS application. If the application doesn't display in a window, press Alt+Enter.

2. Position the application screen in the window to show the information you want to copy.

3. Click on the Control menu at the top-left corner and choose the **Edit Mark** command.

4. Drag the mouse across the rectangular area you want to copy. Drag past an edge to scroll the window to the limit of the DOS screen.

5. Click on the Control menu at the top left and choose the **Edit Copy** command.

T I P   You can avoid having to select the Edit Mark command to mark text to copy using the mouse. Just mark the QuickEdit check box in the dialog box that appears when you choose Settings from the Control menu.

To copy a partial screen of graphics or text characters by using the keyboard, follow these steps:

1. Activate the DOS application. If the application doesn't appear in a window, press Alt+Enter to make the application appear.

2. Position the application screen in the window to show the information you want to copy.

3. Press Alt+space bar to show the Control menu.

4. Select the **Edit** command and then choose **Mark** (see fig. 22.11).

   A rectangular cursor appears at the top-left corner of the application screen. This cursor is used to select the screen area you want to copy.

5. Press the arrow keys to move the cursor to the top-left corner of the rectangular area you want to copy.

6. Press and hold down Shift and press the arrow keys to select a rectangular area that contains the information you want to copy. Figure 22.12 shows a block of cells selected in the Lotus 1-2-3 application.

   You can undo the selection and return to regular Windows NT operation by pressing Esc.

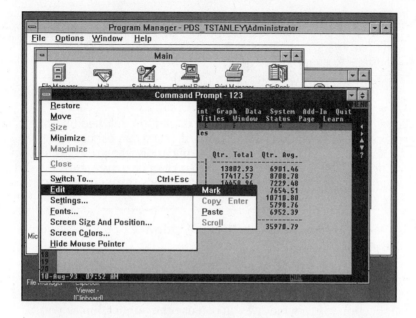

Fig. 22.11

Preparing to
mark an area
to copy.

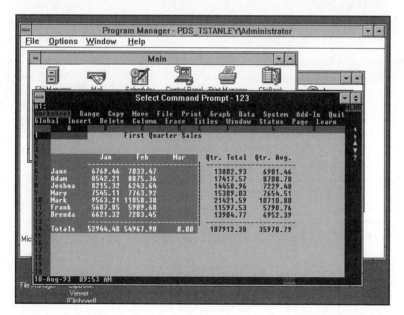

Fig. 22.12

An area marked
for copying.

7. Press Alt+space bar again to display the Control menu.
   Choose the **E**dit **Copy** command.

T I P

After you begin making a selection in the DOS application window, the title bar changes to *Select APPLICATION_NAME*. While in selection mode, you cannot paste, enter data, or use this application's menu. To exit selection mode, press the Esc key.

When you finish these steps, you have copied the marked text or graphics into the Windows NT Clipboard. You can paste text in the Clipboard into any Windows or DOS application when the application is in a mode in which you can type text. You can paste graphics into Windows applications designed to receive graphics through the Clipboard.

Switch DOS Applications between Windowed and Full-Screen Views

To switch a DOS application between full-screen and windowed views, press Alt+Enter. In full-screen view, the application displays as you see the application running under DOS. When the application is in a window, you can use the application as you do in DOS, but you also can change the size of the screen font and use the Windows NT Control menu to copy and paste.

After you either copy or capture text or graphics to the Clipboard, you can save this image or data as a file. This capability enables you to paste the image or data at a later date or send a file of copied data to an associate. If you don't save the image or data, when you next copy or capture a screen, the new image or data overwrites the current Clipboard contents. When you exit Windows NT, the Clipboard also is erased. You save the current clipping by starting the ClipBook Viewer from the Main program group in the Program Manager. Choose the **File** Save **As** command and enter a file name to save the current clipping. The **File** Save **As** dialog box is shown in figure 22.13. Type in the file name under which you want to save this file; note that the file is given the extension CLP. This clipping file can be retrieved by any other ClipBook Viewer so that the contents can be pasted into an application.

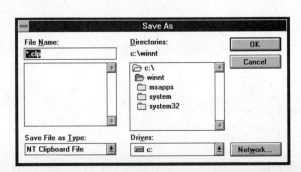

Fig. 22.13

The ClipBook Viewer File Save As dialog box.

Pasting Data into DOS Applications

Now paste the text or graphics from the Clipboard into the Windows or DOS application by following these steps:

1. Switch to the DOS or Windows application in which you want to paste.

2. Move the application's cursor to the location where you want the top-left corner of the pasted data. (This is the application's normal cursor.)

3. If the application is a Windows application, choose **Edit Paste**. If the application is a DOS application, press Alt+space bar to display the Control menu and then choose **Edit Paste**.

Figure 22.14 shows the results of pasting a 1-2-3 worksheet into WordPerfect. When pasting text into a DOS application, such as WordPerfect, notice that the space between Lotus 1-2-3 columns is filled with space characters. If the receiving application uses proportional fonts, you may find that columns of text and numbers do not align correctly. If this happens, insert tabs to align the columns.

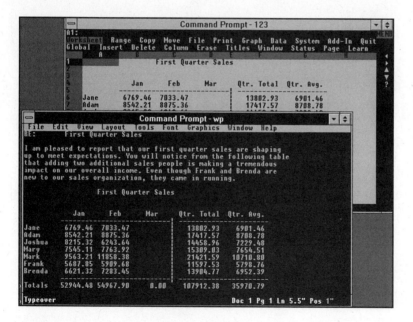

Fig. 22.14

A 1-2-3 worksheet pasted in a WordPerfect document.

Copying Clears the Previous Copy from the Clipboard

Making a copy removes the previous copy from the Clipboard. If you don't make another copy or clear the Clipboard, you can paste the information you copied more than once. You can view the Clipboard contents by opening the ClipBook Viewer in the Main program group.

Applications Handle Multiple Pasted Lines Differently

DOS applications handle multiple lines of pasted data differently. The difference is caused by how the application deals with the carriage return at the end of a line. If you paste multiple lines of data into a Lotus 1-2-3 file, all the lines paste in the same cell, each over the top of the previous line. Therefore, paste one number into one cell at a time into Lotus 1-2-3 for DOS. This problem, however, isn't true for other applications. When you paste a multiple-line entry into Microsoft Excel, each line is pasted into a separate cell. WordPerfect also accepts multiple lines of data. Each line of data pastes into a new line in the WordPerfect document.

Linking DOS and Windows Applications

Copying and pasting data with DOS applications is easy. DOS applications can run in Windows NT, making switching between them easier, and making it possible to select portions of the screen to copy and paste into another application.

Linking Lotus 1-2-3 Spreadsheets to Microsoft Excel Worksheets

You may be using Microsoft Excel for Windows and others in your work area may be using a DOS version of Lotus 1-2-3. Because Microsoft Excel can read and write Lotus 1-2-3 spreadsheets and can read 1-2-3 graphics, you can use Microsoft Excel to link or consolidate 1-2-3 worksheets or to enhance 1-2-3 printouts and charts.

The advantages of linking 1-2-3 spreadsheets to Microsoft Excel worksheets are many. You can create impressive graphs using Microsoft Excel; you can use Microsoft Excel's automatic database form; or you can create automated systems involving integrated Windows applications.

To link Lotus 1-2-3 spreadsheets to an Excel for Windows worksheet, you start by opening the 1-2-3 files, as described in the following steps:

1. Activate Microsoft Excel.

2. Choose the File Open command.

3. Select the drive and directory where the 1-2-3 files are located from the Drives and Directories list boxes.

4. Open the List Files of Type drop-down list box, then choose Lotus 1-2-3 Files (*.WK*) so that you can see the list of Lotus 1-2-3 files.

5. Select the 1-2-3 spreadsheet with which you want to work from the File Name list box, then choose OK. If the worksheet has attached graphs, Excel asks whether you also want to convert these files.

6. Repeat steps 2 through 5 until all the Lotus 1-2-3 spreadsheets you want to link are open.

Microsoft Excel opens Lotus 1-2-3 spreadsheets and graphs. Notice that the 1-2-3 spreadsheets appear in a document window in the same way as Microsoft Excel worksheets. 1-2-3 title bars show the WK3, WK2, or WK1 extension, which indicates the files are 1-2-3 spreadsheets.

You can link open 1-2-3 spreadsheets to an Excel worksheet. To link a 1-2-3 spreadsheet to an Excel worksheet, follow these steps:

1. Activate the 1-2-3 spreadsheet (so that the 1-2-3 spreadsheet is the top document window).

2. Select the cell or range of cells you want to link to an Excel worksheet.

3. Choose the Edit Copy command.

4. Activate the Microsoft Excel worksheet to receive the linked data.

5. Select the cell at the top-left corner of the area where you want the linked data to appear.

6. Choose the Edit Paste Link command.

As shown in figure 22.15, the data from the 1-2-3 spreadsheets, QTR1.WK3 and QTR2.WK1, opened in Microsoft Excel can be linked or consolidated into a Microsoft Excel worksheet. When numbers change in the 1-2-3 spreadsheets, the link sends this change to the Microsoft Excel worksheet. After being linked, the 1-2-3 spreadsheets can be open or on disk for the link to remain. If one of the 1-2-3 files is later retrieved, changed, and saved in Lotus 1-2-3, you need only start Microsoft Excel and open the Microsoft Excel worksheet that contains the link for the new 1-2-3 data to be read in.

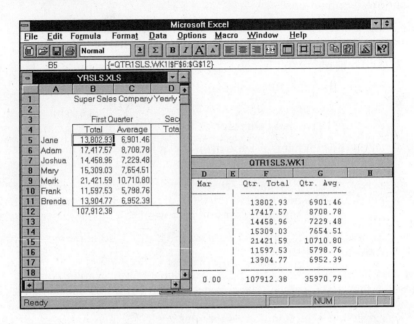

Fig. 22.15

Linking 1-2-3 spreadsheets into a Microsoft Excel worksheet.

Linked cells that contain blanks appear as zeroes (0) in the Microsoft Excel worksheet. You can hide zeroes throughout the Microsoft Excel worksheet by choosing the **O**ptions **D**isplay command and then selecting the **Z**ero Values check box. Hide zeroes selectively by using a custom numeric format that contains no zero portion of the format, as shown in the following example:

$#,##0 ;($#,##0);

Because no format follows the second semicolon, zeroes aren't displayed.

Use care if you save the 1-2-3 spreadsheet from Microsoft Excel. Microsoft Excel saves the worksheet back to the original 1-2-3 format. Microsoft Excel cannot save Excel's enhanced charts to 1-2-3 format because 1-2-3 has no equivalent. If you enhanced the 1-2-3 spreadsheet with Microsoft Excel formatting commands or used formulas or functions not available in 1-2-3, you lose these changes when you save the worksheet back to a 1-2-3 file. To keep the formatting and extra features, save the file in Microsoft Excel format by choosing the **F**ile Save **A**s command, and selecting Normal format from the Save File as **T**ype drop-down list box. Save the file with the same or with a different name.

Make sure you either keep the 1-2-3 spreadsheet name the same or save the spreadsheet before you save the Microsoft Excel worksheet that contains the links. By first saving the 1-2-3 spreadsheet, Microsoft Excel knows the name of the spreadsheet that contains the data to be linked.

If you move or rename a linked 1-2-3 spreadsheet so that the Microsoft Excel worksheet cannot find the file, activate the Microsoft Excel worksheet that contains the links. Choose the **F**ile **L**inks command, select the name of the spreadsheet that was moved or renamed, and choose the **C**hange button. Then type or select the name of the new 1-2-3 worksheet to be linked.

If you need to consolidate (roll-up) multiple Microsoft Excel or 1-2-3 worksheets, make sure you learn about Microsoft Excel's Data Consolidate command. Data Consolidation enables you to total, average, count, or perform other statistics across ranges on multiple Microsoft Excel or 1-2-3 worksheets. The data on the different sheets can be located in different areas of the sheet, can use different item names, and can even have items in different ordering. Microsoft Excel matches item headings and totals, averages, or counts appropriate items and then builds a table that shows the result.

T I P

Linking 1-2-3 Spreadsheets into Word for Windows

Many Windows applications enable you to insert or link data from DOS applications. This capability enables you to incorporate DOS application data into documents from Windows applications. The following example uses Word for Windows to demonstrate how many Windows applications can read and convert files from DOS applications. The receiving Windows application may even be able to link to a DOS application file. Linking enables you to quickly update a Windows document when data in a DOS application file changes.

 NOTE In order to insert 1-2-3 files into Word for Windows, you must have installed the Word for Windows text file converter for Lotus 1-2-3.

Although you can use the copy and paste techniques described previously to copy spreadsheet data to a word processor, a better way is available. In Word for Windows, you can link all or a portion of a Lotus 1-2-3 file to a Word for Windows document. When the worksheet changes, the word processing document can be easily updated.

The 1-2-3 file to which you want to link must be on disk. To link 1-2-3 spreadsheet data from a disk to a Word for Windows document, take the following steps:

1. In the Word for Windows document, position the insertion point where you want the spreadsheet data to appear.

2. Choose the **Insert File** command. The File dialog box appears on-screen.

3. Choose the drive and directory containing the 1-2-3 worksheet from the **Drives** and **Directories** list boxes.

4. Choose All Files (*.*) from the List Files of **Type** drop-down list box.

5. From the File **Name** list, select the 1-2-3 worksheet file.

6. In the **Range** text box, type the range name or range reference (cell addresses) you want to insert.

7. If you want a link to the file so that you can update the data on request, select the **Link** to File check box. If you want to bring in the data without a link to the file, don't select the **Link** check box.

8. Choose OK or press Enter. The Convert File dialog box appears on-screen.

9. Select Lotus 1-2-3 from the Convert **File** From list box, then choose OK.

10. If the Open Spreadsheet dialog box appears on-screen, choose OK.

The 1-2-3 spreadsheet data is inserted into the Word for Windows document. The spreadsheet is inserted as a table, a feature of Word that is similar to a spreadsheet's columns and rows.

If you selected the **Link** check box and the spreadsheet data in the 1-2-3 file changes, you can update the Word for Windows document by selecting the linked data and pressing the Update Field key, F9. Word for Windows rereads and reinserts the spreadsheet data.

Windows applications that have the capability of reading or writing other application files usually require converter or filter files. These files usually are installed during the application installation. If the Windows application doesn't show that it can link to DOS files, check to make sure you installed the appropriate converters or filters.

> **Use Nonproportional Fonts to Align Columns from DOS Applications**
>
> If you paste text columns from a DOS application into a Windows application, the columns may no longer align. The reason for the misalignment probably is that the DOS applications use nonproportional fonts, and Windows applications use proportional fonts. With *proportional* fonts, different characters have different widths. With *nonproportional* fonts, such as Courier, all characters have the same width.
>
> Repair this problem by using one of two techniques. One method is to insert tabs as needed in the rows and then align the columns on new tab settings. The second method is to format the pasted data in Courier or a similar nonproportional font. Because the characters again are the same width, the columns realign.

Sharing Data through Files

If you have large volumes of data to transport between applications, copying and pasting can be too slow. For large volumes of data, use a common file format to transfer information.

In the first of the following two examples, check-register data is exported from Quicken and imported into Microsoft Excel, where financial analysis can be performed and charts created. In the second example, Microsoft Excel chart is printed to disk to create a graph for use in WordPerfect 5.1 documents.

Usually, DOS applications come with a utility application that converts the data file to other formats. Most Windows applications have conversion capability built-in, but you need to make sure that the correct converters or filters are installed for the Windows application.

The following list shows some file formats. These aren't used as a native format by applications but are used as a *lingua franca*, or common language, for exchanging data between applications from different manufacturers. You often can use a file format, such as DBF for dBASE, that might be understood as a common format by the applications involved. The following table lists some file formats through which DOS and Windows applications can transfer data:

CSV, PRN	Comma Separated Values; commas and quotes separate *fields* of data; used to exchange spreadsheet and database data

DIF	Data Interchange Format; used to transfer text and numeric data between spreadsheets
RFT-DCA	IBM document exchange format; used to transfer word processing documents
RTF	Rich Text Format; used to transfer text and formatting between word processing documents
TXT	Text files; tabs used to separate values; use to transfer data between word processors, databases, and spreadsheets
SDF	Column delimited files; each field of data must be within specified character positions; used to transfer data between databases or databases and spreadsheets

Converting Quicken Checkbook Data into Microsoft Excel Spreadsheets

Certain text-file formats have become accepted as vehicles for transporting text and numeric data between incompatible PC applications, and even between PCs and mainframe databases. The following example shows how to transport data from the DOS version of Quicken, a popular check-register application, to Microsoft Excel, where you can analyze or chart the data. This same technique and file format frequently is used to transfer data from a corporate mainframe to Microsoft Excel for analysis.

The file format used as the medium of exchange in this example is *Comma Separated Values* (CSV). CSV is one of the kinds of text files Microsoft Excel reads and directly imports into a worksheet. The file to be imported must end with the extension CSV so that Microsoft Excel knows which converter to use to read the file. In the file, text and numbers are separated by commas. Text or numbers that contain commas are enclosed in quotation marks (" "). The CSV format frequently is used to download mainframe data so that Microsoft Excel can read the file directly.

To create a CSV file from the Quicken application, follow these steps:

1. In Windows NT, or from DOS, open Quicken and use the normal process to prepare a report for printing.

2. After you choose the kind of report you want to print, a line at the bottom of the screen prompts you to press F8 to print. Press F8.

3. Choose the Disk (1-2-3 File) option from the Print Report menu.

4. Type the name for the file. For example, type *QCKN2XCL*. Don't type a file extension.

5. To save the file, press Enter. Quicken saves the file with a PRN extension.

6. Exit from Quicken.

To create a Microsoft Excel file from the Quicken file, follow these steps:

1. Use the Windows NT File Manager to change the file's name from *QCKN2XCL.PRN* to *QCKN2XCL.CSV*.

2. Activate Microsoft Excel.

3. Choose the **File O**pen command and change to the directory that contains the QCKN2XCL.CSV file. If you didn't specify a directory when you saved the file in Quicken, look in the QUICKEN directory.

4. Choose Text Files (*.TXT;*.CSV) from the List Files of **T**ype drop-down list box to list all the files in the directory that have the extension CSV.

5. Select the QCKN2XCL.CSV file and choose OK.

   The file opens in a worksheet with each text title in a cell and each number in a cell.

6. Use this worksheet as you use any Microsoft Excel worksheet.

7. Save the worksheet in Microsoft Excel format by choosing the **File** Save **A**s command, choosing the Normal from the Save File as **T**ype drop-down list. Choose OK.

Importing Microsoft Excel Charts to WordPerfect

You cannot paste graphics into DOS applications. However, an alternative for transferring graphics from Windows applications to DOS applications is to create a graphics file that the DOS application *can* import. You can create a file that contains a Microsoft Excel chart that a DOS application—such as WordPerfect for DOS—can import.

To create a Microsoft Excel chart that WordPerfect can import, you first must set up Windows NT as though you plan to print the chart on an HP plotter. Rather than printing the chart to the plotter, however, you use the Control Panel to redirect the printing information to a disk file. The file created is a Hewlett-Packard Graphics Language, HPGL, file. You then can import this file into WordPerfect. Setting up for this operation is as easy as adding a printer driver; you have to set up for the operation only once.

Begin by choosing the Printers icon from the Control Panel. Choose the **A**dd button and add an HP 7550A Plotter driver. (Chapter 7, "Customizing with the Control Panel," describes how to add new printers and plotters.) Use the original Windows NT installation disks to install the driver software. After you add the plotter driver, choose the **C**onfigure button and select *FILE:* from the **P**orts scrolling list. This selection instructs Windows NT to send the information to print to a disk file rather than to a printer or plotter port. Choose the **S**etup button before you exit from the Printers dialog box. Leave the plotter pen colors at the defaults but clear the **D**raft check box. Choose OK.

To create a Microsoft Excel chart that WordPerfect can import, choose the **F**ile **P**rinter Setup command and select HP Plotter on FILE:. Set the page layout and margins and then print. A dialog box appears, asking for a path name and file name for the file. You can give the file any file extension. The file created is an HPGL printer/plotter file. Many kinds of software and printers can read the HPGL file.

Import the Microsoft Excel chart file into WordPerfect for DOS by using WordPerfect's graphics-import procedures.

Summary

In this chapter, you learned how to run and switch between DOS applications. The chapter also gave an introduction to how Windows NT accommodates DOS applications. You learned how to use copy and paste to transfer text and graphics between DOS and Windows applications. In instances where copying and pasting data is not appropriate, you learned how to transfer entire files.

Chapters 21 and 22 are important for further understanding how to best run DOS applications under Windows NT. Chapter 21 describes how to modify PIFs to change how a DOS application runs under Windows NT. If you have trouble getting DOS applications to run or operate as you suspect they should, turn to the troubleshooting sections in Chapter 32.

Tuning Windows NT

T ips and tricks are available for improving the performance of Windows NT throughout this book. The factors that have the greatest effect can be summarized as follows:

- How you use Windows
- Your hardware
- Memory use
- Hard disk performance

You can do an infinite number of things to increase the performance of Windows NT, but most yield small improvements. There are a few things you can do that will have the largest impact; therefore, it makes sense to focus on them first.

To tune Windows NT, make sure you don't have operating habits that drain performance, such as keeping many applications loaded that you aren't using. Evaluate your hardware and upgrade critical areas, such as memory or hard disk speed. Next, optimize the performance of the hardware by configuring Windows NT's use of memory and hard disk appropriately. Finally, improve the efficiency of Windows NT by conserving resources and fine-tuning Windows NT's internal operating methods.

Working Efficiently in Windows

Computers are often referred to as *systems*. We usually think of computer systems as being made up of hardware and software. But a computer system also includes a third component: you, the user.

The following list offers some general guidelines you can follow to help your computer system running Windows NT operate more efficiently. These guidelines don't require any technical adjustments; they require only that you adjust the way you work.

- Limit the number of applications you run concurrently; each additional application reduces the resources available to the others. Both the speed of your hardware and the amount of memory can severely affect the performance of Windows NT when you are running many applications.

- A fast 80486 or RISC processor can service many more applications simultaneously than the slower 80386. Keep in mind that each loaded application uses some of your computer's processor time, even if the program is idle.

- Limit the display of graphic features in Windows applications. If performance is sluggish and the Windows application you are using has a draft mode, use draft mode. Some applications, such as Word for Windows, enable you to turn off the display of graphical objects, showing only an empty box where the object would appear.

- Limit the number of open windows on the desktop. These windows occupy the computer's memory and your memory—too many document windows slow performance and can confuse you.

- In some applications, such as word processors, document length can affect performance, so having many short documents rather than one long one might be a good idea.

Choosing the Right Hardware

To optimize Windows NT, the first thing you can do beyond being smart in the way you work is to choose the best hardware and ensure that it is configured properly. You should answer the following key questions when choosing hardware components for your computer:

- Is the component 100-percent compatible with Windows NT?

- Are there reliable device drivers for this component?

- Does the component's performance meet the requirements of a powerful operating system such as Windows NT?

By answering these questions, this section will help you select and configure hardware components that will work best with Windows NT.

Choosing Compatible and Reliable Hardware

Each component of a computer requires a device driver to make it work correctly. For example, a VGA video adapter requires a video device driver (sometimes called a *video driver*), a mouse requires a mouse driver, and a printer requires a printer driver. Unlike many previous operating systems, Windows NT even requires a device driver for each type of CPU board.

Windows NT runs on many types of microprocessors, such as Intel 80386, MIPS R4000, Digital Equipment Corporation's Alpha AXP, the SPARC, and Intergraph's Clipper. These processors—and the basic design of the machines built on top of them—are all very different from one another. Windows NT uses a device driver called the *hardware abstraction layer* (HAL) to hide these differences from Windows applications.

Device drivers are critical to the operation of Windows NT. They give Windows applications access to hardware devices while insulating the applications from the details of each model of device. A poorly designed device driver might fail to provide the correct access to the device, causing the system to operate inefficiently or crash. Ensure that high-quality drivers are available for the components you choose for your system.

Most computers sold today are made up of components from different manufacturers. The company whose name is on the front of the case probably makes the case and maybe the main CPU board. But all other peripherals, such as the hard disk, video adapter, and mouse, are probably made by someone else. Windows NT comes with device drivers for most popular hardware components. In most cases, these device drivers were developed and tested by Microsoft, and thus are of high quality. Beware of fly-by-night manufacturers who have spent all their resources on hardware development and marketing materials, and have failed to put any effort into developing device drivers.

The Microsoft Hardware Compatibility List is a great tool to help you determine which hardware components are compatible with Windows NT. Included are listings of compatible systems, SCSI controllers, CD-ROM drives, hard drives, sound boards, video boards, printers, and more. It is strongly recommended that you purchase hardware only if it appears on this list. The Hardware Compatibility List is included in the Windows NT documentation. Updated versions are published frequently and can be obtained by contacting Microsoft (see Chapter 33).

Just because the box says "Windows-compatible" does not mean the product is compatible with Windows NT. Check with the Hardware Compatibility List or the hardware vendor to ensure that the product is 100-percent compatible with Windows NT.

Choosing Powerful Hardware

Windows NT provides you with a large arsenal of features and capabilities. However, it also requires powerful hardware in order to run efficiently. This section provides information on features and capabilities Windows NT requires in the hardware components you select for your system.

Windows NT will run on machines using either the Intel x86 or RISC microprocessors. The system requirements for each are somewhat different and are illustrated in Tables 23.1 and 23.2:

Table 23.1 Hardware requirements for Intel x86 systems		
Component	**Suggested Minimum**	**Recommended**
Processor	25 MHz 80386DX	33 MHz 80486DX
Memory	12M RAM	24M RAM
Video	VGA (640x480x16) (1024x768x256)	SuperVGA
Floppy disk	1.2M or 1.44M	1.2M or 1.44M
Hard disk	One or more hard disks, with 75M free; includes 20M required for 20M paging file	
CD-ROM drive	Optional	CD-ROM drive
Network adapter card	Optional	One or more

RISC-based computer systems, such as the DEC Alpha, Intergraph Clipper, and R4000 have different hardware requirements for Windows NT than Intel machines. Table 23.2 provides the hardware requirements for RISC-based computer systems.

Table 23.2 Hardware requirements for RISC systems		
Component	**Suggested Minimum**	**Recommended**
Processor	Supported RISC-based microprocessor; currently includes MIPS R4000 and DEC Alpha AXP	
Memory	16M RAM	32M RAM
Video	SuperVGA Standard	SuperVGA (1280x1024x256)
CD-ROM drive	SCSI CD-ROM drive	
Hard disk	One or more hard disks, with 95M free; includes 20M required for 20M paging file	
Network adapter card	Optional	One or more

The four components that most affect the speed of your system when running Windows NT are

- Memory
- CPU speed
- Hard disk speed
- Video

Windows NT is a very memory-intensive operating system; the more memory it has available, the better it will perform. Buy the fastest CPU you can afford. In addition, Windows NT relies heavily on the hard disk (see the "Optimizing Disk Access" section later in this chapter), so it is important to have a fast one. Finally, Windows NT is a graphical operating system, and thus really exercises the video subsystem. It is important to choose not only a high-performance video adapter, but also one that has well-written drivers for Windows NT.

Configuring Your Hardware

The performance of Windows NT can be greatly affected by how you configure your hardware, especially the video subsystem and main CPU. Many popular video drivers for Windows NT enable you to specify how many colors your screen uses. For example, the Super VGA driver can be configured for 16-color or 256-color operation. Other drivers have options for 64,000 colors or TrueColor.

The more colors, the slower the display will be. For example, it takes twice as much data per dot on the screen to represent 256 colors (8 bits) as it does to support 16 colors (4 bits). To accomplish most tasks, such as word processing or spreadsheet work, 16 colors is more than enough. If you are doing sophisticated drawing or presentation graphics, however, your work may require 256 colors or more. If you do not require more than 16 colors for your work, you can secure a significant performance gain by using the 16-color version of your video driver.

Using Memory Efficiently

Because Windows NT includes many features that are add-ons in other operating systems, configuring memory is simplified. However, to configure and use your system optimally, it is important to understand how Windows NT uses memory.

The following features are built into Windows NT and do not require user manipulation to operate efficiently. In other operating systems such as Windows 3.1 and MS-DOS, these features are optional and can have many confusing options.

- *Hard disk caching.* Windows NT automatically and efficiently uses all unused memory for disk caching.

- *Memory managers.* Windows NT does not require any additional memory managers (such as EMM386.EXE, QEMM, or HIMEM.SYS). The memory management system in Windows NT is smart enough to automatically provide the memory management services that these DOS-based managers formerly provided, such as EMS (Expanded Memory Services), XMS (eXtended Memory Services), and DPMI (DOS Protected Mode Interface) services.

- *RAM drives.* Because of Windows NT's efficient use of disk caching and its efficient memory manager, the need for a RAM drive is greatly diminished.

The following sections provide detailed information about using memory efficiently. To do this, you must first understand how Windows NT uses memory.

Understanding Memory Usage

This section describes how to use Windows NT in such a way as to optimize its use of the physical memory your machine has. When we discuss memory here, we are talking about RAM (random-access memory), not long-term memory such as your hard drive.

Physical memory is the amount of RAM your machine has. When people say "My computer has 8 megabytes of RAM," it also means that their machine has 8 megabytes of physical memory. Windows NT treats all physical memory on a machine as one big pool. This is different from Windows 3.1 and DOS, which break up a computer's memory to access it. Windows NT is not constrained in this way because it is a 32-bit operating system, based on a flat 32-bit addressing scheme. In figure 23.1, you can see that Windows NT can access much more memory—4000M compared to 64M—and the model it uses is much simpler.

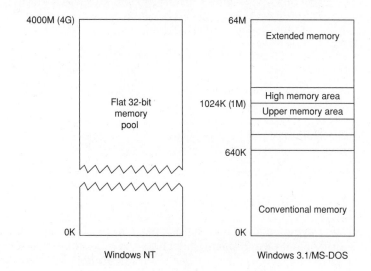

Fig. 23.1

The memory models of Windows NT and Windows 3.1.

Virtual memory refers to the fact that Windows NT can actually allocate more memory for applications than the machine it is running on physically has. The seemingly impossible task of allocating more memory than hard disk space is accomplished by RAM. For example, if you have 16M of physical RAM on your system, Windows NT will use a 28M chunk of your hard disk space to help it pretend you have more than 24M of physical RAM. The hard disk space that Windows NT uses is called a *paging file* or *page file,* and is named PAGEFILE.SYS.

Virtual memory is not a new concept. Other operating systems utilize virtual memory, including Windows 3.1. However, there are some significant differences between the way Windows NT and Windows 3.1 implement and utilize virtual memory. For example, Windows NT allows you to have multiple *non-contiguous* paging files, one on each hard drive in your system; Windows 3.1 supported only one paging file, and it had to be contiguous (all space occupied by the file had to be contained in one uninterrupted chunk).

Another difference between Windows NT and Windows 3.1 in regard to virtual memory is how the two systems use it. On Windows 3.1, virtual memory was optional and used by only parts of the system and applications. On Windows NT, the entire operating system is built with virtual memory in mind. This means that not only is virtual memory not just an option on Windows NT, but it is tightly integrated into every aspect of the system.

For best performance, it is recommended that:

- The total size of all paging files on the system should be equivalent to the system RAM plus 12M. Therefore, a system with 16M of RAM should have at least 28M of paging file space allocated.

- Each local hard drive should have its own paging file. If you have two hard drives on your computer, put a paging file on each one.

Windows NT uses the paging file to provide *backing store* as part of the virtual memory management. To ensure system robustness, Windows NT requires that any accessible memory have space reserved on the backing store. The recommendation of system RAM plus 12M ensures that all memory has preallocated backing store.

The Windows NT virtual memory mechanism allows writes to occur asynchronously, with two outstanding writes allowed for each page file. The first write is always performed to the volume with the most free space. All other writes are then issued, until there are no more pages to write or all the page files have two writes outstanding. Therefore, for maximum performance, each paging file should reside on a separate physical drive. If one of your hard drives is significantly faster than the other, place your paging file on the faster drive.

 NOTE   Previous versions of Windows, such as Windows 3.0 and Windows 3.1, required that the paging file (called a swap file in Windows 3.1) be in contiguous space on the hard drive. This requirement is *not* necessary for Windows NT.

Changing Virtual Memory Settings

You can change the size of your paging file (PAGEFILE.SYS) by using the Virtual Memory button in the System applet in the Control Panel. To change the virtual memory settings:

1. Display the Windows Program Manager and open the Main window.

2. Choose the Control Panel.

3. Choose the System icon to display the System window.

4. Choose the Virtual Memory button to display the Virtual Memory dialog box (see fig. 23.2).

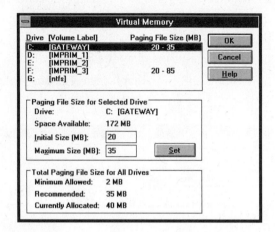

5. In the **D**rive section, select the drive that has paging file parameters you want to modify.

6. Enter values in the **I**nitial Size and Maximum Size text boxes.

7. Choose **S**et to set the parameters for the chosen drive.

8. Repeat steps 5 through 7, if necessary, for each additional drive.

9. Choose OK.

Setting Tasking Options

Windows NT is a preemptively scheduled multitasking operating system. This allows it to run multiple applications, or tasks, simultaneously. For example, one application could be calculating pi to 500 places while the user is playing a game of Solitaire in the foreground using the Solitaire application.

Applications in Windows NT can run at different priority levels. For example, if the user playing Solitaire wanted the cards to redraw and move quickly, Solitaire (the foreground application) should have a higher priority level.

Windows NT usually runs a foreground application at a slightly higher priority than the background applications so that the user has the perception that the background tasks are not degrading system performance. You can change the way Windows NT behaves by following these steps:

1. Display the Windows Program Manager and open the Main window.

2. Choose the Control Panel.

3. Choose the System icon to display the System window.

4. Choose the Tasking button to display the Tasking dialog box (see fig. 23.3).

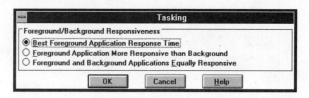

5. Choose an option:

   ■ The **B**est Foreground Application Response Time option, which is the default, gives the highest priority to the foreground application. Applications running in the background may run slower.

   ■ The **F**oreground Application More Responsive than Background option gives background applications a higher priority than the default, but they still run more slowly than foreground applications.

   ■ The Foreground and Background Applications **E**qually Responsive option gives foreground and background applications the same amount of processor time.

6. Choose OK.

Optimizing Disk Access

The efficiency of your Windows NT workstation depends a great deal on the speed of disk access. This section helps you understand which aspects of the disk subsystem affect overall system performance and what you can do to improve the efficiency of disk access.

The most important areas to focus on that affect hard disk performance follow:

- Speed of the hard disk
- Type of file system
- Amount of disk fragmentation

To discuss these items, you must first understand the way that Windows NT accesses the disk and which file systems are available for Windows NT.

Understanding Disk Access

Almost all modern operating systems, including Windows NT, enable users to read and write information to permanent storage devices such as hard disks and floppy diskettes through a mechanism called a *file system*. The file system defines the structure used to store the information.

An analogy to a file system is the kitchen in your house. You use your kitchen to store many things, such as plates, silverware, and food. You have defined a structure in your kitchen that enables you to access what you have stored efficiently. (For example, all glasses are in the cupboard above the sink, and all cooking pans are in the drawer under the range.) The kitchen in a large restaurant probably contains many of the same items, but has a larger and more complex structure. (For example, glasses are stored in palettes and there are too many cooking pans to fit in the drawer under the range.)

Just as you must choose how to organize the items in your kitchen, you must also choose how to organize the files you place on your computer system. If you have a small system that is used primarily for your own files, you will choose the file system equivalent to a home kitchen; on the other hand, if your system is accessed by many users, you would use an industrial-strength file system which is equivalent to a commercial kitchen.

Windows NT comes with several file systems: FAT (small, home kitchen), HPFS, and NTFS (large, commercial kitchen). Each has advantages and disadvantages, and you should choose which one you use based on how your computer will be used.

NTFS versus FAT

Windows NT supports multiple file systems (also called installable file systems), including FAT (File Allocation Table), NTFS (New Technology File Systems), and HPFS (High Performance File System). This section describes the advantages and disadvantages of the FAT file system and NTFS. HPFS is not discussed because it is not widely used and is of limited use to the typical Windows NT user.

MS-DOS uses the FAT file system. Windows NT provides an optimized, high-performance version of the FAT file system that is completely compatible with the MS-DOS FAT file system. Some documentation refers to Windows NT's version of the FAT file system as FastFAT, but it is referred to as FAT in this book. NTFS was designed from the ground up as an integral part of Windows NT. It supports many advanced features that the FAT file system does not.

Advantages of FAT

- Complete compatibility with MS-DOS. The FAT file system can be accessed by both MS-DOS and Windows NT. FAT is the most widely used file system for PCs.

- Fastest file system for Windows NT. The FAT file system trades many of the advanced features of NTFS to gain speed.

Disadvantages of FAT

- Does not support security. Any user can access any file on a FAT partition.

- Files are restricted to 8-character file names with a 3-character file name extension.

- Cannot support files larger than approximately 2 gigabytes.

- For larger partitions (about 400 megabytes and up), the FAT file system's performance begins to degrade in comparison to NTFS.

- Supports removable media. If a removable disk such as a Bernoulli is formatted with NTFS, it cannot be removed without shutting down the machine.

Advantages of NTFS

- Full security. Each file on the system can be associated with a security descriptor. Files can be marked such that they can be read, written to, and executed by one user, but executed only by another.

- Allows extremely large storage media. A single NTFS volume can be approximately 17 *billion gigabytes*.

- File system recovery allows for quick restoration of disk-based data after a system failure.

- Allows file names of up to 256 characters. NTFS automatically generates correct MS-DOS file names (eight-character name and three-character extension) so that files can be shared with users using the FAT file system. NTFS file names use the UNICODE 16-bit character set.

■ Performance is consistent for almost all partition sizes. A 400M NTFS partition provides about the same access speed as a 2G partition.

■ Supports multiple streams of data in each file. This is required if the Windows NT Services for Macintosh are to be used.

Disadvantages of NTFS

■ NTFS volumes can be accessed only by Windows NT. When your computer is running another operating system (such as MS-DOS or OS/2), NTFS volumes are not accessible.

■ If your boot drive (drive C:) is an NTFS volume, you cannot boot MS-DOS from your hard disk.

■ NTFS is not recommended for partitions smaller than about 400M because NTFS uses a large amount of disk space in managing the disk.

■ A floppy disk cannot be formatted with NTFS. Windows NT formats all floppy disks with the FAT file system because the space used by NTFS to manage the disk would not fit on a floppy disk.

Using More than One File System

Windows NT allows you to use more than one file system at one time. A file system can be installed on each logical drive in your system. For example, the C drive might use the FAT file system, and the D and E drives might use NTFS.

The following example illustrates why using more than one file system can help you achieve maximum performance with Windows NT. Suppose your computer has two physical hard disk drives. Drive C is a 120M drive and drive D is a 600M drive. Drive C is less than the 400M minimum recommended for NTFS, but will perform well using the FAT file system. If you formatted drive D as FAT, performance would suffer because the performance of the FAT file system deteriorates as the size of the drive increases beyond about 400M. Thus, formatting drive D as NTFS will yield better performance.

Defragmenting Your Disk

Information written to a hard disk formatted with the FAT file system, HPFS, or NTFS is not necessarily stored in a contiguous (adjacent) block. Fragments of information are more likely spread across the disk wherever the system can find room. The more you use the hard disk, the more fragmented the disk becomes. The drive takes more time to hunt for information located in several places than to fetch it from a single location. Because of this extra time, disk fragmentation can slow the computer's operation considerably.

If you are using the FAT file system on any of your hard disks, use a utility to defragment your disk. Many applications can defragment a hard disk by restructuring files into contiguous blocks and moving free space to the end of the disk. Unfortunately, these applications will not operate under Windows NT because they require direct access to the hard disk hardware. However, if you are using the MultiBoot feature of Windows NT so that you can boot both Windows NT and DOS on your computer, you can run one of these defragmentation utilities under DOS.

To run a defragmentation utility, such as the DEFRAG utility that comes with MS-DOS 6.0, follow these steps:

1. Save all your work.

2. Display the Windows Program Manager.

3. Choose the **File S**hutdown command. The Shutdown Computer window appears (see fig. 23.4).

4. Choose **R**estart when shutdown is complete.

5. Choose OK. Your computer will shut down and then reboot.

6. The MultiBoot screen is displayed as follows:

```
OS Loader V3.1
Please select the operating system to start:
    Windows NT Version 3.1
    MS-DOS
```

```
Use ↑ and ↓ to move the highlight to your choice.
Press Enter to choose.
Seconds until highlighted choice will be started auto-
  matically: 23
```

Use the up- and down-arrow keys to select MS-DOS, then press Enter.

7. To start the Microsoft DEFRAG program, for example, type the following at the MS-DOS prompt (C:\>):

> **DEFRAG *n*: /F**

where *n* is the drive letter. Press Enter. DEFRAG can take several hours to defragment a badly fragmented disk. After it finishes, you are returned to the MS-DOS prompt.

 NOTE If you are using another defragmentation or disk optimization program, consult its documentation for information on how to invoke it.

8. Repeat step 7 for each hard disk you want to defragment.

9. Press Ctrl+Alt+Del to reboot your computer.

10. At the MultiBoot screen, choose Windows NT Version 3.1.

 NOTE You can defragment a disk formatted with NTFS by backing up the entire disk to tape or another drive, deleting everything on the disk, then restoring from the backup copy.

The Performance Monitor

The Windows NT Performance Monitor is a tool that enables you to easily monitor and troubleshoot the performance of your computer or other computers on the network. You can monitor processor, system, thread, memory, and disk performance through logs, charts, and reports. You can also configure the Performance Monitor to alert you to performance problems.

Objects Monitored by the Performance Monitor

You can use the Performance Monitor to monitor just about every part of Windows NT's performance. Each part of Windows NT is associated with an *object*. Each object, in turn, has a *counter* for measuring the activity of a certain aspect of the object.

Within Windows NT are literally hundreds of counters, capable of measuring myriad objects. However, certain objects and counters that yield performance information are more useful than others in most situations. Following is a list of the most useful objects and counters.

Some objects and counters yield performance information that is more useful when tuning a Windows NT workstation. Following is a list of these objects and counters, and their use in tuning Windows NT:

Object	Counter
Processor	*% Processor Time*
	Processor time can be thought of as the fraction of the time that a processor spends doing useful work. The rest of the time the processor is idle.
	Interrupts/sec
	This counter measures the number of interrupts the processor gets each second. A hardware device, such as a serial communications port, interrupts the processor when it requires attention. All normal processing stops when the processor is servicing these interrupts.
System	*R/W Operations/sec*
	This counter represents the number of read and write operations to peripheral devices that occur per second.
	System Up Time
	The System Up Time counter gives the total time in seconds that the system has been operational since it was last started.
	Total Interrupts/sec
	Like the Interrupts/sec counter for the Processor object, this counter gives the rate the system is receiving hardware interrupts.
Memory	*Pages/sec*
	This counter shows how many memory pages are being transferred per second.
PhysicalDisk	*Disk Queue*
	This counter gives the number of requests outstanding on the disk at the time the performance data is collected. If there is a sustained load on the drive, this counter will be consistently high.

Object	Counter
Cache	*Copy Read Hits %*

This counter shows how efficiently the Windows NT disk caching mechanism is working. The higher the percentage of *hits*, the more frequently Windows NT is copying data from memory, instead of having to copy it from disk.

Lazy Write Flushes/sec

Windows NT will delay writing data to the physical disk after an application has told it to do a write operation. It does this so that control can return to the application faster, improving the response for the user. Windows NT then actually writes the data some time later when the system is not busy. This is called a *lazy write*.

The *Lazy Write Flushes/sec* counter shows the frequency at which the cache's lazy write thread has written to disk.

Getting the Most from the Performance Monitor

In the previous section, it was noted that there are just a few performance monitor objects and counters that you can focus on when tuning your Windows NT workstation. This section discusses some of these counters in more detail, providing suggestions on how you can use the information provided by the Performance Monitor.

The *% Processor Time* counter measures how busy the microprocessor in your computer is. You can watch this counter to see how background tasks are affecting the performance of your computer. For example, if you are downloading a file with a communications program in the background and are concerned that your spreadsheet running in the foreground is not getting enough processor time, you can use the *% Processor Time* counter to see how much processor time the communications program is using.

There is always some level of interrupt activity going on in the system. For example, the clock in your computer generates interrupts regularly. But watching the *Interrupts/sec* counter can be useful if you are concerned that a hardware device is adversely affecting system performance.

If you are interested in the overall throughput of your system—that is, the overall amount of data that your system is processing on a consistent basis—the *% Processor Time*, *Total Interrupts/sec*, *Memory pages/sec*, and *Disk Queue* counters are useful. Setting up Performance Monitor to watch all of these counters provides a clear, graphical view of your system's overall throughput.

Although the *System Up Time* counter is not generally useful for tuning Windows NT, it is interesting information and is worth noting. This is particularly true if the Windows NT machine in question is an unattended server; the machine might shut down and restart without anybody noticing. The System Up Time counter would indicate that this had happened.

The *Lazy Write Flushes/sec* counter gives an indication of how successful Windows NT is being at optimizing disk access. This can be useful when you are evaluating the performance of your disk system, or are considering adding more memory (the Lazy Write cache uses physical memory).

Controlling the Performance Monitor Counters

The physical disk object counters are turned off by default. Turning them on imposes an overall system performance penalty of about 2 percent.

To turn on the monitoring of the physical disk performance, follow these steps:

1. Display the Windows Program Manager.

2. Open the Main window.

3. Choose Command Prompt.

4. At the command prompt (C:\>), type

   DISKPERF /Y

   EXIT

5. Restart your computer.

To turn the disk performance monitoring off again, follow the same steps, but replace the /Y parameter for DISKPERF with /N. Note that you must restart your computer for these changes to take effect.

Changing Settings in the Windows NT Configuration Registry

Windows NT stores most configuration information in a database called the Configuration Registry (also called the Registry). Although in almost all cases the information found in the Registry is set correctly by applications and utilities, knowing how to make modifications to entries in the Registry can be useful in tuning Windows NT. This section describes how to modify entries in the Windows NT Configuration Registry using the Registry Editor (RegEdit).

> **CAUTION:** Incorrectly modifying Configuration Registry entries could irreversibly cripple your Windows NT installation, causing loss of data! In almost every case, registry entries should be modified only by the program that uses them. For most system configuration options, you should use the Control Panel to change settings.

Do not modify entries in the Configuration Registry unless you are absolutely, positively sure of what you are doing.

The Windows NT Configuration Registry provides a secure, remotely accessible mechanism for storing system configuration information. The Registry can be thought of as a centralized database for storing operating system, application, and hardware configuration information. The registry combines all the information formerly found in files such as CONFIG.SYS, AUTOEXEC.BAT, WIN.INI, and so on. The information that used to be stored in such files (which were usually scattered all around the system) is now stored in one place: The Registry. Figure 23.5 illustrates this.

Note that some older applications, including most 16-bit Windows applications, may still use .INI files when running on Windows NT. However, eventually all applications running on Windows NT will store their configuration data in the Registry.

The Configuration Registry has a hierarchical structure much like that of the Windows NT directory structure. In the Registry, *Keys* are like directories in that they can contain *SubKeys* (like subdirectories). Just as directories can contain files, registry keys can contain *Values*. The table following the figure illustrates the analogy between the registry and the directory structure.

User Configuration Data
(AUTOEXEC.BAT, WIN INI, Program Mgr Groups, and so on.)

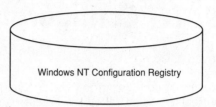

Windows NT Configuration Registry

Application Configuration Data

Network Configuration Data
(PROTOCOL.INI, LANMAN.INI, and so on.)

Hardware Configuration Data
(SYSTEM.INI, CONFIG.SYS, and so on.)

Directory Structure	Configuration Registry
Directory	Key
DOCUMENT\	Serial\
Subdirectory	SubKey
DOCUMENT\BOOK\	Serial\Serial0\
File	Value
DOCUMENT\BOOK\CHAP25.DOC	Serial\Serial0\DosDevices

Values are analogous to files in that they contain data. Values cannot contain other values or keys, just as files cannot contain other files or directories. Values also have a *type* associated with them. For example, if a string is to be stored, it would have the type REG_SZ.

The Registry is designed to be a centralized store of all configuration information for a Windows NT system. It contains four *root keys* that provide access to information about your Windows NT configuration. The four root keys are

Root Key	Contents
HKEY_LOCAL_MACHINE	Contains information about your hardware configuration, such as device drivers. For example, information regarding your display driver is stored here.

Root Key	Contents
HKEY_CLASSES_ROOT	This tree contains the object linking and embedding (OLE) and file association data. This root-tree is really a SubKey of the HKEY_LOCAL_MACHINE root key.
HKEY_USERS	The user environment data (for example, color schemes, program manager groups, and so on) for all active users that have accounts on your computer is contained in this root key.
HKEY_CURRENT_USER	This key contains the user environment data of the currently logged-on user. This key is really a SubKey of the HKEY_USERS root key.

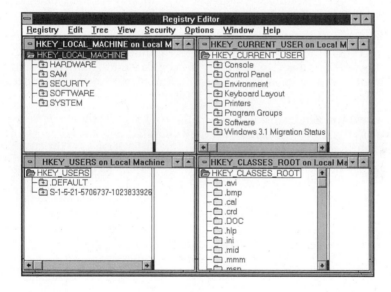

Fig. 23.6

The Registry editor and the four root keys.

As you can see from figure 23.6, each of the predefined root keys occupies its own window within the Registry Editor.

Creating an Icon for the Registry Editor

By default, the icon for the Registry Editor is not visible in the Program Manager. You may want to add an icon yourself, so that you can access it more easily. Add the Registry Editor icon by following these steps:

1. Choose the **File New** command in the Program Manager and select Program **I**tem. The Program Item Properties window appears.

2. In the **D**escription edit box, type **Registry Editor**.

3. In the **C**ommand Line edit box, type **REGEDT32.EXE**.

4. Choose OK to close the Program Item Properties window.

The Registry Editor can now be run by choosing its icon.

Modifying Entries Using the Registry Editor

Although you are discouraged from modifying entries in the Configuration Registry, it is sometimes necessary. To modify an entry using the Registry Editor, follow these steps:

1. Start the Registry Editor by choosing its icon in the Program Manager (note: you must follow the instructions at the beginning of this section to add an icon for the Registry Editor). If you do not want to create an icon, choose **File R**un from Program Manager or File Manager, type **REGEDT32.EXE**, and press OK.

2. Select the window that contains the root key for the entry you want to modify. For example, the value that enables Fifo support in the serial driver is contained in the HKEY_LOCAL_MACHINE root key. To edit this value, you would first select the HKEY_LOCAL_MACHINE window.

3. Choose the SubKey that contains your value in the same manner you would choose subdirectories in the File Manager. Double-clicking on a SubKey "opens" that SubKey, showing additional SubKeys which are children of the current one. For the preceding example, the serial driver's values are in HKEY_LOCAL_MACHINE\System\Serial. This would require opening two SubKeys: System and Serial.

4. After you have selected the appropriate SubKey, choose the value you want to edit, and double-click on it. An Edit Value window appears, allowing you to modify the value. Choose OK to dismiss the Edit value window.

Remember, modifying entries in the Configuration Registry should be done with extreme caution. Make sure that Control Panel or the application that you are interested in does not have a mechanism for allowing you to change settings first. Use the Registry Editor only if you are sure of what you are doing, and you have exhausted all other options.

Summary

In an operating system as powerful as Windows NT, there are invariably many factors that can affect performance. This chapter explained the concepts behind the most important of these factors, and provided tips for tuning Windows NT so that it performs optimally.

There is much more information regarding all of the facets of tuning Windows NT that are beyond the scope of this book. Chapter 27 identifies other resources that you might find helpful when tuning your Windows NT configuration.

Using Windows NT and OS/2 2.1

Windows NT and IBM's OS/2 2.1 (and 2.0) are single-user, multitasking, multithreaded, 32-bit operating systems. The two products are direct competitors. It is important to understand their similarities and differences before deciding how they might apply to you. Many organizations have both systems. It is even possible to have both systems on the same computer. Microsoft does not support such an implementation, but this chapter explains how to do it.

Windows NT versus OS/2

The 32-bit OS/2 had the advantage of being released more than a year before the first release of Windows NT. The second OS/2 release, OS/2 2.1, also beat NT to the market. This should give OS/2 an advantage in stability and reliability, although Microsoft put NT through a long and broadly based beta test cycle.

Many reliability-conscious people go by the philosophy "Never buy version 1.0 of anything." Microsoft cleverly countered this bias by designating the first release of Windows NT as version 3.1. This nomenclature reminds people of the solid and ubiquitous Windows 3.1. However, Windows NT is a new product, not an improved version of Windows 3.1.

Windows 3.1 is not an operating system, but rather a layer of software that gives a graphical user interface to the single-user, single-tasking, single-threaded, 16-bit MS-DOS operating system. Windows NT has much of the look and feel of Windows 3.1, but Windows NT is very different "under the hood" and is more closely related to OS/2. Before the relationship between IBM and Microsoft deteriorated and IBM assumed sole responsibility for OS/2, the Windows NT development effort was slated to become OS/2 3.0.

In the following lists, you can see the features Windows NT and OS/2 2.1 share, and also the important differences.

Similarities

- 32-bit data operations and 32-bit addressing on Intel architecture machines.

- Multitasking, multithreaded operating systems.

- High reliability due to the logical isolation of applications from one another and from the operating system. If one application crashes, it will not bring down the operating system or the other applications.

- Intuitive graphical user interface.

- Compatible with MS-DOS 6, Windows 3.1, and OS/2 1.X, allowing applications written for those environments to run without modification.

- Designed to control local area networks of personal computers by running on network servers.

- Can run multiple DOS and Windows sessions simultaneously.

Differences

- OS/2 runs only on the Intel platforms (386, 486, and Pentium), but Windows NT runs also on the MIPS R4000 and DEC Alpha platforms. The Alpha version is a 64-bit implementation. One of Microsoft's strategic goals is to have a common operating system across multiple platforms that span a wide range of performance values.

- The NT File System (NTFS) is more robust than OS/2's High Performance File System (HPFS). It is transaction-based and recoverable, making it appropriate for use by large organizations in enterprise-critical applications.

- Windows NT has networking capability built into the operating system. For small networks, there is no need to add additional network software.

- OS/2 2.0 was available more than a year before Windows NT. As a result, many organizations adopted it and made a significant investment in OS/2 applications. Windows NT does not support OS/2 2.X applications, so organizations with OS/2 applications may find migration to Windows NT a challenge.

- Windows NT requires more disk space and system memory than OS/2.

- Windows NT is a tightly coupled, symmetric multiprocessing (SMP) operating system. OS/2 2.1 is not an SMP system, although IBM plans to add this capability.

Comparing File Systems

OS/2 and Windows NT support the MS-DOS standard File Allocation Table (FAT) file system. Both also support the OS/2 HPFS, but only Windows NT supports NTFS. Thus, Windows NT can work with any data files created by MS-DOS or OS/2 as well as those created with Windows NT. OS/2 can work with FAT and HPFS data files created by MS-DOS, OS/2, or Windows NT, but cannot work with NTFS files.

FAT

The File Allocation Table file system was introduced with PC-DOS 1.0 in 1981 when it was delivered with the original floppy disk-based IBM PC. Designed to work on a machine with very modest capabilities (no hard disks), it has some serious drawbacks on today's high-capacity machines. Files are accessed through a long chain of physical disk locations, degrading performance for large files. File names are restricted to eight characters with a three-character extension. More importantly, heavy usage tends to fragment the disk holding the file system, causing progressive performance degradation. The chief virtue of the FAT file system is that it will run on anything running DOS, OS/2, or Windows NT. If you want to share files among those three operating systems, use the FAT file system.

HPFS

The High Performance File System was designed for use by systems with hard disks. File access is faster than with FAT. In addition, file names of up to 254 characters are allowed. Because of the file structure, fragmentation is never a problem. HPFS files cannot be read by DOS, but work well with both OS/2 and Windows NT.

NTFS

The NT File System is similar to HPFS in many ways but has some additional capabilities. Like HPFS, NTFS features fast file access, immunity to fragmentation, and the capability to use long file names. In addition, NTFS has a file recovery system that enables the quick restoration of disk files after a system failure. Its 64-bit addressing (on Alpha and future 64-bit processors) enables addressing of up to 18 terabytes (18 billion gigabytes) of memory. New security features include execute-only files. Windows NT also supports the IEEE POSIX operating system standard. Neither DOS nor OS/2 can recognize or use NTFS files.

Comparing Security Features

Windows NT and OS/2 have different approaches to system security, with Windows NT the more stringent of the two. Windows NT has been designed to meet U.S. government security requirements. It is certified as a C2-level secure environment. Every time a person uses Windows NT, he or she must log on and enter a password. Users may exercise only the privileges granted to them by the system administrator. Users cannot delete Windows NT system files or critical configuration data. Process management, local procedure call activity, and thread initiation are all routed through the security subsystem.

In contrast, users can boot OS/2 without identifying or authenticating themselves. Critical system and configuration files, however, are protected from deletion. Password security applies to OS/2's optional Database Manager, but not to other subsystems. Security is enforced on a LAN Manager or LAN Server network by dividing the network into domains. Each domain contains a group of file servers and workstations with similar security needs. Users who are members of a domain would have the privileges granted to that domain.

Comparing Networking Support

Windows NT and OS/2 are similar in their support of the most popular local area networks for personal computers. In addition, Windows
NT offers a built-in peer-to-peer network similar to that included in
Microsoft's Windows for Workgroups. This type of network is appropriate for small installations with a limited number of workstations. OS/2
has no equivalent capability, but the same functions are readily available from third-party peer-to-peer network vendors.

For larger networks, the capabilities of NT and OS/2 are comparable.
Both interface well with the most popular networking environments,
such as LAN Manager, LAN Server, and Novell NetWare.

Comparing System Resource Requirements

Compared to MS-DOS, both Windows NT and OS/2 are large, complex
operating systems. They require a lot of space on disk and in main
memory. They use a lot of CPU cycles to perform an operation because
they do much more than a rudimentary operating system such as DOS
ever attempts to do. To run either one, a system needs a fast clock
speed, plenty of main memory, and huge amounts of disk space.

Microsoft requires that a system have at least 50M of available disk
space before installing Windows NT, and recommends a minimum of
70M. If you install the entire Windows NT operating system, it takes
about 46M, not counting a swap file (PAGEFILE.SYS) that may vary in
size depending on how much free disk space you have.

IBM also requires 50M for OS/2, but is not so squeezed for space as is
Windows NT in that amount. If you install the entire OS/2 operating
system, it takes about 33M, not counting the swap file (SWAPPER.DAT).

Microsoft requires a minimum of 8M of system memory to run NT, but
to run efficiently, it should have at least 12M and preferably 16M. IBM,
on the other hand, claims OS/2 2.1 will run in 4MB. It will, but very
slowly. Much time is spent swapping things out to the swap file on disk.
There is a tremendous difference in performance with 6M, and OS/2 is
very happy in 8M. If you want to run a large number of simultaneous
sessions, you should have 16M.

CPU clock speed is another important determinant of overall system performance. The faster your clock, the snappier the performance will be, whether you are running Windows NT or OS/2. Although they both run acceptably on slower machines, for best results you should have at least a 33 MHz 386. A 486 system will give a noticeable improvement in performance.

Supporting the POSIX Standard

In addition to 32-bit Windows NT applications, Windows NT runs 16-bit MS-DOS, Windows 3.1, and OS/2 1.X applications. To do so it uses a subsystem that creates an environment appropriate for the application. It also has a subsystem for POSIX applications.

POSIX is an internationally recognized standard (IEEE 1003.1) for UNIX and UNIX-like operating systems. It was created to foster the development of applications that are portable across operating systems. Native NT applications are not POSIX-compliant, but NT's POSIX subsystem makes it possible to create and run POSIX applications. IBM's OS/2 2.1 does not support POSIX applications.

Installing Windows NT and OS/2 2.1 on the Same Machine

Although Windows NT and OS/2 2.1 were not designed to work together, it is possible for them to reside on the same machine and share files.

DOS, Windows NT, and OS/2 enable you to divide a hard disk into as many as four partitions. Partitions may be *primary* or *logical*. Primary partitions are bootable and may not be subdivided. A primary partition may not exchange information with any other primary partition. Logical partitions are not bootable, but may be subdivided into one or more logical drives, and may exchange information with whichever primary partition is currently active.

For Windows NT and OS/2 2.1 to be on the same computer, they must each reside in a separate primary partition on the system boot disk. This means that only one of them may be active at a time. To activate the second operating system, you must shut down the first. To share applications and data, place Windows NT and OS/2 into primary partitions that are just large enough to hold them. Assign the remainder of your disk space to a logical partition accessible to both, then place your applications and data on the logical drive (or drives) filling the logical partition. A detailed explanation of how to set up Windows NT and OS/2 2.1 on the same system is given later in this chapter.

Windows NT and OS/2 both provide for cohabitation on a system with other operating systems. Each uses a different technique to accomplish it. Both techniques use a boot control program that asks the user which operating system to activate, then loads and starts whichever one is selected. The Windows NT boot control program is called MultiBoot; the OS/2 program is Boot Manager.

MultiBoot allows character-based OS/2 1.X or any version of MS-DOS to be on the same system as Windows NT. All three operating systems are Microsoft products. This allows an installation to be highly automated because there are a limited number of possibilities, and MultiBoot knows what to expect from each one. The disadvantage of this method is that loading of non-Microsoft operating systems (including IBM's OS/2 2.1) is not supported.

The OS/2 Boot Manager makes no assumptions about the operating systems in the non-OS/2 primary partitions. They could be MS-DOS, an older release of OS/2, SCO UNIX, Windows NT, or something else. By first installing Boot Manager, then OS/2, then Windows NT, in that order, you can make it all work together.

A hard disk can be divided into a maximum of four partitions, and you will need all four to create a system in which both Windows NT and OS/2 2.1 can share data files. Follow these steps to create such a system:

1. Follow the standard OS/2 installation instructions to create a 1M primary partition for Boot Manager, followed by a second primary partition big enough to hold OS/2. You may format the OS/2 partition as either FAT of HPFS, because DOS will never access any files in it.

2. After Boot Manager and OS/2 are installed, verify that they are functioning properly by booting, selecting OS/2 from the Boot Manager menu, then running a few standard OS/2 functions.

3. Use the OS/2 FDISK utility to create a third primary partition large enough to hold Windows NT. From the Options menu, set the new partition as Installable before shutting down OS/2 and rebooting with the Windows NT installation boot disk. When prompted to format the new partition, you may elect to use either the FAT, HPFS, or NTFS format. If you want to place MS-DOS in the same partition as Windows NT, you may do so, but only if the FAT format is used.

4. If you install both DOS and Windows NT in the same partition, MultiBoot will ask you at boot time which one you want. MultiBoot will load and run the one you select.

5. Use either the OS/2 or DOS FDISK utility to create a fourth disk partition. This time, make it logical rather than primary. Assign whatever disk space remains to this new partition. The logical partition is accessible to any of the operating systems residing in the primary partitions, and thus may be used to pass data or programs from one environment to another. The Windows NT security features do not allow you to use FDISK to repartition a disk. Instead, use Disk Administrator from the Administrative Tools group in the Windows NT desktop. If you prefer, you can create the logical partition from the Windows NT Disk Administrator rather than use OS/2 or DOS.

6. After the hard disk has been partitioned and loaded with operating systems, applications, and data, reboot to start Windows NT. Use Windows NT's Disk Administrator to set the OS/2 Boot Manager partition active, then reboot. Boot Manager will be displayed, giving you a choice of OS/2 or Windows NT. Make a selection. If you select OS/2, it will load and start immediately. If you select Windows NT, MultiBoot will appear. If you have installed DOS along with Windows NT, both choices will appear on the MultiBoot menu. Whichever one you select will be loaded.

7. Start working with the operating system you have chosen. Put application and data files in the shared logical partition. When you want to change operating systems, shut down the one you are using and reboot. Select the new operating system from either the Boot Manager or MultiBoot menu. The files that were left in the logical partition by the previous operating system are now available to the new one.

Summary

In this chapter, you learned the similarities and differences between OS/2 2.1 and Windows NT, the two major operating systems on Intel-compatible personal computers. Capabilities and compatibility issues for both were discussed. You learned also how to put OS/2 2.1 and Windows NT on the same computer, a configuration that is not officially supported by either IBM or Microsoft.

Networking with Windows NT

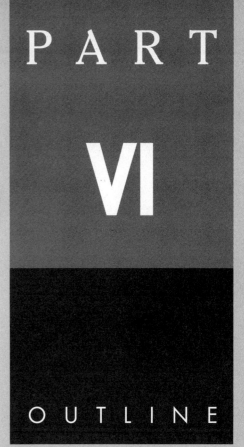

PART

VI

OUTLINE

Networking with Windows NT

Welcome to a new era of networking ease-of-use. Windows NT elevates "point and shoot" networking to another level, by fully integrating network support into the operating system. All of the support in peer-to-peer networks such as Windows for Workgroups and Lantastic—file and directory sharing, electronic mail, and device sharing—are available in Windows NT. That's good news, but there's more.

Windows NT is equally adept at the rigors of client/server networking. The client/server network model differs from the peer-to-peer model, in which each workstation is capable of sharing resources or accessing shared resources. In a client/server network, specific workstations are set aside as resource (file) servers or device (printers, modems, and so on) servers. These network servers are used exclusively for sharing their resources with all the client workstations in the network.

The user version of Windows NT can handle small to medium client/ server networks, in which all servers in the network are Windows NT-compatible servers. For big networks made up of many smaller networks called *domains*, Windows NT Advanced Server is just the ticket. Windows NT Advanced Server can also connect to servers running a different network operating system, such as Novell Netware or Banyan VINES. This connection between dissimilar network operating systems is called a *gateway*.

This chapter serves as an overview of Windows NT networking. The coverage is high-level and conceptual, aimed at providing a condensed introduction to the level of networking support present in the Windows NT User and Advanced Server versions. We'll cover peer-to-peer and client/server networking, security, and resource sharing. The next few chapters cover all of these areas in greater detail, to help you adapt NT to your current networking needs.

Windows NT Networking Strengths

Windows NT networking support is tightly integrated into the operating system. The benefits of a 32-bit protected operating system may not be readily apparent, but can be summed up in one statement: Because all Windows NT subsystems are protected (isolated) from each other, you will reboot significantly less than under Windows 3.1, Windows for Workgroups, or MS-DOS.

Windows NT supports the connection of your Windows NT workstation to most popular networks. Windows NT supports connection to

- DOS, Windows 3.x, and OS/2 using the standard NETBIOS protocol.

- UNIX, VAX, and other operating systems that share the sockets and standard Remote Procedure Call (RPC) protocol.

- Apple computers and mainframes using the XPlatform protocol.

Additionally, Banyan VINES, Novell Netware, Windows for Workgroups, LAN Manager, Sun NFS, and all DOS NETBIOS networks can be connected to and accessed from a Windows NT workstation. Figure 25.1 is a map of the cross-network connections supported by Windows NT.

Possibly the greatest strength of Windows NT is its similarity to Windows 3.1 and Windows for Workgroups. User interface components familiar to Windows users are carried over to Windows NT. To allow easy access to the powerful peer-to-peer and client/server networking support in Windows NT, the familiar Control Panel has been enhanced with new networking tools. The Network tool, which is similar to the one in Windows for Workgroups, makes sharing workgroup resources, joining resources, and connection management (setting and changing passwords) easy. The Server tool enables you to manage and view resources shared by all workgroups and users connected to the network.

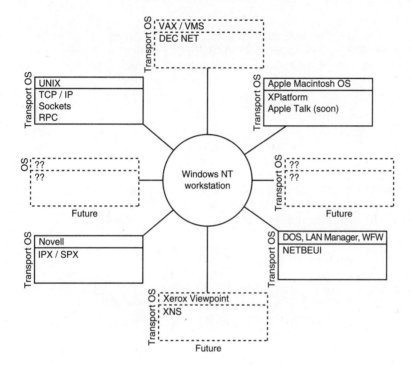

Fig. 25.1

Windows NT network connections.

The Windows NT Advanced Server includes fault-tolerance features such as a distributed naming database, disk mirroring, and (disk) duplexing and striping with parity. These and many other enhancements are built on the base client/server support provided in user-level Windows NT.

In the network applications department, Windows NT includes Microsoft Mail and Microsoft Schedule+. These applications have proven their usefulness in peer-to-peer network environments under Windows for Workgroups, and are fully compatible with their WFW cousins. Microsoft Mail relies on simple MAPI as its command set for handling mail. Mail messages can contain attachments of graphical objects, as long as they are under 32K.

How Windows NT Networking Works

Windows NT networking support by default relies on NDIS 3.0 as its main network transport interface. NDIS uses EtherNet as its native language. NDIS just happens to be the native dialect of Windows for Workgroups and LAN Manager, which goes a long way toward eliminating the hassles normally encountered when connecting stand-alone machines in a workgroup network.

For users who must exist in a mixed hardware environment which does not use NDIS, Windows NT provides integrated support for TCP/IP and NetWare. Windows NT uses the Open Systems Interconnect (OSI) layered network model to compare and integrate TCP/IP, NetWare, VINES, or any other network operating system. Seven layers are defined in the OSI network model, and each represents a level of functionality provided by a network operating system (see figure 25.2). Gateways are used to bridge all layers of dissimilar network models.

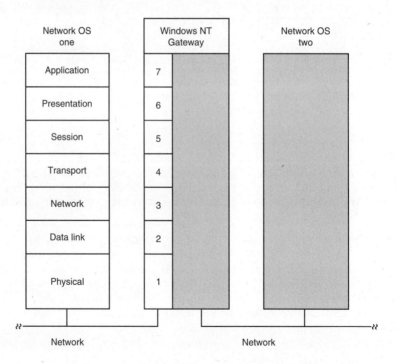

Fig. 25.2

OSI layers and gateways.

Novell NetWare support is available in Windows NT on both the client level and the server level. As a client, a Windows NT workstation can connect to other workstations in any workgroup currently up and running on the network. The mechanisms used to connect a Windows NT client workstation to a Novell server are consistent with those for performing this task in Windows for Workgroups, LANTastic, and others.

Windows NT isn't simply a single user per node network operating system. Broad and robust security mechanisms allow for the definition of new users and groups of users on a local machine.

Windows NT Network Security

Security is usually an issue when dealing with shared resources across a network, whether those resources are files, printers, or directories. From the DOS user's perspective, Windows NT security is tight as a drum. If you are a UNIX user, it's not quite up to the B1 security levels you may be used to. Overall, Windows NT network security is quite robust and flexible, especially when using Windows NT Advanced Server domain security. We discuss domains and domain trust later in this chapter.

The security model used in Windows NT is tightly coupled with the object model that pervades the design of Windows NT. Most functional areas of NT are represented as objects, and security is built into each NT object. Because Windows NT manages processes and threads as objects, security checking is naturally aligned with the creation of these objects. Figure 25.3 is an overview of the Windows NT object model.

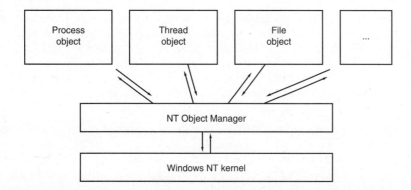

Fig. 25.3

The Windows NT object model.

One implication of this architecture is that security and the tracking and management of access to resources are implemented on a per-process basis, rather than the more common per-data-record method used in UNIX systems. This difference in implementation has little impact on users, but could be more significant to developers migrating to Windows NT from UNIX. There aren't any inherent advantages to either of these two methods of tracking, managing, and accessing resources. Figure 25.4 is an overview of the Windows NT security model.

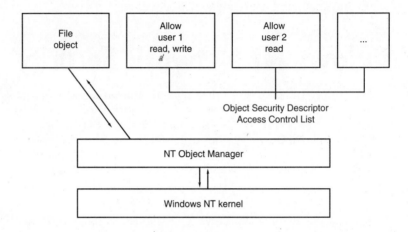

Fig. 25.4

The Windows NT
security model.

Before reading a discussion of NT network security management, you should understand a fundamental concept in the Windows NT networking model: ownership. All shareable resources in NT have an owner. Usually the owner is the creator of the resource if it's a file or directory, or the administrator of the resource if it's hardware, such as a printer or drive.

Resource ownership cannot be given away; it must be taken. For ownership to be transferred between users, the user who wants ownership must first be granted the Take Ownership special access permission. The Take Ownership access permission can be granted only by administrators or the owner of the resource. Only the owner of a resource has the right to change the security and permissions of a given resource.

Each new user defined in the system may be assigned only the privilege levels needed. Furthermore, groups of users may be defined, with privilege and security levels assigned on the group level. By defining groups of users with different privilege and security levels, managing new users becomes as simple as assigning or reassigning a user to the proper group. Figure 25.5 gives you a look at the Group Memberships dialog box, which is used to assign members to a group.

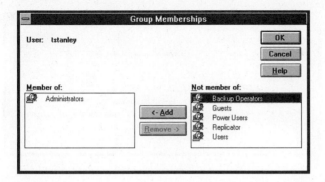

Fig. 25.5

The Group Memberships dialog box.

If you need to keep track of the activity of users or groups, you can, as the administrator, use the Event Logger to build an audit trail of when users log in and out, use resources, and access files. Beyond the obvious security of keeping an audit trail, logged events can provide valuable usage information to help you efficiently manage your resources. In figure 25.6, notice the level of information that can be controlled through the Audit Policy dialog box.

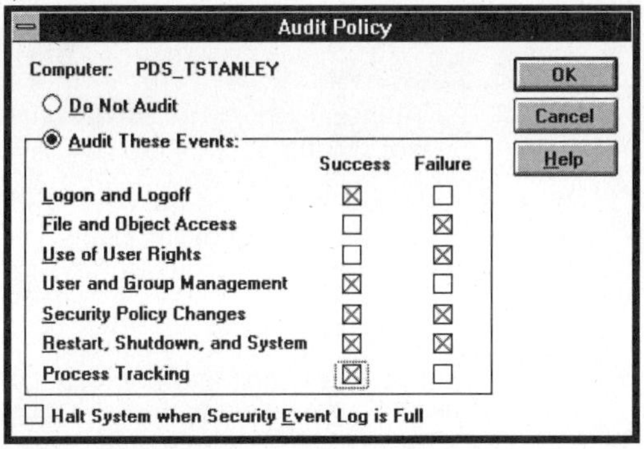

Fig. 25.6

The Audit Policy dialog box.

In user security settings, Windows NT clearly shows its desire to eventually qualify as a U.S. Government B2-level operating system. You, as the administrator, can decide on the level of "paranoia" you want to enforce when defining a user's security policy. This is accomplished in the Account Policy dialog box, shown in figure 25.7.

As the dialog box shows, you can allow the user to define passwords that never expire, or force the passwords to expire in a specified number of days. You can accept blank or empty passwords, or require that all passwords be greater than a minimum length. You can allow passwords to be changed at any time, or restrict changing passwords until a specified number of days have passed. And there's more.

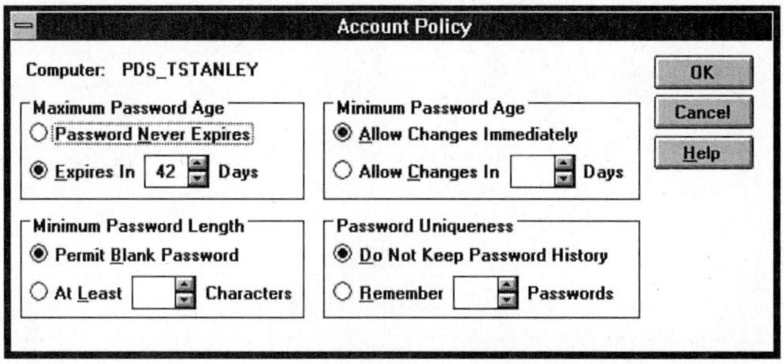

Fig. 25.7

The Account Policy dialog box.

As with much of Windows NT, network security support relies heavily on the presence of NTFS (New Technology File System) to work its magic. Without NTFS, you must forego the ability to set permission levels and security levels on files and directories.

Windows NT relies on the powerful concept of groups and group privileges. These groups can be used to manage local system and network resources. NT has an assortment of predefined group types that represent different levels of privileges for different types of users. The following table lists these predefined groups.

User and Group Type	Definition
Guests	Members are restricted guests of the workgroup or domain.
Users	Members are ordinary (limited) users of the workgroup or domain.
Backup Operators	Members can assign file backup and restore privileges to other users.
Power Users	Members can treat the local computer as their own. This includes managing resources that they own.
Administrators	Members can fully administer the systems, controlling access to all resources.
Replicator	Members can administer domain controller replication.

Permissions give Windows NT a much finer degree of control over how resources are accessed by users. Resource permissions are designed to be used in addition to the standard file attributes (read-only, system, hidden, and archive). Two categories of permissions are available for files and directories: standard permissions and special permissions.

Standard permissions represent a more general level of access control than special permissions. Windows NT defines four standard permission types, as follows.

Permission	Definition
Read	Read files, copy files, execute applications, view a file's attributes, permissions, and owner
Change	Same as read permission, plus the ability to change or delete the original file
Full Control	Full, unrestricted access, along with the ability to change permissions and ownership
No Access	File or directory cannot be accessed

Special permissions are the next logical level of access permission to files and directories. Note that the standard change permission allows a file or directory to be both read and written. This is usually sufficient and desirable, but sometimes write permission is needed, but not read permission. The special permissions address this need by providing a finer granularity of control. Following is a list of the special permissions for files and directories.

Permission	Definition
Read	Read files, copy files, execute applications, view a file's attributes, permissions, and owner
Write	Write to a file, overwrite a file, or append to a file
Execute	Execute an application; to execute a batch file, must have execute and permissions
Delete	Delete a file or move a file to another subdirectory
Change Permissions	Change file or directory permissions or take ownership
Take Ownership	Take ownership of a file or directory

An internal structure called the Access Control List (ACL) is used to manage the list of permissions for a user or a group of users. Each entry in the ACL defines the permissions for a single user or group. These ACL entries are called Access Control Entries (ACE).

You access and manage these permissions using the Windows NT File Manager. See Chapter 30, "Understanding System Security in Windows NT," for a more detailed description of security permissions.

Windows NT has a two-step approach to sharing resources with other users. First, as the resource owner, you can specify which users in your workgroup (or any other user up and running on the network) can have access to the resource. Then, you can set the permission levels for each user or group of users.

Users can share local files and printers with others in the same workgroup easily using the built-in peer-to-peer networking of Windows NT. Although this form of networking is generally relegated to small workgroups due to its marginal performance, the benefit of easily managing and accessing shared peripherals is attractive. Windows NT is shipped with peer-to-peer support for file, peripheral, and application sharing, as well as bundled electronic mail and scheduling software.

Windows NT Client/Server Support

Basic client/server networking support is standard in Windows NT. The level of functionality provided in the desktop version of NT is surprisingly complete. Out of the box, support is provided for NETBIOS, TCP/IP, Telenet, and NetWare, as discussed previously. Remote network access and local and network backup support are also provided. For interdomain connections, you need Windows NT Advanced Server. This advanced version of Windows NT provides support for WANs through the domain network model. In addition to the base Windows NT network support, Macintosh network, disk mirroring (RAID 1 and RAID 5), network server management tools that allow both local and remote network administration and management are provided.

Microsoft achieved a high degree of compatibility between Windows NT (both versions) and Windows for Workgroups by sharing the majority of code between the two products. As a result, Windows NT will find and preconfigure many of the network cards supported by Windows for Workgroups. Unfortunately, Windows NT does not support the number of network cards that Windows for Workgroups does. This is to be expected, however, because recognizing and accessing a network card is dependent on specific device drivers—an operating system component that is always too scarce with new operating systems. Fortunately, device drivers in Windows NT are only moderately complex, which should help increase the number of supported network cards.

Windows NT Advanced Server

The Windows NT Advanced Server provides domain administration tools, advanced fault tolerance, Macintosh support, remote access software, wide-area networking, and conductivity support for minis and mainframes. Designed to be installed independently or on top of the Windows NT user version, Advanced Server installs with the same ease as the user version. You'll notice a few network administration applications above those supplied with the Windows NT user version. The User Manager for Domains application works much like the Windows NT user versions, with the added capability of managing users in other domains (assuming you have the appropriate privileges).

A *domain* is a collection of network servers (whether NT servers, Novell servers, or others) and the groups of network workstations connected to those servers that function as if they are one large network. All workstations and servers in a domain share a common database of user accounts and security policies. Each server in a network domain keeps its own copy of these account and security databases, to ease network management. Domains are usually created and managed on departmental boundaries, such as sales or development.

It's not uncommon for a company to have a number of network domains that need to be connected for resource sharing. Sharing resources across domains must be tightly regulated by standard security measures—unregulated access to a domain's resources could be disastrous. Security and access levels between domains are defined by a concept known as *trust*.

Trust essentially defines the ease with which a user can access resources in another domain. If a no-trust relationship is defined between network domains, a user who wants access to resources in another domain must be able to log on to both network domains. If a full or complete trust relationship is defined between network domains, all shared resources can be freely accessed by any user in the trusted domain.

Trusted relationships between domains are created and managed by the administrator of any Windows NT advanced server in a domain. Trusted relationships between domains must be defined in pairs. The network domain administrator must select another domain, then establish the desired level of trust between two domains. Figure 25.8 illustrates this process. If the administrator defines a partial or full trust relationship between its domain and another, it essentially agrees to vouch for users in its domain who want access to shared resources in the trusted domain.

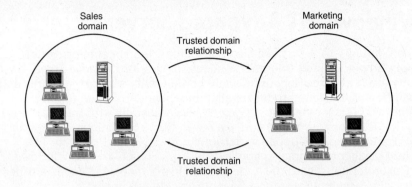

Establishing trusted relation-ships between domains.

Beyond Windows NT Advanced Server

SNA, SQLServer, and Enterprise Message System (EMS) are all waiting in the wings to complement the initial release of Windows NT Advanced Server. These network extensions should be available shortly after the release of version 1.0 and will definitely tip the scales in Microsoft's favor.

Summary

Windows NT may be the first of a new breed of operating systems built from the ground up with networking in mind. As you explore Windows NT network support in the next five chapters, you look in more detail at the issues discussed here: security issues, peer-to-peer networking, client/server networking, workgroups, domains, and gateways.

Creating Workgroups

The basic Windows NT system includes the capability to set up a peer-to-peer network for the sharing of system resources. Printers and hard disk, CD, and floppy disk drives are the principal resources that can be shared by network members. A tape drive on a single workstation can be used to back up the shared disk drives of remote systems.

The clipbook can be used to share pages of text or graphics across systems on the network. The Chat, Mail, and Schedule+ system applications can be used for communications between users on different workstations.

This chapter primarily discusses the procedures used to define and control the sharing of resources among the members of a Windows NT workgroup. The chapter also discusses communications among the members of a workgroup to coordinate the sharing of resources.

Defining a Workgroup

The capability to form workgroups is one of the built-in network features of Windows NT. The discussion of basic Windows NT network features introduces several new terms, which are described in this section.

Understanding Workgroups, Workstations, and Resources

A *workgroup* is a group of networked computers that share information and printers. Windows NT enables each networked computer, called a *workstation*, to share its directories and printers with other workstations in the workgroup and to use directories and printers shared by other workstations on the network.

 NOTE The term *workstation* is used to refer to any computer that executes Windows NT. Windows NT can execute on 386 or higher PC systems, MIPS R4000, and Digital computers. The term workstation is used to refer to any of these systems rather than using the term *PC* or *computer*.

Several workgroups can reside on the same network. Although workgroups are set up to allow member workstations to share resources among themselves, workstations from different workgroups can also share resources.

 NOTE If your computer cannot run Windows, use Workgroup Connections to attach to shared directories and printers in a workgroup.

An analogy to a workgroup is a university library. The library is accessible through the use of a descriptive designation, a library card. The university library consists of a group of libraries, each located on a different campus. Users and faculty members can borrow books and use the facilities of any campus library.

Visiting professors, students from other universities, and independent scholars are also allowed to use the library. This outside access is infrequent and transitory. The members of the university are the primary users of the library.

The library system is analogous to the workgroup network. A user with a library card is like a user with an account on an NT system. Each library on a separate campus is like an NT workstation. Visiting professors are like the NT Guest user account and students from other universities are like workstations on the same NT network; they infrequently access the resources of the workstations of one workgroup.

A *resource* is a device attached to a workstation that can be shared. Examples of resources are disk drives and the directories and files they contain, printers, CD drives, and the clipbook. Tape drives can be shared with the addition of third-party applications. Workstations in a workgroup can share each other's resources equally.

Suppose a workgroup consists of two workstations. Each workstation has two hard disk drives. One drive is not shared and is used for NT system files, local applications, and data. The second drive is used for shared applications and data.

CD drives, as well as hard disk drives, can be shared in a workgroup. When we refer to CD drives, we mean read-only drives. CD drives can't be used for the storage of new data. A CD drive is used typically to store applications, application distributions, or multimedia applications, and is far more likely to be shared than non-shared.

Suppose a second example of a workgroup consists of two workstations. One workstation has a hard disk drive and a CD-ROM drive; the other has a hard disk drive and a printer. The CD-ROM drive is shared between both workstations and is used for read-only applications and multimedia applications. The hard disk drive on both workstations is used for local applications and data and isn't shared.

 **NOTE** You must have at least two workstations networked together to make a workgroup. At least one workstation must run either Windows NT or Windows for Workgroups. The other workstation must be running at least Workgroup Connections. A better alternative for two networked computers is to run at least one Windows NT workstation and one Windows for Workgroups workstation. Even better for two networked computers, however, is to run Windows NT on both computers.

Understanding Resource Sharing

Workstations in a network that share each other's resources should be placed in a logical organization, which is the NT workgroup. You must designate which NT workstations become members of the same group. After you've formed the workgroups, you can set up the resources for sharing. For example, after the disk sharing feature is enabled on each system, you can access the shared disk of another workstation in the workgroup. You can execute applications, read from or write to databases, create documents and spreadsheets, and delete or rename files.

A *local drive* is a disk drive that is one of the hardware components of a workstation. A local disk drive is directly connected to the NT workstation through a short (12 to 18 inches or less) ribbon cable. The drive is usually in the workstation's main enclosure, or it may be in an expansion box.

A *remote drive* is the accessible, local drive of another workstation. The physical connection to a remote drive is through the LAN network cable and the network interface card (NIC). The network interface card and cable, along with the network software, enable the interconnection of workstations and the shared access to resources.

Windows NT system applications have different icons for local and remote disk drives. In the File Manager, for example, icons for all current accessible disk drives appear in the drivebar, which is below the toolbar. (The display of the drivebar in the File Manager is enabled by default.) Although the icons are different, your access to the information on local and remote disk drives can be identical.

Figure 26.1 shows the main window of the File Manager. The name of the current system, BOB486, is shown in the title bar of the Program Manager window, which is behind and above the File Manager window.

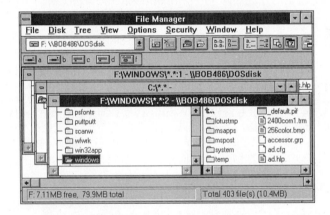

Fig. 26.1

The File Manager window on BOB486.

Drives A and B are local floppy disk drives. Drive D is a local CD-ROM drive. Drives C, E, G, and H are local hard drives. Drive F is a remote hard disk drive. The list box to the left of the toolbar shows a legend for drive F, the currently selected drive. The path for drive F includes a reference to another workstation, BOB386. The slashes preceding BOB386 specify that it is a remote workstation. C$ is the share name of the drive on BOB386. All shared resources on a workstation are assigned a share name.

NOTE The share name C$ can be used to establish a shared drive. However, only members of the group administrators can access the drive referenced through use of the C$ share name.

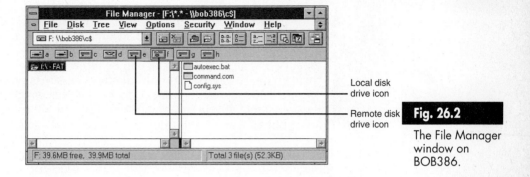

Fig. 26.2

The File Manager window on BOB386.

Figure 26.2 shows the File Manager window for BOB386. BOB386, like BOB486, has two local floppy disk drives, A and B. It also has two local hard disk drives, C and D, and a single remote disk drive, F.

The path for drive F specifies that F is a drive on the BOB486 workstation:

```
\\BOB486\DOSdisk
```

The share name for the local drive on BOB486 (the remote disk drive on BOB386) is DOSdisk. This is a more descriptive name than C$, the share name for the local drive on BOB386 (the remote disk drive on BOB486). You can choose a descriptive share name when a drive is designated available for sharing. A descriptive share name can make it easier for you to locate the correct name for operations that you later perform with the disk drive.

BOB386 and BOB486 are workstation members that are both client and server to one another. A *client* is a workstation that accesses the resources of another workstation. A *server* is a workstation that makes a resource available to another workstation. BOB486 is a server for the drive that appears on BOB386 as drive F. BOB386 is also a server for the drive that appears on BOB486 as drive F. Both systems are clients for access to the other's disk drive.

The default access to shared drives specifies no restrictions. BOB386 and BOB486 have full access to read, change, and delete directories and files on their remote drives. This default implements the equal sharing of resources that is possible in the client-server model.

The BOB386 and BOB486 workstations can be located across the room from one another, in another part of the building, or in an adjoining building if the network cable is run between them. An interconnected group of workstations in close proximity is called a *local area network*, and is the usual configuration for a network of NT workstations.

NOTE A local area network is local only if the interconnected systems are close to one another. Through the use of devices such as bridges, the local area network connection can be extended to any location that can be interconnected through microwave or other frequency transmission techniques. A local area network connected in this way is only logically local. All the capabilities of the network remain the same but all the workstations are not close to each other.

Workstations that need to access each other's resources should be made members of the same workgroup. This is the basic criteria for the formation of workgroups. A workgroup can be defined based on any criteria, however, as long as the workstations are part of the same network.

The administrator controls who is made a member of the workgroup. You need to have administrative access to a machine to change the workgroup it is in. However, you cannot prevent another machine that you do not have administrative access to from joining your workgroup.

Peer-to-Peer Networking

Each workstation running Windows NT or Windows for Workgroups on a workgroup is equal to other workstations on the network. This equality of access to resources is called *peer-to-peer networking*. In such an arrangement, the systems function as both clients and servers to one another.

Suppose two systems are set up as follows:

System A	System B
Local disk	Local disk
Shared disk (local disk of B)	Shared disk (local disk of A)

System A, one of the two workstations, makes its local disk drive available to system B. System A is a disk server for system B. System B is a client of system A because it accesses system A's disk. System B also makes its disk available to system A and is a disk server for system A. System A is a client of system B for access to system B's disk. The peer-to-peer capability of NT allows systems A and B to function as both a client and a server.

The sharing of resources in a peer-to-peer network doesn't have to be equal. Workstations don't have to be both a server and a client of one another. For example, system A could function as a

---

disk server to system B. If system B makes its disks unavailable, it is only a client of system A.

An alternate configuration is one in which a single disk is accessible to multiple NT workstations. For example, another workstation could join workstations A and B for the purpose of sharing access to system A's disk. Both system B and the new workstation, C, become clients of system A. A is a server to both B and C.

Understanding System Administration

A workgroup can have a system administrator for each workstation. A system administrator is the user whose account has the user privileges that enable him or her to use the Administrative applications to control the allocation of the workstation's resources.

Multiple users can use a single workstation at different times with different user rights to control the operations they can perform on the system. If a workstation has multiple accounts, one of the workstation's users can be designated to control the accounts.

If each workstation is used by a single user, however, a system administrator may be designated for the workgroup. Another possibility is to define a workgroup in which some workstations have their own administrator and other workstations share an administrator.

Understanding Workgroup Limitations

There is a practical limit on the number of systems that can be in the same workgroup. One constraint is the speed of the workstation's hardware, including the speed of its disk drives, processor, and system bus. The hardware components of a workstation used as a server may not be fast enough to allow it to serve many workgroup members. The amount of memory available on a workgroup member also constrains the number of systems that it can serve.

Remember that in a workgroup, multiple workstation members function as servers for one another. If all 20 members of a workgroup share a single disk, all 20 members function as servers for disk sharing. The number of members who can work effectively in a workgroup—with some if not all the members functioning as servers as well as clients—is primarily constrained by the speed of the hardware of the workstation members.

In a client-server network system (an alternative to the peer-to-peer model on which Windows NT is based), you can purchase a large, powerful, fast system that is the only server in a group of workstations. If your server system is a Pentium, a MIPS R4000, an Alpha AXP processor, or multiple i486 processors, it can function as a server for several hundred workstations.

In a client-server network, however, individual workstations can't function as servers for one another as they can in a peer-to-peer network. This is an advantage of a peer-to-peer network. You don't need to purchase workstations with the processing and I/O power of a server system.

NOTE   Workstations do not need to be as powerful when they are functioning only as disk servers for one member or a few members of the workgroup. In a workgroup system, if one workstation is to have one or more of its resources shared by as many as perhaps 20 other workgroup members, the workstation must have hardware that is fast enough to allow it to function adequately.

A workstation that meets the minimum hardware requirements for Windows NT—for example, a 386SX 25-MHz system with 12M of memory, an ISA bus, and a 100M disk drive with an average access of 18 milliseconds—may be able to share its disk with two or three other workgroup members if they use the shared disk extensively.

The overall activity on the network through which the workgroup members communicate affects how effectively resources are shared between workgroup members. These two basic factors—the speed of workgroup members and the amount of activity on the network—constrain the maximum number of members in a workgroup. A simple rule for peer-to-peer configured workgroups is to limit the number of members to about 20.

The flexibility of the peer-to-peer network allows powerful Windows NT systems to function as servers for many other workstations very much like in a client-server model. But these systems can still be a client of other workstations in the workgroup. You can initially organize your workstations into workgroups, then later organize them into a configuration that is more centralized.

This type of centralized organization provides some of the features of a client-server network. If you require more of a client-server configuration for your workstations, including the capability to serve dozens or hundreds of clients, you'll want to use the additional features provided by the Windows NT Advanced Server. You can read about these features in the next chapter.

If you limit the members of a workgroup to less than 20, you can allow for the occasional load put on the system by connections to resources from outside your workgroup. A workgroup isn't a security mechanism and it doesn't restrict access to the resources of member workstations. Members of the network can access the resources of workstations outside their own workgroups.

Creating and Attaching to a Workgroup

When you install a basic NT system, you are asked to specify the workgroup that you want to join. If you enter the name of a workgroup that is not currently defined, a new workgroup is created with the workstation on which you're installing NT as its sole member. Later, you can use Network in the Control Panel application to change membership in the workgroup. A workstation can be a member of only one workgroup at a time.

You learned previously that a network can have more than one workgroup. So how do you decide which workstations on a network should be part of a workgroup, and which workstations should be part of the same workgroup? Your criteria for workgroup membership should be based primarily on a requirement for shared resources. You shouldn't place workstations together in the same workgroup if they don't share resources and don't communicate with one another.

You can also define workgroups based on the existing groups in an organization, such as the members of a department. You might define a second workgroup for all first-level managers who deal with similar problems and communicate with one another frequently. You might also form a workgroup consisting of people from different departments who are working on the same project.

Suppose that you can create a workgroup for the sole purpose of sharing a printer. You restrict the workgroup to ten people who work near one another on the same floor. If more than ten members shared the printer, the workload would be too great and the members would have to wait too long for print jobs to be finished. In addition, the number of pages printed per month would exceed the printer manufacturer's recommendations, and your service contract requires that you adhere to the printer manufacturer's recommendations.

Recall that a new workgroup is created the first time you use its name, which occurs either during the installation of a Windows NT system or when you later choose Network in the Control Panel to change the name. Members of the same workgroup are displayed together when you examine the workstations on the network.

Figure 26.3 shows how network information is displayed. The first level of the display is the Microsoft Windows network. The workgroups that are part of the network are indented under the network name. Only a single workgroup, Workgroup2, is defined. Two workstations are part of Workgroup2, BOB386 and BOB486.

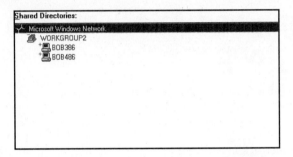

Fig. 26.3

Pictorial representation of workgroups.

This type of network display is part of several dialog boxes that allow connections to remote resources, such as the Connect Network Drive dialog box and the Connect Printer dialog box. (Both of these dialog boxes are explained later in the chapter.)

To designate a workstation as the first member of a new workgroup or to change the membership of a workstation from one workgroup to another, follow these steps:

1. From the Control Panel, choose Network. The Network Settings dialog box appears, as shown in figure 26.4. The current workgroup of the system is Workgroup1.

2. Select the Change button next to the current workgroup name. This displays the Domain/Workgroup Settings dialog box, shown in figure 26.5.

3. Select **W**orkgroup, then change WORKGROUP1 by entering the name of a different workgroup. If the workgroup entered doesn't exist, a new workgroup is created and the workstation becomes its first member.

NOTE You should decide beforehand what workgroup you want to become a member of. When entering the name of a workgroup, it's easy to make a typing error and inadvertently create a new workgroup.

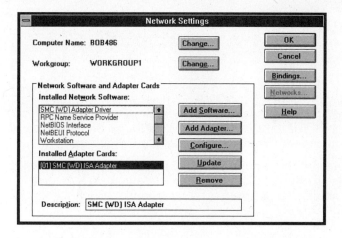

Fig. 26.4

The Network Settings dialog box.

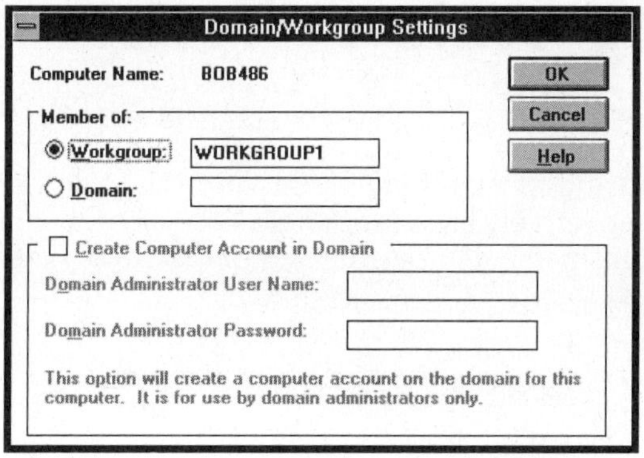

Fig. 26.5

The Domain/ Workgroup Settings dialog box.

4. Select OK when you have changed the workgroup name. This displays a Network Settings message box that verifies your change of workgroup. (Fig. 26.6 shows the message box for a change to Workgroup2.)

Fig. 26.6

The Network Settings workgroup confirmation message box.

5. Confirm the change of workgroup by selecting the OK button. This displays the message box shown in figure 26.7.

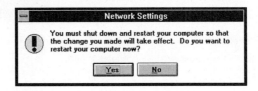

Fig. 26.7

The Network Settings restart message box.

6. Select **Yes** to reboot your workstation so that your shared resources will be available in the new workgroup.

The Domain/Workgroup Settings dialog box, as its name implies, can be used also to specify a domain for your computer. A domain is a more tightly administered group of workstations. You learn about domains in the next chapter.

Logging On to a Workgroup

When you log on to the NT system by pressing Ctrl+Alt+Del, a Welcome logon dialog box appears, as shown in figure 26.8. You must enter a valid username and its matching password in the **U**sername and **P**assword fields, respectively. The **F**rom field lists the defined name for your workstation. This name can be changed only if your system is not part of a workgroup.

Fig. 26.8

The Welcome logon dialog box.

If your username and password are valid, you gain access to the system and are a member of the workgroup defined during the installation of the NT system or through the Domain/Workgroup Settings dialog box. If you enter an invalid username or password, you are prompted to enter the password or change the username. When you reattach to a workgroup, you are reconnected to any shared resources that you previously requested to be automatically reconnected to at logon.

Sharing Workgroup Resources

The resources that can be shared among members of a workgroup are disk drives, their directories and files, printers, CD-ROM drives, and the clipbook. As mentioned, workstations are placed in a workgroup because they need to share at least some resources or because they are in close proximity, which facilitates the sharing of some resources. For example, several workstations that are close to one another and near a printer could become the printer workgroup.

A workstation that has a tape drive can back up the shared disk or directory of another workstation. A tape drive, however, can't be defined as a shared device.

CD-ROM drives are shared in the same way as hard disk drives. They provide access to large amounts of static data and applications, including multimedia applications.

Sharing Directories

The procedure for establishing a disk to be shared is integrated into the File Manager application. You can set up a directory or an entire disk to be shared with other workstation members. You issue one command on the server workstation to enable the disk or directory to be shared. You issue a second command on a client workstation to establish a connection to the disk or directory to be shared. Other commands terminate a connection and disallow a disk or directory from being shared by another workstation member.

 **NOTE** The terminology *setting up a shared directory* is used even when an entire disk is set up to be shared. You should define an entire disk drive to be shared only if other workgroup members require access to all the directories and files of the disk. Otherwise, you should share only the directories that other workgroup members need to access.

When you share an entire disk, you get access to all the files and directories on the disk. If you have write access to the entire shared disk, new files can be placed in any directory on the disk. New directories may also be created on the disk and files placed within them.

When you define an entire disk drive as a shared directory, workgroup members can view it as their drive. A workstation that has only a single local hard drive, for example, could maintain a continuous connection to a remote drive on a second system. As long as the hard drive and the second system are running, the remote disk drive is as available to the workstation as its own local drive.

When a workstation is started, NT automatically attempts to reconnect to its remote drives. If the disk server system is available, the connection is reestablished transparently. If a connection can't be made to a disk drive on a remote system, the Restoring Network Connections dialog box is displayed, as shown in figure 26.9.

Fig. 26.9

The Restoring Network Connections dialog box.

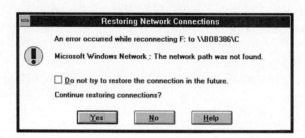

You can allow the system to either continue its attempt to connect to the remote drive or permanently break the connection to the remote disk drive. You may also choose not to have the system continue to attempt to reconnect to the remote disk. The usual reason why the connection can't be restored is that the workstation with the remote drive is turned off.

Setting Up a Shared Directory

To enable a disk for sharing, you must be logged on as an administrator at the server system. Then follow these steps:

1. From the File Manager, choose the **D**isk menu.

2. Choose the Share **A**s command. This displays the Shared Directory dialog box.

3. Select **N**ew Share to display the New Share dialog box, shown in figure 26.10.

4. In the **S**hare Name text box, enter a descriptive name to be associated with the shared disk drive.

5. The **P**ath text box is filled in automatically when you select a shared directory from the shared directory list of the dialog box.

6. In the **C**omment text box, enter a comment (optional). In fig. 26.10, the **C**omment field indicates the type of disk and the workstation on which the disk is located.

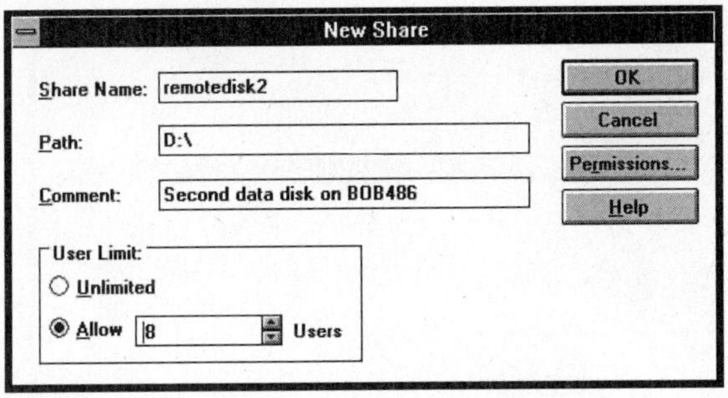

Fig. 26.10

The New Share dialog box.

7. In the User Limit section, the **Allow** option can be used to restrict the users of the shared directory to the number of members of your workgroup. This prevents any other workstations from accessing the disk—if all workstation members are connected. (The preferential method for controlling access is shared directory permissions, which is described at the end of this section.)

> **NOTE**
>
> The Unlimited option is the default. It allows any number of workstations in your network to connect to the drive. This is usually inappropriate for performance as well as security reasons. If workstations outside your workgroup that have no need for the shared directory are allowed to connect to it, their accesses cause the server workstation to respond. This unnecessary activity wastes CPU time on the server workstation—time that could be used for local operations or the remote requests of workgroup members.
>
> An unlimited amount of workstations also negates any security by allowing any workstation in the network to connect to the drive. Although you can use a second mechanism to more precisely control access to files on a shared directory, the user limit should be used to restrict access to the maximum numbers of users who must use the shared directory.

8. Choose OK to make the shared directory available to be connected to by other workstations.

A second mechanism for closely controlling access to files in a shared directory is called *shared directory permissions*. In the New Share dialog box (fig. 26.10), choose the Permissions button. This displays the Access Through Share Permissions dialog box, shown in figure 26.11.

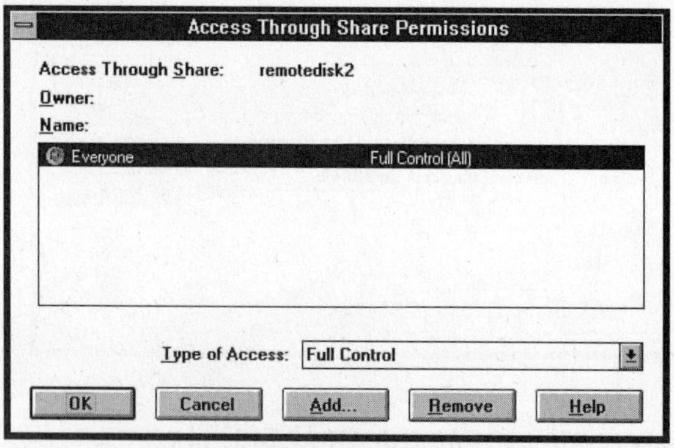

Fig. 26.11

The Access
Through Share
Permissions
dialog box.

You apply permissions to shared directories just as you do to local files
and directories. The default access control list (ACL) entry allows the
Everyone group full access to the shared directory. All local and remote users are part of this group because the Everyone group includes
the Network group, which is all users on other workstations of the network. In figure 26.11, the Everyone group has access to the shared directory on remotedisk2.

The default permissions provide no security because they allow any
workstation to perform any operation to this shared directory. If only
read access is needed to the shared directory, the Type of Access entry
for the Everyone or Network group could be changed to provide only
read access. You can refer to Chapter 29, "Understanding File Security
in Windows NT," which explains file permissions and file security in
detail, to learn how to specify new ACLs for the shared directory.

Connecting a Shared Directory

To set up access to a directory that another workstation has defined to
be shared, follow these steps:

1. From the File Manager, choose the **D**isk menu.

2. Choose Connect **N**etwork Drive to display the Connect Network
   Drive dialog box, shown in figure 26.12.

3. In the **S**hared Directories section, select a shared directory from
   the list. (In fig. 26.12, the APPS shared directory is selected. It is
   located on the BOB386 workstation in workgroup2.)

4. Choose OK. The shared directory appears in the drivebar of the
   File Manager window as a remote disk drive.

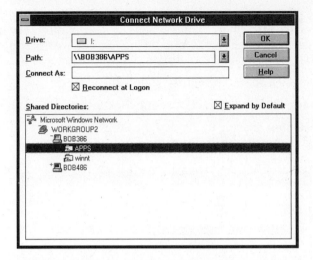

Fig. 26.12

The Connect
Network Drive
dialog box.

Disconnecting from a Shared Directory

To disconnect from a shared directory, follow these steps:

1. From the File Manager, choose the **D**isk menu.

2. Choose **D**isconnect Network Drive to display the Disconnect
   Network Drive dialog box, shown in figure 26.13.

Fig. 26.13

The Disconnect
Network Drive
dialog box.

3. Select the shared directory that you want to disconnect. The system warns you if you attempt to disconnect the shared directory
   when other workgroup members are connected. In the example
   shown in figure 26.13, remote drive D is selected for disconnection.

4. Select the OK button to disconnect from the shared directory.

Stopping Directory Sharing

Workgroup members typically remain connected to the directories that
they need to share. Although they may disconnect from the shared

directories temporarily, the shared directories remain defined to be shared. You use Stop Sharing only when the shared directory must be made inaccessible to all workgroup members. The workstation that has stopped sharing its shared directory still has local access to it.

To stop sharing a shared directory, follow these steps:

1. From the File Manager, choose the **D**isk menu.

2. Choose Stop Sharing to display the Stop Sharing Directory dialog box, shown in figure 26.14.

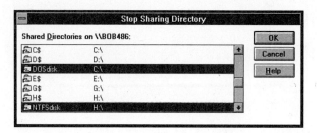

3. Select one or more shared directories. (In the figure, two shared directories on the BOB486 workstation, DOSdisk and NTFSdisk, are selected to be made unavailable to members of the workgroup.)

4. Choose OK. A dialog box appears, informing you of users who are accessing files remotely. You are also warned that removing the shared device may cause currently connected users to lose data.

5. You can choose to cancel the operation if one or more users are connected to the shared drive. Otherwise, choose OK.

Sharing Printers

You can make printers available to workgroup members easily. You might want to make sure the workstations are close to the printer, so that members don't have far to walk to retrieve their print jobs. The sharing of a printer among members of a workgroup can be accomplished when the printer is defined.

Defining a Printer to Share

To make a printer accessible to the members of a workgroup, the printer must be defined with the shared characteristic. You do this when you define the characteristics for the printer, as follows:

1. From the Print Manager, choose **P**rinter.

2. Choose **C**reate Printer to display the Create Printer dialog box (see fig. 26.15).

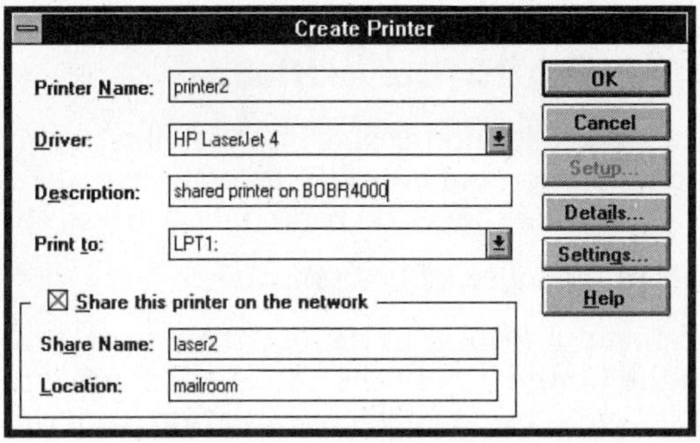

Fig. 26.15

The Create Printer dialog box for a shared printer.

3. Check the box titled **S**hare this printer on the network.

4. In the Sh**a**re Name text box, enter a descriptive name for the printer used by the underlying server mechanism.

5. In the **L**ocation text box, you can enter the location of the workstation and its attached printer.

6. Choose OK.

If you don't initially define a printer to be shared, you can change its characteristics later with the Print Manager, as follows:

1. From the Print Manager, choose **P**rinter.

2. Choose **P**roperties to display the Printer Properties dialog box (see fig. 26.16). The fields are identical to those in the Create Printer dialog box.

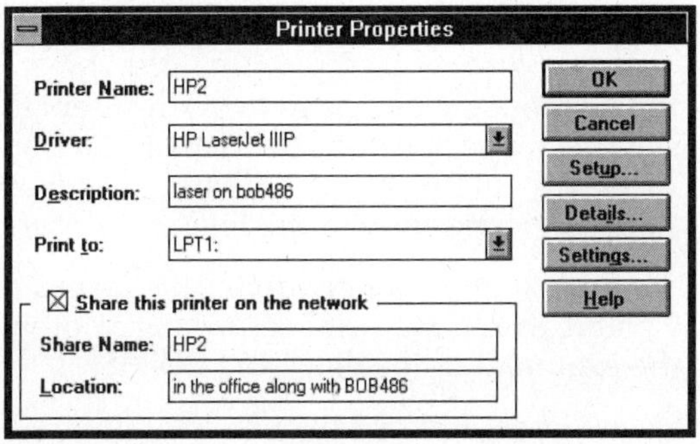

Fig. 26.16

The Printer Properties dialog box for a shared printer.

3. Check the box titled **S**hare this printer on the network. This enables the printer for sharing.

4. Choose OK.

Connecting to a Shared Printer

After a printer has been set up for sharing, you must connect to the printer from each member workstation. To establish access to a printer on another workstation in the workgroup, follow these steps:

1. From the Print Manager, choose **P**rinter.

2. Choose **C**onnect to Printer to display the Connect to Printer dialog box. In the Connect to Printer dialog box in figure 26.17, the printer1 printer on the BOB386 workstation from the workgroup2 workgroup is connected to and made available to the BOB486 workstation.

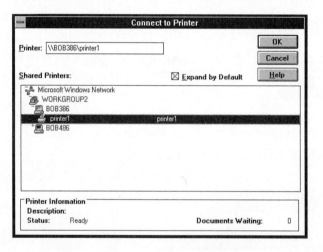

Fig. 26.17

The Connect to Printer dialog box.

3. To display the printers defined as network printers for all the workgroups in the network, check the **E**xpand by Default check box. Or, to display the network printers for a particular workgroup, select a workgroup in the **S**hared Printers region.

4. Choose OK to confirm the connection to the shared printer. The printer is available to receive print requests remotely (from BOB486 in the example) or locally (from BOB386).

Figure 26.18 shows a Microsoft Word document submitted from the BOB486 workstation that is printing on printer1, the remote printer on BOB386.

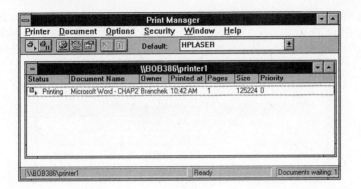

Fig. 26.18

Display of a remote printer in the Print Manager window.

Controlling Access to a Shared Printer

After the printer is connected, you can control access to it through permissions. You can specify permissions to enable only specific users or groups to manage or send requests to the printer. However, to set printer permissions, you must be in the Administrators or Power Users group. See Chapter 31, "Using the Administrative Applications," for more information on specifying file permissions for printers.

The default permissions for a printer grant full control to the Administrators and Power Users groups. The Creator Owner is granted the ability to manage documents in the print queue. All workgroup members are granted the ability to submit requests to the print queue through the Print permission granted to the Everyone group. Figure 26.19 shows the Printer Permissions dialog box for the HPLASER printer on BOB486.

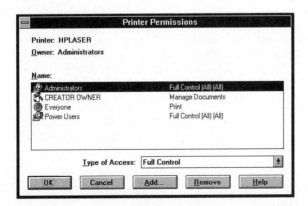

Fig. 26.19

The Printer Permissions dialog box.

If you minimize the printer windows, they are displayed as icons in the Print Manager window. Figure 26.20 shows the three printers available for access from the BOB486 workstation. The icon for the HP2 printer is a local printer icon. The HP2 printer can receive print job requests from only the local workstation.

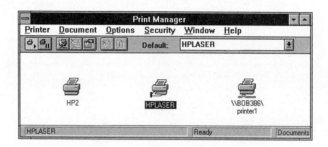

The icon for the HPLASER printer is a local shared printer icon. HPLASER is a local printer physically connected to BOB486, but other workstations in its workgroup can connect to HPLASER and send it print job requests.

The third printer, printer1, is a remote shared printer physically connected to the BOB386 workstation. You can submit print jobs from BOB486 to printer1 on BOB386.

Sharing Tape Drives

Windows NT provides the Backup application so that you can use a tape drive to back up information located on disk drives. Although Windows NT does not allow the direct sharing of tape drives among workgroup members, you can form a workgroup to indirectly share the use of one workstation's tape drive. Then the disks or directories you want backed up can be connected as remote drives of the workgroup member with the tape drive. You can use this technique to back up any drive on any workstation in the workgroup.

Figure 26.21 shows the main window of the Backup application on the BOB486 workstation. Drive F, a remote drive located on the BOB386 workstation, has been selected for backup.

You can add a tape drive to one workstation in the workgroup, then use this workstation only for backup, requiring workgroup members to log on to the workstation to perform a backup. The workstation could have a single hard disk that is only large enough to contain the NT system. You create remote connections from it to all hard drives of the workgroup members. These connections are automatically enabled when the tape drive workstation starts up.

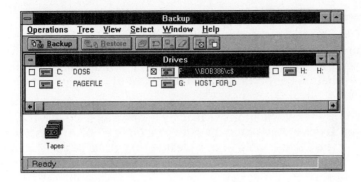

Fig. 26.21

Remote disk drive
in the Backup
main window.

When a member logs on to the backup workstation, you could provide a message that displays a list of the drive letters and the systems on which these drives are located. A member could then back up any drive in the workgroup by simply selecting it from the Backup application.

Another advantage to buying only one tape drive for the workgroup is that you may be able to buy a faster, larger capacity, more expensive tape drive. With a larger capacity drive, you could select all remote drives, then back up their files to one tape cartridge with a single command. A problem in implementing this strategy is that you are limited to a total of 24 letters for referencing your hard drives. You can use *C* to *Z* once to reference the shared drives of the workgroup members. *A* and *B* are used only for floppy drives. To reference more drives, you must disconnect and connect drives to free up drive letters before performing backups.

The example in figure 26.22 shows a backup from a workstation connected to four remote disk drives, or shared directories. All of the remote drives—two from the BOB386 workstation and two from the BOB486 workstation—have been selected for backup. Remote disk drive M is a floppy disk drive. You can remotely connect to a floppy disk drive if a disk is in it when you issue Connect To from the remote workstation.

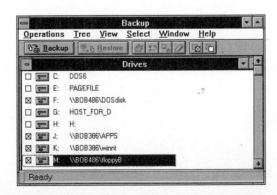

Fig. 26.22

Backup selection
of multiple remote
drives.

Sharing CD Drives

You can set up CD-ROM drives to be shared among members of a workgroup. A CD-ROM drive can be used in a workgroup to keep read-only information continuously available without taking up hard disk space on the local drives of workstation members.

Several types of information are usually located on a CD drive. For example, a CD drive might contain extensive on-line documentation for the use of the system, help in troubleshooting, or large applications such as drawing or CAD programs, which often contain extensive clip-art libraries.

Another use for CD drives is during the installation of new versions of applications. Workgroup members designate the shared drive as the source for the installation. They won't have to change floppy disks as the installation proceeds because the storage capacity of a CD is over 600 megabytes, which is more than enough to store an application on a single CD.

Multimedia applications are stored predominantly on CDs because a large amount of storage space is needed for text, graphics, and full-motion video. For example, you could define a CD drive that contains a multimedia training product that is used separately by each member of the workgroup. A member could use Mail or Chat to signal when he or she has finished using the CD drive, so that the next member may use it. A problem with the shared use of a CD drive for multimedia products, however, is that many require a sound interface card, which is an optional card for most PCs. When buying new systems to be used in a workgroup, you may want to consider buying PC workstations that have built-in sound capabilities.

You set up a CD drive as a shared directory in the same way that you set up any hard drive. Refer to the "Setting Up a Shared Directory" section in this chapter. A data CD disk must be loaded in the drive to connect to the drive from a client workstation. Otherwise, you receive an I/O error message.

Figure 26.23 shows the File Manager window on the BOB386 workstation. The drivebar includes a remotely connected CD drive from BOB486. Note that the icon for the shared CD drive is the same as the icon for a remote hard drive.

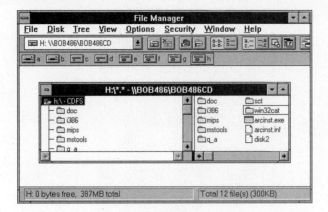

Sharing Clipbook Pages

The clipbook is a *pseudodevice*, which is a software mechanism used like a drive. The clipbook is an extension of the Windows Clipboard, which is a logical structure for the transfer of data between different applications running on a single workstation.

In Windows NT, the clipbook enables data in RAM or the disk memory of one computer to be accessible from another computer. You perform operations with the clipbook using the same sharing procedure you use for disks and printers.

Each page of the clipbook must be set to be shared. To do so, follow these steps:

1. From the ClipBook Viewer, choose **F**ile.

2. Choose **S**hare.

3. Select OK.

Information can be transferred from each workgroup member's local clipboard to a clipbook page. You can transfer any information, including text files, figures, tables, spreadsheets, and pictures in any number of formats.

Figure 26.25 shows one page of the clipbook on the BOB386 remote system that is shared from the clipbook of the BOB486 workstation. The page is expanded to show the graphic (a picture), which is transferred between the workstations. For more information about using the clipbook, see Chapter 15, "Using Desktop Accessories."

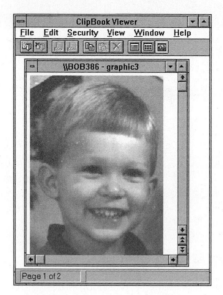

Fig. 26.24

Displaying a
page from a
remote clipbook.

Communicating with Workgroup Members

Several applications are available for communications among members of the workgroup. This section describes three of these applications: Chat, Mail, and Schedule+.

Communicating with Chat

If you are the administrator for all the workstations in a workgroup, you may need to send messages periodically to all workstations. For example, you might send a message to tell workstation users when back-ups will be performed or to notify them of changes to printers or other resources in the workgroup.

Usually, however, no one is assigned the responsibility for the administration of all workstations in the workgroup. Each workstation in the workgroup has its own administrator. When a workstation configuration changes, for example, the user of that workstation must send a message to the other workgroup members to inform them of the change. Coordination in the workgroup is imperative in such a workgroup configuration.

The Chat application enables a workgroup member to type a message that appears simultaneously on each member's screen. The user at the workstation receiving the call selects the Chat icon to display the Chat window. The Chat window's status line displays the connection to the remote system. Anything that is typed appears on both screens, in separate display areas.

In the Chat dialog shown in figure 26.25, the system administrator on BOB486 notifies the user on BOB386 that a tape drive has been added to BOBR4000, the tape backup workstation. The user on BOB386 requests that his local drive C be set up as a remote drive on BOBR4000 so that the local drive can be backed up from BOBR4000

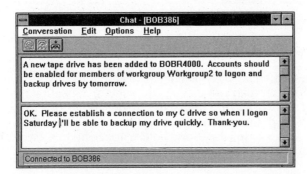

Fig. 26.25
The Chat
window.

With the Chat application, an administrator can notify one or more workstation users of a workgroup event immediately. If necessary, a dialog between the administrator and a user can be initiated to allow an interchange of information. For more information about using Chat, see Chapter 15, "Using Desktop Accessories."

Communicating with Mail

You use the Mail application to leave a message for another member of your workgroup. Mail, unlike Chat, doesn't require that the other workgroup member be logged on to his or her workstation.

Each workgroup has its own Postoffice, and mail cannot be transferred between Postoffices. You can send mail to and receive mail from only other members of your workgroup. You designate a shared directory as the location of the Postoffice. The shared directory must be accessible to all the members in the workgroup.

Figure 26.26 shows a Mail message sent from the administrator of a workgroup to one of the workstation users. You can send the same message to all members of the workgroup. For additional information about using Mail, see Chapter 10, "Using Microsoft Mail."

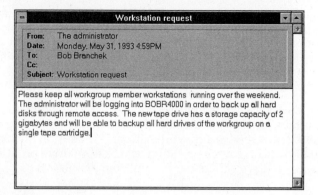

From: The administrator
Date: Monday, May 31, 1993 4:59PM
To: Bob Branchek
Cc:
Subject: Workstation request

Please keep all workgroup member workstations running over the weekend. The administrator will be logging into BOBR4000 in order to back up all hard disks through remote access. The new tape drive has a storage capacity of 2 gigabytes and will be able to backup all hard drives of the workgroup on a single tape cartridge.

Fig. 26.26

A Mail message.

Communicating with Schedule+

You can use Schedule+ to coordinate the activities of your workgroup members. For example, you can use it to set up a meeting time for members of the workgroup to discuss workgroup problems, or you can use it to list the dates and times for regularly scheduled backups of workgroup data. For information about using Schedule+ see Chapter 11, "Using Schedule+."

Summary

Windows NT has peer-to-peer network capabilities to organize groups of workstations for the sharing of resources such as storage devices and printers. NT can also access and share resources among systems that are part of the same network.

You can set up the sharing of hard disks, floppy disks, and read-only CD drives to enable unlimited access to their files and directories by workgroup members. Other workstations in the workgroup can perform the identical operations that a user at the local workstation can, including deleting, renaming, changing, copying, and appending data. Connections to a remote disk can be made transparent and occur automatically each time a workstation is turned on and the NT system is booted.

You can specify one or more printers of a workstation as shareable, which gives workgroup members access to them. The primary purpose of this feature is to reduce the need for a printer at every work-station. High-cost printers such as color printers or high-speed/duplex printers can be placed on a single workstation and shared among workgroup members. You usually share printers among workgroup members who are in close proximity.

A tape drive of a single workstation can be shared indirectly. You can remotely connect the workgroup disks to the workstation member with the tape drive, then back up the remote disks to the workstation's tape drive. This can alleviate the necessity of configuring each workstation with a tape drive to perform backups of its local disk drives.

You use the clipbook as a logical receptacle for the transfer of documents, graphics files, and other data between workgroup members. The clipbook is organized into pages, each of which can have a separate access control. Workstation clipbooks are connected to and disconnected from in the same way as printers and disk drives.

You use system applications to communicate among workgroup members. Chat allows an interactive dialog between workgroup members. Mail allows a message to be stored and read later by workstation members. You can use the Schedule+ application to coordinate the activities and work of workgroup members.

Windows NT basic network features are well integrated and designed for the sharing, control, and coordination of resources among a small number of networked workstations. A small network can evolve into a larger, more centralized configuration with the additional features provided by the Windows NT Advanced Server, which is the subject of the next chapter.

Understanding Windows NT Advanced Server

W indows NT Advanced Server adds several features to the existing Windows NT operating system. One of these is the capability to centralize the creation and maintenance of user accounts. User accounts are stored on a single server workstation and validated when you log on, rather than at each workstation.

The centralization of account information includes the user environment of Windows NT. The basic NT system enables characteristics such as desktop settings and program groups and items to be modified for each workstation user. The Advanced Server enables the user environment information to be stored and maintained on an advanced workstation.

Another feature provided by the Advanced Server enables directories and files to be copied and updated automatically from a server to one or more workstations. These copies are used to improve performance or provide backups.

You also gain additional fault-tolerance features for the storage of information on disks. For example, a continuous copy of all the information on a disk, called a mirrored disk, can be made on a second disk of an Advanced Server workstation. Data can also be stored across multiple disks (called striping) along with error correction information to enable the restoration of data.

The Advanced Server also enables you to fully use features provided with the basic NT system, such as the Remote Access feature. You can use this feature to log on to an Advanced Server system and perform centralized account administration tasks or other administrative operations for the entire network.

Understanding Client-Server Features

The first of the additional features provided with the Advanced Server system is the capability to organize a network of NT workstations in a client-server configuration, rather than a peer-to-peer configuration. You can do this without sacrificing the peer-to-peer capabilities of the basic NT system configuration. The capability to implement features of both client-server and peer-to-peer models enables you to more closely adapt the Windows NT network configuration to meet your work requirements.

Centralizing Network Administration

In a Windows NT workgroup—a peer-to-peer network configuration defined with the basic Windows NT system—you create and administer the user accounts on each workstation. You log on to each workstation, and your username and password are validated at each workstation.

If you administer more than one workstation, you must log on to each one to maintain its account database. This is particularly inconvenient if a user has accounts on several workstations and changes must be made to each.

In a network of NT workstations configured with at least one workstation executing the Advanced Server NT software, you can log on from a workstation to the group of NT systems. This feature enables logon access control to be maintained from one workstation.

Grouping Workstations

The peer-to-peer workgroup configuration also restricts you to a small number of total workstations, approximately 20, in each workgroup. The workstation limit is not imposed by the developers of the NT system; it is a guideline for configuring NT networks.

To extend the 20-workstation limit of the basic NT network, you can use NT workstations with faster processors or multiple processors and large, fast disks, which will perform server tasks faster. This allows more workstations to interact as clients and servers and still have acceptable performance. However, you won't be able to extend your network to a configuration in which your servers support 10,000 NT workstations, which is the limit suggested by Microsoft for an Advanced Server network. The maximum number of workstations in an NT network can be significantly fewer than 10,000, depending on the processing power of the server workstations and other hardware components. In a client-server configuration, such as one that can be implemented with the Windows NT Advanced Server, one NT workstation functions as a server rather than all the workstations functioning as workstations and servers. This unloads multiple workstations from server responsibilities, including the CPU and I/O processing work to service client workstations and disk and printer requests.

You can use a powerful single-processor system such as the Digital Alpha AXP, MIPS R4000 or R4400, or Intel Pentium system for your NT server. You also can use multiple Intel 486 or Pentium systems because of the symmetric multiprocessing capability of Windows NT. Symmetric multiprocessing enables several applications, or parts of a single application, to execute simultaneously.

 **NOTE** Multiple CPU systems are particularly advantageous for use as servers because I/O requests from client systems can be handled while other operations, such as account validation, are performed in a second processor of the system. Multiple server requests can be performed at one time, which greatly increases the number of workstation clients that can be served.

Protecting Data with the Advanced Server

The client-server implementation provided by the Advanced Server provides advantages as a disk server. You can place the applications and data files on the disk of an Advanced Server system. The additional fault-tolerant disk storage technique of mirror sets and stripe sets with parity (discussed in the "Fault-Tolerance Features" section) can be used to decrease the probability that the applications and data are lost or corrupted. These features also provide a type of data backup that isn't available with the basic NT system.

Conventional backups are easier to perform with the Advanced Server system. All applications and data are on the disk of the server. A back-up of the server's disks backs up all data and applications and can be performed at the server.

In the basic workgroup peer-to-peer configuration, you typically don't have a single-disk server system. You must set up one of two configura-tions for backup. In the first configuration, you provide a tape drive for backup on each workstation in the workgroup. Backups are performed from the local workstation to its own tape drive.

An alternate workgroup peer-to-peer configuration is a form of central-ized backup that was discussed in Chapter 26. You designate a single workstation in the workgroup as the backup workstation. You connect all disks in the workgroup as remote disks (up to the 24-disk limit im-posed by using the letters of the alphabet to reference disks). You then can back up the remote disks to a tape drive located on the backup workstation.

With the Windows NT Advanced Server, you gain centralized backup capability without having to connect to the disks of all workstations. You've defined a single server system that is the disk server for the network. The tape drives on this server system back up only its local drives because they contain the applications and data of the users.

You still can allow users to keep applications and data available on local drives. You also can allow them to share the information on the drives with other members of the network through remote connections to shared directories. The Advanced Server enables you to implement the features of both the client-server and peer-to-peer models.

Understanding Domains

A different name is used for the set of interconnected NT systems in the client-server configuration provided by the Windows NT Advanced Server. A *domain* is the group of NT workstations that are part of a Win-dows NT Advanced Server network. The domain is the equivalent of the workgroup set up through the basic features of an NT system. Not all workstations in a domain need to be executing the Windows NT Ad-vanced Server. You need to load and boot the Windows NT Advanced Server software on only a single workstation, which is called the *do-main controller.*

NOTE It may seem obvious, but you must have a workstation that is executing the Windows NT Advanced Server to create a domain. If all your workstations are executing the basic system, you can create only one or more workgroups rather than a domain.

Creating Domains

You create user accounts from a domain controller as one of the centralized administration features of the Advanced Server. The user account is a domain account that enables you to log on to any workstation in the domain, unless you are restricted to logging on to selected workstations for security reasons. Logons to the domain are checked against the entries kept in the account server database on a domain controller.

A more detailed definition for a domain than the one cited earlier is that it is the group of workstations that share a set of user accounts that are stored and validated at logon by a domain controller. The defining component of the domain is the centralized control of account information.

An additional type of group that can be referenced throughout the domain, rather than locally as a single workstation, can be defined on an Advanced Server network. This type of group, called a *global group*, can be used to selectively control access to resources. After a logon is successful, global groups are used to provide access control to the resources of the workstations in the domain. You read about global groups later in this chapter, in "Using Global Groups."

Logging On to a Domain

When you log on to a workstation that is part of a domain, you can log on to the domain or your local workstation, if you have an account on it. Figure 27.1 shows the Welcome logon dialog box for the BOB386 workstation, which is a member of the BRANCH1 domain. The down-arrow button of the **F**rom field is selected to display a choice of logon to either the default domain, BRANCH1, or the local workstation, BOB386.

When users log on to the domain, they have access to any domain resources that were provided by you. The Advanced Server provides close control over the resources of the domain, including the system itself. For example, the hours of allowable access to the domain can be controlled from the domain controller workstation.

Fig. 27.1

The logon dialog box for a work-station in a domain.

Controlling User Access by Time

To better secure the system, you might want to limit the times when a user can gain access to the domain. For example, you could set up a Guest entry that can be used only during business hours.

To restrict hours of access, first choose the User menu from the User Manager. Then choose **P**roperties to display the Users Properties dialog box. Select the H**o**urs button. This displays the Logon Hours dialog box, shown in figure 27.2. You use the cursor to select blocks of hours, then select the **A**llow or **D**isallow buttons to enable or disable the selected hours for access the account, which is shown in the User field.

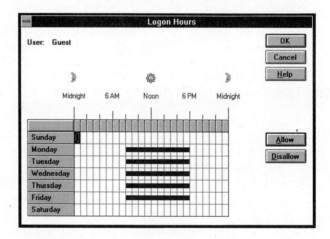

Fig. 27.2

The Logon Hours dialog box.

In figure 27.2, the hours of access to the system are restricted to the hours of 8 A.M. to 6 P.M. on Monday through Friday. No access to the domain is possible on the weekend. If you attempt to log on to the domain using the Guest account outside the allowed hours of access, you receive a Logon Message box that displays the reason for the denial of access. Figure 27.3 shows the Logon Message box for an attempted logon to the domain on a Sunday. For security, the message does not display the allowable hours of access. (If unauthorized users attempt access, you do not want to notify them of the times when they can attempt to break into the domain.)

You can enforce the hours of access to a workstation both at logon and while users are on the system. To do so, choose **P**olicies from the User Manager. Then choose Account to display the Account Policy dialog box. Figure 27.4 shows the Account Policy dialog box for the domain controller workstation. If you check the box at the bottom of the screen, **F**orcibly disconnect remote users from server when logon hours expire, users are logged off their workstations if they attempt to continue working beyond their allowed hours of access.

Controlling User Access by Workstation

The centralized control of the domain provided by the Advanced Server makes it possible to create a list of workstations from which logons are allowed and disallowed for each user account. From the User Properties dialog box, choose the **L**ogon From button. This displays the Logon Workstations dialog box. The default entry for a user account is User May Log On To **A**ll Workstations. Alternately, you can enter the names of the workstations from which a user may log on.

Figure 27.5 shows the Logon Workstations dialog box for the Branchek user account. The Branchek user may log on from only the BOB386, BOB486, and DOS386 workstations.

Fig. 27.5

The Logon
Workstations
dialog box.

You should think of the logon procedure as a log on to the domain that
gives you direct access to a workstation. Unless you have an account at
the local workstation, you cannot log on to the workstation if its name
isn't in the list of workstations in the Logon Workstations dialog box.
Figure 27.6 shows the message box displayed after an unsuccessful
logon attempt with a user account that doesn't have the workstation in
its Logon Workstations list.

Fig. 27.6

The Logon
Message box
for a disabled
workstation.

The message box specifies that you cannot log on from this workstation and suggests that you log on from another workstation. Remember
that you can still log on to the local workstation rather than the domain
if you can select the workstation's name in the From list of the Welcome logon dialog box (refer to fig. 27.1).

Using Global Groups

Global groups are used along with permissions on Windows NT domains
to control access to the resources of an NT system. They supplement the
built-in Network and Everyone groups, which include members of remote
NT workstations. (Global groups and local groups are represented with
different icons.) Several global groups are defined automatically by NT
and are added to built-in local groups.

Understanding Groups

A *global group* is a set of user accounts that is known to all members of a domain. Global groups are defined in addition to the system and user-defined groups of each workstation. Directory and file permission entries that reference local groups apply only to user accounts on a local workstation. Unlike local groups, directory and file permission entries that reference a global group can apply to user accounts on remote workstations as well as the local workstation.

The creation of global groups is the feature of the Windows NT Advanced Server that allows selective access control to workstation resources in a domain. Selective remote access to the resources of a workstation isn't possible in basic NT workgroups. You can't selectively control the access users on individual workstations have to shared files, directories, disks, and other workgroup resources.

In a workgroup network, you can use the two built-in groups—Everyone and Network—to identify users at other workstations. The Network group allows any access to a workstation resource that originates from a user at a remote workstation, rather than the local workstation. The Everyone group includes the accesses of any user on the local or remote workstation.

You'll recall from Chapter 26 that a local workstation is the one that you're sitting in front of and using to enter commands. A remote workstation is any other workstation that you can connect to on a network. Remote workstations are usually part of a workgroup or a domain.

You can't selectively control the remote access to the resources of a workstation with these two groups. Any permission that you set for either Network or Everyone applies to the users at other workstations in the workgroup when they remotely access your system. You can't allow different types of access for users on different workstations because these groups don't provide selectivity.

The remaining groups that you can use with permissions to selectively control resource access in a workgroup are local groups. *Local groups* are user accounts whose members are on the local workstation. The local groups are Users, Power Users, Administrators, Backup Operators, Guests, Interactive, and Creator Owner. Each workstation has its own set of local groups.

Local groups are used to control access to the resources of the local workstation from different user accounts on the local workstation. If you define file permissions that reference the Users group, the permissions apply only to the members of the Users group on the local workstation.

For example, figure 27.7 shows the file permissions for demo.txt. The permissions for demo.txt prohibit access to the file by members of the Users group. If you log on to a remote workstation using the username and password of someone in the Users group, you can access the file. You've denied access to the local Users group, not to members of the Users group on other workstations in the workgroup.

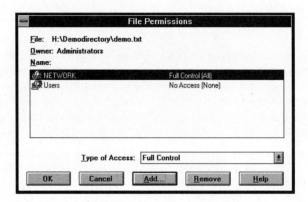

Fig. 27.7

The access control list for the demo.txt file.

The other entry in the access control list allows access to the demo.txt file by the members of the Network group. Any user attempting to access the file from another workstation is a member of the Network group. (Remember that the Network group is one of two groups you can reference when you define access control entries for users on remote workstations.) In an NT workgroup, there is no way to allow a user on one remote workstation to access a file but prevent another user on another remote workstation from accessing the same file.

The only other group that controls access to the resources of a local workstation from users on remote workstations is the Everyone group. The Everyone group includes all users at both the local workstation and remote workstations. You can't use the Everyone group to selectively control access by local and remote users to local system resources.

Visually Differentiating Global Groups from Local Groups

Local and global groups are represented by different icons, as shown in figure 27.8. The local group icon depicts two users in front of a workstation, and pictorially represents the workstation limitation of local groups. The global group icon depicts two users in front of a globe, representing multiple users and user accounts in the domain. The globe represents the cross-workstation definition of a global group.

The local and global group icons appear in applications such as the File Manager and the Print Manager. You can see combinations of global group icons in the permissions entries associated with workstation resources such as files or printers. For example, see figure 27.9, which is the File Permissions dialog box of the File Manager for the demo2.txt file.

```
┌─────────────────────────────────────────────────────┐
│  ─               File Permissions                    │
│                                                       │
│  File:   H:\Demodirectory\demo2.txt                  │
│  Owner: Administrators                                │
│  Name:                                                │
│  ┌─────────────────────────────────────────────────┐ │
│  │ Administrators           Full Control (All)       │ │
│  │ Everyone                 Change (RWXD)            │ │
│  │ Sales Unit Managers      Read (RX)                │ │
│  │ Server Operators         Change (RWXD)            │ │
│  │ SYSTEM                   Full Control (All)       │ │
│  │                                                   │ │
│  └─────────────────────────────────────────────────┘ │
│                                                       │
│      Type of Access:  Read                       ▼   │
│  ┌──────┐ ┌────────┐ ┌───────┐ ┌─────────┐ ┌──────┐  │
│  │  OK  │ │ Cancel │ │ Add...│ │ Remove  │ │ Help │  │
│  └──────┘ └────────┘ └───────┘ └─────────┘ └──────┘  │
└─────────────────────────────────────────────────────┘
```

One of the entries in the list, the Sales Unit Managers group, grants its members the standard file permission read. The global icon to the left of the Sales Unit Managers entry identifies it as a global group. The first entry, which grants Full Control to the Administrators group, is displayed with the local group icon.

You create global groups that are made up of user accounts from the domain in which the user accounts are defined. You can use up to 20 characters (uppercase and lowercase) as part of the global group name, with the exception of the following characters:

    ? + : ; " | = , * < > [ ] / \

Creating Global Groups

You define global groups from a domain controller using the User Manager for Domains application in the Administrative Tools program group. Select New **G**lobal Group from the **U**ser menu to bring up the New Global Group dialog box. You enter the name and a short description of the global group in this dialog box. Use the **A**dd button to add users or groups to the global group, or use the **R**emove button to remove users or groups from the global group.

 NOTE You can define global groups from any workstation in a trusted domain in addition to the domain controller. Trusted domains are discussed in the next section of this chapter, "Multiple Domains."

Figure 27.10 shows the New Global Group dialog box for the new global group called Instructors. The user account for Bob Branchek is automatically made a member of the global group because it was the selected account when New **G**lobal Group was chosen. After you choose OK, the new global group appears in the list of groups at the bottom of the main window of the User Manager for Domains.

Fig. 27.10

The New Global Group dialog box.

The new global group defined in figure 27.10 can have a local user account, such as the Bob Branchek user account, as its member. Local groups also can be members of global groups, and a global group can be a member of a local group. This enables precise control over the access to domain resources.

Some system-defined global groups automatically become members of local groups when a domain is created. The Domain Admins global group automatically becomes a member of the Administrators group. This permits a domain administrator to perform all operations, including administrative ones, for all workstations in the domain.

Figure 27.11 shows the Local Group Properties dialog box for the Administrators group. The members of the Administrators group for the BOB486 workstation include the Domain Admins global group, which was added automatically when the domain was created.

Group Name: Administrators

Description: Members can fully administer the system

Show Full Names

Members:
Administrator
Branchek
Domain Admins

OK

Cancel

Help

Add...

Remove

To prevent the domain administrator from managing the local group, you can delete the Domains Admins global group from the workstation's Administrators group, but you usually wouldn't delete the Domain Admins global group from your local Administrators group. Even if you plan to perform all administrative activity for your workstation, you may want the domain administrator to function as your backup (when you're unavailable or not logged on). You would remove the Domain Admins global group from your local Administrators group only to provide additional security for your workstation by limiting remote administrative access to the workstation.

The Administrator user account is also automatically made a member of the Domain Admins global group. This membership allows the Administrator account to perform the operations of a domain administrator, including the administration of the domain, the domain controller, and all workstations in the domain.

A second global group, Domain Users, is automatically made a member of your local users group. This gives the Domain Users global group the same access as the local users to the resources of the local workstation.

You can remove the Domain Users global group from your workstation's local Users group to provide a more secure system, but at the expense of accessibility. Figure 27.12 shows the Users local group for the BOB486 workstation that includes an entry for the Domain Users global group. The entry can be removed by selecting the Domain Users global group and then choosing the **R**emove button.

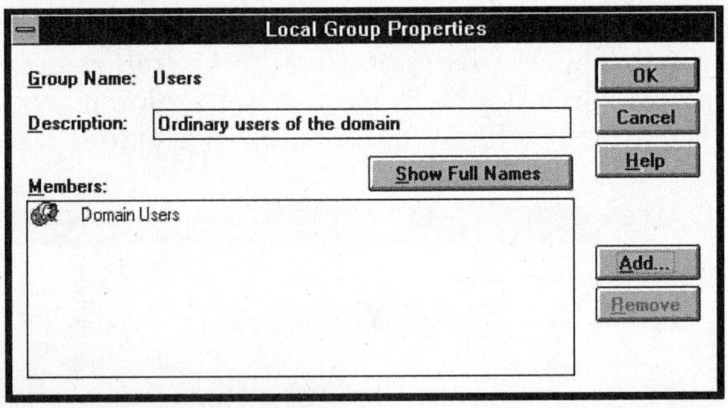

Fig. 27.12

The Local Group
Properties dialog
box for the Users
local group.

Multiple Domains

You can use global groups across multiple domains as well as within
the same domain. You can define the selective control of resources
with global groups across multiple domains that have entered into a
trust relationship.

Domains in a *trust relationship* trust the successful logon to any domain
member to be adequate validation for access to the resources of all
trusted domains. Each domain trusts all other domains with which it
has a trust relationship to perform the account validation—a logon—
for all domains.

A trust relationship provides an extension of the process of account
validation across domains. You log on once and receive access to the
resources of the workstations in the domains that are part of a trust
relationship.

To view or change trust relationships, begin by choosing **P**olicies in the
User Manager for Domains application. Choose **T**rust Relationships to
display the Trust Relationships dialog box. In the example shown in
figure 27.13, the entry in the **T**rusted Domains field shows that
BRANCH1 (the selected domain) trusts the Research domain. The Sales
domain trusts BRANCH1.

Changes can be made to the **T**rusted Domains and **P**ermitted to Trust
this Domain fields. You can add or remove a domain to either of these
fields using their respective set of Add and Remove buttons.

Trust relationships can be created only between Windows NT Advanced Server domains, not Windows NT workgroups. If two domains
must trust one another, entries are made from the domain controllers
of each domain by administrators who are members of each domain's
Domain Admins group.

Domains that are part of a trust relationship use global groups to selectively control access to the resources of workstations. You must add

the global groups from the remote trusted domain to one or more local groups to allow them to be resolved correctly across domains.

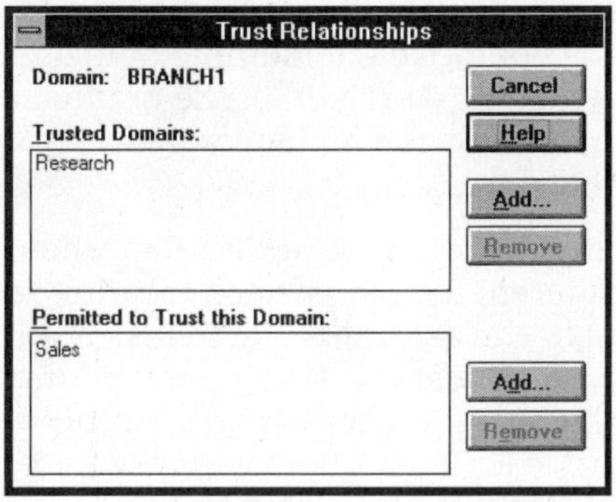

Fig. 27.13

The Trust Relationships dialog box.

To prevent ambiguity, NT applications display the name of the global group preceded by the name of the domain or workstation on which the group was defined. For example, the Instructors global group is preceded by its domain name, Training, in the form Training\ Instructors. Ambiguity would result if the same global group names are defined for different domains of a trust relationship and the global name was shown without the domain name.

Secondary Domain Controllers

More than one workstation in a domain can execute the Windows NT Advanced Server software. In addition to the original domain controller, each Advanced Server workstation maintains copies of the account database for a domain. The domain controller downloads changes in the account database to the other controllers every five minutes to ensure that the copies on the backup domain controllers are valid.

Secondary controllers in a domain are used to replace the primary controller if it fails. If the first controller isn't available, logons at any workstation in the domain can still be verified by a secondary controller. If users also don't have accounts on local workstations, they will be unable to log on if the domain controller is unavailable and there isn't a secondary controller.

Additional controllers also share the load of the primary domain controller for logon validation. Logon requests can be validated from the secondary domain controllers as well as the primary domain controller. When a second workstation in a domain installs the Windows NT Advanced Server system software, the second workstation is defined as a secondary backup controller.

NT Advanced Server Domain Configuration

Large networks can be comprised of multiple domains. You may add a second domain server as the workload of the original domain server increases to the extent that it can no longer provide the necessary throughput on the network.

Multiple domain controllers must be added also when sets of workstations are placed at different locations. Each location requires a domain controller to implement the centralized administration features of the Advanced Server for each location. The separate domains can enter into trust relationships to allow access to each other's resources. Global groups are used to selectively control access to resources among domain users from workstations in different domains.

For example, suppose that a Windows NT network consists of dozens of workstations at two training centers. The training center in Texas has a dozen instructors whose workstations are part of a single domain. The second training center, located in New York, has eight instructors whose workstations are part of another domain. The Txinstructors global group is defined in the Texas domain. A second global group, Nyinstructors, is defined for the New York domain.

The instructors use course material, including student guides and laboratory examples, from the company's course development location in California, which is a third domain. The instructors at both the Texas and New York locations need read access to the student guides and laboratory exercises as they are developed at the California site. The course developers in California don't need access to any of the instructor's workstations in New York or Texas.

To allow access, the three domains are made part of a trust relationship. The instructors from New York and Texas have read access to the course developer's files in California through global groups added to local groups in California. A telecommunications link and bridge at each location allow the three domains to be interconnected.

The Nyinstructors and Txinstructors global groups are added to the newly created local group, Instructors, on the course development workstation in California. The Instructors group isn't one of the built-in groups and should be added before the global groups are defined. The course developer sets the appropriate file permission—read access— to the student guide and laboratory exercise files.

If a continuous network communication connection can be maintained, an alternate configuration could place all workstations at each location in the same domain. Another configuration could define only two domains, one at the New York location and one at the Texas location. The course developer's workstation in California could be part of either domain.

The original configuration uses a domain controller at each location. This configuration is necessary if the network operations cannot be handled by a workgroup configuration. The use of a domain controller at each site is also advantageous because it can be used as the disk server for each site. The disk server benefits the instructors because it results in centralized storage of their course materials as well as centralized account organization.

Directory Replication

The Windows NT Advanced Server includes a feature that enables you to specify directories and files for automatic duplication from an Advanced Server to other workstations. The duplicated directories and files are continuously updated when the original directories and files are changed on the server system.

The directory replication feature saves you from having to manually make copies of master files that are read at local workstations but updated at the server. These files can function as backup copies of the originals, so you still have copies of important files to work with if the server is unavailable.

A second reason for maintaining multiple copies of files across workstations is to improve performance. An individual server may be unable to allow timely read access to all members of a domain. A server may provide poor performance if it must allow all workstations access to a single copy. You can achieve better performance by exporting copies to one or more workstations, then splitting read requests to multiple workstations.

Only the original set of directories and files can be copied on a system executing the Windows NT Advanced Server. This system is called an *export server.* You can designate Windows NT and Windows NT Advanced Server workstations as systems to which directories and files are replicated. These systems are called *import computers*, or import systems. You can define workstations as import computers in a different domain from the export server.

The Advanced Server features provide a simple way to perform replication. Subdirectories and files that you place in the C:\WINNT \SYSTEM32\REPL\EXPORT directory are automatically exported to an import computer in the C:\WINNT\SYSTEM32\REPL\IMPORT directory. To enable directory replication, you must create a special account for each export server and import computer. You use the User Manager for Domains application to create this special account with the following characteristics:

- Password Never Expires
- User Must Change Password at Next Logon disabled
- No hourly restrictions for logon
- A member of Backup Operators, Domain Users, and Replicator groups of the domain
- A member of the Replicator group for each import workstation
- Log On As a Service user right granted to the domain and local Replicator groups

You must also use the Server Manager to set the Directory Replicator service to start automatically using the special user account that you created.

To define a Windows NT Advanced Server system as an export server, begin by choosing the **C**omputer menu of the Server Manager. Choose **P**roperties to display the Properties dialog box. Choose the **R**eplication button to display the Directory Replication dialog box. Select the **E**xport Directories toggle button, then use the **A**dd button to add the name of the system to export files to in the **T**o List field. Choose OK to complete the operation.

Figure 27.14 shows the Directory Replication dialog box for BOB486. The BOB386 NT workstation is defined as the system on which directories and files are replicated. You can automatically replicate directories and files across multiple systems by entering the systems in the **T**o List. The **I**mport Directories toggle button and its corresponding **A**dd button can be used to designate Advanced Server workstations from which export servers will replicate directories and files.

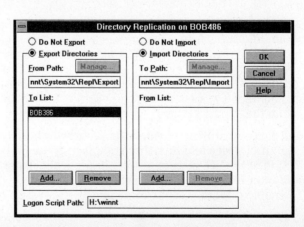

Fig. 27.14

The Directory Replication dialog box for an export server.

Directory replication is enabled also on import workstations. Select the name of the import workstation from the main window of the Server Manager on the domain controller. Then select the **R**eplication button displayed in the Properties dialog box. This displays a Directory Replication dialog box used to specify the replication for an import workstation, as shown in figure 27.15.

Fig. 27.15

The Directory Replication dialog box for an import workstation.

The **I**mport Directories toggle button is selected to allow the entry of an export server in the Fr**o**m List using the A**d**d button. BOB486 is the export server from which directories and files are replicated to the import directories on BOB386.

When the OK button is chosen, the Directory Replication service is started on each system. You can use Services from the Control Panel to ensure that the Directory Service is set up to start automatically each time the system is booted using the special account you created for directory replication.

User Profiles

One feature of the basic NT system enables you to define different Windows environment profiles for users. This gives each user a desktop environment tailored for his or her use. The environment information includes desktop characteristics, the screen saver and colors, printers, shared directories, mouse settings, and the position and size of windows. It also includes program groups and items available when you log on to the system. The basic NT system maintains this information on its local workstation.

The additional features provided by the Advanced Server also enable the user profile information to be maintained in a central location like user accounts. The central maintenance of user profiles provides several benefits. You can log on to any workstation in the domain and use your user profile to provide an identical user environment. You can also create a uniform environment by defining a profile to be used by multiple accounts.

You can use the user profile feature to control system use and improve the security of the system. The user profile can be defined to restrict one or more users in the operations they can perform in some system applications. For example, you can disable the **R**un command from the Program Manager or disallow changes to program groups and items for one user or a set of users. Users are still allowed to make changes in their environment, but only in the range determined by their user profile.

You create a user profile with the User Profile Editor of an Advanced Server system or from the Windows NT Resource kit. You must be part of the Administrators or Domain Admins group to use the User Profile Editor. Your current Windows NT environment is used by the User Profile Editor as a template for the creation of a new profile. Therefore, first set up your NT environment in the way it should be for the users who will later use the profile.

Select the User Profile Editor icon in the Administrative Tools program group to display the User Profile Editor dialog box. You specify additional environment characteristics for the new profile through fields in this dialog box. For example, you enable or disable the use of program groups and allow or disallow users from saving settings they have made during a workstation session.

Figure 27.16 shows the User Profile Editor for the creation of a new user profile. The profile is defined for the Smith user account, which is in the BRANCH1 domain. The **R**un command in the **F**ile menu is disabled, and changes made to the profile can't be saved. No startup groups are defined, and the Administrative Tools, Games, and Startup program groups are unavailable. A user can make changes to unlocked program groups but cannot change the printer connections for the Print Manager. The profile is saved as a file, H:\WINNT\smith.man, which is displayed in the title bar of the dialog box.

You have several options for saving profile settings. From the **F**ile menu of the User Profile Editor dialog box, you can save the profile for the account in which you are currently working. You can specify that the profile will be the default for the system or for the selected user. The last change is saving the profile as a file. This makes it easier to specify the profile for one or more users as well as edit the profile by bringing it into the User Profile Editor with the **O**pen command from the **F**ile menu.

NOTE Program items in a program group you define as a startup group are started automatically when a user logs on with this profile. You probably don't want to choose system groups such as Accessories or Main because they contain many program items. One disadvantage of automatically starting up several applications at logon is that you can exhaust RAM and virtual memory, which causes the system to slow down dramatically. Start automatically only the applications that the workstation can support with its current configuration of RAM and allocated virtual memory space in the page file on disk.

If you save a profile as a file, you must specify the location and name of the file. Begin by choosing **P**roperties in the User Manager for Domains application. Select the P**r**ofile button to display the User Environment Profile dialog box. In the **U**ser Profile Path field, enter the name and location of the profile file. The profile file should be entered on a shared directory so that it can be located and used when a user logs on at any workstation in the domain.

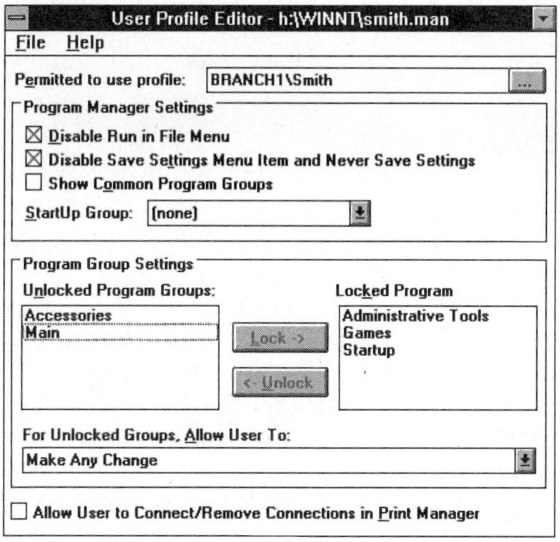

User Profile Editor - h:\WINNT\smith.man
File   Help

P**e**rmitted to use profile: `BRANCH1\Smith` `...`

Program Manager Settings

☒ **D**isable **R**un in File Menu
☒ **D**isable Save Se**t**tings Menu Item and Never Save Settings
☐ Show **C**ommon Program Groups

StartUp Group: `[none]` ⯆

Program Group Settings

Unlocked Program Groups: Loc**k**ed Program

Accessories   Administrative Tools
Main   Games
                                     Startup
          `Lock ->`

          `<-Unlock`

For Unlocked Groups, **A**llow User To:
`Make Any Change` ⯆

☐ Allow User to Connect/Remove Connections in **P**rint Manager

Fig. 27.16

The User Profile Editor dialog box.

You can create the user profile as one of two types of profile files: mandatory or personal. A mandatory profile file has a file type of MAN. Changes made to the user environment during a session for a user account assigned a mandatory profile are always reset to the mandatory profile at the next logon. A mandatory profile can be used by more than one user account.

A personal user profile file is created with a file type of USR. A personal user profile is designed to be used by only one user account. Changes made to a personal profile are saved and are in effect for the next logon.

Fault-Tolerance Features

The features of the basic NT system permit you to create volume sets and stripe sets without error correction. The techniques of volume and stripe sets extend the storage capacity of a single disk to multiple disks, which may be necessary for the storage of a large database file, for example.

The Windows NT Advanced Server system adds two fault-tolerance techniques for disk storage: the creation of mirror sets and the creation of stripe sets with parity. Both of these techniques can be used to decrease the probability that data and applications are irretrievably lost in a Windows NT network.

Striping and mirroring are two of several techniques for the storage of data on multiple disks. This group of techniques is called RAID, or Redundant Array of Independent (or Inexpensive) Disks.

NOTE The *I* in RAID originally meant Inexpensive because the technique was developed to allow multiple inexpensive disks to be used collectively for data storage. The disks were inexpensive when compared to the cost of the single large disks used on mainframe computer systems. The word *Independent* is a better one to use in the RAID acronym to emphasize the use of multiple small disks rather than their cost.

Creating and storing data on volume or stripe sets rather than on a single large-capacity disk also improves I/O performance. Data stored on multiple disks can be accessed faster than data stored on a single disk, because all or part of the data transfer operations can be performed simultaneously.

You can increase performance for disk operations by placing data that you reference at the same time on different disks. The advantage of placing data on different disks is that the disk drives (or the interface board through which the drive is connected to the system) contain enough hardware logic to allow at least part of simultaneous requests to two or more drives to be performed at the same time. With multiple data requests to the same disk drive, each previous request must be completed before the next request is processed.

Another way to increase performance is to place your files and applications on a different disk than the page file used by the Windows NT system. Windows NT uses the page file as a logical extension of RAM, and performs read and write operations to and from it frequently. The less RAM and the smaller page file that you have, the more read and write requests the NT system must make. If your data and application files are on the same disk as the page file, your requests to that disk must contend with the I/O requests to and from the page file.

PC Disk Choices

PC workstations typically have IDE (Integrated Drive Electronics) disk drives. These drives don't allow the simultaneous transfer of data on two or more drives. You can benefit from splitting I/O across separate disk drives only if you use a drive such as a SCSI (Small Computer Systems Interface) drive. Many interface cards used with these drives provide the capability for the simultaneous transfer of at least part of the I/O requests to or from two or more drives.

If you are purchasing PC workstations for Windows NT or Windows NT Advanced Server, there are several advantages to choosing SCSI drives instead of IDE drives. Most IDE controllers support only two drives, but SCSI controllers support up to seven drives. IDE drives are used predominantly on PC systems. SCSI drives are used across computer systems. Other computers are more likely to have a SCSI interface board and software driver, so moving a SCSI disk drive to another computer is easier.

A disadvantage to SCSI drives on PC systems is that they are a little more expensive than IDE drives for the equivalent speed and storage capacity. The interface cards for SCSI disk drives are also more expensive than the interface cards for IDE disk drives. (The price disadvantage of a SCSI controller card can be offset if you also are purchasing a CD and tape drive for your system because the same SCSI interface card may be used also for many CD drives and large-capacity tape drives.) Note, however, that the performance advantage of SCSI disk drives when used for a Windows NT system outweigh these disadvantages.

Mirror Sets

You use the mirroring feature of the Advanced Server to set up a continual backup of a disk drive partition. A disk drive partition is simply a logically contiguous area (one region) of a disk referenced by a letter and treated as a logical disk. A mirror set enables you to designate that a partition of a disk drive—and all data written to it—are automatically copied to the partition of a second disk drive. If the first drive fails and you can't access the data in the original partition, you can use the second, or mirrored, partition.

Mirroring provides a dynamic copy of a partition—the changes to the original partition are continually replicated on the second drive. Although mirroring does provide a type of backup capability, you cannot rely on it completely as a backup copy of your data.

The mirroring feature won't help you recover information from deleted files. If you delete a file from the original partition, for example, it is deleted also from the mirrored copy. You must still rely on a tape backup of files to recover files inadvertently deleted from the mirrored set. Mirroring is considered one of the RAID techniques for data storage on disks and is referenced as RAID level 1.

 NOTE Mirror sets can degrade write performance because all the information in the disk partition is recorded twice. The increase in data reliability through the creation of an immediate copy, however, greatly outweighs the performance disadvantage.

You can break apart mirrored sets without the loss of the data stored in the partitions, and assign the partitions their own drive letter for reference. You can delete a mirrored partition to recover space, just as you can delete any partition.

You create mirrored sets from the **Fault Tolerance** menu of the Disk Administrator on a Windows NT Advanced Server system. This additional menu is available only in the Disk Administrator application from a workstation executing the Advanced Server system. The choices in the **Fault Tolerance** menu are Establish **Mirror**, **Break Mirror**, Create Stripe Set with **Parity**, and **Regenerate**. A discussion of each of these options follows.

Creating a Mirror Set

You use the Establish **Mirror** option to create a mirrored set. First, you create the partition that you want to have mirrored, then you select it from the main window of the Disk Administrator. On a second drive, you select an area of free space that will become the mirror copy by holding the Ctrl key and clicking the free area. Both the original partition and the second area of free space show as selected. The size of the free area must be equal to or greater than the first partition.

Select Establish **M**irror from the **F**ault Tolerance menu to create the mirrored partition in the area of free space, as shown in figure 27.17. (Establish **M**irror can be selected only after a partition on one drive and an area of free space have been selected.) The mirrored partition is created at an equal size to the original and is assigned a drive letter.

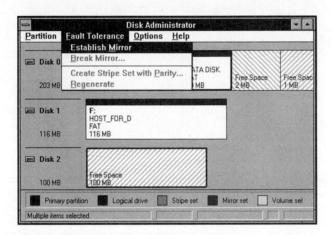

Fig. 27.17

Creating a mirror set.

After you have created the mirror set, it appears in the display of disk regions in the main window of the Disk Administrator. The original partition and its mirror disk region are both assigned the same drive letter and are treated as a single volume. The File Manager shows only a single drive with the storage capacity of the original partition.

Figure 27.18 shows the Disk Administrator window with a mirror set that has been assigned the drive letter G. The status bar at the bottom of the main window indicates that mirror set number zero is selected and is unformatted. The region of free space can be established as part of a mirror set with either a formatted or unformatted partition.

> You should use mirror sets if you can afford the extra disk space that is required. The continuous backup capability can be dramatically useful if the partition of a mirror set is unusable because its hard drive fails. (All hard drives fail eventually.) Even if you back up everything on your disks each day, you will still lose new and changed data written between backups when a drive fails.

T I P

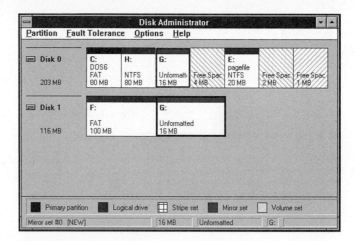

Fig. 27.18

The main window of the Disk Administrator with a mirror set.

Breaking a Mirror Set

You use the **B**reak Mirror option to dissolve a mirror set for two reasons. If the data in one region of the mirror set is unusable, you break the mirror set to reassign the drive letter to the single remaining good partition. You can then use the remaining partition, called an *orphan*, in place of the original. You can also use the free area on another good drive to re-create a new mirrored set.

You use **B**reak Mirror also to discontinue the mirroring of data from an original partition. You might do this simply because you are short of free disk space; you can reestablish the mirrored set when you add another drive to the system. After the mirrored set relationship is broken, you must rely on tape backups of the data in the original partition.

Figure 27.19 shows the selection of **B**reak Mirror that disables a region of a disk as a mirror set. After you select **B**reak Mirror, you must confirm the disabling of the mirror set in the Confirm message box that is displayed.

Stripe Sets

The additional data redundancy feature added by the Advanced Server is a second type of striping. Data in stripe sets is divided into 64K-sized segments, or chunks. Each chunk of data is stored across the number of drives defined for the stripe set. The creation of stripe sets is one of the capabilities of a basic NT system.

The Windows NT Advanced Server system adds another type of disk striping to the disk striping of a basic NT system. This second type of striping adds parity information along with the data stored across

multiple disks. (*Parity* is a form of control information created by performing a mathematical operation on the stored binary data.) The parity information enables you to recover the values of the original data if
it is corrupted by a failure in the recording device or media.

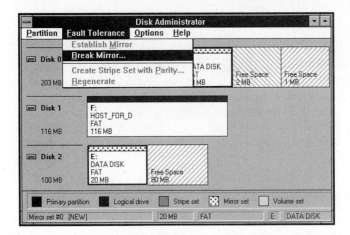

Fig. 27.19

Selecting **B**reak
Mirror from the
Fault Tolerance
menu.

A stripe set with parity can be created in equally-sized areas of free
space on 3 to 32 disks. The parity error detection and correction control information is added to each partition that is part of the striped
set.

Although the information is written across multiple partitions on different disks, the stripe set appears with a single letter for reference. Although there is a cost imposed for both the calculation and storage of
the parity information, read access time is better because the data is
distributed across multiple drives. Disk striping with parity can be used
to improve performance and data reliability.

> One way to get around the 24-drive limitation of NT is to define
> multiple drives as either volume sets or stripe sets. You can use
> more than 24 disks with this technique because each volume or
> stripe set is assigned a single letter.

T I P

Creating a Stripe Set with Parity

You create a stripe set with parity by first selecting areas of free space
on at least three disks in the main window of the Disk Administrator.
Then choose the Fault Tolerance option. In figure 27.20, for example,

three areas of free space on three physical drives (not three lettered partitions on one or two drives) are first selected.

Fig. 27.20

Creation of a stripe set with parity.

Next, choose Create Stripe Set with **P**arity to display the Create Stripe Set With Parity dialog box, shown in figure 27.21. You select the total size of the stripe set in the Create stripe set of total size field. The maximum size for the set is 48M in this example because the smallest of the three areas of free space is 16M. (Stripe set regions are sized approximately equal by the Disk Administrator, and three 16-megabyte disk regions allocate a total storage region of 48 megabytes.)

Fig. 27.21

Create Stripe Set With Parity dialog box.

The completion of the stripe set creation results in three unformatted regions of space referenced by a single drive letter. The total stripe set region is 50 megabytes and is made up of two 17-megabyte regions and one 16-megabyte region. (The Disk Administrator rounds up the total stripe set, so the 48M region was rounded to 50M.)

Figure 27.22 shows the main window of the Disk Administrator after the stripe set has been created. The stripe set is selected and assigned a single drive letter D. The status bar and legend confirm that the selected regions are stripe set 0. Set numbers are placed on striped sets to enable you to differentiate between different stripe sets.

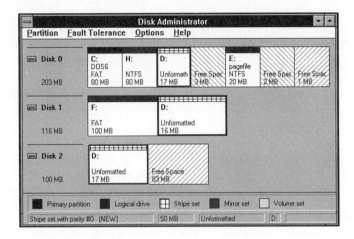

Fig. 27.22

The Disk Administrator window showing stripe set with parity regions.

You can delete a stripe set if you no longer want to maintain the set and the capability it provides. Click any of the three regions of the stripe set, and all of them are selected. Then choose **D**elete from the **P**artition menu of the Disk Administrator. This displays the Confirm message box. You are cautioned that the deletion of the stripe set will result in the loss of data in the partitions.

Regenerating a Stripe Set

You use **R**egenerate in the **F**ault Tolerance menu of the Disk Administrator to recover information in the stripe set if the stripe set is corrupted. Even when an entire partition of the stripe set is lost, your data can be regenerated by using the parity information in the remaining members of the stripe set.

Select the stripe set and an area of free space that is of equal or greater size to recover the data. Next, choose **R**egenerate from the **F**ault Tolerance menu. To initiate the regeneration process, reboot the system. The data will be recovered in the free area as a background operation. A message appears in the status bar of the Disk Administrator when the operation is finished.

Remote Access Service

You can log on to any workstation in the domain from your workstation using the Remote Access Service. A remote logon over a modem, XLS, or other serial link is called a *remote access* and is controlled by the Remote Access Service software. The default installation of Windows NT does not automatically install the Remote Access Service. You can install it from the network in the Control Panel of the main group.

You use the Remote Access Service to log on to an NT system for user or administrative access. You can log on remotely to access a server or workstation system while you're away from the office. If you're traveling on business, for example, your access to the system might be from your hotel room.

 **NOTE** You can optionally use a direct connection—a null modem cable connected between the serial ports of a client and server system—for a remote access connection. This technique is limited to the length of the cable and the dedication of one communications port on each system. The client and server system must be in close physical proximity, such as in the same room or on the same floor, to use this procedure.

The Remote Access Service is installed on your system in a separate common program group created with the group property description Remote Access Service. Two program item applications and a file of information are displayed in this program group. You use the Remote Access application to initiate and maintain the access information from the client system. (A client system is the NT workstation that initiates access to an NT system that establishes itself as a remote access server.)

The Remote Access Service Admin application establishes a workstation as a remote access server. Figure 27.23 shows the Remote Access Service common program group and the icons for its two applications. The Read Me icon is associated with a file containing information about the use of the Remote Access Service.

You select the Remote Access icon to display the Remote Access dialog box. The phone book entries in the dialog box are used to begin a remote access logon to a remote server. The buttons in the toolbar are used to create, modify, delete, and dial phone book entries.

Fig. 27.23

The Remote
Access Service
program group.

Figure 27.24 shows the Remote Access dialog box for the BOB386 workstation. Two entries appear in the phone book. The first contains a
phone number connected to a modem on the BOB486 remote access
server.

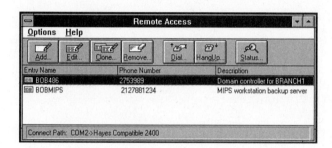

Fig. 27.24

The Remote
Access dialog
box.

Each entry in the phone book contains three basic fields of information.
The Entry Name field contains the name of the remote access server.
The second field contains the phone number associated with a modem
on the remote server. The last field is used for descriptive information
about the remote access server connection.

The Edit Phone Book Entry dialog box is used to change phone book
entries. The dialog box in figure 27.25 shows the first entry in the
phone book for the remote access client BOB486 (see fig. 27.24). The
entry shows that the server to be connected to is the domain controller
for the BRANCH1 domain, whose modem is connected to the local
phone number 275-3989. You are not prompted to enter an account
name and password when you dial this entry because the Automatically logon as current user check box is selected.

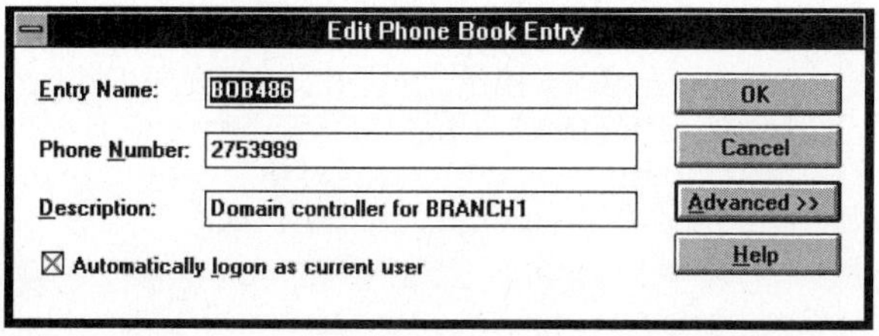

Fig. 27.25

The Edit Phone
Book Entry
dialog box.

To begin a remote access connection, you select an entry from the phone book and the Dial button from the toolbar. This displays a Connect To dialog box whose title includes the system named in the entry field of the selected entry. After you hang up, it's as if you had a direct network attachment, but slower.

The workstation that you connect to must have started the Remote Access Service software from the Remote Access Admin application. Select the Remote Access Admin icon from the Remote Access Service program group. This displays the Remote Access Service dialog box. Select Start Remote Access Service from the Server menu. The started server appears in the main window of the Remote Access Admin dialog box.

Figure 27.26 shows the main window of Remote Access Admin on the \\BOB486 server after the remote access server is started. The word Running in the Condition field shows that the server is operating. One communications port is available for remote access from a remote access client system. No ports are in use because no connection is established from a remote client.

Fig. 27.26

The Remote
Access Admin
main window.

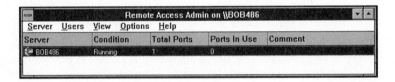

You must perform one additional operation at the Remote Access Server to allow remote access connections. Use the Permissions option in the Users menu to display the Remote Access Permissions dialog box, which is shown in figure 27.27. The accounts in the domain appear by default in the Without Permission list field, which means they are disabled. Select one or more accounts and use the Add or Add All button to move them to the With Permission list.

You can use the No Call Back toggle button to control access to the system from specific phone numbers. This allows an additional level of security by forcing the calls to originate from known phone number locations. Optionally, the remote access client can set the phone number dynamically. This enables you to gain access to the system from different phone numbers even though you have enabled the call back feature. Note that this effectively negates security provided by the call back feature because remote access can be performed from any phone number. It also can save billing charges, however.

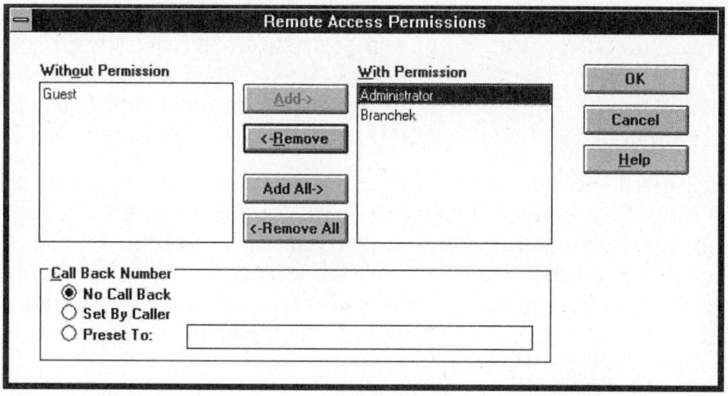

Fig. 27.27

The Remote Access Permissions dialog box.

T I P

If you need access to the system from a different phone number (because you are traveling on business, for example), ask a local administrator to add phone book entries at the server. The server administrator can verify your identity by phone before enabling remote access. Although this is more work, it is also more secure than allowing call back access from any phone number.

Summary

The features of the Windows NT Advanced Server system allow a client-server network configuration to be superimposed on a basic NT peer-to-peer network configuration. You can continue to use the peer-to-peer capabilities while using the client-server capabilities in your network.

The Advanced Server adds the capability to selectively control access to workstation resources. The Advanced Server client-server model also provides centralized storage and maintenance of user accounts. Account names, passwords, workstations at which you can log on, and characteristics of your working environment such as the desktop settings and available applications are maintained on a central server workstation. A backup account server can be used to improve performance and provide additional systems to be used if the primary server fails.

The additional fault-tolerance disk storage techniques of mirror sets and stripe sets with parity can be implemented to lessen the probability of the loss of applications and data. The related directory replication feature, which automatically copies and updates directories and files, can improve performance and provide backup copies.

The features of the Advanced Server complement, rather than replace, the features of the basic NT system. Additional menus are simply added to the Disk Administrator of the basic NT system. The level of integration of the basic features and Advanced Server features enables you to easily change your NT network to a client-server configuration rather than peer-to-peer configuration or a combination of both.

Connecting Windows NT to Network Operating Systems

T he Windows NT system includes the capability to communicate with other Microsoft systems and non-Microsoft systems. You can send messages and share files, directories, and printers when you connect to other Microsoft systems. The built-in connectivity to non-Microsoft systems allows terminal emulation, file transfer, and administrative operations from a Windows NT workstation.

You must install and configure the built-in connectivity to non-Microsoft systems if you didn't do so when the Windows NT system was installed. You can also remove and update network software components.

Both the basic Windows NT system and the Advanced Server provide the capability to connect to other computer systems so that you can share resources. You may create the connection to access information on a remote disk on a non-Windows NT system, for example, or to transfer data between systems. Database files, word processor documents, and electronic mail are the types of information transferred most frequently.

You also can access a non-Windows NT system to use its printers. You submit print jobs from your NT workstation and get the printouts from the remote printer. You also can perform administrative operations through network connections to non-NT systems. You use commands to learn the interconnection status of systems, monitor the flow of control data and user data between connections, and alter the characteristics that affect the connections. You also can change the size of buffers, which are temporary storage spaces in RAM for the data transferred from one system to another.

To save RAM and disk space, applications that allow connections between different systems are not automatically installed by Windows NT. You must install them, then manage the applications and connections to them. This chapter discusses the commands and operations you need to implement and maintain connections between your NT system and non-NT systems.

Many inter-system applications use a command-line interface rather than a graphical user interface. Only 20 years ago, systems used a hardcopy terminal, rather than the video screen, as an interactive interface. The developers of the original interconnection software could implement only a command-line interface because only hardcopy terminals were in widespread use.

The built-in applications in Windows NT allow interconnections with non-NT systems using command-line interfaces. This is true also for the comparable applications of the non-NT systems that you connect to. If you've worked on systems that predominantly use command lines rather than GUIs, such as the UNIX system, you'll feel right at home.

If you've worked with a system only through a GUI, you'll experience the pain and discomfort associated with entering incorrect commands. Fortunately, the interconnection applications have a relatively small number of commands. After you learn them, you can perform network operations quickly and easily.

New interconnection applications are being developed with a front-end GUI that automatically generates a command in a command-line form. This will enable you to use a graphical user interface to send commands to a remote system that only recognizes command lines. The basic Windows NT, however, implements only a small part of interconnection operations to non-Windows NT systems through a GUI.

Built-In Connectivity to Microsoft Systems

It shouldn't be surprising that the connections to non-NT systems that are the least complicated to set up and the simplest to use are connections to other Microsoft systems. The first of these, Windows for Workgroups, provides interconnectivity features that are nearly identical to Windows NT. The workgroups in Windows for Workgroups can be integrated with the workgroups in Windows NT.

Microsoft's LAN Manager client software for DOS and Windows can be connected to a Windows NT system for the sharing of disk and printer resources. The DOS client software uses both a command-line interface and a menu-driven interface for network operations. The LAN Manager client software for Windows is integrated into the Windows GUI.

Communicating with Windows for Workgroups Workstations

You can connect to and share the disk and printer resources of a Windows for Workgroups workstation from a Windows NT system. The operations are nearly identical to connecting to disk and printer resources from one Windows NT workstation to another. The common Windows graphical user interface is used to provide a seamless integration.

Sharing Directories

You use the Share **As** command from the **D**isk menu of the File Manager application on a Windows for Workgroups system to establish a share name. The share name enables you to connect a disk drive from another system. This operation is similar to the operation performed with Share **As** in the **D**isk menu of the File Manager application of a Windows NT system.

The Share Directory dialog box of a Windows for Workgroups workstation is shown in figure 28.1. You use the Access Type section to restrict access to read-only access or access through a password rather than full access. In the Passwords section, you enter the read-only password or the full access password.

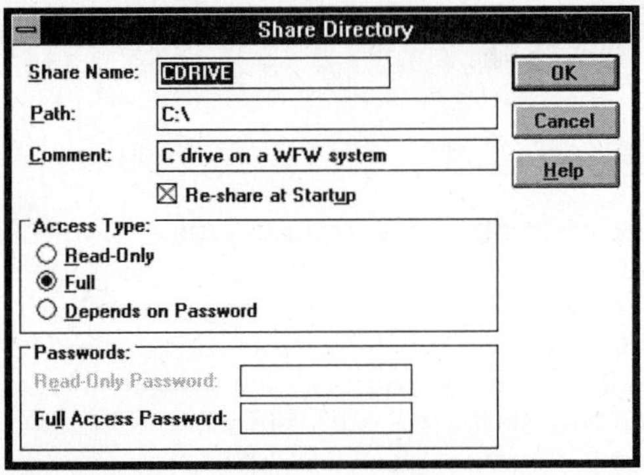

Fig. 28.1

The Share
Directory dialog
box on a
Windows for
Workgroups
system.

You can't specify file permissions for files, directories, or shared directories with Windows for Workgroups as you can with Windows NT. Windows for Workgroups recognizes only the FAT disk format, which doesn't allow the use of file permissions. To control access to resources such as shared directories in a network of Windows for Workgroups workstations, you must use passwords.

In figure 28.1, the share name of the drive is entered as CDRIVE, which is the local C drive of the system. The **F**ull access type toggle button is selected so that full access is granted to any workstation that connects to the drive; you don't need to enter a password to connect to the drive.

The Windows NT workstation uses Connect **N**etwork Drive on the **D**isk menu of the File Manager to create a connection to the shared directory of the Windows for Workgroups system. You connect to a shared directory on a Windows for Workgroups system in the same way you connect to a shared directory of a Windows NT workstation. After the drive is connected, it is available for any type of access.

Figure 28.2 shows the Connect **N**etwork Drive dialog box on a Windows NT workstation. The drive letter for use on the local system is I and the path to the Windows for Workgroups shared directory is \\BOBWFW\CDRIVE. BOBWFW is the name of the Windows for Workgroups system and CDRIVE is the share name of its shared directory. The path is specified using the Universal Naming Convention (UNC), in which the name of the system in a network is typed after a double slash (\\).

You can perform operations with the files on a shared drive after it is connected. Figure 28.3 shows a selected shared directory of a Windows for Workgroups system in the File Manager display of a Windows NT system. Drive I is shown on the drivebar using the remote drive icon.

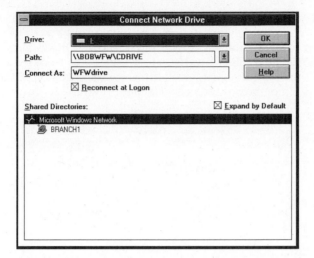

Fig. 28.2

The Connect
Network Drive
dialog box of a
Windows NT
system.

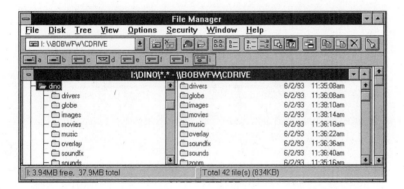

Fig. 28.3

The File Manager
window showing
a shared
directory of a
Windows for
Workgroups
remote system.

The directory of the selected drive is expanded and displays the selected directory of the shared directory, DINO. The Windows for Workgroups BOBWF remote system and the CDRIVE shared directory are shown in the title bar of the drive window. Files and directories on the shared directory can be used as if they were on a local drive.

Sharing Printers

You use Connect Network Printer from the **P**rinter menu of the Print Manager of a Windows for Workgroups workstation to bring up the Connect Network Printer dialog box. You enter the path to the shared printer of a Windows NT system in the **P**ath field of the dialog box. The OK button enables the connection to the shared printer.

Figure 28.4 shows the Connect Network Printer dialog box on a Windows for Workgroups workstation. The local printer port, LPT1:, is connected to the LASER1 shared printer on the BOB486 Windows NT workstation. The LASER1 printer is first defined as a shared printer by selecting the **S**hare this printer on the network check box in the Printer Properties dialog box of the Print Manager on the Windows NT system.

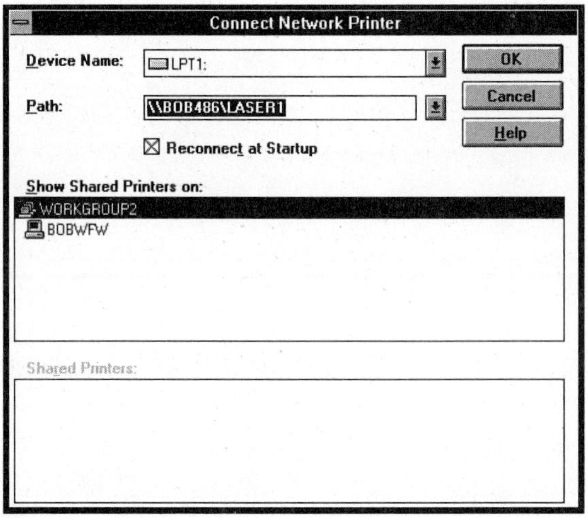

Fig. 28.4

The Connect Network Printer dialog box on a Windows for Workgroups system.

Print requests directed to the LPT1: printer port are automatically directed to the shared printer on the Windows NT system from the Windows for Workgroups system. The main window of the Printer Manager on both systems shows the print job request to the remote printer.

Figure 28.5 shows the Print Manager window on the Windows for Workgroups system that submits a request to the LASER1 remote printer on BOB486. The printer status is `Printing`; NT is in the process of transferring the file to the LASER1 printer.

Fig. 28.5

The Print Manager window showing a remote print request for a Windows for Workgroups system.

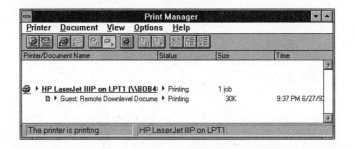

Sharing Information

Windows for Workgroups, like Windows NT, can also share pages of information among network workstations using the clipbook. You use the Share ClipBook Page dialog box on a Windows for Workgroups system to specify a page for sharing.

Figure 28.6 shows the Share ClipBook Page dialog box that defines a ClipBook page as wfw2 and allows full access to any system that connects to it. The Share ClipBook Page dialog box is displayed by selecting the Share Item Now check box in the Paste dialog box when a new page is added to the clipbook. (The Paste dialog box is displayed by choosing Paste from the Edit menu of the ClipBook Viewer.)

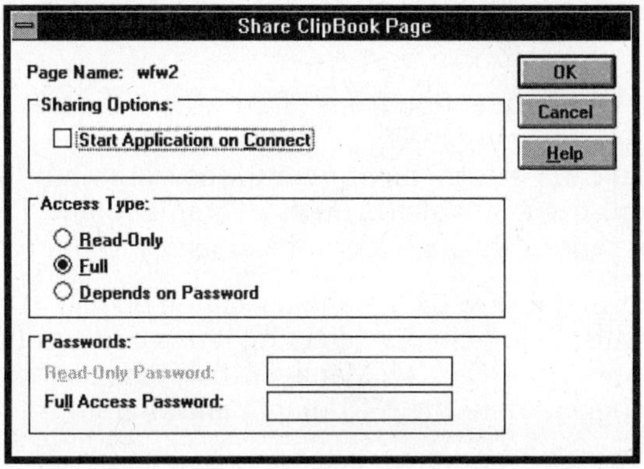

Fig. 28.6

The Share ClipBook Page dialog box on a Windows for Workgroups system.

You use the Connect option in the File menu of the ClipBook Viewer on a Windows NT system to display the Select Computer dialog box. This dialog box enables you to specify the name of the remote system to gain access to its clipbook.

After you select the computer system to connect to a remote clipbook, the shared pages of the clipbook can be displayed through the ClipBook Viewer on a Windows NT system. Figure 28.7 shows the ClipBook Viewer on the BOB486 Windows NT system with a connection to the wfw2 shared page on the BOBWFW Windows for Workgroups workstation. The page is displayed as a thumbnail view, a small representation of the page.

Communicating with LAN Manager Systems

The LAN Manager client software for DOS and Windows connects to an Advanced Server domain controller in the same way as a Windows NT workstation. You log on to the NT domain with a username and a password, just like you do for a Windows NT workstation.

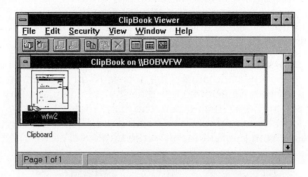

Fig. 28.7

The ClipBook
Viewer on a
Windows NT
workstation.

One way to make a connection from DOS to the NT domain is to issue the NET command from the DOS prompt. This displays a DOS window from which you can perform most operations. Although these and other operations are available through a command line, it's preferable to perform operations through a graphical user interface.

Figure 28.8 shows the DOS LAN Manager dialog box. You perform operations from this dialog box by selecting items or commands from pull-down menus. The DOS LAN Manager dialog box shows that you are not currently logged on to the NT domain and that your local workstation is DOS386.

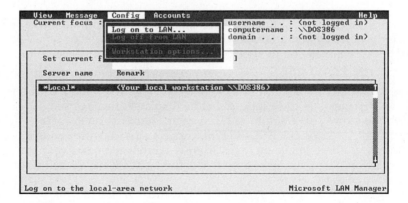

Fig. 28.8

The DOS LAN
Manager dialog
box.

From the **C**onfig menu, you select Log **on** to LAN to display the DOS Log On to Network dialog box. In this dialog box, you enter your username and password. The **D**omain field shows the domain in which your workstation is a member. Figure 28.9 shows a logon to the BRANCH1 NT domain, with the Branchek username and its associated password. A successful logon displays a confirmation message.

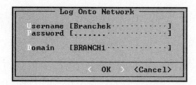

Fig. 28.9

The Log Onto
Network dialog
box for MS-DOS.

The equivalent operation for a LAN Manager client for the Windows
system results in the display of a LAN Manager Logon dialog when Windows is started from DOS. Figure 28.10 shows the LAN Manager Logon
dialog box for a logon to the BRANCH1 domain. The logon name can be
saved and automatically used for subsequent logons.

Fig. 28.10

The Windows
LAN Manager
Logon dialog
box.

NETADMIN is a Windows application provided with the LAN Manager
client software that displays a dialog box equivalent to the DOS LAN
Manager dialog box displayed with the DOS NET command. Figure
28.11 shows the Windows LAN Manager dialog box, titled Microsoft
LAN Manager. The menu bar has the same View, Message, Config, and
Accounts menus of the DOS LAN Manager dialog box, along with an
additional menu, Status.

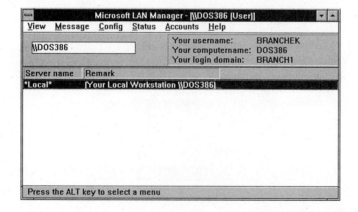

Fig. 28.11

The Windows
LAN Manager
dialog box.

Both the DOS and Windows interfaces enable you to connect to shared
directories that are defined as available for sharing from the NT system. You select the NT workstation in the Set current focus on field of

the DOS or Windows LAN Manager screen. Select **A**vailable resources on the **V**iew menu to display the available resources of the system shown as the current focus. You make a resource available by selecting it from the list of resources and then choosing **U**se resource.

The Resources Available dialog box shows the resources currently used by the local workstation or those that can be selected and made available. In figure 28.12, three disks are available for sharing and one is already available as the local D drive. The laser1 printer is also available for access from the local workstation. Cdrive, the sharename drive on the Windows NT system, is selected and can be made available to the DOS LAN Manager client by selecting **U**se resource.

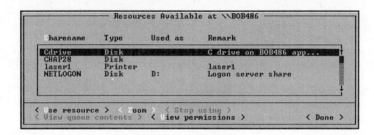

Fig. 28.12

The DOS
Resources
Available
dialog box.

Figure 28.13 shows the equivalent Windows Resources Available dialog box after Cdrive on BOB486 has been made available (see fig. 28.12). Three drives and the laser1 printer are shown. The drive with the Cdrive sharename has been made available on the local system as drive E. The printer remains available as LPT1. The resources in this example were made available through the DOS Available Resources dialog box.

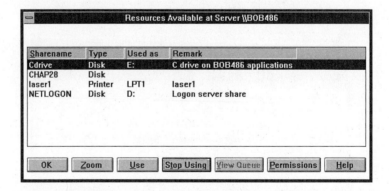

Fig. 28.13

The Windows
Resources
Available
dialog box.

You can use either the DOS or Windows Resources Available dialog box to list, enable, or disable the shared resources of a Windows NT system that the local system has logged onto.

You can work with the resources of a remote workstation after you have made the resources available to your system. For example, you can use the DIR command from a DOS session on a LAN Manager client to list the directories and files of a CD drive that you made available from the Windows NT workstation. The directories and files of the disk can be manipulated as if the drive were a local drive of the DOS workstation.

Figure 28.14 shows a DOS session on a LAN Manager client workstation. The G drive, which is the CD drive on a remote Windows NT system, is set as the default drive for the session. A DIR command is used to display the directories of the remote drive. The volume label for the remote drive is WINDOWS_NT because it is the distribution CD for the Windows NT system.

```
C:\WINDOWS>g:

G:\>dir

 Volume in drive G is WINDOWS_NT
 Directory of G:\

.              <DIR>       01-01-85  12:00a
..             <DIR>       01-01-85  12:00a
ARCINST  EXE      119296  09-28-92   9:03p
ARCINST  INF         194  08-28-92  11:46a
DEMO           <DIR>       03-05-93   8:11p
DISK2               22  02-25-93   3:24p
I386           <DIR>       03-05-93   5:51p
JZSETUP  EXE       77824  11-10-92  10:09a
MIPS           <DIR>       03-05-93   5:51p
        9 file(s)       197336 bytes
                             0 bytes free
```

Fig. 28.14

A directory listing of a remote drive from a DOS LAN Manager client.

You can also access a remote drive of a Windows NT workstation on a Windows LAN Manager client in the same way that you access a local drive. For example, the File Manager can be used to perform operations with the files of a remote drive as well as the files of local drives.

Figure 28.15 shows the main window of the File Manager on a Windows LAN Manager client workstation executing Windows 3.1. The selected drive is G, the remote drive of the BOB486 Windows NT workstation made available through the Resources Available dialog box. The directories and files of the remote CD drive (drive G) are displayed in a separate window just as they would be for a selected local drive.

The path displayed under the drive bar, G:\\BOB486\CDDRIVE, shows that the drive referenced locally as G is located on the remote workstation with a shared name of CDDRIVE. The double slash (\\) that precedes the name of the BOB486 remote system is the convention used to reference a remote system. The directories and files of the remote drive can be manipulated in the same way as those of a local drive.

A remote printer of a Windows NT system is accessed from a LAN Manager client through DOS or Windows transparently. You use the usual DOS PRINT command to print files on a remote printer.

Figure 28.16 shows the config.sys file submitted from a DOS LAN Manager client system to a remote printer on a Windows NT workstation. The normal DOS print command is used to construct the `print config.sys` command line. The command and the confirmation message returned by DOS are identical to a request submitted to a local printer.

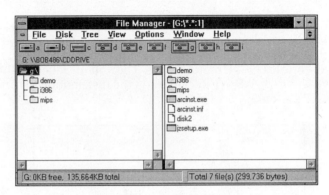

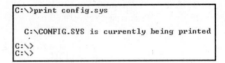

You can print from a Windows LAN Manager client to a printer on a remote Windows NT workstation as transparently as you can from a DOS session. From your application, you first select the remote printer using a printer setup command, then you simply use a print command.

A print operation works transparently for DOS and Windows sessions because the connection to the remote Windows NT printer is made through LPTn:, the local logical print device. Your local application submits print requests normally, and they are redirected to the remote printer from both DOS and Windows sessions. For example, the laser1 remote printer, shown in the previous examples, is mapped to LPT1 (refer to fig. 28.13).

Figure 28.17 shows a remote shared print request listed in the Print Manager window on the laser1 Windows NT printer. The Status and Document Name fields show the downloading from the remote system to the laser1 printer. The number of pages and the size of the document are not shown because they haven't been determined yet. A moment later they will be recorded and will appear in the display.

The Spooling status refers to the process of queuing the print request and the creation of a local copy of the document for printing.

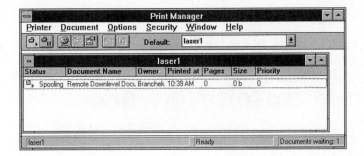

Fig. 28.17

The Windows NT Print Manager display of a document submitted by a LAN Manager client.

You can send a message from a LAN Manager client system to a Windows NT workstation. The message can be sent from either a DOS or Windows client system. You select **S**end a typed message from the **Me**ssage menu of the dialog box displayed with the NET command on a DOS LAN Manager client or from the LAN Manager Administration utility on a Windows system.

Figure 28.18 shows the DOS Send a Message dialog box displayed by the **S**end a typed message option. The message is sent to the BOB486 workstation. If you enter the domain name, the message is sent to all members of the domain. The LAN Manager client sends a message to notify the BOB486 Windows NT server workstation that it is logging off in 15 minutes. The Windows LAN Manager client Send a Message dialog box also allows a file to be sent as a message.

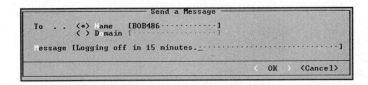

Fig. 28.18

The DOS LAN Manager client Send a Message dialog box.

A Messenger Service dialog box that contains the text of the message sent, the user to whom it was sent, the date, and the time appears on the workstation of the Windows NT system when a message is delivered. Figure 28.19 shows the Messenger Service dialog box on the BOB486 workstation. The message is sent from the DOS386 DOS LAN Manager client through the Send a Message dialog box shown in figure 28.18. The Messenger Service dialog box appears on top of any opened windows on the Windows NT system.

Fig. 28.19

The Windows
NT Messenger
Service dialog
box.

Non-Microsoft Network Software Components and Terminology

To perform network operations with non-Microsoft applications, you must use a command-line interface and a cryptic syntax. You also must determine the meaning of the diagnostic and status information returned by the commands that you issue.

An understanding of two basic terms—protocol and packet—will help you work successfully with network applications on systems other than Windows NT, Windows for Workgroups, and LAN Manager. An understanding of these terms is also useful when you work with the setup and administrative applications of the Microsoft network.

A *protocol* is the set of rules used for communication between systems. For example, a sample (but fictitious) protocol says that the sending system will use a space character to signal that it is about to send data to the receiving system. The sending system then sends 32 characters of data.

All data in this sample protocol is sent in 32-byte segments, regardless of the length of the original data. The 32-byte segments of data are called *packets*, the second term you need to understand. The receiving system is responsible for reassembling the packets back to the original data at its original size.

Although this protocol could be used for the transfer of information between systems, it is too simplistic to be practical. Typical protocols provide for variable-length rather than fixed-length packets. Protocols also perform error checking and a way to differentiate the control information (such as the length of variable-size packets) from the original data.

All protocols also provide a way for the sending and receiving computer systems to recognize one another. Often the protocols use information recorded in the hardware. For example, any computer system that can communicate to another system either has built-in or add-on network hardware components. UNIX workstations, for example, have built-in network hardware components. Most PCs, on the other hand, require the addition of a Network Interface Card (NIC).

Each manufacturer of network hardware components is assigned a unique network number. This network number is embedded in the component (for example, an EtherNet card). Many protocols use the assigned number of the network interface card or built-in network interface to identify the sender and receiver information transferred between computer systems. Two EtherNet cards of the same model from the same manufacturer have different network numbers.

An example of a protocol that uses the EtherNet number assigned with the hardware circuitry of each system is TCP/IP. The TCP/IP acronym references not one but two protocols: Transmission Control Protocol and Internet Protocol. TCP/IP is nearly the de facto network standard. UNIX systems use TCP/IP, and other computer systems adopted TCP/IP to communicate with the large number of UNIX systems. Like English, TCP/IP isn't the best and isn't the worst; it's just used most often as a common language for communication between computer systems.

Multiple protocols are often used together to perform intersystem communications. Different functions that must be performed to allow the transfer of information between computer systems can be defined by different sets of rules. You use several sets of protocols during a data transfer between systems.

An analogy to the use of multiple protocols for the transfer of information between computer systems is the task of checking a book out of the library. You probably only consider the rules that you use for checking out a book: presenting a valid library card, checking out the book at the desk, and returning the book by the due date (or paying a fine if it's not returned on time). This set of rules is analogous to the TCP rules.

The TCP protocol specifies the way in which data is sent between interconnected computer systems. It includes rules for checking whether the data arrives at the destination corrupted, and resending the data if it is corrupted.

In the library example, there are additional rules that you must follow to get to the library. You get in your car, drive on the right side of the road (in most countries), drive within the speed limit, and stop at stop signs and red traffic lights along the way. You must also park in a legal parking spot and put money in the meter, if necessary.

The rules for getting to the library are analogous to the IP rules. The Internet protocol specifies the rules for getting the TCP data to and from the workstations across the network of interconnected systems.

The data to be sent between systems is first placed into a packet that follows the TCP protocol. Then the TCP organized data is placed into the IP form for transmission. Data is often repackaged into several forms before it is sent, then repackaged along the way, and unpacked when it is delivered.

A second analogy can be helpful in understanding this process. Suppose you are on vacation in Hong Kong and purchase an inexpensive but exquisite mother-of-pearl inlaid hardwood table and twelve dining room chairs and arrange to have them shipped to your home. The chairs and table are first placed in individual boxes, numbered 1 of 13, 2 of 13, and so on.

The boxes are loaded on a truck and brought to a dock in Hong Kong. There the boxes are unloaded and placed in a large container along with other merchandise going to the United States. On arrival, your furniture is unloaded, then reloaded into a truck for final delivery to your house. When the furniture is unloaded at the correct destination, you have your furniture.

The individual boxes that contain your table and chairs can be loaded and unloaded at various stages of transport along the way in any order. It doesn't matter if the chair in box 10 is loaded or unloaded before the chair in box 1. It's only important that all the chairs and the table arrive at their destination intact.

The last leg of the transport of your furniture is performed by a trucking company that is a subcontractor to the original shipping company. The rules of their agreement state that you must check the condition of the furniture when it arrives and report any damage to the truck driver who delivers it. According to their rules, the shipping company or the manufacturer in Hong Kong, not the trucking company, is responsible for replacing any damaged furniture.

Network protocols such as TCP/IP typically allow for the delivery of packets of information in a different order than the order in which they were sent. The protocols also allow for the data to be checked when it arrives to see whether it is damaged and request a retransmission of the data if it is corrupted.

Different protocols, like the different transport companies in the shipment of your chairs and table, handle different parts of the operation. The IP protocols don't guarantee that the data will arrive undamaged. TCP is responsible for the retransmission of the data if a packet arrives at its destination corrupted.

Built-In Connectivity to Non-Microsoft Systems

The network capabilities that are available across systems can be organized into the following four categories:

- Messaging
- File sharing and transfer
- Printer sharing
- Administrative capabilities

Some protocols provide some but not all capabilities. The computer industry is just beginning to develop cross-system products for networking. An interest in one or more products that will work uniformly across all systems is quite recent.

New protocols to provide these four network capabilities have not yet been developed. Instead, the manufacturers have half-heartedly repackaged older network protocols such as TCP/IP or their own proprietary protocols. The disadvantage is twofold. One, the proprietary protocols are not implemented across all systems. Two, a single system, such as Windows NT, must support a number of different protocols to be able to communicate with different systems.

Older protocols such as TCP/IP were created when computer systems used only command-line interfaces rather than graphical user interfaces. TCP/IP, like the UNIX systems for which it was originally developed, had applications developed to implement some of the four network capabilities at different times. There was no attempt to use a common syntax to facilitate ease of use across applications.

Because manufacturers view TCP/IP support as an ad hoc solution, they generally provide only a basic command-line interface rather than invest development resources to support all TCP/IP capabilities or the easier to use GUI. A few third-party vendors do provide GUIs for the capabilities provided by TCP/IP, but principally for Windows. These products are not discussed in this chapter because none are currently available for Windows NT. This chapter discusses the network features provided by Windows NT through its TCP/IP command-line interface.

TCP/IP is the most important set of protocols because it can be used for communication between most systems, including Novell's NetWare, IBM's OS/2, Digital's OpenVMS, and most UNIX systems. Unlike Windows NT, these systems either do not include a network communication capability in the basic system or do not have integrated network capabilities as in Windows NT.

Network communication components may be provided by third-party companies or by the same manufacturer of the operating system at an extra cost. Regardless of how the TCP/IP components are provided, the capabilities are basically the same. The commands and features of the Windows NT workstation are similar as well.

Two types of commands are part of the TCP/IP command set. One set performs connectivity operations such as file transfer and remote program execution. You use the second set of commands to perform administrative operations, including the display of diagnostic and status information.

The TCP/IP commands invoke applications that are referred to as utilities. These utility applications evolved over years of use and development and were written by different people at different places. New utilities were added as the need arose. Several utilities perform the same operation because people at different locations simply developed the same or slightly different utilities when they were needed. No attempt was made to follow a common syntax for new commands because no common syntax had been agreed upon.

Multiple commands are available for a second reason. Systems you connect to may have included only one of the several utilities for the same operation. You can use different utilities depending on the system to which you connect.

Messaging

None of the TCP/IP utility applications provided with Windows NT allows a specific message to be sent between Windows NT and a non-Microsoft system in the way it is accomplished from a Windows NT system to another Windows NT system, a Windows for Workgroups system, or a LAN Manager system. The FTP utility does allow a file to be sent to another node; this file can be a text file that is read by the user on the other system as a message.

Sharing and Transferring Files

The TCP/IP utilities of Windows NT allow file transfer between systems. You can use several of these utilities depending on what is available on the system to which you're connected. The TCP/IP file transfer utilities are File Transfer Protocol (FTP), Trivial File Transfer Protocol (TFTP), and Remote Copy Protocol (RCP). FTP is the most useful file transfer utility because it is the most widely implemented and has the most features and options.

The Windows NT TCP/IP software provides only for file transfer, not for the direct access of a remote file from an NT system. You must copy the file from the remote system to the local system to access it from NT applications. You can write your own remote access application in a programming language such as C that uses special file access mechanisms, called *sockets*. Two other TCP/IP utilities—Remote Shell (RSH) and Remote Execute (REXEC)—can be used as part of this capability to start up an application that you communicate with on the remote non-Windows NT system.

The following FTP commands are used for file operations. The remote system must be an FTP server to allow an NT workstation to perform a file transfer.

Command	Purpose
open	Establishes a connection to a remote system; the open command also supplies the name of the IP address of the remote system
put	Send a file to the remote system
get	Receive a file from the remote host
rename	Rename a file on a remote system
user	Send a user name to a remote system (some systems require this before allowing file transfer operations)
pwd	Send a password to a remote system (some systems require this before allowing file transfer operations)
delete	Delete a file
rmdir	Delete a directory on a remote system
dir	Display a list of files in a directory on a remote system
close	Terminate your FTP connection
bye or quit	Exit the FTP utility

Other commands allow operations with multiple files, but they are variations of ones in the preceding list.

Figure 28.20 shows a file transfer operation using FTP from a Windows NT workstation to a remote system. You enable the command-line interface for Windows NT by selecting the Single Command Set icon from the Main program group. Next, you type **ftp** as you would type a SCS command to start the ftp utility. FTP enters command mode and prompts you with the following:

```
ftp>
```

The open command establishes a connection with the remote system, UNIX386. The UNIX386 remote system requires a login using one of its local accounts. A get command and then a put command are used to transfer a file to and from the remote system. The FTP dir command verifies that the local file was transferred to the remote system. Finally, the connection to the remote system is terminated with a close command. You exit FTP with the bye or quit command.

Fig. 28.20

An FTP session with a remote non-Windows NT system.

Sharing Printers

The TCP/IP software of Windows NT has no support for submitting print job requests to a printer on a non-Windows NT remote system.

Performing Administrative Operations

Several TCP/IP utility applications are provided with Windows NT for administrative operations, including the display of diagnostic and status information. The following TCP/IP utility applications are used for administrative operations:

Application	Operation
hostname	Display the name of the current host Windows NT system
nbtstat and netstat	Display network and protocol data structures
arp	Display and change the Internet protocol and EtherNet address tables
route	Change the routing table, which specifies the direction through which data is exchanged between systems that aren't directly connected
ping	Send test data back and forth between connected systems to diagnose network connection problems

In the example shown in figure 28.21, the netstat command is first used to display information about the network software system. The arp command with the -g parameter is used to display the remote system and its Internet and EtherNet addresses. Finally, ping is used to test the capability to send test data to and from the UNIX386 remote system.

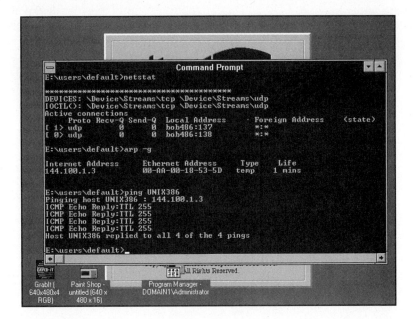

Fig. 28.21

The use of TCP/IP administrative commands.

Telnet

The Telnet utility is a terminal emulator package that allows a remote connection to a system that uses your Windows NT system as a terminal. You can use Telnet to log on to a remote system under the following conditions:

■ The remote system you connect to must use a terminal rather than a workstation for an interface. (Terminals are simple interface devices that, unlike PC or other workstations, have only a CRT display screen, a keyboard, a power supply, and enough logic circuitry to use these devices. With a terminal, all work is performed not locally but through a system you connect to. Several versions of UNIX allow terminals to be used as input devices.)

■ The remote system must have the Telnet utility.

Figure 28.22 shows the Terminal dialog box displayed with the telnet command shown in the Command Prompt window. The Telnet server is first started and the Terminal dialog box is displayed by the Terminal application from the Accessories program group. After the connection is established to the UNIX386 remote system with a connect telnet command and a log in to UNIX386, a command prompt ($) is displayed so that you may issue commands as if a direct local connection were established.

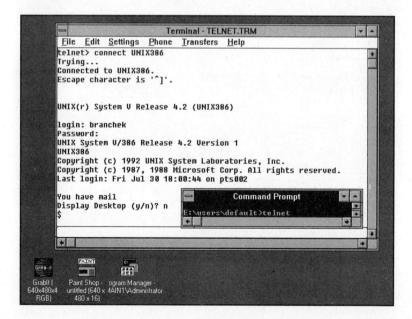

Fig. 28.22

A sample Telnet session.

Network and Protocol Software Installation

The basic NT system doesn't install all the network software that comes with the NT distribution software. You install the NIC driver, which is the software that directly works with your network interface card, the NT workstation client, the NT server, and the NetBEUI and NetBIOS protocols.

To add network software to the system, choose the Network icon in the Control Panel of the Main program group. The Network Settings dialog box is displayed, as shown in figure 28.23. This dialog box enables you to change your workgroup or domain, add or change NIC drivers, add network software, and change network software characteristics.

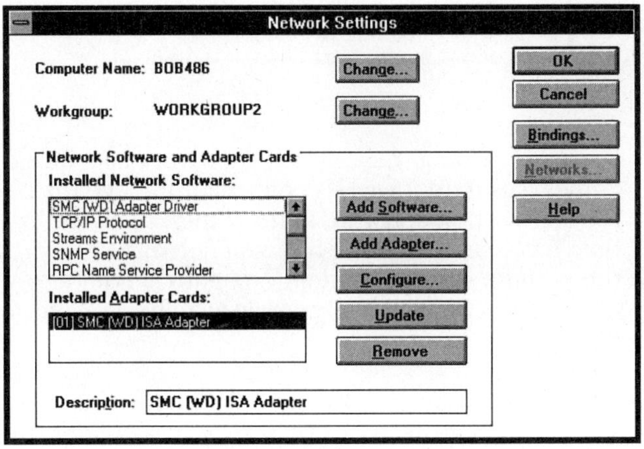

Fig. 28.23

Network Settings dialog box.

Installing Network Software

To add network software, principally other protocol drivers to enable you to create network connections to their operating systems, follow these steps:

1. From the Network Settings dialog box, select Add Software to display the Add Network Software dialog box. See figure 28.24.

2. Select the additional network software to be installed from the Network Software list box.

3. Choose the Continue button to have the network component installed. The Windows NT Setup dialog box is displayed (see fig. 28.25).

Fig. 28.24

The Add
Network
Software dialog
box.

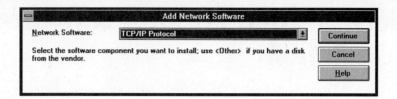

4. Choose Continue to accept the default path, or type a new path in the text box and choose Continue. (See the following note.)

Fig. 28.25

The Windows NT
Setup dialog
box for adding
network
software.

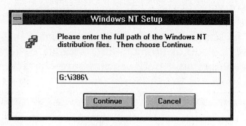

NOTE If you are adding the additional network software that comes with Windows NT, confirm or change the path for the NT distribution software in the Windows NT Setup dialog box. If you are installing optional network software, enter the path for its distribution. The path is the letter designation of the CD drive that contains the basic Windows NT distribution.

You can add the network components to use the features they provide to communicate with systems other than Windows NT or other Microsoft systems. Remember that the optional software components can be installed during the NT system installation or at a later time.

Removing and Updating Network Components

You can remove network software if you no longer will be communicating to another system using one of the installed protocols. To do so, follow these steps:

1. From the Network Settings dialog box, select the protocol from the Installed Network Software list.

2. Choose the **R**emove button. This displays the Network Settings message box (shown in fig. 28.26).

3. Choose **Y**es to confirm the deletion.

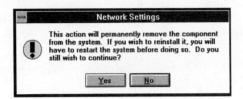

Fig. 28.26

The Network Settings message box.

You can also replace an older version of network software, as follows:

1. From the Network Settings dialog box, select the network software from the Installed Network Software list. The name of the selected software is displayed in the Description field.

2. Choose the Update button. This displays the Windows NT Setup dialog box (see figure 28.27) for updating network software.

3. Choose Continue to accept the default path, or type a new path in the text box and choose Continue.

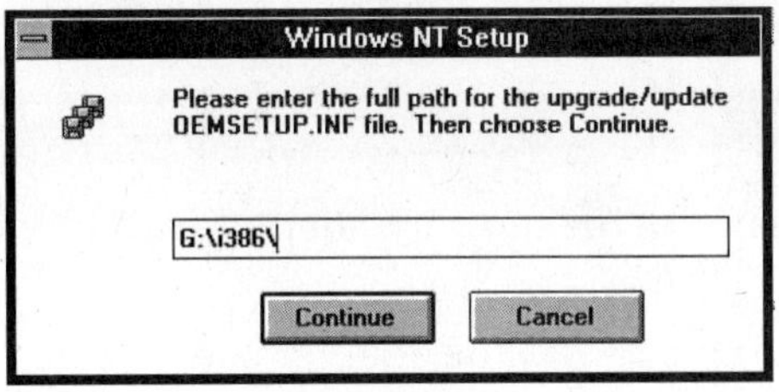

Fig. 28.27

The Windows NT Setup dialog box for updating network software.

You may need to enter additional information in subsequent dialog boxes depending on the network software you are updating. New characteristics may be set identically to the previous version of the network software. Alternatively, you can specify different settings in keeping with the requirements of the new software version.

Configuring Adapter Cards

If your NT workstation has either a built-in network hardware interface or an installed network interface card (NIC), its associated network software is installed during the basic Windows NT installation. You may add or change network interface cards on PC workstations that don't have network interfaces on their motherboard.

The manufacturers of network interface cards that are not built-in use software, referred to as *drivers*, for their NIC. If you change from one NIC to another you must change the driver software. Another reason for changing a network adapter card is to improve network performance. You can change from a slower 8-bit NIC to a faster 16- or 32-bit NIC. Other characteristics of NICs, such as the card's buffer size, can also affect performance.

Adding the Adapter

Before using a new network interface card, you must add the network adapter software and configure its settings. Follow these steps to add the adapter software:

1. From the Network Settings dialog box, choose the Add Adapter button. This displays the Add Network Adapter dialog box, as shown in figure 28.28.

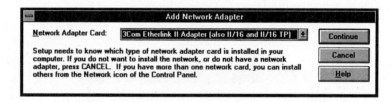

Fig. 28.28

The Add Network Adapter dialog box.

2. Select the name of the network adapter card in the Network Adapter Card list.

3. Choose Continue to add the adapter software and return to the Network Settings dialog box.

Configuring the Adapter

Network adapter cards typically require that an IRQ level and I/O be specified when the adapter software is added. The IRQ level and I/O base address should match the ones specified by the jumper settings on adapter cards or by software settings on software configurable cards. Windows NT can automatically detect and configure a number of adapter cards.

T I P

A network adapter card that can be set through software rather than through small jumpers is more convenient, because you can change the card's characteristics, such as its IRQ or base address, without opening the computer cabinet. This type of card also has a wider range of addresses and IRQ levels. This can be important if you have or plan to have a number of adapter cards in your system.

Ideally, you should check the specifications of all cards that you want to use in your PC workstation to determine if all IRQ and address conflicts can be eliminated. Otherwise, you may have to change one or more cards later so that all the cards work. You should also check that all the interface cards are supported. Microsoft provides a list of supported interface cards, including the network interface cards that can be used with Windows NT.

You should know the factory default settings for your network adapter card and the current settings if you've changed the settings. You also should run any diagnostic program, to quickly learn if the network adapter card functions properly. Most vendors provide setup and diagnostic programs for execution under DOS. If your NT workstation is a PC, you load and execute these diagnostics under DOS to check your board before installing NT.

To configure your network adapter card, follow these steps:

1. From the Network Settings dialog box, select the adapter card from the Installed **A**dapter Cards list.

2. Choose the **C**onfigure button to display the setup dialog box for the selected network adapter card.

3. Change the settings in the Adapter Card Setup dialog box to match the settings of your network card.

4. Choose OK when you have completed the settings. The network adapter is configured on your system.

The Adapter Card Setup dialog box displays different information, depending on the adapter card in your workstation. You use this dialog box to alter the combination of the IRQ level, the I/O address, and the memory address for your network adapter card. Some adapter cards also enable you to specify the transceiver type and whether to map the I/O port in memory.

Figure 28.29 shows the SMC (WD) ISA Adapter Card Setup dialog box for a Western Digital 8003E 8-bit EtherNet adapter card. The values shown for this card can be set either with jumpers on the card or through a software program. The IRQ value is specified as 2 and the

I/O port address is 280. This card also enables you to specify the memory base address. Refer to the network adapter documentation to specify the correct settings.

Many manufacturers repackage network adapter cards that are manufactured by other companies. If your network adapter card doesn't appear in the Installed **A**dapter Cards list (in the Network Settings dialog box), it may be shown under a different name. Check with the vendor, the card's documentation, a diagnostic display of the card's characteristics, or the labeling on the adapter board itself to find its designation.

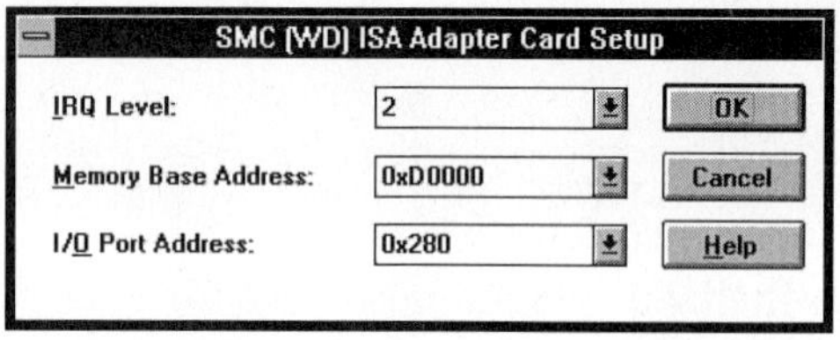

Fig. 28.29

A network adapter card setup dialog box.

For example, the installed network adapter card listed in figure 28.29 is an SMC (WD) ISA adapter. The WD stands for Western Digital, which is the manufacturer of the card, but the card is often sold under the SMC label. The adapter card was purchased from Radio Shack as a Radio Shack adapter card. The DOS diagnostics that come with the card identify it as a Western Digital card.

T I P

The on-line help in the resource kit for Microsoft Windows for Workgroups includes drawings of the jumper settings for many network adapter cards. This information is particularly useful if you can't locate the original documentation for the adapter card and you must change the jumper settings.

Configuring Protocol Software

Windows NT has several software components that can be called *protocol software*. Configuring network protocol software refers to setting its characteristics that function between the network adapter card and high-level network software.

The basic Windows NT system is delivered with three middle-level protocols: NetBEUI, Data Link Control, and TCP/IP. NetBEUI is the primary middle-level interface for Windows NT and is installed automatically when the Windows NT system is installed. TCP/IP is typically used for connection to other computer systems, primarily UNIX. TCP/IP must be installed manually. Data Link Control can be used as a protocol for access to IBM mainframe systems or stand-alone network printers and also must be installed manually.

Configuring Network Bindings

Windows NT automatically specifies which components interact with one another. Several components can interact with a single one. Note, however, that not all components interact with one another.

You can disconnect one or more components connected to a single lower-level component to improve performance, then restore the connections later as necessary. To do so, follow these steps:

1. From the Network Settings dialog box, select the network software in the Installed Network Software list.

2. Choose the **B**indings button to display the Network Bindings dialog box (see fig. 28.30). You use this dialog box to disable or enable a connection, called a *binding*. (The lit lightbulb icon indicates that a binding is enabled.)

3. Select a protocol binding. For example, in figure 28.30, the TCP/IP protocol bound to the adapter driver through the Streams environment protocol is selected.

4. Choose the **D**isable button to disconnect the binding and return to the Network Settings dialog box.

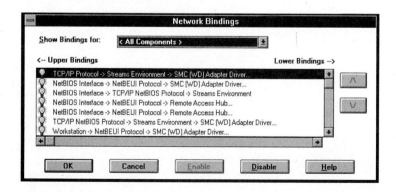

Fig. 28.30

The Network Bindings dialog box.

Redefining the Network Provider Search Order

When more than one network is installed, Windows NT searches for a protocol in the order specified by the Network Provider Search Order. You can change the order, for example, so that the network you use most often is located faster. To do so, follow these steps:

1. From the Network Settings dialog box, choose the **Networks** button. This displays the Network Provider Search Order dialog box.

2. Select the name of the network from the Access Networks In This Order list.

3. Use the **Up** or **Down** button to change the network's order in the list.

4. Choose Continue to change the network provider search order and return to the Network Settings dialog box.

Note that if only the Windows NT Advanced Server network is available, the Networks button is shaded and cannot be chosen.

The search order is changed to improve the performance of network access. The network that is used most frequently or that has the most important network operations should be listed first. Arrange other network providers in order of decreasing importance.

Windows NT always searches for servers, directories, and files using the order specified in the Network Provider Search Order list. When NT tries to locate a software component such as a server, it uses the first entry it finds in a network. If there are conflicting entries for items across networks, you can change the order until you can permanently rename the items to prevent future conflicts.

Summary

Windows NT can connect to computer systems that execute other operating systems. Built-in features allow connections to other Microsoft systems for sharing disk and printer resources. A Windows for Workgroups system can become a member of a Windows NT workgroup for the seamless sharing of resources. Windows and DOS systems require an optional product, the LAN Manager client software, to share the disks and printers of a Windows NT system.

Windows NT has a built-in command-line interface for the use of several TCP/IP utilities. These utilities allow terminal emulation, file transfer, and administrative operations to other operating systems that support TCP/IP. The TCP/IP support allows connection to nearly all other systems because of the widespread support for TCP/IP protocols.

The support for TCP/IP and other protocols isn't installed automatically during the Windows NT system installation. You must use the network setup capability to load and integrate other network software with the default Windows NT network software.

Understanding File Security in Windows NT

Windows NT supports a new file system called the New Technology File System, or NTFS. NTFS stores information along with each file to control access by individuals or groups of users. The access control information stored with each file specifies the operations you can perform with the files.

Operations such as reading or writing a document with a word processor are controlled by the stored access information called file permissions. The read permission, for example, permits the contents of a file to be displayed.

The file permissions are stored with a reference to the individual users or groups of users who have a set of associated permissions. A permission for a file can specify that a single user has Read access to the file. For example, the file permissions for the demo1.txt file in figure 29.1 show that the user who logs onto the system using the *Branchek* account name has Read access to the file. The *Branchek* user may open the file and read it, but cannot change or delete the file.

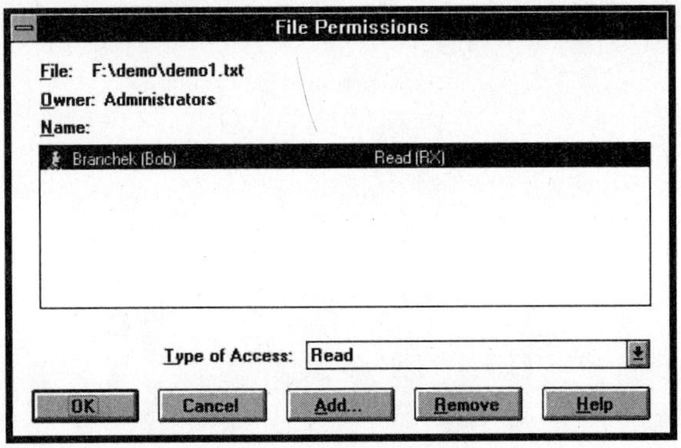

Fig. 29.1

File permissions
for a single user.

The file permissions kept along with a file can define permissions for groups of users rather than an individual user. For example, the SALES group in figure 29.2 shows the file permissions for the demo2.pcx file. The SALES group has the Change permission to the file, which allows any user who is a member of the SALES group to open the file in a word processor and modify its contents.

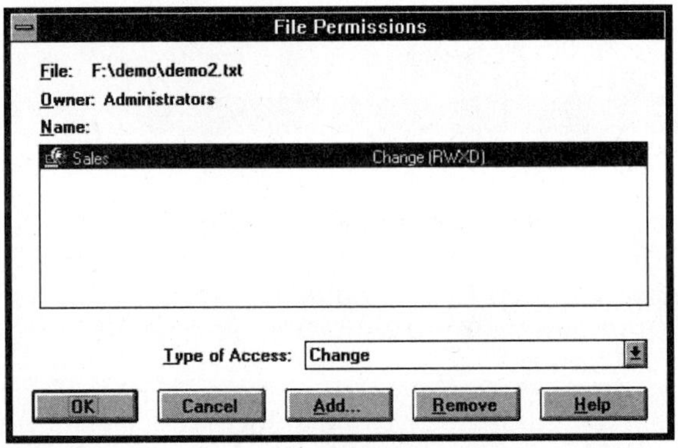

Fig. 29.2

File permissions
for a group.

The file permissions of the NT file system are part of the security mechanisms of the Windows NT system. The permissions permit selective access to files. Users and groups can be assigned different access to files stored on NTFS disks.

One or more users of the system must be able to control the permissions for files. Any user who is a member of the Administrators system group can modify the file permissions stored with a file. (The capability to selectively control access to files at the discretion of a user such as the system administrator is one feature of Windows NT that qualifies it for a C-2 level security rating.)

FAT disks allow information—called *attributes*—to be stored along with files. The file permissions of NT files are different from the file attributes of the DOS, Windows 3.1, and Windows for Workgroups FAT disks. Three attributes can be stored with files: read-only, hidden, and system. If the read-only attribute is specified for a file, the file can be read but cannot be edited or deleted. The system and hidden attributes prevent a file from being displayed in directory listings. For example, the DOS DIR command doesn't display a file that has the hidden or system attribute, unless the command is used with the /A:H or /A:S qualifier.

The file attributes can be changed easily. The DOS ATTRIB command, for example, enables you to add or remove the read-only, hidden, or system attributes. After you remove the attributes from a file, you can display the file with a DIR command without qualifiers, edit the file, or delete the file.

The file permissions of Windows NT NTFS disks enable file access to be closely controlled, unlike the file attributes of FAT disks. File attributes can be changed by anyone who issues the DOS ATTRIB command. Changing the permissions for an NT file, however, can be restricted to a system administrator. In addition, the file permissions of NT allow more control than just the read-only and directory list control access of DOS or Windows files.

Standard Permissions for NTFS files

In addition to the read and change file permissions, there are two additional basic permissions, Full Control and No Access. The Full Control permission enables you to change the file permissions for a file; you can change entries for users or groups to restrict their current access or provide additional access. The No Access permission denies all access to a file. The following list shows the four basic, or standard, file permissions.

Permission	Access
Read	You can read and copy data files; execute program and batch files; and display the owner, attributes, and permissions of files
Change	Same access as the read permission; plus you can change files, append data to files, delete files, and change the attributes of files

continues

Permission	Access
Full Control	Same access as the change permission, plus you can change the ownership and permissions of files
No Access	No access allowed

The Full Access permission also allows the owner of a file to be changed. A file can be owned by an individual user or a group. *Owner*, a system-defined group, normally has the capability to change the file permissions associated with a file. When you create a file, you become its owner and have to ability to change its file permissions.

Two additional terms are used to reference and interpret the information associated with file permissions. The access control list (ACL) is the list of permissions displayed for users or groups in the File Permissions dialog box. Each line in the list that displays one or more file permissions for users or groups is called an access control entry (ACE). Both names of both these terms describe their function: They are the information stored with files that control access.

Displaying Standard File Permissions

The ACL for a file can be displayed through the File Manager. To display the permissions for a file, follow these steps:

1. From the File Manager, select a file.

2. Choose **S**ecurity, then **P**ermissions to display the File Permissions dialog box, which contains the ACL for the selected file.

This procedure was used to display the file permissions in figures 29.1 and 29.2. You can display the permissions for a file also by selecting the file and choosing the Permissions tool on the toolbar. Figure 29.3 shows the Permissions tool.

An access control list for a file usually contains more than one access control entry. In figure 29.4, for example, three access control entries are in the access control list for the TEST1.TXT file. Two entries show the permissions for the Administrators and System groups. These groups of users are responsible for the management and control of the system and its files. Both are granted full control to the file. The third entry references the Everyone group, which is granted Change access to the file. All users are automatically members of the Everyone group.

Fig. 29.3

The Permissions
tool.

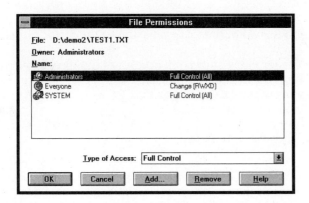

Fig. 29.4

The File Permis-
sions dialog box
containing the
access control list
for the TEST1.TXT
file.

Access control lists and the permissions contained in their entries are associated with directories as well as files. You display the access control list for a directory and its entries in the same way that you display the access control list for a file:

1. From the File Manager, select a directory.

2. Choose **S**ecurity, then **P**ermissions to display the Directory Permissions dialog box. Alternatively, select the Permissions tool from the toolbar.

By default, files inherit their permissions from the directory in which they are created. This simple mechanism protects files by implicitly applying permissions to control access. The permissions for the TEST1.TXT file (see fig. 29.4) were inherited from its directory, which is shown in figure 29.5.

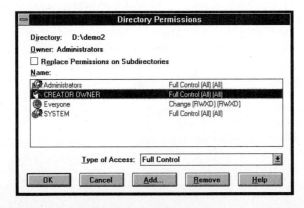

Fig. 29.5

The Directory
Permissions
dialog box,
containing the
access control list
for the demo2
directory.

Compare the permissions for the TEST1.TXT file and its directory, and you can see that the access control entries are identical for the Administrators, System, and Everyone groups. The demo2 directory has an additional access control entry for the Creator Owner system group.

 NOTE The owner of a file or directory can be changed by someone who has Full Control permission to the file or directory.

The Creator Owner entry allows full control of the directory. The owner of the directory, to which this permission applies, appears at the top of the Directory Permissions dialog box in the **O**wner field. The owner of the demo2 directory is Administrators, so anyone who is a member of the Administrators group has full access to the directory. The **O**wner field also appears at the top of a File Permissions dialog box.

NOTE The word ALL that appears in parentheses following the standard file and directory permissions of an access control entry specifies that all special permissions are available for the user or group of the entry. The special permissions are an additional set of permissions.

An ACE entry for a directory file can have two sets of special permissions, both shown in parentheses. The first set is the special permissions for the directory file. The second set is the special permissions that apply to files created in the directory. Special permissions are described in more detail later in this chapter.

Adding, Changing, and Deleting Standard File Permissions

You apply different permissions to files to selectively control access to them by users and groups. You must be the owner of a file or have the Full Control standard permission to add, change, or delete the permissions of a file. To add an entry in the access control list for a file, follow these steps:

1. From the File Manager, select a file.

2. Choose **S**ecurity, then Permissions. Alternatively, select the Permissions tool from the toolbar. The File Permissions dialog box is displayed.

3. Choose the **A**dd button. This displays the Add Users and Groups dialog box, as shown in figure 29.6. You can use this dialog box not only to add users, but also to specify the type of access or the permission.

4. In the **A**dd Names section, type the name of the user for whom you want to add an entry.

5. In the **T**ype of Access drop-down list, select the type of permission. (In fig. 29.6, for example, the permission for the BRANCHEK user is specified as Read.)

6. Choose OK.

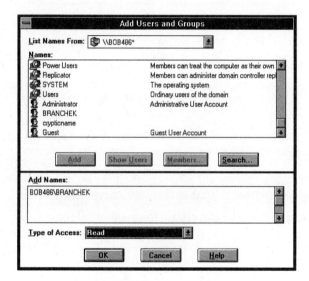

Fig. 29.6

The Add Users and Groups dialog box for adding an access control entry for the BRANCHEK user.

The Add Users and Groups dialog box displays the user in the **A**dd Names field, preceded by the name of the system in which the user account is defined. For example, figure 29.6 shows BOB486, the name of the NT workstation on which the BRANCHEK user is defined.

When you select the OK button in the Add Users and Groups dialog box, the new access control entry is shown (in alphabetical order) in the File Permissions dialog box. Figure 29.7 shows the new entry for the BRANCHEK user for the TEST1.TXT file. Compare this figure with figure 29.4, which shows the access control list for the same file before the BRANCHEK entry was added.

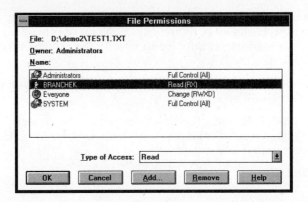

Fig. 29.7

The File Permissions dialog box after an entry for BRANCHEK is added.

You may want to specify a new access control entry for a user or group on a remote NT system. The List Names From field at the top of the Add Users and Groups dialog box displays by default the name of the NT system that you are logged on to. If you are connected to other NT systems, click the down arrow at the end of this field to display the names of the remote systems.

You can select a remote user or group from this list and specify the permissions for a file. Remote users and groups gain access to files and directories on a local NT system if a directory is made available on the remote system as a shared directory. See Chapter 26 for information about how to make files available through shared directories.

You can change an existing entry by first selecting the entry and then changing the permissions in the Type of Access list in the File Permissions dialog box. In figure 29.8, access to the TEST1.TXT file for the BRANCHEK user is changed from Read to Change.

To remove an entry, select it in the access control list in the File Permissions dialog box or the Directory Permissions dialog box and then choose the Remove button. The remove operation, and all other operations including additions and changes, are not permanent until you select the OK button. To abort the operation, choose the Cancel button.

Often, more than one access control entry applies to you and affects your access to a file. You can be a member of more than one group, with different permissions specified for each group. In addition to your membership in groups, you can also have a specific entry by your user name that grants or denies you permissions.

Multiple entries that grant or deny you permissions to files and directories can result in conflicting or redundant permissions, but these are resolved by the NT system. The permissions that apply to you through multiple entries are additive. If you are a member of one group that grants read access and also a member of a group or an entry by your user name that grants you change access, you have the sum of both permissions. The one exception to this rule is if any access entry has the No Access permission.

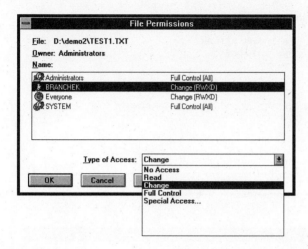

A No Access file permission for an entry that applies to you disallows you any access to the file regardless or any other entries. This is true even if you are a member of a group that specifies full control. The entry that denies you access must be deleted before you have any access to the file.

In figure 29.9, two entries for the file apply to the BRANCHEK user. As a member of the Administrators group, BRANCHEK is specified to have full control. The entry for the BRANCHEK user name, however, is no access, so he cannot access the file even though he is a member of the Administrators group. If the entry for BRANCHEK was a permission other than no access, he would have full control to the TEST1.TXT file from his membership in the Administrators group.

To interpret a user's file access, you need to see the groups to which a user belongs. To do so, use the User Manager administrative tool to display the Group Memberships dialog box. (See Chapter 30 for more information about this dialog box.) In figure 29.10, you can see that the Branchek user is a member of both the Administrators and Guests groups.

If you don't already know the groups a user is a member of, the access control list for a file or directory is difficult to interpret if it contains entries that reference individual users. To simplify the interpretation of the permissions for files and directories, you can create entries that apply only to groups rather than to individual users. Then you make a user a member of a group to which you have granted appropriate file access. You can remove a user from a group to deny the user access to one or more file operations.

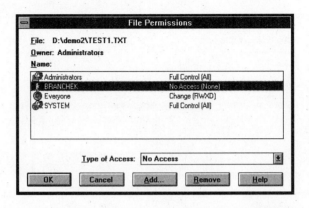

Fig. 29.9

A File Permissions dialog box that contains an access control entry of No Access.

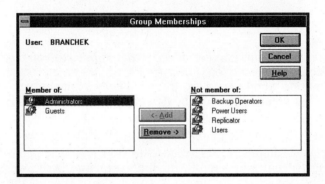

Fig. 29.10

The Group Memberships dialog box used to display a user's membership in groups.

For more selective control over file access, add entries for individual users. To deny a user access to a file but keep the user in the group that has access to the file, add an entry of No Access for that user's user name. The remaining members of the group continue to have access to the file.

Determining a user's access to a file becomes more difficult with each new group or user entry. Therefore, be careful not to define more entries than are necessary to maintain the security of files and directories.

Special File Permissions

Each of the standard permissions is actually one or more of the special permissions, as follows:

This Standard Permission	Contains These Special Permissions
Read	Read and execute
Change	Read, write, execute, and delete
Full Control	All (read, write, execute, delete, change permissions, and take ownership)
No Access	No access allowed

You can maintain adequate protection and still provide access to files using only the four standard permissions. When you need to provide more selective access to files, you must use the special permissions.

Suppose you want to allow a user or group to change a file but not delete it. This is impossible using the standard permissions. The Change standard permission allows both write and delete access. The Full Control standard permission allows all access to a file. Neither of these standard permissions enable you to grant the ability to change a file without also granting the ability to delete a file.

The special permissions, however, enable you to grant write access without delete access. You can also grant the ability to change the permissions and the owner separately instead of granting the Full Control standard permission. The following list describes the special permissions for files.

Special Permission	Access
Read	Read, copy, and list the attributes, permissions, and owner of a file
Write	Open and replace the entire contents of a file or append to a file; no read access
Execute	Execute program; execute a batch file if Read permission is also granted
Delete	Delete or move a file
Change Permissions	Alter file permissions, including taking ownership
Take Ownership	Become the owner; can replace previous owner

Displaying and Changing Special Permissions

The special permissions are displayed in parentheses following the standard permission at the end of each access control entry, which is shown in the access control list of the File Permissions dialog box. To display the special permissions for entries in the access control list of a file, follow these steps. From the File Manager, select a file. Choose **S**ecurity, then **P**ermissions (or select the **P**ermissions tool from the toolbar). The File Permissions dialog box is displayed.

The special permissions follow the standard permission. Figure 29.11, for example, shows that the Change standard permission is made up of the following special permissions: Read (R), Write (W), Execute (X), and Delete (D). The Full Control standard permission is followed by All in parentheses to denote that all special permissions are granted.

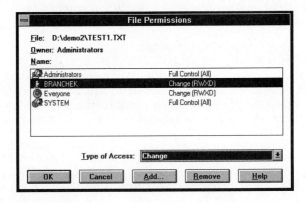

Fig. 29.11

The File Permissions dialog box showing the special permissions for entries in the access control list of a file.

You can display the full name of each special permission by selecting Special Access in the **T**ype of Access list in the File or Directory Permissions dialog box. This displays the Special Access dialog box, which has a check box for each special permission. In the example shown in figure 29.12, the access control entry for the BRANCHEK user has the Read, Write, Execute, and Delete special permissions.

When you display the Special Access dialog box for a file that has a set of standard file permissions defined for it, you see the special permissions that correspond to the standard permissions. The primary function of the Special Access dialog box, however, is not to display the full names of the special permissions for an access control entry. Its primary function is to enable you to specify combinations of special permissions that don't correspond to standard permissions.

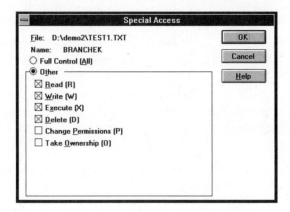

Fig. 29.12

The Special
Access dialog
box.

To specify a combination of special permissions, you simply select or
deselect the check boxes in the Special Access dialog box. For example,
suppose you unchecked all the special permissions except Read to the
TEST1.TXT file for the BRANCHEK entry (see fig. 29.12). The file permission for BRANCHEK is now displayed as `Special Access(R)` in the File
Permissions dialog box, as shown in figure 29.13. (The entry is shown
as Special Access because there is no standard permission that grants
only read access. The *R* represents the read special permission.)

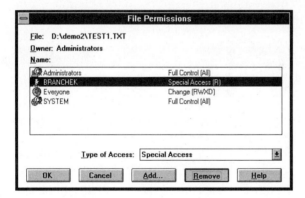

Fig. 29.13

A File Permis-
sions dialog box
containing a
special access
entry.

Deleting Entries

You can use the **R**emove button at the bottom of the File or Directory
Permissions dialog box to delete a selected entry. You must have the
Change special permission, or a standard permission that includes
change permissions, such as Full Control, to remove an access control
entry from the access control list of a file or directory.

For example, the selected entry for BRANCHEK in figure 29.13 can be removed by selecting the **R**emove button. The remove operation, and all other operations including additions and changes, are not permanent until the OK button is chosen. You can use the Cancel button to abort the operation.

Remember, even though you remove an entry that specifically grants a user or a group access to a file, the user or group may still have access to the file through membership in another group. The only way to guarantee that a specific user doesn't have access to a file is to create an entry for the person's user name that specifies no access. No access overrides any access the user still has to the file through a group.

Standard Directory Permissions

You can apply permissions to directories as well as to files. Permissions control the operations that users or groups may perform with the directory and its files. You affect more than access to the directory when you create or change directory permissions. The permissions that you define for a directory also set permissions for the directory's files but do not set permissions for its subdirectories. The permissions for subdirectories are inherited from the ACL entries of its directory. They are not changed because the directory is changed. Table 29.1 shows the standard permissions for directories.

Table 29.1 Standard directory permissions	
Permission	**Access**
List	List file by name, owner, attributes, and permissions, and use any subdirectories in a directory as part of a path specification
Read	Same as list permission but also gives read access to newly created files in the directory
Add	Create files in the directory, but cannot list
Add & read	Both add and read
Change	Create and list files and subdirectories and display and change directory attributes
Full control	All access
No access	No access for newly created files and cannot list files

The list standard permission enables you to list files by name and by their owner, permissions, and attributes. List also enables you to use any of the subdirectories in a directory as part of a path specification. Unlike No Access, if you have only list access to the directory, you are not denied access to the files created in the directory.

You can assign the Read permission—which also allows the display of file names and their owner, permissions, and attributes—for both the directory and its files. Read grants the ability to reference the subdirectories of a directory, allowing the user to read files and execute applications in the directory.

You can assign the Add permission to allow subdirectories and files to be created in a directory without allowing the display of the files in the directory. The user may create new files and execute applications in the directory, but cannot list the directory contents. The Add permission is also like List in that it applies no access to files in the directory.

The Add permission can be the source of confusing error messages. You can't display files in the directory from the File Manager with only the Add permission. From a SCS command line, a DIR command results in a `File not found` error message. An attempt to change your default to the directory results in a `System cannot find the path specified` message. An attempt to display the file in the subdirectory, even if you know its name, results in an `Access is denied` message.

NOTE SCS is the acronym for the Single Command Set. POSIX, OS/2, and most DOS commands can be issued from the SCS command line. See Chapter 22 for more information about SCS.

Use the Add permission to allow a user or group to transfer files into the directory, without the ability to later access the files. The permission is useful for an operator who must be able to restore files to a directory from a backup tape, but needn't access them after they are restored.

The Add & read permission enables you to list and access the characteristics of the directory and its files and examine the contents of files. You can also execute applications in the directory and change a directory's attributes.

The Change permission allows all operations of the Add & read permission as well as the ability to delete the directory, its subdirectories, and its files. Change also allows the user to write and append to files in the directory and to change the attributes of the directory.

The Full Control permission allows all operations to a directory, its subdirectories, and its files.

The No Access permission disallows access to the directory and the files within it and overrides any access to files granted from another group.

Displaying Standard Directory Permissions

You can display standard directory permissions by performing the following steps:

1. From the File Manager, select a directory.

2. Choose **S**ecurity, then **P**ermissions. Alternatively, select the Permissions tool from the toolbar.

The example in figure 29.14 lists the standard directory permissions for a newly created Demo directory on disk D. In the access control list, the Administrators, System, and Creator Owner groups are granted Full Control access. The Everyone group, of which all users are members, is granted the Change permission.

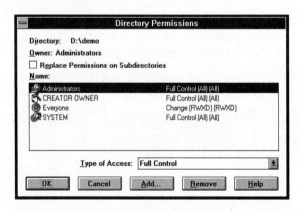

Fig. 29.14

The Directory Permissions dialog box displaying the standard permissions for the Demo directory.

Standard file permissions for a directory are inherited from the directory in which the new directory is created. For example, the Demo directory on disk D is one level below the root. If the root of disk D is selected, as in figure 29.15, you can see that the permissions for the root directory are identical to those of the Demo directory.

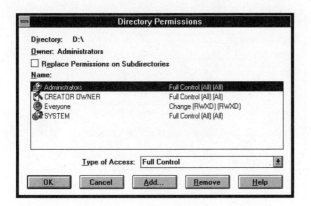

Fig. 29.15

The Directory Permissions dialog box displaying the standard permissions for the root directory.

Adding, Changing, and Deleting Standard Directory Permissions

You may want to apply different permissions to directories to selectively control access to them by users and groups. You must have the Full Control standard permission to change a directory's permissions. With the Full Control permission, you can also add a user or group with specified permissions and delete an entry from the access control list.

You add an entry to the access control list for a directory in the same way that you add an entry for a file. Use the following steps:

1. From the File Manager, select a directory.

2. Choose **S**ecurity, then **P**ermissions. Alternatively, select the Permissions tool from the toolbar.

3. From the Directory Permissions dialog box, choose the **A**dd button. This displays the Add Users and Groups dialog box, which you use not only to add users, but also to change file permissions. (In figure 29.16, for example, a new access control entry for the BRANCHEK user is added and the type of access, or permission, is specified as list.)

4. In the **A**dd Names section, type the name of the user for which you want to add an entry.

5. In the **T**ype of Access drop-down list, select the type of permission.

6. Choose OK.

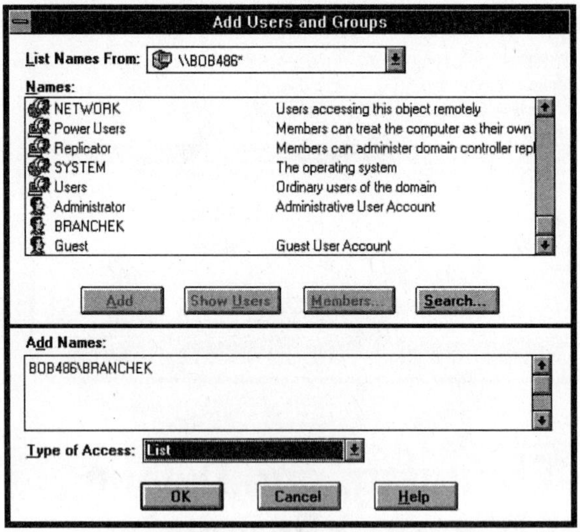

Fig. 29.16

The Add Users and Groups dialog box used to add an access control entry.

For a user or group on a remote NT system, you specify an access control entry for a directory in the same way that you do for a file. Choose **Add** in the Directory Permissions dialog box to display the Add Users and Groups dialog box. Specify the remote system in the **List Names From** field. You then follow the same steps you use to add any entry to a directory. Remote users and groups gain access to files and directories if a directory is made available on the remote system as a shared directory. (See Chapter 26 for more information about shared directories.)

To change an entry in the Directory Permissions dialog box, perform the following steps:

1. In the Directory Permissions dialog box, select the entry to be changed.

2. Select the down arrow at the end of the **Type of Access** list field to display the list of directory permissions.

3. Select a permission from those shown in the **Type of Access** list field.

4. Choose OK.

For example, in the entry for the BRANCHEK user in figure 29.17 for the Demo directory on disk D, the Full Control standard directory permission is selected from the **Type of Access** list. After the OK button is chosen, a subsequent Directory Permissions dialog box for the Demo directory on disk D displays the additional access control entry for BRANCHEK in the access control list.

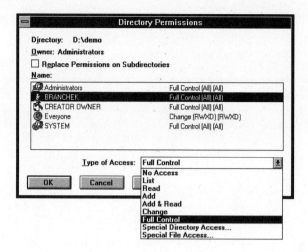

Fig. 29.17

The Directory
Permissions
dialog box that
shows the use of
the Type of
Access field to
change the
standard
permissions.

For a user or group, you remove an access control entry for a directory
with the same procedure you use to remove an entry for a file. Follow
these steps:

1. From the File Manager, select a directory.

2. Choose **S**ecurity, then **P**ermissions. Alternatively, select the
   Permissions tool from the toolbar.

3. From the Directory Permissions dialog box, select the **R**emove
   button.

4. Choose OK.

The remove operation, and all other operations including additions and
changes, are not permanent until you choose the OK button in the Directory Permissions dialog box. (Choose the Cancel button to abort the
operation.)

Special Access Directory Permissions

Standard permissions for directories, like standard permissions for
files, are predefined combinations of special permissions. Although you
may require only the standard permissions to control the security of
directories, you must understand the special directory permissions to
interpret, understand, and then appropriately apply the standard directory permissions. It's also useful to be able to make up your own sets of

special directory permissions to provide more precise access to directories. Table 29.2 shows the special directory permissions and the access they allow.

Table 29.2 Special directory access permissions

Permission	Access
Read	View files and directory attributes
Write	Create new files and change directory attributes
Execute	Traverse (pass through) the directory to gain access to a subdirectory, and view the permissions and owner of the directory
Delete	Delete the directory; with delete access to the files in the directory or subdirectories, all files may be deleted
Change Permissions	Change the directory or file permissions
Take Ownership	Become the owner, replacing the previous owner

There's a complication to understanding the special permissions of directories. Directories, unlike files, have two sets of special permissions. The special directory access permissions control the operations allowed on the directory. The special file access permissions control the operations on the files in the directory.

The special directory access permissions are shown in the first set of parentheses following the standard permissions (see fig. 29.14). The special file access permissions are shown in the second set of parentheses following the standard permissions. Each special file access permission and special directory access permission is represented by an uppercase letter in the parentheses. The All keyword specifies that all special permissions are enabled for either the special file or special directory access permission.

When applied to a directory, the Read special directory permission allows you to display the file names, attributes, owner, and permissions. When applied to a file, Read allows you to display the file attributes, owner, permissions, and contents.

When applied to a directory, the Write special directory permission allows you to create files and directories within the directory, change the directory's attributes, and display the owner and permissions.

When applied to a file, Write allows you to change the file, add to the file, change the file's attributes, and display the file's owner and permissions.

Execute allows you to display the directory's attributes, owner, and permissions and reference its subdirectories as part of a path specification. For files, Execute allows you to display a file's owner, permissions, and attributes. Execute also allows you to execute applications.

The remaining three permissions allow identical control for a file or a directory, although they are specified separately for the directory and for the files within the directory. The Delete permission allows you to delete a directory or file. Change allows you to change the directory or file permissions. Take Ownership allows you to take ownership of a directory or file.

You can display the full name of each set of special permissions by performing the following steps:

1. From the File Manager, select a directory.

2. Choose Security, then Permissions (or choose the Permissions tool from the toolbar). The special permissions are displayed in parentheses following the standard permissions.

If the set of special permissions in an entry of a selected directory doesn't match a standard permission, the words Special Access are shown in place of a standard permission. You can also select Special Access from the Type of Access list to define a nonstandard set of special permissions.

Figure 29.18 shows the Directory Permissions dialog box for the Demo directory on disk D. The access control list contains an entry for the BRANCHEK user that has the Read special directory permission. There isn't a standard directory permission that corresponds to the Read special directory permission. Special Access is shown (in place of a standard permission) to indicate that a nonstandard set of special directory access permissions is specified for the entry.

No special file access permissions in the entry for the BRANCHEK user are present. The NT system doesn't generate a set of special file permissions when a special access permission is defined.

If you change the permissions in an entry for a directory, files already stored in the directory are changed. The corresponding entries for subdirectories in the directories, however, are not changed, nor are the files in the subdirectories unless you check the Replace Permissions on Subdirectory check box in the Directory Permissions dialog box.

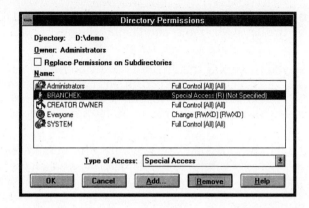

Fig. 29.18

The Directory
Permissions
dialog box
containing an
access entry with
a customized set
of special
directory
permissions.

For example, an entry for the user Branchek with Change permission
exists in the ACL for the Demo directory, the demosub subdirectory,
and the TEST1.TXT file. When the entry for BRANCHEK is changed for
the Demo directory to allow full control, the access control list in the
File Permissions dialog box for the TEST1.TXT file in the Demo directory is automatically changed to Full Control (see fig. 29.19).

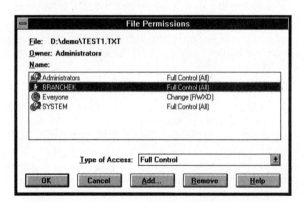

Fig. 29.19

The File Permis-
sions dialog box
after a change of
directory
permissions.

The Directory Permissions dialog box for the demosub subdirectory
shows that the entry for Branchek has not changed (see fig. 29.20).
The permissions for the files located in the demosub subdirectory
are also unchanged. Remember that you can specify a change to the
subdirectories of a changed directory by selecting the Replace Permissions on Subdirectories check box in the Directory Permissions dialog
box. You should carefully consider the impact of changing the permissions for a user or group entry in a directory ACL because of the
changes that propagate to files in the directory.

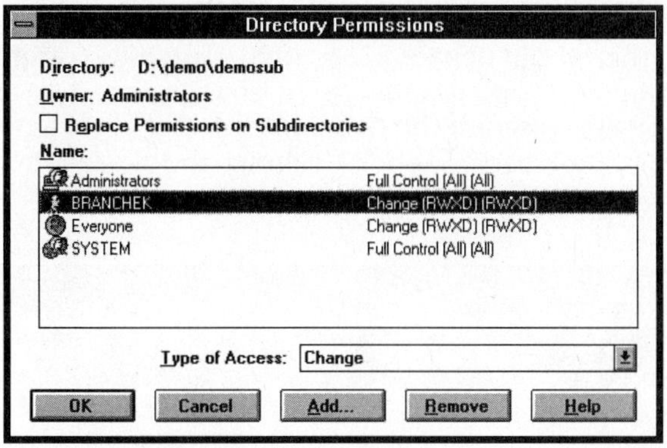

Fig. 29.20

The Directory
Permissions
dialog box after
a change of
directory
permissions
doesn't affect the
permissions for a
directory.

Shared Directory Permissions

Windows NT's built-in network capabilities include accessing directories and files on a remote Windows NT system. Data on a remote disk connected in this way is called a *shared directory*. A shared directory can be an entire disk drive, a directory with several subdirectories, or a single directory. You can apply permissions to the shared directories to provide normal access control. See Chapter 26 for additional information about shared directories.

One advantage to applying permissions to shared directories is that different permissions can be applied to a directory when it's accessed remotely rather than locally. For example, you can allow only Read access for a shared directory on a remove system, but allow change access when the shared directory is accessed locally.

A second advantage of shared directory permissions is that you can apply them to a FAT or an HPFS disk as well as normal NTFS-formatted disks or partitions. FAT-formatted volumes, which have minimal security, can then take advantage of the security provided by shared directory permissions.

You can control the permissions for shared directories only from a user account that is a member of the Administrators or Power Users group. This is a security feature in itself. Only one or a few users should be assigned to either of these groups to prevent too many users from controlling the access to shared directories.

The permissions established on a shared directory are available when the directory is connected remotely. When the shared directory is made available, its permissions apply indirectly to its files, its subdirectories, and the files in the subdirectories. The standard and special permissions applied to files and directories in shared directories remain in effect.

Shared directory permissions don't override file and directory permissions because this would negate the normal protection originally intended. For example, if you grant a group Change access to a shared directory, it doesn't override the Read access applied to a directory under the shared directory. Table 29.3 shows the shared directory permissions and a description of the access they provide.

Table 29.3 Shared directory permissions	
Permission	**Access**
Read	View files, directories, and their attributes; run applications; and use directory path specification
Change	Same as read permission; plus you can create files and directories, delete files and directories, change files and file attributes, and append to files
Full Control	All access and control
No Access	No access

Displaying Shared Directory Permissions

You can display the permissions that are part of an access control entry for a shared directory through the File Manager. To display the access control list that contains all the access control entries for a shared directory, follow these steps:

1. From the File Manager, choose **D**isk.

2. Choose Share **A**s.

3. Select the Permissions button from the Shared Directory dialog box.

The default entry grants everyone full control to the shared directory (see fig. 29.21).

Access control entries for shared directories are displayed in a less complicated way than those for files and directories. Read, Change, Full Control (All), or No Access (None) is displayed following the user or group name for each entry. Shared directory permissions are divided into a set of standard and special permissions, rather than the standard permissions and two sets of special permissions for local directories.

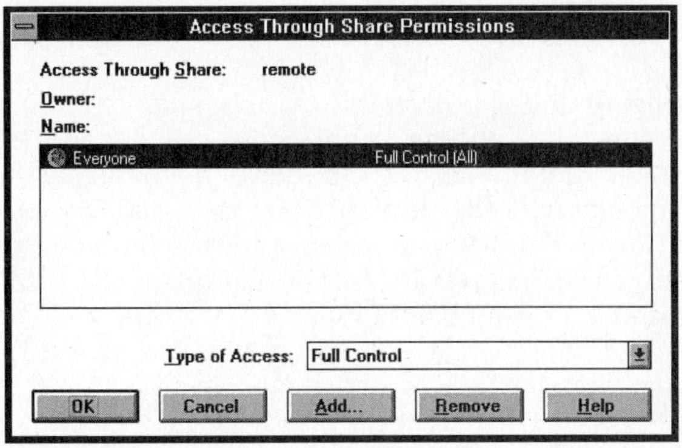

Fig. 29.21

The Access
Through Share
Permissions
dialog box
showing the
default access
control list for a
shared directory.

You can add new access control entries for users or groups as follows:

1. From the File Manager, choose **D**isk, then choose Share **A**s.

2. Select the Permissions button from the Shared Directory dialog box.

3. From the Access Through Share Permissions dialog box, choose the **A**dd button. This displays the Add Users and Groups dialog box, which you use not only to add users but also to change permissions.

4. In the **L**ist Names From field, select the system from which the users and groups are displayed.

5. In the Ad**d** Names section, type the name of the user for whom you want to add an entry.

6. In the **T**ype of Access drop-down list, select the type of permission.

7. Choose OK.

You use the **R**emove button in the Access Through Share Permissions dialog box to delete access control entries for a shared directory.

You can use the Shared Directory capability to apply permissions to a local FAT-structured disk. You treat the local disk as a shared directory that is set up to be available on a remote NT system. You then connect the directory in the same way you connect an actual remote shared directory. You can view the shared directory permissions only through Share **A**s from the **D**isk menu in the File Manager.

Specifying User Limits

The Share Directory dialog box enables you to specify the maximum number of users who can access a shared directory (see fig. 29.22). You use the **Allow** Users field to set the number of users unless the **Unlimited** button is specified. A user limit of 1, for example, increases security by prohibiting any additional access after the intended user gains access to the shared directory. If another user gains access first, however, the intended user is locked out.

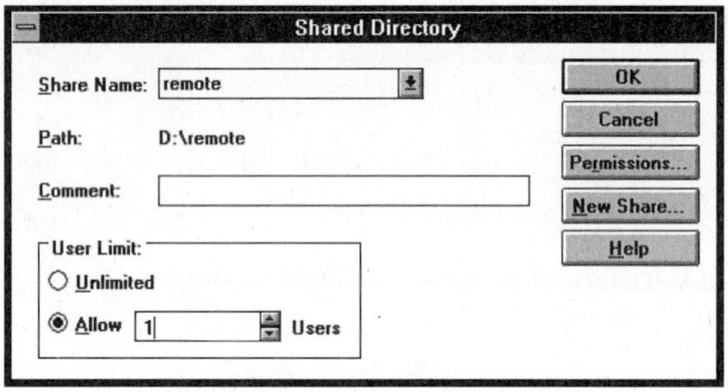

Fig. 29.22

The Shared
Directory
dialog box.

Another reason for limiting the number of users who can gain access to the shared directory is to prevent overloading the machine by remote access. You may find that a single workstation can support only a certain number of remote user accesses without slowing local user operations. Too many remote accesses can affect the performance of the remote operations also.

Changing File and Directory Ownership

The creator of a file or directory becomes its owner. The owner of a file or directory can assign the Full Control standard permission or the take ownership special permission to the file or directory for other users or groups. A member of the Administrators group may also take ownership because this group is granted full control to files and directories by default.

The security of directories and files is assured only if the Full Control standard permission, the Take Ownership special permission, and the change special permissions are not granted to users or groups who should not have them. These permissions provide the ability to grant or deny standard and special permissions to other users and groups. You must audit the use of these permissions to detect their misuse. See Chapter 30 for information about auditing file and directory activity.

Descriptive owner names can present a security problem. Intruders may attempt to gain unauthorized access to the system through an account that has powerful user rights. If they can list the owner names for files or directories and they match the names of accounts, they may attempt to log on to the system using one of the account names.

To change the ownership for a file, do the following:

1. From the File Manager, select a file.

2. Choose **O**wner from the **S**ecurity menu to display the Owner dialog box.

3. Choose the **T**ake Ownership button to change the owner of the file to the current user.

Figure 29.23 shows the Owner dialog box for the TEST1.TXT file.

Fig. 29.23

The Owner dialog box for a file.

If passwords are allowed to be descriptive and chosen by their users, the passwords may be easy to guess. For this reason, you could use the **T**ake Ownership button in the Owner dialog box simply to change the owner name to one that is less descriptive.

Auditing Files and Directories

The ability to audit file and directory operations is a powerful security feature. This mechanism allows operations to be logged whether the operation is successful or unsuccessful. You can log attempted accesses to files or directories for all major operations to detect unauthorized activity. You can also monitor authorized file or directory accesses to correct problems or improve performance.

An examination of unsuccessful operations may show that the file or directory permissions are set improperly. You can use the log entries to determine what changes should be made to file or directory access control to enable valid operations. Unsuccessful unauthorized operations can trigger a search for the source of a security problem. For both of these problems, you can use the auditing mechanism for discovery and correction.

You can also use logged information about successful directory and file operations to improve performance. You can move files and directories that are frequently referenced to faster disks to provide better access. Frequent access to important files can also indicate the need to provide the continuous backup capability of disk mirroring.

Logged successful disk and file accesses may also be unauthorized. A frequent and careful examination of the source of operations may show that they were performed by a user or group who should not have file or directory access for those types of operations. The file permissions can prevent a repeat of the unauthorized operations on a file or directory. Table 29.4 lists the file operations that you can select for auditing.

Table 29.4 File operations you can audit

Operation	Description
Read	Read the file and list the attributes, owner, and permissions
Write	Write to the file, change its attributes, and list its owner and permissions
Execute	Run an application and list its attributes, owner, and permissions
Delete	Delete the file
Change Permissions	Change the file permissions
Take Ownership	Change the owner of the file

If you audit Take Ownership, for example, a change to a file's owner will be logged, as shown in figure 29.23.

Table 29.5 lists the directory operations that may be selected as events for auditing.

Table 29.5 Directory operations you can audit

Operation	Description
Read	List file names and their attributes, owner, and permissions

Operation	Description
Write	Create files and subdirectories in the directory, show the owner and permissions, and change attributes
Execute	Show the owner, permissions, and attributes; use subdirectories in a path specification
Delete	Delete the directory
Change Permissions	Change the directory permissions
Take Ownership	Change the directory owner

Fig. 29.24

The display of a change in file ownership.

Summary

In this chapter, you learned that you can use NT permissions to closely protect files and directories. The permissions are granted or denied to users or groups. The special permissions provide finer control than the standard permissions over the operations allowed for files and directories. The owner of a file or directory may be changed to alter the primary responsibility for its access control.

You can use permissions to control the access to shared directories as well as local files and directories. You can also control the maximum number of users who can connect to a shared directory. Finally, you can audit the type of operations performed on files and directories to detect and correct security problems.

Understanding System Security in Windows NT

M aintaining the security of a Windows NT system involves controlling access to the system and its resources. Security is achieved by protecting the system from an accidental or deliberate loss of information. User accounts, which define the authorized users of the system, are the principal security mechanism. You can control the user's membership in groups in which access to system resources is granted or denied. Typical resources to which access is controlled are files, directories, and printers. To understand the security mechanisms of Windows NT, you begin by learning about the user account mechanism and how it secures the system.

Controlling System Availability

The control of the security of a Windows NT system begins with the control of its availability. You can control the physical access to a system by locking it in an office and restricting access to users who have a key.

Whether the physical access is restricted or not, use of the Windows NT system is restricted to previously defined authorized users of the system. In this way, you can control system use, identify users and optionally audit their activity, and restrict the operations that users may perform.

Starting Windows NT

You must load the NT system from disk to memory before you can attempt to log on to the system. This procedure is called *booting*, or loading, the system and is discussed in Chapter 2, "Operating Windows NT." The initial phase of loading the NT system varies according to the platform on which it has been built. On PCs, for example, a dual boot capability is possible so that users can bring up Windows NT or DOS.

After you have selected the NT system for loading, you see a series of messages about the operations that NT performs. The startup messages vary according to the computer platform. For example, on a PC workstation, NT checks the hardware of your system and displays the workstation's version of NT and amount of RAM. It also checks and displays the format for all disk drives.

> **WARNING:** Never abort the boot procedure. If you power off a system before NT is completely loaded, or any time that it is loaded, the file system can be corrupted. When a file system is corrupted, you must perform a repair operation before you can use the system again.

Logging On

After the Windows NT logo appears, a logon message box prompts you to press Ctrl+Alt+Del to begin the logon dialog, as shown in figure 30.1. (On a DOS system, pressing Ctrl+Alt+Del reboots the PC. Under Windows 3.1, pressing Ctrl+Alt+Del displays a dialog box.) From this dialog box, you can reboot the system, return to the application, or terminate the application. On a Windows NT system, Ctrl+Alt+Del is used solely to initiate a logon.

Fig. 30.1

The logon
message box.

A second dialog box appears after you press Ctrl+Alt+Del during the
boot of the NT system. The dialog box prompts you to enter a
username and password, with the username and system in the From
field entered from the previous logon serving as the default.

You additionally may enter in the From field the name of a domain (a
client-server set of NT workstations). In a domain, your account information is kept on a central server that administers the group of networked workstations. If you're working with a single workstation, the
domain name can simply reference the name of your workstation.

In the example log shown in figure 30.2, the username entered is Administrator, which is the username for an account created automatically
during the installation of Windows NT. After the entry of the domain,
the password is entered. Regardless of the characters you type, only
asterisks appear in the Password field. This prevents anyone from seeing your password and using it later to gain unauthorized access to the
system.

```
┌─────────────────────────────────────────────────┐
│ ▬                     Welcome                      ▲ │
├─────────────────────────────────────────────────┤
│  ▓▓▓▓▓                                             │
│  ▓▓▓▓▓  Username:  [Administrator          ]      │
│  ▓▓▓▓▓  From:      [BOB486              ][▼]      │
│  MICROSOFT.                                        │
│  WINDOWS NT.  Password:  [*******         ]       │
│                                                    │
│          [   OK   ]     [   Help   ]              │
└─────────────────────────────────────────────────┘
```

Fig. 30.2

The Welcome
dialog box.

After you have entered the username and password, they are checked
against the ones recorded for your username and your domain. If they
match the stored entries, the Program Manager window appears. If you
have set Save Settings on Exit, the program groups expanded during
your preceding session are expanded automatically.

The logon procedure is the first and primary level of protection provided by Windows NT. It restricts use of the system to only the users
whom you have authorized to gain access to the system.

As part of this security mechanism, you also can record all system logon attempts. One or two unsuccessful logons followed by a successful logon with the same username probably means the user mistyped the password, forgot it momentarily, or misspelled it. Many more unsuccessful attempts, perhaps five or more within several minutes, may signal a break-in attempt. To interpret the security log information, you should establish a criterion based on published security guidelines, your experience on other computer systems, and an assessment of the security requirements of your environment.

If you have administrative responsibility for the system, you may choose to set up two accounts for yourself. The first account is part of the Administrators group. Through this account, you perform all operations that require the user rights and access granted to an Administrator. A second account can be used for your work on the system, which has fewer user rights and less access to files and directories.

There are two advantages to having a second account for use when you don't require the administrative rights. First, you can't accidentally delete a file, a directory, or an account if you are using an account that doesn't allow it. Second, if you always use an account that gives access to all system resources and enables you to perform all operations, you will have difficulty understanding user problems. If you have never seen an `Access denied` message, for example, you are less likely to understand—and correct—a user request about a similar problem.

Logging Off

You should log off if you have completed your work for the session and will not be using the system. The logoff procedure prepares the system for use by another user. All currently executing applications are terminated and any data cached in RAM is written to the disk.

The most important aspect of a logoff is that it forces a subsequent user to log on before using the system. A logon requires that the user be identified as an authorized user of the workstation. Unauthorized users can't begin to use the system because they won't be able to successfully complete the logon procedure.

NOTE The login of a user to an account allows the user to be identified both as a specific user and a member of one or more groups.

Access to files and directories is granted or denied through file permissions. Although you can assign different file permissions to each file in a directory, you can use the special directory file permissions to grant or deny users or groups

access to the files in directories. Special directory file per-missions are automatically applied to new files created in a directory. By using the special directory file permissions, you avoid having to manually assign permissions to individual files.

If you use special directory file permissions to automatically assign file permissions, you must create enough directories to segregate files that must have different file permissions. Although you must set up more directories, the definition of file permissions is automatic and therefore simpler. File and directory permissions are discussed in Chapter 29, "Understanding File Security in Windows NT."

You can log off the Windows NT system at any time. From the File menu, select Logoff. This displays the Logoff Windows NT message box (see fig. 30.3). Select OK, and your opened applications are closed and the logoff operation continues. (If you select Cancel, the Logoff Windows NT message box is removed from the screen and no logoff is performed.)

Fig. 30.3

The Logoff Windows NT message box.

When the logoff is completed, the screen presents the logon message box (refer to fig. 30.1), prompting the user to press Ctrl+Alt+Del to log on. Another user can log on, or you can log on again to change to another account, for example.

Shutting Down

You can also choose to make the system unavailable by shutting it down. Before turning the power off, however, wait until you are prompted to do so. Otherwise, you risk losing information cached in memory. This information can be data from the applications you have been using as well as control data kept by the Windows NT system.

From the File menu, select Shutdown. This displays the Shutdown Computer message box, shown in figure 30.4. To complete the shutdown, select OK. If you want the computer to automatically reboot after the shutdown, check the Restart when shutdown is complete option, then select OK. To abort the shutdown and return to your session, select Cancel. Any applications that you started previously are still available.

Fig. 30.4

The Shutdown
Computer
dialog box.

NOTE   If you simply want another user to use the workstation, do not shut down the system. Instead, log off to prepare the workstation for use by another user. In this way, a new user won't have to wait for the system to be reloaded and you maintain the security of the system.

Locking a Workstation

You can also lock your workstation. This security feature, which is part of the Desktop screen saver, prevents unauthorized continuance of a session when the screen saver feature has been invoked.

The Windows NT screen saver feature is different from the screen savers used on the DOS and Windows systems. DOS screen savers allow a password to be defined separately for the screen saver application. In the Windows NT system, the passwords established for accounts are used also for the screen saver.

To enable this feature, select the Desktop icon from the Control Panel, or press Ctrl+Alt+Del and select Lock Workstation. This displays the Desktop dialog box, which is shown in figure 30.5. Select the Password protected check box.

When the number of minutes in the **D**elay field of the Desktop dialog box has passed without activity, the screen saver is displayed. Any attempt to use the workstation again displays the Workstation Locked message box, which is shown in figure 30.6.

The message box displays the time and date that the workstation was locked and the accounts that may unlock it. It also specifies the action you must take to resume the system. The example in figure 30.6 indicates that only the administrator or a user in the Administrators group can resume the current session and gain access to the workstation. After you press Ctrl+Alt+Del to unlock the workstation, the Workstation Locked dialog box is displayed.

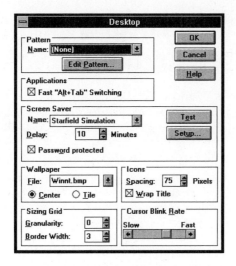

Fig. 30.5

The Desktop
dialog box.

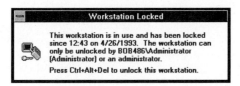

Fig. 30.6

The Worksta-
tion Locked
message box.

In figure 30.7, for example, the dialog box requests a password for the
Administrator account. You can create at least one additional account
that is a member of the Administrators group to enable the restart of a
terminal session if the user who locked the workstation was using an
account in the Administrators group. This feature enables you to regain
control of the system without turning off the power when the user who
initiated the session can't return to resume it. The user who locked the
workstation in figure 30.6, for example, was using an account in the
Administrators group. So if you had created at least one additional
account that is a member of the Administrators group, you could enable the restart of the session.

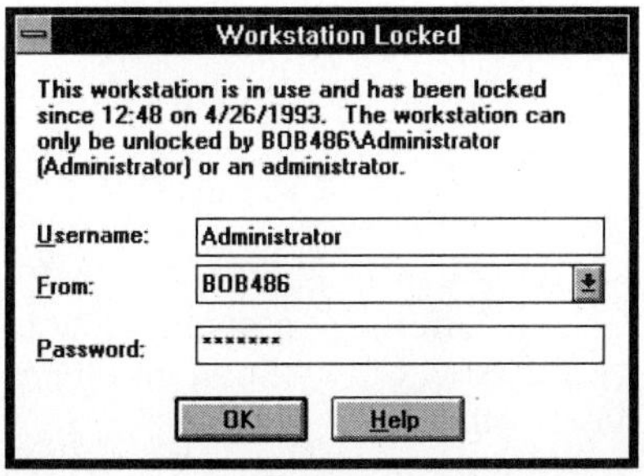

```
┌─────────────────────────────────────────┐
│ ─             Workstation Locked          │
├─────────────────────────────────────────┤
│ This workstation is in use and has been locked │
│ since 12:48 on 4/26/1993.  The workstation can │
│ only be unlocked by BOB486\Administrator      │
│ (Administrator) or an administrator.          │
│                                               │
│ Username:    Administrator                    │
│                                               │
│ From:        BOB486                    ▼      │
│                                               │
│ Password:    *******                          │
│                                               │
│        ┌────────┐   ┌────────┐               │
│        │   OK   │   │  Help  │               │
│        └────────┘   └────────┘               │
└─────────────────────────────────────────┘
```

Fig. 30.7

The Worksta-
tion Locked
dialog box.

Controlling Local System Access with User Accounts

The accounts of a Windows NT system are the basis for nearly all its security protection mechanisms. After you have logged on to a system, your user account determines the types of access you have to system resources. The best example of this is the directory and file permissions (which are discussed in Chapter 29).

The creation and control of accounts is important and demands that you understand the components of accounts and how account operations are performed. You administer accounts through the User Manager program item in the Administrative Tools program group. Double-click the User Manager icon to display the User Management window.

You control the accounts of the local Windows NT system from the User Manager window. The accounts are listed alphabetically in the upper half of the window. The various groups to which users may belong are listed alphabetically in the lower half of the window. In figure 30.8, for example, the Administrator, Branchek, and Guest accounts are displayed, along with seven groups and a brief description of each.

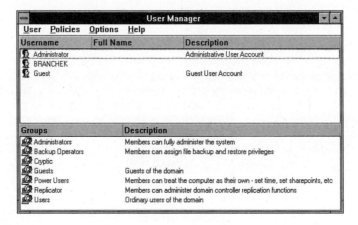

Fig. 30.8

The User Manager window.

NOTE   Before you create an account, you should decide on the account characteristics.

To create an account for a new user, select New User from the User menu. This displays the New User dialog box. Figure 30.9 displays a new account for Mary Smith.

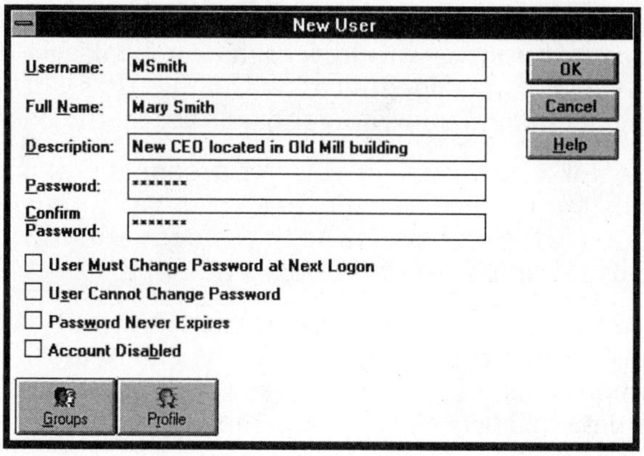

```
┌─────────────────────────────────────────────────────┐
│ ─                        New User                     │
├───────────────────────────────────────────────────────┤
│ Username:     [MSmith                    ]    [  OK  ] │
│                                                         │
│ Full Name:    [Mary Smith                ]    [Cancel] │
│                                                         │
│ Description:  [New CEO located in Old Mill building]  [ Help ] │
│                                                         │
│ Password:     [••••••••        ]                        │
│ Confirm                                                 │
│ Password:     [••••••••        ]                        │
│                                                         │
│  ☐ User Must Change Password at Next Logon             │
│  ☐ User Cannot Change Password                         │
│  ☐ Password Never Expires                              │
│  ☐ Account Disabled                                    │
│                                                         │
│   [  Groups  ]   [  Profile  ]                          │
└─────────────────────────────────────────────────────┘
```

Fig. 30.9

The New User dialog box.

Usernames and Passwords

You can enter up to 20 characters for the username. Duplicate usernames are not allowed. You can form a descriptive username by using the first letter of a user's first name appended to their last name. This method enables users with the same last name to have an easily identifiable username that is still unique. The problem with deriving account names in this way is that it may provide unauthorized users with information that can help them to gain access to the system.

This becomes a security problem only if you allow users with descriptive usernames to define their own passwords. A user will often choose a familiar word or name as their password to make it easier to remember. For example, they may choose the name of their spouse, one of their children, or a pet.

Other members of the same company or organization may attempt an unauthorized access to an NT workstation using the username of an authorized user whose habits they know. Unauthorized users may try the names of the authorized user's spouse, children, pets, or favorite sports team as passwords. (On one major computer manufacturer's system, some devotees of the Adventure game chose as passwords PLUGH and XYZZY, which serve as magic words to gain advantages during the game.)

You can eliminate this problem by defining cryptic usernames and passwords for your NT system. If you don't, unauthorized accesses will likely occur. The use of totally cryptic words for passwords presents another security problem. If a password is too cryptic, you increase the likelihood that a user will write it down. An unauthorized user may read the written username or password and use it to log on to the system.

An analogous problem occurs frequently with Automatic Teller Machine (ATM) cards used to withdraw cash from bank accounts. Users choose a cryptic Personal Identification Number (PIN), have difficulty remembering it, and end up writing the number on the back of the card.

You should enter a password for your NT accounts that can't be guessed easily but is not so cryptic that a user can't remember it. You can also enter a cryptic username so that it does not provide clues for someone to use in an unauthorized logon attempt.

You continue the process of account creation in the New User dialog box by optionally entering information in the Full Name field to identify the user of the account. If you entered a cryptic username, you should always complete this field because it is the only way to identify the user.

You use the **Description** field to provide additional information that you want associated with the account. For example, in an Advanced Server for Windows NT domain of interconnected systems, the **Description** field could identify the location of the user's workstation.

You can use up to 14 characters for a password. Passwords are case-sensitive. The password must be entered identically in the **Password** and **Confirm Password** fields. Choose a minimum of 8 or 9 characters for the password because the number of combinations of 8 or 9 characters is large, making it difficult for an intruder to gain entry to the system.

You may create accounts that don't require passwords. Access to the system can be gained if an unauthorized user learns only the username to such an account. You should consider the creation of accounts without passwords only when access to the workstations is restricted or the system doesn't require security protection.

You select the check boxes at the bottom of the New User dialog box to enable the remaining password and account characteristics. Check the first box if you want the user to change the password at the next logon. (The password you have entered in the **Password** field becomes a temporary password for the account.)

If you require users to change their password at the next logon (which may be their first logon), do not check the second check box, User Cannot Change Password. You must allow users to change their password if you require a password change at the next logon.

You can specify that passwords expire periodically by leaving the Password Never Expires check box blank. It's a good idea to force password changes periodically (for example, every three months). If an unauthorized access has occurred, it may be prevented from continuing by a periodic change in passwords.

When you detect an unauthorized access, review the security log to determine if there were earlier intrusions. Look for logons at times that the authorized user knows he or she did not log on. (This process is similar to checking your monthly credit card charges for unauthorized purchases.)

The last check box in the New User dialog box is Account Disabled. You might disable an account, for example, while a user is on vacation or on a business trip. Unauthorized attempts to gain access to a disabled account are impossible. You can't disable the default Administrator account. This ensures that an account will always be available to control all operations of the system.

You could use the Account Disabled option to create a disabled account that is used as a template for the creation of new accounts. You can create new accounts quickly if most of the information is already filled in. You can also create several template accounts, each for a different group of users.

Groups

Access to system resources such as files, directories, and printers is controlled by entries that reference groups as well as individual users. You may find that the administration of the resource access is more easily controlled by ACL entries that reference groups rather than individual users. Group membership is controlled through the User Manager application.

Two buttons are located in the lower-left corner of the New User dialog box. You select the **G**roups button to display the Group Memberships dialog box. From this window, a user can be made a member of one or more groups. A user is automatically made a member of the Users group, which allows the user minimal capabilities. In figure 30.10, the account for Mary Smith is a member of a single group.

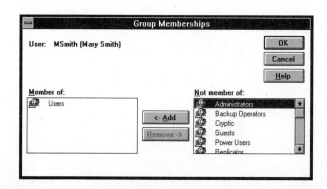

Fig. 30.10

The Group Memberships dialog box.

You can make a user a member of one or more additional groups by selecting a group in the **N**ot member of list and then choosing the **A**dd button. You can remove a user from a group by selecting the group from the **M**ember of list and choosing the **R**emove button.

Membership in groups affects the operations a user may perform on the system and the user's access to files and other system resources. The use of groups can be useful if you later expand your system. If your workstation becomes a member of an Advanced Server for Windows NT network, your user accounts and groups will become the basis of a central server that administers all domain workstations.

Domain user accounts established on, or transferred to, the server can be used to log on to any workstation in the domain. If groups are already established, it is easier to allow or disallow access to files using the existing permissions, which already contain entries for the groups.

Several groups that provide varying degrees of access to resources are already defined by the NT system. These groups are Administrators, Backup Operators, Users, Guests, Power Users, and Replicator.

A member of the Administrators group has complete control over the system. Administrators can perform the following operations:

- Partition or format a hard disk
- Display, initialize, and control security data
- Perform volume backups and restores
- Access system memory locations for debugging
- Become the owner of files
- Unlock a locked workstation
- Assign user rights
- Create, delete, and connect to administrative shares such as disk root directories

(Administrative shares are symbolic names applied to system resources accessible only to members of the Administrators group.)

A member of the Backup Operators group can perform the following tasks:

- Perform volume backups and restores of the system disks
- Bypass the read permission of files for backup and the write permission for restoring files from tape
- Back up files across the network to a workstation that has a tape drive
- Connect to the root directory of hard drives

The Guests group and account allow access to the workstation through an established account other than the Administrator account. The Guests account is created during the installation of the NT system along with the Administrator account. Access to system resources through this group is meant to be specifically assigned by the Administrator. You must set the specific user rights for the Guests account and the permissions assigned to the Guests group. You should define the Guests account with minimal user rights for most systems.

The Power Users group is designed to allow members to perform some administrative capabilities on a system. Operations authorized through this account are

■ Access directories and printers of local and remote NT systems

■ Assign permissions to shared directories on the network

■ Install, share, and manage printers on the network

■ Create, modify, and delete user accounts they've created, and add accounts to groups they've created

■ Change the internal clock

You are automatically added to the Users group when your account is created. The Users group allows normal operations to be performed on the system. Specific operations that may be performed by members of the Users group are

■ Create and delete groups and add or remove user accounts from groups they've created; cannot create a new account

■ Establish personal profiles including desktop colors, mouse and keyboard settings, and personal program groups

■ Connect to resources, such as files or printers, on a network

■ Lock a workstation

You can assign a user to a member of the Replicator group to grant them the ability to log on as a workstation's Replicator Service. You should make only one account a member of this group. After the member is granted the Log On as a Service user right, he or she can perform directory replication functions in a domain of NT systems. Membership in this group may be necessary only for the administrator.

A second set of groups is based on how you are using a system. These groups are not displayed in the **M**ember of and **N**ot member of lists in the Group Memberships dialog box. Users become members of one of these two groups as they gain access to the system. The first group is Interactive Users, which are users who have directly logged onto a workstation. The second is Network Users, which are users who have connected to the system from another in the network.

Two additional groups are Creator Owner and Everyone. The Everyone group contains all users of the system, including members of the Interactive Users and Network Users groups. A member of the Creator Owner group is a user who created or became the owner of a file, directory, or print job.

Groups can be used in the access control list entries for system resources such as files, directories, and printers. Each group in an ACL entry is associated with permissions. You use the permissions to grant or deny access to system resources. Groups provide a convenient way to control the access of multiple users. If the groups have more than a single member, you are controlling the access of multiple users to a resource with a single ACL entry.

Groups are part of the mechanism that provides C2-level security for the Windows NT system. The level of security provided by this specification is discretionary access control to the resources of a system. Discretionary access control allows an individual, ideally the system administrator, to use a mechanism to control the access to system resources. To implement C2-level security, NT uses permissions stored with resources such as directories, files, and printers.

Profiles

Although multiple users can be authorized to use one Windows NT workstation, they all won't use it in the same way. Users may execute different applications and read and write to different data files and documents. The permissions you create may restrict them to only the system resources to which they require access, such as certain files and directories. If this is the case, you should make it easy for them to get to and use these resources.

The user environment profile sets up the environment for users based on the information they access most frequently when they use the workstation. It points them to the information they typically use during a session on the NT workstation. In addition, the user environment profile can execute a set of commands automatically when a user logs on. This is a common feature of multiuser and client-server systems. In Windows NT, for example, you can place commands in a command file that executes automatically at logon to start up an application. These two features eliminate some of the liabilities of sharing the system with other users by allowing their user accounts to be tailored to meet their user requirements.

Select the Profile button in the New User dialog box to display the User Environment Profile dialog box. You use this dialog box to define a command file and its location. The command file is a BAT or CMD file whose contents are executed automatically at logon. You must place the command file in the WINNT root directory on the boot drive.

The command file is called a *script file* and can be used for one user or several. In the example shown in figure 30.11, a script file for the Mary Smith user has the MSmithlogon file name. The file name denotes that the script file is used for only her account.

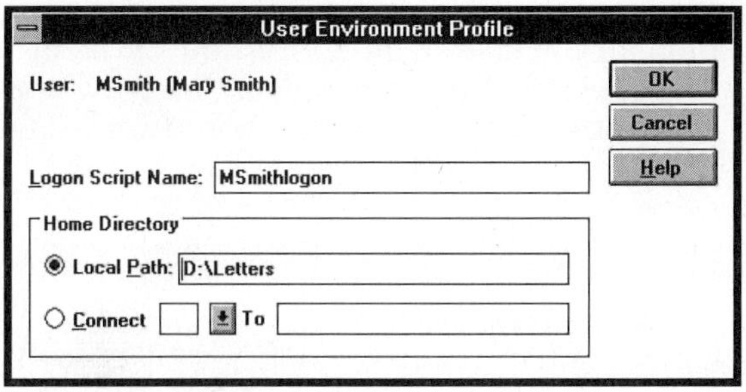

```
┌─────────────────────────────────────────────┐
│═             User Environment Profile         │
│                                               │
│ User:   MSmith (Mary Smith)          ┌──────┐ │
│                                      │  OK  │ │
│                                      ├──────┤ │
│                                      │Cancel│ │
│ Logon Script Name: MSmithlogon       ├──────┤ │
│                                      │ Help │ │
│ ┌Home Directory──────────────────────└──────┘ │
│ │ ⦿ Local Path: D:\Letters                │  │
│ │ ○ Connect  [  ] ⬥ To [            ]     │  │
│ └──────────────────────────────────────────┘ │
└─────────────────────────────────────────────┘
```

Fig. 30.11

The User Environment Profile dialog box.

You use the User Environment Profile dialog box also to define a home directory for a user. The home directory is the default disk and directory used for File Open and Save As dialog boxes from the system and third-party applications. If a working directory isn't defined for an application, the home directory is the default target or destination for file accesses. The home directory entry also becomes the default for the SCS command prompt.

The purpose of the home directory is to automatically set the location for the majority of data files and applications used by users as they logon on to the system. If users don't access files or applications outside this location, they can begin working immediately. In addition, if users don't need to reference another directory, you can set file and directory permissions to restrict them to the home directory.

To enable the entry of a directory on a local system drive, select Local **P**ath and enter the path specification. In the example shown in figure 30.11, Mary Smith's account is directed to drive D and the Letters directory.

If you use the %USERNAME% symbol in place of a subdirectory in the path specification, the NT system replaces the symbol with the logon username. This feature enables you to define a template account in which the user environment profile defines a user's home directory as a subdirectory that matches the username.

You can create new accounts quickly if you don't have to change the home directory specification for each new account. You must create the subdirectory (with the File Manager Create Directory command) with a name that matches the username. The NT system's boot disk contains a USERS directory that is created when the system is installed. You can create the home directory for a user as a subdirectory under this directory.

Select **C**onnect To in the User Environment Profile dialog box to define a home directory on a remote shared directory. You enter the drive letter specification for the shared directory, and a system and directory specification in the Universal Naming Convention (UNC) format. In figure 30.12, the home directory is set to the shared spreadsheets directory referenced as G on the BOB386 system.

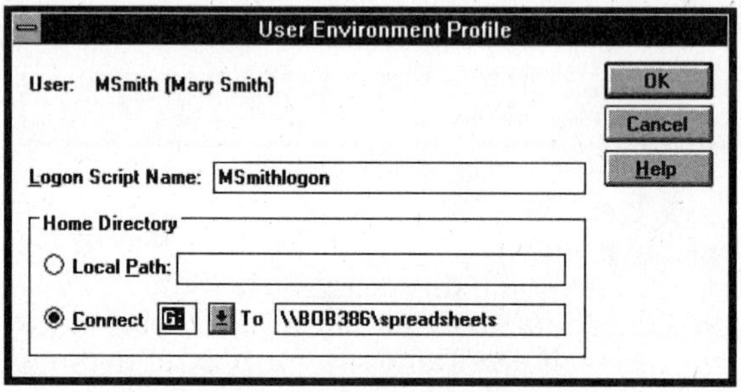

Fig. 30.12

The Connect To field of the User Environment Profile dialog box.

```
┌─────────────────────────────────────────────────────────┐
│ ▄                   User Environment Profile              │
│                                                           │
│   User:   MSmith (Mary Smith)                  ┌───OK───┐ │
│                                                └────────┘ │
│                                                ┌─Cancel─┐ │
│                                                └────────┘ │
│   Logon Script Name:  MSmithlogon              ┌──Help──┐ │
│  ┌─Home Directory────────────────────────────┐ └────────┘ │
│  │ ○ Local Path: [                          ] │           │
│  │                                            │           │
│  │ ◉ Connect [G:] [▲] To [\\BOB386\spreadsheets] │        │
│  └────────────────────────────────────────────┘          │
└─────────────────────────────────────────────────────────┘
```

NOTE The Universal Naming Convention (UNC) format extends the naming format used by systems such as NT and DOS. In the UNC format, the name of the system a shared directory is located on is prefixed with double slashes (\\) and terminated with a single slash (\). The share name associated with the shared directory follows the single slash, which is followed by the file specification.

Changing an Account's Properties

Sometimes you need to change the characteristics of an account. For example, you may want to change the group to which a member belongs. To change the characteristics of an account, select **P**roperties from the **U**ser menu. This displays the User Properties dialog box, shown in figure 30.13.

The User Properties dialog box, which contains the same information as the New User dialog box, is used to change information. For

```
┌─────────────────────────────────────────────────────┐
│ ─              User Properties                        │
├───────────────────────────────────────────────────────┤
│  Username:   MSmith                        ┌──────────┐ │
│                                            │   OK     │ │
│  Full Name:  [Mary Smith              ]    └──────────┘ │
│                                            ┌──────────┐ │
│  Description: [New CEO located in Old Mill building]  │ Cancel   │ │
│                                            └──────────┘ │
│  Password:   [**************]              ┌──────────┐ │
│                                            │  Help    │ │
│  Confirm     [**************]              └──────────┘ │
│  Password:                                              │
│                                                         │
│  ☐ User Must Change Password at Next Logon             │
│  ☒ User Cannot Change Password                         │
│  ☒ Password Never Expires                              │
│  ☐ Account Disabled                                    │
│                                                         │
│  ┌────────┐ ┌────────┐                                 │
│  │ 👥     │ │ 🔧     │                                  │
│  │ Groups │ │ Profile│                                  │
│  └────────┘ └────────┘                                 │
└─────────────────────────────────────────────────────┘
```

Fig. 30.13

The User Properties dialog box.

example, the description, password, password expiration, and ability to change the password for Mary Smith's account are changed through the User Properties dialog box shown in figure 30.13.

Copying an Account

Select **C**opy from the **U**ser menu or press F8 to display the Copy of user name dialog box. You use this dialog box to add a new user account based on the entries of the selected account in the User Manager window. You must supply new entries in the **U**sername, **D**escription, **P**assword, and **C**onfirm Password fields.

Select the **G**roups button to change the groups to which the new user will belong. Select the **P**rofile button to change the characteristics set through the user environment profile. The information in the fields of the Group Memberships and User Environment Profile dialog boxes are copied from the selected user account. You also use the **C**opy command with permanently disabled template accounts, which were discussed in the "Usernames and Passwords" section.

When copying an account to create a new one, you aren't restricted to using only template accounts. Any existing account can be used as a template for the creation of a new account. You should choose the one that is the most similar to the account you want to create.

Changing the Username

To change a username in some multiuser systems, you must delete the account and enter it again. Windows NT, however, allows you to change the username through a simple menu command.

To change only the username for an existing account, select the account and choose **R**ename in the **U**ser menu. This displays the Rename dialog box (see fig. 30.14). For example, suppose you must create an account for Matilde Smith. Because you can't have duplicate usernames, you change Mary Smith's username from MSmith to LSmith (*L* is her middle initial).

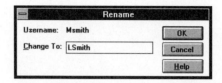

Deleting an Account

The **D**elete option in the **U**ser menu enables you to remove the selected user account. Use this command with caution. When you attempt to delete an account, the message box in figure 30.15 is displayed.

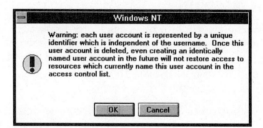

If you delete an account and then create a new one with the same username, a new number serving as an identifier of the account is created. This new identifier will not match the one associated with the old account with the same name. The new account will not have access to resources through old file permission entries that reference the earlier username. The internal identification for a user is a number associated with the username and not the username itself. You can avoid this problem by granting access to resources through file permissions that reference groups rather than usernames.

If you decide to continue the deletion process by selecting OK, you are asked to confirm the deletion of the account with a subsequent dialog box. Select **N**o to retain the account and **Y**es to complete its deletion.

Defining a Group

You can define your own groups in addition to the defined system groups. You choose the criteria for membership in the new group and the permissions to use resources. This increases security because the addition of groups can provide more selective access to resources.

To define a new group, first select a user in the User Manager window. Then choose New Local Group from the User menu. This displays the New Local Group dialog box. The selected user is automatically made a member of the newly created group. Figure 30.16 displays the addition of a new group, Salespersons, of which LSmith is made a member. The group and its description are added to the list of groups in the lower half of the User Manager window.

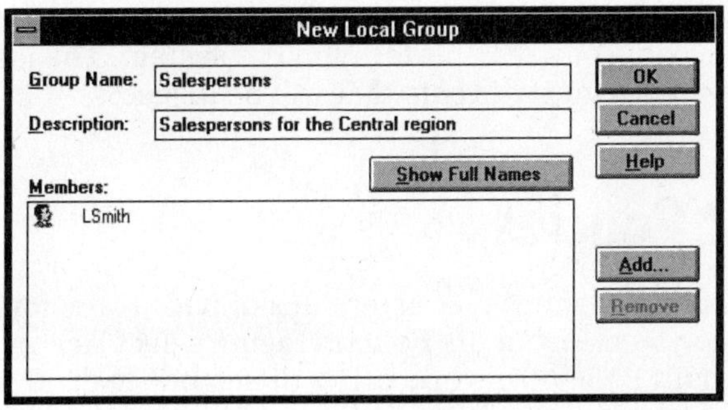

Fig. 30.16

The New Local Group dialog box.

An unlimited number of groups can be created and referenced in access control entries. However, you should create new groups only when they are needed to more closely control access to system resources. The addition of new groups does provide more control, but at the cost of adding complexity to the interpretation of the access users have to resources.

As discussed in Chapter 29, a user's access to a file or directory is the sum of the access specified for each group to which the user is a member (unless No Access is specified for a group to which the user is a member). The more entries you make in the ACLs for resources, the more difficult it is to interpret the access users are granted.

Controlling Local System Access with Policies

Windows NT controls the application of three categories of security rules for the system. These rules, which are collectively called *security policies*, control password characteristics, operations that can be performed by users, and the security events that are audited. The first two policies are applied separately for each user account, and the third policy is applied to the system. The policies are defined from an Administrative application.

You define policies in the **P**olicies menu of the User Manager window. **A**ccount, the first option in the **P**olicies menu, sets password constraints for all user accounts. The User Rights option specifies the operations a user or group may perform on the system. The last option, Au**d**it, defines the security events that will be logged.

Account Policies

The account policy defines characteristics of passwords for all the accounts of the system. From the **P**olicies menu, select **A**ccount to display the Account Policy dialog box. The dialog box is divided into four fields, each of which controls an attribute of the password. For example, you can set the fewest number of characters that can be defined for user passwords. In the example shown in figure 30.17, the password for any accounts cannot be less than 9 characters.

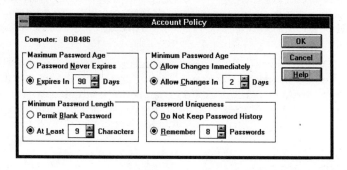

Fig. 30.17

The Account Policy dialog box.

The greater the number of characters used for a password, the more secure an account because an unauthorized user must try more combinations of characters for the password. Although the specification of many characters for a password increases security, it creates the burden of entering a long password every time users log on. A minimum password length of 9 characters is often recommended by security experts because this length provides adequate security without overburdening the users.

In the Maximum Password Age section of the dialog box, you can specify the duration of time before a user must change the password. Remember the benefit of requiring users to choose new passwords. You may prevent unauthorized users who had previously gained access to an account from accessing the account again after the password is changed. If you select the Password Never Expires toggle button, passwords are no longer required to be changed.

The Minimum Password Age section controls the period of time before users are first allowed to change their password. Set the toggle button Allow Changes Immediately to allow users to change their password at any time.

The last section in this dialog box, Password Uniqueness, controls the number of previous passwords that are kept in a password history list for each user. When users attempt to change their password, they cannot change it to an entry in this list.

If you force password expirations but set the Do Not Keep Password History toggle button, users can keep their original password by changing it twice. They change their password to a new one and then immediately change it back to their original password. To prevent this, set the Remember toggle button to at least two passwords.

T I P

If you implement password history lists, you must not allow immediate password changes by setting the Allow Changes Immediately toggle button. In addition, the Allow Changes In selection must be set to at least one day.

Remember, the account password policies apply to all accounts. The Account Policy dialog box cannot be set separately for different accounts.

User Rights

User rights are similar to permissions. Both rights and permissions grant the ability to perform operations. However, permissions apply to objects (such as directories and files), but rights apply to the system.

A right enables a user to perform a specific operation on the system. There are more than two dozen rights, most of which are self-descriptive. Any combination of them may be assigned to a user account. From the **P**olicies menu, you select **U**ser Rights to display the User Rights Policy dialog box, shown in figure 30.18.

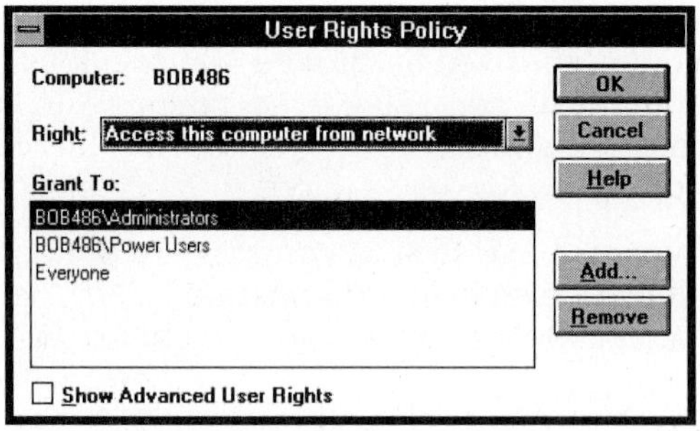

Fig. 30.18

The User Rights Policy dialog box.

A user right can override the file permissions stored on an object. For example, if you grant the user right Backup files and directories, the user can back up files that have an entry in the user's ACL that specifically denies the user read access. You should carefully consider the assignment of user rights for this reason.

You can assign nine standard rights through the User Rights Policy dialog box, as follows:

User Right	Groups Assigned
Access this computer from network	Allows a connection to this computer from a remote system.
Backup files and directories	Grants the right to copy any of the files and directories on the system regardless of their ACL entries.
Change the system time	Grants the right to set the system date and time through the Date/Time application in the Control Panel.
Force shutdown from a remote system	Not currently enabled. Designed to allow an NT server control over the shutdown of the local system.
Log on locally	Allows a normal logon from the workstation.

User Right	Groups Assigned
Manage auditing and security log	Grants the right to define the security events that are logged and to view and reinitialize the log file.
Restore files and directories	Allows a user to restore backed up files and subdirectories to their original directories regardless of the file permissions. You should assign this right along with the Backup files and directories right.
Shut down the system	Allows a user to shut down the local system.
Take ownership of files or other objects	Allows a user to become the owner of objects such as files and directories. An owner normally is granted the Full Control permission for objects.

To display an additional set of user rights in the list of rights, check the **S**how Advanced User Rights check box. Most of the additional rights are designed for use by Windows NT programmers. You need not assign these to a typical user's account. The list of additional rights follows:

Act as part of the operating system

Bypass traverse checking

Create pagefile

Create permanent shared objects

Create token object

Debug programs

Generate security audits

Increase quotas

Increase scheduling priorities

Load and unload device drivers

Lock pages in memory

Log on as a service

Modify firmware environment values

Profile single process

Profile system performance

Receive unsolicited device input

Replace process level token

You can assign advanced user rights to specific users who require the ability to use a feature in an application program they are writing. For example, you can grant the right `Lock pages in memory` to a user who must guarantee that sections of the data in the program will always remain in memory. These pages of memory can be an area into which several cooperating applications read and write data. They are locked into memory to allow a fast exchange of information among the applications.

You should assign no more than the minimum number of user rights that a user requires to successfully complete work on a system. Assigning users more rights than are needed creates the risk that users accidentally or deliberately perform operations that they shouldn't. For example, assigning a user who isn't responsible for backups the right `Backup files and directories` would allow them to make an unauthorized copy of all files on the system.

Approximately half of the rights are preassigned to the system groups. You can manage the user rights by granting a user membership in a group that already has the required user rights. You should assign a specific user right only if the user can't receive it through membership in one or more groups. The following table lists the rights and the groups to which they are assigned:

User Right	Groups Assigned
Access this computer from network	Administrators, Everyone, Power Users
Backup files and directories	Administrators, Backup Operators
Change the system time	Administrators, Power Users
Force shutdown from a remote system	Administrators
Log on locally	Administrators, Backup Operators, Everyone, Guests, Power Users, Users
Manage auditing and security log	Administrators
Restore files and directories	Administrators, Backup Operators

User Right	Groups Assigned
Shut down the system	Administrators, Backup Operators, Everyone, Power Users, Users
Take ownership of files or other objects	Administrators

You can create additional groups that are granted combinations of user rights that are different than the system groups. For example, you can define a group that has all the user rights of a Power User and some of the rights of an Administrator. You can select the name and the abilities of this group to match those of a system from which you're moving applications to the NT system.

Select New Local Group from the User menu to display the Local Group Properties dialog box. Figure 30.19 displays a newly defined group called Operator Manager. The description indicates that members of this group have the user rights of Backup Operators and some of the rights of the Administrators group. You could place users who have some management responsibilities, such as senior operators, in this group. You needn't compromise system security by making them members of the Administrators group, which gives them more rights than they require for their work.

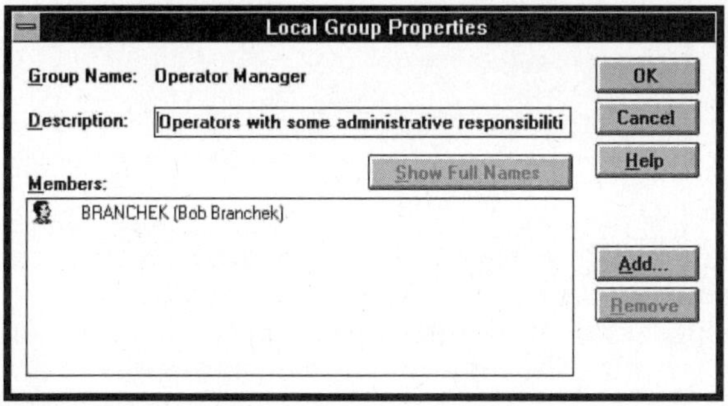

Fig. 30.19

The Local Group Properties dialog box.

Audit Policy

Windows NT enables you to control the system events that will be recorded. You can use an administrative application to examine the recorded system events to determine if one or more system security mechanisms have been compromised. You can then implement a different security strategy to prevent a recurrence of the problem.

You control the auditing of the system through the Audit Policy dialog box by defining the type of operations that will be logged. For example, you can record logons and logoffs of users on the system. You also determine whether to record successful events, unsuccessful events, or both. For example, you can choose to log only unsuccessful attempts to change any of the security policies.

You must first select the **Audit** These Events toggle button in the Audit Policy dialog box to enable the logging of any of the security events. In the example shown in figure 30.20, the boxes are checked for **F**ile and Object Access and **U**se of User Rights to enable both successful and unsuccessful attempts. To audit directory and file access, you must also define the type of access through the Directory and File Auditing dialog boxes, which are displayed by choosing **A**uditing from the **S**ecurity menu of the File Manager. Directory and file auditing can be enabled only on NTFS disks.

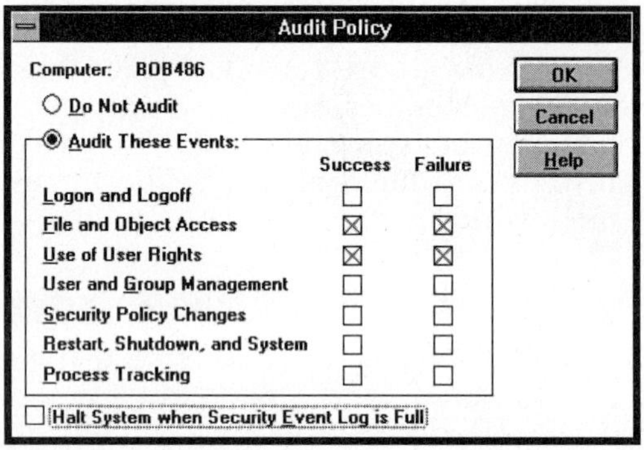

Fig. 30.20

The Audit Policy dialog box.

For a selected file or directory, and user or group, you can select the type of access that may be recorded. In the example shown in figure 30.21, the unsuccessful attempts by users in the Guests group are logged. If you examine the log and find many attempts to access an important file, you may need to learn why a user in the Guests group is repeatedly attempting an unauthorized access to the file.

If you select a different user or group in the **N**ame list of the File Auditing dialog box, the Events to Audit list changes to only the events selected for that user or group. None of the file accesses for any user will be logged if the **D**o Not Audit toggle button is selected in the Audit Policy dialog box of the User Manager (refer to fig. 30.20).

In the Audit Policy dialog box, check Halt System when Security **E**vent Log Is Full to ensure that no audit events are lost. This mechanism forces the system to become unusable if it loses the capability to record security events.

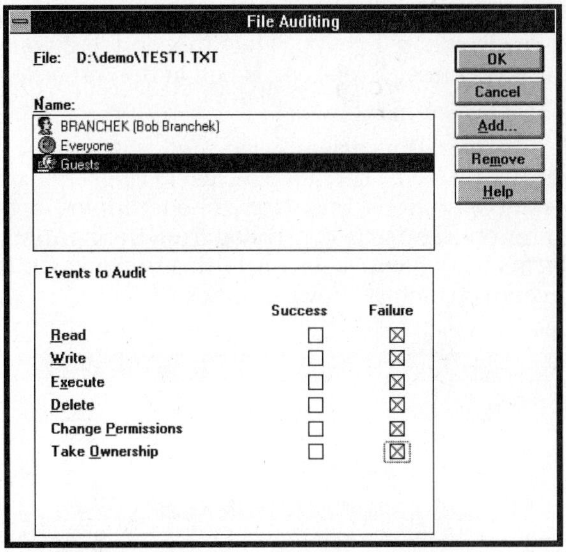

Fig. 30.21

The File
Auditing
dialog box.

If you consider such an action extreme, leave the box unchecked but
define a large enough security log file so that it is unlikely to become
full and lose information about security events. You control the size of
the security log file through the Event Viewer in the Administrative
application. Choose the Log option to display the Event Log Settings
dialog box, which is shown in figure 30.22.

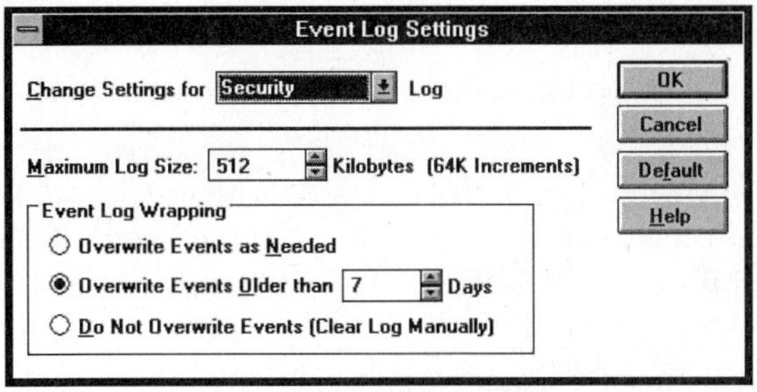

Fig. 30.22

The Event Log
Settings dialog
box.

You use the Event Log Settings dialog box also to set the action the
audit log mechanism will take if the security log file becomes full. You
have several options. You can choose to overwrite events in the log
after the number of days you specify. If you back up the log file, perhaps as part of a full system backup every week, you can safely overwrite events in the security log that are older than seven days. Or you
could select Overwrite Events as Needed to overwrite the oldest events

if new security events must be recorded and the log file is full. The last option is **D**o Not Overwrite Events. Select this option if you've selected Halt System when Security **E**vent Log Is Full in the Audit Policy dialog box.

You can audit the operations users performed with printers on a system. The operations may be specified for users or groups and you may record successful operations, unsuccessful operations, or both. The logging of printer operations is controlled from the Print Manager window. From the **S**ecurity menu, select **A**uditing to display the Printer Auditing dialog box, which is shown in figure 30.23.

```
┌──────────────────────── Printer Auditing ──────────────────────┐
│                                                                  │
│  Printer: Laser                                    [   OK   ]    │
│                                                                  │
│  Name:                                             [ Cancel ]    │
│   BRANCHEK (Bob Branchek)                          [  Add... ]   │
│   Guests                                           [ Remove ]    │
│   INTERACTIVE                                      [  Help  ]    │
│                                                                  │
│  ┌─ Events to Audit ──────────────────────────┐                 │
│  │                          Success    Failure │                 │
│  │   Print                    ☐          ☐     │                 │
│  │   Full Control             ☐          ☒     │                 │
│  │                                             │                 │
│  └─────────────────────────────────────────────┘                │
└──────────────────────────────────────────────────────────────────┘
```

The Printer
Auditing
dialog box.

You use the Printer Auditing dialog box to add, change, delete, and display the auditing of printer operations. In the Events to Audit section, select Print to log the printing of documents on this printer. Select Full Control to enable the recording when

- The job settings for documents are changed

- The printer properties or permissions are changed

- The printer queue is deleted

- The printing of documents is deleted, paused, or restarted

- A printer is set up to be shared

In the example in figure 30.23, only unsuccessful operations categorized as Full Control will be logged for Interactive users.

You may audit only shared printers. In addition to printing local requests, shared printers can print documents from a disk on another
system through a print request made from the remote system. To select
a user (whose printer access will be audited) from a list of users of a
local or remote system, first choose the **A**dd button in the Printer Auditing dialog box. This displays the Add Users and Group dialog box. In
the **L**ist Names From list, select the username.

You use the Event Viewer to view a logged security event (see fig.
30.24). You should read the logged security events periodically to
check for unauthorized operations—including unsuccessful operations.
You may have to change the security policies or issue new procedures
to one or more users to prevent improper use of the system.

Log	View	Options	Help				
Date	Time	Source	Category	Event	User	Computer	
4/27/93	1:32:36 PM	Security	Object Access	560	Administrator	BOB486	
4/27/93	1:32:36 PM	Security	Object Access	560	Administrator	BOB486	
4/27/93	1:32:35 PM	Security	Object Access	560	Administrator	BOB486	
4/27/93	1:23:22 PM	Security	Object Access	562	Administrator	BOB486	
4/27/93	1:23:22 PM	Security	Object Access	561	Administrator	BOB486	
4/27/93	1:23:22 PM	Security	Object Access	560	Administrator	BOB486	
4/27/93	1:23:22 PM	Security	Object Access	562	Administrator	BOB486	
4/27/93	1:23:22 PM	Security	Object Access	561	Administrator	BOB486	
4/27/93	1:23:22 PM	Security	Object Access	560	Administrator	BOB486	
4/27/93	1:18:40 PM	Security	Object Access	562	Administrator	BOB486	
4/27/93	1:18:40 PM	Security	Object Access	561	Administrator	BOB486	
4/27/93	1:18:40 PM	Security	Object Access	560	Administrator	BOB486	

Fig. 30.24

Display of
security events
through the
Event Viewer.

Figure 30.24 displays the events logged over a brief period of time. You
should not log more information than you require to maintain adequate
security on the system. At a minimum, you should audit unsuccessful
logons and logoffs. Record logons and logoffs if you have modems used
for dialing into your system or your workstations aren't in a physically
secure area. Numerous failed logons may indicate attempted break-ins.
You'd like to learn of these before they become successful.

You also should check the Failure box for **F**ile and Object Access
events (in the Audit Policy dialog box) to learn of attempted unauthorized accesses from valid user accounts. These may be errors by someone attempting to access a file in the wrong directory. You can use the
record of the failed attempt to correct the user. An unsuccessful attempt to access a file also may indicate that access to the file is mistakenly denied to the user.

If you attempt to define audit events when auditing is not enabled
through the **P**olicies menu of the User Manager, you receive a message

box. The message indicates that auditing is not turned on and must be enabled by an Administrator account through the User Manager application.

Determine from the security requirements of your system what other events should be logged. You can choose to log comparable events to those logged on another computer system you've worked on. If you have previously worked with only a stand-alone PC system without connections to other systems, you can't immediately appreciate the need for auditing as part of a comprehensive security mechanism. If you are the only user of an NT workstation without connections to other systems, without a dial-in facility, and in a physically secure location, you don't need to enable auditing.

Controlling Shared Disks

Access to remote disks is controlled through shared directories. This subject was discussed in Chapter 29 along with the control of files and directories. The procedure for establishing a disk to be shared is relatively simple because it's integrated into the regular system applications.

You use the File Manager to manage disks, directories, and files both locally and remotely. The four commands from the Manager **D**isk menu that work with network drives are Connect **N**etwork Drive, **D**isconnect Network Drive, Share **A**s, and S**t**op Sharing.

The first step in making a drive or directory accessible from another system in the network is to set it up to be shared. Choose the Share **A**s command from the **D**isk menu or its icon from the toolbar to display the Shared Directory dialog box. In the User Limit section, you can specify the number of users who can access the disk or directory. The example in figure 30.25 shows the Shared Directory dialog box for D, the selected drive.

Fig. 30.25

The Shared Directory dialog box.

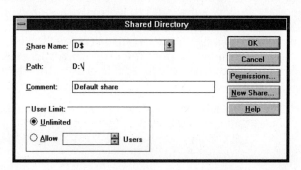

The default value for the User Limit field, **Unlimited**, provides no security because it allows an unlimited number of users to access the disk. If the **A**llow toggle button is selected instead, the default value of 32 is displayed. Enter a value that represents the maximum number of users who must gain access to the shared directory. This mechanism alone would prevent an unauthorized access—if the maximum number of users remain connected to the shared directory. After the number of users connected is less than the limit, however, the system is inadequately protected because any user may now connect to the shared directory.

A second mechanism is required to provide more control over access to information on the shared directory. This second mechanism is permissions. Permissions can be applied to shared directories just as they are to files and directories. The Permissions button in the Shared Directory dialog box is selected to display the Access Through Share Permissions dialog box, which is shown in figure 30.26. The default permissions entry allows the Everyone group full access to the shared object. All users are part of this group, which results in full access to the shared directory.

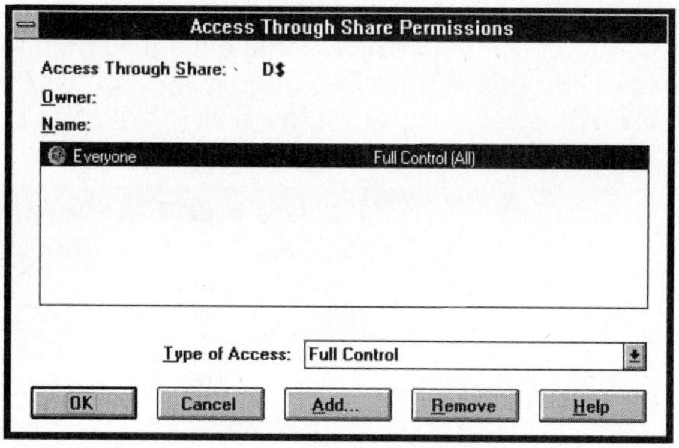

Fig. 30.26

The Access Through Share Permissions dialog box.

You can also define No Access (in the **T**ype of Access list box) for users or groups that should be unable to access the shared directory, unless this conflicts with other permissions. If users are a member of a group that has a permission of No Access, other entries that apply to them cannot grant them any access.

Ensure that you don't have conflicting entries that negate the accesses and protection you are establishing on the shared directory. Recall from previous chapters that permissions on the shared directory do not override the permissions applied to directories and files in the shared directory.

If you want to make the shared drive or directory inaccessible, use **D**isconnect Network Drive from the **D**isk menu of the File Manager. This displays the Disconnect Network Drive dialog box, which enables you to confirm the disconnection of the drive. The shared directory should be disconnected only when no users are accessing the drive. The system will warn you if you attempt to disconnect the shared directory when users are connected.

You should continue the disconnection only if the information on the drive is currently being accessed by an unauthorized user and you want to stop it immediately. Authorized access to the drive will be terminated also and data can be lost by both authorized and unauthorized users.

Controlling Shared Printers

Printers can easily be made available across a network of several computers. The **C**onnect to Printer and **R**emove Printer Connection commands on the **P**rinter menu are used to set up shared network printers. **C**onnect to Printer, or its icon on the toolbar, allows access to a printer on another system in the network. Double-click it to display the Connect to Printer dialog box. Figure 30.27 shows a Connect to Printer dialog box with the HPLASER printer on the BOB486 system selected.

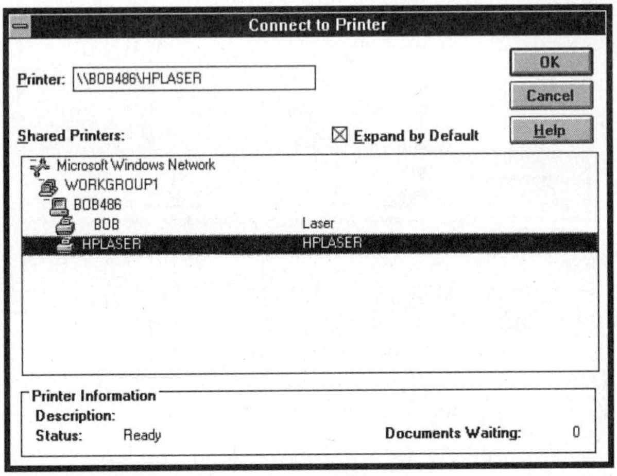

Fig. 30.27

The Connect to Printer dialog box.

After the printer is connected, you control access to it through permissions. You can specify permissions to allow only specific users or groups to manage or send requests to the printer. You must be in the Administrators or Power Users group to set printer permissions.

To define printer permissions, begin by choosing **S**ecurity from the Print Manager. Then choose **P**ermissions to display the Printer Permissions dialog box. The default ACL for a printer grants full control to the Administrators and Power Users groups. The Creator Owner (the owner) is granted the ability to manage documents in the print queue. All users are granted the ability to submit requests to the print queue through the print permission granted to the Everyone group. Figure 30.28 shows the Printer Permissions dialog box for the HPLASER printer on BOB486.

The following table lists the permissions that can be set on a printer and the access they control:

Permission	Access
Print	Print documents on printer
Manage Documents	Change document settings and delete, pause, restart, and resume the printing of documents
Full Control	Set and change all document and printer characteristics
No Access	Cannot use printer

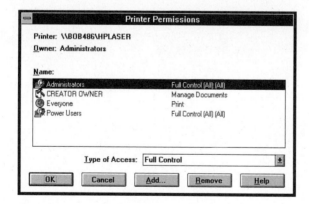

Fig. 30.28

The Printer Permissions dialog box.

The default ACL for a shared printer allows any user to send a document to the printer. You can use the **A**dd button in the Printer Permissions dialog box to add entries that restrict access to the printer. You may allow only certain groups to use a printer and deny all others the print permission. You might want to do this to ensure that the printer is available when needed for certain users.

For example, suppose a user will be printing a form designed in a desktop publishing application on a special stock of paper. You don't want the user to have to wait on the printer and you don't want other users printing on the special paper, so you temporarily restrict access to the printer to only that user. When the user has completed the print job, you allow the other users access to the printer.

Summary

The security of Windows NT is set up and maintained by controlling the access users have to system resources. This is implemented primarily through the creation and maintenance of user accounts. The security policies of the system are defined through the account mechanism, which is administered through the User Manager application.

Precise control is provided by the policies controlling the password characteristics for all accounts, the user rights controlling the operations users can perform to access resources, and the security events that can be logged. They are used along with permissions to control the access for users and groups to resources such as files, directories, shared directories, and printers.

Administering Windows NT

PART

VII

Using the Administrative Applications

W indows NT contains a set of applications that control the administration—that is, the management and control—of the resources of the system. You'll find these applications in the Administrative Tools program group, as shown in figure 31.1.

The User Manager application controls the access and rights users have in the system. The Disk Administrator controls the way information is stored on the primary permanent storage media. Backup ensures that data can be recovered from copies when the original information is corrupted or lost. Both the Event Viewer and the Performance Monitor record and display information about the operations of the system; this information is used to manage the system's resources.

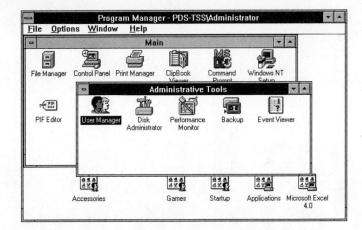

The Administrative Tools program group.

Using the User Manager

The User Manager controls user accounts on the system. Each user must enter a username and password to gain access to Windows NT. This requirement provides security by restricting access to only authorized users. User accounts are created and administered by an individualized password management policy, membership in user groups, user rights to control operations on the system, and auditing control.

The User Manager enables the creation of accounts for each user of the system. User accounts contain information about a user's membership in user groups and the rights users have to perform operations on the system. Auditing information about user activity is also specified through the User Manager. This section describes how to perform operations in the User Manager. To learn about account characteristics that implement security, see Chapter 30, "Understand System Security in Windows NT."

To start the User Manager application, double-click the User Manager icon. This displays the main window, as shown in figure 31.2. Defined user accounts are listed alphabetically below the menu bar. Defined groups are listed at the bottom of the main window. In figure 31.2 there are four user accounts and nine groups. (Use the scroll bar to display the remaining groups.)

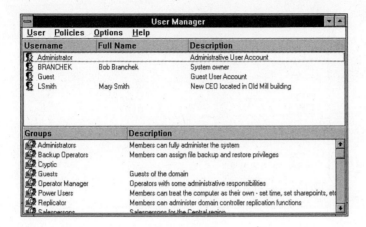

Fig. 31.2

The User
Manager
window.

Managing User Accounts

You use the first option in the User Manager window, **User**, to create, change, rename, delete, or copy user accounts (see fig. 31.3). You can also define a new group and add or remove group members.

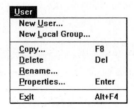

Fig. 31.3

The User menu.

Creating a User Account

To create a new account, follow these steps:

1. From the User Manager window, choose **User**.

2. Choose New **User**. This displays the New User dialog box, which is shown in figure 31.4.

3. In the **Username** field, type the logon name for the user.

4. In the Full **Name** field, type the user's full name.

5. In the **D**escription field, type any descriptive information about the account.

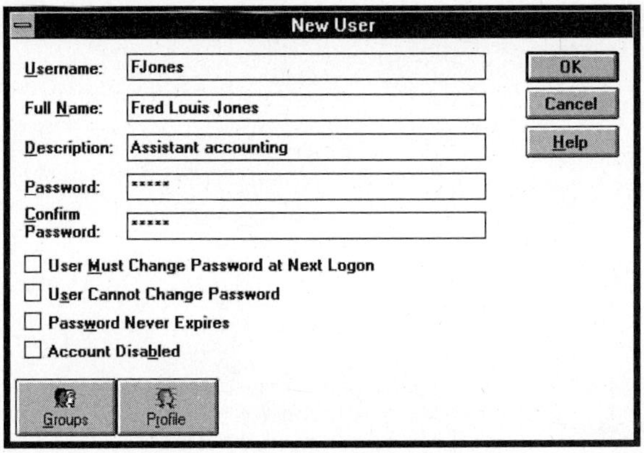

Fig. 31.4

The New User
dialog box.

6. In the **P**assword field and **C**onfirm Password field, enter the user's password. An asterisk appears for each character that you enter in these fields as a security measure to prevent unauthorized users from observing the password.

7. Use the check boxes to define the characteristics for the password.

8. Select the **G**roups button to display the Group Memberships dialog box. You can use this dialog box to control the groups the user will belong to.

9. Select the **P**rofile button to display the User Environment Profile dialog box. You can use this dialog box to define a logon script and a home directory.

10. When you have finished creating the user account, choose OK.

Deleting, Renaming, or Changing a User Account

To delete an account, you must first select it. Then choose **D**elete from the **U**ser menu. In separate message boxes, you must subsequently confirm that you want to delete the account.

To change the username for a selected account, choose **R**ename from the **U**ser menu.

To change the characteristics for a selected account, choose **P**roperties from the **U**ser menu. This displays the User Properties dialog box, which is the same as the New User dialog box except for the title bar and **U**sername field. Figure 31.5 shows the User Properties dialog box for Mary Smith. No entry can be made for the username because it's an existing account.

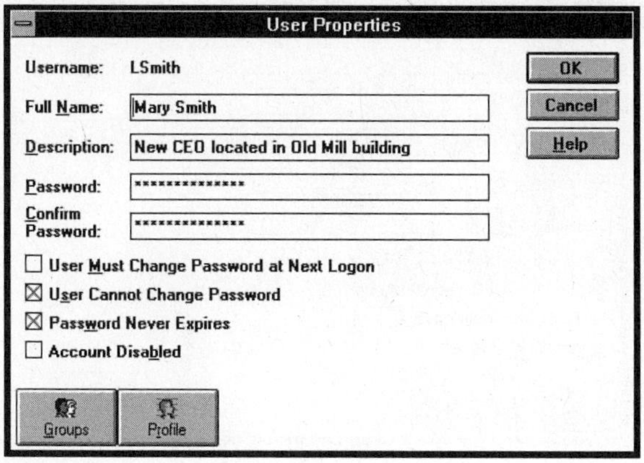

Fig. 31.5

The User
Properties
dialog box.

Copying a User Account

If you're adding a new account that will have similar characteristics as an existing account, you can copy the account. By copying an account, you don't have to type entries in each field that controls account characteristics.

To copy a user account, you must first select it. Then choose **C**opy from the **U**ser menu. This displays the Copy of *username* dialog box, which is similar to the New User and User Properties dialog boxes. You can enter information in all the fields.

Most fields and account characteristics are copied from the account name listed in the title bar of the dialog box. You must type entries into fields that control unique account characteristics, such as the **U**sername, Full **N**ame, **P**assword, and **C**onfirm Password fields. The new account isn't created until you enter information into fields that require entries and select the OK button.

Figure 31.6 shows the Copy of LSmith dialog box. No entries have been typed in this dialog box—the **D**escription field was copied from the LSmith account. The **U**sername, Full **N**ame, and password fields are blank. You must make entries in these fields yourself.

Creating User Groups

New groups are created through the New Local Group dialog box. After a group is created, users can be made a member of the group.

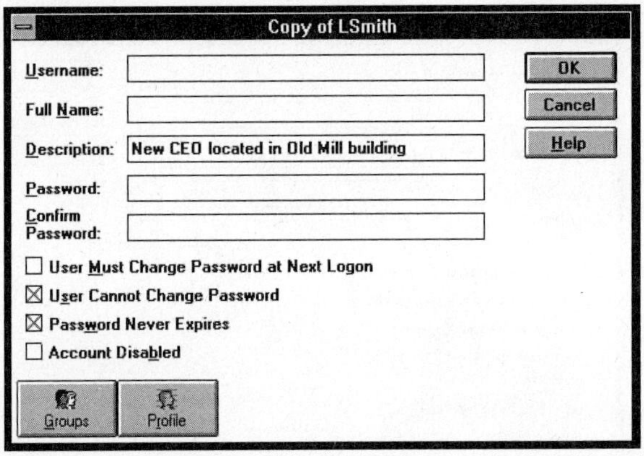

Fig. 31.6

The Copy of *username* dialog box.

To create a new user group, choose **New Local Group** from the **User** menu. This displays the New Local Group dialog box, as shown in figure 31.7. Users who are chosen by you are displayed in the **M**embers section in the lower half of the dialog box. In figure 31.7, a new group called Accounting (along with a description) is defined. The Guest account has been made a member of the new group. Guest became a member of the new local group Accounting because it was the selected account when **New Local Group** was chosen from the **User** menu.

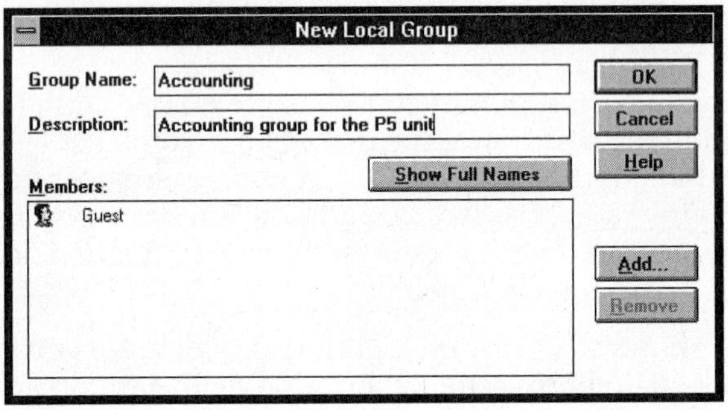

Fig. 31.7

The New Local Group dialog box.

Using Policies

The second option in the User Manager window is **P**olicies. You use the **P**olicies option to set or change the security policies for the system. From the User Manager window, choose **P**olicies to display the Policies menu, shown in figure 31.8.

Fig. 31.8

The Policies
menu.

Setting the Account Policy

You use the **A**ccount option to define the password characteristics that
apply to all user accounts. You cannot define a separate password
policy for different users or groups. To define the account policy,
follow these steps:

1. From the User Manager window, choose **P**olicies.

2. Choose **A**ccount. This displays the Account Policy dialog box
    shown in figure 31.9.

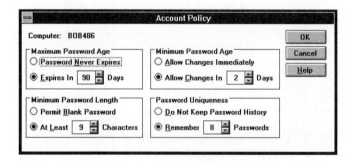

Fig. 31.9

The Account
Policy dialog
box.

3. Make your selections, then choose OK.

A minimum password length of nine characters makes it difficult for an
unauthorized user to attempt to break into accounts by trying different
character combinations. The Password Uniqueness section in the Account Policy dialog box shows the number of previous passwords that
are kept for each user. When users change their password, they cannot
change it to one of the passwords in the history list. This keeps users
from choosing from a small set of passwords each time their password
expires. In the example shown in figure 31.9, the eight most recently
used passwords are kept for all users.

The Minimum Password Age section of the Account Policy dialog box
controls the number of days that must elapse before users are allowed
to change their password. If the **A**llow Changes Immediately toggle
button is selected, users can change their passwords at any time.
In figure 31.9, users can change their passwords every two days.

The Maximum Password Age section of the Account Policy dialog box sets the number of days before passwords expire. Several days before the expiration date, users are notified through a message box that appears when they log on. The Account Policy dialog box in figure 31.9 shows that passwords expire every three months.

Setting the User Rights Policy

User rights control the operations granted or denied to users and groups. To set the user rights policy, follow these steps:

1. From the User Manager window, choose **P**olicies.

2. Choose **U**ser Rights. This displays the User Rights Policy dialog box shown in figure 31.10.

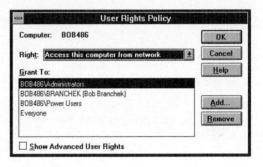

Fig. 31.10

The User Rights Policy dialog box.

3. Use the down arrow at the end of the Right list field to select a user right.

4. The **G**rant To field displays the users and groups who are assigned the right shown in the Right field. To add a user or group to this list, use the **A**dd button to display the Add Users and Groups dialog box. From the **N**ame list, choose the users and groups to add, then select the OK button.

5. Use the **R**emove button to delete a selected entry in the **G**rant To field.

6. To display an additional set of user rights in the Right list field, check the **S**how Advanced User Rights box. Advanced user rights are granted only to user accounts that are system developers who write system applications.

7. When you have finished listing the rights to be granted to a user or group, click OK.

In figure 31.10, the Access this computer from network user right is granted to the BRANCHEK user. The Administrators, Power Users, and Everyone groups were already granted this user right.

Setting the Audit Policy

You use the Audit option to specify the security events for the system that are logged in the security log file of the Event Viewer. You use the Event Viewer to display detailed information about logged events. For each event that you select for auditing, you specify whether you want to record events that are successful, unsuccessful, or both successful and unsuccessful.

You specify the events to be logged based primarily on security. For example, you should log security policy changes to detect attempted alterations of the security measures that you define for your system. You should record logons and logoffs to learn of attempted unauthorized logons to your system.

To set the audit policy, follow these steps:

1. From the User Manager window, choose **P**olicies.

2. Choose Au**d**it. This displays the Audit Policy dialog box shown in figure 31.11.

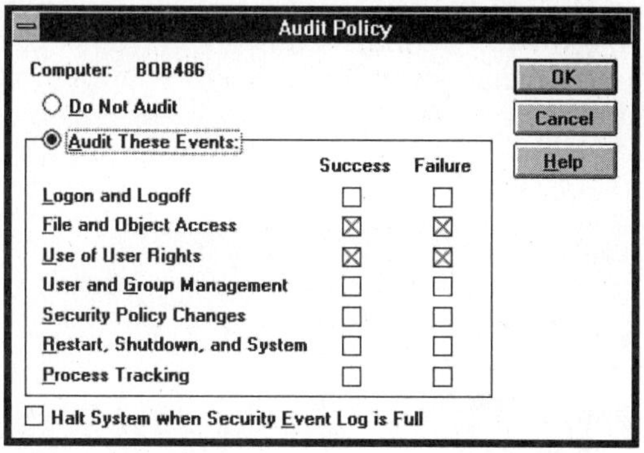

```
┌─────────────────────────────────────────────────────────┐
│ ─                    Audit Policy                        │
├─────────────────────────────────────────────────────────┤
│  Computer:   BOB486                    ┌──────────┐      │
│                                        │    OK    │      │
│  ○ Do Not Audit                        └──────────┘      │
│  ◉ Audit These Events:                 ┌──────────┐      │
│                          Success Failure│  Cancel  │      │
│  Logon and Logoff          □      □    └──────────┘      │
│  File and Object Access    ☒      ☒    ┌──────────┐      │
│  Use of User Rights        ☒      ☒    │   Help   │      │
│  User and Group Management  □      □    └──────────┘      │
│  Security Policy Changes   □      □                      │
│  Restart, Shutdown, and System  □  □                    │
│  Process Tracking          □      □                      │
│                                                          │
│  □ Halt System when Security Event Log is Full          │
└─────────────────────────────────────────────────────────┘
```

Fig. 31.11

The Audit Policy dialog box.

3. To specify events for logging, select the appropriate check boxes in the **A**udit These Events section. If you are unconcerned about recording any of the auditable events, select the **D**o Not Audit toggle button. (If your system is in a physically secure location, you may not require the auditing of security events.)

4. The box at the bottom of the screen can be checked to halt the system when the security event log is full.

5. When you are finished, click OK.

NOTE Select the Halt System when Security Event Log Is Full check box if you do not want the system available when security events can't be recorded in the security log file. (Where security is a major concern, NT systems are often required to prevent a system from being used if security events can't be recorded.)

If this option is checked, you must ensure that adequate space remains in the security log file. Examine the entries in the security log file with the Event Viewer. Then, either copy old entries to another file or delete them to ensure that adequate space is maintained in the security log file.

Saving Policy Settings

You use the Options selection in the User Manager window to set defaults for your current and subsequent use of the User Manager application.

If you choose Confirmation from the Options menu, additional message boxes appear and must be confirmed when various operations are performed in the User Manager application. For example, a delete account operation must be confirmed through two message boxes rather than one. A check mark appears to the left of Confirmation in the Options menu when it is selected.

Choose Save Setting on Exit from the Options menu to keep the current Confirmation setting for the User Manager application.

Using the Disk Administrator

The Disk Administrator application enables you to create and control partitions, volume sets, and stripe sets for disks on the system. The Disk Administrator is similar to the DOS FDISK command, but uses the Windows GUI.

The display in the main window shows the hard disks, their partitions, and the file system of each partition. Disk space is defined as primary partitions, extended partitions, logical drives, stripe sets, mirror sets, volume sets, and free space. Both volume and stripe sets enable regions of free space to be defined as a single logical partition across multiple disks.

The Disk Administrator can be opened only by members of the Administrators group. To start the Disk Administrator application, double-click its icon.

The Disk Administrator displays disk characteristics (for example, partition types) through user-defined colors and patterns. To change the display, use the **O**ptions menu in the Disk Administrator window.

An example of the Disk Administrator main window is shown in figure 31.12. The defined areas of disks 0 and 1 are displayed. Disk 0 has partitions defined as C, D, and F, and three areas of free space. Disk 1 has a single partition defined as G.

Fig. 31.12

The Disk Administrator main window.

Understanding Partitions

A *partition* is an area of a hard disk that can function as a separate storage region. You may define one or more partitions for each hard disk. Windows NT and DOS can be placed in the same primary partition, formatted as a File Allocation Table (FAT) file system. Separate partitions must be defined for other operating systems. For Intel xxx86 processors, the operating system starts from the active partition on the first internal hard disk, displayed in the Disk Manager window as Disk 0.

NT File Systems

Windows NT can directly access and manage files on the following file systems:

- NT File System (NTFS), the native NT file system
- File Allocation Table (FAT) system of DOS
- High Performance File System (HPFS) of OS/2

FAT was developed for DOS in the early 1980s. It is supported as a secondary file system to provide access to DOS files from an NT system. One disadvantage of this file system is its restriction on naming files. The file name for a FAT formatted disk can have a maximum of only 8 characters, with a 3-character extension. A second disadvantage is that there is no provision for file protection when the FAT file system is used on either DOS or an NT system.

Only the FAT format can be used to format floppy disks on Windows NT. A disk formatted for the FAT system can be read and written to on NT, MS-DOS, and OS/2. On a system that can boot both DOS and Windows NT, a FAT partition on a hard disk can be accessed from both systems. FAT or HPFS partitions can be converted to the NTFS file system.

HPFS, the file system for OS/2, is more advanced than the FAT file system. HPFS supports longer file names (up to 254 characters, including spaces) and extended file attributes. It also provides better error correction than the FAT file system. You should format a disk using HPFS only if you will be exchanging files between Windows NT and OS/2 systems.

NTFS is the native file system for Windows NT. Like HPFS, NTFS supports long file names and extended file attributes and provides better error correction than the FAT file system. NTFS can use the security features of NT, including directory and file permissions and the ACLs. These features provide the discretionary access control of NT's C2 security rating. You should select the native file system to be able to take advantage of the NT security mechanisms. NTFS also supports unicode file names, streams, and POSIX links. See Chapter 30 for a description of C2-level security.

The NT file system uses transaction logging to keep track of changes made to a disk's memory structure. Errors made while data is recorded on a disk can't prevent a file from being closed properly.

A program designed for MS-DOS and Windows can access NTFS files when executing on Windows NT because NT provides shortened file names and paths if necessary to allow access to the files.

After you partition a disk and save the changes, you must reboot the system to save the new set of partitions (called the *configuration*). Then the partitions can be formatted with the FORMAT command from a command prompt.

Partitions defined as *unknown* may contain a format and information that isn't recognized by NT. For example, partitions defined by a UNIX system are displayed as Unknown.

Free space is a disk region that hasn't been defined. You may choose to leave a region of the disk free for subsequent use. Free space on a drive may be defined by the Disk Administrator as

A primary partition

Up to three additional partitions

Extended partitions with several logical drives

A volume set

A stripe set

A *primary partition* is an area of a disk marked for use by an operating system and may be made bootable. A primary partition cannot be sub-divided into smaller units.

The system partition for Windows NT is the partition that contains the Windows NT system files. The boot partition contains the initial code to load the Windows NT system; it can be the same partition as the system partition.

You can mark a partition as active using Mark **A**ctive from the **P**artition menu (see fig. 31.13). A system partition must be defined as active on an Intel xxx86-based system for the system to boot. The system partition for a NT xxx86-based system is automatically marked active during the installation of the NT system, so you don't need to mark or change the active partition.

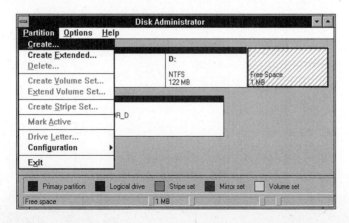

Fig. 31.13

The Partition menu.

NOTE The capability to change the active partition is a carryover from DOS systems. It's designed to allow advanced users to change the system that is started up when the system is turned on.

Although the NT system provides the feature of marking a partition as active, it also provides an alternate feature for changing the system to be booted. This feature is called Flexboot and can be implemented when the NT system is installed. Flexboot enables you to choose between Windows NT and your previous operating system at boot time. Rather than change active partitions, you should use the Flexboot feature to change between NT and another operating system.

An *extended partition* can be subdivided into one or more logical drives. A disk can have up to four partitions but only one can be an extended partition. An extended partition can be defined on a disk without a primary partition. Logical drives, volume sets, or stripe sets may be defined in an extended partition. Up to 24 volumes can be defined for NT, each assigned a letter from C to Z. Drive letters A and B are always used for floppy drives.

You use the **P**artition menu to define, change, or remove disk partitions. The **C**reate and Create **E**xtended options are darkened if a region of free space is selected. The **D**elete and Drive **L**etter options are enabled and display with black rather than gray letters if a formatted region is selected. Menu choices that appear in gray are not available for selection.

To create a partition, choose **C**reate or Create **E**xtended from the **P**artition menu. You use **C**reate to create either a primary partition for a disk or a logical drive in an extended partition. Create **E**xtended is used to create an extended partition for a disk. If you've selected a region of free space in an extended partition, **C**reate displays the Create Logical Drive dialog box, which is shown in figure 31.14.

Fig. 31.14

The Create Logical Drive dialog box.

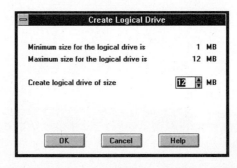

You use the Create logical drive of size field of the Create Logical Drive dialog box to select the size of the logical drive in an extended partition. The size of the logical drive that you can select must be within the range shown in the minimum and maximum size for the logical drive fields, which is 1 to 12 megabytes.

After you select the logical drive size, click OK. You are returned to the Disk Administrator window. Note that the area of the drive that was previously labeled `Free Space` is now labeled `Unformatted`. In the example shown in figure 31.15, the drive letter H is assigned to the logical drive.

Fig. 31.15

The Region Display of the Disk Administrator.

NOTE The logical drive must be formatted with a FORMAT command from a Single Command Set command line before files can be stored on or copied to the logical drive.

Understanding Volume Sets

Volume sets are regions of free space (on one to eight hard disks) that are used as a single disk volume. The NT system controls the use of the storage space in each area of the volume set, using each area in turn until all space is allocated.

NOTE NT is restricted to 24 letters for the reference of hard drive regions, thus restricting an NT system to 24 disks. With volume sets, however, you may assign one drive letter to up to eight disk regions. This dramatically increases the number of disks that can be used on an NT system.

NOTE When you use volume sets, data can be distributed across multiple volumes on different disks. This improves performance by decreasing the time it takes for reading the data; all or at least part of a read operation can occur simultaneously on different disks. If the regions of a volume set are on multiple drives, data access is faster than if it were on a single drive. MS-DOS does not support volume partitions.

continues

continued

The degree of performance benefit that you can achieve with volume sets is limited by the type of disks on which you create the volume.

The performance advantage that you gain from using a volume set is secondary to its primary purpose of providing a larger logical disk volume than that found on individual disks. If you are interested primarily in disk performance, use a stripe set rather than a volume set.

You can create and delete volume sets with Create **V**olume Set and **D**elete from the **P**artition menu. The Disk Administrator creates approximately equal-sized volume partitions on the selected disks and assigns a single drive letter. To create a volume set, follow these steps:

1. Select two or more areas of free space on from 2 to 32 disks from the region display. You select the first region of free space by clicking its display region. Then hold the Ctrl key and select the remaining areas of free space that will become part of the volume set.

2. Select Create **V**olume Set from the **P**artition menu to display the Create Volume Set dialog box. This dialog box shows the minimum and maximum sizes that can be defined for the volume set. The default size of the volume set is equal to the total size of all selected regions of free space.

3. Select the OK button to create the volume set.

In figure 31.16, for example, two areas of free space have been selected. The Create Volume Set dialog box in figure 31.17 shows that the size of the volume set to be created is 17M, which is the total size of the two selected regions of free space

Fig. 31.16

Selected regions for volume set creation.

The volume set is shown in the region display of the Disk Administrator with the two regions assigned identical drive letters, both of which are unformatted. Figure 31.18 shows the volume set created as a result the previous example. Notice that the letter H appears on two regions of the region display.

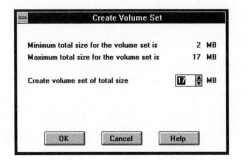

Fig. 31.17

The Create
Volume Set
dialog box.

Fig. 31.18

The region
display
containing a
defined volume
set.

NOTE The two regions referenced with the same drive letter are a
volume set. They are not shown as a volume set using the
color or pattern for a volume until they are formatted. Figure 31.18 shows the region display immediately after the OK
button is selected in the Create Volume Set dialog box.

Volume sets formatted for the native Windows NT file system (NTFS)
can be extended. To extend an NTFS volume set, follow these steps:

1. Select a volume set and an area of free space from the region
   display of the Disk Administrator.

2. Select **Ex**tend Volume Set from the **P**artition menu to display the
   Create Extended Volume Set dialog box.

3. Enter the amount of disk space to be added to the volume set,
   in the range specified in the dialog box.

4. Choose OK.

Understanding Stripe Sets

Stripe sets, like volume sets, provide better performance by placing
data across multiple drives. The data is divided into segments called
chunks. If a stripe set contains three drives, for example, each succes-
sive chunk of user data is placed across the three drives rather than on
a single drive. This is often referred to as *interleaving* data across the

partitions that make up the stripe set. Striping techniques are collectively referred to as *redundant array of inexpensive (*or *independent) disks (RAID)*. Striping is considered RAID 0, the first of six RAID types.

Stripe sets store all files across each of the disk regions of the stripe set. Volume sets, however, do not split individual files across multiple disk drives.

You can use from 2 to 32 disks to form an NT stripe set. Stripe sets are comprised of approximately equal-sized partitions. Stripe sets are created from the **P**artition menu using Create **S**tripe Set. You can delete them by using **D**elete. MS-DOS does not see or support stripe sets.

Creating a stripe set is similar to creating a volume set. Follow these steps:

1. Select two or more areas of free space on 2 to 32 disks from the region display of the Disk Administrator. Select the first area by clicking its display region. Then hold the Ctrl key and select the remaining areas of free space that will become part of the stripe set.

2. Choose Create **S**tripe Set from the **P**artition menu to display the Create Stripe Set dialog box. You choose a size for the stripe set from the range of minimum and maximum sizes specified in the dialog box.

Deleting Partitions, Volume Sets, and Stripe Sets

You use **D**elete from the **P**artition menu to delete partitions, logical drives, volume sets, and stripe sets. NT warns you that you will lose any data stored in an area that is deleted. NT will not allow you to delete an active primary partition or the partition containing NT system files. To delete an extended partition, you first must delete its logical drives. To delete a volume or stripe set, you first must delete all the areas in it.

To delete a partition, volume set, or stripe set, follow these steps:

1. Select the area from the region menu.

2. Choose **D**elete from the **P**artition menu. This displays a Confirm dialog box to enable you to confirm the deletion.

3. Choose **Y**es to delete the partition, volume set, or stripe set.

Other Partition Menu Options

The remaining commands of the Partition menu are Drive Letter, Configuration, and Exit. You can use Drive Letter to assign a letter to a drive rather than accept the default of the next unassigned letter from C through Z. The drive may be formatted or unformatted.

Select Configuration to search for, save, or restore different configurations of disk drive regions. You can assign a unique set of drive letter designations to different types of partitions, such as volume sets or stripe sets. You must reboot your system to implement a change in configuration.

Select Exit from the Partition menu to exit the Disk Administrator application.

Display Control

You select commands from the Options menu to change the display of descriptive information about disk usage (see fig. 31.19). You can change the display of the status bar, the legend, the region, and colors and patterns.

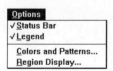

A description of the commands on the Options menu follows:

Option	Description
Status Bar	Displays the type of partition, size, file system, letter designation, and operating label when a partition is selected.
Legend	Uses colors or hash patterns to indicate the type of partition; displayed above the status bar.
Colors and Patterns	Displays the Colors and Patterns dialog box, which you use to select the color or pattern for each type of region.
Region Display	Displays the Region Display Option box, which you use to show the size of regions proportionally or nonproportionally.

In the region display shown in figure 31.20, the status bar shows that the drive partition labeled C on volume set 0 is selected. The status bar also shows the size, format, letter designation, and volume label (unless the volume is unlabeled) for the selected volume set. The legend displays different patterns for the primary partition, logical drives, stripe sets, mirror sets, and volume sets. The Disk Administrator determines the size of the area for the drive region.

Fig. 31.20

The region display in the main window of the Disk Administrator.

To change the color or pattern for partition types in the region display, choose Colors and Patterns from the Options menu. This displays the Colors and Patterns dialog box (see fig. 31.21). You can select both a color and a pattern for each of the regions that can be defined. First select the type of partition in the Color and pattern for field. Then select both a color from the Colors field and a pattern from the Patterns field. Select OK to exit the dialog box and view the changes in the region display.

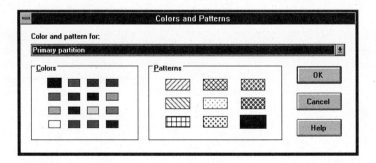

Fig. 31.21

The Colors and Patterns dialog box.

To change the way disk regions are displayed in the Disk Administrator window, choose Region Display from the Options menu. The Region Display Options dialog box appears. You can display regions at their actual size, all at the same size, or at a size determined by the Disk Administrator. In figure 31.22, the display size for the regions in disk 0 are set to be sized by the Disk Administrator.

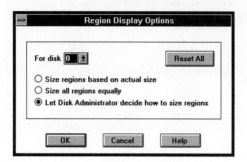

Fig. 31.22

The Region
Display Options
dialog box.

Using Backup

Windows NT comes with a built-in tape backup tool. The Backup administrative tool controls the backup and restore operations used to prevent the loss of data files and programs if the original source—the disks—are unreadable.

You use Backup to back up files to tape and store them off-line. You can then restore the files by copying them from the tape to a hard disk. Associated operations also controlled through the Backup application include erasing tapes and selecting tape drives.

Understanding Backup

To back up and restore files on NT, choose the Backup icon in the Administrative Tools program group to display the Backup window (see fig. 31.23). Files stored in NTFS, HPFS, and FAT formatted regions can be backed up or restored. You can copy files stored on both local and remote drives.

The Backup window has six menus. The first menu, Operations, contains the commands to perform the operations of the Backup application, as shown in figure 31.24. You use the Tree and View menus to control the hierarchical display of files and directories. Options on the Select menu are used to select or deselect directories and files to backup or restore. The Window and Help menus are similar to menus in other programs. The Window menu enables you to control the display of drive and tape information windows. The Help menu contains help for backup commands.

The following table summarizes the operations that you choose
through the Operations menu.

Option	Description
Backup	Copies directories and files from disk to tape
Restore	Copies directories and files from tape to disk
Catalog	Displays directories and files on tape
Erase Tape	Deletes directories and files on tape
Re**t**ension Tape	Winds and rewinds tape to provide uniform tension and remove slack from a 1/4-inch tape cartridge
E**j**ect Tape	Ejects a tape cartridge from a tape drive that provides a software ejection interface
Hardware Setup	Selects a different tape device and driver than the one selected automatically
E**x**it	Exit Backup

You can back up or restore files by volume, directory, or individual file name. You can perform a verification pass during a backup or restore operation to ensure the validity of the copies.

The set of directories and files copied to one or more tape cartridges as the result of a single backup operation is called a *backup set*. Multiple backup sets can be placed on the same tape, either by erasing previous sets or adding to sets.

Backup sets and files can span multiple tapes. A batch file can be created to control subsequent identical backups. The backup or restore operation status, including the file being processed, is dynamically displayed on-screen.

The Backup application supports several types of tape cartridges, including 4-mm, 8-mm, and 1/4-inch tape cartridges. Each of these types of tape cartridges can store up to several gigabytes of data.

Although multiple drives can be connected to the system, only one can be used at a time. The system checks automatically for the correct tape backup device when NT is started and initializes a tape drive when Backup is started.

 **NOTE** You can back up files only from a disk that you normally have access to through user rights or the permissions in the ACLs of files and directories. Members of the Administrators or Backup Operators group can back up files regardless of the permissions in the ACLs of directories and files. Note that if a user is a member of the local Backup Operators group but is not a member of the Backup Operators or Administrators group on a connected remote machine, the user may not have the necessary access to the remote files and directories.

Backing Up Files

To back up files and directories, you must first select them. Then you choose options in the Backup Information dialog box. During the backup, the Backup Status dialog box informs you of the progress of the backup operation. These two dialog boxes are described next, before the list of steps for backing up files.

In the upper section of the Backup Information dialog box, you can choose to append the new backup set or replace the set or sets already on the tape. You can control access to the tape by checking the box for

Restrict Access to Owner or Administrator. You can verify copied files by checking the Verify After Backup check box.

Following is a description of the fields in the Backup Information dialog box:

Field	Description
Append	Adds the backup set to existing sets on tape; Tape Name field and Restrict Access to Owner or Administrator field are unavailable
Backup Local Re**g**istry	Includes a copy of NT registry files
Creation Date	Automatically displays the creation date of the original backup set or the date it was last replaced
Current Tape	Displays the name entered in the Tape Name field; blank if no tape is loaded or the format is unrecognized
Owner	Owner of the first backup of the tape
Replace	Overwrites tape; a caution message appears for confirmation
Restrict Access to Owner or Administrator	Restricts reading, writing, and erasing the tape to the tape owner or the administrator
Tape Name	Tape name of up to 31 characters
Verify After Backup	Compares backed up files on tape and the original on the disk

The next section of the Backup Information dialog box displays the selected drives and backup sets. If more than one drive is selected, you can use the scroll bar to move between tape sets. You can use a maximum of 31 characters to describe each set of backup tapes.

You can perform several different types of backups:

Backup	Description
Copy	All selected files are backed up but not marked on disk
Daily	Selected files that have been modified that day are backed up but are not marked on the disk
Differential	Selected files that have been modified are backed up but are not marked on the disk

Backup	Description
Incremental	Selected files that have been modified that day are backed up and marked on the disk
Normal	Selected files are backed up and marked on the disk

The last section of the Backup Information dialog box enables you to select the type of backup information that will be logged:

Log Option	Description
Don't Log	No information is logged
Full Detail	Logs all information, including the names of all files and directories that were backed up
Summary Only	Logs major operations—loading a tape, starting the backup, and failing to open a file

The second dialog box mentioned, the Backup Status dialog box, displays a status area in which the information continuously updates. The Backup Status dialog box contains information about the number of directories, files, and bytes that are backed up. The summary section of the Backup Status dialog box shows the start and end type for the backup.

The status area at the top of the box also shows the elapsed time in hours, minutes, and seconds; the number of corrupt or skipped files because of read errors or open or locked files; and the selected disk drive, directory path, and file name. A summary section of the tape label and an event log also are displayed.

If you abort a backup operation (by selecting **Abort** in the Backup Status dialog box), the backup of the current file is completed if less than 1M of the file remains to be copied. A message appears allowing you to stop the backup immediately; if you do so and Backup is in the process of copying a file, a message is displayed warning that the file might be corrupt.

CAUTION: Information about corrupted files is recorded in CORRUPT.LST. Check the information in this file before you attempt a restore operation. If the file is not deleted after examining it, you will receive a message about corrupt files when you restore from the backup tape.

To back up the directories and files for a disk, follow these steps:

1. From the main window of Backup, double-click the disk drive from which you want to back up directories and files. Doing so displays the Disk Drive window. In figure 31.25, a separate window displays the directories and files on disk drive D, the selected drive.

2. Click the appropriate check boxes to select the directories and files to back up. You can also use **C**heck and **U**ncheck from the **S**elect menu to change the check box associated with one or more directories on a disk. In figure 31.25, all directories and files on drive D were selected by selecting the check box for drive D in the Drives window.

3. Select **B**ackup from the **O**perations menu or double-click the Backup icon in the toolbar to display the Backup Information dialog box.

4. Select the options in Backup Information dialog box. (See the text preceding the numbered list for details.)

5. Choose OK to begin the backup. The Backup Status dialog box is displayed. If a tape becomes full during the backup process, an Insert New Tape dialog box appears. When the backup process is complete, a message is displayed at the bottom of the Backup Status dialog box.

NOTE   You can stop a backup operation by selecting the **A**bort button in the Backup Status dialog box.

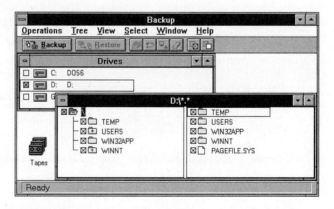

Fig. 31.25

The Backup and Disk Drive windows.

Restoring Files

When you restore files, you retrieve copies of the original information that was previously backed up to tape. You restore files because the original files are lost or corrupted. If you're very fortunate, you'll never have to restore the files from your backup tapes.

To back up the directories and files for a disk, follow these steps:

1. Load into the tape drive the tape that contains the files you want to restore to disks.

2. In the main window of Backup, double-click the Tapes icon to open the Tapes window.

3. Click the appropriate check boxes to select the directories and files to restore. You can also use **C**heck and **U**ncheck from the **S**elect menu to change the check box associated with one or more directories to restore to disk.

4. Select **R**estore from the **O**perations menu or double-click the Restore icon in the toolbar to display the Restore Information dialog box.

5. Choose options in the Restore Information dialog box. The Restore Information dialog box contains the following information about each tape and backup set:

    Tape name

    Descriptive title for the backup set

    Type of backup

    Date and time of backup

    User who performed the backup

In the bottom section of the Restore Information dialog box, you can specify a log file in which information about the restore operation is logged. The following log options are available:

Don't Log	No information is logged
Full Detail	Log all operations; record all files and directories restored
Summary Only	Log major operations: loading tape, starting the restore process, and file creation failures

6. When you have finished making selections in the Restore Informa-
    tion dialog box, choose OK to begin the restoration process. This
    displays the Restore Status dialog box, which informs you of the
    progress of the operation. If a file on the disk is newer than the file
    to be restored, you are prompted about whether you want to con-
    tinue and replace the file. A message appears if you need to insert
    an additional tape.

    The Restore Status dialog box dynamically updates as the restora-
    tion process proceeds to show the directories, files, and bytes
    processed; the elapsed time in hours, minutes, and seconds; and
    the number of corrupt or skipped files. The status area also shows
    the selected drive, directory path, file name, tape label, and event
    log.

 You can stop a restore operation by selecting the **A**bort
button in the Restore Status dialog box.

Using Tape Maintenance Options

NT provides commands to erase a tape and retension it. The **E**rase
Tape command erases the tape from its current position to the end.
The Retension Tape command first moves the tape to the end and then
rewinds it.

You can erase the tape by clicking the Erase Tape button on the
toolbar or selecting **E**rase Tape from the **O**perations menu. Two erase
options are available from the Erase Tape dialog box: a Quick Erase
rewrites only the tape header, whereas a Secure Erase rewrites the
entire tape.

Tapes in 1/4-inch tape cartridges should be retensioned after every 20
uses. You can start a retension operation by choosing Retension Tape
from the **O**perations menu or by clicking the Retension Tape button on
the toolbar. You do not have to retension 4-mm and 8-mm tapes.

Using the Event Viewer

An integrated logging tool is used in Windows NT to log application,
system, and security problems or occurrences, called *events*. The Event
Viewer application controls the logging and subsequent display of information about all events. You use the Event Viewer icon from the
Administrative Tools program group to invoke the application.

You can use the Event Viewer to record the following for each event: the date and time of the occurrence, source, type, category, ID number, user name, and computer system. You can display these events organized by various categories or by their order of occurrence. You also can display events with varying amounts of detail.

Starting the Event Viewer

You start the Event Viewer by double-clicking its icon. The first time you display the Event Viewer, the events from the system log are displayed in the Event Viewer main window (see fig. 31.26).

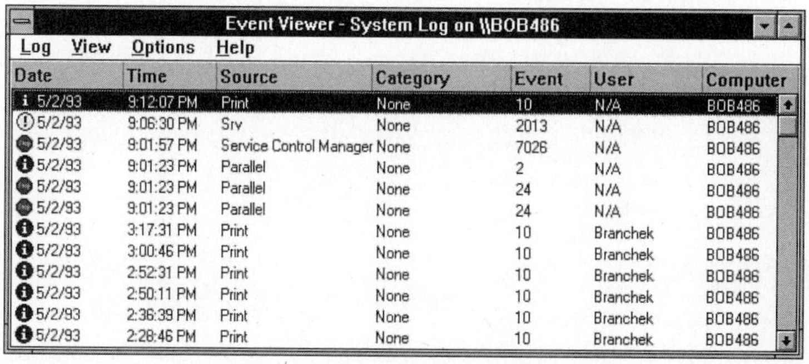

Date	Time	Source	Category	Event	User	Computer
5/2/93	9:12:07 PM	Print	None	10	N/A	BOB486
5/2/93	9:06:30 PM	Srv	None	2013	N/A	BOB486
5/2/93	9:01:57 PM	Service Control Manager	None	7026	N/A	BOB486
5/2/93	9:01:23 PM	Parallel	None	2	N/A	BOB486
5/2/93	9:01:23 PM	Parallel	None	24	N/A	BOB486
5/2/93	9:01:23 PM	Parallel	None	24	N/A	BOB486
5/2/93	3:17:31 PM	Print	None	10	Branchek	BOB486
5/2/93	3:00:46 PM	Print	None	10	Branchek	BOB486
5/2/93	2:52:31 PM	Print	None	10	Branchek	BOB486
5/2/93	2:50:11 PM	Print	None	10	Branchek	BOB486
5/2/93	2:36:39 PM	Print	None	10	Branchek	BOB486
5/2/93	2:28:46 PM	Print	None	10	Branchek	BOB486

Fig. 31.26

The Event Viewer main window.

In figure 31.26, the window is large enough to display one-line listings of twelve system events. The most recent event is listed first and is selected. If you have selected **S**ave Settings on Exit from the **O**ptions menu, the last log viewed is displayed in the Event Viewer window when the Event Viewer is run again.

Understanding the Event Viewer

The Windows NT Event Viewer, unlike other systems, integrates the recording and display of information. This helps you interpret the recorded information in two ways: you use the same commands to collect and display information about the system, security, and application events, and information recorded about events is displayed in the same format rather than three different formats.

Events are things that an administrator should know about that happen during the execution of user or system code. The events are logged in the event log file, which is automatically enabled at system startup.

You can save event logs and examine them later as printed reports. You can disable event logging through the Service icon in the Control Panel.

You control the collection of security audit events (such as logon attempts) from the User Manager application. To select the audit policy for the system, choose Audit from the Policies menu in the User Manager application. This displays the Audit Policy dialog box. Auditable events are set with the check boxes. Figure 31.27 shows the Audit Policy dialog box with all events logged, both successful and unsuccessful.

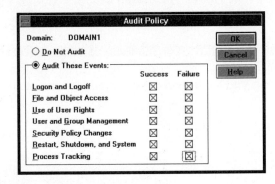

The Audit Policy dialog box.

Using the Log Menu

The Event Viewer Log menu enables you to view events from the system, security, or application logs. Following is a description of the Log menu commands:

Command	Description
System	Displays the system log contents
Security	Displays the security log contents
Application	Displays the application log contents
Open	Opens an archived log file
Save As	Saves a log in a text or log file format
Clear All Events	Empties the selected log file of all recorded events
Log Settings	Defines the maximum size and overwrite event options for log files
Select Computer	Selects an NT workstation to access and display log entries from
Exit	Exits the Event Viewer

Select Log Settings from the Log menu to display the Log Settings dialog box. Through this dialog box, you can set the maximum size for the log file in kilobytes, the period of time that events are kept, and whether to overwrite events when the log file is full. Separate settings are kept for the system, security, and application logs. In figure 31.28, the system log file is set to a maximum size of 512K, and events are set to be overwritten in a week.

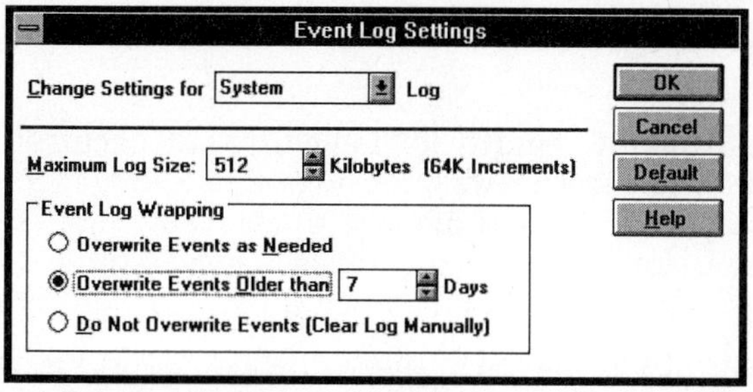

Fig. 31.28

The Event Log Settings dialog box.

The example in figure 31.29 shows eight events from the security log. For each logged event, the following items are displayed:

Event Item	Description
Date	Date of the event
Time	Time of the event
Source	Program (such as an application) or system component (such as a driver) that was logged
Category	Event source; a security event source, for example, can be Login, Logoff, Shutdown, Use of User Rights, File, Print, or Security Changes
Event	Unique number for each source to identify the event
User	Username when error occurred; *** no user specified for system applications
Computer	Name of the computer on which the error occurred
Type	The severity of the error; error, warning, information, success, audit, failure audit displayed as an icon

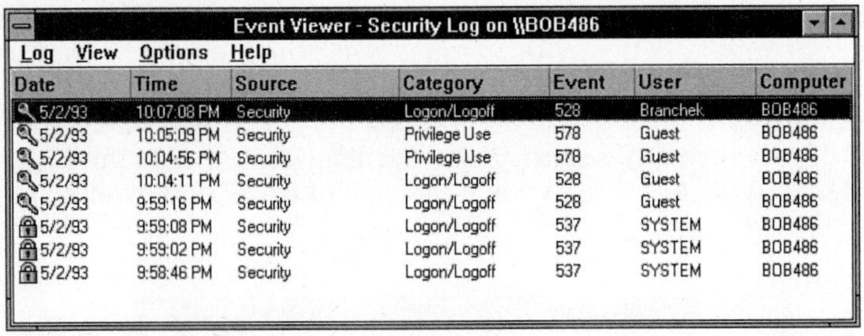

Fig. 31.29

The Security log.

The first event from the security log in figure 31.29 occurred on May 2, 1993 at 10:07 PM. The source was the security auditing mechanism and the event was either a logon or logoff with an event number of 528. The username used to log on was Branchek, who logged on to the BOB486 computer.

The username is not displayed in this summary report for each event, although the computer system has been recorded. To display the detail about an event, double-click the selected event or choose **D**etail from the **V**iew menu. This displays the Event Detail dialog box (see fig. 31.30). You must examine the detail of an event to learn the meaning of the event numbers.

Fig. 31.30

The Event Detail dialog box.

The information at the top of the detail display is similar to an event line in the initial display of events. The **D**escription section of the Event Detail dialog box provides additional information about the event.

Figure 31.30 shows the detail for the first event of type number 537. The Event Detail dialog box shows that the event was an unsuccessful logon under the Branchek username. You can use the scroll bar on the right to display additional information if there is any for this event.

The last section of information in the Event Detail dialog box displays, by default, a byte dump. This information can be interpreted by someone who knows the program code for the Windows NT system component or the application that resulted in this event. Not all events return a dump. You can select the appropriate toggle button to display the dump in words rather than bytes.

Use the **P**revious and **N**ext buttons from the Event Detail dialog box to display the detail for the previous and next events in the current log. **H**elp displays help on the interpretation of events. Click the Close button to remove the Event Detail window.

Using the View Menu

You use the View menu to control other characteristics of the display of events in the main window of the Event Viewer. For example, the most recent events are listed first in the window by default. With the View menu, you can reverse this and display the oldest events first. Following is a description of the View menu commands:

Command	Description
All Events	Select and display all recorded events of the log
Filter Events	Select and display events by characteristics such as date and time and type of event
Newest First	The most recent event is shown at the top of the event display
Oldest First	The earliest event is shown at the top of the event display
Find	Selects the next event by such characteristics as event type, category, or source
Detail	Displays the Event Detail dialog box, which contains detailed information about the selected event
Refresh	Rebuilds the event display in the main window of the Event Viewer with the most recent information

Choosing the **F**ind command in the **V**iew menu displays the Find dialog box, shown in figure 31.31. You can enter various items for an event in the dialog box, such as the source, the category, or any part of the

1098

description. If the event is located, the main Event Viewer window is displayed with the specified event selected. If the event is not located, a `Search failed` message appears to notify you.

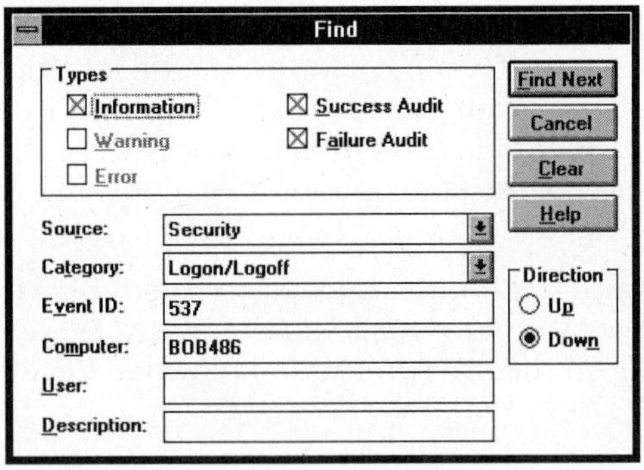

Fig. 31.31

The Find dialog box.

The **R**efresh command from the View menu updates the displayed log. You can select the Filter Events command from the **V**iew menu to restrict the events displayed in the selected log.

Select **F**ilter Events from the **V**iew menu to display the Filter dialog box to select events using a criteria based on one or more items (see fig. 31.32). For example, you can select the events based on the date and time of all events or the first and last events of a range of dates and times.

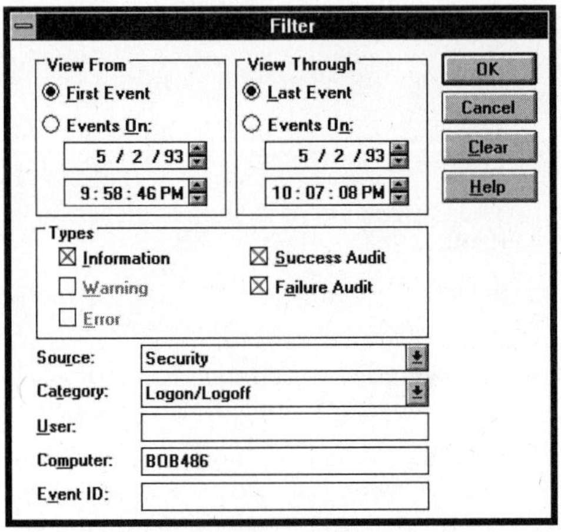

Fig. 31.32

The Filter dialog box.

Information, **W**arning, **E**rror, **S**uccess Audit, and **F**ailure Audit are selected by default. Any of these can be deselected to restrict the events
returned. In addition, you can enter the Source, Category, User,
Computer, and Event ID fields to filter the events displayed.

Events in the system log are typically errors resulting from system
operations and user activity. You expand a selected error in the system
log with a double-click to display the dialog box. For example, the Event
Detail dialog box shown in figure 31.33 shows that disk C is almost full.
You should copy files to other drives, delete unnecessary files, or back
up and delete the original files to provide more free space on drive C.

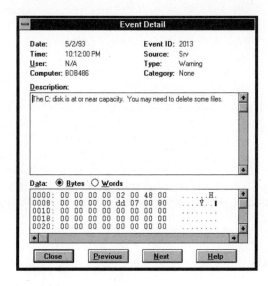

Using Log Files

Use **S**elect Computer from the **L**og menu to access the event log files of
remote NT systems. The **S**elect Computer command displays the Select
Computer dialog box. After you select the system name, the dialog
box is removed from the screen and the Event Viewer main window
appears with the events of the specified system.

Log files can be saved in one of three formats for subsequent viewing:

- Use the log file format if you want to reopen the log file in the
  Event Viewer

- Use a text file format if you want to open the log file subsequently
  in a word processor

■ Use a comma-delimited text file format to allow access from a spreadsheet or flat-file database.

The operation of saving log files is called *archiving*. Files saved in a log file format are given a file type of .EVT. Files saved in a text file format or comma-delimited text file format are given a file type of TXT.

Understanding Maintenance Operations

Use Clear All Events from the Log menu to empty a log file of all recorded events. If you select Clear All Events, a precautionary dialog box is displayed, as shown in figure 31.34. If you answer either **Yes** or **No**, a second message box appears to warn you that the information in the event log will be lost.

The Clear Event Log message box.

The **O**ptions menu command Save **S**ettings on Exit enables the Low Speed Connection to be saved for subsequent sessions of the use of the Event Viewer.

Using the Performance Monitor

You must be able to monitor the use of system resources by applications to properly control the system. Windows NT has an extensive performance monitoring capability. The Performance Monitor administrative tool controls the monitoring and display of system resource use.

You can closely monitor the characteristics of the main resources of the computer system—the CPUs, RAM, and disks—using the Performance Monitor application. For example, you can collect and display the percentage of time that system code and user code use the CPU.

NOTE The Performance Monitor should be used to monitor the performance of both stand-alone and network server systems. You monitor system performance to collect baseline statistics. Then, when you change the system, you can compare performance values.

If you have a stand-alone system and you are satisfied with its performance, you don't need to monitor it. You should still obtain a report to be used as a baseline, however, in case you must monitor the system's performance later.

A server system is more likely to be monitored than a stand-alone system, because network access makes it easier to exhaust the resources of a server system. By monitoring the performance of a server system, you can improve its performance by changing the mechanisms that control its use of resources.

The Performance Monitor graphically displays the performance of one or more computers in a network. Resources or entities that can be monitored are called *objects* and can include processes, threads, processors, and memory. Counters are used with objects to record usage statistics. You can record and later review performance information in a chart.

Additional capabilities of the Performance Monitor enable an administrator to

- Change the update frequency for charts
- Define view alerts
- Automatically execute a program when a counter value exceeds or falls below a user-defined value
- Print alerts, charts, and reports
- Export charts to spreadsheets and database applications

Starting the Performance Monitor

You start the Performance Monitor by double-clicking its icon in the Administrative Tools program group. When the Performance Monitor starts, the chart view is displayed by default.

Logging is not enabled when the Performance Monitor is started, so no information is displayed. The three additional views you can display are alert, log, and report. You can select these views from the toolbar or from the View menu.

Using Chart View

The default source for information is the current activity of the system. This source is shown on the status bar at the bottom-left corner of the

Performance Monitor main window (see fig. 31.35). The alternate source for information is a log file in which previous system activity has been recorded.

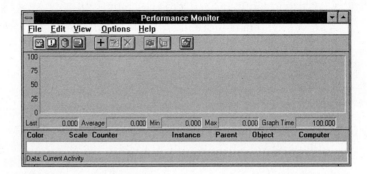

Fig. 31.35

The initial Performance Monitor window.

Selecting a Log File

You can change the source of data by selecting Data From in the Options menu. This displays the Data From dialog box, which is shown in figure 31.36. The default log file is perfmon.log. If you click the button to the right of the Log File field, the Open Input Log File dialog box is displayed, which you use to select a log file.

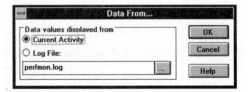

Fig. 31.36

The Data From dialog box.

Selecting a System to Log

When you start the Performance Monitor, the source of data is the current activity of the system, and the view is a chart. No information is displayed, however, because no objects are chosen by default for display. To select objects to be monitored and displayed (or recorded in a log file), use Add to Chart from the Edit menu. An Add to Chart dialog box is displayed, as shown in figure 31.37, to enable you to select the objects for monitoring.

```
┌─────────────────────────────────────────────────────────────────┐
│ □                          Add to Chart                           │
│                                                                   │
│ Computer: │\\BOB486                              │  │...│  │ Add  │ │
│                                                                   │
│ Object:   │Processor                  │▼│  Instance: │0│ │Cancel│ │
│                                                                   │
│ Counter:  ┌─────────────────────────────┐      ┌──┐ │Explain>>│  │
│           │% Privileged Time            │      │  │            │ │
│           │% Processor Time             │      │  │ │ Help │    │ │
│           │% User Time                  │      │  │            │ │
│           │Interrupts/sec               │      └──┘            │ │
│           └─────────────────────────────┘                     │ │
│                                                                   │
│ Color: │████████│▼│  Scale: │1.0│▼│  Width: │───│▼│  Style: │───│▼│ │
│                                                                   │
│ ┌─Counter Definition───────────────────────────────────────────┐ │
│ │Processor Time is expressed as a percentage of the elapsed time that a processor is busy executing a │▲│ │
│ │non-idle thread.  It can be viewed as the fraction of the time spent doing useful work.              │▼│ │
│ └───────────────────────────────────────────────────────────────┘ │
└─────────────────────────────────────────────────────────────────┘
```

Fig. 31.37

The Add to Chart
dialog box.

You can make several choices for the chart view. The first choice is the
system to be logged. The default is the local system. Use the Computer
field to select any interconnected system known to the system.

You select objects for monitoring in the Object field. You select a
counter for an object in the Counter field. Each object has a different
default counter. The default object is Processor, which has the default
% Processor Time counter.

You can select the following objects for a chart view:

   Cache

   LogicalDisk

   Memory

   Netbeui

   Netbeui Resource

   Objects

   Paging File

   PhysicalDisk

   Process

   Processor

   Redirector

   Server

   System

   Thread

Objects have varying numbers of counters that can be displayed. For example, the counters for the Processor object are % Privileged Time, % Processor Time, % User Time, and Interrupts/sec. (For more information about a counter, select it and choose the Explain button.) The resulting chart for an object can display separate lines for each counter. You can also select a color, scale, width, and style for each object counter.

After you select an object counter, use the Add button to add it to the display. Do this for each object counter you want to include, then choose the Done button to display the chart view. In the chart view shown in figure 31.38, the percentage of time the CPU was busy executing code is displayed in graph form.

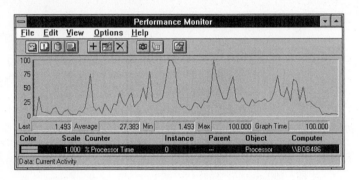

Fig. 31.38

The Performance Monitor chart display.

Editing a Chart

To edit a chart view, use Edit Chart from the Edit menu. This displays the Edit Chart Line dialog box, which is shown in figure 31.39. You can change the color, scale, width, or style of each object counter. Examine the legend at the bottom of the chart view to confirm a change in a line of the chart. The legend (which is above the status line) shows the object counter that each color or style line represents.

The Scale field in the Edit Chart Line dialog box is a multiplier that you can use to make an object counter line fit in the boundaries of the current chart when other object counters have widely varying values. The Instance field specifies which object counter of the identical type is displayed. For the Process object, any number of instances can be displayed, one for each thread. Figure 31.40 shows the % processor time for five instances.

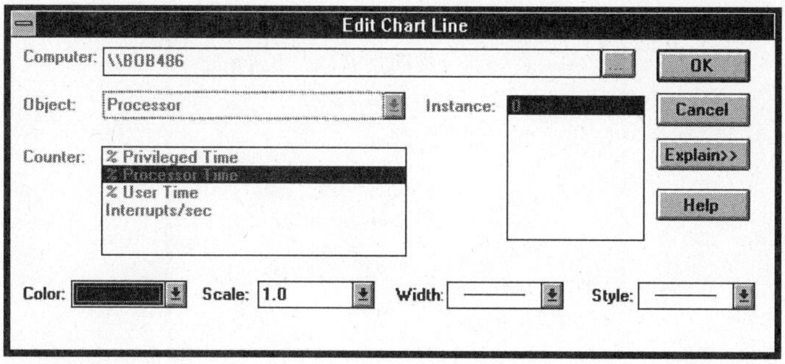

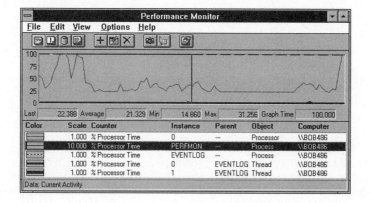

Fig. 31.39

The Edit Chart
Line dialog box.

Fig. 31.40

A chart view of
the % processor
time counter.

In figure 31.40, the processor time used by the Performance Monitor
(shown in the chart view as PERFMON) has a scale of 10. This allows it
to fit in the chart view along with the counter lines for other objects.
The last, average, minimum, and maximum values are shown in boxes
above the legend. The Parent column is used with objects such as
threads to denote their process. For example, in figure 31.40, the processor time for two threads of the EVENTLOG process, and the
EVENTLOG process itself, are displayed.

Changing the Chart Characteristics

You can change characteristics of the Chart view by choosing **C**hart
from the **O**ptions menu. This displays the Chart Options dialog box,
which is shown in figure 31.41.

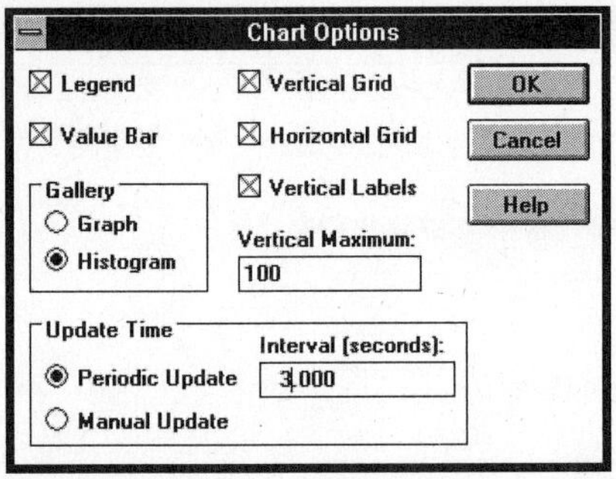

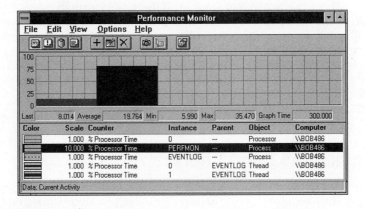

Fig. 31.41

The Chart Options dialog box.

From this dialog box, you can do the following:

- Remove the legend and counter values from the display
- Add a vertical and horizontal grid to the chart
- Increase or decrease the vertical maximum from a default of 100
- Change the time or sample interval
- Change the display or gallery from a default histogram to a bar graph

In figure 31.42, vertical and horizontal grids are selected. The Gallery, or display, is changed from a graph to a histogram. The update interval is changed to three seconds rather than one. The resultant chart view is shown in figure 31.42.

Fig. 31.42

The chart display histogram.

Setting Display Options

To keep the Performance Monitor available for quick reference, choose Always On To**p** from the Options menu. Always On To**p** allows the

Performance Monitor display to appear on top of any window you select. If the Performance Monitor is reduced to an icon, the icon continues to remain on top of any window.

To update the chart data when you want to rather than at the defined
update interval, first choose **C**hart to display the Chart Options dialog
box. Set the **M**anual Update toggle button. Now, whenever you want to
update the chart data immediately, choose **U**pdate Now from the **O**p-
tions menu or click the update icon.

Saving, Resetting, and Opening a Chart

The **F**ile menu enables you to select several options for the chart. **N**ew
Chart reinitializes the chart window; a dialog box gives you the option
of saving or deleting the current chart information. The **O**pen option
enables you to open a previously saved chart from a PMC file. You can
save chart settings to a PMC file using **S**ave Chart Settings or Save
Chart Settings **A**s from the **F**ile menu.

Using Report View

You can display the nformation collected by the Performance Monitor
for object counters in a report rather than in a graphical representation. To create a report, choose **R**eport from the **V**iew menu. A new
report is blank because you haven't selected any object counter information. You select the object counters for a report using **A**dd to Report
from the **E**dit menu.

Only object counter values are displayed in the report. In the Add to
Report dialog box shown in figure 31.43, the % Processor Time counter
for the Processor object on the BOB486 system is added to the report.

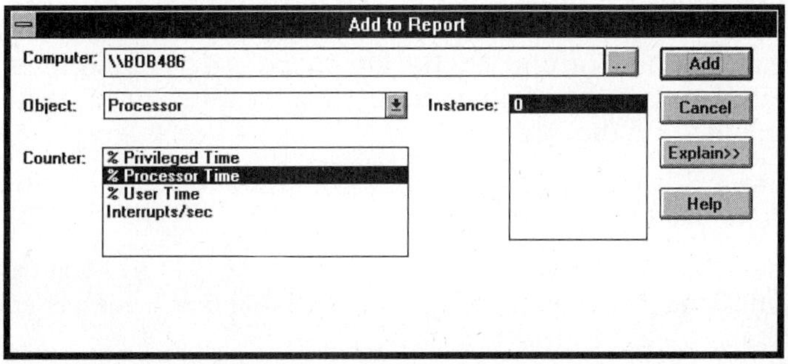

Fig. 31.43

The Add to
Report dialog
box.

After you've selected the object counters, click the Done button to display the report view. The report is organized by objects, with all counters for the same object group together under a column header. Instances of the same object are displayed across the page, rather than in a single column.

The Report view in figure 31.44 shows the counters for each of the three objects specified to be included in the report. The counters for each object are displayed under their object. For the Processor and PhysicalDisk, the last column shows the instance. PhysicalDrive 0 denotes the first hard drive of the system. Instance 0 of the Processor denotes the first and only CPU of the BOB486 computer system.

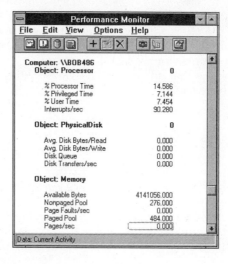

Fig. 31.44

A Performance Monitor report.

Using Alert View

An alert is a line of information returned to the alert view of the Performance Monitor when the value of an object counter is above or below a user-defined value. The entry in the log includes a date and time stamp, the actual object counter value, the criteria for returning it, the object value counter, and the system.

To display an alert view, choose **A**lert from the View menu. The alert view is initialized by default.

To define alter counter value thresholds, choose Add to Alert from the **E**dit menu. This displays the Add to Alert dialog box, which is shown in figure 31.45.

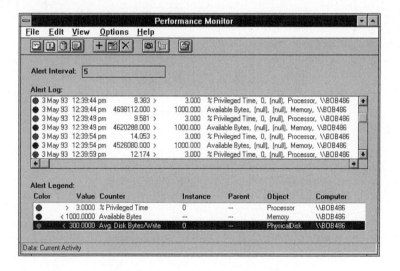

You select the computer, object counter, color, and instance, if appropriate, in a manner similar to what you did for a chart view. Alerts are different in that they result in the display of information only if the object counter value is greater than or less than a value you define. Optionally, you can specify a program to execute either the first time or each time an alert is recorded.

After you've finished adding object counters to the alert log, click the Done button to display the alert view in the Performance Monitor window. Figure 31.46 shows an example of a Performance Monitor alert display.

The legend shows that alerts will be logged if

■ The processor uses more than 3 percent of its time executing kernel mode code (shown as the % Privileged Time counter)

■ The number of available or free bytes of memory drops below 1000

■ The average number of bytes written to the disk is less than 300

You use Alert from the **O**ptions menu to change the automatic monitoring interval. Use Data From in the **O**ptions menu to select the current activity of the system or a log file.

Using Log View

The log view enables you to select objects and their counters to be logged for subsequent display and analysis. You display the log view by selecting **L**og from the **V**iew menu. Like the other views, it is initialized by default; no object counters are defined for it.

To add counter values to a log, choose **A**dd to Log from the **E**dit menu. This displays the Add to Log dialog box, which is shown in figure 31.47. Select objects from this dialog box to add to the log, then click the Done button to display the log view with your selected objects.

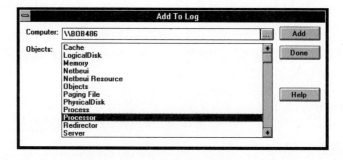

Fig. 31.47

The Add to Log dialog box.

The selected objects appear in the view with all counters collected for each object. To define the log characteristics, choose **L**og from the **V**iew menu. This displays the Log Option dialog box, which you can use to specify the name for the log file, its location, and the interval at which counters will be written to the log file. After logging is started with the **S**tart Log button, you can terminate logging with the **S**topped Log button. Counters for the objects included in the log file are available for subsequent viewing.

In figure 31.48, the log file is created on drive D and is named demoperformance.log. Information is logged for the Cache, PhysicalDisk, and Processor objects every 30 seconds. The File Size field shows the current size of the log file.

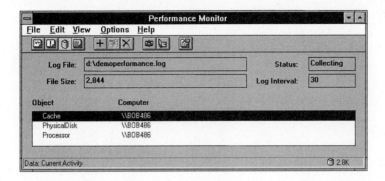

Fig. 31.48

The Performance
Monitor log
display.

After the Done button is selected, the Performance Monitor window
appears with the default chart view. The status line at the bottom of
the window shows that the source of the data is the log file. The graph
time displays the duration for the log.

Summary

The Windows NT administrative applications control access to the
system and its resources. The User Manager application controls access to the system through logons. It also controls access to resources
by users through account characteristics such as user rights.

The Disk Administrator allows partitions to be defined in three different
file systems. The Disk Administrator features of volume sets and striping allow the extension of data across multiple volumes.

Backup is used to provide tape backup copies of code and data, which
increases the integrity of the system. Both the Event Viewer and the
Performance Monitor record and display system, security, and application events that are used to correct problems or improve the
performance of the system. The capabilities of the administrative
tools provide for the comprehensive administration of a Windows
NT system.

Troubleshooting Windows NT

Windows NT is a robust operating system that is easy to use and configure. Sometimes, however, a problem may occur. Most problems have simple and quick solutions; other problems require a bit of research to uncover their source and devise a solution.

If you have a problem when installing or using Windows NT, this chapter is a good place to begin looking for a solution. Each section lists the simplest solution first. If a simple solution doesn't solve the problem, try the next one. If none of the solutions solve the problem, see Chapter 33 for a listing of support resources.

Although problems may be frustrating, working with them can also be educational. So consider these experiences a way to learn more about your computer.

Solving Installation Problems

The installation process for Windows NT usually proceeds flawlessly. In most cases, you simply insert the Windows NT boot diskette in drive A, reboot your computer, and follow the simple instructions on the screen. The Windows NT Setup program automatically figures out your machine's hardware. The only information you typically need to provide is where you want Windows NT installed and the optional components you want to include.

Installation can fail, however, if your computer (or a piece of it) is incompatible or does not have enough resources. This section helps you figure out what went wrong and how you can correct it.

The process of installing Windows NT can be broken down into several phases: preinitialization, text-mode, and GUI setup. When trying to identify an installation problem, it is helpful to be able to identify which phase the problem occurred in. This section outlines the Windows NT setup process.

Preinitialization phase: If you are installing Windows NT from the network or from an unsupported CD-ROM drive, you must first run WINNT.EXE from DOS. This program copies all Windows NT files to a local hard drive so that the Windows NT Setup program can access the files when the text-mode phase is entered. All files are copied into a temporary subdirectory named \WIN_NT.~LS. Note that the preinitialization process does not occur if you are installing from a supported CD-ROM drive or floppy disk.

Text-mode phase: If all Windows NT files are accessible by Windows NT (that is, you have a supported CD-ROM drive or you are installing from floppy disks, or you have completed the preinitialization process), the text-mode phase begins when you boot the computer from the Windows NT Boot or Setup disk. The disk is crammed with a stripped-down version of the Windows NT operating system: everything that is needed to access the most popular CD-ROM drives, format hard disks, and copy files—and not much more.

This miniature Windows NT accomplishes the following tasks:

- It asks whether you want to use the Custom or Express setup.

- It asks where you want Windows NT installed, and whether you want to format the destination drive.

- It copies all essential Windows NT files from the floppy disks or the CD-ROM to the destination directory you specified.

At the end of the text-mode phase, Windows NT Setup instructs you to remove the floppy disk from drive A and reboot the computer using Ctrl+Alt+Del.

GUI setup phase: After the text-mode phase, Windows NT Setup reboots to the GUI (Graphical User Interface) setup. During the GUI setup phase, Windows NT is running.

After asking you to identify yourself and name the computer, the setup program analyzes your hardware configuration. In most cases, it figures out exactly what components you have; you do not need to supply any information. Next, Setup copies the files required to support your hardware from the CD-ROM drive (or temporary directory if your setup required the preinitialization phase). During the GUI setup phase, user accounts, the Emergency Recovery diskette, and Program Manager groups are created.

Failure during the Preinitialization Phase

The preinitialization phase occurs completely in the confines of DOS. Therefore, few things can go wrong. The most common problem during this stage is not having enough disk space to hold all the Windows NT files. The WINNT.EXE program will tell you if you do not have enough disk space to install Windows NT. To solve this problem, you can either make more space available on the hard disk or specify a different hard disk that has the required amount of space.

Setup Doesn't List Your Hardware

If you have hardware that Windows NT Setup doesn't recognize during the installation, you may need a special driver for the hardware. First, however, find out whether the hardware is compatible with a piece of equipment that *is* listed; if the equipment is compatible, choose the name of the compatible equipment during installation.

If the equipment you have is not compatible with any of the equipment listed on the Hardware Compatibility List, a Windows NT-compatible driver may be available from the manufacturer of the equipment.

The Hardware Compatibility List is updated periodically to include newly supported equipment. You can always download the latest HCL (and even drivers) from CompuServe, GEnie, Microsoft OnLine, and some user group bulletin boards.

Failure during the Text-Mode Phase

During the text-mode phase of installation, Windows NT setup asks you whether you want Express or Custom setup and where you want Windows NT installed. It then copies the most essential Windows NT files to this location. It is very unlikely that any problems should occur during the execution of this phase, but if they do, the following sections should provide you with assistance.

The CD-ROM drive is unsupported. Windows NT Setup installs directly only from the most popular SCSI CD-ROM drives. If your CD-ROM drive is not recognized by Windows NT Setup (the make and model are not listed on the Windows NT Hardware Compatibility List), the text-mode phase will fail with the following message:

```
This version of Setup requires a CD-ROM drive connected to a
SCSI adapter recognized by Windows NT. Setup has determined
that no such CD-ROM drives are attached to this computer.
```

First check that your CD-ROM drive is on and the Windows NT CD-ROM is in the drive. If that doesn't solve your problem, you must install with the WINNT.EXE program. See Chapter 18 of the *Windows NT System Guide* for instructions.

The SCSI CD-ROM drive is configured incorrectly. If you receive a `File Copy Errors` message during Windows NT Setup, your CD-ROM drive is probably not configured correctly. Refer to your CD-ROM drive and SCSI adapter manuals to check the following:

- Some SCSI adapters reserve SCSI ID 0 and 1 for hard disks, so verify that your CD-ROM drive is not set for either of these addresses. If you have a CD-ROM drive assigned to ID 0 or 1, see your CD-ROM drive documentation for instructions on how to change the SCSI address of the CD-ROM drive.

- SCSI devices are all hooked together on the *SCSI bus*. The SCSI bus must have terminating resistors, or terminators, installed at each "end" of the bus to operate correctly. If you have only internal or only external SCSI devices, the ends of the bus are probably the SCSI adapter and one of your devices. If you have both internal and external devices, the SCSI adapter is probably in the middle of the bus and should not have a terminator.

The partition used as the destination during preinitialization is inaccessible. When you install Windows NT using the WINNT.EXE program (that is, you go through the preinitialization phase), Windows NT Setup copies all the Windows NT files to a temporary directory on a drive it chooses. Setup could choose a drive that is unsupported by Windows NT and is therefore inaccessible during the text-mode phase. For example, if you are using a disk compression product such as Stacker, Setup may copy the files to your compressed partition. Windows NT version 3.1 cannot access compressed drives (such as MS-DOS 6.0 DoubleSpace drives), so installation fails.

When this type of failure occurs, you receive the following message:

```
Setup is unable to locate the hard drive partition prepared
by the MS-DOS portion of Setup.
```

To get around this problem, use WINNT.EXE with the /T switch. This enables you to specify to WINNT.EXE which drive to use for the temporary files. For example, if you type

WINNT /T N:

Setup will use drive N for the temporary files.

The machine doesn't have enough hard disk space to install Windows NT. Windows NT version 3.1 requires 66M available on the hard drive to install. If this much space is not available, scour the hard disk for files and applications you can delete. Depending on how you use your computer, you may be able to delete some of the following files:

- *Large graphics files that you no longer use.* For example, Windows 3.1 includes a large number of bitmap files (BMP) that may be candidates for deletion.

- *Help files that you no longer need.* If you are comfortable using an application, you may want to delete its online help files. These files usually have the HLP extension.

- *Pagefiles from previous versions of Windows.* If you are upgrading to Windows NT from Windows 3.0 or Windows 3.1, you can delete or shrink the permanent swap file. See your Windows 3.1 manual for instructions on how to change the size of your permanent swap file.

- *Old temporary files.* Many applications litter your TEMP directory with temporary files. You can delete all files in your TEMP directory that have the TMP extension.

The Graphical Portion of Setup Doesn't Appear

The purpose of text-mode setup is to get just enough setup tasks accomplished to start the Windows NT operating system. Setup does the majority of its work when the text-mode phase is completed and Windows NT is running. This phase is called the GUI setup phase because Windows NT—a graphical user interface—is running. The mouse is active, and all the familiar graphic controls (such as buttons, list boxes, and menus) are available.

If something goes wrong between the text-mode phase and the GUI setup phase, it probably means the video driver was specified incorrectly. During text-mode setup, either you choose a video driver (the Custom Setup option) or Setup chooses one for you (the Express Setup option). If the GUI setup phase fails to start, you or Setup most likely chose the wrong video driver. The only way to correct this problem is to start from scratch: Reboot your computer with the Windows NT Setup disk in drive A. This time, however, specify a different video choice. (The VGA 640x486 16 Color option is the one most likely to work.)

Solving Mouse Problems

If the mouse doesn't work or behaves strangely, there is a problem with the connection, the software, or the mouse. Two kinds of mice are generally available: serial and port. A serial mouse attaches to a serial port of the computer. A port mouse attaches to a port built into the system unit or a port on a board you install inside the computer's system unit.

The Mouse Doesn't Work in Windows

A serial mouse must be connected to the COM1 or COM2 port. The port you choose doesn't matter. Make sure that you connect the mouse before you start the computer. (If you plug in the mouse after you start the computer, choose the File Restart command from the Program Manager to reboot.)

If the mouse is connected but still doesn't work, there is probably an interrupt conflict. Serial devices and mouse ports use IRQ interrupts to communicate with the computer, and only a limited number of IRQ interrupts are available. If two devices are fighting for the same interrupt, a conflict develops. Suspect this problem if a lot of equipment is attached to the computer. Check the IRQ interrupts for the other devices and make sure that the mouse doesn't conflict. Windows 3.1 and MS-DOS, by accident, allowed two devices to share an interrupt as long as they didn't try to use it at the same time. Windows NT, however, does not allow interrupt sharing.

The Mouse Pointer Jumps Around or Doesn't Move

If the mouse pointer appears on-screen but doesn't move, the wrong mouse driver is selected, or there is an interrupt conflict. Check the driver first, because an incorrect driver selection is easier to correct.

To check the driver, choose the Windows Setup application in the Main group in the Program Manager. A dialog box appears that lists the equipment you installed during the Windows installation. If the mouse doesn't match the equipment settings, choose Options, then choose Change System Settings. From the Mouse list, select the correct mouse. If this procedure doesn't work, check for an IRQ interrupt conflict. See the preceding section, "The Mouse Doesn't Work in Windows."

If the mouse pointer moves but jumps around on-screen, the mouse may be dirty. To clean the mouse, you can usually remove the ball by following instructions on the bottom of the mouse. Use a solvent to clean the ball, and then replace it. If cleaning doesn't work, an IRQ interrupt conflict is the probable culprit. See the preceding section, "The Mouse Doesn't Work in Windows."

Solving Problems with Booting Windows NT

If you start your computer and Windows NT does not appear or seems to be frozen, there is probably a configuration problem or a hardware problem. Windows NT provides two mechanisms for resolving boot problems: the Last Known Good Configuration and the Emergency Repair disk.

The Last Known Good Configuration

Sometimes a change in the hardware configuration (such as installing a new, but faulty, device driver) can cause Windows NT to fail to boot. Windows NT provides a mechanism that enables you to revert back to what is called the *Last Known Good Configuration.*

Windows NT attempts to use the Last Known Good Configuration automatically when the system is recovering from a Severe or Critical device driver loading error.

You can also ask Windows NT to load the Last Known Good Configuration. To do so, follow these steps:

1. Restart your computer.

2. If your machine is configured to use MultiBoot, choose Windows NT. Otherwise, go to the next step.

3. As soon as the screen clears and OS Loader appears, press and hold down the Spacebar. The Last Known Good Select screen will appear as follows:

```
LAST KNOWN GOOD SELECT
You may choose to boot the system using the Last Known
Good configuration.
If you choose to boot from the Last Known Good configu-
ration, any configuration changes since the system was
successfully booted will be lost.
        Use Current Configuration
        Use Last Known Good Configuration
        Reboot
Use the up and down arrow keys to make your selection.
Press ENTER when you have made your selection
```

4. Follow the instructions on the screen. If you choose "Use Last Known Good Configuration," Windows NT will boot using the configuration that you most recently logged in with.

Restoring the System with the Emergency Repair Disk

If Windows NT suddenly stops working because a file was damaged from a power failure or a configuration error, you can use the Emergency Repair disk to repair your system—if you created an Emergency Repair disk during installation. If you did not create an Emergency Repair disk or you have lost the disk, you must reinstall Windows NT from the original floppy disks or CD-ROM disk.

 NOTE Do not attempt to use an Emergency Repair disk that was created by installing Windows NT on a different computer. The Emergency Repair disk is specific to the computer it was created on and is not interchangeable.

To restore Windows NT using the Emergency Repair disk, follow these steps:

1. Insert your original Windows NT Setup or Boot disk in drive A and reboot your computer.

2. Choose **R**epair from the Setup screen.

3. Follow the instructions on the screen, inserting the Emergency Repair disk or Windows NT disks as requested.

4. When the repair process is complete, follow the instructions on the screen by pressing Ctrl+Alt+Del to restart the system.

The repair process accomplishes the following tasks:

■ A utility called CHKDSK is run to check the integrity of the hard disk that Windows NT is installed on.

■ Each Windows NT system file is checked to make sure it has not been corrupted. If any files are found to be corrupt, original versions are copied from the installation disks or CD-ROM disk.

■ If you choose, the repair process replaces the current configuration information with the default configuration information.

■ The boot loader is reinstalled. The boot loader gets Windows NT running after you start your computer.

Solving Program Manager Problems

The Program Manager is the hometown of the Windows program. When you first start Windows, you see the Program Manager. When you run an application, you start from the Program Manager.

In the Program Manager window, there are group windows (which contain program item icons) and group icons that represent closed group windows. Windows creates some of these group windows as part of the installation process, and you create other group windows. The same is true for program item icons: Windows creates some, and you create others.

Group windows and program item icons are easy to create and delete. To delete a group window or program item icon, just select the icon and press the Delete key. You can accidentally delete an icon in no time at all. Fortunately, deleting a group or icon doesn't delete applications or files; this action deletes only the group or icon.

To create a new group window, follow these steps:

1. In the Program Manager, choose File.

2. Choose New.

3. Select Program Group.

4. Choose OK.

To create a program item icon:

1. From the Program Manager, select the group where you want the icon.

2. Choose File.

3. Choose New.

4. Select Program Item.

5. In the Description text box, enter a name for the icon.

6. In the Command Line text box, enter the application's path and name (choose Browse if you're not sure where the application is located).

7. Choose OK.

Recovering Erased and Lost Files

If you erased system or application files that the computer needs, you must reinstall the application or Windows NT. If you accidentally erased data files, restore them from backup copies.

What? You didn't make backup copies? Stop what you're doing—don't do anything else on the computer—and use a file recovery application, such as the MS-DOS 6.0 UNDELETE command, to recover lost files. Note, however, that these applications do not work while you are running Windows NT; you have to boot MS-DOS. This means you can recover files only on FAT partitions (because MS-DOS cannot access NTFS partitions).

If you lose a file through no fault of your own, such as a power outage, many applications perform an automatic save, which often preserves at least part of your work. Check the application's documentation to see whether the application has the capability of backing up files when a power failure or application failure occurs. These backup files may have odd names and be located in special directories; the documentation can tell you how to find these files.

Troubleshooting Windows Applications

Sometimes while you use an application, you press a key and the wrong thing happens. The first thing to do is to try again. If the incorrect response persists, check this section to try find out what may be happening.

If the system stops responding altogether or crashes, refer to the section in this chapter titled "Responding to an Application Failure." If there is a performance problem, Chapters 19, 22, and 23 offer tips on enhancing the performance of Windows and the system, respectively.

A Keypress Gives You the Wrong Result

If something unexpected happens when you press a key—usually a shortcut key—in an application, a shortcut key conflict probably exists. In many applications, you can assign custom shortcuts to keyboard combinations. If you assigned system-level shortcut keys to an application-level function, you'll get the wrong result when you press the keys. (The Ctrl+Alt+Del combination, for example, reboots a computer. Don't assign this sequence to the function of making selected text bold in the application.) The easiest solution to the problem is to change the shortcut in the application. You can change shortcut keys also in a DOS PIF (program information file) or in the Properties dialog box in the Program Manager (select the program item icon and choose the File Properties command).

If you press a Windows shortcut key and the Windows function doesn't happen, a DOS application may be preempting the shortcut. Check the DOS application's PIF by using the PIF Editor in the Main group in the Program Manager. Alternatively, check the properties of the DOS program item icon in the Program Manager by choosing the File Properties command.

The Application Slows Down

If the application begins running slowly, the computer may lack enough memory to run the application optimally. You need to free memory by closing other applications or by taking other measures (see the section in this chapter titled "Solving Memory Problems"). Suspect low memory if the hard disk's light blinks frequently. This indicates that Windows NT is thrashing (switching applications and data between memory and the hard disk because memory is low).

A full hard disk can also cause an application to slow down. If you suspect the hard disk is nearly full, save all work and use the File Manager to remove unneeded files or transfer files to floppy disks.

Troubleshooting DOS Applications

Windows NT uses PIFs (Program Information Files) to run DOS applications. A PIF includes information about the DOS application's location on disk, as well as setup information that is standardized to work on all computers.

Although the PIF settings enable the DOS application to work on the computer, they don't enable the application to work optimally on the computer. If you have difficulty with a DOS application you may need to adjust the PIF settings for that application. An entire chapter (Chapter 21) is devoted to optimizing DOS application performance by fine-tuning PIF settings.

Installation and Setup Problems

When installing software, you usually must provide information about the equipment or software. Before you start an installation, find out the following:

- The type of equipment you have
- The amount of memory in your system
- The software you previously installed and where on the computer the software is located

Check the application's documentation to see whether you can find a list of information needed during installation. As always, make sure you have enough hard disk space before you begin the installation process and, if possible, shut down all memory-resident applications. If you have difficulty while installing a DOS application, refer to the application's documentation.

A DOS Application Is Frozen

If you're stuck in a DOS application after you marked (selected) text or after you scrolled, you may still be in the Windows editing mode, which prevents you from working with the DOS application. Look at the DOS application's title bar: if the bar still reads Select or Mark, a Windows operation still is incomplete. Complete the operation (by selecting text or choosing the Edit Copy command) or press the Escape key to return control to the application.

You Can't Capture the Screen

If you are unable to capture a DOS screen, check the Reserve Shortcut Key option in the Advanced dialog box in the PIF Editor. See whether the Print Screen key (PrtScrn) or Alt+Print Screen combination (Alt+PrtScrn) is reserved for the application's use. The application may use the key combinations, disabling them for Windows NT.

You Can't Paste Information

If you are unable to paste information you have copied or cut into the Clipboard, check the following:

■ Windows cannot paste graphics in DOS applications. Windows can paste graphics in Windows applications that can accept graphics.

■ Copied text from DOS applications actually may be graphics that appear as text on-screen. If so, Windows cannot copy the graphical text to another DOS application. You may be able to copy and paste the entire screen of the application instead.

■ Some DOS applications cannot handle the fast paste method. If you suspect this is the problem, modify the advanced portion of the PIF to clear the Allow Fast Paste check box. (See Chapter 21, "Customizing PIFs," for more details.)

You Can't Close a DOS Application

When closing a DOS application, you should always use the normal command used to quit that application. If the screen does not return immediately to Windows, press Alt+Spacebar to display the Control menu, then choose **C**lose. You can control how the window or screen for a DOS application reacts when the application closes with the **C**lose Window on Exit setting in the PIF. You can use the **C**lose Window on Exit setting in the PIF to control how the window or screen for a DOS application reacts.

If the Allow **C**lose When Active box is selected in the application PIF, you can close Windows while that DOS application is running. This may result in a loss of data and in damaged program files. This option should rarely be used.

Normally you cannot quit Windows NT when a DOS application is running. If you try to, Windows asks you to close the application first unless this PIF option has been selected. Always close Command Prompt windows before exiting Windows NT.

Normally, whey you try to quit Windows NT when a DOS application is running, Windows asks you to close the application first. If you select the Allow **C**lose When Active box in the application PIF, however, you can close Windows while that DOS application is running. This may result in data loss and damaged program files. This option should rarely be used.

If a DOS application running under Windows NT terminates improperly, it prevents you from exiting the application. When a DOS application crashes and you cannot exit from the frozen application, you can end the application as follows. From the application's Control menu, choose **S**ettings, then choose **T**erminate. This option should be used only as a last resort.

The Application Fails

The computer rarely encounters an internal instruction that it doesn't understand or that conflicts with another instruction. When it does, the application may fail, or crash. When this happens, sometimes you see a message advising you that the application has encountered an unrecoverable error, but sometimes the application may just become unstable and may behave incorrectly.

Although crashes occur rarely, they are the best reason for you to save your files frequently. (Earthquakes also happen rarely, but if you live in southern California, being prepared for tremors is a good idea!)

When an application crashes, you may not lose everything. Windows NT is a robust system and you will almost always be able to recover from the crash just by shutting down the offending application. You lose the data in the application that crashed (unless the application has a file recovery utility), but you will not lose data from other applications running at the same time because Windows NT's robustness ensures that the rest of the system continues to run.

A crash sometimes occurs for no apparent reason, and you must restart the application. If the system crashes frequently, however, suspect a problem. One problem stems from using an older version of an application that is not compatible with Windows NT. If this is the case, call the manufacturer to see if they offer an updated version of the application.

If an application you are using freezes, you can "kill" it by using the **End Task** command in the Task List. To kill a frozen application, follow these steps:

1. Press Ctrl+Esc. The Task List, shown in figure 32.1, appears.

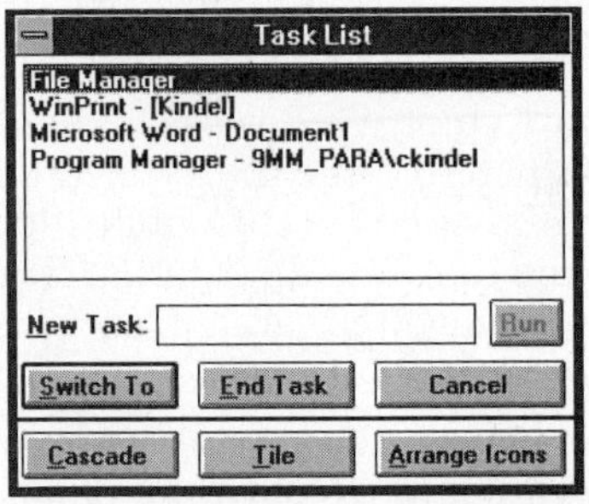

Fig. 32.1

The Task List.

2. Select the name of the application you want to kill in the list.

3. Choose **End Task**.

4. If the application does not disappear immediately, wait a few seconds. Eventually it will either disappear or you will see a Window saying that the task will not end. Keep choosing **E**nd Task. If after several attempts the application still won't go away, your best option is to restart your computer.

Solving Memory Problems

Everything you do on the computer happens in memory, and the computer has only so much memory. If memory becomes full, you will see the `Out of Memory` or `Cannot Allocate Virtual Memory` error. If you see either of these error messages, too many applications are running. Close any applications you're not using. Make sure your paging file is large enough, and that you have enough disk space available for it to grow to its maximum size.

If this problem occurs regularly, consider adding physical memory to your machine. The improvement in speed can be amazing—especially if you jump from having 12M in your system to having 16M or 32M in your system.

Solving Font and Printing Problems

In the days before Windows, printing was an area likely to cause problems for people. Windows simplifies printing by using a common printer driver and by including the Print Manager to manage printing. Occasionally, however, a problem crops up.

The Printer Won't Print

This section provides information about what to do if your printer won't print. The first thing you should do if you are having trouble printing is to make sure that the printer cable is connected and functioning properly. In Windows, all pin connectors must be working. To test the cable, borrow another cable that you know works.

If you still cannot print, try the following:

■ If you selected a printer to emulate, make sure you chose the correct printer. Check the printer's documentation.

- If you have a serial printer, look for an IRQ interrupt conflict. If another serial device, such as a mouse, is using the same IRQ interrupt as the printer, one of the devices won't work. See the section titled "The Mouse Doesn't Work in Windows," or refer to Chapter 7.

The Format Is Wrong or the Output Is Garbled

If the printed pages are formatted incorrectly, check the following:

- The printer can print the fonts and sizes you specified in the application.

- The printer configuration settings are correct. In the Print Manager, choose **Printer Properties** (see Chapter 7).

- The switches on the printer that control settings, such as page length and line feeds, are correct. Check the printer's manual.

If printed text is garbled, try the following:

- Make sure you selected the correct printer as the default. In the Print Manager, use the Default combo box on the tool bar to select the correct printer.

- If the printer contains a cartridge, make sure you selected the correct cartridge. See Chapter 7, "Customizing with the Control Panel," or Chapter 9, "Using the Print Manager," for more information.

- Turn the printer off and then on again to clear the printer's memory of text that may be left over from a previous print.

- Test for a faulty cable by borrowing a cable that you know is functioning correctly.

If you use a serial printer, check the port settings. Choose the Ports application in the Control Panel, then choose **S**ettings. Sometimes, choosing a lower baud rate can improve printing.

If you chose a printer to emulate, try emulating a different model.

Fonts Are Displayed or Printed Incorrectly

Windows NT is equipped with TrueType technology, which shows you the same fonts on-screen that you see when you print—no matter what kind of printer you use. Windows comes with four TrueType fonts: Times New Roman, Arial, Courier New, and Symbol. You can add more easily.

If you use fonts other than TrueType fonts, what you see on-screen may not match what is printed. This can happen when you use printer fonts for which no corresponding screen fonts exist; Windows substitutes the closest TrueType font for the screen display. In many applications, you can select an option to make only printer fonts available or to show fonts on-screen as they appear when printed. Check the application documentation.

If you installed a cartridge in the printer and cannot print the fonts, check that you selected the correct cartridge as follows:

1. In the Print Manager, choose **P**rinter.

2. Choose **P**roperties.

3. Choose **S**etup.

4. In the Fonts Cartridges list, select the correct cartridge.

If the cartridge is correct, try turning off the printer and making sure that the cartridge is properly installed. (Often, firm pressure is needed to insert the cartridge.)

If you have trouble printing soft fonts, try the following:

- Check that you haven't turned off the printer since you downloaded the fonts. If you did turn off the printer, you must download the fonts again.

- Check the font documentation to be sure that you installed the fonts correctly.

- If you changed the port connection, you must download the fonts again.

- If you use many soft fonts at once, try using fewer fonts. Many printers support only a limited number of fonts.

The Printer Loses Text

If the printer loses text, the cable or the port may be at fault. If you use a parallel printer (LPT), suspect the cable and try another one that you know is working. If you use a serial printer (COM), change the port settings as follows:

1. From the Control Panel, choose the Ports application.

2. Choose **S**ettings.

3. Select a lower baud rate from the list.

If this doesn't work, check that all settings are the same in Windows NT and on the printer.

If only part of a page prints, the printer probably has insufficient memory. Graphics often present this kind of problem because their files are large. If possible, split the graphics so that fewer graphic images appear on one page. If you cannot do this, try a lower print resolution. If you run into this problem frequently, find out whether you can add more memory to your printer.

If you know that the printer has enough memory, check that the correct amount of memory is specified as follows:

1. From the Print Manager, choose **P**rinter.

2. Choose **P**roperties.

3. Choose **S**etup.

4. Check the amount of memory in the memory list.

Correcting Paintbrush Printing Problems

If a Paintbrush picture is printed smaller than normal, check the **V**iew Picture command in the **V**iew menu to see whether the picture looks okay. If necessary, choose the **O**ptions **I**mage Attributes command to change the height and width of the image.

When you print, make sure the **U**se Printer Resolution option in the Print dialog box is turned off. Check that the correct scaling is set. (If scaling is set to less than 100 percent, the picture prints smaller than normal.)

Solving Network Problems

If you have trouble connecting to a network or using Windows NT on a network, check this section for solutions. Additionally, Chapters 26 and 28 provide specific information that may help solve problems you have connecting users to the network. If the difficulty is with printing, refer to the preceding section, "Solving Font and Printing Problems."

You Can't Connect to a Network Drive

If you cannot connect to a network drive, try the following test to see whether the network is working correctly:

1. From the Main window in the Program Manager, choose Command Prompt.

2. At the command prompt (for example, C:\>), type the following command:

   NET VIEW

3. You should see a list of at least two computer names: your computer and one or more others.

If this fails, make sure that you use the correct network drivers. From the Control Panel, choose the Network application and make sure the settings are correct.

Determining Which Network Component Didn't Start

The Event Viewer (discussed in Chapter 31) can tell you which Windows NT components failed to start. Usually, it can also tell you why. To determine which network components failed to start, follow these steps:

1. From the Program Manager, open the Administrative Tools window.

2. Choose Event Viewer. A list of events is displayed, with the most recent events at the top. Look for any event with a stop sign icon and a Source of LanmanServer, Server, Svr, Workstation, Wksta, or another network-related component.

3. Double-click the event. The Event Detail window, shown in Figure 32.2, appears.

4. Use the **Next** and **Previous** buttons to view other events.

5. Choose Close to dismiss the Event Detail window.

Solving Object Linking and Embedding Problems

Object linking and embedding (OLE) enables you to create compound documents made up of objects created by different applications. To create a compound document, the applications must be OLE-compatible.

Creating a compound document involves at least two applications: the *client*, or primary, application (into which you embed objects) and the *server*, or secondary, application (which you use to create objects to embed in the client application). Some applications can function as either a client or a server. An object embedded in a client application is linked to the server application you used to create the object.

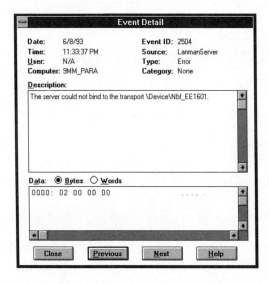

Fig. 32.2

The Event Detail window.

Many Windows applications come with free OLE applications. Word for Windows, for example, includes Microsoft Draw, WordArt, and Equation Editor. After these applets are installed on the computer, they are available to all other applications that support OLE.

The following sections provide information on what you should do if your OLE operations are not working correctly.

The Server Is Unavailable

When you create, edit, or update an embedded object, the server application used to create the object must be available. If you see a warning that the server application is unavailable, you must either wait until the application becomes available or switch to the server application and complete or end the current task. You may be able to just choose Cancel to close the warning dialog box and try again later.

If these simple methods don't help, you may need to reinstall the application that includes the applet you want to use as a server. Installing the application registers the applet in Windows.

Can't Insert an Object or Open a Server Application

If you try to insert a new object into a client and the server application isn't listed or doesn't start when chosen from the list, try one of the following solutions:

■ Make sure the server application wasn't deleted from the computer.

■ If you moved the server application, make sure the directory where the server application is located is in your path environment variable.

■ Some server applications contain a registration file, which has the REG extension. Double-click this file in the File Manager to run it. Running the registration file tells the OLE system where to find the applications components.

Understanding Different Ways of Pasting

When you paste information from one application to another, two things may happen. If you use certain server applications to create the information, copy the information to the Clipboard, and then paste it in a client application, the information is embedded in the client application. You can double-click the information to start the server application. (For some server applications, you can embed objects only by using a special command.)

If you used a non-server application to create the information on the Clipboard and then paste it in another application, the information becomes an unchangeable part of the document.

You Have Problems with Linking

When you link an object from one application to another, to update the link you must first save all changes made to the original document.

If you are trying to paste and link the contents of the clipboard into a document but the Paste Link command is unavailable (grayed out), first save the file you used to create the information. If the Paste Link command is still unavailable, the application you used to create the information may not be a server application. If it is not a server application, you can paste, but not link, the information into the document.

Solving Communication and Port Difficulties

Serial communications take place on the COM ports in Windows NT. Serial communications include printing, faxing, scanning, operating a mouse, and connecting to a distant computer by modem.

You Have Trouble Using a Serial (COM) Port

If you have trouble using a serial port, try the following:

- Check whether another application is using the same port. If so, close the application.

- Check whether the serial driver is initializing the port correctly. Look for events in the Event Viewer with Serial as the Source. See Chapter 31 for more information on using the Event Viewer.

- If you suspect IRQ interrupt conflicts, check the IRQ interrupt settings in the documentation for the serial devices. These default settings often can be changed so that all applications on the computer can exist harmoniously.

You Have Problems Communicating at High Speed

Windows NT can communicate at very high speeds—exceeding 56K baud—through the serial ports. However, some slower machines may experience problems. The following suggestions might help:

■ Check the documentation to make sure the computer is running as fast as possible. (Some computers slow down to prolong battery life or have a Turbo switch.)

■ Add a 16550AF Universal Asynchronous Receiver Transmitter (UART) to the serial port. The 16550AF UART buffers the serial port data, which enables the port to run faster.

Follow these steps to enable Windows NT's use of a 16550AF UART:

1. From the Program Manager, choose **F**ile.

2. Choose **R**un.

3. In the **C**ommand Line edit box, type:

   REGEDT32

4. The Registry Editor appears. Select the HKEY_LOCAL_MACHINE on Local Machine window.

5. Choose SYSTEM by double-clicking it. The SYSTEM tree opens up, making the subtree visible.

6. Select CurrentControlSet.

7. From the CurrentControlSet tree, select Services.

8. From the Services tree, select Serial.

9. From the Serial tree, select Parameters.

10. If necessary, add a key to correspond to the serial port for which you want to enable 16650 buffering. Add the Serial0 key for your first serial port (for example, COM1) and Serial1 for your second port. To add a key, Choose **E**dit Add **K**ey. The Add Key window appears. Type **Serial0** or **Serial1** in the **K**ey Name edit box. Do not enter anything in the **C**lass box. Choose OK.

11. Select the Serial0 or Serial1 key.

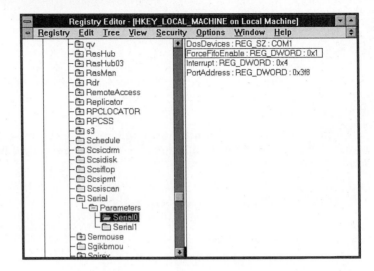

Fig. 32.3

The Registry
Editor.

12. Create the following values for COM1 (Serial0) or COM2 (Serial1):

Value Name	Data Type	COM1 Data	COM2 Data
DosDevices	REG_SZ	COM1	COM2
ForceFifoEnable	REG_DWORD	1	1
Interrupt	REG_DWORD	4	3
PortAddress	REG_DWORD	3f8	2f8

Use the following procedure to add values to a specific key. Select the key, then choose **E**dit Add **V**alue. The Add Value window appears. Type the Value name in the Value Name edit box. Choose the correct Data Type from the Data Type combo box. Choose OK. A value editor window appears; the contents vary with each data type. Enter the appropriate value in the edit box in the value editor window. Press OK.

When you are done, the Registry Editor should look similar to figure 32.3.

NOTE   If you have a 16550 or 16550A UART, do not carry out the preceding steps. These versions of the 16550 have a defect that causes them to lose data when buffering is enabled, which is why buffering support is turned off by default. The 16550 UART usually has a label that indicates whether it is a 16550, 16550A, or 16550AF.

If you experience additional communications difficulties after turning on 16550 buffering, turn it off by changing the ForceFifoEnable value from 1 to 0.

You Can't Communicate through Windows NT Terminal

If the modem won't dial the phone number in Terminal, first make sure that the hardware is connected correctly. Then make sure that the correct serial port is specified by choosing **S**ettings **C**ommunications and checking the **C**onnector option.

If the modem dials but doesn't establish a connection, the settings you chose for the remote computer may be wrong. The system and the remote system must use the same baud rate, data bits, parity setting, stop bits, and flow control. You have to contact someone at the remote site to discover the settings of the remote computer. On your system, change the settings to match the settings of the remote computer by choosing the **S**ettings **C**ommunications command and selecting the appropriate options.

If you dial and connect but cannot send or receive a file, both the computer and the remote computer may not be using the same handshake protocol (which is the flow control method). Find out whether the remote system uses Xon/Xoff and whether the remote system uses hardware handshaking. Use **S**ettings **C**ommunications to change the **F**low Control settings to match the settings of the remote computer.

Summary

Although Windows NT is a stable and robust operating system that usually works well, problems can occur. This chapter explained what to do when you encounter common problems. If none of the solutions described in this chapter solve your problem, contact Microsoft's technical support service as described in Chapter 33. Chapter 33 also identifies other resources that you may find helpful when using and troubleshooting Windows NT.

Help, Support, and Resources

Windows is one of the most popular software applications ever written. To follow the popularity, Windows NT has created much excitement, too. Because of the complexity of NT as a new operating system, a great deal of support is available to aid you in learning and operating Windows NT. The following resources should help you get the most from Windows NT.

Telephone Support

Microsoft offers a number of ways to obtain product support for Windows NT. For the first 30 days that you own Windows NT, Microsoft offers free telephone support for NT installation and setup. You can contact Microsoft Monday through Friday, not including holidays, from 6 a.m. to 6 p.m. Pacific Time.

Additionally, Microsoft has available a toll-free number which gives you access 24 hours per day, 7 days per week, to an automated system called FastTips. FastTips enables you to receive answers to common questions and technical notes by way of recordings or fax.

Microsoft offers technical support by technical support specialists after the first 30 days—at a price. Support calls are $150 per incident. You can apply the charges to your phone bill or use a credit card. This service is available 24 hours per day, 7 days per week.

The following table lists Microsoft phone numbers that you can call for support:

Phone Number	Service
(800) 936-4400	FastTips automated phone service. Free access.
(900) 555-2100	Technical support at $150 per incident, applied to your phone bill.
(206) 635-7022	Technical support at $150 per incident, applied to your credit card.
(206) 635-4948	Technical support for the deaf and hard-of-hearing using a special TT modem. Available Monday through Friday, 6 a.m. to 6 p.m. Pacific Time.
(800) 227-4679	For more information about Windows NT support options. Available Monday through Friday, 6:30 a.m. to 5:00 p.m., Pacific Time.

Support Organizations

Most major cities in the United States have a computer club. Within each club, you usually can find a Windows Special Interest Group (SIG). Although these SIGs normally focus on Windows for DOS, you may find that many also support Windows NT.

Clubs usually have monthly meetings, demonstrate new software, maintain a list of consultants, and have free or low-cost training. To contact your local computer club, check newspaper listings under *computer* or call local computer stores.

The Windows User Group Network (WUGNET) is a national organization devoted to providing its members with information about Windows and Windows applications. WUGNET publishes a substantial bimonthly journal containing tips and articles written by members and consultants. The staff is highly knowledgeable about Windows and Windows applications. Contact WUGNET at the following address:

WUGNET Publications, Inc.
126 E. State St.
Media, PA 19063
(215) 565-1861 voice
(215) 565-7106 fax

WUGNET is also available on CompuServe by typing **GO WUGNET** when you are online with CompuServe. Additionally, you can send CompuServe electronic mail to WUGNET at the addresses 76702,1356 and 76702,1023. Send MCI electronic mail to the address 311-5246.

Computer Bulletin Board Forums

Computer bulletin boards are databases from which you can retrieve information over the telephone line using Terminal, the communication application that comes with Windows. Some bulletin boards contain a wealth of information about Windows and Windows applications. Microsoft provides information about Windows NT using two outside services, CompuServe and Internet, and its own service, the Microsoft Download Service.

Information from CompuServe

CompuServe contains forums where Windows and Windows applications can be discussed. You can submit questions to Microsoft operators who will return an answer within a day. After you become a CompuServe member, you can access the Microsoft user forums. To gain access to one of these areas, type one of the following GO commands at the CompuServe prompt symbol (!), then press Enter.

Type	To access
GO WINNT	Support for Windows NT
GO MSSQL	Support for Microsoft SQL Server
GO MSWORKGRP	Support for Microsoft Mail
GO MSNETWORKS	Support for Microsoft LAN Manager
GO MSAPP	Support for Microsoft applications
GO MSWIN32	Receive information about Win32
GO MSDR	Information related to software development
GO WINEXT	Support for Windows NT extensions and drivers
GO WINSDK	Support for the Windows Software Development Kit

To access CompuServe, you must sign up as a CompuServe member and receive an access ID and password. For more information, contact CompuServe, representative 230, at (800) 848-8199.

Information from Internet

You can access the Windows NT Driver Library and the Windows NT Knowledge Base by using the Internet service. The Windows NT Driver Library enables you to download driver files available for Windows NT. The Knowledge Base gives you access to many technical documents. You can search through the Knowledge Base using keywords, or you can list the technical documents.

Access Microsoft through Internet at the address **gowinnt.microsoft.com**.

Information from the Microsoft Download Service

The Microsoft Download Service is an electronic bulletin board system that you can access for technical notes and other information about Windows NT. Access Microsoft Download Service from your computer using communications software, such as Terminal. The settings for your communications software should be 1200, 2400, or 9600 baud, no parity, 8 data bits, and one stop bit. The phone number is (206) 936-6735.

PART

VIII

Appendixes

Installing Windows NT

Windows NT is easier to install and configure than some other operating systems with which you may have had experience, such as UNIX. Windows NT is easier because it's a smart operating system that knows more about its contours, configuration, and requirements than your previous operating system knew about itself—and a great deal more about itself than you will ever know. At the same time, installation can be a bit difficult simply because Windows NT is huge and demanding of resources.

Mistakes—or rather, poor choices made during installation—can usually be remedied with the administrative tools after Windows NT is up and running. Some errors you can make during installation are serious enough that you have to reinstall Windows NT. Although performing the original installation is interesting, watching it a second time can be tedious in the extreme. Therefore, it's worth it to make sure you are doing precisely what you want to do.

The mechanical process of Windows NT installation is simpler than installing Windows 3.1 on an MS-DOS machine. Windows NT doesn't have to figure out which disk cache program you are using; you are going to be using Windows NT's built-in disk caching. Windows NT doesn't care what TSRs you are running; you won't be running them prior to booting Windows NT each morning as you might have done under MS-DOS before booting Windows 3.1. Windows NT doesn't care what network software you were running under DOS; you'll be running

Windows NT network software from now on, (except on those occasions, rarer and rarer, when you are tempted to boot MS-DOS).

Installation is mostly automatic. Windows NT asks some questions, then starts working on its own and doesn't need you until it's ready to establish the first user account in order to log you into your first session. So, if you're installing from CD-ROM, after answering the preliminary question prompts, go get a cup of coffee and come back when Windows NT Setup gets to the first login account screen. Otherwise, be so kind as to feed the nice machine the disk it asks for when it asks for it!

 **NOTE**   Instructions in this Appendix are based on preliminary information provided by Microsoft. It is possible that by the time you install Windows NT, some information will have changed. The latest information will always be the information provided with your installation package for Windows NT from Microsoft.

Basics of Installation

To install from CD-ROM on an Intel-based machine conforming to the minimum standards in the next section, perform the following steps:

1. Insert the CD-ROM in the CD-ROM drive.

2. Insert the Windows NT Setup disk in the boot floppy drive.

3. Restart your machine and follow the instructions on-screen.

Alternatively, you can install from within MS-DOS by running the WINNT program from the \i386 directory of the CD-ROM or network server from which you are installing Windows NT.

Installing from diskettes is similar to installing from CD-ROM. Simply perform steps 2 and 3. Follow the prompts on the screen to replace one diskette with another.

To install Windows NT on a RISC-based system, reboot your machine. From the ARC screen, choose Run a Program. The program you want to run is CD:\mips\setupldr.

The Setup program tells you anything else you need to do at Setup time for either type of machine, including preserving an alternate boot partition for MS-DOS on Intel machines.

Minimal Installation

The hardware requirements for an Intel-based computer on which to install and run Windows NT are more rigorous than the requirements for running MS-DOS or certain other operating systems. The following minimum hardware requirements for your Intel-based computer must be met or exceeded for you to be able to install Windows NT without major difficulty.

- Your Intel-based computer's central processing unit must be at least an Intel 386 level, preferably a 386DX/33 MHz or better.

- Your Intel-based computer must possess at least 12M of memory, preferably 16 to 20M.

- Your Intel-based computer should have a VGA or better display.

- Your computer should have at least 90M of free disk space (Windows NT requires 70M).

Alternatively, you can install Windows NT on an ARC-compliant RISC workstation with 16M of memory.

A Bit More than the Minimum

Aside from these Microsoft-prescribed minimum requirements, certain items are both optional and desirable. Some of these are discussed in more detail elsewhere in this book; briefly, they are the following:

- *More disk space than the minimum.* Really, about 200M for the Windows NT system, swap file, and programs is a realistic single-user system.

- *More RAM.* 32M won't hurt at all.

- *A tape drive for backups.* Do you know how many floppy disks 200M is?

- *A CD-ROM drive.* Everyone needs a CD-ROM drive!

- *A network card.* Every person or team who has more than one computer in the work environment needs a network. In the old days, we called the practice of running in sneakers from machine to machine with floppy disks in our hands the "NikeNet." Those days departed with individual programs that, even when compressed, fill more than one high-density floppy.

■ *An uninterruptable power supply (UPS).* This makes recovery much easier after an unexpected powerdown, in view of Windows NT support for this function. UPS systems have come down a great deal in price recently, and might continue to do so as Windows NT aids in rendering them more common, hence, more economical.

Planning Your Installation

Although you can install many options during Windows NT Setup, most of these options can also be installed after Windows NT is up and running.

Questions you must ask yourself, and then answer, include the following:

■ How are hard disks to be formatted so that you will get maximum use from the sets of applications you want to use?

■ Is this to be a stand-alone machine, or is it to reside on a network?

■ If on a network, is it to be accessed by other network users?

■ Is more than one user going to log onto this machine from the keyboard?

■ Who is going to administer this machine?

The technical details involved in setting up according to your requirements are prosaic. The issue that must be resolved in each of these instances is, "How am I going to get any work done after I have installed this neat, new operating system?"

Other Operating Systems and Disk Partitioning

Are you such a power MS-DOS user that you often boot MS-DOS rather than Windows NT? Or are all your really useful tools Windows 3.x tools? Do you have a huge collection of OS/2 character-mode applications? When you purchased your tape drive, did it turn out to be one currently supported by Windows NT?

Windows NT provides a Boot Loader mechanism whereby it is possible to leave other operating system(s) on your machine and occasionally boot the other operating system(s), rather than Windows NT. You will be asked if you want to install the Boot Loader to enable you to preserve and to boot an operating system (such as MS-DOS) that is already installed when you run Windows NT Setup.

It is not necessary to be able to boot MS-DOS to run MS-DOS applications. Windows NT is able to successfully run the vast majority of MS-DOS applications. Exceptions to this include:

- Certain programs that perform hardware access, such as some communications programs and most special I/O hardware programs such as EPROM burners, in-circuit emulators, and FAX and RS-422 cards.

- Programs that depend on device drivers which are incompatible with Windows NT, such as third-party dynamic disk volume compression/decompression software.

- Programs that take advantage of well-known but unapproved programming shortcuts which are available, though frowned on, to programmers providing software to run under the nonsecure Windows or MS-DOS environments.

If your work style includes such programs, you might need to be able to restart your machine and bring up MS-DOS "classic."

> **WARNING:** If you need to boot MS-DOS, make sure you leave the boot volume with its original FAT file system. In our enthusiasm to install Windows NT when we first obtained it, we neglected this critical step, only to discover the self-evident fact that MS-DOS won't boot off of a volume reformatted to NTFS.

Windows NT itself can coexist with a number of disk drive formats. Each logical disk drive present in your computer can be one of the following:

- Formatted as an MS-DOS-style, 16-bit FAT drive, and accessible to both MS-DOS and Windows NT.

- Formatted as an OS/2-style HPFS drive, and accessible to both OS/2 and Windows NT.

- Formatted as a Windows NT-style NTFS drive, and accessible only to Windows NT.

- Formatted to some other operating system's specification, such as UNIX, that you want to have installed on your computer.

Windows NT Setup will try to persuade you to convert all fixed disks to NTFS drives. There are some sound reasons for this. In particular, Windows NT file security applies fully only to NTFS drives. Furthermore, MS-DOS and OS/2 applications running under Windows NT can still use files from an NTFS volume. (Windows NT provides MS-DOS and OS/2 applications with an appropriate compatible file name.) If this is to be a multiuser

Windows NT installation, you've crossed the line: You should go with the program and format all disks to NTFS. See Chapters 28, 29, and 30 for more information about Windows NT file security as it pertains to multiple users.

Also, NTFS is a more efficient file system for large disks. FAT was originally designed for floppy disks! NTFS volumes perform disk access much faster than FAT volumes. If you want high performance, you want NTFS.

Remember that security also covers issues such as file system recovery abilities. Your FAT partition files are not secured in the same way NTFS files are via the UPS support provided with Windows NT. If you want maximum recoverability, NTFS is the choice.

However, this option might not serve the single user who wants to continue to boot MS-DOS on his or her personal computer and still be able to access all drives. It doesn't serve the user whose tape drive is unsupported under Windows NT. It is possible that a single-user installation with an unsupported tape drive will be quite usable in the absence of full Windows NT security with all disks formatted FAT style, thus allowing old-fashioned MS-DOS tape backups to continue on all partitions, including the Windows NT partitions.

Another problem with NTFS and file security is that occasionally an MS-DOS application running under Windows NT wants to access files in a way not compatible with Windows NT security. Because this file security is disabled on FAT volumes, the user of a workstation that is also a server might want to have an unshared FAT volume at his or her disposal to be used only locally to run certain MS-DOS programs.

WARNING: Any FAT volume—even if it's not shared and is totally inaccessible over the network—nonetheless is *fully accessible* to any local user, regardless of privilege level. Once again, the only way to achieve full system security is to format to NTFS.

T I P   If you are upgrading an MS-DOS or OS/2 machine to Windows NT, you are not committing yourself to an irrevocable step if you *do not* allow Windows NT Setup to convert all disks to NTFS during installation. You can always convert logical drives from FAT or HPFS to NTFS later using the well-named CONVERT command from the Windows NT Command Prompt.

> **WARNING:** If you *do* permit Windows NT Setup to convert disks to NTFS, Windows NT cannot convert such disks back to FAT or HPFS volumes.

Note that in the current release of Windows NT, removable media such as floppy disks and removable hard drives are not formatted to NTFS, but to FAT. Floppy disks formatted by Windows NT remain readable to MS-DOS and OS/2 systems.

Summary of Operating System and File System Issues during Setup

There are many factors that go into your decision to stay with FAT or HPFS partitions, or to convert to NTFS. The following section summarizes once again what your choices and liabilities are regarding file systems on your Windows NT workstation.

■ Converting a FAT disk volume to NTFS means that MS-DOS no longer boots from that volume; however, MS-DOS applications running under Windows NT will be able to access that volume's files (and the files on any other NTFS volume to which the user has access).

■ Ditto converting an HPFS volume to NTFS: OS/2 no longer boots from such a volume, but OS/2 applications running under Windows NT will be able to access files on that volume.

■ If you need full Windows NT multiuser file security, failure recovery, or long file names, you must convert to NTFS, either during Setup or at any later time via the CONVERT utility after Windows NT is set up and running.

■ If you convert to NTFS, you can't switch back without deleting the NTFS volume and reformatting it (thereby losing all data contained in that volume in the process). If you do not convert, you can always do so later.

■ Alternatively, one volume formatted to the alternative operating system that you often use, with the rest of your disk volumes being formatted to NTFS, seems a good choice. This sort of arrangement is best performed after Setup by using the CONVERT command from the Command Prompt. Remember that users logging in locally have full access to any non-NTFS partition.

It looks like the safe advice is, "Don't switch to NTFS until you are sure what you want to do."

T I P
After you have converted a volume to NTFS and you decide to delete it (for instance, to reformat it for use by MS-DOS), you may discover that MS-DOS FDISK is powerless to delete NTFS volumes. Instead, run Windows NT Disk Administrator and delete the volume by means of that tool. See Chapter 31 for more information about the Disk Administrator. Remember that removing a partition destroys all data on that partition.

Setting Options during Installation

In those instances where Windows NT is polite enough to ask, don't install anything you don't want right now; you can always install it later. This applies, for instance, to network installation, tape backup, and user groups and accounts.

On the other hand, if this is to be a dedicated Windows NT machine and you are the type who "wants it all," answer "yes" to everything and go for it. Windows NT is very clever with the hardware and generally sets everything up correctly, even if you don't know what it is doing when it does it. Options can generally be tuned, adjusted, reinstalled, disabled, and so on after you get the hang of the system.

Windows NT Setup installs the default PAGEFILE.SYS virtual memory swapfile on the C:\ root directory. You can change this location to another volume after Windows NT is running by using the Program Manager's Main/Control Panel/System/Virtual Memory tool. See Chapters 7 and 23 for more information about Windows NT virtual memory.

Windows NT Setup wants to set you up with network software from the beginning. Of course, if you don't have a network, or lack a network card in this particular machine, this installation and the accompanying automatic configuration of the Registration Database carried out at Setup time is superfluous. However, it's also harmless.

Having the network software installed with no network produces an error message at bootup which can be nonchalantly clicked away into the oblivion of an Event Log entry. You can install the network now, even with no network hardware present, and disable the network installation later; you can install now and ignore the absence of network hardware; you can defer installation until a later date, even if the hardware is already present. See Chapters 25 and 28 for more information on Windows NT network support.

Tape drive support and UPS support are other features about which it is not necessary to make any decision at installation. They are easy enough to install from the Administrative Tools program group after Windows NT is up and running.

Creating Accounts during Installation

You use Setup to install Windows NT for a single-user workstation. In this case, pretty much all you have to do during Setup is provide the name of one user account along with its password. The Administration and Guest accounts are established at the same time automatically.

This final Setup step of installing the first user account is very important. In general, you won't want to log on as Administrator, because your ability to do damage by simple mistakes is so much greater than if you log onto your own machine as a less-privileged user. Later, when Windows NT is up and running, you will want to adjust the privileges of your personal login account to the level of trust you want to bestow upon yourself in day-to-day operations.

By the way, Windows NT doesn't compel you at Setup time to give a password to the pre-established Administrator account. Although it's certainly the best idea to give Administrator a password in a multiuser or workplace environment, if you have only a single-user Windows NT installation, why give Administrator a password? It's always easier to log on via a carriage return. You can add the Administrator password at a later date by logging in as Administrator and changing your password with the User Manager.

WARNING: If you do give Administrator a password, don't forget the password. Without it, you will have to reinstall NT. There is no Microsoft-provided method for accessing the most important administrative aspects of a Windows NT system without the Administrator password. There is no Microsoft-provided method for recovering lost passwords.

> **T I P** It's a good idea to create at least one other account that has Administration privileges. That way, you have a better chance of remembering the password to one of the accounts! If you remember the password for one Administrator-privileged account, you can use it to change the password for the account whose password you have forgotten. For more information about creating accounts and groups, modifying accounts and groups, and assigning permissions to them, see Chapter 31.

Installation Troubleshooting

Installation should be fairly straightforward. If something *does* go wrong, *first* make sure you are reading the instructions in the documentation accompanying the Windows NT distribution. The installation documentation provided with the disks and/or CD-ROM is *always* the latest information on installation. *Next*, try again, and make sure you understand any questions that Setup asks you during installation.

Is It a Hardware Problem?

Often, an installation problem is a hardware problem. Is the hardware on which you are attempting to install Windows NT supported hardware? Although problems of this sort were common during prerelease testing, every indication is that Microsoft has moved quickly both to support previously unsupported hardware and to fix bugs in the support for the approved hardware.

Video Adapter

Is your video adapter jumpered correctly? Windows NT runs a test on the video adapter during Setup. If you have your adapter jumpered wrong, it can lead to some odd results during Setup (at least in the latest release). Make sure the jumper shunts (usually a small black "plug" connecting two copper pins, easy to slide on and off and used by the manufacturer to provide options to the end user) are firmly in place on the correct pairs of pins, as shown in the manual for the adapter, to obtain the settings corresponding to the requirements of your Windows NT installation. In some cases, dip switches may be used rather than jumpers.

Port and IRQ Conflicts

To which port is your mouse attached? Are separate devices jumpered claiming the same IRQ? If up to now under DOS you have been barely holding together your computer's IRQ and port usage—in other words, carefully choosing which software you run during a session to avoid manually any potential conflicts—such a setup might no longer work under Windows NT. Windows NT attempts to determine from the very first what hardware is located at what I/O address and uses which interrupt(s). In case of failed Setup sessions, try removing the more exotic option cards in your system, such as custom I/O hardware, EPROM burners, in-circuit emulators, and so on, if they are present. Eventually, to reinstall such devices, you might have to either rejumper them, or to rejumper some conflicting standard peripheral (mouse, network card, tape drive, and so on).

SCSI Problems

A common user error having to do with hardware in installation is the incorrectly-terminated SCSI CD-ROM unit. This is an electrical issue extraneous to operating systems and to software in general: The last SCSI device on a chain of one or more SCSI devices *must* have a resistor terminator. Many users have discovered that, in some instances, incorrectly installed CD-ROM devices have worked flawlessly under MS-DOS and Windows 3.x. No such luck under Windows NT—and it *was* luck that it worked before under MS-DOS and Windows. Be sure your SCSI devices are properly terminated; read your SCSI card manual and your CD-ROM drive manual for more information.

In some instances, the same problem may affect SCSI hard drives, in which case the remedy is the same as for CD-ROMs.

Microsoft recommends against jumpering your CD-ROM drive for device 0 or 1 in view of the fact that some SCSI BIOS extensions reserve 0 and 1 for SCSI hard disks.

Once Again the Minimum

If Windows NT installs but does not boot, check to make sure your system meets the minimum requirements. For instance, if insufficient disk space exists for the PAGEFILE.SYS swap file to be created, Windows NT will not boot successfully. The same thing happens if you have insufficient RAM.

Documentation Discrepancies

The problems you might encounter might be complicated by another factor. As of the preliminary release of Windows NT, to which we had access while writing this book, not all of Microsoft's suggestions in the installation documentation are entirely accurate.

If you're installing the first commercial release of Windows NT, let's face it: You're a pioneer. And as the saying goes, you can always tell the pioneers by the arrows in their backs. If Windows NT Setup isn't happy with something, read the manual. If the manual is wrong, try something other than what the manual suggests.

For instance: The manual said that a Trantor 130B controller for a CD-ROM drive *must* be jumpered to IRQ5 for installation. Setup aborted when our Trantor 130B was thus jumpered. Setup succeeded when the Trantor 130B was returned to its default, "No-IRQ" jumpering, and furthermore, is working just fine up to now under Windows NT. We do, however, get an event log message for each bootup that a device is configured for an incorrect interrupt. But it works—that's how it installed itself—and we figure it will install itself correctly in the next release, Microsoft having either changed the documentation or the Setup program in the interim, so for now we're toughing it out. If we get *really* motivated, we might go as far as to use the Registry Editor to change the CD-ROM entry having to do with IRQ and see what happens. Nah, we'll wait and let Microsoft solve it.

> **T I P**
>
> Although it's true you can install Windows NT on a disk that already has an MS-DOS partition (provided that there is enough room left for Windows NT to be installed), don't absolutely count on the MS-DOS partition being usable when you are done. It should be, but you might make mistakes. When installing Windows NT on a disk already containing data, or reinstalling a later release of Windows NT, *back up everything you want to keep!*

Avoiding Reinstallation

It's possible that you will do enough damage during some future login session with Administration privileges that your Windows NT system will become unusable. We know—we've done it. One easy way to do this is to change to an inappropriate video driver via the Control Panel.

If you are unlucky enough to have made an unfortunate change that prevents Windows NT from booting successfully, there is a way of returning to the last known good configuration; that is, rebooting under the last configuration that successfully completed the bootup process. Here is what to do:

When the words "OS Loader" appear on the screen at powerup (or after choosing Windows NT from the Boot Loader screen), hold down the space bar. You are offered the choice of booting from the last known good configuration.

The moral is, when you change the *default*, whatever happens next is *your fault*. Keep good, current tape backups so that if you ever have to reinstall Windows NT—knock on wood—you don't have to individually reinstall and reconfigure every piece of software you have used or picked up since you first installed it.

Enjoy Windows NT

Have fun using Windows NT! In the majority of instances, it's going to be easy for you to install, learn to use, and administer. Windows NT looks to us like the most powerful and most pleasant-to-use virtual memory, multitasking, GUI-based operating system in the marketplace to date. Windows NT seems to superbly serve the diverse requirements of a wide spectrum of individual and workplace users.

Understanding MultiBoot

When a Windows NT computer boots, a small program called the *boot loader* is run. This program is responsible for "boot strapping" Windows NT into memory. The boot loader also enables you to choose an operating system other than Windows NT (such as MS-DOS) to run. This feature, which enables you to select the operating system to boot, is called *MultiBoot*. The boot loader and MultiBoot are controlled by a hidden initialization file called BOOT.INI, which is in the root directory of your C drive.

Modifying Settings in BOOT.INI (MultiBoot)

The BOOT.INI file contains the settings used to control the operating systems that you have available on your computer, the default operating system to boot, and how long your system should pause, enabling you to select the operating system to load. The following sections describe the contents of the BOOT.INI file and show you how to manually modify the BOOT.INI file.

Opening the BOOT.INI File

The BOOT.INI file is an ASCII text file that you can edit with any text editor. You can, for example, use the Notepad application that comes with Windows NT to edit the contents of this file. Or, use EDIT from a Command Prompt window to edit the file.

Normally you cannot see the BOOT.INI file because it is a hidden system file. To change it, you must first change its file attributes using the ATTRIB command. Use the following steps to make BOOT.INI editable:

1. Choose the Command Prompt from the Main window in the Program Manager. The Command Prompt window appears.

2. At the prompt, type the following:

```
ATTRIB -H -S -R C:\BOOT.INI
```

Changing the Contents of BOOT.INI

When you open BOOT.INI, you will find it contains the following sections and entries:

```
[Boot Loader]
timeout=30
default=scsi(0)disk(0)rdisk(0)partition(1)\winnt
[operating systems]
scsi(0)disk(0)rdisk(0)partition(1)\winnt="Windows NT Version
3.1" /NODEBUG
c:\="MS-DOS"
```

The [Boot Loader] section of BOOT.INI is used to configure how MultiBoot behaves. Values in this section indicate the default operating system and the amount of time that MultiBoot pauses before loading the default operating system. The timeout entry determines the number of seconds the MultiBoot screen waits before making the default choice. If you want the default choice to start immediately, without even displaying a choice, use a timeout value of 0.

The default entry determines the default operating system to load if no user input is made within the timeout period. Note that the value to the right of the default entry varies from system to system.

The [operating systems] section defines which operating systems are installed on the system (that is, which entries are in the MultiBoot list). The syntax for an entry in this section is

Operating System Location="*String to display*" *options*

In the syntax, *Operating System Location* is the location where the operating system resides, for example, **C:**. MultiBoot uses this location to know where to find the operating system to boot.

String to display is the name of the operating system that MultiBoot displays on the screen. You must enclose *String to display* in quotes as shown.

There are many reasons why you would want to change the default BOOT.INI settings. For example, you may want to use Windows NT infrequently and use MS-DOS the rest of the time. In this case, you would want MS-DOS to boot by default. BOOT.INI should be changed to the following:

```
[Boot Loader]
timeout=15
default=c:\
[operating systems]
c:\="MS-DOS 6.0"
scsi(0)disk(0)rdisk(0)partition(1)\winnt="Windows NT
Version 3.1" /NODEBUG
scsi(0)disk(0)rdisk(0)partition(1)\winnt="Windows NT
Version 3.1 (DEBUG)" /DEBUG
```

Note that in addition to changing the order of the operating systems, another line was added. This line loads a special version of NT called the *debugging* version. This version is needed only if you are developing device drivers for Windows NT. You probably won't need it, but it does illustrate that you can add entries and change the labels that appear on the MultiBoot screen.

Saving the BOOT.INI File

After you have changed the contents of BOOT.INI, save the file. You will see the effect of the changes the next time you boot the computer. However, before you reboot your computer, you must set the file attributes that you removed before editing the file.

If you want to hide BOOT.INI after you have finished editing it, follow these steps:

1. Choose Command Prompt from the Main window in Program Manager. A Command Prompt window appears.

2. At the prompt type

   ATTRIB +H +S +R C:\BOOT.INI

BOOT.INI is now hidden and read-only.

 You do not have to hide BOOT.INI or make it read-only, but doing so helps prevent accidental erasure.

Symbols

A

Q–R

QBASIC command, 772
QEMM memory manager, 862
Quick Edit Mode options, 817
Quicken, 854-855

RAID (Redundant Array of Independent Disks), 34, 954-955, 1082
RAM (Random-Access Memory), 126, 862
RCP (Remote Copy Protocol), 984
read directory permission, 1013
read file permission, 1001
Read special directory permission, 1018
read-only files, 158
read-only program groups, 109
reading mail (Mail), 336-337
reading message responses, 413
rearranging toolbar buttons (File Manager), 162-163
Receive Binary File (Transfers menu) command, 564
Receive Text File (Transfers menu) command, 562
receiving files
  binary files (Terminal), 564-565
  text files (Terminal), 562-563
recording
  logon attempts, 1032
  sound files, 637-638
recovering files, 1122
  NTFS, 33
Rectangle/square tool, 683, 686-688
rectangles, 510, 683, 686-688
recurring
  appointments, 392-396
  tasks, 404-405
Recurring Appointment dialog box, 392, 396
Recurring Task box, 404

redefining
  Network Provider Search Order, 996
  program groups, 112
redrawing charts (Graph), 720
Reduced Instruction Set Computer, see RISC
reducing text, 449
Redundant Array of Independent Disks (RAID), 954-955
Refresh command
  View menu, 1098
  Window menu, 156
REGEDIT program, 24
Registration Database Editor program, 24
Registry, 175-176
  Editor, 1136-1137
    icon creation, 877-878
    modifying Registry entries, 878
  Keys, 875
  modifying, 875-878
  root keys, 876
  SubKeys, 875
  Values, 875
reminders (Schedule+), 391-392
remote printers, 977
Remote Access Admin dialog box, 964
Remote Access dialog box, 962
Remote Access Permissions dialog box, 964
Remote Access Service, 962-965
Remote Copy Protocol (RCP), 984
remote disks, 1058-1060
remote drives, 906, 977
remote echoing, 548
Remote Execute (REXEC), 985
remote files, 746
remote groups, 1006
Remote Procedure Call (RPC) protocol, 892
Remote Shell (RSH), 985
remote users, 1006

X-Y-Z

Word Processing Is Easy
When You're Using Que!

Using Word for Windows 2, Special Edition

Ron Person & Karen Rose

Complete coverage of program basics and advanced desktop publishing hints. Includes Quick Start lessons and a tear-out Menu Map.

Version 2

$27.95 USA
0-88022-832-6, 900 pp., $7^3/8$ x $9^1/4$

Word for Windows 2 QuickStart

Elaine J. Marmel

This step-by-step tutorial to learning the basics of Word for Windows 2 provides illustrations to support the text, and teaches users how to use pull-down menus, dialog boxes, and multiple windows.

Version 2

$21.95 USA
0-88022-920-9, 620 pp., $7^3/8$ x $9^1/4$

Easy Word for Windows

Shelley O'Hara

The revolutionary how-to book that introduces beginners to word processing in the windows environment. Includes before and after screen shots to illustrate each task.

Versions 1 & 2

$19.95 USA
0-88022-922-5, 224 pp., 8 x 10

More Word Processing Titles from Que

Word for Windows 2 Quick Reference

Trudi Reisner
Versions 1 & 2

$9.95 USA
0-88022-950-0, 160 pp., $4^3/4$ x 8

Microsoft Word Quick Reference

Que Development Group
Through Version 5.5

$9.95 USA
0-88022-720-6, 160 pp., $4^3/4$ x 8

Using Ami Pro 3, Special Edition

James Meade
Version 3

$27.95
1-56529-067-4, 600 pp., $7^3/8$ x $9^1/4$

Easy Ami Pro

Shelley O'Hara
Version 2

$19.95 USA
0-88022-977-2, 224 pp., 8 x 10

Look Your Best with Ami Pro

Que Development Group
Version 2

$24.95
1-56529-028-3, 500 pp., 8 x 10

To Order, Call (800) 428-5331 OR (317) 573-2500

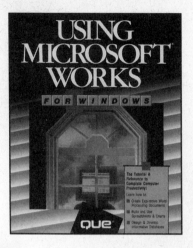